uk:athletics

BRITISH ATHLETICS
1999

Compiled by the
National Union of Track Statisticians

Editors: Rob Whittingham & Peter Matthews
Assistant Editors: Ian Hodge, Liz Sissons,
Tony Miller and Martin Rix.

Published by: Umbra Software Limited,
Unit 1, Bredbury Business Park,
Bredbury Park Way, Bredbury, Stockport SK6 2SN
Tel: 0161 406 6320   Fax: 0161 406 6732

ISBN 1 898258 08 2

Front Cover: IWAN THOMAS. Champion - AAA, European, Commonwealth, World Cup.

All photos by: All photographs provided by Mark Shearman,
22 Grovelands Road, Purley, Surrey CR8 4LA
Tel: 0181-660 0156   Fax: 0181-660 3437
His help is greatly appreciated.

Distributed by: Old Bakehouse Publications,
The Old Bakehouse, Church Street,
Abertillery, Gwent NP13 1EA
Tel: 01495 212600   Fax: 01495 216222

Printed in
Great Britain by: J.R. Davies (Printers) Limited,
The Old Bakehouse, Church Street, Abertillery, Gwent NP13 1EA
Tel: 01495 212600   Fax: 01495 216222

CONTENTS

NATIONAL UNION OF TRACK STATISTICIANS AND COMPILERS

Honorary President: Norris D McWhirter CBE

Vice Presidents: Peter E May   Leonard F Gebbett   Richard Hymans   Martin H James
Patrick E Brian Colin Young Andrew Huxtable Tim G Lynch-Staunton

Honorary Members: Roberto L Quercetani, John Bromhead

Executive Committee: Les Crouch (Chairman)   Dr Shirley E Hitchcock (Hon Sec)
John M Powell (Treasurer)

Stanley Greenberg	Peter J Matthews	Melvyn F Watman	Lionel Peters
Elizabeth Sissons	Bob Sparks	Alfred P Wilkins	Colin Young
Sally Gandee	Dr. Tim Grose	Joe Barrass	Justin Clouder

Annual

General Editors - Rob Whittingham, Peter Matthews

Assistant Editors - Ian Hodge, Liz Sissons, Tony Miller, Martin Rix

Records - Bob Sparks All Time Lists and Index - Martin Rix, Tony Miller

Results - Brian Hatch, Brian Webster and Peter Matthews

Men's Lists - Ian Hodge (HJ, PV and overall), Joe Barrass (sprints),
Tim Grose (800m to 10,000m), Steve Mitchell (5000m, 10,000m), John Walsh (Marathon),
Shirley Hitchcock (hurdles), Bill Myers (LJ, TJ),Tony O'Neill (throws).

Under 20 & Under 17 Men - Ian Hodge with above compilers

Under 15 Men - Ian Hodge   Under 13 Men - Martin Rix

Women's Lists - Liz Sissons, Tony Miller (Under 17 and others),
John Brant (Under 15), Bill Green (Under 13)

Walks - John Powell   Relays - Keith Morbey   Multi-Events - Alan Lindop

Also acknowledgements for specific help to Arnold Black (Scotland), John Glover and
Alan Keys (Northern Ireland) and various other NUTS members.

ABBREVIATIONS & NOTES

A	-	mark set at altitude over 1000m	
a	-	automatic timing only known to one tenth of a second	
D	-	performance made in a Decathlon	
dh	-	downhill	
e	-	estimated time	
et	-	extra trial	
ex	-	exhibition	
h	-	heat	
H	-	performance made in a Heptathlon	
hc	-	handicap race	
i	-	indoor	
jo	-	jump off	
m	-	position in race when intermediate time taken	
mx	-	performance in mixed race	
O	-	performance made in an Octathlon	
o	-	over age	
P	-	performance made in a Pentathlon	
Q	-	qualifying round	

q	-	quarter final
r	-	race number
s	-	semi final
t	-	track
u	-	unofficial time
un	-	unconfirmed performance
w	-	wind assisted (> 2.0 m/sec)
W	-	wind assisted (over 4m/sec in decathlon/heptathlon)
x	-	relay team may include outside age-group members
+	-	intermediate time
*	-	legal performance where best is wind assisted
"	-	photo electric cell time
#	-	Unratified (may not be ratifiable)
&	-	as yet unratified
§	-	now competes for another nation
¶	-	drugs ban

AGE GROUP DESIGNATIONS

U13 - Under 13 (born 1.9.85 or later) U15 - Under 15 (born 1.9.83 to 31.8.85)
U17 - Under 17 (born 1.9.81 to 31.8.83) U20 - Under 20 (born 1.1.79 to 31.8.81)
Vxx - Veteran (age 40 or over Men) Vxx - Veteran (age 35 or over Women)

Care must be taken with very young age groups for athletes with an unknown date of birth from Northern Ireland since their age groups differ slightly.

Italics indicates the athlete competes for a British club but is not eligible to represent Britain.

MULTI - EVENTS

Pentathlon, Heptathlon and Decathlon lists show the complete breakdown of individual performances in the following order:

Pentathlon (women) - 100mH, SP, HJ, LJ, 800m; Junior: LJ, SP, 75mH, HJ, 800m
Heptathlon (women) - 100mH, HJ, SP, 200m (1st day); LJ, JT, 800m (2nd day) (80mH - Inters)
Decathlon (men)   - 100m, LJ, SP, HJ, 400m (1st day); 110mH, DT, PV, JT, 1500m (2nd day)

Totals which include performances made with following winds in excess of 4 m/s are denoted by W. The date shown is the second day of competition.

RANKING LISTS:

These show the best performances in each event recorded during the 1998 season.
For each performance the following details are shown:

Performance; wind reading (where appropriate); name (with, where appropriate, age-group category); date of birth (DDMMYY); position in competition; venue; date.

The following numbers are used, although strength of performance or lack of information may vary the guidelines -

50 perfomances   100 athletes for each standard event

Age Groups - 40 Under 20, 30 Under 17, 20 Under 15, 10 Under 13

In the junior men, athletes are shown in older age groups if their performances merit this, e.g. an U15 can appear in the U17 list etc. For junior women, athletes are shown in their age group as per womens rules, although juniors of any age will be shown in the main list on merit.

INDEX

Club details and previous personal bests, where better than those recorded in 1998, are shown in the index for all athletes in the main lists.

VENUES

Major venues for athletics in Britain - the name by which the stadium is denoted in this book is shown in capitals. Most are 8-lane synthetic tracks, unless shown.

LONDON (xx)

B	Barn Elms Sports Centre, Barnes	ME	Mile End Stadium, Poplar (formerly East London)
BP	Battersea Park (6l)	Nh	Terence McMillan Stadium, Newham, Plaistow
Col	Colindale, Hendon Police Track, Peel Centre (6l)	PH	Parliament Hill Fields, Hampstead
CP	Crystal Palace, Nat. Sports Cen. Norwood	SP	Southwark Park, Surrey Quays (7l)
Cr	Croydon Sports Arena	TB	Tooting Bec
Elt	Sutcliffe Park, Eltham	WF	Waltham Forest, Walthamstow
FP	Finsbury Park	WL	West London, Linford Christie Stadium,
Ha	Haringey, New River Sports Centre, Wood Green		Wormwood Scrubs
He	Barnet Copthall Stadium, Hendon	WP	Wimbledon Park (6l)

ABERDARE, Michael Sobell Sports Centre
ABERDEEN, Chris Anderson Stdm, Balgowrie
ABINGDON, Tilsley Park Sports Complex
ALDERSHOT Military Stadium (Army) (7l)
ANDOVER, Charlton Sports Centre (6l)
ANNAN, Everholm Sports Complex
ANTRIM Stadium
ASHFORD, Julie Rose Stadium
ASHTON-UNDER-LYNE, Richmond Park Stadium (6l)
AYR, Dam Park Stadium
BANGOR
BARKING, Mayesbrook Park, Dagenham
BARRY, Jenner Park
BASILDON Bowl, Gloucester Park
BASINGSTOKE, Down Grange (6l)
BATH, University Track, Claverton Down Road
BEBINGTON, The Oval, Wirral
BEDFORD Athletic Stadium, Barkers Lane

BELFAST, Mary Peters Track, Upper Malone
BIRMINGHAM, Alexander Stadium, Perry Park
(Un) University Track, Edgbaston
BLACKBURN, Witton Park
BLACKPOOL, Stanley Park
BOLTON, Leverhulme Park (6l)
BOURNEMOUTH, Kings Park (7l)
BRACKNELL, Sport and Leisure Centre (6l)
BRAINTREE, Leisure Centre, Panfield Lane
BRAUNTON, North Devon Track (6l)
BRECON Penlan Track
BRIERLEY HILL, The Dell, Dudley
BRIGHTON Withdean Stadium
BRISTOL, Whitchurch Stadium
BROMLEY, Norman Park (6l)
BURY, Market Street Track (6l)
BURY ST EDMONDS, W. Suffolk Athletics Arena
CAMBRIDGE University Track, Wilberforce Rd

CANNOCK Sports Stadium, Pye Green Road
CANVEY ISLAND, Castle Point Tr, Waterside Farm (6l)
CARDIFF Athletic Stadium, Leckwith Road
CARLISLE, Sheepmount Stadium (6l)
CARMARTHEN Track, Johnstown (6l)
CARSHALTON, Sutton Arena
CHELTENHAM, Prince of Wales Stadium (6l)
CLECKHEATON, Pr. Mary Pl. Fields, Liversedge
COATBRIDGE Outdoor Centre
COLCHESTER, Garrison Arena
COLWYN BAY, Eirias Park
CONNAH'S QUAY, Deeside Arena
CORBY, Rockingham Triangle
COSFORD (RAF) - Indoor and outdoor arenas
COVENTRY, Univ. of Warwick Sports Centre
CRAWLEY Leisure Centre, Haslett Avenue
CREWE, Cumberland Athletics Track (7l)
CUDWORTH, Dor. Hyman Sports Cen, Barnsley
CWMBRAN Stadium
DARTFORD, Central Park (6l)
DERBY, Moorways Stadium
DOUGLAS, National Sports Centre, Isle of Man (6l)
DUMFRIES, David Keswick Stadium
DUNDEE, Caird Park
EAST KILBRIDE, John Wright Sports Centre
EDINBURGH, Meadowbank Sports Centre
ENFIELD, Q. E. II Stadium, Carterhatch Lane
FELTHAM Arena, Shakespeare Avenue (6l)
GALASHIELS, Tweedbank Sports Complex
GATESHEAD International Stadium
GLASGOW, Crownpoint Sports Park
      Indoors: Kelvin Hall
GLASGOW (S), Scotstoun Leisure Centre
GLOUCESTER, Blackbridge Athletic Track (6l)
GRANGEMOUTH Sports Stadium, Falkirk
GRANTHAM, South Kesteven Stadium
GREAT YARMOUTH, Wellesley Recr Ground (6l)
GREENOCK, Ravenscraig Stadium
GRIMSBY, K George V Stadium, Weelsby Rd
GUILDFORD, Spectrum Sports Centre
HARLOW Sports Centre (6l)
HARROW, Bannister Sports Cen, Harrow Weald (7l)
HAYES Stadium, Judge Heath Lane
HEMEL HEMPSTEAD, Dacorum Athletic Track
HEXHAM, Tynedale Athletics Park (6l)
HIGH WYCOMBE, Wycombe Sports Centre (6l)
HOO, Deangate Ridge Stadium, Rochester
HORNCHURCH Stadium, Havering, Upminster (6l)
HORSHAM, Broadbridge Heath Leisure Centre (6l)
HULL, Costello Stadium, Anlaby Park
ILFORD, Cricklefield Sports Ground (6l)
INVERNESS, Queen's Park
IPSWICH, Northgate Sports Centre (6l)
JARROW, Monkton Stadium
JERSEY Athletics Track, St Clement, CI
KEIGHLEY, Greenshead Athletics Track
KETTERING Leisure Village
KINGSTON, Kingsmeadow Centre (ex Norbiton)
KINGS LYNN, Lynnsports Dow Track (6l)
KIRKBY Sports Centre, Knowsley
LEAMINGTON, Edmondscote Track
LEEDS, South Leeds Stadium
      (B) Beckett Park Headingley (7l)
LEICESTER, Saffron Lane Sports Centre
LINCOLN, Yarborough Leisure Centre (6l)
LINWOOD Sports Complex, Paisley
LIVERPOOL, Wavertree Athletics Centre
LIVINGSTON, Craigwood Sports Centre
LOUGHBOROUGH University, Ashby Road
LUTON, Stockwood Park

MANCHESTER, Wythenshawe Park
    (BV) Belle Vue
MANSFIELD, Berry Hill Track
MELKSHAM, Christie Miller Sports Centre
MILTON KEYNES, Stantonbury Fields
MIDDLESBROUGH, Clairville Stadium (7l)
NEATH, Court Herbert (6l)
NEWCASTLE -upon-Tyne, Lightfoot Cen, Walker
NEWPORT Stadium, Langland Way
NORTHAMPTON, Sixfields Stadium
NORWICH, Norfolk Athletics Track, Un. E. Anglia
NOTTINGHAM, Harvey Hadden Stadium (7l)
OLDHAM, Westwood Park
OXFORD University Track, Iffley Road (6l)
PERIVALE, Stockdove Way, Greenford, Mx
PETERBOROUGH, Embankment Track
PITREAVIE Athletics Track, Dunfermline (6l)
PLYMOUTH, Brickfields Stad, Devonport(R.N)
PORTSMOUTH, Mountbatten Cen, Alex. Park
    (RN) HMS Temeraire, Burnaby Road (7l)
READING, Palmer Park Sports Stadium (6l)
REDDITCH, Abbey Stadium
REDRUTH, Royal Duchy Track, Carn Brea, Pool
ROTHERHAM, Herringthorpe Stadium
RUGBY, Ken Marriott Leisure Centre
ST. ALBANS, Westminster Lodge (6l)
ST. IVES, St. Ivo Outdoor Complex (6l)
ST. PETER PORT, Osmond Priaulx Field, Guernsey (6l)
SALFORD, Cleavley Athletics Track, Eccles
SALISBURY Leisure Centre, The Butts
SANDOWN, Fairway Athletics Centre, Isle of Wight
SCUNTHORPE, Quibell Park
SHEFFIELD, Don Valley Stadium Attercliffe
    (W) Woodbourne Road, Attercliffe
SOLIHULL, Norman Green Sports Centre
SOUTHAMPTON Sports Centre, Bassett (6l)
SOUTHEND-on-Sea, Garon Park
STOCKPORT, Woodbank Park Track (6l)
STOKE-on-Trent, Northwood Stadium, Hanley
STREET, Millfield School (6l)
STRETFORD, Trafford Athletic Stad, Longford Park (6l)
SUNDERLAND, Silksworth Sports Complex
SUTTON COLDFIELD,Wyndley Leisure Centre
SWANSEA, Morfa Stadium, Landore
SWINDON, Thamesdown Tr., County Road (6l)
TAMWORTH
TELFORD, Oakengates Leisure Centre
THURROCK, Blackshots Stadium, Grays (7l)
WAKEFIELD, Thornes Park Track
WALTON-on-Thames, Stompond Lane (6l)
WARE, Wodson Stadium
WARLEY, Hadley Stadium, Smethwick
WARRINGTON, Victoria Park, Knutsford Rd
WATFORD, Woodside Stadium, Garston
WELWYN Garden City, Gosling Stadium
WHITEHAVEN, Copeland Athletic Stadium (6l)
WHITLEY BAY, Churchill Playing Fields (6l)
WIGAN, Robin Park
WINDSOR, Vansittart Road (6l)
WISHAW Sports Centre
WOKING, Blackmore Crescent, Sheerwater (6l)
WOLVERHAMPTON Aldersley Stadium
WOODFORD, Ashton Pl Fields,Woodford Br.
WORCESTER, Nunnery Wood Sports Centre
WORTHING, West Park, Shaftesbury Avenue
WREXHAM, Queensway Stadium
YATE, Broad Lane Track, Gloucester
YEOVIL Recreation Centre, Chilton Grove
YORK, Huntingdon Stadium (6l)
DUBLIN (B) Belfield & (S) Morton Stadium, (Santry)

INTRODUCTION - by Rob Whittingham

Another year has passed and the Annual continues to catalogue the progress of British Athletics. This year has been good for medals with better than expected totals in both European and Commonwealth Championships. It has also seen a year of transition for the governing body with the new UK Athletics taking over in 1999. It is very good to report that the new board is supporting the annual and that Reebok have offered sponsorship. For readers on the web a new site www.ukathletics.org will provide extra information.

I always thank the main contributors to the annual and special thanks this year go to Liz Sissons who completed the Women's lists in the most difficult of circumstances. This effort was supplemented by Peter Matthews and all the assistant editors, with Peter again enabling the annual to be published early. Tony Miller and Ian Hodge helped with all the lists and Martin Rix has made great efforts to ensure all the records and all-time lists are as accurate as possible.

Also all the specialist compilers have continued to provide excellent service.

I also thank, as ever, the people at Umbra - Geoff Blamire, my partner, for his assistance with computer facilities, Julie and Mary for all the typing and checking and other staff members who help in various ways.

I also thank Marty, who again has checked the typesetting and put up with the endless production of the book.

Each year seems to bring it's own problems and this year has been no exception. The seemingly simple question of nationality has created great problems with the Commonwealth Games. Consider the Thomas brothers, who having gained British nationality, competed in the British trials and having failed to win selection, represented Sierra Leone at the Commonwealth Games. There is no simple way of deciding how to represent this in the main lists, I hope the readers approve of the compromise shown.

During the year I deal with several hundred pieces of correspondence. I reply personally to as many as possible but some receive no response. I hope readers will continue to give their comments and additions but realise a reply may not always be given.

As usual any corrections are always welcome.

Rob Whittingham
March 1999

7 Birch Green   Glossop   SK13 8PR
e-mail rob@umbra.co.uk

BAF & OTHER ADDRESSES

UK Athletics
Athletics House
30a Harborne Road
Edgbaston
Birmingham   B15 3AA
Tel: 0121 456 5098

AAA of England
Edgbaston House
3 Duchess Place
Hagley Road
Birmingham B16 8NM
Tel: 0121 452 1500

SCOTLAND
Scotland A.F.
Caledonia House
South Gyle
Edinburgh
Tel: 0131 317 7320

WALES
A.A. of Wales
Morfa Stadium Landore
Swansea
West Glamorgan SA1 7DF
Tel: 01792 456237

NORTHERN IRELAND
Northern Ireland A.A.F.
Honorary Secretary: J.Allen
Athletics House
Old Coach Road
Belfast BT9 5PR
Tel: 01232 381222

Midland Counties A.A.
Edgbaston House
3 Duchess Place
Hagley Road
Birmingham
B16 8NM
Tel: 0121 452 1500

North of England A.A.
Studio 106, EMCO House
5/7 New York Road
Leeds LS2 7PJ
Tel: 01532 461835

South of England A.A.
Suite 106 City of London Fruit Exchange
Brushfield St
London E1 6EU
Tel: 0171 247 2963

Commonwealth Games Councils:
England
General Secretary: Miss A.Hogbin
1 Wandsworth Plain
London SW18 1EH
Tel: 0181 871 2677

Northern Ireland
Honorary Secretary: R.J.McColgan MBE
22 Mountcoole Park, Cave Hill
Belfast BT14 8JR
Tel: 01232 716558

Scotland
Honorary Secretary: G.A.Hunter OBE
139 Old Dalkeith Road
Little France
Edinburgh EH16 4SZ
Tel: 0131 664 1070

Wales
Honorary Secretary: M.John MBE
Pennant
Blaenau, Ammanford
Dyfed SA18 3BZ
Tel: 0269 850390

British Athletics League
Honorary Secretary: D. Jeacock
16 Church Street
Wotton Bassett
Wilts SN4 7BQ

National Young Athletes' League
Honorary Secretary: N. Bailey
15 Chaseley Avenue
Cannock
Staffs WS11 1JG
Tel: 01543 574624

Supporters Club - British Athletics Club
Honorary Secretary: Mrs M.Pieri
11 Railway Road
Newbury, Berks RG14 7PE
Tel: 01635 33400

Sports Council
The Sports Council
16 Upper Woburn Place
London WC1H OQP
Tel: 0171 388 1277

Athletics Weekly
Editor: Nigel Walsh
Bretton Court, Bretton
Peterborough PE3 8DZ
Tel: 01733 261144

National Union of Track Statisticians
Secretary: Dr. S. Hitchcock
2 Chudleigh Close
Bedford
MK40 3AW

MAJOR OUTDOOR FIXTURES IN 1999

APRIL

19	Flora London Marathon	London

MAY

1-3	BUSA Championships	Bedford
8-9	County Championships	Various
8-9	District Championships (Scotland)	Various
30-31	Inter-Counties	Bedford

JUNE

13-14	European Cup Combined Events	ITA
19	U20/U23 International	Mannheim, GER
19-20	South Championships	Watford
19-20	North Championships	Leeds
19-20	Welsh Championships	Colwyn Bay
19-20	European Cup	Paris, FRA
26	Scottish Championships	Glasgow
27	IAAF Permit	Gateshead

JULY

3-4	AAA U23/U20 Championships	Bedford
9-10	English Schools Championships	Bury St Edmunds
18	U23 International v FRA v SPA	Hexham
23-25	AAA Championships	Birmingham
24	U20 International	Albertville, FRA
29-1 Aug	European U23 Championships	Gothenburg, SWE

AUGUST

7	British Grand Prix II	Sheffield
5-8	European U20 Championships	Riga, LAT
9	Welsh Games	Wrexham
14-15	AAA U17/U15 Championships	Sheffield
14-15	U20/U23 International Combined Events	Stuttgart, GER
21	U19 International	Berlin, GER
21-22	Midland Championships	Stoke
21-22	NI Championships	Belfast
20-29	World Championships	Seville, SPA
28	GBR 'A' v FRA 'A'	

SEPTEMBER

4	GBR v USA	Glasgow
11	Grand Prix Final	Munich, GER

BEST AUTHENTIC PERFORMANCES (MEN)

(as at 31st December 1998)

W = World, E = European, C = Commonwealth, A = UK All-Comers, N = UK, J = Junior

100m	W,C	9.84	Donovan Bailey	CAN	27 Jul 96	Atlanta
	E,N	9.87	Linford Christie		15 Aug 93	Stuttgart
	A	10.03	Jon Drummond	USA	15 Jul 94	London (CP)
	WJ	10.05 #	Davidson Ezinwa	NGR	4 Jan 90	Bauchi
	WJ,EJ,NJ	10.06	Dwain Chambers		25 Jul 97	Ljubljana
200m	W	19.32	Michael Johnson	USA	1 Aug 96	Atlanta
	E	19.72 A	Pietro Mennea	ITA	12 Sep 79	Mexico City
	C	19.68	Frank Fredericks	NAM	1 Aug 96	Atlanta
	A	19.85	Michael Johnson	USA	6 Jul 90	Edinburgh
	N	19.87 A&	John Regis		31 Jul 94	Sestriere
		19.94	John Regis		20 Aug 93	Stuttgart
	WJ	20.07 #	Lorenzo Daniel	USA	18 May 85	Starkville
		20.13	Roy Martin	USA	16 Jun 85	Indianapolis
	EJ,NJ	20.29	Christian Malcolm		19 Sep 98	Kuala Lumpur
300m	W	31.48	Danny Everett	USA	3 Sep 90	Jerez de la Frontera
		31.48	Roberto Hernández	CUB	3 Sep 90	Jerez de la Frontera
	E,C,A,N	31.56	Doug Walker	Sco	19 Jul 98	Gateshead
	WJ	32.08	Steve Lewis	USA	28 Sep 88	Seoul
	EJ,NJ	32.53	Mark Richardson		14 Jul 91	London (Ha)
400m	W	43.29	Butch Reynolds	USA	17 Aug 88	Zürich
	E	44.33	Thomas Schönlebe	GER	3 Sep 87	Rome
	C	44.17	Innocent Egbunike	NGR	19 Aug 87	Zürich
	A	43.98	Michael Johnson	USA	10 Jul 92	London (CP)
	N	44.36	Iwan Thomas		13 Jul 97	Birmingham
	WJ	43.87	Steve Lewis	USA	28 Sep 88	Seoul
	EJ	45.01	Thomas Schönlebe	GER	15 Jul 84	Berlin
	NJ	45.36	Roger Black		24 Aug 85	Cottbus
600m	W	1:12.81	Johnny Gray	USA	24 May 86	Santa Monica
	E	1:14.5	Wilson Kipketer	DEN	13 Aug 97	Zürich
	C	1:13.2	John Kipkurgat	KEN	23 Mar 74	Pointe-à-Pierre
	A,N	1:14.95	Steve Heard		14 Jul 91	London (Ha)
	NJ	1:16.79	Andrew Lill		24 Jul 90	Mansfield
800m	W,E	1:41.11	Wilson Kipketer	DEN	24 Aug 97	Cologne
	C,N	1:41.73 "	Sebastian Coe	Eng	10 Jun 81	Florence
	A	1:43.22	Steve Cram		31 Jul 86	Edinburgh
	WJ	1:43.64	Japheth Kimutai	KEN	13 Aug 97	Zürich
	EJ	1:45.45	Andreas Busse	GER	7 Jun 78	Ostrava
	NJ	1:45.64	David Sharpe		5 Sep 86	Brussels
1000m	W,E,C,N	2:12.18	Sebastian Coe	Eng	11 Jul 81	Oslo
	A	2:12.88	Steve Cram		9 Aug 85	Gateshead
	WJ	2:16.84	Ali Hakimi	TUN	28 Jul 95	Lindau
	EJ	2:18.31	Andreas Busse	GER	7 Aug 77	Dresden
	NJ	2:18.98	David Sharpe		19 Aug 86	Birmingham
1500m	W	3:26.00	Hicham El Guerrouj	MAR	14 Jul 98	Rome
	E	3:28.95	Fermin Cacho	SPA	13 Aug 97	Zürich
	C	3:29.46	Daniel Komen	KEN	16 Aug 97	Monaco
	A	3:30.72	Noureddine Morceli	ALG	15 Jul 94	London (CP)
	N	3:29.67	Steve Cram		16 Jul 85	Nice
	WJ	3:32.91 #	Noah Ngeny	KEN	16 Aug 97	Monaco
		3:33.24	William Chirchir	KEN	12 Aug 98	Zürich
	EJ	3:35.51	Reyes Estévez	SPA	16 Aug 95	Zürich
	NJ	3:36.6	Graham Williamson		17 Jul 79	Oslo

Event		Time	Athlete	Nat	Date			Venue
1 Mile	W	3:44.39	Noureddine Morceli	ALG	5	Sep	93	Rieti
	E,C,N	3:46.32	Steve Cram	Eng	27	Jul	85	Oslo
	A	3:49.49	Steve Cram		12	Sep	86	London (CP)
	WJ	3:50.41	Noah Ngeny	KEN	16	Jul	97	Nice
	EJ,NJ	3:53.15	Graham Williamson		17	Jul	79	Oslo
2000m	W	4:47.88	Noureddine Morceli	ALG	3	Jul	95	Paris
	E,N	4:51.39	Steve Cram		4	Aug	85	Budapest
	C	4:48.74	John Kibowen	KEN	1	Aug	98	Hechtel
	A	4:48.36	Hicham El Guerrouj	MAR	19	Jul	98	Gateshead
	WJ	4:59.14	Ali Sief-Saïdi	ALG	29	Jun	97	Villeneuve d'Ascq
	EJ	5:04.4	Harald Hudak	GER	30	Jun	76	Oslo
	NJ	5:06.56	Jon Richards		7	Jul	82	Oslo
3000m	W,C	7:20.67	Daniel Komen	KEN	1	Sep	96	Rieti
	E	7:29.34	Isaac Viciosa	SPA	9	Jul	98	Oslo
	A,N	7:32.79	Dave Moorcroft		17	Jul	82	London (CP)
	WJ	7:35.52	Philip Mosima	KEN	12	Jul	96	London (CP)
	EJ	7:43.20	Ari Paunonen	FIN	22	Jun	77	Cologne
	NJ	7:48.28	Jon Richards		9	Jul	83	Oslo
2 Miles	W,C	7:58.61	Daniel Komen	KEN	19	Jul	97	Hechtel
	E	8:13.2 i#	Emiel Puttemans	BEL	18	Feb	73	Berlin
	E,A,N	8:13.51	Steve Ovett		15	Sep	78	London (CP)
	WJ	8:25.2	Jim Ryun	USA	13	May	66	Los Angeles
	EJ,NJ	8:28.31	Steve Binns		31	Aug	79	London (CP)
5000m	W	12:39.36	Haile Gebreselassie	ETH	13	Jun	98	Helsinki
	E	12:54.70	Dieter Baumann	GER	13	Aug	97	Zürich
	C	12:39.74	Daniel Komen	KEN	22	Aug	97	Brussels
	A	13:06.72	William Sigei	KEN	15	Jul	94	London (CP)
	N	13:00.41	Dave Moorcroft		7	Jul	82	Oslo
	WJ	12:53.72	Philip Mosima	KEN	5	Jun	96	Rome
	EJ,NJ	13:27.04	Steve Binns		14	Sep	79	London (CP)
10000m	W	26:22.75	Haile Gebreselassie	ETH	1	Jun	98	Hengelo
	E	27:13.81	Fernando Mamede	POR	2	Jul	84	Stockholm
	C	26:27.85	Paul Tergat	KEN	22	Aug	97	Brussels
	A	27:20.38	Aloÿs Nizigama	BUR	7	Jul	95	London (CP)
	N	27:18.14 &	Jon Brown		28	Aug	98	Brussels
		27:23.06	Eamonn Martin		2	Jul	88	Oslo
	WJ	27:11.18	Richard Chelimo	KEN	25	Jun	91	Hengelo
	EJ	28:22.48	Christian Leuprecht	ITA	4	Sep	90	Koblenz
	NJ	29:21.9	Jon Brown		21	Apr	90	Walnut
20km	W	56:55.6	Arturo Barrios	MEX	30	Mar	91	La Flèche
	E	57:18.4	Dionisio Castro	POR	31	Mar	90	La Flèche
	C,N	57:28.7	Carl Thackery	Eng	31	Mar	90	La Flèche
	A	58:39.0	Ron Hill		9	Nov	68	Leicester
1 Hour	W	21,101 m	Arturo Barrios	MEX	30	Mar	91	La Flèche
	E	20,944 m	Jos Hermens	HOL	1	May	76	Papendal
	C,N	20,855 m	Carl Thackery	Eng	31	Mar	90	La Flèche
	A	20,472 m	Ron Hill		9	Nov	68	Leicester
	NJ	18,221 m	Eddie Twohig		16	Jun	81	Leamington
25km	W	1:13:55.8	Toshihiko Seko	JAP	22	Mar	81	Christchurch, NZ
	E	1:14:16.8	Pekka Päivärintä	FIN	15	May	75	Oulu
	C,A,N	1:15:22.6	Ron Hill	Eng	21	Jul	65	Bolton
30km	W	1:29:18.78	Toshihiko Seko	JAP	22	Mar	81	Christchurch, NZ
	E,C,A,N	1:31:30.4	Jim Alder	Sco	5	Sep	70	London (CP)
Half Marathon	W,C	59:17	Paul Tergat	KEN	4	Apr	98	Milan
	E	59:43	António Pinto	POR	15	Mar	98	Lisbon
	A	60:02	Benson Masya	KEN	18	Sep	94	Tyneside

Event		Mark	Name		Date	Venue
Half	N	60:09 #	Paul Evans		15 Jan 95	Marrakech
Marathon		60:59	Steve Jones		8 Jun 86	Tyneside
	WJ	61:00	John Gwako	KEN	28 Sep 97	Grevenmacher
	NJ	66:41	Stuart Jones		12 Jun 88	Weaverham
Marathon	W	2:06:05	Ronaldo da Costa	BRA	20 Sep 98	Berlin
	E	2:07:12	Carlos Lopes	POR	20 Apr 85	Rotterdam
	C	2:06:54	Ondoro Osoro	KEN	11 Oct 98	Chicago
	A	2:07:55	António Pinto	POR	13 Apr 97	London
	N	2:07:13	Steve Jones		20 Oct 85	Chicago
	WJ	2:12:49	Negash Dube	ETH	18 Oct 87	Beijing
		2:12:49	Tesfaye Dadi	ETH	9 Oct 88	Berlin
	NJ	2:23:28	Eddie Twohig		28 Mar 82	Wolverhampton
2km St	W,C	5:14.43	Julius Kariuki	KEN	21 Aug 90	Rovereto
	E	5:18.36	Alessandro Lambruschini	ITA	12 Sep 89	Verona
	A	5:19.68	Samson Obwocha	KEN	19 Jul 86	Birmingham
	N	5:19.86	Mark Rowland		28 Aug 88	London (CP)
	WJ,EJ	5:25.01	Arsenios Tsiminos	GRE	2 Oct 80	Athens
	NJ	5:29.61	Colin Reitz		18 Aug 79	Bydgoszcz
3km St	W,C	7:55.72	Bernard Barmasai	KEN	24 Aug 97	Cologne
	E	8:07.62	Joseph Mahmoud	FRA	24 Aug 84	Brussels
	A	8:08.11	Patrick Sang	KEN	7 Jul 95	London (CP)
	N	8:07.96	Mark Rowland		30 Sep 88	Seoul
	WJ	8:07.69	Paul Kosgei	KEN	7 Jul 97	Stockholm
	EJ	8:29.50	Ralf Pönitzsch	GER	19 Aug 76	Warsaw
	NJ	8:29.85	Paul Davies-Hale		31 Aug 81	London (CP)
110m H	W,E,C,N	12.91	Colin Jackson	Wal	20 Aug 93	Stuttgart
	A	13.03	Colin Jackson		4 Sep 94	Sheffield
	WJ	13.23	Renaldo Nehemiah	USA	16 Aug 78	Zürich
	EJ,NJ	13.44	Colin Jackson		19 Jul 86	Athens
200m H	W,E	22.55	Laurant Ottoz	ITA	31 May 95	Milan
	C	22.59	Darryl Wohlsen	AUS	14 Mar 96	Brisbane
	A,N	22.63	Colin Jackson		1 Jun 91	Cardiff
	NJ	24.02	Paul Gray		13 Sep 87	London (CP)
400m H	W	46.78	Kevin Young	USA	6 Aug 92	Barcelona
	E	47.37	Stéphane Diagana	FRA	5 Jul 95	Lausanne
	C	47.10	Samuel Matete	ZAM	7 Aug 91	Zürich
	A	47.67	Kevin Young	USA	14 Aug 92	Sheffield
	N	47.82	Kriss Akabusi		6 Aug 92	Barcelona
	WJ	48.02	Danny Harris	USA	17 Jun 84	Los Angeles
	EJ	48.74	Vladimir Budko	RUS	18 Aug 84	Moscow
	NJ	50.22	Martin Briggs		28 Aug 83	Schwechat
High	W	2.45	Javier Sotomayor	CUB	27 Jul 93	Salamanca
Jump	E	2.42	Patrik Sjöberg	SWE	30 Jun 87	Stockholm
		2.42 i#	Carlo Thränhardt	GER	26 Feb 88	Berlin
	(C,N)	2.38 i#	Steve Smith	Eng	4 Feb 94	Wuppertal
	C	2.38	Troy Kemp	BAH	12 Jul 96	Nice
	A	2.41	Javier Sotomayor	CUB	15 Jul 94	London (CP)
	N,WJ,EJ,NJ	2.37	Steve Smith		20 Sep 92	Seoul
	N	2.37	Steve Smith		22 Aug 93	Stuttgart
	WJ,EJ	2.37	Dragutin Topic	YUG	12 Aug 90	Plovdiv
Pole	W,E	6.15 i#	Sergey Bubka	UKR	21 Feb 93	Donetsk
Vault		6.14 A	Sergey Bubka	UKR	31 Jul 94	Sestriere
	C	6.03	Okkert Brits	RSA	18 Aug 95	Cologne
	A	6.05	Sergey Bubka	UKR	10 Sep 93	London (CP)
	N	5.80	Nick Buckfield		27 May 98	Hania
	WJ,EJ	5.80	Maksim Tarasov	RUS	14 Jul 89	Bryansk
	NJ	5.50	Neil Winter		9 Aug 92	San Giuliano Teime

Event		Mark		Athlete	Country	Date			Place
Long	W	8.95		Mike Powell	USA	30	Aug	91	Tokyo
Jump	E	8.86	A	Robert Emmiyan	ARM	22	May	87	Tsakhkadzor
	C	8.62		James Beckford	JAM	5	Apr	97	Orlando
	A	8.54		Mike Powell	USA	10	Sep	93	London (CP)
	N	8.23		Lynn Davies		30	Jun	68	Berne
	WJ	8.34		Randy Williams	USA	8	Sep	72	Munich
	EJ	8.24		Volodymyr Ochkan	UKR	21	Jun	87	St. Petersburg
	NJ	7.98		Stewart Faulkner		6	Aug	88	Birmingham
Triple	W,E,C,N	18.29		Jonathan Edwards	Eng	7	Aug	95	Gothenburg
Jump	A	18.00		Jonathan Edwards		27	Aug	95	London (CP)
	WJ,EJ	17.50		Volker Mai	GER	23	Jun	85	Erfurt
	NJ	16.58		Tosi Fasinro		15	Jun	91	Espoo
Shot	W	23.12		Randy Barnes	USA	20	May	90	Los Angeles (Ww)
	E	23.06		Ulf Timmermann	GER	22	May	88	Hania
	C,N	21.68		Geoff Capes	Eng	18	May	80	Cwmbrân
	A	22.28	#	Brian Oldfield	USA	18	Jun	75	Edinburgh
		21.75		John Godina	USA	17	Aug	97	London (CP)
	WJ	21.05	i#	Terry Albritton	USA	22	Feb	74	New York
		20.65	#	Mike Carter	USA	4	Jul	79	Boston
		20.39	A	Janus Robberts	RSA	7	Mar	98	Germiston
	EJ	20.20		Udo Beyer	GER	6	Jul	74	Leipzig
	NJ	19.46		Carl Myerscough		6	Sep	98	Blackpool
Discus	W,E	74.08		Jürgen Schult	GER	6	Jun	86	Neubrandenburg
	C	67.88		Jason Tunks	CAN	14	May	98	Abilene
	A	68.32		John Powell	USA	30	Aug	82	London (CP)
	N	66.64		Perris Wilkins		6	Jun	98	Birmingham (Un)
	WJ	65.62	#	Werner Reiterer	AUS	15	Dec	87	Melbourne
	(WJ),EJ	63.64		Werner Hartmann	GER	25	Jun	78	Strasbourg
	NJ	60.97		Emeka Udechuku		5	Jul	98	Bedford
Hammer	W,E	86.74		Yuriy Sedykh	UKR/RUS	30	Aug	86	Stuttgart
	C	77.58		Sean Carlin	AUS	11	Feb	94	Adelaide
	A	85.60		Yuriy Sedykh	UKR/RUS	13	Jul	84	London (CP)
	N	77.54		Martin Girvan		12	May	84	Wolverhampton
	WJ,EJ	78.14		Roland Steuk	GER	30	Jun	78	Leipzig
	NJ	67.48		Paul Head		16	Sep	84	Karlovac
Javelin	W,E	98.48		Jan Zelezny	CZE	25	May	96	Jena
	C,N	91.46		Steve Backley	Eng	25	Jan	92	Auckland (NS)
	A	95.66		Jan Zelezny	CZE	29	Aug	93	Sheffield
	WJ,EJ	82.52		Harri Haatainen	FIN	25	May	96	Leppävirta
	NJ	79.50		Steve Backley		5	Jun	88	Derby
Pent.	W,A	4282		Bill Toomey	USA	16	Aug	69	London (CP)
	E	4273		Rein Aun	EST	18	Jul	68	Tartu
	C,N	3840		Barry King	Eng	20	May	70	Santa Barbara
	NJ	2970		Wayne Dubrose		2	Jun	74	London (Ha)
Dec.	W	8891		Dan O'Brien	USA	5	Sep	92	Talence
	E,C,N	8847		Daley Thompson	Eng	9	Aug	84	Los Angeles
	A	8663		Daley Thompson		28	Jul	86	Edinburgh
	WJ,EJ	8397		Torsten Voss	GER	7	Jul	82	Erfurt
	NJ	8082		Daley Thompson		31	Jul	77	Sittard
(1986 Javelin)									
	E,C,N	8811	#	Daley Thompson	Eng	28	Aug	86	Stuttgart
	WJ,EJ	8114	#	Michael Kohnle	GER	25	Aug	89	Varazdin
	NJ	7488	#	David Bigham		9	Aug	90	Plovdiv

4x100m	W	37.40	United States	8 Aug 92	Barcelona
		37.40	United States	21 Aug 93	Stuttgart
	E,N	37.77	UK National Team	22 Aug 93	Stuttgart
	C	37.69	Canada	3 Aug 96	Atlanta
	A	38.39	UK National Team	5 Aug 89	Gateshead
	WJ	39.00 A	United States	18 Jul 83	Colorado Springs
	(EJ),NJ	39.21	UK National Team	20 Sep 92	Seoul
	EJ	39.25	West Germany	28 Aug 83	Schwechat
4x200m	W	1:18.68	Santa Monica T.C. USA	17 Apr 94	Walnut
	E	1:21.10	Italy	29 Sep 83	Cagliari
	C	1:20.79	Jamaica	24 Apr 88	Walnut
	A,N	1:21.29	UK National Team	23 Jun 89	Birmingham
	NJ	1:25.40 i#	UK National Team	2 Mar 96	Liévin
		1:27.6	Borough of Enfield	13 Jun 82	London (He)
4x400m	W	2:54.20	United States	22 Jul 98	Uniondale
	E,N	2:56.60	UK National Team	3 Aug 96	Atlanta
	C	2:56.75	Jamaica	10 Aug 97	Athens
	A	2:59.85	UK National Team	19 Aug 96	Gateshead
	WJ	3:01.90	United States	20 Jul 86	Athens
	(EJ),NJ	3:03.80	UK National Team	12 Aug 90	Plovdiv
	EJ	3:04.58	East Germany	23 Aug 81	Utrecht
4x800m	WECAN	7:03.89	UK National Team Eng	30 Aug 82	London (CP)
	NJ	7:26.2	BMC Junior Squad	2 Sep 95	Oxford
4x1500m	W,E	14:38.8	West Germany	16 Aug 77	Cologne
	C	14:40.4	New Zealand	22 Aug 73	Oslo
	A	15:04.7	Italy	5 Jun 92	Sheffield
	N	14:56.8 a#	BMC National Squad	23 Jun 79	Bourges
		15:04.6	UK National Team	5 May 76	Athens (NF)
	NJ	15:52.0	BMC Junior Squad	30 Apr 97	Watford
4x1mile	W,E	15:49.08	Ireland	17 Aug 85	Dublin (B)
	C	15:59.57	New Zealand	1 Mar 83	Auckland
	A	16:21.1	BMC National Squad	10 Jul 93	Oxford
	N	16:17.4	Bristol A.C./Western Kentucky U	25 Apr 75	Des Moines
	NJ	16:56.8	BMC Junior Squad	10 Jul 93	Oxford

Track Walking

1500m	W,E	5:12.0	Algis Grigaliunas	LIT	12 May 90	Vilnius
	C	5:19.1	Dave Smith	AUS	7 Feb 83	Melbourne
	A,N	5:46.2 a	Roger Mills		29 Aug 75	London (CP)
	N	5:19.22 i#	Tim Berrett §		9 Feb 90	East Rutherford
1 Mile	W,E	5:36.9	Algis Grigaliunas	LIT	12 May 90	Vilnius
	C	5:54.6 i#	Marcel Jobin	CAN	16 Feb 80	Houston
	C,A,N	5:58.9 mx	Andy Penn	Eng	13 Aug 97	Rugby
	N	5:56.39 i#	Tim Berrett §		2 Feb 90	New York
	NJ	6:09.2	Phil Vesty		23 Jun 82	Leicester
3000m	W,E	10:47.11	Giovanni DeBenedictis	ITA	19 May 90	S. G. Valdarno
	C	10:56.22	Andrew Jachno	AUS	7 Feb 91	Melbourne
	A	11:19.00 i#	Axel Noack	GER	23 Feb 90	Glasgow
		11:19.9	Tim Berrett	CAN	20 Apr 92	Tonbridge
	N	11:24.4	Mark Easton		10 May 89	Tonbridge
	WJ,EJ	11:13.2	Jozef Pribilinec	SVK	28 Mar 79	Banská Bystrica
	NJ	11:54.23	Tim Berrett §		23 Jun 84	London (CP)

14

5000m	W	18:05.49		Hatem Ghoula	TUN	1 May 97	Tunis
	E	18:07.08	i#	Mikhail Shchennikov	RUS	14 Feb 95	Moscow
		18:17.22		Robert Korzeniowski	POL	3 Jul 92	Reims
	C	18:51.39		Nick A'Hern	AUS	21 Feb 98	Auckland (NS)
	A	18:56.27	i#	Axel Noack	GER	23 Feb 90	Glasgow
	A,N	19:35.0		Darrell Stone		16 May 89	Brighton
	WJ,EJ	19:19.3		Mikhail Shchennikov	RUS	9 Aug 86	Chemnitz
	NJ	20:16.40		Philip King		26 Jun 93	Lübeck
10km	W,E	38:02.60		Jozef Pribilinec	SVK	30 Aug 85	Banská Bystrica
	C	38:06.6		Dave Smith	AUS	25 Sep 86	Sydney
	A	39:26.02		Guillaume Leblanc	CAN	29 Jun 90	Gateshead
	N	40:06.65		Ian McCombie		4 Jun 89	Jarrow
	WJ,EJ	38:54.75		Ralf Kowalsky	GER	24 Jun 81	Cottbus
	NJ	41:52.13		Darrell Stone		7 Aug 87	Birmingham
(Road)	NJ	41:47		Darrell Stone		26 Sep 87	Paris
1 Hour	W	15,577 m		Bernardo Segura	MEX	7 May 94	Fana
	E	15,447 m		Jozef Pribilinec	SVK	6 Sep 86	Hildesheim
	C	15,300 m		Dave Smith	AUS	6 Sep 86	Hildesheim
	A	14,383 m		Anatoliy Solomin	UKR	26 Aug 77	Edinburgh
	N	14,324 m	#	Ian McCombie		7 Jul 85	London (SP)
		14,158 m		Mark Easton		12 Sep 87	Woodford
	NJ	13,487 m		Darrell Stone		12 Sep 87	Woodford
20km	W	1:17:25.6		Bernardo Segura	MEX	7 May 94	Fana
	E	1:18:35.2		Stefan Johansson	SWE	15 May 92	Fana
	C	1:20:12.3		Nick A'Hern	AUS	8 May 93	Fana
	A	1:24:07.6	#	Phil Vesty		1 Dec 84	Leicester
		1:24:22.0		José Marín	SPA	28 Jun 81	Brighton
	N	1:23:26.5		Ian McCombie		26 May 90	Fana
	WJ	1:22:16.0		Li Mingcai	CHN	3 Mar 90	Donetsk
	EJ	1:22:42		Andrey Perlov	RUS	6 Sep 80	Donetsk
	NJ	1:31:34.4		Gordon Vale		28 Jun 81	Brighton
2 Hours	W,E	29,572 m		Maurizio Damilano	ITA	4 Oct 92	Cuneo
	C	28,800 m	#	Guillaume Leblanc	CAN	16 Jun 90	Sept Iles
		27,123 m		Willi Sawall	AUS	24 May 80	Melbourne
	A,N	27,262 m	#	Chris Maddocks		31 Dec 89	Plymouth
	A	26,265 m		Jordi Llopart	SPA	28 Jun 81	Brighton
	N	26,037 m		Ron Wallwork		31 Jul 71	Blackburn
30km	W,E	2:01:44.1		Maurizio Damilano	ITA	4 Oct 92	Cuneo
	C	2:04:55.7		Guillaume Leblanc	CAN	16 Jun 90	Sept Iles
	A,N	2:11:54	#	Chris Maddocks		31 Dec 89	Plymouth
	A	2:17:26.4		Jordi Llopart	SPA	28 Jun 81	Brighton
	N	2:19:18		Chris Maddocks		22 Sep 84	Birmingham
50km	W,E	3:40:57.9		Thierry Toutain	FRA	29 Sep 96	Héricourt
	C	3:43:50.0		Simon Baker	AUS	9 Sep 90	Melbourne
	A	4:03:52		Gerhard Weidner	GER	1 Jun 75	Woodford
	N	4:05:44.6		Paul Blagg		26 May 90	Fana

Race Walking - Fastest Recorded Times

20km	W	1:17:25.6 t	Bernardo Segura	MEX	7 May 94	Fana
	E	1:18:13	Pavol Blazek	SVK	16 Sep 90	Hildesheim
	C	1:19:22	Dave Smith	AUS	19 Jul 87	Hobart
	A	1:21:42	José Marin	SPA	29 Sep 85	St. John's, IoM
	N	1:22:03	Ian McCombie		23 Sep 88	Seoul
	WJ	1:19:38	Yu Guohui	CHN	10 Mar 96	Zhuhai
	EJ	1:21:40	Ralf Kowalsky	GER	7 Aug 81	Jena
	NJ	1:26:13	Tim Berrett §		25 Feb 84	Dartford
30km	W,E	2:01:44.1 t	Maurizio Damilano	ITA	4 Oct 92	Cuneo
	C	2:04:55.7 t	Guillaume Leblanc	CAN	16 Jun 90	Sept Iles
	A	2:07:47	Simon Baker	AUS	31 Jul 86	Edinburgh
	N	2:07:56	Ian McCombie		27 Apr 86	Edinburgh
	NJ	2:30:46	Phil Vesty		31 Jul 82	London (VP)
50km	W,E	3:37:41	Andrey Perlov	RUS	5 Aug 89	St. Petersburg
	C	3:43:13	Simon Baker	AUS	28 May 89	L'Hospitalet
	A	3:47:31	Hartwig Gauder	GER	28 Sep 85	St. John's, IoM
	N	3:51:37	Chris Maddocks		28 Oct 90	Burrator
	WJ	4:00:04	Hao Huanquan	CHN	10 Apr 94	Beijing
	EJ	4:07:23	Aleksandr Volgin	RUS	27 Sep 86	Zhytomyr
	NJ	4:18:18	Gordon Vale		24 Oct 81	Lassing

RECORDS set in 1998

200m	NJ	20.44	Christian Malcolm		1 Aug 98	Annecy
	EJ,NJ	20.29	Christian Malcolm		19 Sep 98	Kuala Lumpur
300m	E,C,A,N	31.56	Doug Walker	Sco	19 Jul 98	Gateshead
1500m	W	3:26.00	Hicham El Guerrouj	MAR	14 Jul 98	Rome
	WJ	3:33.24	William Chirchir	KEN	12 Aug 98	Zürich
2000m	A	4:52.86 i#	Haille Gebreselassie	ETH	15 Feb 98	Birmingham
	C	4:51.30	Daniel Komen	KEN	5 Jun 98	Milan
	A	4:48.36	Hicham El Guerrouj	MAR	19 Jul 98	Gateshead
	C	4:48.74	John Kibowen	KEN	1 Aug 98	Hechtel
3000m	E	7:29.34	Isaac Viciosa	SPA	9 Jul 98	Oslo
5000m	W	12:39.36	Haile Gebrselassie	ETH	13 Jun 98	Helsinki
10000m	W	26:22.75	Haile Gebrselassie	ETH	1 Jun 98	Hengelo
	N	27:18.14	Jon Brown		28 Aug 98	Brussels
H. Mar	W,E	59:43	António Pinto	POR	15 Mar 98	Lisbon
	W,C	59:17	Paul Tergat	KEN	4 Apr 98	Milan
Mar	W	2:06:05	Ronaldo da Costa	BRA	20 Sep 98	Berlin
	C	2:06:54	Ondoro Osoro	KEN	11 Oct 98	Chicago
PV	N	5.80	Nick Buckfield		27 May 98	Hania
SP	NJ	18.31 i#	Carl Myerscough		8 Feb 98	Birmingham
	WJ	20.39 A	Janus Robberts	RSA	7 Mar 98	Germiston
	NJ	18.11	Carl Myerscough		13 Jun 98	Mannheim
	NJ	18.50	Carl Myerscough		13 Jun 98	Mannheim
	NJ	19.24	Carl Myerscough		4 Jul 98	Bedford
	NJ	19.46	Carl Myerscough		6 Sep 98	Blackpool
DT	NJ	58.52	Carl Myerscough		4 Apr 98	San Diego
	C	67.88	Jason Tunks	CAN	14 May 98	Abilene
	NJ	60.21	Emeka Udechuku		16 May 98	Enfield
	N	66.64	Perris Wilkins		6 Jun 98	Birmingham (Un)
	NJ	60.52	Emeka Udechuku		5 Jul 98	Bedford
	NJ	60.97	Emeka Udechuku		5 Jul 98	Bedford

Relays

4x400m	W	2:54.20	United States		22 Jul 98	Uniondale

Track Walking

5000 m	C	18:51.39 #	Nick A'Hern	AUS	21 Feb 98	Auckland (NS)

BEST AUTHENTIC PERFORMANCES (WOMEN)

(as at 31st December 1998)

100m	W	10.49	Florence Griffith Joyner	USA	16	Jul	88	Indianapolis
	E	10.73	Christine Arron	FRA	19	Aug	98	Budapest
	C	10.74	Merlene Ottey	JAM	7	Sep	96	Milan
	A	11.02	Merlene Ottey	JAM	14	Jul	89	London (CP)
	N	11.10	Kathy Smallwood/Cook		5	Sep	81	Rome
	WJ,EJ	10.88 #	Marlies Oelsner/Göhr	GER	1	Jul	77	Dresden
		10.89	Kathrin Krabbe	GER	20	Jul	88	Berlin
	NJ	11.27 A	Kathy Smallwood/Cook		9	Sep	79	Mexico City
200m	W	21.34	Florence Griffith Joyner	USA	29	Sep	88	Seoul
	E	21.71	Marita Koch	GER	10	Jun	79	Chemnitz
		21.71 #	Marita Koch	GER	21	Jul	84	Potsdam
		21.71	Heike Drechsler	GER	29	Jun	86	Jena
		21.71 #	Heike Drechsler	GER	29	Aug	86	Stuttgart
	C	21.64	Merlene Ottey	JAM	13	Sep	91	Brussels
	A	22.23	Merlene Ottey	JAM	9	Sep	94	London (CP)
	N	22.10	Kathy Cook		9	Aug	84	Los Angeles
	WJ,EJ	22.19	Natalya Bochina	RUS	30	Jul	80	Moscow
	NJ	22.70 A	Kathy Smallwood/Cook		12	Sep	79	Mexico City
300m	W,E	35.00	Marie-José Pérec	FRA	27	Aug	91	Tokyo
		34.1	Marita Koch	GER	6	Oct	85	Canberra
	C,A,N	35.46	Kathy Cook	Eng	18	Aug	84	London (CP)
	A	35.46	Chandra Cheeseborough	USA	18	Aug	84	London (CP)
	WJ,EJ	36.24	Grit Breuer	GER	29	Aug	90	Split
	WJ,EJ,NJ	36.2	Donna Murray/Hartley		7	Aug	74	London (CP)
	NJ	36.46	Linsey Macdonald		13	Jul	80	London (CP)
400m	W,E	47.60	Marita Koch	GER	6	Oct	85	Canberra
	C	48.63	Cathy Freeman	AUS	29	Jul	96	Atlanta
	A	49.33	Tatjána Kocembová	CZE	20	Aug	83	London (CP)
	N	49.43	Kathy Cook		6	Aug	84	Los Angeles
	WJ,EJ	49.42	Grit Breuer	GER	27	Aug	91	Tokyo
	NJ	51.16	Linsey Macdonald		15	Jun	80	London (CP)
600m	W	1:22.63	Anna Fidelia Quirot	CUB	25	Jul	97	Guadalajara
	E	1:23.5	Doina Melinte	ROM	27	Jul	86	Poiana Brasov
	C	1:26.0	Charlene Rendina	AUS	12	Mar	79	Adelaide
	C,N	1:26.0	Kelly Holmes	Eng	13	Aug	95	Gothenburg
	A	1:25.90	Delisa Walton-Floyd	USA	28	Aug	88	London (CP)
	NJ	1:27.33	Lorraine Baker		13	Jul	80	London (CP)
800m	W,E	1:53.28	Jarmila Kratochvílová	CZE	26	Jul	83	Munich
	C	1:55.29	Maria Lurdes Mutola	MOZ	24	Aug	97	Cologne
	A	1:57.14	Jarmila Kratochvílová	CZE	24	Jun	85	Belfast
	N	1:56.21	Kelly Holmes		9	Sep	95	Monaco
	WJ	1:57.18	Wang Yuan	CHN	8	Sep	93	Beijing
	EJ	1:57.45 #	Hildegard Ullrich	GER	31	Aug	78	Prague
		1:59.17	Birte Bruhns	GER	20	Jul	88	Berlin
	NJ	2:01.11	Lynne MacDougall		18	Aug	84	London (CP)
1000m	W,E	2:28.98	Svetlana Masterkova	RUS	23	Aug	96	Brussels
	C	2:29.66	Maria Lurdes Mutola	MOZ	23	Aug	96	Brussels
	A	2:32.08 i#	Maria Lurdes Mutola	MOZ	10	Feb	96	Birmingham
	A,N	2:32.55	Kelly Holmes		15	Jun	97	Leeds
	WJ,EJ	2:35.4 a	Irina Nikitina	RUS	5	Aug	79	Podolsk
		2:35.4	Kathrin Wühn	GER	12	Jul	84	Potsadam
	NJ	2:38.58	Jo White		9	Sep	77	London (CP)

Event	Cat	Time	Name	Nat	Date	Place
1500m	W	3:50.46	Qu Yunxia	CHN	11 Sep 93	Beijing
	E	3:52.47	Tatyana Kazankina	RUS	13 Aug 80	Zürich
	C	3:57.41	Jackline Maranga	KEN	8 Aug 98	Monaco
	A,N	3:58.07	Kelly Holmes		29 Jun 97	Sheffield
	WJ	3:51.34	Lang Yinglai	CHN	18 Oct 97	Shanghai
	(EJ),NJ	3:59.96	Zola Budd/Pieterse		30 Aug 85	Brussels
	EJ	4:03.45	Anita Weyerman	SWZ	3 Jul 96	Lausanne
1 Mile	W,E	4:12.56	Svetlana Masterkova	RUS	14 Aug 96	Zürich
	C,N,WJ,EJ,NJ	4:17.57	Zola Budd/Pieterse	Eng	21 Aug 85	Zürich
	A	4:19.59	Mary Slaney	USA	2 Aug 85	London (CP)
2000m	W,E,A	5:25.36	Sonia O'Sullivan	IRE	8 Jul 94	Edinburgh
	C,N	5:26.93	Yvonne Murray	Sco	8 Jul 94	Edinburgh
	WJ,EJ,NJ	5:33.15	Zola Budd/Pieterse		13 Jul 84	London (CP)
3000m	W	8:06.11	Wang Junxia	CHN	13 Sep 93	Beijing
	E,A	8:21.64	Sonia O'Sullivan	IRE	15 Jul 94	London (CP)
	C,N,NJ	8:28.83	Zola Budd/Pieterse	Eng	7 Sep 85	Rome
	WJ,EJ	8:28.83 #	Zola Budd/Pieterse		7 Sep 85	Rome
	WJ	8:36.45	Ma Ningning	CHN	6 Jun 93	Jinan
	EJ	8:40.08	Gabriela Szabo	ROM	10 Aug 94	Helsinki
5000m	W	14:28.09	Jiang Bo	CHN	23 Oct 97	Shanghai
	E	14:31.48	Gabriela Szabo	ROM	1 Sep 98	Berlin
	C	14:44.05	Elana Meyer	RSA	22 Jul 95	Hechtel
	A	14:47.64	Sonia O'Sullivan	IRE	7 Jul 95	London (CP)
	N	14:45.51	Paula Radcliffe		22 Aug 97	Brussels
	WJ	14:39.96 #	Yin Linli	CHN	23 Oct 97	Shanghai
		14:45.90	Jiang Bo	CHN	24 Oct 95	Nanjing
	(EJ),NJ	14:48.07	Zola Budd/Pieterse		26 Aug 85	London (CP)
	EJ	14:56.22	Annemari Sandell	FIN	8 Jul 96	Stockholm
10000m	W	29:31.78	Wang Junxia	CHN	8 Sep 93	Beijing
	E	30:13.74	Ingrid Kristiansen	NOR	5 Jul 86	Oslo
	C,N	30:48.58	Paula Radcliffe	Eng	4 Apr 98	Lisbon
	A	30:52.51	Elana Meyer	RSA	10 Sep 94	London (CP)
	WJ	30:39.41	Lan Lixin	CHN	19 Oct 97	Shanghai
	EJ	31:40.42	Annemari Sandell	FIN	27 Jul 96	Atlanta
	NJ	34:31.41 #	Tanya Povey		3 Jun 98	Amherst
1 Hour	W,C	18,340 m	Tegla Loroupe	KEN	7 Aug 98	Borgholzhausen
	E	18,084 m	Silvana Cruciata	ITA	4 May 81	Rome
	A,N	16,460 m i#	Bronwen Cardy-Wise		8 Mar 92	Birmingham
		16,364 m	Alison Fletcher		3 Sep 97	Bromley
	NJ	14,580 m	Paula Simpson		20 Oct 93	Bebington
20km	W	1:06:48.8	Izumi Maki	JAP	19 Sep 93	Amagasaki
	E	1:06:55.5 #	Rosa Mota	POR	14 May 83	Lisbon
	C,A,N	1:15:46	Caroline Hunter-Rowe	Eng	6 Mar 94	Barry
25km	W,E	1:29:29.2	Karolina Szabó	HUN	22 Apr 88	Budapest
	C,A,N	1:35:16	Caroline Hunter-Rowe	Eng	6 Mar 94	Barry
30km	W,E	1:47:05.6	Karolina Szabó	HUN	22 Apr 88	Budapest
	C,A,N	1:55:03	Caroline Hunter-Rowe	Eng	6 Mar 94	Barry
Half Marathon	W,E	66:40 #	Ingrid Kristiansen	NOR	5 Apr 87	Sandnes
	W	66:43	Masako Chiba	JAP	19 Jan 97	Tokyo
	E,C,N	67:11	Liz McColgan	Sco	26 Jan 92	Tokyo
	A	68:42	Liz McColgan		11 Oct 92	Dundee
	WJ	69:05	Delillah Asiago	KEN	5 May 91	Exeter
	NJ	77:52	Kathy Williams		28 Mar 82	Barry
Marathon	W,C	2:20:47	Tegla Loroupe	KEN	19 Apr 98	Rotterdam
	E,A	2:21:06	Ingrid Kristiansen	NOR	21 Apr 85	London
	N	2:25:56	Véronique Marot		23 Apr 89	London
	WJ	2:27:30	Ai Dongmei	CHN	4 Oct 97	Beijing
	NJ	2:50:09	Siobhan Quenby		16 Oct 83	Milan

2km St	W,E	6:11.84	Marina Pluzhnikova	RUS	25	Jul	94	St. Petersburg
(3'0")	C	6:30.8	Mary Fien	AUS	4	Dec	96	Sydney
	A,N	6:53.7 (2'6")	Sharon Dixon		8	May	94	Horsham
		7:04.7 mx#	Sally Young		14	Jul	93	Sutton
		7:05.76	Veronica Boden		17	Jul	94	Bedford
	WJ,EJ	6:31.31	Yelena Sayko	UKR	13	Jul	97	Kiev
	(WJ)	6:31.04 mx#	Mellisa Rollison	AUS	27	Nov	98	Brisbane
	NJ	7:27.99	Lois Joslin		2	May	98	Bath
3km St	W,E	9:57.62	Svetlana Rogova	RUS	19	Jul	98	Uniondale
(3'0")	C	10:18.28	Karen Harvey	CAN	19	Jul	98	Uniondale
	A,N	10:52.6(2'6")	Tanya Blake		22	Aug	93	Horsham
	NJ	12:11.1(2'6")	Lindsey Oliver		22	Aug	93	Horsham
100m H	W,E	12.21	Yordanka Donkova	BUL	20	Aug	88	Stara Zagora
	C	12.52	Michelle Freeman	JAM	10	Aug	97	Athens
		12.52	Michelle Freeman	JAM	12	Aug	98	Zürich
	A	12.51	Ginka Zagorcheva	BUL	12	Sep	86	London (CP)
	N	12.80	Angie Thorp		31	Jul	96	Atlanta
	WJ	12.84	Aliuska López	CUB	16	Jul	87	Zagreb
	EJ	12.88	Yelena Ovcharova	UKR	25	Jun	95	Villeneuve d'Ascq
	NJ	13.25	Diane Allahgreen		21	Jul	94	Lisbon
400m H	W	52.61	Kim Batten	USA	11	Aug	95	Gothenburg
	E,C,N	52.74	Sally Gunnell	Eng	19	Aug	93	Stuttgart
	A	53.69	Sandra Farmer-Patrick	USA	10	Sep	93	London (CP)
	WJ	54.93 #	Li Rui	CHN	22	Oct	97	Shanghai
		55.20	Leslie Maxie	USA	9	Jun	84	San Jose
	EJ	55.26	Ionela Tirlea	ROM	12	Jul	95	Nice
	NJ	57.27	Vicki Jamison		28	Jul	96	Bedford
High	W,E	2.09	Stefka Kostadinova	BUL	30	Aug	87	Rome
Jump	C	1.99 i#	Debbie Brill	CAN	23	Jan	82	Edmonton
		1.98	Debbie Brill	CAN	2	Sep	84	Rieti
		1.98	Vanessa Ward	AUS	12	Feb	89	Perth
		1.98	Alison Inverarity	AUS	17	Jul	94	Ingolstadt
	A	2.03	Ulrike Meyfarth	GER	21	Aug	83	London (CP)
		2.03	Tamara Bykova	RUS	21	Aug	83	London (CP)
	N	1.95	Diana Elliott/Davies		26	Jun	82	Oslo
		1.95 i#	Debbie Marti		23	Feb	97	Birmingham
	WJ,EJ	2.01 #	Olga Turchak	KZK	7	Jul	86	Moscow
		2.01	Heike Balck	GER	18	Jun	89	Chemnitz
	NJ	1.91	Lea Haggett		2	Jun	91	Hania
		1.91	Susan Jones		31	Aug	97	Catania
Pole	W,C	4.59	Emma George	AUS	21	Mar	98	Brisbane
Vault	E	4.51	Daniela Bártová	CZE	9	Jun	98	Bratislava
	A,N	4.31	Janine Whitlock		30	May	98	Bedford
	WJ,EJ	4.31	Monika Götz	GER	9	May	98	Troisdorf
		4.31	Yvonne Buschbaum	GER	21	Aug	98	Budapest
	NJ	3.75 &	Tracy Bloomfield		9	Aug	98	London (He)
		3.72	Tracy Bloomfield		24	May	98	London (Ha)
Long	W,E	7.52	Galina Chistyakova	RUS	11	Jun	88	St. Petersburg
Jump	C,N,NJ	6.90	Beverly Kinch	Eng	14	Aug	83	Helsinki
	A	7.14	Galina Chistyakova	RUS	24	Jun	89	Birmingham
	WJ,EJ	7.14 #	Heike Daute/Drechsler	GER	4	Jun	83	Bratislava
		6.98	Heike Daute/Drechsler	GER	18	Aug	82	Potsdam
Triple	W,E	15.50	Inessa Kravets	UKR	10	Aug	95	Gothenburg
Jump	C,N	15.16 i#	Ashia Hansen	Eng	28	Feb	98	Valencia
		15.15	Ashia Hansen	Eng	13	Sep	97	Fukuoka
	A	14.94	Ashia Hansen		29	Jun	97	Sheffield
	WJ,EJ	14.62	Tereza Marinova	BUL	25	Aug	96	Sydney
	NJ	13.05	Michelle Griffith		16	Jun	90	London (CP)

Event	Cat	Mark	Name	Nat	Date	Venue
Shot	W,E	22.63	Natalya Lisovskaya	RUS	7 Jun 87	Moscow
	C	19.74	Gael Mulhall/Martin	AUS	14 Jul 84	Berkeley
	A	21.95	Natalya Lisovskaya	RUS	29 Jul 88	Edinburgh
	N	19.36	Judy Oakes		14 Aug 88	Gateshead
	WJ,EJ	20.54	Astrid Kumbernuss	GER	1 Jul 89	Orimattila
	NJ	17.10	Myrtle Augee		16 Jun 84	London (CP)
Discus	W,E	76.80	Gabriele Reinsch	GER	9 Jul 88	Neubrandenburg
	C	68.72	Daniele Costian	AUS	22 Jan 94	Auckland
	A	73.04	Ilke Wyludda	GER	5 Aug 89	Gateshead
	N	67.48	Meg Ritchie		26 Apr 81	Walnut
	WJ,EJ	74.40	Ilke Wyludda	GER	13 Sep 88	Berlin
	NJ	54.78	Lynda Whiteley/Wright		4 Oct 82	Brisbane
Hammer	W,E	73.80 #	Olga Kuzenkova	RUS	15 May 98	Tolyatti
		73.14	Mihaela Melinte	ROM	16 Jul 98	Poiana Brasov
	C	67.16	Debbie Sosimenko	AUS	10 Aug 98	Sydney
	A	65.24	Debbie Sosimenko	AUS	15 Jul 95	Birmingham
	N	64.90	Lorraine Shaw		10 Jun 95	Bedford
	WJ,EJ	65.48	Mihaela Melinte	ROM	25 Feb 94	Bucharest
	NJ	57.97	Rachael Beverley		25 Jul 98	Birmingham
Javelin	W,E	80.00	Petra Felke	GER	9 Sep 88	Potsdam
	C,N	77.44	Fatima Whitbread	Eng	28 Aug 86	Stuttgart
	A	75.62	Fatima Whitbread		25 May 87	Derby
	WJ,EJ	71.88	Antoaneta Todorova	BUL	15 Aug 81	Zagreb
	NJ	60.14	Fatima Whitbread		7 May 80	Thurrock
Hept.	W	7291	Jackie Joyner-Kersee	USA	24 Sep 88	Seoul
	E	7007	Larisa Nikitina	RUS	11 Jun 89	Bryansk
	C,N	6736	Denise Lewis	Eng	1 Jun 97	Götzis
	A	6419	Birgit Clarius	GER	21 Jul 91	Sheffield
	WJ,EJ	6465	Sybille Thiele	GER	28 Aug 83	Schwechat
	NJ	5833	Joanne Mulliner		11 Aug 85	Lons-le-Saunier
4x100m	W,E	41.37	East Germany		6 Oct 85	Canberra
	C	41.94	Jamaica		1 Sep 91	Tokyo
		41.94	Jamaica		22 Aug 93	Stuttgart
	A	41.87	East Germany		5 Aug 89	Gateshead
	N	42.43	UK National Team		1 Aug 80	Moscow
	WJ,EJ	43.33 #	East Germany		20 Jul 88	Berlin
		43.48	East Germany		31 Jul 88	Sudbury
	NJ	44.16	UK National Team		12 Aug 90	Plovdiv
4x200m	W,E	1:28.15	East Germany		9 Aug 80	Jena
	C,N	1:31.57	UK National Team	Eng	20 Aug 77	London (CP)
	A	1:31.49	Russia		5 Jun 93	Portsmouth
	NJ	1:38.34 i#	UK National Team		19 Aug 72	Bracknell
		1:42.2	London Olympiades AC		19 Aug 72	Bracknell
4x400m	W,E	3:15.17	U.S.S.R.		1 Oct 88	Seoul
	C	3:21.21 #	Canada		11 Aug 84	Los Angeles
		3:21.30	Jamaica		10 Aug 97	Athens
	A	3:20.79	Czechoslovakia		21 Aug 83	London (CP)
	N	3:22.01	UK National Team		1 Sep 91	Tokyo
	WJ,EJ	3:28.39	East Germany		31 Jul 88	Sudbury
	NJ	3:35.10	UK National Team		25 Aug 85	Cottbus
4x800m	W,E	7:50.17	U.S.S.R.		5 Aug 84	Moscow
	C	8:20.73	UK National Team	Eng	5 Jun 93	Portsmouth
	A	7:57.08	Russia		5 Jun 93	Portsmouth
	N	8:19.9	UK National Team		5 Jun 92	Sheffield
	NJ	8:39.6	BMC Junior Squad		17 Jul 96	Watford

4x1500m	W	17:18.10	#	Villanova Univ	USA/IRE	27	Apr	90	Philadelphia
	W,E	17:22.30		Providence Univ	IRE	26	Apr	91	Philadelphia
	C,A,N	17:41.0		BMC National Squad	Eng	30	Apr	97	Watford
	NJ	18:38.0		BMC Junior Squad		30	Apr	97	Watford
4x1Mile	WECAN	19:17.3		BMC National Squad	Eng	10	Jul	93	Oxford
	NJ	20:16.2		BMC Junior Squad		11	Jun	97	Watford

Track Walking

1500m	W,C	5:50.51		Kerry Saxby-Junna	AUS	20	Jan	91	Sydney
	E	5:53.0		Sada Eidikyte	LIT	12	May	90	Vilnius
	A	6:04.5	i#	Beate Anders/Gummelt	GER	4	Mar	90	Glasgow
	A,N,NJ	6:58.5	i#	Carol Tyson		5	Sep	76	Gateshead
1 Mile	W, E	6:16.72	i#	Sada Eidikyte	LIT	12	May	90	Vilnius
		6:19.31		Ileana Salvador	ITA	15	Jun	91	Siderno
	C	6:47.9		Sue Cook	AUS	14	Mar	81	Canberra
	A	6:30.7	i#	Beate Anders/Gummelt	GER	4	Mar	90	Glasgow
	A,N	7:14.3		Carol Tyson		17	Sep	77	London (PH)
	NJ	7:31.6		Kate Horwill		22	Aug	93	Solihull
3000m	W,E	11:44.00	i#	Alina Ivanova	RUS	7	Feb	92	Moscow
		11:48.24		Ileana Salvador	ITA	29	Aug	93	Padua
	C	11:51.26		Kerry Saxby-Junna	AUS	7	Feb	91	Melbourne
	A	12:32.37		Yelena Nikolayeva	RUS	19	Jun	88	Portsmouth
	N	12:49.16		Betty Sworowski		28	Jul	90	Wrexham
	WJ,EJ	12:21.7	i#	Susana Feitór	POR	19	Feb	94	Braga
		12:24.47		Claudia Iovan	ROM	24	Jul	97	Ljubljana
	NJ	13:03.4		Vicky Lupton		18	May	91	Sheffield
5000m	W,C	20:03.0	#	Kerry Saxby-Junna	AUS	11	Feb	96	Sydney
		20:13.26		Kerry Saxby-Junna	AUS	25	Feb	96	Hobart
	E	20:07.52	#	Beate Anders/Gummelt	GER	23	Jun	90	Rostock
		20:21.69		Annarita Sidoti	ITA	1	Jul	95	Cesenatico
	A	21:08.65		Yelena Nikolayeva	RUS	19	Jun	88	Portsmouth
	N	21:52.4	#	Vicky Lupton		9	Aug	95	Sheffield (?)
		22:01.53		Lisa Kehler		26	Jul	98	Birmingham
	WJ,EJ	20:31.4		Irina Stankina	RUS	10	Feb	96	Adler
	NJ	22:36.81		Vicky Lupton		15	Jun	91	Espoo
(Road)	N	21:36		Vicky Lupton		18	Jul	92	Sheffield
10km	W,E	41:56.23		Nadezhda Ryashkina	RUS	24	Jul	90	Seattle
	C	41:57.22		Kerry Saxby-Junna	AUS	24	Jul	90	Seattle
	A,N	45:18.8		Vicky Lupton		2	Sep	95	Watford
	WJ	42:49.7		Gao Hongmiao	CHN	15	Mar	92	Jinan
	EJ	44:51.67		Claudia Iovan	ROM	14	Jun	96	Bucharest
	NJ	47:04		Vicky Lupton		30	Mar	91	Sheffield (W)
1 Hour	W	13,194 m		Victoria Herazo	USA	5	Dec	92	Santa Monica
	E	12,644 m		Giuliana Salce	ITA	25	Apr	86	Ostia
	C	12,805 m		Wendy Muldoon	AUS	25	Jun	94	Melbourne
	A,N,NJ	11,590 m		Lisa Langford/Kehler		13	Sep	86	Woodford
20km	W,E	1:35:29.5		Monica Gunnarsson	SWE	10	Jul	91	Borås
	C	1:39:54.2		Linn Murphy	NZ	21	Nov	93	Auckland
	A,N	1:56:59.7		Cath Reader		21	Oct	95	Loughborough
2 Hours	W,C	22,747 m		Carolyn Vanstan	AUS	20	Jun	92	Melbourne
	E	22,239 m		Jana Zarubova	CZE	12	Oct	85	Prague
	A,N	20,502 m		Cath Reader		21	Oct	95	Loughborough
30km	W,E	2:56:36.0		Cinzia Chianda	ITA	18	Oct	86	Limbiate
50km	W,E	5:13:49.8		Zofia Turosz	POL	13	Oct	85	Warsaw
	C,N	5:26:59		Sandra Brown	Eng	27	Oct	90	Etrechy

Road Walking - Fastest Recorded Times

10km	W,E	41:04	Yelena Nikolayeva	RUS	20 Apr 96	Sochi
	C	41:30	Kerry Saxby-Junna	AUS	27 Aug 88	Canberra
	A	44:04	Sari Essayah	FIN	23 Jul 91	Sheffield
	N	45:03	Lisa Kehler		19 Sep 98	Kuala Lumpur
	WJ,EJ	41:55	Irina Stankina	RUS	11 Feb 95	Adler
	NJ	47:04 t	Vicky Lupton		30 Mar 91	Sheffield (W)
20km	W	1:27:30	Liu Hongyu	CHN	1 May 95	Beijing
	E	1:28:13	Erica Alfridi	ITA	9 Mar 97	Cassino
	C	1:29:40	Kerry Saxby-Junna	AUS	13 May 88	Värnamo
	A,N	1:40:45	Irene Bateman		9 Apr 83	Basildon
	WJ	1:29:26	Wang Liping	CHN	1 May 95	Beijing
	EJ	1:34:31	Tatyana Titova	RUS	4 Oct 87	Alushta
	NJ	1:52:03	Vicky Lupton		13 Oct 91	Sheffield
50km	WECAN	4:50:51	Sandra Brown	Eng	13 Jul 91	Basildon

RECORDS set in 1998

100m	E	10.73		Christine Arron	FRA	19 Aug 98	Budapest
1500m	C	3:57.41		Jackline Maranga	KEN	9 Aug 98	Monaco
5000m	E	14:31.48		Gabriela Szabo	ROM	1 Sep 98	Berlin
10000m	C,N	30:48.58		Paula Radcliffe	Eng	4 Apr 98	Lisbon
	NJ	35:07.62	#	Tanya Povey		22 May 98	Gainesville
	NJ	34:31.41	#	Tanya Povey		3 Jun 98	Amherst
1 Hour	W,C	18,340 m		Tegla Loroupe	KEN	7 Aug 98	Borgholzhausen
Mar	W,C	2:20:47		Tegla Loroupe	KEN	19 Apr 98	Rotterdam
2kSt	NJ	7:27.99	#	Lois Joslin		2 May 98	Bath
3kSt	W,C	10:19.6		Karen Harvey	CAN	16 Apr 98	Walnut
	W,E	9:57.62		Svetlana Rogova	RUS	19 Jul 98	Uniondale
	C	10:18.28		Karen Harvey	CAN	19 Jul 98	Uniondale
100mH	C	12.52		Michelle Freeman	JAM	12 Aug 98	Zürich
PV	E	4.41	i#	Daniela Bártová	CZE	4 Feb 98	Erfurt
	E	4.42	i#	Vala Flosadóttir	ISL	6 Feb 98	Bielefeld
	E	4.43	i#	Daniela Bártová	CZE	14 Feb 98	Prague
	E	4.44	i#	Vala Flosadóttir	ISL	14 Feb 98	Eskilstuna
	WJ,EJ	4.20	i#	Monika Götz	GER	15 Feb 98	Sindelfingen
	W,C	4.57		Emma George	AUS	21 Feb 98	Auckland (NS)
	N	4.25	i#	Janine Whitlock		1 Mar 98	Valencia
	E	4.45	i#	Anzhela Balakhonova	UKR	1 Mar 98	Valencia
	E	4.46	i#	Daniela Bártová	CZE	6 Mar 98	Berlin
	N	4.28	i#	Janine Whitlock		8 Mar 98	Sindelfingen
	E	4.48	i#	Daniela Bártová	CZE	8 Mar 98	Sindelfingen
	W,C	4.58		Emma George	AUS	14 Mar 98	Melbourne
	W,C	4.59		Emma George	AUS	21 Mar 98	Brisbane
	WJ,EJ	4.22		Monika Götz	GER	9 May 98	Troisdorf
	WJ,EJ	4.31		Monika Götz	GER	9 May 98	Troisdorf
	E	4.37		Anzhela Balakhonova	UKR	16 May 98	Kiev
	N	4.25		Janine Whitlock		17 May 98	Loughborough
	NJ	3.72		Tracey Bloomfield		24 May 98	London (Ha)
	N	4.30		Janine Whitlock		27 May 98	Cottbus
	E	4.40		Daniela Bártová	CZE	27 May 98	Cottbus
	E	4.50		Daniela Bártová	CZE	27 May 98	Cottbus
	A,N	4.31		Janine Whitlock		30 May 98	Bedford
	E	4.51		Daniela Bártová	CZE	9 Jun 98	Bratislava
	NJ	3.75	&	Tracey Bloomfield		9 Aug 98	London (He)
	WJ,EJ	4.31		Yvonne Buschbaum	GER	21 Aug 98	Budapest
TJ	C,N	15.16	i#	Ashia Hansen	Eng	28 Feb 98	Valencia
HT	C	66.71		Debbie Sosimenko	AUS	14 Mar 98	Melbourne
	W, E	73.80	#	Olga Kuzenkova	RUS	15 May 98	Tolyatti
	W, E	73.14		Mihaela Melinte	ROM	16 Jun 98	Poiana Brasov
	NJ	57.97		Rachael Beverley		25 Jul 98	Birmingham
	C	67.16		Debbie Sosimenko	AUS	10 Aug 98	Sydney
5000mWT	N	22:01.53		Lisa Kehler		26 Jul 98	Birmingham
10kmWR	N	45:18		Lisa Kehler		15 May 98	Rotterdam
	N	45:03		Lisa Kehler		19 Sep 98	Kuala Lumpur

22

NATIONAL RECORDS OF THE UNITED KINGDOM (MEN)

(as at 31st December 1998)

These are the best authentic performances for the four home countries of the U.K.
E = England S = Scotland W = Wales NI = Northern Ireland

100m	E	9.87		Linford Christie	15 Aug 93	Stuttgart, GER
	S	10.11		Allan Wells	24 Jul 80	Moscow, RUS
	W	10.12		Christian Malcolm	29 Jul 98	Annecy, FRA
	NI	10.46		Mark Forsythe	17 Jun 89	Tel Aviv, ISR
200m	E	19.87	A&	John Regis	31 Jul 94	Sestriere, ITA
		19.94		John Regis	20 Aug 93	Stuttgart, GER
	S	20.21		Allan Wells	28 Jul 80	Moscow, RUS
	W	20.29		Christian Malcolm	19 Sep 98	Kuala Lumpur, MAL
	NI	20.81		Paul McBurney	24 Aug 94	Victoria, CAN
300m	S	31.56		Dougie Walker	19 Jul 98	Gateshead
	E	31.67		John Regis	17 Jul 92	Gateshead
	W	32.06		Jamie Baulch	31 May 97	Cardiff
	NI	33.77		Simon Baird	24 Jun 85	Belfast
400m	W	44.36		Iwan Thomas	13 Jul 97	Birmingham
	E	44.37		Roger Black	3 Jul 96	Lausanne, SWZ
		44.37		Mark Richardson	9 Jul 98	Oslo, Nor
		44.37		Mark Richardson	8 Aug 98	Monaco, MON
	S	44.93		David Jenkins	21 Jun 75	Eugene, USA
	NI	45.85		Paul McBurney	13 Jul 97	Birmingham
600m	E	1:14.95		Steve Heard	14 Jul 91	London (Ha)
	S	1:15.4		Tom McKean	21 Jul 91	Grangemouth
	W	1:17.8	i	Bob Adams	20 Dec 69	Cosford
		1:18.02		Glen Grant	2 Aug 78	Edmonton, CAN
	NI	1:18.3	i	Joe Chivers	14 Dec 74	Cosford
		1:20.1		Kenneth Thompson	24 May 80	Belfast
800m	E	1:41.73	"	Sebastian Coe	10 Jun 81	Florence, ITA
	S	1:43.88		Tom McKean	28 Jul 89	London (CP)
	W	1:45.44		Neil Horsfield	28 Jul 90	Wrexham
	NI	1:46.94		Mark Kirk	20 Jul 87	Belfast
1000m	E	2:12.18		Sebastian Coe	11 Jul 81	Oslo, NOR
	S	2:16.82		Graham Williamson	17 Jul 84	Edinburgh
	W	2:17.36		Neil Horsfield	9 Aug 91	Gateshead
	NI	2:19.05		Mark Kirk	5 Aug 87	Oslo, NOR
1500m	E	3:29.67		Steve Cram	16 Jul 85	Nice, FRA
	S	3:33.83		John Robson	4 Sep 79	Brussels, BEL
	NI	3:34.76		Gary Lough	9 Sep 95	Monaco, MON
	W	3:35.08		Neil Horsfield	10 Aug 90	Brussels, BEL
1 Mile	E	3:46.32		Steve Cram	27 Jul 85	Oslo, NOR
	S	3:50.64		Graham Williamson	13 Jul 82	Cork, IRE
	W	3:54.39		Neil Horsfield	8 Jul 86	Cork, IRE
	NI	3:55.0		Jim McGuinness	11 Jul 77	Dublin (B), IRE
2000m	E	4:51.39		Steve Cram	4 Aug 85	Budapest, HUN
	S	4:58.38		Graham Williamson	29 Aug 83	London (CP)
	NI	5:02.61		Steve Martin	19 Jun 84	Belfast
	W	5:05.32		Tony Simmons	4 Jul 75	London (CP)
3000m	E	7:32.79		Dave Moorcroft	17 Jul 82	London (CP)
	S	7:45.81		John Robson	13 Jul 84	London (CP)
	W	7:46.40		Ian Hamer	20 Jan 90	Auckland, NZ
	NI	7:49.1		Paul Lawther	27 Jun 78	Oslo, NOR

Event		Time/Dist		Athlete	Date			Venue
2 Miles	E	8:13.51		Steve Ovett	15	Sep	78	London (CP)
	S	8:19.37		Nat Muir	27	Jun	80	London (CP)
	W	8:20.28		David James	27	Jun	80	London (CP)
	NI	8:30.6		Paul Lawther	28	May	77	Belfast
5000m	E	13:00.41		Dave Moorcroft	7	Jul	82	Oslo, NOR
	W	13:09.80		Ian Hamer	9	Jun	92	Rome, ITA
	S	13:17.9		Nat Muir	15	Jul	80	Oslo, NOR
	NI	13:27.63		Dermot Donnelly	1	Aug	98	Hechtel, BEL
10000m	E	27:18.14	&	Jon Brown	28	Aug	98	Brussels, BEL
		27:23.06		Eamonn Martin	2	Jul	88	Oslo, NOR
	W	27:39.14		Steve Jones	9	Jul	83	Oslo, NOR
	S	27:43.03		Ian Stewart	9	Sep	77	London (CP)
	NI	28:38.56		Dermot Donnelly	29	Jun	97	Sheffield
20km	E	57:28.7		Carl Thackery	31	Mar	90	La Flèche, FRA
	S	59:24.0		Jim Alder	9	Nov	68	Leicester
1 Hour	E	20,855 m		Carl Thackery	31	Mar	90	La Flèche, FRA
	S	20,201 m		Jim Alder	9	Nov	68	Leicester
	W	18,898 m		Mike Rowland	7	Aug	73	Stockholm, SWE
25km	E	1:15:22.6		Ron Hill	21	Jul	65	Bolton
	S	1:15:34.3		Jim Alder	5	Sep	70	London (CP)
30km	S	1:31:30.4		Jim Alder	5	Sep	70	London (CP)
	E	1:31:56.4		Tim Johnston	5	Sep	70	London (CP)
	W	1:33:49.0		Bernie Plain	1	Dec	73	Bristol
Half Marathon	E	60:09	#	Paul Evans	15	Jan	95	Marrakesh, MAR
		61:03		Nick Rose	15	Sep	85	Philadelphia, USA
	W	60:59		Steve Jones	8	Jun	86	Tyneside
	S	61:34	#	Paul Evans	15	Mar	92	Lisbon, POR
		62:28		Allister Hutton	21	Jun	87	Tyneside
	NI	62:16		Jim Haughey	20	Sep	87	Philadelphia, USA
Marathon	W	2:07:13		Steve Jones	20	Oct	85	Chicago, USA
	E	2:08:33		Charlie Spedding	21	Apr	85	London
	S	2:09:16		Allister Hutton	21	Apr	85	London
	NI	2:13:06		Greg Hannon	13	May	79	Coventry
2km St	E	5:19.86		Mark Rowland	28	Aug	88	London (CP)
	S	5:21.77		Tom Hanlon	11	Jun	92	Caserta, ITA
	W	5:23.6		Roger Hackney	10	Jun	82	Birmingham
	NI	5:31.09		Peter McColgan	5	Aug	86	Gateshead
3km St	E	8:07.96		Mark Rowland	30	Sep	88	Seoul, SKO
	S	8:12.58		Tom Hanlon	3	Aug	91	Monaco, MON
	W	8:18.91		Roger Hackney	30	Jul	88	Hechtel, BEL
	NI	8:27.93		Peter McColgan	25	Jun	91	Hengelo, HOL
110m H	W	12.91		Colin Jackson	20	Aug	93	Stuttgart, GER
	E	13.00		Tony Jarrett	20	Aug	93	Stuttgart, GER
	S	13.80		Ross Baillie	19	Sep	98	Kuala Lumpur, MAL
	NI	14.19		C.J. Kirkpatrick	16	Jun	73	Edinburgh
200m H	W	22.63		Colin Jackson	1	Jun	91	Cardiff
	E	22.79		John Regis	1	Jun	91	Cardiff
	S	23.76		Angus McKenzie	22	Aug	81	Edinburgh
	NI	24.81		Terry Price	31	Aug	92	Belfast
400m H	E	47.82		Kriss Akabusi	6	Aug	92	Barcelona, SPA
	W	49.16		Paul Gray	18	Aug	98	Budapest, HUN
	NI	49.60		Phil Beattie	28	Jul	86	Edinburgh
	S	50.43		Charles Robertson-Adams	17	Aug	97	London (CP)

Event		Mark		Name	Date	Venue
High	E	2.38	i	Steve Smith	4 Feb 94	Wuppertal, GER
Jump		2.37		Steve Smith	20 Sep 92	Seoul, SKO
		2.37		Steve Smith	22 Aug 93	Stuttgart, GER
	S	2.31		Geoff Parsons	26 Aug 94	Victoria, CAN
	W	2.24		John Hill	23 Aug 85	Cottbus, GER
	NI	2.20		Floyd Manderson	14 Jul 85	London (CP)
		2.20		Floyd Manderson	21 Jun 86	London (CP)
		2.20		Floyd Manderson	16 Aug 86	Leiden, HOL
Pole	E	5.80		Nick Buckfield	27 May 98	Hania, GRE
Vault	W	5.60		Neil Winter	19 Aug 95	Enfield
	NI	5.25		Mike Bull	22 Sep 73	London (CP)
	S	5.21		Graham Eggleton	10 Jul 82	Grangemouth
Long	W	8.23		Lynn Davies	30 Jun 68	Berne, SWZ
Jump	E	8.15		Stewart Faulkner	16 Jul 90	Belfast
	NI	8.14		Mark Forsythe	7 Jul 91	Rhede, GER
	S	7.86		Darren Ritchie	15 Jun 96	Birmingham
Triple	E	18.29		Jonathan Edwards	7 Aug 95	Gothenburg, SWE
Jump	S	16.17		John Mackenzie	17 Sep 94	Bedford
	W	15.90		David Wood	16 Sep 84	Karlovac, CRO
	NI	15.78		Michael McDonald	31 Jul 94	Corby
Shot	E	21.68		Geoff Capes	18 May 80	Cwmbrân
	W	20.45		Shaun Pickering	17 Aug 97	London (CP)
	S	18.93		Paul Buxton	13 May 77	Los Angeles(Ww), USA
	NI	16.35		Mike Atkinson	18 Jul 81	Dublin (S), IRE
		16.35		John Reynolds	16 Aug 86	Leiden, HOL
Discus	E	66.64		Perris Wilkins	6 Jun 98	Birmingham (Un)
	W	60.43		Lee Newman	12 Aug 98	Enfield
	S	59.84	#	Colin Sutherland ¶	10 Jun 78	San Jose, USA
		58.58		Darrin Morris	22 Jun 91	Enfield
	NI	51.76		John Moreland	1 Jul 95	Antrim
Hammer	NI	77.54		Martin Girvan	12 May 84	Wolverhampton
	E	77.30		David Smith	13 Jul 85	London (CP)
	S	75.40		Chris Black	23 Jul 83	London (CP)
	W	68.64		Shaun Pickering	7 Apr 84	Stanford, USA
Javelin	E	91.46		Steve Backley	25 Jan 92	Auckland(NS), NZ
	W	81.70		Nigel Bevan	28 Jun 92	Birmingham
	NI	70.34	#	Damien Crawford	20 Jul 91	Hayes
		67.60		Dean Smahon	9 Jul 94	King's Lynn
	S	69.20		Roddy James	28 Apr 89	Des Moines, USA
Dec.	E	8847		Daley Thompson	9 Aug 84	Los Angeles, USA
	S	7885	h	Brad McStravick	6 May 84	Birmingham
		7856		Brad McStravick	28 May 84	Cwmbrân
	NI	7874		Colin Boreham	23 May 82	Götzis, AUT
	W	7308	h	Clive Longe	29 Jun 69	Kassel, GER
		7268		Paul Edwards ¶	14 Aug 83	Bonn, GER
4x100m	E	37.98		D. Braithwaite, J. Regis, M. Adam, L. Christie	(UK) 1 Sep 90	Split, CRO
	W	38.73		K. Williams, D. Turner, C. Malcolm, J. Henthorn	21 Sep 98	Kuala Lumpur, MAL
	S	39.24		D. Jenkins, A. Wells, C. Sharp, A. McMaster	12 Aug 78	Edmonton, CAN
	NI	40.71		J. McAdorey, I. Craig, P. Brizzell, M. Allen	22 Jun 96	Belfast

4x400m	E	2:57.53	R. Black, D. Redmond, (UK)			
			J. Regis, K. Akabusi	1 Sep 91	Tokyo, JAP
	W	3:01.86	P. Gray, J. Baulch,		
			D. Turner, I. Thomas	21 Sep 98	Kuala Lumpur, MAL
	S	3:04.68	M. Davidson, T. McKean,		
			D. Strang, B. Whittle	3 Feb 90	Auckland, NZ
	NI	3:07.27	B. Forbes, M. Douglas,		
			E. King, P. McBurney	21 Sep 98	Kuala Lumpur, MAL

Track Walking

3000m	E	11:24.4	Mark Easton	10 May 89	Tonbridge
	W	11:45.77	Steve Johnson	20 Jun 87	Cwmbrân
	S	11:53.3	Martin Bell	9 Aug 95	Birmingham
	NI	13:15.0	David Smyth	5 Sep 70	Plymouth
5000m	E	19:22.29 i	Martin Rush	8 Feb 92	Birmingham
		19:35.0	Darrell Stone	16 May 89	Brighton
	W	20:08.04 i	Steve Barry	5 Mar 83	Budapest, HUN
		20:22.0	Steve Barry	20 Mar 82	London (WL)
	S	20:13.0	Martin Bell	2 May 92	Enfield
	NI	23:50.0	Jimmy Todd	28 Aug 68	Ballyclare
10km	E	40:06.65	Ian McCombie	4 Jun 89	Jarrow
	W	41:13.62	Steve Barry	19 Jun 82	London (CP)
	S	41:13.65	Martin Bell	22 Jul 95	Cardiff
	NI	47:37.6	David Smyth	26 Apr 70	Bournemouth
1 Hour	E	14,324 m #	Ian McCombie	7 Jul 85	London (SP)
		14,158 m	Mark Easton	12 Sep 87	Woodford
	W	13,987 m	Steve Barry	28 Jun 81	Brighton
	S	13,393 m	Bill Sutherland	27 Sep 69	London (He)
	NI	12,690 m #	David Smyth	26 Apr 70	Bournemouth
		12,646 m	David Smyth	23 Sep 67	London (PH)
20km	E	1:23:26.5	Ian McCombie	26 May 90	Fana, NOR
	W	1:26:22.0	Steve Barry	28 Jun 81	Brighton
	S	1:38:53.6	Alan Buchanan	6 Jul 75	Brighton
2 Hours	E	27,262 m #	Chris Maddocks	31 Dec 89	Plymouth
		26,037 m	Ron Wallwork	31 Jul 71	Blackburn
30km	E	2:11:54 #	Chris Maddocks	31 Dec 89	Plymouth
		2:19:18	Chris Maddocks	22 Sep 84	Birmingham
50km	E	4:05:44.6	Paul Blagg	26 May 90	Fana, NOR
	W	4:54:55	Bob Dobson	22 May 93	Maisons-Alfort, FRA
	S	4:56:53.0	Bob Coates	9 Apr 72	Leicester

Road Walking

10km	E	40:17	Chris Maddocks	30 Apr 89	Burrator
	W	40:35	Steve Barry	14 May 83	Southport
	S	42:08	Martin Bell	4 Mar 89	Kenilworth
	NI	44:49 #	David Smyth	20 Jun 70	Clevedon
		51:53	Arthur Agnew	6 Aug 80	Helsinki, FIN
		51:53	G. Smyth	6 Aug 80	Helsinki, FIN
20km	E	1:22:03	Ian McCombie	23 Sep 88	Seoul, SKO
	W	1:22:51	Steve Barry	26 Feb 83	Douglas
	S	1:25:42	Martin Bell	9 May 92	Lancaster
	NI	1:39:01	David Smyth	Jul 67	Cardiff
30km	E	2:07:56	Ian McCombie	27 Apr 86	Edinburgh
	W	2:10:16	Steve Barry	7 Oct 82	Brisbane, AUS
	S	2:22:21	Martin Bell	8 May 94	Cardiff
	NI	2:41:15	David Smyth	26 Apr 69	Winterbourne
50km	E	3:51:37	Chris Maddocks	28 Oct 90	Burrator
	W	4:11:59	Bob Dobson	22 Oct 81	Lassing, AUT
	S	4:13:18	Graham White	27 Jun 98	Stockport
	NI	4:45:48	David Smyth	3 May 69	Bristol

NATIONAL RECORDS OF THE UNITED KINGDOM (WOMEN)

(as at 31st December 1998)

100m	E	11.10	Kathy Smallwood/Cook	5 Sep 81	Rome, ITA
	W	11.39	Sallyanne Short	12 Jul 92	Cwmbrân
	S	11.40	Helen Golden/Hogarth	20 Jul 74	London (CP)
	NI	11.91 #	Joan Atkinson	1 Sep 61	Sofia, BUL
		11.93	Vicki Jamison	2 Aug 97	Belfast
200m	E	22.10	Kathy Cook	9 Aug 84	Los Angeles, USA
	W	22.80	Michelle Scutt	12 Jun 82	Antrim
	S	22.98	Sandra Whittaker	8 Aug 84	Los Angeles, USA
	NI	23.62	Linda McCurry	8 Aug 78	Edmonton, CAN
300m	E	35.46	Kathy Cook	18 Aug 84	London (CP)
	W	36.01	Michelle Probert/Scutt	13 Jul 80	London (CP)
	S	36.46	Linsey Macdonald	13 Jul 80	London (CP)
	NI	38.20	Linda McCurry	2 Aug 78	Edmonton, CAN
400m	E	49.43	Kathy Cook	6 Aug 84	Los Angeles, USA
	W	50.63	Michelle Scutt	31 May 82	Cwmbrân
	S	50.71	Allison Curbishley	18 Sep 98	Kuala Lumpur, MAL
	NI	52.54	Stephanie Llewellyn	9 Jul 95	Cwmbrân
		52.4	Stephanie Llewellyn	1 Jul 95	London (He)
600m	E	1:26.0	Kelly Holmes	13 Aug 95	Gothenburg, SWE
	W	1:26.5	Kirsty McDermott/Wade	21 Aug 85	Zürich, SWZ
	S	1:27.4 i	Linsey Macdonald	12 Dec 81	Cosford
		1:29.88	Anne Clarkson/Purvis	25 Sep 82	Brisbane, AUS
	NI	1:29.46	Jo Latimer	19 May 93	Birmingham
800m	E	1:56.21	Kelly Holmes	9 Sep 95	Monaco, MON
	W	1:57.42	Kirsty McDermott/Wade	24 Jun 85	Belfast
	S	2:00.15	Rosemary Stirling/Wright	3 Sep 72	Munich, GER
	NI	2:01.83	Amanda Crowe	18 Sep 98	Kuala Lumpur, MAL
1000m	E	2:32.55	Kelly Holmes	15 Jun 97	Leeds
	W	2:33.70	Kirsty McDermott/Wade	9 Aug 85	Gateshead
	S	2:37.05	Christine Whittingham	27 Jun 86	Gateshead
	NI	2:48.59	Jane Ewing	26 Jun 90	Antrim
1500m	E	3:58.07	Kelly Holmes	29 Jun 97	Sheffield
	W	4:00.73	Kirsty Wade	26 Jul 87	Gateshead
	S	4:01.20	Yvonne Murray	4 Jul 87	Oslo, NOR
	NI	4:10.68	Amanda Crowe	21 Sep 98	Kuala Lumpur, MAL
1 Mile	E	4:17.57	Zola Budd	21 Aug 85	Zürich, SWZ
	W	4:19.41	Kirsty McDermott/Wade	27 Jul 85	Oslo, NOR
	S	4:22.64	Yvonne Murray	22 Jul 94	Oslo, NOR
	NI	4:32.99	Amanda Crowe	30 Aug 98	Glasgow (S)
2000m	S	5:26.93	Yvonne Murray	8 Jul 94	Edinburgh
	E	5:30.19	Zola Budd	11 Jul 86	London (CP)
	W	5:45.81 i	Kirsty Wade	13 Mar 87	Cosford
		5:50.17	Susan Tooby/Wightman	13 Jul 84	London (CP)
	NI	5:57.24	Ursula McKee/McGloin	25 Jun 90	Antrim
3000m	E	8:28.83	Zola Budd	7 Sep 85	Rome, ITA
	S	8:29.02	Yvonne Murray	25 Sep 88	Seoul, SKO
	W	8:47.59	Angela Tooby/Tooby-Smith	5 Jul 88	Stockholm, SWE
	NI	9:16.25	Ursula McKee/McGloin	7 Jun 90	Helsinki, FIN
5000m	E	14:45.51	Paula Radcliffe	22 Aug 97	Brussels, BEL
	S	14:56.94	Yvonne Murray	7 Jul 95	London (CP)
	W	15:13.22	Angela Tooby/Tooby-Smith	5 Aug 87	Oslo, NOR
	NI	16:54.47	Ann Terek	23 Jul 95	Cardiff

10000m	E	30:48.58	Paula Radcliffe	4 Apr 98	Lisbon, POR
	S	30:57.07	Liz McColgan	25 Jun 91	Hengelo, HOL
	W	31:55.30	Angela Tooby/Tooby-Smith	4 Sep 87	Rome, ITA
	NI	36:19.98	Teresa Kidd	25 Aug 85	Dublin (S), IRE
Half	S	1:07:11	Liz McColgan	26 Jan 92	Tokyo, JAP
Marathon	E	1:09:39	Andrea Wallace	21 Mar 93	Bath
	W	1:09:56	Susan Tooby/Wightman	24 Jul 88	Tyneside
	NI	1:15:57 #	Moira O'Boyle/O'Neill	23 Mar 86	Cavan, IRE
		1:16:23	Moira O'Neill	24 Sep 88	Londonderry
Marathon	E	2:25:56	Véronique Marot	23 Apr 89	London
	S	2:26:52	Liz McColgan	13 Apr 97	London
	W	2:31:33	Susan Tooby/Wightman	23 Sep 88	Seoul, SKO
	NI	2:37:06	Moira O'Neill	31 Oct 88	Dublin, IRE
100m H	E	12.80	Angie Thorp	31 Jul 96	Atlanta, USA
	W	12.91	Kay Morley-Brown	2 Feb 90	Auckland, NZ
	NI	13.29	Mary Peters	2 Sep 72	Munich, GER
	S	13.35	Pat Rollo	30 Jul 83	London (CP)
400m H	E	52.74	Sally Gunnell	19 Aug 93	Stuttgart, GER
	NI	55.91	Elaine McLaughlin	26 Sep 88	Seoul, SKO
	W	56.43	Alyson Layzell	16 Jun 96	Birmingham
	S	57.43	Liz Sutherland	6 Jul 78	Düsseldorf, GER
High	E	1.95	Diana Elliott/Davies	26 Jun 82	Oslo, NOR
Jump		1.95 i	Debbie Marti	23 Feb 97	Birmingham
	NI	1.92	Janet Boyle	29 Sep 88	Seoul, SKO
	S	1.91	Jayne Barnetson	7 Jul 89	Edinburgh
	W	1.84	Sarah Rowe	22 Aug 81	Utrecht, HOL
		1.84	Sarah Rowe	31 May 82	Cwmbrân
Pole	E	4.31	Janine Whitlock	30 May 98	Bedford
Vault	W	3.90 i	Rhian Clarke	8 Mar 97	Paris, FRA
		3.90	Rhian Clarke	31 May 97	Cardiff
	S	3.85 A#	Alison Murray/Jessee	16 Jun 98	Albuquerque, USA
		3.60	Alison Murray/Jessee	1 Jun 96	Cardiff
	NI	2.60	Elaine Murphy	3 May 98	Bath
		2.60	Elaine Murphy	27 Jun 98	Belfast
Long	E	6.90	Bev Kinch	14 Aug 83	Helsinki, FIN
Jump	W	6.52	Gillian Regan	28 Aug 82	Swansea
	S	6.43 #	Moira Walls/Maguire	18 Sep 70	Bucharest, ROM
		6.43	Myra Nimmo	27 May 73	Edinburgh
	NI	6.11	Thelma Hopkins	29 Sep 56	Budapest, HUN
		6.11	Michelle Rea	11 Aug 90	Maia, POR
Triple	E	15.16 i	Ashia Hansen	28 Feb 98	Valencia, SPA
Jump		15.15	Ashia Hansen	13 Sep 97	Fukuoka, JAP
	S	12.89	Karen Hambrook/Skeggs	17 May 92	London (CP)
	W	12.14	Jayne Ludlow	21 May 94	Istanbul, TUR
	NI	11.79	Michelle Rea	16 Jun 91	Grangemouth
Shot	E	19.36	Judy Oakes	14 Aug 88	Gateshead
	S	18.99	Meg Ritchie	7 May 83	Tucson, USA
	W	19.06 i	Venissa Head	7 Apr 84	St. Athan
		18.93	Venissa Head	13 May 84	Haverfordwest
	NI	16.40 i	Mary Peters	28 Feb 70	Bucharest, ROM
		16.31	Mary Peters	1 Jun 66	Belfast (PP)
Discus	S	67.48	Meg Ritchie	26 Apr 81	Walnut, USA
	W	64.68	Venissa Head	18 Jul 83	Athens, GRE
	E	60.82	Shelley Drew	25 Jul 98	Birmingham
	NI	60.72	Jackie McKernan	18 Jul 93	Buffalo, USA

Event		Mark		Name	Date	Location
Hammer	E	64.90		Lorraine Shaw	10 Jun 95	Bedford
	W	56.60		Sarah Moore	12 Jul 97	Birmingham
	S	53.37		Catherine Garden	1 Aug 98	Dessau, GER
	NI	48.90		Julie Kirkpatrick	15 Jun 96	Dublin (S), IRE
Javelin	E	77.44		Fatima Whitbread	28 Aug 86	Stuttgart, GER
	S	62.22	#	Diane Royle	18 May 85	Stretford
		61.94		Diane Royle	2 Sep 84	Birmingham
	W	59.40		Karen Hough	28 Aug 86	Stuttgart, GER
	NI	49.10		Alison Moffitt	16 Jun 96	Dublin (S), IRE
Hept.	E	6736		Denise Lewis	1 Jun 97	Götzis, AUT
	S	5803		Jayne Barnetson	20 Aug 89	Kiev, UKR
	W	5642		Sarah Rowe	23 Aug 81	Utrecht, HOL
	NI	5065	h	Catherine Scott	13 Sep 87	Tullamore, IRE
		4564		Wendy Phillips	18 Jul 82	Birmingham
4x100m	E	42.43		H. Oakes, K. Cook, (UK)		
				B. Callender, S. Lannaman	1 Aug 80	Moscow, RUS
	S	45.37		J. Booth, K. Hogg,		
				J. Neilson, S. Whittaker	8 Jun 86	Lloret de Mar, SPA
		45.2		A. MacRitchie, S. Pringle, (ESH)		
				H. Hogarth, E. Sutherland	27 Jun 70	London (CP)
	W	45.37		H. Miles, S. Lewis,		
				S. Short, C. Smart	2 Aug 86	Edinburgh
	NI	46.36		K. Graham, H. Gourlay,		
				J. Robinson, R. Gaylor	31 Aug 85	Tel Aviv, ISR
4x400m	E	3:22.01		L. Hanson, P. Smith, (UK)		
				S. Gunnell, L. Keough	1 Sep 91	Tokyo, JAP
	S	3:32.92		S. Whittaker, A. Purvis,		
				A. Baxter, L. Macdonald	9 Oct 82	Brisbane, AUS
	W	3:35.60		C. Smart, K. Wade,		
				D. Fryar, M. Scutt	4 Jul 82	Dublin (S), IRE
	NI	3:40.12		Z. Arnold, V. Jamison,		
				J. Latimer, S. Llewellyn	22 Jun 96	Belfast

Track Walking

Event		Mark		Name	Date	Location
3000m	E	12:49.16		Betty Sworowski	28 Jul 90	Wrexham
	S	13:16.23		Verity Snook	27 May 96	Bedford
	W	14:28.2		Karen Dunster	18 May 91	Portsmouth
5000m	E	21:52.4	#	Vicky Lupton	9 Aug 95	Sheffield (?)
		22:01.53		Lisa Kehler	26 Jul 98	Birmingham
	S	23:22.52		Verity Snook	19 Jun 94	Horsham
	W	24:32.92		Karen Nipper	21 Jul 84	Lyngby, DEN
10km	E	45:18.8		Vicky Lupton	2 Sep 95	Watford
	S	47:10.07		Verity Larby/Snook	19 Jun 93	Horsham
	W	50:25.0	mx	Lisa Simpson	1 Apr 87	Hornchurch
		51:00.0		Karen Nipper	21 Feb 81	Leicester
1 Hour	E	11,590 m		Lisa Langford/Kehler	13 Sep 86	Woodford
20km	E	1:56:59.7		Cath Reader	21 Oct 95	Loughborough

Road Walking

Event		Mark	Name	Date	Location
5km	E	21:36	Vicky Lupton	18 Jul 92	Sheffield
	S	22:45	Verity Snook	25 Aug 94	Victoria, CAN
	W	23:35	Lisa Simpson	31 Oct 87	Cardiff
10km	E	45:03	Lisa Kehler	19 Sep 98	Kuala Lumpur, MAL
	S	46:06	Verity Snook	25 Aug 94	Victoria, CAN
	W	49:33	Lisa Simpson	14 Mar 87	Ham
20km	E	1:40:45	Irene Bateman	9 Apr 83	Basildon
	S	1:54:15	Verity Snook	7 Sep 96	Horsham

BRITISH INDOOR RECORDS
(as at 7 March 1999)

MEN

50m	5.65	Jason Gardener	21 Feb 99	Liévin, FRA
60m	6.46	Jason Gardener	7 Mar 99	Maebashi, JAP
200m	20.25	Linford Christie	19 Feb 95	Liévin, FRA
300m	32.90	Ade Mafe	31 Jan 92	Karlsruhe, GER
400m	45.39	Jamie Baulch	9 Feb 97	Birmingham
800m	1:44.91	Sebastian Coe	12 Mar 83	Cosford
1000m	2:17.86	Matthew Yates	22 Feb 92	Birmingham
1500m	3:34.20	Peter Elliott	27 Feb 90	Seville, SPA
1 Mile	3:52.02	Peter Elliott	9 Feb 90	East Rutherford, USA
2000m	5:05.20	John Gladwin	15 Mar 87	Cosford
3000m	7:43.31	John Mayock	23 Feb 97	Birmingham
5000m	13:21.27	Nick Rose	12 Feb 82	New York, USA
50m Hurdles	6.40	Colin Jackson	5 Feb 99	Budapest, HUN
60m Hurdles	7.30	Colin Jackson	6 Mar 94	Sindelfingen, GER
High Jump	2.38	Steve Smith	4 Feb 94	Wuppertal, GER
Pole Vault	5.61	Nick Buckfield	3 Feb 96	Birmingham
Long Jump	8.05	Barrington Williams	11 Feb 89	Cosford
	8.05 #	Stewart Faulkner	27 Feb 90	Seville, SPA
Triple Jump	17.64	Jonathan Edwards	15 Feb 98	Birmingham
Shot	20.98	Geoff Capes	16 Jan 76	Los Angeles, USA
	20.98 #	Geoff Capes	14 Feb 76	Winnipeg, CAN
Heptathlon	5978	Alex Kruger	12 Mar 95	Barcelona, SPA
	(7.16, 7.23, 14.79, 2.16, 8.36, 4.90, 2:48.66)			
5000m Walk	19:22.29	Martin Rush	8 Feb 92	Birmingham
4 x 200m Relay	1:22.11	UK National Team	3 Mar 91	Glasgow
	(Linford Christie, Darren Braithwaite, Ade Mafe, John Regis)			
4 x 400m Relay	3:03.20	UK National Team	7 Mar 99	Maebashi, JAP
	(Allyn Condon, Solomon Wariso, Adrian Patrick, Jamie Baulch)			

WOMEN

50m	6.21	Wendy Hoyte	22 Feb 81	Grenoble, FRA
60m	7.13	Beverly Kinch	23 Feb 86	Madrid, SPA
200m	22.83	Katharine Merry	14 Feb 99	Birmingham
300m	37.46 A	Sharon Colyear/Danville	14 Mar 81	Pocatello, USA
400m	51.69	Phylis Smith	23 Feb 97	Birmingham
800m	2:01.12	Jane Colebrook/Finch	13 Mar 77	San Sebastián, SPA
1000m	2:38.95	Kirsty Wade	1 Feb 87	Stuttgart, GER
1500m	4:06.87	Zola Budd	25 Jan 86	Cosford
1 Mile	4:23.86	Kirsty Wade	5 Feb 88	New York, USA
2000m	5:40.86	Yvonne Murray	20 Feb 93	Birmingham
3000m	8:34.80	Liz McColgan	4 Mar 89	Budapest, HUN
5000m	15:03.17	Liz McColgan	22 Feb 92	Birmingham
50m Hurdles	7.03	Yvette Wray/Luker	21 Feb 81	Grenoble, FRA
60m Hurdles	8.01	Jacqui Agyepong	12 Mar 95	Barcelona, SPA
High Jump	1.95	Debbie Marti	23 Feb 97	Birmingham
Pole Vault	4.29	Janine Whitlock	14 Feb 99	Birmingham
Long Jump	6.70	Sue Hearnshaw/Telfer	3 Mar 84	Gothenburg, SWE
	6.70	Jo Wise	9 Mar 97	Paris, FRA
Triple Jump	15.16	Ashia Hansen	28 Feb 98	Valencia, SPA
Shot	19.06	Venissa Head	7 Apr 84	St. Athan
Pentathlon	4363	Kim Hagger	4 Feb 84	Vittel, FRA
	(8.44, 1.82, 11.89, 6.31, 2:27.08)			
3000m Walk	13:12.01	Julie Drake	12 Mar 93	Toronto, CAN
4 x 200m Relay	1:33.96	UK National Team	23 Feb 90	Glasgow
	(Paula Dunn, Jennifer Stoute, Linda Keough, Sally Gunnell)			
4 x 400m Relay	3:32.25	UK National Team	9 Mar 97	Paris, FRA
	(Phylis Smith, Sally Gunnell, Michelle Thomas, Donna Fraser)			

UK ALL TIME LISTS - MEN
as at 31 December 1998

100 METRES

9.87	Linford Christie	15 Aug	93
10.03 A†	Dwain Chambers	11 Sep	98
10.06		25 Jul	97
10.04	Darren Campbell	19 Aug	98
10.09	Jason Livingston ¶	13 Jun	92
10.11	Allan Wells	24 Jul	80
10.12	Darren Braithwaite	15 Jul	95
10.12	Christian Malcolm	29 Jul	98
10.13	Marlon Devonish	17 Sep	98
10.15	Michael Rosswess	15 Sep	91
10.15	John Regis	29 May	93
10.17	Ian Mackie	25 Aug	96
10.20	Cameron Sharp	24 Aug	83
10.20	Elliot Bunney	14 Jun	86
10.21 A	Ainsley Bennett	8 Sep	79
10.21	Jamie Henderson	6 Aug	87
10.22	Mike McFarlane	20 Jun	86
10.23	Marcus Adam	26 Jul	91
10.23	Jason John	15 Jul	94
10.23	Terry Williams	22 Aug	94
10.25	Jason Gardener	21 Jul	94
10.26	Daley Thompson	27 Aug	86
10.26	Ernest Obeng	1 Aug	87
10.21	for GHA	11 Aug	80
10.28	Julian Golding	22 Jul	97
10.29	Peter Radford (10.31?)	13 Sep	58
10.29	Colin Jackson	28 Jul	90
10.30	Clarence Callender	26 Jul	91
10.31	Doug Walker	11 Jun	97
10.32	Buster Watson	1 Jul	83
10.32	Donovan Reid	4 Aug	84
10.32	Lincoln Asquith	11 Aug	86
10.32	Lenny Paul	29 May	93
10.32	Toby Box	28 Jun	95
10.32	Daniel Money	29 Aug	97
10.32	Josephus Thomas	25 Jul	98
10.29	for SLE	16 Sep	98
10.33	Brian Green	15 Jul	72
10.33	Solomon Wariso	19 Jun	94
10.34	Drew McMaster	9 Jul	83
10.34	Barrington Williams	5 Aug	88
10.34	Kevin Williams	11 Jun	97
10.35 A	Barrie Kelly	13 Oct	68
10.35	Brian Taylor	29 May	93
10.35	Owusu Dako	8 Jul	96
10.35	Mark Richardson	2 May	98
10.36	David Jenkins	24 Jun	72
10.36	Allyn Condon	15 Jun	96
10.37	Micky Morris	23 Aug	87
10.37	Steve Gookey	20 Jul	91
10.38	Adrian Patrick	11 Aug	96
10.39	Ray Burke	13 Jun	92
10.40	Trevor Hoyte	11 Aug	79
10.40	Jim Evans	24 Jul	82
10.40	Paul White	31 Aug	95
10.40	Doug Turner	26 Jun	97
10.40	Uvie Ugono	20 Jun	98

wind assisted

10.00	Ian Mackie	18 Jul	98
10.01	Doug Walker	18 Jul	98
10.02	Allan Wells	4 Oct	82
10.07	Cameron Sharp	4 Oct	82
10.07	John Regis	28 Aug	90
10.07	Toby Box	11 Jun	94
10.07	Michael Rosswess	11 Jun	94
10.08	Mike McFarlane	27 May	84
10.08	Jason John	11 Jun	94
10.10	Donovan Reid	26 Jun	83
10.10	Christian Malcolm	18 Jul	98
10.11	Drew McMaster	26 Jun	83
10.12	Buster Watson	27 May	84
10.14	Ernest Obeng	20 Jun	87
10.14	Marcus Adam	28 Jan	90
10.16	Daniel Money	21 Jun	97
10.17	Terry Williams	23 Aug	94
10.17	Jason Gardener	7 Sep	97
10.17	Owusu Dako	5 Jul	98
10.19	Josephus Thomas	23 Apr	98
10.20	Lincoln Asquith	6 Jul	85
10.22	Jamie Henthorn	29 Aug	97
10.22	Danny Joyce	30 Aug	97
10.25	Lenny Paul	14 Jul	91
10.26	Peter Little	21 May	80
10.26	Doug Turner	13 Jul	96
10.27	Barrington Williams	2 Jul	88
10.27	Clarence Callender	22 Jun	91
10.28	Du'aine Ladejo	23 May	98
10.29	Trevor Cameron	11 Jun	94
10.29	Allyn Condon	5 Jul	98
10.30	Kevin Williams	27 Jul	97
10.31	Jim Evans	22 Aug	81
10.32	Brian Green	16 Jun	72
10.32	Harry King	22 Aug	81
10.32	Uvie Ugono	23 Apr	98
10.33	Steve Gookey	20 Jul	91
10.34	Phil Davies	13 Jul	86
10.34	Jason Fergus	5 Jun	94
10.35	Nigel Walker	26 Aug	89
10.35	Ross Baillie	18 Jul	98
10.36	Les Piggot	15 Jul	72
10.36	Mark Lewis-Francis	16 Aug	98
10.36	Joselyn Thomas	23 Apr	98
10.37	Earl Tulloch	22 Aug	81
10.37	Courtney Rumbolt	25 Jun	88

hand timing

10.1	David Jenkins	20 May	72
10.1	Brian Green	3 Jun	72
10.1	Ernest Obeng (for GHA)	2 Aug	79

hand timing - wind assisted

10.0	Allan Wells	16 Jun	79
10.0	Drew McMaster	1 Jun	80
10.0	Jason Gardener	11 Jun	98

200 METRES

	19.87 A	John Regis	31 Jul 94	
	19.94		20 Aug 93	
	20.09	Linford Christie	28 Sep 88	
	20.18	Julian Golding	19 Sep 98	
	20.21	Allan Wells	28 Jul 80	
	20.29	Christian Malcolm	19 Sep 98	
	20.35	Doug Walker	26 Jul 98	
	20.36	Todd Bennett	28 May 84	
	20.41	Marcus Adam	13 Jun 92	
	20.42 A	Ainsley Bennett	12 Sep 79	
	20.84		31 Aug 80	
10	20.43	Mike McFarlane	7 Oct 82	
	20.43	Doug Turner	9 Jun 96	
	20.47	Cameron Sharp	9 Sep 82	
	20.47	Darren Braithwaite	13 May 95	
	20.48	Darren Campbell	2 Aug 98	
	20.50	Terry Williams	24 Aug 94	
	20.50	Tony Jarrett	16 Jul 95	
	20.50	Solomon Wariso	16 Jul 95	
	20.51	Michael Rosswess	28 Sep 88	
	20.53 i	Allyn Condon	8 Feb 98	
	20.63		19 Jul 97	
20	20.54	Ade Mafe	25 Aug 85	
	20.56	Roger Black	4 May 96	
	20.57	Owusu Dako	16 Jul 95	
	20.62	Buster Watson	5 Jun 83	
	20.62	Donovan Reid	28 May 84	
	20.62	Mark Richardson	24 Aug 97	
	20.65	Marlon Devonish	25 Aug 97	
	20.66 A	Dick Steane	15 Oct 68	
	20.66	David Jenkins	27 Aug 73	
	20.70	Chris Monk	20 Aug 73	
30	20.72	Toby Box	24 Aug 94	
	20.73 A	Ralph Banthorpe	15 Oct 68	
	20.75	Dave Clark	20 Jan 90	
	20.76	Andy Carrott	5 Jul 88	
	20.76	Clarence Callender	24 Jun 91	
	20.77	Drew McMaster	9 Jul 83	
	20.79	Phil Goedluck	6 Aug 94	
	20.79	Paul White	27 May 96	
	20.81	Mike St. Louis	21 Jun 86	
	20.81	Paul McBurney	24 Aug 94	
40	20.83	Martin Reynolds	22 Jul 70	
	20.83	Claude Moseley	23 Aug 81	
	20.84	Brian Green	4 Sep 71	
	20.84	Earl Tulloch	25 May 81	
	20.84	Jamie Baulch	24 Aug 94	
	20.85	Richard Ashby	25 Aug 85	
	20.86	Lincoln Asquith	28 Aug 83	
	20.86	Roger Hunter	5 May 84	
	20.86	Gus McCuaig	28 May 84	
	20.86	Jason John	1 Jul 95	
50	20.87	Mark Smith	28 Jul 90	
	20.87	Iwan Thomas	30 Aug 97	
	20.88	Daley Thompson	18 Aug 79	
	20.88	Phil Brown	28 May 84	
	20.89	Mark Forsythe	12 Aug 90	

wind assisted (* 220 yards time less 0.12)

20.10	Marcus Adam	1 Feb 90	
20.11	Allan Wells	20 Jun 80	
20.26	Ade Mafe	1 Feb 90	
20.36	Doug Turner	27 Jul 97	
20.48	Michael Rosswess	9 Sep 90	
20.49	Josephus Thomas	23 Apr 98	
20.51	Jason John	2 Jul 93	
20.55	Buster Watson	10 Aug 85	
20.61	Martin Reynolds	22 Jul 70	
20.61	Marlon Devonish	25 Apr 97	10
20.62	Adrian Patrick	10 Jun 95	
20.64	Drew McMaster	23 Aug 80	
20.70 *	David Jones	20 May 61	
20.70	Trevor Hoyte	14 Sep 79	
20.73	Phil Goedluck	23 Apr 95	
20.75	Daniel Money	26 May 97	
20.76	Paul McBurney	26 May 97	
20.84	Nigel Stickings	9 Jul 93	
20.85	Phil Brown	28 May 84	
20.85	Mark Smith	1 Jul 90	20
20.88	Trevor Cameron	12 Jun 94	
20.89	Tim Bonsor	10 Aug 78	
20.89	David Grindley	13 Jun 93	

hand timing (* 220 yards time less 0.1)

20.3	David Jenkins	19 Aug 72
20.4 *	Peter Radford	28 May 60
20.6	Donovan Reid	1 Jul 84
20.7 *	Menzies Campbell	10 Jun 67
20.7	Martin Reynolds	2 Aug 70
20.7	Brian Green	3 Jun 72
20.7	Drew McMaster	16 Aug 80
20.7	Claude Moseley	28 Aug 81

wind assisted

20.4	Buster Watson	11 Aug 85
20.5	Roger Black	6 Jul 96
20.6	Ainsley Bennett	22 Jun 74
20.6	Mark Richardson	6 Jul 96

300 METRES

31.56	Doug Walker	19 Jul 98	
31.67	John Regis	17 Jul 92	
31.87	Mark Richardson	19 Jul 98	
32.06	Jamie Baulch	31 May 97	
32.08	Roger Black	8 Aug 86	
32.14	Todd Bennett	18 Aug 84	
32.23	Solomon Wariso	19 Jul 98	
32.26	Mark Hylton	19 Jul 98	
32.32	Derek Redmond	16 Jul 88	
32.36	Iwan Thomas	19 Jul 98	10
32.44	David Jenkins	4 Jul 75	
32.45	David Grindley	19 Jun 93	
32.59	Kriss Akabusi	14 Jul 91	
32.61	Brian Whittle	16 Jul 88	

during 400m

32.06 +	Roger Black	29 Aug 91
32.08 +	Iwan Thomas	5 Aug 97
32.26 +	Derek Redmond	1 Sep 87
32.35 +	David Grindley	26 Jun 93

400 METRES

	44.36	Iwan Thomas	13	Jul	97
	44.37	Roger Black	3	Jul	96
	44.37	Mark Richardson	9	Jul	98
	44.47	David Grindley	3	Aug	92
	44.50	Derek Redmond	1	Sep	87
	44.57	Jamie Baulch	3	Jul	96
	44.66	Du'aine Ladejo	16	Jun	96
	44.68	Solomon Wariso	26	Jul	98
	44.93	David Jenkins	21	Jun	75
10	44.93	Kriss Akabusi	7	Aug	88
	45.22	Brian Whittle	25	Sep	88
	45.24	Mark Hylton	12	Aug	98
	45.26	Phil Brown	26	May	85
	45.27	Todd Bennett	7	Aug	88
	45.30	Ade Mafe	23	Jul	93
	45.33	Paul Sanders	15	Jun	91
	45.42	Sean Baldock	13	Jul	97
	45.47	David McKenzie	12	Jun	94
	45.48	John Regis	17	Apr	93
20	45.49	Glen Cohen	21	May	78
	45.63	Adrian Patrick	5	Jul	95
	45.64	Paul Harmsworth	7	Aug	88
	45.65	Alan Bell	14	Jun	80
	45.67	Roger Hunter	19	May	85
	45.74	Steve Heard	26	May	85
	45.75	Robbie Brightwell	19	Oct	64
	45.76	Guy Bullock	16	Jun	96
	45.81	Terry Whitehead	14	Jun	80
	45.84	Richard Knowles	18	May	97
30	45.85	Paul McBurney	13	Jul	97
	45.88	Wayne McDonald	17	Aug	91
	45.91 A	Martin Winbolt-Lewis	17	Oct	68
	45.92	Mark Thomas	27	Jun	87
	45.94	Jared Deacon	13	Jul	97
	45.94	Paul Slythe	26	Jul	98
	45.97	Steve Scutt	14	Sep	79
	46.03	Peter Crampton	8	Aug	87
	46.04	Alan Slack	27	Jun	85
	46.08	Tim Graham	19	Oct	64
40	46.08	Rod Milne	15	Jun	80
	46.10	Peter Gabbett	7	Sep	72
	46.11	Martin Reynolds	4	Sep	72
	46.15	Ainsley Bennett	29	Aug	75
	46.16	Gary Armstrong	15	Jul	72
	46.16	Claude Moseley	1	Jul	83
	46.18	Garry Cook	14	Jun	80
	46.19	Roy Dickens	28	May	84
	46.20	David Nolan	9	Jun	96
	46.22	Mark Sesay	25	May	97
50	46.24	Mel Fowell	15	Jun	80
	46.27	Richard Ashton	6	Aug	78
	46.31	Neil Jackson	14	Jun	80
	46.31	Kent Ulyatt	10	Sep	95

hand timing (* 440 yards time less 0.3)

45.6 *	Robbie Brightwell	14	Jul	62
45.7	Adrian Metcalfe	2	Sep	61
45.9	Colin Campbell	2	Jul	68
46.0	Garry Cook	20	May	81

600 METRES

1:14.95	Steve Heard	14	Jul	91
1:15.0 +	Sebastian Coe	10	Jun	81
1:15.4	Garry Cook	30	Jul	84
1:15.4	Tom McKean	21	Jul	91
1:15.6	David Jenkins	3	Aug	74
1:15.94	Brian Whittle	28	Jul	92

800 METRES (* 880 yards time less 0.70)

1:41.73"	Sebastian Coe	10	Jun	81	
1:42.88	Steve Cram	21	Aug	85	
1:42.97	Peter Elliott	30	May	90	
1:43.84	Martin Steele	10	Jul	93	
1:43.88	Tom McKean	28	Jul	89	
1:43.98	David Sharpe	19	Aug	92	
1:44.09	Steve Ovett	31	Aug	78	
1:44.55	Garry Cook	29	Aug	84	
1:44.59	Tony Morrell	2	Jul	88	
1:44.65	Ikem Billy	21	Jul	84	10
1:44.65	Steve Heard	26	Aug	92	
1:44.92	Curtis Robb	15	Aug	93	
1:45.05	Matthew Yates	26	Aug	92	
1:45.12	Andy Carter	14	Jul	73	
1:45.14	Chris McGeorge	28	Jun	83	
1:45.14	John Gladwin	22	Jul	86	
1:45.31	Rob Harrison	21	Jul	84	
1:45.35	Kevin McKay	16	Aug	92	
1:45.44	Neil Horsfield	28	Jul	90	
1:45.47	Brian Whittle	20	Jul	90	20
1:45.6	Graham Williamson	12	Jun	83	
1:45.64	Paul Herbert	5	Jun	88	
1:45.66	Paul Forbes	8	Jun	83	
1:45.69	Steve Crabb	17	Aug	88	
1:45.69	Craig Winrow	21	Jun	96	
1:45.71	Andy Hart	19	Sep	98	
1:45.76	Frank Clement	10	Jul	76	
1:45.81	David Strang	12	Jul	96	
1:46.05	Mark Sesay	18	May	97	
1:46.10	Gary Marlow	10	Jul	87	30
1:46.1	Colin Campbell	26	Jul	72	
1:46.16	Gareth Brown	2	Jul	84	
1:46.20	David Warren	29	Jun	80	
1:46.21	Pete Browne	14	Jul	73	
1:46.26	Phil Lewis	27	Jan	74	
1:46.3 a	Chris Carter	4	Sep	66	
1:46.37	Andrew Lill	28	Jun	92	
1:46.4	Paul Walker	22	Jul	97	
1:46.51	John Boulter	18	Jun	66	
1:46.6	Derek Johnson	9	Aug	57	40
1:46.63	Peter Hoffman	11	Jun	78	
1:46.64	Dave Moorcroft	25	Jul	82	
1:46.65	Steve Caldwell	31	May	82	
1:46.70 *	John Davies I	3	Jun	68	
1:46.70	Atle Douglas (NOR?)	9	Jun	88	
1:46.72	Mal Edwards	13	Sep	87	
1:46.8	Bob Adams	9	Aug	69	
1:46.8	Dave Cropper	1	Jul	73	
1:46.8	Dave McMeekin	6	Jun	74	
1:46.86	Bradley Donkin	19	Sep	98	50
1:46.92	Colin Szwed	7	Aug	82	

1000 METRES

2:12.18	Sebastian Coe	11 Jul	81
2:12.88	Steve Cram	9 Aug	85
2:15.91	Steve Ovett	6 Sep	79
2:16.30	Peter Elliott	17 Jan	90
2:16.34	Matthew Yates	6 Jul	90
2:16.82	Graham Williamson	17 Jul	84
2:16.99	Tony Morrell	28 Aug	88
2:17.14	John Gladwin	6 Jul	90
2:17.20	Rob Harrison	18 Aug	84
2:17.36	Neil Horsfield	9 Aug	91
2:17.43	Gareth Brown	18 Aug	84
2:17.45	Chris McGeorge	20 Aug	84
2:17.63	Kevin McKay	14 Jul	89

1500 METRES (+ during 1 mile)

3:29.67	Steve Cram	16 Jul	85
3:29.77	Sebastian Coe	7 Sep	86
3:30.77	Steve Ovett	4 Sep	83
3:31.86	John Mayock	22 Aug	97
3:32.34	Anthony Whiteman	16 Aug	97
3:32.69	Peter Elliott	16 Sep	90
3:33.34	Steve Crabb	4 Jul	87
3:33.79	Dave Moorcroft	27 Jul	82
3:33.83	John Robson	4 Sep	79
3:34.00	Matthew Yates	13 Sep	91
3:34.01	Graham Williamson	28 Jun	83
3:34.1 +	Tony Morrell	14 Jul	90
3:34.50	Adrian Passey	4 Jul	87
3:34.53	Mark Rowland	27 Jul	88
3:34.59	Kevin McKay	24 Aug	97
3:34.76	Gary Lough	9 Sep	95
3:35.08	Neil Horsfield	10 Aug	90
3:35.26	John Gladwin	5 Sep	86
3:35.28	Jack Buckner	1 Jul	86
3:35.66	Frank Clement	12 Aug	78
3:35.74	Rob Harrison	26 May	86
3:35.94	Paul Larkins	10 Jul	87
3:36.53	David Strang	15 Jul	94
3:36.81	Mike Kearns	26 Jul	77
3:37.55	Colin Reitz	27 Jun	85
3:37.64	Brendan Foster	2 Feb	74
3:37.88	Jason Dullforce	17 Jul	92
3:37.97	Rod Finch	30 Jul	93
3:37.99	Rob Denmark	5 Jun	95
3:38.05	Glen Grant	12 Aug	78
3:38.06	Tim Hutchings	31 Aug	84
3:38.08	Tom Hanlon	28 Jun	92
3:38.1	Jim McGuinness	1 Aug	77
3:38.2 a	James Espir	11 Jul	80
3:38.22	Peter Stewart	15 Jul	72
3:38.31	Matt Barnes	23 Jul	93
3:38.52	Ray Smedley	15 Jul	72
3:38.56	Curtis Robb	26 Jun	93
3:38.64	Simon Fairbrother	17 Jun	92
3:38.65	Ian Stewart II	8 Aug	81
3:38.66	Glen Stewart	26 May	96
3:38.68	John Kirkbride	15 Jul	72
3:38.7	Jim Douglas	27 Jun	72
3:38.78	Mark Scruton	17 Jun	84
3:38.8	Paul Lawther	12 Jun	77
3:38.9	Ian Hamer	5 Aug	89
3:38.93	Brian Treacy	28 Aug	94
3:39.0	David Lewis	9 Aug	83
3:39.06	Andy Keith	5 Jun	93
3:39.10	Alan Simpson	15 Aug	64
3:39.1	Neil Caddy	14 Aug	96
3:39.1	Rob Hough	14 May	97

ONE MILE

3:46.32	Steve Cram	27 Jul	85
3:47.33	Sebastian Coe	28 Aug	81
3:48.40	Steve Ovett	26 Aug	81
3:49.20	Peter Elliott	2 Jul	88
3:49.34	Dave Moorcroft	26 Jun	82
3:50.32	John Mayock	5 Jul	96
3:50.64	Graham Williamson	13 Jul	82
3:51.02	John Gladwin	19 Aug	87
3:51.31	Tony Morrell	14 Jul	90
3:51.57	Jack Buckner	29 Aug	84
3:51.76hc	Steve Crabb	14 Aug	87
3:52.20		1 Jul	89
3:51.90	Anthony Whiteman	16 Jul	98
3:52.44	John Robson	11 Jul	81
3:52.75	Matthew Yates	10 Jul	93
3:52.99	Mark Rowland	10 Sep	86
3:53.20	Ian Stewart II	25 Aug	82
3:53.64	Kevin McKay	22 Jul	94
3:53.82	Gary Staines	12 Aug	90
3:53.85	Rob Harrison	15 Jul	86
3:54.2	Frank Clement	27 Jun	78
3:54.30	David Strang	22 Jul	94
3:54.39	Neil Horsfield	8 Jul	86
3:54.53	Tim Hutchings	31 Jul	82
3:54.9	Adrian Passey	20 Aug	89
3:55.0	Jim McGuinness	11 Jul	77
3:55.3	Peter Stewart	10 Jun	72
3:55.38	Rob Denmark	12 Aug	90
3:55.41	Colin Reitz	31 Jul	82
3:55.68	Alan Simpson	30 Aug	65
3:55.8	Geoff Smith	15 Aug	81
3:55.84	Neil Caddy	25 Aug	96
3:55.9	Brendan Foster	10 Jun	72
3:55.91	Gary Lough	27 Aug	95
3:55.96	David Lewis	23 Aug	83
3:56.0	Jim Douglas	10 Jun	72
3:56.04	Mike Downes	25 Aug	82
3:56.1	Neill Duggan	11 Jun	66
3:56.19	Ian Hamer	5 Jul	91
3:56.29 i	Andy Keith	22 Jan	94
3:56.36	Steve Martin	5 Aug	86
3:56.38	Mike McLeod	31 Aug	79
3:56.5	John Kirkbride	10 Jun	72
3:56.5	Paul Davies-Hale	20 Aug	89
3:56.6	Walter Wilkinson	31 May	71
3:56.65	Paul Larkins	17 Jul	87
3:56.7	James Espir	15 Aug	81
3:56.71	Chris McGeorge	5 Jul	88
3:56.8	Ian McCafferty	11 Jun	69
3:56.83	Simon Fairbrother	17 Aug	90
3:56.9 a	Ron Speirs	30 Apr	77

2000 METRES

	4:51.39	Steve Cram	4 Aug 85	
	4:52.82	Peter Elliott	15 Sep 87	
	4:53.06	Jack Buckner	15 Sep 87	
	4:53.69	Gary Staines	15 Sep 87	
	4:57.71	Steve Ovett	7 Jul 82	
	4:58.38	Graham Williamson	29 Aug 83	
	4:58.84	Sebastian Coe	5 Jun 82	
	4:59.57	Nick Rose	3 Jun 78	
	5:00.37	Tim Hutchings	29 Aug 83	
10	5:00.91	John Mayock	9 Sep 96	
	5:01.09	Eamonn Martin	19 Jun 84	
	5:01.48	Paul Larkins	5 Jun 88	
	5:02.35	Sean Cahill	4 Aug 85	
	5:02.61	Steve Martin	19 Jun 84	
	5:02.8 a	Frank Clement	10 Sep 78	
	5:02.86	David Moorcroft	19 Jul 86	
	5:02.93	Brendan Foster	4 Jul 75	
	5:02.98	Ian Stewart I	4 Jul 75	
	5:02.98	Gary Lough	11 Aug 96	
20	5:02.99	Neil Caddy	11 Aug 96	
	5:03.16	David Bedford	8 Jul 72	
	5:03.8	Lawrie Spence	26 May 78	
	5:04.11	Rob Denmark	11 Aug 96	
	5:04.16	Eddie Wedderburn	15 Jul 83	
	5:04.51	Steve Harris	29 Aug 83	
	5:04.53	David Lewis	26 Jun 83	
	5:04.56	Geoff Smith	26 Jun 83	
	5:04.75	Dave Clarke	15 Jul 83	
	5:04.85	Billy Dee	15 Jul 83	

3000 METRES (+ during 2 Miles)

	7:32.79	Dave Moorcroft	17 Jul 82	
	7:35.1	Brendan Foster	3 Aug 74	
	7:36.40	John Nuttall	10 Jul 96	
	7:39.55	Rob Denmark	1 Aug 93	
	7:40.4	Nick Rose	27 Jun 78	
	7:40.43	Jack Buckner	5 Jul 86	
	7:40.94	Eamonn Martin	9 Jul 83	
	7:41.3	Steve Ovett	23 Sep 77	
	7:41.79	Gary Staines	14 Jul 90	
10	7:42.26	Graeme Fell	9 Jul 83	
	7:42.47	David Lewis	9 Jul 83	
	7:42.77	Billy Dee	18 Jul 92	
	7:43.03	Tim Hutchings	14 Jul 89	
	7:43.1 +	Steve Cram	29 Aug 83	
	7:43.31 i	John Mayock	23 Feb 97	
	7:47.28		23 Jul 95	
	7:43.61	Anthony Whiteman	27 Jun 98	
	7:43.90	Ian Stewart II	26 Jun 82	
	7:44.40	Colin Reitz	9 Jul 83	
	7:44.76	Paul Davies-Hale	20 Jul 85	
20	7:45.2 +	Geoff Turnbull	12 Sep 86	
	7:45.29	Dennis Coates	9 Sep 77	
	7:45.41	Jon Brown	1 Aug 98	
	7:45.81	John Robson	13 Jul 84	
	7:46.22 i	Mark Rowland	27 Feb 90	
	7:49.82		28 Jul 89	
	7:46.39	Adrian Royle	28 Jun 83	
	7:46.40	Ian Hamer	20 Jan 90	

7:46.4	David Bedford	21 Jun 72	
7:46.6 +	Dave Black	14 Sep 73	
7:46.83	Ian Stewart I	26 May 76	
7:46.85 i	Ricky Wilde	15 Mar 70	30
7:46.95	David James	26 May 80	
7:47.12	Simon Mugglestone	27 Jun 88	
7:47.54	Paul Larkins	14 Jul 89	
7:47.56	Dick Callan	15 Jul 83	
7:47.6	Dick Taylor	6 Sep 69	
7:48.00	Richard Nerurkar	15 Jul 92	
7:48.09	Adrian Passey	28 Jul 89	
7:48.18	Mike McLeod	9 Jul 78	
7:48.28	Jon Richards	9 Jul 83	
7:48.28	Ian Gillespie	25 May 97	40
7:48.6 +	Nat Muir	27 Jun 80	
7:48.66	Julian Goater	26 May 80	
7:48.76	Neil Caddy	2 Aug 98	
7:48.81	Tim Redman	18 Aug 84	
7:49.1	Paul Lawther	27 Jun 78	
7:49.45	Gary Lough	30 May 95	
7:49.47	Roger Hackney	13 Jul 84	
7:49.64	Barry Smith	26 Jul 81	
7:49.72	Ray Smedley	9 Jul 78	
7:49.80	Steve Jones	13 Jul 84	50
7:49.83 i	Andy Keith	6 Feb 94	
7:50.04	Karl Keska	2 Aug 98	
7:50.20	Jon Solly	8 Aug 86	
7:50.38	Mark Scrutton	15 Jul 83	
7:50.69	Sean Cahill	23 May 85	
7:50.8	Ken Newton	3 Jun 82	
7:50.82 i	Matthew Yates	4 Mar 93	

2 MILES

8:13.51	Steve Ovett	15 Sep 78	
8:13.68	Brendan Foster	27 Aug 73	
8:14.93	Steve Cram	29 Aug 83	
8:15.53	Tim Hutchings	12 Sep 86	
8:15.98	Geoff Turnbull	12 Sep 86	
8:16.75	Dave Moorcroft	20 Aug 82	
8:17.12	Jack Buckner	12 Sep 86	
8:18.4 i	Nick Rose	17 Feb 78	
8:22.41		15 Sep 78	
8:18.98	Eamonn Martin	16 Jul 88	10
8:19.37	Nat Muir	27 Jun 80	
8:20.28	David James	27 Jun 80	
8:20.66	David Lewis	7 Sep 84	
8:21.09	Barry Smith	27 Jun 80	
8:21.86	David Black	14 Sep 73	
8:21.97	Rob Denmark	9 Aug 91	
8:22.0	Ian Stewart I	14 Aug 72	
8:22.65	Ian Hamer	17 Jul 92	
8:22.7 i	Graeme Fell	19 Feb 82	
8:22.98	Geoff Smith	27 Jun 80	
8:23.16	Gary Staines	9 Aug 91	20
8:23.80	Billy Dee	9 Aug 91	
8:23.92	Ray Smedley	6 Aug 76	
8:24.58	Adrian Royle	16 May 82	
8:24.82	Eddie Wedderburn	16 Jul 88	
8:25.02	Tony Simmons	6 Aug 76	
8:25.52	Colin Reitz	19 Aug 86	

5000 METRES

13:00.41	Dave Moorcroft	7 Jul	82
13:09.80	Ian Hamer	9 Jun	92
13:10.15	Jack Buckner	31 Aug	86
13:10.24	Rob Denmark	9 Jun	92
13:11.50	Tim Hutchings	11 Aug	84
13:14.28	Gary Staines	15 Aug	90
13:14.6 a	Brendan Foster	29 Jan	74
13:15.59	Julian Goater	11 Sep	81
13:16.70	John Nuttall	8 Jun	95
13:17.21	David Bedford	14 Jul	72
13:17.21	Keith Cullen	19 Jul	97
13:17.84	Eamonn Martin	14 Jul	89
13:17.9	Nat Muir	15 Jul	80
13:18.06	Ian Gillespie	19 Jul	97
13:18.6	Steve Jones	10 Jun	82
13:18.91	Nick Rose	28 Jun	84
13:19.03	Jon Brown	5 Aug	98
13:19.66	Ian McCafferty	14 Jul	72
13:20.06	Steve Ovett	30 Jun	86
13:20.09	Adrian Passey	19 Jul	97
13:21.13	David Lewis	4 Jul	85
13:21.14	Barry Smith	7 Jun	81
13:21.2	Tony Simmons	23 May	76
13:21.60	Paul Davies-Hale	8 Jul	88
13:21.73	Geoff Turnbull	5 Sep	86
13:21.83	Mark Rowland	1 Jun	88
13:22.17 i	Geoff Smith	12 Feb	82
13:26.33		8 Aug	81
13:22.39	Jon Solly	7 Jul	86
13:22.54	Dave Clarke	28 Jun	83
13:22.8 a	Ian Stewart I	25 Jul	70
13:23.26	Mike McLeod	24 Jun	80
13:23.36	Richard Nerurkar	10 Aug	90
13:23.48	John Doherty	1 Jun	85
13:23.52	Dave Black	29 Jan	74
13:23.71	Steve Binns	1 Jun	88
13:25.38	Paul Evans	28 Jun	95
13:26.0	Bernie Ford	30 Jul	77
13:26.19	Adrian Royle	4 Jul	83
13:26.2	Dick Taylor	13 Jun	70
13:26.37	Karl Keska	18 Apr	98
13:26.74	Craig Mochrie	25 Aug	89
13:26.97	John Mayock	9 Jun	92
13:27.14	Dick Callan	25 Aug	82
13:27.41	Billy Dee	10 Jul	92
13:27.63	Dermot Donnelly	1 Aug	98
13:27.75	Rod Finch	1 Aug	98
13:28.15	Malcolm Prince	14 Sep	79
13:28.29	Simon Mugglestone	8 Jul	88
13:28.58	Steve Cram	3 Jun	89
13:28.7 a	Charlie Spedding	13 Aug	78
13:28.99	Steve Emson	4 Sep	79
13:29.8 a	Allan Rushmer	25 Jul	70
13:29.91	John Downes	4 Jul	94
13:29.93	Mark Roberts	10 Jun	84
13:30.79	Steve Harris	18 Jun	83
13:30.8	Ricky Wilde	5 Jul	72
13:30.88	Tony Milovsorov	10 Jun	84
13:31.3 a	Neil Coupland	21 Jun	77

10000 METRES

27:18.14	Jon Brown	28 Aug	98
27:23.06	Eamonn Martin	2 Jul	88
27:30.3	Brendan Foster	23 Jun	78
27:30.80	David Bedford	13 Jul	73
27:31.19	Nick Rose	9 Jul	83
27:34.58	Julian Goater	26 Jun	82
27:36.27	David Black	29 Aug	78
27:39.14	Steve Jones	9 Jul	83
27:39.76	Mike McLeod	4 Sep	79
27:40.03	Richard Nerurkar	10 Jul	93
27:43.03	Ian Stewart I	9 Sep	77
27:43.59	Tony Simmons	30 Jun	77
27:43.74	Bernie Ford	9 Sep	77
27:43.76	Geoff Smith	13 Jun	81
27:47.16	Adrian Royle	10 Apr	82
27:47.79	Paul Evans	5 Jul	93
27:48.73	Gary Staines	6 Jul	91
27:51.76	Jon Solly	20 Jun	86
27:53.52	Keith Cullen	4 Apr	98
27:55.66	Steve Binns	9 Jul	83
27:55.77	Dave Clarke	25 May	82
27:57.77	Ian Hamer	13 Sep	91
27:59.12	Allister Hutton	30 May	86
27:59.24	Carl Thackery	16 Jul	87
27:59.33	Steve Harris	22 Jul	86
28:00.62	Jim Brown	1 Aug	75
28:00.64	Billy Dee	13 Sep	91
28:03.34	Rob Denmark	11 Jun	94
28:04.04	Andy Bristow	17 Aug	90
28:04.2	Ian Robinson	20 Apr	96
28:05.2	Dave Murphy	10 Apr	81
28:06.13	Barry Smith	7 Aug	81
28:06.6	Dick Taylor	22 Jun	69
28:07.43	John Nuttall	25 Aug	95
28:07.57	Tim Hutchings	7 Jul	90
28:08.12	Charlie Spedding	23 Jul	83
28:08.44	David Lewis	5 Jun	88
28:09.39	Mark Dalloway	5 Jun	88
28:11.07	Karl Harrison	20 Jun	86
28:11.71	Lachie Stewart	18 Jul	70
28:11.85	Lawrie Spence	29 May	83
28:13.04	Gerry Helme	29 May	83
28:13.13	Colin Moore	29 Jun	90
28:13.36	Jack Buckner	13 Sep	91
28:14.08	Jon Richards	20 Jun	86
28:14.65	Mike Tagg	10 Aug	71
28:14.89	Bernie Plain	1 Aug	75
28:15.58	Martin McLoughlin	20 Jun	86
28:16.0	Mike Baxter	23 May	74
28:16.73	Neil Coupland	11 Jun	77
28:17.00	Justin Hobbs	29 Jun	94
28:18.6	John Davies II	11 Apr	79
28:18.68	Terry Thornton	17 Aug	90
28:18.8	Nick Lees	7 May	79
28:19.97	Kevin Forster	29 May	83
28:20.29	Steve Kenyon	7 Aug	81
28:21.48	Roger Matthews	18 Jul	70
28:22.48	Paul Dugdale	10 Jul	93
28:22.53	Tony Staynings	11 Apr	80

10 KILOMETRES ROAD

27:34	Nick Rose	1 Apr 84
27:53	Mike O'Reilly	19 Oct 86
27:55	Mark Scrutton	5 Mar 84
27:56	John Doherty	4 Jul 86
27:58	Steve Harris	5 Apr 86
27:59	Steve Jones	28 Apr 84
28:02	Steve Binns	15 Apr 89
28:03	Jon Solly	5 Apr 86
28:03	Jack Buckner	28 Feb 87
28:05	Jon Brown	17 Oct 93
28:06	Geoff Smith	2 Mar 85
28:07	Colin Reitz	28 Apr 84
28:07	Peter Whitehead	4 Jul 96
28:09	Dave Moorcroft	16 May 82
28:10	Adrian Leek	10 Mar 84
28:10	Dave Clarke	5 May 85
28:11	Jon Richards	5 May 85
28:12	Dave Murphy	19 May 85
28:13	Allister Hutton	28 Apr 84
28:13	Paul Evans	8 Jan 95
28:14	Karl Harrison	5 May 85
28:14	David Lewis	5 Apr 86
28:14	Eamonn Martin	30 Apr 89
28:17	Paul Davies-Hale	21 Apr 85
28:17	Colin Moore	5 May 85
28:18	Steve Kenyon	15 Sep 85
28:19	Peter Tootell	28 Apr 84
28:19	Nigel Gates	5 May 85
28:19	Terry Greene	4 Apr 87
28:21	Bod Westwood	28 Apr 84
28:21	Andrew Pearson	5 Nov 95

course measurement uncertain

27:56	Steve Harris	4 Dec 83
28:00	Dave Lewis	5 Nov 83
28:00	Roger Hackney	4 Dec 83
28:01	Barry Smith	4 Dec 83
28:01	Steve Kenyon	21 Sep 86
28:04	Dave Bedford	27 Mar 77

downhill

27:20	Jon Brown	24 Sep 95
27:57	Malcolm East	25 Sep 82

10 MILES ROAD

46:02	Richard Nerurkar	17 Oct 93
46:11	Gary Staines	10 Oct 93
46:26	Carl Thackery	7 Apr 91
46:35	Paul Evans	21 Sep 97
46:41	Roger Hackney	6 Apr 86
46:42	Dave Murphy	28 Apr 84
46:43	Steve Kenyon	28 Aug 82
46:43	Nick Rose	25 Apr 87
46:48	Geoff Smith	2 May 82
46:49	Steve Jones	2 Apr 89
47:00	Paul Davies-Hale	10 Oct 93

intermediate times

46:10 +	Paul Evans	14 Sep 97
46:21 +	Nigel Adams	15 Sep 91
46:21 +	Carl Thackery	15 Sep 91
46:23 +	Allister Hutton	1 Jan 85

course measurement uncertain

45:13	Ian Stewart I	8 May 77
45:37	Barry Smith	22 Mar 81
45:44	Mike McLeod	9 Apr 78
46:03	Colin Moore	29 Aug 83
46:08	Nick Rose	26 Apr 81
46:11	Steve Kenyon	20 Jun 81
46:14	Charlie Spedding	12 Oct 86
46:17	Brendan Foster	9 Apr 78

downhill and measurement uncertain

46:05	Allister Hutton	3 Apr 82

HALF MARATHON

1:00:59	Steve Jones	8 Jun 86
1:01:03	Nick Rose	15 Sep 85
1:01:04	Carl Thackery	12 Apr 87
1:01:06	Richard Nerurkar	14 Apr 96
1:01:17	David Lewis	20 Sep 92
1:01:18	Paul Evans	14 Sep 97
1:01:28	Steve Brooks	23 Mar 97
1:01:31	Steve Kenyon	8 Jun 86
1:01:39	Geoff Smith	25 Sep 83
1:01:39	Paul Davies-Hale	15 Sep 91
1:01:49	Jon Brown	14 Sep 97
1:01:53	Nigel Adams	15 Sep 91
1:01:56	Mark Flint	22 Aug 93
1:01:57	Gary Staines	14 Sep 97
1:02:07	Kevin Forster	5 Apr 87
1:02:07	Martyn Brewer	20 Sep 87
1:02:07	Andrew Pearson	14 Sep 97
1:02:08	Steve Harris	20 Oct 85
1:02:11	Dave Clarke	5 Apr 92
1:02:15	Dave Murphy	16 Sep 84
1:02:16	Jim Haughey	20 Sep 87
1:02:16	Dave Long II	15 Mar 92
1:02:19	Dave Long I	11 Dec 81
1:02:22	Colin Moore	26 May 85
1:02:24	Jimmy Ashworth	8 Jun 86
1:02:25	Barry Royden	18 Sep 94
1:02:28	Terry Greene	12 Apr 86
1:02:28	Allister Hutton	21 Jun 87
1:02:30	Tony Milovsorov	21 Jun 87
1:02:33	Steve Brace	15 Sep 91
1:02:33	Billy Dee	4 Apr 93
1:02:33	Peter Whitehead	5 May 95
1:02:36	Roger Hackney	10 Sep 89
1:02:37	Rob Denmark	18 Sep 94
1:02:39	Neil Tennant	8 May 88
1:02:39	Mike McLeod	18 Jun 89
1:02:40	Dave Swanston	20 Sep 92

intermediate time

1:02:36 +	Ron Hill	23 Jul 70

course measurement uncertain

1:00:09	Paul Evans	15 Jan 95
1:01:47	Dave Long II	17 Mar 91
1:02:08	Ray Smedly	28 Mar 82
1:02:09	Steve Anders	25 Sep 88
1:02:19	Mike Carroll	3 Jun 90
1:02:23	Charlie Spedding	15 Mar 87

MARATHON

	2:07:13	Steve Jones	20	Oct	85
	2:08:33	Charlie Spedding	21	Apr	85
	2:08:36	Richard Nerurkar	13	Apr	97
	2:08:52	Paul Evans	20	Oct	96
	2:09:08	Geoff Smith	23	Oct	83
	2:09:12	Ian Thompson	31	Jan	74
	2:09:16	Allister Hutton	21	Apr	85
	2:09:24	Hugh Jones	9	May	82
	2:09:28	Ron Hill	23	Jul	70
10	2:09:28	John Graham	23	May	81
	2:09:43	Mike Gratton	17	Apr	83
	2:09:54	Tony Milovsorov	23	Apr	89
	2:10:12	Gerry Helme	17	Apr	83
	2:10:13	Jon Brown	19	Oct	97
	2:10:30	Dave Long II	21	Apr	91
	2:10:35	Steve Brace	21	Jan	96
	2:10:39	Mike O'Reilly	5	Dec	93
	2:10:48	Bill Adcocks	8	Dec	68
	2:10:50	Eamonn Martin	18	Apr	93
20	2:10:51	Bernie Ford	2	Dec	79
	2:10:52	Kevin Forster	17	Apr	88
	2:10:55	Chris Bunyan	18	Apr	83
	2:11:06	Dave Buzza	31	Oct	93
	2:11:18	Dave Murphy	12	Jun	83
	2:11:22	Dave Cannon	6	Sep	80
	2:11:25	Paul Davies-Hale	29	Oct	89
	2:11:25	Gary Staines	20	Oct	96
	2:11:35	Malcolm East	20	Apr	81
	2:11:36	Kenny Stuart	15	Jan	89
30	2:11:40	Steve Kenyon	13	Jun	82
	2:11:43	Jimmy Ashworth	29	Sep	85
	2:11:44	Jim Dingwall	17	Apr	83
	2:11:50	Fraser Clyne	2	Dec	84
	2:11:54	Martin McCarthy	17	Apr	83
	2:11:58	Mark Hudspith	2	Apr	95
	2:12:04	Jim Alder	23	Jul	70
	2:12:07	Jon Solly	14	Oct	90
	2:12:07	Mark Flint	17	Apr	94
	2:12:12	Dennis Fowles	13	May	84
40	2:12:12	Andy Green	25	Apr	93
	2:12:13	John Wheway	17	Apr	88
	2:12:17	Dave Long I	16	Jan	82
	2:12:19	Don Faircloth	23	Jul	70
	2:12:23	Peter Whitehead	2	Apr	95
	2:12:32	Trevor Wright	3	Dec	78
	2:12:33	Tony Simmons	7	May	78
	2:12:37	Carl Thackery	25	Oct	92
	2:12:41	Derek Stevens	16	Jun	84
	2:12:50	Jeff Norman	7	May	78
50	2:13:06	Greg Hannon	13	May	79

2000 METRES STEEPLECHASE

5:19.86	Mark Rowland	28	Aug	88
5:21.77	Tom Hanlon	11	Jun	92
5:23.56	Tom Buckner	17	Jul	92
5:23.6	Roger Hackney	10	Jun	82
5:23.71	Colin Walker	28	Aug	88
5:23.87	Colin Reitz	28	Jun	84
5:24.91	Eddie Wedderburn	19	Aug	86

	5:26.24	Paul Davies-Hale	26	Aug	85
	5:26.64	Nick Peach	19	Aug	86
	5:26.82"	David Lewis	12	Jun	83	10
	5:30.6	Dennis Coates	23	Apr	78
	5:30.86	Tony Staynings	26	May	76
	5:31.04	John Hartigan	17	Aug	90
	5:31.09	Peter McColgan	5	Aug	86
	5:31.43	John Bicourt	26	May	76

3000 METRES STEEPLECHASE

	8:07.96	Mark Rowland	30	Sep	88
	8:12.11	Colin Reitz	5	Sep	86
	8:12.58	Tom Hanlon	3	Aug	91
	8:15.16	Graeme Fell	17	Aug	83
	8:18.32	Eddie Wedderburn	5	Jul	88
	8:18.91	Roger Hackney	30	Jul	88
	8:18.95	Dennis Coates	25	Jul	76
	8:20.83	Paul Davies-Hale	10	Jun	84
	8:22.48	John Davies II	13	Sep	74
	8:22.82	John Bicourt	8	Jun	76	10
	8:23.90	Justin Chaston	18	Jul	94
	8:24.64	Spencer Duval	16	Jul	95
	8:25.15	Colin Walker	28	Jun	92
	8:25.50	Tom Buckner	28	Aug	92
	8:26.05	Keith Cullen	21	Aug	95
	8:26.33	Rob Hough	6	Jul	96
	8:26.4	Andy Holden	15	Sep	72
	8:26.6	Gordon Rimmer	4	Jun	80
	8:27.21	Tony Staynings	15	Jun	80
	8:27.8	Steve Hollings	5	Aug	73	20
	8:27.93	Peter McColgan	25	Jun	91
	8:28.6	David Bedford	10	Sep	71
	8:29.46	Julian Marsay	14	Jul	79
	8:29.72	David Lewis	29	May	83
	8:30.6 a	Peter Griffiths	17	Jul	77
	8:30.8	Gerry Stevens	1	Sep	69
	8:31.09	Ian Gilmour	16	Jul	78
	8:31.22	David Lee	19	Jun	92
	8:32.00	Steve Jones	8	Aug	80
	8:32.06	David Camp	10	Aug	74	30
	8:32.13	Barry Knight	25	Jul	82
	8:32.4 a	Maurice Herriott	17	Oct	64
	8:32.76	Christian Stephenson	26	Jul	98
	8:33.0	John Jackson	13	Aug	69
	8:33.8 a	Gareth Bryan-Jones	23	Jul	70
	8:33.8	Peter Morris	4	Aug	73
	8:33.83	Richard Charleston	24	May	80
	8:33.89	Nick Peach	21	Jun	86
	8:33.97	John Hartigan	20	Jul	90
	8:34.77	Kevin Capper	18	Aug	85	40
	8:34.83	Ken Baker	1	Jul	84
	8:35.49	Micky Morris	14	Aug	76
	8:35.52	Neil Smart	28	Aug	89
	8:35.6	Ron McAndrew	9	Jul	71
	8:35.8	John Wild	3	Aug	77
	8:36.2 a	Bernie Hayward	26	Jan	74
	8:36.55	Mick Hawkins	16	Jul	95
	8:37.0	Ernie Pomfret	15	Jul	67
	8:37.59	Dave Baptiste	28	Aug	89
	8:37.68	Darren Mead	26	Jun	93	50

110 METRES HURDLES

12.91	Colin Jackson	20 Aug 93	
13.00	Tony Jarrett	20 Aug 93	
13.29	Jon Ridgeon	15 Jul 87	
13.42	David Nelson	27 Aug 91	
13.43	Mark Holtom	4 Oct 82	
13.44	Hugh Teape	14 Aug 92	
13.51	Nigel Walker	3 Aug 90	
13.52	Andy Tulloch	11 Aug 94	
13.53	Paul Gray	22 Aug 94	
13.60	Wilbert Greaves	21 Aug 85	10
13.60	Neil Owen	28 Jun 95	
13.69	Berwyn Price	18 Aug 73	
13.72	David Hemery	1 Aug 70	
13.75	Lloyd Cowan	17 Jul 94	
13.79	Alan Pascoe	17 Jun 72	
13.80	Ross Baillie	19 Sep 98	
13.82	Damien Greaves	21 Jun 97	
13.86	Ken Campbell	23 Aug 94	
13.96	Steve Buckeridge	31 May 86	
14.02	Mark Lambeth	9 Jul 95	20
14.03	Brett St Louis	27 Jun 87	
14.03	Brian Taylor	19 May 96	
14.04	Daley Thompson	28 Aug 86	
14.08	Paul Brice	26 Aug 83	
14.09	Colin Hamplett	11 Aug 90	
14.10	Graham Gower	15 Jul 72	
14.10	Bob Danville	4 Jul 76	
14.10	Jamie Quarry	25 Jun 94	
14.11	Neil Fraser	11 Jul 87	
14.11	Ererton Harrison	31 Jul 91	30
14.12	Matthew Clements	17 May 98	
14.13	Mark Stern	22 Jun 96	
14.14	Mike Hogan	5 Sep 63	
14.14	Max Robertson	7 Jun 86	
14.14	Martin Nicholson	12 Jun 94	
14.16 A	Mike Parker	16 Oct 68	
14.26		17 Oct 64	
14.16	Martyn Hendry	25 Aug 97	
14.17	Colin Bovell	23 Jul 94	
14.18	Chris Breen	13 Jul 75	
14.18	James Archampong	21 Jul 94	40
14.19	C. J. Kirkpatrick	16 Jun 73	
14.20 A	Stuart Storey	16 Oct 68	
14.20	Kevin Lumsdon	16 Jul 94	
14.21	David Wilson	15 Jul 72	
14.21	Alan Cronin	13 Jul 75	
14.21	Mark Whitby	14 Jun 85	
14.23	Alan Tapp	14 Jun 86	
14.24	Kieran Moore	7 Jun 86	
14.25	Ben Warmington	31 Jul 98	
14.26	Peter Hildreth	14 Sep 58	50
14.26	Phil Barthropp	24 Jun 84	
14.26	Dominic Bradley	1 Aug 98	
14.28	Gus McKenzie	25 May 80	
14.28	Glenn MacDonald	22 Aug 82	
14.28	Nick Dakin	12 Jun 93	

wind assisted

13.49	Nigel Walker	3 Jun 89	
13.65	Berwyn Price	25 Aug 75	
13.66	David Hemery	18 Jul 70	
13.96	Mike Robbins	28 Mar 98	
13.97	Brett St Louis	30 Jul 88	
13.99	Bob Danville	14 Aug 76	
14.06	Tony James	22 Aug 81	
14.07	Dominic Bradley	24 May 98	
14.08	David Wilson	15 Jul 72	
14.11	Mark Stern	20 Jun 93	10
14.14	James Archampong	25 May 96	
14.16	Mark Hatton	14 Jul 79	
14.17	C. J. Kirkpatrick	13 Jul 74	
14.19	Alan Cronin	25 Aug 75	
14.19	Norman Ashman	15 Aug 92	
14.22	Phil Barthropp	1 Jul 84	
14.22	Dave Sweetman	24 May 98	
14.23	Gus McKenzie	21 May 80	
14.23	John Wallace	26 Jul 86	
14.23	Greg Dunson	10 Jun 89	20
14.24	Ben Warmington	5 Jul 98	
14.25	Stuart Storey	18 Jul 70	
14.25	Glenn MacDonald	13 Jun 82	
14.25	Anthony Brannen	30 Apr 95	
14.25	Chris Rawlinson	28 Jun 97	

hand timing

13.5	Berwyn Price	1 Jul 73	
13.6	David Hemery	5 Jul 69	
13.7	Alan Pascoe	5 Jul 69	
13.7	C. J. Kirkpatrick	29 Jun 74	
13.8	Martin Nicholson	25 Jun 94	
13.9	Mike Parker	2 Oct 63	
13.9	David Wilson	29 Jun 74	
13.9	Brian Taylor	8 May 93	
14.1	Stuart Storey	2 Aug 67	
14.1	Colin Bovell	17 Jul 94	10
14.1 y	Laurie Taitt	13 Jul 63	
14.2		2 Oct 63	
14.2	Bob Birrell	6 Sep 61	
14.2	Andy Todd	27 Oct 67	
14.2	Mark Whitby	12 May 84	
14.2	James Hughes	2 Jul 94	
14.2	Anthony Brannen	6 May 95	
14.2	Chris Rawlinson	3 May 97	
14.2 y	Rodney Morrod	13 Jun 64	

wind assisted

12.8	Colin Jackson	10 Jan 90	
13.4	Berwyn Price	7 Jul 76	
13.5	Neil Owen	2 Jun 96	
13.5	Andy Tulloch	2 Jun 96	
13.7	Lloyd Cowan	27 Apr 95	
14.0	Laurie Taitt	13 Sep 62	
14.0 y	Bob Birrell	9 Sep 61	
14.1	Donald Finlay	8 Sep 37	
14.1	Neil Fraser	30 May 87	
14.1	James Archampong	6 Jul 96	

400 METRES HURDLES

47.82	Kriss Akabusi	6 Aug 92	
48.12 A	David Hemery	15 Oct 68	
48.52		2 Sep 72	
48.59	Alan Pascoe	30 Jun 75	
48.73	Jon Ridgeon	6 Sep 92	
49.03 A	John Sherwood	15 Oct 68	
49.88		13 Aug 69	
49.07	Gary Cadogan	22 Jul 94	
49.11	Gary Oakes	26 Jul 80	
49.16	Paul Gray	18 Aug 98	
49.25	Max Robertson	28 Aug 90	
10 49.26	Peter Crampton	8 Aug 94	
49.49	Mark Holtom	20 Jul 85	
49.60	Phil Beattie	28 Jul 86	
49.65	Bill Hartley	2 Aug 75	
49.69	Chris Rawlinson	13 Jul 97	
49.79	Anthony Borsumato	27 Jun 98	
49.82	Martin Gillingham	14 Aug 87	
49.82	Gary Jennings	27 Jun 95	
49.86	Martin Briggs	6 Jun 84	
49.95	Steve Sole	24 Jul 83	
20 50.01	Phil Harries	5 Jun 88	
50.05	Lawrence Lynch	15 Jun 96	
50.16	Paul Thompson	17 May 96	
50.1 a	John Cooper	16 Oct 64	
50.19	Steve Coupland	12 Jun 94	
50.20	Matt Douglas	17 Sep 98	
50.31	Tony Williams	27 Jun 95	
50.37	Bob Danville	27 Jul 82	
50.38	Andy Todd	18 Sep 69	
50.43	Charles Robertson-Adams	17 Aug 97	
30 50.49	Eddie Betts	13 Jul 97	
50.52	Paul Hibbert	30 Jun 96	
50.57	Blair Young	14 Mar 98	
50.58	Colin O'Neill	29 Jan 74	
50.58	Mike Whittingham	7 Aug 82	
50.68	Peter Warden	18 Jun 66	
50.70	Noel Levy	8 Jul 94	
50.71	Steve Hawkins	4 Jun 89	
50.79	Mark Davidson	17 Jun 89	
50.79	Lloyd Cowan	3 Jun 95	
40 50.82 "	Paul Atherton	12 Jun 83	
50.91		6 Jun 84	
50.84	Mark Whitby	6 Jun 84	
50.86	Wilbert Greaves	18 May 80	
50.88	Greg Dunson	7 Jun 92	
50.91	Brian Whittle	5 Jun 93	
50.94	Trevor Burton	17 Jul 87	
50.97	Dave Savage	15 Jun 96	
50.98	Tom Farrell	15 Jun 60	
50.98	Stan Devine	14 Jul 82	
51.04	Peter Kelly	12 Jun 76	
50 51.08	Tim Gwynne	30 May 94	

hand timing

49.9	Andy Todd	9 Oct 69
50.5	Wilbert Greaves	12 Feb 80
50.7	Steve Black	20 Aug 74
50.7	Stewart McCallum	21 Mar 76
50.8	Dave Schärer	26 Jun 71

HIGH JUMP

2.38 i	Steve Smith	4 Feb 94	
2.37		20 Sep 92	
2.37 i	Dalton Grant	13 Mar 94	
2.36		1 Sep 91	
2.32 i	Brendan Reilly	24 Feb 94	
2.31		17 Jul 92	
2.31	Geoff Parsons	26 Aug 94	
2.28 i	John Holman	28 Jan 89	
2.24		27 May 89	
2.28	Ben Challenger	31 May 98	
2.26	James Brierley	3 Aug 96	
2.25	Floyd Manderson	20 Aug 88	
2.24	Mark Naylor	28 Jun 80	
2.24	John Hill	23 Aug 85	10
2.24	Phil McDonnell	26 Aug 85	
2.23	Mark Lakey	29 Aug 82	
2.23 i	David Abrahams	12 Mar 83	
2.19		7 Oct 82	
2.21	Fayyaz Ahmed	29 Jun 86	
2.21	Steve Chapman	30 Jul 89	
2.20	Brian Burgess	11 Jun 78	
2.20	Trevor Llewelyn	15 Jul 83	
2.20	Byron Morrison	14 Jul 84	
2.20 i	Henderson Pierre	10 Jan 87	
2.18		16 Aug 86	
2.20	Alex Kruger	18 Jun 88	20
2.20	Ossie Cham	21 May 89	
2.20 i	Warren Caswell	10 Mar 90	
2.18		2 Sep 90	
2.20	Colin Bent	16 Jun 96	
2.20 i	Stuart Ohrland	1 Feb 97	
2.17		27 Aug 94	
2.20	Stuart Smith	13 Apr 97	
2.20	David Barnetson	3 Aug 97	
2.19 i	Mike Robbins	3 Feb 96	
2.17		5 Aug 95	
2.18	Tim Foulger	23 Sep 79	
2.18	Rupert Charles	25 Jul 82	
2.18	Steve Ritchie	15 Jul 89	30
2.18	Hopeton Lindo	23 Jul 89	
2.18	Andrew Lynch	9 Jul 95	
2.18 i	Tim Gilhooly	9 Mar 97	
2.15		31 May 97	
2.16 i	Mike Butterfield	23 Jan 76	
2.16 i	Claude Moseley	13 Apr 80	
2.16		19 Jul 81	
2.16 i	David Watson	13 Mar 82	
2.15		19 Aug 84	
2.16	Andy Hutchinson	2 Sep 84	
2.16	Mike Powell	3 Sep 88	
2.16	John Wallace	29 Jul 90	
2.16	Richard Aspden	7 Jul 95	40
2.16	Rob Brocklebank	7 Jul 95	
2.16	Ian Holliday	8 Aug 98	
2.15	16 athletes		
	including 4 indoors		

POLE VAULT

	Mark	Athlete	Date	
	5.80	Nick Buckfield	27 May 98	
	5.65	Keith Stock	7 Jul 81	
	5.60	Neil Winter	19 Aug 95	
	5.59	Brian Hooper	6 Sep 80	
	5.52	Mike Edwards	13 May 93	
	5.50	Paul Williamson	6 Jul 96	
	5.50	Kevin Hughes	29 Jul 98	
	5.45 i	Andy Ashurst	16 Feb 92	
	5.40		19 Jun 88	
10	5.45	Mike Barber	27 Jul 97	
	5.40 A	Jeff Gutteridge ¶	23 Apr 80	
	5.40		5 Jun 83	
	5.40 i	Matt Belsham	10 Feb 96	
	5.35		26 Jun 93	
	5.40	Tim Thomas	2 Aug 97	
	5.35	Ian Tullett	26 Jul 98	
	5.30	Dean Mellor	17 Jun 95	
	5.26	Mark Johnson	31 Aug 91	
	5.25	Mike Bull	22 Sep 73	
	5.25	Allan Williams	29 Aug 77	
	5.25	Daley Thompson	15 Jun 86	
20	5.21	Graham Eggleton	10 Jul 82	
	5.20	Billy Davey	5 Jun 83	
	5.20	Warren Siley	4 Aug 90	
	5.20	Mark Hodgkinson	24 Aug 96	
	5.20	Ben Flint	2 Aug 97	
	5.20	Neil Young	2 Aug 97	
	5.20	Christian Linskey	24 May 98	
	5.18	Steve Chappell	15 Jun 78	
	5.11	Andrew Gayle	10 Aug 91	
	5.10	Darren Wright	12 Jun 88	
30	5.10	Paul Phelps	9 Jul 89	
	5.10	Mark Grant	20 May 95	
	5.10	Mark Davis	9 Jun 96	
	5.02	Bob Kingman	29 Aug 94	
	5.02 i	Craig Guite	11 Jan 97	
	4.90		28 Jul 96	
	5.01	Paul Hoad	16 Aug 86	
	5.00	Richard Gammage	19 Aug 84	
	5.00	Brian Taylor	5 May 91	
	5.00	Dan Gilby	20 Jul 91	
	5.00	Paul Wray	26 Jul 91	
40	5.00	Alex Greig	31 May 92	
	5.00	Barry Thomas	23 Aug 92	
	5.00	Ian Wilding	1 Jun 96	
42	5.00	Andrew Weston	29 Jul 98	
	4.98 A	Dick Williamson	17 Apr 78	
	4.90	15 athletes including 3 indoors		

LONG JUMP

	8.23	Lynn Davies	30 Jun 68	
	8.15	Stewart Faulkner	16 Jul 90	
	8.14	Mark Forsythe	7 Jul 91	
	8.11	Nathan Morgan	24 Jul 98	
	8.10	Fred Salle	9 Sep 94	
	8.08	Roy Mitchell	27 Sep 80	
	8.05 i	Barrington Williams	11 Feb 89	
	8.01		17 Jun 89	
	8.03	Steve Phillips	5 Aug 98	
	8.01	Daley Thompson	8 Aug 84	
	8.00	Derrick Brown	7 Aug 85	10
	7.98	Alan Lerwill	29 Jun 74	
	7.94 i	Paul Johnson	10 Mar 89	
	7.85		3 Jun 89	
	7.91	John King	26 Sep 87	
	7.90	Ian Simpson	3 Jun 89	
	7.87	Keith Fleming	7 Jun 87	
	7.86	Darren Ritchie	15 Jun 96	
	7.84	Wayne Griffith	25 Aug 89	
	7.79	John Morbey	11 Jul 64	
	7.89 for BER		8 Aug 66	
	7.79	Geoff Hignett	31 May 71	
	7.79	Don Porter	13 Jul 75	20
	7.78 i	George Audu	13 Feb 98	
	7.72		23 May 98	
	7.77	Len Tyson	25 Jul 82	
	7.76	Carl Howard	31 Jul 93	
	7.75	Ken Cocks	2 Jul 78	
	7.75	Trevor Hoyte	6 May 84	
	7.75	Michael Morgan	30 Jul 94	
	7.74	Fred Alsop	6 Jun 64	
	7.74 i	Phil Scott	17 Feb 73	
	7.68		27 May 73	
	7.74 i	Aston Moore	10 Jan 81	
	7.74	John Herbert	14 Jul 85	30
	7.74	David Burgess	4 Jul 87	
	7.73	Jason Canning	20 Apr 88	
	7.72	Femi Abejide	20 Jun 86	
	7.71	Billy Kirkpatrick	2 Jun 78	
	7.71 i	Keith Connor	20 Feb 81	
	7.71	Chris Davidson	21 Jun 97	
	7.70	Kevin Liddington	27 Aug 88	
	7.68	Garry Slade	1 Aug 92	
	7.67	Dave Walker	14 Sep 68	
	7.67	Onochie Onourah	15 Jun 96	40
	7.66	Tony Henry	12 Jun 77	
	7.66	Barry Nevison	7 Jul 85	
	7.66	John Shepherd	18 Jun 88	
	7.66	Julian Flynn	3 May 97	
	7.65 i	John Munroe	11 Feb 95	
	7.64		24 Jun 95	
	7.64	Gus Udo	6 Sep 80	
	7.64	Eddie Starrs	11 Jul 81	
	7.64 i	Enyinna Chukukere	6 Mar 94	
	7.63	Henry Walters	15 Aug 81	

wind assisted

	Mark	Athlete	Date	
	8.17	Mark Forsythe	11 Jun 89	
	8.16	Roy Mitchell	26 Jun 76	
	8.15	Alan Lerwill	29 May 72	
	8.12	Derrick Brown	14 Jun 86	
	8.11	Daley Thompson	7 Aug 78	
	8.04	Ian Simpson	3 Jun 89	
	7.96	Colin Jackson	17 May 86	
	7.94	John Herbert	25 Jul 82	
	7.94	John King	20 Jun 86	
	7.94	Chris Davidson	21 Jun 97	10
	7.93	David Burgess	15 Jun 86	
	7.91	Steve Ingram	18 Jun 94	

TRIPLE JUMP

18.29	Jonathan Edwards	7 Aug 95
17.57 A	Keith Connor	5 Jun 82
17.30		9 Jun 82
17.41	John Herbert	2 Sep 85
17.21	Tosi Fasinro	27 Jul 93
17.18	Francis Agyepong	7 Jul 95
17.10	Larry Achike	18 Sep 98
17.06	Julian Golley	10 Sep 94
17.01	Eric McCalla	3 Aug 84
16.87	Mike Makin	2 Aug 86
16.86	Aston Moore	16 Aug 81
16.75	Vernon Samuels	7 Aug 88
16.58	Femi Akinsanya	15 Jun 96
16.46	Fred Alsop	16 Oct 64
16.35	Phillips Idowu	21 Jun 98
16.32	Tayo Erogbogbo	21 Aug 95
16.30	Femi Abejide	27 Jun 85
16.29 i	David Johnson	1 Mar 78
16.18		22 Jun 75
16.26	Joe Sweeney	3 Aug 91
16.22	Derek Boosey	15 Jun 68
16.20	Rez Cameron	5 Jun 88
16.18	Tony Wadhams	6 Jul 69
16.17	John Mackenzie	17 Sep 94
16.16	Conroy Brown	19 Sep 81
16.15	Wayne Green	10 Jul 88
16.15	Michael Brown	23 Jul 89
16.13	Steven Anderson	11 Jun 83
16.10	Alan Lerwill	28 Aug 71
16.09	Courtney Charles	17 Jun 90
16.08	Craig Duncan	21 Jun 86
16.02	Peter Akwaboah	15 Jun 89
15.98	Frank Attoh	5 Sep 80
15.97	Mike Ralph	23 Jul 64
15.97	Carl Howard	6 May 95
15.95	Derek Browne	12 Jun 93
15.92	John Slaney	15 Oct 77
15.92	Lawrence Lynch	13 Jul 85
15.91 i	Akin Oyediran	3 Mar 84
15.91	Dave Emmanuel	31 Aug 91
15.90	David Wood	16 Sep 84
15.88	John Phillips	14 May 78
15.87	Chris Colman	15 Jul 78
15.87	Stewart Faulkner	22 Aug 87
15.86 i	Donovan Perkins	23 Jan 81
15.86	Joe Allison	24 Aug 85

wind assisted

18.43	Jonathan Edwards	25 Jun 95
17.81	Keith Connor	9 Oct 82
17.30	Tosi Fasinro	12 Jun 93
17.29 A	Francis Agyepong	29 Jul 95
17.24		2 Jul 95
17.02	Aston Moore	14 Jun 81
16.82	Vernon Samuels	24 Jun 89
16.65	Fred Alsop	13 Aug 65
16.49	Tony Wadhams	16 Sep 69
16.44	Tayo Erogbogbo	31 May 97
16.38	Femi Abejide	10 Jun 89
16.38	Courtney Charles	22 Jul 90

SHOT

21.68	Geoff Capes	18 May 80
20.85 i	Mark Proctor	25 Jan 98
20.04		1 Jul 98
20.45	Shaun Pickering	17 Aug 97
20.43	Mike Winch	22 May 74
20.33	Paul Edwards ¶	9 Jul 91
19.56	Arthur Rowe	7 Aug 61
19.49	Matt Simson	28 Aug 94
19.46	Carl Myerscough	6 Sep 98
19.44 i	Simon Williams	28 Jan 89
19.17		18 May 91
19.43	Bill Tancred	18 May 74
19.18	Jeff Teale ¶	7 Aug 68
19.01	Billy Cole	21 Jun 86
18.94	Bob Dale	12 Jun 76
18.93	Paul Buxton	13 May 77
18.88	Mark Edwards	14 Jul 98
18.85	Lee Newman	2 Jun 96
18.62	Martyn Lucking	2 Oct 62
18.59 i	Alan Carter	11 Apr 65
18.26		1 May 65
18.50	Mike Lindsay	2 Jul 63
18.46	Roger Kennedy	22 May 77
18.46 i	Simon Rodhouse	20 Feb 82
18.20		25 Jul 82
18.40	Stephan Hayward	9 Jun 96
18.35	Peter Tancred	9 Jul 74
18.34	Richard Slaney	3 Jul 83
18.14 i	Neal Brunning ¶	26 Jan 92
17.45		17 Aug 91
18.05	John Watts	19 Aug 72
18.04	Andy Vince	30 Apr 83
17.96	Nigel Spratley	28 Aug 94
17.95	Graham Savory	4 Jun 88
17.92	Nick Tabor	9 Apr 83
17.87	Bill Fuller	15 Jul 72
17.87 i	Ian Lindley	15 Mar 81
17.58		25 May 81
17.87 i	Antony Zaidman	22 Jan 83
17.22		4 Jul 81
17.79	John Alderson	31 Jul 74
17.78	Steve Whyte	11 Feb 89
17.62	Neil Gray	7 Jun 89
17.55	David Callaway	1 Aug 93
17.54	Eric Irvine	16 Aug 86
17.47	Carl Jennings	13 Sep 87
17.45	Abi Ekoku	3 Feb 90
17.44	Hamish Davidson	3 Jun 78
17.41	Lee Wiltshire	1 May 94
17.41	Jamie Cockburn	12 May 96
17.40	Barry King	11 Apr 70
17.40	Allan Seatory	27 Apr 75
17.36 i	Chris Ellis	8 Dec 84
17.26		10 Sep 86
17.30	Mark Aldridge	19 Sep 82
17.25	Tony Satchwell	2 Jun 84
17.25	Emeka Udechuku	20 Sep 97
17.14	Gary Sollitt	1 Jun 97
17.13	John Turton	29 Apr 77

DISCUS

66.64	Perris Wilkins	6 Jun 98	
65.16	Richard Slaney	1 Jul 85	
64.94	Bill Tancred	21 Jul 74	
64.60	Robert Weir	26 Jul 97	
62.80	Glen Smith	12 Apr 97	
62.36	Peter Tancred	8 May 80	
61.86	Paul Mardle	13 Jun 84	
61.62	Peter Gordon	15 Jun 91	
61.14	Simon Williams	18 Apr 92	
61.10	Kevin Brown	30 Aug 97	10
61.00	Allan Seatory	6 Oct 74	
60.97	Emeka Udechuku	5 Jul 98	
60.92	Graham Savory	10 May 86	
60.48	Lee Newman	10 May 97	
60.42	Mike Cushion	16 Aug 75	
60.19	Carl Myerscough	8 Aug 98	
60.08	Abi Ekoku	16 May 90	
59.84	Colin Sutherland ¶	10 Jun 78	
59.76	John Hillier	27 Jul 74	
59.70	John Watts	14 Jul 72	20
58.64	Steve Casey	19 May 91	
58.58	Darrin Morris	22 Jun 91	
58.34	Geoff Capes	29 Sep 73	
58.08	Mike Winch	7 Sep 75	
57.58	Arthur McKenzie	17 Aug 69	
57.12	Paul Edwards ¶	10 Aug 88	
57.10	Dennis Roscoe	3 May 80	
57.00	Gerry Carr	17 Jul 65	
56.71	Roy Hollingsworth	14 Sep 63	
56.66	Gary Herrington	15 Jun 96	30
56.46	Paul Reed	24 Apr 96	
56.42	Paul Buxton	6 Aug 76	
56.40	Guy Dirkin	1 Aug 75	
55.68	Neville Thompson	12 Jun 93	
55.68	Leith Marar	24 Jul 96	
55.60	Jeff Clare	25 Jul 88	
55.52	Jamie Murphy	29 Jul 95	
55.42	Geoff Tyler	3 May 80	
55.34	Nick Woolcott	27 Jul 88	
55.32	Mike Lindsay	4 May 60	40
55.08	Mark Proctor	9 Jul 97	
55.04	Denzil McDonald	28 Aug 95	
54.78	Colin Bastien	29 Mar 87	
54.38	Shaun Pickering	26 Aug 89	
54.36	Matt Symonds	24 Jun 95	
54.27	Mark Pharoah	27 Nov 56	
54.16	Scott Hayes	23 Mar 97	
54.01	Eric Cleaver	21 Oct 62	
53.76	John Turton	18 May 79	
53.76	Robert Russell	8 Sep 96	50
53.64 A	Barry King	7 May 66	
53.54	Tony Satchwell	30 Sep 73	
53.48	George Patience	11 Jul 87	
53.46	Neal Brunning ¶	1 May 91	
53.24	Andy Drzewiecki	8 Aug 76	
53.06	Mark Davies	20 Jun 92	
53.02	Nick Tabor	3 May 80	
52.81	Peter Nimmo	3 Apr 65	
52.38	Michael Jemi-Alade	30 Jun 87	

HAMMER

77.54	Martin Girvan	12 May 84	
77.30	Dave Smith I	13 Jul 85	
77.02	Matt Mileham	11 May 84	
75.40	Chris Black	23 Jul 83	
75.10	Dave Smith II	27 May 96	
75.08	Robert Weir	3 Oct 82	
74.02	Paul Head	30 Aug 90	
74.02	Mick Jones	18 Sep 98	
73.86	Barry Williams	1 Jul 76	
73.80	Jason Byrne	19 Sep 92	10
73.20	Paul Dickenson	22 May 76	
71.60	Shane Peacock	24 Jun 90	
71.28	Peter Vivian	25 Jun 95	
71.00	Ian Chipchase	17 Aug 74	
70.88	Howard Payne	29 Jun 74	
70.30	Stewart Rogerson	14 Aug 88	
70.28	Paul Buxton	19 May 79	
70.24	John Pearson	11 May 97	
70.09	Bill Beauchamp	19 Jul 98	
69.52	Jim Whitehead	23 Sep 79	20
68.64	Shaun Pickering	7 Apr 84	
68.18	Ron James	2 Jun 82	
67.82	Steve Whyte	15 Apr 89	
67.45	Steve Pearson	27 Jun 98	
67.32	Gareth Cook	1 Jun 91	
66.97	Chris Howe	6 Jun 98	
65.36	Russell Devine	23 Apr 94	
65.30	Karl Andrews	2 Jul 94	
64.95	Mike Ellis	4 Jun 59	
64.80	Bruce Fraser	30 Sep 73	30
64.64	Iain Park	22 Jul 98	
64.54	Michael Petra	30 May 79	
64.36	Andrew Tolputt	27 Jun 87	
63.98	Craig Ellams	13 Jul 97	
63.74	Mark Sterling	18 Jul 84	
63.20	Peter Gordon	17 Sep 82	
63.16	Graham Callow	29 May 89	
62.88	Anthony Swain	13 Apr 97	
62.70	Paul Barnard	19 Jul 95	
62.60	Peter Weir	2 Aug 87	40
62.60	Rob Earle	1 Aug 95	
62.56	Adrian Palmer	6 Aug 94	
62.54	Tony Elvin	25 May 70	
62.43	Simon Bown	18 Jul 98	
62.42	Malcolm Fenton	16 May 82	
62.40	Lawrie Nisbet	5 Jul 86	
62.32	Peter Aston	6 Sep 75	
62.28	Lawrie Bryce	13 Oct 73	
62.24	Phil Scott	16 Jun 76	
62.24	Tony Kenneally	18 May 85	50
62.20	Steve Minnikin	11 May 96	
62.16	Geoff Whaley	30 Apr 80	
62.10	Chris Melluish	7 Sep 74	
62.01	Mike Floyd	26 Apr 98	
62.00	Eric Berry	26 Aug 74	
61.72	Peter Seddon	10 May 67	
61.70	John Urquhart	18 Jul 98	
61.62	Matthew Bell	31 Aug 98	
61.61	Graham Holder	20 Jun 98	

JAVELIN

	91.46	Steve Backley	25 Jan 92	
	86.94	Mick Hill	13 Jun 93	
	85.67	Mark Roberson	19 Jul 98	
	83.84	Roald Bradstock	2 May 87	
	83.06	Nick Nieland	15 Jun 96	
	82.38	Colin Mackenzie	7 Aug 93	
	81.70	Nigel Bevan	28 Jun 92	
	80.98	Dave Ottley	24 Sep 88	
	78.54	Gary Jenson	17 Sep 89	
10	77.84	Peter Yates	21 Feb 87	
	76.66 i	Stuart Faben	3 Mar 96	
	74.24		29 Jul 95	
	75.52	Marcus Humphries	25 Jul 87	
	75.32	Steve Harrison	9 Jul 95	
	75.28	Nigel Stainton	5 Aug 89	
	75.21	David Parker	13 Jun 98	
	74.90	Darryl Brand	27 Jun 86	
	74.72	Chris Crutchley	13 Jul 86	
	74.70	Myles Cottrell	16 May 92	
	73.88	Keith Beard	12 May 90	
20	73.26	David Messom	25 Apr 87	
	72.92	Stefan Baldwin	8 May 93	
	71.86	Tony Hatton	3 May 93	
	71.14	Dan Carter	11 Jul 98	
	70.90	Shane Lewis	6 Jun 98	
	70.30	Tim Newenham	11 Jun 89	
	70.12	Paul Morgan	12 Sep 87	
	70.10	Richard Hooper	21 May 89	
	70.00	Paul Bushnell	22 Jul 90	
	70.00	Phil Parry	2 Jul 94	
30	69.90	Ken Hayford	5 Jul 87	
	69.90	Tony Smith	6 Jul 96	
	69.20	Roddy James	28 Apr 89	
	69.02	Kevin Murch	2 Sep 89	
	68.91	Stuart Loughran	26 Jul 98	
	68.84	James Hurrion	12 Jul 91	
	68.74	Jon Clarke	14 Jun 86	
	68.74	Tony Norman	23 May 87	
	68.70	Robert Mullen	2 Jul 96	
	68.53	Phill Sharpe	16 May 98	
40	68.38	James Drennen	12 Jul 91	
	68.30	Mark Lawrence	31 Jul 88	
	68.10	Paul Edgington	12 Oct 86	
	68.08	Tim Kitney	13 Sep 98	
	68.02	Mark Francis	12 Jul 97	
	67.62	Allan Holloway	25 Jun 89	
	67.60	Dean Smahon	9 Jul 94	
	67.48	Rob Laing	31 May 87	
	67.44	John Guthrie	17 May 89	
	67.22	Richard Atkinson	14 Aug 93	
50	67.16	Damien Crawford	12 Jul 92	

rough tailed model

82.60	Colin Mackenzie	1 Jun 91	
79.54	Gary Jenson	19 Jun 91	
76.10	Keith Beard	18 May 91	
70.34	Damien Crawford	20 Jul 91	
70.16	James Hurrion	19 Jul 91	
69.94	Tony Smith	22 Jun 91	
67.92	Bruce Craven	7 Sep 91	

DECATHLON (1985 Tables)

8847	Daley Thompson	9 Aug 84		
8131	Alex Kruger	2 Jul 95		
7980	Simon Shirley	24 Aug 94		
	8036 for AUS	29 Sep 88		
7922 w	Brad McStravick	28 May 84		
	7885	6 May 84		
7904	David Bigham	28 Jun 92		
7901	Peter Gabbett	22 May 72		
7889	Eugene Gilkes	18 May 86		
7874	Colin Boreham	23 May 82		
7861	Anthony Brannen	30 Apr 95		
7787	Brian Taylor	30 May 93	10	
7766	Barry Thomas	2 Sep 95		
7748	Eric Hollingsworth	30 May 93		
7740	Greg Richards	7 Jun 87		
7713	James Stevenson	5 Jun 93		
7708	Fidelis Obikwu	28 May 84		
7663	Rafer Joseph	24 Aug 94		
7654 w	Jamie Quarry	24 May 98		
	7610	24 Aug 94		
7643 w	Tom Leeson	8 Sep 85		
	7565	11 Aug 85		
7635 w	Du'aine Ladejo	24 May 98		
	7633	18 Sep 98		
7596	Mike Corden	27 Jun 76	20	
7594	Mark Bishop	3 Sep 89		
7579	Mark Luscombe	8 May 88		
7571	Alexis Sharp	17 Apr 98		
7535	Duncan Mathieson	24 Jun 90		
7515	Ken Hayford	9 Jun 85		
7500	Barry King	22 May 72		
7500	Pan Zeniou	2 Aug 81		
7480	Dean Macey	22 Aug 96		
7439	Kevan Lobb	19 Aug 84		
7431	Alan Drayton	8 Aug 78	30	
7425	Anthony Southward	16 Jun 96		
7425 w	Paul Field	21 May 95		
	7295	2 Jul 95		
7367	John Garner	8 May 88		
7363	Mike Bull	27 Jan 74		
7363	Nick Phipps	27 Jun 76		
7335	Stewart McCallum	19 Aug 73		
7308	Clivé Longe	29 Jun 69		
7295	Stephen Rogers	4 Jun 95		
7275	Buster Watson	18 Jun 78		
7268	Paul Edwards ¶	14 Aug 83	40	
7240	Paul Allan	25 Aug 91		
7221	Andy Lewis	19 Jun 94		
7198	Robert Betts	7 Aug 83		
7172	Dave Kidner	20 Aug 72		
7159	Roger Hunter	20 Jul 97		
7147	Justin Whitfield	12 May 85		
7136	Billy Jewers	3 Sep 89		
7112	Gavin Sunshine	30 Jul 93		
7094	Paul Howard	31 May 92		
7089 w	John Howell	18 Jun 78	50	
	7062	2 Jul 78		
7078	Steve Leader	19 Jun 94		
7076	Rob Laing	30 Jul 89		

3000 METRES TRACK WALK

11:24.4	Mark Easton	10 May	89
11:28.4	Phil Vesty	9 May	84
11:29.6 i	Tim Berrett	21 Jan	90
11:54.23		23 Jun	84
11:31.0	Andi Drake	22 Jul	90
11:32.2	Ian McCombie	20 Jul	88
11:33.4	Steve Partington	12 Jul	95
11:35.5	Andy Penn	10 May	97
11:39.0 i+	Martin Rush	8 Feb	92
11:49.48		1 Jul	84
11:44.68	Roger Mills	7 Aug	81
11:45.1 [10]	Chris Maddocks	9 Aug	87
11:45.77	Steve Johnston	20 Jun	87
11:47.12 i	Philip King	26 Feb	95
11:49.64		29 May	95
11:49.0	Darrell Stone	10 Jul	90
11:51.1	Paul Nihill	5 Jun	71
11:52.51	Sean Martindale	28 Jul	90
11:53.3	Martin Bell	9 Aug	95
11:53.46	Steve Barry	21 Aug	82
11:54.7	Mike Parker	20 Apr	82
11:55.0	Phil Embleton	24 May	71

10000 METRES TRACK WALK

40:06.65	Ian McCombie	4 Jun	89
40:53.60	Phil Vesty	28 May	84
40:55.6	Martin Rush	14 Sep	91
41:06.57	Chris Maddocks	20 Jun	87
41:10.11	Darrell Stone	16 Jul	95
41:13.62	Steve Barry	19 Jun	82
41:13.65	Martin Bell	22 Jul	95
41:14.3	Mark Easton	5 Feb	89
41:14.61	Steve Partington	16 Jul	95
41:18.64 [10]	Andi Drake	5 Jun	88
41:49.06	Sean Martindale	26 Jun	90
41:55.5	Phil Embleton	14 Apr	71
41:59.10	Andy Penn	27 Jul	91
42:06.35	Gordon Vale	2 Aug	81
42:08.57	Paul Blagg	28 Aug	89
42:23.0	Mike Parker	2 Feb	86
42:28.0	Philip King	17 May	95
42:34.6	Paul Nihill	28 May	72
42:35.6	Ken Matthews	1 Aug	60

track short

40:54.7	Steve Barry	19 Mar	83

20 KILOMETRES ROAD WALK

1:22:03	Ian McCombie	23 Sep	88
1:22:12	Chris Maddocks	3 May	92
1:22:51	Steve Barry	26 Feb	83
1:23:34	Andy Penn	29 Feb	92
1:23:34	Martin Rush	29 Feb	92
1:23:58	Darrell Stone	24 Feb	96
1:24:04	Mark Easton	25 Feb	89
1:24:04.0t	Andi Drake	26 May	90
1:24:07.6t	Phil Vesty	1 Dec	84
1:24:09 [10]	Steve Partington	24 Sep	94
1:24:25	Tim Berrett	21 Apr	90
1:24:50	Paul Nihill	30 Jul	72
1:25:42	Martin Bell	9 May	92
1:25:53.6t	Sean Martindale	28 Apr	89
1:27:00	Roger Mills	30 Jun	80
1:27:16	Les Morton	25 Feb	89
1:27:35	Olly Flynn	3 Oct	76
1:27:46	Brian Adams	11 Oct	75
1:27:59	Phil Embleton	3 Apr	71
1:28:02	Paul Blagg	27 Feb	82 [20]
1:28:15	Ken Matthews	23 Jul	60
1:28:26	Chris Harvey	29 Sep	79
1:28:30	Allan King	11 May	85
1:28:34	Chris Smith	11 May	85
1:28:37	Dave Jarman	30 Jun	80
1:28:46	Jimmy Ball	4 Apr	87
1:28:46	Steve Taylor	20 Dec	92
1:28:50	Amos Seddon	3 Aug	74
1:29:07	Philip King	20 Aug	95
1:29:11	Chris Cheeseman	21 May	94 [30]
1:29:19	Stuart Phillips	31 May	92
1:29:24	George Nibre	6 Apr	80
1:29:27	Graham White	19 Apr	97
1:29:29 +	Steve Johnson	16 Apr	89
1:29:37	John Warhurst	28 Jul	73
1:29:42	Dennis Jackson	10 May	86
1:29:48	Mike Parker	8 May	82
1:29:48	Martin Young	31 Mar	96
1:29:49	Peter Marlow	3 Aug	74

50 KILOMETRES ROAD WALK

3:51:37	Chris Maddocks	28 Oct	90
3:57:48	Les Morton	30 Apr	89
3:59:55	Paul Blagg	5 Sep	87
4:03:08	Dennis Jackson	16 Mar	86
4:03:53	Mark Easton	25 Apr	98
4:06:14	Barry Graham	20 Apr	85
4:07:23	Bob Dobson	21 Oct	79
4:07:57	Ian Richards	20 Apr	80
4:08:41	Adrian James	12 Apr	80
4:09:15	Don Thompson	10 Oct	65 [10]
4:09:22	Mike Smith	27 Mar	89
4:10:23	Darrell Stone	6 May	90
4:10:23	Chris Cheesman	20 Apr	97
4:10:42	Amos Seddon	9 Mar	80
4:11:32	Paul Nihill	18 Oct	64
4:12:00	Sean Martindale	16 Oct	93
4:12:02	Martin Rush	28 Jul	91
4:12:37	John Warhurst	27 May	72
4:12:50	Darren Thorn	6 May	90
4:13:18	Graham White	27 Jun	98 [20]
4:13:25	Allan King	16 Apr	83
4:14:03	Tom Misson	20 Jun	59
4:14:25	Dave Cotton	15 Jul	78
4:14:37	Steve Hollier	27 Jun	98
4:15:14	Shaun Lightman	13 Oct	73
4:15:22	Brian Adams	17 Sep	78
4:15:52	Ray Middleton	27 May	72
4:16:30	Karl Atton	20 Apr	97
4:16:47	George Nibre	9 Mar	80
4:17:24	Andi Drake	18 Oct	87 [30]

4 x 100 METRES RELAY

37.77   UK   22 Aug 93
Jackson, Jarrett, Regis, Christie
37.98   UK   1 Sep 90
Braithwaite, Regis, Adam, Christie
38.05   UK   21 Aug 93
John, Jarrett, Braithwaite, Christie
38.08   UK   8 Aug 92
Adam, Jarrett, Regis, Christie
38.09   UK   1 Sep 91
Jarrett, Regis, Braithwaite, Christie
38.09 A   UK   12 Sep 98
Condon, Devonish, Golding, Chambers
38.14   UK   10 Aug 97
Braithwaite, Campbell, Walker, Golding
38.20   England   21 Sep 98
Chambers, Devonish, Golding, Campbell
38.25   UK   9 Aug 97
Chambers, Campbell, Braithwaite, Golding
10 38.28   UK   1 Oct 88
Bunney, Regis, McFarlane, Christie
38.34   UK   9 Sep 89
Callender, Regis, Adam, Christie
38.36   UK   31 Aug 91
Jarrett, Regis, Braithwaite, Christie
38.39   UK   5 Aug 89
Jarrett, Regis, Adam, Christie
38.46   UK   10 Sep 94
Braithwaite, Jarrett, Regis, Christie
38.47   UK   9 Aug 97
Campbell, Devonish, Braithwaite, Golding
38.47   UK   22 Aug 98
Condon, Campbell, Devonish, Chambers
38.52   UK   1 Oct 88
Bunney, Regis, McFarlane, Christie
38.52   UK   22 Aug 98
Condon, Campbell, Walker, Golding
38.53   UK   26 Jun 93
John, Jarrett, Regis, Christie
20 38.56   UK   27 Jun 98
Condon, Campbell, Walker, Golding
38.62   UK   1 Aug 80
McFarlane, Wells, Sharp, McMaster
38.62   England   20 Sep 98
Gardener, Devonish, Chambers, Campbell
38.64   UK   7 Aug 91
Livingston ¶, Regis, Callender, Rosswess
38.64   UK   7 Aug 92
Jarrett, Regis, Adam, Christie
38.64   UK   15 Jul 94
John, Braithwaite, Regis, Christie
38.67   England   3 Feb 90
Callender, Regis, Adam, Christie
38.67   UK   1 Jun 96
K. Williams, Braithwaite, John, Campbell
38.68   UK   11 Aug 84
Thompson, Reid, McFarlane, Wells
38.71   UK   31 Aug 86
Bunney, Thompson, McFarlane, Christie
30 38.72   UK   25 Jun 94
John, Wariso, Regis, Christie

4 x 400 METRES RELAY

2:56.60   UK   3 Aug 96
Thomas, Baulch, Richardson, Black
2:56.65   UK   10 Aug 97
Thomas, Black, Baulch, Richardson
2:57.53   UK   1 Sep 91
Black, Redmond, Regis, Akabusi
2:58.22   UK   1 Sep 90
Sanders, Akabusi, Regis, Black
2:58.68   UK   23 Aug 98
Hylton, Baulch, Thomas, Richardson
2:58.86   UK   6 Sep 87
Redmond, Akabusi, Black, Brown
2:59.13   UK   11 Aug 84
Akabusi, Cook, Bennett, Brown
2:59.13   UK   14 Aug 94
McKenzie, Whittle, Black, Ladejo
2:59.46   UK   22 Jun 97
Black, Baulch, Thomas, Richardson
2:59.49   UK   31 Aug 91 10
Mafe, Redmond, Richardson, Akabusi
2:59.71 A   UK   13 Sep 98
Hylton, Baulch, Baldock, Thomas
2:59.73   UK   8 Aug 92
Black, Grindley, Akabusi, Regis
2:59.84   UK   31 Aug 86
Redmond, Akabusi, Whittle, Black
2:59.85   UK   19 Aug 96
Baulch, Hylton, Richardson, Black
3:00.19   UK   9 Aug 97
Hylton, Black, Baulch, Thomas
3:00.25   UK   27 Jun 93
Ladejo, Akabusi, Regis, Grindley
3:00.34   UK   25 Jun 95
Thomas, Patrick, Richardson, Black
3:00.46   UK   10 Sep 72
Reynolds, Pascoe, Hemery, Jenkins
3:00.58   UK   30 Jun 91
Sanders, Akabusi, Whittle, Black
3:00.68   UK   11 Sep 82 20
Jenkins, Cook, Bennett, Brown
3:00.82   England   21 Sep 98
Slythe, Wariso, Hylton, Richardson
3:00.93   UK   19 Jun 92
Redmond, Akabusi, Ladejo, Black
3:00.95   UK   28 Jun 98
Black, Baulch, Thomas, Richardson
3:01.03   UK - Under 23   19 Jul 92
McKenzie, Grindley, Richardson, Ladejo
3:01.12   UK   28 Jun 87
Harmsworth, Whittle, Bennett, Black
3:01.20   UK   7 Aug 92
Richardson, Akabusi, Black, Ladejo
3:01.21 A   UK   20 Oct 68
Winbolt-Lewis, Campbell, Hemery, Sherwood
3:01.22   UK   12 Aug 95
McKenzie, Patrick, Hylton, Richardson
3:01.26   UK   9 Sep 72
Reynolds, Pascoe, Hemery, Jenkins
3:01.26   UK   5 Aug 86 30
Akabusi, Black, Bennett, Brown

UNDER 20

100 METRES

10.06	Dwain Chambers	25	Jul	97
10.12	Christian Malcolm	29	Jul	98
10.21	Jamie Henderson	6	Aug	87
10.25	Jason Livingston ¶	9	Aug	90
10.25	Jason Gardener	21	Jul	94
10.29	Peter Radford (10.31?)	13	Sep	58
10.32	Mike McFarlane	6	Aug	78
10.34	Lincoln Asquith	25	Aug	83
10.37	Darren Campbell	26	Jul	91
10.38	Elliot Bunney	22	Aug	85
10.39	Jason John	28	Jul	90
10.41	Jamie Henthorn	28	Jul	95
10.43	Julian Golding	20	Jul	94
10.44	Steve Gookey	3	Aug	90
10.44	Jason Fergus	16	Sep	92
10.45	Luke Davis	21	Jul	97
10.46	Marcus Adam	6	Aug	87

wind assisted

10.12	Christian Malcolm	18	Jul	98
10.22	Lincoln Asquith	26	Jun	83
10.28	Darren Campbell	26	Jul	91
10.29	Mike McFarlane	7	Aug	78
10.29	Elliot Bunney	27	May	84
10.29	Trevor Cameron	11	Jun	94
10.34	Darren Braithwaite	25	Jun	88
10.34	Julian Golding	17	Sep	94
10.36	Mark Lewis-Francis	16	Aug	98
10.37	Courtney Rumbolt	25	Jun	88
10.37	Allyn Condon	3	Jul	93

hand timing

10.3	Martin Reynolds	29	Jun	68

200 METRES

20.29	Christian Malcolm	19	Sep	98
20.54	Ade Mafe	25	Aug	85
20.67	David Jenkins	4	Sep	71
20.73 A	Ralph Banthorpe	15	Oct	68
20.78	John Regis	29	Sep	85
20.80	Mike McFarlane	1	Jul	79
20.85	Richard Ashby	25	Aug	85
20.86	Lincoln Asquith	28	Aug	83
20.86	Roger Hunter	5	May	84
20.87	Donovan Reid	7	Oct	82
20.87	Mark Smith	28	Jul	90
20.87	Darren Campbell	19	Sep	92

wind assisted

20.61	Darren Campbell	11	Aug	91
20.73	Julian Golding	17	Sep	94
20.85	Mark Smith	1	Jul	90

hand timing

20.6	David Jenkins	19	Sep	71

wind assisted

20.7	Lincoln Asquith	2	Jul	83

300 METRES

32.08	Roger Black	8	Aug	86

400 METRES

45.36	Roger Black	24	Aug	85
45.41	David Grindley	10	Aug	91
45.45	David Jenkins	13	Aug	71
45.53	Mark Richardson	10	Aug	91
45.83	Mark Hylton	16	Jul	95
46.03	Peter Crampton	8	Aug	87
46.13	Guy Bullock	31	Jul	93
46.22	Wayne McDonald	17	Jun	89
46.32	Derek Redmond	9	Sep	84
46.46	Adrian Metcalfe	19	Sep	61
46.48	Roger Hunter	20	May	84
46.53	Mark Thomas	15	Sep	84
46.54	Michael Parper	7	Jun	97
46.56	Roy Dickens	6	Sep	80
46.59	Carl Southam	17	Sep	92
46.63	Melvin Fowell	18	Aug	79
46.64	Alloy Wilson	31	Jul	98
46.65	Darren Bernard	20	May	88
46.66	Du'aine Ladejo	9	Aug	90
46.77	Paul Dunn	31	May	82
46.78	Roger Jenkins	2	Sep	74

hand timing

45.7	Adrian Metcalfe	2	Sep	61
46.6	Todd Bennett	1	Aug	81

800 METRES (* 880 yards time less 0.70)

1:45.64	David Sharpe	5	Sep	86
1:45.77	Steve Ovett	4	Sep	74
1:46.46	John Gladwin	7	Jul	82
1:46.63	Curtis Robb	6	Jul	91
1:46.70*	John Davies I	3	Jun	68
1:47.0	Ikem Billy	12	Jun	83
1:47.02	Chris McGeorge	8	Aug	81
1:47.08	Atle Douglas	22	Aug	87
1:47.22	Kevin McKay	5	Jun	88
1:47.27	Tom Lerwill	22	Aug	96
1:47.35	Peter Elliott	23	Aug	81
1:47.53	Graham Williamson	1	Aug	79
1:47.56	Julian Spooner	24	Apr	79
1:47.69	Simon Lees	5	Sep	98
1:47.70	Darryl Taylor	13	Jul	84
1:47.71	Dane Joseph	15	Sep	78
1:47.73	Colin Szwed	9	Sep	77
1:47.75	Garry Cook	3	Jul	77

1000 METRES

2:18.98	David Sharpe	19	Aug	86
2:19.92	Graham Williamson	8	Jul	79
2:20.0	Steve Ovett	17	Aug	73
2:20.02	Darryl Taylor	18	Aug	84
2:20.37	Johan Boakes	17	Jun	84
2:21.17	Curtis Robb	16	Sep	90
2:21.41	Stuart Paton	17	Sep	82
2:21.7 A	David Strang	26	Jan	87
2:21.71	Kevin Glastonbury	18	Jun	77
2:22.3	Chris McGeorge	19	Jul	81
2:22.69	Gary Staines	17	Sep	82

1500 METRES

3:36.6 +	Graham Williamson	17	Jul	79
3:40.09	Steve Cram	27	Aug	78
3:40.68	Brian Treacy	24	Jul	90
3:40.72	Gary Taylor	8	Jul	81
3:40.90	David Robertson	28	Jul	92
3:41.59	Chris Sly	22	Jul	77
3:42.2	Paul Wynn	9	Aug	83
3:42.5	Colin Reitz	8	Aug	79
3:42.67	Matthew Hibberd	28	Jul	92
3:42.7	David Sharpe	17	Oct	85
3:42.86	Stuart Paton	29	Aug	82
3:42.89	Alistair Currie	17	Jul	84
3:43.1 a	Paul Lawther	31	Jan	74
3:43.24	Nick Hopkins	15	Jun	85
3:43.37	Davey Wilson	4	Jul	87
3:43.39	Johan Boakes	30	May	87

ONE MILE

3:53.15	Graham Williamson	17	Jul	79
3:57.03	Steve Cram	14	Sep	79
3:58.68	Steve Flint	26	May	80
3:59.4	Steve Ovett	17	Jul	74
4:00.31	Johan Boakes	5	Aug	86
4:00.6	Simon Mugglestone	16	Sep	87
4:00.67	Brian Treacy	22	Aug	90
4:01.0	David Sharpe	3	May	86
4:01.5	Tony Leonard	12	Sep	77
4:01.5	Gary Staines	19	Sep	82

2000 METRES

5:06.56	Jon Richards	7	Jul	82

3000 METRES

7:48.28	Jon Richards	9	Jul	83
7:51.84	Steve Binns	8	Sep	79
7:56.28	John Doherty	13	Jul	80
7:59.55	Paul Davies-Hale	8	Aug	81
8:00.1 a	Micky Morton	11	Jul	78
8:00.7	Graham Williamson	29	Jul	78
8:00.73	David Black	24	Jul	71
8:00.8	Steve Anders	1	Aug	78
8:00.88	Paul Taylor	12	Jun	85
8:01.2	Ian Stewart I	7	Sep	68
8:01.26	Darius Burrows	21	Aug	94
8:01.43	Nat Muir	28	Aug	77
8:01.44	Colin Reitz	16	May	79

5000 METRES

13:27.04	Steve Binns	14	Sep	79
13:35.95	Paul Davies-Hale	11	Sep	81
13:37.4	David Black	10	Sep	71
13:43.82	Simon Mugglestone	24	May	87
13:44.64	Julian Goater	14	Jul	72
13:48.74	Jon Richards	28	May	83
13:48.84	John Doherty	8	Aug	80
13:49.1 a	Nat Muir	21	Aug	77
13:53.30	Ian Stewart I	3	Aug	68
13:53.3 a	Nick Lees	21	Aug	77
13:54.2	Mick Morton	1	Jul	78
13:54.52	Keith Cullen	8	Jun	91

10000 METRES

29:21.9	Jon Brown	21	Apr	90
29:38.6	Ray Crabb	18	Apr	73

2000 METRES STEEPLECHASE

5:29.61	Colin Reitz	18	Aug	79
5:31.12	Paul Davies-Hale	22	Aug	81
5:32.84	Tom Hanlon	20	Jul	86
5:34.8 a	Micky Morris	24	Aug	75
5:38.01	Ken Baker	1	Aug	82
5:38.2	Spencer Duval	8	Jul	89
5:39.3 a	Graeme Fell	11	Jul	78
5:39.93	Eddie Wedderburn	9	Sep	79
5:40.2	Paul Campbell	31	Jul	77
5:40.2	John Hartigan	27	Jun	84
5:40.87	Andrew Rodgers	25	Aug	83
5:40.9	Alastair O'Connor	25	Aug	90

3000 METRES STEEPLECHASE

8:29.85	Paul Davies-Hale	31	Aug	81
8:42.75	Colin Reitz	6	Jun	79
8:43.21	Kevin Nash	2	Jun	96
8:44.68	Alastair O'Connor	12	Aug	90
8:44.91	Ken Baker	30	May	82
8:45.65	Spencer Duval	17	Jun	89
8:47.49	Tom Hanlon	8	Jun	86
8:48.43	Graeme Fell	16	Jul	78
8:50.14	Dave Long I	13	Jul	73
8:51.02	Tony Staynings	14	Jul	72
8:54.15	Stuart Kefford	18	Sep	92

110 METRES HURDLES (3'3")

13.77	Kevin Lumsdon	8	Aug	92
14.01	Jamie Quarry	13	Jul	91
14.06	Neil Owen	4	Jul	92
14.07	Leo Barker	12	Jul	97
14.08	Liam Collins	12	Jul	97
14.13	Derek Wilson	25	Jun	83
14.14	James Hughes	30	May	93
14.15	Mark Purser	13	Jul	91
14.16	Robert Newton	11	Jul	98
14.16	Ben Warmington	9	Aug	98
wind assisted				
13.92	Matthew Clements	27	Aug	94
14.10	Simon McAree	9	Jul	94
14.11	Tony Gill	13	Jul	96
hand timing				
13.8	Jon Ridgeon	13	Jul	84
13.8	Paul Gray	16	Jul	88
14.0	Paul Brice	25	Jun	83
14.0	Colin Jackson	27	Aug	84
14.0	Neil Owen	2	Aug	92
14.0	James Hughes	11	May	93
14.0	Damien Greaves	8	Jul	95
wind assisted				
13.6	Mark Holtom	9	Jul	77
13.8	Paul Brice	9	Jul	83
13.8	Colin Jackson	15	Jul	84
13.8	Brett St Louis	11	Jul	87
13.9	Tony Jarrett	12	Jul	86

110 METRES HURDLES (3'6")

13.44	Colin Jackson	19	Jul	86
13.46	Jon Ridgeon	23	Aug	85
13.72	Tony Jarrett	24	May	87
13.91	David Nelson	21	Jun	86
13.97	Paul Gray	30	Jul	88
14.01	Ross Baillie	25	Aug	96
14.03	Brett St Louis	27	Jun	87
14.04	Damien Greaves	25	Aug	96
14.06	Mark Holtom	7	Aug	77
14.08	Paul Brice	26	Aug	83
14.14	Neil Owen	17	Sep	92
14.18	James Archampong	21	Jul	94
14.21	Berwyn Price	12	Sep	70
14.24	Nigel Walker	17	Sep	82

wind assisted

13.42	Colin Jackson	27	Jul	86
13.82	David Nelson	5	Jul	86

hand timing wind assisted

14.1	Neil Owen	20	Jun	92

400 METRES HURDLES

50.22	Martin Briggs	28	Aug	83
50.70	Noel Levy	8	Jul	94
51.07	Philip Beattie	20	Aug	82
51.15 A	Andy Todd	18	Oct	67
51.70		23	Sep	67
51.31	Gary Oakes	9	Sep	77
51.48	Bob Brown	19	Jun	88
51.51	Max Robertson	24	Jul	82
51.55	Mark Whitby	26	Aug	83
51.63	Mark Rowlands	21	Jun	97
51.66	Paul Goacher	2	Aug	80
51.71	Matthew Elias	7	Jun	97
51.73	Matt Douglas	29	Jul	95
51.91	Peter Campbell	19	Jun	88
51.97	Bel Blik	17	Aug	85
52.13	Richard McDonald	29	Jul	98

hand timing

51.5	Max Robertson	10	Jul	82
51.5	Matthew Elias	6	Jun	98
52.1	Michael Bryars	30	Apr	83
52.2	Phil Harries	20	Jul	85

HIGH JUMP

2.37	Steve Smith	20	Sep	92
2.27	Brendan Reilly	27	May	90
2.26	James Brierley	3	Aug	96
2.25	Geoff Parsons	9	Jul	83
2.24	John Hill	23	Aug	85
2.23	Mark Lakey	29	Aug	82
2.23 i	Ben Challenger	1	Mar	97
2.21		24	Aug	96
2.22	Dalton Grant	3	Jul	85
2.20	Byron Morrison	14	Jul	84
2.18	Ossie Cham	14	Jun	80
2.18	Alex Kruger	26	Jun	82
2.18	Steve Ritchie	15	Jul	89
2.18	Hopeton Lindo	23	Jul	89
2.17	Stuart Ohrland	27	Aug	94
2.17	Mike Robbins	5	Aug	95

POLE VAULT

5.50	Neil Winter	9	Aug	92
5.30	Matt Belsham	16	Sep	90
5.21	Andy Ashurst	2	Sep	84
5.20	Billy Davey	5	Jun	83
5.20	Warren Siley	4	Aug	90
5.20	Nick Buckfield	31	May	92
5.20	Ben Flint	2	Aug	97
5.20	Christian Linskey	24	May	98
5.10	Brian Hooper	1	Oct	72
5.10	Mike Edwards	20	Jun	87
5.10	Mark Davis	9	Jun	96
5.05	Ian Tullett	22	Aug	87
5.05	Dean Mellor	7	Jul	90
5.02	Paul Williamson	29	May	93
5.00	Keith Stock	3	Jul	76
5.00	Bob Kingman	2	May	92
5.00	Tim Thomas	17	Jun	92
5.00	Mike Barber	1	Jul	92
5.00 ns	Ian Wilding	16	Jul	94
5.00	Neil Young	18	May	96

LONG JUMP

7.98	Stewart Faulkner	6	Aug	88
7.91	Steve Phillips	10	Aug	91
7.90	Nathan Morgan	25	Jul	97
7.84	Wayne Griffith	25	Aug	89
7.76	Carl Howard	31	Jul	93
7.73	Jason Canning	20	Apr	88
7.72	Daley Thompson	21	May	77
7.70	Kevin Liddington	27	Aug	88
7.66	Barry Nevison	7	Jul	85
7.62	Colin Mitchell	11	Jul	78
7.61	Darren Gomersall	19	Jul	87

wind assisted

8.04	Stewart Faulkner	20	Aug	88
7.97	Nathan Morgan	13	Jul	96
7.96	Colin Jackson	17	May	86
7.82	Kevin Liddington	25	Jun	89
7.72	John Herbert	15	Jun	80

TRIPLE JUMP

16.58	Tosi Fasinro	15	Jun	91
16.53	Larry Achike	24	Jul	94
16.24	Aston Moore	11	Jun	75
16.22	Mike Makin	17	May	81
16.13	Steven Anderson	11	Jun	83
16.03	John Herbert	23	Jun	81
15.95	Keith Connor	30	Aug	76
15.94	Vernon Samuels	27	Jun	82
15.93	Tayo Erogbogbo	17	Sep	94
15.92	Lawrence Lynch	13	Jul	85
15.88	Julian Golley	28	Jul	90
15.87	Stewart Faulkner	22	Aug	87

wind assisted

16.81	Tosi Fasinro	15	Jun	91
16.67	Larry Achike	24	Jul	94
16.43	Mike Makin	14	Jun	81
16.34	Phillips Idowu	27	Jul	97
16.31	Aston Moore	9	Aug	75
16.07	Vernon Samuels	14	Aug	82

SHOT (7.26kg)

19.46	Carl Myerscough	6 Sep 98
18.21 i	Matt Simson	3 Feb 89
18.11		27 Aug 89
17.78 i	Billy Cole	10 Mar 84
17.72		2 Jun 84
17.36 i	Chris Ellis	8 Dec 84
17.10		7 Jul 85
17.26 i	Geoff Capes	16 Nov 68
16.80		30 Jul 68
17.25	Emeka Udechuku	20 Sep 97
17.22	Antony Zaidman	4 Jul 81
16.61	Simon Williams	10 Aug 86
16.60	Alan Carter	11 May 63
16.48	Martyn Lucking	24 Aug 57
16.47	Paul Buxton	25 May 75
16.21	Mike Lindsay	29 Jul 57
16.20 i	Nigel Spratley	19 Mar 89
16.04		20 May 89
16.18	Tony Satchwell	23 Apr 72
16.10	Martin Fletcher	19 Jun 88
16.03	Jon Wood	26 Sep 70
15.94	Andy Vince	5 May 78
15.94	Mitchell Smith	23 Mar 85

SHOT (6.25kg)

21.03	Carl Myerscough	13 May 98
19.47	Matt Simson	20 May 89
19.15	Billy Cole	19 May 84
18.66 i	Simon Williams	15 Nov 86
18.52		11 Jul 86
18.20 i	Chris Ellis	16 Feb 85
18.13		14 Jul 84
17.81	Antony Zaidman	16 May 81
17.74	Emeka Udechuku	9 Aug 98
17.58	Nigel Spratley	28 May 89
17.32	Andy Vince	15 May 77
17.31	Mitchell Smith	11 Jun 85
17.30	Jamie Cockburn	20 Sep 92
17.26	Neil Gray	19 May 84
17.26 i	Neal Brunning ¶	9 Dec 89
17.08		21 Aug 88
17.22	Richard Slaney	20 Jul 75

DISCUS (2kg)

60.97	Emeka Udechuku	5 Jul 98
60.19	Carl Myerscough	8 Aug 98
55.10	Glen Smith	31 Aug 91
53.42	Paul Mardle	25 Jul 81
53.40	Robert Weir	10 Aug 80
53.32	Paul Buxton	9 Aug 75
53.02	Simon Williams	16 Aug 86
52.94	Lee Newman	29 Aug 92
52.84	Jamie Murphy	14 Jun 92
52.14	Robert Russell	4 Jul 93
51.70	Richard Slaney	27 Jul 75
51.66	Neal Brunning ¶	30 Jul 89
51.10	Mike Lindsay	29 May 57
51.08	Peter Weir	1 Aug 82
50.74	Tony Satchwell	21 Aug 72

DISCUS (1.75kg)

64.35	Emeka Udechuku	21 Jun 98
61.81	Carl Myerscough	18 Aug 98
60.76	Glen Smith	26 May 91
56.64	Jamie Murphy	19 May 90
56.10	Lee Newman	4 Jul 92
56.00	Simon Williams	17 May 86
55.94	Mark Davies	19 Aug 90
55.44	Neal Brunning ¶	8 Jul 89
55.00	Robert Russell	16 May 93
54.50	Paul Mardle	27 Jun 81
53.84	Bob Weir	14 Sep 80
53.50	Colin Bastien	8 Jun 85
53.24	Matt Symonds	21 Jun 87

HAMMER (7.26kg)

67.48	Paul Head	16 Sep 84
67.10	Jason Byrne	6 Aug 89
66.14	Martin Girvan	21 Jul 79
65.86	Robert Weir	6 Sep 80
65.30	Karl Andrews	2 Jul 94
64.14	Ian Chipchase	25 Sep 71
63.84	Andrew Tolputt	7 Sep 86
63.72	Gareth Cook	10 Jul 88
62.82	Mick Jones	29 Aug 82
62.02	Peter Vivian	1 Jul 89
61.34	Ron James	22 Apr 78
61.22	Malcolm Croad	25 Aug 92
61.10	Vaughan Cooper	5 May 84

HAMMER (6.25kg)

74.92	Jason Byrne	17 Dec 89
73.28	Robert Weir	14 Sep 80
72.66	Paul Head	2 Sep 84
71.84	Gareth Cook	28 May 88
70.36	Andrew Tolputt	21 Sep 86
69.10	Karl Andrews	3 Aug 94
68.84	Eric Berry	Jul 73
67.80	Martin Girvan	7 Jul 79
67.52	Vaughan Cooper	19 May 84
67.48	Mick Jones	2 Jun 82
66.38	Tony Kenneally	10 Jul 82
65.82	Dave Smith I	4 Jul 81

JAVELIN

79.50	Steve Backley	5 Jun 88
75.21	David Parker	13 Jun 98
74.54	Gary Jenson	19 Sep 86
74.24	Mark Roberson	18 Jul 86
73.76	Nigel Bevan	29 Aug 87
71.74	Myles Cottrell	29 Jul 89
71.14	Dan Carter	11 Jul 98
69.62	Stefan Baldwin	8 Jul 89
68.84	James Hurrion	12 Jul 91
68.74	Jon Clarke	14 Jun 86
68.53	Phill Sharpe	16 May 98
68.38	James Drennen	12 Jul 91
68.30	Mark Lawrence	31 Jul 88
68.08	Tim Kitney	13 Sep 98

rough tailed

70.16	James Hurrion	19 Jul 91

DECATHLON (1985 Tables)

8082	Daley Thompson	31	Jul	77
7488	David Bigham	9	Aug	90
7480	Dean Macey	22	Aug	96
7299	Eugene Gilkes	24	May	81
7274	James Stevenson	24	Jun	90
7247	Brian Taylor	7	May	89
7169	Barry Thomas	5	Aug	90
7126	Fidelis Obikwu	16	Sep	79
7112	Gavin Sunshine	30	Jul	93
7018	Jamie Quarry	30	Jun	91
6958	Roy Mitchell	29	Sep	74
6936	Anthony Brannen	24	May	87
6925	Roger Hunter	4	Jun	95
6839	Mark Bushell	30	Apr	95
6812	Nigel Skinner	19	Aug	84
6809	Rafer Joseph	26	Jul	87
6801 w	Kevan Lobb	18	Jun	78

Junior implements

7134	Dean Macey	17	Sep	95
6958 w	Roger Hunter	18	Sep	94

3000 METRES TRACK WALK

11:54.23	Tim Berrett	23	Jun	84
12:01.89 i	Philip King	21	Feb	93
12:02.0		12	May	92
12:02.04	Phil Vesty	24	Jul	82
12:16.5	David Hucks	5	Aug	84
12:19.8	Gordon Vale	11	Mar	81
12:23.2	Martin Rush	18	Sep	83
12:23.53	Darrell Stone	19	Sep	87
12:24.45	Richard Dorman	5	Sep	80
12:25.8	Gareth Holloway	17	Jun	89
12:29.3	Ian Ashforth	19	May	85

5000 METRES TRACK WALK

20:16.40	Philip King	26	Jun	93
20:33.4 +	Darrell Stone	7	Aug	87
20:55.4	Tim Berrett	9	Jun	84
21:00.5 +	Phil Vesty	19	Jun	82
21:10.5 +	Gordon Vale	2	Aug	81

10000 METRES TRACK WALK

41:52.13	Darrell Stone	7	Aug	87
42:06.35	Gordon Vale	2	Aug	81
42:46.3	Phil Vesty	20	Mar	82
42:47.7	Philip King	2	May	92
43:04.09	Tim Berrett	25	Aug	83
43:42.75	Martin Rush	29	May	83
43:54.25	Gareth Brown	7	Aug	87
44:22.12	Gareth Holloway	5	Jun	88
44:22.38	Jon Vincent	1	Apr	89
44:30.0	Andy Penn	15	Mar	86

Road

41:47	Darrell Stone	26	Sep	87
42:29	Steve Hollier	10	Dec	95
42:39	Martin Rush	7	May	83
42:40	Tim Berrett	18	Feb	84

UNDER 17

100 METRES

10.49	Mark Lewis-Francis	16	Aug	98
10.60	Tyrone Edgar	16	Aug	98
10.64	Jon Barbour	12	Jul	97
10.66	Ben Lewis	7	Sep	97
10.67	Michael Nartey	28	Sep	91
10.69	Mike McFarlane	13	Aug	76
10.70	Steve Green	15	Jul	72
10.71	Luke Davis	12	Jul	96
10.71	Tim Benjamin	16	Aug	98
10.72	Peter Little	6	Aug	77
10.72	Trevor Cameron	7	Aug	93
10.73	Danny Joyce	17	Aug	91
10.75	Elliot Bunney	28	May	83
10.75	Dwain Chambers	28	May	94

overage

10.51	Lincoln Asquith	4	Oct	80

wind assisted

10.36	Mark Lewis-Francis	16	Aug	98
10.38	Kevin Mark	3	Jul	93
10.44	Luke Davis	13	Jul	96
10.51	Tim Benjamin	4	Jul	98
10.56	Dwain Chambers	9	Jul	94
10.57	Trevor Cameron	3	Jul	93
10.58	Tyrone Edgar	16	Aug	98
10.62	Elliot Bunney	25	Jun	83
10.62	Jamie Nixon	7	Jul	85

hand timing

10.5	Michael Powell	17	Sep	78

200 METRES

20.92	Ade Mafe	27	Aug	83
21.19	Tim Benjamin	31	Jul	98
21.24	Peter Little	21	Aug	77
21.25	Mark Richardson	24	Jul	88
21.44	Roger Hunter	2	Aug	81
21.51	Darren Campbell	15	Sep	90
21.51	Ben Lewis	19	Jul	97
21.53	Steve Eden	2	Aug	81
21.56	Trevor Cameron	8	Aug	93
21.58	Christian Malcolm	9	Jul	95
21.62	Tyrone Edgar	24	May	98
21.63	Richard Ashby	7	Aug	83
21.64	Elliot Bunney	7	Aug	83
21.65	Uvie Ugono	7	Aug	94
21.66	Marcus Adam	12	Aug	84

wind assisted

20.98	Tim Benjamin	18	Jul	98
21.17	Mark Richardson	20	Aug	88
21.25	Trevor Cameron	25	Sep	93
21.32	Graham Beasley	9	Jul	94
21.38	Elliot Bunney	13	Aug	83
21.38	Ben Lewis	12	Jul	97
21.41	Roger Hunter	19	Jul	81
21.41	Richard Ashby	13	Aug	83
21.41	Christian Malcolm	1	Jul	95

hand timing wind assisted

21.0	Peter Little	30	Jul	77

400 METRES

46.43	Mark Richardson	28	Jul	88
46.74	Guy Bullock	17	Sep	92
47.81	Mark Hylton	17	Jul	93
47.86	Kris Stewart	13	Jul	96
48.05	David Naismith	10	Aug	96
48.11	Gary Thomas	18	Sep	82
48.25	Adrian Patrick	2	Sep	89
48.34	Richard McNabb	27	Aug	95
48.35	James Hilston	6	Aug	95
48.36	David Simpson	29	May	89
48.41	Mark Tyler	11	Aug	84
48.46	Phil Harvey	24	Jun	79
48.63	Wayne McDonald	19	Jul	86

hand timing

47.6	Kris Stewart	3	Aug	96
48.2	David Simpson	8	Jul	89
48.3	David McKenzie	21	Sep	86
48.4	Steve Ovett	20	Aug	72
48.4	Chris Thompson	1	Aug	81

800 METRES

1:49.9	Mark Sesay	18	Jul	89
1:50.7	Peter Elliott	16	Sep	79
1:50.90	Craig Winrow	21	Aug	88
1:51.0	Chris McGeorge	1	Jul	78
1:51.05	Mal Edwards	20	Sep	74
1:51.3	Julian Spooner	3	Aug	77
1:51.4	Kevin McKay	19	Aug	85
1:51.6	Neil Horsfield	31	Aug	83
1:51.6	David Gerard	21	Jul	84
1:51.8	Paul Burgess	14	Jul	87
1:51.9 +	Johan Boakes	17	Jun	84
1:52.0	Paul Causey	21	Jul	84

1000 METRES

2:20.37	Johan Boakes	17	Jun	84

1500 METRES

3:47.7	Steve Cram	14	May	77
3:48.49	Johan Boakes	28	Jun	84
3:49.9	Kelvin Newton	20	Jun	79
3:51.1	Jason Lobo	30	Aug	85
3:51.4	Darren Mead	26	Jul	85
3:51.7	Martin Forder	19	Sep	86
3:51.8	Mark Sesay	22	Aug	89
3:52.0	Stuart Poore	6	Sep	89
3:52.47	Simon Young	4	Aug	90
3:52.6	Glen Stewart	19	Sep	87
3:52.78	Clifton Bradeley	2	Aug	81
3:52.9	Steve Johnson	8	Jul	89
3:53.0	Mark Bateman	31	Aug	74

ONE MILE

4:06.7	Barrie Williams	22	Apr	72
4:09.5	Colin Clarkson	29	Aug	77
4:09.6	Alistair Currie	9	Jun	81

2000 METRES

5:28.2 +	Kevin Steere	10	Jul	71

3000 METRES

8:13.42	Barrie Moss	15	Jul	72
8:15.34	Kevin Steere	30	Aug	71
8:19.08	Darren Mead	26	Aug	85
8:19.38	Johan Boakes	24	Jun	84
8:24.2	Simon Goodwin	16	Jul	80
8:24.2	Jason Lobo	13	Aug	86
8:25.2	Colin Clarkson	3	Aug	77
8:26.3	Paul Williams	10	Aug	83
8:26.6	Jon Dennis	23	Apr	86
8:26.92	Jon Richards	5	Sep	80
8:29.09	Steve Fury	18	Aug	84
8:29.4	Darrell Smith	16	Jul	83

overage

8:23.6	Ian Stewart II	14	Dec	77

5000 METRES

14:41.8	Nick Lees	24	Aug	74
14:46.8	Paul Williams	15	Dec	71

overage

14:30.6	Nick Lees	11	Dec	74
14:45.4	Ray Crabb	15	Dec	71

1500 METRES STEEPLECHASE

4:11.2	Steve Evans	15	Jul	74
4:12.3	Chris Sly	15	Jul	74
4:13.1	John Crowley	15	Jul	74
4:13.2	David Lewis	1	Jul	78
4:13.7	Danny Fleming	31	Jul	77
4:13.9	Eddie Wedderburn	31	Jul	77
4:14.0	Dave Robertson	8	Jul	89
4:14.4	Stephen Arnold	7	Sep	85
4:15.0	David Caton	9	Jun	84
4:15.0	Spencer Duval	12	Jul	86
4:15.2	Garrie Richardson	8	Jul	89
4:15.3	John Wilson	26	Jul	75

overage

4:13.2	Darren Mead	16	Oct	85

2000 METRES STEEPLECHASE

5:55.0	David Lewis	20	Aug	78
5:58.8	Chris Thompson	22	Jun	97

3000 METRES STEEPLECHASE

9:16.6	Colin Reitz	19	Sep	76

100 METRES HURDLES (3'0")

12.68	Matthew Clements	8	Aug	93
12.90	Steve Markham	17	Aug	91
12.97	Jon Snade	8	Aug	93
12.97	Andy Turner	16	Aug	97
12.98	Robert Newton	16	Aug	97
12.99	Dominic Girdler	11	Jul	98
13.01	Hugh Teape	3	Aug	80
13.05	Brett St Louis	4	Aug	85
13.07	Jon Ridgeon	7	Aug	83
13.07	David O'Leary	3	Aug	96
13.09	Damien Greaves	8	Jul	94
13.09	Chris Baillie	16	Aug	97
13.10	Ricky Glover	17	Aug	91
13.11	Robert Hollinger	16	Aug	97
13.11	Nathan Palmer	8	Aug	98

wind assisted

12.47	Matthew Clements	9	Jul	94
12.70	Damien Greaves	9	Jul	94
12.88	Nick Csemiczky	13	Jul	91
12.90	Ricky Glover	13	Jul	91
12.90	Ben Warmington	8	Jul	95
12.96	Nathan Palmer	15	Aug	98
12.96	Dominic Girdler	15	Aug	98
12.99	Neil Owen	1	Jul	90
13.01	Berian Davies	30	Jul	89

hand timing

12.8	Brett St Louis	28	Jul	85
12.8	Richard Dunn	29	Jun	91
12.9	Hugh Teape	31	Aug	80

wind assisted

12.6	Brett St Louis	20	Jul	85
12.9	Jon Ridgeon	9	Jul	83
12.9	Dominic Girdler	13	Sep	98

110 METRES HURDLES (3'0")

13.71	Matthew Clements	19	May	94
14.16	Ben Warmington	12	Jul	95
14.19	Ross Baillie	19	May	94

hand timing

13.6	Jon Ridgeon	16	Jul	83

110 METRES HURDLES (3'3")

15.44	Ian Cawley	6	Aug	95

wind assisted

13.92	Matthew Clements	27	Aug	94
14.61	Damien Greaves	27	Aug	94
15.42	Ian Cawley	6	Aug	95

hand timing

14.5	Kieran Moore	30	Aug	80
14.7	Max Robertson	20	Sep	80

110 METRES HURDLES (3'6")

15.39	Jon Kell	7	Aug	82

400 METRES HURDLES (2'9")

52.81	Richard McDonald	10	Aug	96
53.14	Martin Briggs	2	Aug	80
53.26	Nange Ursell	11	Jul	98
53.30	Mark Rowlands	31	Jul	94
53.55	Charles Robertson-Adams	31	Jul	94
53.58	Noel Levy	13	Jul	91
53.64	Dean Park	17	May	94
53.69	Max Robertson	2	Aug	80
53.69	Bob Brown	9	Aug	86
53.71	Andrew Bargh	11	Jul	92
53.82	Robert Taylor	9	Aug	86
53.98	Paul Martin	11	Jul	92
53.98	Austin Ferns	12	Jul	97

hand timing

53.2	Phil Beattie	24	May	80
53.8	Carl McMullen	20	Jul	96

400 METRES HURDLES (3'0")

53.06	Phil Beattie	2	Aug	80
53.31	Richard McDonald	28	Jul	96

hand timing

54.0	Bob Brown	1	Jul	86

HIGH JUMP

2.23	Mark Lakey	29	Aug	82
2.15	Ossie Cham	14	Jul	79
2.15	Brendan Reilly	7	May	89
2.15	Stanley Osuide	1	Sep	91
2.12	Femi Abejide	11	Jul	81
2.11	Leroy Lucas	6	Aug	83
2.11 i	Ken McKeown	12	Jul	98
	2.11	18	Jul	98
2.10	Dalton Grant	18	Sep	82
2.10	Tim Blakeway	29	Aug	87
2.10	James Brierley	16	May	93
2.10	Martin Lloyd	28	Sep	96
2.09	Steve Smith	10	Sep	89
2.08	Ross Hepburn	29	Jul	78
2.08	Nick Hay	19	Aug	84
2.08	Sean McLean	14	Jul	91

overage

2.13 i	Colin McMaster	1	Dec	96

POLE VAULT

5.20	Neil Winter	2	Sep	90
5.15	Christian Linskey	23	Aug	96
4.90	Warren Siley	8	Sep	89
4.80	Billy Davey	14	Sep	80
4.76	Nick Buckfield	11	Jun	89
4.72	Ian Lewis	24	Aug	85
4.70	Richard Smith	7	Jun	97
4.66	Mike Edwards	24	Aug	85
4.60	Ben Flint	10	Jun	95
4.53	Keith Stock	5	Sep	73
4.50	Christian North	26	Aug	90
4.50	Mike Barber	15	Sep	90
4.50	Neil Young	5	Jun	93
4.50	Chris Type	4	Jul	98
4.48	Mark Hodgkinson	17	Sep	88

LONG JUMP

7.53	Brian Robinson	21	Jul	97
7.32	Kevin Liddington	16	May	87
7.25	Alan Slack	12	Jun	76
7.21	Hugh Teape	17	May	80
7.20	Hugh Davidson	21	Jun	80
7.19	Onochie Onuorah	8	Jul	89
7.18	Barry Nevison	1	May	83
7.17	Hugh Whyte	15	Jul	79
7.15	Matthew John	29	Jun	86
7.14	Stewart Faulkner	17	Aug	85
7.13	Mark Findlay	24	Sep	94

wind assisted

7.60	Brian Robinson	21	Jul	97
7.40	Matthew John	10	May	86
7.27	David Mountford	25	Jul	98
7.25	Nathan Morgan	27	Aug	94
7.25	Mark Awanah	25	Jul	98
7.23	Onochie Onuorah	26	May	90
7.23	Andy Turner	20	Sep	97
7.22	Paul Hanson	7	Jul	78
7.18	Nicki Gordon	12	Sep	93
7.18	Kevin Hibbins	21	Jul	96
7.16	Marcellas Peters	18	Jun	94

TRIPLE JUMP

15.65	Vernon Samuels	18	Jul	81
15.50	Junior Campbell	18	May	86
15.45	Steven Anderson	2	Aug	81
15.28	Larry Achike	22	Jun	91

note resident but not British citizen at this time

15.14	Marvin Bramble	8	Aug	93
15.14	Stephen Shalders	18	Jul	98
14.94	Hugh Teape	17	May	80
14.93	Mark Whitehead	26	Aug	85
14.90	Lawrence Lynch	21	Jul	84
14.84	Peter Vaughan	2	May	83
14.83	Malwyn Gordon	10	Jul	98

overage

14.88	Ian Timbers	5	Oct	80

wind assisted

15.40	Stephen Shalders	18	Jul	98
15.25	Marvin Bramble	3	Jul	93
15.08	Lawrence Lynch	29	Apr	84
15.06	Craig Duncan	7	Aug	82
15.01	Malwyn Gordon	15	Aug	98
14.93	Chris Tomlinson	18	Jul	98
14.88	Carl Howard	13	Jul	90
14.87	Darren Gomersall	3	Aug	85
14.84	Nick Leech	8	Jul	78

SHOT (7.26kg)

17.30	Carl Myerscough	3	Aug	96
16.03	Chris Ellis	11	Sep	82
15.81	Matt Simson	16	Aug	86

SHOT (6.25kg)

16.80	Chris Ellis	13	Sep	81
16.36	Neal Brunning ¶	31	Aug	87
16.26	Emeka Udechuku	23	Apr	95

overage

16.62 i	Emeka Udechuku	16	Dec	95

SHOT (5kg)

21.20	Carl Myerscough	22	Sep	96
19.22	Chris Ellis	4	Jun	82
18.90	Neal Brunning ¶	6	Sep	87
18.44	Matt Simson	27	Jul	86
18.43	Emeka Udechuku	28	May	95
18.25	Billy Cole	1	Aug	81
17.91	Antony Zaidman	28	May	78
17.76	George Brocklebank	22	Jul	79
17.36	Piers Selby	10	Jul	92
17.30	Jason Mulcahy	7	Jul	89
17.24	Mark Edwards	20	Aug	91
17.14	Bill Fuller II	9	Jul	93
17.09	Adrian Cluskey	21	Sep	97
17.04	Jeff Clare	18	Jul	81
17.01	James Muirhead	7	Sep	87

overage

18.73	Matt Simson		Nov	86
17.37 i	Guy Litherland	15	Dec	85
17.30 i	Simon Williams	1	Dec	84

downhill

18.90	Matt Simson	23	Aug	86

DISCUS (2kg)

50.60	Carl Myerscough	28	Jul	96
48.96	Emeka Udechuku	19	Aug	95
46.64	Guy Litherland	29	Jun	85
46.52	Chris Symonds	19	Sep	87

DISCUS (1.75kg)

54.70	Emeka Udechuku	18	Jun	95
52.50	Paul Mardle	7	Jul	79
51.16	Chris Symonds	6	Sep	87

DISCUS (1.5kg)

62.22	Emeka Udechuku	10	Jul	95
58.14	Carl Myerscough	12	May	96
56.14	Chris Symonds	6	Sep	87
55.94	Simon Williams I	9	Sep	84
55.90	Guy Litherland	14	Sep	85
55.72	Keith Homer	27	Jun	82
55.52	Glen Smith	14	May	88
55.36	Neal Brunning ¶	7	Jun	87
54.18	Matt Symonds	21	Jul	84
53.98	Felice Miele	10	Jul	98
53.80	Paul Mardle	19	May	79
52.84	Simon Williams II	31	Aug	97
52.76	Julian Willett	17	Jun	89
52.76	James South	1	Sep	91
52.62	Ashley Knott	22	Sep	91
52.40	Guy Dirkin	28	Jun	69

downhill

56.98	Neal Brunning ¶	11	Jul	87

HAMMER (7.26kg)

59.94	Andrew Tolputt	30	Sep	84
57.04	Peter Vivian	27	Jun	87
56.66	Paul Head	5	Sep	81

HAMMER (6.25kg)

66.70	Andrew Tolputt	2	Sep	84
64.00	Matthew Sutton	22	Aug	98
62.52	Paul Head	16	May	81

HAMMER (5kg)

76.28	Andrew Tolputt	11	Aug	84
73.90	Paul Head	29	Aug	81
73.76	Matthew Sutton	14	Jun	98
73.00	Nick Steinmetz	17	Jul	93
71.34	Tony Kenneally	7	Sep	80
70.82	Jason Byrne	20	Jun	87
68.62	Peter Vivian	16	May	87
67.64	Gareth Cook	22	Sep	85
67.48	Chris Howe	24	Jun	84
67.21	Ross Thompson	22	Aug	98
66.92	Paul Murden	8	May	85
66.74	Matthew Sutton	14	Sep	97
66.30	Malcolm Croad	21	Jul	90
65.70	Ross Kidner	26	May	97
64.82	Vaughan Cooper	13	May	82
64.40	Jonathan Bond	14	May	89
64.32	Neil Homer	18	Aug	84
64.18	Charles Beresford	1	May	89

JAVELIN (800g -1986 model)

68.26	David Parker	19 May	96
61.00	Phill Sharpe	6 Jul	97

JAVELIN (800g Original model)

72.78	Gary Jenson	10 Sep	83
69.84	Colin Mackenzie	12 May	79
66.14	David Messom	14 May	81
65.32	Marcus Humphries	26 Aug	78

JAVELIN (700g)

73.56	David Parker	20 Jul	96
72.48	Gary Jenson	3 Jul	83
70.30	Colin Mackenzie	6 Jul	79
68.88	Phill Sharpe	19 Jul	97
68.26	Ian Marsh	30 Jul	77
68.18	James Hurrion	3 Jun	90
66.88	David Messom	4 Jul	81
66.86	Michael Williams	16 Jul	79
66.52	Marcus Humphries	17 Sep	78
66.00	Dan Carter	1 Sep	96
65.92	Tim Kitney	10 Aug	96
65.68	Tim Eldridge	18 Aug	91
65.16	Mark Wells	31 May	77
64.92	Jason Beaumont	11 Jun	83
64.92	Paul Bushnell	20 Sep	85
64.80	Justin Rubio	1 Sep	85
64.68	Paul Godwin	20 May	90

DECATHLON (Senior Implements)

6484	David Bigham	27 Sep	87
6299	Tom Leeson	21 Sep	80
overage			
5943	John Ball	8 Oct	78

DECATHLON (Junior Implements)

6554	Jim Stevenson	25 Sep	88
6093	Robert Hughes	28 May	89

DECATHLON (U17 Implements)

6706	David Bigham	28 Jun	87
6047	Jeremy Lay	30 Jun	85

OCTATHLON

5550	Dominic Girdler	20 Sep	98
5426	John Holtby	20 Sep	98
5423	Leo Barker	17 Sep	95
5378	Matthew Lewis	20 Sep	92
5311	Dean Macey	18 Sep	94
5238	Neil Scrivener	21 Sep	97
5208	Fyn Corcoran	18 Sep	94
5158	Edward Coats	25 Aug	96
5149	Paul Hourihan	19 Sep	93
5144	Marc Newton	17 Sep	95
5136	Jamie Russell	20 Sep	98
5121	Chris Hindley	20 Sep	92
5102	Matt Douglas	22 Aug	93
with 100m			
5531	Jim Stevenson	18 Sep	88
5304	Tom Leeson	28 Sep	80
5194	Bryan Long	26 Sep	76

3000 METRES TRACK WALK

12:04.9	Philip King	18 May	91
12:35.94	David Hucks	30 Aug	82
12:50.9	Jon Vincent	8 Jul	87
12:50.67 i	Stuart Monk	18 Feb	95
12:52.9		12 Jul	95
13:03.5	Ian Ashforth	16 Sep	84
13:05.8	Sean Maxwell	8 Aug	76
13:08.4	Ian McCombie	8 Aug	76
13:09.74	Kirk Taylor	2 Jun	84
13:10.6	Niall Troy	23 Jul	78
13:11.5	Nigel Whorlow	30 Aug	97
overage			
12:44.8	Gordon Vale	11 Oct	78

5000 METRES TRACK WALK

20:46.5	Philip King	29 Sep	91
21:52.7	Stuart Monk	22 Jul	95
22:17.5	Russell Hutchings	27 Sep	86
22:32.5	Gareth Holloway	27 Sep	86
22:35.0	Ian Ashforth	6 Jun	84
22:37.0	Jon Bott	27 Sep	86
22:42.0	Martin Young	20 Aug	88
22:42.19	Jon Vincent	6 Jun	86
22:53.7	Tim Berrett	28 Jun	81
22:53.8	David Hucks	10 Mar	82
22:55.0	Lloyd Finch	14 Nov	98
22:57.7	Michael Kemp	31 Aug	96
23:01.0	Karl Atton	19 Apr	88
23:16.1	Thomas Taylor	31 May	97
overage			
22:42.2	Michael Kemp	13 Oct	96
22:48.0hc	Matthew Hales	13 Nov	96
22:51.1	Thomas Taylor	12 Oct	97

Road

21:33	Jon Vincent	1 Nov	86
22:04	Gareth Holloway	14 Sep	86
22:05	Karl Atton	19 Mar	88
22:16	Stuart Monk	11 Feb	95
22:25	Russell Hutchings	1 Nov	86
22:30	Gordon Vale	15 Oct	77
overage			
21:31	Gareth Holloway	1 Nov	86
21:35	Jon Bott	1 Nov	86
22:11	Gordon Vale	21 Oct	78
22:12	Nathan Kavanagh	22 Oct	83

10000 METRES TRACK WALK

43:56.5	Philip King	2 Feb	91
45:47.0	Ian Ashforth	12 Sep	84
46:11.0	Jon Vincent	20 May	87
overage			
46:01.0	Thomas Taylor	21 Oct	97
46:34.0	Karl Atton	3 Dec	88
46:36.0	Gordon Vale	26 Nov	78

Road

43:49	Philip King	29 Jun	91
45:43	Jon Vincent	7 Mar	87

UNDER 15

100 METRES
10.93	Mark Lewis-Francis	12	Jul	97
11.05	Jamie Nixon	21	Jul	84
11.11	Tristan Anthony	17	Aug	97
11.21	Kevin Mark	13	Jul	91
11.22	Chris Blake	7	Aug	93
11.23	Ray Burke	11	Aug	84
11.23	Charles Gordon	12	Aug	90
11.24	Mike Williams II	19	Jul	86

wind assisted
11.00	Steve Wiggans	9	Jul	94
11.04	Joe Brown	13	Jul	96
11.05	Ray Burke	11	Aug	84
11.06	Duncan Game	5	Jul	86
11.06	Paul Chantler	9	Jul	94
11.11	Andrew Rose	13	Jul	96
11.17	Tony Cairns	5	Jul	86

hand timing
11.0	Norman Ellis	23	Jul	89
11.1	Michael Hitchen	24	Apr	77
11.1	Malcolm James			77
11.1	Ray Burke	25	Aug	84
11.1	Duncan Game	29	Jun	86
11.1	Michael Williams II	31	Aug	86
11.1	Jeffrey Anderson	3	Jul	89
11.1	Matthew Clements	23	Aug	92

hand timing wind assisted
11.0	Malcolm James	24	Jun	77
11.0	Ian Strange	24	Jun	77
11.0	John Burt	6	Sep	80
11.0	Hilton Thompson	6	Aug	89
11.0	Jeffrey Anderson	6	Aug	89
11.0	Matthew Clements	15	Sep	91

200 METRES
22.30	Jamie Nixon	29	Sep 84
22.31	Mike Williams II	10	Aug 86
22.35	Tristan Anthony	12	Jul 97
22.40	Ben Lewis	8	Jul 95
22.54	Matthew Clements	16	Aug 92
22.65	Daniel Angus	12	Jul 96
22.69	Chris Blake	8	Aug 93
22.74	L. Oboh	11	Jul 98
22.79	Jermaine Williams	16	Aug 92

wind assisted
22.26	Steven Daly	9	Jul 94
22.39	André Duffus	9	Jul 94
22.40	Tom Hyde	15	Aug 98
22.46	Robert Allenby	9	Jul 94
22.48	Daniel Angus	13	Jul 96

hand timing
22.2	Mike Williams II	12	Jul 86
22.3	Tony Cairns	12	Jul 86
22.4	Duncan Game	29	Jun 86
22.6	Stuart Lawrenson	27	Jun 76

overage
22.4	Ade Mafe	11	Nov 81

wind assisted
21.9	Tony Cairns	21	Jun 86

400 METRES
49.8	Mark Tyler	25	Aug 82
49.9	David McKenzie	11	Aug 85
49.97		23	Jun 85
49.96	Craig Erskine	18	Jul 98
49.98	Ryan Preddy	11	Jul 98
50.0	Simon Heaton	7	Jul 79
50.1	Ade Mafe	6	Sep 81
50.3	Malcolm James	29	Aug 77
50.65	Ian Lowthian	29	Jul 95
50.7	Cephas Howard	19	May 91
50.99		13	Jul 91
50.78	Mike Snow	12	Jul 97
50.88	Aaron Evans	17	Aug 96
50.9	Alan Leonard	30	Aug 78
50.9	Noel Goode	7	Jul 79
51.00	Paul Roberts	22	Jul 84
51.0	Marc Newton	30	Jul 94

overage
50.5 i	Cephas Howard	14	Dec 91

800 METRES (*880yards less 0.7)
1:56.1	Craig Winrow	12	Jul 86
1:56.6	Paul Burgess	13	Jul 85
1:57.1	Delroy Smith	12	Jul 86
1:57.12	Michael Combe	14	Aug 93
1:57.2 a	Tony Jarman	15	Sep 78
1:57.5	Noel Goode	11	Jul 79
1:57.5	Ryan Preddy	7	Jun 98
1:57.7	Eric Kimani	15	Sep 81
1:57.7	Mark Sesay	11	Aug 87
1:57.87	Austin Finn	7	Jul 91
1:58.1	Piers Counsell	12	Jul 86
1:58.2	Ketan Desai	6	Aug 97
1:58.3 *	Dave Dutton	6	Aug 66

overage
1:53.6	David Gerard	9	Nov 83
1:57.7	Stephen Gilbey	17	Oct 73

1000 METRES
2:38.2	Eric Kimani	11	Sep 81

1500 METRES
4:03.0	Glen Stewart	28	Aug 85
4:03.0	Scott West	28	Aug 90
4:03.52	Mike Isherwood	17	Sep 82
4:03.56	Richard Youngs	17	Sep 82
4:03.6	Doug Stones	7	Jul 79
4:03.7	David Gerard	31	Jul 83
4:05.7	Ben Mabon	1	Sep 85
4:05.8	Graham Green	19	Jun 79
4:05.9	Glen Coppin	25	Jun 97
4:06.0	Eric Kimani	29	Jul 81
4:06.41	Mohammed Farah	12	Jul 97
4:06.5	Paul Hemmings	18	Jul 82
4:06.8	Richard Green	7	Jun 70

ONE MILE
4:21.9	Glen Stewart	11	Sep 85

2000 METRES
5:45.8	Richard Slater	16	Jun 74

3000 METRES

8:47.0	Ben Mabon	16	Jul	85
8:47.48	Mohammed Farah	5	Jul	97
8:48.8	Dale Smith	14	Aug	85
8:51.1	Mark Slowikowski	4	Jun	80
8:54.6	Gary Taylor	14	Sep	77
8:54.6	David Bean	22	Jul	79
8:56.0	Paul Ryder	29	Aug	79
8:56.4	Stuart Bond	10	Sep	91
8:57.0	Philip Hennessy	28	Jul	82
8:57.6	Chris Taylor	16	Jul	69

overage

8:56.9	David Gerard	12	Oct	83

80 METRES HURDLES (2'9")

10.71	Matthew Clements	15	Aug	92
11.04	Leon McRae	8	Jul	95
11.07	Robert Hollinger	8	Jul	95
11.10	Seb Bastow	13	Jul	96
11.10	Chris Tye-Walker	12	Jul	97
11.20	Tony Lashley	13	Jul	91

wind assisted

11.00	Tom Benn	9	Jul	94
11.02	Nick Dowsett	10	Jul	93
11.12	Sam Allen	10	Jul	93

hand timing

11.0	Austin Drysdale	22	Jun	75
11.1	Ricky Glover	8	Jul	89
11.1	Tom Bradwell	13	Jul	90

hand timing wind assisted

11.0	Tim Greenwood	29	Jun	97

100 METRES HURDLES (3'0")

13.3	Matthew Clements	23	Aug	92

HIGH JUMP

2.04	Ross Hepburn	22	Aug	76
2.01	Ken McKeown	10	Aug	96
1.97	Andrew Lynch	29	Aug	88
1.97	Wayne Gray	3	Sep	95
1.96	Chuka Enih-Snell	29	Aug	98
1.95	Mark Lakey	14	Sep	80
1.94	Brian Hall	16	Aug	97
1.93	Ewan Gittins	21	Jul	84
1.91	Mark Smith	15	Jul	89
1.91	Edward Willers	9	Jul	94
1.91	Matthew Brereton	9	Jul	94
1.91	Jamie Russell	22	Sep	96

overage

1.94 i	Paul Byrne	10	Dec	77

POLE VAULT

4.31	Richard Smith	28	Aug	95
4.30	Neil Winter	8	Jul	88
4.30	Christian Linskey	18	Jun	94
4.18	Ian Lewis	24	May	83
4.00	Jimmy Lewis	9	Sep	79
3.90	Peter Eyre	2	Jul	89
3.90	Martin Parley	6	Jun	92
3.90	Steve Francis	11	Sep	93
3.90	Andrew Corey	17	Aug	96
3.85	Steven Brown	2	Jun	96

overage

4.40	Neil Winter	1	Oct	88

LONG JUMP

6.79	Onochie Onuorah	17	Sep	88
6.77	Barry Nevison	30	Aug	81
6.74	Kevin Hibbins	17	Jun	95
6.71	Mark Awanah	17	Aug	97
6.62	Martin Giraud	25	May	92
6.59	Danny Smith	29	Aug	87
6.58	Tony Allen	8	Aug	82
6.55	Jonathan Moore	17	May	98
6.54	Jordan Lau	11	Jul	98
6.52	Julian Danquah	7	Jul	67
6.52	Ian Strange	24	Jun	77

overage

6.59 i	David Gilkes	19	Dec	92
6.59 i	Marcellas Peters	11	Dec	93

wind assisted

7.12	Onochie Onuorah	17	Sep	88
6.72	David Gilkes	6	Apr	92
6.68	Jordan Lau	16	Aug	98
6.63	Ian Strange			77

downhill

6.77	Eric Wood	25	Aug	58

TRIPLE JUMP

13.86	Jamie Quarry	10	Jul	87
13.79	Paul Dundas	11	Jun	88
13.77	Eugene Hechevarria	16	Sep	78
13.71	Larry Achike	10	Jun	89

note resident but not British citizen at this time

13.69	Vernon Samuels	25	Aug	79
13.60	Steven Anderson	9	Jun	79
13.60	Steve Folkard	11	Jul	80
13.57	Errol Burrows	11	Jul	80
13.56	Delroy Ricketts	18	Jun	88
13.55	Darren Yeo	15	Jul	89
13.55	Michael Duberry	14	Jul	90

wind uncertain

13.83	Vernon Samuels	30	Jun	79

wind assisted

13.92	Eugene Hechevarria	7	Jul	78
13.87	Vernon Samuels	20	Sep	79
13.83	Chris Tomlinson	12	Jul	96
13.73	Donovan Fraser	6	Jul	79
13.69	Kevin O'Shaughnessy	7	Jul	78

SHOT (4kg)

18.71	Chris Ellis	14	Jun	80
16.54	Geoff Hodgson	7	Jul	72
16.39	Pete Waterman	2	Jul	94
16.39	Gregg Beard	25	Aug	97
16.29	Neal Brunning ¶	11	Sep	85
16.20	Carl Saggers	9	Sep	98
16.14	Andrew Monaghan	19	Sep	70
16.11	Billy Cole	6	Jul	79
16.05	John Nicholls	29	Jun	80
16.01	Ian McLaughlin	18	Sep	91
15.96	James Muirhead	14	Sep	85
15.95	Spencer English	3	Aug	86

overage

16.36 i	Billy Cole	1 Nov	79
15.94 i	Phil Adams	14 Dec	86

SHOT (5kg)

15.62	Chris Ellis	18 Jun	80

overage

15.93	Chris Ellis	7 Dec	80

DISCUS (1.25kg)

53.08	Emeka Udechuku	5 Sep	93
50.80	Paul Mardle	3 Sep	77
50.32	Chris Symonds	23 Jul	85
50.04	Keith Homer	11 Jul	80
49.36	James Muirhead	12 May	85
49.32	Jucan Douglas	16 Sep	79
49.22	Spencer English	1 Jun	86
48.84	Witold Leonowicz	23 Aug	80
48.78	Neville Lynch	7 Sep	80
48.76	Ben Walker	15 Aug	92
48.30	Alan Rudkin	22 Aug	93
48.02	Matt Symonds	26 Jun	82

DISCUS (1.5kg)

44.20	Matt Symonds	18 Sep	82
44.10	Keith Homer	30 Aug	80

HAMMER (4kg)

70.78	Andrew Tolputt	9 Jul	82
67.24	Peter Vivian	22 Sep	85
65.42	Matthew Sutton	29 Sep	96
64.28	Jason Byrne	22 Sep	85
63.68	Paul Binley	29 Sep	85
63.30	Richard Fedder	26 Aug	79
63.16	Tony Kenneally	29 May	78
62.06	Nick Steinmetz	4 Aug	91
61.32	John Barnes	8 Jun	96
61.08	Neil Curtis	11 Sep	88
60.52	Ian McLaughlin	21 Aug	91
60.15	Carl Saggers	16 Aug	98
59.94	Mike Rowlatt	2 Sep	90

HAMMER (5kg)

60.10	Andrew Tolputt	5 Sep	82
58.00	Peter Vivian	22 Sep	85

overage

58.06	Jason Byrne	27 Oct	85

HAMMER (6.25kg)

48.86	Peter Vivian	22 Sep	85

JAVELIN (600g)

62.70	Paul Godwin	20 May	89
60.56	David Messom	6 Jul	79
60.56	Clifton Green	3 Jul	94
60.34	Richard Lainson	18 Aug	96
59.88	James Hurrion	17 Sep	88
59.52	Paul Brice	19 Aug	79
58.94	Dan Carter	7 Aug	94
58.74	Philips Olweny	6 Aug	95
58.58	Justin Rubio	11 Jun	83
58.58	Rhys Williams	10 Aug	96
58.48	Andrew Ravenscroft	9 Aug	80

JAVELIN (700g)

58.76	Dan Carter	29 Aug	94
55.10	Michael Williams	24 Jul	77

PENTATHLON (80H,SP,LJ,HJ,800)

3272	Chris Dack	20 Sep	97
3187	Mark Newton	27 Aug	94
3163	Kevin Drury	27 Aug	94
3129	Mark Awanah	24 Aug	97
3039	Chuka Enih-Snell	23 Aug	98
3037	Edward Dunford	19 Sep	98
3024	Tom Benn	17 Sep	94
3014	Chris Jenkins	21 Sep	96
2995	Marcellas Peters	18 Sep	93
2993	Sam Allen	18 Sep	93
2989	Ian Leaman	18 Sep	93

(100,SP,LJ,HJ,800)

3199	Onochie Onuorah	17 Sep	88
3085 w	Cephas Howard	21 Sep	91
3035	Ricky Glover	16 Sep	89

OCTATHLON (Under 15 implements)

3933	Aidan Turnbull	1 Oct	95

DECATHLON (Under 15 implements)

5341	Jamie Quarry	28 Jun	87

3000 METRES TRACK WALK

12:44.64	Lloyd Finch	24 May	98
13:19.57	Philip King	29 May	89
13:35.0	Russell Hutchings	7 Sep	85
13:45.0	John Murphy	14 May	95
13:51.0	Robert Mecham	12 May	92
13:58.0	Jon Vincent	7 Sep	85
14:03.0	Neil Simpson	1 Apr	89
14:03.5	Nathan Kavanagh	20 Sep	81
14:13.0	Karl Atton	15 Mar	86
14:15.3	Matthew Hales	14 May	94

overage

12:59.7	Philip King	10 Oct	89

Road

12:55	Lloyd Finch	21 Jun	98
13:20	Jonathan Deakin	18 Sep	88
13:29	Robert Mecham	20 Apr	92
13:32	Russell Hutchings	10 Nov	84
13:38	Philip King	1 Apr	89
13:39	Neil Simpson	6 May	89
13:43	Nathan Kavanagh	21 Feb	81

overage

13:30	Ben Allkins	1 Dec	90

5000 METRES TRACK WALK

22:54.0	Lloyd Finch	15 Jul	98
23:53.9	Philip King	27 Jun	89
24:22.0	Robert Mecham	14 Jul	92

overage

23:17.0	Philip King	17 Dec	89
24:03.6	John Murphy	15 Oct	95

Road

23:56	Philip King	24 Sep	89

overage

23:15	Philip King	9 Dec	89

UNDER 13

100 METRES
11.6	Tristan Anthony	28	Aug	95
11.8	Cephas Howard	2	Jul	89
11.9	Stephen Buttler	26	Sep	87

200 METRES
24.0	Stephen Buttler	26	Jul	87
24.1	Tristan Anthony	30	Jul	95
24.4	Cephas Howard	3	Sep	89

400 METRES
55.1	Cephas Howard	2	Jul	89
56.1	Andrew French	4	Jul	92
56.5	Craig Erskine	22	Sep	96

800 METRES
2:04.1	Ben Mabon	8	Jul	83
2:06.4	Eric Kimani	11	Aug	79
2:11.0	Brendan Waters	17	Jun	89

1500 METRES
4:18.4	Eric Kimani	26	Sep	79
4:20.5	Ben Mabon	18	Jun	83
4:22.3	David Gerard	12	Aug	81
4:23.9	Mark Slowikowski	12	Jul	78

3000 METRES
9:31.4	Ben Mabon	19	Jul	83
9:41.4	Mark Slowikowski	21	May	78
9:49.5	John Tilley	9	Jul	86
overage				
9:41.2	Graham Green	26	Oct	77

75 METRES HURDLES (2'3")
11.7	Stephen Cotterill	16	Jul	78
11.7	Sean Ashton	12	Sep	98

80 METRES HURDLES (2'6")
11.9	Matthew Clements	27	Aug	90
12.1	Sean Ashton	27	May	98

80 METRES HURDLES (2'9")
12.6	James Dunford	27	Sep	98
12.92	Sam Allen	18	Aug	91

HIGH JUMP
1.68	Sam Allen	22	Sep	91
1.68	James Dunford	29	Sep	98
1.67	Glen Carpenter	3	Jul	83
1.67	Jamie Dalton	28	Jun	92

POLE VAULT
3.40	Neil Winter	27	Jul	86
3.20	Ian Lewis	8	Sep	81
2.80	Philip Wade	11	Sep	94

LONG JUMP
5.74 w?	Edward Dunford	21	Sep	97
5.65	Sam Allen	14	Sep	91
5.64	Kevin Hibbins	18	Jul	93

TRIPLE JUMP
12.57	Rigsby Agoreyo	9	Aug	69
11.78	Edward Dunford	27	Sep	97

SHOT (3.25kg)
13.36	Chris Hughes	21	Aug	91
13.11	Tony Quinn	28	Aug	93
12.46	Paul Beard	31	Aug	86

SHOT (4kg)
11.99	Mark Griffiths		78

DISCUS (1kg)
42.38	Ben Barnes	1	Sep	91
38.92	Chris Hughes	28	Jul	91
38.50	Carl Saggers	15	Sep	96

DISCUS (1.25kg)
33.88	Chris Symonds		83

HAMMER (3.25kg)
44.38	Ross Thompson	4	Sep	94
36.96	Edward Dunford	24	Sep	97

HAMMER (4kg)
38.72	Adrian Johnson	30	Sep	84
38.64	Ross Thompson	14	Aug	94

JAVELIN (400g)
43.02	Max Shale	8	Aug	93
42.29	Edward Dunford	27	Sep	97
41.86	James Dunford	29	Sep	98

JAVELIN (600g)
39.62	P. Shearing	23	May	76

PENTATHLON (75H,SP,LJ,HJ,800)
2562	Edward Dunford	28	Sep	97

2000 METRES TRACK WALK
9:40.0	Luke Finch	12	Nov	97
9:40.3	Thomas Taylor	19	Jun	93
9:51.0	Lloyd Finch	11	Aug	96

2000 METRES ROAD WALK
9:16	Lloyd Finch	28	Sep	96
9:38	Luke Finch	12	Sep	98

2500 METRES ROAD WALK
12:01	Grant Ringshaw	14	Sep	80
12:11	Gareth Brown	14	Sep	80

3000 METRES TRACK WALK
15:02.62	Lloyd Finch	21	Sep	96
15:15.5	Robert Mecham	25	Jul	89
overage				
14:47.0	Gareth Brown	11	Nov	80
14:51.0	Grant Ringshaw	10	Dec	80
Road				
14:44	Martin Young	22	Sep	84
14:48	John Griffiths	22	Oct	83
overage				
14:31 hc	Martin Young	16	Dec	84
14:35	Lloyd Finch	10	Nov	96

UK ALL TIME LISTS - WOMEN

100 METRES

11.10	Kathy Cook	5 Sep 81	
11.15	Paula Thomas	23 Aug 94	
11.16	Andrea Lynch	11 Jun 75	
11.20	Sonia Lannaman	25 Jul 80	
11.20	Heather Oakes	26 Sep 80	
11.22 A	Bev Callender	8 Sep 79	
11.35		22 Jul 81	
11.27	Stephanie Douglas	26 Jul 91	
11.29	Bev Kinch	6 Jul 90	
11.31	Wendy Hoyte	4 Oct 82	
10 11.31	Shirley Thomas	3 Jul 83	
11.31	Simmone Jacobs	24 Sep 88	
11.32	Joan Baptiste	24 Aug 83	
11.32	Joice Maduaka	16 Sep 98	
11.34	Katharine Merry	25 Jun 94	
11.35	Sharon Danville	20 Aug 77	
11.36 A	Della Pascoe	14 Oct 68	
11.39 A	Val Peat	14 Oct 68	
11.39	Sallyanne Short	12 Jul 92	
11.40	Helen Golden	20 Jul 74	
20 11.40	Marcia Richardson	29 Aug 98	
11.41	Jayne Christian	27 May 84	
11.45	Helen Barnett	26 Aug 83	
11.46 A	Donna Hartley	22 Mar 75	
11.46	Eleanor Cohen	30 Jul 82	
11.47	Mary Agyepong	20 Jun 87	
11.48	Carmen Smart	26 Aug 89	
11.48	Geraldine McLeod	26 May 96	
11.48	Andrea Coore	1 Jun 97	
11.49	Sophia Smith	25 Aug 96	
30 11.50	Sandra Whittaker	14 Jun 86	
11.50	Helen Miles	5 Aug 88	
11.51	Kaye Scott	28 May 83	
11.51	Sarah Oxley	21 Jun 97	
11.52	Pippa Windle	6 Jun 86	
11.53	Sharon Williams	31 Aug 95	
11.54	Dorothy Hyman	15 Oct 64	
11.54	Janis Neilson	24 May 87	
11.54	Aileen McGillivary	27 Jun 92	
11.55	Anita Neil	1 Sep 72	
40 11.57	Michelle Scutt	2 Sep 84	
11.5 a	Daphne Slater	15 Oct 64	
11.59	Chris Bloomfield	28 Aug 93	
11.59	Rebecca Drummond	8 Jul 95	
11.60	Phylis Smith	24 May 87	
11.60	Danaa Callow	22 Aug 94	
11.60	Shani Anderson	30 Jun 96	

hand timing

10.9	Andrea Lynch	28 May 77
11.1	Sonia Lannaman	29 Jun 80
11.1	Heather Oakes	29 Jun 80
11.1	Joan Baptiste	16 Jul 85
11.2	Helen Golden	29 Jun 74
11.2	Sharon Danville	25 Jun 77
11.2	Bev Kinch	14 Jul 84
11.2	Geraldine McLeod	21 May 94

wind assisted

10.93	Sonia Lannaman	17 Jul 77	
11.01	Heather Oakes	21 May 80	
11.08	Kathy Cook	24 Aug 83	
11.13	Bev Kinch	6 Jul 83	
11.13	Shirley Thomas	27 May 84	
11.13	Paula Thomas	20 Aug 88	
11.18	Wendy Hoyte	4 Oct 82	
11.18	Simmone Jacobs	11 Jun 97	
11.19	Bev Callender	21 May 80	
11.23	Joan Baptiste	24 Aug 83	10
11.23	Jayne Andrews	17 Jul 84	
11.27	Katharine Merry	11 Jun 94	
11.32	Donna Fraser	25 Apr 97	
11.34	Sandra Whittaker	22 May 83	
11.36	Sallyanne Short	26 Aug 89	
11.36	Marcia Richardson	12 Jul 98	
11.37	Val Peat	17 Jul 70	
11.37	Kaye Scott	22 May 83	
11.37	Helen Barnett	11 Sep 83	
11.39	Pippa Windle	24 Jul 87	20
11.40	Phylis Smith	3 Jun 90	
11.41	Helen Miles	20 Aug 88	
11.43	Dorothy Hyman	2 Sep 60	
11.43	Aileen McGillivary	10 Jul 93	
11.43	Clova Court	26 May 97	
11.45	Michelle Scutt	12 Jun 82	
11.45	Rebecca White	4 Jul 98	
11.45	Abi Oyepitan	4 Jul 98	
11.46	Geraldine McLeod	9 Jul 93	
11.48	Jakki Harman	23 Jul 88	30
11.48	Angie Thorp	7 Jul 96	
11.50	Margot Wells	15 Jul 78	
11.50	Rebecca Drummond	9 Jul 94	
11.50	Samantha Davies	18 Jul 98	
11.51	Anita Neil	17 Jul 70	
11.53	Sharon Tunaley	16 Aug 86	
11.53	Ellena Ruddock	25 May 98	
11.55	Daphne Slater	15 Oct 64	
11.55	Liz Sutherland	18 Jul 70	
11.55	Maxine Ascroft	30 Jun 79	40
11.55	Ena Waldo	30 Jul 88	
11.55	Donna Hoggarth	29 Aug 92	
11.55	Shani Anderson	30 Aug 97	
11.56	Sue Hearnshaw	23 Jun 84	
11.57	Rosalee Wilson	21 May 80	
11.58	Liz Johns	17 Jul 71	
11.58	Janine MacGregor	13 Sep 81	
11.58	Danaa Callow	11 Jun 94	
11.59	Lynne Draper	20 Aug 88	
11.59	Maria Bolsover	4 Jul 98	50

hand timing - wind assisted

10.8	Sonia Lannaman	22 May 76
11.1	Sharon Danville	22 May 76
11.1	Bev Kinch	9 May 87
11.2	Margaret Williams	15 May 76

60

200 METRES

22.10	Kathy Cook	9 Aug	84
22.58	Sonia Lannaman	18 May	80
22.69	Paula Thomas	26 Aug	94
22.72	Bev Callender	30 Jul	80
22.73	Jenni Stoute	3 Aug	92
22.75	Donna Hartley	17 Jun	78
22.77	Katharine Merry	21 Jun	97
22.80	Michelle Scutt	12 Jun	82
22.86	Joan Baptiste	9 Aug	84
10 22.92	Heather Oakes	28 Aug	86
22.95	Simmone Jacobs	25 Apr	96
22.96 i	Donna Fraser	23 Feb	97
23.25		29 Jun	97
22.98	Sandra Whittaker	8 Aug	84
23.10	Diane Smith	11 Aug	90
23.14	Helen Golden	7 Sep	73
23.14	Helen Burkart	17 Jul	82
23.15	Andrea Lynch	25 Aug	75
23.17	Stephanie Douglas	12 Jun	94
23.18	Joslyn Hoyte-Smith	9 Jun	82
20 23.20	Sarah Oxley	21 Jun	97
23.23	Sarah Wilhelmy	13 Jun	98
23.24	Sallyanne Short	28 Jun	92
23.29	Verona Elder	17 Jun	78
23.29	Aileen McGillivary	25 Jul	93
23.30	Sally Gunnell	13 Jun	93
23.33	Linsey Macdonald	9 Jun	82
23.33	Allison Curbishley	8 Jun	98
23.34	Val Peat	19 Sep	69
23.35	Melanie Neef	2 Jul	95
30 23.36	Shirley Thomas	10 Jun	84
23.36	Louise Stuart	4 Aug	90
23.37	Joice Maduaka	30 May	98
23.40	Dorothy Hyman	18 Aug	62
23.40	Sharon Danville	9 Sep	77
23.40	Phylis Smith	6 Jun	92
23.40	Catherine Murphy	16 Jul	95
23.42 A	Lillian Board	17 Oct	68
23.52		3 Aug	68
23.42	Debbie Bunn	17 Jun	78
23.43	Sue Hearnshaw	16 Jun	84
40 23.46	Janine MacGregor	22 Aug	81
23.47 A	Angela Bridgeman	10 May	86
23.47	Geraldine McLeod	24 Aug	94
23.48	Wendy Hoyte	7 Jun	75
23.48	Denise Ramsden	21 Aug	76
23.48	Margaret Williams	21 Aug	76
23.49	Wendy Addison	16 Jun	84
23.51	Eleanor Cohen	16 Jul	78
23.51	Linda Keough	8 Jul	89

wind assisted

22.48	Michelle Scutt	4 Jul	82
22.69	Bev Callender	24 Jun	81
22.90	Andrea Lynch	11 Jun	75
22.90	Donna Fraser	25 Apr	97
22.90	Allison Curbishley	17 Jul	98
22.97	Helen Golden	26 Jul	74
23.00	Joslyn Hoyte-Smith	13 Jun	82
23.11	Linsey Macdonald	5 Jul	80

23.14	Shirley Thomas	28 May	84
23.15	Margaret Williams	22 Jul	70 10
23.19	Sallyanne Short	29 Jan	90
23.20	Sarah Wilhelmy	18 Jul	98
23.32	Louise Stuart	4 Jun	89
23.36	Lorna Boothe	30 Mar	80
23.39 A	Angela Bridgeman	12 Apr	86
23.41	Louise Fraser	16 Jun	91

hand timing

22.9	Heather Oakes	3 May	80
22.9	Helen Barnett	6 Aug	83
23.0	Helen Golden	30 Jun	74
23.1	Andrea Lynch	21 May	77
23.1	Linda Keough	5 Jul	89
23.2	Dorothy Hyman	3 Oct	63
23.2	Margaret Williams	2 Aug	70
23.3	Sharon Danville	30 Jun	74
23.3	Linsey Macdonald	8 May	82
23.3	Louise Stuart	25 Aug	91 10
23.4 A	Lillian Board	5 Oct	68
23.4	Pippa Windle	2 Aug	87
23.4	Marcia Richardson	1 Aug	93
23.4	Geraldine McLeod	1 Aug	93
23.4	Louise Fraser	1 Jul	95

wind assisted

23.1	Margaret Williams	14 Jul	74
23.1	Sharon Danville	17 Sep	77
23.1	Linda McCurry	2 Jul	78
23.2	Debbie Bunn	2 Jul	78
23.2	Sybil Joseph	1 Jun	85
23.3	Angela Bridgeman	15 Aug	82
23.3	Janis Nelson	1 Jun	86

300 METRES

35.46	Kathy Cook	18 Aug	84
36.01	Michelle Scutt	13 Jul	80
36.44	Sally Gunnell	30 Jul	93
36.45	Joslyn Hoyte-Smith	5 Jul	80
36.46	Linsey Macdonald	13 Jul	80
36.65	Joan Baptiste	18 Aug	84
36.69	Helen Barnett	9 Sep	83
36.92	Phylis Smith	11 Aug	96
36.95	Jenni Stoute	21 Jul	91
36.97	Donna Hartley	4 Jul	75 10
37.30	Verona Elder	26 May	76
37.31	Donna Fraser	12 Jul	96
37.33	Melanie Neef	8 Jul	94
37.40	Tracy Lawton	18 Aug	84
37.42	Angela Bridgeman	25 Sep	82
37.45	Jane Parry	18 Aug	84
37.46	Linda Forsyth	30 Aug	82
37.46 iA	Sharon Danville	14 Mar	81
37.47	Allison Curbishley	11 Aug	96

hand timing

36.2	Donna Hartley	7 Aug	74
37.0	Linda Keough	22 Jul	89

during 400

37.4 +	Georgina Oladapo	18 Jun	95

400 METRES

49.43	Kathy Cook	6 Aug 84	
50.40	Phylis Smith	3 Aug 92	
50.63	Michelle Scutt	31 May 82	
50.71	Allison Curbishley	18 Sep 98	
50.75	Joslyn Hoyte-Smith	18 Jun 82	
50.85	Donna Fraser	17 Sep 98	
50.93	Lorraine Hanson	26 Aug 91	
50.98	Linda Keough	26 Aug 91	
51.02	Katharine Merry	30 Aug 98	
51.04	Sally Gunnell	20 Jul 94	10
51.16	Linsey Macdonald	15 Jun 80	
51.18	Melanie Neef	6 Aug 95	
51.28	Donna Hartley	12 Jul 75	
51.41	Sandra Douglas	2 Aug 92	
51.53	Jenni Stoute	12 Aug 89	
51.70	Verona Elder	10 Jun 78	
51.93	Janine MacGregor	28 Aug 81	
51.97	Linda Forsyth	31 May 82	
52.12 A	Lillian Board	16 Oct 68	
53.00		2 Sep 68	
52.13	Helen Barnett	28 Jun 84	20
52.20	Ann Packer	17 Oct 64	
52.26	Pat Beckford	14 Aug 88	
52.43	Gladys Taylor	2 Sep 84	
52.48	Georgina Oladapo	16 Jun 96	
52.52	Sybil Joseph	14 Sep 85	
52.54	Stephanie Llewellyn	9 Jul 95	
52.57 A	Janet Simpson	16 Oct 68	
52.65	Jane Parry	11 Jun 83	
52.67	Tracy Lawton	8 Jul 84	
52.71	Loreen Hall	18 Jun 88	30
52.75	Sandra Leigh	12 Jul 91	
52.77	Michelle Pierre	20 Jul 97	
52.79	Angela Piggford	2 Jul 89	
52.80	Sian Morris	18 Jun 83	
52.83	Ruth Patten	10 Jul 79	
52.85	Jannette Roscoe	3 Sep 74	
52.88	Michelle Thomas	11 Jun 97	
52.89	Janet Smith	6 Aug 88	
52.97	Vicki Jamison	1 Aug 98	
52.98	Karen Williams	6 Aug 78	40
52.98	Dyanna Clarke	28 Jul 79	
52.99	Angela Bridgeman	24 Jul 82	
53.01 i	Marilyn Neufville	14 Mar 70	
53.08	Bev Callender	21 Aug 76	
53.12	Joy Grieveson	14 Sep 63	
53.23	Tracy Joseph	15 Jun 91	
53.24	Rosemary Wright	28 Aug 71	
53.25	Dawn Kitchen	16 Jun 90	
53.26	Natasha Danvers	21 Jun 98	
53.28 A	Diane Modahl	2 May 92	50
53.31	Liz Barnes	21 Jun 75	

hand timing

51.2	Donna Hartley	28 Jul 78
51.4	Verona Elder	22 May 76
52.2	Liz Barnes	22 May 76
52.4	Stephanie Llewellyn	1 Jul 95
52.6	Marilyn Neufville	20 Jun 70
52.8	Lillian Board	9 Jul 67

600 METRES

1:26.0 +	Kelly Holmes	13 Aug 95
1:26.18	Diane Modahl	22 Aug 87
1:26.5 +	Kirsty Wade	21 Aug 85
1:26.7	Ann Griffiths	22 Jan 90
1:26.8	Shireen Bailey	16 Jun 85

800 METRES

1:56.21	Kelly Holmes	9 Sep 95	
1:57.42	Kirsty Wade	24 Jun 85	
1:58.65	Diane Modahl	14 Jul 90	
1:58.97	Shireen Bailey	15 Sep 87	
1:59.05	Christina Cahill	4 Aug 79	
1:59.67	Lorraine Baker	15 Aug 86	
1:59.76	Paula Fryer	17 Jul 91	
1:59.81	Ann Griffiths	10 Aug 94	
2:00.10	Tanya Blake	31 May 98	
2:00.15	Rosemary Wright	3 Sep 72	10
2:00.20	Anne Purvis	7 Jul 82	
2:00.30	Cherry Hanson	25 Jul 81	
2:00.39	Bev Nicholson	28 Aug 88	
2:00.55mx	Zola Budd	21 Jun 86	
2:00.6 a	Jane Finch	9 Jul 77	
2:00.80	Yvonne Murray	10 Jul 87	
2:01.1 a	Ann Packer	20 Oct 64	
2:01.11	Lynne MacDougall	18 Aug 84	
2:01.2	Joan Allison	1 Jul 73	
2:01.2	Christine Whittingham	26 Aug 78	20
2:01.24	Chris Benning	28 Jul 79	
2:01.35	Liz Barnes	10 Jul 76	
2:01.36	Gillian Dainty	31 Aug 83	
2:01.40	Janet Bell	10 Jul 87	
2:01.48	Lesley Kiernan	11 Jun 77	
2:01.50	Lillian Board	18 Sep 69	
2:01.52 i	Hayley Parry	15 Feb 98	
	2:02.18	11 Jun 97	
2:01.65	Teena Colebrook	21 Jul 84	
2:01.66	Pat Cropper	12 Aug 71	
2:01.67	Sonya Bowyer	24 Jun 95	30
2:01.7	Ann Middle	28 Aug 91	
2:01.82	Linda Keough	1 Aug 93	
2:01.83	Amanda Crowe	18 Sep 98	
2:01.86	Helen Daniel	10 Jul 87	
2:01.87	Dawn Gandy	19 Jun 88	
2:01.93	Sue Bevan	19 Jul 91	
2:02.0	Margaret Coomber	1 Jul 73	
2:02.0	Jo White	13 Aug 77	
2:02.0	Lynne Robinson	26 Jul 89	
2:02.34	Lynn Gibson	14 Aug 92	40
2:02.39	Emma Davies	17 Sep 98	
2:02.47	Abigail Hunte	16 Jul 95	
2:02.6	Evelyn McMeekin	20 Aug 78	
2:02.69	Natalie Tait	16 Jul 95	
2:02.70	Janet Marlow	15 Jun 80	
2:02.79	Sue Morley	27 Jul 85	
2:02.83	Mary Kitson	21 Jul 91	
2:02.89	Wendy Sly	30 Jul 83	
2:02.9	Sheila Carey	10 Sep 71	
2:02.91	Carol Sharp	7 Jul 82	50
2:02.92	Debbie Russell	2 Aug 85	

1000 METRES

2:32.55	Kelly Holmes	15 Jun 97	
2:33.70	Kirsty Wade	9 Aug 85	
2:34.92	Christina Cahill	9 Aug 85	
2:35.32	Shireen Bailey	19 Jul 86	
2:35.51	Lorraine Baker	19 Jul 86	
2:35.86	Diane Modahl	29 Aug 93	
2:37.05	Christine Whittingham	27 Jun 86	
2:37.29	Yvonne Murray	14 Jul 89	
2:37.61	Bev Hartigan	14 Jul 89	
2:37.82	Gillian Dainty	11 Sep 81	10
2:38.44	Evelyn McMeekin	23 Aug 78	
2:38.58	Jo White	9 Sep 77	
2:38.67	Lynne MacDougall	19 Jul 86	
2:38.83	Lynn Gibson	29 Aug 93	
2:39.23	Teena Colebrook	24 Jul 90	
2:39.29	Ann Griffiths	16 Sep 90	
2:39.42	Mary Cotton	26 May 76	

1500 METRES

3:58.07	Kelly Holmes	29 Jun 97	
3:59.96	Zola Budd	30 Aug 85	
4:00.57	Christina Cahill	6 Jul 84	
4:00.73	Kirsty Wade	26 Jul 87	
4:01.20	Yvonne Murray	4 Jul 87	
4:01.38	Liz McColgan	4 Jul 87	
4:01.53	Chris Benning	15 Aug 79	
4:02.32	Shireen Bailey	1 Oct 88	
4:03.17	Alison Wyeth	7 Aug 93	
4:04.14	Wendy Sly	14 Aug 83	10
4:04.81	Sheila Carey	9 Sep 72	
4:05.66	Bev Hartigan	20 Jul 90	
4:05.75	Lynn Gibson	20 Jul 94	
4:05.81	Paula Radcliffe	1 Jun 98	
4:05.96	Lynne MacDougall	20 Aug 84	
4:06.0	Mary Cotton	24 Jun 78	
4:06.24	Christine Whittingham	5 Jul 86	
4:07.11	Janet Marlow	18 Aug 82	
4:07.28	Joanne Pavey	29 Jun 97	
4:07.59	Ann Griffiths	9 Jun 92	20
4:07.69	Teena Colebrook	19 Aug 90	
4:07.90	Gillian Dainty	16 Jun 84	
4:08.98	Hayley Parry	17 Aug 97	
4:09.26	Lisa York	13 Jun 92	
4:09.29	Angela Davies	20 Jul 94	
4:09.37	Joyce Smith	7 Sep 72	
4:09.46	Karen Hargrave	4 Sep 89	
4:09.5	Penny Yule	6 Aug 80	
4:10.07	Maxine Newman	28 Jun 92	
4:10.10	Cherry Hanson	30 Aug 81	30
4:10.21	Kathy Carter	31 Jul 82	
4:10.32	Lynne Robinson	30 Jul 94	
4:10.41	Jo White	10 Jun 84	
4:10.66	Joan Allison	2 Feb 74	
4:10.68	Amanda Crowe	21 Sep 98	
4:10.7 mx	Sonia Bowyer	16 Jul 96	
4:10.75	Sonia McGeorge	20 Jul 90	
4:10.76	Ruth Partridge	16 Jun 84	
4:11.00	Sue Morley	6 Jul 85	
4:11.12	Bridget Smyth	26 May 85	40
4:11.23	Paula Fudge	31 Jul 81	
4:11.24 i	Nicky Morris	7 Jan 89	
4:11.46	Ursula McGloin	20 Jan 90	
4:11.51	Jane Shields	4 Sep 83	
4:11.57	Sue Parker	18 Jun 96	
4:11.75	Debbie Peel	31 Jul 82	
4:11.82	Una English	28 Jun 82	
4:11.85	Jo Dering	28 Jul 90	
4:11.94	Lorraine Baker	5 Jul 90	
4:12.19	Gill Settle	26 May 85	50

ONE MILE

4:17.57	Zola Budd	21 Aug 85	
4:19.41	Kirsty Wade	27 Jul 85	
4:22.64	Christina Cahill	7 Sep 84	
4:22.64	Yvonne Murray	22 Jul 94	
4:24.57	Chris Benning	7 Sep 84	
4:24.87	Alison Wyeth	6 Jul 91	
4:24.94	Paula Radcliffe	14 Aug 96	
4:26.11	Liz McColgan	10 Jul 87	
4:26.16	Teena Colebrook	14 Jul 90	
4:26.52	Bev Hartigan	14 Aug 92	10
4:27.80	Lisa York	14 Aug 92	
4:28.04	Kelly Holmes	30 Aug 98	
4:28.07	Wendy Sly	18 Aug 84	
4:28.8	Karen Hargrave	20 Aug 89	
4:29.15	Sue Morley	18 Aug 84	
4:30.08	Lynne MacDougall	7 Sep 84	
4:30.29	Jane Shields	9 Sep 83	
4:30.77	Joanne Pavey	30 Aug 97	
4:30.89	Ruth Partridge	18 Aug 84	
4:31.17	Lynn Gibson	1 Jul 94	20
4:31.24 i	Jo White	5 Feb 83	
4:31.45	Shireen Bailey	17 Sep 89	
4:31.65	Gillian Dainty	26 Jun 82	
4:31.83	Angela Davies	1 Jul 94	
4:32.00	Carole Bradford	18 Aug 84	
4:32.32	Debbie Gunning	5 Jul 91	
4:32.82	Monica Joyce	10 May 81	
4:32.91	Lynne Robinson	14 Aug 92	
4:32.99	Amanda Crowe	30 Aug 98	
4:33.01	Una English	14 Aug 92	30

2000 METRES

5:26.93	Yvonne Murray	8 Jul 94	
5:30.19	Zola Budd	11 Jul 86	
5:33.85	Christina Cahill	13 Jul 84	
5:37.00	Chris Benning	13 Jul 84	
5:38.50	Alison Wyeth	29 Aug 93	
5:39.20	Paula Radcliffe	29 Aug 93	
5:40.24	Liz McColgan	22 Aug 87	
5:42.15	Wendy Sly	17 Sep 82	
5:43.24	Sue Morley	13 Jul 84	
5:45.0 i	Bev Hartigan	20 Feb 93	10
5:45.15	Debbie Gunning	29 Aug 93	
5:45.34	Lisa York	10 Jul 92	
5:45.45	Ruth Partridge	13 Jul 84	
5:45.81 i	Kirsty Wade	13 Mar 87	
5:46.40	Sonia McGeorge	29 Aug 93	
5:46.54	Una English	10 Jul 92	

3000 METRES

8:28.83	Zola Budd	7 Sep	85
8:29.02	Yvonne Murray	25 Sep	88
8:34.80 i	Liz McColgan	4 Mar	89
8:38.23		15 Jul	91
8:35.28	Paula Radcliffe	13 Aug	97
8:37.06	Wendy Sly	10 Aug	83
8:38.42	Alison Wyeth	16 Aug	93
8:44.46	Chris Benning	22 Aug	84
8:45.69	Jane Shields	10 Aug	83
8:47.36	Jill Hunter	17 Aug	88
10 8:47.59	Angela Tooby	5 Jul	88
8:47.7	Kirsty Wade	5 Aug	87
8:47.71	Lisa York	31 Jul	92
8:48.72	Karen Hargrave	28 Jan	90
8:48.74	Paula Fudge	29 Aug	78
8:49.89	Christina Cahill	20 Jul	85
8:50.52	Debbie Peel	7 Aug	82
8:51.33	Sonia McGeorge	29 Aug	90
8:51.40	Ruth Partridge	7 Aug	82
8:52.79	Ann Ford	28 Aug	77
20 8:53.52 i	Nicky Morris	4 Mar	89
8:59.46		24 Jun	89
8:55.53	Joyce Smith	19 Jul	74
8:56.09	Andrea Wallace	10 Jul	92
8:56.39	Sue Morley	21 Jul	84
8:57.17	Susan Wightman	6 Jun	84
8:57.2	Kathy Carter	7 Apr	84
8:58.2	Joanne Pavey	4 May	98
8:58.44	Kathryn Binns	26 May	80
8:58.59	Andrea Whitcombe	26 Jul	91
8:59.39	Regina Joyce	8 May	81
30 8:59.45	Jo Dering	11 Aug	90
8:59.65	Gillian Dainty	20 Jul	83
9:00.21	Carole Bradford	9 Jul	85
9:00.3	Bridget Smyth	20 Apr	91
9:00.68	Alison Wright	23 Jun	81
9:01.67	Melissa Watson	27 Jun	88
9:02.25	Julie Holland	11 Aug	90
9:02.47	Laura Adam	4 Jun	94
9:03.35	Philippa Mason	19 Jul	86
9:03.51	Rhona Makepeace	25 Feb	92
40 9:03.88 i	Bev Hartigan	17 Feb	90
9:04.27	Sarah Young	2 Aug	98
9:04.4	Sarah Bentley	22 Jun	96
9:04.98	Lynne Harvey	25 Aug	82
9:05.02	Sue Crehan	19 Aug	87
9:05.03	Hilary Hollick	25 May	81
9:05.14	Jill Harrison	13 Jul	85
9:05.4	Mary Cotton	29 Jul	84
9:05.49	Zahara Hyde	29 Jul	91
9:05.65	Kerry Robinson	18 Apr	82
50 9:05.80	Teena Colebrook	21 Apr	90

5000 METRES

14:45.51	Paula Radcliffe	22 Aug	97
14:48.07	Zola Budd	26 Aug	85
14:56.94	Yvonne Murray	7 Jul	95
14:59.56	Liz McColgan	22 Jul	95
15:00.37	Alison Wyeth	7 Jul	95
15:09.98	Jill Hunter	18 Jul	92
15:13.22	Angela Tooby	5 Aug	87
15:14.51	Paula Fudge	13 Sep	81
15:21.45	Wendy Sly	5 Aug	87
15:28.63	Andrea Wallace	2 Jul	92 [10]
15:29.04	Sonia McGeorge	27 May	96
15:31.78	Julie Holland	18 Jul	90
15:32.19	Susan Wightman	26 May	85
15:32.34	Jane Shields	5 Jun	88
15:34.16	Jill Harrison	26 May	85
15:34.40	Lucy Elliott	2 Jun	97
15:38.84	Ann Ford	5 Jun	82
15:40.14	Helen Titterington	17 Jul	89
15:41.11	Angela Hulley	18 Jul	90
15:41.68	Debbie Peel	27 Jun	85 [20]
15:43.03	Andrea Whitcombe	25 Jul	98
15:45.03	Lynne MacDougall	29 Jun	97
15:45.08	Sarah Young	25 Jul	98
15:48.1 mx	Tara Krzywicki	5 Aug	98
15:49.6	Kathryn Binns	5 Apr	80
15:50.59	Angela Davies	3 Jun	98
15:50.85	Liz Talbot	1 Aug	98
15:51.62	Carol Greenwood	26 May	85
15:52.2	Ruth Partridge	23 Aug	89
15:53.84	Heather Heasman	6 Jul	96 [30]
15:53.86	Sarah Bentley	22 Jul	95

10000 METRES

30:48.58	Paula Radcliffe	4 Apr	98
30:57.07	Liz McColgan	25 Jun	91
31:07.88	Jill Hunter	30 Jun	91
31:53.36	Wendy Sly	8 Oct	88
31:55.30	Angela Tooby	4 Sep	87
31:56.97	Yvonne Murray	24 Aug	94
32:20.95	Susan Wightman	2 Jul	88
32:21.61	Andrea Wallace	6 Jun	92
32:24.63	Sue Crehan	4 Jul	87
32:32.42	Vikki McPherson	15 Jul	93 [10]
32:36.09	Helen Titterington	29 Aug	89
32:41.29	Jenny Clague	20 Jun	93
32:42.0	Jane Shields	24 Aug	88
32:42.84	Angela Hulley	6 Aug	89
32:44.06	Suzanne Rigg	27 Jun	93
32:47.78	Julie Holland	31 Aug	90
32:57.17	Kathy Binns	15 Aug	80
32:58.2	Claire Lavers	20 Apr	91
33:05.43	Elspeth Turner	1 Jun	88
33:10.25	Shireen Barbour	5 Jul	86 [20]
33:10.94	Marina Stedman	28 Jul	86
33:17.88	Karen Macleod	1 Jul	89
33:19.19	Bernadette Madigan	27 Apr	85
33:19.48	Heather Heasman	6 Jun	92
33:21.46	Louise Watson	14 Jun	96
33:23.25	Zahara Hyde	12 Jun	94
33:26.79	Amanda Wright	6 Jun	92
33:27.69	Jill Harrison	22 Jun	86
33:30.0	Annette Bell	10 Aug	91
33:30.27	Angela Joiner	4 Apr	98 [30]
33:34.03	Lynn Everington	26 May	86
33:34.7	Priscilla Welch	2 Jun	84

10 KILOMETRES ROAD

	Time	Name	Date
	30:39	Liz McColgan	11 Mar 89
	31:29	Wendy Sly	27 Mar 83
	31:42	Jill Hunter	21 Jan 89
	31:47	Paula Radcliffe	29 Mar 97
	31:56	Andrea Wallace	4 Aug 91
	32:14	Angela Tooby	31 Mar 84
	32:15	Priscilla Welch	23 Mar 85
	32:20	Zola Budd	2 Mar 85
	32:24	Yvonne Murray	2 Nov 97
10	32:27	Ruth Partridge	11 Mar 89
	32:31	Heather Heasman	6 Nov 94
	32:35	Suzanne Rigg	15 Aug 92
	32:38	Jane Shields	23 Mar 85
	32:38	Marian Sutton	28 Sep 97
	32:41	Jill Harrison	21 Feb 87
	32:43	Teresa Dyer	1 Jan 93
	32:44	Carole Bradford	14 Oct 85
	32:44	Paula Fudge	13 Mar 88
	32:46	Kirsty Wade	28 Feb 87
20	32:46	Amanda Wright	25 Feb 96
	32:47	Chris Benning	15 Mar 87
	32:52	Susan Wightman	29 Oct 89

course measurement uncertain

31:43	Zola Budd	6 May 84
32:03	Paula Fudge	29 Aug 82
32:29	Yvonne Danson	13 Nov 94
32:36	Mary Cotton	5 Aug 84
32:41	Susan Wightman	4 Mar 84

10 MILES ROAD

	51:41	Jill Hunter	20 Apr 91
	51:51	Angie Hulley	18 Nov 89
	52:00	Liz McColgan	5 Oct 97
	52:15	Marian Sutton	5 Oct 97
	53:42	Suzanne Rigg	10 Oct 93
	53:44	Paula Fudge	21 Sep 85
	53:44	Andrea Wallace	7 Mar 93
	53:49	Véronique Marot	25 Aug 85
	53:50	Yvonne Murray	6 Oct 96
10	53:51	Priscilla Welch	5 Apr 87

intermediate time

53:00 +	Andrea Wallace	5 May 91

course measurement uncertain

Time	Name	Date
53:17	Joyce Smith	12 Oct 80
53:44	Sarah Rowell	10 Mar 84

downhill

53:42	Karen Macleod	11 Apr 93

HALF MARATHON

	1:07:11	Liz McColgan	26 Jan 92
	1:09:39	Andrea Wallace	21 Mar 93
	1:09:41	Maria Sutton	14 Sep 97
	1:09:56	Susan Wightman	24 Jul 88
	1:10:54	Alison Wyeth	29 Mar 98
	1:11:17	Véronique Marot	21 Jun 87
	1:11:33	Vikki McPherson	14 Sep 97
	1:11:36	Ann Ford	30 Jun 85
	1:11:37	Paula Fudge	24 Jul 88
10	1:11:38	Sally Ellis	20 Mar 88

MARATHON

2:25:56	Véronique Marot	23 Apr 89	
2:26:51	Priscilla Welch	10 May 87	
2:26:52	Liz McColgan	13 Apr 97	
2:28:06	Sarah Rowell	21 Apr 85	
2:28:38	Sally-Ann Hales	21 Apr 85	
2:29:03	Marian Sutton	19 Oct 97	
2:29:29	Sally Eastall	8 Dec 91	
2:29:43	Joyce Smith	9 May 82	
2:29:47	Paula Fudge	30 Oct 88	
2:30:38	Ann Ford	17 Apr 88	10
2:30:51	Angie Hulley	23 Sep 88	
2:30:53	Yvonne Danson	17 Apr 95	
2:31:33	Susan Wightman	23 Sep 88	
2:31:33	Andrea Wallace	12 Apr 92	
2:31:45	Lynn Harding	23 Apr 89	
2:32:53	Gillian Castka	2 Dec 84	
2:33:04	Sheila Catford	23 Apr 89	
2:33:07	Nicky McCracken	22 Apr 90	
2:33:16	Karen Macleod	27 Aug 94	
2:33:22	Carolyn Naisby	6 Dec 87	20
2:33:24	Sally Ellis	23 Apr 89	
2:33:38	Lynda Bain	21 Apr 85	
2:34:11	Sally Goldsmith	3 Mar 96	
2:34:19	Jill Harrison	23 Apr 89	
2:34:21	Suzanne Rigg	24 Sep 95	
2:34:26	Heather MacDuff	16 Oct 88	
2:35:03	Sandra Branney	23 Apr 89	
2:35:05	Carol Gould	26 Oct 80	
2:35:10	Sue Crehan	17 Apr 88	
2:35:18	Karen Holdsworth	29 Sep 85	30
2:35:18	Debbie Noy	13 Oct 91	
2:35:32	Rose Ellis	23 Apr 89	
2:35:39	Hayley Nash	27 Aug 94	
2:35:53	Julie Coleby	13 May 84	
2:36:06	Margaret Lockley	13 May 84	
2:36:12	Kathryn Binns	12 Jun 82	
2:36:21	Glynis Penny	17 Apr 83	
2:36:29	Danielle Sanderson	7 Aug 94	
2:36:31	Julia Gates	20 Apr 86	
2:36:32	Marina Stedman	23 Apr 89	40
2:36:34	Lorna Irving	1 Aug 86	
2:36:40	Teresa Dyer	17 Apr 94	
2:36:52	Gillian Horovitz	20 Jun 92	
2:37:06	Moira O'Neill	31 Oct 88	
2:37:14	Cath Mijovic	22 Oct 95	
2:37:26	Caroline Horne	21 Apr 85	
2:37:36	Sandra Mewett	17 Jan 88	
2:37:37	Anne Roden	20 Apr 92	
2:37:49	Alison Gooderham	17 Apr 88	
2:38:17	Inez McLean	3 Feb 85	50

2000 METRES STEEPLECHASE (2'6")

6:53.7	Sharon Dixon	8 May 94
7:00.7	Sally Young	8 May 94

(3'0" barriers)

Time	Name	Date
7:04.7mx	Sally Young	14 Jul 93
7:05.1	Veronica Boden	17 Jul 94

3000 METRES STEEPLECHASE (2'6")

Time	Name	Date
10:52.6	Tanya Blake	22 Aug 93

100 METRES HURDLES

	12.80	Angie Thorp	31 Jul 96
	12.82	Sally Gunnell	17 Aug 88
	12.87	Shirley Strong	24 Aug 83
	12.90	Jacqui Agyepong	25 Jun 95
	12.91	Kay Morley-Brown	2 Feb 90
	13.03	Lesley-Ann Skeete	3 Aug 90
	13.03	Diane Allahgreen	11 Jul 97
	13.04	Clova Court	9 Aug 94
	13.05	Judy Simpson	29 Aug 86
10	13.07	Lorna Boothe	7 Oct 82
	13.08	Sam Farquharson	4 Jul 94
	13.11	Sharon Danville	22 Jun 76
	13.11	Keri Maddox	29 Aug 98
	13.16	Wendy Jeal	27 Aug 86
	13.18	Denise Lewis	25 May 96
	13.20	Natasha Danvers	2 May 98
	13.24	Kim Hagger	31 Aug 87
	13.26	Michelle Campbell	3 Aug 90
	13.29	Mary Peters	2 Sep 72
20	13.32	Sam Baker	29 Aug 93
	13.34	Judy Vernon	7 Sep 73
	13.34	Melanie Wilkins	15 Jul 95
	13.35	Pat Rollo	30 Jul 83
	13.36	Louise Fraser	17 Aug 91
	13.44	Judith Robinson	1 Jul 89
	13.45	Lorna Drysdale	20 Jul 74
	13.46	Tessa Sanderson	25 Jul 81
	13.46	Nathalie Byer	26 Aug 83
	13.47	Heather Ross	16 Jun 84
30	13.49	Blondelle Caines	17 Jul 77
	13.50 A	Yvette Wray	8 Sep 79
	13.57		15 Jul 79
	13.52	Rachel King	26 Jul 97
	13.52	Julie Pratt	5 Jul 98
	13.52	Liz Fairs	25 Jul 98
	13.53	Ann Simmonds	4 Sep 72
	13.53	Lynne Green	27 Jun 88
	13.54	Debbie Brennan	7 Aug 88
	13.57	Bethan Edwards	29 Aug 92
	13.58	Lauraine Cameron	19 Jun 90
40	13.59	Jane Hale	19 May 96
	13.60	Elaine McMaster	7 Oct 82
	13.60	Joanne Mulliner	25 Jul 87
	13.62	Gillian Evans	1 Jul 83
	13.62	Jill Kirk	3 Jul 83
	13.62	Sarah Claxton	18 Jul 98
	13.68	Heather Platt	7 Jul 85
	13.70	Yinka Idowu	14 Jun 92
	13.71	Margot Wells	4 Aug 82
	13.73	Ann Girvan	7 Aug 82
50	13.74	Kerry Hill	6 Jun 86
	13.75	Sue Reeve	21 Jul 70
	13.75	Maureen Prendergast	5 May 84
	13.78	Lynne Ilott	20 Jul 74
	13.78	Katy Sketchley	20 Jun 98
	13.79	Manndy Laing	6 Aug 83
	13.79	Joss Harwood	22 Jul 89
	13.80	Sue Longden	31 Jul 77
	13.80	Jenny Kelly	29 Aug 98

wind assisted

12.78	Shirley Strong	8 Oct 82	
12.80	Sally Gunnell	29 Jul 88	
12.84 A	Kay Morley-Brown	8 Aug 90	
12.90	Lorna Boothe	8 Oct 82	
13.01	Lesley-Ann Skeete	1 Feb 90	
13.06	Sharon Danville	14 Jul 84	
13.07	Keri Maddox	27 Jun 98	
13.08	Michelle Campbell	26 May 95	
13.12	Pat Rollo	27 May 84	
13.22	Heather Ross	27 May 84	10
13.23	Melanie Wilkins	30 Jun 96	
13.28	Sarah Claxton	5 Jul 98	
13.36	Judith Robinson	11 Jul 87	
13.39	Debbie Brennan	29 Jul 88	
13.39	Lauraine Cameron	1 Jul 90	
13.44	Yvette Wray	21 May 80	
13.44	Kerry Hill	27 May 84	
13.44	Rachel King	28 May 98	
13.48	Elaine McMaster	12 Jun 82	
13.48	Joanne Mulliner	25 Jul 87	20
13.48	Julie Pratt	5 Jul 98	
13.54	Jill Kirk	7 Jun 86	
13.56	Ann Girvan	15 Jul 84	
13.57	Katy Sketchley	14 Jun 98	
13.62	Yinka Idowu	17 Sep 94	
13.63	Heather Platt	1 Jul 84	
13.66	Maureen Prendergast	14 Apr 84	
13.71	Sue Longden	21 May 80	
13.71	Manndy Laing	12 Jun 82	
13.72	Myra Nimmo	20 Jul 74	30
13.72	Kate Forsyth	6 Jul 97	
13.74	Claire St. John	21 May 80	
13.74	Natasha Mighty	30 Apr 94	
13.76	Julie Vine	28 Jul 90	
13.78	Jane Low	10 Sep 83	
13.79	Vikki Schofield	4 May 96	
13.79	Pauline Richards	23 May 98	
13.80	Lisa Gibbs	30 Apr 94	

hand timing

13.0	Judy Vernon	29 Jun 74	
13.0	Blondelle Caines	29 Jun 74	
13.1	Melanie Wilkins	2 Jul 95	
13.2	Pat Rollo	11 Jun 83	
13.3	Ann Symonds	29 Jul 72	
13.3	Debbie Brennan	16 Jul 89	
13.4	Christine Bell	2 Aug 70	
13.5	Pat Pryce	26 Jul 72	
13.5	Liz Sutherland	29 Mar 76	
13.5	Sue Longden	26 Jun 76	10
13.5	Yvette Wray	7 Jun 80	
13.5	Jill Kirk	7 Aug 83	

wind assisted

12.7	Kay Morley-Brown	10 Jan 90
12.9	Judy Vernon	18 May 74
13.1	Mary Peters	19 Aug 72
13.2	Ann Symonds	19 Aug 72
13.2	Liz Sutherland	8 May 76
13.3	Kerry Hill	9 May 87
13.5	Myra Nimmo	24 Jul 74

400 METRES HURDLES

	Time	Name	Date
	52.74	Sally Gunnell	19 Aug 93
	54.63	Gowry Retchakan	3 Aug 92
	55.69	Natasha Danvers	19 Jul 98
	55.91	Elaine McLaughlin	26 Sep 88
	56.04	Sue Chuck	10 Aug 83
	56.05	Wendy Cearns	13 Aug 89
	56.06	Christine Warden	28 Jul 79
	56.15	Jacqui Parker	27 Jul 91
	56.26	Louise Fraser	7 Jun 92
10	56.38	Keri Maddox	18 Sep 98
	56.42	Vicki Jamison	21 Jun 98
	56.43	Alyson Layzell	16 Jun 96
	56.46	Yvette Wray	11 Jul 81
	56.61	Louise Brunning	16 Jun 96
	56.70	Lorraine Hanson	13 Aug 89
	56.72	Gladys Taylor	6 Aug 84
	57.00	Simone Laidlow	6 Aug 88
	57.07	Verona Elder	15 Jul 83
	57.38	Sarah Dean	27 Jul 91
20	57.41	Jennifer Pearson	6 Aug 88
	57.43	Liz Sutherland	6 Jul 78
	57.49	Maureen Prendergast	16 Jun 84
	57.52	Clare Sugden	3 Jun 90
	57.55	Sharon Danville	8 May 81
	57.76	Aileen Mills	5 Aug 86
	57.79	Susan Cluney	15 Jun 80
	57.81	Margaret Southerden	10 Jul 82
	57.86	Teresa Hoyle	29 Jul 83
	58.02	Vyvyan Rhodes	28 Jun 92
30	58.04	Clare Bleasdale	16 Jul 94
	58.09	Stephanie McCann	12 Jun 94
	58.16	Diane Fryar	9 Jul 83
	58.19	Sara Elson	4 Jul 92
	58.28	Carol Dawkins	14 Sep 85
	58.31	Jannette Roscoe	19 Jul 75
	58.31	Fiona Laing	18 Sep 81
	58.35	Debbie Skerritt	11 Jul 81
	58.41	Lynn Parry	19 Jun 88
	58.43	Jane Low	24 Aug 94
40	58.44	Maggie Still	19 Jun 88
	58.51	Julie Vine	17 Jun 90
	58.54	Sinead Dudgeon	26 Jul 98
	58.55	Jackie Stokoe	19 Jul 75
	58.62	Sharon Allen	3 May 97
	58.68	Kay Simpson	15 Jul 83
	58.68	Vicky Lee	5 Aug 86
	58.79	Sheila Peak	25 Jul 87
	58.83	Sue Smith	23 Jun 79
	59.00	Debbie Church	12 Jun 86
50	59.04	Allison Curbishley	31 Jul 93
	59.07	Clare Wise	26 Jul 98

hand timing

Time	Name	Date
57.5	Vicky Lee	28 Jun 86
57.8	Teresa Hoyle	26 Jul 86
58.0	Fiona Laing	28 Aug 81
58.2	Debbie Skerritt	6 Jun 81
58.6	Jane Finch	21 Sep 80
58.8	Veronica Boden	28 Jun 87
58.8	Allison Curbishley	5 May 96

HIGH JUMP

1.95	Diana Davies	26 Jun 82	
1.95 i	Debbie Marti	23 Feb 97	
1.94		9 Jun 96	
1.94	Louise Gittens	25 May 80	
1.94 i	Jo Jennings	13 Mar 93	
1.91		20 Sep 98	
1.92	Barbara Simmonds	31 Jul 82	
1.92	Judy Simpson	8 Aug 83	
1.92	Janet Boyle	29 Sep 88	
1.92 i	Julia Bennett	10 Mar 90	
1.89		11 Jun 94	
1.92	Lea Haggett	15 Jun 96	
1.92 i	Susan Jones	28 Feb 98	10
1.91		31 Aug 97	
1.91	Ann-Marie Cording	19 Sep 81	
1.91	Gillian Evans	30 Apr 83	
1.91	Jayne Barnetson	7 Jul 89	
1.90	Kim Hagger	17 May 86	
1.90	Sharon Hutchings	1 Aug 86	
1.89 i	Michelle Dunkley	16 Feb 97	
1.88		20 Sep 98	
1.88 i	Debbie McDowell	17 Jan 88	
1.82		7 May 88	
1.88 i	Kerry Roberts	16 Feb 92	
1.86		6 Jun 92	
1.88 i	Kelly Thirkle	16 Feb 92	
1.85		10 Aug 91	
1.87	Barbara Lawton	22 Sep 73	20
1.87	Moira Maguire	11 May 80	
1.87	Louise Manning	6 May 84	
1.87	Rachael Forrest	7 Jul 95	
1.86	Claire Summerfield	7 Aug 82	
1.86	Jennifer Farrell	11 May 86	
1.86	Catherine Scott	8 May 87	
1.86	Michelle Marsella	31 May 87	
1.85	Brenda Flowers	20 Aug 77	
1.85	Gillian Cadman	3 Jun 78	
1.85	Julie Peacock	8 Jul 94	30
1.85	Hazel Melvin	3 Aug 97	
1.84	Sarah Rowe	22 Aug 81	
1.84	Ursula Fay	6 Aug 83	
1.84	Tonia Schofield	20 Aug 83	
1.84	Denise Lewis	19 May 96	
1.83	Linda Hedmark	4 Jul 71	
1.83	Val Rutter	19 Jun 74	
1.83 i	Ros Few	25 Feb 75	
1.83	Denise Hinton	8 Aug 80	
1.83	Joanne Brand	4 Jun 83	40
1.83	Rhona Scobie	4 Aug 85	
1.83	Marion Hughes	19 Jul 86	
1.83	Tracey Clarke	2 Aug 87	
1.83	Kay Fletcher	17 Jun 89	
1.83	Lee McConnell	30 May 98	
1.83	Julie Crane	30 May 98	
1.82	Mary Peters	2 Sep 72	
1.82	Wendy Phillips	19 Jul 80	
1.82	Elaine Hickey	9 Aug 80	
1.82	Natasha Danvers	24 May 98	50

POLE VAULT

4.31	Janine Whitlock	30 May	98
3.91	Emma Hornby	27 Jun	98
3.90	Kate Staples	26 May	96
3.90 i	Rhian Clarke	8 Mar	97
3.90		31 May	97
3.85 A	Allison Murray-Jessee	16 Jun	98
3.60		4 Aug	98
3.80	Lucy Webber	21 Jun	98
3.80	Paula Wilson	25 Jul	98
3.75	Louise Schramm	19 Jul	98
3.75	Tracey Bloomfield	9 Aug	98
10 3.72	Linda Stanton	11 Jun	95
3.60 A	Krissy Owen	9 May	98
3.52		18 Apr	98
3.60	Fiona Harrison	25 May	98
3.60	Clare Ridgley	25 May	98
3.60	Alison Davies	29 Jul	98
3.55	Kimberly Rothman	17 Jun	98
3.50	Noelle Bradshaw	25 Jul	98
3.41	Hilary Smith	20 Sep	98
3.40 i	Claire Adams	26 Feb	95
3.30		18 Jun	95
3.40	Maria Newton	10 May	98
20 3.40	Danielle Codd	4 Jul	98
3.40	Becky Ridgley	5 Jul	98
3.40	Laura Patterson	30 Aug	98
3.35	Lindsay Hodges	5 Sep	98
3.30	Kate Alexander	20 Jul	96
3.30	Stacey Dicker	7 Sep	96
3.20 i	Samantha Stapleton	3 Aug	94
3.20		17 Aug	96
3.20	Larissa Lowe	26 May	96
3.20	Rebecca Roles	31 Aug	96
3.20	Jenny Cunnane	5 Oct	97
30 3.20 i	Suzanne Woods	15 Mar	98
3.20		10 Jun	98
3.20	Ellie Spain	13 Sep	98
3.15	Sarah Hartley	9 Aug	97
3.10	Dawn-Alice Wright	10 Jul	94
3.10	Leanne Mellor	21 Aug	94
3.10 i	Susie Drummie	4 Feb	95
3.00		4 Feb	95
3.10	Fiona Peake	27 Apr	96
3.10 ns	Katharine Horner	4 Jun	96
3.00		25 Mar	95
3.10	Jo Hughes	29 Jul	98
3.10	Kate Rowe	31 Aug	98
40 3.10 i	Kathryn Dowsett	19 Dec	98
3.00		16 Aug	98
3.05	Amy Rennison	4 Aug	98
3.03	Anna Watson	13 Sep	98
3.01 i	Louise Gauld	16 Dec	98
3.00	Claudia Filce	20 May	95
3.00	Kirsty Armstrong	27 Jul	96
3.00	Liz Hughes	1 Sep	96
3.00	Bonny Elms	19 Jul	97
3.00 i	Kia Knuk	28 Feb	98
3.00		19 Apr	98
3.00	Ruth Anness	25 Apr	98
50 3.00	Jayne Collins	9 May	98
3.00	Penny Hall	16 Aug	98
3.00	Eirion Owen	12 Sep	98

LONG JUMP

6.90	Bev Kinch	14 Aug	83
6.88	Fiona May	18 Jul	90
6.83	Sue Hearnshaw	6 May	84
6.76	Mary Rand	14 Oct	64
6.75	Joyce Oladapo	14 Sep	85
6.73	Sheila Sherwood	23 Jul	70
6.73	Yinka Idowu	7 Aug	93
6.70	Kim Hagger	30 Aug	86
6.70 i	Jo Wise	9 Mar	97
6.63		19 Sep	98
6.69	Sue Reeve	10 Jun	79 10
6.67	Denise Lewis	28 May	95
6.63	Mary Agyepong	17 Jun	89
6.55	Ann Simmonds	22 Jul	70
6.52	Gillian Regan	29 Aug	82
6.52	Georgina Oladapo	16 Jun	84
6.52	Sarah Claxton	31 Jul	98
6.51 i	Ruth Howell	23 Feb	74
6.49		16 Jun	72
6.47 A	Ashia Hansen	26 Jan	96
6.27		26 Jun	94
6.45	Carol Zeniou	12 May	82
6.45	Margaret Cheetham	18 Aug	84 20
6.44	Sharon Danville	15 Jun	77
6.44	Barbara Clarke	13 Sep	81
6.43	Myra Nimmo	27 May	73
6.40	Judy Simpson	26 Aug	84
6.40	Sharon Bowie	28 Jun	86
6.39	Moira Walls	22 Jul	70
6.39	Maureen Chitty	28 Jun	72
6.39	Sue Longden	12 Sep	76
6.39	Tracy Joseph	27 Jun	98
6.37	Kelly Wenlock	24 Apr	82 30
6.36	Andrea Coore	19 Jul	98
6.34 i	Barbara-Anne Barrett	20 Feb	71
6.31		14 Aug	71
6.33 i	Barbara Lawton	21 Nov	70
6.33	Glenys Morton	19 Jul	81
6.33	Joanne Mulliner	13 Sep	86
6.33	Jo Dear	19 May	93
6.32	Helen Garrett	7 Jun	87
6.32	Jo Willoughby	28 May	89
6.31	Lorraine Campbell	19 May	85
6.28	Janet Robson	4 May	77 40
6.28	Ruth Irving	9 May	98
6.28	Vikki Schofield	16 Jul	95
6.27	Alix Stevenson	13 Jun	70
6.27	Anita Neil	29 Aug	70
6.27	Sandra Green	14 Jun	80
6.27	Allison Manley	16 Aug	80
6.27	Liz Ghojefa	23 Jul	95
6.26	Maria Smallwood	14 Jun	80
6.25 i	Evette Finikin	3 Feb	89
6.25	Mandy Bell	16 May	92 50
6.25	Lisa Armstrong	15 Jul	92
6.24	Karen Murray	16 Jul	77
6.24	Gladys Taylor	28 Jul	79

wind uncertain

6.43	Moira Maguire	18 Sep	70

wind assisted

7.00	Sue Hearnshaw	27 May 84
6.98	Fiona May	4 Jun 89
6.93	Bev Kinch	14 Aug 83
6.84	Sue Reeve	25 Jun 77
6.80	Joyce Oladapo	22 Jun 85
6.77	Denise Lewis	1 Jun 97
6.69	Jo Wise	30 Jul 88
6.65	Mary Agyepong	4 Jun 89
6.57	Ann Simmonds	22 Aug 70
6.56	Judy Simpson	30 Aug 86
6.54	Ruth Howell	16 Jun 72
6.54	Myra Nimmo	19 Jun 76
6.53	Sarah Claxton	12 Jul 97
6.49	Margaret Cheetham	4 Sep 83
6.48	Moira Maguire	17 May 70
6.44	Tracy Joseph	21 Jun 97
6.41	Allison Manley	28 Jul 79
6.40	Barbara-Anne Barrett	17 Jul 71
6.39	Alix Stevenson	6 Jun 70
6.39	Carolyn Ross	19 Apr 87
6.38	Joanne Mulliner	1 Jun 85
6.38	Jo Willoughby	6 Aug 89
6.38	Ann Danson	7 Aug 94
6.36	Karen Murray	9 Jul 77
6.34	Janet Frank-Lynch	8 Jul 78
6.34	Jill Moreton	8 Jul 78
6.32	Diana Davies	22 May 88
6.32	Liz Ghojefa	16 Jul 94
6.29	Evette Finikin	1 May 89
6.29	Karen Skeggs	17 Jun 89
6.29	Julie Hollman	1 Jun 97

TRIPLE JUMP

15.16 i	Ashia Hansen	28 Feb 98
15.15		13 Sep 97
14.08	Michelle Griffith	11 Jun 94
13.95	Connie Henry	27 Jun 98
13.64	Rachel Kirby	7 Aug 94
13.56	Mary Agyepong	5 Jun 92
13.46	Evette Finikin	26 Jul 91
13.03	Shani Anderson	4 May 96
13.03	Kate Evans	26 Apr 97
12.94	Lorna Turner	9 Jul 94
12.89	Karen Skeggs	17 May 92
12.67	Caroline Stead	1 Jun 96
12.64	Liz Ghojefa	4 Sep 93
12.61	Kerensa Denham	14 Jun 98
12.61	Debbie Rowe	29 Aug 98
12.55	Pamela Anderson	29 Jun 96
12.50	Julia Johnson	21 Jun 98
12.47	Anna-Maria Thorpe	13 Sep 98
12.45	Lea Haggett	11 Nov 95
12.42	Liz Gibbens	2 Jul 95
12.41 i	Judy Kotey	28 Feb 98
12.33		17 May 98
12.27	Nikki Barr	17 May 98
12.26	Jodie Hurst	14 Jun 97
12.22	Mary Rand	18 Jun 59
12.22	Allison Forbes	9 Sep 89
12.22	Liz Patrick	4 May 98
12.18	Justina Cruickshank	26 May 96
12.15 i	Fiona Davidson	22 Jan 95
11.91		29 Jun 96
12.14	Jayne Ludlow	21 May 94
12.13 i	Margaret Still	21 Jan 96
12.03		2 Jun 96
12.11 i	Caroline Warden	21 Jan 96
12.06		1 May 94
12.10	Jane Falconer	29 Aug 93
12.03	Stephanie Aneto	17 May 97
11.91	Lisa Brown	30 Jul 95
11.88	Rachel Atkinson	9 May 98
11.87	Kirsty Payne	15 Aug 98
11.86	Kerry Jury	19 Jul 98
11.85	Lauraine Cameron	16 Jul 94
11.85	Jo Morris	30 Jun 96
11.85	Hayley Warrilow	13 Jun 98
11.84	Jayne Green	7 Sep 91
11.83	Marcia Richardson	4 Sep 93
11.79	Michelle Rea	16 Jun 91
11.79	Michelle Dunkley	7 Sep 96
11.78	Marcia Walker	5 Jul 97
11.76	Stephanie Dobson	10 Sep 94
11.76	Lucy Clements	9 Jun 96
11.74	Mandy Bell	16 May 92
11.72 i	Catherine Burrows	18 Feb 95
11.71	Helen Garrett	7 Aug 93
11.70	Clare O'Rourke	18 Jun 86
11.69	Kathryn Blackwood	9 Jul 94
11.68 i	Syreeta Williams	16 Feb 97
11.67 i	Jessie Aru	7 Mar 93
11.67	Linda Davidson	17 Jul 93
11.67	Rebecca White	10 May 98
11.66	Milly Clements	29 Jun 97
11.65	Kelly Sotherton	30 Aug 97

wind assisted

12.93	Karen Skeggs	13 Jun 92
12.76	Debbie Rowe	8 Jun 97
12.61	Judy Kotey	5 Jul 98
12.55	Lauraine Cameron	30 Aug 93
12.42	Jodie Hurst	5 May 97
12.42	Nikki Barr	28 Jun 97
12.37	Jane Falconer	30 Aug 93
12.31	Caroline Warden	23 Jul 94
12.21	Justina Cruickshank	19 May 96
12.20	Rachel Atkinson	28 Jul 96
12.18	Michelle Rea	29 Jun 91
12.07	Jo Morris	13 Jul 96
12.07	Rachel Peacock	18 Jul 98
12.06	Fiona Davidson	2 Jun 96
12.06	Stephanie Aneto	7 Jun 97
11.98	Ruth Irving	25 Feb 95
11.96	Lisa Brown	24 Jun 95
11.94	Milly Clements	8 Jun 97
11.93	Jessie Aru	15 May 93
11.81	Linda Davidson	18 Apr 93
11.80	Kathryn Blackwood	4 Jul 93
11.79	Catherine Burrows	27 May 95

SHOT

19.36	Judy Oakes	14 Aug 88
19.06 i	Venissa Head	7 Apr 84
18.93		13 May 84
19.03	Myrtle Augee	2 Jun 90
18.99	Meg Ritchie	7 May 83
17.53	Angela Littlewood	24 Jul 80
17.45	Yvonne Hanson-Nortey	28 Jul 89
16.57	Maggie Lynes	20 Jul 94
16.40 i	Mary Peters	28 Feb 70
16.31		1 Jun 66
16.29	Brenda Bedford	26 May 76
10 16.05	Janis Kerr	15 May 76
15.85 i	Alison Grey	12 Feb 94
15.69		11 Jun 94
15.81	Tracy Axten	19 Jul 98
15.80	Sharon Andrews	30 Jul 93
15.76	Jo Duncan	5 Jul 98
15.75 i	Caroline Savory	23 Feb 83
15.50		19 Jun 83
15.60 i	Justine Buttle	27 Feb 88
15.45		25 Aug 88
15.48	Mary Anderson	8 Sep 85
15.46	Vanessa Redford	14 Jun 80
15.45	Susan King	27 Mar 83
20 15.41	Fatima Whitbread	29 Apr 84
15.32 i	Helen Hounsell	13 Feb 82
14.91		22 May 82
15.27	Julie Dunkley	21 Jun 98
15.27	Denise Lewis	21 Aug 98
15.23	Judy Simpson	18 Jun 88
15.21	Uju Efobi	18 Jun 88
15.18	Suzanne Allday	18 May 64
15.18 i	Lana Newton	Jan 79
15.09		6 Sep 78
15.10	Christina Bennett	25 Apr 98
15.09	Jayne Berry	22 Jul 93
30 15.08	Janet Kane	3 Jun 79
15.08	Susan Tudor	30 May 82
15.00 i	Philippa Roles	19 Dec 98
14.60		4 Sep 96
14.98 i	Sandra Smith	21 Dec 85
14.95		18 Aug 85
14.88 i	Jenny Kelly	10 Mar 90
14.73		18 May 91
14.88	Debbie Callaway	15 May 93
14.77	Gay Porter	11 Apr 70
14.76 i	Carol Parker	14 Dec 91
14.71		1 Sep 90
14.75 i	Cynthia Gregory	12 Dec 81
14.70		29 Aug 81
40 14.71 i	Nicola Gautier	26 Jan 97
14.68	Eleanor Gatrell	18 Jul 98
14.67	Rosemary Payne	23 Apr 74
14.66 i	Terri Salt	7 Jan 84
14.64 i	Vickie Foster	8 Feb 98
14.61		25 Jul 98
14.62	Kathryn Farr	7 Jun 92
14.59	Dawn Grazette	19 May 91
14.53	Emma Beales	12 Sep 92

DISCUS

67.48	Meg Ritchie	26 Apr 81	
64.68	Venissa Head	18 Jul 83	
60.82	Shelley Drew	25 Jul 98	
60.72	Jackie McKernan	18 Jul 93	
58.56	Debbie Callaway	19 May 96	
58.18	Tracy Axten	31 May 97	
58.02	Rosemary Payne	3 Jun 72	
57.32	Lynda Wright	16 Jun 84	
56.24	Sharon Andrews	12 Jun 94	
56.06	Kathryn Farr	27 Jun 87	10
55.52	Jane Aucott	17 Jan 90	
55.42	Lesley Bryant	12 Sep 80	
55.06	Janet Kane	17 Jun 78	
55.04	Lorraine Shaw	14 May 94	
54.72	Karen Pugh	27 Jul 86	
54.68	Emma Beales	10 Jun 95	
54.46	Ellen Mulvihill	14 May 86	
54.46	Janette Picton	17 Aug 90	
54.24	Nicola Talbot	15 May 93	
54.14	Philippa Roles	25 Jul 98	20
53.96	Julia Avis	27 Apr 86	
53.66	Rosanne Lister	22 Jun 91	
53.44	Judy Oakes	20 Aug 88	
53.21	Emma Merry	26 Jun 98	
53.16	Sarah Winckless	18 Jun 94	
52.52	Alison Grey	18 Jun 94	
52.46	Vanessa Redford	4 Jul 82	
52.31	Lauren Keightley	18 Jul 98	
51.82	Catherine Bradley	20 Jul 85	
51.60	Dorothy Chipchase	20 Jul 73	30
51.18	Angela Sellars	12 Aug 90	
51.12	Joanne Brand	26 May 86	
50.98	Sarah Henton	30 Aug 97	
50.57	Brenda Bedford	24 Aug 68	
50.06	Joanne Essex	7 May 89	
50.04	Morag Bremner	27 Apr 86	
49.92	Fiona Condon	10 Apr 82	
49.84	Janis Kerr	15 May 77	
49.84	Denise Sturman	12 Apr 81	
49.66	Gay Porter	19 Aug 70	40
49.58	Jackie Wright	2 Aug 75	
49.48	Gwen Bird	20 Jul 91	
49.44	Myrtle Augee	14 May 95	
49.30	Amanda Barnes	18 Jun 82	
49.20	Jane Tabor	5 Apr 86	
49.12	Jean Robertson	14 Jul 74	
49.00	Tracey Jackson	26 Jun 84	
48.98	Angela Littlewood	6 Jun 82	
48.84	Uju Efobi	14 May 95	
48.76	Rachel Hopgood	27 May 96	50
48.64	Helen Cowe	17 Sep 94	
48.62	Vickie Foster	8 Jun 93	
48.54	Sandra Browne	3 Jul 88	
48.08	Donna Williams	12 Jul 96	
48.06	Yvonne Hanson-Nortey	13 Aug 89	
48.02	Natalie Hart	19 May 90	
48.01	Hilda Atkins	20 Feb 66	
downhill			
51.04	Fiona Condon	7 Jul 79	
47.88	BELINDA HOCKLEY	31 MAR 86	70
47.78	LYNN SMITH	4 SEP 83	
47.70	SUSAN ALLDAY	7 JUN 58 NR	

HAMMER

	Mark	Name	Date
	64.90	Lorraine Shaw	10 Jun 95
	61.70	Lyn Sprules	12 Jul 97
	57.97	Rachael Beverley	25 Jul 98
	57.95	Diana Holden	18 Jul 98
	57.56	Liz Pidgeon	18 Apr 98
	56.76	Esther Augee	15 May 93
	56.60	Sarah Moore	12 Jul 97
	55.60	Ann Gardner	9 May 98
	54.72	Helen Arnold	26 Jul 97
10	53.37	Catherine Garden	1 Aug 98
	52.84	Fiona Whitehead	29 Jun 93
	52.28	Samantha Burns-Salmond	3 May 97
	51.62	Julie Lavender	15 May 94
	51.25	Zoe Derham	26 Jul 98
	50.62	Janet Smith	16 Aug 97
	50.50	Sarah Harrison	2 Aug 97
	50.38	Irene Duffin	31 May 97
	50.34	Jean Clark	27 Jul 97
	49.48	Suzanne Last	8 Jun 97
20	49.10	Lindsey Jones	25 Aug 97
	49.10	Carys Parry	16 Aug 98
	48.90	Julie Kirkpatrick	15 Jun 96
	48.58	Andrea Jenkins	19 Jul 97
	48.38	Mhairi Walters	5 Sep 98
	48.32	Helen McCreadie	9 Jun 96
	48.18	Suzanne Roberts	1 Jun 97
	47.87	Philippa Roles	19 Jul 98
	47.70	Angela Bonner	11 May 96
	47.52	Vicki Clark	1 Aug 98
30	47.10	Karen Chambers	11 Sep 93
	47.08	Lesley Brannan	23 May 96
	47.06	Caroline Manning	22 Jul 95
	46.86	Leanne Taylor	12 Jun 97
	46.66	Christina Bennett	9 May 98
	46.64	Myrtle Augee	5 Jul 95
	46.00	Diane Smith	24 Aug 96
	45.82	Vicki Scott	20 Jun 98
	45.46	Vickie Foster	10 Aug 97
	44.93	Jenny Cunnane	22 Aug 98
40	44.90	Joanne Eley	3 Aug 96
	44.64	Debbie Callaway	10 Aug 96
	44.48	Helen Wilding	20 Jun 98
	44.46	Kim Thompson	18 Jun 94
	44.00	Natasha Smith	9 May 98
	43.60	Rachel Stott	13 Apr 97
	43.52	Helen Cowe	6 Jul 93
	43.52	Cheryl Cunnane	7 May 95
	43.44	Janette Brown	7 Jul 98
	43.10	Lucy Marshall	15 Aug 98
50	43.02	Claire Burnett	25 May 96
	42.92	Sheena Parry	25 May 97
	42.86	Louise Kay	27 Jul 96
	42.80	Julie Delasaux	15 Jun 97
	42.49	Jenny Earle	12 Jul 98
	42.48	Imogen Martin	20 May 95
	42.46	Lucy Mills	3 Aug 91
	42.42	Tracy Shorts	9 Jun 96
	42.38	Sally Giles	22 Jun 96
NR	42.32	ANNETTE O'CONOR	10 MAR 90
60	42.32	LOUISE CAMPBELL	9 JUN 96

JAVELIN

	77.44	Fatima Whitbread	28 Aug 86
	73.58	Tessa Sanderson	26 Jun 83
	62.32	Sharon Gibson	16 May 87
	62.22	Diane Royle	18 May 85
	60.12	Shelley Holroyd	16 Jun 96
	60.00	Julie Abel	24 May 87
	59.40	Karen Hough	28 Aug 86
	59.36	Kirsty Morrison	4 Sep 93
	58.60	Jeanette Rose	30 May 82
10	58.39	Lorna Jackson	6 Jun 98
	57.90	Anna Heaver	1 Jul 87
	57.84	Mandy Liverton	3 Jun 90
	57.82	Karen Martin	19 Sep 98
	56.96	Nicky Emblem	1 Feb 90
	56.50	Caroline White	8 Jun 91
	56.50	Denise Lewis	11 Aug 96
	55.70	Lynn Hayhoe	31 May 92
	55.60	Sue Platt	15 Jun 68
	55.38	Catherine Garside	19 May 84
20	55.36	Jackie Zaslona	30 Aug 80
	55.30	Clova Court	27 Aug 91
	55.04	Joanne Harding	24 May 87
	54.50	Karen Costello	11 Jun 94
	54.19	Rosemary Morgan	25 Apr 64
	54.02	Janeen Williams	29 Mar 80
	53.88	Sharon Avann	21 Jul 73
	53.32	Maxine Jervis	27 Aug 78
	53.04	Kelly Morgan	17 May 98
	52.58	Shona Urquhart	17 Jun 83
30	52.48	Gail Hornby	22 Jun 90
	52.40	Noelle Bradshaw	30 Jun 93
	52.16	Sandra O'Toole	5 Apr 78
	52.14	Amanda Caine	25 May 87
	52.14	Jo Burton	25 Jun 94
	52.10	Anne Norton	19 Aug 73
	52.00	Lucy Stevenson	16 Aug 92
	51.92	Goldie Sayers	17 May 98
	51.76	Lucy Burrell	11 Jun 94
	51.56	Jean Lintern	6 Aug 72
40	51.50	Pru French	9 Jul 72
	51.48	Claire Faragher	14 Apr 91
	51.32	Yvonne Fountain	22 Sep 74
	51.08	Karen Slaughter	7 Jul 91
	50.84	Shara Spragg	17 Jun 78
	50.82	Anne Finch	25 Jul 70
	50.80	Maxine Bennett	15 Jun 86
	50.80	Janine King	4 May 96
	50.58	Tina Fletcher	14 Aug 88
	50.48	Caroline Hatton	11 Jun 89
50	50.48	Michelle Fields	15 May 93
	50.38	Jacqui Barclay	13 May 84
	50.34	Katie Amos	3 May 98
	50.32	Katie Granger	12 Sep 93
	50.12	Karen Miller	25 Jul 87
	50.04	Kim Lisbon	19 Feb 84
	50.02	Angelique Pullen	31 Aug 85
	49.84	Janette McClean	26 Aug 90
	49.78	Mary Bloomfield	7 Aug 83
	49.72	Michelle Poole	2 Mar 86
	49.50	AVRIL WILLIAMS	16 JUL 60
71	49.38	TRACEY AVERIES	20 MAY 84
	49.36	JENNIFER KEMP	18 AUG 98
	49.28	GINA D'ARCY	15 AUG 8?
	49.24	YVONNE GREGORY	4 SEP 77

HEPTATHLON (1985 Tables)

6736	Denise Lewis	1 Jun	97
6623	Judy Simpson	30 Aug	86
6259	Kim Hagger	18 May	86
6125	Tessa Sanderson	12 Jul	81
6094	Joanne Mulliner	7 Jun	87
6022	Clova Court	27 Aug	91
6005 w	Kerry Jury	24 May	98
5719		3 Aug	97
5826	Jenny Kelly	3 Jul	94
5816 w	Julie Hollman	24 May	98
5595		13 Jul	97
10 5803	Jayne Barnetson	20 Aug	89
5776	Kathy Warren	12 Jul	81
5747 w	Julia Bennett	5 May	96
5496		21 May	95
5702	Yinka Idowu	21 May	95
5700	Vikki Schofield	5 May	96
5691 w	Pauline Richards	24 May	98
5563		5 Jul	98
5642	Sarah Rowe	23 Aug	81
5633	Marcia Marriott	18 May	86
5632	Emma Beales	1 Aug	93
5618 w	Sarah Damn	5 May	96
5392		30 Apr	95
20 5594	Gillian Evans	22 May	83
5585	Kelly Sotherton	13 Jul	97
5555 w	Diana Bennett	24 May	98
5550		1 Jun	97
5548	Val Walsh	18 May	86
5517	Shona Urquhart	21 Aug	88
5497	Nicola Gautier	30 Aug	98
5495	Charmaine Johnson	24 May	92
5493	Sally Gunnell	28 May	84
5455	Claire Phythian	19 May	95
5446	Manndy Laing	7 Aug	83
30 5434 w	Debbie Woolgar	8 Jul	90
5380		18 Jun	89
5424	Lisa Gibbs	1 Aug	93
5409	Uju Efobi	19 Jun	94
5391 w	Jackie Kinsella	22 Jun	86
5331		19 Jul	86
5389	Sarah Owen	15 Aug	82
5384	Sue Longden	8 May	82
5358 w	Chloe Cozens	24 May	98
5220		1 Aug	98
5353	Emma Lindsay	23 Aug	94
5351	Wendy Laing	1 Aug	93
5339	Tracy Joseph	4 Aug	96
40 5297	Kim Crowther	24 Aug	86
5273 w	Debbie Marti	11 Aug	85
5216		7 Jul	85
5258	Anne Hollman	26 May	96
5244	Val Lemoignan	19 Apr	84
5242	Allison Manley	28 Mar	81
5237	Danielle Freeman	19 Jul	98
5215	Katherine Livesey	1 Jun	97
5208	Michelle Stone	30 Sep	84
5208	Mary Anderson	24 Aug	86
5190	Wendy Jeal	2 Jun	91

3000 METRES TRACK WALK

12:49.16	Betty Sworowski	28 Jul	90
12:59.3	Vicky Lupton	13 May	95
13:02.5mx	Lisa Kehler	17 Jun	98
13:11.0		6 Jul	90
13:12.01 i	Julie Drake	12 Mar	93
13:16.0		11 Dec	90
13:13.3	Carolyn Partington	12 Jul	95
13:16.23	Verity Snook	27 May	96
13:25.2	Carol Tyson	6 Jul	79
13:28.0	Helen Elleker	22 Jul	90
13:37.1	Bev Allen	16 May	87
13:42.10	Sylvia Black	23 May 90	10
13:43.0	Melanie Wright	5 Jul	94
13:44.0	Ginney Birch	19 Jun	84
13:46.3 +	Marion Fawkes	30 Jun	79
13:48.0	Sarah Brown	16 May	87
13:52.0	Lillian Millen	7 May	83
13:56.0	Irene Bateman	20 Sep	80
13:57.8	Jill Barrett	2 Jun	84

5000 METRES TRACK WALK

21:52.4	Vicky Lupton	9 Aug	95
21:57.68	Lisa Kehler	25 Jun	90
22:02.06	Betty Sworowski	28 Aug	89
22:37.47	Julie Drake	17 Jul	93
22:41.19	Carolyn Partington	16 Jul	95
22:51.23	Helen Elleker	25 Jun	90
23:11.2	Carol Tyson	30 Jun	79
23:15.04	Bev Allen	25 May	87
23:19.2	Marion Fawkes	30 Jun	79
23:20.00	Ginney Birch	25 May 85	10
23:22.52	Verity Snook	19 Jun	94
23:34.43	Sylvia Black	5 Jul	92
23:35.54	Nicky Jackson	25 May	87
23:38.3	Irene Bateman	28 Jun	81
23:46.7	Lillian Millen	28 Jun	81
23:47.6	Melanie Wright	29 May	94
23:50.96	Catherine Charnock	26 Jul	98
23:51.1	Jill Barrett	5 May	84
23:55.27	Susan Ashforth	25 May	85
24:00.0	Sarah Brown	21 May 91	20
24:09.66	Elaine Callanin	16 Jul	95

5k Road - *where superior to track time*

21:36	Vicky Lupton	18 Jul	92
21:50	Betty Sworowski	6 May	90
21:55 hc	Lisa Kehler	13 Jul	98
22:45 +	Verity Snook	25 Aug	94
22:51	Marion Fawkes	29 Sep	79
22:59	Carol Tyson	29 Sep	79
23:00 +	Bev Allen	1 Sep	87
23:13	Sylvia Black	13 Feb	93
23:24	Melanie Wright	9 Apr	95
23:25	Irene Bateman	29 Sep 79	10
23:35	Lisa Simpson	31 Oct	87
23:38	Jill Barrett	12 May	84
23:42	Lillian Millen	23 Apr	83
23:45 hc	Elaine Callanin	28 Jan	95
23:54	Vicky Lawrence	26 Sep	87
23:57	Sarah Brown	6 Dec	80

72

10000 METRES TRACK WALK

45:18.8	Vicky Lupton	2 Sep 95	
45:53.9	Julie Drake	26 May 90	
46:23.08	Betty Sworowski	4 Aug 91	
46:25.2	Helen Elleker	26 May 90	
47:10.07	Verity Snook	19 Jun 93	
47:56.3	Ginney Birch	15 Jun 85	
47:58.3	Bev Allen	21 Jun 86	
48:11.4	Marion Fawkes	8 Jul 79	
48:20.0	Carolyn Partington	7 May 94	
48:34.0mx	Lisa Kehler	15 Mar 86	10
48:34.5	Carol Tyson	22 Aug 81	
48:35.8	Melanie Wright	2 Sep 95	
48:56.5	Sarah Brown	18 Apr 91	
48:57.6	Irene Bateman	20 Mar 82	
49:27.0	Sylvia Black	22 Apr 95	
49:39.0	Karen Ratcliffe	22 May 91	
49:41.0	Elaine Callanin	22 Apr 95	
50:10.2	Brenda Lupton	17 Mar 84	
50:25.0mx	Lisa Simpson	1 Apr 87	
50:28.0	Andrea Crofts	21 Jul 92	20
50:46.0	Judy Farr	25 Mar 78	
50:50.0	Nicky Jackson	21 Jun 86	
50:52.3	Kim Braznell	31 Aug 96	
51:00.0	Karen Nipper	21 Feb 81	
51:03.0	Liz Corran	22 Apr 95	
51:03.0	Karen Kneale	22 Apr 95	
51:06.1	Lillian Moore	20 Mar 82	

track short

48:52.5	Irene Bateman	19 Mar 83
50:11.2	Jill Barrett	19 Mar 83

Road - *where superior to track time*

45:03	Lisa Kehler	19 Sep 98	
45:59	Betty Sworowski	24 Aug 91	
46:06	Verity Snook	25 Aug 94	
46:26	Carolyn Partington	1 Jul 95	
47:58	Nicola Jackson	27 Jun 87	
47:59	Sylvia Black	29 Mar 92	
48:18	Melanie Wright	9 May 92	
48:30	Karen Ratcliffe	16 Apr 94	
48:36	Kim Braznell	25 Apr 98	
48:47	Irene Bateman	20 Jun 81	10
49:02	Catherine Charnock	27 Jun 98	
49:10	Vicky Lawrence	14 Mar 87	
49:12	Elaine Callanin	20 Jun 81	
49:14	Carolyn Brown	29 Mar 92	

20 KILOMETRES ROAD WALK

1:40:45	Irene Bateman	9 Apr 83	
1:42:02 hc	Lillian Millen	9 Apr 83	
1:44:42		2 Apr 83	
1:42:47	Vicky Lupton	1 Jul 95	
1:43:50	Betty Sworowski	22 Feb 88	
1:43:52	Sylvia Black	14 Jun 97	

50 KILOMETRES ROAD WALK

4:50:51	Sandra Brown	13 Jul 91	
5:01:52	Lillian Millen	16 Apr 83	
5:13:03 +	Irene Corlett	29 Apr 84	
5:22:04	Cath Reader	2 May 93	

4 x 100 METRES RELAY

42.43	UK	1 Aug 80		Oakes, Cook, Callender, Lannaman
42.66	UK	11 Sep 82		Hoyte, Cook, Callender, S.Thomas
42.71	UK	10 Aug 83		Baptiste, Cook, Callender, S.Thomas
42.72	UK	3 Sep 78		Callender, Cook, Danville, Lannaman
43.02	UK	26 Sep 80		Oakes, Cook, Callender, Scutt
43.03	UK	15 Aug 81		Hoyte, Cook, Callender, S.Thomas
43.06	UK	10 Aug 83		Baptiste, Cook, Callender, S.Thomas
43.11	UK	11 Aug 84		Jacobs, Cook, Callender, Oakes
43.15	England	9 Oct 82		Hoyte, Cook, Callender, Lannaman
43.18	UK	4 Aug 79	10	Barnett, Hoyte, Cook, Oakes
43.18	UK	20 Aug 83		Baptiste, Cook, Callender, S.Thomas
43.19	UK	20 Sep 80		Oakes, Cook, Callender, Scutt
43.21	UK	18 Aug 82		Hoyte, Cook, Callender, S.Thomas
43.26 A	UK Students	13 Sep 79		Wray, Cook, Patten, Callender
43.30	UK	30 Aug 86		P. Thomas, Cook, Baptiste, Hoyte
43.3	UK	1 Jul 80		Oakes, Cook, Callender, Lannaman
43.32	UK	5 Jun 80		Oakes, Cook, Callender, Lannaman
43.32	UK	1 Sep 90		Douglas, Kinch, Jacobs, P.Thomas
43.35	UK	17 Aug 85		Andrews, Baptiste, Joseph, Oakes
43.36	UK	13 Jul 80	20	Oakes, Cook, Callender, Lannaman
43.36	UK	23 Jun 81		Hoyte, Cook, Callender, S.Thomas
43.37	UK	30 Aug 82		Hoyte, Cook, Callender, S.Thomas
43.38	UK	8 Aug 86		P. Thomas, Cook, Baptiste, Oakes
43.39	England	2 Aug 86		P. Thomas, Cook, Baptiste, Oakes
43.43	UK	31 Aug 91		Douglas, Kinch, Jacobs, P.Thomas
43.44	UK	30 Jul 76		Hoyte, Ramsden, Danville, Lynch
43.44	UK	31 Aug 86		P. Thomas, Cook, Baptiste, Hoyte
43.46	UK	19 Jun 88		Miles, Baptiste, Jacobs, P.Thomas
43.46	UK	25 Jun 94		Douglas, Merry, Jacobs, P.Thomas
43.46	England	28 Aug 94	30	Douglas, McLeod, Jacobs, P.Thomas

4 x 400 METRES RELAY

3:22.01   UK   1 Sep 91
  Hanson, Smith, Gunnell, Keough
3:23.41   UK   22 Aug 93
  Keough, Smith, Joseph, Gunnell
3:23.89   UK   31 Aug 91
  Smith, Hanson, Keough, Gunnell
3:24.14   UK   14 Aug 94
  Neef, Keough, Smith, Gunnell
3:24.23   UK   8 Aug 92
  Smith, Douglas, Stoute, Gunnell
3:24.25   UK   30 Jun 91
  Gunnell, Hanson, Stoute, Keough
3:24.36   UK   5 Jun 93
  Smith, Joseph, Stoute, Gunnell
3:24.78   UK   1 Sep 90
  Gunnell, Stoute, Beckford, Keough
3:25.20   UK   7 Aug 92
  Douglas, Smith, Stoute, Gunnell
10 3:25.50   UK   12 Aug 95
  Neef, Llewellyn, Hanson, Oladapo
3:25.51   UK   11 Aug 84
  Scutt, Barnett, Taylor, Hoyte-Smith
3:25.66   UK   23 Aug 98
  Fraser, Jamison, Merry, Curbishley
3:25.78   UK   9 Aug 97
  Curbishley, Pierre, Thomas, Fraser
3:25.82   UK   11 Sep 82
  Cook, Macdonald, Taylor, Hoyte-Smith
3:25.87   UK   19 Jun 82
  Forsyth, Hoyte-Smith, Elder, Scutt
3:26.27   UK   10 Aug 97
  Curbishley, Pierre, Thomas, Fraser
3:26.48   UK   22 Jun 97
  Curbishley, Fraser, Thomas, Gunnell
3:26.54   UK   6 Aug 89
  Keough, Stoute, Piggford, Gunnell
3:26.6 a UK   17 Aug 75
  Roscoe, Taylor, Elder, Hartley
20 3:26.89   UK   1 Oct 88
  Keough, Stoute, Piggford, Gunnell
3:26.89   UK   13 Aug 95
  Neef, Llewellyn, Hanson, Oladapo
3:27.04   UK   21 Aug 93
  Keough, Smith, Joseph, Gunnell
3:27.06   England   28 Aug 94
  Smith, Joseph, Keough, Gunnell
3:27.09   UK   30 Jul 76
  Barnes, Taylor, Elder, Hartley
3:27.17   UK   3 Sep 78
  Williams, Hoyte-Smith, Elder, Hartley
3:27.19   England   12 Aug 78
  Patten, Hoyte-Smith, Elder, Hartley
3:27.25   UK   13 Aug 94
  Neef, Keough, Smith, Gunnell
3:27.27   UK   16 Aug 81
  Forsyth, Scutt, Elder, Hoyte-Smith
3:27.29   UK   21 Aug 83
  Scutt, Bridgeman, Hoyte-Smith, Cook
30 3:27.33   UK   26 Jun 94
  Neef, Joseph, Smith, Gunnell

UNDER 20

100 METRES

11.27 A	Kathy Smallwood	9	Sep	79
	11.42	11	Aug	79
11.30	Bev Kinch	5	Jul	83
11.36 A	Della James	14	Oct	68
11.43	Shirley Thomas	7	Aug	82
11.45	Sonia Lannaman	1	Sep	72
11.45	Simmone Jacobs	6	Jul	84
11.52	Katharine Merry	16	Sep	92
11.53	Marcia Richardson	21	Jul	91
11.54	Wendy Clarke	8	Jun	75
11.59	Heather Hunte	9	Sep	77
11.59	Stephi Douglas	23	Jul	88
11.59	Rebecca Drummond	8	Jul	95

wind assisted

11.13	Bev Kinch	6	Jul	83
11.25	Shirley Thomas	20	Aug	81
11.26	Simmone Jacobs	27	May	84
11.40	Katharine Merry	3	Jul	93
11.43	Dorothy Hyman	2	Sep	60
11.45	Stephi Douglas	25	Jun	88
11.45	Rebecca White	4	Jul	98
11.45	Abi Oyepitan	4	Jul	98
11.47	Helen Golden	17	Jul	70
11.50	Rebecca Drummond	9	Jul	94
11.50	Samantha Davies	18	Jul	98
11.53	Wendy Clarke	22	Aug	75
11.53	Sharon Dolby	16	Aug	86

hand timing

11.3	Sonia Lannaman	9	Jun	74
11.3	Heather Hunte	15	Jul	78
11.3	Heather Hunte	15	Jul	78
11.4	Della James	2	Aug	67
11.5	Anita Neil	19	Jul	68
11.5	Victoria Shipman	3	Aug	96

wind assisted

11.2	Wendy Clarke	22	May	76
11.3	Helen Golden	30	May	70
11.3	Linsey Macdonald	3	May	80
11.4	Anita Neil	30	Jun	68
11.4	Helen Barnett	16	May	76
11.4	Jane Parry	5	Jul	80

200 METRES

22.70 A	Kathy Smallwood	12	Sep	79
	22.84	5	Aug	79
23.10	Diane Smith	11	Aug	90
23.20	Katharine Merry	13	Jun	93
23.23	Sonia Lannaman	25	Aug	75
23.23	Sarah Wilhelmy	13	Jun	98
23.24	Sandra Whittaker	12	Jun	82
23.28	Simmone Jacobs	28	Aug	83
23.33	Linsey Macdonald	9	Jun	82
23.35	Donna Murray	26	May	74
23.42	Debbie Bunn	17	Jun	78
23.46	Shirley Thomas	31	May	82
23.48	Wendy Clarke	7	Jun	75
23.51	Sharon Colyear	26	May	74
23.54	Jane Parry	30	Jul	83

wind assisted

23.01	Simmone Jacobs	28 May	84
23.11	Linsey Macdonald	5 Jul	80
23.16	Donna Murray	27 Jul	74
23.20	Sarah Wilhelmy	18 Jul	98
23.42	Helen Golden	22 Jul	70

hand timing

23.1	Sonia Lannaman	7 Jun	75
23.3	Donna Murray	9 Jun	74
23.3	Sharon Colyear	30 Jun	74
23.3	Linsey Macdonald	8 May	82
23.4	Helen Barnett	17 Jul	76

wind assisted

22.9	Donna Murray	14 Jul	74
23.2	Debbie Bunn	2 Jul	78
23.3	Angela Bridgeman	15 Aug	82
23.4	Michelle Probert	9 Jul	77
23.4	Hayley Clements	10 Aug	85

400 METRES

51.16	Linsey Macdonald	15 Jun	80
51.77	Donna Murray	30 Jul	74
52.54	Donna Fraser	10 Aug	91
52.65	Jane Parry	11 Jun	83
52.80	Sian Morris	18 Jun	83
52.98	Karen Williams	6 Aug	78
52.99	Angela Bridgeman	24 Jul	82
53.01 i	Marilyn Neufville	14 Mar	70
53.08	Loreen Hall	29 Jul	84
53.14	Michelle Probert	28 Jul	79
53.20	Verona Bernard	8 Jul	72
53.48	Lillian Board	22 Sep	67
53.52	Ruth Kennedy	25 Sep	74
53.59	Janine MacGregor	11 Jul	78

hand timing

52.6	Marilyn Neufville	20 Jun	70
52.8	Lillian Board	9 Jul	67
52.9	Verona Bernard	15 Sep	72
53.3	Tracey Burges	5 Sep	81
53.5	Ruth Kennedy	30 Jun	74

600 METRES

1:27.33	Lorraine Baker	13 Jul	80

800 METRES (*880yds less 0.7)

2:01.11	Lynne MacDougall	18 Aug	84
2:01.66	Lorraine Baker	26 Jun	82
2:02.00	Diane Edwards	14 Sep	85
2:02.0	Jo White	13 Aug	77
2:02.18	Lynne Robinson	18 Jul	86
2:02.8 a	Lesley Kiernan	2 Sep	74
2:02.88 i	Kirsty McDermott	22 Feb	81
	2:04.01	29 Jul	81
2:03.11	Janet Prictoe	19 Aug	78
2:03.18	Paula Newnham	17 Jul	78
2:03.53	Christine McMeekin	25 Aug	75
2:04.30	Bridget Smyth	19 Aug	86
2:04.6	Janet Lawrence	26 Jul	77
2:04.7*	Rosemary Stirling	13 Aug	66
2:04.85	Louise Parker	28 Jul	79

1000 METRES

2:38.58	Jo White	9 Sep	77

1500 METRES

3:59.96	Zola Budd	30 Aug	85
4:05.96	Lynne MacDougall	20 Aug	84
4:11.12	Bridget Smyth	26 May	85
4:13.40	Wendy Smith	19 Aug	78
4:14.40	Janet Lawrence	20 Aug	77
4:14.50	Wendy Wright	20 Jun	87
4:14.56	Andrea Whitcombe	22 Aug	90
4:14.58	Ruth Smeeth	16 Jul	78
4:14.73	Mary Stewart	2 Feb	74
4:15.1	Yvonne Murray	18 Jul	82
4:15.39	Lisa York	26 Aug	89
4:15.55	Sandra Arthurton	29 Jul	78
4:16.10	Katie Fairbrass	29 May	83

ONE MILE

4:17.57	Zola Budd	21 Aug	85

3000 METRES

8:28.83	Zola Budd	7 Sep	85
8:51.78	Paula Radcliffe	20 Sep	92
9:03.35	Philippa Mason	19 Jul	86
9:04.14	Yvonne Murray	28 May	83
9:06.16	Helen Titterington	19 Jun	88
9:07.02	Carol Haigh	24 Jun	85
9:09.14	Lisa York	19 Jul	89
9:10.9	Julie Holland	7 Apr	84
9:12.28	Hayley Haining	20 Jul	91
9:12.97	Bernadette Madigan	30 Jun	79
9:13.81	Andrea Whitcombe	12 Aug	90
9:14.10	Maxine Newman	19 Jul	89

5000 METRES

14:48.07	Zola Budd	26 Aug	85
15:51.62	Carol Haigh	26 May	85
15:52.55	Yvonne Murray	29 May	83
16:11.61 i	Jenny Clague	22 Feb	92

100 METRES HURDLES

13.25	Diane Allahgreen	21 Jul	94
13.30	Sally Gunnell	16 Jun	84
13.32	Keri Maddox	21 Jul	91
13.45	Natasha Danvers	6 Aug	95
13.46	Nathalie Byer	26 Aug	83
13.47	Sam Baker	30 Jun	91
13.49	Angie Thorp	30 Jun	91
13.50	Lesley-Ann Skeete	6 Jun	86
13.52	Julie Pratt	5 Jul	98
13.56	Wendy McDonnell	3 Jun	79
13.57	Bethan Edwards	29 Aug	92
13.58	Lauraine Cameron	19 Jun	90

wind assisted

13.24	Lesley-Ann Skeete	7 Jun	86
13.28	Sarah Claxton	5 Jul	98
13.39	Lauraine Cameron	1 Jul	90
13.45	Louise Fraser	30 Jul	89
13.45	Sam Baker	30 Jun	91
13.46	Wendy McDonnell	30 Jun	79
13.48	Julie Pratt	5 Jul	98

hand timing wind assisted

13.1	Sally Gunnell	7	Jul	84
13.3	Keri Maddox	14	Jul	90
13.4	Judy Livermore	27	May	79
13.4	Sam Baker	14	Jul	90

400 METRES HURDLES

57.27	Vicki Jamison	28	Jul	96
58.02	Vyvyan Rhodes	28	Jun	92
58.37	Alyson Evans	1	Sep	85
58.68	Kay Simpson	15	Jul	83
58.76	Simone Gandy	28	May	84
59.00	Diane Heath	19	Jul	75
59.01	Sara Elson	24	Aug	89
59.04	Allison Curbishley	31	Jul	93
59.12	Tracy Allen	29	Jul	89
59.13	Sue Morley	12	Aug	79
59.39	Tracey Duncan	29	Jul	98
59.52	Debbie Church	25	Jul	81
59.56	Lucy Elliott	26	Jul	85

hand timing

58.3	Simone Gandy	14	Jul	84
58.7	Sara Elson	18	Jun	89
59.0	Tracy Allen	9	Jul	88
59.3	Michelle Cooney	13	Jul	85
59.4	Diane Wade	21	Jul	79

HIGH JUMP

1.91	Lea Haggett	2	Jun	91
1.91	Susan Jones	31	Aug	97
1.90	Jo Jennings	29	Sep	88
1.89	Debbie Marti	2	Jun	84
1.89 i	Michelle Dunkley	16	Feb	97
1.87		7	Jul	95
1.88	Jayne Barnetson	3	Aug	85
1.87	Louise Manning	6	May	84
1.87	Rachael Forrest	7	Jul	95
1.86	Barbara Simmonds	9	Sep	79
1.86	Claire Summerfield	7	Aug	82
1.86	Michele Wheeler	31	May	87
1.85	Gillian Hitchen	3	Jun	78
1.85	Sharon McPeake	22	Sep	81
1.85	Julia Bennett	15	Apr	89

POLE VAULT

3.75	Tracey Bloomfield	9	Aug	98
3.70	Rhian Clarke	10	Aug	96
3.60	Fiona Harrison	25	May	98
3.51 i	Clare Ridgley	17	Feb	96
3.50		6	May	96
3.40	Danielle Codd	4	Jul	98
3.40	Becky Ridgley	5	Jul	98
3.40	Laura Patterson	30	Aug	98
3.35	Lindsay Hodges	5	Sep	98
3.20	Rebecca Roles	31	Aug	96
3.20	Ellie Spain	13	Sep	98
3.15	Sarah Hartley	9	Aug	97
3.10	Dawn-Alice Wright	10	Jul	94
3.10	Leanne Mellor	21	Aug	94
3.10	Fiona Peake	27	Apr	96
3.10 ns	Katharine Horner	4	Jun	96

LONG JUMP

6.90	Bev Kinch	14	Aug	83
6.82	Fiona May	30	Jul	88
6.68	Sue Hearnshaw	22	Sep	79
6.63	Yinka Idowu	21	May	89
6.55	Joyce Oladapo	30	Jul	83
6.52	Georgina Oladapo	16	Jun	84
6.52	Sarah Claxton	31	Jul	98
6.47	Jo Wise	30	Jul	88
6.45	Margaret Cheetham	18	Aug	84
6.43	Moira Walls	18	Sep	70
6.43	Myra Nimmo	27	May	73
6.35	Sharon Bowie	1	Jun	85

wind assisted

6.93	Bev Kinch	14	Aug	83
6.88	Fiona May	30	Jul	88
6.71	Yinka Idowu	15	Jun	91
6.69	Jo Wise	30	Jul	88
6.53	Sarah Claxton	12	Jul	97
6.49	Margaret Cheetham	4	Sep	83
6.48	Moira Walls	17	May	70
6.41	Ann Wilson	30	Jun	68

TRIPLE JUMP

13.05	Michelle Griffith	16	Jun	90
12.50	Julia Johnson	21	Jun	98
12.43	Shani Anderson	26	Jun	93
12.42	Liz Gibbens	2	Jul	95
12.41 i	Judy Kotey	28	Feb	98
12.33		17	May	98
12.27	Lorna Turner	26	May	91
12.22	Mary Bignal	18	Jun	59
12.20	Jodie Hurst	8	Jun	96
12.18	Justina Cruickshank	26	May	96
12.14	Jayne Ludlow	21	May	94
12.10	Jane Falconer	30	Aug	93
12.10	Pamela Anderson	2	Jul	95

wind assisted

12.61	Judy Kotey	5	Jul	98
12.48	Lorna Turner	30	Jun	91
12.44	Shani Anderson	9	Jul	94
12.37	Jane Falconer	30	Aug	93
12.21	Justina Cruickshank	19	May	96

SHOT

17.10	Myrtle Augee	16	Jun	84
16.24 i	Judy Oakes	26	Feb	77
16.05		26	Aug	77
15.72 i	Alison Grey	29	Feb	92
15.26		13	Jul	91
15.60 i	Justine Buttle	27	Feb	88
15.45		25	Aug	88
15.48	Mary Anderson	8	Sep	85
15.45	Susan King	27	Mar	83
15.27	Julie Dunkley	21	Jun	98
14.75 i	Cynthia Gregory	12	Dec	81
14.70		29	Aug	81
14.71 i	Nicola Gautier	26	Jan	97
14.66 i	Terri Salt	7	Jan	84
14.60	Philippa Roles	4	Sep	96

DISCUS

54.78	Lynda Whiteley	4	Oct 82
53.10	Kathryn Farr	19	Jul 86
52.58	Emma Merry	22	Aug 93
52.31	Lauren Keightley	18	Jul 98
51.82	Catherine Bradley	20	Jul 85
51.60	Philippa Roles	24	Jul 97
51.24	Jane Aucott	11	Jun 86
51.12	Janette Picton	6	Jun 82
50.44	Karen Pugh	8	Jul 83
50.34	Angela Sellars	27	Jul 86
50.30	Julia Avis	19	Sep 82
49.74	Shelley Drew	10	May 92

downhill

51.04	Fiona Condon	7	Jul 79

HAMMER

57.97	Rachael Beverley	25	Jul 98
55.44	Lyn Sprules	19	Jul 94
54.72	Helen Arnold	26	Jul 97
53.34	Diana Holden	13	Aug 94
51.62	Julie Lavender	15	May 94
51.25	Zoe Derham	26	Jul 98
50.52	Catherine Garden	3	Aug 97
50.50	Sarah Harrison	2	Aug 97
49.48	Sam Burns-Salmond	13	Aug 95
49.10	Carys Parry	16	Aug 98

JAVELIN

60.14	Fatima Whitbread	7	May 80
59.40	Karen Hough	28	Aug 86
59.36	Kirsty Morrison	4	Sep 93
57.84	Mandy Liverton	3	Jun 90
57.82	Shelley Holroyd	9	Aug 92
57.80	Julie Abel	5	Jun 83
56.96	Nicky Emblem	1	Feb 90
55.72	Karen Martin	25	Jul 92
55.38	Catherine Garside	19	May 84
55.04	Tessa Sanderson	26	Sep 74
53.32	Maxine Jervis	27	Aug 78
53.04	Kelly Morgan	17	May 98
52.52	Lorna Jackson	8	May 93
52.48	Gail Hornby	22	Jun 90

HEPTATHLON (1985 Tables)

5833	Joanne Mulliner	11	Aug 85
5642	Sarah Rowe	23	Aug 81
5496	Yinka Idowu	3	Sep 89
5493	Sally Gunnell	28	May 84
5484	Denise Lewis	30	Jun 91
5459	Jenny Kelly	30	Jul 88
5391 w	Jackie Kinsella	22	Jun 86
5331		19	Jul 86
5377	Uju Efobi	18	Jul 93
5358 w	Chloe Cozens	24	May 98
5220		1	Aug 98
5311	Nicola Gautier	21	Sep 97
5299	Emma Beales	26	Aug 90
5273 w	Debbie Marti	11	Aug 85
5216		7	Jul 85
5246	Val Walsh	7	Aug 83
5237	Danielle Freeman	19	Jul 98

3000 METRES TRACK WALK

13:03.4	Vicky Lupton	18	May 91
13:47.0	Julie Drake	5	Jul 88
13:53.0 e+	Lisa Langford	23	Aug 85
14:04.1	Susan Ashforth	19	May 85
14:09.81	Amy Hales	19	Sep 98
14:10.2	Carol Tyson	5	Sep 76
14:11.8	Carolyn Brown	18	Sep 92
14:12.0	Jill Barrett	11	Jun 83
14:12.8	Nicola Jackson	5	May 84
14:17.96 i	Katie Ford	28	Feb 98

5000 METRES TRACK WALK

22:36.81	Vicky Lupton	15	Jun 91
23:31.67	Lisa Langford	23	Aug 85
23:55.27	Susan Ashforth	25	May 85
23:56.9	Julie Drake	24	May 88
24:02.15	Nicola Jackson	27	May 84
24:08.4	Jill Barrett	28	May 83
24:19.0	Vicky Lawrence	13	Jun 87
24:24.31	Andrea Crofts	4	Jun 89
24:27.73	Carolyn Brown	29	Aug 92
24:28.60	Debbie Wallen	26	Jul 98
24:34.6	Tracey Devlin	17	Sep 89
24:35.0	Joanne Pope	16	Dec 90
24:35.16	Angela Hodd	25	May 87

Road - *where superior to track time*

23:05	Lisa Langford	2	Nov 85
23:18	Julie Drake	27	Feb 88
23:35	Lisa Simpson	31	Oct 87
23:44	Nicky Jackson	12	May 84
23:46	Jill Barrett	14	May 83
23:54	Vicky Lawrence	26	Sep 87
23:57	Sarah Brown	6	Dec 80
24:13	Gill Edgar	3	May 81
24:15	Carol Tyson	31	Jul 76

10,000 METRES TRACK WALK

47:04.0	Vicky Lupton	30	Mar 91
48:34.0mx	Lisa Langford	15	Mar 86
49:48.7	Julie Drake	7	Feb 88
50:25.0mx	Lisa Simpson	1	Apr 87
51:00.0	Karen Nipper	21	Feb 81
51:31.2	Helen Ringshaw	17	Mar 84
52:09.0	Elaine Cox	8	Apr 78
52:10.4	Sarah Brown	20	Mar 82
52:48.5	Kate Horwill	22	Aug 92

short

50:11.2	Jill Barrett	19	Mar 83

Road - *where superior to track time*

49:10	Vicky Lawrence	14	Mar 87
49:14	Carolyn Brown	29	Mar 92
49:26	Julie Drake	21	May 88
49:33	Lisa Simpson	14	Mar 87
49:47	Jill Barrett	24	Sep 83
51:15	Nicola Jackson	18	Nov 84

Note: LJ, Hep. Although Idowu competed for UK Juniors, she was a Nigerian citizen at the time.

UNDER 17

100 METRES

11.45	Sonia Lannaman	1	Sep	72
11.59	Simmone Jacobs	25	Aug	83
11.60	Katharine Merry	28	Jul	90
11.61	Diane Smith	9	Aug	90
11.69	Jane Parry	6	Jun	81
11.70	Linsey Macdonald	24	May	80
11.73	Etta Kessebeh	20	Aug	81
11.77	Hayley Clements	26	Jul	85
11.78	Tatum Nelson	16	May	94
11.79	Janet Smith	26	Jul	85
11.80	Sharon Dolby	26	Jul	85
11.81	Lisa Goreeph	6	Jun	82

wind assisted

11.50	Rebecca Drummond	9	Jul	94
11.61	Linsey Macdonald	16	Jun	79
11.62	Kathleen Lithgow	25	Jun	88
11.62	Donna Maylor	4	Jul	98
11.63	Sharon Dolby	10	Aug	85

hand timing

11.6	Denise Ramsden	19	Jul	68
11.6	Linsey Macdonald	25	May	80
11.6	Jane Parry	2	Aug	80
11.7	Michelle Probert	8	Aug	76

wind assisted

11.3	Linsey Macdonald	3	May	80
11.4	Sonia Lannaman	3	Jun	72
11.4	Jane Parry	5	Jul	80
11.5	Sharon Dolby	20	Jul	85

200 METRES

23.10	Diane Smith	11	Aug	90
23.28	Simmone Jacobs	28	Aug	83
23.42	Debbie Bunn	17	Jun	78
23.43	Linsey Macdonald	20	Aug	80
23.50	Katharine Merry	20	Jul	91
23.60	Michelle Probert	12	Sep	76
23.66	Jane Parry	15	Jun	80
23.69	Donna Fraser	1	Jul	89
23.79	Sharon Colyear	5	Sep	71
23.90	Angela Bridgeman	20	Aug	80
23.95	Helen Golden	30	Aug	69
23.97	Lisa Goreeph	31	Jul	82

wind assisted

23.11	Linsey Macdonald	5	Jul	80
23.41	Katharine Merry	15	Jun	91
23.64	Jane Parry	5	Jul	80
23.70	Sonia Lannaman	16	Jun	72
23.85	Helen Golden	1	Sep	69

hand timing (* 220 yards less 0.1)

23.8 *	Marilyn Neufville	27	Jul	68
23.8	Janet Smith	1	Jun	85
23.9	Fay Nixon	24	Jul	76
23.9	Hayley Clements	1	Jun	85

wind assisted

23.2	Debbie Bunn	2	Jul	78
23.4	Hayley Clements	10	Aug	85
23.6	Janet Smith	10	Aug	85

300 METRES

36.46	Linsey Macdonald	13	Jul	80
38.21	Lesley Owusu	27	Aug	95
38.49	Kim Wall	24	May	98
38.60	Karlene Palmer	12	Jul	97
38.75	Gaby Howell	24	May	98
38.95	Maria Bolsover	8	Jul	95
39.04	Heather McKay	19	Jun	98
39.07	Nicola Sanders	24	May	98
39.22	Jenny Meadows	11	Jul	97
39.25	Rebecca White	17	Aug	96
39.34	Ruth Watson	12	Jul	96
39.40	Sophie Cocker	15	Aug	92
39.42	Alison Shingler	26	May	91

hand timing

38.2	Marilyn Neufville	6	Sep	69
38.4	Kim Wall	10	May	98
38.6	Fay Nixon	10	Sep	77
38.7	Katharine Merry	1	Sep	91
39.2	Allison Curbishley	30	Aug	92
39.2	Jenny Meadows	16	Aug	97

400 METRES

51.16	Linsey Macdonald	15	Jun	80
53.08	Loreen Hall	29	Jul	84
53.75	Linda Keough	8	Aug	80
54.01	Angela Bridgeman	16	Aug	80
54.25	Emma Langston	19	Jun	88
54.57	Lesley Owusu	9	Sep	95
54.84	Carol Candlish	25	Jul	81
54.86	Ruth Kennedy	20	Jul	73
55.03	Donna Fraser	6	Aug	88
55.13	Carolyn Wells	23	Aug	80

hand timing

53.7	Linda Keough	2	Aug	80
54.4	Marilyn Neufville	23	Aug	69
54.6	Evelyn McMeekin	15	Sep	73
54.6	Ruth Kennedy	19	Sep	73
54.7	Gaby Howell	30	May	98

overage

54.2	Marilyn Neufville	9	Oct	69

600 METRES

1:27.33	Lorraine Baker	13	Jul	80

800 METRES

2:02.0	Jo White	13	Aug	77
2:03.66	Lesley Kiernan	26	Aug	73
2:03.72	Lorraine Baker	15	Jun	80
2:04.85	Louise Parker	28	Jul	79
2:06.5	Emma Langston	10	Aug	88
2:06.53	Lynne Robinson	6	Jul	85
2:06.8	Jayne Heathcote	31	May	87
2:07.0	Bridget Smyth	27	Jun	84
2:07.3	Amanda Alford	7	May	80
2:07.32	Amanda Pritchard	22	Jun	96
2:07.53	Sandra Arthurton	17	Sep	78
2:07.57	Mary Sonner	13	Sep	70
2:07.6	Natalie Tait	9	Jul	88
2:07.7	Karen Hughes	7	May	80
2:07.7	Michelle Wilkinson	31	Aug	88

1000 METRES

2:38.58	Jo White	9 Sep 77	

1500 METRES

4:15.20	Bridget Smyth	29 Jul 84
4:15.55	Sandra Arthurton	29 Jul 78
4:16.8	Jo White	30 Jul 77
4:21.88	Jeina Mitchell	20 Jul 91
4:22.25	Karen Hughes	24 May 81
4:22.25	Clare Keller	7 Jul 85
4:22.51	Elise Lyon	31 Jul 82
4:23.11	Gillian Stacey	2 Sep 89
4:23.25	Denise Kiernan	20 Aug 77
4:23.37	Dawn Hargan	14 Jun 87
4:23.6	Janette Howes	5 Sep 81

1 MILE

4:46.0	Sandra Arthurton	13 May 78

3000 METRES

9:28.9	Bridget Smyth	21 Apr 84
9:30.0	Yvonne Murray	4 Jul 81
9:32.20	Nicky Slater	28 Aug 93
9:33.1	Alison Hollington	6 Jun 81
9:34.5	Louise Watson	28 Aug 88
9:34.79	Helen Titterington	28 Jun 86
9:36.8	Karen Hughes	4 Jun 80
9:38.1	Elise Lyon	12 Sep 81
9:38.2	Amanda Alford	7 Mar 79
9:39.9	Sharon Willicombe	8 Jul 88
9:40.0	Julie Adkin	12 Sep 87
overage		
9:26.4	Jo White	7 Dec 77

80 METRES HURDLES (2'6")

11.02	Helen Worsey	15 Aug 98
11.07	Amanda Parker	7 Jun 86
11.12	Sam Farquharson	7 Jun 86
11.13	Claire St. John	2 Jun 79
11.16	Ann Girvan	4 Jul 81
11.16	Stephi Douglas	27 Jul 85
11.20	Ann Wilson	11 Aug 66
11.20	Louise Brunning	25 Jul 87
11.22	Sharon Davidge	18 Jul 98
11.23	Rachel Rigby	25 Jul 87
11.25	Louise Fraser	25 Jul 87
11.26	Liz Fairs	17 Jul 93
11.29	Nina Thompson	7 Aug 88
overage		
11.10 A	Sue Scott	15 Oct 68
wind assisted		
10.96	Helen Worsey	11 Jul 98
11.00	Sharon Davidge	11 Jul 98
11.03	Wendy McDonnell	20 Aug 77
11.11	Liz Fairs	9 Jul 94
hand timing		
11.0	Wendy McDonnell	2 Jul 77
11.1	Ann Wilson	18 Sep 66
11.1	Angela Thorp	7 Jul 89
11.1	Liz Fairs	29 May 93

wind assisted

10.9	Ann Wilson	16 Jul 66
10.9	Wendy McDonnell	9 Jul 77
10.9	Sam Farquharson	20 Jul 85
11.0	Stephi Douglas	20 Jul 85
11.1	Claire St. John	16 Jul 79

100 METRES HURDLES (2'9")

13.73	Ann Girvan	7 Aug 82
13.88	Natasha Danvers	28 Aug 93
13.98	Claire St John	11 Aug 79
14.04	Lauraine Cameron	7 Aug 88
14.24	Pamela St Ange	2 Oct 82
14.24	Angela Thorp	9 Jul 89
14.39	Michelle Stone	18 Aug 84
14.40	Vicki Jamison	22 Jun 93
14.51	Susan Jones	29 May 94
14.52	Louise Brunning	26 Jun 88
wind assisted		
13.67	Ann Girvan	4 Jul 82
13.76	Natasha Danvers	27 Aug 94
14.10	Sue Mapstone	25 Aug 73
14.27	Heather Ross	27 Aug 78
hand timing		
13.7	Ann Girvan	29 Aug 81
14.1	Pamela St Ange	7 Aug 83
14.2	Nnenna Njoku	26 Jun 71
wind assisted		
13.7	Nathalie Byer	4 Sep 82
13.9	Angela Thorp	9 Sep 89
14.1	Heather Ross	2 Jul 78

300 METRES HURDLES

41.98	Rachael Kay	3 Aug 97
41.99	Natasha Danvers	10 Jul 93
42.58	Syreeta Williams	12 Jul 97
42.67	Vicki Jamison	17 Jul 93
42.87	Nusrat Ceesay	12 Jul 97
42.91	Allison Curbishley	18 Aug 91
43.03	Val Theobalds	13 Aug 89
43.06	Claire Griffiths	18 Aug 91
43.08	Yewande Ige	13 Jul 96
43.12	Keri Maddox	6 Aug 88
43.28	Denise Bolton	5 Sep 93
43.37	Katherine Porter	11 Jul 98
43.38	Dextene McIntosh	31 Jul 94
43.38	Wendy Davidson	8 Aug 98
43.44	Jo Mersh	13 Jul 91
43.53	Catherine Murphy	21 Jul 90
hand timing		
41.8	Rachael Kay	17 Aug 97
42.4	Keri Maddox	8 May 88
42.4	Syreeta Williams	17 Aug 97
42.5	Louise Brunning	8 May 88
42.8	Rachel Stafford	8 Jul 89
42.8	Vyvyan Rhodes	8 Jul 89
42.9	Val Theobalds	17 Jun 89
43.1	Tricia Byford	17 Jun 89
43.1	Charlotte Knowles	8 Jul 89
43.4	Jo Mersh	15 Jun 91

400 METRES HURDLES

60.87	Karin Hendrickse	31	Jul	82
60.93	Rachael Kay	21	Jul	97
61.02	Claire Edwards	8	Sep	91
61.04	Allison Curbishley	26	Jul	92
61.10	Vicki Jamison	26	Jun	93
61.27	Kay Simpson	25	Jul	81
61.32	Debra Duncan	27	Jul	85
61.33	Denise Kiernan	17	Jul	77
61.59	Donna Pert	31	Jul	82
61.81	Joanna Douglas	27	Jul	85

hand timing

59.7	Keri Maddox	9	Jul	88
60.8	Jayne Puckeridge	9	Jul	88
61.5	Julie Lindsey	1	Sep	79

HIGH JUMP

1.89	Debbie Marti	2	Jun	84
1.85	Louise Manning	11	Sep	82
1.85	Jayne Barnetson	21	Jul	84
1.84	Ursula Fay	6	Aug	83
1.83	Jo Jennings	26	Jul	85
1.83	Tracey Clarke	2	Aug	87
1.82	Elaine Hickey	9	Aug	80
1.82	Kerry Roberts	16	Jul	83
1.82	Susan Jones	20	May	94
1.81	Barbara Simmonds	22	Jul	78
1.80	Carol Mathers	10	Jun	73
1.80	Susan Brown	28	Jul	79
1.80	Lea Haggett	3	Sep	88

POLE VAULT

3.60	Fiona Harrison	25	May	98
3.44	Clare Ridgley	10	Sep	94
3.35	Lindsay Hodges	5	Sep	98
3.30 mx	Rhian Clarke	4	Jul	93
3.25		11	Sep	93
3.20	Rebecca Roles	31	Aug	96
3.20	Ellie Spain	13	Sep	98
3.15	Sarah Hartley	9	Aug	97
3.15	Laura Patterson	7	Sep	97
3.05	Amy Rennison	4	Aug	98
3.03	Anna Watson	13	Sep	98

LONG JUMP

6.45	Margaret Cheetham	18	Aug	84
6.32	Georgina Oladapo	23	Jul	83
6.27	Fiona May	14	Jun	86
6.26	Jo Wise	31	May	87
6.25	Sue Hearnshaw	9	Jul	77
6.24	Sarah Claxton	15	Jun	96
6.23	Sue Scott	27	Jul	68
6.22	Ann Wilson	18	Sep	66
6.22	Michelle Stone	28	Apr	84
6.18	Sheila Parkin	4	Aug	62

wind assisted

6.49	Margaret Cheetham	23	Sep	84
6.47	Fiona May	28	Jun	86
6.41	Sue Hearnshaw	9	Jul	77
6.34	Sarah Claxton	12	Jul	96
6.33	Sue Scott	27	Aug	68

TRIPLE JUMP

12.14	Jayne Ludlow	21	May	94
11.82	Julia Johnson	30	Jun	96
11.71	Hayley Warrilow	30	Jun	96
11.68 i	Syreeta Williams	16	Feb	97
11.45		22	Jun	97
11.64	Rachel Peacock	19	Jul	97
11.59	Tolu Jegede	30	Jun	96
11.48	Emma Hughes	10	Aug	96
11.44	Donna Quirie	8	Aug	93
11.44	Rachel Hogg	23	May	98
11.41	Shani Anderson	8	Sep	91

wind assisted

12.07	Rachel Peacock	18	Jul	98
11.69	Claire Quigg	18	Jul	98
11.68	Rachel Hogg	18	Jul	98
11.50	Pamela Anderson	8	Aug	93

SHOT

15.08	Justine Buttle	16	Aug	86
14.40	Susan King	17	May	81
14.04	Mary Anderson	6	May	84
14.03 i	Terri Salt	19	Mar	83
13.77		17	Sep	83
13.94	Jenny Bloss	13	May	67
13.89 i	Alison Grey	11	Feb	89
13.83		20	May	89
13.68 i	Philippa Roles	26	Feb	94
13.65		6	Aug	94
13.64	Cynthia Gregory	20	Aug	80
13.58 i	Natalie Hart	19	Mar	88
13.49	Lana Newton	11	Jul	75
13.46	Julie Dunkley	22	Jun	96

overage

14.20 i	Terri Salt	10	Dec	83

DISCUS

51.60	Emma Merry	27	Jun	90
49.56	Jane Aucott	3	Aug	85
48.88	Philippa Roles	13	Aug	94
48.84	Karen Pugh	7	Aug	82
47.58	Catherine Bradley	14	Jul	84
47.54	Lauren Keightley	12	Jul	95
47.50	Sarah Symonds	16	May	90
47.24	Amanda Barnes	3	Aug	85
46.76	Fiona Condon	6	Aug	77
46.55	Emma Carpenter	5	Sep	98
46.34	Janette Picton	26	Mar	79

HAMMER

48.66	Zoe Derham	16	Aug	97
47.68	Diana Holden	31	Jul	91
46.98	Helen Arnold	29	Jul	95
46.82	Carys Parry	30	Aug	97
45.58	Julie Lavender	13	Sep	92
44.70	Rachael Beverley	15	Jul	95
43.64	Catherine Garden	30	Apr	95
43.36	Vicki Clark	16	Aug	97
43.10	Lucy Marshall	15	Aug	98
42.14	Louise Kay	22	Jul	94

JAVELIN

56.02	Mandy Liverton	11 Jun	89
53.42	Karen Hough	15 Jul	84
53.22	Kirsty Morrison	15 Aug	92
51.92	Goldie Sayers	17 May	98
51.50	Shelley Holroyd	22 Jul	89
50.82	Nicky Emblem	19 Jun	87
50.04	Kim Lisbon	19 Feb	84
50.02	Angelique Pullen	31 Aug	85
49.24	Jacqui Barclay	7 Aug	82
49.00	Kelly Morgan	27 Apr	96
48.34	Fatima Whitbread	29 Aug	77
48.00	Claire Taylor	17 Jun	92

HEPTATHLON (1985 Tables) with 80mH

5037	Michelle Stone	1 Jul	84
5031	Yinka Idowu	18 Sep	88
4915	Denise Lewis	24 Jul	88
4861	Clover Wynter-Pink	26 Jun	94
4841	Rebecca Lewis	18 Sep	94
4839	Jackie Kinsella	21 Jul	85
4830 w	Katherine Livesey	22 Sep	96
4790		28 Jul	96
4794	Claire Phythian	22 May	88
4780	Danielle Freeman	23 Jun	96
4746	Chloe Cozens	22 Sep	96
4742	Julie Hollman	26 Sep	93
4673	Denise Bolton	19 Sep	93

with 100mH

5071	Debbie Marti	5 Jun	83

HEPTATHLON (1985 Tables) Senior

5208	Michelle Stone	30 Sep	84
5184	Claire Phythian	20 Aug	89
4815 w	Julie Hollman	2 May	93
4807		30 May	93
4784	Jackie Kinsella	12 May	85
4721	Joanne Taylor	21 Sep	80

3000 METRES TRACK WALK

14:04.1	Susan Ashforth	19 May	85
14:09.81	Amy Hales	19 Sep	98
14:17.96 i	Katie Ford	28 Feb	98

5000 METRES TRACK WALK

23:55.27	Susan Ashforth	25 May	85
24:22.3	Vicky Lawrence	21 Jun	86
24:34.6	Tracey Devlin	17 Sep	89
24:45.4	Karen Eden	9 Jul	78
24:57.5	Angela Hodd	24 Jun	86
25:13.8	Carla Jarvis	2 Jun	91
25:15.3	Vicky Lupton	3 Sep	88
25:18.5	Jill Barrett	16 Aug	80

overage

25:08.0	Julie Drake	22 Dec	85

Road - *where superior to track time*

23:57	Sarah Brown	6 Dec	80
24:20	Karen Eden	3 Dec	78

10000 METRES TRACK WALK

51:00.0	Karen Nipper	21 Feb	81

UNDER 15

100 METRES

11.67	Katharine Merry	13 May	89
11.86	Hayley Clements	2 Jul	83
11.89	Joanne Gardner	20 Aug	77
11.92	Jane Parry (U13)	20 Aug	77
11.95	Tatum Nelson	7 Aug	93
12.00	Diane Smith	15 Sep	89
12.02	Renate Chinyou	28 Aug	88
12.02	Sarah Wilhelmy	28 May	94
12.07	Margaret Cheetham	29 Jul	83
12.09	Libby Alder	8 Jul	95
12.10 A	Helen Seery	25 Jul	96
12.10	Lesley Owusu	7 Aug	93

wind assisted

11.47	Katharine Merry	17 Jun	89
11.67	Tatum Nelson	10 Jul	93
11.78	Jane Parry	8 Aug	78
11.84	Janis Walsh	26 May	74
11.88	Sarah Claxton	9 Jul	94
11.97	Yvonne Anderson	16 Jun	79
11.97	Renate Chinyou	20 Aug	88
12.06	Rachel Redmond	12 Jul	96

hand timing

11.8	Janis Walsh	7 Jul	74
11.8	Joanne Gardner	2 Jul	77
11.9	Sonia Lannaman	9 Aug	69
11.9	Linsey Macdonald	26 Aug	78
11.9	Jane Perry	22 Apr	79
11.9	Etta Kessebeh	11 Jul	80

wind assisted

11.7	Diane Smith	30 Jul	89
11.8	Sonia Lannaman	30 May	70
11.8	Debbie Bunn (U13)	28 Jun	75
11.8	Delmena Doyley	6 Jul	79

200 METRES

23.72	Katharine Merry	17 Jun	89
23.90	Diane Smith	3 Sep	89
24.05	Jane Parry	16 Jul	78
24.39	Hayley Clements	3 Jul	83
24.44	Rachael Kay	8 Jul	95
24.51	Tatum Nelson	8 Aug	93
24.54	Sarah Wilhelmy	31 Jul	94
24.58	Simmone Jacobs	25 Jul	81
24.58	Donna Fraser	22 Aug	87
24.59	Janet Smith	30 Jul	83
24.63	Dawn Flockhart	4 Jul	81

wind assisted

23.54	Katharine Merry	30 Jul	89
23.99	Sarah Wilhelmy	9 Jul	94
24.25	Vernicha James	11 Jul	98
24.35	Tatum Nelson	27 Jun	93
24.41	Lesley Owusu	9 Jul	93

hand timing

23.8	Janis Walsh	23 Jun	74
24.1	Sonia Lannaman	29 Aug	70

wind assisted

23.6	Jane Parry (U13)	9 Jul	77
23.8	Diane Smith	9 Sep	89

300 METRES
41.1	Maria Bolsover	10	Apr	94

400 METRES
56.7	Jane Colebrook	25	Jun	72

600 METRES
1:36.47	Sarah Willicombe	12	Aug	90

800 METRES
2:06.5	Rachel Hughes	19	Jul	82
2:08.7	Emma Langston	12	Jul	86
2:09.58	Sally Ludlam	8	Jun	75
2:09.6	Isabel Linaker	1	Aug	90
2:09.77	Lorraine Baker	19	Aug	78
2:09.80	Hannah Curnock	15	Aug	92
2:10.1	Lesley Kiernan	9	Jul	71
2:10.3	Carol Pannell	9	Jul	71
2:10.6	Christina Boxer	10	Jul	71
2:10.6	Natalie Tait	12	Jul	86
2:10.66	Amanda Pritchard	15	Jul	94
2:10.76	Carolyn Wells	19	Aug	78
2:10.9	Emma Ward	30	Jun	96
2:10.96	Hayley Haining	7	Jun	86

1000 METRES
2:51.4	Hayley Haining	20	Aug	86

1500 METRES
4:23.45	Isabel Linaker	7	Jul	90
4:27.9	Joanne Davis	9	Jul	88
4:29.0	Claire Allen	8	Jul	89
4:29.1	Valerie Bothams	16	Jul	89
4:29.6	Lynne MacDougall	16	Jul	79
4:29.9	Heidi Hosking	9	Jul	88
4:30.4	Claire Nicholson	18	Jun	87
4:31.12	Karen Hughes	31	Aug	79
4:31.45	Amanda Alford	22	Jul	78
4:31.6	Michelle Lavercombe	13	Jun	81
4:31.70	Jenny Mockler	4	Aug	96
4:32.0	Elise Lyon	2	Apr	80
4:32.0	Jojo Tulloch	13	Jul	85
4:32.0	Julie Adkin	13	Aug	86

ONE MILE
4:54.7	Hannah Curnock	9	Sep	92

3000 METRES
10:00.6	Louise Silva	7	Mar	79

75 METRES HURDLES (2'6")
10.93	Rachel Halstead-Peel	27	Jul	85
11.00	Louise Fraser	27	Jul	85
11.00	Danielle Selley	20	Jun	98
11.01	Nathalie Byer	16	Aug	80
11.08	Nicola Hall	29	May	94
11.08	Sara McGreavy	12	Jul	97
11.09	Catherine Murphy	6	Aug	88
11.09	Orla Bermingham	25	Aug	90
11.11	Symone Belle	30	Aug	98
11.13	Lydia Chadwick	7	Jun	86
11.13	Naomi Hodge-Dallaway	30	Jul	95
11.14	Serena Bailey	30	Jul	95

wind assisted
10.99	Symone Belle	11	Jul	98
11.01	Naomi Hodge-Dallaway	8	Jul	95
11.05	Helen Worsey	13	Jul	96
11.06	Kate Forsyth	10	Jul	93
11.07	Melissa Harris	11	Jul	98
11.09	Luisa Giles	13	Jul	96

hand timing
11.0	Wendy McDonnell	31	Aug	75
11.0	Lydia Chadwick	12	Jul	86
11.0	Nina Thompson	4	Jul	87

wind assisted
10.7	Orla Bermingham	14	Jul	90
10.8	Nathalie Byer	12	Jul	80
10.8	Ann Girvan	12	Jul	80

HIGH JUMP
1.83	Ursula Fay	5	Jun	82
1.81	Debbie Marti	18	Sep	82
1.81	Lea Haggett	6	Jun	86
1.80	Jo Jennings	19	Aug	84
1.79 i	Julia Charlton	24	Feb	80
1.78		13	Jul	80
1.79	Aileen Wilson	4	Jul	98
1.78	Claire Summerfield	28	Jul	79
1.75	Anne Gilson	2	Jun	73
1.75	Claire Smith	8	Aug	82
1.75	Jane Falconer	10	Jun	89
1.74	Lorinda Matthews	19	Aug	77
1.74	Janice Anderson	27	Jun	87
1.74	Katharine Merry	18	Sep	88

POLE VAULT
3.50	Fiona Harrison	24	Aug	96
2.80	Cariann Cutts	30	Aug	98
2.70	Jo-Anne Nightingale	20	Aug	97
2.65	Rhian Clarke	18	Aug	91
2.65	Daisy Nisbit	16	Aug	97

overage
2.80	Rhian Clarke	2	Oct	91

LONG JUMP
6.34	Margaret Cheetham	14	Aug	83
6.30	Fiona May	7	Jul	84
6.07	Georgina Oladapo	21	Jun	81
5.98	Sandy French	22	Jul	78
5.93	Jackie Harris	10	Jul	87
5.88	Sue Scott	11	Aug	66
5.86	Tammy McCammon	18	Aug	91
5.85	Kim Hagger	20	Aug	76
5.81	Yvonne Hallett	24	Aug	86
5.80	Monique Parris	23	May	98

overage
5.93 i	Sue Scott	19	Nov	66

wind assisted
6.49	Margaret Cheetham	4	Sep	83
6.05	Katharine Merry	18	Sep	88
6.02	Michelle Stone	10	Jul	82
5.99	Sandy French	8	Jul	78

TRIPLE JUMP
10.06	Megan Lishman	17	Aug	97

SHOT (3.25kg)

14.27	Susan King	19	May	79
13.69	Gloria Achille	21	Jun	80
13.61	Justine Buttle	4	Aug	84
13.22	Emily Steele	23	Jul	89
13.11	Amy Wilson	2	Sep	95
13.08	Ashley Morris	11	Aug	84
13.05	Tracy Page	21	Jun	86
13.04	Navdeep Dhaliwal	17	May	92
12.97	Alison Grey	23	Aug	87
12.96	April Kalu	23	Jun	96
12.95	Cynthia Gregory	7	Jul	78
12.91	Terri Salt	24	Jul	81
12.86	Lucy Rann	28	May	95
12.85	Philippa Roles	15	Aug	92

overage

13.50 i	Philippa Roles	19	Dec	92
13.45 i	Susan Coyne	28	Oct	82
13.43 i	Navdeep Dhaliwal	19	Dec	92

SHOT (4kg)

12.16	Susan King	9	Sep	79

DISCUS

44.12	Philippa Roles	30	Aug	92
41.92	Catherine Garden	12	Sep	93
40.92	Sandra McDonald	24	Jun	78
40.84	Natalie Kerr	24	Jul	94
40.54	Claire Smithson	25	May	97
40.44	Catherine MacIntyre	12	Sep	82
40.34	Natalie Hart	23	Mar	86
40.22	Emma Merry	27	Aug	88
40.18	Kelly Mellis	17	Sep	94
40.14	Clare Tank	29	Aug	88
39.76	Alix Gallagher	6	Jun	87
39.38	Charladee Clarke	1	Sep	85
39.38	Alex Hajipavlis	13	Aug	95

HAMMER (3.25kg)

35.74	Rachael Beverley	11	Sep	93
35.46	Kirsty Walters	20	Sep	98

HAMMER (4kg)

38.00	Catherine Garden	14	Mar	93

JAVELIN

48.40	Mandy Liverton	31	Aug	87
46.98	Kirsty Morrison	30	Jun	90
43.16	Shelley Holroyd	27	Jun	87
43.08	Karen Hough	4	Sep	82
42.70	Emily Steele	23	Sep	89
41.56	Goldie Sayers	12	Jul	96
41.50	Kelly Morgan	9	Jul	94
41.22	Maxine Worsfold	12	Jul	80
41.06	Heather Derbyshire	15	Aug	93
40.86	Julie Hawkins	28	Aug	77
40.80	Jenny Foster	16	Aug	92
40.74	Anna Bloxsome	16	Aug	87
40.72	Val Price	11	Aug	76
40.56	Julie Abel	3	Aug	80
40.54	Clover Wynter-Pink	10	Jul	92

PENTATHLON (with 800m & 75m hdls)

3518	Katharine Merry	18	Sep	88
3509	Aileen Wilson	20	Sep	98
3333	Jackie Harris	27	Jun	87
3296	Claire Everett	19	Sep	93
3225	Amy Nuttell	26	Jun	94
3216	Sally Gunnell	23	Aug	80
3213	Julie Hollman	22	Sep	91
3195	Julia Charlton	10	May	80
3193	Sam Foster	26	Jun	94
3186	Lauraine Cameron	16	Aug	86
3175	Linda Wong	14	Sep	80
3167	Sandy French	5	Aug	78
3162	Claire Phythian	20	Sep	87
3153	Katie Budd	16	Sep	90

with 80mH

3444	Jane Shepherd	16	Jul	83
3350	Claire Smith	3	Jul	82
3295	Paula Khouri	16	Jul	83
3283	Jackie Kinsella	16	Jul	83

2500 METRES TRACK WALK

11:50.0	Susan Ashforth	12	Sep	84
12:17.0	Karen Eden	3	Sep	77

Road - *where superior to track time*

12:03	Nikola Ellis	5	May	84
12:04	Vicky Lawrence	5	May	84

3000 METRES TRACK WALK

14:56.4	Sarah Bennett	26	Sep	93
15:00.0	Susan Ashforth	19	Jun	84
15:00.6	Sally Wish	16	Sep	72
15:06.69	Kelly Mann	30	May	98
15:14.6	Amy Hales	31	Aug	96
15:16.4	Natalie Watson	31	Aug	96
15:18.3	Vicky Lawrence	17	Jul	83
15:19.0	Tracey Devlin	28	Mar	87
15:26.63	Nicola Phillips	20	Sep	97
15:28.0	Kim Macadam	3	Sep	83
15:30.0	Nikola Ellis	1	Sep	84
15:31.0	Philippa Savage	3	Sep	88

overage

15:16.0	Helen Ringshaw	11	Nov	80

short track

15:18.7	Sharon Tonks	19	Mar	83

Road - *where superior to track time*

14:47	Amy Hales	23	Jun	96
14:48	Nikola Ellis	16	Sep	84
14:55	Lisa Langford	6	Dec	80
14:58	Carolyn Brown	19	Aug	87
14:59	Julie Snead	16	Sep	84
15:07	Stephanie Cooper	10	Dec	83

overage

14:19	Susan Ashforth	20	Oct	84
14:41	Ruth Sugg	7	Nov	81
14:41	Lisa Langford	7	Nov	81

5000 METRES TRACK WALK

26:52.0	Nina Howley	14	Sep	92

Road - *where superior to track time*

26:20	Tracey Devlin	14	Feb	87

UNDER 13

75 METRES
9.8	Amy Spencer	19	Jul	98
9.83		6	Sep	98
9.9	Cherie Pierre	21	Jul	96
9.9	Charlene Lashley	17	May	98

wind assisted
9.96	Joanne Wainwright	8	Sep	96

80 METRES
10.2	Jane Riley	1	Jun	85
10.2	Helen Seery	20	May	89
10.3	Katharine Merry	6	Jun	87
10.3	Emma Ania	7	Sep	91

100 METRES (y = 100 yards)
11.92	Jane Parry	20	Aug	77
12.1	Katharine Merry	26	Sep	87
11.1y	Sonia Lannaman	10	Aug	68
12.3	Joanne Gardner	24	Aug	75
12.3	Debbie Bunn	30	Aug	75
12.4	Lorraine Broxup	13	Jun	76
12.4	Sarah Claxton	31	Aug	92
12.5	Rachael Kay	26	Sep	93

wind assisted
11.8	Debbie Bunn	28	Jun	75
12.3	Barbara Parham	7	Jul	73
12.3	Susan Croker	17	Jun	78
12.3	Gail Hayes	7	Jul	78
12.4	Janis Walsh	15	Jun	72

150 METRES
19.1	Emma Ania	7	Sep	91
19.2	Helen Seery	19	Feb	89
19.2	Amy Spencer	28	Jun	98
19.3	Alanna Wain	29	Jun	97
19.4	Vernicha James	31	Aug	96
19.5	Karlene Palmer	1	Aug	93
19.5	Cherie Pierre	2	Jun	96
19.5	Justine Roach	29	Jun	97

course measurement uncertain
19.1	Kelly Massey	17	Aug	97
19.2	Kelly Rea	30	Apr	95
19.2	Rebecca Smith	30	Apr	95
19.4	Lisa Parry	17	Aug	97

200 METRES
24.2	Jane Parry	28	May	77
25.4	Katharine Merry	21	Jun	87
25.4	Myra McShannon	8	May	88
25.6	Debbie Bunn	5	Jul	75
25.6	Joanne Gardner	24	Aug	75
25.6	Jane Riley	30	Jun	85
25.7	Jane Bradbeer	1	Aug	81
25.7	Donna Fraser	28	Sep	85
25.87	Amy Spencer	2	Aug	98
25.95	Sandy French	20	Aug	76

wind assisted
23.6	Jane Parry	9	Jul	77

600 METRES
1:37.5	Hannah Wood	17	Jul	94
1:38.5	Jennifer Meadows	4	Apr	93
1:38.9	Emma Ward	17	Jul	94
1:39.7	Charlotte Moore	16	Aug	97
1:40.9	Amanda O'Shea	25	Jul	92

800 METRES
2:14.8	Janet Lawrence	10	Jul	71
2:15.05	Rachel Hughes	11	Sep	81
2:16.8	Angela Davies	25	Jul	83
2:17.20	Emma Langston	7	Sep	84
2:17.6	Michelle Wilkinson	22	Jun	85
2:17.9	Melissa Rooney	20	Jun	81
2:18.1	Lileath Rose	19	Jun	76
2:18.50	Jennifer Meadows	3	Jul	93
2:18.6	Jayne Heathcote	11	Jun	83
2:18.7	Charlotte Moore	14	Sep	97

1000 METRES
3:00.1	Charlotte Moore	25	Aug	97
3:08.2	Kelly Deacon	14	May	95
3:09.1	Abby Lyons	29	Jun	97
3:09.2	Catherine Draper	29	Jun	97
3:09.4	Hannah Curnock	18	Jul	90

1200 METRES
3:52.9	Emma Hunt	17	May	98
3:56.5	Michelle Jessop	28	Jun	98
3:57.3	Megan Wright	3	May	98

1500 METRES
4:36.9	Rachel Hughes	20	Jul	81
4:39.3	Charlotte Moore	2	Aug	97
4:42.1	Stacey Washington	18	Jul	84
4:43.0	Julie Adkin	18	Jul	84
4:44.0	Paula Matheson	20	Jul	76
4:44.2	Clare Keller	13	Jun	81
4:44.7	Deborah Russell	18	Jul	76
4:44.9	Susan Jordan	20	Sep	81
4:46.8	Amanda Alford	11	Sep	76
4:47.1	Susan Byrom	29	Jun	85

overage
4:35.5	Rachel Hughes	2	Dec	81

70 METRES HURDLES
11.0	Katharine Merry	20	Sep	87
11.0	Justine Roach	13	Sep	97
11.1	Sarah Claxton	14	Jun	92
11.1	Emma Makin	26	May	98
11.17	Anne-Marie Massey	3	Sep	95
11.2	Claire Stuart	19	Jun	88
11.24	Alana Watson	8	Sep	96
11.3	Katie Challoner	22	Sep	91
11.3	Nicola Hall	23	Aug	92
11.3	Caroline Pearce	1	Aug	93
11.3	Naomi Hodge-Dallaway	30	Aug	93
11.3	Jennifer Molloy	25	Aug	96
11.3	Anna Salter	9	Aug	97

wind assisted
11.21	Sandra Gunn	4	Sep	88
11.26	Catriona Burr	4	Sep	88

84

75 METRES HURDLES
11.3	Katharine Merry	26	Sep	87
11.6	Jenny Vanes	26	Sep	87

HIGH JUMP
1.69	Katharine Merry	26	Sep	87
1.68	Julia Charlton	6	Aug	78
1.65	Debbie Marti	20	Sep	80
1.65	Jane Falconer	20	Sep	87
1.63	Lindsey Marriott	11	Aug	79
1.63	Paula Davidge	13	Sep	81
1.60	Denise Wilkinson	17	Jul	76
1.59	Julie O'Dell	28	Jul	74
1.59	Julia Cockram	18	May	80
1.59	Beverley Green	30	Aug	86

overage
1.62 i	Claire Summerfield	20	Nov	77

POLE VAULT
2.30	Lauren Stoney	5	Aug	96

LONG JUMP
5.71	Sandy French	20	Aug	76
5.45	Sarah Wilhelmy	31	Aug	92
5.43	Margaret Cheetham	19	Sep	81
5.42	Katharine Merry	7	Jun	87
5.40	Kerrie Gray	1	Sep	84
5.38	Toyin Campbell	6	Aug	77
5.35	Deborah Bunn	7	Sep	75
5.34	Fiona May	12	Jun	82
5.33	Kathryn Dowsett	7	Sep	91
5.32	Ann Flannery	18	Sep	82

wind assisted
5.55	Katharine Merry	10	Jul	87

SHOT (2.72kg)
11.04	Amy Wilson	12	Sep	93
10.91	Catherine Garden	8	Sep	91
10.60	Lucy Rann	29	Aug	93
10.56	Candace Schofield	17	Aug	97
10.52	Faye Brennan	18	Aug	96
10.50	Lynne Stewart	12	Jul	97
10.48	Julie Robin	1	Jul	89
10.48	Natalie Kerr	9	Aug	92
10.47	Navdeep Dhaliwal	1	Sep	90
10.46	Sandra Biddlecombe	4	Jul	90

overage
11.57 i	Navdeep Dhaliwal	12	Dec	90

SHOT (3.25kg)
12.20	Susan King	3	Sep	77
10.77	Michele Morgan	19	Jun	82
10.54	Claire Burnett	1	Sep	85
10.49	Alison Grey	3	Aug	85

overage
10.68 i	Rebecca Hyams	21	Dec	85
10.64 i	Roxanne Blackwood	10	Nov	86

DISCUS (0.75kg)
39.44	Catherine Garden	8	Sep	91
37.64	Sandra Biddlecombe	4	Jul	90
32.70	Claire Smithson	26	Aug	95
32.52	Candace Schofield	7	Sep	97

31.46	Sian Howe	21	Sep	96
30.54	Eleanor Garden	10	Sep	89
29.76	Navdeep Dhaliwal	19	Aug	90
29.62	Helen Gates	3	Jul	93
29.48	Rebecca Roles	16	May	92
29.35	Lauren Therin	18	Jun	98

DISCUS (1kg)
34.22	Catherine Garden	25	Aug	91
31.34	Sandra Biddlecombe	9	Sep	90
30.54	Fiona Condon	15	Sep	73
30.02	Alison Moffitt	6	Jul	82
29.88	Iona Doyley	2	Sep	78
29.58	Claire Smithson	28	Aug	95
29.42	Eleanor Garden	27	Aug	89

overage
33.86	Fiona Condon	13	Oct	73

JAVELIN (400gm)
36.06	Samantha Redd	1	Sep	96
33.90	Lauren Therin	6	Sep	98
33.46	Emma Claydon	26	Jul	92
33.32	Melanie Vaggers	27	Sep	94
32.60	Candace Schofield	10	Aug	97
32.38	Eve Russell	30	Jul	95
31.87	Georgina Field	31	Aug	98
31.58	Louise Telford	20	Aug	94
31.50	Sarah Ashdown	29	Sep	96
31.30	Helen Davis	14	Sep	97

JAVELIN (600gm)
32.02	Claire Lacey	20	Sep	87
31.60	Emma Langston	2	Sep	84
31.44	Alison Moffitt	6	Jul	82
31.28	Eve Russell	2	Sep	95
31.04	Shelley Holroyd		Jun	85

PENTATHLON
2811	Katharine Merry	20	Sep	87
2551	Sarah Wilhelmy	2	Aug	92
2505	Caroline Pearce	26	Sep	93
2451	Seonaid Ferry	17	Jul	94
2419	Donna Medlock	7	Aug	94

Under 15 implements
2607	Jane Shepherd	6	Jun	81
2604	Alison Kerboas	19	Sep	93
2541	Jane Falconer	23	Aug	87

1000 METRES TRACK WALK
5:11.1	Amy Hales	4	Sep	94

2000 METRES TRACK WALK
10:09.0	Kelly Mann	10	Sep	95
10:17.0	Sarah Bennett	27	Sep	92
10:19.0	Joanne Ashforth	7	Sep	85
10:31.0	Claire Walker	7	Sep	85
10:31.0	Jo Pickett	25	Apr	92

2500 METRES TRACK WALK
12:48.9	Claire Walker	20	Jul	85
12:50.5	Victoria Lawrence	4	Jul	82

overage
12:49.0	Karen Eden	11	Oct	75

UK CLUB RELAY RECORDS

MEN

Seniors

4 x 100m	39.49	Haringey	1 Jun 91
4 x 200m	1:23.5	Team Solent	19 Jul 87
4 x 400m	3:04.48	Team Solent	29 Jun 90
1600m Medley	3:20.8	Wolverhampton & Bilston	1 Jun 75
4 x 800m	7:24.4*	North Staffs and Stone	27 Jun 65
4 x 1500m	15:12.6	Bristol	5 Aug 75

* = 4 x 880y time less 2.8sec

Under 20

4 x 100m	41.30	Victoria Park	14 Aug 76
4 x 200m	1:27.6	Enfield	13 Jun 82
4 x 400m	3:15.3	Enfield	5 Sep 82
1600m Medley	3:31.6	Cardiff	14 Aug 71
4 x 800m	7:35.3	Liverpool H	14 Aug 90
4 x 1500m	16:04.3	Blackburn	15 Sep 79
4 x 110H	1:04.8	Oundle Sch	19 May 79

Under 17

4 x 100m	42.22	Thames V H	24 Jun 89
4 x 200m	1:31.2	Hercules-W.	12 Jul 78
4 x 400m	3:23.1	Enfield	1 Oct 80
1600m Medley	3:36.1	Thurrock	13 Jun 84
4 x 800m	7:52.1	Clydebank	29 Aug 87
4 x 1500m	16:27.0	Liverpool H	14 Sep 88

Under 15

4 x 100m	44.62	Sale	29 Aug 93
4 x 200m	1:36.9	Belgrave	19 Sep 93
4 x 400m	3:31.5	Ayr Seaforth	5 Sep 82
1600m Medley	3:48.4	Blackheath	29 Sep 86
4 x 800m	8:13.28	Clydebank	2 Sep 89
4 x 1500m	17:52.4	Stretford	22 Oct 85

Under 13

4 x 100m	50.5	Blackheath	12 Sep 93
4 x 200m	1:49.7	Braintree	29 Aug 94
4 x 400m	4:04.5	Blackheath	12 Sep 93
1600m Medley	4:13.7	Blackheath	28 Sep 86
4 x 800m	9:29.8	Sale	28 Jun 88

WOMEN

Seniors

4 x 100m	43.79	Hounslow	18 Sep 82
4 x 200m	1:35.15	Stretford	14 Jul 91
4 x 400m	3:31.62	Essex Ladies	31 May 92
1600m Medley	3:50.6	Coventry Godiva	5 May 84
3 x 800m	6:32.4	Cambridge H	29 Jun 74
4 x 800m	8:41.0	Cambridge H	26 May 75

Under 20

4 x 100m	47.66	Essex Ladies	27 Sep 97
4 x 200m	1:47.3	Millfield School	11 May 96
4 x 400m	3:51.6	Birchfield	23 Aug 98
3 x 800m	7:33.2	Essex Ladies	12 Jun 94

Under 17

4 x 100m	47.52	Hounslow	2 Oct 82
4 x 200m	1:42.2	London Oly.	19 Aug 72
4 x 400m	3:52.1	City of Hull	3 Jul 82
1600m Medley	4:07.8	Warrington	14 Aug 75
3 x 800m	6:46.5	Haslemere	15 Sep 79
	6:46.5	Bromley L	1 Jul 84
4 x 800m	8:53.1	Havering	24 May 80

Under 15

4 x 100m	48.5	Haringey	15 Sep 79
4 x 200m	1:44.0	Bristol	15 Sep 79
3 x 800m	6:39.8	Havering	13 Sep 78
4 x 800m	9:21.4	Sale	5 Aug 78

Under 13

4 x 100m	53.16	Wigan	5 Sep 93
4 x 200m	1:52.5	Mitcham	24 Jul 82
3 x 800m	7:18.0	Mid Hants	14 Sep 83
4 x 800m	10:02.4	Warrington	16 Sep 75

AAA INDOOR CHAMPIONSHIPS   Birmingham   7 - 8 February 1998

MEN

60 Metres (7 Feb)
1. DARREN BRAITHWAITE   6.57
2. DWAIN CHAMBERS   6.58
3. JASON GARDENER   6.61
4. JASON LIVINGSTON   6.66
5. JOSEPHUS THOMAS   6.67
6. KEVIN WILLIAMS   6.70

200 Metres (8 Feb)
1. JULIAN GOLDING   20.46
2. ALLYN CONDON   20.53
3. JAMIE HENTHORN   21.26
4. DOUG TURNER   21.35
5. STEPHEN TOPLISS   21.65

400 Metres (8 Feb)
1. SOLOMON WARISO   45.71
2. SEAN BALDOCK   46.11
3. PAUL SLYTHE   47.48
4. LAWRENCE BAIRD   47.60
5. BRIAN FORBES   47.94

800 Metres (8 Feb)
1. Wilson Kirwa   KEN   1:47.85
2. James Nolan   IRE   1:48.11
3. Einars Tupurutis   LAT   1:48.43
4. BRADLEY DONKIN   1:48.94
5. JASON DUPUY   1:50.35

WOMEN

60 Metres (7 Feb)
1. JOICE MADUAKA   7.34
2. Lena Barry   IRE   7.48
3. DONNA FRASER   7.49
4. SHANI ANDERSON   7.52
5. AILEEN McGILLIVARY   7.58

200 Metres (8 Feb)
1. DONNA FRASER   23.15
2. SARAH WILHELMY   23.54
3. JOICE MADUAKA   23.54
4. CATHERINE MURPHY   23.91
5. ELLENA RUDDOCK   24.41

400 Metres (8 Feb)
1. VICKI JAMIESON   53.04
2. KELLY SOTHERTON   54.59
3. VICTORIA DAY   55.05
4. KERRI MADDOX   55.33
5. KIM GOODWIN   55.95

800 Metres (8 Feb)
1. HAYLEY PARRY   2:02.91
2. EMMA DAVIES   2:07.90
3. MICHELLE FAHERTY   2:09.47
4. ALICE BEECROFT   2:10.02
5. JENNIFER WARD   2:12.92

1500 Metres (8 Feb)
1. JOSEPH MILLS   3:50.30
2. BRADFORD GLENTON   3:50.61
3. TONY JOHNSTON   3:51.20
4. BRUNO WITCHALLS   3:51.86
5. ALASDAIR DONALDSON   3:53.10

3000 Metres (8 Feb)
1= DAVID TAYLOR   8:00.37
1= RODNEY FINCH   8:00.37
3. JULIAN MOORHOUSE   8:00.63
4. STUART POORE   8:05.12
5. ROBERT SCANLON   8:08.67

60 Metres Hurdles (7 Feb)
1. TONY JARRETT   7.59
2. ANDREW TULLOCH   7.66
3. DAMIEN GREAVES   7.83
4. MATTHEW CLEMENTS   7.91
5. MARTYN HENDRY   8.10

High Jump (7 Feb)
1. BEN CHALLENGER   2.27
2. Antoine Burke   IRE   2.24
3. DAVID BARNETSON   2.18
4. Mark Mandy   IRE   2.18
5. MARTIN LLOYD   2.08

Pole Vault (7 Feb)
1. NICK BUCKFIELD   5.30
2. KEVIN HUGHES   5.30
3. CHRISTIAN LINSKEY   5.00
4. MARK DAVIS   4.90
5. MARK GRANT   4.80

1500 Metres (7 Feb)
1. SHIRLEY GRIFFITHS   4:23.56
2. AMANDA PARKINSON   4:24.61
3. Pauline Thom   IRE   4:25.46
4. CAROLINE SLIMIN   4:30.24
5. SARAH SINGLETON   4:36.03

3000 Metres (22 Feb Birm)
1. SARAH SINGLETON   9:35.04
2. VAL BOTHAMS   9:36.50
3. SUSAN HARRISON   9:39.18
4. JENNIE COX   9:42.72

60 Metres Hurdles (7 Feb)
1. DIANE ALLAHGREEN   8.21
2. DENISE LEWIS   8.40
3. RACHEL KING   8.41
4. CLOVA COURT   8.44
5. ELIZABETH FAIRS   8.50

High Jump (8 Feb)
1. SUSAN JONES   1.89
2. DEBORA MARTI   1.89
3. MICHELLE DUNKLEY   1.89
4. DALIA MIKNEVICUTE   1.83
5. Sharon Foley   IRE   1.83

Long Jump (7 Feb)
1. CHRIS DAVIDSON   7.43
2. STEVEN PHILLIPS   7.27
3. ANTHONY MALCOLM   7.12
4. Mark Krumle   IRE   7.10
5. GARY SMITH   7.10

Triple Jump (8 Feb)
1. JULIAN GOLLEY   16.49
2. FRANCIS AGYEPONG   16.31
3. FEMI AKINSANYA   16.07
4. TOSI FASINRO   15.46
5. CHARLES MADEIRA-COLE   15.30

Shot (8 Feb)
1. SHAUN PICKERING   18.95
2. CARL MYERSCOUGH   18.31
3. STEPHEN WHYTE   17.03
4. GARY SOLLITT   16.89
5. EMEKA UDECHUKU   16.82

Heptathlon (7-8 Feb)
1. Joe Naughton   IRE   5384
2. PAUL JONES   4954
3. BEN ROBERTS   4892
4. ANDREW WESTON   4819
5. STEPHEN GARLAND   4812

3000 Metres Walk (8 Feb)
1. MARTIN BELL   12:08.61
2. Pierce O'Callaghan   IRE   12:12.67
3. ANDREW DRAKE   12:23.13
4. James Costin   IRE   12:51.69

Pole Vault (8 Feb)
1. JANINE WHITLOCK   4.11
2. RHIAN CLARKE   3.80
3. EMMA HORNBY   3.60
4. LINDA STANTON   3.60

Long Jump (8 Feb)
1. DENISE LEWIS   6.29
2. TRACY JOSEPH   6.21
3. JULIE HOLLMAN   6.05
4. DONITA BENJAMIN   5.76

Triple Jump (7 Feb)
1. ASHIA HANSEN   14.19
2. KERENSA DENHAM   12.19
3. ELIZABETH GIBBENS   11.96
4. Siobhan Hoey   IRE   11.95

Shot (8 Feb)
1. JUDY OAKES   18.23
2. JOANNE DUNCAN   14.67
3. VICKIE FOSTER   14.64
4. CAROL PARKER   14.22

Pentathlon (8 Feb)
1. JULIA BENNETT   4297
2. DIANA BENNETT   4166
3. JENNIFER KELLY   3916
4. JENNY BROWN   3416

GB&NI v FRA v GER (U20) (Indoors)   Birmingham 28 February 1998

MEN

60 Metres Race 1
1. MARK LEWIS-FRASER   6.80
2. CHRISTIAN MALCOLM   6.82

60 Metres Race 2
1. CHRISTIAN MALCOLM   6.81
2. MARK LEWIS-FRASER   6.83

200 Metres Race 1
1. Kevin Hanjohr   GER   21.78
2. JAMES CHATT   21.89

200 Metres Race 2
1. Stefan Holz   GER   21.30
2. TIM BENJAMIN   21.52
4. JAMES CHATT   21.89

400 Metres Race 1
1. MATTHEW ELIAS   47.98

400 Metres Race 2
1. Marc Alex. Scheer GER   47.54
2. KRIS STEWART   gst   48.34
3. ALLOY WILSON   48.38

800 Metres
1. GARETH BEARD   1:54.37
2. ROSS FITTALL   1:54.93

WOMEN

60 Metres Race 1
1. REBECCA WHITE   7.56
6. MARIA BOLSOVER   7.76

60 Metres Race 2
1. Anne Reucher   GER   7.53
2. REBECCA WHITE   7.56
3. MARIA BOLSOVER   7.60

200 Metres Race 1
1. SARAH WILHELMY   23.59

200 Metres Race 2
1. SARAH ZAWADA   24.61

400 Metres Race 1
1. Hedda Jacob   GER   56.31
2. ABIGAIL NAUGHER   56.91
4. JENNIFER MEADOWS   gst   57.44
5. KAREN GEAR   gst   58.53

400 Metres Race 2
1. Kerstin Seitz   GER   55.60
2. CAREY EASTON   56.22
4. LUCY CHAFFE   gst   57.50

800 Metres
1. Verena Joos   GER   2:10.11
2. JOANNA ROSS   2:11.15
4. SIMONE HARDY   2:13.27

1500 Metres
1. Wolfram Müller   GER   3:53.72
4. ANDREW INGLE   3:57.59
5. CHRIS BOLT   4:00.86

3000 Metres
1. Michael May   GER   8:26.71
4. IAIN MURDOCH   8:38.63
6. GARETH PRICE   8:52.83

60 Metres Hurdles Race 1
1. David Cissoko   FRA   8.03
2. CHRIS BAILLIE   8.15
4. BEN WARMINGTON   8.29

60 Metres Hurdles Race 2
1. David Cissoko   FRA   8.01
2. CHRIS BAILLIE   8.18
5. BEN WARMINGTON   8.27

High Jump
1. COLIN McMASTER   2.14
3. DANNY GRAHAM   2.09

Pole Vault
1. Lars Borgeling   GER   5.10
5. CHRISTIAN LINSKEY   4.80
6. SCOTT SIMPSON   4.60

1500 Metres
1. Sandy Wäzek   GER   4:35.37
2. JENNIFER MOCKLER   4:38.20
5. CAMILLA WAITE   4:58.36

3000 Metres
1. Melanie Schulz   GER   9:39.99
5. JEANETTE SHORTALL   10:42.48
6. LUCY KIRBY   10:46.06

60 Metres Hurdles Race 1
1. SARAH CLAXTON   8.39
4. JULIE PRATT   8.64

60 Metres Hurdles Race 2
1. SARAH CLAXTON   8.38
4. JULIE PRATT   8.60

High Jump
1. Gaelle Naire   FRA   1.85
2. CHLOE COZENS   1.76
4. GILLIAN BLACK   1.70

Pole Vault
1. Annika Becker   GER   4.00
5. TRACY BLOOMFIELD   3.40
6. LAURA PATTERSON   3.10

Long Jump
1. Aurelie Felix   FRA   6.01
3. DANIELLE FREEMAN   5.79
6. AMIEE CUTLER   5.57

Long Jump
1. Leslie Djhone   FRA   7.51
5. STUART WELLS   6.94
6. DOMINIQUE RICHARDS   6.68

Triple Jump
1. Alexander Karge   GER   15.34
3. NICHOLAS THOMAS   15.58
5. TOSIN OKE   15.09

Shot
1. CARL MYERSCOUGH   17.44
3. EMEKA UDECHUKU   16.57

5k Walk
1. Marcus Hackbusch   GER 21:22.25
4. MICHAEL KEMP   22:11.44
5. THOMAS TAYLOR   23:27.28

4 x 400 Metres Relay
1. GREAT BRITAIN & NI   3:13.88
    (CARSON, CAINES, WILSON, ELIAS)

Match Result
1. GREAT BRITAIN & NI   104
2. Germany   97
3. France   83

Triple Jump
1. Henny Gastel   GER   12.69
3. JUDY KOTEY   12.41
6. HAYLEY WARRILOW   11.66

Shot
1. Nadine Banse   GER   16.34
3. JULIE DUNKLEY   14.19
6. CLAIRE SMITHSON   11.42

3k Walk
1. Sabine Zimmer   GER 12:59.72
3. KATIE FORD   14:17.96
6. AMY HALES   14:44.35

4 x 400 Metres Relay
1. Germany   3:45.66
3. GREAT BRITAIN & NI   3:47.28
    (NAUGHER, CHAFFE, GEAR, MEADOWS)

Match Result
1. Germany   126
2. France   82
3. GREAT BRITAIN & NI   77

Overall Match Result
1. Germany   223
2. GREAT BRITAIN & NI   181
3. France   165

International Ekiden Marathon Relay   Yokohama, Japan 1 February 1998

Women
1. Japan   2:15:07
2. Kyushu   2:17:48
3. China   2:18:00
10. GREAT BRITAIN & NI 2:21:59

(JOINER, SUTTON, MACDOUGALL,
HEASMAN, PERCIVAL, STACEY)

AAA INDOOR JUNIOR CHAMPIONSHIPS Birmingham 21 - 22 February 1998

MEN Under 20

60	Christian Malcolm	6.82
200	Christian Malcolm	21.43
400	Alloy Wilson	47.84
800	Gareth Beard	1:53.13
1500	Andrew Ingle	3:59.77
3000	Iain Murdoch	8:48.29
60H	Chris Baillie	8.10
HJ	Colin McMaster	2.10
PV	Christian Linskey	4.70
LJ	Stuart Wells	7.13
TJ	Nicholas Thomas	15.20
SP	Emeka Udechuku	17.02
3kW	David Kidd (IRE)	12:45.85
Pent	Ben Roberts	3254

3000 at Birmingham 7 February

Under 17

Mark Lewis-Francis		6.79
Tim Benjamin		21.51
Gary Ankers		50.45
Aaron McIndoe		2:00.08
Stephen Bates		4:05.40
Nathan Palmer		8.23
Ken McKeown		2.07
Chris Type		4.20
Chris Tomlinson		6.95
Stephen Shalders		14.42
Gregory Beard		15.26
James Anthony		3360

Under 15

Darren Watson		7.50
Ryan Preddy		23.35
Ryan Preddy		50.72
Edward Bailey		2:08.79
Tim Sinclaire		8.80
Chuka Enih-Snell		1.91
Michael Parker		3.00
Alan Ruddock		5.70
Carl Saggers		15.74
Edward Dunford		2615

WOMEN Under 20

60	Rebecca White	7.55
200	Rebecca White	24.17
400	Carey Easton	55.29
800	Joanna Ross	2:11.20
1500	Camilla Waite	4:53.57
60H	Sarah Claxton	8.53
HJ	Chloe Cozens	1.75
PV	Laura Patterson	3.25
LJ	Danielle Freeman	5.96
TJ	Jody Kotey	12.07
SP	Julie Dunkley	14.30
3kW	Katie Ford	15:01.32
Pent	Danielle Freeman	3430

Pentathlons at Birmingham 31 January

Under 17

Natalie Smellie			7.66
Sarah Zawada			24.30
	300	Nicola Sanders	39.95
Catherine Riley			2:15.11
Jennifer Mockler			4:35.33
Helen Worsey			8.53
Lorraine Marsh (IRE)			1.66
Kia Wnuk			2.90
Aimee Cutler			5.70
Mary McLoone (IRE)			11.67
Claire Smithson			12.72
Samantha Adamson			3331

Under 15

Danielle Selley		7.77
Sarah Bell		25.59
Jennifer Tunstill		2:26.41
Danielle Selley		8.94
Aileen Wilson		1.75
Monique Parris		5.76
Gillian Austin		10.76
Danielle Selley		3229

EUROPEAN INDOOR CHAMPIONSHIPS Valencia, Spain 27 Feb - 1 Mar 1998

MEN

60 Metres (28 Feb)

1.	Angelos Pavlakakis	GRE	6.55
2.	JASON GARDENER		6.59
3.	Stephane Cali	FRA	6.60
4.	Marcin Krzywannski	POL	6.61
5.	Ryszard Pilarczyk	POL	6.64
6.	Georgios Theodoridis	GRE	6.68

5s2 DWAIN CHAMBERS		6.66
7s2 DARREN BRAITHWAITE		6.68

200 Metres (1 Mar)

1.	Sergey Osovich	UKR	20.40
2.	Anninos Marcoullides	CYP	20.65
3.	ALLYN CONDON		20.68
4.	JULIAN GOLDING		20.84
5.	DOUG TURNER		21.51
6.	Prodromos Katsantonis	CYP	22.49

400 Metres (1 Mar)

1.	Ruslan Mashchenko	RUS	45.90
2.	Ashraf Saber	ITA	45.99
3.	Robert Mackowiak	POL	46.00
4.	Tomasz Czubak	POL	47.18
5.	Carlos Silva	POR	47.32
6.	SEAN BALDOCK		50.05

3h2 SOLOMON WARISO		48.41
4h3 PAUL SLYTHE		47.62

800 Metres (1 Mar)

1.	Nils Schumann	GER	1:47.02
2.	Marko Koers	NED	1:47.20
3.	Vebjorn Rodal	NOR	1:47.40
4.	James Nolan	IRE	1:47.81
5.	David Matthews	IRE	1:48.37
6.	Ivan Komar	BLR	1:50.94

1500 Metres (28 Feb)

1.	Rui Silva	POR	3:44.57
2.	Kader Chekhemani	FRA	3:44.89
3.	Andrey Zadorozhniy	RUS	3:44.93
4.	Andres Diaz	ESP	3:45.18
5.	Leszek Zblewski	POL	3:45.67
6.	Branko Zorko	CRO	3:46.00

3000 Metres (1 Mar)

1.	JOHN MAYOCK		7:55.09
2.	Manuel Pancorbo	ESP	7:55.23
3.	Alberto Garcia	ESP	7:55.24
4.	Isaac Viciosa	ESP	7:55.45
5.	Sergey Lebed	UKR	7:55.62
6.	Ovidio Olteanu	ROM	7:56.09

7s1 IAN GILLESPIE		8:03.28

60 Metres Hurdles (1 Mar)

1.	Igor Kazanov	LAT	7.54
2.	Tomasz Scigaczewski	POL	7.56
3.	Mike Fenner	GER	7.58
4.	Jonathan Nsenga	BEL	7.59
5.	Dan Philibert	FRA	7.60
6.	Yevgeniy Pechenkin	RUS	7.66
7.	ANDY TULLOCH		7.66

5s1 TONY JARRETT		7.61
4h2 DAMIEN GREAVES		7.77

High Jump (1 Mar)

1.	Artur Partyka	POL	2.31
2.	Vyacheslav Voronin	RUS	2.31
3.	Tomas Janku	CZE	2.29
4.	Jan Janku	CZE	2.26
5.	Lambros Papakostas	GRE	2.26
6=	Elvir Krehmic	BOS	2.22
6=	Dragutin Topic	YUG	2.22
10= BEN CHALLENGER			2.22

Pole Vault (28 Feb)

1.	Tim Lobinger	GER	5.80
2.	Michael Stolle	GER	5.80
3.	Danny Ecker	GER	5.75
4.	Montxu Miranda	ESP	5.70
5.	Javier Garcia	ESP	5.60
6.	Martin Voss	DEN	5.60
17=Q NICK BUCKFIELD			5.55

89

Long Jump (28 Feb)
1. Aleksey Lukashevich UKR 8.06
2. Carlos Calado POR 8.05
3. Emmanuel Bangue FRA 8.05
4. Aleksey Musikhin RUS 8.00
5. Yago Lamela ESP 7.95
6. Romuald Ducros FRA 7.84

Triple Jump (1 Mar)
1. JONATHAN EDWARDS 17.43
2. Charles Friedek GER 17.15
3. Serge Helan FRA 17.02

WOMEN

60 Metres (28 Feb)
1. Melanie Paschke GER 7.14
2. Frederique Bangue FRA 7.18
3. Odiah Sidibe FRA 7.22
4. Katerina Thanou GRE 7.23
5. Katerina Koffa GRE 7.24
6. Irina Pukha UKR 7.28

8s1 JOICE MADUAKA 7.43

200 Metres (1 Mar)
1. Svetlana Goncharenko RUS 22.46
2. Melanie Paschke GER 22.50
3. Katerina Koffa GRE 22.86
4. Birgit Rockmeier GER 23.24
5. DONNA FRASER 23.53
6. Natalya Voronova RUS 24.99

400 Metres (1 Mar)
1. Grit Breuer GER 50.45
2. Ionela Tirlea ROM 50.56
3. Helena Fuchsova CZE 51.22
4. Ester Goossens NED 51.82
5. Irina Rosikhina RUS 52.73
6. Hana Benesova CZE 54.89

800 Metres (1 Mar)
1. Ludmila Formanova CZE 2:02.30
2. Malin Ewerlof SWE 2:03.61
3. Judit Varga HUN 2:03.81
4. Stella Jongmans NED 2:03.82
5. Petya Strashilova BUL 2:05.74
6. Stephanie Graf AUT 2:07.99

3h1 HAYLEY PARRY 2:04.37

1500 Metres (28 Feb)
1. Theresia Kiesl AUT 4:13.62
2. Lidia Chojecka POL 4:14.93
3. Violeta Szekely ROM 4:15.54

4. Rogel Nachum ISR 16.93
5. Raul Chapado ESP 16.87
6. Yuriy Osipenko UKR 16.86
7. FRANCIS AGYEPONG 16.57

16QJULIAN GOLLEY 16.19

Shot (28 Feb)
1. Oliver- Sven Buder GER 21.47
2. Mika Halvari FIN 20.59
3. Arsi Harju FIN 20.53
4. Dragan Peric YUG 20.21

4. Silvia Kuhnemund GER 4:15.64
5. Luminita Gogirlea ROM 4:16.68
6. Maite Zuniga ESP 4:18.41

3000 Metres (1 Mar)
1. Gabriela Szabo ROM 8:49.96
2. Fernanda Ribeiro POR 8:51.42
3. Marta Dominguez ESP 8:57.52
4. Jelena Celnoa LAT 9:00.78
5. Chrisoula Iakovou GRE 9:01.06
6. Zaiha Dahmani FRA 9:02.77

60 Metres Hurdles (1 Mar)
1. Patricia Girard FRA 7.85
2. Svetlana Laukhova RUS 8.01
3. DIANE ALLAHGREEN 8.02
4. Anna Leszczynska-Lazor POL 8.15
5. Maria Jose Mardomingo ESP 8.16
6. Caren Sonn GER 8.24

High Jump (28 Feb)
1. Monica Iagar ROM 1.96
2. Alina Astafei GER 1.94
3. Yelena Yelesina RUS 1.94
4. Yelena Gulyayeva RUS 1.92
5. Zuzana Kovacikova CZE 1.92
6. SUSAN JONES 1.92

9. DEBBI MARTI 1.85
11. MICHELLE DUNKLEY 1.85

Pole Vault (1 Mar)
1. Anzhela Balakhonova UKR 4.45
2. Daniela Bartova CZE 4.40
3. Vala Flosadottir ISL 4.40
4. JANINE WHITLOCK 4.25
5. Nicole Rieger GER 4.25
6. Zsuzsa Szabo HUN 4.15

23Q RHIAN CLARKE 3.60

5. Roman Virastyuk UKR 20.19
6. Miroslav Menc CZE 20.17

14QSHAUN PICKERING 18.82
16QMARK PROCTOR 18.66

Heptathlon (28 Feb-1 Mar)
1. Sebastian Chmara POL 6415
2. Dezso Szabo HUN 6249
3. Lev Lododin RUS 6226
4. Tomas Dvorak CZE 6175
5. Jon Arnar Magnusson ISL 6170
6. Aleksandr Averbukh RUS 6144

Long Jump (1 Mar)
1. Fiona May ITA 6.91
2. Tatyana Ter-Mesrobyan RUS 6.72
3. Linda Ferga FRA 6.67
4. Magdalena Khristova BUL 6.60
5. Niki Xanthou GRE 6.55
6. Monica Toth ROM 6.39

Triple Jump (28 Feb)
1. ASHIA HANSEN 15.16
2. Sarka Kasparkova CZE 14.76
3. Yelena Lebedyenko RUS 14.32
4. Olga Vasdeki GRE 14.29
5. Rodica Mateescu ROM 14.27
6. Betty Lise FRA 14.26

Shot (28 Feb)
1. Irina Korzhanenko RUS 20.25
2. Vita Pavlysh UKR 20.00
3. Corrie De Bruin NED 18.97
4. Krystyna Danilczjk POL 18.81
5. Nadine Kleinert GER 18.42
6. JUDY OAKES 18.42

Pentathlon (27 Feb)
1. Urszula Wlodarczyk POL 4808
2. Irina Belova RUS 4631
3. Karin Specht GER 4523
4. Tiia Hautala FIN 4473
5. Marie Collonville FRA 4300
6. Helena Vinarova CZE 4238

8. JULIA BENNETT 4226

Coca-Cola International Cross Country   Belfast 25 January 1998

MEN 8k
1. Laban Chege KEN 26:16
2. Yann Millon FRA 26:18
3. Robert Stefko SVK 26:29
4. Peter Matthews IRE 26:31
5. KEITH CULLEN 26:36
6. GLYNN TROMANS 26:40
12. PHIL MOWBRAY 27:13
13. STEWART BELL 27:16
14. STEVE BROOKS 27:18
15. ROBERT QUINN 27:20

WOMEN 4.8k
1. Marianna Chirila ROM 17:59
2. Susan Chepkemei KEN 17:59
3. PAULA RADCLIFFE 18:00
4. Lucia Subano KEN 18:22
5. VICKI McPHERSON 18:30
6. MARA MYERS 18:35
7. Rekiya Maraoui MAR 18:40
8. LIZ TALBOT 18:44
9. LUCY WRIGHT 18:51
10. VICTORIA WILKINSON 18:54

MEN Match Result
1. ENGLAND 35
2. GREAT BRITAIN 37
3. IRELAND 37
4. SCOTLAND 62

WOMEN Match Result
1. KENYA 19
2. GREAT BRITAIN 25
3. ENGLAND 36
4. SCOTLAND 46

UK CHAMPIONSHIPS & WORLD CROSS COUNTRY TRIALS
Cardiff 1 March 1998

MEN (12km)

1.	KEITH CULLEN	35.02
2.	ANDREW PEARSON	35.04
3.	GLYNN TROMANS	35.35
4.	SPENCER DUVAL	35.41
5.	CHRIS ROBISON	35.46
6.	DERMOT DONNELLY	35.47
7.	JOHN NUTTALL	35.50
8.	ROBERT QUINN	35.54
9.	RICHARD NERURKAR	35.57
10.	JUSTIN PUGSLEY	36.11
11.	PAUL RODEN	36.17
12.	BARRY ROYDEN	36.34

MEN (4km)

1.	ROBERT WHALLEY	10.25
2.	PHILIP MOWBRAY	10.27
3.	JULIAN MOORHOUSE	10.32
4.	MIKE OPENSHAW	10.35
5.	GLEN STEWART	10.37
6.	JAMES STARLING	10.39
7.	NICK COMMERFORD	10.45
8.	KEITH ANDERSON	10.49
9.	KEVIN McKAY	10.49
10.	M. CARROLL	10.50
11.	ROBERT SCANLON	10.50
12.	ADRIAN CALLAN	10.50

JUNIOR MEN (8km)

1.	SAM HAUGHIAN	23.56
2.	GAVIN THOMPSON	24.24
3.	SIMON BURTON	24.28
4.	ANDREW BECKWITH	24.34
5.	CHRIS THOMPSON	24.38
6.	ABDUSALAM MOHAMMED	24.40
7.	NICK MAPP	24.41
8.	DAVID STANLEY	24.46
9.	STEVEN VERNON	24.56
10.	CHRISTOPHER LIVESEY	24.56
11.	RYAN FAULKNER	25.04
12.	JAMIE HENDRY	25.12

WOMEN (8km)

1.	LIZ TALBOT	26.22
2.	VIKKY McPHERSON	26.22
3.	LUCY WRIGHT	26.35
4.	ANGELA JOINER	26.38
5.	BEV HARTIGAN	27.11
6.	SARAH BENTLEY	27.23
7.	MARA MYERS	27.23
8.	TARA KRZYWICKI	27.24
9.	HAYLEY NASH	27.25
10.	AMANDA WRIGHT	27.30
11.	LUCY ELLIOT	27.33
12.	HEATHER HEASMAN	27.34

WOMEN (4km)

1.	ANGELA DAVIES	11.59
2.	AMANDA CROWE	12.13
3.	HELEN PATTINSON	12.16
4.	NICOLA SLATER	12.22
5.	AMANDA PARKINSON	12.26
6.	ELINOR DOUBELL	12.30
7.	SARAH SINGLETON	12.33
8.	LYNN GIBSON	12.34
9.	KATE SKORUPSKA	12.35
10.	SHEILA FAIRWEATHER	12.37
11.	HAYLEY PARKINSON	12.42
12.	VICTORIA WILKINSON	12.45

JUNIOR WOMEN (6km)

1.	LOUISE KELLY	21.20
2.	AMBER GASCOIGNE	21.22
3.	CAROLINE WALSH	21.24
4.	KAREN FLETCHER	21.42
5.	REBECCA EVERETT	21.58
6.	SONIA THOMAS	21.59
7.	SUSAN PARTRIDGE	22.08
8.	CHARLEY COFFEY	22.16
9.	LISA WORDEN	22.17
10.	CLARE CAMPBELL	22.28
11.	LOUISE THOMPSON	22.37
12.	CARLEY WILSON	22.54

ENGLISH CROSS COUNTRY CHAMPIONSHIPS Leeds 14 March 1998

MEN (14.2k)

1.	DOMINIC BANNISTER	44:45
2.	BARRY ROYDEN	45:14
3.	JUSTIN PUGSLEY	45:20
4.	MARK HUDSPITH	45:24
5.	IAN HUDSPITH	45:39
6.	PAUL RODEN	45:47
7.	MIKE SIMPSON	46:03
8.	RICHARD FINDLOW	46:09
9.	NICK FRANCIS	46:14
10.	STEVE GREEN	46:16

Team

1.	Bingley Harriers	140
2.	Tipton Harriers	179
3.	Morpeth Harriers	256

MEN Under 20 (10k)

1.	ANDREW GRAFFIN	31:31
2.	ALLEN GRAFFIN	31:36
3.	Karim Bouchamia ALG	31:40
4.	JASON WARD	32:11
5.	NICK TALBOT	32:18
6.	DANIEL HYDE	32:26

Team

1.	Aldershot Farnham & D.	65
2.	Sale Harriers	155
3.	Morpeth Harriers	170

MEN Under 17 (6.1k)

1.	LEE McCASH	19:40
2.	STEVE VERNON	19:49
3.	ROBERT MAYCOCK	19:59
4.	CHRIS BOLT	20:15
5.	GERRARD SHARP	20:26
6.	GARY BLACKMAN	20:35

Team

1.	Blackheath Harriers	93
2.	Sale Harriers	124
3.	Holmfirth Harriers	139

WOMEN (8k)

1.	MARA MYERS	28:59
2.	LUCY ELLIOTT	29:07
3.	TARA KRZYWICKI	29:14
4.	HEATHER HEASMAN	29:23
5.	ANNE BUCKLEY	29:49
6.	LORETTA SOLLARS	30:16
7.	ELINOR DOUBELL	30:26
8.	ANN TASWELL	30:37
9.	PENNY THACKRAY	30:43
10.	RACHEL JORDAN	30:44

Team

1.	Shaftesbury Barnet H	49
2.	Charnwood	96
3.	Leeds City	132

WOMEN Under 20 (5k)

1.	AMY WATERLOW	18:07
2.	VICTORIA WILKINSON	18:21
3.	JILLY INGMAN	18:29
4.	EMMA BROOKER	18:49

Team

1.	Bristol AC	79
2.	Sale Harriers	123

WOMEN Under 17 (5k)

1.	JANE POTTER	18:53
2.	CLARE CAMPBELL	19:09
3.	HATTI DEAN	19:18
4.	CARLEY WILSON	19:21

Team

1.	Liverpool H & AC	88

WOMEN Under 15 (3.6k)

1.	LOUISE WHITTAKER	13:28
2.	LOUISE DAMEN	13:37
3.	KIRSTY WATERSON	13:46

Team

1.	Bristol AC	68

WOMEN Under 13 (3k)

1.	COURTNEY BIRCH	10:52
2.	CHARLOTTE MOORE	10:57
3.	HELEN LEE	11:24

Team

1.	Liverpool Pembroke & Sefton	85

WORLD CROSS COUNTRY CHAMPIONSHIPS Marrakech, Morocco   21-22 March 1998

SENIOR MEN (12km) 22 Mar

1.	Paul Tergat	KEN	34:01
2.	Paul Koech	KEN	34:06
3.	Assefa Mezegebu	ETH	34:28
4.	Thomas Nyariki	KEN	34:37
5.	Wilson Boit Kipketer	KEN	34:38
6.	Christopher Kelong	KEN	34:41
7.	Ismael Kirui	KEN	34:41
8.	Mohammed Mourhit	BEL	34:44
9.	Domingos Castro	POR	34:46
10.	Fabián Roncero	ESP	34:50

38.	GLYNN TROMANS	36:19
44.	KEITH CULLEN	36:25
59.	ANDREW PEARSON	36:41
75.	JOHN NUTTALL	37:06
87.	CHRIS ROBISON	37:26
111.	SPENCER DUVAL	38:16

Men's Teams

1.	Kenya	12
2.	Ethiopia	57
3.	Morocco	60
10.	GREAT BRITAIN & N.I.	216

SENIOR WOMEN (8km) 21 Mar

1.	Sonia O'Sullivan	IRL	25:39
2.	PAULA RADCLIFFE		25:42
3.	Gete Wami	ETH	25:49
4.	Merima Denboba	ETH	25:56
5.	Jackline Maranga	KEN	25:56
6.	Julia Vaquero	ESP	26:06
7.	Jane Omoro	KEN	26:07
8.	Leah Malot	KEN	26:16
9.	Ayelech Worku	ETH	26:17
10.	Sally Barsosio	KEN	26:27

13.	HAYLEY HAINING	26:40
25.	VIKKI McPHERSON	27:18
34.	LIZ TALBOT	27:28
53.	LUCY WRIGHT	28:09
59.	ANGELA JOINER	28:21

Women's Teams

1.	Kenya	30
2.	Ethiopia	37
3.	GREAT BRITAIN & N.I.	74

JUNIOR MEN (8km) 22 Mar

1.	Million Wolde	ETH	22:47
2.	Richard Limo	KEN	22:50
3.	Haylu Mekonhen	ETH	22:51
4.	Yibeltal Admasu	ETH	22:53
5.	Douglas Mumanyi	KEN	22:54
6.	Kiyara Kamzee	KEN	22:55
7.	Titus Kipkemboi	KEN	23:02
8.	Alene Emere	ETH	23:06
9.	Yitbarek Eshetu	ETH	23:14
10.	Adil El Kaouch	MAR	23:17

45.	GAVIN THOMPSON	25:07
46.	CHRIS THOMPSON	25:08
69.	ANDREW BECKWITH	25:35
76.	DAVID STANLEY	25:41
82.	NICK MAPP	25.50
dnf	SAM HAUGHIAN	

Junior Men's Teams

1.	Ethiopia	16
2.	Kenya	20
3.	Morocco	62
11.	GREAT BRITAIN & N.I.	236

SENIOR MEN (4km) 21 Mar

1.	John Kibowen	KEN	10:43
2.	Daniel Komen	KEN	10:46
3.	Paul Kosgei	KEN	10:50
4.	Benjamin Limo	KEN	10:59
5.	John Kosgei	KEN	11:04
6.	Brahim Boulami	MAR	11:06
7.	Marc Davis	USA	11:08
8.	Kipkurui Misoi	KEN	11:10
9.	Hicham Bouaouiche	MAR	11:11
10.	Maru Daba	ETH	11:11

35.	PHILIP MOWBRAY	11:29
37.	ROB WHALLEY	11:29
42.	MIKE OPENSHAW	11:33
55.	JULIAN MOORHOUSE	11:43
59.	IAN GILLESPIE	11:49
70.	ANTHONY WHITEMAN	12:00

Men's Teams

1.	Kenya	10
2.	Morocco	42
3.	Ethiopia	60
9.	GREAT BRITAIN & N.I.	169

SENIOR WOMEN (4km) 22 Mar

1.	Sonia O'Sullivan	IRL	12:20
2.	Zahra Ouaziz	MAR	12:34
3.	Kutre Dulecha	ETH	12:37
4.	Anita Weyermann	SUI	12:45
5.	Restituta Joseph	TAN	12:46
6.	Beatrice Omwanza	KEN	12:47
7.	Rodica Nagel	FRA	12:48
8.	Elva Dryer	USA	12:51
9.	Amy Rudolph	USA	12:51
10.	Samukeliso Moyo	ZIM	12:51

46.	HELEN PATTINSON	13:35
61.	NICOLA SLATER	13:47
64.	AMANDA CROWE	13:52
69.	SARAH BENTLEY	13:54
76.	AMANDA PARKINSON	14:10
dnf	ANGELA DAVIES	

Women's Teams

1.	Morocco	57
2.	Ethiopia	58
3.	United States	68
11.	GREAT BRITAIN & N.I.	240

JUNIOR WOMEN (6km) 21 Mar

1.	Yimenashu Taye	ETH	19:32
2.	Jeruto Kiptum	KEN	19:34
3.	Worknesh Kidane	ETH	19:34
4.	Alemgena Bezabeh	ETH	19:46
5.	Vivian Cheruiyot	KEN	19:47
6.	Margaret Chepkemboi	KEN	19:48
7.	Agnes Kiprop	KEN	19:57
8.	Meryma Hashim	ETH	19:59
9.	Emiko Kojima	JPN	20:02
10.	Emilie Mondor	CAN	20:16

51.	CAROLINE WALSH	21:52
59.	LOUISE KELLY	22:02
66.	KAREN FLETCHER	22:06
86.	REBECCA EVERETT	22:44
89.	CLARE THOMAS	22:50
dnf	AMBER GASCOIGNE	

Junior Women's Teams

1.	Ethiopia	16
2.	Kenya	20
3.	Japan	68
13.	GREAT BRITAIN & NI	262

AAA HALF MARATHON CHAMPIONSHIPS
Wilmslow   29 March 1998

MEN

1.	IAN HUDSPITH	64:22
2.	PAUL RODEN	64:24
3.	MARK HUDSPITH	64:36

Team

1.	Morpeth Harriers	37

WOMEN

1.	HEATHER HEASMAN	75:59
2.	AMANDA WRIGHT	76:06
3.	BEVERLEY JENKINS	76:40

Team

1.	Salford Harriers	18

EKIDEN RELAY
Seoul, Korea 12 April 1998

WOMEN

1.	Russia	2:21:16
2.	Japan	2:25:20
3.	Japan B	2:26:31
10.	GREAT BRITAIN & N.I.	2:33:33

(FAIRWEATHER, SKORUPSKA, KRZYWICKI, THACKRAY, GROVES, WILKINSON, PARKINSON)

EUROPEAN CHALLENGE 10000 METRES
Lisbon, Portugal 4 April 1998

MEN
1. Fabián Roncero ESP 27:14.44
2. António Pinto POR 27:15.76
3. Dieter Baumann GER 27:32.31
10. KEITH CULLEN 27:53.52
20. GLYNN TROMANS 28:31.71
22. ANDREW PEARSON 29:01.05
25. DERMOT DONNELLY 29:27.40

Team
1. Portugal 1:22:46.26
2. Spain 1:22:51.22
3. Germany 1:23:48.95
4. GREAT BRITAIN & N.I. 1:25:26.28

WOMEN
1. Fernanda Ribeiro POR 30:48.06
2. PAULA RADCLIFFE 30:48.58
3. Marina Bastos POR 32:20.51
8. VICKI McPHERSON 32:38.48
15. ANGELA JOINER 33:30.27
17. SARAH BENTLEY 33:59.69
18. BEV HARTIGAN 34:21.91

Team
1. Portugal 1:35:29.46
2. GREAT BRITAIN & N.I. 1:36:57.33
3. Spain 1:38:08.22

EUROPEAN RACE WALKING CUP
Dudince, Slovakia
25 April 1998

MEN 50k
1. Tomasz Lipiec POL 3:42:57
2. Jesus Angel Garcia ESP 3:43:17
3. Giovanni Perricelli ITA 3:44:17
28. MARK EASTON 4:03:53

MEN 20k
1. Francisco Fernandez ESP 1:20:31
2. Robert Korzeniowski POL 1:20:40
3. Aigars Fadejevs LAT 1:20:44
39. MARTIN BELL 1:29:01

WOMEN 10k
1. Nadezhda Ryashkina RUS 43:06
2. Maria Urbanik-Rosza HUN 43:08
3. Claudia Iovan ROM 43:12
27. LISA KEHLER 45:54

LONDON MARATHON 26 April 1998

MEN
1. Abel Antón ESP 2:07:57
2. Abd. El Mouaaaziz MAR 2:08:07
3. António Pinto POR 2:08:13
4. Julio Rey ESP 2:08:33
5. Abebe Mekonnen ETH 2:09:52
6. Robert Stefko SVK 2:09:53
7. Diego Garcia ESP 2:10:35
8. JON BROWN 2:11:10
9. Steve Moneghetti AUS 2:11:40
10. Kenjiro Jitsui JPN 2:12:46

16. MARK HUDSPITH 2:14:19
21 BILLY BURNS 2:16:11
24. STEVE BRACE 2:16:34
26. ALAN CHILTON 2:17:07
29. MALCOLM PRICE 2:17:43
31. STEVE GREEN 2:18:11
33. BARRY ROYDEN 2:19:57
34. NICK JONES 2:20:22

WOMEN
1. Christina McKiernan IRE 2:26:26
2. LIZ McCOLGAN 2:26:54
3. Joyce Chepchumba KEN 2:27:22
4. Marleen Renders BEL 2:27:30
5. Lidia Simon ROM 2:28:41
6. Sonja Oberem GER 2:29:39
7. Adriana Fernandez MEX 2:29:46
8. Wang Yanfang CHN 2:30:47
9. Malgorzata Sobanska POL 2:32:02
10. MARIAN SUTTON 2:32:14

15. DEBBIE PERCIVAL 2:39:54
20. NICOLA BROWN 2:43:18
21. TRACY SWINDELL 2:43:41
22. RUTH KINGSBOROUGH 2:44:33
24. ANITA MELLODEW 2:46:17
27. SANDRA BRANNEY 2:48:47
28. JOANNA LODGE 2:50:10
30. LISA HOLLICK 2:51:16

IAAF WORLD ROAD RELAY
Manaus, Brazil
18 - 19 April 1998
(5000,10000,5000,10000,5000, 7195)

MEN (19 Apr)
1. Kenya 2:01:13
John Kibowen 13:44, Paul Koech 28:40,
Benjamin Limo 14:04, Thomas Nyariki 29:33,
John Kosgei 14:28, Paul Kosgei 20:44
2. Ethiopia 2:03:47
3. Brazil 2:04:50
11. GREAT BRITAIN & N.I. 2:09:59
JULIAN MOORHOUSE 14:30, DALE
LAUGHLIN 31:11, JAMES STARLING
15:10, IAN HUDSPITH 31:39, JUSTIN
PUGSLEY 15:18, GLEN STEWART 22:11

WOMEN (18 Apr)
1. Ethiopia 2:21:15
2. Kenya 2:21:49
3. Romania 2:24:13

EIGHT NATIONS WALKING CUP Senigallia, Italy 31 May 1998

MEN 20k
1. Arturo Di Mezza ITA 1:21:36
2. Sandor Urbanik HUN 1:22:16
3. Andrey Stadnichuk RUS 1:22:25
10. ANDREW DRAKE 1:28:01
16. STEVEN HOLLIER 1:34:26
MARTIN BELL dnf

Team
1. Italy 137
2. Russia 135
4. GREAT BRITAIN & N.I. 78

MEN 35k
1. Marco Giungi ITA 2:35:26
2. Sylvain Caudron FRA 2:37:13

3. Rene Piller FRA 2:37:13
14. MARK EASTON 2:47:28
19. CHRIS CHEESEMAN 2:56:13
GRAHAM WHITE dnf
LES MORTON dsq

Team
1. France 144
2. Italy 142
6. GREAT BRITAIN & N.I. 74

WOMEN 10k
1. Yelena Gruzinova RUS 44:01
2. Maria Urbanik-Rosza HUN 44:04
3. Erica Alfridi ITA 44:31

17. KIM BRAZNELL 49:10
18. LISA CRUMP 49:51
20. KAREN KNEALE 52:05
VIKKI LUPTON 52:05

JUNIOR WOMEN 5k
1. Lyudmila Yefimkina RUS 22:49
2. Natalya Fedoskina RUS 22:58
19. SARAH BENNETT 24:59
21. AMY HALES 25:17
25. DEBORAH WALLEN 25:50

Team
1. Italy 140
2. Hungary 139
5. GREAT BRITAIN & N.I.

Throws International   Halle, Germany 16 May 1998

MEN

Shot
1. Oliver Sven Buder   GER   20.19
2. MARK PROCTOR   19.50
3. SHAUN PICKERING   19.20

Discus
1. Virgilijus Alekna   LIT   68.86
2. Michael Alekna   GER   67.18
8. GLEN SMITH   60.16
9. PERRIS WILKINS   58.54

Hammer
1. Holger Klose   GER   79.70
2. Karsten Kobs   GER   78.90
4. PAUL HEAD   72.56

6. MICK JONES   71.90

Javelin
1. Boris Henry   GER   86.26
2. Peter Blank   GER   79.48
3. MARK ROBERTSON   77.88
7. STUART FABEN   64.72

WOMEN

Shot
1. Krystyna Zabawska   POL   19.24
2. Valentina Fedyuschina   UKR   18.79
3. JUDY OAKES   18.46

Discus
1. Anastasia Kelesidou   GRE   66.18

2. Anna Söderberg   SWE   63.56
8. SHELLEY DREW   57.94

Hammer
1. Lyudmila Gubkina   BLR   67.30
2. Kirsten Münchow   GER   66.10
8. LYN SPRULES   58.20
12. DIANA HOLDEN   54.80
13. LORRAINE SHAW   52.70

Javelin
1. Rita Ramanauskaite   LIT   61.34
2. Dörte Bärby   GER   61.20
6. LORNA JACKSON   53.72
7. KIRSTY MORRISON   51.44

SLO v Eng v HUN v IRE v CZE   Ljubljana, Slovenia 31 May 1998
Note This should not be considered as a true International

MEN

100 Metres
1. Olapade Adeniken   NGR   10.43
2. OWUSU DAKO   10.48

200 Metres
1. Gary Ryan   IRE   21.24
3. ADRIAN PATRICK   21.63

300 Metres
1. Zefeny Dombi   HUN   33.57
2. SOLOMON WARISO   35.08

400 Metres
1. IWAN THOMAS   45.29
2. JARED DEACON   46.70
3. IAN McGURK   47.57
4. CHRIS CARSON   47.67

800 Metres
1. James Nolan   IRE   1:47.40
4. BRADLEY DONKIN   1:49.01
5. PAUL WALKER   1:49.60
6. GRANT GRAHAM   1:49.60

110 Metres Hurdles
1. TONY JARRETT   13.69

400 Metres Hurdles
1. Tom McGuirk   IRE   50.27
4. GARY CADOGAN   51.29
5. MARK STERN   53.20

Long Jump
1. NATHAN MORGAN   8.04
3. CHRIS DAVIDSON   7.81

Discus
1. Robert Fazekas   HUN   64.57
4. GLEN SMITH   59.66

Hammer
1. Adrian Annus   HUN   78.55
2. PAUL HEAD   69.73

Javelin
1. Gregor Högler   AUT   81.18
2. MARK ROBERTSON   77.40

WOMEN

100 Metres
1. MARCIA RICHARDSON   11.66
2. JOICE MADUAKA   11.78

200 Metres
1. MARCIA RICHARDSON   24.22
4. TRACEY JOSEPH   24.67

400 Metres
1. MICHELLE THOMAS   53.39

800 Metres
1. Oznur Dursun   TUR   2:05.82
3. MICHELLE FAHERTY   2:10.46

100 Metres Hurdles
1. ANGIE THORP   13.69

400 Metres Hurdles
1. GOWRY RETCHAKAN   56.29

High Jump
1. Cigdem Arsian   TUR   1.86
2. SUSAN JONES   1.75

Pole Vault
1. Katalin Donáth   HUN   3.85
3. LUCY WEBBER   3.60

Long Jump
1. Ksenija Predikaka   SLO   6.38
2. TRACEY JOSEPH   6.26

Triple Jump
1. Anja Valant   SLO   13.80
4. KATIE EVANS   12.58

Hammer
1. CATHERINE GARDEN   49.94

AAA COMBINED EVENTS CHAMPIONSHIPS
Derby 30 - 31 May 1998

MEN - Decathlon
1. RAFER JOSEPH   7126
2. Joe Naughton   IRE   6870
3. WILLIAM WYNNE   6700
4. LEO BARKER   6468
5. DOMINIC SHEPHERD   6334
6. STEPHEN GARLAND   6296

WOMEN - Heptathlon
1. CLOVA COURT   5639
2. KIMBERLEY CROWTHER   4680
3. NATALIE BUTLER   4561
4. KATE ROGERS   4559
5. JIMENEZ JOSEPH   4259
6. LISA CARYL   4083

NATIONAL WALKS CHAMPIONSHIPS
Brighton 8 June 1998

MEN (20 Miles)
1. LES MORTON   2:43:01
2. ALLAN KING   2:46:57
3. DON BEARMAN   2:49:19
4. KARL ATTON   2:49:56
5. GARETH BROWN   2:50:58
6. MIKE SMITH   2:55:07

Team
1. Coventry   23
2. Steyning   28
3. Leicester WC   56

U20 Men (10k)
1. MICHAEL KEMP   46:52
2. THOMAS TAYLOR   48:15
3. MATTHEW HALES   49:34

WOMEN (5k)
1. KIM BRAZNELL   24:45
2. DEBORAH WALLEN   25:24
3. AMY HALES   25:52
4. SALLY WARREN   25:57
5. NICOLA HUCKERBY   26:16
6. SARAH BENNETT   26:23

Team
1. Birchfield   15
2. Steyning   25
3. Aldershot   27

94

GB & NI v FRANCE U23   Hexham   14 June 1998

MEN

100 Metres
1.	DWAIN CHAMBERS		10.43
2.	JAMIE HENTHORN		10.44
3.	DANIEL MONEY	gst	10.44
5.	UVIE UGONO	gst	10.50

200 Metres
1.	MARLON DEVONISH	21.11
2.	MARK FINDLAY	21.28

400 Metres
1.	MARK HYLTON		46.87
2.	DANIEL CAINES	gst	47.37
5.	SEAN BALDOCK		47.79
6.	GEOFF DEARMAN	gst	48.48

800 Metres
1.	ALASDAIR DONALDSON		1:51.04
3.	RICHARD GIRVAN		1:51.78
4.	ANDREW YOUNG	gst	1:52.09
6.	NEIL SPEIGHT	gst	1:55.20
7.	NICK McCORMICK	gst	1:58.67

1500 Metres
1.	MICHAEL EAST	gst	3:57.59
3.	ALAN TATHAM	gst	3:58.54
4.	ANDREW GRAFFIN		3:59.02
5.	JAMES THIE		3:59.07
8.	CHRIS DAVIES	gst	4:00.19

3000 Metres
1.	V. Laurent	FRA	8:13.33
3.	ALLEN GRAFFIN		8:22.29
4.	ANDREW CAINE		8:27.18
5.	NATHAN LANE		8:30.62

3000 Metres Steeplechase
1.	BEN WHITBY	gst	8:41.79
4.	CRAIG WHEELER		8:58.49
5.	STUART STOKES		9:00.44
6.	SIMON WURR	gst	9:23.48

110 Metres Hurdles wind 2.0
1.	DAMIEN GREAVES		13.85
4.	DOMINIC BRADLEY		14.38
5.	DUNCAN MALINS	gst	15.02
	ROSS BAILLIE		dnf

400 Metres Hurdles
1.	REMI EDU	52.45
3.	MATT DOUGLAS	53.04

High Jump
1.	BEN CHALLENGER	2.15
3.	ROB BROCKLEBANK	2.00

Pole Vault
1.	Romain Mesnil	FRA	5.10
3.	BEN FLINT		4.80

Long Jump
1.	NATHAN MORGAN	7.67
3.	JAN IRVING	6.82

Triple Jump
1.	Colomba Fofana	FRA	15.48
3.	CHARLES MADEIRA-COLE		15.04
4.	PHILLIP IDOWU		14.38

Shot
1.	Y. Naire	FRA	17.54
3.	BRUCE ROBB		15.04
4.	IAIN McMULLEN		14.08

Discus
1.	Y. Naire	FRA	55.90
3.	BRUCE ROBB		49.42
4.	ANDREW ROLLINGS		44.25

Hammer
1.	Nicolas Figere	FRA	67.22
4.	MIKE FLOYD		60.13
5.	JOHN URQUART		58.93

Javelin
1.	Laurent Dorique	FRA	74.30
3.	STUART LOUGHRAN		62.55
4.	MARK FRANCIS		59.68

5000 Metres Walk
1.	F. Delree	FRA	21:26.34
3.	STEVE HOLLIER		21:42.44
4.	SCOTT TAYLOR		23:31.15

4 x 100 Metres Relay
1.	GB SENIORS	gst	40.09
2.	GREAT BRITAIN & NI		40.11

4 x 400 Metres Relay
1.	GREAT BRITAIN & NI	3:11.65
3.	GREAT BRITAIN & NI B	3:13.54

Match Result
1.	France	122
2.	GREAT BRITAIN & NI	102

WOMEN

100 Metres wind 1.4
1.	S. Citte	FRA	11.57
2.	ELLENA RUDDOCK		11.67
4.	MALGORZATA ROSTEK		11.95
5.	SARAH OXLEY	gst	12.02
7.	VICTORIA SHIPMAN	gst	12.12

200 Metres wind 5.0
1.	F. Feraez	FRA	23.21w
3.	ZOE WILSON		24.28w
4.	SUSAN WILLIAMS		24.34w

400 Metres
1.	ALLISON CURBISHLEY	53.47
2.	LESLEY OWUSU	54.80

800 Metres
1.	Laetitia Valdonado	FRA	2:08.61
2.	EMMA DAVIES		2:08.88
4.	KELLY McNIECE	gst	2:12.21
5.	KERRY SMITHSON		2:13.60

1500 Metres
1.	SUSAN SCOTT	gst	4:31.89
3.	ELLEN O'HARE		4:33.57
5.	EMMA FORD		4:37.40

3000 Metres
1.	JILLY INGMAN	gst	9:35.96
2.	AMY WATERLOW		9:38.10
4.	SHEILA FAIRWEATHER		9:42.44
5.	HAYLEY PARKINSON	gst	9:45.73

100 Metres Hurdles wind 3.1
1.	RACHEL KING	13.72w
3.	ELIZABETH FAIRS	13.86w

400 Metres Hurdles
1.	VICKI JAMISON	56.98
2.	SINEAD DUDGEON	60.34

High Jump
1.	SUSAN JONES	1.80
2.	LEE McCONNELL	1.70

Pole Vault
cancelled

Long Jump
1.	Sarah Gautreau	FRA	6.27
3.	ADELE FORESTER		5.44
4.	JULIE HOLLMAN		4.47

Triple Jump
1.	M-Véronique Mazarin	FRA	12.59
3.	JODIE HURST		11.77
4.	ELIZABETH GIBBENS		11.56

Shot
1.	CHRISTINA BENNETT	14.82
2.	ELEANOR GATRELL	14.14

Discus
1.	PHILIPPA ROLES	52.76
4.	ELEANOR GARDEN	39.88

Hammer
1.	Manuela Montebrun	FRA	55.54
2.	LIZ PIDGEON		55.17
4.	CATHERINE GARDEN		52.57

Javelin
1.	Sarah Walter	FRA	48.56
3.	KATIE AMOS		47.75
4.	TAMARA FRANCIS		41.83

3000 Metres Walk
1.	M. Fabiella	FRA	14:22.36
2.	DEBBIE WALLEN		14:23.48
3.	SALLY WARREN		15:06.06

4 x 100 Metres Relay
1.	France	46.57
2.	GREAT BRITAIN & NI	46.68
3.	GREAT BRITAIN & NI B	47.57

4 x 400 Metres Relay
1.	GREAT BRITAIN & NI	3:42.62

Match Result
1.	France	110
2.	GREAT BRITAIN & NI	99

EUROPEAN CUP SUPER LEAGUE St Petersburg, Russia 27 - 28 June 1998
MEN

100 Metres wind -0.4 (27 Jun)
1.	Stephane Cali	FRA	10.32
2.	Aleksandr Porkhomovskiy	RUS	10.40
3.	COLIN JACKSON		10.41
4.	Carlo Boccarini	ITA	10.52
5.	Marc Blume	GER	10.61
6.	Ivan Slehobr	CZE	10.61
7.	Sami Lansivuori	FIN	10.67
8.	Frutos Feo	ESP	10.71

200 Metres wind 1.4 (28 Jun)
1.	DOUG WALKER		20.42
2.	Christophe Cheval	FRA	20.61
3.	Alessandro Attene	ITA	20.69
4.	Martin Morkes	CZE	20.85
5.	Javier Navarro	ESP	21.01
6.	Daniel Bittner	GER	21.02
7.	Aleksandr Porkhomovskiy	RUS	21.02
8.	Janne Hautaniemi	FIN	21.32

400 Metres (27 Jun)
1.	MARK RICHARDSON		45.81
2.	Jan Podebradsky	CZE	46.10
3.	Dimitriy Golovastov	RUS	46.50
4.	Marc Foucan	FRA	46.58
5.	Marco Vaccari	ITA	46.62
6.	David Canal	ESP	47.16
7.	Jens Dautzenberg	GER	47.50
8.	Petri Pohjonen	FIN	47.79

800 Metres (28 Jun)
1.	Andrea Longo	ITA	1:45.40
2.	Lukas Vydra	CZE	1:45.92
3.	ANDY HART		1:46.19
4.	Wilson Kirwa	FIN	1:46.30
5.	Sergey Kozhevnikov	RUS	1:46.61
6.	Nico Motchebon	GER	1:46.92
7.	David Divad	FRA	1:47.14
8.	Andres Diaz	ESP	1:47.62

1500 Metres (27 Jun)
1.	Giuseppe D'Urso	ITA	3:44.58
2.	Reyes Estevez	ESP	3:44.91
3.	JOHN MAYOCK		3:45.09
4.	Nadir Bosch	FRA	3:45.12
5.	Rudiger Stenzel	GER	3:45.12
6.	Lukas Vydra	CZE	3:45.71
7.	Vyacheslav Shabunin	RUS	3:46.67
8.	Juha Kukkamo	FIN	3:48.20

3000 Metres (27 Jun)
1.	Dieter Baumann	GER	7:41.92
2.	Manuel Pancorbo	ESP	7:42.24
3.	ANTHONY WHITEMAN		7:43.61
4.	Abdellah Behar	FRA	7:44.59
5.	Jan Pesava	CZE	7:46.72
6.	Samuli Vasala	FIN	7:52.97
7.	Salvatore Vincenti	ITA	7:59.69
8.	Sergey Drygin	RUS	8:01.65

5000 Metres (28 Jun)
1.	Alberto Garcia	ESP	13:37.45
2.	Mustapha Essaid	FRA	13:37.79
3.	Stephane Franke	GER	13:38.90
4.	Jan Pesava	CZE	13:45.04
5.	Vyacheslav Shabunin	RUS	13:57.77
6.	KARL KESKA		13:59.30
7.	Lucianco Di Pardo	ITA	14:18.58
8.	Santtu Makinen	FIN	14:28.63

3000 Metres Steeplechase (28 Jun)
1.	Alessandro Lambruschini	ITA	8:32.96
2.	Andre Green	GER	8:34.21
3.	Mohamed Belabbes	FRA	8:35.12
4.	Vladimir Pronin	RUS	8:38.33
5.	Alberto Genoves	ESP	8:41.17
6.	BEN WHITBY		8:42.12
7.	Michael Nejedly	CZE	8:42.25
8.	Ville Hautala	FIN	8:42.46

110 Metres Hurdles 0.0 (28 Jun)
1.	COLIN JACKSON		13.17
2.	Falk Balzer	GER	13.22
3.	Jean-Marc Grava	FRA	13.63
4.	Emiliano Pizzoli	ITA	13.68
5.	Sergey Manakov	RUS	13.68
6.	Tomas Dvorak	CZE	13.92
7.	Antti Haapakoski	FIN	14.04
8.	Carlos Sala	ESP	14.08

400 Metres Hurdles (27 Jun)
1.	Ruslan Mashchenko	RUS	48.49
2.	Fabrizio Mori	ITA	48.57
3.	Steffen Kolb	GER	49.43
4.	Jan Podebradsky	CZE	49.66
5.	TONY BORSUMATO		49.79
6.	Petteri Pulkkinnen	FIN	50.38
7.	Jimmy Coco	FRA	50.48
8.	Iigo Monreal	ESP	50.71

High Jump (27 Jun)
1.	Sergey Klyugin	RUS	2.28
2.	BEN CHALLENGER		2.28
3.	Tomas Janku	CZE	2.25
4=	Martin Buss	GER	2.20
4=	Ivan Bernasconi	ITA	2.20
6.	Arturo Ortiz	ESP	2.20
7.	Didier Detchenique	FRA	2.15
8.	Mika Polku	FIN	2.15

Pole Vault (28 Jun)
1.	Yevgeniy Smiryagin	RUS	5.60
2=	Javier Garcia	ESP	5.50
2=	Heikki Vääräniemi	FIN	5.50
4.	Danny Ecker	GER	5.50
5=	Andrea Giannini	ITA	5.40
5=	Jean Galifone	FRA	5.40
7.	Stephan Janacek	CZE	5.30
	MIKE EDWARDS		nh

Long Jump (27 Jun)
1.	Kirill Sosunov	RUS	8.38
2.	Milan Kovar	CZE	8.14
3.	NATHAN MORGAN		7.85
4.	Thorsten Heide	GER	7.85
5.	Paolo Camossi	ITA	7.79
6.	Emmanuel Bangue	FRA	7.78
7.	Yago Lamela	ESP	7.75
8.	Niklas Rorarius	FIN	7.62

Triple Jump (28 Jun)
1.	JONATHAN EDWARDS		17.29
2.	Jiri Kuntos	CZE	16.91
3.	Hrvoje Verzl	GER	16.74
4.	Raul Chapado	ESP	16.60
5.	Johan Meriluoto	FIN	16.44
6.	Colomba Fofana	FRA	16.40
7.	Fabrizio Donato	ITA	16.32
8.	Andrey Kurennoy	RUS	15.95

Shot (27 Jun)
1.	Mika Halvari	FIN	20.79
2.	Oliver-Sven Buder	GER	19.97
3.	Manuel Martinez	ESP	19.86
4.	Petr Stehlik	CZE	18.59
5.	Corrado Fantini	ITA	18.41
6.	MARK PROCTOR		17.98
7.	Rocky Vaitanacki	FRA	17.82
8.	Pavel Chumachenko	RUS	17.28

Discus (28 Jun)
1.	Dmitriy Shevchenko	RUS	65.14
2.	Jurgen Schult	GER	64.37
3.	Diego Fortuna	ITA	62.49
4.	BOB WEIR		59.75
5.	Libor Malina	CZE	59.29
6.	Jean-Claude Retel	FRA	59.13
7.	Harri Uurainen	FIN	58.57
8.	Jose Luis Valencia	ESP	57.27

Hammer (28 Jun)
1.	Heinz Weis	GER	79.68
2.	Ilya Konovalov	RUS	79.68
3.	Enrico Sgrulletti	ITA	78.13
4.	Vladimir Maska	CZE	74.24
5.	Gilles Dupray	FRA	73.63
6.	MICK JONES		72.28
7.	Olli-Pekka Karjalainen	FIN	68.94
8.	Jose Manuel Perez	ESP	66.90

Javelin (28 Jun)
1.	Boris Henry	GER	84.72
2.	Sergey Makarov	RUS	84.37
3.	Aki Parviainen	FIN	84.33
4.	MICK HILL		83.50
5.	Carlo Sonego	ITA	77.02
6.	Gaetan Siakinou	FRA	76.38
7.	Patrick Landmesser	CZE	75.25
8.	Raimundo Fernandez	ESP	68.58

4 x 100 Metres Relay (27 Jun)
1.	GREAT BRITAIN & NI	38.56
	(CONDON, CAMPBELL, WALKER, GOLDING)	
2.	France	38.90
3.	Russia	39.13
4.	Italy	39.22
5.	Germany	39.60
6.	Spain	39.60
7.	Czech Republic	39.67
8.	Finland	39.69

4 x 400 Metres Relay (28 Jun)
1.	GREAT BRITAIN & NI	3:00.95
	(BLACK, BAULCH, THOMAS, RICHARDSON)	
2.	Italy	3:03.45
3.	France	3:03.57
4.	Russia	3:03.83
5.	Germany	3:04.49
6.	Czech Republic	3:05.69
7.	Spain	3:06.73
8.	Finland	3:08.39

Match Result
1.	GREAT BRITAIN & NI	111
2.	Germany	108.5
3.	Russia	102
4.	Italy	101
5.	France	89.5
6.	Czech Republic	87
7.	Spain	67.5
8.	Finland	52.5

WOMEN

100 Metres wind 1.2 (27 Jun)
1. Irina Privalova   RUS   11.04
2. Christine Arron   FRA   11.14
3. Andrea Philipp   GER   11.26
4. Alenka Bikar   SLO   11.54
5. Tatyana Lukyanenko   UKR   11.57
6. MARCIA RICHARDSON   11.57
7. Manuela Levorato   ITA   11.57
8. Pavlina Vostatkova   CZE   11.61

200 Metres wind -0.9 (28 Jun)
1. Erika Suchovska   CZE   22.96
2. Sylviane Felix   FRA   22.96
3. Melanie Paschke   GER   22.98
4. Yekaterina Leshchova   RUS   23.06
5. KATHARINE MERRY   23.22
6. Manuela Levorato   ITA   23.34
7. Tatyana Lukyanenko   UKR   23.43
8. Tina Matul   SLO   24.36

400 Metres (27 Jun)
1. Helena Fuchsova   CZE   51.33
2. Irina Rosikhina   RUS   51.48
3. ALLISON CURBISHLEY   51.48
4. Uta Rohlander   GER   51.76
5. Patrizia Spuri   ITA   52.65
6. Viviane Dorsile   FRA   53.64
7. Galina Misiruk   UKR   54.69
8. Brigita Langerholc   SLO   54.73

800 Metres (27 Jun)
1. Larisa Mikhaylova   RUS   1:58.01
2. Irina Lishchinskaya   UKR   1:59.15
3. Ludmila Formanova   CZE   1:59.44
4. Heike Meissner   GER   2:00.12
5. Patricia Djate-Taillard FRA 2:00.16
6. TANYA BLAKE   2:02.06
7. Claudia Salvarini   ITA   2:02.99
8. Jolanda Ceplak   SLO   2:03.70

1500 Metres (28 Jun)
1. Olga Komyagina   RUS   4:05.88
2. PAULA RADCLIFFE   4:05.92
3. Andrea Suldesova   CZE   4:06.25
4. Frederique Quentin   FRA   4:10.21
5. Sylvia Kuhnemund   GER   4:11.15
6. Sara Palmas   ITA   4:12.44
7. Sonja Roman   SLO   4:14.85
8. Natalya Ivanova   UKR   4:19.57

3000 Metres (28 Jun)
1. Olga Yegorova   RUS   9:04.03
2. Blandine Bitzner-Ducret FRA 9:06.74
3. Luminita Zaituc   GER   9:10.18
4. Elisa Rea   ITA   9:11.54
5. Helena Javornik   SLO   9:12.13
6. Andrea Suldesova   CZE   9:13.99
7. ANGELA DAVIES   9:17.03
8. Yelena Gorodnychova   UKR   9:21.62

5000 Metres (27 Jun)
1. PAULA RADCLIFFE   15:06.87
2. Krist. da Fonseca-Wollheim GER 15:10.33
3. Joalsiae Llado   FRA 15:17.58
4. Helena Javornik   SLO 15:27.50
5. Mariya Pantyukhova   RUS 15:37.82
6. Maria Guida   ITA 15:38.68
7. Natalya Berkut   UKR 15:57.24
8. Petra Drajzajtlova   CZE 16:08.71

100 Metres Hurdles 0.0 (28 Jun)
1. Brigita Bukovec   SLO   12.89
2. Patricia Girard   FRA   12.89
3. Tatyana Reshetnikova   RUS   13.06
4. Heike Blassneck   GER   13.22
5. Andrea Novotna   CZE   13.36
6. ANGIE THORP   13.45
7. Margaret Macchiut   ITA   13.53
8. Tatyana Tereshchuk   UKR   13.67

400 Metres Hurdles (27 Jun)
1. Tatyana Tereshchuk   UKR   54.15
2. Yekaterina Bakhvalova RUS   54.72
3. Silvia Rieger   GER   54.93
4. Florence Delaune   FRA   57.01
5. VICKY JAMISON   57.51
6. Laura Rocco   ITA   58.02
7. Meta Macus   SLO   58.42
8. Martina Blazkova   CZE   59.19

High Jump (28 Jun)
1. Zuzana Kovacikova   CZE   1.98
2. Alina Astafei   GER   1.95
3. Yelena Gulyayeva   RUS   1.95
4. Viktoria Styopina   UKR   1.92
5. JO JENNINGS   1.89
6. Francesca Bradamante   ITA   1.89
7. Marie Collonville   FRA   1.89
8. Britta Bilac   SLO   1.86

Pole Vault (27 Jun)
1. Daniela Bartova   CZE   4.35
2. JANINE WHITLOCK   4.30
3. Nicole Rieger   GER   4.20
4. Lyudmila Prikhodko   UKR   3.80
5. Caroline Ammel   FRA   3.80
6. Francesca Dolcini   ITA   3.60
7. Teja Melink   SLO   3.60
    Yelena Belyakova   RUS   nh

Long Jump (28 Jun)
1. Fiona May   ITA   7.08
2. Lyudmila Galkina   RUS   6.84
3. Linda Ferga   FRA   6.75
4. Susan Tiedtke   GER   6.59
5. Sarka Kasparkova   CZE   6.52
6. Yelena Khlopotnova   UKR   6.40
7. SARAH CLAXTON   6.32
8. Ksenija Predikaka   SLO   6.16

Triple Jump (27 Jun)
1. Fiona May   ITA   14.65
2. Sarka Kasparkova   CZE   14.63
3. Yelena Govorova   UKR   14.13
4. CONNIE HENRY   13.95
5. Yelena Donkina   RUS   13.92
6. Sylvie Borda   FRA   13.71
7. Nkechi Madubuko   GER   13.10
8. Anja Valant   SLO   13.00

Shot (28 Jun)
1. Irina Korzhanenko   RUS   20.65
2. JUDY OAKES   18.38
3. Stephanie Storp   GER   18.38
4. Mara Rosolen   ITA   18.16
5. Natasa Erjavec   SLO   16.96
6. Laurence Manfredi   FRA   16.77
7. Zdenka Silhava   CZE   16.27
8. Nadezhda Lukyniv   UKR   15.49

Discus (27 Jun)
1. Natalya Sadova   RUS   64.18
2. Anja Mollenbeck   GER   60.80
3. Yelena Antonova   UKR   59.28
4. Agnese Maffeis   ITA   58.78
5. Isabelle Devaluez   FRA   57.48
6. SHELLEY DREW   56.10
7. Zdenka Silhava   CZE   54.24
8. Natasa Erjavec   SLO   46.52

Hammer (27 Jun)
1. Olga Kuzenkova   RUS   65.89
2. Kirsten Munchow   GER   64.86
3. Cecile Lignot   FRA   61.12
4. Ester Balassini   ITA   59.48
5. LORRAINE SHAW   58.02
6. Jana Lejskova   CZE   53.33
7. Natalya Kunitskaya   UKR   51.00
8. Simona Kozmus   SLO   47.43

Javelin (27 Jun)
1. Tanja Damaske   GER   62.30
2. Nikola Tomeckova   CZE   60.82
3. Oksana Makarova   RUS   58.38
4. Claudia Coslovich   ITA   57.69
5. Nadine Auzeil   FRA   56.56
6. LORNA JACKSON   54.56
7. Evfemija Storga   SLO   54.02
8. Olga Ivankova   UKR   53.72

4 x 100 Metres Relay (27 Jun)
1. Russia   42.49
2. Germany   42.59
3. France   42.61
4. Ukraine   44.48
5. Italy   44.58
6. Czech Republic   45.70
7. Slovenia   45.76
    GREAT BRITAIN & NI   dq
(RICHARDSON, MADUAKA, RUDDOCK, WHITLOCK)

4 x 400 Metres Relay (28 Jun)
1. Russia   3:25.52
2. Czech Republic   3:28.05
3. GREAT BRITAIN & NI   3:28.07
(JAMISON, FRASER, THOMAS, CURBISHLEY)
4. Italy   3:30.14
5. France   3:30.27
6. Germany   3:30.36
7. Ukraine   3:31.60
8. Slovenia   3:40.39

Match Result
1. Russia   124
2. Germany   108
3. France   93
4. Czech Republic   89
5. GREAT BRITAIN & NI   81
6. Italy   78
7. Ukraine   64
8. Slovenia   45

HUN v Eng v CZE v IRE v SLO Budapest, Hungary 5 July 1998

MEN

100 Metres wind -0.4
1. DARREN CAMPBELL   10.36
4. EDWARD WHITE   10.70

100 Metres Invitation wind 0.6
1. DARREN CAMPBELL   10.33

200 Metres wind 2.1
1. Tyree Washington USA/gst 20.40w
6. EDWARD WHITE   21.38w

400 Metres
1. IWAN THOMAS   WAL/gst 45.37
5. GUY BULLOCK   47.89

800 Metres
1. James Nolan   IRE 1:48.86
2. CRAIG WINROW   1:51.46

110 Metres Hurdles Race 1 1.4
1. TONY JARRETT   13.43

110 Metres Hurdles Race 2 1.7
1. Mark Crear   USA/gst 13.28
3. TONY JARRETT   13.45

400 Metres Hurdles
1. Neil Gardener   JAM/gst 49.76
2. GARY CADOGAN   51.56

Triple Jump
1. Zsolt Czingler   HUN 17.07
2. JULIAN GOLLEY   16.51

Hammer (IAAF GP Event)
1. Vasiliy Sidorenko RUS 80.26
15. MICHAEL JONES   70.12

WOMEN

100 Metres wind 1.3
1. Cheryl Taplin   USA/gst 11.41
3. SIMMONE JACOBS   11.71

200 Metres wind 0.0
1. Ionela Tirlea   ROM/gst 22.94
2. SIMMONE JACOBS   23.80

400 Metres
1. Helena Fuchsová   CZE 51.40
2. DONNA FRASER   52.49

800 Metres
1. Judit Varga   HUN 2:04.92
3. EMMA DAVIES   WAL/gst 2:06.52

1500 Metres
1. Olga Komyagina RUS/gst 4:12.97
2. HELEN PATTINSON   4:17.31

400 Metres Hurdles
1. Ionela Tirlea   ROM/gst 55.64
4. NATASHA DANVERS   58.14

High Jump
1. Dóra Györffy   HUN 1.90
2. MICHELLE DUNKLEY   1.80

Pole Vault
1. Eszter Szemerédi HUN 4.15
   EMMA HORNBY   nh
   RHIAN CLARKE   WAL/gst   nh

Long Jump
1. Valentina Gotovska LAT/gst 6.42
2. CORINNE HENRY   6.06

Discus
1. Irina Yatchenko   BLR/gst 61.21
3. SHELLEY DREW   57.80

4. JACKIE McKERNAN gst   57.10

Javelin
1. Nikola Tomecková CZE 61.78
5. KAREN MARTIN   54.65

Match Result
1. Hungary   63
2. Czech Republic   62
3. ENGLAND   54
4. Slovakia   41
5. Ireland   32

This is not considered a true
International Match

EUROPEAN CUP COMBINED EVENTS
Bressanone, Italy 4 - 5 July 1998

MEN Decathlon
1. Sebastian Chmara   POL 8067
2. Francisco Benet   ESP 8000
3. Jaime Peñas   ESP 7811
4. Aleksandr Yurkov   UKR 7748
5. Vladimir Mikhailenko UKR 7712
6. Beniamino Poserina ITA 7667
7. JAMIE QUARRY   7504
8. RAFER JOSEPH   7392
9. ALEXIS SHARP   7112
10. DU'AINE LADEJO   7003

Team
1. Spain   22,927
2. Ukraine   22,806
3. Poland   22,494
6. GREAT BRITAIN & NI 22,008

WOMEN Heptathlon
1. Gertrud Bacher   ITA 6091
2. Karin Perignelli ITA 6008
3. Katerina Nekolná CZE 5941
4. Inga Michailová   CZE 5796
5. Deborah Feltrin   ITA 5770
6. KERRY JURY   5686
9. CLOVA COURT   5656
12. PAULINE RICHARDS   5563
13. JULIE HOLLMAN   5557

Team
1. Italy   17,869
2. Czech Republic   17,415
3. GREAT BRITAIN & NI 16,905

HOME COUNTIES COMBINED EVENTS
Wrexham 1 - 2 August 1998

MEN Decathlon
1. Joe Naughton   IRE 6860
2. ROGER HUNTER   ENG 6812
3. LEO BARKER   ENG 6457
4. PAUL JONES   WAL 6389
5. Darragh O'Farrell IRE 6336
6. BILL WYNN   ENG 6269

Team
1. ENGLAND   19,538
2. Ireland   19,060
3. WALES   14,805

WOMEN Heptathlon
1. DIANA BENNETT   ENG 5425
2. KATHERINE LIVESEY ENG 5015
3. KIM CROWTHER   ENG 4858
4. AMANDA WALE   WAL 4546
5. Orna O'Donoghue   IRE 4434
6. LISA THOMPSON   WAL 4357

Team
1. ENGLAND   15,298
2. WALES   13,132
3. Ireland   12,165
4. NORTHERN IRELAND 11,859

SPAIN v GB & NI v FRANCE U20　Alicante, Spain　18 July 1998

MEN

100 Metres wind 3.8
1. CHRISTIAN MALCOLM　10.10w
3. JONATHAN BARBOUR　10.52w
7. CHRIS LAMBERT　10.69w

200 Metres wind 2.6
1. TIM BENJAMIN　20.98w
2. JOHN STEWART　21.16w
7. BEN LEWIS　22.46w

400 Metres Race A
1. ALLOY WILSON　47.31
2. DAVID NAISMITH　47.99

400 Metres Race B
1. CHRIS CARSON　47.58
2. ADAM BUCKLEY　47.93

800 Metres
1. Aissat Nicolas　FRA　1:50.60
3. CHRIS MOSS　1:50.93
5. PAUL FISHER　1:52.94

1500 Metres
1. Joussef El Nasri　ESP　3:45.13
2. RICHARD VINT　3:49.72
6. CHRIS LIVESEY　3:56.27

3000 Metres
1. Alvaro Jimenez　ESP　8:22.43
4. ANDREW BECKWITH　8:27.05
5. DAVID HIBBERT　8:34.16

5000 Metres
1. Ivan Galan　ESP　14:46.09
4. STEPHEN HEPPLES　15:06.95
5. OLIVER LAWS　15:15.23

3000 Metres Steeplechase
1. Adrian Pena　ESP　8:54.50
4. CHRIS THOMPSON　9:07.99
7. IAIN MURDOCH　9:19.36

110 Metres Hurdles wind 0.7
1. Desire Delric　FRA　14.20
2. ROBERT NEWTON　14.57
　 BEN WARMINGTON　disq

400 Metres Hurdles
1. Jean Roberto Harris FRA　52.64
3. RICHARD McDONALD　53.16
5. AUSTIN FERNS　54.14

High Jump
1. DANIEL GRAHAM　2.11
4. MARTIN LLOYD　2.00

Pole Vault
1. Gildas Verbist　FRA　5.20
2. CHRISTIAN LINSKEY　5.10
5. SCOTT SIMPSON　4.50

Long Jump
1. Leslie Djhone　FRA　7.73
3. STUART WELLS　7.37
6. NICHOLAS TAYLOR　6.53

Triple Jump
1. Sébastien Pincemail FRA　15.96w
2. NICHOLAS THOMAS　15.70
　 JONATHAN WALLACE　nm

Shot
1. EMEKA UDECHUKU　16.92
6. GRAEME ALLAN　13.57

Discus
1. EMEKA UDECHUKU　58.08
3. LUKE ROSENBERG　45.31

Hammer
1. Nicolas Figere　FRA　67.59
3. ANDREW GRIERSON　59.12
5. ROSS KIDNER　53.09

Javelin
1. DAN CARTER　68.45
2. PHILLIP SHARPE　65.31

10000 Metres Walk
1. Juan Molina　ESP　43:57.42
3. THOMAS TAYLOR　47:31.97
5. MICHAEL KEMP　48:30.78

4 x 100 Metres Relay
1. France　40.17
2. GREAT BRITAIN & NI　40.29
(LAMBERT, BENJAMIN, MALCOLM, BARBOUR)

4 x 400 Metres Relay
1. GREAT BRITAIN & NI　3:10.76
(NAISMITH, BUCKLEY, CARSON, WILSON)

Match Result
1. France　166
2. GREAT BRITAIN & NI　147
3. SPAIN　128

WOMEN

100 Metres Race A wind 3.0
1. ABIODUN OYEPITAN　11.50w
2. SAMANTHA DAVIES　11.50w

100 Metres Race B wind 3.0
1. MARIA BOLSOVER　11.77w

200 Metres wind 4.2
1. Muriel Hurtis　FRA　22.87w
2. SARAH WILHELMY　23.20w
3. MELANIE PURKISS　23.67w
5. REBECCA WHITE　24.05w

400 Metres Race A
1. CAREY EASTON　54.78
2. KIM WALL　55.39

400 Metres Race B
1. Laure Kouassi　FRA　55.55
2. KAREN GEAR　56.20
4. ABIGAIL NAUGHER　57.93

800 Metres
1. Natalia Rodriguez　ESP　2:07.65
3. EMMA WARD　2:12.53
5. WENDY DAVIS　2:14.57

1500 Metres
1. TOMI KEMP　4:29.30
4. CAROLINE WALSH　4:32.60

3000 Metres
1. Vanesa Veiga　ESP　9:25.81
3. LOUISE KELLY　9:28.64
4. AMBER GASCOIGNE　9:36.83

100 Metres Hurdles wind 1.9
1. SARAH CLAXTON　13.62
2. JULIE PRATT　13.70

400 Metres Hurdles
1. TRACEY DUNCAN　59.56
2. RACHAEL KAY　59.62

High Jump
1. Anne Jardin　FRA　1.82
2. GILLIAN BLACK　1.80
5. AILEEN WILSON　1.74

Pole Vault
1. Amandine Homo　FRA　3.90
4. TRACEY BLOOMFIELD　3.45
7. DANIELLE CODD　3.30

Long Jump
1. Celia Harmenil　FRA　6.36w
2. SARAH CLAXTON　6.27w
6. SYREENA PINEL　5.88

Triple Jump
1. Yasmina Soualha　FRA　12.84w
6. JULIA JOHNSON　12.08
7. JUDY KOTEY　11.74w

Shot
1. Amadji Ndiave　FRA　14.45
3. JULIE DUNKLEY　14.23
6. JULIE McCORRY　12.63

Discus
1. Milina Robert-Michon FRA　55.80
2. LAUREN KEIGHTLEY　52.31
5. JOANNA BRADLEY　41.53

Hammer
1. Manuela Montebrun FRA　55.08
4. CARYS PARRY　48.85
5. ZOE DERHAM　47.69

Javelin
1. Bina Ramesh　FRA　54.59
3. KELLY MORGAN　48.68
5. GOLDIE SAYERS　46.25

5000 Metres Walk
1. Vanesa Espinosa　ESP　23:33.0
4. KATIE FORD　25:25.4
6. SARAH BENNETT　26:01.4

4 x 100 Metres Relay
1. France　44.40
2. GREAT BRITAIN & NI　44.54
(OYEPITAN, WILHELMY, DAVIES, WHITE)

4 x 400 Metres Relay
1. GREAT BRITAIN & NI　3:40.75
(NAUGHER, GEAR, WALL, EASTON)

Match Result
1. France　152
2. GREAT BRITAIN & NI　139
3. Spain　107

AAA CHAMPIONSHIPS Birmingham 24 - 26 July 1998
Including European & Commonwealth Trials

MEN

100 Metres wind -1.7 (25 Jul)
1. DARREN CAMPBELL 10.22
2. DWAINE CHAMBERS 10.23
3. MARLON DEVONISH 10.26
4. JASON GARDENER 10.30
5. JOSEPHUS THOMAS 10.32
6. OWUSU DAKO 10.36
7. MARCUS ADAM 10.58
8. KEVIN WILLIAMS 10.67

200 Metres wind -1.5 (26 Jul)
1. DOUG WALKER 20.35
2. DOUG TURNER 20.55
3. JULIAN GOLDING 20.88
4. JOHN REGIS 20.89
5. ALLYN CONDON 20.93
6. MARCUS ADAM 20.99
7. OWUSU DAKO 21.20
8. ANDREW WALCOTT 21.35

400 Metres (26 Jul)
1. IWAN THOMAS 44.50
2. MARK RICHARDSON 44.62
3. SOLOMON WARISO 44.68
4. ROGER BLACK 44.71
5. MARK HYLTON 45.30
6. SEAN BALDOCK 45.50
7. PAUL SLYTHE 45.94
8. JAMIE BAULCH 46.17

800 Metres (26 Jul)
1. JASON LOBO 1:49.68
2. GRANT GRAHAM 1:49.73
3. EDDIE KING 1:49.74
4. PHILIP TULBA-MORRISON 1:50.07
5. NOEL EDWARDS 1:50.14
6. MATTHEW SHONE 1:50.45
7. BRAD DONKIN 1:50.67
   PAUL WALKER dnf

1500 Metres (25 Jul)
1. JOHN MAYOCK 3:39.38
2. ANTHONY WHITEMAN 3:39.52
3. MATT YATES 3:40.38
4. KEVIN McKAY 3:40.78
5. MICHAEL OPENSHAW 3:43.50
6. IAN GRIME 3:44.06
7. VINCE WILSON 3:44.63
8. GARY LOUGH 3:44.99

3000 Metres (Sheffield 16 Aug)
1. NICK COMERFORD 8:11.98
2= ALLEN GRAFFIN 8:12.41
2= DAVID TAYLOR 8:12.41
4. ANDREW GRAFFIN 8:15.40
5. MARTIN PALMER 8:25.93

5000 Metres (25 Jul)
1. KARL KESKA 13:41.61
2. JON BROWN 13:41.72
3. KEITH CULLEN 13:43.15
4. KRIS BOWDITCH 13:43.86
5. ROD FINCH 13:49.46
6. IAN GILLESPIE 13:51.24
7. GLYNN TROMANS 13:53.59
8. ROB DENMARK 13:53.86

10000 Metres (Bedford 4 Jul)
1. DERMOT DONNELLY 28:43.17
2. CARL THACKERY 28:52.71
3. ROB DENMARK 29:17.72
4. MARK HUDSPITH 29:22.88
5. DAVID TAYLOR 29:24.15
6. ROBERT QUINN 29:25.55
7. DAVID TUNE 29:29.23
8. ADRIAN MUSSETT 29:40.96

3000 Metres Steeplechase (26 Jul)
1. CHRISTIAN STEPHENSON 8:32.76
2. SPENCER DUVAL 8:36.37
3. CRAIG WHEELER 8:42.83
4. BEN WHITBY 8:47.69
5. Andrew Colvin AUS 8:48.23
6. LEE HURST 8:49.63
7. ANDY COLEMAN 8:52.35
8. ANDREW MORGAN-LEE 8:57.56

110 Metres Hurdles -1.3 (26 Jul)
1. COLIN JACKSON 13.37
2. TONY JARRETT 13.42
3. DAMIEN GREAVES 13.88
4. ROSS BAILLIE 13.90
5. LLOYD COWAN 14.03
6. NEIL OWEN 14.33
7. KEN CAMPBELL 14.42
8. MARTYN HENDRY 14.63

400 Metres Hurdles (25 Jul)
1. PAUL GRAY 49.81
2. ANTHONY BORSUMATO 49.85
3. CHRIS RAWLINSON 50.20
4. MATT DOUGLAS 50.41
5. GARY JENNINGS 51.11
6. EDDIE BETTS 51.63
7. LAWRENCE LYNCH 51.71
8. BLAIR YOUNG 52.00

High Jump (25 Jul)
1. DALTON GRANT 2.20
2= BRENDAN REILLY 2.15
2= STANLEY OSUIDE 2.15
2= STUART OHRLAND 2.15
5. IAN HOLLIDAY 2.15
6. GEOFF PARSONS 2.10
7. COLIN BENT 2.10
8. RICHARD ASPDEN 2.10

Pole Vault (26 Jul)
1. KEVIN HUGHES 5.40
2. MATT BELSHAM 5.35
3. IAN TULLETT 5.35
4. PAUL WILLIAMSON 5.20
5. DEAN MELLOR 5.10
6= MIKE EDWARDS 5.00
6= BEN FLINT 5.00
8. TIM THOMAS 5.00

Long Jump (24 Jul)
1. NATHAN MORGAN 8.11
2. CHRIS DAVIDSON 7.71
3. STEVE PHILLIPS 7.48
4. JULIAN FLYNN 7.43w
5. JOHN MUNROE 7.38

6. ANDREW LEWIS 7.30
7. BARRINGTON WILLIAMS 7.29
8. STUART WELLS 7.20

Triple Jump (26 Jul)
1. JONATHAN EDWARDS 17.12
2. ONOCHIE ACHIKE 16.42
3. JULIAN GOLLEY 16.28
4. FEMI AKINSANYA 16.16
5. TAYO EROGBOGBO 16.12
6. PHILLIPS IDOWU 15.90
7. ALVIN WALKER 15.56
8. TOSI FASINRO 15.46

Shot (26 Jul)
1. MARK PROCTOR 19.50
2. SHAUN PICKERING 18.87
3. MARK EDWARDS 18.52
4. STEPHAN HAYWARD 18.03
5. MATT SIMSON 17.20
6. GARY SOLLITT 16.52
7. DAVID CALLAWAY 16.32

Discus (25 Jul)
1. ROBERT WEIR 62.82
2. GLEN SMITH 60.56
3. EMEKA UDECHUKU 57.90
4. PERRIS WILKINS 57.89
5. LEE NEWMAN 57.47
6. KEVIN BROWN 57.40
7. LEITH MARAR 53.62
8. GARY HERRINGTON 52.52

Hammer (26 Jul)
1. MICK JONES 72.13
2. PAUL HEAD 69.46
3. BILL BEAUCHAMP 66.56
4. DAVE SMITH 65.51
5. SHANE PEACOCK 64.53
6. CHRIS HOWE 64.28
7. JOHN PEARSON 63.72
8. STEVE PEARSON 62.74

Javelin (26 Jul)
1. STEVE BACKLEY 84.78
2. MICK HILL 81.55
3. MARK ROBERSON 78.93
4. NICK NIELAND 75.69
5. STUART FABEN 68.93
6. STUART LOUGHRAN 68.91
7. NIGEL BEVAN 67.96
8. STEPHEN HARRISON 67.69

10000 Metres Walk (26 Jul)
1. MARTIN BELL 41:48.81
2. STEVE PARTINGTON 42:27.21
3. ANDI DRAKE 42:46.26
4. MARK EASTON 44:04.41
5. MARTIN YOUNG 44:21.63
6. JAMIE O'RAWE 44:32.81
7. RICHARD OLDALE 44:55.16
8. STEVEN HOLLIER 45:08.97

WOMEN

100 Metres wind 0.9 (25 Jul)
1.	JOICE MADUAKA	11.40
2.	MARCIA RICHARDSON	11.46
3.	SIMMONE JACOBS	11.56
4.	ELLENA RUDDOCK	11.74
5.	CHRISTINE BLOOMFIELD	11.78
6.	SAMANTHA DAVIES	11.84
7.	ABIODUN OYEPITAN	11.86
8.	JOANNA HILL	11.89

200 Metres wind -1.2 (26 Jul)
1.	KATHARINE MERRY	23.46
2.	JOICE MADUAKA	23.48
3.	MARCIA RICHARDSON	23.71
4.	CHRISTINE BLOOMFIELD	24.25
5.	ELLENA RUDDOCK	24.30
6.	CATHERINE MURPHY	24.45
7.	JOANNA HILL	24.52
8.	NICOLE CROSBY	24.72

400 Metres (26 Jul)
1.	ALLISON CURBISHLEY	50.92
2.	DONNA FRASER	51.47
3.	MICHELLE THOMAS	53.25
4.	DAWN HIGGINS	53.79
5.	MICHELLE PIERRE	53.79
6.	VICKY DAY	53.80
7.	HELEN FROST	54.28
8.	LOURETTA THORNE	54.98

800 Metres (25 Jul)
1.	DIANE MODAHL	2:02.73
2.	TANYA BLAKE	2:03.83
3.	AMANDA CROWE	2:05.40
4.	JOANNE FENN	2:06.10
5.	BEV BLAKEMAN	2:06.48
6.	EMMA DAVIES	2:06.63
7.	RACHEL NEWCOMBE	2:07.03
8.	MICHELLE FLAHERTY	2:08.92

1500 Metres (25 Jul)
1.	LYNN GIBSON	4:12.72
2.	HELEN PATTINSON	4:12.87
3.	ANGELA DAVIES	4:13.55
4.	HAYLEY PARKINSON	4:14.19
5.	DEBBIE GUNNING	4:19.21
6.	KERRY SMITHSON	4:20.25
7.	SUSAN SCOTT	4:20.37
8.	SARAH BULL	4:21.02

3000 Metres (Sheffield 15 Aug)
1.	AMANDA PARKINSON	9:34.74
2.	DEBORAH SULLIVAN	9:36.90
3.	JILLY INGMAN	9:53.98
4.	LOUISE WATSON	10:03.28
5.	PAULA GOWING	10:24.58

5000 Metres (25 Jul)
1.	ANDREA WHITCOMBE	15:43.03
2.	SARAH YOUNG	15:45.08
3.	TARA KRZYWICKI	15:53.28
4.	BIRHAN DAGNE	15:55.81
5.	VIKKI McPHERSON	15:56.04
6.	AMY WATERLOW	15:57.45
7.	LUCY WRIGHT	15:59.51
8.	LIZ TALBOT	16:06.88

10000 Metres (Bedford 5 Jul)
1.	TARA KRZYWICKI	34:37.04
2.	HAYLEY NASH	34:45.57
3.	ANGELA JOINER	34:47.41
4.	MARA MYERS	34:52.57
5.	JILL BOLTZ	34:55.25
6.	DAWN JAMES	35:14.76
7.	ZAHARA HYDE	35:24.46
8.	LOUISE WATSON	35:33.72

100 Metres Hurdles -0.9 (25 Jul)
1.	KERI MADDOX	13.20
2.	CLOVA COURT	13.34
3.	LIZ FAIRS	13.52
4.	MELANIE WILKINS	13.65
5.	DENISE LEWIS	13.73
6.	RACHEL KING	13.76
7.	KATIE SKETCHLEY	14.06
8.	KERRY JURY	14.11

400 Metres Hurdles (26 Jul)
1.	NATASHA DANVERS	56.27
2.	GOWRY RETCHAKAN	56.57
3.	KERRI MADDOX	56.76
4.	VICKI JAMISON	57.58
5.	SINEAD DUDGEON	58.54
6.	JACQUI PARKER	58.68
7.	CLARE WISE	59.07
8.	JENNIE MATTHEWS	59.28

High Jump (26 Jul)
1.	JO JENNINGS	1.88
2.	SUSAN JONES	1.85
3.	MICHELLE DUNKLEY	1.85
4.	DENISE LEWIS	1.82
5.	JULIE CRANE	1.76
6.	LEE McCONNELL	1.76
7.	HAZEL MELVIN	1.76
8.	GILLIAN BLACK	1.73

Pole Vault (25 Jul)
1.	JANINE WHITLOCK	4.10
2.	RHIAN CLARKE	3.80
3.	PAULA WILSON	3.80
4.	EMMA HORNBY	3.70
5.	LUCY WEBBER	3.70
6.	LINDA STANTON	3.70
7.	TRACEY BLOOMFIELD	3.60
8.	LOUISE SCHRAMM	3.50

Long Jump (25 Jul)
1.	DENISE LEWIS	6.44
2.	TRACEY JOSEPH	6.24
3.	ANDREA COORE	6.23
4.	JO WISE	6.23
5.	DONITA BENJAMIN	6.09
6.	JACQUI WHITE	5.95
7.	RUTH IRVING	5.85
8.	ANN DANSON	5.83

Triple Jump (25 Jul)
1.	CONNIE HENRY	13.90
2.	MICHELLE GRIFFITH	13.84
3.	KERENSA DENHAM	12.42
4.	CAROLINE STEAD	12.23
5.	RACHEL KIRBY	12.22
6.	DEBORAH ROWE	12.08
7.	JODIE HURST	12.07
8.	ELIZABETH PATRICK	11.99

Shot (25 Jul)
1.	JUDY OAKES	17.82
2.	MYRTLE AUGEE	17.39
3.	MAGGIE LYNES	15.73
4.	TRACY AXTEN	15.43
5.	JOANNE DUNCAN	15.24
6.	JULIE DUNKLEY	14.63
7.	VICKIE FOSTER	14.61
8.	CHRISTINA BENNETT	14.42

Discus (25 Jul)
1.	SHELLEY DREW	60.82
2.	JACQUI McKERNAN	57.09
3.	PHILIPPA ROLES	54.14
4.	TRACY AXTEN	54.03
5.	EMMA MERRY	52.30
6.	DEBBIE CALLAWAY	51.59
7.	LORRAINE SHAW	51.16
8.	JUDY OAKES	49.94

Hammer (25 Jul)
1.	LORRAINE SHAW	60.71
2.	LYN SPRULES	59.20
3.	RACHAEL BEVERLEY	57.97
4.	LIZ PIDGEON	55.61
5.	DIANA HOLDEN	55.26
6.	ANN GARDNER	52.96
7.	SARAH MOORE	52.12
8.	CATHERINE GARDEN	50.49

Javelin (25 Jul)
1.	LORNA JACKSON	57.89
2.	SHELLEY HOLROYD	54.16
3.	KAREN MARTIN	53.17
4.	KIRSTY MORRISON	51.29
5.	DENISE LEWIS	51.28
6.	NOELLE BRADSHAW	47.29
7.	KATIE AMOS	46.88
8.	CAROLINE WHITE	45.35

5000 Metres Walk (26 Jul)
1.	Gillian O'Sullivan	IRE	21:52.68
2.	LISA KEHLER		22:01.53
3.	VICKY LUPTON		23:32.48
4.	CATHERINE CHARNOCK		23:50.96
5.	SHARON TONKS		24:20.07

10000 Metres Walk
(Basildon 26 Sep)
1.	PAM PHILLIPS	64:08.9

WORLD JUNIOR CHAMPIONSHIPS Annecy, France 28 July - 2 August 1998

MEN

100 Metres wind 1.6 (29 Jul)
1. CHRISTIAN MALCOLM   10.12
2. Amar Johnson   USA   10.34
3. Dwight Thomas   JAM   10.40

200 Metres wind -0.2 (1 Aug)
1. CHRISTIAN MALCOLM   20.44
2. Jairo Duzant   AHO   20.92
3. Russell Frye   USA   20.94
6s1 TIM BENJAMIN   21.59

400 Metres (31 Jul)
1. Nduka Awazie   NGR   45.54
2. Casey Vincent   AUS   45.55
3. Fawzi Al Shammari   KUW   45.89
4. ALLOY WILSON   46.64
7s2 DAVID NAISMITH   47.73

800 Metres (31 Jul)
1. William Chirchir   KEN   1:47.23
2. Wilfed Bungei   KEN   1:47.53
3. Paskar Owor   UGA   1:48.20
6. CHRIS MOSS   1:48.77
6h6 SIMON LEES   1:53.79

1500 Metres (2 Aug)
1. Adil El Kaouch   MAR   3:42.43
2. Benjamin Kipkurui   KEN   3:42.67
3. Robert Witt   POL   3:43.47
8h3 CHRIS BOLT   3:52.10

5000 Metres (2 Aug)
1. Million Wolde   ETH   13:47.49
2. Kipchumba Mitei   KEN   13:49.60
3. Ahmed Baday   MAR   13:49.86
14. SAM HAUGHIAN   14:32.66

10000 Metres (30 Jul)
1. Benson Barus   KEN   29:24.28
2. Salim Kipsang   KEN   29:36.80
3. Alene Emere   ETH   29:47.60

3000 Metres Steeplechase (1 Aug)
1. Reuben Kosgei   KEN   8:23.76
2. Abraham Cherono   KEN   8:32.24
3. El Moustapha Mellouk   MAR   8:34.91
5h1 CHRIS THOMPSON   9:07.37
7h2 IAIN MURDOCH   9:07.09

110 Metres Hurdles -0.2 (2 Aug)
1. Stanislav Olijars   LAT   13.51
2. Sharif Paxton   USA   14.10
3. Florian Seibold   GER   14.21
4. BEN WARMINGTON   14.33
7s2 ROBERT NEWTON   14.69

400 Metres Hurdles (31 Jul)
1. Periklis Iakovakis   GRE   49.82
2. Osiris Martinez   CUB   50.17
3. Peter Bate   AUS   50.83
7s1 RICHARD McDONALD   52.13

High Jump (31 Jul)
1. Alfredo Deza   PER   2.21
2. Yin Xueli   CHN   2.21
3. Aleksandr Veryutin   BLR   2.21
8. MARTIN LLOYD   2.10
23=Q ED WILLERS   2.05

Pole Vault (2 Aug)
1. Pavel Gerasimov   RUS   5.55
2. Lars Borgeling   GER   5.50
3= Paul Burgess   AUS   5.20
3= Adam Ptacek   CZE   5.20
3= Giuseppe Gibiliso   ITA   5.20
12. CHRISTIAN LINSKEY   5.00

Long Jump (30 Jul)
1. Petar Datchev   BUL   8.14
2. Abdulrahman Al-Nubi   QAT   8.11
3. Felipe Melis   CUB   7.91
32Q DARREN THOMPSON   6.50

Triple Jump (1 Aug)
1. Ionut Punga   ROM   16.94
2. Ivaylo Rusenov   BUL   16.65
3. Gregory Yeldell   USA   16.44
18Q JOHN WALLACE   15.53
22Q NICHOLAS THOMAS   15.40

Shot (1 Aug)
1. Mikulas Konopka   SVK   18.50
2. Janus Robberts   RSA   18.15
3. CARL MYERSCOUGH   18.12
13Q EMEKA UDECHUKU   16.42

Discus (30 Jul)
1. Zoltan Kovago   HUN   59.36
2. EMEKA UDECHUKU   57.99
3. Gabor Mate   HUN   56.96
6. CARL MYERSCOUGH   55.75

Hammer (1 Aug)
1. Olli-Pekka Karjalainen   FIN   72.40
2. Yuriy Voronkin   RUS   69.66
3. Wojciech Kondratowicz   POL   68.93

Javelin (2 Aug)
1. DAVID PARKER   72.85
2. Gerhardus Pienaar   RSA   71.16
3. Yukifumi Murakami   JPN   70.72
8. DAN CARTER   66.10

Decathlon (29/30 Jul)
1. Aki Heikkinen   FIN   7476
2. Thomas Poge   GER   7332
3. Jaakko Ojaniemi   FIN   7246

10 Kilometres Walk (30 Jul)
1. Roman Rasskazov   RUS   41:55
2. Liu Yunfeng   CHN   42:01
3. Mario Flores   MEX   42:04
27. MICHAEL KEMP   49:40

4 x 100 Metres Relay (2 Aug)
1. Jamaica   39.70
    (Slowly, Collin, Paul, Bailey)
2. United States   39.71
3. Germany   39.99
h2 GREAT BRITAIN & NI   dq

4 x 400 Metres Relay (2 Aug)
1. Australia   3:04.74
    (Daniel, Batman, Russell, Vincent)
2. United States   3:05.06
3. Jamaica   3:05.31
5. GREAT BRITAIN & NI   3:06.32
    (NAISMITH, CAINES, CARSON, WILSON)

WOMEN

100 Metres wind 1.7 (29 Jul)
1. Shakedia Jones   USA   11.19
2. Angela Williams   USA   11.27
3. Joan Uduak Ekah   NGR   11.50

200 Metres wind -1.1 (1 Aug)
1. Muriel Hurtis   FRA   23.22
2. Shakedia Jones   USA   23.39
3. SARAH WILHELMY   23.56
6q4 REBECCA WHITE   24.40

400 Metres (31 Jul)
1. Natalya Nazarova   RUS   52.02
2. Nakiya Johnson   USA   52.09
3. Yudalis Diaz   CUB   52.39
8s1 CAREY EASTON   54.70

800 Metres (31 Jul)
1. Olga Mikayeva   RUS   2:05.34
2. Jebet Langat   KEN   2:05.43
3. Naomi Misoi   KEN   2:05.77

1500 Metres (2 Aug)
1. Lan Lixin   CHN   4:10.05
2. Yimenashu Taye   ETH   4:11.97
3. Bouchra Benthami   MAR   4:12.76

3000 Metres (30 Jul)
1. Yin Lili   CHN   8:57.09
2. Yimenashu Taye   ETH   9:01.70
3. Edna Kiplagat   KEN   9:05.45
7h1 AMBER GASCOIGNE   9:43.55

5000 Metres (2 Aug)
1. Yin Lili   CHN   15:29.65
2. Faith Jemutai   KEN   15:34.48
3. Meryma Hashim   ETH   15:39.57
10. LOUISE KELLY   16:20.51

100 Metres Hurdles -1.0 (2 Aug)
1. JULIE PRATT   13.75
2. Sun Hongwei   CHN   13.75
3. Susanna Kallur   SWE   13.77
6h3 SARAH CLAXTON   14.00

400 Metres Hurdles (31 Jul)
1. Li Yulian   CHN   55.93
2. Allison Beckford   JAM   57.19
3. Sun Hongwei   CHN   57.43
5s2 TRACEY DUNCAN   59.39
7s1 RACHAEL KAY   60.12

High Jump (1 Aug)
1. Marina Kuptsova RUS 1.88
2. Marie Norrman SWE 1.88
3= Nevena Lendjel CRO 1.84
3= Tatyana Yefimenko KGZ 1.84

Pole Vault (29 Jul)
1. Monika Götz GER 4.20
2= Maria Sanchez ESP 4.10
2= Monika Pyrek POL 4.10
22=Q TRACEY BLOOMFIELD 3.50

Long Jump (31 Jul)
1. Peng Fengmei CHN 6.59
2. Lu Xin CHN 6.57
3. Maria Chiara Baccini ITA 6.55
4. SARAH CLAXTON 6.52

Triple Jump (2 Aug)
1. Baya Rahouli ALG 14.04
2. Maria Solomon ROM 13.75
3. Marija Martinovic YUG 13.47

Shot (31 Jul)
1. Nadesda Ostapchuk BLR 18.23
2. Du Xianhui CHN 17.69
3. Nadine Banse GER 16.94
20Q JULIE DUNKLEY 13.82

Discus (1 Aug)
1. Liu Fengying CHN 60.66
2. Milina Robert-Michon FRA 55.01
3. Lacramioara Ionescu ROM 54.64
15Q LAUREN KEIGHTLEY 44.62

Hammer (29 Jul)
1. Bianca Achilles GER 61.79
2. Sini Poyry FIN 61.76
3. Maureen Griffin USA 60.14
13Q RACHEL BEVERLEY 54.64

Javelin (29 Jul)
1. Osleidys Menendez CUB 68.17
2. Liang Lili CHN 61.72
3. Wei Jianhua CHN 59.10
18Q KELLY MORGAN 46.58
22Q GOLDIE SAYERS 45.54

Heptathlon (31 Jul/1 Aug)
1. Shen Shengfei CHN 5815
2. Susanna Rajamaki FIN 5721
3. Viorica Tigau ROM 5720
15= CHLOE COZENS 5220

5 Kilometres Walk (1 Aug)
1. Sabine Zimmer GER 21:14
2. Yolanta Dukure LAT 21:17
3. Xue Ailing CHN 21:28

4 x 100 Metres Relay (2 Aug)
1. United States 43.52
(Williams, Soley, Combs, Jones)
2. France 44.07
3. Jamaica 44.61
4. GREAT BRITAIN & NI 44.65
(Oyepitan, Wilhelmy, Davies, White)

4 x 400 Metres Relay (2 Aug)
1. Jamaica 3:32.29
(Hall, Gayle, Downer, Beckford)
2. Russia 3:32.35
3. United States 3:32.85

GERMANY v GB & NI v FRANCE U23 Dessau, Germany 1 August 1998

MEN

100 Metres Race A wind -1.0
1. Frederic Krantz FRA 10.47
2. JAMIE HENTHORN 10.52
3. MICHAEL TIETZ 10.59

100 Metres Race B
3. BRENDON GHENT 10.91

200 Metres wind -1.6
1. Frederic Krantz FRA 20.85
2. JAMIE HENTHORN 21.01
5. KEVIN FARRELL 21.52

400 Metres Race A
1. GEOFF DEARMAN 46.46
5. PETER BREND 47.70

400 Metres Race B
2. LAWRENCE BAIRD 47.85

800 Metres
1. ALASDAIR DONALDSON 1:51.58
4. ANDREW YOUNG 1:52.49

1500 Metres
1. MICHAEL EAST 3:56.31
5. ANDREW DIXON 3:58.18

5000 Metres
1. ALLEN GRAFFIN 14:23.50
5. CHRIS DAVIES 14:42.72

3000 Metres Steeplechase
1. Ralf Assmus GER 8:37.22
4. CRAIG WHEELER 8:45.90
6. STUART STOKES 9:04.16

110 Metres Hurdles wind 0.0
1. Jerome Crews GER 13.53
3. DAMIEN GREAVES 13.97
5. ROSS BAILLIE 14.10

400 Metres Hurdles
1. MATT DOUGLAS 50.87
6. ANDY BARGH 53.08

High Jump
1. Charles Mwinkau FRA 2.15
3. RICHARD ASPDEN 2.08
4. ANDREW PENK 2.08

Pole Vault
1. Nicolas Jolivet FRA 5.30
4. BEN FLINT 5.10
5. NEIL YOUNG 5.00

Long Jump
1. Rémi Robert FRA 7.50
4. JAN IRVING 7.18
6. DAVID CLERIHEW 6.63

Triple Jump
1. Tobias Pöss GER 16.18
3. PHILLIPS IDOWU 15.93
4. CHARLES MADEIRA-COLE 15.72

Shot
1. Peter Sack GER 18.23
5. BRUCE ROBB 14.71
6. IAIN McMULLAN 14.48

Discus
1. Patrick Stang GER 55.98
5. BRUCE ROBB 48.42
6. ANDREW ROLLINS 43.54

Hammer
1. Stefan Paukner GER 69.36
4. MICHAEL FLOYD 61.63
6. JOHN URQUHART 59.57

Javelin
1. Laurent Dorique FRA 75.95
5. STUART LOUGHRAN 63.03
6. GREG MARKHAM 57.10

10000 Metres Walk
1. Andre Höhne GER 44:26.99
4. STEVE HOLLIER 46:35.30
6. SCOTT TAYLOR 50:03.69

4 x 100 Metres Relay
1. France 39.31
2. GREAT BRITAIN & NI 40.20
(BAILLIE, HENTHORN, TIETZ, FARRELL)

4 x 400 Metres Relay
1. Germany 3:08.22
3. GREAT BRITAIN & NI 3:13.93
(BARGH, DONALDSON, GHENT, BAIRD)

Match Result
1. Germany 152
2. France 150
3. GREAT BRITAIN & NI 117

WOMEN

100 Metres Race A wind -0.6
1. Sandra Citté FRA 11.43
2. MALGORZATA ROSTEK 11.82
6. ELLENA RUDDOCK 11.88

100 Metres Race B wind -0.7
3. TATUM NELSON 11.98

200 Metres wind 0.0
1. Sabrina Mulrain GER 22.84
5. NICOLE CROSBY 24.42
6. ZOE WILSON 24.70

400 Metres Race A
1. Nicole Marahrens GER 52.92
2. VICKY JAMISON 52.97
5. LESLEY OWUSU 54.84

400 Metres Race B
1. LOURETTA THORNE 54.32
3. KAREN GEAR 55.41

800 Metres
1. Claudia Gesell GER 2:03.57
3. EMMA DAVIES 2:04.88
5. SUSAN SCOTT 2:07.77

1500 Metres
1. KERRY SMITHSON 4:23.83
4. ELLEN O'HARE 4:31.34

5000 Metres
1. Sylvia Nussbeck GER 16:27.48
2. SHEILA FAIRWEATHER 16:34.61
3. JILLY INGHAM 16:35.86

100 Metres Hurdles wind -1.0
1. LIZ FAIRS 13.56
6. RACHEL KING 13.90

400 Metres Hurdles
1. Ulrike Urbansky GER 56.35
2. NATASHA DANVERS 57.18
5. SINDEAD DUDGEON 59.38

High Jump
1. Daniela Rath GER 1.84
3. MICHELLE DUNKLEY 1.81
4. JULIE CRANE 1.78

Pole Vault
1. Nastja Ryshich GER 4.20
4. RHIAN CLARKE 3.70
6. CLAIRE RIDGELEY 3.50

Long Jump
1. Sarah Gautreau FRA 6.34
5. DEBORAH HARRISON 5.83
6. MICHELLE DUNKLEY 5.65

Triple Jump
1. Nathalie Jacques-Gustave FRA 13.37
5. ELIZABETH PATRICK 11.85
6. ELIZABETH GIBBENS 11.45

Shot
1. Ilona Beyer GER 16.74
3. CHRISTINA BENNETT 14.65
5. ELEANOR GATRELL 14.43

Discus
1. Nadine Beckel GER 55.65
4. PHILIPPA ROLES 53.91
6. NAVDEEP DHALIWAL 42.88

Hammer
1. Susane Keil GER 63.33
4. ELIZABETH PIDGEON 55.78
5. CATHERINE GARDEN 53.37

Javelin
1. Simone Mathies GER 54.39
4. KATIE AMOS 49.77
6. KATHERINE EVANS 42.47

5000 Metres Walk
1. Melanie Seeger GER 22:04.46
4. SALLY WARREN 25:36.61
   DEBBIE WALLEN dq

4 x 100 Metres Relay
1. France 44.46
3. GREAT BRITAIN & NI 45.60
(ROSTEK, RUDDOCK, WILSON, NELSON)

4 x 400 Metres Relay
1. France 3:35.36
2. GREAT BRITAIN & NI 3:40.10
(DUDGEON, OWUSU, THORNE, JAMISON)

Match Result
1. Germany 171
2. France 128
3. GREAT BRITAIN & NI 99

EUROPEAN CHAMPIONSHIPS Budapest, Hungary 18 - 23 August 1998
MEN

100 Metres wind 0.3 (19 Aug)
1. DARREN CAMPBELL 10.04
2. DWAIN CHAMBERS 10.10
3. Haralambos Papadias GRE 10.17
4. Stefano Tilli ITA 10.20
5. MARLON DEVONISH 10.24
6. Aleksandr Porkhomovskiy RUS 10.29
7. Marcin Krzywanski POL 10.29
8. Marcin Nowak POL 10.36

200 Metres wind -1.0 (21 Aug)
1. DOUG WALKER 20.53
2. DOUG TURNER 20.64
3. JULIAN GOLDING 20.72
4. Geir Moen NOR 20.78
5. Rodrigue Nordin FRA 20.83
6. Christophe Cheval FRA 20.91
7. Prodromos Katsantonis CYP 21.24
   Troy Douglas NED dq

400 Metres (21 Aug)
1. IWAN THOMAS 44.52
2. Robert Mackowiak POL 45.04
3. MARK RICHARDSON 45.14
4. Tomasz Czubak POL 45.43
5. Piotr Haczek POL 45.46
6. Ashraf Saber ITA 45.67
7. David Canal ESP 45.93
4s2 SOLOMON WARISO 45.59

800 Metres (23 Aug)
1. Nils Schumann GER 1:44.89
2. Andre Bucher SUI 1:45.04
3. Likas Vydra CZE 1:45.23
4. James McElroy IRL 1:45.46
5. Balázs Koranyi HUN 1:45.78
6. Wojciech Kaldowski POL 1:46.60

Marathon (22 Aug)
1. Stefano Baldini ITA 2:12:01
2. Danilo Goffi ITA 2:12:11
3. Vincenzo Modica ITA 2:12:53
4. Jose Ramon Ray ESP 2:13:17
5. Alejandro Gomez ESP 2:13:23
6. Antonio Peña ESP 2:13:53
7. Giovanni Rugerio ITA 2:13:59
8. RICHARD NERURKAR 2:14:02
28. DAVE BUZZA 2:19:28
30. MARK HUDSPITH 2:19:58

European Cup (team result)
1. Italy 8:51:01
2. Spain 8:55:31
3. Portugal 8:59:52

3000 Metres Steeplechase (23 Aug)
1. Damian Kallabis GER 8:13.10
2. Alessandro Lambruschini ITA 8:16.70
3. Jim Svenoy NOR 8:18.97
4. Luis Martin ESP 8:20.54
5. Luciano Di Pardo ITA 8:20.96
6. Ramiro Moran ESP 8:24.06
7. Elisio Martin ESP 8:26.60
8. Rafal Wojcik POL 8:27.74

110 Metres Hurdles 1.5 (22 Aug)
1. COLIN JACKSON 13.02
2. Falk Balzer GER 13.12
3. Robin Korving NED 13.20
4. Florian Schwarthoff GER 13.23
5. Artur Kohutek POL 13.29
6. TONY JARRETT 13.32
7. Mike Fenner GER 13.38
8. Jonathan Nsenga BEL 13.54
7s2 ANDY TULLOCH 13.79

1500 Metres (20 Aug)
1. Reyes Estevez ESP 3:41.31
2. Rui Silva POR 3:41.84
3. Fermin Cacho ESP 3:42.13
4. ANTHONY WHITEMAN 3:42.27
5. JOHN MAYOCK 3:42.58
6. MATTHEW YATES 3:42.63
7. Rudiger Stenzel GER 3:42.75
8. A'kader Chekhmani FRA 3:42.92

5000 Metres (22 Aug)
1. Isaac Viciosa ESP 13:37.46
2. Manuel Pancorbo ESP 13:38.03
3. Mark Carroll IRL 13:38.15
4. Mustapha Essaid FRA 13:39.85
5. Abdellah Behar FRA 13:40.26
6. Samuli Vasala FIN 13:40.68
7. Driss El Himer FRA 13:41.36
8. Miroslav Vanko SVK 13:41.92
9. KARL KESKA 13:42.58
17. ROD FINCH 14:09.87

10000 Metres (18 Aug)
1. Antonio Pinto POR 27:48.62
2. Dieter Baumann GER 27:56.75
3. Stephane Franke GER 27:59.90
4. JON BROWN 28:02.33
5. Bruno Toledo ESP 28:15.17
6. Enrique Molina ESP 28:19.54
7. Rachid Berradi ITA 28:22.31
8. Kamiel Maase NED 28:26.37
11. KEITH CULLEN 28:34.34

400 Metres Hurdles (20 Aug)
1. Pawel Januszewski POL 48.17
2. Rusian Mashchenko RUS 48.25
3. Fabrizio Mori ITA 48.71
4. Carlos Silva POR 49.02
5. Vadim Zadoynov MOL 49.10
6. Laurent Ottoz ITA 49.15
7. Jiri Muzik CZE 50.51
8. Vladislav Shiryayev RUS 50.94
6s1 PAUL GRAY 50.34
6h1 TONY BORSUMATO 50.91
7h2 CHRIS RAWLINSON 51.11

High Jump (21 Aug)
1. Artur Partyka POL 2.34
2. DALTON GRANT 2.34
3. Sergey Klyugin RUS 2.32
4. Martin Buss GER 2.32
5. Dimitrios Kokotis GRE 2.30
6. Steinar Hoen NOR 2.30
7. Stefan Holm SWE 2.27
8. Staffan Strand SWE 2.27
9= BRENDAN REILLY 2.24

Pole Vault (22 Aug)
1. Maksim Tarasaov RUS 5.81
2. Tim Lobinger GER 5.81
3. Jean Galfione FRA 5.76
4. Danny Ecker GER 5.76
5. Khalid Lachheb FRA 5.60
6. Andrej Tiwontschik GER 5.50
7. Pavel Burlachenko RUS 5.50
8. Heikki Vääräniemi FIN 5.50
18=Q NICK BUCKFIELD 5.30

Long Jump (19 Aug)
1. Kirill Sosunov RUS 8.28
2. Bogdan Tarus ROM 8.21
3. Petar Dachev BUL 8.06
4. Simone Bianchi ITA 8.02
5. Mattias Sunneborn SWE 8.01
6. Gregor Cankar SLO 8.00
7. Paulo Camossi ITA 7.98
8. Yago Lamela ESP 7.93
24Q NATHAN MORGAN 7.67
32Q STEVEN PHILLIPS 7.51

Triple Jump (23 Aug)
1. JONATHAN EDWARDS 17.99
2. Denis Kapustin RUS 17.45
3. Rostislav Dimitrov BUL 17.26w
4. Aleksandr Glavatskiy BLR 17.22
5. Vasiliy Sokov RUS 17.16w
6. Charles Friedek GER 17.04
7. Zsolt Czingler HUN 17.03

WOMEN
100 Metres wind 2.0 (19 Aug)
1. Christine Arron FRA 10.73
2. Irina Privalova RUS 10.83
3. Ekaterini Thanou GRE 10.87
4. Zhanna Pintusevich UKR 10.92
5. Melanie Paschke GER 11.07
6. Petja Pendareva BUL 11.12
7. Anzhela Kravchenko UKR 11.16
8. Frederique Bangue FRA 11.27
7s1 JOICE MADUAKA 11.49

8. Rogel Nachum ISR 16.99
17Q JULIAN GOLLEY 16.32
21Q ONOCHIE ACHIKE 16.13

Shot (18 Aug)
1. Aleksandr Bagach UKR 21.17
2. Oliver-Sven Buder GER 20.98
3. Yuriy Belonog UKR 20.92
4. Dragan Peric YUG 20.65
5. Paulo Dal Soglio ITA 20.50
6. Miko Halvari FIN 20.33
7. Manuel Martínez ESP 20.02
8. Michael Mertens GER 19.67
24Q SHAUN PICKERING 17.80
MARK PROCTOR 3nt

Discus (23 Aug)
1. Lars Riedel GER 67.07
2. Jürgen Schult GER 66.69
3. Virgilijus Alekna LIT 66.46
4. Róbert Fazekas HUN 65.13
5. Diego Fortuna ITA 64.26
6. Vladimir Dubrovshchik BLR 63.96
7. Andreas Seelig GER 63.15
8. ROBERT WEIR 61.92
15Q GLEN SMITH 58.97
30Q PERRIS WILKINS 53.16

Hammer (19 Aug)
1. Tibor Gécsek HUN 82.87
2. Balázs Kiss HUN 81.26
3. Karsten Kobs GER 80.13
4. Heinz Weis GER 80.04
5. Szymon Ziolkowski POL 78.16
6. Hristos Polyhroniou GRE 77.97
7. Igor Astapkovich BLR 77.81
8. Adrián Annus HUN 77.29

Javelin (23 Aug)
1 STEVE BACKLEY 89.72
2 MICK HILL 86.92
3 Raymond Hecht GER 86.63
4 Sergey Makarov RUS 86.45
5 Juha Laukkanen FIN 84.78
6 MARK ROBERSON 84.15
7 Peter Blank GER 83.66
8 Matti Narhi FIN 82.59

Decathlon (19/20 Aug)
1. Erkki Nool EST 8667
2. Eduard Hämäläinen FIN 8587
3. Lev Lobodin RUS 8571
4. Jon Arnar Magnússon ISL 8552
5. Tomás Dvorák CZE 8506
6. Román Sebrle CZE 8477
7. Deszö Szabó HUN 8392
8. Mike Maczey GER 8174

200 Metres wind -0.7 (21 Aug)
1. Irina Privalova RUS 22.62
2. Zhanna Pintusevich UKR 22.74
3. Melanie Paschke GER 22.78
4. Natalya Voronova RUS 22.80
5. Nora Ivanova BUL 23.02
6. Sabrina Mulrain GER 23.04
7. Gabi Rockmeier GER 23.08
8. Erika Suchovska CZE 23.18
5s2 KATHARINE MERRY 23.38
7h1 SARAH WILHELMY 24.11

20 Kilometres Walk (18 Aug)
1. Ilya Markov RUS 1:21:10
2. Aigars Fadejevs LAT 1:21:29
3. Francisco Fernández ESP 1:21:39
4. Andrea Erm GER 1:21:53
5. Sándor Urbanik HUN 1:22:12
6. Ivan Trotskiy BLR 1:22:46
7. Denis Langlllois FRA 1:23:02
8. Yevgeniy Shmalyuk RUS 1:23:32

50 Kilometres Walk (21 Aug)
1. Robert Korzeniowski POL 3:43:51
2. Valentin Kononen FIN 3:44:29
3. Andrey Plotnikov RUS 3:45:53
4. Mikel Odriozola ESP 3:47:24
5. Tomasz Lipiec POL 3:48:05
6. Santiago Pérez ESP 3:48:17
7. Arturo Di Mezza ITA 3:48:49
8. Denis Trautmann GER 3:49:46

4 x 100 Metres Relay (23 Aug)
1. GREAT BRITAIN & NI 38.52
(CONDON, CAMPBELL, WALKER, GOLDING)
2. France 38.87
(Lubin, Krantz, Cheval, Guims)
3. Poland 38.98
(Krzywanski, Nowak, Blacerzak, Pilarczyk)
4. Greece 39.07
(Yenovelis, Alexopoulos, Panayotopoulos, Papadias)
5. Germany 39.09
(Schneider, Crews, Milde, M Blume)
6. Sweden 39.32
(Lüvgren, Ghansah, T Eriksson, Karlsson)
7. Netherlands 39.79
(Ungerer, Snoek, van Balkom, Tilburg)
8. Italy 39.85
(Scuderi, Colombo, Attene, Floris)

4 x 400 Metres Relay (23 Aug)
1. GREAT BRITAIN & NI 2:58.68
(HYLTON, BAULCH, THOMAS, RICHARDSON)
2. Poland 2:58.88
(Rysiukewicz, Czubak, Haczek, Mackowiak)
3. Spain 3:02.47
(Andrés, Trull, A Martinez, Canal)
4. Italy 3:02.48
(Pirovano, Vaccari, Nuti, Saber)
5. Switzerland 3:02.91
(Clerc, Widmer, Rohr, Rusterholz)
6. Germany 3:03.19
(Letzelter, Ehrnsperger, Goller, Dautzenberg)
7. Czech Republic 3:04.37
(Podebradsky, Stejfa, Blaha, Muzik)
France disq.
(Hilaire, Foucan, Mango, Diagana)

400 Metres (21 Aug)
1. Grit Breuer GER 49.93
2. Helena Fuchsova CZE 50.21
3. Olga Kotlyarova RUS 50.38
4. Uta Rohländer GER 50.48
5. ALLISON CURBISHLEY 51.05
6. DONNA FRASER 51.54
7. Olena Rurak UKR 51.92
8. Patrizia Spuri ITA 51.94

800 Metres (20 Aug)
1. Yelena Afanasyeva RUS 1:58.50
2. Malin Ewerlöf SWE 1:59.61
3. Stephanie Graf AUT 2:00.11
4. Violeta Szekely ROM 2:00.56
5. Tzvetelina Kirilova BUL 2:00.66
6. Heike Meissner GER 2:01.36
7. Natalya Duknova BLR 2:02.14
   Larisa Mikhailova RUS dnf
5s1 DIANE MODAHL 2:00.08

1500 Metres (23 Aug)
1. Svetlana Masterkova RUS 4:11.91
2. Carla Sacramento POR 4:12.62
3. Anita Weyermann SUI 4:13.06
4. Anna Jakubczak POL 4:13.33
5. Violeta Szekely ROM 4:14.66
6. Lidia Chojecka POL 4:15.00
7. Andrea Suldesova CZE 4:15.04
8. Maite Zuñiga ESP 4:15.10

5000 Metres (23 Aug)
1. Sonia O'Sullivan IRL 15:06.50
2. Gabriela Szabo ROM 15:08.31
3. Marta Dominguez ESP 15:10.54
4. Olivvera Jevtic YUG 15:16.61
5. Annemari Sandell FIN 15:20.78
6. Blandine Bitzner-Ducret FRA 15:38.61
7. Valerie Vaughan IRL 15:39.99
8. Teresa Recio ESP 15:40.54

10000 Metres (19 Aug)
1. Sonia O'Sullivan IRL 31:29.33
2. Fernanda Ribeiro POR 31:32.42
3. Lidia Simon ROM 31:32.64
4. Olivera Jevtic YUG 31:34.26
5. PAULA RADCLIFFE 31:36.51
6. Julia Vaquero ESP 31:46.47
7. Annemari Sandell FIN 32:22.50
8. Irina Mikitenko GER 32:30.67

Marathon (23 Aug)
1. Manuela Machado POR 2:27:10
2. Madina Biktagirova RUS 2:28:01
3. Maura Viceconte ITA 2:28:31
4. Franca Fiacconi ITA 2:28:59
5. Marleen Renders BEL 2:29:43
6. Rocio Rios ESP 2:29:53
7. Lyubov Morgunova RUS 2:30:07
8. Tatyana Razdrogina RUS 2:30:09

European Cup (team result)
1. Russia 9:58:43
2. Italy 10:10:14
3. Germany 10:15:23

100 Metres Hurdles 0.5 (23 Aug)
1. Svetla Dimitrova BUL 12.56
2. Brigita Bukovec SLO 12.65
3. Irina Korotya RUS 12.85
4. Nicole Ramalalanirina FRA 12.87
5. Patricia Girard FRA 12.89
6. Heike Blassneck GER 13.02
7. Julie Baumann SUI 13.15
8. Linda Ferga FRA 13.22

400 Metres Hurdles (21 Aug)
1. Ionela Tirlea ROM 53.37
2. Tatyana Tereshchuk UKR 54.07
3. Silvia Rieger GER 54.45
4. Gudrun Arnardottir ISL 54.59
5. Ester Goossens NED 54.62
6. Ulrike Urbansky GER 55.38
7. Anna Knoroz RUS 55.47
8. Susan Smith IRL 55.61
6h3 NATASHA DANVERS 57.19

High Jump (23 Aug)
1. Monica Dinescu ROM 1.97
2. Donata Jancewicz POL 1.95
3. Alina Astafei GER 1.95
4. Sigrid Kirchmann AUT 1.92
5. Venelina Veneva BUL 1.92
6. Yelena Gulyayeva RUS 1.92
7. Viktoriya Styopina UKR 1.92
8. Pia Zinck DEN 1.89

Pole Vault (21 Aug)
1. Anzhela Balakhonova UKR 4.31
2. Nicole Humbert GER 4.31
3. Yvonne Buschbaum GER 4.31
4= Nastja Ryshich GER 4.15
4= Monique de Wilt NED 4.15
4= Gabriela Mihalcea ROM 4.15
7. Monika Pyrek POL 4.15
8. Zsuzsa Szabü HUN 4.15
17=Q JANINE WHITLOCK 4.00
   EMMA HORNBY nh

Long Jump (22 Aug)
1. Heike Drechsler GER 7.16
2. Fiona May ITA 7.11
3. Lyudmila Galkina RUS 7.06w
4. Tünde Vaszi HUN 6.82w
5. Erica Johansson SWE 6.75w
6. Zita Ajkler HUN 6.64
7. Linda Ferga FRA 6.64
8. Susan Tiedtke GER 6.62

Triple Jump (20 Aug)
1. Olga Vasdeki GRE 14.55
2. Sárka Kaspárková CZE 14.53
3. Tereza Marinova BUL 14.50
4. Rodica Mateescu ROM 14.46
5. Tatyana Lebedyeva RUS 14.25
6. Olena Govorova UKR 14.24
7. Natalya Safronova BLR 14.01
8. Yelena Donkina RUS 13.92
20Q CONNIE HENRY 13.77

Shot (20 Aug)
1. Vita Pavlysh UKR 21.69
2. Irina Korzhanenko RUS 19.71
3. Yanina Korolchik BLR 19.23
4. Svetlana Krivelyova RUS 19.08
5. Katarzyna Zakowicz POL 18.77
6. Nadine Kleinert GER 18.48
7. Corrie de Bruin NED 18.28
8. Tatyana Khorkhulyova BLR 18.17

Discus (21 Aug)
1. Franka Dietzsch GER 67.49
2. Natalya Sadova RUS 66.94
3. Nicoleta Grasu ROM 65.94
4. Ellina Zvereva BLR 65.92

5. Ekaterini Voggoli GRE 63.56
6. Ilke Wyludda GER 63.46
7. Anastasia Kelesidou GRE 62.95
8. Irina Yatchenko BLR 61.20
25Q SHELLEY DREW 53.13

Hammer (22 Aug)
1. Mihaela Melinte ROM 71.17
2. Olga Kuzenkova RUS 69.28
3. Kirsten Münchow GER 65.61
4. Simone Mathes GER 64.05
5. Katalin Divós HUN 63.74
6. Lyudmila Gubkina BLR 63.03
7. Kamilia Skolimowska POL 62.68
8. Alla Davydova RUS 62.36
11. LORRAINE SHAW 58.19
12. LYN SPRULES 57.68

Javelin (19 Aug)
1. Tanja Damaske GER 69.10
2. Tatyana Shikolenko RUS 66.92
3. Mikaela Ingberg FIN 64.92
4. Trine Hattestad NOR 63.16
5. Heli Rantanen FIN 62.34
6. Steffi Nerius GER 62.08
7. Claudia Coslovich ITA 60.73
8. Nikolett Szabó HUN 60.56

Heptathlon (21/22 Aug)
1. DENISE LEWIS 6559
2. Urszula Wlodarczyk POL 6460
3. Natalya Sazanovich BLR 6410
4. Remigija Nazarovienė LIT 6394
5. Irina Belova RUS 6375
6. Sabine Braun GER 6259
7. Karin Specht GER 6239
8. Maria Collonvillé FRA 6218

10 Kilometres Walk (20 Aug)
1. Anna Sidoti ITA 42:49
2. Erica Alfridi ITA 42:54
3. Susana Feitor POR 42:55
4. Maria Urbanik HUN 42:59
5. Maria Vasco ESP 43:02
6. Katarzyna Radtke POL 43:09
18. LISA KEHLER 45:42

4 x 100 Metres Relay (22 Aug)
1. France 42.59
   (Benth, Bangué, Félix, Arron)
2. Germany 42.68
(Paschke, G Rockmeier, B Rockmeier, Philipp)
3. Russia 42.73
   (Ekk, Malchugina, Voronova, Privalova)
4. Ukraine 43.58
5. Greece 44.01
6. Finland 44.10

4 x 400 Metres Relay (23 Aug)
1. Germany 3:23.03
   (Feller, Rohländer, Rieger, Breuer)
2. Russia 3:23.56
(Khrushchelyova, Goncharenko, Bakhvalova, Kotlyarova)
3. GREAT BRITAIN & NI 3:25.66
(FRASER, JAMISON, MERRY, CURBISHLEY)
4. Romania 3:27.24
5. Czech Republic 3:27.54
6. France 3:27.61

AAA 10 MILE CHAMPIONSHIPS
Erewash 23 August 1998

MEN
1. GLYNN TROMANS   47:25
2. Benson Masya   KEN   48:12
3. DAVID TUNE   48:19

Team
1. Morpeth Harriers   70

WOMEN
    ALISON WYETH   55:55
1. MARIA BRADLEY   55:59
2. JILL BOLTZ   56:29
3. MIRANDA HEATHCOTE   56:35

Team
1. Border Harriers   71

RWA CHAMPIONSHIPS
Holmewood 29 August 1998

MEN 50k
1. TIM WATT   4:32:00
2. MIKE SMITH   4:49:40
3. CHRIS BERWICK   4:58:08
4. BRIAN ADAMS   5:11:11
5. ROBERT DOBSON   5:15:43
6. STEVE ARNOLD   5:38:30
7. GEORGE SMOLENSKI   5:45:54
8. IAN RICHARDS   5:46:47

Team
1. Leicester   14

WOMEN 20k
1. VICKY LUPTON   1:44:35
2. CATHERINE CHARNOCK   1:45:24
3. MARY WALLEN   2:04:01
4. JO HESKETH   2:06:48
5. GILL TROWER   2:10:27
6. JEANETTE BLEACH   2:17:53
7. PAM FICKEN   2:18:37
8. SHEILA BULL   2:21:35

Team
1. Steyning   15

SPAR BRITISH CHALLENGE - GB & NI v USA Glasgow 30 August 1998

MEN

100 Metres wind -1.8
1. Tim Harden   USA   10.32
3. DARREN CAMPBELL   10.37
4. DWAIN CHAMBERS   10.39
6. JASON GARDENER   10.57

200 Metres wind -1.7
1. DOUG TURNER   20.63
3. JOHN REGIS   21.22
4. JULIAN GOLDING   21.24

400 Metres
1. IWAN THOMAS   45.13
4. MARK HYLTON   45.75
5. JAMIE BAULCH   46.50

1 Mile
1. David Krummenacker USA   4:01.90
2. MATT YATES   4:03.65
3. KEVIN McKAY   4:05.07
6. GARY LOUGH   4:15.01

2 Miles
1. JOHN MAYOCK   8:54.16
2. NEIL CADDY   8:54.43
5. KARL KESKA   9:11.07

WOMEN

200 Metres wind -1.7
1. Toyah Brown   USA   23.66
3. JOICE MADUAKA   23.72
4. DONNA FRASER   23.73
5. SARAH WILHELMY   23.94

400 Metres
1. ALLISON CURBISHLEY   50.73
2. KATHARINE MERRY   51.02
6. MICHELLE THOMAS   53.77

110 Metres Hurdles wind -2.5
1. COLIN JACKSON   13.40
3. TONY JARRETT   13.78
6. ANDY TULLOCH   14.11

400 Metres Hurdles
1. Eric Thomas   USA   48.84
3. PAUL GRAY   50.05
4. ANTHONY BARSUMATO   50.22
6. MATT DOUGLAS   50.79

Long Jump
1. Kareem Streete-Thompson USA 8.07
2. CHRIS DAVIDSON   7.43
3. STEVE PHILLIPS   7.37

Triple Jump
1. JULIAN GOLLEY   16.63
3. LARRY ACHIKE   16.36

Shot
1. John Godina   USA   21.23
3. MARK PROCTOR   19.84
4. SHAUN PICKERING   17.90

1 Mile
1. KELLY HOLMES   4:28.04
2. PAULA RADCLIFFE   4:31.72
3. AMANDA CROWE   4:32.99

Women Match Result
1. GREAT BRITAIN & NI   36
2. United States   25

Discus
1. Adam Setcliff   USA   63.53
2. ROBERT WEIR   60.16
4. GLEN SMITH   57.60

Javelin
1. STEVE BACKLEY   85.13
2. MARK ROBERSON   gst   84.37
3. MICK HILL   82.57

4 x 100 Metres Relay
1. United States   38.47
    (Streete-Thompson, McCall, Johnson, Harden)
2. GREAT BRITAIN & NI   39.20
    (CONDON, REGIS, GOLDING, CHAMBERS)

4 x 400 Metres Relay
1. United States   3:04.96
    (Young, Woody, Wheeler, Campbell)
2. GREAT BRITAIN & NI   3:05.29
    (SLYTHE, HYLTON, BAULCH, THOMAS)
3. GREAT BRITAIN B   3:07.48
    (McBURNEY, DEACON, BORSUMATO, DOUGLAS)

Men Match Result
1. United States   107
2. GREAT BRITAIN & NI   105

Overall Match Result
1. GREAT BRITAIN & NI   141
2. United States   132

IAAF WORLD CUP Johannesburg, South Africa 11 - 13 September 1998

MEN

100 Metres wind -0.2 (11 Sep)
1. Obadele Thompson AME 9.87
2. Seun Ogunkoya AFR 9.92
3. DWAIN CHAMBERS 10.03
4. Tim Harden USA 10.03
5. Matt Shirvington AME 10.07
6. Haralambos Papadias EUR 10.15
7. Marc Blume GER 10.30
8. Zhou Wei ASI 10.37

200 Metres wind 1.3 (13 Sep)
1. Frank Fredericks AFR 19.97
2. Gentry Bradley USA 20.38
3. Troy Douglas EUR 20.40
4. Koji Ito ASI 20.40
5. DOUG TURNER 20.51
6. Sebastian Keitel AME 20.62
7. Darryl Wohlsen OCE 20.75
8. Manuel Milde GER 20.85

400 Metres (12 Sep)
1. IWAN THOMAS 45.33
2. Jerome Young USA 45.37
3. Troy McIntosh AME 45.45
4. Clement Chukwu AFR 45.56
5. Ashraf Saber EUR 46.54
6. Sugath Tillakaratne ASI 46.70
7. Patrick Dwyer OCE 46.99
8. Stefan Letzelter GER 47.12

800 Metres (11 Sep)
1. Nils Schumann GER 1:48.66
2. Mark Everett USA 1:48.73
3. Norberto Téllez AME 1:48.92
4. Japheth Kimutai AFR 1:49.16
5. Andre Bucher EUR 1:49.55
6. ANDY HART 1:50.07
7. Shaun Farrell OCE 1:50.69
8. Cheng Bin ASI 1:53.11

1500 Metres (12 Sep)
1. Laban Rotich AFR 3:40.87
2. Rui Silva EUR 3:40.95
3. ANTHONY WHITEMAN 3:40.99
4. Mohamed Suleiman ASI 3:46.93
5. Hamish Christensen OCE 3:48.64
6. Marc Ostendarp GER 3:49.56
7. Jason Pyrah USA 3:52.10
8. Steve Agar AME 3:57.36

3000 Metres (13 Sep)
1. Dieter Baumann GER 7:56.24
2. Isaac Viciosa EUR 7:56.47
3. Thomas Nyariki AFR 7:59.46
4. Pablo Olmedo AME 8:10.58
5. Toshinari Takaoka ASI 8:12.19
6. Dan Browne USA 8:15.88
7. NEIL CADDY 8:16.81
8. Alan Bunce OCE 8:20.98

5000 Metres (11 Sep)
1. Daniel Komen AFR 13:46.57
2. Shaun Creighton OCE 13:53.66
3. Dieter Baumann GER 13:58.40
4. Pablo Olmedo AME 14:01.66
5. KEITH CULLEN 14:13.32
6. Dan Browne USA 14:22.48
7. Abdellah Béhar EUR 14:24.41
Gulab Chand ASI dnf

3000 Metres Steeplechase (12 Sep)
1. Damlan Kallabis GER 8:31.25
2. Bernard Barmasai AFR 8:31.85
3. Saad Al-Asmari ASI 8:39.69
4. Alessandro Lambruschini EUR 8:54.10
5. CHRISTIAN STEPHENSON 8:55.67
6. Wander do Prado Moura AME 8:59.06
7. Pascal Dobert USA 9:08.36
8. Stephen Thurston OCE 9:37.13

110 Metres Hurdles 2.0 (13 Sep)
1. Falk Balzer GER 13.10
2. COLIN JACKSON 13.11
3. Anier Garcia AME 13.14
4. Robin Korving EUR 13.25
5. Chen Yanhao ASI 13.49
6. Rod Zuyderwyk OCE 13.78
7. Shawn Bownes AFR 21.33
8. Reggie Torian USA 30.29

400 Metres Hurdles (11 Sep)
1. Samuel Matete AFR 48.08
2. Mubarak Al-Nubi ASI 48.17
3. Dinsdale Morgan AME 48.40
4. Pawel Januszewski EUR 48.49
5. Joey Woody USA 48.55
6. Steffen Kolb GER 49.77
7. ANTHONY BORSUMATO 49.86
8. Zid Abou Hamed OCE 50.50

High Jump (13 Sep)
1. Charles Austin USA 2.31
2. Javier Sotomayor AME 2.28
3. Sergey Klyugin EUR 2.28
4. Martin Buss GER 2.25
5. Zhou Zhongge ASI 2.15
6= Nick Moroney OCE 2.10
6= DALTON GRANT 2.10
6= Hamad Abdulrahman AFR 2.10

Pole Vault (12 Sep)
1. Maksim Tarasov EUR 5.85
2. Tim Lobinger GER 5.80
3. Jeff Hartwig USA 5.70
4. Igor Potapovich ASI 5.60
5. Riaan Botha AFR 5.60
6. MIKE EDWARDS 5.40
7. Paul Burgess OCE 5.20
8. Edgar Diaz AME 5.00

Long Jump (11 Sep)
1. Ivan Pedroso AME 8.37
2. Jail Taurima OCE 8.32
3. Hatem Hassine Mersal AFR 8.26
4. Kirill Sosunov EUR 8.08
5. Roland McGhee USA 7.79
6. Masaki Morinaga ASI 7.76
7. Kofi Amoah Prah GER 7.75
8. STEVE PHILLIPS 7.66

Triple Jump (12 Sep)
1. Charles Friedek GER 17.42
2. Denis Kapustin EUR 17.32
3. Yoelbi Quesada AME 17.25
4. Andrew Owusu AFR 17.21
5. LaMark Carter USA 17.20
6. Andrew Murphy OCE 16.89
7. LARRY ACHIKE 16.69w
8. Duan Qifeng ASI 14.09

Shot (11 Sep)
1. John Godina USA 21.48
2. Aleksandr Bagach EUR 20.45
3. Oliver-Sven Buder GER 20.42
4. Burger Lambrechts AFR 20.29
5. MARK PROCTOR 19.66
6. Yoger Medina AME 19.08
7. Justin Anlezark OCE 18.26
8. Bilal Saad Mubarak ASI 18.21

Discus (12 Sep)
1. Virgilijus Alekna EUR 69.66
2. Lars Riedel GER 67.47
3. Frantz Kruger AFR 65.73
4. John Godina USA 65.15
5. ROBERT WEIR 64.39
6. Alexis Elizalde AME 62.53
7. Li Shaojie ASI 61.37
8. Ian Winchester OCE 60.56

Hammer (12 Sep)
1. Tibor Gécsek EUR 82.68
2. Heinz Weis GER 80.13
3. Andrey Abduvaliyev ASI 79.40
4. Alberto Sánchez AME 73.71
5. MICK JONES 72.89
6. Jud Logan USA 70.51
7. Chris Harmse AFR 68.34
8. Justin McDonald OCE 59.62

Javelin (13 Sep)
1. STEVE BACKLEY 88.71
2. Sergey Makarov EUR 86.96
3. Raymond Hecht GER 84.92
4. Marius Corbett AFR 83.53
5. Emeterio González AME 80.72
6. Adrian Hatcher OCE 73.75
7. Zhang Lianbiao ASI 68.35
Ed Kaminski USA dns

4 x 100 Metres (12 Sep)
1. GREAT BRITAIN & NI 38.09
(CONDON, DEVONISH, GOLDING, CHAMBERS)
2. USA 38.25
3. Africa 38.29
4. Americas 38.33
5. Oceania 38.78
6. Europe 38.80
7. Germany 38.89
8. Asia 39.35

4 x 400 Metres (13 Sep)
1. USA 2:59.28
(Everett, Pettigrew, Woody, Young)
2. GREAT BRITAIN & NI 2:59.71
(HYLTON, BAULCH, BALDOCK, THOMAS)
3. Americas 2:59.77
4. Africa 3:01.08
5. Germany 3:03.65
6. Asia 3:03.94
7. Europe 3:03.95
8. Oceania 3:08.57

Men Team Result
1. Africa 110
2. Europe 109
3. Germany 102
4. Americas 97
5. United States 94
6. GREAT BRITAIN & NI 89
7. Asia 64
8. Oceania 53

Women Team Result
1. United States 96
2. Europe 94
3. Africa 88
4. Russia 87
5. Americas 81
6. Germany 75
7. Asia 45
8. Oceania 42
(Note no British competitors)

CASTLE WALKS U20
Budapest, Hungary
7 September 1998

MEN 10k
1. Milos Batovsky SVK 43:59
8. MATTHEW HALES 46:44
12. TOM TAYLOR 47:45
13. MICHAEL KEMP 48:02
19. NIGEL WHORLOW 50:57

Team
1. Slovakia 69
4. GREAT BRITAIN & NI 48

WOMEN 5k
1. Zuzana Blazekova SVK 24:04
8. DEBBIE WALLEN 25:11
9. SARAH BENNETT 25:15
12. KATIE FORD 25:38
16. AMY HALES 25:17

Team
1. Slovakia 55
3. GREAT BRITAIN & NI 40

IAAF WORLD HALF-MARATHON CHAMPIONSHIPS
Zurich, Switzerland 27 September 1998

MEN
1. Paul Koech KEN 60:01
2. Hendrick Ramaala RSA 60:24
3. Khalid Skah MAR 60:24

Men Team
1. South Africa 3:02:21
2. Kenya 3:03:07
3. Ethiopia 3:05:18

No British competitors in men's race

WOMEN
1. Tegla Loroupe KEN 68:29
2. Elana Meyer RSA 68:32
3. Lidia Simon ROM 68:58
4. Olivera Jevtic YUG 70:02
5. Annemari Sandell FIN 70:04
6. Joyce Chepchumba KEN 70:10
7. Julia Vaquero ESP 70:33
8. Cristina Pomacu ROM 70:39
9. Yukiko Okamoto JPN 70:50
10. Leah Malot KEN 71:04
11. Albertina Dias POR 71:08
12. Alina Ivanova RUS 71:18
52. LIZ TALBOT 75:06
64. DEBBIE PERCIVAL 76:25
67. ALISON WYETH 76:44
71. MARIA BRADLEY 77:25
79. SUE REINSFORD 79:30

Women Team
1. Kenya 3:29:43
2. Romania 3:32:19
3. Spain 3:34:18
15. GREAT BRITAIN & NI 3:48:15

COMMONWEALTH GAMES Kuala Lumpur, Malaysia 16 - 21 September 1998

MEN
100 Metres wind -0.1 (17 Sep)
1. Ato Boldon TRI 9.88
2. Frank Fredericks NAM 9.96
3. Obadele Thompson BAR 10.00
4. Matt Shirvington AUS 10.03
5. DARREN CAMPBELL ENG 10.08
6. Eric Nkansah GHA 10.18
7. Chris Donaldson NZL 10.19
8. MARLON DEVONISH ENG 10.22
5s1 DWAIN CHAMBERS ENG 10.18
5s2 CHRISTIAN MALCOLM WAL 10.33
5q4 KEVIN WILLIAMS WAL 10.43
7q3 JAMIE HENTHORN WAL 10.52
7q2 IAN CRAIG NIR 10.71
8q2 ELLIOTT BUNNEY SCO 10.72
6h1 KEVIN FURLONG IOM 11.41

200 Metres wind -0.2 (19 Sep)
1. JULIAN GOLDING ENG 20.18
2. CHRISTIAN MALCOLM WAL 20.29
3. JOHN REGIS ENG 20.40
4. Anninos Marcoullides CYP 20.43
5. Daryl Wohlsen AUS 20.48
6. Matt Shirvington AUS 20.53
7. Chris Donaldson NZL 20.62
8. DOUG WALKER SCO 20.69

5s2 DOUG TURNER WAL 20.64
8s1 ALLYN CONDON ENG 21.06
5q3 JAMES HENTHORN WAL 21.02
6q4 IAN CRAIG NIR 21.51
4h1 PAUL McBURNEY NIR 21.65

400 Metres (18 Sep)
1. IWAN THOMAS WAL 44.52
2. MARK RICHARDSON ENG 44.60
3. Sugath Tillakeratne SRI 44.64
4. JAMIE BAULCH WAL 45.30
5. Andre Malherbe RSA 45.45
6. Greg Haughton JAM 45.49
7. Davian Clarke JAM 45.55
8. Kennedy Ochieng KEN 45.56
5s1 MARK HYLTON ENG 45.54
7s1 PAUL McBURNEY NIR 46.50
8s2 SOLOMON WARISO ENG 47.80
7q3 BRIAN FORBES NIR 47.41

800 Metres (19 Sep)
1. Japheth Kimutai KEN 1:43.82
2. Hezekiel Sepeng RSA 1:44.44
3. Johan Botha RSA 1:44.57
4. Savieri Ngidhi ZIM 1:45.18
5. ANDY HART ENG 1:45.71
6. BRADLEY DONKIN ENG 1:46.86

7. Crispen Mutakanyi ZIM 1:46.97
8. Kennedy Ngetich UGA 1:48.13
6s2 JASON LOBO ENG 1:47.96
5h4 GRANT GRAHAM SCO 1:49.25
3h5 RICHARD GIRVAN NIR 1:49.33
3h3 EDDIE KING NIR 1:49.38

1500 Metres (21 Sep)
1. Laban Rotich KEN 3:39.49
2. JOHN MAYOCK ENG 3:40.46
3. ANTHONY WHITEMAN ENG 3:40.70
4. John Kibowen KEN 3:42.71
5. KEVIN McKAY ENG 3:43.22
6. Hamish Christensen NZL 3:43.93
7. Stephen Agar CAN 3:44.17
8. Terrance Armstrong BER 3:44.57
9. CHRISTIAN STEPHENSON WAL 3:44.82

5000 Metres (19 Sep)
1. Daniel Komen KEN 13:22.57
2. Tom Nyariki KEN 13:28.09
3. Richard Limo KEN 13:37.42
4. KARL KESKA ENG 13:40.24
5. KEITH CULLEN ENG 13:44.69
6. Lee Troop AUS 13:56.32
7. KRIS BOWDITCH ENG 14:02.36
8. Allan Bunce NZL 14:02.98
8s1 IAN GILLESPIE SCO 14:50.34

10000 Metres (16 Sep)
1. Simon Maina KEN 28:10.00
2. William Kalya KEN 29:01.68
3. Steve Moneghetti AUS 29:02.76
4. Tsunaki Kalamore RSA 29:05.80
5. DERMOT DONNELLY NIR 29:05.96
6. Abel Chimukoko ZIM 29:10.53
7. Lee Troop AUS 29:34.23
8. Makhosonke Fika RSA 29:46.41
9. GLYNN TROMANS ENG 30:04.95

Marathon (20 Sep)
1. Thabiso Moqhali LES 2:19:15
2. Simon Basiligitwa TAN 2:19:42
3. Andea Geway Suja TAN 2:19:50
4. DAVID TAYLOR ENG 2:20:30
5. Frank Pooe RSA 2:21:12
6. Julius Kimutai KEN 2:21:57
7. Patrick Carroll AUS 2:22:14
8. Thabiso Ralekhetia LES 2:22:47
10. KEITH ANDERSON ENG 2:23:07
15. DALE RIXON WAL 2:26:50
17. STEVE BRACE WAL 2:29:21
21. WILLIAM BURNS ENG 2:31:16
   DAVE CAVERS SCO dnf

3000 Metres Steeplechase (17 Sep)
1. John Kosgei KEN 8:15.34
2. Bernard Barmasai KEN 8:15.37
3. Kipkurui Misoi KEN 8:18.24
4. Joël Bourgeois CAN 8:34.50
5. Chris Unthank AUS 8:37.24
6. CHRISTIAN STEPHENSON WAL 8:42.95
7. BEN WHITBY ENG 8:44.24
8. CRAIG WHEELER ENG 8:57.29
   SPENCER DUVAL ENG dnf

110 Metres Hurdles -0.1 (20 Sep)
1. TONY JARRETT ENG 13.47
2. Steve Brown TRI 13.48
3. Shaun Bownes RSA 13.53
4. PAUL GRAY WAL 13.62
5. Kyle Vander-Kuyp AUS 13.67
6. ANDREW TULLOCH ENG 13.67
7. Gregory Hines JAM 13.85
8. ROSS BAILLIE SCO 13.85
5s3 MATTHEW DOUGLAS NIR 15.13
6s3 KEVIN FURLONG IOM 15.22

400 Metres Hurdles (19 Sep)
1. Dinsdale Morgan JAM 48.28
2. Rohan Robinson AUS 48.99
3. Ken Harnden ZIM 49.06
4. Abou Hamed AUS 49.11
5. Victor Houston BAR 49.21
6. Kamel Thompson JAM 49.81
7. Eric Keter KEN 49.98
8. Wayne Whyte JAM 51.10
4s1 ANTHONY BORSUMATO ENG 50.15
4s2 MATTHEW DOUGLAS NIR 50.20
6s2 GARY JENNINGS ENG 50.94
8s1 MATTHEW ELIAS WAL 52.34

High Jump (19 Sep)
1. DALTON GRANT ENG 2.31
2. BEN CHALLENGER ENG 2.28
3. Tim Forsyth AUS 2.28
4. Khemraj Naiko MRI 2.28
5. BRENDAN REILLY ENG 2.24

6. Gavin Lendis RSA 2.24
7. Kum Zee Loo MAS 2.20
8. Mike Ponikvar CAN 2.20

Pole Vault (20 Sep)
1. Riaan Botha RSA 5.60
2. Paul Burgess AUS 5.50
3. Kersley Gardenne MRI 5.35
4. MATT BELSHAM ENG 5.25
5. KEVIN HUGHES ENG 5.15
6. Marcus Popp CAN 5.05
7. NEIL YOUNG NIR 4.80
   IAN TULLETT ENG nh
(2dqDenis Petushinskiy NZL 5.55)

Long Jump (20 Sep)
1. Peter Burge AUS 8.22
2. Jai Taurima AUS 8.22
3. Wendell Williams TRI 7.95
4. Shane Hair AUS 7.82
5. Mark Awere GHA 7.73
6. Chris Wright BAH 7.70
7. STEVE PHILLIPS ENG 7.64
8. CHRIS DAVIDSON ENG 7.62

Triple Jump (18 Sep)
1. LARRY ACHIKE ENG 17.10
2. Andrew Owusu GHA 17.03
3. Remy Limo KEN 16.89
4. JULIAN GOLLEY ENG 16.83
5. Ndabez. Mdhlongwa ZIM 16.51
6. Gable Garenamotse BOT 16.05
7. FEMI AKINSANYE ENG 16.02
8. Zaki Sadri MAS 15.94

Shot (21 Sep)
1. Burger Lambrechts RSA 20.01
2. Michalis Louca CYP 19.52
3. SHAUN PICKERING WAL 19.33
4. Clay Cross AUS 19.16
5. Janus Robberts RSA 19.15
6. Aaron Neighbour AUS 18.77
7. Justin Anlezark AUS 18.49
8. Ian Winchester NZL 18.35
9. STEPHAN HAYWARD SCO 16.89
10. MARK PROCTOR ENG 16.78
12. MARK EDWARDS ENG 16.59

Discus (17 Sep)
1. ROBERT WEIR ENG 64.42
2. Frantz Kruger RSA 63.93
3. Jason Tunks CAN 62.22
4. GLEN SMITH ENG 60.49
5. Ian Winchester NZL 60.06
6. Frits Potgeiter RSA 59.01
7. LEE NEWMAN WAL 56.28
8. PERRIS WILKINS ENG 55.39

Hammer (18 Sep)
1. Stuart Rendell AUS 74.71
2. MICHAEL JONES ENG 74.02
3. Chris Harmse RSA 72.83
4. PAUL HEAD ENG 70.36
5. DAVID SMITH ENG 69.77
6. Philip Jensaen NZL 69.63
7. John Stoikos CAN 65.07
8. STEVE WHYTE SCO 61.57

Javelin (21 Sep)
1. Marius Corbett RSA 88.75
2. STEVE BACKLEY ENG 87.38
3. MICK HILL ENG 83.80

4. MARK ROBERSON ENG 80.98
5. Andrew Currey AUS 80.05
6. Diggory Brooks NZL 75.55
7. James Goulding FIJ 73.68
8. NIGEL BEVAN WAL 73.06

Decathlon (17/18 Sep)
1. Jagan Hames AUS 8490
2. Scott Ferrier AUS 8307
3. Mike Smith CAN 8144
4. Doug Pirini NZL 8007
5. Peter Banks AUS 7859
6. Mike Nolan CAN 7703
7. DU'AINE LADEJO ENG 7633
8. Dominic Johnson STL 7587
9. ALEXEI SHARP SCO 7542
10. JAMIE QUARRY SCO 7482
   BARRY THOMAS ENG dnf
   RAFER JOSEPH ENG dnf

20 Kilometres Walk (17 Sep)
1. Nick A'Hern AUS 1:24:59
2. Arturo Huerta CAN 1:25:49
3. Nathan Doakes AUS 1:26:06
4. DARRELL STONE ENG 1:26:37
5. David K Rotich KEN 1:26:57
6. Teoh Boon Lim MAS 1:27:47
7. MARTIN BELL SCO 1:28:20
8. Julius Sawe KEN 1:29:23
10. CHRIS MADDOCKS ENG 1:30:21
12. ANDREW DRAKE ENG 1:32:04
13. STEPHEN PARTINGTON IOM 1:32:15

50 Kilometres Walk (21 Sep)
1. Govindaswamy Saravanan MAS 4:10:05
2. Duane Cousins AUS 4:10:30
3. Dominic McGrath AUS 4:12:50
4. STEVE HOLLIER ENG 4:18:41
5. MARK EASTON ENG 4:22:23
6. GRAHAM WHITE SCO 4:30:17
7. Kannian Pushparajan MAS 4:31:22
8. CHRIS CHEESEMAN ENG 4:38:36

4 x 100 Metres Relay (22 Sep)
1. ENGLAND 38.20
(CHAMBERS, DEVONISH, GOLDING, CAMPBELL)
2. Canada 38.46
3. Australia 38.69
4. WALES 38.73
(WILLIAMS, TURNER, MALCOLM, HENTHORN)
5. Cameroon 39.29
6. Sierra Leone 39.79
7. Ghana 40.00
8. Mauritius 42.70

4 x 400 Metres Relay (22 Sep)
1. Jamaica 2:59.03
2. ENGLAND 3:00.82
(SLYTHE, WARISO, HYLTON, RICHARDSON)
3. WALES 3:01.86
(GRAY, BAULCH, TURNER, THOMAS)
4. South Africa 3:02.21
5. Australia 3:02.96
6. Zimbabwe 3:03.02
7. Sri Lanka 3:04.11
8. Canada 3:04.84
7s1 NORTHERN IRELAND 3:07.27
(FORBES, DOUGLAS, E KING, McBURNEY)

WOMEN

100 Metres wind -0.3 (17 Sep)
1. Chandra Sturrup BAH 11.06
2. Philomena Mensah CAN 11.19
3. Tania Van Heer AUS 11.29
4. Lauren Hewitt AUS 11.37
5. Vida Nsiah GHA 11.39
6. Nova Peris-Kneebone AUS 11.41
7. JOICE MADUAKA ENG 11.50
8. Myriam Mani CMR 11.63
5s2 MARCIA RICHARDSON ENG 11.47
6s1 SIMMONE JACOBS ENG 11.71
8s1 MALGORZATA ROSTEK SCO 11.83

200 Metres wind 0.1 (19 Sep)
1. Nova Peris-Kneebone AUS 22.77
2. Juliet Campbell JAM 22.79
3. Lauren Hewitt AUS 22.83
4. Melinda Gainsford AUS 23.04
5. Heide Seyerling RSA 23.07
6. Vida Nsiah GHA 23.17
7. Philomena Mensah CAN 23.38
8. Monica Twum GHA 23.73
5s2 JOICE MADUAKA ENG 23.50
5s1 SIMMONE JACOBS ENG 23.73
6s1 MARCIA RICHARDSON ENG 23.82
5h4 STEPHANIE LLEWELLYN WAL 26.07

400 Metres (18 Sep)
1. Sandie Richards JAM 50.17
2. ALLISON CURBISHLEY SCO 50.71
3. DONNA FRASER ENG 51.01
4. Damayanthi Darsha SRI 51.06
5. Lee Naylor AUS 52.15
6. Veronica Bawuah GHA 52.70
7. Melissa Straker BAR 52.84
8. LaDonna Antoine CAN 52.93
7s2 MICHELLE THOMAS ENG 53.32
4h2 MICHELLE PIERRE ENG 53.92
5h3 STEPHANIE LLEWELLYN WAL 56.05

800 Metres (19 Sep)
1. Maria Mutola MOZ 1:57.60
2. Tina Paulino MOZ 1:58.39
3. DIANE MODAHL ENG 1:58.81
4. Mardrea Hyman JAM 1:59.71
5. Julia Sakara ZIM 2:00.60
6. Tamsin Lewis AUS 2:01.71
7. Lwiza John TAN 2:01.92
8. Gladys Wamuyu KEN 2:02.74
5s1 AMANDA CROWE NIR 2:01.83
7s1 RACHEL NEWCOMBE WAL 2:03.28
7s2 EMMA DAVIES WAL 2:05.03

1500 Metres (21 Sep)
1. Jackline Maranga KEN 4:05.27
2. KELLY HOLMES ENG 4:06.10
3. Julia Sakara ZIM 4:07.82
4. Naomi Mugo KEN 4:07.95
5. Cindy O'Krane CAN 4:08.88
6. AMANDA CROWE NIR 4:10.68
7. Leah Pells CAN 4:10.71
8. Tania Hodgkinson NZL 4:10.94
9. HELEN PATTINSON ENG 4:12.61
10. LYNN GIBSON ENG 4:13.35

5000 Metres (17 Sep)
1. Katie Anderson AUS 15:52.74
2. ANDREA WHITCOMBE ENG 15:56.85
3. Samukeliso Moyo ZIM 15:57.57
4. Restituta Joseph TAN 15:59.15
5. SARAH YOUNG ENG 15:59.79
6. Hamis Hussein TAN 16:01.25
7. Anne Cross AUS 16:14.98

10000 Metres (20 Sep)
1. Esther Wanjiru KEN 33:40.13
2. Kylie Risk AUS 33:42.11
3. Clare Fearnley AUS 33:52.13
4. VIKKI McPHERSON SCO 34:05.11
5. Margaret Okayo KEN 34:27.39
6. SARAH BENTLEY ENG 34:40.65
7. HAYLEY NASH WAL 35:20.14
8. ANGELA JOINER ENG 35:22.80
9. SALLY GOLDSMITH ENG 36:02.11

Marathon (20 Sep)
1. Heather Turland AUS 2:41:24
2. Lisa Dick AUS 2:41:48
3. Elizabeth Mongudhi NAM 2:43:28
4. GILLIAN HOROVITZ ENG 2:46:58
5. Leanne McPhillips NZL 2:49:36
6. DANIELLE SANDERSON ENG 2:50:54
7. Sarah Mahlangu RSA 2:59:38
8. Nthamane Malepa LES 3:02:14

100 Metres Hurdles -0.2 (21 Sep)
1. Gillian Russell JAM 12.70
2. Sriyani Kulawansa SRI 12.95
3. Katie Anderson CAN 13.04
4. Lesley Tashlin CAN 13.11
5. Bridgette Foster JAM 13.19
6. KERI MADDOX ENG 13.30
7. Debbie Edwards AUS 13.49
   Corien Botha RSA dsq
5s2 ANGIE THORP ENG 13.51
6s2 RACHEL KING WAL 13.73
6s1 ELIZABETH FAIRS ENG 13.79

400 Metres Hurdles (18 Sep)
1. Andrea Blackett BAR 53.91
2. GOWRY RETCHAKAN ENG 55.25
3. Karlene Haughton CAN 55.53
4. KERI MADDOX ENG 56.38
5. NATASHA DANVERS ENG 56.39
6. VIKKI JAMISON NIR 56.62
7. Mary Kapula VAN 59.87

High Jump (20 Sep)
1. Hestrie Storbeck RSA 1.91
2. JO JENNINGS ENG 1.91
3. Alison Inverarity AUS 1.88
4= MICHELLE DUNKLEY ENG 1.88
4= Lisa Bruty AUS 1.88
6. Nicole Forrester CAN 1.85
7. SUSAN JONES ENG 1.85
8. JULIE CRANE WAL 1.80

Pole Vault (19 Sep)
1. Emma George AUS 4.20
2. Elmarie Gerryts RSA 4.15
3. Trista Bernier CAN 4.15
4. JANINE WHITLOCK ENG 4.10
5. Rachel Dacy AUS 4.00
6. Jenny Dryburgh NZL 3.90
7= Melina Hamilton NZL 3.90
7= Cassandra Kelly AUS 3.90
7= Tracey Shepherd AUS 3.90
11. RHIAN CLARKE WAL 3.80
12. PAULA WILSON ENG 3.70
14. ALISON MURRAY- JESSEE SCO 3.50
15. EMMA HORNBY ENG 3.50

Long Jump (19 Sep)
1. JOANNE WISE ENG 6.63
2. Jackie Edwards BAH 6.59
3. Nicole Boegman AUS 6.58
4. Lacena Golding JAM 6.57
5. TRACY JOSEPH ENG 6.35
6. Chantal Brunner NZL 6.35
7. Frith Maunder NZL 6.20
8. Alice Falaiye CAN 6.13

Triple Jump (21 Sep)
1. ASHIA HANSEN ENG 14.32
2. Françoise Mbango CMR 13.95
3. CONNIE HENRY ENG 13.94
4. Natasha Gibson TRI 13.78
5. MICHELLE GRIFFITH ENG 13.77
6. Michelle Hastick CAN 13.64

Shot (18 Sep)
1. JUDY OAKES ENG 18.83
2. MYRTLE AUGEE ENG 17.16
3. Veronica Abrahamse RSA 16.52
4. Beatrice Faumuina NZL 16.41
5. Tania Lutton NZL 16.03
6. Helen Toussis AUS 15.65
7. MAGGIE LYNES ENG 15.18
8. Natalia Brown JAM 12.45

Discus (20 Sep)
1. Beatrice Faumuina NZL 65.92
2. Lisa-Marie Vizaniari AUS 62.14
3. Alison Lever AUS 59.90
4. SHELLEY DREW ENG 56.13
5. JACQUI McKERNAN NIR 55.16
6. PHILIPPA ROLES WAL 54.10
7. EMMA MERRY ENG 52.32
8. TRACY AXTEN ENG 51.58

Hammer (16 Sep)
1. Debbie Sosimenko AUS 66.56
2. LORRAINE SHAW ENG 62.66
3. Caroline Wittrin CAN 61.67
4. Karyne Perkins AUS 60.65
5. Denise Passmore AUS 59.10
6. Caroline Fournier MRI 59.02
7. LYN SPRULES ENG 59.01
8. Michelle Fournier CAN 57.78
11. RACHEL BEVERLEY ENG 55.34
12. SARAH MOORE WAL 47.79

Javelin (19 Sep)
1. Louise McPaul AUS 66.96
2. KAREN MARTIN ENG 57.82
3. KIRSTY MORRISON ENG 56.34
4. LORNA JACKSON SCO 52.97
5. SHELLEY HOLROYD ENG 50.64
6. Iloia Suaniu SAM 43.51
7. Lindy Leveaux SEY 42.94

Heptathlon (16/17 Sep)
1. DENISE LEWIS ENG 6513
2. Jane Jamieson AUS 6354
3. Joanne Henry NZL 6096
4. Catherine Bond-Mills CAN 5875
5. KERRY JURY ENG 5692
6. Marsha Mark TRI 5529
7. PAULINE RICHARDS SCO 5456
8. CLOVA COURT ENG 5421

10 Kilometres Walk (19 Sep)
1. Jane Saville AUS 43:57
2. Kerry Saxby-Junna AUS 44:27

3. LISA KEHLER ENG 45:03
4. Janice McCaffrey CAN 46:36
5. Annastasia Raj MAS 46:41
6. CAROLYN PARTINGTON IOM 48:09
7. VICKY LUPTON ENG 48:27
8. KIM BRAZNELL ENG 51:15
10. KAREN KNEALE IOM 52:25

4 x 100 Metres Relay (21 Sep)
1. Australia 43.39
2. Jamaica 43.49
3. ENGLAND 43.69
(RICHARDSON, FRASER, JACOBS, MADUAKA)

4. Ghana 43.81
5. Canada 44.23
6. Cameroon 45.26

4 x 400 Metres Relay (21 Sep)
1. Australia 3:27.28
2. ENGLAND 3:29.28
(THOMAS, PIERRE, DAY, FRASER)
3. Canada 3:29.97
4. Jamaica 3:34.74
5. Cameroon 3:35.50
6. Uganda 3:36.33
Barbados dnf
Malaysia dnf

ULTRA RUNNING
100K
River Shumanto, Japan
18 October 1998

EKIDEN RELAY Chiba, Japan 23 November 1998

MEN
1. Murzin RUS 6:30:06
2. Tyupin RUS 6:34:10
3. Kashapov RUS 6:36:33
6. SIMON PRIDE 6:59:38

WOMEN
1. CAROLYN HUNTER-ROWE 8:16:07
2. Flay NZL 8:19:11
3. Venancio BRA 8:21:55

MEN (10k,5k,10k,5k,12.195k)
1. Japan 2:00:19
2. Australia 2:00:39
3. New Zealand 2:01:29
15. GREAT BRITAIN 2:05:45
(DAVE TUNE, ROB BIRCHALL,
CARL WARREN, NICK COMERFORD,
MARK STEINLE)

WOMEN (10k,5k,10k,5k,4.767k, 7.428k)
1. Japan 2:16:11
2. China 2:19:25
3. Romania 2:20:15
7. GREAT BRITAIN 2:21:47
(JO THOMPSON, AMANDA PARKINSON,
MIRANDA HEATHCOTE, KATE RAMSEY,
PENNY THACKRAY, VICKY PINCOMBE)

EUROPEAN CROSS COUNTRY CHAMPIONSHIPS
Ferrara, Italy 13 December 1998

SENIOR MEN 9.6km
1. Sergey Lebed UKR 28:07
2. Mohammed Mourhit BEL 28:08
3. Driss El Himer FRA 28:16
4. Günther Weidlinger AUT 28:17
5. Carsten Jørgensen DEN 28:18
6. Eduardo Henriques POR 28:25
7. Giuliano Battocletti ITA 28:36
8. Manuel Pancorbo ESP 28:40
9. Julio Rey ESP 28:41
10. KEITH CULLEN 28:41
11. Paulo Guerra POR 28:42
12. Gabriele De Nard ITA 28:43
13. Martín Fiz ITA 28:43
14. João Junqueira POR 28:43
15. Umberto Pusterla ITA 28:43
18. DOMINIC BANNISTER 28:51
22. CHRISTIAN STEPHENSON 29:01
41. NEIL CADDY 29:28
47. GLYNN TROMANS 29:41
51. GLEN STEWART 29:46

Team
1. Italy 53
2. Portugal 55
3. Spain 68
4. GREAT BRITAIN & NI 91
5. France 92

SENIOR WOMEN 5.6km
1. PAULA RADCLIFFE 18:07
2. Annemari Sandell FIN 18:10
3. Olivera Jevtic YUG 18:11
4. Fernanda Ribeiro POR 18:19
5. Helena Sampaio POR 18:26
6. Yanna Belkacem FRA 18:42
7. Albertina Dias POR 18:46
8. Luisa Larraga ESP 18:49
9. Zahia Dahmani FRA 18:50
10. Fatima Yvelain FRA 18:52
11. Ana Dias POR 18:52
12. Cristina Iloc ROM 18:53
13. Constantina Dita ROM 18:53
14. Charlotte Audier FRA 18:54
15. Una English IRL 18:56
26. ALISON WYETH 19:15
28. HAYLEY NASH 19:20
37. LUCY ELLIOT 19:43
39. HELEN PATTISON 19:46

Team
1. Portugal 16
2. France 25
3. Romania 41
4. Spain 54
5. GREAT BRITAIN & NI 57

UNDER 20 MEN 5.6km
1. Youssef El Nasri ESP 16:50
2. Ovidiu Tat ROM 16:51
3. Gareth Turnbull IRL 16:55
4. SAM HAUGHIAN 16:57
9. PETER RILEY 17:15
17. CHRIS THOMPSON 17:27
40. CHRIS LIVESEY 17:45
53. DANIEL ROWEN 17:59

Team
1. Spain 28
2. GREAT BRITAIN & NI 30
3. Romania 36

UNDER 20 WOMEN 3.6km
1. Katalin Szentgyörgyi HUN 11:51
2. Ines Monteiro POR 11:58
3. Sonja Stolic YUG 12:03
14. KELLY KAFFEL 12:28
22. SONIA THOMAS 12:39
24. SUSANNE PARTRIDGE 12:41
39. CLAIRE COLMER 12:56
60. LOUISE KELLY 13:23

Team
1. Turkey 20
2. Belgium 46
3. Romania 49
7. GREAT BRITAIN & NI 60

REGIONAL CHAMPIONSHIPS

MEN

	SCOTLAND Edinburgh, 17-18 July		WALES Cwmbran, 20 June		NORTHERN IRELAND Belfast, 27 June	
100	Ian Mackie	10.00w	Colin Jackson	10.47	Ian Craig	11.1
200	Michael Afilaka	21.16w	Christian Malcolm	21.01	Paul McBurney	21.52
400	Andrew Mitchell	47.51	Iwan Thomas	45.45	Brian Forbes	47.80
800	Grant Graham	1:48.13	Matthew Shone	1:50.89	Richard Girvan	1:50.81
1500	Glen Stewart	3:55.88	Christian Stephenson	3:46.2	Eddie King	3:46.37
5000	Glen Stewart	14:40.24	Mark Morgan	14:28.11	Pauric McKinney (IRE)	14:37.98
10000	Robert Quinn	29:36.54	Andres Jones	30:21.4	Donal Gallagher	31:37.0
3kSt	Christian Nicolson	8:56.40	Donald Naylor	9:21.1	Martin Kearns	9:26.25
110H	Ross Baillie	13.99w	James Archampong	15.00	Sean Carroll	14.80
400H	Blair Young	51.35	Philip Harries	57.50	Brian Liddy (IRE)	52.03
HJ	Geoff Parsons	2.10	Andrew Penk	1.95	Glenn Morante (AUS)	2.00
PV	Neil Young	4.80	Andrew Penk	4.70	Brendan McConville	4.15
LJ	Jamie Quarry	7.07	Andrew Wooding	7.03	Stuart Finnie	6.60
TJ	Alvin Walker	15.40	Charles Madeira-Cole	15.40	John Donnelly	14.30
SP	Stephan Hayward	17.95	Shaun Pickering	19.14	John Farrelly (IRE)	15.20
DT	Lee Newman	59.38	Lee Newman	56.54	John Moreland	46.51
HT	Steve Whyte	61.71	Graham Holder	61.61	Adrian Palmer	58.05
JT	Phil Parry	65.12	Shane Lewis	67.96	Nigel Carlisle	53.89
Dec	Stephen Robertson	5846	Paul Jones	6389	Brendan McConville	6017
10kW			Martin Bell	43:47.6	3kW Pierce O'Callaghan (IRE)	12:01.0
Dec	Scotstoun, Glasgow 2-3 May		10000 Barry 24 June		10000 Antrim 29 August	
			Dec Wrexham 1-2 August		Dec Antrim 29-30 August	

WOMEN

100	Malgorzata Rostek	11.63	Catherine Murphy	12.12	Tamsin Stephens	13.1
200	Allison Curbishley	22.90w	Catherine Murphy	23.8	Marissa Smith	24.85
400	Lisa Vannet	54.92	Alyson Layzell	53.81	Stephanie Llewellyn	54.69
800	Susan Scott	2:07.89	Rachel Newcombe	2:06.89	Kelly McNeice	2:10.96
1500	Hayley Parkinson	4:21.83	Ceri Thomas	4:39.7	Pauline Thom	4:29.92
5000	Katie Skorupska	16:46.08	Hayley Nash	16:53.07	3000 Sharon Hatch	9:55.20
10000			Hayley Nash	34:28.8	Janice McCartney	43:03.4
100H	Katie Sketchley	13.73w	Rachel King	13.81	Tamsin Stephens	15.49
400H	Sinead Dudgeon	59.53	Abigail Jones	66.66		
HJ	Lee McConnell	1.75	Julie Crane	1.80	Carrie Donnelly	1.60
PV	Alison Murray-Jessee	3.20	Rhian Clarke	3.70	Emma Hornby	3.91
LJ	Ruth Irving	5.92	Aimee Cutler	5.75	Danea Herron	4.93
TJ	Kerensa Denham	12.53	Susanne Bunting	10.89	Siobhan Hoey (IRE)	12.25
SP	Navdeep Dhaliwal	12.78	Philippa Roles	13.91	Julie McCorry	12.98
DT	Ailish O'Brien (IRE)	48.23	Philippa Roles	50.61	Jackie McKernan	53.16
HT	Mhairi Walters	46.40	Sarah Moore	52.39	Nicola Coffey (IRE)	49.79
JT	Lorna Jackson	55.79	Caroline White	47.16	Alison Moffitt	44.30
Hep	Pauline Richards	5393	Amanda Wale	4546	Tamsin Stephens	4250
Hep	Scotstoun, Glasgow 2-3 May		10000 Barry 24 June		10000 Antrim 29 August	
			Hep Wrexham 1-2 August		Hep Antrim 29-30 August	

AREA CHAMPIONSHIPS

	SOUTH — Watford, 20-21 June		MIDLANDS — Birmingham, 22-23 August		NORTH — Liverpool, 20-21 June	
MEN						
100	Josephus Thomas	10.39	Michael Tietz	10.51	Dominic Bradley	11.03
200	Marcus Adam	20.77	Andrew Walcott	21.43	Jared Deacon	21.40
400	Adrian Patrick	46.78	Daniel Bruce	49.22	Guy Bullock	46.36
800	Anthony Draper	1:51.17	Robert Scanlon	1:53.7	Stuart Bailey	1:52.68
1500	Stephen Sharp	3:48.86	Robert Scanlon	3:53.43	Terence West	3:52.48
3000	Patrick Davoren (IRE)	8:14.4	Darius Burrows	8:18.7		
5000	Dale Laughlin	14:26.35	Martin Palmer	14:44.64	Paul Taylor	14:12.17
10000	William Foster	30:36.03			Greg Hull	31:07.2
3kSt	Andy Coleman	9:00.88	David Anderson	10:23.23	Lee Hurst	8:55.04
110H	Jamie Quarry	14.16w	Robert Newton	14.58	Dominic Bradley	14.35
400H	Edward Betts	52.01	Paul Hibbert	53.28	Anthony Williams	51.67
HJ	Brendan Reilly	2.15	Stuart Smith	2.00	Richard Dent	2.10
PV	Kevin Hughes	5.36	Christian North	4.70	Duncan Pearce	4.70
LJ	John Munroe	7.13	Steve Phillips	7.79w	Jan Irving	7.13
TJ	Tosi Fasinro	16.63w	Paul Weston	15.34	David Sanderson	14.60w
SP	David Callaway	16.61	Laine Snook	15.12	John Nicholls	14.62
DT	Perris Wilkins	57.62	Kevin Brown	57.57	Paul Reed	51.06
HT	Paul Head	69.93	Stephen Pearson	65.27	Mike Floyd	61.55
JT	Daniel Carter	69.30	Michael Tarran	58.69	Greg Markham	59.13
10kW	Mark Easton	45:15.6	Martin Young	46:40.79	10kW cancelled	
Dec	Stephen Garland	6503	Par Eregbona	6340	Roger Hunter	5837
3kW	Darrell Stone	12:31.50				

SOUTH:
3000 Brighton 19 August
10000 Bedford 29 August
Dec Enfield 1-2 August
10kW London (BP) 29 April

MIDLANDS:
3000 Solihull 29 July
10kW Solihull 23-24 May

NORTH:
10000 Blackpool 6 September
Dec Derby 30-31 May

	SOUTH		MIDLANDS		NORTH	
WOMEN						
100	Marcia Richardson	11.61	Ellena Ruddock	11.85	Rebecca White	12.25
200	Sarah Wilhelmy	23.25	Ellena Ruddock	25.09	Rebecca White	24.24
400	Natasha Danvers	53.26	Helen Frost	54.6	Kim Goodwin	56.45
800	Joanne Fenn	2:08.60	Vicki Andrews	2:12.18	Bev Blakeman	2:06.65
1500	Andrea Whitcombe	4:18.24	Claudia Minguez	4:40.66	Kerry Smithson	4:26.36
3000	Jenny Brown	9:52.8	Kate Ramsay	9:50.57		
5000	Alison Fletcher	17:17.1	Tara Krzywicki	16:12.2	Sarah Young	16:29.89
100H	Melanie Wilkins	13.47w	Keri Maddox	13.7	Elizabeth Fairs	14.19
400H	Jacqui Parker	57.70	Keri Maddox	58.31	Nicola Sutton	59.94
HJ	Dalia Mikneviciute	1.80	Julie Crane	1.75	Susan Jones	1.75
PV	Lucy Webber	3.80	Dawn-Alice Wright	2.90	Lisa Stanton	3.65
LJ	Tracy Joseph	6.28	Syreena Pinel	5.65	Ruth Irving	6.01
TJ	Michelle Griffith	13.42	Deborah Rowe	12.52w	Hilde Kaland (NOR)	12.27w
SP	Judy Oakes	17.88	Carol Parker	14.22	Nicola Gautier	13.74
DT	Shelley Drew	59.95	Rebecca Hardy	44.12	Susan Backhouse	41.99
HT	Lyn Sprules	59.40	Ann Gardner	52.78	Suzanne Roberts	46.91
JT	Kirsty Morrison	53.31	Sharon Gibson	46.40	Jenny Kemp	45.92
3kW	Deborah Wallen	16:03.33				
5kW			Melanie Wright	25:37.69	Carolyn Partington	23:32.03
Hept	Clover Wynter-Pink	4754	Hannah Stares	4119	Kim Crowther-Price	4680

SOUTH:
3000 Brighton 19 August
5000 Enfield 2 August
Hept Enfield 1-2 August

MIDLANDS:
3000 Solihull 24 May
5kW Soilhull 24 May

NORTH:
Hept Derby 30-31 May

AGE CHAMPIONSHIPS

Under 20 MEN
Bedford, 4-5 July

100	Christian Malcolm	10.17w
200	Christian Malcolm	20.32w
400	Alloy Wilson	48.04
800	Chris Moss	1:50.09
1500	Chris Livesey	3:53.79
5000	Samuel Haughian	14:39.00
3kSt	Chris Thompson	9:06.20
110H	Ben Warmington	14.24w
400H	Richard McDonald	52.63
HJ	Martin Lloyd	2.09
PV	Christian Linskey	5.00
LJ	Stuart Wells	7.38w
TJ	Jonathan Wallace	15.76w
SP	Carl Myerscough	19.24
DT	Emeka Udechuku	60.97
HT	Andrew Grierson	54.12
JT	David Parker	72.95
10kW	Thomas Tayor	45:56.16

Sheffield 15 August

3000	David Hibbert	8:27.93

Derby 30-31 May

Dec	Darren Hatton	6477

Under 17
Sheffield, 15-16 August

	Mark Lewis-Francis	10.49
	Tim Benjamin	21.15w
	Aaron Evans	49.13
	Matthew Thomson	1:56.79
	Richard Ward	4:00.89
1500St	Mark Griffith	4:22.89
100H	Nathan Palmer	12.96w
	Nange Ursell	55.32
	Kenneth McKeown	2.00
	Chris Type	4.35
	Darrell Aldridge	7.14
	Stephen Shalders	15.38
	Gregg Beard	16.49
	James Rumbold	47.03
	Matthew Sutton	71.45
	Richard Lainson	54.70
5kW	Colin Griffin (IRE)	23:41.47

Derby 30 May

	Stephen Bates	8:53.65

Birmingha 22-23 August

Oct	Dominic Girdler	5210

Under 15
Sheffield, 15-16 August

	Tom Hyde	11.27
	Tom Hyde	22.40w
	Craig Erskine	51.84
	Chris Stoves	2:03.47
	Amanuel Tshaye	4:17.85
80H	Edward Dunford	11.45
	Chuka Enih-Snell	1.95
	Alan Jervis	3.50
	Jordan Lau	6.68
	Andrew Harris	12.78
	Carl Saggers	15.64
	Carl Saggers	43.36
	Carl Saggers	60.15
	James Deacon-Brown	53.46
3kW	Lloyd Finch	13:29.59

Derby 30 May

	Phil Nicholls	9:12.72

Birmingham 22-23 August

Pen	Chuka Enih-Snell	3039

Under 20 WOMEN
Bedford, 4-5 July

100	Rebecca White	11.45w
200	Sarah Wilhelmy	23.31w
400	Carey Easton	55.90
800	Emma Ward	2:12.08
1500	Caroline Walsh	4:30.37
3000	Amber Gascoigne	9:46.06
100H	Sarah Claxton	13.28w
400H	Rachael Kay	60.83
HJ	Aileen Wilson	1.79
PV	Rachel Dacy (AUS)	3.70
LJ	Sarah Claxton	6.34w
TJ	Judy Kotey	12.61w
SP	Julie Dunkley	14.81
DT	Lauren Keightley	49.58
HT	Rachael Beverley	56.35
JT	Kelly Morgan	50.32
5kW	Katie Ford	25:30.29

Derby 30-31 May

Hept	Danielle Freeman	4915

Under 17
Birmingham, 15-16 August

	Donna Maylor	11.76w
	Kim Wall	24.52w
300	Kim Wall	38.55
	Claire Taylor	2:12.52
	Emma Ward	4:38.32
	*Collette Fagan	10:33.75
	* Derby 30/31 May	
80H	Helen Worsey	11.02
300H	Wendy Davidson	44.27
	Deirdre Ryan (IRE)	1.73
	Lindsay Hodges	3.20
	Aimee Cutler	5.84
	Rachel Peacock	11.47
	Claire Smithson	12.73
	Emma Carpenter	41.30
	Lucy Marshall	43.10
	Michelle Lonsdale	41.93
	Sheena O'Keefe (IRE)	24:35.02

Birmingham 22-23 August

Hept	Nichola Sanders	4298

Under 15
Birmingham, 15-16 August

	Danielle Selley	12.15
	Cherie Pierre	25.03w
	Lisa Dobriskey	2:12.79
	Charlotte Moore	4:44.12
75H	Danielle Selley	11.08
	Aileen Wilson	1.75
	Zainah Ceesay	5.55
	Gillian Austin (IRE)	11.58
	Angela Lockley	33.66
	Samantha Redd	39.81
3kW	Natalie Evans	15:41.71

Birmingham 22-23 August

Pen	Aileen Wilson	3027

UK MERIT RANKINGS 1998 Compiled by Peter Matthews

This is the 31st successive year that I have compiled annual merit rankings of British athletes. As usual they are based on an assessment of form during the outdoor season. The major factors by which the rankings are determined are win-loss record, performances in the major meetings, and sequence of marks.

I endeavour to be as objective as possible, but form can often provide conflicting evidence, or perhaps an athlete may not have shown good enough results against leading rivals, or in very important competition, to justify a ranking which his or her ability might otherwise warrant.

I can only rank athletes on what they have actually achieved. Much depends on having appropriate opportunities. It is obviously harder for an athlete living in a remote part of the UK than one who is close to the major centres of competition, and it may be hard to break into the élite who get the invitations for the prestige meetings. Difficulties also arise when athletes reach peak form at different parts of the season or, through injury, miss significant competition. Once again it should be pointed out that the rankings are by no means necessarily the order in which I think the athletes would have finished in an idealised contest, but simply my attempt to assess what has actually happened in 1998.

I hope that I have not missed many performances, but I would be very pleased to receive any missing results at 10 Madgeways Close, Great Amwell, Herts SG12 9RU.

For each event the top 12 are ranked. On the first line is shown the athletes name, then their date of birth followed, in brackets, by the number of years ranked in the top 12 (including 1998) and their ranking last year (1997), and finally, their best mark prior to 1998. The following lines include their best six performances of the year (followed, for completeness, by significant indoor marks indicated by 'i', although indoor form, the subject of a separate assessment, is not considered in the rankings). Then follow placings at major meetings, providing a summary of the athlete's year at the event.

Abbreviations include

AAA v LC	AAA v Loughborough Students
BedG	Bedford Games
BGP	British Grand Prix at Sheffield
BL	British League
B.Univs	British Universities at Bath
CAU	Inter-Counties at Bedford
CG	Commonwealth Games
Cork	Cork City Sports
Cup	BAL Cup Final at Bedford (also major clashes in semis – sf)
E.Clubs	European Clubs Cup
ECh	European Championships at Budapest
ECp	European Cup
E.Sch	English Schools
GhG	BUPA Games at Gateshead
GPF	Grand Prix Final at Moscow
HCI	Home Countries International
IR	Inter-regional at Birmingham
IS	Inter-Services
JIvFS	Junior international v France and Spain at Alicante
Jnr IA	Junior Inter-area
U23D	Under 23 international v Germany, France at Dessau
U23H	Under 23 international v France at Hexham
v USA	UK v USA at Glasgow
WCp	World Cup at Johannesburg
WG	Welsh Games at Cardiff
WJ	World Junior Championships

BRITISH MERIT RANKINGS 1998 - MEN

100 METRES
1. **Darren Campbell** 12.9.73 (7y, 3) 10.13 '97   10.04, 10.08, 10.11, 10.13, 10.18, 10.18
   4 Sydney, 3 E.Clubs, 2 Hengelo, 3 Helsinki, 2 ECp inv, 2B Lille, 1/1 Budapest, 1 AAA, 1 ECh, 7 Lausanne, 3 v USA, 5 CG, BL1: 1,2,-,-
2. **Dwain Chambers** 5.4.78 (3y, 4) 10.06 '97   10.03rA, 10.10, 10.15, 10.18, 10.23, 10.24
   7 Doha, 5 Hania, 1 U23H, 3 ECp inv, 2 AAA, 1 BGP, 5h Zürich, 2 ECh, 4 v USA, 3 WCp, 5s1 CG
3. **Marlon Devonish** 1.6.76 (2y, 5) 10.22/10.13w '97   10.13, 10.15w, 10.21, 10.22, 10.22, 10.24
   1 BedG, 2C Lille, 1 GhG, 3 AAA, 2 BGP, 5 ECh, 8 CG
4. **Christian Malcolm** 3.6.79 (2y,11) 10.24 '97   10.10w, 10.12, 10.17w, 10.18, 10.22w, 10.26w
   1D AAA v LC, 1 Mannheim, 1 BL2 (2), 1 AAA-J, 2 Welsh, 1 JlvFS, 1 WJ, 6h Zürich, 8B Lausanne, 5s2 CG
5. **Ian Mackie** 27.2.75 (3y, 2) 10.17 '96   10.00w, 10.16w, 10.31, 10.38, 10.47, 10.65
   5 Doha, 6B Lille, 1 Scot, 2 BedG, 5 GhG
6. **Doug Walker** 28.7.73 (1y, -) 10.31 '97   10.01w, 10.17w, 10.27w, 10.37w, 10.38w; 10.8
   1 Leeds, 2 Scot, 1 BL1 (3), 1 WG
7. **Jason Gardener** 18.9.75 (4y, 6) 10.25 '94, 10.17w '97   10.17w, 10.29w, 10.30, 10.33, 10.33, 10.33; 10.0w
   3 Jena, 1 Caorle, 1 ECp inv, 3= BedG, 3 GhG, 4 AAA, 3 BGP, 2 WG, 6 v USA
8. **Owusu Dako** 23.5.73 (3y, -) 10.35/10.30w '96, 10.3 '97   10.17w, 10.36, 10.37, 10.39, 10.41, 10.44
   1 AAA v LC, 2 Ljubljana, 1 BL1 (2), 3= BedG, 6 GhG, 6 AAA, 5 BGP
9. **Colin Jackson** 18.2.67 (4y, -) 10.29 '90   10.31, 10.32, 10.41, 10.45, 10.45w, 10.47
   4 Milan, 4 Athens, 3 ECp, 1 Welsh, 4 WG
10. **Allyn Condon** 24.8.74 (3y, 12) 10.36/10.33w '96   10.29w, 10.42, 10.49w, 10.58, 10.59, 10.59; 10.4, 10.5; 1r1 BedG, 5 BedG, 4 GhG, 4 BGP, BL1: 1B,-,1B,-
11. **Daniel Money** 7.10.76 (2y, 9) 10.32, 10.16w '97   10.18w, 10.23w, 10.35w, 10.44w?,10.52w, 10.65
   2 AAA v LC, 1 Cork, 3r1 BedG, 3 Leeds, 6 Bedford, BL1: 4,1B,2,-
12. **Jason Livingston** 17.3.71 (5y, 7) 10.09 '92   10.24w, 10.27w, 10.29w, 10.31, 10.39, 10.39w
   2B Doha, 3 Caorle, 7 BedG, 1r2 Cork, 3 BL1 (3), 7 GhG, 6s2 AAA, 5 WG
nr   **Josephus Thomas** SLE 11.7.71 10.39/10.20w '97, 10.2 '96   10.19w, 10.29, 10.31, 10.32, 10.39, 10.42w; 10.2w, 10.3, 10.3w; 1 Middx, 1 South, 1 IS, 5 AAA, 3 WG, 6s1 CG, BL2: -,-,1,1

The successors to Linford Christie took a while to get into their stride, with relatively modest form in the opening months of the season, but from the AAAs were in great form, with Campbell winning there and at the Europeans to take top ranking. There is a case for Gardener being higher, but Walker beat him when they met, and he was 1-1 with Mackie, who beat Walker, when the Scots ran very fast times with a wind of +2.9 in their championships. Just missing out is Kevin Williams, 5-0 over Jamie Henthorn and 1-1 v Livingston. Including Josephus Thomas, the 10th best performer is at 10.31, which equals the record high set in 1997.

200 METRES
1. **Doug Walker** 28.7.73 (5y, 2) 20.49 '97   20.35, 20.38, 20.42, 20.47w, 20.53, 20.59; 20.4w
   1 CAU, 1 Bed G, 1 Coimbra, 1 ECp, 1 AAA, 1 ECh, 8 CG, BL1: -,1,1,-
2. **Julian Golding** 17.2.75 (5y, 1) 20.38 '97   20.18, 20.34, 20.39, 20.51, 20.57w, 20.61; 20.46i, 20.57i
   2 Kalamata, 1 Hania, 5 St Denis, 4 Bratislava, 2 Turku, 6 Lille, 3 AAA, 4 BGP, 3 ECh, 4 v USA, 1 CG
3. **Christian Malcolm** 3.6.79 (2y, 5) 20.83/20.48w '97   20.29, 20.32w, 20.44, 20.53, 20.56, 20.62
   2 AAA v LC, 1 BL2 (2), 2 Leeds, 1 Mannheim, 1 Welsh, 1 AAA-J, 1 WJ, 2 CG
4. **Doug Turner** 2.12.66 (4y, 4) 20.43 '96, 20.36w '97   20.51A, 20.55, 20.63, 20.63, 20.64, 20.64
   1 sf Derby, 2 IR, 2 AAA, 6 BGP, 1 WG, 1 BL2 (4), 2 ECh, 1 v USA, 5 WCp, 5s2 CG
5. **John Regis** 13.10.66 (13y, -) 19.87A '94, 19.94 '93   20.40, 20.49, 20.56, 20.56, 20.58, 20.78
   5 Doha, 2 Sundsvall, 3 Turku, 4 AAA, 2 WG, 1 BL1 (4), 2 Cup, 3 v USA, 3 CG
6. **Darren Campbell** 12.9.73 (5y, 11) 20.84 '97, 20.55w '93   20.48, 20.70; 21.4w, 21.5
   1 Sundsvall, 3 BGP
7. **Allyn Condon** 24.8.74 (4y, 10) 20.63 '97   20.71, 20.83, 20.90, 20.93, 21.01, 21.06; 20.53i, 20.59i, 20.68i, 20.69i, 20.72i;   1 AAA v LC, 2 Milan, 6 Bratislava, 7 Athens, 2 BL1 (3), 5 AAA, 3 WG, 1 Cup, 8s1 CG
8. **Marcus Adam** 28.2.68 (10y, 8) 20.41 '92, 20.10w '90   20.73, 20.77, 20.78, 20.80, 20.87, 20.99
   1 South, 1B BL2 (3), 1 IR, 6 AAA, 2 Hechtel, 6 WG
9. **Solomon Wariso** 11.11.66 (6y, -) 20.50 '95   20.76, 20.95, 21.31; 20.9, 21.1; 20.86i, 20.93i, 21.26i
   6 Walnut, 3 Leiden, BL2: -,2,1,-
10. **Owusu Dako** 23.5.73 (5y, 7) 20.57 '95   20.99, 21.06, 21.20, 21.41   7 AAA, 1B BL1 (4)
11. **Mark Richardson** 26.7.72 (1y, -) 20.62 '97, 20.6w '96   20.77; 1 Irvine
12. **Marlon Devonish** 1.6.76 (3y, 6) 20.65/20.61w '97   20.92, 21.07, 21.11w;   2 Irvine, 1 U23H, 2 Rhede
–   **Adrian Patrick** 15.6.73 (2y, -) 21.02/20.9 '96, 20.62w '95   20.90w, 20.99w, 21.63, 21.65; 20.9, 21.1, 21.4
   1B AAA v LC, 2 CAU, 3 Ljubljana, 1 BL3 (4)
–   **Jamie Henthorn** 20.2.77 (0y, -) 21.12 '95, 21.0w '97   21.01, 21.02, 21.13, 21.26, 21.38, 21.47; 21.3; 20.99i, 21.26i;   1 B.Univs, 2 BL2 (3), 3 IR, 6s1 AAA, 2 U23D, 4 WG, 5qf CG

Golding dropped a place from his 1997 top ranking, but ended the year in superb form, running, in Kuala Lumpur, the two fastest times of the year by a British athlete. His Commonwealth gold showed him at his peak, but he had only just made the British team for Budapest with his 3rd at the AAAs, and was third at the Europeans. Winning in great style there and indeed undefeated prior to his knee operation was the Scot, Walker, and he thoroughly deserved top ranking and a position well up in the world top ten. Remarkably he came back from his arthroscopic surgery to make the Commonwealth final. Malcolm was a brilliant world junior champion and improved yet further to take Commonwealth silver in a European junior record. He also took the Welsh record from Doug Turner, another to have a fine season. Turner started his outdoor campaign late, but soon took 2nd at both AAAs and Europeans. He was 3-1 against Commonwealth bronze medallist Regis, who made a welcome return to top form and now rates as the best of all-time in the UK rankings at this event. Campbell only ran four 200m races, but beat Golding, Turner and Regis.

400 METRES
1. **Iwan Thomas** 5.1.74 (5y, 1) 44.36 '97   44.38, 44.50, 44.50, 44.52, 44.52, 44.54, 44.61, 44.77
   4/4/3/ in S.Africa, 1 Ljubljana, 3 Bratislava, 1 Welsh, 1 Budapest, 2 Oslo, 5 Rome, 1AAA, 2 BGP, 4 Monaco, 5 Zürich, 1 ECh, 3 Brussels, 1 v USA, 3 GPF,1 WCp, 1 CG
2. **Mark Richardson** 26.7.72 (9y, 2) 44.47 '97   44.37, 44.37, 44.48, 44.53, 44.60, 44.62, 44.62, 44.88
   1 Cottbus, 1 Helsinki, 1 ECp, 1 Oslo, 2 Rome, 2AAA, 1 BGP, 3 Monaco, 4 Zürich, 3 ECh, 4 Lausanne, 1 GPF, 2 CG
3. **Roger Black** 31.3.66 (13y, 4) 44.37 '96   44.71, 45.18, 45.20, 45.36, 45.38, 45.51
   1 Bratislava, 2 Helsinki, 7 Rome, 4 AAA, 3 BGP
4. **Solomon Wariso** 11.11.66 (1y, -) 0   44.68, 45.23, 45.59, 45.70, 46.11, 46.27; 45.71i
   2 Barcelona, 3 AAA, 3 Stockholm, dq ECh, dq Brussels, 8s2 CG
5. **Jamie Baulch** 3.5.73 (5y, 3) 44.57 '96   44.83, 45.30, 45.64, 45.67, 45.88, 45.93
   3 Doha, 3 Jena, 4 Bratislava, 5 Helsinki, 8 Nuremberg, 8 AAA, 7 Lausanne, 5 v USA, 4 CG
6. **Mark Hylton** 24.9.76 (5y, 5) 45.57 '96   45.24, 45.30, 45.54, 45.63, 45.75, 45.97
   2 Seville, 5 Bratislava, 1 U23H, 5 Turin, 4 Lucerne, 1 BL3 (3), 5 AAA, 5 BGP, 1B Zürich, 4 v USA, 5s1 CG
7. **Sean Baldock** 3.12.76 (2y, 6) 45.42 '97
   . 45.45, 45.50, 46.38, 46.47, 46.80, 47.03; 46.11i, 46.59i; 1 E.Clubs, 5 U23H, 2 Tallinn, 1 Jona, 6 AAA
8. **Paul Slythe** 5.9.74 (2y, 12) 46.52 '96   45.94, 46.17, 46.23, 46.26, 46.29, 46.7
   3 South, 2 Cork, 1 Hechtel, 7 AAA, 1 Chaux-de-Fonds, BL2: -,1,2,-
9. **Paul McBurney** 14.3.72 (3y, 7) 45.85 '97   45.90, 46.25, 46.46, 46.49, 46.50, 46.57
   4 Leeds, 5s2 AAA, 1 WG, 1 Cup, 7s1 CG, BL1: -,-,1,1
10. **Jared Deacon** 15.10.75 (4y, 8) 45.94 '97   46.32, 46.48, 46.59, 46.70, 46.70, 46.72
    1 AAA v LC, 1 CAU, 1 BedG, 2 Ljubljana, 1 Cork, 6s2 AAA, 7 BGP, 1 BL3 (4)
11. **Adrian Patrick** 15.6.73 (6y, 11) 45.63 '95   46.31, 46.31, 46.5, 46.78, 46.8, 46.88
    2 Leeds, 1 South, 1B BL3 (3), 5s1 AAA, 2 WG, 1 Brighton
12. **Geoff Dearman** 4.8.77 (1y, -) 46.65 '97   46.46, 46.77, 46.8, 46.93, 46.98, 47.01
    2 B.Univs, 1B AAA v LC, 2 CAU, 6g U23I, 6s1 AAA, 1 U23D, 3 WG, 2 Brighton, 2 Cup, BL1: 1,2,3,3
– **Du'aine Ladejo** 14.2.71 (6y, -) 44.66 '96
    46.12, 46.73, 46.90; 47.41i

Even though Richardson beat him 6-3, there can be no doubt about Thomas retaining his top ranking, with his superb quartet of titles: AAA, European, World Cup and Commonwealth. Thomas and Richardson rank 2nd and 3rd in the world for 1998; the best ever for British 400m men – one has to go back to 1961 (1st Adrian Metcalfe, 4th Robbie Brightwell) for anything comparable. Black had a consistent series of races, and it was surely a bad mistake not to select him for the Europeans – but it was sad that he did not continue to help the British and English teams through to the end of the year. He tied the 400m record of 13 years in the rankings of David Jenkins. Wariso's great form at the AAAs was not maintained at the Championships, but was just enough to get him 4th ranking. Baulch left it late, but his CG form just gets him the nod over Hylton; they were 2-2 on win-loss.

800 METRES
1. **Andy Hart** 13.9.69 (3y, 4) 1:46.36 '97   1:45.71, 1:46.19, 1:46.77, 1:47.0, 1:47.0, 1:47.13
   3 Batt.Pk, 3 ECp, 5 GhG, 7 BGP, 1 Tooting, 4h ECh, 1 Solihull, 6 WCp, 5 CG
2. **Bradley Donkin** 6.12.71 (2y, -) 1:48.25 '96   1:46.86, 1:47.5, 1:47.65, 1:48.3, 1:48.32, 1:49.01, 1:48.91i
   3 AAA v LC, 4 CAU, 4 Ljubljana, 3 Leeds, 2 North, 5 Cork, 7 AAA, 1 Watford, 3 Tooting, 6 CG
3. **Jason Lobo** 18.9.69 (3y,11) 1:47.29 '97   1:47.48, 1:47.74, 1:47.96, 1:48.21, 1:48.23, 1:48.41
   2 AAA v LC, 4 Leeds, 2 Istanbul, 2 BL1 (3), 4 GhG, 1 AAA, 8 BGP, 6s2 CG
4. **Grant Graham** 27.12.72 (2y, -) 1:49.2 '96   1:47.85, 1:48.13, 1:48.94, 1:49.25, 1:49.60, 1:49.73
   1 CAU, 6 Ljubljana, 1 Scot, 2 AAA, 10 BGP, 5h CG
5. **Paul Walker** 2.12.73 (4y, 3) 1:46.4 '97   1:47.91, 1:48.53, 1:48.68, 1:48.82, 1:48.85, 1:49.1
   5 Ljubljana, 2 Stockholm, 2 Scot, 3 Celle, 1 BL1 (3), dnf AAA
6. **Eddie King** 26.11.75 (2y, 7) 1:48.22 '97   1:48.51, 1:48.95, 1:49.01, 1:49.38, 1:49.71, 1:49.74
   4 Wyth, 2 Leeds, 1 Tønsberg, 3 Cardiff, 3 AAA, 3h3 CG, BL1: 1,-,-,1
7. **Phillip Tulba** 20.9.73 (1y, -) 1:49.88 '97   1:48.31, 1:48.43, 1:48.71, 1:49.2, 1:49.38, 1:50.07
   1 Swindon, 6B Oslo, 2 Cardiff, 4 AAA, 4 Watford

8. **Matt Shone** 10.7.75 (1y, -) 1:50.2 '97   1:48.33, 1:48.39, 1:48.6, 1:49.21, 1:49.63, 1:49.8
    2B Wyth, 5 Leeds, 7B Swindon, 1 Welsh, 4 Cardiff, 1 IR, 6 AAA, 2 Watford, 3 Solihull, BL3: 3,2,1,-
9. **Chris Moss** 17.6.79 (1y, -) 1:49.98 '97   1:48.43, 1:48.77, 1:49.78, 1:49.92, 1:50.09, 1:50.3
    1D Wyth, 2B Swindon, 1 AAA-J, 3 JIvFS, 6 WJ, 4 Solihull
10. **Simon Lees** 19.11.79 (1y, -) 1:50.5 '97   1:47.69, 1:48.03, 1:48.88, 1:50.82, 1:51.68
    1 Mid-J, 3 Wyth, 2 AAA-J, 6h6 WJ, 2 Solihull
11? **Anthony Whiteman** 13.11.71 (3y, 5) 1:47.16 '97   1:47.5, 1:48.4; 1 BL2 (2), 4 Batt.Pk
12. **Alasdair Donaldson** 21.6.77 (1y, -) 1:49.05 '97   1:48.6, 1:49.18, 1:49.49, 1:49.58, 1:50.0, 1:50.01
    1 B.Univs, 1 AAA v LC, 1 BL1 (2), 1 Leeds, 1 U23H, 8 Istanbul, 4 Cork, 3 Scot, 2h4 AAA, 1 U23D, 1 Cup. 1B Solihull
nr **James McIlroy** IRE 30.12.76 1:51.8 '97   1:45.32, 1:45.46, 1:45.83, 1:46.7, 1:46.81, 1:46.87
    2 Dublin, 1 Wyth, 2 Batt.Pk, 1 Tallinn, 4 Nice, 1 GhG, 4 ECh, 6 Brussels

Hart had a fine year to retain top ranking, and both he and Donkin broke through with pbs at the Commonwealth Games. The overall standard is depressingly low compared to past glories, but an encouraging feature was the progress of two juniors. Moss beat Lees at the AAA and fared far better at the World Juniors, but Lees had better form at the start and end of the season, with pbs for both in the BMC finals at Solihull. Whiteman could well be higher, but is difficult to rank – he had two good times, but did not contest the major races at this distance. One great new talent emerged – the most exciting British middle-distance runner since Curtis Robb, but James McElroy was snapped up by Ireland, so although he has a British passport, he is not ranked.
The 10th best of 1:48.31 is better than 1994 (1:48.38) but otherwise the worst since 1980.

1500 METRES - 1 MILE

1. **John Mayock** 26.10.70 (8y, 1) 3:31.86 '97, 3:50.32M '96   3:32.82, 3:33.90, 3:34.60, 3:34.71, 3:51.99M,
    3:53.72M, 3:53.81M, 3:36.74; 1 Hexham, 7 St Denis, 2 Bratislava, 3 ECp, 6 Oslo, 10 Rome, 2 GhG, 1 AAA,
    7 Paris, 2 E.Carr, 10 Monaco, 5 ECh, 6 Brussels, 9 GPF, 2 CG
2. **Anthony Whiteman** 13.11.71 (3y, 2) 3:32.34/3:54.59M '97   3:32.69, 3:51.90M, 3:52.09M, 3:35.30, 3:36.78,
    3:39.52; 4 Bellinzona, 4 Nuremberg, 3 Nice, 2 AAA, 3 E.Carr, 7 Zürich, 4 ECh, 1 WCp, 3 CG
3. **Matthew Yates** 4.2.69 (7y, 4) 3:34.00 '91, 3:52.75M '93   3:37.04, 3:38.36, 3:38.97, 3:39.5, 3:40.38, 3:40.78
    5 Barakaldo, 11 Nice, dnf GhG, 3 AAA, 7 Hechtel, 2 Watford, 6 ECh, 2 v USA, 12 Berlin
4. **Kevin McKay** 9.2.69 (10y, 3) 3:34.59 '97, 3:53.64M '94   3:37.22, 3:40.78, 3:58.52M, 3:43.22, 3:44.42,
    3:46.18; 4 Hengelo, 5 GhG, 4 AAA, 18 Hechtel, 1 Cup, 3 v USA, 5 CG, BL1: 1,-,1,-
5. **Michael Openshaw** 8.4.72 (2y, 6) 3:41.38/4:03.7M '97   3:39.7, 3:57.2M, 3:40.18, 3:43.50, 3:43.60,
    4:08.33M; 1 CAU, 2 Hexham, 3 Batt.Pk, 3 Rhede, 5 AAA
6. **Neil Caddy** 18.3.75 (4y, 8) 3:39.1/3:55.84M '96   3:39.89, 3:58.49M, 3:58.5M, 3:40.9, 3:42.34, 3:42.66
    1 Wyth, 5 Batt.Pk, 2 Exeter, 2 Rhede, 4 GhG, 3 WG, 3 Bath
7. **Gary Lough** 6.7.70 (5y, -) 3:34.76 '95, 3:55.91M '95   3:57.58M, 3:40.8, 3:43.33, 3:44.55, 3:44.99, 3:46.1
    2B BL1 (2), 2 Lough, dnf Swindon, 12 Cork, 8 AAA, 9 E.Carr, 5 WG, 3 Watford, 6 v USA
8. **Spencer Barden** 31.3.73 (2y, 9) 3:40.10 '97, 4:02.1M '96   3:39.64, 3:58.5M, 3:59.86M, 4:00.73M, 3:44.8,
    3:46.85; 3 Hexham, 2 Barcelona, 8 GhG, 9 WG, 2 BL2 (4), 3 Meilen, 5 Solihull
9. **Ian Gillespie** 18.5.70 (3y, 5) 3:39.8/3:58.4M '97   3:57.6M, 4:01.84M, 3:46.11; 1B BL1 (2), 1 Exeter
10. **Tom Mayo** 2.5.77 (1y, -) 3:43.4 '96   3:41.2, 3:42.33, 4:00.02M, 3:43.98, 3:46.81
    10 AAA, 4 Watford, 16 Rieti, 4 Solihull
11. **Phillip Tulba** 20.9.73 (1y, -) 3:44.5 '97   3:59.7M, 3:42.3, 3:42.96, 3:45.0, 3:45.19, 4:06.20M
    1 B.Univs, 1 AAA v LC, 8 Batt.Pk, 8 Cork, 1 Tooting, 11 Solihull
12. **Christian Stephenson** 22.7.74 (1y, -) 3:49.90/4:02.9M '97   4:01.7M, 3:43.85, 4:02.2M, 3:44.82, 3:45.75,
    3:46.2; 3 Exeter, 1 Welsh, 2 Cardiff, 1 IR, 7 Bath, 9 CG
-   **Grant Graham** 27.12.72 (0y, -) 3:43.2 '95   3:41.5, 3:44.09; 6 Batt.Pk, 11 Cork
nr **James McIlroy** IRE 30.12.76 3:59.48M, 3:46.00, 3:49.83; 2 Dublin, 1 ECp 2A, 1 Irish, 2 Solihull

M = 1 mile time (1500m times in brackets).
Mayock and Whiteman remain 1-2 for the third successive year, but it was close with Mayock just having the edge, 3-1 on win-loss. Yates and McKay swap places. Openshaw, Caddy and Barden moved up slightly from 1997, but maintained their positions against each other, with Lough returning to split them. The 10th best was 3:41.5 – in 1991 it was 3:41.52, but otherwise this was the worst since 1979.

3000 METRES   (Not ranked this year)

Anthony Whiteman 13.11.71 7:57.59i 95, 7:57.65 '97   7:43.61, 8:03.3; 3 ECp
Jon Brown 27.2.71 7:51.72 '93   7:45.41; 5 Hechtel
Neil Caddy 18.3.75 7:58.14i/8:03.59 '96   7:48.76, 8:54.43M , 8:16.8; 6 BGP, 2 v USA, 7 WCp
Karl Keska 7.5.72 7:56.74 '97   7:50.04, 8:01.2; 7 BGP, 5 v USA
Ian Gillespie 18.5.70 7:48.28 '97 7:51.34; 7:52.61i, 7:53.79i, 8:03.28i; 6 Caorle
Spencer Barden 31.3.73 7:53.2 '97   7:55.50; 8 BGP
Kris Bowditch 14.1.75 7:57.7 '97   7:56.12; 2 Cardiff
John Mayock 26.10.70 7:43.31i '97, 7:47.28 '95   8:54.16M; 7:47.43i, 7:48.80i, 7:50.10i, 7:55.09i, 7:58.57i
1 v USA

5000 METRES

1. **Karl Keska** 7.5.72 (2y, 10) 13:37.54 '97   13:26.37, 13:33.67, 13:40.24, 13:41.61, 13:42.58, 13:59.30
   1 Walnut, 9 Eugene, 6 ECp, 1 AAA, 9 ECh, 4 CG
2. **Jon Brown** 27.2.71 (7y, -) 13:19.78 '93   13:19.03, 13:41.72, 13:+?;   2 AAA, 12 Stockholm
3. **Keith Cullen** 13.6.72 (3y, 1) 13:17.21 '97   13:22.31, 13:31.07, 13:33.89, 13:43.15, 13:44.69, 14:13.32
   10 Nuremberg, 3 AAA, 9 Hechtel, 8 Brussels, 5 WCp, 5 CG
4. **Dermot Donnelly** 23.9.70 (3y, 12) 13:45.97 '97   13:27.63, 13:35.3; 2 Batt.Pk, 13 Hechtel
5. **Rod Finch** 5.8.67 (1y, -) 13:59.6 '97   13:27.75, 13:41.44, 13:49.46, 13:52.94, 14:09.87
   1 AAA v LC, 6 Cork, 5 AAA, 14 Hechtel, 17 ECh
6. **Kris Bowditch** 14.1.75 (3y, 6) 13:42.00 '97   13:36.24, 13:43.68, 13:50.91, 13:51.8, 14:01.9, 14:02.36
   8 Walnut, 12 Cork, 4 AAA, 21 Hechtel, 3 Watford, 7 CG
7. **Ian Gillespie** 18.5.70 (3y, 2) 13:18.06 '97   13:28.57, 13:44.08, 13:51.24
   dnf Eugene, 9 Lisbon, 19 Rome, 6 AAA, 8h CG
8. **Spencer Barden** 31.3.73 (3y, 7) 13:43.84 '97   13:45.31, 13:54.13, 13:54.39, 14:04.6
   2 AAA v LC, 8 Cork, 1 Lough, 9 AAA
9. **Rob Denmark** 23.11.68 (8y, 4) 13:10.24 '92   13:48.48, 13:53.86, 13:54.4;   4 Batt.Pk, 9 Cork, 8 AAA
10. **Julian Moorhouse** 13.11.71 (1y, -) 14:07.8 '96   13:48.5, 14:03.01, 14:12.59;   2 North, 12 AAA, 2 Watford
11. **Matthew Clarkson** 25.1.66 (1y, -) 13:57.91 '97   13:52.4, 13:56.15, 14:05.86, 14:16.9
   4 AAA v LC, 10 AAA, 4 Watford, BL1: -,1,-,1
12. **Glynn Tromans** 17.3.69 (2y, -) 13:48.0 '97   13:53.59, 14:21.54; 15 Cork, 7 AAA
   Nick Comerford 23.4.66 (0y, -) 14:11.63 '97   13:52.7, 14:01.19, 14:04.47   3 Batt.Pk, 11 AAA, 3 Solihull

Keska leaps up from 10th to 1st; he did not have a sensational season, but a good, solid one. Brown ran the fastest time, but was beaten by Keska at the AAAs. Cullen was next best ahead of Donnelly, who made big improvements on the Northern Irish record in each of his two 5000m races and was unfortunate not to get a championship race at this distance. The standard in depth is again way below what it was in previous decades. The 10th best standard, under 13:40 each year 1977-92, was 13:48.5, and only 15 men broke 14 minutes – compared to a peak of 49 in 1988.

10,000 METRES

1. **Jon Brown** 27.2.71 (6y, 1) 27:27.47 '97   27:18.14, 28:02.33; 4 ECh, 4 Brussels
2. **Keith Cullen** 13.6.72 (1y, -)   27:53.52, 28:34.34; 10 Eur Chall., 11 ECh
3. **Dermot Donnelly** 23.9.70 (3y, 6) 28:38.56 '97   28:43.17, 29:05.96, 29:27.40
   25 Eur Challenge, 1 AAA, 5 CG
4. **Glynn Tromans** 17.3.69 (2y, 5) 28:35.32 '97   28:31.71, 30:04.95; 20 Eur Challenge, 9 CG
5. **Carl Thackery** 14.10.62 (6y, -) 27:59.24 '87   28:52.71; 2 AAA
6. **Andrew Pearson** 14.9.71 (4y, -) 28:32.0 '96   29:01.05; 22 Eur Challenge
7. **Robert Quinn** 10.12.65 (2y, -) 29:14.23 '95   29:20.72, 29:25.55, 29:36.54, 29:43.88
   11r2 Eur Challenge, 12 Prague, 6 AAA, 1 Scot
8. **Rob Denmark** 23.11.68 (4y, 3) 28:03.34 '94   29:17.72; 3 AAA
9. **Mark Hudspith** 19.1.69 (2y, -) 29:02.38 '92   29:22.88; 4 AAA
10. **David Taylor** 9.1.64 (2y , 9) 29:11.79 '97   29:24.15; 5 AAA
11. **David Tune** 29.10.70 (1y, -) 29:41.54 '97   29:39.23; 7 AAA
12. **Adrian Mussett** 14.4.72 (1y, -) 29:54.49 '97   29:40.96; 8 AAA

Brown is top for the third successive year. After 4th in the Europeans, he beat the easy winner there, António Pinto, in Brussels, when he took Eamonn Martin's UK record. Cullen broke 28 minutes on his debut at the event and Donnelly ran well to win the AAA title and place an unnoticed (by BBC TV) 5th at the Commonwealth Games. Making a welcome return is Carl Thackery, last ranked in this event in 1991. For the third successive year the 10th best was the worst since 1965 (allowing for 6 miles conversions in the 1960s). 29:08.66 in 1996, 29:17.65 in 1997 and 29:24.15 in 1998. In 1986 it was 28:11.07.

MARATHON

1. **Jon Brown** 27.2.71 (2y, 3) 2:10:13 '97   8 London 2:11:10
2. **Richard Nerurkar** 6.1.64 (6y, 1) 2:08:36 '97   8 EC 2:14:02
3. **David Taylor** 9.1.64 (2y, 5) 2:13:27 '97   4 CG 2:20:30
4. **Dave Buzza** 6.12.62 (5y, 7) 2:11:06 '93   14 Boston 2:14:59, 28 EC 2:19:28
5. **Mark Hudspith** 19.1.69 (4y, -) 2:11:58 '95   16 London 2:14:19, 30 EC 2:19:58
6. **David Cavers** 9.4.63 (2y, 9) 2:16:18 '97   12 Rotterdam 2:16:06, dnf CG
7. **Keith Anderson** 10.8.57 (1y, -)   18 Boston 2:17:08, 10 CG 2:23:07
8. **Steve Brace** 7.7.61 (9y, -) 2:10:35 '96   24 London 2:16:34, 17 CG 2:29:21
9 **Billy Burns** 13.12.69 (1y, -)   21 London 2:16:11, 21 CG 2:31:16
10. **Steve Green** 28.7.70 (1y, -) 2:19:58 '96   12 Monaco 2:17:16, 31 London 2:18:11
11. **Dale Rixon** 8.7.66 (3y, -) 2:13:41 '96   8 Sacramento 2:18:11, 15 CG 2:26:50
12. **Alan Chilton** 16.4.71 (1y, -) 2:20:09 '97   26 London 2:17:07
-    **Malcolm Price** 18.6.62 (1y, -) 2:20:14 '97 29 London 2:17:43

The 10th best time at 2:17:43 is again well short of the record 2:12:51 in 1983, when 102 men ran under 2:20, compared to just 14 in 1998. Taylor's time is obviously much slower than the others, but he obtains his high ranking by a fine run in very tough conditions in Kuala Lumpur. Anderson also ran well there, and is the highest newcomer – at the age of 41!

3000 METRES STEEPLECHASE
1. **Christian Stephenson** 22.7.74 (1y, -) 8:54.8 '96   8:32.76, 8:41.76, 8:42.95, 8:44.34, 8:46.44, 8:55.67A
   1 Wyth, 1 AAA, 15 Stockholm, 5 WCp, 6 CG
2. **Ben Whitby** 6.1.77 (1y, -) 8:59.09 '96   8:41.79, 8:42.12, 8:44.24, 8:47.69, 8:49.80, 8:51.5
   1 CAU, 1 U23H, 6 ECp, 4 AAA. 7 CG
3. **Craig Wheeler** 14.6.76 (1y, -) 8:55.44 '97   8:42.83, 8:43.36, 8:45.90, 8:49.47, 8:52.29, 8:56.4
   4 AAA v LC, 2 CAU, 2 Wyth, 4 U23H, 3 AAA, 4 U23D, 8 CG
4. **Spencer Duval** 5.1.70 (8y, 2) 8:24.64 '95   8:36.37, 8:49.6, 8:58.34, 9:09.76
   1 IR, 2 AAA, 3 Watford, dnf CG
5. **Brian Montgomery** 19.7.74 (1y, -) 8:54.1 '96   8:43.71, 8:44.01, 8:46.18, 9:02.46
   1 Seattle, 13 Portland, 7 Dedham, dnf AAA
6. **Lee Hurst** 29.7.72 (3y, 5) 8:48.34 '96   8:49.63, 8:53.90, 8:55.04, 8:55.62, 8:56.56, 8:58.38
   1 AAA v LC, 3 E.Clubs, 1 North, 6 AAA, 3 Cup, BL1: 1,-,2,1
7. **Andy Coleman** 29.9.74 (2y, 12) 8:55.95 '97   8:52.35, 8:52.7, 8:53.27, 9:00.88;   1 South, 7 AAA, 4 Watford
8. **Stuart Stokes** 15.12.76 (2y, 11) 8:55.64 '97   8:56.39, 8:56.92, 8:57.15, 8:58.59, 9:00.44, 9:01.16
   1 B.Univs, 3 Wyth, 5 U23H, 9 AAA, 6 U23D, 1 Cup
9. **Andy Morgan-Lee** 1.3.69 (2y, 7) 8:50.40 '96   8:53.81, 8:55.0, 8:56.9, 8:57.56, 9:00.3, 9:06.36
   5 Wyth, 1 sf Enf, 8 AAA, 4 Cup, BL2: 1,-,1,-
10 **John Brown** ?? (1y, -) 9:26.1 '97   8:55.6, 8:57.87, 9:04.55;   11 AAA, 5 Watford
11. **Martin Yelling** 7.2.72 (2y, 10) 8:54.63 '97   8:57.03, 8:59.9, 9:22.73;   3 CAU, 4 Wyth, 7 South, dnf h1 AAA
12. **Mike Jubb** 20.6.70 (2y, 9) 8:50.37 '96   8:58.00, 9:03.1; 2 AAA v LC, 4 CAU
nr **Andrew Colvin** AUS 23.8.72 (1y, -) 9:21.75 '97   8:48.23, 8:53.97, 8:58.36, 8:59.22, 9:01.59, 9:02.8
   5 AAA, 2 Cup, BL1: 2,1,1,2

Sadly, last year's no. one, Robert Hough, missed the whole season through injury. But, in a unique situation all of the top three ranked for the first time at the event. These three, Stephenson, Whitby and Wheeler, made notable advances, but as they now rank 33, 72 and 74 on the UK all-time list, and many of those ranked ran much slower, it can be seen that the overall picture remains bleak. The 10th best standard declined again to 8:55.74, the worst since 1965; the best was 8:37.59 in 1989, and it was under 8:50 each year 1970-96 (apart from 8:50.2 in 1976).

110 METRES HURDLES
1. **Colin Jackson** 18.2.67 (15y, 1) 12.91 '93, 12.8w '90   13.02, 13.02, 13.07, 13.09, 13.10, 13.11A, 13.12,
   13.14, 13.15, 13.16, 13.16, 13.17, 13.17, 13.18, 13.18, 13.20, 13.21, 13.24;   dnf Doha, 1 Chemnitz, 1 Jena,
   1 Cottbus, 1 Milan, 1 Dortmund, 1 Helsinki, 1 Athens, 1 ECp, 1 Bellinzona, 2 Linz, 1 Nuremberg, 1 GhG,
   4 Goodwill, 1 AAA, 3 BGP, 1 ECh, 2 Lausanne, 2 Brussels, 1 v USA, 2 Berlin, 2 WCp, 1 Tokyo
2. **Anthony Jarrett** 13.8.68 (13y, 2) 13.00 '93   13.25, 13.32, 13.32, 13.32, 13.33, 13.33w, 13.39, 13.40
   1 Ljubljana, 2 Bratislava, 1 Ostrava, 1 Tallinn, 1 Turku, 1/3 Budapest, 2 Salamanca, 2 GhG, 2 AAA
   dnf Zürich, 6 ECh, 1 Thurrock, 3 v USA, 1 CG
3. **Paul Gray** 25.5.69 (9y, 6) 13.53 '94   13.54, 13.62, 13.76, 13.81w; 13.8, 13.8
   1 Leeds, 3 GhG, 4 CG, BL2: 1,1,1,-
4. **Andrew Tulloch** 1.4.67 (12y, 3) 13.52 '94, 13.5w '96   13.57, 13.63, 13.67, 13.72, 13.79, 13.81
   1 Florø, 2 E.Clubs, 7 Bratislava, 6 GhG, 7s2 ECh, 6 v USA, 6 CG
5. **Ross Baillie** 26.9.77 (3y, 5) 13.92/13.90w '97   13.80, 13.82w, 13.83w, 13.85, 13.90, 13.99w
   dnf U23H, 2 Rhede, 1 BL1 (3), 1 Scot, 4 AAA, 5 U23D, 1 Cup, 8 CG
6. **Damien Greaves** 19.9.77 (4y, 4) 13.82 '97   13.84w, 13.85, 13.88, 13.89w, 13.90w, 13.94
   1 U23H, 1 Rhede, 2 Cork, 7 GhG, 3 AAA, 3 U23D, 2 Cup, 3h3 CG, BL1: 1,1,-,1
7. **Lloyd Cowan** 8.7.62 (10y, 8) 13.75 '94   13.97w, 14.03, 14.13w, 14.16w, 14.18w, 14.22
   2 South, 1 IR; 5 AAA, 3 Cup, 2 Thurrock, BL1: -,2,2,2
8. **Neil Owen** 18.10.73 (6y, -) 13.60 '95, 13.5w '96   14.10w, 14.17, 14.22w, 14.24, 14.24w, 14.31w
   3 South, 6 AAA, 4B C-de-Fonds, 2 Brighton, 4 Cup; BL1: -,-,4,3
9. **Ken Campbell** 30.9.72 (5y, -) 13.86 '94   13.89w, 14.16w, 14.21w, 14.22, 14.25w, 14.32
   2 BedG, 3 Leeds, 1 Maia, 3 Istanbul, 1 B Turku, 2 Scot, 7 AAA, BL1: 3,4,3,4
10. **Matthew Clements** 17.9.77 (2y, 7) 14.13 '97   14.12, 14.38w, 14.52w; 1 B.Univs, 1 AAA v LC
11. **Dominic Bradley** 22.12.76 (1y, -) 15.21, 15.0 '96   14.07w, 14.16w, 14.24w, 14.26, 14.32, 14.35; 14.3w
   4 B.Univs, 1D AAA v LC, 1 CAU, 2 Leeds, 4 U23H, 1 North, 3 Cork, 2 IR, 4h2 AAA, 1 Nth IC
12. **Martyn Hendry** 10.4.75 (2y, 9) 14.16 '97   14.24w, 14.28w, 14.31w, 14.39, 14.40, 14.40
   2 B.Univs, 2 AAA v LC, 4 Cork, 3 Scot, 8 AAA, BL1: 2,3,5,5
   Jamie Quarry 15.11.72 (1y, 10) 14.10 '94   14.16w, 14.29w, 14.36w, 14.51, 14.68; 14.4w, 14.5
   1 South, 2 sf Crawley, BL2: 3,2,-,1

Jackson was again superb to gain top ranking ahead of Jarrett, who overcame his nerves to gain a much deserved gold medal at the Commonwealth Games. The brilliance of this pair is shown as Jackson has now ranked in the world's top ten for 13 successive seasons and Jarrett for 11, although the latter only just makes it this year (I rank him 10th). Jackson is UK No. 1 for a record 11 times and his 15 years in the rankings takes him clear of Berwyn Price's previous record of 14. Both Gray and Tulloch ran seasonal bests in Kuala Lumpur, as did Baillie, who as usual was closely matched by Greaves (2-2 on win loss).

400 METRES HURDLES
1. **Paul Gray** 25.5.69 (4y, 4) 50.14 '97   49.16, 49.76, 49.81, 50.05, 50.34, 50.6
    3B Jena, 3 Leeds, 1 AAA, 4 BGP, 1 WG, 6s1 ECh, 3 v USA, BL2: 1,-,1,-
2. **Anthony Borsumato** 13.12.73 (2y, 9) 50.83 '97   49.79, 49.85, 49.86A, 49.96, 50.15, 50.22
    1 BL1 (1), 2 AAA v LC, 2 Leeds, 5 ECp, 2 AAA, 6 BGP, 6h1 ECh, 4 v USA, 7 WCp, 4h1 CG
3. **Chris Rawlinson** 19.5.72 (4y, 1) 49.69 '97   49.81, 50.20, 50.64, 50.89, 51.11, 51.52
    1 B.Univs, 1 AAA v LC, 1 BL1 (3), 3 AAA, 7h2 ECh
4. **Matthew Douglas** 26.11.76 (4y, 7) 50.72 '97   50.20, 50.41, 50.79, 50.87, 50.90, 50.9
    1 CAU, 5 E.Clubs, 3 U23H, 4 AAA, 1 U23D, 2 Cup, 6 v USA, 4h2 CG, BL1: 2,1,3B,1
5. **Gary Jennings** 21.2.72 (6y, 2) 49.82 '95   50.12, 50.81, 50.84, 50.94, 50.96, 51.06
    4 Leeds, 2 Tarare, 5 AAA, 8 BGP, 2 WG, 1 Cup, 6h2 CG, BL1: 3,-,2,1B
6. **Lawrence Lynch** 1.11.67 (9y, -) 50.05 '96   51.2, 51.28, 51.3, 51.6, 51.71, 52.1
    1 IR, 7 AAA, 3 WG, BL2: -,2,2,1
7. **Blair Young** 5.4.71 (1y, -) 52.17 '97   50.57, 51.22, 51.23, 51.35, 51.37, 51.65
    3 AUS Ch, 7 BL1 (3), 2 Jona, 1 Scot, 8 AAA
8. **Eddie Betts** 18.2.71 (4y, 8) 50.49 '97   51.55, 51.63, 51.84, 52.08, 52.45, 52.52
    1 South, 2B Tarare, 6 AAA, BL1: -,-,3,2
9. **Remi Edu** 14.12.78 (1y, -) 54.05 '96   51.3, 51.37, 52.28, 52.35, 52.45, 54.00
    2 B.Univs, 1B AAA v LC, 1 U23H, 2 BL1 (2), 1 Leeds
10. **Paul Thompson** 22.3.72 (3y, 6) 50.16 '96   51.05, 51.28, 51.42, 52.0, 52.25;   3 BL1 (2), 4 Tallinn, 3h2 AAA
11. **Gary Cadogan** 8.10.66 (6y, 3) 49.07 '94   51.01, 51.29, 51.56;   4 Ljubljana, 2 Tartu, 6 Budapest
12. **Tony Williams** 1.5.72 (4y, -) 50.31 '95   51.16, 51.67, 52.10, 53.02, 53.46, 54.8
    1 North, 2 sf Crawley, BL1: -,-,1B,4

Gray improved markedly to take top ranking, with Borsumato also making a breakthrough to rank second. Cadogan ran three times – but never in Britain, a sign of the times; and several others had very thin seasons. 10th best of 51.2 was the 3rd best ever, but only three more men beat 52.0.

HIGH JUMP
1. **Dalton Grant** 8.4.66 (15y, 1) 2.36 '91, 2.37i '94   2.34, 2.31, 2.28, 2.27, 2.25, 2.25; 2.27i, 2.26i
    7 Seville, 5 Athens, 4= Nice, 3= GhG, 1 AAA, 6 Eberstadt, 8 Stockholm, 2 BL2 (4), 4 L'kusen,
    9 Zürich, 2 ECh, 6= WCp, 1 CG
2. **Ben Challenger** 7.3.78 (3y, 4) 2.21 '96, 2.23i '97   2.28, 2.28, 2.28, 2.26, 2.26, 2.25; 2.27i
    1 AAA v LC, 2 E.Clubs, 1 BL1 (2), 1 Tallinn, 1 U23H, 2 ECp, 1 Cup, 2 CG
3. **Brendan Reilly** 23.12.72 (9y, 3) 2.31 '92, 2.32i '94   2.28, 2.25, 2.24, 2.24, 2.24, 2.20; 2.22i
    1 South, 1 Cork, 2 GhG, 2= AAA, 1 WG, 9= ECh, 8 Berlin, 5 CG, BL1: 1,-,1,1
4. **Steve Smith** 29.3.73 (9y, 2) 2.37 '92, 2.38i '94   2.30, 2.24; 2.36i, 2.27i, 2.27i, 2.20i;   2 Ostrava, 4 Athens
5. **Stuart Ohrland** 6.9.75 (5y, 7=) 2.17 '94, 2.20i '97   2.15, 2.11, 2.10, 2.10, 2.10, 2.10
    1 B.Univs, 1 Essex, 6 AAA v LC, 5= CAU, 2 South, 1 IR, 2= AAA, 2 WG, 3 Cup, BL1: 8,4,2,nh
6. **Ian Holliday** 9.12.73 (2y, -) 2.15 '96   2.16, 2.15, 2.10, 2.10, 2.09, 2.05; 2.12i
    7 AAA v LC, 5 AAA, 1 Nth IC, 4 Cup, BL1: -,3,5=,2
7. **Stanley Osuide** 30.11.74 (3y, -) 2.15 '91   2.15, 2.15, 2.15, 2.10, 2.05, 2.00
    2 Essex, 3 BedG, 2= AAA, 2 Cup, BL1: -,7,9, -
8. **Geoff Parsons** 14.8.64 (16y, -) 2.31 '94   2.16, 2.15, 2.14, 2.12, 2.10, 2.10;   1 BedG, 1 Scot, 2 Cork, 6 AAA
9. **Martin Lloyd** 18.6.80 (1y, -) 2.13 '97   2.15, 2.14, 2.10, 2.10, 2.10, 2.15i
    2 AAA v LC, 1 Sth-J, 4 CAU, 2 BedG, 4 Mannheim, 4 JI v FS, 1 AAA-J, 8 WJ
10. **Colin Bent** 12.4.70 (4y, 7=) 2.20 '96   2.12, 2.10, 2.10, 2.10, 2.05, 2.05
    1 CAU, 4 Cork, 1 IS, 7 AAA, BL1: 2,5,-,-
11. **Danny Graham** 3.8.79 (2y, -) 2.15 '96   2.13, 2.11, 2.10, 2.09, 2.08, 2.08; 2.10i, 2.09i
    1 Nth-J, 9 CAU, 2 North, 2 AAA-J, 1 JI v F.S, 2 Nth IC, 1 Jnr IA, BL2: 1,1,-,1
12. **Jason McDade** 3.4.80 (1y, -) 2.12 '97   2.15, 2.12, 2.07, 2.06, 2.06, 2.05;   2 E.Sch
nr **Mark Mandy** IRE 19.11.72 2.25 '95, 2.26i '97   2.15, 2.10, 2.10, 2.10, 2.10, 2.00; 2.23i, 2.20i, 2.18i
    3 CAU, 4= Tallinn, 5= Cork, 1 Irish, nh AAA, BL1: 5=,2,-,-

Grant is top ranked for the sixth time (previously 1988-91 and 1997). Challenger made great progress to rank second, even though he missed two months through injury, and Reilly was third, not quite matching his abilities with heights cleared, but getting very close in Budapest to 2.32. Smith's unfortunate injury meant that he only had two outdoor competitions before his season was brought to an end. There was a big gap after the top five to the men around 2.15-2.16 at best. Osuide ranked for the first time since 1992, and Parsons returned for his record 16th year in these rankings (Grant has 15).

POLE VAULT

1. **Nick Buckfield** 5.6.73 (7y, 1) 5.75 '97   5.80, 5.50, 5.40, 5.32, 5.30; 5.55i, 5.42i
   6= Walnut, 3 Hania, dnq 17= ECh
2. **Kevin Hughes** 30.4.73 (6y, 3) 5.41 '97   5.50, 5.40, 5.36, 5.35, 5.30, 5.30
   1 AAA v LC, 1 CAU, 1 BedG, 1 South, 1 Cork, 1 BL2 (3), 1 AAA, 2 WG, 6 CG, 1 sq Stafford
3. **Matt Belsham** 11.10.71 (8y, -) 5.35 '93, 5.40i '96   5.35, 5.30, 5.25, 5.20, 5.10, 5.10
   nh/2 Arles, nh BedG, 4 Cork, 2 AAA, 3 WG, 2 Cup, 5 CG, BL1: 2,2,-,-
4. **Michael Edwards** 19.10.68 (13y, 6) 5.52 '93   5.50, 5.40A,5.38, 5.30, 5.30, 5.30, 5.30
   10A Arles, 2 E.Clubs, nh ECp, nh IR, 6= AAA, 4 WG, 1 Cup, 6 WCp, BL1: 1,3=,1,1
5. **Ian Tullett** 15.8.69 (11y, -) 5.30 '92   5.35, 5.20, 5.20, 5.20, 5.10, 5.10
   11/4 Arles, 3 Bed G, 2 South, 2 Cork, 2 IR, 3 AAA, nh WG, nh CG, BL1: 3,1,2,3
6. **Paul Williamson** 16.6.74 (5y, 2) 5.50 '96   5.30, 5.20, 5.20, 5.20, 5.15, 5.00
   3A Arles, nh BedG, 3 Cork, 1 IR, 4 AAA, nh WG, 3 Cup, 2 Hasselt, BL1: 6=,3=,4,4=
7. **Christian Linskey** 14.6.80 (3y, 8) 5.15 '96   5.20, 5.10, 5.10, 5.10, 5.05, 5.00
   2 AAA v LC, nh/1 Arles, 2 BedG, 11 Mannheim, nh Cork, 1 AAA-J, 3 JI v FS, 12 WJ, 1 Jnr IA, 7 Cup, BL1: nh,5,-,-
8. **Dean Mellor** 25.11.71 (9y, 7) 5.30 '95   5.20, 5.10, 5.02, 5.00, 5.00, 5.00
   12/5 Arles, 3 IR, 5 AAA, BL4: 1,1,1,1
9. **Ben Flint** 16.9.78 (2y, 9=) 5.20 '97   5.16, 5.15, 5.10, 5.10, 5.00, 4.80
   3 AAA v LC, 7 Arles, 3 U23H, 6= AAA, 1 E.Sch, 4 U23D, 3 Hasselt
10. **Tim Thomas** 18.11.73 (4y, 4) 5.40 '97   5.20, 5.10, 5.00, 4.80, 4.80, 4.80; 5.20i
    1 BL3 (1), 14/6 Arles, nh Bed G, 3 IR, 8 AAA, 5 WG, 1 Bath, 1 Hasselt
11. **Neil Young** 20.2.77 (2y, 9=) 5.20 '97   5.10, 5.00, 5.00, 4.80, 4.80, 4.70
    1 Scot, 1 Irish, 1 WG, 5 U23D, 6 Singapore, 8 CG, BL1: -,-,8=,2
12. **Michael Barber** 19.10.73 (6y, 5=) 5.45 '97   5.00, 5.00, 5.00, 4.90, 4.80, 4.60; 5.20dh sq
    nh Cork, 4 IR, 9 AAA, 4 Cup, 2 sq Stafford, BL1: -,9,3,-
–   **Neil Winter** 21.3.74 (6y, -) 5.60 '95   5.10, 5.00;   nh Welsh, 2 BL1 (4), 2 Bath, nh Mid

Although his season was ruined by injury, Buckfield is top for the fourth successive year, with his fourth British record. Hughes had his best ever season and was the top British vaulter for most of the summer from Belsham. Edwards had a disaster in the European Cup but recovered most creditably from that to end the year in good form with 5.40 at the World Cup. All the top 12 had ranked before.

LONG JUMP

1. **Nathan Morgan** 30.6.78 (4y, 3) 7.90 '97, 7.97w '96   8.11, 8.04, 8.04w (7.67), 7.93 (7.85), 7.86w, 7.67
   1 Ljubljana, 1 BL1 (2), 1 U23H, 3 ECp, 1 IR, 1 AAA, dnq 24 ECh
2. **Steve Phillips** 17.3.72 (8y, 1) 7.91 '91, 8.00w '97   8.03, 7.87w, 7.79w, 7.75, 7.72, 7.70; 7.72i
   1 AAA v LC, 2 CAU, 2 BedG, 4 Rhede, 1 sf Derby, 3 AAA, dnq 32 ECh, 1 Mid, 3 v USA, 8 WCp, 7 CG
3. **Chris Davidson** 4.12.75 (3y, 2) 7.71/7.94w '97   7.89w, 7.81w, 7.71, 7.65, 7.63w, 7.62
   1 B.Univs, 1 CAU, 3 Ljubljana, 2 Cork, 2 AAA, 2 Cup, 2 v USA, 8 CG, BL1: 1,2,2,3
4. **George Audu** 18.1.77 (1y, -) 7.38/7.51w '97   7.83w, 7.72, 7.67, 7.67; 4 NCAA
5. **Julian Flynn** 3.7.72 (3y, 4) 7.66/7.71w '97   7.53, 7.49, 7.45w (7.39), 7.43, 7.43, 7.37
   2 AAA v LC, 5 E.Clubs, 3 Cork, 4 AAA, 1 Cup, BL1: -,4,3,2
6. **Barrington Williams** 11.9.55 (12y, 12) 8.05i/8.01 '89   7.48, 7.38, 7.32, 7.29, 7.24w, 7.18
   2 IR, 7 AAA, 3 Mid, 3 Cup, BL1: 3,3,5,1
7. **Stuart Wells** 26.7.79 (2y, 9) 7.56 '97   7.47, 7.38w, 7.37, 7.36, 7.35, 7.32
   1 Sth-J, 3 AAA v LC, 3 Bed-G, 5 Mannheim, 1 AAA-J, 2 E.Sch, 3 JI v FS, 8 AAA, 1 BL4 (4)
8. **Darren Thompson** 6.11.79 (1y, -) 7.36 '97   7.56, 7.34, 7.23w, 7.20w (7.19), 7.11
   4 AAA v LC, 1 BedG, 2 AAA-J, 1 E.Sch, dnq WJ
9. **John Munroe** 6.1.69 (5y, 5) 7.64, 7.65i '95   7.38, 7.31w, 7.23, 7.14, 7.14, 7.13
   4 CAU, 5 BedG, 1 South, 5 AAA, BL1: 2,5,9,4
10. **Andrew Lewis** 9.3.68 (2y, 6) 7.54 '97   7.30, 7.28w, 7.19;   4 BedG, 1 BL3 (3), 6 AAA
11. **Essop Merrick** 24.5.74 (2y, 11) 7.27/7.53w '97   7.59w, 7.37, 7.10; 1 BL2 (4), 2 Mid, 4 Cup
12   **Onochie Onuorah** 16.10.73 (5y, 8) 7.67 '96, 7.81w '95   7.58w, 7.56, 7.01, 6.84
     2 Sydney, 6 Canberra, 2 sf Derby, 15 AAA
-    **Fred Salle** 10.9.64 (10y, 1) 8.10 '94   7.47, 7.17;   1 BL1 (3), 9 AAA

After ranking 2nd and 3rd as a teenager, Morgan takes over top ranking. Unfortunately injury cut short his season, just when he was beginning to look the most likely jumper for many years to take the 32 year-old British record of Lynn Davies. Williams, 43 this year, leaps up to 6th, great for him, easily the oldest jumper ever in the top ten, but the distances achieved for such rankings show our very weak standards in this event.

TRIPLE JUMP

1. **Jonathan Edwards** 10.5.66 (12y, 1) 18.29/18.43w '95   18.01, 17.99, 17.75, 17.65, 17.60, 17.37A, 17.29,
   17.22; 17.64i, 17.43i, 17.26i, 17.23i;   1 Pietersburg, 1 Leeds, 1 Helsinki, 1 Tallinn, 1 ECp, 1 Oslo, 1 Rome,
   1 GhG, 1 Goodwill, 1 AAA, 1 BGP, 1 Stockholm, nj Monaco, 1 Zürich, 1 ECh, 2 Lausanne
2. **Onochie Achike** 31.1.75 (7y, 8) 16.53/16.67w '94   17.10, 17.07, 16.85w, 16.79w, 16.73, 16.72w
   1 AUS Ch, 3 Florø, 1 BL1 (2), 3 Leeds, 2 Tallinn, 3 GhG, 2 AAA, 4 BGP, dnq 21 ECh, 6 Cup, 3 v USA, 7 WCp, 1 CG
3. **Julian Golley** 12.9.71 (9y, 3) 17.06 '94   16.89, 16.89, 16.88, 16.83, 16.75, 16.72w
   1 AAA v LC, 1 CAU, 2 Leeds, 3 Tallinn, 2 Budapest, 5 Oslo, nj Rome, 4 GhG, 3 AAA, 3 BGP, 4 Stockholm,
   dnq 17 ECh, 11 Berlin, 5 Lausanne, 1 v USA, 4 CG
4. **Femi Akinsanya** 29.11.69 (6y, 5) 16.58 '96   16.32w, 16.16, 16.05, 16.04, 16.02, 16.00; 16.16i, 16.07i
   2 CAU, 3 South, 2 Jona, 4 AAA, 7 CG, BL3: 1,1,1,1
5. **Tayo Erogbogbo** 8.3.75 (5y, 4) 16.32 '95, 16.44w '97   16.43w, 16.12, 15.95w (15.85), 15.88, 15.79, 15.67
   5 Tallinn, 1 Jona, 5 AAA, 1 Cup, BL1: -,2,3,1
6. **Tosi Fasinro** 28.3.72 (9y, 7) 17.21/17.30w '93   16.63w (16.05), 15.46, 15.31; 16.10i, 15.46i
   1 BL2 (1), 1 South, 8 AAA
7. **Phillips Idowu** 30.12.78 (2y, 6) 15.86/16.34w '97   16.35, 15.93, 15.90, 15.72, 15.57, 15.53w
   1 B.Univs, 7 E.Clubs, 4 U23H, 2 South, 6 AAA, 3 U23D, BL1: 4,3,2,2
8. **Charles Madeira-Cole** 29.11.77 (2y, 10) 15.59 '97   15.81w (15.79), 15.75, 15.72, 15.44w, 15.42, 15.41;
   15.82i;   2 AAA v LC, 6 CAU, 4 Leeds, 3 U23H, 1 Welsh, 9 AAA, 4 U23D, 2 Cup, BL1: 2,4,1,3
9. **Alvin Walker** 30.4.65 (1y, -) 15.45 '96   15.71w, 15.56, 15.42, 15.40, 15.25, 15.20w
   5 CAU, 1 Scot, 1 IS, 7 AAA, BL1: 1,-,5,4
10. **Jonathan Wallace** 1.1.79 (2y, 9) 15.68 '97   15.82, 15.76w (15.37), 15.53, 15.26, 15.08,14.81
    5 AAA v LC, 1 Mid-J, 1 AAA-J, 1 E.Sch, nj JI v FS, dnq 18 WJ, 1 Jnr IA, BL1: -5,-6
11. **Nicholas Thomas** 4.4.79 (1y, -) 15.14i '97, 15.12 '96   15.70, 15.63w, 15.40, 15.29, 15.20, 15.18; 15.28i
    1 Sth-J, 6 South, 2 AAA-J, 2 JI v FS, dnq 23 WJ, BL2: 1,9,-,3
12. **Paul Weston** 6.10.67 (1y, -) 15.46 '92   15.64w, 15.34, 15.34, 15.26w, 15.16, 15.08
    7 CAU, 2 IR, 10 AAA, 1 Mid
-   **Francis Agyepong** 16.6.65 (15y, 2) 17.18/17.29Aw/17.24w '95
    16.89i, 16.57i, 16.31i, 16.27i, 16.17i, 16.12i

Edwards was again the best in the world and UK no.1 for the 9th time. Before injury ended his season a little early,
he won 14/16 outdoors and 4/5 indoors, with 17 performances over 17m. Achike took full advantage of Edwards'
absence to win Commonwealth gold, but was pushed hard all year by Golley; they were 4-4 on win-loss. Agyepong
is missing from the rankings for the first time since 1982 as he did not compete outdoors. Fasinro competed only three
times but had a big jump to beat Idowu's season's best at the Southern. Idowu had the long jumps, but was only just
ahead of Madeira-Cole, 4-3 on win-loss.

SHOT

1. **Mark Proctor** 15.1.63 (8y, 3) 19.67 '96, 20.18i '97   20.04, 19.96, 19.86, 19.84, 19.66, 19.50; 20.85i
   2 Halle, 1 Arles, 5 Bratislava, 5 Ostrava, 6 ECp, 1 IS, 3 GhG, 1 AAA, 1 BL1 (4), dnq ECh, 2 Cup, 3 v USA, 10 CG
2. **Shaun Pickering** 14.11.61 (16y, 1) 20.45 '97   20.00, 19.67, 19.47, 19.34, 19.33, 19.24;   6 Walnut, 3 Halle,
   1 E.Clubs, 9 Hengelo, 1 BL2 (2), 1 Welsh, 2 Dutch, 4 GhG, 2 AAA, 1 WG, dnq 24 ECh, 4 v USA, 3 CG
3. **Carl Myerscough** 21.10.79 (2y, -) 17.66 '97   19.46, 19.24, 18.50, 18.28, 18.12, 18.06; 18.31i
   1 AAA v LC, 1 Mannheim, 1 AAA-J, 3 WJ
4. **Mark Edwards** 2.12.74 (3y, 5) 18.42 '97   18.88, 18.52, 18.45, 18.13, 18.02, 17.94
   3 Tallinn, 3 AAA, 2 WG, 12 CG
5. **Matthew Simson** 28.5.70 (12y, 2) 19.49 '94   18.44, 17.99, 17.64, 17.20, 16.41
   3 Gainesville, 5 AAA, 3 Cup, BL1: 1,-,-,2
6. **Stephan Hayward** 30.7.74 (4y, 4) 18.40 '96   18.03, 17.98, 17.95, 17.67, 17.40, 17.39; 17.70i
   1 CAU, 1 Scot, 4 AAA, 4 Cup, 9 CG, BL1: 2,1,1,-
7. **Gary Sollitt** 13.1.72 (5y, 12) 17.14 '97   17.04, 16.90, 16.84, 16.73, 16.52, 16.29; 17.01i, 16.89i
   1 Hants, 2 AAA v LC, 2 South, 2 IR, 6 AAA, 5 Cup, BL2: 1,2,1,-
8. **David Callaway** 4.9.63 (11y, 10) 17.55 '93   16.71, 16.61, 16.58, 16.51, 16.49, 16.41
   2 Hants, 3 AAA v LC, 2 CAU, 1 South, 1 IR, 2 sf Derby, 7 AAA, 7 Cup, BL1: 4,2,3,3
9. **Emeka Udechuku** 10.7.79 (2y, 11) 17.25 '97   16.92, 16.42, 16.35, 16.27, 16.18, 16.17; 17.02i, 16.82i,
   16.80i, 16.79i, 16.66i;   1 B.Univs, 6 Arles, 6 Mannheim, 2 AAA-J, 1 JI v FS, dnq 13 WJ, BL2: 2,3,-,1
10 **Lee Newman** 1.5.73 (2y, 6) 18.85 '96   16.64, 16.48, 15.90, 15.42, 15.33; 16.51i, 16.41i 6 E.Clubs, BL1: 3,4,-,4
11. **Guy Marshall** 24.9.71 (1y, -) 16.00 '95   16.65, 15.27; 1 sf Derby, 6 BL1 (4)
12. **Steve Whyte** 14.3.64 (10y, 9) 17.78 '89   15.90, 15.86, 15.30, 14.78; 17.03i, 16.68i, 16.55i, 16.31i; 6 Cup, BL1: -,4,4,5

Although Pickering ended, fittingly, with the major honour, a Commonwealth bronze medal, Proctor returns to the top
ranking that he held once before, in 1995. Our two big men were both most disappointing at the Europeans, but Proctor,
apart from injury in Kuala Lumpur, achieved his best level of consistency otherwise, beat Pickering 4-2 and had 15
outdoor competitions (and 1 indoor) over 19m to 10 for Pickering, whose 16 years in the rankings matches the record
set by Mike Winch. Myerscough made superb improvement, taking the British junior record from Matt Simson's 18.11
up to 19.46 by three mighty improvements. In only one change from last year, Marshall just makes the 12.

DISCUS

1. **Robert Weir** 4.2.61 (10y, 1) 64.60 '97   64.42, 64.39, 63.62, 62.82, 61.92, 61.69
   4 ECp, 1 AAA, 2 Lough 7/8, 1 Leamington, 8 ECh, 2 v USA, 5 WCp, 1 CG, BL1: -,1,2,1
2. **Glen Smith** 21.5.72 (8y, 2) 62.80 '97   62.44, 61.46, 61.34, 60.62, 60.58, 60.56
   7 La Jolla, 1 Balboa (training comp?), 8 Halle, 4 Ljubljana, 1 Lough 10/6, 5 Nuremberg, 1 IR, 2 AAA,
   1 Hechtel, 1 Lough 7/8, dnq 15 ECh, 4 v USA, 4 CG, BL1: -,1,3,2
3. **Perris Wilkins** 12.11.68 (3y, 4) 65.22 '97   66.64, 62.30, 61.59, 60.26, 59.82, 58.65
   9 Halle, 1 CAU, 1 BedG, 1 South, 2 IR, 4 AAA, 4 Hechtel, 6 Lough 7/8, 2 Leamington, dnq 30 ECh, 8 CG
4. **Emeka Udechuku** 10.7.79 (2y, 7) 55.22 '97   60.97, 60.21, 59.48, 58.08, 57.99, 57.90;   1 B.Univs,
   1 AAA v LC, 2 BedG, 2 Lough 10/6, 4 Mannheim, 1 AAA-J, 1 JI v FS, 3 AAA, 2 WJ, 7 Lough 7/8, 2 Tooting, BL2: 1,1,-,1
5. **Carl Myerscough** 21.10.79 (2y, 8) 55.66 '96   60.19, 60.18, 60.03, 59.90, 59.62, 59.06
   3 AAA v LC, 1 Mannheim, 2 AAA-J, 6 WJ, 3 Lough 7/8
6. **Kevin Brown** 10.9.64 (14y, 3) 61.10 '97   60.67, 59.59, 59.02, 59.01, 58.91, 58.59, 58.09
   9 La Jolla, 3 Balboa, 2 Lisse, 2 AAA v LC, 2 CAU, 4 E.Clubs, 3 Lough 10/6, 6 AAA, 4 Lough 7/8, 1 Mid, BL1: 2,3,4,3
7. **Lee Newman** 1.5.73 (6y, 5) 60.48 '97   60.43, 59.51, 59.38, 59.37, 58.81, 58.58
   3 Lisse, 3 CAU, 1 Welsh, 1 Scot, 5 AAA, 5 Lough 7/8, 1 Tooting, 1 Singapore, 7 CG, BL1: 1,2,-,4
8. **Leith Marar** 7.11.68 (6y, 9) 55.68 '96   54.91, 54.33, 54.26, 53.98, 53.96, 53.90
   4 AAA v LC, 4 CAU, 3 BedG, 2 South, 7 AAA
9. **Gary Herrington** 31.3.61 (10y, 11) 56.66 '96   53.40, 52.70, 52.63, 52.52, 52.05, 51.91
   5 CAU, 4 BedG, 4 IR, 1 sf Derby, 2 Police, 8 AAA, 3 Eur Police
10. **Paul Reed** 2.6.62 (8y, -) 56.46 '96   53.01, 52.48, 52.40, 52.31, 52.20, 52.15
    1 North, 3 IR, 1 Police, 9 AAA, 5 Eur Police, BL3: 1,1,1,-
11. **Mark Proctor** 15.1.63 (2y, -) 55.08 '97   54.50, 52.60, 51.47, 51.09, 51.03, 47.08;   1 IS, 5 BL1 (4), 2 Cup
12. **Peter Gordon** 2.7.51 (16y, -) 61.62 '91   54.20, 54.09, 52.38, 51.33, 51.24, 50.99;   2 North, 1 Eur Vets
–   **Neville Thompson** 28.3.55 (18y, 10) 55.68 '93   52.11, 50.84, 50.66, 50.24, 49.90, 49.29
    6 CAU, 2 sf Derby, 3 Cup, BL1: 4,5,5,6

Weir is top for the sixth successive year and 8th in all, a record for the event all the more remarkable for the fact that he missed eight seasons in mid career to play American Football. He most deservedly ended the year with Commonwealth gold. Last year we had a record five British men over 60 metres, in 1998 we had seven (although no more over 55m). Smith was 2nd, with his most consistent season. Wilkins just takes third, although unable to match his record throws in big events he started quite well and had a 2-1 advantage over both Udechuku and Brown. Udechuku won the battle of the brilliant juniors, setting three British junior records, and beating Myerscough 3-2. Brown edged Newman 4-3. After the top seven there was a big gap. At the age of 47 Peter Gordon returns to the rankings for the first time since 1993, and sets a record for a 21-year span in the rankings, beating the 19 years of Thompson, who just misses this year.

HAMMER

1. **Michael Jones** 23.7.63 (17y, 3) 72.48 '96   74.02, 73.47, 73.28, 73.14, 72.89, 72.88
   1 Col 26/4, 6 Halle, 2 E.Clubs, 6 ECp, 1 sf Liverpoool, 1 AAA, 1 Cup, 1 Thurrock, 5 WCp, 2 CG, BL1: -,1,-,1
2. **Paul Head** 1.7.65 (16y,1) 74.02 '90   73.11, 72.56, 71.16, 70.36, 70.11, 69.93
   4 Halle, 3 Ljubljana, 1 South, 2 AAA, 2 Cup, 2 Thurrock, 4 CG, BL1: -,2,-,2
3. **David Smith** 2.11.74 (5y, 2) 75.10 '96   73.50, 73.36, 70.94, 70.85, 70.84, 69.77
   1 CAU, 6 Rehlingen, 1 Leeds, 4 AAA, 5 CG, BL1: 1,3,1,2
4. **Bill Beauchamp** 9.9.70 (4y, 7) 66.36 '97   70.09, 69.44, 69.22, 68.81, 68.20, 67.36
   2 Col 26/4, 1 AAA v LC, 2 CAU, 2 South, 1 IR, 1 sf Enfield, 3 AAA, BL1: 3,4,2,4
5. **Chris Howe** 17.11.67 (10y, 5) 65.22 '97   66.64, 65.27, 65.25, 65.24, 65.13, 64.28, 63.84
   2 Essex, 3 CAU, 2 Leeds, 2 sf Enfield, 6 AAA, 3 Cup, 4 Thurrock, BL2: 1,1,1,1
6. **John Pearson** 30.4.66 (10y, 4) 70.24 '97   66.66, 66.59, 65.78, 65.06, 64.84, 64.78
   3 Col 26/4, 2 IR, 7 AAA, 2 Mid
7. **Steve Pearson** 13.9.59 (8y, 8) 66.10 '97   67.45, 66.84, 65.27, 64.96, 64.92, 64.75;   4 Col 26/4, 1 Staffs,
   2 AAA v LC, 4 CAU, 2 WL 21/6, 1 Wyth, 2 sf Liverpool, 8 AAA, 1 Mid, 4 Cup, 3 Thurrock, BL1: 4,6,3,5
8. **Shane Peacock** 5.3.63 (13y, 6) 71.60 '90   66.35, 64.53, 64.51, 64.49, 64.46, 63.51
   5 AAA, 5 Cup, BL1: 2,5,4,6
9. **Steve Whyte** 14.3.64 (3y, -) 67.82 '89   66.98, 63.83, 62.40, 62.00, 61.71, 61.57
   3 Leeds, 1 WL 21/6, 2 Wyth, 1 Scot, 9 AAA, 6 Cup, 8 CG, BL1: -,9,6,7
10. **Iain Park** 16.7.74 (2y, -) 62.68 '96   64.64, 63.46, 63.31, 63.24, 62.71, 62.61
    5 Col 26/4, 2 BL2 (1), 6 CAU, 4 Scot, 12 AAA
11. **Michael Floyd** 26.9.76 (1y, -) 60.74 '97   62.01, 61.63, 61.55, 61.43, 61.14, 60.76
    1B Col 26/4, 1 B.Univs, 3 AAA v LC, 5 CAU, 4 U23H, 1 North, 3 Wyth, 5 IR, 10 AAA, 4 U23D, BL1: -,-,5,9
12. **Craig Ellams** 24.11.72 (2y, 9) 63.98 '97   62.82, 62.70, 62.52, 61.54, 61.43, 61.39
    9 Col 26/4, 2 Staffs, 3 sf Liverpool, 11 AAA, 3 Mid, BL3: 1,1,1,-
-   **Simon Bown** 21.11.74 (1y, 11) 62.10 '97   62.43, 62.01, 61.94, 61.57, 61.16, 61.16
    2B Col 26/4, 1 Essex, 3 South, 3 IR, 13 AAA, BL1: 5,7,7,10

Jones has made a habit of producing his best in the biggest meetings, and did so again in 1998 with a pb at the Commonwealth Games. In his 17th year in the rankings, he is ranked no.1 for the first time – never has any athlete taken so long to reach the top. Jones has a terrific record over the years: 2 years at 2nd (1988 and 1991), 8 years at no. 3, 2 at no. 4, and his first place this year was clear cut, over the previous top men, Head and Smith. Beauchamp, ranked 4th, made the most progress of the established men. 5th to 8th were very closely matched. While British strength at distance events has declined, that at the throws is getting much better; here the 10th best of 66.35 is a new record (previous best 65.24 in 1994).

JAVELIN
1. **Steve Backley** 12.2.69 (12y, 1) 91.46 '92   89.89, 89.72, 89.22, 88.80, 88.71A, 87.58, 87.48, 87.45, 87.38, 85.79; 15 comps, all at 82.79 or better; 1 Soini, 1 Leeds, 2 Tartu, 2 Helsinki, 2 Oslo, 1 GhG, 1 AAA, 1 BGP, 1 Stockholm, 1 ECh, 3 Lausanne, 1 Brussels, 1 v USA, 1 WCp, 2 CG
2. **Michael Hill** 22.10.64 (15y, 2) 86.94 '93   86.92, 83.94, 83.80, 83.50, 82.85, 82.57
    2 Auckland, 1 Melbourne, 1 Sydney, 7 Soini, 2 Leeds, 4 Tartu, 4 ECp, 7 Oslo, 3 GhG, 2 AAA, 2 BGP, 4 Stockholm, 2 ECh, 6 Lausanne, 3 Brussels, 3 v USA, 3 CG
3. **Mark Roberson** 13.3.67 (13y, 3) 80.92 '88   85.67, 84.37, 84.15, 80.98, 80.78, 79.63
    4 Auckland, 6 Melbourne, 4 Sydney, 3 Halle, 1 CAU, 2 Ljubljana, 3 Leeds, 2 Karlstad, 2 GhG, 3 AAA, 4 BGP, 6 ECh, 1 Cup, 2 v USA, 4 CG, BL1: -,1,1,1
4. **Nick Nieland** 31.1.72 (7y, 4) 83.06 '96   78.68, 75.69, 75.56, 75.47, 75.03, 74.31
    4 Leeds, 3 Karlstad, 3 Lucerne, 2 BL1 (3), 5 Nuremberg, 4 AAA
5. **David Parker** 28.2.80 (3y, 8) 71.06 '97   75.21, 72.95, 72.89, 72.85, 72.22, 71.57
    2 CAU, 1 AAA-J, 1 E.Sch, 1 WJ,.1 Jnr IA, 4 Cup, 3 Jnr Lg F, BL1: -,2,-,2
6. **Nigel Bevan** 3.1.68 (12y, 7) 81.70 '92   76.26, 73.06, 71.82, 67.96, 66.58, 66.04
    2 Welsh, 7 AAA, 3 BL1 (4), 2 Cup, 8 CG
7   **Colin Mackenzie** 30.6.63 (17y, 4) 82.60 roughened tail '91, 82.38 '93 78.73, 74.16A, 73.52; 4 Johannesburg
8. **Stuart Faben** 28.2.75 (4y, 6) 74.24 '95, 76.66i '96   74.20, 71.75, 71.55, 69.93, 69.78, 67.46
    11 Halle, 5 E.Clubs, 4 Karlstad, 2 Tallinn, 5 AAA, 1 WG, 3 Cup, BL1: -,5,3,4
9. **Dan Carter** 15.4.80 (1y, -) 63.28 '97   71.14, 70.34, 69.30, 68.45, 67.75, 67.64
    1 Sth-J, 1 South, 2 AAA-J, 2 E.Sch, 1 JI v FS, 8 WJ
10. **Stuart Loughran** 19.2.76 (1y, -) 64.08 '96   68.91, 67.38, 66.07, 65.05, 63.86, 63.85
    3 CAU, 6 Leeds, 3 U23H, 3 Welsh, 2 IR, 6 AAA, 2 WG,3 U23D
11. **Steve Harrison** 19.12.72 (4y, 10) 75.32 '95   72.85, 69.19, 67.69; 1 B.Univs, 8 AAA
12. **Shane Lewis** 22.8.72 (3y, -) 69.68 '94   70.90, 67.96, 65.51, 62.99; 1 Welsh, 9 AAA, BL3: 1,1,-,-
-   **Phill Sharpe** 6.3.81 (0y, -) 61.00 '97   68.53, 68.38, 68.13, 67.63, 65.31, 65.00
    4 CAU, 8 Mannheim, 3 AAA-J, 4 E.Sch, 2 JI v FS, 1 Nth IC, 1 Jnr Lg F, BL1: 1,6,-,6
-   **Tim Kitney** 26.4.80 (0y, -) 65.78 '99   68.08, 67.52, 66.88, 66.74, 65.51, 63.79
    4 AAA-J, 3 E.Sch, 10 AAA, 7 BL1 (4), 2 Jnr IA, 2 Thurrock, 2 Jnr Lg F
Backley is number one for the 9th time and Hill 2nd for the 11th time, as Backley regained the world number one ranking. Both are ranked in the world top ten for the tenth time. Roberson joined them in world class, breaking out of the 79-80m range suddenly into 84-85m. Mackenzie competed three times to April before injury. The top eight are the same as last year, with little change in position except that Parker, world junior champion, moves up three places. Another junior, Carter, also makes the rankings, with two more, Sharpe and Kitney not far away. All these four remain juniors next year.

DECATHLON
1= **Du'aine Ladejo** 14.2.71 (1y, -) 0   7635w, 7633, 7003;   4 Arles, 24 ECp, 7 CG
1= **Jamie Quarry** 15.11.72 (6y, 2) 7610 '94   7654w, 7504, 7482;   3 Arles, 10 ECp, 10 CG
3. **Alexis Sharp** 31.10.72 (2y , 4) 7354 '97   7571, 7542, 7112; 1 Azusa, 22 ECp, 9 CG
4. **Rafer Joseph** 21.7.68 (9y, 1) 7663 '94   7447, 7392, 7126; 2 Azusa, 1 AAA, 12 ECp, dnf French, dnf CG
5. **Barry Thomas** 28.4.72 (9y, 3) 7766 '95   7479w; 6 Arles, dnf CG
6. **Anthony Southward** 31.1.71 (4y, 6) 7425 '96   7385; dnf Arles, 1 Sale
7. **Alex Kruger** 18.11.63 (11y, -) 8131 '95   7052w; 10 Arles
8. **Roger Hunter** 10.3.76 (3y , 7) 7159 '97   6901w, 6810; 11 Arles, 9 AAA, 2 HCl
9. **Bill Wynn** (Gilles) 15.2.73 (3y, 11) 6800w/6790 '96   6700, 6283; 3 AAA, 6 HCl
10. **Paul Jones** 11.4.78 (1y, -) 6238w/5672 '97   6696w, 6389; 12 Arles, 4 HCl
11. **Darren Hatton** 21.3.79 (1y, -)   6508w, 6477; (Jnr Imps: 6543, 6397);   13 Arles, 1 AAA-J, 3 E.Sch
12. **Leo Barker** 26.12.78 (1y, -) 6617 '96   6468, 6456; 4 AAA, 3 HCl
–   **Stephen Garland** 12.1.73 (1y, -) 6428 '97   6503, 6346, 6296, 5845 (1 Hr);   4 Hexham, 6 AAA, 1 South
nr **Pierre Faber** RSA 9.1.72 7581 '96   7247; 1 Vienna
nr **Joe Naughton** IRE 17.10.74 6860 '97   6996, 6983w, 6870, 6860; 1 Irish, 2 AAA, 5 ECp 2,1 HCl
Ladejo ranks top at his new event – but jointly as he lost 2-1 to Quarry, only just behind at Arles but clearly ahead at the top meeting, the Commonwealth Games. Kruger's 15-year span in the rankings is a new record for the event. It was again a most disappointing year for decathlon in Britain, with only seven men over 7000 points, the same as 1996 and 1997; the 10th best standard of 6696 is the lowest since 1977.

20 KILOMETRES WALK

1. **Darrell Stone** 2.2.68 (10y, 2) 1:23:58 '96, 1:23:27 sh? '93 1:26:37, 1:31:44
    dq RWA, dq Stockport, 3 CGT, 4 CG
2. **Martin Bell** 9.4.61 (8y, 6) 1:25:42 '92 1:27:22, 1:27:30, 1:29:17, 1:29:18, 1:29:20
    1 Manx, 1 RWA, 39 ECp, dnf 7N, dnf Stockport, 2 Szeged, 7 CG
3. **Andi Drake** 6.2.65 (7y, -) 1:24:04.0t '90 1:28:01, 1:28:18, 1:28:44, 1:30:25, 1:32:04
    2 RWA, 1 Burrator, 10 7N, 1 CGT, 12 CG
4. **Chris Maddocks** 28.3.57 (16y, 7) 1:22:12 '92 1:29:40, 1:30:21, 1:32:09; 2 CGT, 1 Sutton Pk, 10 CG
5. **Andy Penn** 31.3.67 (9y, 1) 1:23:34 '92 1:31:06; 2 Manx
6. **Steve Partington** 17.9.65 (13y, 4) 1:24:09 '94 1:31:50, 1:32:15; 4 Manx, 13 CG
7. **Chris Cheeseman** 11.12.58 (5y, 9) 1:29:11 '94 1:31:58; 3 RWA
8. **Steve Hollier** 27.2.76 (1y, -) 1:37:20 '96 1:32:20, 1:34:26; 16 7N, 4 CGT
9. **Les Morton** 1.7.58 (12y, 11) 1:27:16 '89, 1:26:31sh '93 1:32:53, 1:34:24, 1:34:32;
    dq RWA, 5 CGT, 3 Sutton Pk, 5 Dublin
10. **Gareth Brown** 10.5.68 (3y, -) 1:30:15 '89 1:33:07, 1:33:10 ,1:33:45; 5 Manx, 6 CGT, 3 Dublin
11. **Richard Oldale** 26.1.66 (2y, -) 1:33:17 '96 1:33:22, 1:33:43; dq RWA, 1 Yorks, 2 Sutton Pk
12. **Jamie O'Rawe** 3.2.73 (3y, 10) 1:32:27 '97 1:33:00, 1:33:03, 1:35:47, 1:37:11
    2 Burrator, 1 Colchester, 7 CGT, 8 Dublin

The difficulty in this event was how to rank Stone. He came out clearly ahead in the most important race – a fine 4th in Kuala Lumpur, but he did little else – so should he rank ahead of Bell and Drake who were consistent throughout the year? Perhaps he should – and he did record the fastest time as well. Good to see the return of Drake, last ranked in 1991.

50 KILOMETRES WALK

1. **Mark Easton** 24.5.63 (4y, -) 4:06:01 '95 28 ECp 4:03:53, 1 CGT 4:05:17, 5 CG 4:22:23, dnf Podebrady
2. **Steve Hollier** 27.2.76 (1y, -) 0   4 CGT 4:14:37, 4 CG 4:18:41, 3 Burrrator 4:20:13, 9 Podebrady 4:28:00
3. **Chris Cheeseman** 11.12.58 (3y, 4) 4:10:23 '97 2 CGT 4:10:54, 1 Burrator 4:17:17, 8 CG 4:38:36
4. **Graham White** 28.3.59 (4y, -) 4:14:59 '95 3 CGT 4:13:18, 6 CG 4:30:17
5. **Les Morton** 1.7.58 (14y, 3) 3:57:48 '89 2 Burrator 4:17:44, 5 CGT 4:18:17
6. **Karl Atton** 14.9.71 (3y, 5) 4:16:30 '97 6 CGT 4:24:08
7. **Allan King** 3.12.56 (7y, 7) 4:13:25 '83 4 Burrator 4:22:33
8. **Tim Watt** 19.9.66 (4y, 8) 4:20:43 '95 18 Spanish 4:27:08, 1 RWA 4:32:00
9. **Mike Smith** 20.4.63 (6y, -) 4:09:22 '89 2 RWA 4:49:40
10. **Chris Berwick** 1.5.46 (15y, 9) 4:23:22 '86 3 RWA 4:58:08

CGT Commonwealth Games Trial at Stockport.

Easton had an excellent year to gain his first ever walks top ranking (previous best 2nd at 20km 1990-1). He was, however, beaten in Kuala Lumper by Hollier, who had an exciting first season at 50km – it is great to welcome a young walker (he is 22) to the higher levels. 10th best at 4:55:36 is the second worst since 1966.

BRITISH MERIT RANKINGS 1998 - WOMEN

100 METRES

1. **Joice Maduaka** 30.9.73 (2y, 9) 11.76 '97, 11.74w '95 11.32,11.35, 11.40, 11.40w, 11.44, 11.46
    1 AAA v LC, 4 Cottbus, 2 Ljubljana, 2 BedG, 1 Leeds, 2 South, 1 ECp inv, 1 AAA, 7s1 ECh, 7 CG
2. **Marcia Richardson** 10.2.72 (8y, 3) 11.42 '96, 11.39w '94 11.36w, 11.40, 11.41w, 11.45, 11.46, 11.47
    1 Ljubljana, 1 South, 6 ECp, 1 Jona, 2 AAA, 3 Hechtel, 2 WG, 1 Cup, 5s2 CG, BL1: 1,1,1
3. **Simmone Jacobs** 5.9.66 (16y, 1) 11.31 '88, 11.18w '97 11.34w, 11.46, 11.51, 11.56, 11.62, 11.71
    2 Tallinn, 1 Cork, 3 Budapest, 3 AAA, 3 Cup, 6s1 CG
4. **Katharine Merry** 21.9.74 (10y, 4) 11.34/11.27w '94 11.43, 11.56, 11.65, 11.84, 11.94
    4 Helsinki, 5 Turku, 8 Nuremberg
5. **Ellena Ruddock** 23.2.76 (1y, -) 11.70 '95 11.53w, 11.61w, 11.67, 11.70, 11.73w, 11.74
    1 CAU, 2 U23H, 4 ECp inv, 2 IR, 4 AAA, 6 U23D, 1 Mid
6. **Abi Oyepitan** 30.12.79 (1y,-) 12.06 '96 11.45w, 11.50w, 11.63w, 11.67w, 11.69w, 11.76w, 11.78; 11.7
    1 Sth-J, 2 AAA-J, 1 E.Sch, 7 AAA, 2 BL1 (3), 1 Jnr IA, 2 Ports, 1 Jnr Lg F
7. **Christine Bloomfield** 12.2.68 (2y, -) 11.59 '93 11.75w, 11.77, 11.78, 11.83, 11.97; 11.7, 11.7w
    4 Jona, 2 sf Enfield, 5 AAA, 1 Ports, BL2: 1,1,1
8. **Samantha Davies** 20.9.79 (1y, -) 12.29 '97, 12.24w '95 11.50w, 11.52w, 11.63w, 11.64w, 11.65w, 11.80
    2B AAA v LC, 2 Mid-J, 1B BedG, 1J Cork, 3 AAA-J, 2 JI v FS, 6 AAA, 2 Jnr Lg F
9. **Andrea Coore** 23.4.69 (2y, 6) 11.48 '97 11.61, 11.71, 11.81, 11.82, 11.83; 11.7, 11.7, 11.8
    3 Istanbul, 1 IR, 5s2 AAA, 2 Cup, BL1: 1,1,1
10. **Aileen McGillivary** 13.8.70 (7y, 12) 11.54 '92, 11.43w '93 11.66, 11.68, 11.70w, 11.74, 11.86, 11.88; 11.8w
    5 Cork, 2 Scot, 5s1 AAA, 6 Cup, BL1: 2,2,-
11. **Joanna Clark/Hill** 11.2.73 (1y, -) 12.02/12.00w '97, 11.9w? '96 11.67, 11.67w, 11.75, 11.77, 11.77, 11.82
    2 CAU, 5 BedG, 3 South, 5 Scot, 8 AAA, BL1: 5,5,-

12. **Malgorzata Rostek** 25.3.77 (1y, -) 11.8w/11.83 '96   11.63, 11.65w, 11.66, 11.69, 11.71w, 11.75
  dnf B.Univs, 3 CAU, 7 Bed G, 4 Leeds, 4 U23H, 4 Polish, 1 Scot, 8s1 AAA, 4 U23D, 8s1 CG, BL1: 6,6,3
– **Donna Fraser** 7.11.72 (2y, 7) 11.66/11.32w '97   11.58w, 11.71w, 11.82, 11.90, 11.94, 11.95; 11.2w
  3 BedG, 4 South, 3 ECp inv, 3 WG
– **Sarah Wilhelmy** 2.2.80 (0y, -) 11.83 '95   11.71; 11.6w; 1 BedG
– **Rebecca White** 5.6.80 (0y, -) 12.00 '97   11.45w, 11.70w, 11.85w, 12.20, 12.25, 12.25
  6 AAA v LC, 2 Nth-J, 1 North, 1 AAA-J, 3 Jnr IA

While women's sprint standards remained generally depressed, Maduaka made major progress, from 9th to 1st at 100m and ran pbs at both Europeans and Commonwealth Games. She is followed by Richardson and Jacobs, who is ranked for an event record 16th time. The highest newcomer is Oyepitan, most unfortunate not to be able to run in the individual event at the World Juniors, due to all her best races being wind assisted. Davies and White (who beat them both at the AAA Juniors but did not otherwise fare so well) also suffered from this. There was little between those ranked 7-12.

200 METRES
1. **Katharine Merry** 21.9.74 (8y, 1) 22.77 '97   22.93, 23.22, 23.23, 23.32, 23.33, 23.38
  1 AAA v LC, 5 ECp, 3 GhG, 1 AAA, 4 BGP, 5s2 ECh
2. **Sarah Wilhelmy** 2.2.80 (2y, 7) 23.44 '97   23.20w, 23.21w, 23.23, 23.25, 23.25, 23.31w
  2 AAA v LC, 1 BedG, 2 Mannheim, 1 South, 2 Cork, 1 AAA-J, 2 JI v FS, 3 WJ, 7h1 ECh, 5 v USA
3. **Joice Maduaka** 30.9.73 (3y, -) 23.81 '95   23.37, 23.37, 23.38, 23.48, 23.50, 23.53
  1B AAA v LC, 2 BedG, 2 South, 6 GhG, 2 AAA, 8 BGP, 3 v USA, 5s2 CG
4. **Allison Curbishley** 3.6.76 (1y, -) 23.4 '97   22.90w, 23.33, 23.46, 23.95; 2 Prague, 1 Scot, 3 WG
5. **Simmone Jacobs** 5.9.66 (15y, 2) 22.95 '96   23.03w, 23.28w, 23.71, 23.73, 23.80, 23.90
  5 E.Clubs, 2 Tallinn, 3 Cork, 2 Budapest, 7 GhG, 5s1 CG
6. **Donna Fraser** 7.11.72 (7y, 3) 23.25/22.90w '97, 22.96i '97   23.39w, 23.40, 23.50, 23.63, 23.73, 23.84;
  23.5w; 23.15i, 23.32i, 23.36i. 23.39i; 1 Irvine, 3 BedG, dnr South, 4 GhG, 4 WG, 4 v USA
7. **Marcia Richardson** 10.2.72 (7y, 5) 23.53 '95, 23.4 '93   23.55, 23.71, 23.73, 23.82, 24.08, 24.22; 23.6,
  23.8; 1 Ljubljana, 3 AAA, 1 Cup, 6s1 CG, BL1: -,1,1
8. **Catherine Murphy** 21.9.75 (5y, 10) 23.40 '95   24.22, 24.45, 24.49, 24.51; 23.6w?, 23.8, 23.9, 24.0; 23.91i,
  24.00i, 24.05i; 6 Irvine, 2 Leeds, 1 Welsh, 6 AAA, BL1: 2,2,2
9. **Joanna Clark/Hill** 11.2.73 (1y, -) 24.61 '96, 24.2/24.47w '97   23.62w, 23.93, 23.98w, 24.04, 24.22
  3 CAU, 3 South, 2 Scot, 7 AAA, BL1: 4,3,-
10. **Melanie Purkiss** 11.3.79 (1y, -) 24.04 '97   23.67w, 23.94, 24.10, 24.37w; 24.2, 24.4
  5 AAA-J, 3 JI v FS, 1 Jnr IA, 1 BL4 (3), 2 Cup
11. **Rebecca White** 5.6.80 (1y,-) 24.28 '97   23.82w, 24.02, 24.05, 24.05, 24.20w, 24.24; 24.17i
  1 Nth-J, 1 Leeds, 3 Mannheim, 1 North, 2 AAA-J, 1 E.Sch, 5 JI v FS, 6q4 WJ, 2 Jnr IA
12. **Clova Court** 10.2.60 (5y, 11) 23.57 '90   23.88, 24.01, 24.19; 24.1; 3 BL1 (3)

Merry is top for the fourth time, followed by Wilhelmy, who shoots up from 7th and who remains a junior in 1999. Jacobs is ranked for an event record 15th time. The 10th best on legal marks, 23.94, is the worst since 1981.

400 METRES
1. **Allison Curbishley** 3.6.76 (3y, 1) 50.78 '97   50.71, 50.73, 50.77, 50.92, 50.97, 51.05
  2 Jena, 2 Cottbus, 2 Milan, 1 U23H, 3 ECp, 1 GhG, 1 AAA, 2 BGP, 5 ECh, 1 v USA, 2 CG
2. **Donna Fraser** 7.11.72 (6y, 2) 50.87 '97   50.85, 51.01, 51.19, 51.47, 51.50, 51.54
  2 Walnut, 2 Bratislava, 2 Budapest, 3 GhG, 2 AAA, 3 BGP, 6 ECh, 3 CG
3. **Katharine Merry** 21.9.74 (1y, -) 54.0 '94   51.02, 51.7, 52.76; 1 WG, 2 v USA
4. **Michelle Thomas** 16.10.71 (2y, 6) 52.88 '97   52.92mx, 53.23, 53.23, 53.25, 53.28, 53.30
  1B AAA v LC, 6 Hania, 1 Ljubljana, 2 Tallinn, 3 AAA, 7 BGP, 6 v USA, 7s1 CG
5. **Vicki Jamison** 19.5.77 (2y, 9) 53.85 '97   52.97, 53.31, 53.63; (52.87R); 53.04i, 53.28i, 54.22i
  1 AAA v LC, 1 BedG, 2 U23D
6. **Natasha Danvers** 19.9.77 (1y, -) 0   53.26, 53.60, 53.84; (52.6R, 52.9R); 1 South
7. **Lorraine Hanson** 22.4.65 (9y, 5) 50.93 '91   53.59, 53.85, 53.90, 54.06, 54.18, 54.22
  1 CAU, 2 BedG, 1 BL1 (1), 3 Leeds, 6 GhG, 2h4 AAA, 8 BGP, 2 WG
8. **Dawn Higgins** 10.12.75 (1y, -) 57.8 '97   53.79, 54.20, 54.26, 54.35, 54.47, 54.59
  1 B.Univs, 2 AAA v LC, 2 Leeds, 2 Welsh, 1 BL4 (1), 2 IR, 4 AAA, 5 WG
9. **Michelle Pierre** 30.9.73 (4y, 3) 52.77 '97   53.52, 53.67, 53.78, 53.79, 53.92, 54.05
  3 BedG, 8 Bratislava, 2 South, 7 Lucerne, 3 IR, 5 AAA, 4 WG, 4h2 CG
10. **Vicky Day** 19.6.72 (2y, 11) 54.08 '95   53.73, 53.80, 54.12, 54.29, 54.33, 54.36
  3 AAA v LC, 4 BedG, dnr South, 1 IR, 6 AAA, 3 WG, BL2: -,1,1
11. **Alyson Layzell** 16.12.66 (1y, -) 54.7 '95   53.81, 54.7; 55.0i, 55.4i, 55.54i, 56.53i; 1 Welsh
12. **Helen Frost** 12.3.74 (2y, -) 54.32 '92   54.25, 54.28, 54.6, 55.1, 55.3, 55.71; 4 IR, 7 AAA, 1 BL1 (3), 1 Mid
- **Lesley Owusu** 21.12.78 (1y, -) 54.53 '96   54.26, 54.57, 54.80, 54.8, 54.84, 54.96
  2 U23H, 2 BL1 (2), 5 U23D, 2h1 AAA
- **Carey Easton** 16.11.79 (1y, -) 55.20 '97   54.28, 54.53, 54.70, 54.70, 54.78, 55.17
  4 AAA v LC, 5 BedG, 6 Leeds, 1 AAA-J, 1 JI v FS, 8s1 WJ, 1 Jnr IA

Curbishley and Fraser were again 1st and 2nd and made further progress with highly impressive seasons – 5th and 6th in European and then both gaining Commonwealth medals. In her rare outings at this distance, Merry showed her huge potential. After the top three there was a big gap, but the overall standard improved from 1997. Danvers, difficult to rank but ahead of Pierre at the Southern, and Higgins are the highest newcomers.

800 METRES

1. **Diane Modahl** 17.6.66 (14y, 3) 1:58.65 '90 1:58.81, 1:59.77, 2:00.08, 2:00.17, 2:00.52, 2:00.97
   8 Hengelo, 2 Milan, 4 Helsinki, 6 Athens, 5 Goodwill, 1 AAA, 5 Stockholm, 6 Monaco, 5s1 ECh, 1 Solihull, 3 CG
2. **Tanya Blake** 16.1.71 (2y, 4) 2:01.9mx '97 2:00.10, 2:02.06, 2:02.15, 2:02.72, 2:02.83, 2:03.83
   2 Eugene, 6 ECp, 4 Linz, 2 AAA, dnf Malmö
3. **Amanda Crowe** 21.10.73 (2y, 6) 2:04.2 '97 2:01.83, 2:02.7mx, 2:04.31, 2:04.98, 2:05.40, 2:06.64
   1 CAU, 1 Leeds, 6 Lucerne, 3 Belfast, 3 AAA, 5s1 CG
4. **Emma Davies** 9.10.78 (1y, -) 2:06.50 '97 2:02.39, 2:04.88, 2:05.03, 2:06.23, 2:06.52, 2:06.63
   1 AAA v LC, 2 Leeds, 2 U23H, 2 Welsh, 3 Budapest, 1 Jona, 6 AAA, 3 U23D, 7s2 CG
5. **Lynn Gibson** 6.7.69 (6y, 7) 2:02.34 '92 2:04.61, 2:04.9, 2:05.08, 2:05.1, 2:05.8, 2:06.10
   3 Batt Pk, 3 Tallinn, 1 Swindon, 4 Cardiff, 2 Watford
6. **Joanne Fenn (Mersh)** 19.10.74 (2y, 8) 2:05.63 '97 2:05.2, 2:05.88, 2:06.10, 2:06.12, 2:06.7, 2:06.77
   1 South, 2 Swindon, 2 Jona, 4 AAA, 3 WG, 3 Watford, 3 Namur, BL2: 2,2,1
7. **Rachel Newcombe** 25.2.67 (1y, -) 2:07.3 '97 2:03.28, 2:03.58, 2:04.75, 2:06.89, 2:07.03, 2:07.6
   4 Wyth, 1 Welsh, 1 Cardiff, 2 IR, 7 AAA, 7s1 CG, BL2: 1,1,2
8. **Bev Blakeman** 4.4.74 (1y, -) c. 2:18 '97 2:05.33, 2:06.48, 2:06.5, 2:06.65, 2:07.1, 2:07.65
   2 N.East, 4 CAU, 2 Wyth, 1 North, 3 IR, 5 AAA, 6 Watford, 2 Solihull
9. **Angela Davies** 21.10.70 (3y, -) 2:03.67 '94 2:04.6, 2:05.30, 2:07.3, 2:07.41, 2:07.6
   3 Cardiff, 1 Watford, 4 Solihull
10. **Vicky Sterne** 12.10.68 (4y, 10) 2:04.63 '96 2:04.81, 2:06.38, 2:07.44, 2:07.9, 2:07.94, 2:08.03
    6 Leeds, 3 Swindon, 2 Cardiff, 1 IR, 3h2 AAA, 7 Watford, BL1: 2,-,1
11. **Hayley Parry** 17.2.73 (3y, 2) 2:02.18 '97 2:03.46, 2:06.76, 2:09.07; 2:01.52i, 2:02.91i, 2:04.37i
    3 Walnut, 1 Berne, 4 IR, 5 BL4 (3)
12. **Claire Raven** 15.6.72 (2y, 5) 2:03.15 '97 2:04.98, 2:07.78, 2:08.36, 2:08.78, 2:09.3, 2:12.37
    3 AAA v LC, 1 Wyth, 6 Cork, 4 Swindon, 7h3 (fell) AAA, 1B Hechtel, dnf Watford, 3 BL2 (3)

Injury meant that Kelly Holmes did not contest an 800m race, and clear No.1 was Modahl, on top for a record seventh time and first since 1993. Blake returned from America to claim 2nd ranking before injury ended her season and Crowe's Northern Ireland record in Kuala Lumpur ensured her the third ranking. 4th to 7th are very close, with the top newcomers to the rankings, the Welsh women Davies and Newcombe, helped by their fast pbs at the Commonwealth Games. Gibson had the best competitive record of this group, 2-0 v Fenn, but contested no 800m championships.

1500 METRES

1. **Kelly Holmes** 19.4.70 (5y, 1) 3:58.07 '97 4:06.10, 4:28.04M; 1 v USA, 2 CG
2. **Paula Radcliffe** 17.12.73 (5y, 2) 4:06.84 '95, 4:24.94M '96 4:05.81, 4:05.92, 4:31.72M
   3 Hengelo, 2 ECp, 2 v USA
3. **Amanda Crowe** 21.10.73 (1y, -) 4:28.03 '97 4:10.68, 4:12.11, 4:32.99M, 4:32.71
   2 GhG, 9h2 AAA, dnf Hechtel, 3 v USA, 6 CG
4. **Helen Pattinson** 2.1.74 (1y, -) 4:16.84 '96, 4:41.65M '97 4:12.61, 4:12.87, 4:14.53, 4:14.84, 4:15.0, 4:17.05
   1 Wyth, 3 Rhede, 1 Swindon, 3 Budapest, 5 GhG, 2 AAA, 5 Hechtel, 1 Stretford 1/9, 2 Solihull, 9 CG
5. **Lynn Gibson** 6.7.69 (5y, 6) 4:05.75/4:31.17M '94 4:12.72, 4:13.35, 4:14.72, 4:14.84, 4:18.17, 4:22.46
   2 Wyth, 6 GhG, 1 AAA, 1 Solihull, 10 CG
6. **Angela Davies** 21.10.70 (6y, 5) 4:09.29 '94 4:13.55, 4:14.10, 4:14.36, 4:16.1, 4:16.37, 4:16.84
   1 Rhede, 1 Jona, 4 GhG, 3 AAA, 3 Hechtel
7. **Amanda Parkinson** 21.7.71 (2y, 12) 4:12.9mx '95, 4:18.6 '97 4:14.19, 4:16.60, 4:19.96, 4:20.1, 4:20.5,
   4:21.34; 8 GhG, 4 AAA, 4 Stretford 1/9, 4 Solihull
8. **Debbie Gunning** 31.8.65 (7y, -) 4:12.69 '90, 4:32.32M '91 4:16.75, 4:19.21, 4:19.49, 4:21.71, 4:25.5,
   4:27.51; 1 BL2 (1), 2 South, 2 Jona, 5 AAA
9. **Kerry Smithson** 13.9.76 (1y, -) 4:31.3 '97 4:17.6, 4:18.2, 4:20.2, 4:20.25, 4:21.10, 4:21.54; 6 Wyth,
   1 North, 4 Swindon, 2 Cardiff, 1 IR, 6 AAA, 1 Watford, 1 U23D, 1 Cup, 2 Stret 1/9, 5 Solihull, BL1: 1,1,1
10. **Joanne Colleran** 1.9.72 (1y, 11) 4:20.03 '97 4:18.17, 4:19.0mx, 4:19.4, 4:19.59, 4:21.8, 4:23.97
    7h2 AAA, 3 Stretford 1/9, 3 Solihull
11. **Andrea Whitcombe** 8.6.71 (1y, -) 4:14.56 '90 4:18.24, 4:20.7, 4:27.6, 4:29.03; 1 South, dnf Watford
12. **Shirley Griffiths** 23.6.72 (2y, -) 4:15.68 '96, 4:44.60M '96 4:20.3, 4:20.62, 4:21.74, 4:23.50, 4:24.17, 4:27.3;
    4:44.16Mi, 4:23.56i; 5 AAA v LC, 3 Wyth, 1 BL3 (1), 2 Swindon, 3 Cardiff, dnf ht AAA, 3 Watford

Holmes returned in time to rank top for the fifth successive year. She beat Radcliffe, who had the two fastest times of the year, in Glasgow and went on to Commonwealth silver. Crowe had a fine first season at the event to rank third and Pattinson progressed very well, setting a 1500m pb three times. Neither of 1997's 3-4, Jo Pavey and Hayley Parry, raced at the distance in 1998. The 10th best declined yet again – to the worst since 1976 – 4:18.24. That was run by Whitcombe, but she had not been near ranking when she ran four seconds faster than that in 1990.

3000 METRES (Not ranked)

Paula Radcliffe 17.12.73 8:35.28 '97   8:38.84, 9:08.83+, 9:12.54; 1 BGP
Joanne Pavey 20.9.73 9:05.87 '97   8:58.2, 9:12.10; 1 Millfield, 10 Hengelo
Sarah Young 2.1.70 9:25.1mx '97   9:04.27, 9:08.6mx, 9:49.62M, 9:10.7, 9:20.2mx, 9:35.2+
2 Millfield, 8 Cork, 7 BGP, 1 Stretford 18/8
Kelly Holmes 19.4.70 9:08.7 '95 9:10.23; 1 Bedford
Andrea Whitcombe 8.6.71 8:58.59 '91   9:10.7mx, 9:14.9, 9:26.9mx, 9:35.8+; 1 Watford
Liz Talbot 5.12.74 9:29.8 '95   9:15.25, 9:31.2, 9:35.6+, 9:43.3; 1 Swindon
Lucy Wright 17.11.69 9:17.3 '97   9:16.1mx, 9:16.93, 9:58.92M, 9:28.2, 9:34.30, 9:35.7+
5 Millfield, 12 Cork, 2 IR, 8 BGP, 2 Stretford 18/8
Heather Heasman 27.9.63 9:22.1mx '91   9:16.5mx, 9:28.1mx, 9:28.2mx, 9:35.4+
Debbie Gunning 31.8.65 9:12.12 '94   9:16.6, 9:17.39, 9:29.9; 3 Millfield, 2 Swindon, 2 BL2 (2)
Angela Davies 21.10.70 9:14.1 '94   9:17.03, 9:25.0; 7 ECp
No longer a championship event. M = 2 Miles.

5000 METRES (Previously ranked 1982-90, 1992 and 1995-7)

1. **Paula Radcliffe** 17.12.73 (4y, 1) 14:45.51 '97   14:51.27, 15:06.87, 15:06.96, 15:22.76+
    4 St Denis, 1 ECp, 2 Stockholm
2. **Andrea Whitcombe** 8.6.71 (4y, 6) 16:00.0 '96   15:43.03, 15:53.43, 15:56.85; 3 Wyth, 1 AAA, 2 CG
3. **Sarah Young** 2.1.70 (2y, 7) 16:10.15 '97   15:45.08, 15:53.81, 15:59.79, 16:29.89
    4 Wyth, 1 North, 2 AAA, 5 CG
4. **Tara Krzywicki** 9.3.74 (1y,-) 0   15:48.1mx, 15:53.28, 16:00.1, 16:00.84, 16:12.2, 16:21.26
    1 B.Univs, 6 Wyth, 1 Batt Pk, 3 AAA, 1 Watford, 1 Birmimgham
5. **Angela Davies** 21.10.70 (1y, -) 0   15:50.59; 1 Wyth
6. **Liz Talbot** 5.12.74 (2y, -) 16:24.86 '95   15:50.85, 15:52.61, 16:06.88;   2 Wyth, 8 AAA, 7 Hechtel
7. **Birhane Dagne** ex ETH 7.10.77 (1y, -) 16:17.5mx '95   15:55.81, 16:22.8; 1 CP, 4 AAA
8. **Vikki McPherson** 1.6.71 (3y, 5) 15:56.8mx '97   15:56.04, 16:07.7mx, 16:30.8; 1 So'ton, 5 AAA, 3 Birmingham
9. **Amy Waterlow** 29.7.78 (1y, -) 0   15:57.45, 16:19.72, 16:27.47;   3 B.Univs, 10 Wyth, 6 AAA
10. **Lucy Wright** 17.11.69 (2y, 12) 16:25.72 '97   15:59.51, 16:03.30, 16:20.5;   7 Wyth, 7 AAA, 2 Birmingham
11. **Heather Heasman** 27.9.63 (4y, 10) 15:53.84 '96   15:57.24, 16:08.32, 16:42.23; 5 Wyth, 3 North, 9 AAA
12. **Lynne MacDougall** 18.2.65 (2y, 4) 15:45.03 '97   16:01.41, 16:04.10, 16:21.8; 4 Prague, 7 Turku, 1 Glasgow

Radcliffe is top for the fourth time, and was again a class apart from the rest. However, there was an encouraging improvement in standards overall. Whitcombe and Young ran consistently well, excelling at the Commonwealth Games and they are followed by Krzywicki, desperately unfortunate not to be selected for Kuala Lumpur, where she could well have picked up a medal. Eleven women under 16 minutes is a new record, compared to 5 in 1997, 6 in 1996 and 8 in 1995.

10000 METRES

1. **Paula Radcliffe** 17.12.73 (1y, -) 0   30:48.58, 31:36.51; 2 Eur Challenge, 5 ECh
2. **Vikki McPherson** 1.6.71 (6y, 1) 32:32.42 '93   32:38.48, 34:05.11; 8 Eur Challenge, 4 CG
3. **Angela Joiner** 14.2.69 (1y, -) 0   33:30.27, 34:47.41, 35:22.80;   15 Eur Challenge, 3 AAA, 8 CG
4. **Sarah Bentley** 21.5.67 (2y, 4) 34:06.29 '97   33:59.69, 34:40.65; 17 Eur Challenge, 6 CG
5. **Tara Krzywicki** 9.3.74 (1y, -) 0   34:37.04; 1 AAA
6. **Hayley Nash** 30.5.63 (2y, -) 34:07.24 '92   34:28.8, 34:45.57, 35:20.14; 1 Welsh, 2 AAA, 7 CG
7. **Sally Goldsmith** 18.1.61 (2y, -) 34:28.13 '96   34:16.89, 36:02.11; 3 Italian, 9 CG
8. **Bev Hartigan** 10.6.67 (1y, -) 0   34:21.91; 18 Eur Challenge
9. **Tanya Povey** 13.4.79 (1y, -) 0   34:31.41, 35:07.62; 1 SEC, 7 NCAA
10. **Sheila Fairweather** 24.11.77 (1y, -) 0   34:39.98; 1 B.Univs
11. **Birhane Dagne** 7.10.77 ex ETH (1y, -)   34:38.11; 1 Palafrugell
12. **Katie Skorupska** 3.11.78 (1y, -) 0   34:40.00; 2 B.Univs

Although she was disappointed by her performance at the Europeans, Radcliffe had a most distinguished first season at the event, running a British record on her debut. The most difficult problem is whether to rank Joiner 3rd (clear on time) or 6th. There are eight newcomers to the rankings.

MARATHON

1. **Liz McColgan** 24.5.64 (6y, 1) 2:26:52 '97   2 London 2:26:54
2. **Marian Sutton** 7.10.63 (8y, 2) 2:29:03 '97   10 London 2:32:14, 10 Chicago 2:35:41
3. **Debbie Percival** 22.4.62 (2y, 6) 2:39:05 '97   15 London 2:39:54, 8 Frankfurt 2:40:25
4. **Gillian Horovitz** 7.6.55 (12y, 11) 2:36:52 '92   16 Boston 2:41:15, 19 New York 2:46:36, 4 CG 2:46:58
5. **Danielle Sanderson** 26.10.62 (5y, 5) 2:36:29 '94   6 CG 2:50:54
6. **Nicola Brown** 17.3.74 (1y, -) 0   19 London 2:43:18
7. **Tracy Swindell** 8.11.66 (3y, 7) 2:40:22 '97   20 London 2:43:41
8. **Ruth Kingsborough** 25.10.67 (1y, -) 2:46:53 '97   21 London 2:44:33
9. **Amanda Wright** 14.7.68 (2y, 9) 2:40:43 '97   7 Belgrade 2:44:49
10. **Anita Mellowdew** 1.12.70 (1y, -) 2:55:21 '97   23 London 2:46:17
11. **Sandra Branney** 30.4.54 (4y, -) 2:35:03 '89   24 London 2:48:47

McColgan is top for a record seventh time and Sutton is 2nd for the third successive year. Branney returns after last ranking in 1989. The 10th best of 2:48:47 is the worst since 1980.

100 METRES HURDLES
1. **Keri Maddox** 4.7.72 (9y, 9) 13.24/13.20w '93   13.07w, 13.11, 13.15, 13.20, 13.20, 13.21
   1 CAU, 1 Cork, 1 IR, 1 AAA, 6 BGP, 1 Mid, 1 Cup, 6 CG, BL1: 1,1,1
2. **Clova Court** 10.2.60 (8y, 4) 13.04 '94   13.20, 13.34, 13.37w, 13.38, 13.42, 13.42w
   2 CAU, 3 Cork, 2 IR, 7 GhG, 2 AAA, 8 BGP, 5 WG, 2 BL1 (3), 2 Cup
3. **Angela Thorp** 7.12.72 (8y, 2) 12.80 '96   13.43, 13.45, 13.48, 13.51, 13.58, 13.59; 13.4
   1 Ljubljana, 1 Leeds, 4/3 Talllinn, 6 ECp, 1 BL2 (2), 5h2 CG
4. **Natasha Danvers** 19.9.77 (5y, 8) 13.45 '95, 13.33w '97   13.20, 13.32, 13.66, 13.67, 13.71
   2 Westwood, 2 Pac-10
5. **Julie Pratt** 20.3.79 (2y, 10) 13.75, 13.61w '97   13.48w, 13.52, 13.57, 13.61, 13.64, 13.70
   1 Essex-J, 1 AAA v LC, 1 Sth-J, 1 BedG, 3 Mannheim, 2 AAA-J, 2 JI v FS, 1 WJ, 2 Jnr IA, 1 Jnr Lg F, BL2: 1,-,1
6. **Liz Fairs** 1.12.77 (1y, -) 14.10 '96   13.52, 13.56, 13.66, 13.68w, 13.76w, 13.79; 13.7w
   1 B.Univs, 2 AAA v LC, 3 CAU, 7 Leeds, 3 U23H, 1 North, 3 AAA, 1 U23D, 6h1 CG, BL3: -,1,1
7. **Denise Lewis** 27.8.72 (7y, 5) 13.18 '96   13.42w, 13.57, 13.59, 13.73, 13.77, 13.95; 13.9
   6 GhG, 5 AAA, 2 WG
8. **Melanie Wilkins** 18.1.73 (5y, 6) 13.34/13.1 '95, 13.23w '96   13.47w, 13.49w,13.50w, 13.65, 13.70, 13.75w
   3 AAA v LC, 4 CAU, 6 Celle, 1 South, 1 sf Crawley, 4 AAA, 3 WG, BL1: 3,2,4
9. **Sarah Claxton** 23.9.79 (2y, 11) 13.84, 13.65w '97   13.28w, 13.62, 13.77, 13.77w, 13.78, 13.81; 13.7w
   2 Essex-J, 2 Sth-J, 2 BedG, 2 South, 1 AAA-J, 1 JI v FS, 6h3 WJ, 1 Jnr IA
10. **Rachel King** 11.5.76 (2y, 7) 13.52 '97
    13.44w, 13.52w, 13.72w, 13.73, 13.74, 13.76; 1D AAA v LC, 3 Leeds, 1 U23H, 1 Welsh, 3 IR, 6 AAA, 6
    U23D, 4 WG, 6h2 CG
11. **Katy Sketchley** 9.7.73 (3y, 12) 13.86, 13.72w '96   13.57w, 13.73w, 13.78, 13.85w, 13.85w, 13.97w; 13.7w;
    2D AAA v LC, 5 CAU, 4 Ljubljana, 2 Maia, 3 South, 1 Scot, 2sf Crawley, 7 AAA, 6 WG, 4 Cup, BL4: 1,1,-
12. **Jenny Kelly** 20.6.70 (1y, -) 14.04, 13.95w '96   13.80, 13.83w, 13.91, 13.91w, 13.93w, 13.94w; 13.9,
    13.9w; 5 BedG, 4 South, 4 IR, 3 Cup, BL1: 2,3,3

Maddox has long been a most promising hurdler, but until this year has never ranked higher than third; now, when also running most successfuly at 400mh, she was undefeated by a British athlete and takes over at the top. Her great rival Court is second, and there is then little to choose between the next group, with remarkably little head-to-head action. Top juniors Pratt and Claxton were 3-3 on win-loss, but Pratt won the World Junior title, while Claxton exited in the heats. Top newcomer is Fairs. Missing the whole season were the 1997 no.1 Diane Allahgreen and the 1994-5 no. 1 Jackie Agyepong.

400 METRES HURDLES
1. **Gowry Retchakan** 21.6.60 (10y, 4) 54.63 '92   55.25, 56.29, 56.4, 56.57, 56.7, 56.86
   1 Middx, 1 CAU, 1 Ljubljana, 1 Tallinn, 4 Lucerne, 2 AAA, 2 WG, 2 CG, BL2: 1,-,1
2. **Natasha Danvers** 19.9.77 (2y, 5) 56.84 '97   55.69, 56.27, 56.35, 56.39, 56.58, 56.94
   1 Pac-10, 3 NCAA, 4 Budapest, 4 GhG, 1 AAA, 2 U23D, 6h3 ECh, 5 CG
3. **Keri Maddox** 4.7.72 (3y, 6) 57.69 '97   56.38, 56.76, 56.95, 57.15, 57.22, 57.59
   1 AAA v LC, 6 BedG, 3 Leeds, 2 Rhede, 2 Cork, 3 AAA, 3 WG, 1 Mid, 2 Cup, 4 CG, BL1: 1,-,1
4. **Vicki Jamison** 19.5.77 (4y, 3) 57.27 '96   56.42, 56.62, 56.92, 56.98, 57.16, 57.18
   1 Leeds, 1 U23H, 5 ECp. 6 GhG, 4 AAA, 4 WG, 6 CG
5. **Alyson Layzell** 16.12.66 (5y, 2) 56.43 '96   57.31, 58.08, 58.36; 1 BedG, 2 Leeds, 3 Cork
6. **Lorraine Hanson** 22.4.65 (7y, -) 56.70 '89   57.46, 58.61, 59.01, 59.6, 60.8, 62.02;   4 Cork, 2 Mid, 1 Cup
7. **Jackie Parker** 15.10.66 (10y, -) 56.15 '91   57.70, 58.68, 58.86, 58.9, 58.94, 59.5
   1B AAA v LC, 2 BedG, 1 South, 1 IR, 1 sf Crawley, 6 AAA, BL4: 1,1,-
8. **Sinead Dudgeon** 9.7.76 (2y, -) 58.80 '96   58.54, 58.55, 59.17, 59.2, 59.34, 59.38
   2 CAU, 2 U23H, 5 Leeds, 1 Scot, 5 AAA, 5 U23D, 3 Cup, BL1: -,1,2
9. **Clare Wise** 22.8.69 (1y, -) 60.83 '96   59.07, 59.32, 59.51, 59.62, 59.8, 60.50
   3 South, 3 IR, 2 sf Crawley, 7 AAA, 2 Exeter, BL1: 2,2,-
10. **Jenny Matthews** (Pearson) 3.7.62 (12y, -) 57.41 '88   58.72, 59.28, 59.8, 59.85, 60.1, 60.3
    5 CAU, dnf South, 8 AAA, 1 Eur Vets, BL3: -,1,1
11= **Christine Amede** 7.8.63 (2y, 11) 60.06 '97   59.43, 59.56, 59.82, 59.87, 60.0, 60.2
    2 Middx, 3 BedG, 2 South, 3h2 AAA, 4 Cup, BL1: 3,3,3
11= **Nicola Sutton** 4.3.74 (1y, -) 60.42 '92   59.40, 59.56, 59.8, 59.94, 59.97, 61.04
    1 B.Univs, 2 AAA v LC, 4 Leeds, 1 North, 5 Cork, 1 Exeter
-   **Tracey Duncan** 16.5.79 (1y, -) 60.3, 60.47 '96   59.39. 59.56, 60.6, 60.74, 60.9, 60.95
    2 B.Univs, 3 AAA v LC, 4 BedG, 2 AAA-J, 1 JI v FS, 5s2 WJ, 2 BL2 (3)

Retchakan, ranked second for six successive years 1990-5 behind Sally Gunnell, achieved a wonderful climax to her career with the Commonwealth silver medal. She retires having ranked top for the first time, at the age of 38. She prepared meticulously and was justly rewarded with much her fastest time of the year in KL. There Maddox, Danvers and Jamison finished 4-5-6. Danvers and Maddox were 1-1, but Danvers had the better set of times and results overall.

131

HIGH JUMP

1. **Jo Jennings** 20.9.69 (10y, 3) 1.94i '93, 1.90 '88   1.91, 1.90, 1.89, 1.88, 1.88, 1.88
   1 Yorks, 1 CAU, 1 Leeds, 5 ECp, 1 IR, 1 AAA, 2= WG, 1 BL2 (3), 1 Thurrock, 2 CG
2. **Michelle Dunkley** 26.1.78 (4y, 4) 1.87 '95, 1.89i '97   1.88, 1.86, 1.86, 1.85, 1.85, 1.81; 1.89i, 1.86i
   2= B.Univs, 2= AAA v LC, 3 BedG, 2 Istanbul, 3 Celle, 3 Budapest, 2 IR, 3 AAA, 5 WG, 3 U23D, 2 Thurrock, 4=CG
3. **Susan Jones** 8.6.78 (5y, 2) 1.91 '97   1.85, 1.85, 1.85, 1.83, 1.82, 1.81; 1.92i, 1.89i
   1 AAA v LC, 2 CAU, 2 Ljubljana, 1 U23H, 1 North, 3 IR, 2 AAA, 2= WG, 3 Thurrock, 7 CG, BL2: -,1,2
4. **Denise Lewis** 27.8.72 (6y, 7) 1.84 '96   1.83, 1.83, 1.82, 1.82, 1.80; 1.70i;   4 AAA, 2= WG
5. **Lee McConnell** 9.10.78 (2y, 10) 1.80 '97   1.83, 1.82, 1.80, 1.76, 1.76, 1.75
   1 B.Univs, 2= AAA v LC, 3 CAU, 1 BedG, 9 Prague, 2 U23H, 1 Scot, 6 AAA, BL1: 1,2,-
6. **Julie Crane** 26.9.76 (3y, -) 1.81 '94   1.83, 1.80, 1.80, 1.80, 1.80, 1.75
   4 B.Univs, 5 AAA v LC, 2 Bed G, 3 Leeds, 1 Welsh, 4 IR, 5 AAA, 1 WG, 4 U23D, 1 Mid, 8 CG
7. **Julia Bennett** 26.3.70 (11y, 5) 1.89 '94, 1.92i '90   1.83, 1.82, 1.80, 1.80, 1.76, 1.75; 1.84i, 1.83i
   1 Surrey, 2 sf Crawley
8. **Hazel Melvin** 19.11.73 (6y, 6) 1.85 '97   1.80, 1.80, 1.76, 1.75, 1.72, 1.70; 1.80i, 1.75i
   4 Turku, 2 Scot, 7 AAA, BL1: 2,3,-
9. **Gillian Black** 27.10.79 (2y, 9) 1.81 '97   1.80, 1.78, 1.76, 1.75, 1.75, 1.75
   7 CAU, 2 Leeds, 2 AAA-J, 2 JI v FS, 8 AAA, 1 Jnr IA, BL1: 3=,-,3
10. **Kerry Jury** 19.11.68 (3y, 8) 1.81 '97   1.79, 1.76, 1.75, 1.75, 1.75, 1.75
    2 Yorks, 2 North, 1 Nth IC, BL3: 1,-,1
11. **Natasha Danvers** 19.9.77 (1y, -) 1.65 '93   1.82, 1.78, 1.73, 1.73; 2 Pac-10, 15= NCAA
12. **Aileen Wilson** 30.3.84 (1y, -) 1.72 '97   1.79, 1.78, 1.75, 1.74, 1.74, 1.72; 1.78i, 1.75i, 1.75i
    1 Mid U15, 6 BedG, 1 AAA-J, 5 JI v FS, 2 Celtic Int, 1 AAA U15
–   **Julie Peacock** (Major) 19.8.70 (4y, -) 1.85 '94   1.80, 1.75, 1.75; 1 sf Crawley, BL1: -,1,1
–   **Debbie Marti** 14.5.68 (13y, 1) 1.94 '96, 1.95i '97   1.89i, 1.85i
nr   **Dalia Mikneviciuté** (ex-Lit) 5.9.70 1.89 '97   1.80, 1.80; 1.86i, 1.85i, 1.84i, 1.83i;   3 E.Clubs, 1 South
Jennings has been second once and third three times, initially in 1988 – now she is to top for the first time and ended in fine style with the Commonwealth silver medal. Dunkley was 3-3 with Jones, but had the better marks and, like Jennings, set a outdoor pb in KL. Missed was Debbie Marti, top ranked six times in the previous seven years – who competed twice indoors, but not at all outdoors.

POLE VAULT

1. **Janine Whitlock** 11.8.73 (4y, 1) 4.11 '97   4.31, 4.30, 4.30, 4.25, 4.22, 4.20; 4.28i, 4.25i; in all 17 outdoors
   and 9 indoor competitions at 4.00 or better;   1 AAA v LC, 1/2 Arles, 4 Cottbus, 1 BedG, 5= Milan, 1 Leeds,
   3= Ostrava, 2 ECp, 1 Linz, 1 IR, 1 AAA, 4 BGP, dnq 17= ECh, 4 CG
2. **Rhian Clarke** 19.4.77 (6y, 2) 3.90 '97   3.82, 3.82, 3.80, 3.80, 3.70, 3.70; 3.80i
   2/3 Stellenbosch, 9 Modesto, 4B Arles, 3 Leeds, 1 Welsh, 4 Kingston, 2 AAA, 4 U23D, 6= WG, 1 BL2 (3), 11 CG
3. **Emma Hornby** 12.12.73 (3y, 7) 3.60 '97   3.91, 3.81, 3.80, 3.80, 3.71, 3.70
   1 Coventry, 10/7 Arles, 2 BedG, 1 BL1 (1), 1 Derby, 1 NI, 1 Stoke, 2 IR, 4 AAA, 6= WG, dnq nh ECh, 1 Cup, 15 CG
4. **Paula Wilson** 20.11.69 (5y, 4) 3.75 '97   3.80, 3.80, 3.70, 3.70, 3.70, 3.60
   2 Coventry, 11/9 Arles, nh BedG, 2 Derby, 2 Stoke, 3 AAA, 2 WG, 12 CG, BL1: 4,-,1
5. **Lucy Webber** 5.2.72 (1y, -) 3.30i/3.00 '97   3.80, 3.72, 3.71, 3.70, 3.70, 3.70
   2 AAA v LC, 8/6 Arles, 3 BedG, 3 Ljubljana, 1 South, 6 Kingston, 3 IR, 5 AAA, 3= WG, 1 Enfield, 8 Salgotarján
6. **Tracey Bloomfield** 13.9.79 (1y, -) 3.15 '97   3.75, 3.72, 3.70, 3.60, 3.60, 3.60
   3 AAA v LC, 1 South-J, 1 CAU, 8 Mannheim, 2 South, 4 AAA-J, 5 Kingston, 4 JI v FS, 7 AAA, dnq 21= WJ, 1 Jnr IA
7. **Linda Stanton** 22.6.73 (6y, 5) 3.72 '95   3.70, 3.70, 3.65, 3.62, 3.60, 3.60
   13/8 Arles, 4 BedG, 2 Leeds, 1 North, 6 AAA, 3= WG, 2 Cup, BL1: 2,3,2
8. **Louise Schramm** 18.12.71 (5y, 3) 3.70 '97
   3.75, 3.70, 3.65, 3.50, 3.50, 3.50
   1 Surrey, 9=B Arles, 2 Woking, 6 BedG, 3 Kingston, 1 sf Crawley, 8 AAA
9. **Clare Ridgley** 11.9.77 (6y, 6) 3.55 '97
   3.60, 3.50, 3.50, 3.50, 3.50, 3.50
   1 B.Univs, 4 AAA v LC, 3 CAU, 5 BedG, 4 IR, 2sf Crawley, 9 AAA, 6 U23D, 4 Cup, BL4: 1,2,1
10. **Alison Murray-Jessee** 13.1.67 (3y, 9) 3.60A '96,3.81iA   3.85A, 3.83A, 3.60, 3.50, 3.50, 3.45A, 3.60Ai, 3.50Ai
    1 BL1 (2), 1 Scot, 15 AAA, 5 WG, 14 CG
11. **Fiona Harrison** 30.11.81 (3y, 11) 3.50 '96   3.60, 3.50, 3.50, 3.40, 3.00; 3.30i
    nh Yorks, 1 North-J, 11 Mannheim, 2 CAU
12. **Alison Davies** 6.4.61 (1y, -) 3.10 '97   3.60, 3.50, 3.45, 3.40, 3.35, 3.30;   10 AAA
–   **Kimberly Rothman** 6.9.64 (1y, 8) 3.50 '97   3.55, 3.40, 3.40, 3.40, 3.35, 3.30; 3.40i, 3.40i
    2 Surrey, 3 Woking, 3 South, 12= AAA, 4 Enfield, 3 Cup, BL1: -,2,4
–   **Noelle Bradshaw** 18.12.63 (1y, 12) 3.30 '97   3.50, 3.40, 3.40, 3.40, 3.40, 3.40
    1 Woking, 5 South, 7 Kingston, 5 IR, 3 sf Crawley, 11 AAA, BL1: 3,4,3

After seven more UK records indoors, Whitlock added another three outdoors, but after a superb 2nd in the European Cup her form declined a little. She remained, however, a class apart amongst British women and on the edge of the world top ten. Although Hornby, who improved markedly, achieved the EC qualifying standard, Clarke was superior and ranks second. The biggest improvement was made by Webber, the highest newcomer, and by the new British junior record holder, Bloomfield. Standards at this new event continued to rise with the 10th best 3.60, compared to 3.40 in 1997, 3.30 in 1996 and 3.10 in 1995.

LONG JUMP
1. **Joanne Wise** 15.3.71 (9y, 1) 6.57 '92, 6.70i '97, 6.69w '88   6.63, 6.58, 6.43w, (6.33), 6.39, 6.31, 6.23
   1 Cork, 6 Linz, 6 GhG, 4 AAA, 1 BL2 (3), 1 CG
2. **Denise Lewis** 27.8.72 (7y, 2) 6.67 '95, 6.77w '97   6.59, 6.52, 6.44, 6.34, 6.15; 6.30i, 6.29i
   7 GhG, 1 AAA
3. **Sarah Claxton** 23.9.79 (2y, 3) 6.41/6.53w '97   6.52, 6.40w, 6.34w, 6.32, 6.31, 6.29
   1 AAA v LC, 1 Sth-J, 7 ECp, 1 AAA-J, 1 E.Sch, 2 JI v FS, 4 WJ, 1 Jnr IA
4. **Tracy Joseph** 29.11.69 (2y, 4) 6.34/6.44w '97   6.39, 6.38w (6.34), 6.37w, 6.35, 6.35, 6.32
   2 AAA v LC, 1 CAU, 2 Ljubljana, 1 South, 2 Cork, 2 AAA, 1 Cup, 5 CG
5. **Andrea Coore** 23.4.69 (3y, 5) 6.34 '97   6.36, 6.31, 6.25, 6.23, 6.15, 6.12w
   6 Jena, 4 Istanbul, 5 Cork, 2 IR, 1 sf Crawley, 3 AAA, 1 Cup, nj CG, BL4: 1,-,1
6. **Julie Hollman** 16.2.77 (2y, 7) 6.08/6.29w '97   6.29w, 6.17, 6.12w, 6.03, 6.01, 5.94; 6.05i
   1 B.Univs, 4 U23H, 2 South, 4 Cork, 2 Cup, BL1: 1,-,1
7. **Donita Benjamin** 7.3.72 (1y, -) 5.93, 6.22w '97   6.28w, 6.18w, 6.17w, 6.09, 6.09, 6.07; 3 CAU, 1 IS, 5 AAA
8. **Ruth Irving** 20.7.74 (7y, -) 6.28 '94   6.26, 6.21w, 6.01, 5.99, 5.92, 5.85; 5.90i
   2 CAU, 1 North, 6 Cork, 3 BL1 (2), 1 Scot, 7 AAA
9. **Ashia Hansen** 5.12.71 (5y, 11) 6.47A '96, 6.27 '94   6.23, 5.95w; 4 E.Clubs, 2 BL1 (1)
10. **Ann Brooks/Danson** 4.5.71 (5y, 12) 6.16 '95, 6.38w '94   6.04w, 6.01w, 5.99w, 5.95, 5.82, 5.82w
    3 AAA v LC, 4 CAU, 1 IR, 8 AAA, BL3: 1,1,1
11. **Liz Ghojefa** 24.2.69 (6y, 9) 6.27 '95, 6.32w '94   6.16, 5.92w?, 5.86w, 5.79w, 5.76w
    3 B.Univs, 1 Surrey, 7 AAA v LC, 5 CAU
12. **Connie Henry** 15.4.72 (1y, -) 6.05 '91, 6.12w '93   6.06, 5.99, 5.89, 5.88
    7 Budapest, 2 sf Crawley, BL1: 4,1,-
– **Danielle Freeman** 11.2.80 (1y, 10) 6.15/6.20w '97   6.05, 5.85w; 5.96i, 5.79i
    8 AAA v LC, 3 AAA-J, 2 E.Sch
Returning steadily to form, Wise ended the year with a surprise Commonwealth gold, and that ensured her of retaining top ranking. Indeed the first five places remain the same as in 1997, with Claxton third for the third successive time – yet still a junior.

TRIPLE JUMP
1. **Ashia Hansen** 5.12.71 (8y, 1) 15.15 '97   14.32, 13.91, 13.39; 15.16i, 14.85i, 14.73i, 14.48i, 14.47i, 14.31i, 14.30i; 1 Cup, 1 CG
2. **Connie Henry** 15.4.72 (6y, 4) 13.55 '96   13.95, 13.95, 13.94, 13.90, 13.86, 13.81; 1 AUS Ch, 1 AAA v LC, 1 CAU, 3 E.Clubs, 2 Tallinn, 4 ECp, 3 BL1 (2), 1 AAA, 2 Waldshut, dnq 20 ECh, 1 Thurrock, 3 CG
3. **Michelle Griffith** 6.10.71 (9y, 2) 14.08 '94   13.94, 13.84, 13.83, 13.77, 13.71, 13.45w
   1 South, 1 sf Enfield, 2 AAA, 2 Waldshut, 5 CG, BL1: 1,1,-
4. **Katie Evans** 4.2.74 (4y, 3) 13.03 '97   12.65w, 12.61w, 12.58w, 12.56, 12.53, 12.46
   2 AAA v LC, 2 CAU, 4 Ljubljana, 1 Derby, 1 IR, nj AAA, nj Mid, BL1: 2,2,-
5. **Debbie Rowe** 8.9.72 (5y, 6) 12.76w/12.60 '97   12.69w (12.61), 12.58, 12.52w, 12.39, 12.36, 12.34w; 12.43i
   1 B.Univs, 3 AAA v LC, 3 CAU, 1 BedG, 2 Derby, 3 IR, 6 AAA, 1 Mid, 2 Cup, BL1: 3,5,-
6. **Kerensa Denham** 8.3.74 (3y, 9) 12.51 '96   12.61, 12.53, 12.44, 12.42, 12.29w, 12.22
   2 Kent, 2 South, 1 Scot, 3 AAA, BL2: 1,1,-
7. **Caroline Stead** 14.9.71 (5y, 8) 12.67 '96   12.26, 12.24, 12.23, 12.19, 12.15, 12.14
   4 South, 5 IR, 2 sf Enfield, 4 AAA, 2 Thurrock, BL2: 2,2,1
8. **Karen Skeggs** 26.10.69 (9y, 5) 12.89/12.93w '92
   12.44, 12.35w (12.17), 12.23, 12.13, 12.04, 11.85; 1 Kent, 4 CAU, 3 South, BL3: -,1,1
9. **Jodie Hurst** 21.6.77 (2y, 7) 12.26/12.42w '97   12.20, 12.20, 12.10, 12.07, 12.07w, 11.79
   4 B.Univs, 3 BedG, 3 U23H, 7 AAA, 2 Mid, BL3: 1,2,-
10. **Judy Kotey** 20.5.80 (2y, 11) 12.21/12.37i/12.36w '97   12.61w, 12.55w, 12.33, 12.20, 12.05, 12.01; 12.41i, 12.13i; 4 AAA v LC, 1 Sth-J, 4 BedG, 1 AAA-J, 2 E.Sch, 7 JI v FS, 1 Jnr IA
11. **Julia Johnson** 21.9.79 (2y, 12) 12.05/12.06w ' 97   12.50, 12.27w (12.00), 12.26, 12.23, 12.21w, 12.08
    5 AAA v LC, 2 AAA-J, 1 E.Sch, 6 JI v FS, 9 AAA, 2 Jnr IA, 3 Thurrock
12. **Anna-Maria Thorpe** 15.7.71 (1y, -)   12.47, 12.42, 11.90, 11.74, 11.46
After her brilliant world indoor record when winning European gold, Hansen missed most of the season through injury, but returned just in time to collect Commonwealth gold and rank first for the fourth successive year. Henry overtook Griffith to rank second; they were 2-2, with the order decided by their close 3-5 in Kuala Lumpur. There was a huge gulf after the top three. They had similar marks, but Evans beat Rowe 6-2.

SHOT

1. **Judy Oakes** 14.2.58 (22y, 1) 19.36 '88   18.83, 18.79, 18.46, 18.38, 18.35, 18.28, 18.27; 18.56i, 18.42i, 18.32i
   3 Halle, 1 BL4 (1), 1 Arles, 1 South, 2 ECp, 6 Goodwill, 1 AAA, 1 Thurrock, 1 CG
2. **Myrtle Augee** 4.2.65 (17y, 2) 19.03 '90   17.69, 17.39, 17.22, 17.16, 17.03, 16.95
   2 Arles, 2 South, 1 sf Crawley, 2 AAA, 1 Plate, 2 Thurrock, 2 CG
3. **Maggie Lynes** 19.2.63 (12y, -) 16.57 '94   15.73, 15.55, 15.37, 15.29, 15.18, 15.17
   3 South, 1 IR, 3 AAA, 5 Thurrock, 7 CG; BL2: 2,2,-
4. **Tracy Axten** 20.7.63 (4y, 3) 15.74 '97   15.81, 15.45, 15.43, 15.28, 15.22, 15.04
   5 CAU, 6 E.Clubs, 5 South, 2 IR, 1 Police, 2 sf Crawley, 4 AAA, 4 Eur Police, 4 Thurrock, BL1: 6,1,1
5. **Joanne Duncan** 27.12.66 (5y, 4) 15.18, 15.42i '97   15.76, 15.41, 15.24, 15.15, 15.12, 15.07
   1 AAA v LC, 1 CAU, 6 South, 1 sf Enfield, 5 AAA, 3 Thurrock, BL2: 1,1,1
6. **Julie Dunkley** 11.9.79 (2y, 10) 14.36 '97   15.27, 15.04, 15.00, 14.81, 14.81, 14.80;   3 AAA v LC, 7 Arles,
   4 South, 1 AAA-J, 1 E.Sch, 3 JI v FS, 6 AAA, dnq 18 WJ, 1 Jnr IA, 1 Cup, 6 Thurrock, BL1: 2,-,3
7. **Denise Lewis** 27.8.72 (3y, 8) 14.55 '97   15.27, 15.09, 14.72, 14.45, 13.66;   2 WG, BL1: 1,3,-
8. **Christina Bennett** 27.2.78 (2y, 11) 14.27/14.59i '97   15.10, 14.82, 14.70, 14.65, 14.65, 14.62
   1 B.Univs, 2 AAA v LC, 8 South, 3 sf Crawley, 8 AAA, 3 U23D, 2 Plate, 7 Thurrock
9. **Vickie Foster** 1.4.71 (3y, 7) 14.45 '97   14.61, 14.53, 14.50, 14.48, 14.38, 14.32; 14.64i
   4 AAA v LC, 4 CAU, 7 South, 4 sf Crawley, 7 AAA, BL1: 5,2,2
10. **Carol Parker** 22.9.69 (11y, 6) 14.76i '91, 14.71 '90   14.57, 14.48, 14.33, 14.24, 14.22, 14.13; 14.54i
    3 IR, 9 AAA, 1 Mid, BL2: 3,3,2
11. **Eleanor Gatrell** 5.10.76 (1y, -) 13.96 '97   14.68, 14.43, 14.23, 14.14, 14.13, 14.11; 14.27i
    2 B.Univs, 5 AAA v LC, 4 U23H, 9 South, 10 AAA, 5 U23D
12. **Philippa Roles** 1.3.78 (3y, -) 14.60 '96   14.54, 14.36, 14.22, 14.20, 14.05, 13.92; 15.00i
    3 B.Univs, 3 CAU, 1 Welsh, 2 sf Enfield, 4 IR, 3 WG, BL4: 2,1,1
- **Pauline Richards** 30.6.68 (0y, -) 13.18 '95
  14.51, 14.47, 14.38, 14.04, 13.93, 13.66

Going from strength to strength, Judy Oakes achieves a record 16th number one ranking, with Augee taking her 16th successive year in the top 4. Oakes had 14 competitions, with her worst mark of 17.82 still better than Augee's best. Augee in turn was 2 metres better than the next group of three, very closely matched and ranked in their AAA order. The 10th best of 14.65 (including indoors) is a new record (previously 14.64 in 1991).

DISCUS

1. **Shelley Drew** 8.8.73 (7y, 1) 60.80 '97   60.82, 60.35, 59.95, 58.32, 57.94, 57.87;   7 La Jolla 28/3, 2 Balboa
   4/4, 8 Halle, 1 CAU, 1 South, 6 ECp, 3 Budapest, 1 IR, 1 AAA, 6 BGP, 2 Lough 7/8, dnq 27 ECh, 4 CG
2. **Jacqueline McKernan** 1.7.65 (14y, 2) 60.72 '93   58.05, 58.02, 57.92, 57.10, 57.09, 57.02
   1 Balboa 4/4 (training comp?), 2 La Jolla 11/4, 1 AAA v LC, 2 CAU, 1 NI, 4 Budapest, 2 AAA, 7 BGP, 1 WG,
   1 Lough 7/8, 1 Singapore, 5 CG
3. **Philippa Roles** 1.3.78 (4y, 4) 51.60 '97   54.14, 54.10, 53.91, 53.81, 53.69, 53.66
   3 Balboa 4/4, 1 B.Univs, 2 AAA v LC, 3 CAU, 1 U23H, 1 Welsh, 2 IR, 3 AAA, 2 U23D, 3 WG, 3 Lough 7/8,
   2 Singapore, 6 CG, BL4: 1,1,-
4. **Tracy Axten** 20.7.63 (10y, 3) 58.18 '97   54.03, 53.73, 53.33, 53.10, 51.85, 51.81
   6 E.Clubs, 3 South, 5 IR, 1sf Crawley, 1 Police, 4 AAA, 1 Cup, 3 Eur Police, 8 CG, BL1: 2,1,1
5. **Debbie Callaway** 15.7.64 (15y, 6) 58.56 '96   54.94, 54.18, 52.43, 52.16, 51.59, 51.58
   3 AAA v LC, 4 CAU, 2 South, 3 IR, 2 sf Crawley, 6 AAA, 4 Lough 7/8, BL1: 1,2,3
6. **Emma Merry** 2.7.74 (9y, 5) 52.58 '93   53.21, 52.57, 52.35, 52.32, 52.30, 51.92
   2 B.Univs, 4 AAA v LC, 5 CAU, 4 Tallinn, 4 IR, 5 AAA, 4 WG, 5 Lough 7/8, 7 CG, BL2: 1,1,-
7. **Lorraine Shaw** 2.4.68 (5y, -) 55.04 '94   51.96, 51.74, 51.57, 51.16, 49.13
   1 sf L'pool, 7 AAA, 5 WG, BL1 (3), 2 Cup
8. **Lauren Keightley** 2.8.79 (2y, 9) 48.82 '97   52.31, 49.58, 48.89, 48.56, 48.12, 47.18
   1 Sth-J, 6 AAA v LC, 6 CAU, 4 Mannheim, 6 South, 1 AAA-J, 2 JI v FS, 9 AAA, dnq 15 WJ, 1 Jnr IA
9. **Judy Oakes** 14.2.58 (12y, 11) 53.44 '88   51.71, 49.94, 49.14;   2 BL4 (1) 8 AAA
10. **Nicola Talbot** 17.2.72 (6y, 10) 54.24 '93   47.37, 47.00, 46.30, 45.11, 44.89, 44.25
    5 AAA v LC, 3 BL1 (2), 6 IR, 10 AAA
11. **Sarah Henton** 4.5.73 (3y, 8) 50.98 '97   47.96, 47.34, 46.92, 45.01, 44.50, 43.35
    3 B.Univs, 7 AAA v LC, 4 BL1 (1), 4 South, 2 sf Liverpool, 11 AAA; BL1: 4,4,-
12. **Vickie Foster** 1.4.71 (1y, -) 48.62 '93   47.02, 47.01, 46.92, 46.66, 46.41, 46.31
    7 CAU, 5 South, BL1: 3,5,4

Drew 1st and McKernan 2nd is the same as in 1997, but Drew was well clear this time. McKernan sets an event record with 16 years ranked. The 10th best is 47.96, the worst since 1985, but that is a little misleading as 9th is 51.71 (which is better than the record for 10th!). Roles and Axten swap places from 1997, as do Callaway and Merry. Callaway beat Merry 4-1, but Merry got the CG spot through a higher AAA placing.

HAMMER

1. **Lorraine Shaw** 2.4.68 (5y, -) 64.90 '95 63.30, 63.13, 62.66, 61.19, 61.11, 60.71
   1 Col 26/4, 13 Halle, 1 BedG, 5 ECp, 1 AAA, 1 WG, 1 Col 1/8, 11 ECh, 1 Cup, 2 CG, BL1: 1,-,1
2. **Lyn Sprules** 11.9.75 (6y, 1) 61.70 '97 61.66, 60.64, 60.29, 60.03, 59.40, 59.20
   8 Halle, 1 Leeds, 1 South, 2 AAA, 12 ECh, 7 CG
3. **Rachael Beverley** 23.7.79 (3y, 4) 56.46 '97 57.97, 56.35, 56.14, 56.03, 55.73, 55.68
   2 Col 26/4, 1 B.Univs, 1 AAA v LC, 1 CAU, 4 BedG, 1 AAA-J, 3 AAA, dnq 13 WJ, 11 CG, BL1: 2,-,2
4. **Elizabeth Pidgeon** 27.4.77 (3y, 7) 54.44 '97 57.56, 57.04, 56.95, 56.50, 56.38, 55.96
   13 NCAA, 2 U23H, 2 South, 2 IR, 2 sf Enfield, 4 AAA, 4 U23D, BL2: -,1,1
5. **Diana Holden** 12.2.75 (8y, 3) 55.86 '97 57.95, 57.79, 56.36, 56.27, 56.18, 55.85
   4 Col 26/4, 4 B.Univs, 12 Halle, 2 Bed G, 2 Leeds, 3 South, 1 BL3 (2), 1 IR, 5 AAA, 2 WG, 2 Col 1/8, 2 Thurrock
6. **Sarah Moore** 15.3.73 (7y, 3) 56.60 '97 55.99, 55.74, 55.39, 54.94, 54.74, 54.20
   3 Col 26/4, 2 Lisse, 3 Bed G, 3 Leeds, 1 Welsh, 3 IR, 7 AAA, 4 WG, 1 BL4 (3), 4 Singapore, 12 CG
7. **Ann Gardner** 11.10.68 (7y, 6) 55.00 '96 55.60, 54.92, 54.70, 54.08, 52.96, 52.78
   6 Col 26/4, 3 Lisse, 2 AAA v LC, 2 CAU, 6 BedG, 4 IR, 6 AAA, 1 Mid
8. **Catherine Garden** 4.9.78 (1y, -) 50.52 '97 53.37, 52.57, 52.52, 52.38, 51.78, 51.76
   5 Col 26/4, 3 B.Univs, 4 AAA v LC, 3 CAU, 4 Leeds, 4 U23H, 2 Scot, 8 AAA, 5 U23D
9. **Zoe Derham** 24.11.80 (1y, -) 48.66 '97 51.25, 50.03, 49.98, 49.46, 49.41, 49.41
   3B Col 26/4, 1 Mid-J, 5 AAA v LC, 3 AAA-J, 5 JI v FS, 1J/1J Col 1/8, 1 Jnr IA
10. **Irene Duffin** 10.8.60 (5y, 12) 50.38 '97 50.35, 49.99, 49.60, 49.43, 49.35, 48.37
    7 Col 26/4, 4 CAU, 5 E.Clubs, 4 South, 11 AAA, 4 Cup, BL1: 4,1,5
11. **Esther Augee** 1.1.64 (6y, 8) 56.76 '93 49.95, 49.65, 49.44, 49.42, 48.85, 48.70
    8 South, 9 AAA, 3 Thurrock, BL2: 2,2,2
12. **Janet Smith** 7.10.64 (3y, 10) 50.62 '97 50.20, 49.70, 49.53, 49.48, 49.09, 48.64
    2B Col 26/4, 5 CAU, 8 BedG, 5 South, 10 AAA, 4 Col 1/8, 5 Thurrock, BL1: 6,3,4
nr **Olivia Kelleher** IRE 9.10.75 (6y, 2) 57.92 '97 54.38, 53.92, 53.79, 53.75, 53.69, 53.68
    2B Col 26/4, 2 B.Univs, 3 AAA v LC, 5 BedG, 1 sf Enfield, 1 Irish, 3 Col 1/8, dnq ECh, 2 Cup, 1 Thurrock, BL1: -,2,3

Returning after her long absence with a serious back injury, Shaw ranks top for the fifth time. Like Shaw, Sprules made the European final, but was some way short of the medals at the Commonwealth Games. Ranking 3-5 are Beverley, improving her British junior record, Pidgeon and Holden, who all made substantial progress. These three were closely matched, with Beverley 2-1 against Holden and 1-0 v Pidgeon; Pidgeon 2-1 v Holden.

JAVELIN

1. **Lorna Jackson** 9.1.74 (6y, 8) 58.20 '96 58.39, 57.89, 56.76, 56.71, 55.79, 55.10
   6 Halle, 1 CAU, 1 Karlstad, 6 ECp, 1 Scot, 1 AAA, 1 Cup, 4 CG, BL1: 1,1,1
2. **Karen Martin** 24.11.74 (7y, 2) 55.72 '92 57.82, 57.72, 55.89, 55.67, 55.66, 55.44
   1 AAA v LC, 2 CAU, 1 IS, 5 Budapest, 3 AAA, 2 CG
3. **Kirsty Morrison** 28.10.75 (6y, 4) 59.36 '93 56.34, 56.30, 56.13, 55.66, 55.32, 54.36
   3 Alicante, 7 Halle, 3 Karlstad, 1 South, 4 AAA, 1 Thurrock, 3 CG, BL2: -,1,1
4. **Shelley Holroyd** 17.5.73 (10y, 5) 60.12 '96 54.16, 52.61, 51.52, 51.42, 50.96, 50.87
   4 AAA v LC, 3 CAU, 2 BL2 (2), 1 IR, 2 AAA, 5 CG
5. **Kelly Morgan** 17.6.80 (1y, -) 49.00 '96 53.04, 51.69, 50.84, 50.32, 49.30, 48.63
   2 AAA v LC, 2 BL1 (1), 1 AAA-J, 1 E.Sch, 18 dnq WJ
6. **Denise Lewis** 27.8.72 (4y, 9) 56.50 '96 51.28, 51.22, 50.16; 5 AAA
7. **Sharon Gibson** 31.12.61 (19y, 3) 62.32 '87 54.26, 50.33, 49.48, 48.95, 48.64, 47.22
   2 Alicante, 1 sf Derby, 9 AAA, 1 Mid
8. **Katie Amos** 13.11 78 (1y, -) 47.20 '97 50.34, 49.77, 49.20, 48.31, 48.02, 47.82
   1 B.Univs, 6 AAA v LC, 5 CAU, 3 U23H, 2 South, 3 IR, 7 AAA, 4 U23D, 2 Thurrock, BL2: 2,-,3
9. **Noelle Bradshaw** 18.12.63 (7y, 11) 52.40 '93 48.60, 48.21, 47.52, 47.29, 46.96, 46.68
   4 CAU, 3 South, 4 IR, 6 AAA, BL1: 3,2,3
10. **Goldie Sayers** 16.7.82 (1y, -) 45.10 '97 51.92, 48.90, 48.63, 47.84, 47.13, 46.39
    3 AAA v LC, 8 CAU, 2 AAA-J, 1 E.Sch-I, 5 JI v FS, 22 dnq WJ
11. **Caroline White** 8.10.68 (11y, -) 56.50 '91 49.13, 48.99, 47.32, 47.16, 47.01, 46.46
    7 CAU, 1 Welsh, 2 IR, 2 sf Derby, 8 AAA, 2 Cup, BL2: 1,3,-
12. **Nicola Emblem** 27.3.71 (3y, -) 56.96 '90 50.75, 50.38, 49.68; in USA

Jackson achieved her first top ranking, beating Martin 2-1 and Morrison 3-1; with Martin beating Morrison at both AAAs and Commonwealth Games, where these two kept Jackson out of the medals. Sixth is Lewis, ranked in the top seven at five individual events as well as the heptathlon.

HEPTATHLON

1. **Denise Lewis** 27.8.72 (10y, 1) 6736 '97   6559, 6513; 1 ECh, 1CG
2. **Kerry Jury** 19.11.68 (9y, 3) 5719 '97   6005w, 5692, 5686;   2 Arles, 6 ECp, 5 CG
3. **Clova Court** 10.2.60 (9y, 2) 6022 '91   5656, 5639, 5421;   1 AAA, 9 ECp, 8 CG
4. **Julie Hollman** 16.2.77 (2y, 5) 5595 '97   5816w, 5557; 3 Arles, 13 ECp
5. **Pauline Richards** 30.6.68 (4y, -) 5420 '94   5691w, 5563, 5456, 5390;   1 Scot, 5 Arles, 12 ECp, 7 CG
6. **Jenny Kelly** 20.6.70 (10y, 4) 5826 '94   5608w, 5584; 6 Arles, 4 French
7. **Diana Bennett** 14.6.74 (6y, 7) 5550 '97   5555w, 5504, 5466, 5425;   8 Arles, 5 French, 1 HCl, 2 Dutch
8. **Julia Bennett** 26.3.70 (7y, 8) 5747'w '96, 5496 '95   5604w; 7 Arles
9. **Nicola Gautier** 21.3.78 (3y, 9) 5311 '97   5497, 5368; 6 French, 3 Dutch
10. **Chloe Cozens** 9.4.80 (1y, -) 5002 '97   5358w, 5220, 5129, 4298;   10 Arles, 16 WJ, 1 E.Sch
11. **Danielle Freeman** 11.2.80 (1y, -) 0   5237, 4915; dnf Arles, 1 AAA-J, 1 Cartagena
12. **Katherine Livesey** 15.12.79 (2y, 11) 5215 '97   5015, 4887, 4707;   1 Wrexham, 2 HCl, 2 E.Sch

While not back to her best through injury, Lewis had a great year with double gold and the top highest scores in the world in 1998. Eight British women over 5500 points broke the record of seven set in 1997 and the 10th best of 5358 is also a new record. A measure of the improvement is shown by the fact that Gautier is ninth for the third successive year, but her best each year has progressed: 5213, 5311, 5497.

WALKS

3000m and 5000m performances are on the track, unless indicated by R for road marks (+ indicates intermediate time). All distances above 10k are on the road unless shown by t. Previous bests are shown for track 5000m and road or track 10km and 20km. Priority is given to form at the standard international distance of 10 kilometres, although performances at other distances are also taken into account.

1. **Lisa Kehler** 15.3.67 (14y, 1) 21:57.68 '90, 45:42 '87
   3km: 13:02.5mx, 13:14.48+   5km: 22:01.53, 22:08.69; 21:55R, 22:40+R, 22:45+R
   10km: 45:03, 45:18, 45:42, 45:54, 46:25, 47:10; 1 RWA, 27 ECp, 1 R'dam, 1 CGT, 18 ECh, 3 CG
2. **Victoria Lupton** 17.4.72 (10y, 2) 21:52.4 '95, 45:18.8t '95, 1:42:47 '95
   3km: 13:38.7, 13:43.73, 13:50.71, c.13:51+, 13:56.6; 13:39R?; 1 Yorks, 1 CAU
   5km: 23:32.48; 22:35R, 23:54R, 24:20+R; 1 North, 2 AAA
   10km: 47:41, 48:27, 48:38, 48:45, 49:15, 49:49. 1/1 Sheffield, 1 Leamington, 2 RWA, dq 7N, 2 CGT, 7 CG;
   10M: 1:21:15; 1 RWA.   20km: 1:44:35; 1 RWA
3. **Carolyn Partington** 27.6.66 (6y, 10) 22:41.19 '95, 46:26 '95, 1:48:46 '97
   3km: 13:50.58, 14:00.3; 1 Douglas,1 IR   5000m: 23:32.03; 1 North
   10km: 48:09, 48:24, 49:50, 50:14; 1 Burrator, dnf 7N, 2 Stockport, 6 CG
4. **Kim Braznell** 28.2.56 (6y, 6) 24:16.4 '95, 49:39 '95, 1:46:02 '97
   5km: 24:35; 1 RWA
   10km: 48:36, 48:55, 49:10, 49:27, 50:40, 51:15; 2 Leamington, 3 RWA, 1 Sheffield 25/4, 17 7N, 3 CGT, 8 CG
5. **Catherine Charnock** 3.5.75 (2y, 8) 25:00.22 '96, 52:42 '96
   3km: c.14:01e+, 14:02.5, 14:21.55; 2 CAU   5km: 23:50.96, 23:51.92, 24:09.02; 2 IR, 2 North, 4 AAA
   10km: 49:02, 49:05, 49:14, 49:20, 50:00; 4 Sheffield 25/4, 3 Stockport, 4 CGT, 2 Dublin
   10M: 1:29:55; 3 RWA.   20km: 1:45:24, 1:50:39; 1 York, 2 RWA
6. **Lisa Crump** 30.3.76 (2y, 5) 25:57.5 '96, 50:34 '97   3km: 14:25.22; 2 Yorks
   10km: 49:51, 50:01, 50:15, 50:31, 50:42, 50:51; 2/2/3 Sheffield, 4 RWA, 19 7N. 5 CGT;   10M: 1:26:21; 2 RWA
7. **Karen Kneale** 23.4.69 (5y, 7) 24:40.69 '96, 49:37 '96
   3km: 14:22.2, 14:54.08; 2 Douglas, 2 IR
   10km: 50:05, 50:39, 50:55, 51:25, 52:05, 52:25; 3 Manx, 6 RWA, 2 Sheffield 25/4, 20 &N, 1 Isle of Man, 10 CG
8. **Sharon Tonks** 18.4.70 (1y, -) 25:35.15 '89, 52:39 '94
   3km: 14:23.2, c.14:27+; 14:37.80i   5km: 24:20.07, 24:45.77, 24:59.80; 1 Mid, 2 IR, 5 AAA
   10km: 51:55, 51:56, 52:02; 7 RWA, 7 CGT, 4 Dublin
9. **Nikki Huckerby** 27.2.78 (2y, 9) 25:01.55 '97, 52:23 '96
   3km: 14:24R?   5km: 24:56.69, 25:29.19; 25:08R, 25:09R, 26:16R; 2 Mid, 4 IR, 5 RWA
   10km: 51:07, 53:30; 5 RWA
10. **Melanie Wright** 5.4.64 (8y, -) 23:47.0 '94, 48:18 '92, 47:40sh '93, 1:59:33 '86
   5km: 25:37.69; 3 Mid   10km: 52:03, 52:20, 52:52, 53:29; 5 Sheffield 25/4, 8 RWA, 6 Stockport, 8 CGT
   10M: 1:34:32; 4 RWA
11. **Deborah Wallen** 28.5.79 (1y, -) 26:06.47 '96, 55:19 '96
   3km: 14:23.48, 14:46.03, 14:56.1+; 2 U23 H, dq U23D
   5km: 24:28.60; 24:36R, 25:11R, 25:24R; 2 RWA (1-J); 6 AAA, 8 JI Budapest   10km: 52:24; 9 RWA

Kehler walked marvellously to set British road bests, first at Rotterdam and then at the Commonwealth Games, where she gained a bronze medal, just as she had back in 1990. She is top for a record fifth time and was a long way clear of Partington and Lupton, closely matched for 2nd and 3rd rankings.

With thanks to Tony Miller, Alan Lindop, Ian Hodge, Tony O'Neill, Martin Rix, Matthew Fraser-Moat, John Powell, Bob Sparks and Rob Whittingham for their comments.

1998 LISTS - MEN

50 METRES - Indoors

| 5.75 + | Darren Braithwaite | 20.01.69 | h2 | Lievin, FRA | 22 Feb |
| 5.9 | Jonathan Edwards | 10.05.66 | 1 | Gateshead | 15 Jan |

55 METRES - Indoors

| 6.35 | Ray Coker | 28.07.73 | 5r1 | Gainesville, USA | 15 Jan |

60 METRES - Indoors

6.56	Jason Gardener		18.09.75	2h1	Stuttgart, GER	1 Feb
	6.58			2	Sindelfingen, GER	8 Mar
	6.59			2	Valencia, SPA	28 Feb
	6.60			1h1	Dortmund, GER	30 Jan
	6.61			1	Birmingham	25 Jan
	6.61			3	Birmingham	7 Feb
	6.62			2	Dortmund, GER	30 Jan
	6.62			2h2	Valencia, SPA	27 Feb
	6.62			2h1	Sindelfingen, GER	8 Mar
	6.63			1	Birmingham	3 Jan
	6.63			3s1	Valencia, SPA	27 Feb
	6.64			5	Stuttgart, GER	1 Feb
	6.66			1s2	Birmingham	25 Jan
	6.70			7	Birmingham	15 Feb
	6.71			1s1	Birmingham	7 Feb
	6.73			4h2	Stockholm, SWE	19 Feb
6.57	Darren Braithwaite		20.01.69	1	Birmingham	7 Feb
	6.65			3	Birmingham	15 Feb
	6.67			2s2	Birmingham	7 Feb
	6.67			4h2	Lievin, FRA	22 Feb
	6.67			1h3	Valencia, SPA	27 Feb
	6.68			7s2	Valencia, SPA	27 Feb
	6.69			2h1	Stockholm, SWE	19 Feb
	6.70			4=	Stockholm, SWE	19 Feb
	6.71			2	Tampere, FIN	4 Feb
6.58	Dwain Chambers	U23	5.04.78	2	Birmingham	7 Feb
	6.61			2	Birmingham	25 Jan
	6.64			1s2	Birmingham	7 Feb
	6.64			2h1	Valencia, SPA	27 Feb
	6.66			5s2	Valencia, SPA	27 Feb
	6.67			h	Dortmund, GER	30 Jan
	6.71			1s4	Birmingham	25 Jan
	6.71			6	Dortmund, GER	30 Jan
6.64	Allyn Condon		24.08.74	1	Sheffield	11 Jan
	6.71			2	Birmingham	3 Jan
6.66	Jason Livingston ¶		17.03.71	1s4	Birmingham	7 Feb
	6.66			4	Birmingham	7 Feb
	6.69			5=	Birmingham	15 Feb
	6.70			3rB	Madrid, SPA	3 Feb
	6.71			1h1	Chemnitz, GER	23 Jan
	6.74			5h3	Stuttgart, GER	1 Feb
6.67	Josephus Thomas		11.07.71	5	Birmingham	7 Feb
	6.68			1s3	Birmingham	7 Feb
	6.72			3	Birmingham	25 Jan
6.69	Kevin Williams		15.12.71	2s4	Birmingham	7 Feb
	6.70			6	Birmingham	7 Feb
	6.73			4	Birmingham	25 Jan
	6.74			2s4	Birmingham	25 Jan

6.70	Terence Stamp		18.02.70	2s3	Birmingham	7	Feb
	6.72			7	Birmingham	7	Feb
6.72	Daniel Money	U23	7.10.76	3s3	Birmingham	7	Feb
	6.73			1rB	Birmingham	7	Feb
	6.74			1h12	Birmingham	25	Jan
6.73	Tony Jarrett		13.08.68	3	Tampere, FIN	4	Feb
(10)							
6.73	Jonathan Edwards		10.05.66	4	Tampere, FIN	4	Feb
6.73	Doug Bignall		20.10.74	3s4	Birmingham	7	Feb
6.74	Marlon Devonish	U23	1.06.76	4s3	Birmingham	7	Feb

57 performances to 6.74 by 13 athletes

6.77	Christian Malcolm	U20	3.06.79	1rB	Birmingham	25	Jan
6.77	Akinola Lashore		28.03.73	2rB	Birmingham	7	Feb
6.77	Joselyn Thomas		11.07.71	1	Birmingham	25	Feb
6.77	Matthew Clements	U23	17.09.77	1	Glasgow	14	Mar
6.78	Jamie Henthorn	U23	20.02.77	2rB	Birmingham	25	Jan
6.78	Brendon Ghent	U23	7.09.76	1	Birmingham	1	Mar
6.79	Mark Lewis-Francis	U17	4.09.82	1	Birmingham	21	Feb
(20)							
6.82	Tremayne Rutherford		19.06.72	2h12	Birmingham	25	Jan
6.82	Uvie Ugono	U23	8.03.78	2s2	Birmingham	25	Jan
6.82	Julian Golding		17.02.75	5s4	Birmingham	7	Feb
6.82	Akeem Ogunyemi		4.06.74	3s2	Birmingham	7	Feb
6.84	Michael Tietz	U23	14.09.77	4rB	Birmingham	25	Jan
6.84	Tony Leigh		27.12.65	7s4	Birmingham	7	Feb
6.85	McLean Okotie		31.07.69	2	Bedford	25	Jan
6.85	Owusu Dako		23.05.73	2s1	Birmingham	25	Jan
6.85	Solomon Wariso		11.11.66	3rC	Stuttgart, GER	1	Feb
6.85	Mark McIntyre		14.10.70	5s3	Birmingham	7	Feb
(30)							
6.85	Steve Phillips		17.03.72	1h2	Birmingham	1	Mar
6.86	David Samuyiwa		4.08.72	3r2	Birmingham	3	Jan
6.86	Ray Salami		11.04.75	3s2	Birmingham	25	Jan
6.87	Bola Ojex		26.08.72	5s2	Birmingham	25	Jan
6.88	Damien Greaves	U23	19.09.77	4r2	Birmingham	3	Jan
6.88	Jonathon Oparka	U20	29.01.80	1	Glasgow	17	Jan
6.88	David Turnbull	U20	10.06.79	1	Glasgow	25	Jan
6.88	Ian Clarke		6.11.72	3h4	Birmingham	7	Feb
6.88	Ayo Falola		29.07.68	4s2	Birmingham	7	Feb
6.89	Aiah Yambasu		10.11.73	3h1	Birmingham	7	Feb
(40)							
6.89	Elisha Newell	U20	10.06.79	1s2	Birmingham	21	Feb
6.89	Andy Hughes		10.07.67	2	Birmingham	25	Feb
6.90	John Skeete	U23	8.09.78	6s3	Birmingham	7	Feb
6.90	Dominic Bradley	U23	22.12.76	1	Sheffield	20	Dec
6.91	Ed White		16.11.73	5s3	Birmingham	25	Jan
6.92	Nigel Stickings		1.04.71	5rB	Birmingham	3	Jan
6.92	Tim Barton		3.10.70	2	Birmingham	1	Mar
6.93	Stephen Tucker		30.12.62	2	Glasgow	18	Jan
6.93	Alloy Wilson	U20	25.01.80	4	Birmingham	21	Feb
6.93	Tim Benjamin	U17	2.05.82	1s2	Birmingham	21	Feb
(50)							
6.93	James Chatt	U20	11.02.80	2s2	Birmingham	21	Feb
6.93	Gavin Neblett	U20	27.12.79	3s2	Birmingham	21	Feb
6.93	Graham Beasley	U23	24.10.77	2	Glasgow	14	Mar
6.94	Mark Findlay	U23	20.03.78	1h11	Birmingham	25	Jan
6.94	Sunny Adepegba		6.06.71	7s2	Birmingham	25	Jan
6.94	Darren Burley	U20	13.01.80	2s1	Birmingham	21	Feb
6.94	Richard Rubenis		10.11.73	4	Birmingham	1	Mar
6.95	Jim Watson		4.10.67	2	Glasgow	17	Jan
6.95	Patrick Osborne		5.06.74	6s4	Birmingham	25	Jan

6.96	Darren Scott		7.03.69	2	Sheffield	18	Jan
	(60)						
6.96	Michael Afilaka		16.11.71	6s3	Birmingham	25	Jan
6.96	Tristan Anthony	U17	16.12.82	3	Birmingham	21	Feb
6.96	Darren Chin	U20	30.06.81	3s1	Birmingham	21	Feb
6.96	Tim Miller	U23	2.12.77	1s2	Glasgow	14	Mar
6.97	Dave Nolan		25.07.69	1h3	Sheffield	18	Jan
6.97	Luke Grinnell	U20	21.03.79	1	Birmingham	1	Mar
6.98	Nick Thomas	U20	4.04.79	1s3	Birmingham	21	Feb
6.99	Steve Fletcher		16.12.68	3	Sheffield	18	Jan
6.99	John Regis		13.10.66	2h8	Birmingham	25	Jan
6.99	Daniel Caines	U20	15.05.79	1	Birmingham	1	Feb
	(70)						
6.99	Daniel Plummer	U20	4.01.81	4s1	Birmingham	21	Feb
6.99	Dominique Richards	U20	12.09.79	5s1	Birmingham	21	Feb
6.99	Arif Shah	U23	29.11.78	2s2	Glasgow	14	Mar

Hand Timing

6.8	Tremayne Rutherford		(6.82)	1B1	London (CP)	14	Jan
6.8	Uvie Ugono	U23	(6.82)	2B1	London (CP)	14	Jan
6.8	Ian Clarke		(6.88)	1B1	London (CP)	11	Feb
6.8	Akeem Ogunyemi		(6.82)	4A1	London (CP)	11	Feb
6.8	Onochie Onuorah		16.10.73	2A3	London (CP)	16	Dec
6.9	Jamie Paul		17.07.70	1B3	London (CP)	14	Jan
6.9	James Chatt	U20	(6.93)	3B1	London (CP)	14	Jan
6.9	Patrick Osborne		(6.95)	3B2	London (CP)	14	Jan
6.9	Tyrone Swaray	U23	7.11.77	1B2	London (CP)	11	Feb
6.9	Ed White		(6.91)	4B2	London (CP)	16	Dec
6.9	Paul Nwaolise		31.05.73	1C2	London (CP)	16	Dec
6.9	Kevin Ellis	U23	18.06.76	2r1	Sheffield	20	Dec

unidentified athlete

6.9	Peter			2	London (CP)	14	Jan

Foreign

6.82	Carl Afilaka (TRI)		13.07.68	2h6	Birmingham	7	Feb
6.8	Haroun Korjie (SLE)		17.02.72	2A1	London (CP)	11	Feb

100 METRES X'60

10.03 Art-0.2	Dwain Chambers	U23	5.04.78	3	Johannesburg, RSA	11	Sep
	reaction time 0.063 but start allowed						
10.10	0.3			2	Budapest, HUN	19	Aug
10.15	0.3			1s1	Budapest, HUN	19	Aug
10.18	0.0			5s1	Kuala Lumpur, MAL	17	Sep
10.23	-1.7			2	Birmingham	25	Jul
10.24	-1.1			1	Sheffield	2	Aug
10.24	-0.4			3q1	Kuala Lumpur, MAL	16	Sep
10.26	-0.2			1q3	Budapest, HUN	18	Aug
10.28	0.6			2h5	Budapest, HUN	18	Aug
10.30	-1.1			5h2	Zurich, SWZ	12	Aug
10.33	0.0			3h3	Nuremberg, GER	11	Jul
10.36	0.4			7	Doha, QAT	7	May
10.38	0.5			5	Nuremberg, GER	11	Jul
10.39	-1.8			4	Glasgow (S)	30	Aug
10.04	0.3	Darren Campbell	12.09.73	1	Budapest, HUN	19	Aug
10.08	-0.1			5	Kuala Lumpur, MAL	17	Sep
10.11	0.5			1s2	Budapest, HUN	19	Aug
10.13	-0.5			2q4	Kuala Lumpur, MAL	16	Sep
10.18	-0.3			7	Lausanne, SWZ	25	Aug

(Campbell)	10.18	-0.5				4s2	Kuala Lumpur, MAL	17 Sep
	10.19	0.9				1	Thessaloniki, GRE	27 Jul
	10.20	-1.1				4h3	Zurich, SWZ	12 Aug
	10.22	-1.7				1	Birmingham	25 Jul
	10.23	-0.3				1h6	Kuala Lumpur, MAL	16 Sep
	10.26	-0.1				1q2	Budapest, HUN	18 Aug
	10.27	1.0				2rB	Villeneuve d'Ascq, FRA	11 Jul
	10.27	-0.9				2s1	Birmingham	25 Jul
	10.29	-0.5				5h1	Stockholm, SWE	5 Aug
	10.31	-0.5				4	Sydney, AUS	28 Feb
	10.31	0.0				2	Hengelo, HOL	1 Jun
	10.33	0.6				1r2	Budapest, HUN	5 Jul
	10.35	-0.4				1	Sundsvall, SWE	29 Jun
	10.35	1.2				1h1	Birmingham	24 Jul
	10.36	-0.5				3	Helsinki, FIN	13 Jun
	10.36	-0.4				1r1	Budapest, HUN	5 Jul
	10.37	-1.2				2rB	St. Petersburg, RUS	27 Jun
	10.37	-1.8				3	Glasgow (S)	30 Aug
	10.40	-0.3				1h4	Budapest, HUN	18 Aug
10.12	1.6		Christian Malcolm	U20	3.06.79	1	Annecy, FRA	29 Jul
	10.18	-1.2				1s2	Annecy, FRA	29 Jul
	10.27	0.0				3q2	Kuala Lumpur, MAL	16 Sep
	10.31	0.2				1q2	Annecy, FRA	28 Jul
	10.33	-0.5				5s2	Kuala Lumpur, MAL	17 Sep
	10.36	1.4				8rB	Lausanne, SWZ	25 Aug
	10.39	0.4				1h2	Annecy, FRA	28 Jul
	10.39	-0.9				6h1	Zurich, SWZ	12 Aug
10.13	0.0		Marlon Devonish	U23	1.06.76	4s1	Kuala Lumpur, MAL	17 Sep
	10.21	0.3				2s1	Budapest, HUN	19 Aug
	10.22	0.0				2q2	Kuala Lumpur, MAL	16 Sep
	10.22	-0.1				8	Kuala Lumpur, MAL	17 Sep
	10.24	-0.9				1s1	Birmingham	25 Jul
	10.24	-1.1				5h3	Zurich, SWZ	12 Aug
	10.24	0.3				5	Budapest, HUN	19 Aug
	10.26	-1.7				3	Birmingham	25 Jul
	10.28	-0.3				1q1	Budapest, HUN	18 Aug
	10.29	0.2				1h2	Kuala Lumpur, MAL	16 Sep
	10.32	-1.1				2	Sheffield	2 Aug
	10.36	-2.2				1	Gateshead	19 Jul
	10.38	-0.8				1h2	Budapest, HUN	18 Aug
	10.40	0.1				1rC	Irvine, USA	2 May
10.28	1.5		Julian Golding		17.02.75	3r3	Kalamata, GRE	23 May
	10.39	1.4				3r1	Hania, GRE	27 May
10.29	-0.5		Josephus Thomas	*(for SLE)*	11.07.71	4q4	Kuala Lumpur, MAL	16 Sep
	10.31	0.0		*(for SLE)*		6s1	Kuala Lumpur, MAL	17 Sep
	10.32	-1.7				5	Birmingham	25 Jul
	10.39	-1.2				1	Watford	20 Jun
10.30	-1.7		Jason Gardener		18.09.75	4	Birmingham	25 Jul
	10.33	0.6				2h2	Jena, GER	24 May
	10.33	-1.2				1rB	St. Petersburg, RUS	27 Jun
	10.33	0.7				1h6	Birmingham	24 Jul
	10.34	1.9				3	Jena, GER	24 May
	10.36	-0.2				1s2	Birmingham	25 Jul
	10.36	-1.1				3	Sheffield	2 Aug
10.31	0.4		Ian Mackie		27.02.75	5	Doha, QAT	7 May
	10.38	1.5				1h3	Edinburgh	18 Jul
10.31	2.0		Jason Livingston ¶		17.03.71	2h1	Jena, GER	24 May
	10.39	0.8				2rB	Doha, QAT	7 May
10.31	-0.4		Colin Jackson		18.02.67	4r3	Athens, GRE	17 Jun
	10.32	0.2				4	Milan, ITA	5 Jun

10.35	0.6	Mark Richardson		26.07.72	1r1	Irvine, USA	2	May
10.36	-1.7	Owusu Dako		23.05.73	6	Birmingham	25	Jul
10.37	1.9				1h5	Birmingham	24	Jul
10.39	-1.6				1	Birmingham	6	Jun
10.38	1.6	Linford Christie		2.04.60	1	Bedford	29	Aug
10.40	-1.2	Uvie Ugono	U23	8.03.78	2	Watford	20	Jun

83 performances to 10.40 by 14 athletes *plus 2 for SLE*

10.42	-1.1	Allyn Condon		24.08.74	4	Sheffield	2	Aug
10.43	2.0	Danny Joyce		9.09.74	1	Bedford	24	May
10.43	0.6	Kevin Williams		15.12.71	5q4	Kuala Lumpur, MAL	16	Sep
10.45	1.7	Marcus Adam		28.02.68	1h1	Gava, SPA	24	May
10.45	-0.8	Du'aine Ladejo		14.02.71	1D	Bressanone, ITA	4	Jul
10.46	2.0	McLean Okotie		31.07.69	2	Bedford	24	May
(20)								
10.46	-1.2	Akinola Lashore		28.03.73	3	Watford	20	Jun
10.46	-0.2	Jamie Henthorn	U23	20.02.77	3h3	Kuala Lumpur, MAL	16	Sep
10.49	1.9	Jamie Paul		17.07.70	3h5	Birmingham	24	Jul
10.49	0.1	Mark Lewis-Francis	U17	4.09.82	1	Sheffield	16	Aug
10.51	1.9	Michael Tietz	U23	14.09.77	1	Birmingham	22	Aug
10.52 i		Darren Braithwaite		20.01.69	4	Tampere, FIN	4	Feb
10.52	1.6	Joselyn Thomas		11.07.71	2	Bedford	29	Aug
10.54	1.9	Kevin Farrell	U23	31.10.77	3h4	Birmingham	24	Jul
10.55	0.3	Mark Findlay	U23	20.03.78	2s3	Watford	20	Jun
10.56	-1.2	Jason John		17.10.71	2	Watford	16	May
(30)								
10.56	2.0	Graeme Welsh		8.10.75	5	Bedford	24	May
10.56	1.1	Ian Craig		20.08.69	4r2	Tel Aviv, ISR	19	Jul
10.57	1.9	Brendon Ghent	U23	7.09.76	2	Birmingham	22	Aug
10.58	0.6	Roger Black		31.03.66	5	Irvine, USA	2	May
10.59	1.5	Brian Doyle	U23	12.03.77	2h3	Edinburgh	18	Jul
10.59	1.6	Ed White		16.11.73	4	Bedford	29	Aug
10.60	0.6	Mark Hylton	U23	24.09.76	6	Irvine, USA	2	May
10.60	1.9	John Regis		13.10.66	4	Tonsberg, NOR	20	Jun
10.60	1.9	Doug Bignall		20.10.74	4h4	Birmingham	24	Jul
10.60	0.1	Tyrone Edgar	U17	29.03.82	2	Sheffield	16	Aug
(40)								
10.61		Ray Coker		28.07.73	2h4	Atlanta, USA	23	May
10.61	1.9	Toby Box		9.09.72	5h4	Birmingham	24	Jul
10.61	-1.0	Jason Fergus		11.10.73	2	London (He)	8	Aug
10.61	1.5	Chris Lambert	U20	6.04.81	1	London (He)	30	Aug
10.62	1.6	Peter Maitland		21.01.73	5	Bedford	29	Aug
10.63	0.7	Dominic Bradley	U23	22.12.76	3h6	Birmingham	24	Jul
10.65	-1.5	Daniel Money	U23	7.10.76	1rB	Birmingham	6	Jun
10.65	-0.5	Andrew Walcott		11.01.75	6h1	Nuremberg, GER	11	Jul
10.67	1.2	John Stewart	U20	30.12.79	1	Leeds	23	May
10.67		Andy Hughes		10.07.67	1	Copenhagen, DEN	23	Jun
(50)								
10.67	-0.9	Terence Stamp		18.02.70	5s1	Birmingham	25	Jul
10.68	1.9	Tim Barton		3.10.70	3	Birmingham	22	Aug
10.70	0.0	David Samuyiwa		4.08.72	3h1	Watford	20	Jun
10.70	-0.1	Elliot Bunney		11.12.66	2h1	Kuala Lumpur, MAL	16	Sep
10.71	0.1	Tim Benjamin	U17	2.05.82	3	Sheffield	16	Aug
10.72	0.6	Jamie Baulch		3.05.73	3h3	Cwmbran	20	Jun
10.74	-1.0	Tremayne Rutherford		19.06.72	1rB	Bedford	30	May
10.74	1.5	David Bandele		11.09.71	3h3	Edinburgh	18	Jul
10.75	1.8	Henry Richards	U20	15.05.81	1h1	Bedford	4	Jul
10.75	1.2	Akeem Ogunyemi		4.06.74	4h1	Birmingham	24	Jul
(60)								
10.76	1.0	Onochie Onuorah		16.10.73	4	Sydney, AUS	10	Jan
10.76		Luke Davis	U20	1.01.80	1	Marsa, MLT	16	Apr
10.76	1.6	Seni Edu		4.03.74	7	Bedford	29	Aug

10.76	1.5	Matthew Russell	U20	20.01.81	2	London (He)	30 Aug
10.77	-1.6	Ayo Falola		29.07.68	1	Cape Town, RSA	24 Jan
10.77	-1.2	Richard Johnson		13.10.71	2h3	Watford	20 Jun
10.78	-0.4	Paul White		1.09.74	6	Bedford	30 May
10.79	1.2	James Miller	U20	29.03.80	2	Leeds	23 May
10.79	0.0	Mark McIntyre		14.10.70	4h1	Watford	20 Jun
10.79	0.1	Mark Allen		23.09.66	5h	Tel Aviv, ISR	19 Jul
	(70)						
10.80	1.9	Sunny Adepegba		6.06.71	6h4	Birmingham	24 Jul
10.81		Richard Pinnock		31.10.70	2r2	Birmingham	18 Jul
10.81	1.5	James Chatt	U20	11.02.80	3	London (He)	30 May
10.82	1.5	Ray Salami		11.04.75	6rC	Bedford	30 May
10.82		Tony Noel			1	Bedford	6 Jun
10.82	1.8	David Turnbull	U20	10.06.79	2h1	Bedford	4 Jul
10.83	1.3	Darren Burley	U20	13.01.80	2	London (Ha)	24 May
10.84	-1.2	Jim Watson		4.10.67	5	Watford	16 May
10.84	0.0	Alexis Sharp		31.10.72	D	Bressanone, ITA	4 Jul
10.84	1.5	Fraser Sharp	U23	11.03.78	4h3	Edinburgh	18 Jul
	(80)						
10.84	-0.6	Peter Oshagbemi	U20	26.01.81	2	Dublin (S), IRE	8 Aug
10.84	0.9	Michael Arkle		31.03.73	1	Hexham	30 Aug
10.87	1.3	George Audu	U23	18.01.77	1	Harrisonburg, USA	16 May
10.87	1.5	Mark Avis		22.10.71	5h3	Edinburgh	18 Jul
10.88	-1.1	Michael Afilaka		16.11.71	3r2	Watford	16 May
10.88	1.5	Rohan Samuel		30.01.66	7rC	Bedford	30 May
10.88	-1.2	Aiah Yambasu		10.11.73	4h3	Watford	20 Jun
10.88	1.0	Daniel Bonich	U23	22.11.78	2h4	Watford	20 Jun
10.88	1.8	Nana Wilson	U20	14.01.79	4h1	Bedford	4 Jul
10.89		Paul Nwaolise		31.05.73	1	Gateshead	9 May
	(90)						
10.89	1.9	Graham Hedman	U20	6.02.79	5=h5	Birmingham	24 Jul
10.89	1.9	Leighton Green	U23	10.01.78	5=h5	Birmingham	24 Jul
10.89	0.7	John Skeete	U23	8.09.78	4h6	Birmingham	24 Jul
10.89	1.7	Chris Stobart	U17	27.03.82	1	York	25 Jul
10.91	-0.6	Andrew Bull		26.06.69	1	Cudworth	9 May
10.91	1.0	Ejike Wodu		15.12.74	3h4	Watford	20 Jun
10.92	-1.0	Sam Omonua	U23	16.06.76	3rB	Bedford	30 May
10.92	1.5	Will MacGee		9.06.68	8rC	Bedford	30 May
10.92	0.7	Joshua Wood		19.04.74	5h6	Birmingham	24 Jul
10.92	-0.2	Tyrone Swaray	U23	7.11.77	10s2	Birmingham	25 Jul
	(100)						
10.92	0.1	Luke Bowling	U17	4.11.81	4	Sheffield	16 Aug
10.92	1.9	Bola Ojex		26.08.72	5	Birmingham	22 Aug
10.93	1.2	Nick Long	U20	1.02.79	3	Leeds	23 May
10.93	0.0	Jamie Quarry		15.11.72	D	Bressanone, ITA	4 Jul
10.93		Andrew Parker	U20	1.08.80	1	Barry	14 Jul
10.95	1.3	Steve Surety	U20	18.02.80	4	London (Ha)	24 May
10.95	0.0	Elisha Newell	U20	10.06.79	5h1	Watford	20 Jun
10.95	1.5	O. Akpofure	U17	9.11.81	2	Exeter	11 Jul
10.96	0.5	Tony Leigh		27.12.65	1h	Crewe	9 May
10.97		Liam Collins	U23	23.10.78	2	Gateshead	9 May
	(110)						
10.97	1.9	Mark Dunwell		13.03.70	6	Birmingham	22 Aug
10.97		Ross Linnett	U20	6.10.79	1	Gateshead	29 Aug
10.97	1.0	Leroy Campbell		10.08.66	2	Watford	12 Sep
10.98	1.0	Gary Jones		6.01.72	4h4	Watford	20 Jun
10.99	-0.5	Tokunbo Olabinri		27.02.62	4	Sydney, AUS	31 Jan
10.99	1.5	Duncan Malins	U23	12.06.78	1	Crawley	10 May
10.99	1.7	Alex Golding	U17	3.12.81	2	York	25 Jul

Wind Assisted

10.00	2.9	Ian Mackie		(10.31)	1	Edinburgh	18	Jul
		10.16	2.8		2	Bedford	5	Jul
10.01	2.9	Doug Walker		28.07.73	2	Edinburgh	18	Jul
		10.17	3.7		1	Edinburgh	4	Jul
		10.27	2.1		1	Cardiff	4	Aug
		10.37	3.6		1h2	Edinburgh	18	Jul
		10.38			1	Leeds	7	Jun
10.10	3.8	Christian Malcolm	U20	(10.12)	1	Alicante, SPA	18	Jul
		10.17	3.1		1	Bedford	4	Jul
		10.22	4.1		1s1	Bedford	4	Jul
		10.26	3.3		1	Bruges, BEL	23	Aug
		10.36	3.2		1h2	Bedford	4	Jul
		10.39	2.5		1h2	Cwmbran	20	Jun
10.15	2.8	Devonish	U23	(10.13)	1	Bedford	5	Jul
		10.25	2.1		1h7	Birmingham	24	Jul
10.17	2.8	Owusu Dako		(10.36)	3=	Bedford	5	Jul
10.17	2.8	Jason Gardener		(10.30)	3=	Bedford	5	Jul
		10.29	2.1		2	Cardiff	4	Aug
		10.40	4.0		4=	Padua, ITA	7	Jun
10.18	3.7	Daniel Money	U23	(10.65)	2	Edinburgh	4	Jul
		10.23	4.6		1	Cork, IRE	27	Jun
		10.35	2.8		6	Bedford	5	Jul
10.19	2.7	Josephus Thomas		(10.29)	1	Fullerton, USA	23	Apr
10.20	6.4	Elliot Bunney		(10.70)	1h1	Edinburgh	18	Jul
		10.24	2.9		3	Edinburgh	18	Jul
10.24	3.7	Jason Livingston ¶		(10.31)	3	Edinburgh	4	Jul
		10.27	3.5		1rB	Chemnitz, GER	20	May
		10.29	2.6		1rB	Cork, IRE	27	Jun
		10.39	2.8		7	Bedford	5	Jul
10.28	6.0	Du'aine Ladejo		(10.45)	1D	Arles, FRA	23	May
10.28	2.3	Campbell		(10.04)	3	Belgrade, YUG	31	May
10.29	2.4	Chambers	U23	(10.03A)	5r2	Kalamata, GRE	23	May
		10.34	3.5		1h3	Birmingham	24	Jul
		10.37	2.4		8	St. Denis, FRA	4	Jun
10.29	2.8	Allyn Condon		(10.42)	5	Bedford	5	Jul
10.30	3.6	Jamie Henthorn	U23	(10.46)	1	Bath	2	May
		10.37	3.9		1s1	Bath	2	May
		10.40	2.2		1rB	Cardiff	4	Aug
10.30	3.8	Marcus Adam		(10.45)	1r2	Palma de Mallorca, SPA	28	May
10.32	2.7	Uvie Ugono	U23	(10.40)	2r1	Fullerton, USA	23	Apr
10.35	4.3	Danny Joyce		(10.43)	1h3	Bedford	24	May
10.35	6.4	Ross Baillie	U23	26.09.77	3h1	Edinburgh	18	Jul
10.36	2.7	Joselyn Thomas		(10.52)	4	Fullerton, USA	23	Apr
10.36	4.7	Mark Lewis-Francis	U17	(10.49)	1s1	Sheffield	16	Aug
10.40	4.6	Jason John		(10.56)	6	Cork, IRE	27	Jun
		45 performances to 10.40 by 22 athletes						
10.45	3.1	Jon Barbour	U20	3.11.80	2	Bedford	4	Jul
10.46	4.3	Brendon Ghent	U23	(10.57)	2h3	Bedford	24	May
10.49	2.2	Nathan Morgan	U23	30.06.78	2B	Cardiff	4	Aug
10.50	3.6	Matthew Clements	U23	17.09.77	2	Bath	2	May
10.51	3.6	Graeme Welsh		(10.56)	2h2	Bedford	24	May
10.51	2.9	Tim Benjamin	U17	(10.71)	1s2	Bedford	4	Jul
10.52	3.1	Dominic Bradley	U23	(10.63)	1s2	Bath	2	May
10.52	5.0	Chris Lambert	U20	(10.61)	1h3	Bedford	4	Jul
10.53	2.6	Ed White		(10.59)	2rB	Cork, IRE	27	Jun
10.54	3.5	Terence Stamp		(10.67)	2h3	Birmingham	24	Jul
10.55	3.6	Tim Barton		(10.68)	3h2	Bedford	24	May

143

10.55	3.5	Jason Fergus		(10.61)	3h3	Birmingham	24	Jul
10.58	4.3	Tyrone Edgar	U17	(10.60)	1s2	Sheffield	16	Aug
10.59	3.6	Graham Beasley	U23	24.10.77	4	Bath	2	May
10.59	2.1	Tyrone Swaray	U23	(10.92)	3h7	Birmingham	24	Jul
10.60	2.2	Peter Maitland		(10.62)	4rB	Cardiff	4	Aug
10.61	2.6	Darren Scott		7.03.69	3rB	Cork, IRE	27	Jun
10.62	3.9	Lawrence Baird	U23	14.12.77	2s1	Bath	2	May
10.63	4.1	Matthew Russell	U20	(10.76)	2s1	Bedford	4	Jul
10.63	2.8	Darren Braithwaite		(10.52i)	8	Bedford	5	Jul
10.65	2.2	David Samuyiwa		(10.70)	4h1	Bedford	24	May
10.67	2.9	James Chatt	U20	(10.81)	4s2	Bedford	4	Jul
10.67	6.4	John Skeete	U23	(10.89)	4h1	Edinburgh	18	Jul
10.67	2.9	Ayo Falola		(10.77)	3h2	Birmingham	24	Jul
10.68	4.1	Darren Burley	U20	(10.83)	3s1	Bedford	4	Jul
10.69	4.1	Henry Richards	U20	(10.75)	4s1	Bedford	4	Jul
10.69	2.9	Jim Watson		(10.84)	6	Edinburgh	18	Jul
10.70	2.6	Mark McIntyre		(10.79)	5rB	Cork, IRE	27	Jun
10.70	2.9	Ray Salami		(10.82)	4h2	Birmingham	24	Jul
10.70	4.7	Luke Bowling	U17	(10.92)	2s1	Sheffield	16	Aug
10.71	4.4	Mark Woodhouse		1.11.75	1s3	Bath	2	May
10.71	4.5	Darren Wall	U20	6.04.80	1rB	Bedford	4	Jul
10.71	4.5	Dominique Richards	U20	12.09.79	2rB	Bedford	4	Jul
10.73	4.3	Paul Nwaolise		(10.89)	4h3	Bedford	24	May
10.75	3.5	Gavin Eastman	U20	28.06.80	2h3	Exeter	10	Jul
10.76	6.0	Jamie Quarry		(10.93)	2D	Arles, FRA	23	May
10.77	4.5	David Turnbull	U20	(10.82)	3rB	Bedford	4	Jul
10.77	3.5	Marlon Dickson	U23	17.11.78	4rB	Edinburgh	4	Jul
10.77	4.7	Alex Golding	U17	(10.99)	3s1	Sheffield	16	Aug
10.78		Michael Afilaka		(10.88)	5h3	Bedford	24	May
10.78	5.7	Alexis Sharp		(10.84)	7h	Maia, POR	14	Jun
10.79	3.1	Tim Miller	U23	2.12.77	3s2	Bath	2	May
10.80	2.6	Andrew Parker	U20	(10.93)	3h2	Cwmbran	20	Jun
10.80	3.5	Bola Ojex		(10.92)	5rB	Edinburgh	4	Jul
10.82	3.9	Rowland Ifill		11.11.75	3s1	Bath	2	May
10.82	2.3	Ian Clarke		6.11.72	4h4	Bedford	24	May
10.82	3.2	Darren Chin	U20	30.06.81	1h2	Exeter	10	Jul
10.83	5.0	Graham Hedman	U20	(10.89)	4h3	Bedford	4	Jul
10.83	6.4	Stephen Tucker		30.12.62	5h1	Edinburgh	18	Jul
10.83	4.7	Daniel Angus	U17	15.07.82	4s1	Sheffield	16	Aug
10.84	4.3	Andy Lewis		9.03.68	2h3	Bath	2	May
10.84	3.5	Marcellus Pusey	U20	28.04.79	3h3	Exeter	10	Jul
10.84	4.3	Chris Stobart	U17	(10.89)	3s2	Sheffield	16	Aug
10.85	2.2	Gary Jones		(10.98)	6h1	Bedford	24	May
10.88	3.9	Charles Madeira-Cole	U23	29.11.77	4s1	Bath	2	May
10.88	3.5	Mark Phills		26.07.64	8h3	Birmingham	24	Jul
10.89	3.2	Steven Daly	U20	29.12.79	3h4	Bedford	4	Jul
10.90	4.3	Dwayne Grant	U17	17.07.82	4s2	Sheffield	16	Aug
10.90	4.7	Darrell Aldridge	U17	20.06.83	5s1	Sheffield	16	Aug
10.91	3.6	Kevin Ellis	U23	18.06.76	5h2	Bedford	24	May
10.91	3.2	Ross Linnett	U20	(10.97)	4h2	Bedford	4	Jul
10.92	2.1	Liam Collins	U23	(10.97)	1	Hexham	16	May
10.92	4.3	Mark Wallace	U17	3.10.81	5s2	Sheffield	16	Aug
10.97	2.7	Rob Kerry	U20	20.03.80	1h1	Exeter	10	Jul
10.97	2.9	Ben Green	U23	30.03.76	7h2	Birmingham	24	Jul
10.97	2.7	Chris Dack	U17	28.11.82	2h1	Sheffield	16	Aug
10.98	4.3	Ricky Alfred	U23	20.12.77	6h3	Bedford	24	May
10.98	2.9	Jason Bale	U20	12.12.79	7	Exeter	11	Jul

Hand Timing

Time	Wind	Name	Cat		Pos	Venue	Date	
10.0 w	2.7	Jason Gardener		(10.30)	4	Ostrava, CZE	11	Jun
10.4 w					1	Bath	30	May
10.2 w	3.3	Ayo Falola		(10.77)	1	Bellville, RSA	31	Jan
10.7					1	Woodford	15	Jul
10.2 w	2.4	Josephus Thomas		(10.29)	1	Enfield	9	May
10.3	1.3				1	Watford	4	Jul
10.3 w	3.4				1	Liverpool	8	Aug
10.3 w		Paul White		(10.78)	1	Loughborough	9	May
10.7					1	Loughborough	25	Apr
10.3 w	2.4	Joselyn Thomas		(10.52)	3	Enfield	9	May
10.3 w	2.9	Campbell		(10.04)	1	Cwmbran	10	May
10.4		Allyn Condon		(10.42)	1	Stretford	14	Jul
10.4		Akinola Lashore		(10.46)	1	Harrow	30	Aug
10.4		Jamie Paul		(10.49)	1	London (B)	20	Sep
10.4 w	4.4	Jason Fergus		(10.61)	1	London (WF)	9	May

13 performances to 10.4 by 10 athletes including 9 wind assisted

Time	Wind	Name	Cat		Pos	Venue	Date	
10.5	0.3	Alexis Sharp		(10.84)	D	Azusa, USA	16	Apr
10.5		Doug Turner		2.12.66	1	Derby	19	Jul
10.5		Jon Barbour	U20	(10.45w)	1r1	Ashford	15	Aug
10.5 w	4.4	John Skeete	U23	(10.89)	2	London (WF)	9	May
10.8					1	Portsmouth	4	Jul
10.5 w		Rohan Samuel		(10.88)	1	London (WL)	21	Jun
10.7	1.4				3s1	Enfield	9	May
10.6	1.4	Akeem Ogunyemi		(10.75)	2s1	Enfield	9	May
10.6		Dominic Bradley	U23	(10.63)	1	Ormskirk	11	Jul
10.6		Tony Noel		(10.82)	2	Birmingham	5	Aug
10.6		Patrick Osborne		5.06.74	1	London (FP)	23	Aug
10.6 w		Tremayne Rutherford		(10.74)	1rB	Basildon	2	May
10.6 w	2.8	Matthew Russell	U20	(10.76)	1	London (WF)	9	May
10.7 w?					1	London (Col)	6	Jun
10.6 w		Daniel Bonich	U23	(10.88)	1	Woking	16	May
10.6 w		Mark Walcott		24.11.73	1	Worcester	9	Jul
10.6 w		Geoff Dearman	U23	4.08.77	1	Milton Keynes	16	Aug
10.6 w?		Gary Jones		(10.98)	3	London (B)	20	Sep
10.7		Adrian Patrick		15.06.73	1r1	London (Elt)	2	May
10.7	1.4	Richard Johnson		(10.77)	4s1	Enfield	9	May
10.7		Joshua Wood		(10.92)	1	Hayes	6	Jun
10.7	1.2	Solomon Wariso		11.11.66	3rB	Cardiff	6	Jun
10.7	-1.3	Steve Topliss/Webb	U23	17.07.78	1rB	Watford	6	Jun
10.7		Sunny Adepegba		(10.80)	2	London (Col)	24	Jun
10.7		Trevor Painter		10.08.71	3	Wigan	4	Jul
10.7		James Chatt	U20	(10.81)	2	London (TB)	25	Jul
10.7		Dominique Richards	U20	(10.71w)	1r2	London (TB)	25	Jul
10.7	1.2	Richard Pinnock		(10.81)	1	Barking	8	Aug
10.7 w		Mark Woodhouse		(10.71w)	3	Loughborough	25	Apr
10.7 w		Tony Waddington		30.06.75	1r2	London (Elt)	2	May
10.7 w		Tim Miller	U23	(10.79w)	1	Newport	3	May
10.7 w	2.8	Steve Surety	U20	(10.95)	3	London (WF)	9	May
10.7 w	2.3	Elisha Newell	U20	(10.95)	2	Enfield	9	May
10.7 w	4.4	Mark Brown	U23	3.11.76	3	London (WF)	9	May
10.7 w	4.4	Emmanuel Tawiah	U23	11.07.77	4	London (WF)	9	May
10.7 w	2.8	Nick Thomas	U20	4.04.79	2	London (WF)	9	May
10.7 w		Graham Hedman	U20	(10.89)	1rB	London (Col)	6	Jun
10.7 w		James Miller	U20	(10.79)	1	Derby	13	Jun
10.7 w	4.0	Ian Clarke		(10.82w)	3	Bebington	4	Jul
10.8					1	Enfield	14	Jun
10.7 w	4.0	O. Akpofure	U17	(10.95)	1h2	Exeter	11	Jul

145

10.7 w		Andrew Parker	U20	(10.93)	1	Yate	26	Jul
10.8					1	Neath	14	Jun
10.8		Dan Donovan		8.10.70	1	Basingstoke	2	May
10.8		Darren Wall	U20	(10.71w)	1	Southampton	2	May
10.8		Alex Fugallo		28.01.70	1rB	Basingstoke	2	May
10.8		Rupert Lambert		26.06.74	2B	Basingstoke	2	May
10.8		Ross Bacchus	U20	6.06.81	1	Havering	6	May
10.8	-0.2	Doug Walker		(10.01w)	1h1	Edinburgh	9	May
10.8		Graham Beasley	U23	(10.59w)	3	Loughborough	13	May
10.8		Ben Green	U23	(10.97w)	1	Ashford	16	May
10.8		I. Dobson			2	Loughborough	20	May
10.8		Bola Ojex		(10.92)	1	Birmingham (Un)	6	Jun
10.8		Simon Duberley		2.09.67	2	Hayes	6	Jun
10.8		Pierre Adedze		3.06.69	3	Hayes	6	Jun
10.8		Tyrone Swaray	U23	(10.92)	1	St. Albans	6	Jun
10.8		Jason Bale	U20	(10.98w)	1	Rugby	9	Jun
10.8		Michael Arkle		(10.84)	2	Middlesbrough	14	Jun
10.8		Aiah Yambasu		(10.88)	1r2	Bournemouth	4	Jul
10.8		Matthew Clements	U23	(10.50w)	2	Woodford	15	Jul
10.8		Alastair Gordon	U23	16.04.78	1	Carshalton	25	Jul
10.8		Ross Linnett	U20	(10.97)	1	Wakefield	26	Jul
10.8		Kevin Ellis	U23	(10.91w)	1	Newport	8	Aug
10.8		Derek Morgan		4.04.69	1	Gloucester	8	Aug
10.8		Paul Nwaolise		(10.89)	2r2	Ashford	15	Aug
10.8		Henry Tosh	U20	26.01.80	1	Yate	23	Aug
10.8		Darren Scott		(10.61w)	1	Blackpool	13	Sep
10.8 w		Neil Jones	U20	22.10.79	1	Whitehaven	2	May
10.8 w	2.8	Alloy Wilson	U20	25.01.80	4	London (WF)	9	May
10.8 w	2.3	Darren Chin	U20	(10.82w)	4	Enfield	9	May
10.8 w		Leroy Campbell		(10.97)	2	Loughborough	9	May
10.8 w		Matthew Lewis		11.11.75	3	Loughborough	20	May
10.8 w		Leighton Green	U23	(10.89)	2	London (Col)	6	Jun
10.8 w		Gary Craig		15.02.75	4	Wigan	4	Jul
10.8 w		Carl McMullen	U20	9.11.79	1	Lancaster	4	Jul
10.8 w	3.4	Chris Stobart	U17	(10.89)	1	Blackpool	1	Aug

doubtful timing

10.2 w		David Samuyiwa		(10.70)	1	Bournemouth	30	Jul
10.4 w		Solomon Povey	U20	8.02.80	2	Bournemouth	30	Jul
10.5 w		Pierre Adedze		(10.8)	3	Bournemouth	30	Jul
10.5 w		Tim Slocombe	U23	15.11.77	4	Bournemouth	30	Jul
10.6 w		Paul Campbell	U20	26.03.80	1	Wigan	4	Jul
10.7		Paul McKee	U23	15.10.77	1	Londonderry	28	Jun
10.7 w		Chris Stobart	U17	(10.89)	2	Wigan	4	Jul
10.7 w		Ian Cawley	U23	21.11.78	5	Bournemouth	30	Jul

Additional Under 20 (1 - 45 above)

10.9		Antonio Matarazzo		27.03.80	2	Birmingham (Un)	6	Jun
10.9		Angus	U17	(10.83w)	1	Barnsley	28	Jun
10.9 w	3.1	Alastair Mark	U17	8.12.81	1h3	Exeter	10	Jul
11.0					1	Corby	20	Jun
11.13	1.5			8.12.81	6	Exeter	11	Jul
10.9 w	4.0	Chris Carson		26.10.79	3	Cannock	13	Sep

Additional Under 17 (1 - 13 above)

11.00 w	4.7	Bradley Gelman		18.01.82	6s1	Sheffield	16	Aug
11.0		Grant		(10.90w)	1	Enfield	7	Jun
11.17	0.1				7	Sheffield	16	Aug

146

11.0		Ryan Power		20.11.82	1	Antrim	20 Aug
11.0		Karl Forde		15.04.83	1	Worcester	12 Sep
11.02	1.5				3	Exeter	11 Jul
11.0		Tom Roe		25.06.82	1	Great Yarmouth	
11.0 w		Ian Monckton		14.07.83	1	Telford	9 May
11.0 w	3.5	Andrew Rose		17.08.82	1	London (WF)	9 May
11.0 w		Neil Rochester		4.10.81	2	Telford	9 May
	(20)						
11.0 w	5.1	Seriashe Childs		2.09.82	2	Aberdare	31 Aug
11.01	1.7	Angus		(10.83w)	3	York	25 Jul
11.06 w		Mark Suggitt		7.11.81	1	Gateshead	9 May
11.06 w	3.2	Leroy Slue		11.12.81	3	London (Ha)	23 May
11.06 w	8.5	Bomene Barikor		22.05.82	3s1	Gran Canaria, SPA	23 Jul
11.06 w	4.0	Gary Carr		24.09.82	4h5	Sheffield	16 Aug
11.1		Andrew Norman		27.01.82	1	Exeter	13 Jun
11.1		Lee Bryan		24.11.81	1	Swansea	28 Jun
11.1		Tristan Anthony		16.12.82	1	Bury St. Edmonds	13 Sep
11.1 w	3.1	Martin Houlihan		19.09.81	3h3	Exeter	10 Jul
11.17	1.5	Wallace		(10.92w)	7	Exeter	11 Jul
11.18	1.7	Ben Inatimi		6.07.83	4	York	25 Jul
	(30)						
11.18	1.7	Dack		(10.97w)	5	York	25 Jul
11.18 w	2.8	Matt Hopton	U15	2.03.84	1	Exeter	11 Jul
11.32	1.4				2	Sheffield	16 Aug
11.19	1.7	Michael Pardo		29.07.82	1h2	Edinburgh	19 Jun

Under 15 (1 above)

11.27	1.4	Tom Hyde	7.10.83	1	Sheffield	16 Aug
11.31 w	2.6	Leon Cameron	10.09.83	2s1	Exeter	10 Jul
11.34	1.4	Andrew McCullagh	10.09.83	3	Sheffield	16 Aug
11.35 w	2.6	Gavin Dublin	5.10.83	3s1	Exeter	10 Jul
11.46	1.7			1	London (He)	30 Aug
11.37 w	5.8	Chris Dawkins	3.09.83	1h3	Exeter	10 Jul
11.59	1.5			4s2	Exeter	10 Jul
11.37 w	3.4	Steven Langley	16.12.83	2h3	Sheffield	16 Aug
11.38 w	2.6	Leroy Evelyn	23.09.83	4s1	Exeter	10 Jul
11.39	1.5	Koby Gyasi	18.10.83	1s2	Exeter	10 Jul
11.4		Daniel Crawford	23.02.84	1rB	London (Ha)	7 Jun
	(10)					
11.4 w	4.0	Jordon Lau	23.09.83	1	London (WF)	9 May
11.44 w	5.8	Lee Miller	20.01.84	2h3	Exeter	10 Jul
11.60	1.7			2	London (He)	30 Aug
11.46 w	2.6	Kingslee Maclean-Daley	1.12.83	5s1	Exeter	10 Jul
11.47	1.0	Darren Watson	9.09.83	1	Birmingham	5 Sep
11.5		Laurence Oboh	14.05.84	1	Bournemouth	19 Jul
11.51 w	2.6	Thomas Phillips	12.10.83	1h4	Exeter	10 Jul
11.54	1.5			3s2	Exeter	10 Jul
11.52	1.5	Delvyn Williams	8.12.83	2s2	Exeter	10 Jul
11.56 w	2.3	Kelvin Peltier-Emile	13.12.83	2h2	Sheffield	16 Aug
11.58	1.4			5	Sheffield	16 Aug
11.59 w	2.3	Adrian Dillon	10.09.83	3h2	Sheffield	16 Aug
11.60 w	5.8	Neil Wheeler	6.09.83	4h3	Exeter	10 Jul
	(20)					
11.6		Ryan Preddy	30.01.84	1	Worcester	9 May
11.6		Craig Erskine	26.09.83	1	Greenock	24 May
11.6		Stephen Berthier	19.07.84	1	London (Ha)	7 Jun

Under 13

12.3	Bob Thanda	22.09.85	1	Watford	29 Jul
12.4	James Dunford	14.01.86	1	Swindon	19 Jul
12.4	J. Dixon		1	Stevenage	13 Sep
12.58			1	Bedford	7 Jun

147

12.48 w	2.4	Joel Kangudi			1	Birmingham	5	Sep
12.5		Scott Johnson		4.12.85	1	Bath	19	Jul
12.5		N. Thornton			1	Sheffield (W)	19	Jul

Foreign

10.2 w	2.4	Sanusi Turay (SLE)		14.04.68	2	Enfield	9	May
		10.47dq 0.0			1h1	Watford	20	Jun
		perf valid but disqualified for taking the name of another athlete						
10.5 w	2.4	Haroun Korjie (SLE)		17.02.72	4	Enfield	9	May
		10.58 w 3.7			5	Edinburgh	4	Jul
		10.66 1.2			4s1	Watford	20	Jun
10.55 w	2.1	Paul Brizzell (IRE)	U23	3.10.76	1	Dublin (S), IRE	17	May
		10.65			1	Antrim	23	May
10.77	1.2	Carl Afilaka (TRI)		13.07.68	5h1	Birmingham	24	Jul
10.8 w	3.0	Francis Keita (SLE)		23.07.70	3	Enfield	5	Aug
10.95		Gary Munroe (CAN)		12.04.69	4	Copenhagen, DEN	23	Jun

150 METRES

15.6		Graham Beasley	U23	24.10.77	1r3	Bournemouth	5	Apr
15.8		Jason Fergus		11.10.73	1	Havering	15	Mar

200 METRES

20.18	-0.2	Julian Golding		17.02.75	1	Kuala Lumpur, MAL	19	Sep
		20.34	-0.7		1s2	Kuala Lumpur, MAL	19	Sep
		20.39	-1.2		1h1	Budapest, HUN	20	Aug
		20.46 i			1	Birmingham	8	Feb
		20.51	0.1		1q4	Kuala Lumpur, MAL	18	Sep
		20.57 i			1	Birmingham	15	Feb
		20.61	1.3		1r2	Hania, GRE	27	May
		20.61	-0.2		1s1	Budapest, HUN	21	Aug
		20.63 i			1r1	Lievin, FRA	22	Feb
		20.63	1.0		4	Sheffield	2	Aug
		20.65	1.8		4	Bratislava, SVK	9	Jun
		20.69 i			1s3	Birmingham	8	Feb
		20.72	-1.0		3	Budapest, HUN	21	Aug
		20.84 i			4	Valencia, SPA	1	Mar
		20.88	-1.5		3	Birmingham	26	Jul
		20.90 i			1h2	Valencia, SPA	28	Feb
		20.90	-0.3		2r1	Kalamata, GRE	23	May
		20.93	-0.4		1h4	Birmingham	25	Jul
		20.94 i			2s2	Valencia, SPA	1	Mar
		20.94	-0.1		2h5	Kuala Lumpur, MAL	18	Sep
		20.95	-0.2		2	Turku, FIN	1	Jul
		20.95	0.0		6	Villeneuve d'Ascq, FRA	11	Jul
20.29	-0.2	Christian Malcolm	U20	3.06.79	2	Kuala Lumpur, MAL	19	Sep
		20.44	-0.2		1	Annecy, FRA	1	Aug
		20.53	0.1		2q4	Kuala Lumpur, MAL	18	Sep
		20.56	-0.5		2s1	Kuala Lumpur, MAL	19	Sep
		20.62	1.0		1s2	Annecy, FRA	1	Aug
		20.73	0.7		1h6	Annecy, FRA	31	Jul
		20.85	-0.2		1q3	Annecy, FRA	31	Jul
		20.92	0.4		2h6	Kuala Lumpur, MAL	18	Sep
		20.93	0.0		1	Mannheim, GER	13	Jun
20.35	-1.5	Doug Walker		28.07.73	1	Birmingham	26	Jul
		20.38	1.0		1	Sheffield	2	Aug
		20.42	1.4		1	St. Petersburg, RUS	28	Jun
		20.53	-1.0		1	Budapest, HUN	21	Aug
		20.59	-0.4		1	Bedford	30	May
		20.67	-0.6		3h4	Budapest, HUN	20	Aug

(Walker)	20.67	0.0		1q1	Kuala Lumpur, MAL 18 Sep
	20.68	-0.5		4s1	Kuala Lumpur, MAL 19 Sep
	20.69	-0.2		8	Kuala Lumpur, MAL 19 Sep
	20.71	-0.6		1s1	Birmingham 26 Jul
	20.74	-1.8		1s2	Budapest, HUN 21 Aug
	20.77	0.8		2h8	Kuala Lumpur, MAL 18 Sep
	20.83	1.3		1	Coimbra, POR 10 Jun
20.40 -0.2	John Regis		13.10.66	3	Kuala Lumpur, MAL 19 Sep
	20.49	-0.7		2s2	Kuala Lumpur, MAL 19 Sep
	20.56	1.8		1	London (He) 8 Aug
	20.56	1.7		3	La Chaux de Fonds, SWZ 16 Aug
	20.58	-0.1		2q2	Kuala Lumpur, MAL 18 Sep
	20.78	0.1		2h2	Kuala Lumpur, MAL 18 Sep
	20.81	0.9		2	Tonsberg, NOR 20 Jun
	20.89	-1.5		4	Birmingham 26 Jul
	20.89	1.1		2	Bedford 29 Aug
	20.94	1.7		1r3	Fullerton, USA 23 Apr
	20.95	0.3		5	Doha, QAT 7 May
	20.95	0.1		2	Sundsvall, SWE 29 Jun
	20.99	-0.6		2s1	Birmingham 26 Jul
20.48 1.0	Darren Campbell		12.09.73	3	Sheffield 2 Aug
	20.70	0.1		1	Sundsvall, SWE 29 Jun
20.51 A 1.3	Doug Turner		2.12.66	5	Johannesburg, RSA 13 Sep
	20.55	-1.5		2	Birmingham 26 Jul
	20.63	-0.8		1h3	Budapest, HUN 20 Aug
	20.63	-1.7		1	Glasgow (S) 30 Aug
	20.64	1.0		2	Budapest, HUN 21 Aug
	20.64	-0.7		5s2	Kuala Lumpur, MAL 19 Sep
	20.68	0.0		2q1	Kuala Lumpur, MAL 18 Sep
	20.76 i			2	Birmingham 25 Jan
	20.77 i			4	Birmingham 15 Feb
	20.79	1.0		6	Sheffield 2 Aug
	20.80	0.3		1s2	Birmingham 26 Jul
	20.83	-0.1		1h3	Kuala Lumpur, MAL 18 Sep
	20.88	0.7		1h2	Birmingham 25 Jul
	20.89	-1.8		2s2	Budapest, HUN 21 Aug
	20.92 i			1s2	Birmingham 25 Jan
	20.93 i			2s3	Valencia, SPA 1 Mar
20.53 i	Allyn Condon		24.08.74	2	Birmingham 8 Feb
	20.59 i			1	Birmingham 25 Jan
	20.68 i			3	Valencia, SPA 1 Mar
	20.69 i			1s1	Valencia, SPA 1 Mar
	20.71	0.2		2	Milan, ITA 5 Jun
	20.72 i			1s1	Birmingham 8 Feb
	20.76 i			1s1	Birmingham 25 Jan
	20.76 i			3	Birmingham 15 Feb
	20.83 i			2r2	Lievin, FRA 22 Feb
	20.83	1.1		1	Bedford 29 Aug
	20.85 i			1	Birmingham 3 Jan
	20.87 i			1h1	Valencia, SPA 28 Feb
	20.90	0.3		3q3	Kuala Lumpur, MAL 18 Sep
	20.93	-1.5		5	Birmingham 26 Jul
	20.98 i			1h2	Birmingham 25 Jan
20.73 0.4	Marcus Adam		28.02.68	2	Hechtel, BEL 1 Aug
	20.77	0.5		1	Watford 21 Jun
	20.78			1	Birmingham 18 Jul
	20.80	1.2		1h1	Birmingham 25 Jul
	20.87			1s1	Watford 21 Jun
	20.99	-1.5		6	Birmingham 26 Jul
	21.00	-0.6		3s1	Birmingham 26 Jul

Time	Wind	Name	Cat	DOB	Pos	Venue	Date
20.76	1.4	Solomon Wariso		11.11.66	6	Walnut, USA	19 Apr
20.86 i					1s3	Birmingham	25 Jan
20.93 i					3	Birmingham	25 Jan
20.95	0.6				1	Eagle Rock, USA	9 May
20.77	1.2	Mark Richardson		26.07.72	1	Irvine, USA	2 May
(10)							
20.92	1.2	Marlon Devonish	U23	1.06.76	2	Irvine, USA	2 May
20.99 i		Jamie Henthorn	U23	20.02.77	1s2	Birmingham	8 Feb
21.01	-1.6				2	Dessau, GER	1 Aug
20.99		Akinola Lashore		28.03.73	2s1	Watford	21 Jun
20.99	1.7	Owusu Dako		23.05.73	1rB	London (He)	8 Aug
		106 performances to 21.00 by 14 athletes including 25 indoors					
21.01	1.4	Jason Fergus		11.10.73	3	Belgrade, YUG	31 May
21.05	-1.2	Dwain Chambers	U23	5.04.78	4rB	Kalamata, GRE	23 May
21.06	0.5	Ed White		16.11.73	2	Watford	21 Jun
21.07	-1.0	Jamie Baulch		3.05.73	2	Cwmbran	20 Jun
21.14	-0.4	Danny Joyce		9.09.74	1rB	Bedford	30 May
21.19	1.6	Tim Benjamin	U17	2.05.82	2h7	Annecy, FRA	31 Jul
(20)							
21.20		Mark Findlay	U23	20.03.78	3s1	Watford	21 Jun
21.20	-0.1	Paul McBurney		14.03.72	6	Singapore, SIN	5 Dec
21.21	1.8	Elliot Bunney		11.12.66	3	London (He)	8 Aug
21.26		Josephus Thomas		11.07.71	1	Cosford	1 Jul
21.27	0.6	Ayo Falola		29.07.68	1	Cape Town, RSA	24 Jan
21.28		Seni Edu		4.03.74	4s1	Watford	21 Jun
21.29	1.7	Andrew Walcott		11.01.75	2rB	London (He)	8 Aug
21.30 i		Brendon Ghent	U23	7.09.76	2s2	Birmingham	25 Jan
21.45	-0.7				1	Bedford	30 Aug
21.31 i		Steve Topliss/Webb	U23	17.07.78	2s1	Birmingham	8 Feb
21.56	0.0				2	Liverpool	20 Jun
21.31		Andy Hughes		10.07.67	1	Copenhagen, DEN	23 Jun
(30)							
21.32 A	0.0	Iwan Thomas		5.01.74	3	Potchefstroom, RSA	26 Jan
21.33	-2.1	Daniel Money	U23	7.10.76	1rB	Birmingham	6 Jun
21.34	-0.4	Jamie Paul		17.07.70	3h4	Birmingham	25 Jul
21.40	0.0	Jared Deacon		15.10.75	1	Liverpool	20 Jun
21.45 i		Darren Braithwaite		20.01.69	4	Birmingham	25 Jan
21.87	1.5				4h1	Watford	21 Jun
21.45	-0.4	Kevin Farrell	U23	31.10.77	2h3	Birmingham	25 Jul
21.46	-0.4	Darren Scott		7.03.69	2rB	Bedford	30 May
21.46	1.5	Richard Johnson		13.10.71	3s2	Watford	21 Jun
21.47	1.8	Michael Afilaka		16.11.71	5	London (He)	8 Aug
21.48	-0.9	Jason John		17.10.71	1	Watford	16 May
(40)							
21.49	1.9	Marlon Dickson	U23	17.11.78	1h1	Watford	21 Jun
21.49	0.8	Ian Craig		20.08.69	5h8	Kuala Lumpur, MAL	18 Sep
21.50		Kevin Williams		15.12.71	1rB	Birmingham	18 Jul
21.51	-0.4	Sunny Adepegba		6.06.71	3rB	Bedford	30 May
21.51	1.5	David Samuyiwa		4.08.72	3h4	Watford	21 Jun
21.51	1.8	Alex Fugallo		28.01.70	6	London (He)	8 Aug
21.52	1.7	Toby Box		9.09.72	3rB	London (He)	8 Aug
21.53	1.8	Daniel Caines	U20	15.05.79	2	Bath	4 May
21.53	1.8	Michael Tietz	U23	14.09.77	7	London (He)	8 Aug
21.56	-0.6	Chris Lambert	U20	6.04.81	1	London (He)	30 Aug
(50)							
21.57	1.8	Graham Beasley	U23	24.10.77	3	Bath	4 May
21.59	-0.4	Paul White		1.09.74	6	Bedford	30 May
21.62		John Stewart	U20	30.12.79	1	Gateshead	9 May
21.62	1.6	Tyrone Edgar	U17	29.03.82	1	London (Ha)	24 May
21.63 i		James Chatt	U20	11.02.80	2	Birmingham	22 Feb
21.76	0.0				2	London (He)	30 Aug

150

21.63		Adrian Patrick		15.06.73	3	Ljubljana, SLO	31	May
21.66		Ray Salami		11.04.75	7s1	Watford	21	Jun
21.66	0.2	Mark Allen		23.09.66	4rB	Tel Aviv, ISR	20	Jul
21.68	1.0	Dominique Richards	U20	12.09.79	2	London (Ha)	23	May
21.69	0.0	Michael Arkle		31.03.73	1	Cudworth	1	Aug
	(60)							
21.70 i		Nigel Stickings		1.04.71	4s2	Birmingham	8	Feb
21.70	1.0	Darren Wall	U20	6.04.80	3	London (Ha)	23	May
21.71	1.0	Darren Burley	U20	13.01.80	4	London (Ha)	23	May
21.71	-0.4	Tremayne Rutherford		19.06.72	7	Bedford	30	May
21.72 i		David Turnbull	U20	10.06.79	1h3	Birmingham	22	Feb
21.72	-1.4	Graeme Welsh		8.10.75	3rB	Watford	16	May
21.74	1.7	Terence Stamp		18.02.70	5rB	London (He)	8	Aug
21.75	1.9	Ben Watkins	U23	12.11.78	3h1	Watford	21	Jun
21.75		Peter Maitland		21.01.73	2r2	Birmingham	18	Jul
21.77	1.5	Alastair Gordon	U23	16.04.78	6s2	Watford	21	Jun
	(70)							
21.79	-0.9	Jim Watson		4.10.67	5	Watford	16	May
21.81 i		Joselyn Thomas		11.07.71	2h7	Birmingham	25	Jan
21.85 i		Sean Baldock	U23	3.12.76	1	Glasgow	15	Mar
		21.92	1.8		6	Bath	4	May
21.86	1.8	Matthew Bridle	U23	11.08.76	4	Bath	4	May
21.87	-2.4	Tokunbo Olabinri		27.02.62	1h2	Sydney, AUS	7	Feb
21.87	0.0	Mark Lloyd		28.09.71	4	Liverpool	20	Jun
21.89	-1.4	Ben Lewis	U20	6.03.81	4rB	Watford	16	May
21.89	-0.6	Steve Surety	U20	18.02.80	3	London (He)	30	Aug
21.92	1.5	David Bandele		11.09.71	6h4	Watford	21	Jun
21.94	1.8	Matthew Lewis		11.11.75	7	Bath	4	May
	(80)							
21.97	-0.6	Jason Livingston ¶		17.03.71	4rB	Cardiff	4	Aug
21.97	1.7	Dan Donovan		8.10.70	7rB	London (He)	8	Aug
21.98		Andrew Parker	U20	1.08.80	1	Barry	14	Jul
21.98	-1.3	Mark Lewis-Francis	U17	4.09.82	1	Birmingham	6	Sep
21.99	-0.7	Ian McGurk		17.10.71	1	Glasgow (S)	10	May
22.00		Ross Linnett	U20	6.10.79	2	Gateshead	9	May
22.01 i		Ray Coker		28.07.73	1	Gainesville, USA	6	Feb
22.02 i		Tristan Anthony	U17	16.12.82	1	Birmingham	28	Feb
		22.20	1.6		3	London (Ha)	24	May
22.02	1.6	Dwayne Grant	U17	17.07.82	1h1	Sheffield	15	Aug
22.03	1.7	Simon Duberley		2.09.67	6h2	Watford	21	Jun
	(90)							
22.03	-3.5	Chris Carson	U20	26.10.79	3	London (He)	9	Aug
22.06	0.0	Andrew Bull		26.06.69	3	Cudworth	1	Aug
22.08 i		Geoff Dearman	U23	4.08.77	1h3	Birmingham	1	Feb
22.09	-1.7	Larry Achike		31.01.75	1	Sydney, AUS	4	Jan
22.09 i		Daniel Plummer	U20	4.01.81	2h3	Birmingham	22	Feb
22.11	1.9	Simon Duncan	U23	20.05.77	6h1	Watford	21	Jun
22.12	-0.5	Brian Doyle	U23	12.03.77	1h2	Glasgow (S)	10	May
22.12	1.7	Chris Bennett	U20	18.10.80	7	Bedford	29	Aug
22.15 i		Richard Rubenis		10.11.73	2	Birmingham	1	Mar
22.15	-1.2	Graham Hedman	U20	6.02.79	1rD	Bedford	30	May
	(100)							
22.15	-0.3	Will MacGee		9.06.68	4h3	Watford	21	Jun
22.16	-3.5	Paul Campbell	U20	29.01.80	4	London (He)	9	Aug
22.18 i		Lee Bryan	U17	24.11.81	1	Birmingham	1	Mar
		22.59			1	Solihull	24	May
22.19 i		Mark McIntyre		14.10.70	3h1	Birmingham	1	Feb
22.19	1.7	Leighton Green	U23	10.01.78	7h2	Watford	21	Jun
22.20		Tony Noel			1	Bedford	6	Jun

Wind Assisted

20.32	3.4	Malcolm	U20	(20.29)	1	Bedford	5	Jul
20.47	3.4	Walker		(20.35)	1	Bedford	25	May
20.49	2.7	Josephus Thomas		(21.26)	2r1	Fullerton, USA	23	Apr
20.57	2.6	Golding		(20.18)	5	St. Denis, FRA	4	Jun
20.90	3.4	Adrian Patrick		(21.63)	2	Bedford	25	May
	20.99	3.8			1h1	Bedford	25	May
20.98	2.6	Tim Benjamin	U17	(21.19)	1	Alicante, SPA	18	Jul

7 performances to 21.00 by 6 athletes

21.05	2.8	Brendon Ghent	U23	(21.30i)	2r2	Fullerton, USA	23	Apr
21.10	2.7	Joselyn Thomas		11.07.71	5r1	Fullerton, USA	23	Apr
21.15		Jamie Paul		(21.34)	2	Ashford	9	May
21.16	2.9	Michael Afilaka		(21.47)	1	Edinburgh	17	Jul
21.16	2.6	John Stewart	U20	(21.62)	2	Alicante, SPA	18	Jul
21.19	6.0	Darren Scott		(21.46)	2h2	Bedford	25	May
21.35	3.4	Ben Lewis	U20	(21.89)	3	Bedford	5	Jul
21.38	3.8	Graham Beasley	U23	(21.57)	2h1	Bedford	25	May
21.38	3.4	Chris Lambert	U20	(21.56)	4	Bedford	5	Jul
21.48	3.8	David Samuyiwa		(21.51)	3h1	Bedford	25	May
21.55	2.9	Tyrone Edgar	U17	(21.62)	2	Sheffield	15	Aug
21.55	2.9	Andrew Parker	U20	(21.98)	2	Bruges, BEL	23	Aug
21.57	3.3	Darren Burley	U20	(21.71)	2h2	Exeter	10	Jul
21.60	6.0	Mark Woodhouse		1.11.75	4h2	Bedford	25	May
21.62		Chris Davidson		4.12.75	3	Ashford	9	May
21.63	3.3	James Chatt	U20	(21.76)	3h2	Exeter	10	Jul
21.65	3.4	Darren Wall	U20	(21.70)	6	Bedford	5	Jul
21.66	2.9	John Skeete	U23	8.09.78	3	Edinburgh	17	Jul
21.66	2.9	Jim Watson		(21.79)	4	Edinburgh	17	Jul
21.68	3.4	Tristan Anthony	U17	(22.02i)	7	Bedford	5	Jul
21.72		Matthew Lewis		(21.94)	1h5	Bath	3	May
21.77	2.7	Sean Baldock	U23	(21.85i)	1s3	Bath	4	May
21.77	4.2	Ben Green	U23	(22.19)	4h3	Bedford	25	May
21.78	2.5	Andrew Bull		(22.06)	1	Cudworth	10	May
21.89	3.8	David Turnbull	U20	(21.72i)	4h1	Bedford	25	May
21.90	3.8	Simon Duberley		(22.03)	5h1	Bedford	25	May
21.91	2.9	Gary Jones		6.01.72	5	Edinburgh	17	Jul
21.93	3.3	Michael Bradbury	U20	30.12.80	4h2	Exeter	10	Jul
21.93	2.9	Dwayne Grant	U17	(22.02)	3	Sheffield	15	Aug
21.94	3.3	Ben Nutley	U20	14.11.79	5h2	Exeter	10	Jul
21.95	5.3	Graham Hedman	U20	(22.15)	2rB	Bedford	5	Jul
22.01	2.9	Jim Beattie		22.07.73	6	Edinburgh	17	Jul
22.03	3.8	Nicholas Dawson	U23	11.05.78	2h6	Bath	3	May
22.04		Daniel Angus	U17	15.07.82	1	Gateshead	10	May
22.07	5.3	Spencer Brew	U20	17.08.79	3rB	Bedford	5	Jul
22.09	4.2	Dalton Powell		20.08.63	5h3	Bedford	25	May
22.11	6.0	Leon McRae	U20	3.11.80	5h2	Bedford	25	May
22.14	4.0	Will MacGee		(22.15)	4h1	Edinburgh	17	Jul
22.15	3.3	Danny Bruce	U23	29.09.76	2h1	Bath	3	May
22.16	2.4	Andrew Bargh	U23	21.08.76	1	Portsmouth	9	May
22.16		Mark Suggitt	U17	7.11.81	2	Gateshead	10	May
22.17	4.2	Mark Collins		29.07.73	6h3	Bedford	25	May
22.18	2.9	Alex Golding	U17	3.12.81	4	Sheffield	15	Aug
22.19	2.8	Lee Bryan	U17	(22.18i)	3h3	Exeter	11	Jul
22.20	2.6	Matthew Jones	U20	5.12.80	5h1	Exeter	10	Jul

Hand Timing

20.4 w	2.7	Walker		(20.35)	1	Edinburgh	4 Jul
20.7		Turner		(20.51A)	1	Derby	19 Jul
		20.8 w 3.5			1	Liverpool	8 Aug
20.9	-1.6	Adrian Patrick		(21.63)	1	Bracknell	10 May
20.9	0.1	Malcolm	U20	(20.29)	1	Cardiff	6 Jun
20.9	1.0	Wariso		(20.76)	1	Watford	4 Jul
		6 performances to 21.0 by 5 athletes including 2 wind assisted					
21.1		Jamie Paul		(21.34)	1	Bromley	15 Aug
21.1 w		Jason Gardener		18.09.75	1rB	Bath	30 May
21.2	1.8	Elliot Bunney		(21.21)	1rB	Edinburgh	4 Jul
21.3	2.0	Andy Hughes		(21.31)	1	Loughborough	10 Jun
21.3 w	4.2	Kevin Farrell	U23	(21.45)	1	Bebington	4 Jul
		21.4 0.6			1	Barking	8 Aug
21.3 w	3.5	Paul Slythe		5.09.74	2r1	Liverpool	8 Aug
		21.4			1	Hoo	14 Jun
21.4		Daniel Caines	U20	(21.53)	1	Mansfield	19 Apr
21.4	-0.2	Steve Topliss/Webb	U23	(21.31i)	1r1	Watford	6 Jun
21.4	0.3	Uvie Ugono	U23	8.03.78	2rB	Watford	4 Jul
21.4	1.8	McLean Okotie		31.07.69	3rB	Edinburgh	4 Jul
21.4		Nathan Morgan	U23	30.06.78	2	Derby	19 Jul
21.4		Brendon Ghent	U23	(21.30i)	1	Telford	15 Aug
21.4 w	2.7	Jason John		(21.48)	3	Edinburgh	4 Jul
21.4 w		Dominique Richards	U20	(21.68)	1	London (TB)	25 Jul
		21.6			1	London (TB)	19 Aug
21.4 w		Andrew Parker	U20	(21.98)	1	Newport	9 Aug
		21.8			1	Neath	14 Jun
21.5		Geoff Dearman	U23	(22.08i)	1	Milton Keynes	16 Aug
21.5 w	4.2	Andrew Bull		(22.06)	2	Bebington	4 Jul
		21.7 0.6			3	Barking	8 Aug
21.5 w		Neil Sharp		21.08.75	1	Cleckheaton	15 Aug
21.6		Mark Lloyd		(21.87)	1	Bebington	2 May
21.6		John Stewart	U20	(21.62)	1	Middlesbrough	14 Jun
21.6	1.8	Sean Baldock	U23	(21.85i)	4rB	Edinburgh	4 Jul
21.6		Guy Bullock		15.10.75	1	Ormskirk	11 Jul
21.6	-2.5	Mark Hylton	U23	24.09.76	1rB	Newport	8 Aug
21.6	0.6	David Bandele		(21.92)	2	Barking	8 Aug
21.6 w		Jon Barbour	U20	3.11.80	2	London (TB)	25 Jul
21.7		Steve McCourt		6.05.71	1	Kingston	18 Apr
21.7		Mark Woodhouse		(21.60w)	1	Loughborough	25 Apr
21.7		Tony Leigh		27.12.65	2	Stoke	16 May
21.7		Elisha Newell	U20	10.06.79	1	Dartford	16 May
21.7	1.7	Ben Lewis	U20	(21.89)	1	Birmingham	29 May
21.7		Matt Douglas	U23	26.11.76	1	Watford	29 Jul
21.7		Tony Noel		(22.20)	1	Birmingham	5 Aug
21.7	-0.4	Tim O'Dell		29.05.70	3	Enfield	23 Aug
21.8		Du'aine Ladejo		14.02.71	1rB	Woodford	25 Apr
21.8		Ben Nutley	U20	(21.94w)	1rB	London (Elt)	2 May
21.8		Simon Duberley		(22.03)	2	Dartford	16 May
21.8	-0.2	Sam Omonua	U23	16.06.76	4	Enfield	16 May
21.8		Mark Lewis-Francis	U17	(21.98)	1	Stafford	17 May
21.8		Ben Green	U23	(22.19)	1	Kingston	6 Jun
21.8		Darren Jackson	U23	21.10.78	1	Watford	13 Jun
21.8		Matthew Clements	U23	17.09.77	2	Woodford	15 Jul
21.8 w		Trevor Painter		10.08.71	1	Wigan	4 Jul
21.9		Chris Rawlinson		19.05.72	2	Loughborough	25 Apr
21.9		Dan Donovan		(21.97)	1	Basingstoke	2 May

21.9		Tim Barton		3.10.70	1	Coventry	2 May
21.9		Tony Waddington		30.06.75	2	London (Elt)	2 May
21.9		Joselyn Thomas		(21.81i)	2	Enfield	9 May
21.9		Graham Hedman	U20	(22.15)	1	London (Col)	6 Jun
21.9		Paul Sampson	U23	12.07.77	1	Sheffield	14 Jun
21.9		Corri Henry	U23	9.12.76	1	Lincoln	14 Jun
21.9		Brian Doyle	U23	(22.12)	1	Greenock	14 Jun
21.9		David Turnbull	U20	(21.72i)	2	Greenock	14 Jun
21.9		John Skeete	U23	(21.66w)	1	London (FP)	28 Jun
21.9		Ross Linnett	U20	(22.00)	1	Wakefield	26 Jul
21.9		Paul Campbell	U20	(22.16)	2	Wakefield	26 Jul
21.9		Lawrence Baird	U23	14.12.77	1	Blackpool	8 Aug
21.9		Dominic Bradley	U23	22.12.76	1	Stretford	1 Sep
21.9 w	4.2	Michael Bradbury	U20	(21.93w)	4	Bebington	4 Jul
22.0		Graeme Read	U20	24.10.79	1	York	19 Apr
22.0		Brian Cannon		6.09.75	2	Basildon	2 May
22.0		Tim Miller	U23	2.12.77	1	Newport	3 May
22.0		Mike Rey		19.07.68	2	Bracknell	10 May
22.0		Daniel Bonich	U23	22.11.78	2	Woking	16 May
22.0		Chris Carson	U20	(22.03)	1	Pitreavie	21 May
22.0		Tyrone Swaray	U23	7.11.77	1	St. Albans	6 Jun
22.0		Nick Thomas	U20	4.04.79	1	London (FP)	28 Jun
22.0		Carl McMullen	U20	9.11.79	1	Lancaster	4 Jul
22.0		Ray Burke		11.11.69	2	Bournemouth	4 Jul
22.0	1.8	Liam Collins	U23	23.10.78	7rB	Edinburgh	4 Jul
22.0		Richard David	U23	15.08.77	2	Sutton	15 Jul
22.0		Joshua Wood		19.04.74	1r2	London (TB)	25 Jul
22.0	0.6	Richard Pinnock		31.10.70	4	Barking	8 Aug
22.0		Nicholas Dawson	U23	(22.03w)	1	Portsmouth (RN)	15 Aug
22.0		Stephen Tucker		30.12.62	1	Glasgow	18 Aug
22.0		James Hilston	U20	25.02.79	2	London (TB)	19 Aug
22.0		Brian Forbes		6.09.74	2	Belfast	26 Aug
22.0		Ian Lowthian	U20	10.10.80	2	Derby	20 Sep
22.0 w	3.5	Chris Bennett	U20	(22.12)	2	Portsmouth	9 May
22.0 w	3.5	Gavin Eastman	U20	28.06.80	2rB	Bebington	4 Jul

Additional Under 17 (1 - 9 above)

22.1	1.8	Martin Houlihan		19.09.81	2	Leeds	23 May
22.1	1.8	Angus		(22.04w)	1	Leeds	23 May
22.1		Luke Bowling		4.11.81	1	Peterborough	19 Jul
22.2	1.8	Golding		(22.18w)	3	Leeds	23 May
		22.36	1.0		2h1	Exeter	10 Jul
	(10)						
22.2		Alastair Mark		8.12.81	1	Corby	20 Jun
22.3		Robbie Attwell		17.10.81	2	Cardiff	26 Apr
22.3	1.8	Vincent Davis		1.11.81	4	Leeds	23 May
		22.32	1.0		1h1	Exeter	10 Jul
22.3		David Smith		15.10.81	2	Carlisle	4 Jul
		22.48	1.3		3h2	Exeter	10 Jul
22.40	1.3	Suggitt		(22.16w)	2h2	Exeter	10 Jul
22.40 w	4.0	Tom Hyde	U15	7.10.83	1	Sheffield	15 Aug
		23.11	1.8		3	Exeter	11 Jul
22.4		Michael Snow		5.09.82	1	Corby	9 May
22.42 w	4.9	Ben Inatimi		6.07.83	4	Exeter	11 Jul
22.47 w	2.9	Bruce Gibb		10.10.81	6	Sheffield	15 Aug
		22.51	1.6		4h1	Sheffield	15 Aug
22.48	1.6	Leroy Slue		11.12.81	4	London (Ha)	24 May
	(20)						

Time	Wind	Name		DOB	Pos	Venue	Date
22.50	1.6	Stuart Conolly		9.02.83	3h1	Sheffield	15 Aug
22.5		Andrew Corey		15.10.81	2	Stafford	17 May
22.5		Gary Hunter		10.09.81	1	Wrexham	17 May
22.5	1.8	Gary Ankers		2.06.82	5	Leeds	23 May
22.5		Andrew Norman		27.01.82	1	Exeter	13 Jun
22.5		Scott Thompson		21.02.82	1	Pitreavie	8 Aug
		22.76	-0.6		1	Grangemouth	23 Aug
22.55 w		Aaron Evans		15.02.82	1	Ashford	10 May
22.57	0.7	Kevin Ashley		12.09.81	2h3	Sheffield	15 Aug
22.59		Michael Pardo		29.07.82	1	Glasgow (S)	10 May
22.60	1.3	Adam Paulley		5.10.81	4h2	Exeter	10 Jul
	(30)						
22.66		Adam Rogers		10.04.83	1	Gateshead	29 Aug
22.74	1.8	Laurence Oboh	U15	14.05.84	1	Exeter	11 Jul
22.80		Ryan Power		20.11.82	1	Tullamore, IRE	12 Jul
22.80 w	2.8	Neil Rochester		4.10.81	6h3	Exeter	10 Jul

Additional Under 15 (1 - 2 above)

Time	Wind	Name		DOB	Pos	Venue	Date
22.9		Ryan Preddy		30.01.84	1	Gloucester	29 Aug
		23.35 i			1	Birmingham	22 Feb
22.98 w	5.3	Darren Watson		9.09.83	1h4	Exeter	10 Jul
		23.09	1.8		2	Exeter	11 Jul
23.0		Matt Hopton		2.03.84	1	Bracknell	19 Jul
23.12 w	4.0	Steven Langley		16.12.83	3	Sheffield	15 Aug
		23.64	1.8		4	Exeter	11 Jul
23.15 w	4.0	Andre Flemmings		6.01.84	4	Sheffield	15 Aug
23.22 w	4.2	Craig Erskine		26.09.83	1	Grangemouth	11 Jul
		23.5			1	Pitreavie	21 May
		23.66	0.6		3	Dublin (S), IRE	8 Aug
23.33 w	5.3	Marcus Jeffrey		7.01.84	2h4	Exeter	10 Jul
23.37 w	4.0	Craig Bradshaw		14.04.84	5	Sheffield	15 Aug
		23.59	1.3		1h2	York	25 Jul
	(10)						
23.44 w	2.6	David Whattley		5.09.83	3s2	Exeter	10 Jul
		23.5			1	Bracknell	19 Jul
23.44 w	2.6	Martin Roberts		20.09.83	4s2	Exeter	10 Jul
23.47 w	5.3	Matthew Roberts		8.07.84	4h4	Exeter	10 Jul
23.53	1.4	Andrew Harris		21.09.83	1	London (He)	30 Aug
23.55 w	4.0	Mike Groves		21.03.84	6	Sheffield	15 Aug
		23.7			1	Cwmbran	13 Sep
23.6 w	4.1	Jonathon White		23.10.83	2h2	Exeter	10 Jul
23.68 w	3.1	Matthew Harman		8.11.83	4h2	Sheffield	15 Aug
23.70	-2.5	Leon Cameron		10.09.83	1	Birmingham	6 Sep

Under 13

Time		Name		DOB	Pos	Venue	Date
25.5		Bob Thanda		22.09.85	1	Stevenage	13 Sep
25.5		J. Dixon			2	Stevenage	13 Sep
		25.52			1	Bedford	9 Aug
25.9		Sean Ashton			1	Telford	12 Sep

Foreign

Time	Wind	Name		DOB	Pos	Venue	Date
20.81 w	*4.2*	*Paul Brizzell (IRE)*	*U23*	*3.10.76*	*1*	*Dublin (S), IRE*	*17 May*
		20.93	*-0.1*		*1*	*Tallinn, EST*	*19 Jun*
21.50	*-1.4*	*Sanusi Turay (SLE)*		*14.04.68*	*1rB*	*Watford*	*16 May*

300 METRES

31.56	Doug Walker		28.07.73	1	Gateshead	19	Jul
31.87	Mark Richardson		26.07.72	2	Gateshead	19	Jul
32.23	Solomon Wariso		11.11.66	3	Gateshead	19	Jul
32.26	Mark Hylton	U23	24.09.76	4	Gateshead	19	Jul
32.36	Iwan Thomas		5.01.74	5	Gateshead	19	Jul
32.51	Roger Black		31.03.66	6	Gateshead	19	Jul
33.13	Jared Deacon		15.10.75	7	Gateshead	19	Jul
33.20	Du'aine Ladejo		14.02.71	8	Gateshead	19	Jul
33.93	John Stewart	U20	30.12.79	2	Hexham	31	Aug
34.06 i	Chris Rawlinson		19.05.72	1	Birmingham	25	Feb
(10)							
34.12 i	Matt Douglas	U23	26.11.76	1rB	Birmingham	25	Feb
34.15 i	Geoff Dearman	U23	4.08.77	2	Birmingham	25	Feb
34.5	Adam Buckley	U20	6.12.80	1	Bebington	5	Apr
34.5	Darren Scott		7.03.69	1	Blackpool	27	Sep
34.6	James Chatt	U20	11.02.80	1	Tonbridge	13	Apr
34.7	Peter Brend	U23	2.02.77	1	Braunton	12	Apr

unofficial intermediate time

32.7 i+	Solomon Wariso	11.11.66	1m	Birmingham	8	Feb

400 METRES

44.37	Mark Richardson	26.07.72	1	Oslo, NOR		9	Jul
	44.37		3	Monaco, MON		8	Aug
	44.48		4	Zurich, SWZ		12	Aug
	44.53		1	Helsinki, FIN		13	Jun
	44.60		2	Kuala Lumpur, MAL	18	Sep
	44.62		2	Rome, ITA		14	Jul
	44.62		2	Birmingham		26	Jul
	44.88		1	Moscow, RUS		5	Sep
	45.03		1s1	Kuala Lumpur, MAL	17	Sep
	45.05		1	Sheffield		2	Aug
	45.14		3	Budapest, HUN		21	Aug
	45.17		1	Cottbus, GER		27	May
	45.22		4	Lausanne, SWZ		25	Aug
	45.40		1s2	Birmingham		25	Jul
	45.41		2s1	Budapest, HUN		20	Aug
	45.54		2q2	Kuala Lumpur, MAL	16	Sep
	45.81		1	St. Petersburg, RUS	27	Jun
	46.05		1h4	Budapest, HUN		19	Aug
	46.19		1h6	Kuala Lumpur, MAL	16	Sep
44.38	Iwan Thomas	5.01.74	4	Monaco, MON		8	Aug
	44.50		2	Oslo, NOR		9	Jul
	44.50		1	Birmingham		26	Jul
	44.52		1	Budapest, HUN		21	Aug
	44.52		1	Kuala Lumpur, MAL	18	Sep
	44.54		5	Zurich, SWZ		12	Aug
	44.61		1s2	Kuala Lumpur, MAL	17	Sep
	44.77		5	Rome, ITA		14	Jul
	44.82		1s2	Budapest, HUN		20	Aug
	44.95		3	Brussels, BEL		28	Aug
	44.96		3	Moscow, RUS		5	Sep
	45.13 A		4	Roodepoort, RSA		16	Mar
	45.13		1	Glasgow		30	Aug
	45.2 A		4	Pietersburg, RSA		11	Mar
	45.22		2	Sheffield		2	Aug
	45.26		1q3	Kuala Lumpur, MAL	16	Sep
	45.29		1	Ljubljana, SLO		31	May
	45.33 A		1	Johannesburg, RSA	12	Sep

(Thomas)	45.37			1	Budapest, HUN	5	Jul
	45.44			2s2	Birmingham	25	Jul
	45.44			2h2	Budapest, HUN	19	Aug
	45.45			1	Cwmbran	20	Jun
	45.53			3	Cape Town, RSA	20	Mar
	45.70			3	Bratislava, SVK	9	Jun
	46.24			1h3	Birmingham	24	Jul
44.68	Solomon Wariso		11.11.66	3	Birmingham	26	Jul
	45.23			3	Stockholm, SWE	5	Aug
	45.59			4s2	Budapest, HUN	20	Aug
	45.70			3s2	Birmingham	25	Jul
	45.71 i			1	Birmingham	8	Feb
	46.11			3q4	Kuala Lumpur, MAL	16	Sep
	46.27			4h1	Budapest, HUN	19	Aug
44.71	Roger Black		31.03.66	4	Birmingham	26	Jul
	45.18			7	Rome, ITA	14	Jul
	45.20			2	Helsinki, FIN	13	Jun
	45.36			1	Bratislava, SVK	9	Jun
	45.38			1s1	Birmingham	25	Jul
	45.51			3	Sheffield	2	Aug
44.83	Jamie Baulch		3.05.73	2s2	Kuala Lumpur, MAL	17	Sep
	45.30			4	Kuala Lumpur, MAL	18	Sep
	45.64			1q1	Kuala Lumpur, MAL	16	Sep
	45.67			7	Lausanne, SWZ	25	Aug
	45.88			4s2	Birmingham	25	Jul
	45.93			4	Bratislava, SVK	9	Jun
	46.08			3	Doha, QAT	7	May
	46.11			5	Helsinki, FIN	13	Jun
	46.14			2h5	Kuala Lumpur, MAL	16	Sep
	46.17			8	Birmingham	26	Jul
45.24	Mark Hylton	U23	24.09.76	1rB	Zurich, SWZ	12	Aug
	45.30			5	Birmingham	26	Jul
	45.54			5s1	Kuala Lumpur, MAL	17	Sep
	45.63			3s1	Birmingham	25	Jul
	45.75			4	Glasgow	30	Aug
	45.97			4q1	Kuala Lumpur, MAL	16	Sep
	46.06			5	Bratislava, SVK	9	Jun
	46.13			5	Sheffield	2	Aug
	46.39			4	Lucerne, SWZ	2	Jul
45.45	Sean Baldock	U23	3.12.76	2s1	Birmingham	25	Jul
	45.50			6	Birmingham	26	Jul
	46.11 i			2	Birmingham	8	Feb
	46.38			1	Belgrade, YUG	31	May
45.90	Paul McBurney		14.03.72	3q4	Kuala Lumpur, MAL	16	Sep
	46.25			5s2	Birmingham	25	Jul
45.94	Paul Slythe		5.09.74	7	Birmingham	26	Jul
	46.17			1	Hechtel, BEL	1	Aug
	46.23			1h1	Birmingham	24	Jul
	46.26			1	La Chaux de Fonds, SWZ	16	Aug
	46.29			4s1	Birmingham	25	Jul
46.12	Du'aine Ladejo		14.02.71	1D	Kuala Lumpur, MAL	17	Sep
46.31	(10) Adrian Patrick		15.06.73	1h1	Watford	21	Jun
	46.31			5s1	Birmingham	25	Jul
46.32	Jared Deacon		15.10.75	6s2	Birmingham	25	Jul
46.34	Tim O'Dell		29.05.70	7s2	Birmingham	25	Jul
46.36	Guy Bullock		15.10.75	1	Liverpool	20	Jun

93 performances to 46.40 by 14 athletes including 2 indoors

| 46.46 | Geoff Dearman | U23 | 4.08.77 | 1 | Dessau, GER | 1 | Aug |

46.61	Richard Knowles		12.11.75	2h3	Birmingham	24	Jul
46.64	Alloy Wilson	U20	25.01.80	7	Annecy, FRA	31	Jul
46.8	Allyn Condon		24.08.74	1	Stretford	1	Sep
46.89	Blair Young		5.04.71	2	Brisbane, AUS	15	Feb
46.92	Anthony Borsumato		13.12.73	1	Birmingham	6	Jun
	(20)						
47.08	Trevor Painter		10.08.71	2	Liverpool	20	Jun
47.09	Chris Carson	U20	26.10.79	3	Bedford	29	Aug
47.13	Daniel Caines	U20	15.05.79	1	London (He)	9	Aug
47.17	David Naismith	U20	15.12.79	3	Liverpool	20	Jun
47.19	Ian McGurk		17.10.71	1	Edinburgh	26	Apr
47.41	Brian Forbes		6.09.74	4h3	Kuala Lumpur, MAL	16	Sep
47.43	Matthew Lewis		11.11.75	1rB	Birmingham	6	Jun
47.44	Peter Brend	U23	2.02.77	1h3	Watford	21	Jun
47.46	Neil Jennings	U23	18.09.77	2	Gateshead	9	May
47.49	Paul Gray		25.05.69	2	Cwmbran	20	Jun
	(30)						
47.5	Matt Douglas	U23	26.11.76	1	Loughborough	13	May
	47.90			6	Watford	21	Jun
47.5	Roger Jordan		26.05.72	1	London (TB)	25	Jul
47.51	Andrew Mitchell		30.07.76	1	Edinburgh	18	Jul
47.52	Anders Lustgarten		9.02.74	1	Westwood, USA	21	Mar
47.56 i	Lawrence Baird	U23	14.12.77	2s2	Birmingham	7	Feb
	47.85			2rB	Dessau, GER	1	Aug
47.63	Tony Williams		1.05.72	2	Watford	16	May
47.75	Ian Horsburgh	U23	10.01.78	3	Watford	16	May
47.81	Richard Workman		31.05.71	4	Liverpool	20	Jun
47.82	Remi Edu	U23	14.12.78	5	Watford	21	Jun
47.83 i	Matthew Elias	U20	25.04.79	1h3	Birmingham	7	Feb
	(40)						
47.9	Ian Lowthian	U20	10.10.80	1	Blackpool	6	Sep
47.92	Paul McKee	U23	15.10.77	1	Tullamore, IRE	5	Jul
47.93	Adam Buckley	U20	6.12.80	2rB	Alicante, SPA	18	Jul
47.98 i	Kent Ulyatt		10.04.72	4s2	Birmingham	7	Feb
47.99	Richard Clifford	U23	28.07.78	3	Edinburgh	18	Jul
48.03	John Regis		13.10.66	2	Fullerton, USA	23	Apr
48.04	Kris Stewart	U20	11.04.80	1	Edinburgh	19	Jun
48.07 i	Michael Parper	U23	20.05.78	3s1	Birmingham	7	Feb
	48.49			3rB	Birmingham	6	Jun
48.10 i	Chris Rawlinson		19.05.72	1h3	Birmingham	25	Jan
48.1	Ruben Tabares	U23	22.10.78	2	Crawley	19	Jul
	(50)						
48.11	Dan Donovan		8.10.70	4	Bedford	30	May
48.11	Peter Maitland		21.01.73	5	Cardiff	4	Aug
48.19	Justin Bird		3.05.71	5	Edinburgh	18	Jul
48.20	Tom Nimmo		9.05.71	6	Edinburgh	18	Jul
48.2	Shane King		8.02.74	1	Whitehaven	9	May
48.2	Wayne Ellwood		26.09.74	2	Blackpool	8	Aug
	48.47			1	Watford	12	Sep
48.2	Alastair Gordon	U23	16.04.78	3	Brighton	19	Aug
48.23	Chris Bennett	U20	18.10.80	1	London (He)	31	Aug
48.3	Lawrence Lynch		1.11.67	1	Enfield	16	May
48.3	Marcus Adam		28.02.68	4	Watford	4	Jul
	(60)						
48.31	Gary Jennings		21.02.72	3	Loughborough	17	May
48.34	Alex Fugallo		28.01.70	1rB	Watford	16	May
48.39	Paul Curtis	U20	29.05.80	3	London (He)	9	Aug
48.4	Nick Buckfield		5.06.73	1	Sheffield (W)	16	May
48.4	Michael Riddell	U20	3.08.79	1	Bracknell	6	Jun
48.4	Craig Hurst		30.12.70	2	Watford	6	Jun
48.4	Eddie Williams		1.10.70	1	London (WL)	2	Aug

Time	Name	Cat	DOB	Pos	Venue	Date
48.42 A	Gary Cadogan		8.10.66	5	Potchefstroom, RSA	26 Jan
48.42	Eddie Betts		18.02.71	2h1	Watford	21 Jun
48.50	Lea Farmer	U20	22.01.80	1	Bruges, BEL	23 Aug
(70)						
48.5	Tim Slocombe	U23	15.11.77	1	London (Elt)	2 May
48.5	Mark Rivers		8.10.73	1	London (TB)	16 May
48.80				3h3	Watford	21 Jun
48.5	Joe Lloyd		9.04.73	1	Stoke	16 May
48.77				3	Cwmbran	20 Jun
48.5	Hugh Kerr	U23	4.01.76	1	Ayr	24 May
48.65				7	Edinburgh	18 Jul
48.5	Gary Stevenson	U20	12.09.79	2	Ayr	24 May
48.61				4	Bath	4 May
48.5	Tim Benjamin	U17	2.05.82	1	Aberdare	31 Aug
48.57 i	Darren Scott		7.03.69	4	Birmingham	1 Feb
48.9				1	Stretford	4 Aug
48.58	Scott Keenan	U20	31.07.81	2	Edinburgh	19 Jun
48.60 i	Mark Ponting	U23	28.04.77	3s4	Glasgow	14 Mar
48.89				2s1	Bath	3 May
48.6	Alexis Sharp		31.10.72	D	Azusa, USA	16 Apr
(80)						
48.6	Christopher Lawton		6.01.73	1	Ilford	25 Jul
48.6	Matt Kloiber		22.11.71	1	Watford	12 Aug
48.62	Alasdair Donaldson	U23	21.06.77	1rB	London (He)	8 Aug
48.63	Matthew Aldwinkle		23.08.74	2h2	Bedford	24 May
48.63	Corri Henry	U23	9.12.76	1rB	Birmingham	18 Jul
48.69	Graham Hedman	U20	6.02.79	2	London (He)	31 Aug
48.7	Dave Deacon		19.03.65	2	Gateshead	24 Jun
48.82				2	Poznan, POL	7 Sep
48.71	Paul Campbell	U20	26.03.80	1	Gateshead	9 May
48.73	Mark Collins		29.07.73	3rB	Bedford	30 May
48.73	Aaron Evans	U17	15.02.82	1	Exeter	11 Jul
(90)						
48.74	Lee Wiscombe	U20	12.07.80	2	Gateshead	9 May
48.77	Sandy Scott	U23	1.09.76	3s2	Bath	3 May
48.78	Stuart Tolcher	U23	18.10.77	1	Portsmouth	10 May
48.8	Philip Octave	U23	12.06.78	1	Bromley	15 Aug
48.8	Chris Harris		2.03.72	1	London (TB)	29 Aug
48.82	Kermitt Bentham		16.04.60	3rB	Watford	16 May
48.83	Nick Budden		17.11.75	6h3	Birmingham	24 Jul
48.84 i	Richard McDonald	U20	11.01.80	2	Glasgow	31 Jan
48.90	James Hilston	U20	25.02.79	2h4	Watford	21 Jun
48.9	David McKenzie		3.09.70	1	Basingstoke	2 May
(100)						
48.9	Danny Bruce	U23	29.09.76	2	Loughborough	13 May
48.9	Barry Middleton		10.03.75	1	Glasgow	14 Jun
49.09				1	Inverness	2 Aug
48.9	Lee Fairclough		23.06.70	1	Welwyn	15 Aug
48.98	Vince Wilson		1.04.73	3	Gateshead	9 May
49.00	Dean Park	U23	23.09.77	4rB	Birmingham	6 Jun
49.00	Andrew Gillespie		16.10.71	1	Bedford	30 Aug
49.0 i	Nigel Stickings		1.04.71	1rB	Birmingham	1 Feb
49.05 i				1	Birmingham	4 Jan
49.0	Richard David	U23	15.08.77	2	Kingston	9 May
49.0	Tony Draper		23.04.74	1	Bromley	15 Jul
49.0	Jamie Paul		17.07.70	1	London (Elt)	29 Jul
(110)						
49.01 i	Douglas Thom		13.04.68	2h2	Birmingham	7 Feb
49.01	Gary Ankers	U17	2.06.82	2	Exeter	11 Jul
49.03	Dave Savage		13.11.72	6	Watford	16 May
49.05 i	Pete Clarke		9.07.65	3rB	Birmingham	25 Jan

Additional Under 20 (1 - 22 above)

49.1	Colin Young		11.12.79	1	Nottingham	9	May
49.1	Carl McMullen		9.11.79	1	Wigan	23	Aug
49.16	Chris Page		13.11.80	1	Carmarthen	23	May
49.19	Paul Roberts	U17	15.09.81	3	Exeter	11	Jul
49.20	Nick Hamilton		13.03.79	4	Fribourg,SWZ	9	Aug
49.2	Simon Lees		19.11.79	1	Leamington	9	May
49.2	Ian Tinsley		23.01.81	1	Bebington	9	May
49.2	Lee Bryan	U17	24.11.81	1	Telford	26	Jul
(30)							
49.21	Geoffrey Djan	U17	21.07.82	4	Exeter	11	Jul
49.26	Jonathan Simpson	U17	27.05.82	1	Edinburgh	19	Jun
49.48	Tristan Anthony	U17	16.12.82	3	Sheffield	15	Aug
49.5	Steve Surety		18.02.80	2	Reading	16	May
49.5	Tom Roe	U17	25.06.82	1	Peterborough	26	Jul
	49.77			4	Sheffield	15	Aug
49.5	Tony O'Connor			2	Telford	26	Jul
49.6	Simon Bullock		22.11.80	1	Birmingham	2	May
49.67	Michael Snow	U17	5.09.82	1	Solihull	24	May
49.67	Alex Guthrie		6.07.79	1rB	Inverness	2	Aug

Additional Under 17 (1 - 10 above)

49.77	Robbie Attwell		17.10.81	5	Exeter	11	Jul
49.96	Craig Erskine	U15	26.09.83	3	Ayr	18	Jul
49.98	Ryan Preddy	U15	30.01.84	1	Exeter	11	Jul
50.04	Dominic Girdler		6.03.82	1O	Hull	19	Sep
50.13	Tom Lavender		7.12.81	2	Gateshead	9	May
50.15	Mike Charville		7.05.82	3	Gateshead	9	May
50.18	David Teague		20.01.82	3	Dublin, IRE	8	Aug
50.3	Simon Tunnicliffe		2.03.83	1	Tamworth	31	Aug
50.34	John Holtby		27.03.82	2	York	25	Jul
50.40	Andrew Corey		15.10.81	1	Oudenaarda, BEL	22	Aug
(20)							
50.40	Vernon Small		1.01.82	2	Birmingham	6	Sep
50.4	Lee Holehouse		23.12.81	3h1	Exeter	10	Jul
	50.46			2	Solihull	24	May
50.4	Nic Andrews		3.10.81	1	Exeter	25	Aug
50.46	Colin Joyce		21.10.81	8	Exeter	11	Jul
50.49	Bruce Gibb		10.10.81	2	Edinburgh	19	Jun
50.5	Jeffrey Christie		24.09.82		Bromsgrove	26	Jun
50.54	David Moulton		7.09.81	1rB	Sheffield	15	Aug
50.62	Russell Nicholls		8.03.83	1rB	Birmingham	6	Sep
50.67 i	Emmanuel Farrugia		19.07.82	2	Birmingham	21	Feb
50.7	Matt Peleszok		17.10.81	1	Stafford	17	May
	50.82			3	Solihull	24	May
(30)							
50.9	Neil Palmer		1.10.81	4	Birmingham	21	Jun
50.94	Gary Carr		24.09.82	3	Edinburgh	19	Jun
51.00	Adam Rogers		10.04.83	3	York	25	Jul
51.0	Ben Caldwell		3.03.82	1	Cleckheaton	8	Aug

Additional Under 15 (1 - 2 above)

51.67	Jonathon Hall		18.11.83	2	Edinburgh	20	Jun
51.86	Daniel Petros		8.08.85	2	Sheffield	15	Aug
51.86	Martin Davolls		9.04.85	1	Birmingham	6	Sep
52.0	Liam Frost		13.05.84	1	Nottingham	24	Jun
	52.40			3	Exeter	11	Jul
52.4	Philip Duggleby		20.09.83	1	Stretford	4	Aug
	52.86			2s1	Exeter	10	Jul
52.76 i	Neil Simpson		11.09.83	2	Birmingham	21	Feb

52.8	Lee Whitehead	7.03.84	1	Bury	7	Jun
	52.96		3s2	Exeter	10	Jul
52.87	Stephen Gill	25.09.84	2h2	Exeter	10	Jul
(10)						
52.9	Mark Holloway	6.10.83	1	Bracknell	19	Jul
53.0	T. Gallagher		1	Bury St. Edmonds	13	Jun
53.0	Andrew Pearce	13.10.83	1	Jarrow	20	Jun
	53.04		3h1	Exeter	10	Jul
53.01	Ben Ottaway	4.01.84	2h1	Exeter	10	Jul
53.01	Adam Davies	27.07.84	3	Glasgow	30	Aug
53.04	Chris Stoves	20.02.84	4	Glasgow	30	Aug
53.17	Brett Hipkiss	3.12.83	1h3	Exeter	10	Jul
53.2	Simon Rees	23.01.84	2	Stockport	19	Jul
53.21	Denee De Emmony		1	London (He)	30	Aug
53.30	Eddie Bailey	14.02.84	3	Birmingham	6	Sep
(20)						
53.48	Ricky Preston	18.09.83	2	York	25	Jul
53.52	Fajo Onibuje	25.09.83	4s1	Exeter	10	Jul
53.54	Liam McGowan	27.01.84	4h1	Exeter	10	Jul
53.56	John Wells	19.04.84	5s1	Exeter	10	Jul
53.6	Robert Smith	25.01.84	1	Southampton	11	Aug
53.6	Graham Blackman	25.03.85	1	Nottingham	23	Aug
53.6	David Lewis	27.01.84	1	Mansfield	11	Sep

Under 13

58.0	James Dunford	14.01.86	1	Watford	23	Sep
58.2	Bob Thanda	22.09.85	1	Stevenage	31	May

Foreign

48.05	*Robert Fanning (IRE)*	*U23*	*31.10.78*	*2h4*	*Bedford*	*24*	*May*
48.3	*Kamel Talhaoui (ALG)*		*18.03.71*	*1*	*Watford*	*6*	*Jun*

600 METRES

1:17.8	Andy Hart	13.09.69	1	Watford	10	Jun

Under 17

1:22.9	Jonathan Simpson	27.05.82	1	Grangemouth	3	Jun
1:23.0	Andrew Fulford	23.06.82	1	Swindon	19	Apr

800 METRES

1:45.71	Andy Hart	13.09.69	5	Kuala Lumpur, MAL	19	Sep
	1:46.19		3	St. Petersburg, RUS	28	Jun
	1:46.77		7	Sheffield	2	Aug
	1:47.0		3	London (BP)	14	Jun
	1:47.0		1	London (TB)	8	Aug
	1:47.13		1	Solihull	5	Sep
	1:47.34		4s1	Kuala Lumpur, MAL	18	Sep
	1:47.74		5	Gateshead	19	Jul
	1:47.90		4h1	Budapest, HUN	21	Aug
	1:48.70		1h3	Kuala Lumpur, MAL	17	Sep
1:46.86	Bradley Donkin	6.12.71	6	Kuala Lumpur, MAL	19	Sep
	1:47.5		3	London (TB)	8	Aug
	1:47.65		4s2	Kuala Lumpur, MAL	18	Sep
	1:48.3		1	Watford	5	Aug
	1:48.32		2h2	Kuala Lumpur, MAL	17	Sep
	1:48.94 i		4	Birmingham	8	Feb
1:47.48	Jason Lobo	18.09.69	8	Sheffield	2	Aug
	1:47.74		4	Gateshead	19	Jul
	1:47.96		6s2	Kuala Lumpur, MAL	18	Sep

(Lobo)	1:48.21			4	Nivelles, BEL	9 Aug
	1:48.23			3h1	Kuala Lumpur, MAL	17 Sep
	1:48.41			1h2	Birmingham	25 Jul
	1:48.72			2	Jambes, BEL	7 Aug
1:47.5	Anthony Whiteman		13.11.71	4	London (BP)	14 Jun
	1:48.4			1	Cardiff	6 Jun
1:47.69	Simon Lees	U20	19.11.79	2	Solihull	5 Sep
	1:48.03			1	Solihull	24 May
	1:48.88			3	Manchester	3 Jun
1:47.8	John Mayock		26.10.70	5	London (BP)	14 Jun
1:47.85	Grant Graham		27.12.72	10	Sheffield	2 Aug
	1:48.13			1	Edinburgh	18 Jul
	1:48.94			1h3	Birmingham	25 Jul
1:47.91	Paul Walker		2.12.73	1h1	Birmingham	25 Jul
	1:48.53			1rB	Sydney, AUS	28 Feb
	1:48.68			3	Celle Ligure, ITA	25 Jun
	1:48.82			2	Edinburgh	18 Jul
	1:48.85			1	Edinburgh	4 Jul
1:48.28	Matthew Yates		4.02.69	9	Lisbon, POR	20 Jun
1:48.31	Phillip Tulba		20.09.73	6rB	Oslo, NOR	9 Jul
	1:48.43			2	Cardiff	15 Jul
	1:48.71			1	Swindon	24 Jun
1:48.33	(10) Matt Shone		10.07.75	2h1	Birmingham	25 Jul
	1:48.39			3	Solihull	5 Sep
	1:48.6			2	Watford	5 Aug
1:48.43	Chris Moss	U20	17.06.79	4	Solihull	5 Sep
	1:48.77			6	Annecy, FRA	31 Aug
1:48.5	Kevin McKay		9.02.69	8	London (BP)	14 Jun
	1:48.86			2	Manchester	3 Jun
1:48.51	Eddie King		26.11.75	3	Cardiff	15 Jul
	1:48.95			1	Tonsberg, NOR	20 Jun
1:48.6	Alasdair Donaldson	U23	21.06.77	1	Loughborough	9 Jul
1:48.68	Vince Wilson		1.04.73	7	Gateshead	19 Jul
1:48.99	Noel Edwards		16.12.72	2h2	Birmingham	25 Jul
	53 performances to 1:49.00 by 17 athletes including 1 indoors					
1:49.0	Mark Griffin		16.02.75	1rB	London (BP)	14 Jun
1:49.05	Craig Winrow		22.12.71	2	Swindon	24 Jun
1:49.1	Dominic Hall		21.02.71	2rB	London (BP)	14 Jun
1:49.13	(20) Andy Young	U23	20.06.77	3	Swindon	24 Jun
1:49.20	Dave Locker		28.03.75		, USA	
1:49.33	Richard Girvan	U23	26.07.76	3h5	Kuala Lumpur, MAL	17 Sep
1:49.51	Stuart Bailey	U23	6.08.78	4h1	Birmingham	25 Jul
1:49.57	Neil Kirk	U23	14.09.78	4h2	Birmingham	25 Jul
1:49.6	Tony Draper		23.04.74	2	Cardiff	6 Jun
1:49.67	Jason Dupuy		31.01.71	2h3	Birmingham	25 Jul
1:49.68	Peter Hackley		19.02.71	5h1	Birmingham	25 Jul
1:49.7	Justin Swift-Smith		28.08.74	10	London (BP)	14 Jun
1:49.71	Robin Hooton		5.05.73	1rB	Swindon	24 Jun
1:49.8	(30) Grant Cuddy	U23	6.01.77	11	London (BP)	14 Jun
1:49.8	Tony Thompson	U23	9.11.77	1rB	Watford	5 Aug
1:49.81	David Stanley	U20	16.01.79	6h1	Birmingham	25 Jul
1:50.02	James Mayo		24.02.75	3rB	Swindon	24 Jun
1:50.2	Joe Mills		9.07.72	8	Utrecht, HOL	29 Aug
1:50.46	Neil Speaight	U23	9.09.78	5	Loughborough	17 May
1:50.6	Michael Openshaw		8.04.72	2	Stretford	14 Jul
1:50.62	David Bullock		18.12.74	4rB	Solihull	5 Sep
1:50.65	Simon Bullock	U20	22.11.80	2	Solihull	24 May
1:50.77	Terry Feasey	U23	5.08.77	6rB	Solihull	5 Sep

1:50.8	Andi Knight		26.10.68	6rB	London (BP)	14	Jun
1:50.8	David Thornton		27.07.73	3	Stretford	18	Aug
1:50.8	Mick Morris		16.07.74	.2	Gateshead	29	Aug
1:50.81	Ian Campbell		6.09.71	2rB	Prague, CZE	8	Jun
1:50.82 i	Andrew Blackmore	U23	12.07.76	2	Fort Worth, USA	21	Feb
	short track ?						
1:50.82	Mark Wiscombe		25.01.74	8r3	Tessenderlo, BEL	30	Aug
1:50.83	Ian Scott	U20	27.10.79	4	Sacramento, USA	13	Jun
1:50.9	Rob Scanlon		13.04.74	4	Stretford	18	Aug
1:51.05	Garth Watson		20.04.73	2rB	Birmingham	6	Jun
1:51.27	Rupert Waters		3.01.72	1rC	Swindon	24	Jun
	(50)						
1:51.28	Steve Rees-Jones		24.12.74	5rB	Manchester	3	Jun
1:51.30	Matthew Morris		5.04.75	8	Loughborough	17	May
1:51.30	Michael Combe	U23	24.12.78	3rB	Birmingham	6	Jun
1:51.3	Neil Caddy		18.03.75	1	Exeter	9	Aug
1:51.36	John Rogers		30.07.73	6	Dublin (S), IRE	26	Jul
1:51.40	Ross Fittall	U20	4.09.79	9r3	Tessenderlo, BEL	30	Aug
1:51.4	Neil Beasley		28.09.73	1	Bedford	10	May
1:51.41	Paul Fisher	U20	17.05.79	1	Bedford	14	Jun
1:51.43	James Tonner		3.06.75	6	Edinburgh	18	Jul
1:51.44	Tom Mayo	U23	2.05.77	2rC	Swindon	24	Jun
	(60)						
1:51.6	Andrew Prophett		10.06.74	1	Stoke	16	May
1:51.6	Christian Stephenson		22.07.74	2rB	Cardiff	6	Jun
1:51.6	Tom Ranger	U23	20.11.77	4	Jarrow	27	Jun
1:51.65	Eddie Williams		1.10.70	2r2	Edinburgh	4	Jul
1:51.7	Jon McCallum		19.11.75	1rC	Watford	5	Aug
1:51.80	Keri Idessane		1.12.69	5rB	Birmingham	6	Jun
1:51.84 i	Adam Mole		31.08.75	3h2	Birmingham	7	Feb
1:51.9	Stuart Austin	U20	21.03.79	3rB	Cardiff	6	Jun
1:51.9	Paul Gilbert	U20	21.06.81	2rC	Watford	5	Aug
1:51.94	Andrew Walling		3.04.73	3rC	Manchester	3	Jun
	(70)						
1:52.04	Paul Burgess		10.11.70	4rC	Manchester	3	Jun
1:52.1	Paul Roberts		24.12.69	3	Enfield	16	May
1:52.1	Terry West		19.11.68	1	Middlesbrough	6	Jun
1:52.1	Steve Kneller		9.11.71	1	Watford	24	Jun
1:52.2	Steve Lowe	U23	10.01.76	1rB	Stretford	19	May
1:52.21	Matt Kloiber		22.11.71	10rB	Swindon	24	Jun
1:52.24	Andy Keith		25.12.71	5	Dedham, USA	23	May
1:52.24	Andrew Graffin	U23	20.12.77	2rB	Cardiff	15	Jul
1:52.3	Gareth Beard	U20	28.02.79	1	Birmingham (Un)	6	Jun
1:52.3	Martin Airey		28.10.70	5	Watford	26	Aug
	(80)						
1:52.32	Chris Bolt	U20	21.09.80	11r3	Tessenderlo, BEL	30	Aug
1:52.36	James Parker	U20	28.10.79	9	Loughborough	17	May
1:52.4	Alan Tatham	U23	29.04.76	2	Loughborough	13	May
1:52.4	Louis Wells	U23	6.02.78	1	Enfield	6	Jun
1:52.4	Dean Clark		20.12.73	4	Watford	1	Jul
1:52.4	Gavin Thompson	U20	9.04.80	1	Crawley	12	Jul
1:52.5	Jonathan Burrell		24.11.75	2	Stoke	16	May
1:52.5	Gavin Maley	U23	19.05.78	1r2	Sheffield (W)	16	May
1:52.5	Paul Causey		15.01.68	7	Stretford	14	Jul
1:52.5	Marcus Bridges		18.03.71	2rD	Watford	5	Aug
	(90)						
1:52.5	Michael Skinner	U20	21.11.79	1	Brighton	19	Aug
1:52.60	Clive Gilby		24.02.66	4	Watford	21	Jun
1:52.6	Nick Davy		26.12.74	2	Enfield	6	Jun
1:52.6	Brad Glenton		2.11.69	3	London (Elt)	4	Jul
1:52.6	Chris Livesey	U20	8.08.80	8	Stretford	18	Aug

163

1:52.66	Kevin Corr	U20	17.04.79	1	Cudworth	1 Aug
1:52.7	Kriss Haggerty	U23	2.12.76	1	Bracknell	10 May
1:52.7	Ian Tinsley	U20	23.01.81	1	Bebington	10 May
1:52.7	Michael East	U23	20.01.78	1	Hayes	6 Jun
1:52.7	Tatum Johnson	U23	20.10.76	4	Cardiff	6 Jun
	(100)					
1:52.7	Andrew Brown	U23	17.06.77	6rC	Watford	5 Aug
1:52.7	Steven Neill		11.08.66	1rB	Stretford	18 Aug
1:52.7	Brendan Smith	U23	20.07.77	9	Stretford	18 Aug
1:52.7	Matt Davies		23.07.71	6	Watford	26 Aug
1:52.73	Paul Cooper		30.01.75	3r2	London (He)	8 Aug
1:52.8	Matthew Lawson		22.07.71	2rB	Watford	1 Jul
1:52.8	Steve Sharpe		31.12.75	6	Watford	1 Jul
1:52.9	Matt Hibberd		23.06.73	3	Loughborough	13 May
1:52.9	Gavin MacPherson	U23	17.09.77	2rB	Stretford	19 May
1:52.9	Chris Mulvaney	U20	25.05.81	1	Stretford	1 Sep
	(110)					
1:53.0	Roger Morley	U23	20.09.77	3rD	Watford	5 Aug

Additional Under 20 (1 - 18 above)

1:53.1	Brian Stopher	U20	8.04.80	4rD	Watford	5 Aug
1:53.1	Jon Stewart	U20	22.05.80	2rB	Stretford	18 Aug
	(20)					
1:53.2	Paul Morby		15.01.79	1	Leamington	9 May
1:53.4	Stephen Holmes		17.10.80	8rD	Watford	5 Aug
1:53.5	David Gow		9.02.79	1	Antrim	23 Jun
1:53.66	Richard Sinclair		25.06.79	4	Solihull	24 May
1:53.80	Nathan Dosanjh		13.02.79	2rC	Cardiff	15 Jul
1:53.8	Chris Thompson		17.04.81	2	Stretford	28 Apr
1:53.8	Mark Best		9.09.79	4	Street	4 May
1:53.86	Simon Eyre		30.10.80	1	London (Ha)	24 May
1:53.95	Andrew Fulford	U17	23.06.82	6rC	Swindon	24 Jun
1:53.97	Dafydd Solomon/Clarke		18.09.79	2rE	Solihull	5 Sep
	(30)					
1:54.0	Nic Andrews	U17	3.10.81	1	Ayr	18 Jul
1:54.0	Rob Jefferies		4.10.79	1	Derby	8 Aug
1:54.01	Raymond Adams	U17	5.11.81	6	Belfast	26 Aug
1:54.30	Stuart Reid			5rD	Manchester	3 Jun
1:54.3	Will Barry		4.09.79	4rB	Stretford	14 Jul
1:54.4	Simon Burton		23.04.79	6rC	London (BP)	14 Jun
1:54.5	Richard Blagrove	U17	29.12.81	1	Stretford	29 Apr
1:54.8	Steven Frost	U17	12.12.81	3	Ayr	18 Jul
1:54.8	Glenn Parsons		5.04.80	1	Hemel Hempstead	5 Aug
1:54.8	Craig Houston		9.07.80	1rB	Jarrow	22 Aug
	(40)					
1:54.88	Andrew Evans		2.10.80	5	Solihull	24 May
1:54.93	Andrew Ingle		19.02.80	3	London (Ha)	24 May
1:54.98	Barry Woodward		20.11.80	6	Solihull	24 May
1:55.0	Jamie Hendry		12.05.79	2	Glasgow	11 Aug

Additional Under 17 (1 - 5 above)

1:55.1	Joe Collins		28.05.82	1	Watford	24 Jun
1:55.1	Matt Thomson		20.09.81	4rE	Watford	5 Aug
1:55.1	David Moulton		7.09.81	2	Watford	23 Sep
1:55.21	Aaron McIndoe		15.05.82	1	Edinburgh	20 Jun
1:55.6	Alasdair McLean-Foreman		10.11.81	9	Street	4 May
	(10)					
1:55.73	Andrew Sherman		28.09.81	4rD	Swindon	24 Jun
1:56.6	Michael Coulthard		28.12.82	1	Carlisle	13 Jun
1:56.7	Richard Ward		5.05.82	5	Carshalton	20 Sep
1:57.1	Nick McCormick		11.09.81	1	Gateshead	13 Jun
1:57.31	Peter Bridger		6.09.81	4	London (Ha)	24 May
1:57.4	Andrew Baddeley		20.06.82	1	Bebington	17 Jun

1:57.5	Ryan Preddy	U15	30.01.84	1	Hereford	7	Jun
1:57.55	Malcolm Hassan		27.11.82	1	Leeds	23	May
1:57.56	Colin Joyce		21.10.81	1h3	London (Ha)	23	May
1:57.6	Stephen Bates		5.11.81	1	Rotherham	21	Jun
(20)							
1:57.8	Ketan Desai		1.12.82	1h3	Exeter	10	Jul
1:58.0	Daniel Coleman		5.07.82	1	Derby	7	Jun
1:58.0	Graham Nichol		11.01.82	1	Belfast	16	Aug
1:58.4	Matthew Simpkins		9.05.82	1	Corby	15	Aug

Under 15 (1 above)

1:59.92	Chris Stoves		20.02.84	1	Cudworth	1	Aug
2:01.1	Daniel Bothwick		22.02.84	1	Bath	12	Aug
2:01.8	Alex Spencer		25.10.83	1	Stretford	18	Aug
2:02.90	Oliver Barrett		25.12.84	1	Enfield	30	Aug
2:03.01	Richard Dowse		3.01.85	3	Cudworth	1	Aug
2:03.48	Tom Bolton		24.11.83	5r7	Solihull	5	Sep
2:03.5	David Lewis		27.01.84		Rotherham	9	Aug
2:04.0	S. Marriott			2	Stretford	18	Aug
2:04.17	Adam Davies		27.07.84	3	Exeter	11	Jul
(10)							
2:04.3	Andrew Jenner		2.02.84	1	Kingston	20	Jun
2:04.3	Robert Tobin		20.12.83	2	Kingston	20	Jun
2:04.34	Ian Munro		5.09.83	1	Grangemouth	23	Aug
2:04.39	Eddie Bailey		14.02.84	2	Birmingham	6	Sep
2:05.0	Kirk Lee		17.07.84	2	Blackpool	13	Jun
2:05.28	Craig Kelly		20.03.84	5s2	Exeter	10	Jul
2:05.37	Jospeh Godsell		27.10.83	2h1	Sheffield	16	Aug
2:05.51 i	Chris Bodys		29.12.83	1	Glasgow	8	Feb
2:05.64	Gavin Page		25.06.84	3h3	Exeter	10	Jul
2:05.73	Robin MacIntosh		2.03.85	2	Grangemouth	23	Aug
(20)							
2:05.8	Morton Agnew		07.84		Tullamore, IRE	12	Jul
2:05.85	Simon Manning		9.08.84	3	York	25	Jul
2:05.86	Craig Farrar		11.10.83	2s1	Exeter	10	Jul

unconfirmed

| 2:01.7 | Paul Brown | | 8.10.83 | 1 | Loughborough | 9 | May |

Under 13

2:11.3	Ahmed Ali		31.03.86	1	London (WF)	10	May
2:11.8	Michael Smart		18.11.85	1	Worthing	9	Aug
2:14.6	Bob Thanda		22.09.85	1	Watford	8	Jul
2:15.6	Michael Hall-Evans		14.03.86	1	Tamworth	19	Jul
2:16.6	Paul Lipman		2.09.85	1	Welwyn	31	Aug

Foreign

1:45.32	*James McIlroy (IRE)*	*U23*	*30.12.76*	*4*	*Nice, FRA*	*16*	*Jul*
1:49.64	*Colm McLean (IRE)*	*U20*	*7.06.80*	*5*	*Tallinn, EST*	*19*	*Jun*
1:49.9	*Des English (IRE)*		*6.06.67*			*30*	*Aug*
1:50.65	*Gareth Turnbull (IRE)*	*U20*	*14.05.79*	*3*	*Belfast*	*26*	*Aug*
1:52.4	*Cor Datema (HOL)*		*19.09.71*	*4*	*Watford*	*4*	*Jul*
1:52.60	*Pat Davoren (IRE)*		*13.03.72*	*1*	*Crawley*	*9*	*May*
1:53.1	*Conor Sweeney (IRE)*	*U17*	*28.12.81*		*Dublin (S), IRE*		*Jun*

1000 METRES

2:18.82	Anthony Whiteman		13.11.71	2	Jena, GER	24	May
2:20.41	Grant Graham		27.12.72	10	Stockholm, SWE	5	Aug
2:20.9	Jason Lobo		18.09.69	1	Stretford	18	Aug
2:21.8	Kevin McKay		9.02.69	2	Stretford	18	Aug
2:22.33	Andy Hart		13.09.69	3	Hamilton, NZ	18	Feb
2:22.4	Bradley Donkin		6.12.71	3	Stretford	18	Aug
2:22.7	Matt Dixon	U23	26.12.78	4	Stretford	18	Aug

1500 METRES

3:32.69	Anthony Whiteman	13.11.71	7	Zurich, SWZ	12	Aug
3:35.30			4	Nuremberg, GER	10	Jul
3:36.78			4	Bellinzona, SWZ	1	Jul
3:39.52			2	Birmingham	26	Jul
3:40.70			3	Kuala Lumpur, MAL	21	Sep
3:40.99 A			3	Johannesburg, RSA	12	Sep
3:41.7 +e			1m	Brussels, BEL	28	Aug
3:41.71			3h1	Budapest, HUN	18	Aug
3:42.27			4	Budapest, HUN	20	Aug
3:32.82	John Mayock	26.10.70	10	Monaco, MON	8	Aug
3:33.90			6	Brussels, BEL	28	Aug
3:34.60			9	Moscow, RUS	5	Sep
3:34.71			6	Oslo, NOR	9	Jul
3:36.74			10	Rome, ITA	14	Jul
3:37.05			7	St. Denis, FRA	4	Jun
3:39.37 i			5	Stockholm, SWE	19	Feb
3:39.38			1	Birmingham	26	Jul
3:39.49 +			2m	Bratislava, SVK	9	Jun
3:40.08 i			8	Lievin, FRA	22	Feb
3:40.46			2	Kuala Lumpur, MAL	21	Sep
3:41.68			1h1	Birmingham	25	Jul
3:41.69			2h1	Budapest, HUN	18	Aug
3:42.58			5	Budapest, HUN	20	Aug
3:37.04	Matthew Yates	4.02.69	12	Berlin, GER	1	Sep
3:38.36			7	Hechtel, BEL	1	Aug
3:38.97			3h2	Budapest, HUN	18	Aug
3:39.5			2	Watford	5	Aug
3:40.38			3	Birmingham	26	Jul
3:40.78			5	Barakaldo, SPA	1	Jul
3:42.61			2	Monzon, SPA	8	Aug
3:42.63			6	Budapest, HUN	20	Aug
3:43.33			2h1	Birmingham	25	Jul
3:37.22	Kevin McKay	9.02.69	4	Hengelo, HOL	1	Jun
3:40.78			4	Birmingham	26	Jul
3:43.22			5	Kuala Lumpur, MAL	21	Sep
3:39.64	Spencer Barden	31.03.73	2	Barcelona, SPA	17	Jun
3:39.7	Michael Openshaw	8.04.72	3	London (BP)	14	Jun
3:40.18			3	Rhede, GER	19	Jun
3:39.89	Neil Caddy	18.03.75	2	Rhede, GER	19	Jun
3:40.9			5	London (BP)	14	Jun
3:42.34			3	Cardiff	4	Aug
3:42.66			1	Manchester	3	Jun
3:40.8	Gary Lough	6.07.70	3	Watford	5	Aug
3:43.33			5	Cardiff	4	Aug
3:41.2	Tom Mayo U23	2.05.77	4	Watford	5	Aug
3:42.33			16	Rieti, ITA	30	Aug
3:41.5	Grant Graham	27.12.72	6	London (BP)	14	Jun
	(10)					
3:41.9	Brad Glenton	2.11.69	5	Watford	5	Aug
3:42.3	Phillip Tulba	20.09.73	8	London (BP)	14	Jun
3:42.96			8	Cork, IRE	27	Jun
3:42.55	Andy Hart	13.09.69	1	Swindon	24	Jun

51 performances to 3:43.50 by 13 athletes including 2 indoors

3:43.5	Terry Feasey U23	5.08.77	7	Watford	5	Aug
3:43.66	Steve Sharp	31.12.75	3	Swindon	24	Jun
3:43.82	Jon McCallum	19.11.75	4h1	Birmingham	25	Jul
3:43.85	Christian Stephenson	22.07.74	2	Cardiff	15	Jul
3:44.06	Ian Grime	29.09.70	6	Birmingham	26	Jul
3:44.3	Steve Green	18.02.71	10	London (BP)	14	Jun

166

3:44.63	Vince Wilson		1.04.73	7	Birmingham	26 Jul
	(20)					
3:44.78	Stuart Poore		30.12.72	3	Cardiff	15 Jul
3:44.79	Rob Scanlon		13.04.74	5	Swindon	24 Jun
3:44.86	Michael East	U23	20.01.78	6	Swindon	24 Jun
3:44.87	Christian Nicolson		19.09.73	5	Fayetteville, USA	18 Apr
3:45.3	Andrew Graffin	U23	20.12.77	2rB	Watford	5 Aug
3:45.32	Terry West		19.11.68	2	Loughborough	17 May
3:45.4	Joe Mills		9.07.72	1rB	London (BP)	14 Jun
3:45.43	David Bullock		18.12.74	4	Loughborough	17 May
3:45.6	Stuart Bailey	U23	6.08.78	1	Stretford	1 Sep
3:45.69	Rod Finch		5.08.67	4	Manchester	3 Jun
	(30)					
3:45.7	Andy Keith		25.12.71	5	Dedham, USA	13 Jun
3:45.7	Jon Stewart	U20	22.05.80	2	Stretford	1 Sep
3:45.8	James Thie	U23	27.06.78	4rB	Watford	5 Aug
3:45.90	Matt Dixon	U23	26.12.78	5	Cardiff	15 Jul
3:45.92	Mark Griffin		16.02.75	9	Cape Town, RSA	20 Mar
3:46.1	Steven Neill		11.08.66	11	Watford	5 Aug
3:46.11	Ian Gillespie		18.05.70	1rB	Birmingham	6 Jun
3:46.21	Justin Swift-Smith		28.08.74	1rB	Loughborough	17 May
3:46.21	John Nuttall		11.01.67	2rB	Loughborough	17 May
3:46.37	Eddie King		26.11.75	1	Belfast	27 Jun
	(40)					
3:46.4	Brendan Smith	U23	20.07.77	3	Stretford	1 Sep
3:46.5	Julian Moorhouse		13.11.71	3rB	London (BP)	14 Jun
3:46.5	Matt Davies		23.07.71	6rB	Watford	5 Aug
3:46.5	Chris Livesey	U20	8.08.80	5rB	Watford	5 Aug
3:46.8	Nick Comerford		23.04.66	2	Cwmbran	20 Jun
3:46.8	Andy Renfree		18.05.75	8rB	Watford	5 Aug
3:47.0	Chris Thompson	U20	17.04.81	9rB	Watford	5 Aug
3:47.07	Chris Bolt	U20	21.09.80	11	Cardiff	15 Jul
3:47.24	Darius Burrows		8.08.75	5rB	Loughborough	17 May
3:47.24	Paul Fisher	U20	17.05.79	1	London (He)	30 Aug
	(50)					
3:47.36	Paul Morby	U20	15.01.79	6	Loughborough	17 May
3:47.42	Keith Cullen		13.06.72	12	Swindon	24 Jun
3:47.48	James Ellis-Smith		11.09.72	6rB	Loughborough	17 May
3:47.5	Mick Morris		16.07.74	1	Stretford	4 Aug
3:47.5	Sam Illidge	U23	4.02.77	5	Stretford	1 Sep
3:47.63	Karl Keska		7.05.72	1	London (He)	8 Aug
3:47.65 i	Ian Campbell		6.09.71	4	Ghent, BEL	1 Feb
	3:49.09			8rB	Loughborough	17 May
3:47.82	Simon Lees	U20	19.11.79	8	Loughborough	17 May
3:48.00	Dominic Bannister		1.04.68	9	Loughborough	17 May
3:48.1	Mark Morgan		19.08.72	1	Watford	6 Jun
	(60)					
3:48.18	Jason Boothroyd		26.11.69	9	Berne, SWZ	13 Jun
3:48.2	Craig Wheeler	U23	14.06.76	3	Stretford	4 Aug
3:48.2	Lee Garrett	U23	2.09.78	10rB	Watford	5 Aug
3:48.3	Chris Moss	U20	17.06.79	1	Watford	9 Sep
3:48.5	Martin Airey		28.10.70	11rB	Watford	5 Aug
3:48.56	Alan Tatham	U23	29.04.76	10	Loughborough	17 May
3:48.78	Kevin Farrow		8.09.75	3	Columbia, USA	17 May
3:48.80	Kris Bowditch		14.01.75	1	San Luis Obispo, USA	22 Mar
3:48.8	Ben Whitby	U23	6.01.77	2	Watford	6 Jun
3:48.90	Jason Lobo		18.09.69	2	Bedford	29 Aug
	(70)					
3:48.92	Bruno Witchalls		22.03.75	7rB	Loughborough	17 May
3:48.92	Dermot Donnelly		23.09.70	2	Belfast	27 Jun
3:48.99	Phil Mowbray		19.03.73	3	London (He)	8 Aug

3:49.0 i	Tony Johnston		23.08.68	2	Birmingham	25	Jan
3:49.0	Allen Graffin	U23	20.12.77	1	Tonbridge	25	Jul
3:49.04	Rob Denmark		23.11.68	10	Manchester	3	Jun
3:49.18	Clive Gilby		24.02.66	3	Watford	16	May
3:49.26	Matthew Smith		26.12.74	1	Dedham, USA	9	May
3:49.30	Kim Critchley		15.07.73	11	Manchester	3	Jun
3:49.5	Clayton Bannon	U23	15.03.77	12rB	Watford	5	Aug
(80)							
3:49.52	Ben Reese	U23	29.03.76	3	Knoxville, USA	10	Apr
3:49.64	James Tonner		3.06.75	4	Watford	16	May
3:49.72	Richard Vint	U20	16.02.79	2	Alicante, SPA	18	Jul
3:50.1	Nigel Stirk		13.03.72	5	Loughborough	10	Jun
3:50.55	Eric Crowther		23.01.75	2rB	Swindon	24	Jun
3:50.59	Dave Locker		28.03.75	8	Knoxville, USA	10	Apr
3:50.6	James Trapmore		31.07.75	1	Watford	10	Jun
3:50.61	Peter Hackley		19.02.71	4	London (He)	8	Aug
3:51.04	Matthew Morris		5.04.75	3rB	Manchester	3	Jun
3:51.10	Michael James			5h2	Birmingham	25	Jul
(90)							
3:51.38	Richard Sinclair	U20	25.06.79	4rB	Manchester	3	Jun
3:51.48	David Stanley	U20	16.01.79	5	Watford	21	Jun
3:51.60 i	Alasdair Donaldson	U23	21.06.77	2h2	Birmingham	7	Feb
3:51.7	Paul Burgess		10.11.70	4	Cardiff	6	Jun
3:51.7	Matt Shone		10.07.75	1	Newport	8	Aug
3:51.8	Alistair Moses	U23	5.07.78	2	Watford	10	Jun
3:51.89	Scott Hughes	U23	20.11.78	5rB	Manchester	3	Jun
3:51.9	Mark Wiscombe		25.01.74	3	Watford	29	Apr
3:51.93	Stewart Reid		15.11.73	1	Edinburgh	9	May
3:52.3	Andrew Prophett		10.06.74	4	Watford	6	Jun

Additional Under 20 (1 - 11 above)

3:52.37	Gareth Price		27.11.79	1	London (He)	9	Aug
3:52.4	Michael Skinner		21.11.79	2rC	Watford	5	Aug
3:52.50	Nathan Dosanjh		13.02.79	4rB	Swindon	24	Jun
3:52.55	Chris Mulvaney		25.05.81	2	London (He)	9	Aug
3:52.7	Sam Haughian		9.07.79	2	Newport	8	Aug
3:53.6	Richard Ward	U17	5.05.82	2	London (TB)	19	Aug
3:53.62	Robert Maycock		21.02.81	7rB	Manchester	3	Jun
3:53.8	Angus Maclean		20.09.80	5	Cardiff	6	Jun
3:54.1	David Hibbert		31.01.79	1rB	Stretford	23	Jun
(20)							
3:54.3	Gavin Thompson		9.04.80	1	Crawley	24	Jun
3:54.57	Simon Burton		23.04.79	9rB	Manchester	3	Jun
3:55.2	Andrew Beckwith		22.04.79	10rC	Watford	5	Aug
3:55.54	Gareth Beard		28.02.79	12rB	Manchester	3	Jun
3:55.6	Brian Stopher		8.04.80	2rB	Watford	10	Jun

Additional Under 17 (1 above)

3:57.21	Raymond Adams		5.11.81	1	Sheffield	2	Aug
3:57.5	Lee McCash		22.10.81	4rB	Stretford	4	Aug
3:57.67	Mohammed Farah		13.03.83	2	Sheffield	2	Aug
3:58.24	Nick McCormick		11.09.81	1	York	25	Jul
3:58.30	Malcolm Hassan		27.11.82	2	York	25	Jul
3:58.41	Matt Thomson		20.09.81	2	Ayr	18	Jul
3:59.39	Richard King		5.04.82	1	Exeter	11	Jul
3:59.76	Matthew Simpkins		9.05.82	3	Exeter	11	Jul
3:59.99	Adam Bowden		5.08.82	1	Birmingham	6	Sep
(10)							
4:00.8	Mark Griffith		25.11.81	2rE	Watford	5	Aug
4:01.42	Stephen Bates		5.11.81	5	Exeter	11	Jul
4:01.5	Andrew Baddeley		20.06.82		Stretford	19	May

4:01.73	Andrew Sherman	28.09.81	2	London (Ha)	24 May
4:02.2	Anthony Waters	18.07.82	1	Aberdare	16 Aug
4:02.22	Alasdair McLean-Foreman	10.11.81	3	London (Ha)	24 May
4:02.4	Tom Hopkins	1.08.82	1	Crawley	24 Jun
4:02.56	Ian Boneham	30.09.82	3	York	25 Jul
4:02.8	Martyn Cryer	16.10.81	2	Blackpool	13 Jun
4:02.90	Gareth Suffling	13.11.81	4h2	Exeter	10 Jul
(20)					
4:03.2	Tom Carter	20.08.82	1	Stretford	18 Aug
4:03.43	Daniel Beynon	23.01.82	4	Ayr	18 Jul
4:03.67	Jamie Paterson	5.04.82	5	Ayr	18 Jul
4:04.14	Matthew Jones	10.10.82	3	Birmingham	6 Sep
4:04.91	Andrew Fulford	23.06.82	7	Sheffield	2 Aug
4:05.1	Andrew Mallows	18.01.82		Loughborough	10 Jun
4:05.14	Lee Browell	16.02.82	4	York	25 Jul
4:06.07	David Baldwin	17.03.82	4	Birmingham	6 Sep
4:06.45	Graham Nichol	11.01.82	1	Edinburgh	9 May
4:06.5	Edward Jackson	4.04.82	1	Harrow	30 Aug
(30)					
4:06.61	Chris Iddon	8.10.82	2	Cudworth	1 Aug
4:07.25	Ian Lawton	13.12.81	3	Cudworth	1 Aug
4:07.31	Nick Andrews	13.01.83	8	Sheffield	2 Aug
4:07.32	Lee Turner	30.06.82	7h2	Exeter	10 Jul
4:07.39	Steve Thompson	5.12.82	4	London (Ha)	24 May
4:07.4	Edward Prickett	28.01.83	1	Crawley	22 Jul
4:07.5	Aaron McIndoe	15.05.82	1	Grangemouth	13 Sep

Under 15

4:12.0	Tim Egerton	19.01.84	8	Stretford	23 Jun
4:12.1	Steven Ablitt	16.11.83	1	Ipswich	20 Jun
4:15.09	Tom Wade	31.12.83	2	York	25 Jul
4:16.1	Jonathan Graham	10.10.83	1	Jarrow	20 Jun
4:16.17	Amanuel Tshaye	5.11.83	2	Exeter	11 Jul
4:16.47	Phil Nicholls	29.09.83	1	Stoke	20 Jun
4:17.11	Chris Reynolds	23.01.85	4	Exeter	11 Jul
4:17.26	Terry Hawkey	6.01.84	5	Exeter	11 Jul
4:17.30	Colin Hawkins	23.03.84	6	Exeter	11 Jul
4:18.16	Stephen Enright	5.09.84	4	York	25 Jul
(10)					
4:19.1	Daniel Bothwick	22.02.84	1	Worcester	9 Jul
4:19.3	Joe Grant		1	Antrim	30 May
4:19.34	Rory Smith	12.12.84	5	York	25 Jul
4:19.46	Ian Carter	19.09.83	2	London (Ha)	24 May
4:20.0	Malcolm Riley	6.01.84	1	Watford	10 Jun
4:20.4	Thomas Bark	18.10.83	2	Corby	20 Jun
4:20.5	Tom Bolton	24.11.83	2	Basingstoke	31 May
4:20.84	Tom Holden	2.02.84	1h2	Solihull	23 May
4:21.29	Chris Davies	2.09.83	1	Cwmbran	21 Jun

Under 13

4:31.8	Ahmed Ali	31.03.86	1	Basildon	17 May
4:32.9	Michael Smart	18.11.85	1	Watford	29 Jul
4:35.3	Sam Hall		1	Watford	27 May
4:37.4	Tom Snow		2	Watford	26 Aug
4:38.6	James Horsman	27.09.85	3	Watford	26 Aug

Foreign

3:43.46	Colm McLean (IRE)	U20	7.06.80	10	Cork, IRE	27 Jun
3:43.99	Pat Davoren (IRE)		13.03.72	4	Swindon	24 Jun
3:45.0	Cor Datema (HOL)		19.09.71	1rB	Watford	5 Aug
3:46.00	James McIlroy (IRE)	U23	30.12.76	2	Dublin (S), IRE	3 May
3:47.62	Gareth Turnbull (IRE)	U20	14.05.79	7	Loughborough	17 May
3:57.44	Conor Sweeney (IRE)	U17	28.12.81	1	Tullamore, IRE	6 Jun

1 MILE

3:51.90	Anthony Whiteman		13.11.71	3	Nice, FRA	16	Jul
	3:52.09			3	Sheffield	2	Aug
	3:57.8 +			1m	Brussels, BEL	28	Aug
3:51.99	John Mayock		26.10.70	2	Sheffield	2	Aug
	3:53.72			7	Paris, FRA	29	Jul
	3:53.81			2	Bratislava, SVK	9	Jun
	3:54.8			1	Hexham	29	May
	3:56.88			2	Gateshead	19	Jul
3:57.2	Michael Openshaw		8.04.72	2	Hexham	29	May
3:57.58	Gary Lough		6.07.70	9	Sheffield	2	Aug
3:57.6	Ian Gillespie		18.05.70	1	Exeter	16	Jun
	4:01.84			1	Eugene, USA	15	May
3:58.49	Neil Caddy		18.03.75	4	Gateshead	19	Jul
	3:58.5			2	Exeter	16	Jun
	4:00.7			3	Bath	12	Aug
	4:01.6			1	Londonderry	4	Jul
3:58.5	Spencer Barden		31.03.73	3	Hexham	29	May
	3:59.86			8	Gateshead	19	Jul
	4:00.73			5	Solihull	5	Sep
3:58.52	Kevin McKay		9.02.69	5	Gateshead	19	Jul
3:58.80 i	Andy Keith		25.12.71	1	Boston, USA	14	Feb
3:59.7	Phillip Tulba		20.09.73	1	London (TB)	19	Aug
	(10)						
3:59.91	Darius Burrows		8.08.75	3	Solihull	5	Sep
4:00.02	Tom Mayo	U23	2.05.77	4	Solihull	5	Sep
4:01.7	Andy Hart		13.09.69	6	Bath	12	Aug
4:01.7	Christian Stephenson		22.07.74	7	Bath	12	Aug
	26 performances to 4:02.00 by 14 athletes including 1 indoors						
4:02.05	Andrew Graffin	U23	20.12.77	6	Solihull	5	Sep
4:02.1	Glen Stewart		7.12.70	4	Hexham	29	May
4:02.9	Steve Green		18.02.71	5	Hexham	29	May
4:03.0	Brad Glenton		2.11.69	8	Bath	12	Aug
4:03.2	Nick Comerford		23.04.66	9	Bath	12	Aug
4:03.3	Vince Wilson		1.04.73	6	Hexham	29	May
	(20)						
4:03.65	Matthew Yates		4.02.69	2	Glasgow (S)	30	Aug
4:03.9	James Thie	U23	27.06.78	11	Bath	12	Aug
4:04.0	Allen Graffin	U23	20.12.77	12	Bath	12	Aug
4:04.50	Rob Scanlon		13.04.74	7	Solihull	5	Sep
4:04.7	Christian Nicolson		19.09.73	4	Exeter	16	Jun
4:07.03 i	Matthew Smith		26.12.74	1	Boston, USA	23	Jan
4:07.32	Steven Neill		11.08.66	12	Solihull	5	Sep
4:07.39	Ian Grime		29.09.70	11	Sheffield	2	Aug
4:07.9	Ian Campbell		6.09.71	8	Hexham	29	May
4:08.3	Peter Hackley		19.02.71	9	Hexham	29	May
	(30)						
4:08.6	Terry Feasey	U23	5.08.77	2	London (TB)	19	Aug
4:08.70 i	Dave Locker		28.03.75	8	Indianapolis, USA	14	Feb
4:08.75	Brendan Smith	U23	20.07.77	15	Solihull	5	Sep
4:09.24	Julian Moorhouse		13.11.71	1rB	Solihull	5	Sep
4:09.33	Sam Haughian	U20	9.07.79	2rB	Solihull	5	Sep
4:09.96	Jason Dupuy		31.01.71	2	Bedford	25	May

Foreign

3:59.48	*James McIlroy (IRE)*	*U23*	*30.12.76*	*2*	*Solihull*	*5*	*Sep*
4:07.4	*Gareth Turnbull (IRE)*	*U20*	*14.05.79*	*7*	*Hexham*	*29*	*May*
4:08.08	*Pat Davoren (IRE)*		*13.03.72*	*13*	*Solihull*	*5*	*Sep*

3000 METRES

7:43.61	Anthony Whiteman		13.11.71	3	St. Petersburg, RUS	27	Jun
7:45.41	Jon Brown		27.02.71	5	Hechtel, BEL	1	Aug
7:47.43 i	John Mayock		26.10.70	4	Budapest, HUN	6	Feb
7:48.80 i				6	Stuttgart, GER	1	Feb
7:50.10 i				1	Sindelfingen, GER	8	Mar
7:55.09 i				1	Valencia, SPA	1	Mar
7:58.57 i				3h2	Valencia, SPA	27	Feb
7:48.76	Neil Caddy		18.03.75	6	Sheffield	2	Aug
7:50.04	Karl Keska		7.05.72	7	Sheffield	2	Aug
7:51.34	Ian Gillespie		18.05.70	6	Caorle, ITA	13	Jun
7:52.61 i				1	Roxbury, USA	20	Feb
7:53.79 i				6	New York, USA	13	Feb
7:55.50	Spencer Barden		31.03.73	8	Sheffield	2	Aug
7:56.12	Kris Bowditch		14.01.75	2	Cardiff	15	Jul
7:58.15 i	Matthew Smith		26.12.74	2	Boston, USA	14	Feb
7:59.89 i				6	Indianapolis, USA	14	Mar
8:08.36				9	Cardiff	15	Jul
7:58.92	Michael Openshaw		8.04.72	1	Manchester	3	Jun
	(10)						
7:59.07	Rod Finch		5.08.67	1	Rhede, GER	19	Jun
7:59.44	Julian Moorhouse		13.11.71	9	Sheffield	2	Aug
7:59.59	Jon Wild		30.08.73	3	Cardiff	15	Jul
7:59.6	Matthew Clarkson		25.01.66	1	Stretford	14	Jul
7:59.97	Phil Mowbray		19.03.73	2	Manchester	3	Jun
	22 performances to 8:00.00 by 15 athletes including 9 indoors						
8:00.37 i	Dave Taylor		9.01.64	1=	Birmingham	8	Feb
8:12.41				2=	Sheffield	16	Aug
8:00.38	Dermot Donnelly		23.09.70	3	Manchester	3	Jun
8:01.65	Nick Comerford		23.04.66	3	Cardiff	4	Aug
8:02.08 i	Andy Keith		25.12.71	3	Boston, USA	31	Jan
8:02.88	Stuart Poore		30.12.72	1	Swindon	24	Jun
	(20)						
8:03.22	Allen Graffin	U23	20.12.77	5	Cardiff	15	Jul
8:03.55	Spencer Newport		5.10.66	6	Cardiff	15	Jul
8:04.06	Darius Burrows		8.08.75	7	Rhede, GER	19	Jun
8:07.31	Ian Grime		29.09.70	5	Manchester	3	Jun
8:07.69	Glen Stewart		7.12.70	6	Manchester	3	Jun
8:08.06	Paul Green		7.04.72	7	Manchester	3	Jun
8:08.27	Glynn Tromans		17.03.69	4	Swindon	24	Jun
8:08.67 i	Rob Scanlon		13.04.74	5	Birmingham	8	Feb
8:08.92	David Miles		16.11.65	10	Cardiff	15	Jul
8:09.3	Mark Hudspith		19.01.69	1	Jarrow	27	Jul
	(30)						
8:09.65 i	Andy Wedlake		30.11.71	7	Boston, USA	31	Jan
8:11.90				7	Dedham, USA	23	May
8:10.20	Richard Taylor		5.12.73	5	Swindon	24	Jun
8:10.2	Steve Green		18.02.71	1	Stretford	19	May
8:10.64	Andy Coleman		29.09.74	11	Cardiff	15	Jul
8:11.22	Jim Campbell		17.06.70	8	Manchester	3	Jun
8:12.68	Mike Proudlove		26.01.70	10	Manchester	3	Jun
8:13.0	Craig Wheeler	U23	14.06.76	3	Stretford	14	Jul
8:13.1	Ian Hudspith		23.09.70	2	Jarrow	27	Jul
8:13.18	Eric Crowther		23.01.75	13	Manchester	3	Jun
8:13.28 i	Ben Whitby	U23	6.01.77	6	Birmingham	8	Feb
	(40)						
8:14.21 i	Darren Spawforth		1.08.69	3	Birmingham	25	Jan
8:14.6	Brad Glenton		2.11.69	2	Brighton	19	Aug
8:15.16	Matt O'Dowd	U23	13.04.76	6	Swindon	24	Jun
8:15.2	Carl Warren		28.09.69	4	Stretford	14	Jul

8:15.40	Andrew Graffin	U23	20.12.77	4	Sheffield	16	Aug
8:15.62 i	Phillip Tulba		20.09.73	4	Birmingham	25	Jan
8:15.83	Christian Nicolson		19.09.73		Fayetteville, USA	17	Apr
8:16.12	James Thie	U23	27.06.78	7	Swindon	24	Jun
8:16.4	Gary Lough		6.07.70	1	Loughborough	20	May
8:16.62	Adrian Marriott		24.09.72	8	Swindon	24	Jun
(50)							
8:16.9	Dave Tune		29.10.70	5	Stretford	14	Jul
8:16.91	Chris Thompson	U20	17.04.81	9	Swindon	24	Jun
8:17.10 i	Rob Whalley		11.02.68	5	Birmingham	25	Jan
8:17.3	Ian Mitchell	U23	10.03.76	6	Stretford	14	Jul
8:17.40	Richard Gardiner		11.06.73	12	Cardiff	15	Jul
8:17.62	Chris Davies	U23	19.10.76	9	Cardiff	4	Aug
8:18.2	Paul Freary		3.04.68	3	Stretford	19	May
8:18.6	Ben Reese	U23	29.03.76	1	Stretford	23	Jun
8:18.82 i	Ben Noad	U23	6.05.76	2	Boston, USA	28	Feb
8:18.98 i	Nathaniel Lane	U23	10.04.76	5	Ames, USA	28	Feb
(60)							
8:19.2	Michael East	U23	20.01.78	4	Brighton	19	Aug
8:19.22	Matthew Vaux-Harvey	U23	30.03.76	14	Cardiff	15	Jul
8:19.47	Mark Flint		19.02.63	15	Manchester	3	Jun
8:19.5	Chris Livesey	U20	8.08.80	4	Stretford	19	May
8:19.53	Dave Dudley		2.05.65	16	Manchester	3	Jun

Additional Under 20 (1 - 2 above)

8:25.52 i	Graeme Reid		14.04.79	1	Glasgow	25	Jan
	8:28.05			6rB	Manchester	3	Jun
8:27.05	Andrew Beckwith		22.04.79	4	Alicante, SPA	18	Jul
8:27.53	David Hibbert		31.01.79	1	Sheffield	15	Aug
8:29.1	Peter Riley		6.07.79	3	Stretford	28	Apr
8:29.92	Nick Mapp		18.03.79	2	Sheffield	15	Aug
8:31.22	Iain Murdoch		10.07.80	3	Sheffield	15	Aug
8:32.51	Stephen Hepples		6.01.80	4	Exeter	11	Jul
8:32.7	Paul Fisher		17.05.79	2	London (He)	9	Aug
(10)							
8:33.28	Matthew Watson		23.02.80	2	Cudworth	10	May
8:33.51	Mohammed Farah	U17	13.03.83	1	Ayr	18	Jul
8:33.9	Mark Brown		1.08.79	3	Gateshead	5	Aug
8:35.08	Daniel Dalmedo		14.03.80	11rB	Swindon	24	Jun
8:35.8	Michael Skinner		21.11.79	1	London (He)	23	Aug
8:36.48	Angus Maclean		20.09.80	12rB	Swindon	24	Jun
8:36.7	Alan Old		1.12.79	4	Gateshead	5	Aug

Additional Under 17 (1 above)

8:39.88	Richard Ward		5.05.82	2	Ayr	18	Jul
8:41.8	Martyn Cryer		16.10.81	1	Stretford	18	Aug
8:45.11	Lee McCash		22.10.81	1	Leeds	23	May
8:53.65	Stephen Bates		5.11.81	1	Derby	30	May
8:53.7	Richard Williams		22.10.81	1	Watford	27	May
8:54.58	Simon Stygall		20.09.82	3	Exeter	11	Jul
8:55.50	Matthew Jones		10.10.82	6	Bruges, BEL	23	Aug
8:55.83	Gareth Suffling		13.11.81	1	Enfield	1	Aug
8:56.09	Paul Arcari		10.10.82	1	Edinburgh	20	Jun
(10)							
8:56.15	Malcolm Hassan		27.11.82	1	Gateshead	9	May
8:56.3	Adam Bowden		5.08.82	1	Watford	24	Jun
8:56.4	Stephen Murphy		6.01.83	1	Watford	13	May
8:56.53	Craig Poole		28.03.83	2	Edinburgh	20	Jun
8:57.50	Andrew Baddeley		20.06.82	2	Leeds	23	May
8:57.5	Nicholas Goodliffe		12.05.82	5	Stretford	18	Aug
8:58.1	Edward Jackson		4.04.82	1	Watford	1	Jul

8:59.17	Mark Hood		6.09.81	1	Cudworth	1 Aug
8:59.3	Daniel Ledgerwood		24.03.83	1	London (He)	17 May
8:59.35	Sam Turner		3.03.82	4	Leeds	23 May
	(20)					
8:59.99	Kevin Pace		21.10.81	2	Gateshead	9 May
9:00.0	Ian Boneham		30.09.82	1	Birmingham	28 Jun
9:00.3	Bruce Raeside		2.12.81	1	Bingham	20 Jun
9:00.81	Dave Green		24.12.82	2	Stoke	20 Jun
9:01.20	Nick Andrews		13.01.83	3	Stoke	20 Jun
9:01.36	Kerr Johnstone		3.09.82	2	Derby	30 May
9:01.4	Russell Parrington		7.01.82	1	Stretford	4 Aug
9:01.6	Mark Harris		2.06.82	2	Bingham	20 Jun

Under 15

9:05.4	Colin Hawkins		23.03.84	2	Watford	23 Sep
9:12.72	Phil Nicholls		29.09.83	1	Derby	30 May
9:13.7	Tim Egerton		19.01.84		Stretford	1 Sep
9:17.60	Jonathan Graham		10.10.83	1	York	25 Jul
9:20.8	Gavin Page		25.06.84	1	Mansfield	7 Aug
9:21.5	Steven Ablitt		16.11.83	2	Mansfield	7 Aug
9:29.82	Robert Spencer		4.10.83	3	York	25 Jul
9:30.5	Michael Targatt		1.02.84	1	Watford	29 Jul
9:31.37	Chris Reynolds		23.01.85	1	Enfield	1 Aug
9:33.8	Neil Siner		27.01.84	1	Bebington	9 May
	(10)					
9:34.03	Terry Dymond		24.10.83	4	Derby	30 May
9:35.1	Tom Bedford		12.12.83	1	Norwich	28 Jun
9:35.67	Ray Edgar		15.05.84	4	York	25 Jul
9:35.98	Mohammed Osman		26.06.84	2	Enfield	1 Aug
9:37.28	Tom Bolton		24.11.83	3	Enfield	1 Aug
9:38.0	Glen Raggett		30.07.84	1	Brighton	19 Jul
9:38.3	James Henry		31.07.84	1	Stretford	4 Aug

Under 13

9:51.1	Sam Hall			1	Watford	23 Sep
9:51.7	James Horsman		27.09.85	2	Watford	23 Sep
10:07.9	Gary Harrison			1	Watford	12 Aug
10:21.0	Tom Snow			1	Woodford	20 May
10:26.1	Oliver Freeman		11.01.86	1	Kingston	26 Jul

Foreign

8:14.4	*Pat Davoren (IRE)*		*13.03.72*	*1*	*Brighton*	*19 Aug*
8:17.60	*David Burke (IRE)*		*68*	*14*	*Manchester*	*3 Jun*
8:18.0	*Andrew Colvin (AUS)*		*23.08.72*	*3*	*Brighton*	*19 Aug*

2 MILES

| 8:54.16 | John Mayock | | 26.10.70 | 1 | Glasgow (S) | 30 Aug |
| 8:54.43 | Neil Caddy | | 18.03.75 | 2 | Glasgow (S) | 30 Aug |

4000 METRES

11:03.2	Rob Whalley		11.02.68	1	Street	4 May
11:19.7	Martin Hula		2.01.66	2	Street	4 May
11:20.7	Michael East	U23	20.01.78	3	Street	4 May
11:21.6	Gavin Pavey		13.09.71	4	Street	4 May
11:22.6	Richard Gardiner		11.06.73	5	Street	4 May
11:24.8	Daniel Hyde	U23	5.10.77	6	Street	4 May
11:29.1	Andres Jones	U23	3.02.77	7	Street	4 May

5000 METRES

13:19.03	Jon Brown	27.02.71	12	Stockholm, SWE	5 Aug
13:41.72			2	Birmingham	25 Jul
13:22.31	Keith Cullen	13.06.72	9	Hechtel, BEL	1 Aug
13:31.07			8	Brussels, BEL	28 Aug
13:33.89			10	Nuremberg, GER	11 Jul
13:43.15			3	Birmingham	25 Jul
13:44.69			5	Kuala Lumpur, MAL	19 Sep
13:26.37	Karl Keska	7.05.72	1	Walnut, USA	18 Apr
13:33.67			9	Eugene, USA	31 May
13:40.24			4	Kuala Lumpur, MAL	19 Sep
13:41.61			1	Birmingham	25 Jul
13:42.58			9	Budapest, HUN	22 Aug
13:59.30			6	St. Petersburg, RUS	28 Jun
13:27.63	Dermot Donnelly	23.09.70	13	Hechtel, BEL	1 Aug
13:35.3			2	London (BP)	14 Jun
13:27.75	Rod Finch	5.08.67	14	Hechtel, BEL	1 Aug
13:41.44			6	Cork, IRE	27 Jun
13:49.46			5	Birmingham	25 Jul
13:52.94			1	Loughborough	17 May
13:28.57	Ian Gillespie	18.05.70	19	Rome, ITA	14 Jul
13:44.08			9	Lisbon, POR	20 Jun
13:51.24			6	Birmingham	25 Jul
13:36.24	Kris Bowditch	14.01.75	8	Walnut, USA	18 Apr
13:43.68			4	Birmingham	25 Jul
13:50.91			21	Hechtel, BEL	1 Aug
13:51.8			3	Watford	5 Aug
13:45.31	Spencer Barden	31.03.73	8	Cork, IRE	27 Jun
13:54.13			9	Birmingham	25 Jul
13:54.39			2	Loughborough	17 May
13:48.48	Rob Denmark	23.11.68	9	Cork, IRE	27 Jun
13:53.86			8	Birmingham	25 Jul
13:54.4			4	London (BP)	14 Jun
13:48.5	Julian Moorhouse	13.11.71	2	Watford	5 Aug
(10)					
13:52.4	Matthew Clarkson	25.01.66	4	Watford	5 Aug
13:56.15			10	Birmingham	25 Jul
13:52.7	Nick Comerford	23.04.66	3	London (BP)	14 Jun
13:53.55	Glen Stewart	7.12.70	11	Cork, IRE	27 Jun
13:53.59	Glynn Tromans	17.03.69	7	Birmingham	25 Jul
13:57.1	Jim Campbell	17.06.70	5	London (BP)	14 Jun
	39 performances to 14:00.00 by 15 athletes				
14:00.43	Christian Nicolson	19.09.73	16	Turku, FIN	1 Jul
14:01.5	Nick Weatheridge	11.10.72	5	Watford	5 Aug
14:02.41	Matthew Smith	26.12.74	8rB	Walnut, USA	17 Apr
14:02.41	Phil Mowbray	19.03.73	2	Solihull	5 Sep
14:04.13	Neil Caddy	18.03.75	13	Birmingham	25 Jul
(20)					
14:04.4	Gary Staines	3.07.63	7	Watford	5 Aug
14:05.11	Darius Burrows	8.08.75	14	Birmingham	25 Jul
14:05.45	Stuart Poore	30.12.72	3	Loughborough	17 May
14:06.73	Andrew Graffin U23	20.12.77	7	Loughborough	17 May
14:07.57	Spencer Newport	5.10.66	17	Birmingham	25 Jul
14:07.73	Rob Whalley	11.02.68	9	Loughborough	17 May
14:08.84	Ben Noad U23	6.05.76	6	Philadelphia, USA	23 Apr
14:09.50	Carl Thackery	14.10.62	11	Loughborough	17 May
14:10.21	David Miles	16.11.65	19	Birmingham	25 Jul
14:11.4	Ian Hudspith	23.09.70	1	Jarrow	15 Jul
(30)					
14:11.5	Mark Hudspith	19.01.69	2	Jarrow	15 Jul

174

14:12.17	Paul Taylor		9.01.66	1	Liverpool	20	Jun
14:12.83	Matt O'Dowd	U23	13.04.76	12	Loughborough	17	May
14:14.5	Adrian Marriott		24.09.72	12	Watford	5	Aug
14:17.2	Sam Haughian	U20	9.07.79	1	Southampton	11	Jul
14:18.00	Martin Palmer	U23	5.04.77	5	Solihull	5	Sep
14:18.2	Dale Laughlin		28.12.66	9	London (BP)	14	Jun
14:19	Andrew Pearson		14.09.71	3	Hexham	29	May
14:19	Adrian Passey		2.09.64	4	Hexham	29	May
14:19.13	Robert Quinn		10.12.65	2	Glasgow (S)	10	May
(40)							
14:19.68	Allen Graffin	U23	20.12.77	13	Loughborough	17	May
14:20.1	David Hibbert	U20	31.01.79	14	Watford	5	Aug
14:20.3	Richard Taylor		5.12.73	1	Rugby	14	Jun
14:21.1	Malcolm Price		18.06.62	3	Jarrow	15	Jul
14:21.14	Andy Wedlake		30.11.71	3	Dedham, USA	27	Jun
14:21.21	Chris Robison		16.03.61	3	Glasgow (S)	10	May
14:21.21	Kim Critchley		15.07.73	1	Edinburgh	4	Jul
14:21.5	Brad Glenton		2.11.69	2	Southampton	11	Jul
14:21.7	Steve Green		28.07.70	1	Bury	8	Aug
14:23.0	Martin Hula		2.01.66	16	Watford	5	Aug
(50)							
14:23.26	Ian Grime		29.09.70	17	Cork, IRE	27	Jun
14:24.07	Adrian Callan		28.11.62	4	Glasgow (S)	10	May
14:24.72	Paul Green		7.04.72	2	Edinburgh	4	Jul
14:26.7	Simon Wilkinson	U23	27.08.77	17	Watford	5	Aug
14:27.4	Mark Morgan		19.08.72	1	Stoke	16	May
14:27.7	Dan Leggate		5.10.74	18	Watford	5	Aug
14:27.82	Billy Jenkins		13.07.71	5	Glasgow (S)	10	May
14:29.0	Stuart Bell		29.07.67	9	Hexham	29	May
14:29.0	Andy Magnall		1.03.62	1	London (He)	6	Jun
14:29.1	Andres Jones	U23	3.02.77	1	Cwmbran	10	Jun
(60)							
14:29.4	Barry Royden		15.12.66	1	Hoo	14	Jun
14:29.46	Nathaniel Lane	U23	10.04.76	2	Knoxville, USA	10	Apr
14:29.8	Colin Moore		25.11.60	2	Bury	8	Aug
14:29.87	Jon Wild		30.08.73	22	Birmingham	25	Jul
14:30.4	Christian Stephenson		22.07.74	1	Watford	4	Jul
14:31.0	Brian Rushworth		14.12.62	10	Hexham	29	May
14:31.8	Ben Whitby	U23	6.01.77	1	Derby	4	Jul
14:31.87	Nick Francis		29.08.71	2	Edinburgh	4	Jul
14:32.4	Dave Tune		29.10.70	1	Enfield	6	Jun
14:32.6	Guy Amos		15.06.63	1	Norwich	13	May
(70)							
14:33.0	Andy Morgan-Lee		1.03.69	1	Stretford	18	Aug
14:33.3	Darren Hiscox		21.03.72	3	Cwmbran	10	Jun
14:33.3	Mark Flint		19.02.63	1	Cosford	3	Jul
14:33.3	Gary Nagel		4.06.62	4	Jarrow	15	Jul
14:33.56	Alaister Russell		17.06.68	3	Birmingham	6	Jun
14:33.9	Jerome Brooks		9.08.73	13	London (BP)	14	Jun
14:33.9	Ian Mitchell	U23	10.03.76	2	Stretford	18	Aug
14:34.1	Carl Warren		28.09.69	14	London (BP)	14	Jun
14:34.3	John Brown		2.02.69	1	Ormskirk	11	Jul
14:34.45	Nigel Stirk		13.03.72	16	Loughborough	17	May
(80)							
14:34.6	Lee Hurst		29.07.72	3	Stretford	18	Aug
14:35.0	Tommy Murray		18.05.61	11	Hexham	29	May
14:35.3	Adrian Mussett		14.04.72	1	Bury St. Edmonds	15	Aug
14:35.5	Matthew Vaux-Harvey	U23	30.03.76	17	Watford	5	Aug
14:35.7	Julian Emery		18.10.68	2	Exeter	16	Jun
14:35.9	Stephen Platts		12.03.66	20	Watford	5	Aug
14:36.10	Rob Birchall		14.06.70	3	Watford	16	May

14:36.8	Paul Freary		3.04.68	1	Stretford	2 May
14:37.4	Chris Knight		3.01.69	2	Hoo	14 Jun
14:37.5	Graeme Croll		1.02.66	1	Grangemouth	17 May
	(90)					
14:37.5	Chris Davies	U23	19.10.76	2	Derby	4 Jul
14:38.0	Billy Burns		13.12.69	12	Hexham	29 May
14:38.01	Dave Dudley		2.05.65	1	Bedford	25 May
14:38.44	Tony Duffy	V40	26.06.56	1	Blackburn	14 Jun
14:38.9	Terry Wall		12.06.70	5	Jarrow	15 Jul
14:39.1	Allan Adams		11.09.72	1	Glasgow	11 Aug
14:39.4	Richard Gardiner		11.06.73	1	Watford	4 Jul

Additional Under 20 (1 - 2 above)

14:40.40	Graeme Reid		14.04.79	6	Glasgow (S)	10 May
14:44.41	Chris Lindsey		11.02.79	3	Bath	3 May
14:51.60	Oliver Laws		18.03.80	1	Solihull	23 May
14:55.88	Andrew Beckwith		22.04.79	21	Loughborough	17 May
14:59.83	Peter Riley		6.07.79	1	Leeds	23 May
15:01.63	Stephen Hepples		6.01.80	4	Bedford	4 Jul
15:07.00	Nick Mapp		18.03.79	6	Bedford	4 Jul
15:07.42	Robert Maycock		21.02.81	6	Watford	16 May
	(10)					
15:13.5	Gary Blackman		24.09.80	3	Leamington	10 May
15:16.51	Daniel Dalmedo		14.03.80	8	Bedford	4 Jul
15:18.62	Daniel Rowen		30.12.79	2	Solihull	23 May
15:22.47	Glen Cornish		27.10.79	4	Leeds	23 May

Foreign

13:54.04	David Eadie (AUS)		21.12.70		Melbourne	13 Mar
14:12.7	Andrew Colvin (AUS)		23.08.72	11	Watford	5 Aug
14:15.6	John Burke (IRE)		18.05.70	13	Watford	5 Aug
14:17	Kassa Tadesse ETH)		21.08.74	2	Hexham	29 May
14:20.82	Hagai Chepkwony (KEN)		13.08.69	14	Loughborough	17 May
14:26.8	Svein Risa (NOR)		7.03.74	1	Exeter	16 Jun
14:31.5	Pamenos Ballantyne (STV)		9.12.73	12	London (BP)	14 Jun
14:32.62	Pat O'Keefe (IRE)		5.03.75	2	Birmingham	6 Jun
15:07.3	Abdusalam Mohammed	U20	20.03.79	1	Feltham	25 Jul

10000 METRES

27:18.14	Jon Brown	27.02.71	4	Brussels, BEL	28 Aug
	28:02.33		4	Budapest, HUN	18 Aug
27:53.52	Keith Cullen	13.06.72	10	Lisbon, POR	4 Apr
	28:34.34		11	Budapest, HUN	18 Aug
28:31.71	Glynn Tromans	17.03.69	20	Lisbon, POR	4 Apr
28:43.17	Dermot Donnelly	23.09.70	1	Bedford	4 Jul
	29:05.96		5	Kuala Lumpur, MAL	16 Sep
	29:27.40		25	Lisbon, POR	4 Apr
28:52.71	Carl Thackery	14.10.62	2	Bedford	4 Jul
29:01.05	Andrew Pearson	14.09.71	22	Lisbon, POR	4 Apr
29:17.72	Rob Denmark	23.11.68	3	Bedford	4 Jul
29:20.72	Robert Quinn	10.12.65	11rB	Lisbon, POR	4 Apr
	29:25.55		6	Bedford	4 Jul
	29:36.54		1	Edinburgh	17 Jul
	29:43.88		12	Prague, CZE	8 Jun
29:22.88	Mark Hudspith	19.01.69	4	Bedford	4 Jul
29:24.15	Dave Taylor	9.01.64	5	Bedford	4 Jul
	(10)				
29:39.23	Dave Tune	29.10.70	7	Bedford	4 Jul
29:40.96	Adrian Mussett	14.04.72	8	Bedford	4 Jul
29:42.08	Ian Hudspith	23.09.70	11	Prague, CZE	8 Jun
29:43.14	David Miles	16.11.65	9	Bedford	4 Jul

29:46.45	Tommy Murray		18.05.61	2	Edinburgh	17	Jul
29:51.2	Kris Bowditch		14.01.75	1	Azusa, USA	11	Apr
	23 performances to 30:00.00 by 16 athletes						
30:07.82	Spencer Newport		5.10.66	10	Bedford	4	Jul
30:13.15	Nathaniel Lane	U23	10.04.76		Philadelphia, USA	23	Apr
30:14.11	Spencer Barden		31.03.73	1	Bath	4	May
30:14.47	Bill Foster	V40	9.08.58	3	Cesenatico, ITA	12	Sep
(20)							
30:17.03	Alaister Russell		17.06.68	3	Edinburgh	17	Jul
30:19.66	Adrian Marriott		24.09.72	11	Bedford	4	Jul
30:21.19	Andy Wedlake		30.11.71	5	Montreal, CAN	10	Jul
30:21.4	Andres Jones	U23	3.02.77	1	Barry	24	Jun
30:22.88	Ian Grime		29.09.70	1	Bedford	29	Aug
30:35.15	Martin Hula		2.01.66	1	Bedford	24	May
30:46.19	Stuart Bell		29.07.67	1	Wrexham	17	May
30:49.8	Mark Steinle		22.11.74	1	Crawley	19	Jul
30:51.33	Wayne Oxborough		10.11.66	2	Bedford	29	Aug
30:52.87	Rod Finch		5.08.67	3	Bedford	29	Aug
(30)							
30:56.72	Nick Francis		29.08.71	4	Bedford	29	Aug
30:58.33	Brian Scally		9.05.66	4	Edinburgh	17	Jul
31:00.90	John Cunningham		19.09.63	5	Edinburgh	17	Jul
31:05.69	Nigel Gates	V45	18.05.53	13	Bedford	4	Jul
31:06.70	Sandy Moss		21.09.72	2	Bath	4	May
31:07.2	Greg Hull		16.11.65	1	Blackpool	6	Sep
31:11.2	Kevin Holland		11.09.75	1	Basingstoke	14	Jun
31:12.2	Gareth Deacon		8.08.66	2	Derby	19	Jul
31:13.71	Charles Woodd		16.11.71	5	Bedford	24	May
31:17.7	Ian Archbold		10.06.65	1	Bolton	15	Aug
(40)							
31:18.06	Charles Herrington		28.07.71	1	Bedford	14	Jun
31:18.8	Nick Milovsorov		16.03.64	1	Aberdeen	25	Jun
31:18.85	Robert Holladay		10.01.75	4	Bath	4	May
31:19.50	Malcolm Price		18.06.62	6	Bedford	24	May

Foreign

29:58.3	*Pamenos Ballantyne (STV)*		*9.12.73*	*1*	*Derby*	*19*	*Jul*
30:28.38	*Svein Risa (NOR)*		*7.03.74*	*6*	*Ravnanger, NOR*	*2*	*Aug*
30:34.13	*Kassa Tadesse (ETH)*		*21.08.74*	*2*	*Bedford*	*29*	*Aug*

10 KILOMETRES Road

28:58	Richard Nerurkar		6.01.64	6	Brunssum, HOL	5	Apr
29:02				1	Eastleigh	15	Mar
29:15				1	Datchet	28	Jun
29:19				1	Sheffield	29	Mar
29:06	Dermot Donnelly		23.09.70	1	Belfast	31	Oct
29:07	Spencer Newport		5.10.66	1	Dewsbury	8	Feb
29:16				4	Swansea	6	Sep
29:08	Keith Cullen		13.06.72	13	Bolzano, ITA	31	Dec
29:09				1	Barnsley	1	Nov
29:15	Stuart Bell		29.07.67	2	Dewsbury	8	Feb
29:15	Dave Tune		29.10.70	3	Swansea	6	Sep
29:16	Chris Robison		16.03.61	3	Dewsbury	8	Feb
29:17	Malcolm Price		18.06.62	4	Dewsbury	8	Feb
29:20	Glynn Tromans		17.03.69	2	Barnsley	1	Nov
29:22	Michael Openshaw		8.04.72	1	Leeds	6	Dec
	14 performances to 29:25 by 10 athletes						
29:28	Christian Stephenson		22.07.74	4	Cardiff	27	Sep
29:32	Alan Chilton		16.04.71	5	Swansea	6	Sep
29:32	Matt O'Dowd	U23	13.04.76	5	Cardiff	27	Sep

29:33	Adrian Passey		2.09.64	18	Marseille, FRA	1 May
29:36	Jon Wild		30.08.73	1	Fort Worth, USA	28 Feb
29:38	Allan Adams		11.09.72	6	Dewsbury	8 Feb
29:38	Andres Jones	U23	3.02.77	6	Cardiff	27 Sep
29:39	David Miles		16.11.65	7	Cardiff	27 Sep
29:40	Paul Freary		3.04.68	7	Dewsbury	8 Feb
29:40	James Starling		13.08.67	2	Eastleigh	15 Mar
	(20)					
29:40	Mark Morgan		19.08.72	7	Swansea	6 Sep
29:41	Stuart Poore		30.12.72	3	Eastleigh	15 Mar
29:41	Colin Moore		25.11.60	4	Barnsley	1 Nov
29:42	Tommy Murray		18.05.61	1	Troon	13 May
29:45	Steve Brooks		8.06.70		Duisburg, GER	15 Feb
29:45	Richard Findlow		4.12.66	8	Cardiff	27 Sep
29:45	Nick Weatheridge		11.10.72	2	Basingstoke	18 Oct
29:46	Steve Green		28.07.70	5	Barnsley	1 Nov
29:47	Adrian Mussett		14.04.72	9	Swansea	6 Sep
29:47	Eric Crowther		23.01.75	3	Basingstoke	18 Oct
	(30)					
29:49	Matthew Smith		26.12.74	9	Cardiff	27 Sep
29:49	Kim Critchley		15.07.73	2	Leeds	6 Dec
29:50	Nick Comerford		23.04.66	1	Barry	19 Apr

short (236m)

28:52	Glen Stewart	7.12.70	1	Glasgow	7 Mar
29:13	Billy Jenkins	13.07.71	2	Glasgow	7 Mar
29:22	Tommy Murray	18.05.61	3	Glasgow	7 Mar

Foreign

29:28	*Kassa Tadesse (ETH)*	*21.08.74*	*3*	*Cardiff*	*27 Sep*

10 MILES Road

47:01	Paul Evans	13.04.61	8	Newry	20 Sep
47:25	Glynn Tromans	17.03.69	1	Erewash	23 Aug
47:46	Dave Tune	29.10.70	12	Newry	20 Sep
	48:19		3	Erewash	23 Aug
48:14	Peter Whitehead	3.12.64	7	Tilberg, HOL	7 Jun
48:15	Alan Chilton	16.04.71	14	Newry	20 Sep
48:25	Mark Steinle	22.11.74	4	Erewash	23 Aug
48:30	Spencer Newport	5.10.66	18	Newry	20 Sep
48:34	Malcolm Price	18.06.62	19	Newry	20 Sep
48:37	Andrew Pearson	14.09.71	3	Portsmouth	13 Sep
48:41	Dale Laughlin	28.12.66	1	Chelmsford	17 May
	11 performances to 48:45 by 10 athletes				
48:51	Gary Staines	3.07.63	6	Portsmouth	13 Sep
48:56	Nick Jones	10.07.74	7	Portsmouth	13 Sep
49:03	Paul Freary	3.04.68	1	Sale	2 Aug
49:06	Mark Morgan	19.08.72	20	Newry	20 Sep
49:11	Tommy Murray	18.05.61	21	Newry	20 Sep
49:18	Larry Matthews	11.08.65	6	Erewash	23 Aug
49:26	Tim Dickinson	14.10.72	8	Portsmouth	13 Sep
49:28	Allan Adams	11.09.72	2	Sale	2 Aug
49:31	Graeme Croll	1.02.66	23	Newry	20 Sep
49:32	Billy Nixon	9.02.68	2	Woking	1 Mar

	(20)					
49:36	Martin Rees	V45	28.02.53	3	Woking	1 Mar
49:40	Vince Garner		2.07.66	4	Woking	1 Mar
49:45	Keith Anderson	V40	10.08.57	15	Flint, USA	22 Aug
49:46	Tony Graham		15.10.63	9	Portsmouth	13 Sep
49:49	Mark Croasdale		10.01.60	10	Portsmouth	13 Sep

49:49	Mark Hudspith	19.01.69	1	Carlisle	21	Nov
49:50	Ian Archbold	10.06.65	9	Erewash	23	Aug
49:54	Bashir Hussain	20.12.64	1	Llandudno	1	Nov
49:56	Darren Hiscox	21.03.72	26	Newry	20	Sep

Downhill

48:38	Tommy Murray	18.05.61	1	Motherwell	5	Apr

Foreign

49:46	*John Burke (IRE)*	*18.05.70*	*8*	*Erewash*	*23*	*Aug*

HALF MARATHON

1:03:23	Paul Evans	13.04.61	4	Egmond aan Zee, HOL	11	Jan
1:03:25			3	Glasgow	23	Aug
1:04:12			5	South Shields	4	Oct
1:04:40			25	The Hague, HOL	29	Mar
1:03:25	Richard Nerurkar	6.01.64	1	Hardelot, FRA	5	Jul
1:03:45			3	Perpignan, FRA	31	May
1:04:13	Mark Steinle	22.11.74	5	South Shields	4	Oct
1:04:14	Dave Taylor	9.01.64	6	Glasgow	23	Aug
1:04:22	Ian Hudspith	23.09.70	1	Wilmslow	29	Mar
1:04:24	Malcolm Price	18.06.62	3	Reading	15	Mar
1:04:24	Paul Roden	18.04.65	2	Wilmslow	29	Mar
1:04:34	Steve Brooks	8.06.70	9	Egmond aan Zee, HOL	11	Jan
1:04:36	Mark Hudspith	19.01.69	3	Wilmslow	29	Mar
1:04:43	Alan Chilton	16.04.71	4	Reading	15	Mar
(10)						
1:04:46	Dave Cavers	9.04.63	5	Reading	15	Mar
1:04:49	Steve Brace	7.07.61	4	Wilmslow	29	Mar
1:04:50	Tony O'Brien	14.11.70	7	Glasgow	23	Aug
1:04:55	Paul Freary	3.04.68	5	Wilmslow	29	Mar

18 performances to 1:05:00 by 14 athletes

1:05:13	Dave Tune		29.10.70	8	South Shields	4	Oct
1:05:15	Nick Weatheridge		11.10.72	9	South Shields	4	Oct
1:05:21	Dale Rixon		8.07.66	1	Gloucester	26	Jul
1:05:23	Matt O'Dowd	U23	13.04.76	10	South Shields	4	Oct
1:05:30	Colin Moore		25.11.60	11	South Shields	4	Oct
1:05:40	David Miles		16.11.65	12	South Shields	4	Oct
(20)							
1:05:43	Brian Rushworth		14.12.62	13	South Shields	4	Oct
1:05:46	Rob Birchall		14.06.70	2	Lake Vyrnwy	27	Sep
1:05:53	Steve Green		28.07.70	1	Camberley	22	Feb
1:05:58	Nick Jones		10.07.74	6	Wilmslow	29	Mar
1:06:01	Tony Graham		15.10.63	3	Lake Vyrnwy	27	Sep
1:06:01	Adrian Callan		28.11.62	19	Strasbourg, FRA	25	Oct
1:06:03	Carl Thackery		14.10.62	1	Sheffield	26	Apr
1:06:04	Andrew Pearson		14.09.71	15	South Shields	4	Oct
1:06:05	John Ferrin		20.02.67	20	Strasbourg, FRA	25	Oct
1:06:14	Larry Matthews		11.08.65	16	South Shields	4	Oct
(30)							
1:06:15	Mark Flint		19.02.63	11	Glasgow	23	Aug
1:06:18	Darren Hiscox		21.03.72	9	Reading	15	Mar
1:06:18	Ian Pierce		13.11.75	7	Wilmslow	29	Mar
1:06:20	Tommy Murray		18.05.61	12	Glasgow	23	Aug
1:06:24	Billy Burns		13.12.69	9	Liverpool	30	Aug
1:06:28	Barry Royden		15.12.66	1	Paddock Wood	5	Apr
1:06:28	Adrian Mussett		14.04.72	1	Norwich	14	Jun

unofficial intermediate times

1:03:52 +	Jon Brown	27.02.71		London	26	Apr
1:05:49 +	Billy Burns	(1:06:24)		London	26	Apr
1:05:49 +	Barry Royden	(1:06:28)		London	26	Apr

1:02:50	*John Mutai (KEN)*	*U23*	*22.04.76*	*2*	*South Shields*	*4*	*Oct*
1:04:02	*Kassa Tadesse (ETH)*		*21.08.74*	*2*	*Reading*	*15*	*Mar*
1:05:32	*Jamie Lewis (IRE)*		*8.03.69*	*1*	*Portsmouth*	*8*	*Mar*

MARATHON

2:11:10	Jon Brown		27.02.71	8	London	26	Apr
2:14:02	Richard Nerurkar		6.01.64	8	Budapest, HUN	22	Aug
2:14:19	Mark Hudspith		19.01.69	16	London	26	Apr
	2:19:58			30	Budapest, HUN	22	Aug
2:14:59	Dave Buzza		6.12.62	14	Boston, USA	20	Apr
	2:19:28			28	Budapest	22	Aug
2:16:06	Dave Cavers		9.04.63	12	Rotterdam, HOL	19	Apr
2:16:11	Billy Burns		13.12.69	21	London	26	Apr
2:16:34	Steve Brace		7.07.61	24	London	26	Apr
2:17:07	Alan Chilton		16.04.71	26	London	26	Apr
2:17:08	Keith Anderson	V40	10.08.57	18	Boston, USA	20	Apr
2:17:16	Steve Green		28.07.70	12	Monaco, MON	22	Nov
	2:18:11			31	London	26	Apr
(10)							
2:17:43	Malcolm Price		18.06.62	29	London	26	Apr
2:18:11	Dale Rixon		8.07.66	8	Sacramento, USA	6	Dec
2:18:44	Scott Cohen		6.12.64	4	Florence, ITA	29	Nov
2:19:57	Barry Royden		15.12.66	33	London	26	Apr
2:20:13	Tony Graham		15.10.63	25	New York, USA	1	Nov
2:20:22	Nick Jones		10.07.74	34	London	26	Apr
2:20:30	Dave Taylor		9.01.64	4	Kuala Lumpur, MAL	20	Sep
2:21:09	Chris Parkes		17.04.64	1	Stoke	6	Sep
2:21:16	Darren Hiscox		21.03.72	35	London	26	Apr
2:21:38	Graham Hill		23.06.65	36	London	26	Apr

23 performances to 2:22:00 by 20 athletes

2:23:23	Bashir Hussain		20.12.64	1	Manchester	11	Oct
2:23:27	Spencer Newport		5.10.66	42	London	26	Apr
2:23:36	Andy Arrand		20.01.66	2	Manchester	11	Oct
2:23:58	Mich Hannay		10.10.61	45	London	26	Apr
2:24:49	Jon Solly		28.06.63	16	Belgrade, YUG	25	Apr
2:24:54	Ieuan Ellis		11.05.60	47	London	26	Apr
2:25:38	Billy Nixon		9.02.68	48	London	26	Apr
2:25:41	Tony Duffy	V40	26.06.56	49	London	26	Apr
2:25:57	Paul Froud		6.04.66	50	London	26	Apr
2:26:11	Paul Bennett	V40	18.01.58	51	London	26	Apr
(30)							
2:26:30	Darren Hale		2.10.59	5	Manchester	11	Oct
2:26:48	Mike Thompson		14.09.68	53	London	26	Apr
2:26:48	Shaun Milford		13.07.63	54	London	26	Apr
2:26:51	Greg Dell		20.11.64	55	London	26	Apr
2:26:56	Duncan Hurdwell		24.04.62	57	London	26	Apr
2:27:00	Simon Kinson		3.12.70	58	London	26	Apr
2:27:01	Seb Shepley		23.11.67	59	London	26	Apr
2:27:11	Alan Shepherd		28.04.69	60	London	26	Apr
2:27:28	John Cox		17.09.63	1	Abingdon	18	Oct
2:27:41	Brian Rushworth		14.12.62	62	London	26	Apr
(40)							
2:27:55	Mark Burnhope		20.03.60	63	London	26	Apr
2:28:00	Ronnie James		14.12.64	2	Abingdon	18	Oct
2:28:14	John Ross			2	Belfast	4	May
2:28:22	Paul Cadwallader		23.10.62	1	Leeds	17	May
2:28:28	Dave Thomson		18.09.59	68	London	26	Apr
2:28:46	Vince Stamp		22.11.59	71	London	26	Apr
2:28:48	Howard Parsell		13.11.60	72	London	26	Apr

Time	Name	Cat	DOB		Place	Date
2:28:53	Martin Ferguson		17.09.64	24	Florence, ITA	29 Nov
2:29:02	Paul Daly		27.10.68	73	London	26 Apr
2:29:04	Simon Pride		20.07.67	1	Elgin	6 Sep
	(50)					
2:29:17	Bill Gristwood		20.03.59	5	Dublin, IRE	26 Oct
2:29:19	Robin Bentley		17.02.65	74	London	26 Apr
2:29:32	Brian Scally		9.05.66	1	Greenock	13 Sep
2:29:52	Donal Gallagher		5.12.72	75	London	26 Apr
2:29:52	Billy Crowley		1.01.63	76	London	26 Apr
2:29:54	Alan Ruben	V40	9.03.57		Boston, USA	20 Apr
2:30:09	Andy Holt		23.02.64	78	London	26 Apr
2:30:11	Jerry Greeves		14.09.67	79	London	26 Apr
2:30:16	Chris Ling		5.08.63	80	London	26 Apr
2:30:17	Darren Bilton		9.03.72	4	Manchester	11 Oct
	(60)					
2:30:40	Mike Higginbottom	V40	9.08.54	5	Manchester	11 Oct
2:30:41	Richard Jordan	V40	14.07.57	81	London	26 Apr
2:30:44	Colin Pitts		5.04.60	82	London	26 Apr
2:30:46	Mike Girvan	V40	16.03.54	1	Lochaber	17 May
2:30:54	Michael Cotton		17.04.68	84	London	26 Apr
2:30:54	Alan Beavers			2	Leeds	17 May
2:30:56	Richard Ironmonger		11.07.67	1	Sheffield	26 Apr
2:30:58	Nick Milovsorov		16.03.64	85	London	26 Apr
2:31:05	Paul Richards		13.02.65	2	Sheffield	26 Apr
2:31:18	Lee Harris		20.10.69	88	London	26 Apr
	(70)					
2:31:24	John Kerr	V45	1.06.49	89	London	26 Apr
2:31:30	Paul Smith	V40	12.08.54	90	London	26 Apr
2:31:33	Mark Croasdale		10.01.60	2	Washington, USA	25 Oct
2:31:34	Lee Martin		21.05.64	91	London	26 Apr
2:31:35	Toby Tanser		21.07.68	47	Boston, USA	20 Apr
2:31:39	David Forrest		17.05.68	92	London	26 Apr
2:31:39	Alan Clarkson			1	Wolverhampton	6 Sep
2:31:58	Richie Bullen		6.10.60	93	London	26 Apr
2:32:06	Alan Turnbull		22.07.66	94	London	26 Apr
2:32:10	Ian O'Neill		30.12.65	95	London	26 Apr
	(80)					
2:32:11	Alex Rowe	V40	10.04.57	6	Manchester	11 Oct
2:32:19	David Laing		1.01.66	96	London	26 Apr
2:32:21	Mike Bradley	V40	27.05.57	97	London	26 Apr
2:32:29	Carl Barker		23.05.59	3	Sheffield	26 Apr
2:32:30	Paul Young		21.08.59	4	Sheffield	26 Apr
2:32:30	Mike McGeoch	V40	15.08.55	7	Dublin, IRE	26 Oct
2:32:31	S. Dickinson			5	Sheffield	26 Apr
2:32:32	Steve Moore	V50	17.12.47	101	London	26 Apr
2:32:36	Gary Matthews		9.04.60	7	Manchester	11 Oct
2:32:40	Paul Kinsella		8.10.63	8	Manchester	11 Oct
	(90)					
2:32:43	Gary Gerrard		7.07.63	3	Washington, USA	25 Oct
2:33:06	Peter Sibbett		18.12.62	105	London	26 Apr
2:33:11	Shaun Winstanley			3	Leeds	17 May
2:33:13	Keith Newton		14.03.63	106	London	26 Apr
2:33:22	Richard Sales		28.05.62	101	New York, USA	1 Nov
2:33:24	Martin Farran		8.05.61	6	Sheffield	26 Apr
2:33:26	Leigh Beard		3.04.69	109	London	26 Apr
2:33:32	K. Butler			9	Manchester	11 Oct
2:33:44	Ray Dzikowski		6.03.63	110	London	26 Apr
2:33:46	Fraser Clyne	V40	23.08.55	2	Lochaber	18 May

Foreign

2:13:37	John Mutai (KEN)	U23	22.04.76	2	Seville, SPA	22	Feb
2:15:37	Pamenos Ballantyne (STV)		9.12.73	1	Port of Spain, TRI	25	Jan
2:23:33	Tommy Hughes (IRE)		8.01.60	1	Belfast	4	May
2:23:59	Sam Mully (KEN)		4.09.64	46	London	26	Apr
2:27:18	Ben Ballantyne (STV)		23.03.70	61	London	26	Apr
2:32:28	Derrick Baard (RSA)		17.12.70	98	London	26	Apr

100 KILOMETRES

6:55:48	Steve Moore	V50	17.12.47	11	Torhout, BEL	19	Jun
6:57:33				1	Greenwich	10	May
7:05:11				1	Winschoten, HOL	12	Sep
6:57:28	Simon Pride		20.07.67	13	Torhout, BEL	19	Jun
6:59:38				6	Nakamura, JAP	18	Oct

24 HOURS (Track)

226.934 km	Walter Hill			1	London (TB)	11	Oct
218.016 km	Adrian Stott	V40	5.08.54	2	London (TB)	11	Oct
213.844 km	Geoff Oliver	V65	8.08.33	3	London (TB)	11	Oct
209.214 km	Andy Bottomley		15.04.61	1	Doncaster	24	May
205.990 km	Bernard Jarvis	V50	28.10.44	2	Doncaster	24	May
200.432 km	John Lucas			4	London (TB)	11	Oct
200.255 km	Richard Brown	V50	18.11.46	2	Surgeres, FRA	9	May

24 HOURS (Road)

240.291 km	Willie Sichel	V45	1.10.53	3	Niort, FRA	8	Nov
234.083 km	Don Ritchie	V50	6.07.44	11	Marquette, FRA	30	Aug
210.199 km	James Zarei	V50	13.01.44	26	Marquette, FRA	30	Aug
200.280 km	Martin Eccles	V40	16.01.57	30	Marquette, FRA	30	Aug

1500 METRES STEEPLECHASE - Under 17

4:19.28	Mark Griffith	25.11.81	1	Exeter	11	Jul
4:19.54	Daniel Moore	8.11.81	2	Exeter	11	Jul
4:22.58	Tom Hopkins	1.08.82	1	London (Ha)	23	May
4:24.26	Adam Bowden	5.08.82	3	Exeter	11	Jul
4:24.87	Andrew Sherman	28.09.81	2	Sheffield	16	Aug
4:27.76	Grant Ritchie	25.12.81	1	Edinburgh	19	Jun
4:27.78	Michael Glover	20.12.81	3	Sheffield	16	Aug
4:28.1	Richard Williams	22.10.81	2	London (He)	17	May
4:29.24	Manuel Lovell	10.04.82	3	London (Ha)	23	May
4:29.79	Russell Parrington	7.01.82	1	York	25	Jul
(10)						
4:30.39	Stewart Payne	15.03.82	4	Sheffield	16	Aug
4:31.17	Royston Green	4.01.82	5	Sheffield	16	Aug
4:31.40	Ian Wilson	6.02.82	5	Exeter	11	Jul
4:31.47	James Williams	17.07.82	5	Ayr	18	Jul
4:31.9	David Taylor	28.10.81	1	Stoke	13	Jun
4:32.23	Philip Downes	4.10.81	2	York	25	Jul
4:32.7	Richard Lomas	5.09.81	1	Middlesbrough	17	May
4:33.8	Stephen Murphy	6.01.83	1	Norwich	28	Jun
4:34.4	Sam Myers	16.08.82	1	Middlesbrough	17	May
4:35.67	David Ragan	26.03.83	4	London (Ha)	23	May
(20)						
4:35.9	Ricky Soos	28.06.83	1	Solihull	23	May
4:37.48	Matthew Hill	15.12.82	1	Birmingham	5	Sep
4:37.68	Stephen Nicholls	1.04.83	7h2	Exeter	10	Jul
4:38.9	Greg Atkins	20.10.81	2	Portsmouth	13	Jun
4:39.2	Frank Flegg		1	Carmarthen	23	May
4:39.42	Robert Barton	5.11.82	6h1	Sheffield	15	Aug

4:39.5	Michael Jones		1.02.82	2	Carmarthen	23 May
4:39.88	Neil Gamester		15.02.83	5	London (Ha)	23 May
4:39.9	Andrew Gargan		10.10.81	1	Antrim	17 May

2000 METRES STEEPLECHASE

5:40.6	Spencer Duval		5.01.70	1	Stretford	23 Jun
5:46.85	Iain Murdoch	U20	10.07.80	1	London (He)	9 Aug
5:48.2	Lee Hurst		29.07.72	1	Stretford	4 Aug
5:50.6	Ray Plant		13.05.68	1	Stoke	27 Jun
5:54.51				2	Cudworth	1 Aug
5:52.28	Mark Warmby	U23	12.12.78	1	Exeter	11 Jul
5:53.11	Rob Berry		29.07.69	1	Cudworth	1 Aug
5:54.1	Simon Wurr	U23	7.01.77	1	Jarrow	22 Apr
5:54.47	Steve Cairns		3.11.67	1	Cosford	25 Apr
5:54.64	Gary Blackman	U20	24.09.80	2	London (He)	9 Aug
5:55.39	Tom Kingsnorth	U20	15.10.79	2	Exeter	11 Jul

(10)

5:56.3	Michael East	U23	20.01.78	1	Sandown, IOW	6 Sep
5:57.05	Chris Thompson	U20	17.04.81	1	London (He)	31 Aug
5:57.2	Mark Hirsch		31.03.63	1	Leamington	9 May
5:58.07	Chris Davies	U23	19.10.76	2	Cosford	25 Apr
5:58.1	Darren Barton		11.10.69	1	Hayes	15 Jul
6:00.8	Delroy Simon	U23	27.11.78	2	Hayes	15 Jul
6:01.5	Mike Proudlove		26.01.70	2	Manchester	23 Jun
6:02.6	Jon Pavis		4.10.66	3	Manchester	23 Jun

Additional Under 20 (1 - 4 above)

6:03.25	Andrew Franklin		13.09.80	2	London (He)	31 Aug
6:08.3	Dave Baxter		16.01.79	1	Wigan	19 Apr
6:08.35	Matt Lemon		6.02.80	3	London (He)	9 Aug
6:10.07	Andrew Thomas		29.01.81	3	London (He)	31 Aug
6:10.55	Chris Pickering		23.09.79	4	Exeter	11 Jul
6:10.60	Ian Ratcliffe		28.05.79	4	London (He)	9 Aug

(10)

6:10.7	John Rice		29.08.81	1	Stretford	19 May
6:10.84	Glen Cornish		27.10.79	1	Cudworth	9 May
6:11.22	Mark Griffith	U17	25.11.81	4	London (He)	31 Aug
6:11.56	Joe Kidger		16.03.80	5	London (He)	31 Aug

3000 METRES STEEPLECHASE

8:32.76	Christian Stephenson		22.07.74	1	Birmingham	26 Jul
8:41.76				1	Manchester	3 Jun
8:42.95				6	Kuala Lumpur, MAL	17 Sep
8:44.34				15	Stockholm, SWE	5 Aug
8:46.44				1h1	Birmingham	24 Jul
8:55.67 A				5	Johannesburg, RSA	12 Sep
8:36.37	Spencer Duval		5.01.70	2	Birmingham	26 Jul
8:49.6				3	Watford	5 Aug
8:41.79	Ben Whitby	U23	6.01.77	1	Hexham	14 Jun
8:42.12				6	St. Petersburg, RUS	28 Jun
8:44.24				7	Kuala Lumpur, MAL	17 Sep
8:47.69				4	Birmingham	26 Jul
8:49.80				2h2	Birmingham	24 Jul
8:51.5				1	Bedford	24 May
8:42.83	Craig Wheeler	U23	14.06.76	3	Birmingham	26 Jul
8:43.36				2	Manchester	3 Jun
8:45.90				4	Dessau, GER	1 Aug
8:49.47				1h2	Birmingham	24 Jul

8:43.71	Brian Montgomery		19.07.74	1	Seattle, USA	2 May
	8:44.01			7	Dedham, USA	27 Jun
	8:46.18			13	Portland, USA	16 May
8:49.63	Lee Hurst		29.07.72	6	Birmingham	26 Jul
	8:53.90			5h2	Birmingham	24 Jul
	8:55.04			1	Liverpool	20 Jun
	8:55.62			3	Belgrade, YUG	31 May
8:52.35	Andy Coleman		29.09.74	7	Birmingham	26 Jul
	8:52.7			4	Watford	5 Aug
	8:53.27			3h2	Birmingham	24 Jul
8:53.81	Andy Morgan-Lee		1.03.69	4h2	Birmingham	24 Jul
	8:55.0			1	Enfield	19 Jul
8:55.6	John Brown		2.02.69	5	Watford	5 Aug
8:55.74	Simon Bell		26.12.66	7h2	Birmingham	24 Jul

32 performances to 8:56.00 by 10 athletes

8:56.3	Kevin Nash	U23	6.02.77	6	Watford	5 Aug
8:56.39	Stuart Stokes	U23	15.12.76	1	Bedford	29 Aug
8:56.40	Christian Nicolson		19.09.73	1	Edinburgh	18 Jul
8:56.55	Steve Cairns		3.11.67	3	Poznan, POL	6 Sep
8:57.03	Martin Yelling		7.02.72	4	Manchester	3 Jun
8:57.4	Colin Palmer		27.07.67	7	Watford	5 Aug
8:58.00	Mike Jubb		20.06.70	2	Loughborough	17 May
8:58.15	Iain Murdoch	U20	10.07.80	3	Loughborough	17 May
9:00.38	Andy Fooks		26.04.75	2	Bath	4 May
9:01.1	Ray Plant		13.05.68	1	Derby	4 Jul
	(20)					
9:01.19	Bruno Witchalls		22.03.75	2	Watford	21 Jun
9:03.15	Carl Warren		28.09.69	3	Edinburgh	4 Jul
9:03.46	Jon Pavis		4.10.66	3	Birmingham	6 Jun
9:03.61	Donald Naylor		5.09.71	9h2	Birmingham	24 Jul
9:03.90	Mick Hawkins		24.10.61	2	Liverpool	20 Jun
9:04.1	Spencer Newport		5.10.66	1	Liverpool	8 Aug
9:05.20	Rob Berry		29.07.69	3	Liverpool	20 Jun
9:05.73	Andrew Robinson	U23	20.04.78	5	Loughborough	17 May
9:05.86	Chris Davies	U23	19.10.76	3	Bath	4 May
9:06.20	Chris Thompson	U20	17.04.81	1	Bedford	4 Jul
	(30)					
9:07.47	Andrew Sharkey		13.12.74	4	Birmingham	6 Jun
9:07.6	Andrew Hennessy	U23	24.08.77	1	Oxford	16 May
9:08.10	Martin Roscoe		19.09.64	5	Bedford	24 May
9:09.9	Oliver Norman		6.09.73	4	London (He)	8 Aug
9:10.21	Matthew Plano	U23	8.10.76	6	Manchester	3 Jun
9:11.0	Chris Knight		3.01.69	6	Bedford	24 May
9:11.5	Jason Lendon		17.03.75	3	Sheffield (W)	16 May
9:12.05	Darren Barton		11.10.69	11h2	Birmingham	24 Jul
9:12.66	Ewan Malloch	U23	4.08.76	2	Oxford	30 Jun
9:12.81	Andy Beevers		3.05.73	5	Liverpool	20 Jun
	(40)					
9:13.25	Simon Wurr	U23	7.01.77	12h2	Birmingham	24 Jul
9:13.31	Matt O'Dowd	U23	13.04.76	4	Bath	4 May
9:13.8	Billy Jenkins		13.07.71	1	Greenock	26 Apr
9:14.83	Dave Mitchinson	U23	4.09.78	9	Loughborough	17 May
9:15.0	Huw Lobb	U23	29.08.76	2	Oxford	16 May
9:16.67	Pat Miller		21.02.67	5	Birmingham	6 Jun
9:17.2	Colin Johnston		10.03.73	5	London (He)	8 Aug
9:17.5	Mike Proudlove		26.01.70	2	Derby	4 Jul
9:17.87	Wayne Aylesbury		24.03.64	2	Cudworth	9 May
9:19.8	Delroy Simon	U23	27.11.78	2	Cardiff	6 Jun
	(50)					
9:23.4	Mark Hirsch		31.03.63	7	London (He)	8 Aug
9:24.47	Sandy Moss		21.09.72	5	Watford	16 May

184

9:24.8	Jeff Pyrah		6.07.72	1	Grangemouth	17 May
9:24.88	Jason Ward	U23	15.09.78	4	Cudworth	9 May
9:24.9	James Austin		9.08.65	2	Grangemouth	17 May
9:25.1	Michael Hutchinson		5.10.65	1	Bolton	15 Aug
9:25.29	Tom Kingsnorth	U20	15.10.79	3	Bedford	4 Jul
9:26.1	Mike Hoey		29.04.69	1	Bournemouth	10 May
9:26.2	Paul Northrop		15.01.70	2	Barking	7 Aug
9:26.82	Edward Barnett	U20	6.02.79	4	Bedford	4 Jul
	(60)					
9:27.22	Danny Duke		23.12.68	3	Edinburgh	4 Jul
9:27.70	Tony Forrest	U23	22.12.76	9	Bedford	24 May
9:27.80	Tom Buckner		16.04.63	1	Portsmouth	10 May
9:27.+	Tim Watson		28.06.73	1	Portsmouth	2 Aug
9:28.40	Chris Sampson		30.09.75	10	Bedford	24 May
9:29.74	Orlando Edwards		11.10.73	1	Watford	16 May
9:29.8	Alexander Bowden		16.11.73	1	Douglas, IOM	8 Aug
9:29.9	Phil Cook		7.05.69	2	Enfield	16 May

Additional Under 20 (1 - 4 above)

9:31.6	Stephen Patmore		9.07.79	1	Rotherham	6 Jun
9:33.12	Gary Blackman		24.09.80	5	Bedford	4 Jul
9:35.2	Niall Cameron		19.12.79	2	Edinburgh	9 May
9:42.4	Andrew Thomas		29.01.81	4	Enfield	23 Aug
9:47.4	Matt Lemon		6.02.80	2	Enfield	16 May
9:49.0	Joe Kidger		16.03.80	5	Enfield	6 Jun
	(10)					
9:49.96	Ian Ratcliffe		28.05.79	7	Bedford	4 Jul
9:50.6	Jamie McDonald		11.06.79	1	Grangemouth	2 Aug
9:50.61	Dave Baxter		16.01.79	2	Watford	16 May
9:51.5	Lee Wolstencroft		19.07.81	1	Bolton	6 Jun
9:55.1	Richard Kay		4.04.79	3	Stoke	16 May

Foreign

8:48.23	*Andrew Colvin (AUS)*		*23.08.72*	*5*	*Birmingham*	*26 Jul*
9:07.1	*Svein Risa (NOR)*		*7.03.74*	*1*	*Yate*	*14 Jun*
9:49.5	*Abdusalam Mohammed*	*U20*	*20.03.79*	*4*	*Watford*	*6 Jun*

50 METRES HURDLES - Indoor

7.39	Mike Robbins		19.06.76	1	Fort Worth, USA	21 Feb

60 METRES HURDLES - Indoor

7.50	Tony Jarrett	13.08.68	1	Birmingham	15 Feb
7.50			2	Lievin, FRA	22 Feb
7.52			1h4	Valencia, SPA	28 Feb
7.53			2h2	Lievin, FRA	22 Feb
7.54			1	Ostrava, CZE	29 Jan
7.59			1	Birmingham	7 Feb
7.61			2h1	Ostrava, CZE	29 Jan
7.61			4s1	Valencia, SPA	1 Mar
7.65			4	Maebashi, JAP	7 Mar
7.71			3h1	Stockholm, SWE	19 Feb
7.72			1h1	Birmingham	7 Feb
7.55	Andy Tulloch	1.04.67	1s2	Valencia, SPA	1 Mar
7.56			1h1	Valencia, SPA	28 Feb
7.66			2	Birmingham	7 Feb
7.66			7	Valencia, SPA	1 Mar
7.66			1h3	Sindelfingen, GER	8 Mar
7.70			1h2	Birmingham	7 Feb
7.73			5	Sindelfingen, GER	8 Mar

(Tulloch)	7.75				3	Piraeus, GRE	21 Feb
	7.78				1h1	Birmingham	25 Jan
	7.79				1	Birmingham	25 Jan
7.77	Damien Greaves	U23	19.09.77		4h2	Valencia, SPA	28 Feb
	7.83				3	Birmingham	7 Feb
	7.87				8	Birmingham	15 Feb
	7.91				2	Birmingham	25 Jan
	7.92				2h2	Birmingham	7 Feb
	7.95				3	Ghent, BEL	1 Feb
7.88	Matthew Clements	U23	17.09.77		1	Glasgow	14 Mar
	7.91				4	Birmingham	7 Feb
	7.92				3	Birmingham	25 Jan
	7.99				1	Birmingham	4 Jan
8.00	Martyn Hendry		10.04.75		2	Glasgow	14 Mar
	32 performances to 8.00 by 5 athletes						
8.08	Dominic Bradley	U23	22.12.76		1	Sheffield	20 Dec
8.10	Chris Baillie	U20	21.04.81		1	Birmingham	21 Feb
8.12	Duncan Malins	U23	12.06.78		3	Glasgow	14 Mar
8.18	Mensah Elliott	U23	29.08.76		5	Glasgow	14 Mar
8.19	Paul Gripton	U23	9.11.76		6	Glasgow	14 Mar
(10)							
8.20	Ben Warmington	U20	20.03.79		2	Birmingham	21 Feb
8.23	Lloyd Cowan		8.07.62		4h1	Birmingham	7 Feb
8.26	Chris Rawlinson		19.05.72		1	Birmingham	25 Feb
8.28	Chris Low	U20	24.04.80		3	Glasgow	25 Jan
8.31	Greg Dunson		2.12.63		1	Birmingham	10 Feb
8.35	Chris Hargrave	U20	27.02.79		3	Birmingham	4 Jan
8.40	Alexis Sharp		31.10.72		4	Glasgow	25 Jan
8.40	Robert Newton	U20	10.05.81		3	Birmingham	21 Feb
8.41	Duncan Mathieson		8.03.69		1H	Glasgow	15 Feb
8.43	Nathan Hart		1.07.73		3h1	Glasgow	14 Mar
(20)							
8.45	Rafer Joseph		21.07.68		1P	Bedford	18 Jan
8.48	Paul Jones	U23	11.04.78		4h1	Birmingham	25 Jan
8.50	Ben Roberts	U20	15.01.80		1P	Birmingham	31 Jan
8.53	Adrian Caines		13.11.74		1	Birmingham	1 Mar

Hand Timing

8.4	Richard Sear	U20	21.08.79		1	London (CP)	10 Jan

Foreign

8.3	*Pascal Renaud (FRA)*		*20.04.70*		*1*	*London (Ha)*	*1 Feb*

70 METRES HURDLES - Under 13 (2'3")

11.3	Sean Ashton		1	Leicester	13 Jun

75 METRES HURDLES - Under 13 (2'3")

11.7	Sean Ashton		1	Telford	12 Sep

75 METRES HURDLES - Under 13 (2'6")

12.4		Barry O'Brien	21.04.86	1	Grangemouth	28 Jun
		12.49 -0.7		1	Grangemouth	11 Jul

80 METRES HURDLES - Under 13 (2'6")

12.1	1.1	Sean Ashton		1r2	Peterborough	27 May
12.6		James Dunford	14.01.86	1P	Woking	2 Aug

80 METRES HURDLES - Under 15 (2'9")

11.25 w 2.7	Minh Ho	3.01.84	1h2	Exeter	10	Jul
11.8			1	Liverpool	7	Jun
11.34 1.3	James Francis-Famous	14.12.83	1h1	Exeter	10	Jul
11.42 w 2.7	Kenneth Frempong	17.07.84	2h2	Exeter	10	Jul
11.7			1	London (TB)	22	Jul
11.45 0.7	Edward Dunford	15.09.84	1	Sheffield	15	Aug
11.49 1.3	Matthew Roberts	8.07.84	1	London (He)	30	Aug
11.52 w 2.9	Michael Hudson	13.03.84	2	Exeter	11	Jul
11.9			2	Cannock	19	Jul
11.53	Nick Hiscott	19.09.83	1	Brecon	4	Jul
11.63 w 2.9	Tim Sinclair	26.12.83	4	Exeter	11	Jul
11.7			1	Kingston	13	Jun
11.72 1.1			1	London (Ha)	24	May
11.67 w 4.8	Richard Myers	21.12.83	1h3	Exeter	10	Jul
11.69 -0.7	Martin Roberts	20.09.83	1P	Hull	19	Sep
(10)						
11.69 w 2.9	David Hughes	31.05.84	5	Exeter	11	Jul
11.69 w 3.2	Mark Garner	2.11.83	1h2	Sheffield	15	Aug
11.73 -0.4			2P	Hull	19	Sep
11.70 1.4	Ross Tressider	8.11.83	1h1	London (He)	30	Aug
11.7	Greg Smith	29.01.84	1	Bournemouth	9	May
11.80 1.1			2	London (Ha)	24	May
11.71 1.3	Ramon Durrani	9.10.83	2	London (He)	30	Aug
11.77 0.7	Matthew Walden	30.11.83	3	Sheffield	15	Aug
11.80 -1.5	Chuka Enih-Snell	2.03.84	1P	Birmingham	23	Aug
11.8	Richard Fitzgerald	6.06.84	1P	Hoo	8	Aug
11.81 0.7	Oliver Brewer	14.09.83	5	Sheffield	15	Aug
11.83 1.3	Dean Walker	15.03.84	3h1	Exeter	10	Jul
(20)						
11.84 0.7	Matthew Williams	31.01.84	6	Sheffield	15	Aug
11.85 w 3.2	Ross Elliott	6.09.83	3h2	Sheffield	15	Aug

doubtful timing

11.6	Adam Crickmore	26.01.84	1	Newport	18	Jul

Under 13

12.6	James Dunford	14.01.86	2P	Exeter	27	Sep

100 METRES HURDLES - Under 17 (3'0")

12.9 w?	Dominic Girdler	6.03.82	1	Cwmbran	13	Sep
12.96 w 2.4			2	Sheffield	15	Aug
12.99 2.0			1	Exeter	11	Jul
12.96 w 2.4	Nathan Palmer	16.06.82	1	Sheffield	15	Aug
13.1 w?			2	Cwmbran	13	Sep
13.11 -2.1			1	Dublin (S), IRE	8	Aug
13.11 w 2.4	Nange Ursell	1.10.81	3	Sheffield	15	Aug
13.19 1.8			2h3	Sheffield	15	Aug
13.29 w 2.4	William Beattie	22.10.82	4	Sheffield	15	Aug
13.47 1.8			3h3	Sheffield	15	Aug
13.3	Allan Scott	27.12.82	1	Glasgow (S)	7	Jun
13.34 0.7			1h1	Edinburgh	19	Jun
13.45 2.0	Jonathon Crawshaw	28.09.81	2	Exeter	11	Jul
13.53 2.0	Chris Tye-Walker	20.09.82	3	Exeter	11	Jul
13.58 1.9	David Brackstone	13.03.82	2h2	Sheffield	15	Aug
13.61 w 2.6	James Peet	2.12.82	3h1	Exeter	10	Jul
13.97 1.3			7	Exeter	11	Jul
13.70 2.0	Phillip Walsh	26.10.81	4	Exeter	11	Jul
(10)						
13.77 0.5	Martin Taylor	31.01.82	2	Edinburgh	19	Jun

13.77 w	3.7	Dominic Saban		27.02.82	1h2	Exeter	10 Jul
14.02	1.3				3	London (Ha)	24 May
13.8		Seb Bastow		11.10.81	1	Liverpool	7 Jun
13.95	-2.7				1	Birmingham	6 Sep
13.81 w	3.7	Lee Rowley		28.02.82	2h2	Exeter	10 Jul
13.85	2.0				6	Exeter	11 Jul
13.82	0.3	Gareth Rees		15.01.82	1	Cudworth	1 Aug
13.82	0.3	Chris Dack		28.11.82	2	Cudworth	1 Aug
13.83		Chris Lomas		22.04.82	1	Bedford	10 Jun
13.86	1.9	Scott Ensbury		4.01.82	4h2	Sheffield	15 Aug
13.90	1.9	James Anthony		30.03.82	5h2	Sheffield	15 Aug
13.9		Tim Greenwood		22.11.82	1	Oxford	13 Jun
(20)							
13.9		Steven Green		15.01.83	1O	Carn Brea	27 Jun
13.98 w	2.6				4h1	Exeter	10 Jul
14.15	1.8				5h3	Sheffield	15 Aug
13.93 w	3.7	Lolimar Pagkatipunan		17.11.82	3h2	Exeter	10 Jul
13.94	0.8	Alex Zulewski		6.06.82	4h1	Sheffield	15 Aug
14.10 w	3.7	Robert Lloyd		15.04.83	4h2	Exeter	10 Jul
14.1		Tennyson Mawema		12.12.82	1r2	Bournemouth	2 Aug
14.12 w	2.7	James Tattershall		25.11.81	3	Leeds (South)	23 May

doubtful timing

13.5		Peter Reed		31.12.81	1	Hereford	10 May

overage doubtful timing

13.6		Chris Low	U20	24.04.80	1	Arbroath	16 Jun

110 METRES HURDLES - Under 20 (3'3")

14.16	1.3	Robert Newton		10.05.81	2	Exeter	11 Jul
14.16	-0.9	Ben Warmington		20.03.79	1	London (He)	9 Aug
14.24 w	4.4	Andrew Turner		19.09.80	2h2	Exeter	10 Jul
14.49	1.3				3	Exeter	11 Jul
14.26	1.2	Jason McDade		3.04.80	1	London (He)	30 Aug
14.34	1.2	Mohammed Sillah-Freckleton		11.09.80	2	London (He)	30 Aug
14.38 w	2.8	Stevie Scott		5.06.79	1h1	London (Ha)	24 May
14.40	1.4				1	London (Ha)	24 May
14.42		Chris Baillie		21.04.81	1	Barry	14 Jul
14.45		Chris Low		24.04.80	2	Barry	14 Jul
14.46 w	2.2	John Monds		24.03.80	1	Leeds	23 May
14.81	1.3				8	Exeter	11 Jul
14.57	1.4	Dan Brewer		10.08.80	2	London (Ha)	24 May
(10)							
14.64	1.3	Colin Roberts		20.01.81	6	Exeter	11 Jul
14.69	1.9	Luke Gittens		4.01.81	1	Carmarthen	23 May
14.69 w	3.2	Chris Hodson		11.11.80	4h1	Exeter	10 Jul
14.79	1.3				7	Exeter	11 Jul
14.74 w	3.2	Dwayne Stoddart		29.12.80	5h1	Exeter	10 Jul
15.17	1.0				4h1	London (He)	30 Aug
14.83 w	3.2	Simon Hunt		22.07.81	6h1	Exeter	10 Jul
14.97	1.4				6	London (Ha)	24 May
14.85	1.9	Matthew Butler		4.04.80	2	Carmarthen	23 May
14.85	1.4	Marc Wareham		9.08.80	4	London (Ha)	24 May
14.91 w	3.2	Lee Tindall		19.02.80	7h1	Exeter	10 Jul
15.07	1.4				7	London (Ha)	24 May
14.93 w	3.2	Patrick Brown		2.09.79	8h1	Exeter	10 Jul
15.10					1	Gateshead	9 May
14.98	-3.4	Richard McDonald		11.01.80	1r3	Loughborough	17 May
(20)							
15.07		Shaun Robson		21.06.80	5	Barry	14 Jul
15.12		Craig McCarthy		13.10.80	2	Gateshead	9 May
15.12	1.3	Neil Thompson		23.04.79	1D	Hexham	17 May

15.14	1.1	Stephen McDonnell		24.07.80	4	Tullamore, IRE	12	Jul
15.15	-3.4	Ben Roberts		15.01.80	2r3	Loughborough	17	May
15.17	1.0	Tyrone Carr		30.07.80	4h2	London (Ha)	24	May
15.20		John Dannan		5.12.80	1	Bedford	10	Jun
15.27	0.3	Robert Hollinger		11.10.80	D	Hull	20	Sep
15.29 w	4.4	Pat Crowley		4.11.80	7h2	Exeter	10	Jul
15.30	0.6	John Heanley		25.09.80	D	Hull	20	Sep

overage

14.12	1.3	Liam Collins	U23	23.10.78	1	Exeter	11	Jul

Hand Timing

14.1 w		Ben Warmington		(14.16)	1	Cannock	13	Sep
14.4	1.7	Andrew Turner		(14.49)	2	Nottingham	13	Jun
14.7 w	2.8	Matthew Butler		(14.85)	1	Aberdare	31	Aug
14.8		John Monds		(14.81)	1	Telford	26	Jul
14.8		Andrew Hicks		30.07.79	1	Worcester	12	Sep
14.8 w	2.8	Ben Roberts		(15.15)	2	Aberdare	31	Aug
14.9					1	Colwyn Bay	10	May
15.0	.	Richard Sear		21.08.79	2	London (WF)	19	Apr
15.0		Lee Tindall		(15.07)	1	Portsmouth	13	Jun
15.0		Paul Crossley		30.03.79	2	Peterborough	26	Jul
15.0		David O'Leary		3.08.80	2	Derby	20	Sep
15.1	1.6	Craig McCarthy		(15.12)	2	Birmingham	21	Jun
15.1		Patrick Brown		(15.10)	1	York	19	Jul
15.1		Robert Hollinger		(15.27)	1	Hull	23	Aug
15.1		Steve Surety		18.02.80	1	Woodford	23	Aug
15.1 w		Austin Ferns		12.01.81	2r2	Cannock	13	Sep
15.2		Tim Dalton		18.01.79	4	London (He)	23	Aug

Under 17

15.4		David Brackstone		13.03.82	3	Derby	20	Sep

110 METRES HURDLES

13.02	1.9	Colin Jackson		18.02.67	1s1	Budapest, HUN	22	Aug
13.02	1.5				1	Budapest, HUN	22	Aug
13.07	-1.4				1	Nuremberg, GER	11	Jul
13.09	0.8				2	Lausanne, SWZ	25	Aug
13.10	-1.1				1	Bellinzona, SWZ	1	Jul
13.11 A	2.0				2	Johannesburg, RSA	13	Sep
13.12	-0.7				1	Helsinki, FIN	13	Jun
13.14	1.2				1	Chemnitz, GER	20	May
13.15	-0.5				1	Athens, GRE	17	Jun
13.16	0.0				1	Jena, GER	24	May
13.16	0.2				2	Brussels, BEL	28	Aug
13.17	0.0				1	St. Petersburg, RUS	28	Jun
13.17	0.9				4	New York, USA	20	Jul
13.18	0.0				1	Milan, ITA	5	Jun
13.18	-0.6				2	Linz, AUT	5	Jul
13.20	-0.6				2	Berlin, GER	1	Sep
13.21	0.0				1	Cottbus, GER	27	May
13.24	-0.5				1	Dortmund, GER	7	Jun
13.24	1.5				3	Sheffield	2	Aug
13.30	0.9				1h1	Jena, GER	24	May
13.31	-1.5				1h3	Budapest, HUN	21	Aug
13.36	-0.8				1h3	Birmingham	26	Jul
13.37	-1.3				1	Birmingham	26	Jul
13.40	-2.5				1	Glasgow	30	Aug
13.42	-2.0				1	Gateshead	19	Jul
13.51	-1.4				1	Tokyo, JAP	19	Sep
13.74	-1.7				1h1	Tokyo, JAP	19	Sep

13.25	1.1	Tony Jarrett		13.08.68	1	Turku, FIN	1	Jul
	13.32	0.6			2	Bratislava, SVK	9	Jun
	13.32	1.5			6	Budapest, HUN	22	Aug
	13.32	-0.2			1h2	Kuala Lumpur, MAL	19	Sep
	13.33	-2.0			3s2	Budapest, HUN	22	Aug
	13.39	0.6			1h2	Birmingham	26	Jul
	13.40	2.0			1	Ostrava, CZE	11	Jun
	13.42	-1.3			2	Birmingham	26	Jul
	13.43	1.4			1r1	Budapest, HUN	5	Jul
	13.45	1.7			3r2	Budapest, HUN	5	Jul
	13.47	-0.1			1	Kuala Lumpur, MAL	20	Sep
	13.48 i				1	Tampere, FIN	4	Feb
	13.51	0.0			1h4	Budapest, HUN	21	Aug
	13.52	0.4			1	Tallinn, EST	19	Jun
	13.65	-2.0			2	Gateshead	19	Jul
	13.69	-3.3			1	Ljubljana, SLO	31	May
	13.78	-2.5			3	Glasgow	30	Aug
13.54	-0.2	Paul Gray		25.05.69	2h2	Kuala Lumpur, MAL	19	Sep
	13.62	-0.1			4	Kuala Lumpur, MAL	20	Sep
	13.76	-2.0			3	Gateshead	19	Jul
13.57	-0.3	Andy Tulloch		1.04.67	2h1	Kuala Lumpur, MAL	19	Sep
	13.63	1.8			2	Belgrade, YUG	31	May
	13.67	-0.1			6	Kuala Lumpur, MAL	20	Sep
	13.72	0.6			7	Bratislava, SVK	9	Jun
	13.79	-2.0			7s2	Budapest, HUN	22	Aug
	13.81				4h2	Budapest, HUN	21	Aug
	13.86	-0.4			1	Floro, NOR	23	May
13.80	-0.3	Ross Baillie	U23	26.09.77	3h1	Kuala Lumpur, MAL	19	Sep
	13.85	-0.1			8	Kuala Lumpur, MAL	20	Sep
	13.90	-1.3			4	Birmingham	26	Jul
13.85	2.0	Damien Greaves	U23	19.09.77	1	Hexham	14	Jun
	13.88	-1.3			3	Birmingham	26	Jul
	13.94	-0.3			1	Rhede, GER	19	Jun
	13.95	-0.3			1h1	Birmingham	26	Jul
	13.97	0.0			3	Dessau, GER	1	Aug

62 performances to 14.00 by 6 athletes including 1 indoors

14.03	-1.3	Lloyd Cowan		8.07.62	5	Birmingham	26	Jul
14.12	-2.2	Matthew Clements	U23	17.09.77	1	Loughborough	17	May
14.17	0.5	Neil Owen		18.10.73	4r2	La Chaux de Fonds, SWZ	16	Aug
14.22	0.2	Ken Campbell		30.09.72	1rB	Turku, FIN	1	Jul
	(10)							
14.25	0.2	Ben Warmington	U20	20.03.79	3h4	Annecy, FRA	31	Jul
14.26	1.9	Dominic Bradley	U23	22.12.76	1	Cudworth	1	Aug
14.30		Mike Robbins	U23	14.03.76	1	Hattiesburg, USA	14	Mar
14.30	0.4	Duncan Malins	U23	12.06.78	1	Bedford	30	May
14.34	1.3	Matt Douglas	U23	26.11.76	1	Singapore, SIN	5	Sep
14.39	0.5	Martyn Hendry		10.04.75	2	Gava, SPA	24	May
14.40	0.3	Sean Carroll		8.08.74	1h1	Watford	21	Jun
14.43	1.8	Dave Sweetman		27.01.71	2h2	Bedford	24	May
14.51	0.0	Jamie Quarry		15.11.72	1D	Kuala Lumpur, MAL	18	Sep
14.56	-1.2	Robert Newton	U20	10.05.81	4h2	Annecy, FRA	31	Jul
	(20)							
14.59	0.6	Mensah Elliott	U23	29.08.76	5h2	Birmingham	26	Jul
14.59	-2.7	Paul Gripton	U23	9.11.76	2	Birmingham	23	Aug
14.63	-1.3	Du'aine Ladejo		14.02.71	1D	Bressanone, ITA	5	Jul
14.65	1.5	Kirk Harries		7.08.74	2r2	London (He)	8	Aug
14.66	1.2	Chris Hargrave	U20	27.02.79	1h3	Bedford	24	May
14.68	0.3	Richard Sear	U20	21.08.79	3h1	Watford	21	Jun
14.69	-0.7	Tony Gill	U23	19.09.77	2	Liverpool	20	Jun
14.71	1.4	Chris Baillie	U20	21.04.81	2h1	Bedford	5	Jul

14.73	-2.2	Greg Dunson		2.12.63	4	Loughborough	17	May
14.77	-1.5	Paul Thompson		22.03.72	5	Birmingham	6	Jun
	(30)							
14.79	1.5	Nick Cooper	U23	4.02.77	3r2	London (He)	8	Aug
14.80		James Archampong	U23	14.03.76	4	Birmingham	18	Jul
14.85	-2.2	Martin Nicholson		9.12.70	7	Loughborough	17	May
14.88	-0.8	Liam Collins	U23	23.10.78	4h3	Birmingham	26	Jul
14.89		Ciaran Doherty		14.01.75	2	Belfast	27	Jun
14.90	-2.6	Chris Rawlinson		19.05.72	4	Watford	16	May
14.91	-1.7	Adrian Caines		13.11.74	1r2	Birmingham	6	Jun
14.95	1.8	Nathan Hart		1.07.73	5h2	Bedford	24	May
14.96	1.4	Dan Brewer	U20	10.08.80	3h1	Bedford	5	Jul
14.98	1.9	Anthony Southward		31.01.71	2	Cudworth	1	Aug
	(40)							
15.04	0.4	Rafer Joseph		21.07.68	1D	Bressanone, ITA	5	Jul
15.09	-0.3	Jason McDade	U20	3.04.80	1D	Wrexham	2	Aug
15.12	1.2	Andrew David		9.09.69	3h3	Bedford	24	May
15.14	1.8	Gary McCracken	U23	23.01.78	6h2	Bedford	24	May
15.18	0.4	Ererton Harrison		8.04.66	6	Bedford	30	May
15.21	0.2	Alexis Sharp		31.10.72	D	Azusa, USA	17	Apr
15.22	-0.4	Kevin Furlong		19.05.70	6h3	Kuala Lumpur, MAL	19	Sep
15.30	1.4	Matthew Butler	U20	4.04.80	4h1	Bedford	5	Jul
15.32		Perry Batchelor		11.12.75	1	Cosford	18	Jul
15.37		G. Evans			1	Copenhagen, DEN	23	Jun
	(50)							
15.39	-2.0	Stevie Scott	U20	5.06.79	2r2	Watford	16	May
15.46	1.5	Mark Bushell	U23	22.10.76	4r2	London (He)	8	Aug
15.48	1.8	Josef Bailey	U23	2.12.77	7h2	Bedford	24	May
15.51	-0.2	Adam Tibbets	U23	14.12.78	5r2	Bedford	30	May
15.52	-2.3	Mark Sweeney	U23	26.02.77	1D	Birmingham	23	Aug
15.54	0.3	Chris Dorgu		11.12.69	5h1	Watford	21	Jun
15.54	1.9	John Monds	U20	24.03.80	4	Cudworth	1	Aug
15.56	-2.2	Chris Low	U20	24.04.80	6r2	Loughborough	17	May
15.59	1.4	Lee Tindall	U20	19.02.80	5h1	Bedford	5	Jul
15.61		Ian Cawley	U23	21.11.78	1	Portsmouth	26	Jun
	(60)							
15.65	0.3	Nigel Hayman		25.09.74	6h1	Watford	21	Jun
15.68	1.5	Ian Neely		29.12.74	5r2	London (He)	8	Aug

Wind Assisted

13.33	2.1	Jackson		(13.02)	1h	Chemnitz, GER	20	May
13.33	2.1	Jarrett		(13.25)	2	Salamanca, SPA	10	Jul
13.81	2.1	Gray		(13.54)	1	Leeds	7	Jun
13.82	2.4	Baillie	U23	(13.80)	1	Cork, IRE	27	Jun
13.83	2.4				1	Bedford	29	Aug
13.99	3.5				1	Edinburgh	18	Jul
13.84	3.1	Damien Greaves	U23	(13.85)	1	London (He)	8	Aug
13.89	2.4				2	Bedford	29	Aug
13.90	2.4				2	Cork, IRE	27	Jun
13.89	4.2	Ken Campbell		(14.22)	1	Maia, POR	14	Jun
13.96	4.2	Mike Robbins	U23	(14.30)	1	Monroe, USA	28	Mar
13.97	3.1	Lloyd Cowan		(14.03)	2	London (He)	8	Aug
		12 performances to 14.00 by 8 athletes						
14.07	4.6	Dominic Bradley	U23	(14.26)	1	Bedford	24	May
14.10	3.1	Neil Owen		(14.17)	3	London (He)	8	Aug
14.16	2.9	Jamie Quarry		(14.51)	1	Watford	21	Jun
14.22	4.6	Dave Sweetman		(14.43)	2	Bedford	24	May
14.24	4.2	Martyn Hendry		(14.39)	1h2	Bath	3	May
14.24	3.9	Ben Warmington	U20	(14.25)	1	Bedford	5	Jul
14.29	4.6	Mensah Elliott	U23	(14.59)	3	Bedford	24	May

14.35	4.5	Liam Collins	U23	(14.88)	1rB	Edinburgh	4	Jul
14.40	3.9	Robert Newton	U20	(14.56)	2	Bedford	5	Jul
14.47	5.0	Tony Gill	U23	(14.69)	6	Edinburgh	4	Jul
14.52	4.6	Richard Sear	U20	(14.68)	4	Bedford	24	May
14.52	2.9	Ererton Harrison		(15.18)	6	Watford	21	Jun
14.55	4.6	Chris Baillie	U20	(14.71)	5	Bedford	24	May
14.63	4.6	Kirk Harries		(14.65)	6	Bedford	24	May
14.65	4.5	Nick Cooper	U23	(14.79)	2rB	Edinburgh	4	Jul
14.75	2.5	Perry Batchelor		(15.32)	4h1	Bedford	24	May
14.76	3.6	Mohammed Sillah-Freckleton	U20	11.09.80	2h2	Bedford	5	Jul
14.87	2.5	Stevie Scott		(15.39)	4h3	Watford	21	Jun
14.88	3.1	Adrian Caines		(14.91)	6	London (He)	8	Aug
14.91	3.2	Barry Thomas		28.04.72	4D	Arles, FRA	24	May
14.98	2.8	Rafer Joseph		(15.04)	D	Azusa, USA	17	Apr
14.98	4.6	Ben Roberts	U20	15.01.80	1D	Arles, FRA	24	May
15.05	2.4	Paul Hibbert		31.03.65	6	Bedford	29	Aug
15.10	2.7	William Wynn		15.02.73	4h2	Watford	21	Jun
15.13	3.3	Mark Sweeney	U23	(15.52)	5h1	Bath	3	May
15.16	3.4	Luke Gittens	U20	4.01.81	5	Bruges, BEL	23	Aug
15.27	2.5	Adrian Carter		7.02.68	5h3	Watford	21	Jun
15.28	3.0	Alex Kruger		18.11.63	4D	Arles, FRA	24	May
15.30	2.5	Lee Tindall	U20	(15.59)	6h3	Watford	21	Jun
15.31	4.3	Steve Gutteridge		5.07.71	2=D	Arles, FRA	24	May
15.31	2.5	Ian Cawley	U23	(15.61)	7h3	Watford	21	Jun
15.35	2.5	Richard Hunter		12.01.71	5h1	Bedford	24	May
15.35	4.6	Paul Jones	U23	11.04.78	2D	Arles, FRA	24	May
15.35	3.6	Chris Low	U20	(15.56)	4h2	Bedford	5	Jul
15.37	3.6	Anthony Bliss		7.03.70	2	Crawley	10	May
15.44	2.4	Mike Coker	V40	16.01.57	8	Bedford	29	Aug
15.45	3.4	Stephen McDonnell	U20	24.07.80	7	Bruges, BEL	23	Aug
15.49	3.5	Duncan Mathieson		8.03.69	5	Edinburgh	18	Jul
15.51	4.5	Colin Hogg		22.05.67	4rB	Edinburgh	4	Jul
15.52	4.5	Ian Neely		(15.68)	5rB	Edinburgh	4	Jul
15.63	4.3	Roger Hunter	U23	10.03.76	4D	Arles, FRA	24	May

Hand Timing

13.8	2.0	Gray		(13.54)	1	Cardiff	6	Jun
13.8	1.4				1	Watford	4	Jul
13.9		Jarrett		(13.25)	1	Thurrock	31	Aug
3 performances to 14.0 by 2 athletes								
14.3	1.4	Mensah Elliott	U23	(14.59)	2	Watford	4	Jul
14.6		Chris Hargrave	U20	(14.66)	1	London (TB)	16	May
14.6		Greg Dunson		(14.73)	1	Cosford	1	Jul
14.6		Du'aine Ladejo		(14.63)	1	Harrow	30	Aug
14.6 w	3.2	Anthony Southward		(14.98)	2	Bebington	4	Jul
14.7	-0.1				2	Liverpool	18	Jul
14.7		Nick Cooper	U23	(14.79)	3	Thurrock	31	Aug
14.7 w	2.7	James Archampong	U23	(14.80)	1	Newport	8	Aug
14.8	1.6	Ciaran Doherty		(14.89)	1	Londonderry	28	Jun
14.8	-0.1	Liam Collins	U23	(14.88)	3	Liverpool	18	Jul
14.8 w	4.0	Gary McCracken	U23	(15.14)	1	Lloret de Mar, SPA	20	Jun
14.9		Kevin Furlong		(15.22)	1	Douglas, IOM	13	May
14.9 w	2.7	Anthony Brannen		16.09.68	2	Newport	8	Aug
15.0	1.2				2	Watford	6	Jun
14.9 w	4.1	Andrew David		(15.12)	3	Liverpool	8	Aug
15.1					2	Woodford	25	Apr
15.0		Ererton Harrison		(15.18)	1	Brighton	16	May

15.0 w	3.2	Leo Barker	U23	26.12.78	3	Bebington	4	Jul
		15.1			1	Woodford	25	Apr
15.1	1.9	Adrian Carter		(15.27w)	2	Enfield	9	May
15.1		Ian Cawley	U23	(15.61)	1	Reading	14	Jun
15.1		Perry Batchelor		(15.32)	2	Derby	19	Jul
15.1	-0.3	Mark Bishop		12.02.67	1r2	Barking	8	Aug
15.1 w	2.2	Andrew Bargh	U23	21.08.76	1r2	Liverpool	8	Aug
		15.2 1.6			2r2	Watford	4	Jul
15.2	2.0	William Wynn		(15.10w)	2D	Derby	30	May
15.2	1.2	Chris Dorgu		(15.54)	4	Watford	6	Jun
15.2	1.4	Ayo Falola		29.07.68	1rB	Cardiff	6	Jun
15.3		Ben Roberts	U20	(14.98w)	1	Newport	3	May
15.3		Mark Roberts		1.09.69	1	Walton	16	May
15.3		Adam Tibbets	U23	(15.51)	2	Loughborough	10	Jun
15.3		Philip McIlfatrick	V40	5.02.54	2	Londonderry	28	Jun
15.3	1.4	Mike Coker	V40	(15.44w)	4	Watford	4	Jul
15.3		Barry Marsden		11.06.64	1	Southend	15	Aug
15.3 w	2.7	Sean Saxon		11.12.71	3	Newport	8	Aug
		15.4 1.2			5	Watford	6	Jun
15.4		Roger Honey	V40	10.02.55	1	Woodford	18	Apr
15.4		Mohammed Sillah-Freckleton	U20	(14.76w)	1	Walton	19	Apr
15.4		Anthony Bliss		(15.37w)	1	Basingstoke	2	May
15.4		Nigel Hayman		(15.65)	2	London (TB)	16	May
15.4		Clarence Allen		1.04.64	3	London (TB)	16	May
15.4	1.6	Sebastian Rosato		19.11.72	3r2	Watford	4	Jul
15.4		Paul Jones	U23	(15.35w)	1rB	Brecon	5	Jul
15.4	-0.2	Roger Hunter	U23	(15.63w)	2D	Wrexham	2	Aug
15.4		John Monds	U20	(15.54)	1	Colwyn Bay	5	Sep
15.4 w	2.2	Rob Laing		30.07.66	3r2	Liverpool	8	Aug
		15.6			1m2	Ormskirk	11	Jul
15.5		Stuart Caudery		19.11.66	2	London (BP)	16	May
15.5		Adrian Ferrand		5.02.68	1	London (Nh)	16	May
15.5	2.0	Richard Hunter		(15.35w)	4D	Derby	30	May
15.5		Chris Hodson	U20	11.11.80	1	King's Lynn	6	Jun
15.5		Mark Sweeney	U23	(15.52)	4	Derby	19	Jul
15.5		Andy Hodge		18.12.68	2	Bromley	15	Aug
15.5		Richard Scott		14.09.73	2	Southend	15	Aug
15.6		Scott Exley	U23	9.02.78	1	Bournemouth	9	May
15.6		John Hadler		18.08.69	2	Brighton	16	May
15.6		Barry Thomas		(14.91w)	4	Sheffield (W)	16	May
15.6		Steve Gutteridge		(15.31w)	1	London (PH)	6	Jun
15.6		Paul Crossley	U20	30.03.79	1	Luton	4	Jul
15.6		Dean Leslie	U23	9.01.78	2r2	Barking	8	Aug
15.6 w	3.2	Steve Leader		24.11.66	4	Bebington	4	Jul
15.6 w	2.2	John Franklin		1.03.66	4r2	Liverpool	8	Aug

doubtful timing

14.6		Leroy Gould		16.06.64	1r2	Basildon	2	May

Foreign

15.3		*Pascal Renaud (FRA)*		*20.04.70*	*1*	*London (EL)*	*2*	*May*
15.53	*2.0*	*Joe Naughton (IRE)*		*17.10.74*	*5D*	*Derby*	*31*	*May*

200 METRES HURDLES

22.69	Colin Jackson		18.02.67	1	Nantes, FRA	8	Sep

300 METRES HURDLES

36.87 i	Gary Cadogan		8.10.66	3	Tampere, FIN	4	Feb

400 METRES HURDLES

49.16	Paul Gray	25.05.69	3h3	Budapest, HUN	18	Aug
49.76			4	Sheffield	2	Aug
49.81			1	Birmingham	26	Jul
50.05			3	Glasgow	30	Aug
50.34			6s1	Budapest, HUN	19	Aug
50.6			1	Watford	4	Jul
50.72			1h3	Birmingham	25	Jul
51.04			1	Cardiff	4	Aug
51.05			3r2	Jena, GER	24	May
51.44			3	Leeds	7	Jun
49.79	Anthony Borsumato	13.12.73	5	St. Petersburg, RUS	27	Jun
49.85			2	Birmingham	26	Jul
49.86 A			7	Johannesburg, RSA	11	Sep
49.96			1	Watford	16	May
50.15			4h1	Kuala Lumpur, MAL	17	Sep
50.22			4	Glasgow	30	Aug
50.28			6	Sheffield	2	Aug
50.51			2	Leeds	7	Jun
50.63			1	Gateshead	10	May
50.91			6h1	Budapest, HUN	18	Aug
50.96			1h4	Birmingham	25	Jul
51.03			2	Loughborough	17	May
49.81	Chris Rawlinson	19.05.72	1	Loughborough	17	May
50.20			3	Birmingham	26	Jul
50.64			2	Celle Ligure, ITA	25	Jun
50.89			1h2	Birmingham	25	Jul
51.11			7h2	Budapest, HUN	18	Aug
50.12	Gary Jennings	21.02.72	2	Tarare, FRA	18	Jul
50.81			1r2	London (He)	8	Aug
50.84			8	Sheffield	2	Aug
50.94			6h2	Kuala Lumpur, MAL	17	Sep
50.96			3	Tallinn, EST	19	Jun
51.06			1h1	Birmingham	25	Jul
51.10			5	Birmingham	26	Jul
51.12			1	Bedford	29	Aug
50.20	Matt Douglas	U23 26.11.76	4h2	Kuala Lumpur, MAL	17	Sep
50.41			4	Birmingham	26	Jul
50.79			6	Glasgow	30	Aug
50.87			1	Dessau, GER	1	Aug
50.90			2	Watford	16	May
50.9			1	Birmingham	6	Jun
51.10			2h3	Birmingham	25	Jul
51.17			2	Bedford	29	Aug
51.36			1	London (He)	8	Aug
50.57	Blair Young	5.04.71	3	Melbourne, AUS	14	Mar
51.22			5	Brisbane, AUS	21	Mar
51.23			2h1	Birmingham	25	Jul
51.35			1	Edinburgh	18	Jul
51.37			2	Jona, SWZ	12	Jul
51.01	Gary Cadogan	8.10.66	2	Tartu, EST	11	Jun
51.29			4	Ljubljana, SLO	31	May
51.05	Paul Thompson	22.03.72	1	Seattle, USA	16	May
51.28			1rC	Walnut, USA	19	Apr
51.42			4	Tallinn, EST	19	Jun
51.16	Tony Williams	1.05.72	1rB	Celle Ligure, ITA	25	Jun
51.2	Lawrence Lynch	1.11.67	2	Watford	4	Jul
51.28			2h4	Birmingham	25	Jul
51.3			1	Enfield	19	Jul

(10)

51.3	Remi Edu	U23	14.12.78	2	Birmingham	6	Jun
51.37				1	Bedford	30	May
51.5	Matthew Elias	U20	25.04.79	1	Cardiff	6	Jun
52.34				8h1	Kuala Lumpur, MAL	17	Sep

61 performances to 51.5 by 12 athletes

51.55	Eddie Betts		18.02.71	2h2	Birmingham	25	Jul
52.13	Richard McDonald	U20	11.01.80	7s1	Annecy, FRA	29	Jul
52.18	Paul Hibbert		31.03.65	3h3	Birmingham	25	Jul
52.34	Ian Neely		29.12.74	2	Bedford	30	May
52.38	Dave Savage		13.11.72	2	Liverpool	20	Jun
52.47	Andrew Bargh	U23	21.08.76	2	Watford	20	Jun
52.47	Barry Middleton		10.03.75	4h3	Birmingham	25	Jul
52.6	Mark Stern		22.05.72	1	Bournemouth	4	Jul
52.90				1h3	Bedford	25	May
	(20)						
52.62	Greg Dunson		2.12.63	2r2	Loughborough	17	May
52.65	Mike Robbins	U23	14.03.76	1	Monroe, USA	28	Mar
52.72	Richard Scott		14.09.73	3	Watford	20	Jun
52.92	Berian Davies		22.04.73	3	Bedford	25	May
53.04	Douglas Thom		13.04.68	4	Watford	16	May
53.1	Ruben Tabares	U23	22.10.78	1	Bromley	14	Jun
54.11				1	Exeter	11	Jul
53.12	James Hillier	U23	3.04.78	1	Dublin (S), IRE	19	Jun
53.3	Gary Telfer		10.01.65	2	Enfield	19	Jul
53.41				2r2	London (He)	8	Aug
53.3	John McIlwham		29.02.72	1	Blackpool	6	Sep
53.74				4h2	Birmingham	25	Jul
53.39	David Gifford		9.03.73	5h3	Birmingham	25	Jul
	(30)						
53.42	Andrew Hicks	U20	30.07.79	3r2	Loughborough	17	May
53.5	Mark Davidson		15.11.68	1	Aberdeen	6	Jun
55.33				2	Edinburgh	10	May
53.77	Howard Moscrop	V40	16.12.57	1	Cesenatico, ITA	12	Sep
53.80	Austin Ferns	U20	12.01.81	2	Bedford	5	Jul
53.8	Andrew Kennard		2.01.66	3	Enfield	19	Jul
54.60				6	Watford	20	Jun
53.9	Robert Lewis	U23	2.09.78	1	Bromley	15	Aug
54.15				1	Bedford	30	Aug
53.92	Lee Wiscombe	U20	12.07.80	3	Bedford	5	Jul
53.94	Ayo Falola		29.07.68	3h1	Watford	20	Jun
53.95	Dean Park	U23	23.09.77	3h2	Watford	20	Jun
54.02	Tim Dalton	U20	18.01.79	1	London (He)	30	Aug
	(40)						
54.03	Jon Goodwin	U23	22.09.76	3	Loughborough	17	May
54.08	John Bell		10.09.73	3r2	Birmingham	6	Jun
54.15	Jon Cuff	U20	30.03.80	4	Bedford	5	Jul
54.22	Mark Rowlands	U23	18.04.78	5h2	Birmingham	25	Jul
54.3	Carl Foster		24.10.75	2	Enfield	6	Jun
54.96				1	Cudworth	9	May
54.4	Mark Green		28.06.71	2	Stoke	16	May
54.4	Phil Harries		7.04.66	1	Scunthorpe	4	Jul
54.5	Carl McMullen	U20	9.11.79	1	Whitehaven	2	May
55.37				3r3	Loughborough	17	May
54.57	Mike Coker	V40	16.01.57	1	Calais, FRA	20	Jun
54.7	Mark Anderson	U23	5.11.77	2	Watford	6	Jun
55.43				3h3	Bath	2	May
	(50)						
54.80	Paul Armstrong	U20	20.10.79	6	Bedford	5	Jul
54.8	Steve Evans	U23	29.05.78	1	Colwyn Bay	7	Jun
54.8	Glenn Gray		21.04.68	1	Stevenage	4	Jul
54.94				7h2	Birmingham	25	Jul

54.8	David Walker	U23	24.11.78	2	Newport	8	Aug
55.71				h	Cudworth	1	Aug
54.90	Paul Beaumont		27.03.63	2	Cosford	1	Jul
54.9	Simon Wilson		30.04.74	2	Ashford	9	May
54.9	Matt Birchall		1.11.71	3	Enfield	16	May
54.97				5	Liverpool	21	Jun
54.9	Martin Holgate		2.11.65	4	Enfield	19	Jul
54.92	Nange Ursell	U17	1.10.81	1h2	Bedford	4	Jul
54.93	Scott Chisholm	U23	20.10.77	1rB	Inverness	2	Aug
	(60)						
54.97	Dale Daborn		14.11.66	3	Cosford	1	Jul
55.00	Tony Seston	U20	21.12.80	3h2	Bedford	4	Jul
55.0	Leon McRae	U20	3.11.80	3	London (Ha)	23	May
55.70				2h1	London (Ha)	23	May
55.07	Anthony Pamah		11.11.63	4h2	Watford	20	Jun
55.07	N. Edwards			4	Cosford	1	Jul
55.2	Stephen Pratt		6.02.71	2	Walton	16	May
55.3	Robert Osborne		22.10.75	1	St. Ives	29	Apr
55.3	Stephen Hudson	U23	13.08.76	1	Loughborough	10	Jun
55.3	Gareth Lewis	U23	5.10.78	1	Kingston	14	Jun
55.35	Shaun Robson	U20	21.06.80	1	Barry	14	Jul
	(70)						
55.43	Paul Crossley	U20	30.03.79	3	London (He)	30	Aug
55.48	David O'Leary	U20	3.08.80	1	Stoke	20	Jun
55.5	Martin Thomas	U23	21.09.78	6	Cardiff	6	Jun
55.56	Chris Herring	U20	3.03.81	2	Gateshead	10	May
55.6	Richard Gawthorpe	U20	28.01.81	1	Derby	13	Jun
55.6	Dave Griffin		5.12.63	3r2	Liverpool	8	Aug
55.6	Mark Nitsch	U23	3.03.78	1	Peterborough	31	Aug
55.69	Mark Barrow		30.06.68	7	Liverpool	20	Jun
55.72	Martin Purvis		26.10.71	3	Edinburgh	18	Jul
55.8	Gary Stevenson	U20	12.09.79	1	Greenock	26	Apr
	(80)						
55.89	Robert Gascoigne		5.10.74	4r2	Bedford	30	May
55.9	Patrick Brown	U20	2.09.79	3	Wakefield	2	May
55.9	Stephen White		2.10.75	2	Loughborough	13	May
55.9	Ian Wells		18.02.62	2	London (BP)	25	Jul
55.92				4r2	London (He)	8	Aug
55.94	Tim Lang		8.12.73	3h2	Bath	2	May
56.0	Rowland Ifill		11.11.75	2	Loughborough	10	Jun
56.0	Michael Strain	U20	11.09.79	1	Grangemouth	2	Aug

Additional Under 20 (1 - 19 above)

56.05	Bradley Yiend		25.10.80	4h2	Exeter	10	Jul
	(20)						
56.07	Gavin Jones		4.03.80	2	Barry	14	Jul
56.3	Tim Knox-Hook		17.12.80	2	Enfield	9	May
56.32	Stephen McDonnell		24.07.80	6	Dublin (S), IRE	25	Jul
56.36	Tristan Anthony	U17	16.12.82	3h1	Bedford	4	Jul
56.40	Robert Doubal		16.04.80	3	Barry	14	Jul
56.4	Trevor Agard		12.03.80	1	Enfield	13	Jun
56.4	Dale Garland		13.10.80	1	Portsmouth	13	Jun
56.5	Ben Caldwell	U17	3.03.82	1	Bolton	6	Jun
56.8	Daniel Jackson		17.04.79	3	London (PH)	6	Jun
56.8	Justin Smith		13.06.79	1	Yeovil	26	Jul
	(30)						
56.9	Drew Hall		31.08.81	2	Antrim	20	Jun
57.0	John Shenava		5.02.81	3	Grangemouth	17	May

Additional Under 17 (1 - 3 above)

58.1	Graeme Lammie		3.10.81	1rB	Glasgow (S)	14	Jun
58.4	Brian McPhail		6.05.82	3	Grangemouth	17	May

Foreign

53.5	*Colin Byrne (IRE)*	*U20*	*9.02.79*	*1*	*Exeter*	*6*	*Jun*
53.72	*Nicholas Ring (IRE)*	*U23*	*76*	*4*	*Dublin, IRE*	*26*	*Jul*
53.75	*Nigel Keogh (IRE)*		*18.07.67*	*5*	*Dublin, IRE*	*26*	*Jul*
53.8	*Paul Conroy*		*24.08.71*	*1*	*Enfield*	*6*	*Jun*
54.22				*5*	*Bedford*	*30*	*May*

400 METRES HURDLES - Under 17

53.26	Nange Ursell	1.10.81	1	Exeter	11	Jul
54.64	Jeffrey Christie	24.09.82	3	Ayr	18	Jul
54.85	Graeme Lammie	3.10.81	4	Ayr	18	Jul
55.50	Ben Caldwell	3.03.82	2h3	Exeter	10	Jul
55.51	John Cole	13.11.81	3	Exeter	11	Jul
56.09	Gareth Rees	15.01.82	1	Cudworth	1	Aug
56.16	Chris Lomas	22.04.82	5	Exeter	11	Jul
56.5	Leighton Lewis	10.09.81	1	Carmarthen	13	Jun
56.79	Richard Castillo	3.12.81	4	Sheffield	16	Aug
56.8	Ben Hooper	10.09.82	1	Yeovil	13	Jun
(10)						
56.85	James Tattershall	25.11.81	3h2	Exeter	10	Jul
56.90	Ben Tromans	8.12.81	2	Birmingham	5	Sep
57.13	David Lockwood	24.11.81	3	York	25	Jul
57.26	Ian Ward	3.04.82	1h1	Exeter	10	Jul
57.33	Adam D' Arcy	25.05.82	2h1	Exeter	10	Jul
57.4	Ross Kirby	16.12.81	1	Bracknell	19	Jul
58.23			5	Sheffield	16	Aug
57.53	Matthew Dewsberry	9.10.81	4h2	Exeter	10	Jul
57.59	Aaron Hamilton	7.08.82	4	York	25	Jul
57.6	Andrew Griffiths	26.09.81	2	Swansea	28	Jun
57.6	Danny Glover	3.03.82	1	Ashford	5	Jul
57.70			5h2	Exeter	10	Jul
(20)						
57.66	Daniel Brandwood	1.10.82	2h2	York	25	Jul
57.79	Lee Grice	17.04.82	1	Birmingham	6	Sep
57.85	Richard Smith	12.10.82	4h3	Exeter	10	Jul
58.05	Brian McPhail	6.05.82	1	Inverness	9	Jun
58.21	Adrian Hemery	6.08.82	2h4	Exeter	10	Jul
58.26	Russell Billingham	13.10.81	4h1	Exeter	10	Jul

overage

55.89	Drew Hall	U20	31.08.81	2	Tullamore, IRE	6	Jun
57.9	Paul McMullan	U20	11.07.81	2	Antrim	30	May

HIGH JUMP

2.36 i	Steve Smith	29.03.73	1	Balingen, GER	8	Feb
2.30			4	Athens, GRE	17	Jun
2.27 i			1	Stange, NOR	24	Jan
2.27 i			4=	Arnstadt, GER	30	Jan
2.24			2	Ostrava, CZE	11	Jun
2.20 i			3=	Berlin, GER	6	Mar
2.34	Dalton Grant	8.04.66	2	Budapest, HUN	21	Aug
2.31			1	Kuala Lumpur, MAL	19	Sep
2.28			4	Leverkusen, GER	9	Aug
2.27 i			2	Arnstadt, GER	31	Jan
2.27			5	Athens, GRE	17	Jun
2.26 i			2	Piraeus, GRE	21	Feb
2.25 i			2	Stockholm, SWE	19	Feb
2.25			4=	Nice, FRA	16	Jul
2.25			9	Zurich, SWZ	12	Aug
2.24 i			8=	Wuppertal, GER	6	Feb

(Grant)	2.24 i			7	Banska Bystrica, SVK	11	Feb
	2.24			6	Eberstadt, GER	26	Jul
	2.24			Q	Budapest, HUN	19	Aug
	2.22 i			2	Ostrava, CZE	29	Jan
	2.22			2	Viersen, GER	30	Aug
	2.21			3=	Buhl, GER	28	Aug
	2.20 i			10=	Balingen, GER	8	Feb
	2.20			3=	Gateshead	19	Jul
	2.20			1	Birmingham	25	Jul
2.28	Ben Challenger 6TH	U23	7.03.78	2	Belgrade, YUG	31	May
	2.28			2	St. Petersburg, RUS	27	Jun
	2.28			2	Kuala Lumpur, MAL	19	Sep
	2.27 i			1	Birmingham	7	Feb
	2.26			1	Tallinn, EST	19	Jun
	2.26			1	Bedford	29	Aug
	2.25			1	Loughborough	17	May
	2.24 i			Q	Valencia, SPA	28	Feb
	2.22 i			10=	Valencia, SPA	1	Mar
	2.21 i			2	Ghent, BEL	1	Feb
	2.20 i			1	Birmingham	25	Jan
	2.20			1	Birmingham	6	Jun
2.28	Brendan Reilly		23.12.72	1	London (He)	8	Aug
	2.25			2	Gateshead	19	Jul
	2.24			Q	Budapest, HUN	19	Aug
	2.24			9=	Budapest, HUN	21	Aug
	2.24			5	Kuala Lumpur, MAL	19	Sep
	2.22 i			6	Lievin, FRA	22	Feb
	2.21 i			4=	Sindelfingen, GER	8	Mar
	2.20 i			5	Berlin, GER	6	Mar
	2.20			1	Cardiff	4	Aug
	2.20			8	Berlin, GER	1	Sep
2.20 i	David Barnetson		1.07.71	1	Glasgow	25	Jan
	2.05			8	Prague, CZE	8	Jun
48 performances to 2.20 by 5 athletes including 20 indoors							
2.16	Geoff Parsons		14.08.64	1	London (Elt)	4	Jul
2.16	Ian Holliday 42		9.12.73	2	London (He)	8	Aug
2.15 i	Martin Lloyd 56	U20	18.06.80	1	London (CP)	14	Feb
	2.15			2	Loughborough	17	May
2.15 i	Tony Gilhooly	U23	26.03.76	1	Glasgow	15	Mar
	2.10			1	Edinburgh	10	May
2.15	Ed Willers 57	U20	18.09.79	1	Street	13	May
(10)							
2.15	Stuart Ohrland		6.09.75	2=	Birmingham	25	Jul
2.15	Stanley Osuide		30.11.74	2=	Birmingham	25	Jul
2.15	Jason McDade 58	U20	3.04.80	1	London (He)	30	Aug
2.14 i	Colin McMaster	U20	15.01.80	1	Birmingham	28	Feb
	2.05			5	Loughborough	17	May
2.13 i	Mike Robbins	U23	14.03.76	1	Fort Worth, USA	20	Feb
	2.10			2	Austin, USA	4	Apr
2.13	Danny Graham	U20	3.08.79	1	London (He)	9	Aug
2.12 i	Mark Latham 75	U23	13.01.76	1	Birmingham	1	Mar
	2.10			1	Burton	2	May
2.12	Colin Bent		12.04.70	1	Cosford	1	Jul
2.11 i	Ken McKeown 56	U17	6.03.82	1	Grangemouth	12	Jul
	2.11			1	Ayr	18	Jul
2.10 i	Richard Aspden	U23	15.10.76	1	Bedford	25	Jan
	2.10			3	Watford	21	Jun
(20)							
2.10	Daniel Turner	U23	27.11.78	1	Crawley	2	May
2.10	Andrew Lynch		28.06.74	3	Watford	16	May
2.10	Rob Brocklebank	U23	12.10.76	2	Bedford	25	May

2.10	Richard Dent	U23	2.11.78	1	Liverpool	20 Jun
2.10	Andrew Penk	U23	19.09.78	2	Birmingham	18 Jul
2.10	Stuart Smith	U23	2.08.76	9=	Birmingham	25 Jul
2.10	Kevin McKinson	U20	6.09.80	1	London (TB)	25 Jul
2.07 i	Jamie Russell	U17	1.10.81	2	Birmingham	21 Feb
2.05				1	Leeds	23 May
2.07	Simon Bannister	U20	16.04.81	1	Peterborough	13 Jun
2.07	Robert Mitchell	U20	14.09.80	3	Exeter	11 Jul
(30)						
2.06	James Alix	U17	24.12.81	1	Exeter	10 Jul
2.06	Stuart Livingstone	U20	29.08.79	1	Inverness	2 Aug
2.05	David Nolan		16.05.75	2	Bath	4 May
2.05	John Wallace		9.10.68	2	Gateshead	9 May
2.05	James Brierley	U23	31.07.77	1	Oxford	16 May
2.05	Darren Joseph	U23	10.04.78	4	Watford	16 May
2.05	Tim Knox-Hook	U20	17.12.80	1	Sheffield (W)	16 May
2.05	Michael Leigh	U23	14.12.77	2	Sheffield (W)	16 May
2.05	Ian Massey	U23	9.09.76	2=	Liverpool	20 Jun
2.05	Mark Smith		14.09.74	1	Watford	4 Jul
(40)						
2.05	Lee Spike	U20	20.02.80	3	Watford	4 Jul
2.05	Dan Plank	U17	27.04.82	2	Ayr	18 Jul
2.04	Du'aine Ladejo		14.02.71	3D	Kuala Lumpur, MAL	17 Sep
2.03 i	Luke Crawley	U17	5.09.81	1	Birmingham	1 Mar
1.91				8	Sheffield	16 Aug
2.03	Aaron Robb	U23	24.04.76	1	Grangemouth	17 May
2.03	Brian Hall	U17	17.11.82	1	Stretford	13 Jun
2.03	Bomene Barikor	U17	22.05.82	3	Exeter	10 Jul
2.02	Alex Kruger		18.11.63	D	Arles, FRA	23 May
2.02	Brendan McConville	U20	3.01.79	1D	Antrim	29 Aug
2.01	Marlon Huggins		11.02.71	1	Kingston	9 May
(50)						
2.00 i	Paul Dovell	U23	5.05.77	2	Antwerp, BEL	10 Jan
2.00 i	Ben Davies	U20	24.08.81	6	Birmingham	25 Jan
2.00				1	Bath	30 May
2.00 i	Duncan McInnes	U23	1.05.78	6	Glasgow	25 Jan
2.00				1	Glasgow (S)	10 May
2.00	Nathan Hart		1.07.73	4	Bath	4 May
2.00	Tom Costello	U23	16.12.76	2	Oxford	16 May
2.00	Tony Kuiper	U20	25.10.79	1	Enfield	6 Jun
2.00	Alun Davies	U20	23.08.80	1	Carmarthen	14 Jun
2.00	Chris Petts	U20	22.01.80	1	Ashford	21 Jun
2.00	Stuart Judge		29.11.73	2	Derby	4 Jul
2.00	Ben Smith	U17	12.06.82	4	Exeter	10 Jul
(60)						
2.00	James Hind	U23	24.05.77	1	Leamington	15 Aug
2.00	Darren Slater	U20	1.01.80	2	Bromley	15 Aug
2.00	Simon Thomas	U20	4.03.81	1	Southend	15 Aug
2.00	Gareth Dyball	U20	16.03.81	6	Bedford	29 Aug
1.99	Dominic Girdler	U17	6.03.82	1O	Hull	20 Sep
1.98 i	Duncan Mathieson		8.03.69	H	Glasgow	14 Feb
1.97	David Warren	U20	5.12.79	1	Carlisle	29 Mar
1.97	Robert Paul	U20	12.11.80		Enfield	30 Jun
1.97	Simon Whittingham	U23	18.09.78	1	London (WF)	25 Jul
1.97	Neil Thompson	U20	23.04.79	1	Carlisle	31 Aug
(70)						
1.96 i	Paul Gilding		2.10.75	P	Horsham	7 Mar
1.95				2	Basingstoke	2 May
1.96	Gavin Fordham	U20	1.02.79	1	London (TB)	16 May
1.96	Steve Linsell		13.10.63	1	Mansfield	7 Aug
1.96	Kim Harland	U17	21.02.82	1	Dublin (S), IRE	8 Aug

1.96		Chuka Enih-Snell	U15 5TH	2.03.84	1	Aberdare	29	Aug
1.95	i	Daniel Slessor	U23	5.10.78	2	Sheffield	17	Jan
1.95					9	Birmingham	6	Jun
1.95	i	Derek Kidd	U20	12.03.79	4	Glasgow	18	Jan
1.95					1	Linwood	18	Apr
1.95	i	Shawn Baptiste	U20	16.04.81	P	Bedford	18	Jan
1.95					4	Dartford	21	Jun
1.95	i	James Hardie	U17	16.04.82	2	Glasgow	29	Jan
1.91					5	Sheffield	16	Aug
1.95	i	Barry Millar	U20	1.04.81	2	Glasgow	31	Jan
		(80)						
1.95	i	Mark Elliott	U20	12.08.80	4	Glasgow	31	Jan
1.95					1	Glasgow (S)	10	May
1.95	i	Chris Giblin	U20	20.06.81	3	Birmingham	1	Feb
1.95	i	Ian Gidley		13.11.70	3	Birmingham	1	Mar
1.95		Andrew Squire	U20	30.09.79	1	Tamworth	19	Apr
1.95		Mark Sweeney	U23	26.02.77	5	Bath	4	May
1.95		Barry Thomas		28.04.72	6	Bath	4	May
1.95		Andy Hodge		18.12.68	3	Enfield	16	May
1.95		James Anthony	U17	30.03.82	1	Carmarthen	23	May
1.95		Gerard Plunkett	U20	30.06.80		Grimsby		May
1.95		N. Watson			1	St. Ives	14	Jun
		(90)						
1.95		Paul Burraway		30.11.68	1	Walton	14	Jun
1.95		Jon Roberts	U23	28.09.77	2	Cosford	1	Jul
1.95		James Leaver		15.09.75	5	Watford	4	Jul
1.95		Stuart Back	U23	12.05.77	6	Watford	4	Jul
1.95		Steve Bonnett	U23	13.07.78	4	Derby	4	Jul
1.95		David Franks	U23	27.04.78	1	Wigan	4	Jul
1.95		Stuart Brown		27.11.72	1	Brecon	5	Jul
1.95		Robert Curzon	U23	7.12.78	1	Derby	19	Jul
1.95		Anthony Southward		31.01.71	D	Sale	22	Jul
1.95		S. Rance			3	London (WL)	25	Jul
		(100)						
1.95		Gavin Fisher	U23	18.11.77	1	London (WP)	25	Jul
1.95		Greg Dunson		2.12.63	7	London (He)	7	Aug
1.95		Brad Knowles	U23	17.11.76	2	Leamington	15	Aug
1.95		Martin Ohrland	U20	19.11.79	2	Enfield	23	Aug
1.95		Andrew Palmer	U23	13.04.77	7	Bedford	29	Aug
1.95		Alexis Sharp		31.10.72	D	Kuala Lumpur, MAL	17	Sep

Additional Under 17 (1 - 13 above)

1.94		Chris Dack		28.11.82	4	Sheffield	16	Aug
1.93		Shane Booth		16.01.82	1	Grimsby	27	Sep
1.92		Matt Little		22.07.83	1	Oxford	19	Jul
1.91		Jon Liddle		13.09.81	1	Yeovil	10	May
1.91		Paul Tohill		9.10.82	1	Tullamore, IRE	6	Jun
1.90		Richard Brown		13.05.82	1	Barking	19	Apr
1.90		Paul Doherty		22.01.83	3	Grangemouth	17	May
		(20)						
1.90		Christopher Binns		7.05.82	2	Leeds (South)	23	May
1.90		Roger Owens		26.10.81	2	Carmarthen	23	May
1.90		Alex Rowswell		18.03.82	1	Yeovil	28	Jun
1.90		Rhodri Parry		24.11.81	2	Brecon	4	Jul
1.90		Gavin Gunputhram		21.03.82	1	Ashford	5	Jul
1.90	i	Darren Locke		16.10.81	2	Grangemouth	12	Jul
1.90		David Espin		27.01.83	1	Mansfield	7	Aug
1.90		Tom Salter		7.01.83	1	Cannock	29	Aug

Additional Under 15 (1 above)

1.89	Colin Bailey	15.11.83	1P	Hull	19	Sep
1.87	Chris Bailey	28.09.83	1	London (He)	30	Aug
1.86	Edward Dunford	15.09.84	2P	Hull	19	Sep
1.85	Martin Aram	2.12.83	1	Douglas, IOM	16	Jun
1.85	Calvin Hall		2	Swindon	9	Jul
1.85	Mark Bidwell	4.09.84	1	Mansfield	9	Aug
1.81	Mark Crowley	15.11.83	2	Exeter	10	Jul
1.81	Jamie Creighton	15.09.83	3	Exeter	10	Jul
1.80	Matthew Thurgood	29.12.83	1	Great Yarmouth	21	Jun
	(10)					
1.80	Samuel Hood	17.10.83	2	Brecon	4	Jul
1.78	Ian Fenn	3.12.83	1	Brighton	19	Jul
1.77	Andrew Dickson	30.11.83	1	St. Ives	9	May
1.77	Josie McCall	12.11.83	1	Glasgow (S)	15	Aug
1.76	Gordon Clarke		1	Tullamore, IRE	6	Jun
1.75 i	Neil Hay	10.05.84	2	Birmingham	21	Feb
1.75	Mike Cross	19.12.83	1	London (Elt)	26	Apr
1.75	Brett Williams	23.10.83	1	Sheffield	26	Apr
1.75	Greg Goodrem	14.09.83	1	Luton	21	Jun
1.75	Mike Taylor		3	Brecon	4	Jul
	(20)					
1.75	D. Sham		3	Swindon	19	Jul
1.75	Barry Furse	13.05.84	1	Carn Brea	2	Aug
1.75	Iain Ramsay	10.09.83	1	Grangemouth	23	Aug

Under 13

1.68	James Dunford	14.01.86	1	Exeter	29	Sep
1.60	John Fletcher	15.07.86	1	Hull	12	Apr
1.60	Keith Higham	7.11.85	1	Carlisle	20	Jun
1.60	Yassin Kargbo		1	London (WL)	24	Jun
1.60	Paige Gallimore	18.01.86	1	Kingston	26	Jul

Foreign

2.23 i	Mark Mandy (IRE)		19.11.72	1	Nenagh, IRE	15	Feb
	2.15			2	Birmingham	6	Jun
2.10	Samson Oni (NIG)	U20	25.06.81	2	London (He)	9	Aug
2.05	Ginturas Varanauskas (LIT)		17.04.72	4	Edinburgh	4	Jul
2.05	Olu Robbin-Cocker (SLE)		27.11.75	2	Blackpool	6	Sep
2.03 i	Joe Naughton (IRE)		17.10.74	1P	Bedford	18	Jan
	2.01			1D	Derby	30	May
2.00	Pierre Faber (RSA)		9.01.72	3	Bath	4	May
1.95	Adam Read (AUS)		13.06.71	3	Inverness	2	Aug

POLE VAULT

5.80	Nick Buckfield	5.06.73	3	Hania, GRE	27	May
	5.55 i		17=Q	Valencia, SPA	27	Feb
	5.50		2	Modesto, USA	9	May
	5.42 i		4	Birmingham	15	Feb
	5.40		6=	Walnut, USA	19	Apr
	5.32		2	Irvine, USA	2	May
	5.30 i		1	Birmingham	7	Feb
	5.30		17=	Budapest, HUN	19	Aug
5.50	Mike Edwards	19.10.68	1	Waco, USA	21	Mar
	5.40 A		6	Johannesburg, RSA	12	Sep
	5.38			Arlington, USA	19	Jun
	5.30			Stephensville, USA	2	Apr
	5.30		1	Watford	16	May
	5.30		1	Watford	24	Jun
	5.30		1	Bedford	29	Aug

(Edwards)	5.28 i			5	Oklahoma City, USA	17 Feb
	5.22 Ai			4	Reno, USA	14 Feb
	5.20 i			1	Birmingham	1 Mar
	5.20			1	London (He)	8 Aug
5.50	Kevin Hughes 7TH		30.04.73	1	Watford	29 Jul
	5.40			1	Birmingham	26 Jul
	5.36			1	Watford	20 Jun
	5.35			1	Loughborough	17 May
	5.30 i			2	Birmingham	7 Feb
	5.30			1	Bedford	24 May
	5.30			1	Cork, IRE	27 Jun
	5.25 A			1	El Paso, USA	26 Dec
	5.20 i			1	Ghent, BEL	1 Feb
	5.20			4	Barcelona, SPA	17 Jun
	5.20			1	Watford	4 Jul
	5.20			1	Jona, SWZ	12 Jul
	5.20			1	Meilen, SWZ	29 Aug
	5.30 et				Bedford	30 May
5.35	Matt Belsham		11.10.71	2	Birmingham	26 Jul
	5.30			2	Watford	16 May
	5.25			5	Kuala Lumpur, MAL	20 Sep
	5.20			2	Bedford	29 Aug
5.35	Ian Tullett 13TH		15.08.69	3	Birmingham	26 Jul
	5.20			3	Watford	16 May
	5.20			2	Cork, IRE	27 Jun
	5.20			2	Birmingham	18 Jul
5.30	Paul Williamson		16.06.74	3	Arles, FRA	23 May
	5.20			1	Walnut, USA	18 Apr
	5.20			4	Birmingham	26 Jul
	5.20			3	Bedford	29 Aug
5.20 i	Tim Thomas		18.11.73	1	Birmingham	3 Jan
	5.20			1	Hasselt, BEL	22 Aug
5.20	Christian Linskey 25TH	U20 8TH	14.06.80	1	Arles, FRA	24 May
5.20	Dean Mellor		25.11.71	3	Birmingham	18 Jul
	49 performances to 5.20 by 9 athletes including 9 indoors and 1 extra trial					
5.16	Ben Flint	U23	16.09.78	1	Exeter	11 Jul
(10)						
5.10	Neil Young	U23	20.02.77	1	Cardiff	4 Aug
5.10	Neil Winter		21.03.74	2	London (He)	8 Aug
5.00	Mark Davis	U23	1.03.77	1	Corby	9 May
5.00	Mike Barber		19.10.73	3	Edinburgh	4 Jul
5.00	Andrew Weston 42		4.12.73	2	Watford	29 Jul
4.90	Christian North		2.02.74	2	Tamworth	6 Jun
4.90	Tom Richards	U23	13.11.78	5	Bedford	29 Aug
4.85 i	Mark Grant		17.05.71	2	Birmingham	3 Jan
4.80 i	Mark Johnson		7.09.64	2	Wakefield	10 Jan
	4.80			1	Enfield	16 May
4.80 i	Andrew Penk 75	U23	19.09.78	3=	Birmingham	25 Jan
	4.70			3	Bedford	24 May
(20)						
4.80	Rafer Joseph		21.07.68	D	Azusa, USA	17 Apr
4.80	Matt Weaver		14.11.73	2	Watford	4 Jul
4.80	Ashley Swain 76	U20	3.10.80	2	Exeter	11 Jul
4.80	Chris Wills 77	U23	18.05.76	1	Halesowen	13 Jul
4.75	Barry Thomas		28.04.72	3=D	Arles, FRA	24 May
4.75	Scott Simpson 81	U20 79	21.07.79		Birmingham (Un)	26 Jun
4.70 i	Craig Guite	U23	19.08.77	3	Wakefield	10 Jan
	4.62			4	Alicante, SPA	10 Apr
4.70	Duncan Pearce		21.10.70	4	Watford	16 May
4.70	Martin Densley 105	U20 82	1.05.81	1	Enfield	13 Jun
4.70	Leigh Walker 106	U23	17.08.77	3	Watford	20 Jun

4.65	Jamie Quarry		15.11.72	5=D	Arles, FRA	24 May
4.61	Richard Gammage		21.11.62	2	Cosford	18 Jul
4.60 i	Dave Gordon		20.03.68	9	Birmingham	25 Jan
4.60				8	Watford	16 May
4.60 i	Steve McLennan	U23	17.11.78	1	Horsham	25 Jan
4.20				4	Enfield	9 May
4.60 i	Richard Smith 4.70 -97	U20	17.01.81	1	Horsham	25 Jan
4.60				5	Bedford	5 Jul
4.60 i	Robert Thickpenny	U23	17.07.76	2	Horsham	21 Feb
4.50				5	Watford	20 Jun
4.60	Bob Kingman		21.02.73	6=	Watford	16 May
4.60	Rufus Cooper 4.70 -97	U20	24.02.79	1	London (Ha)	23 May
4.60	Paul Beswick		5.12.68	3	Cardiff	6 Jun
4.60	Mark Hodgkinson		20.07.72	7	Birmingham	6 Jun
	(40)					
4.60	Gavin Showell		29.09.72	1	Tamworth	14 Jun
4.60	Alex Kruger		18.11.63	2	Liverpool	20 Jun
4.60	Doug Hamilton		19.05.61	2	Edinburgh	18 Jul
4.60	Egryn Jones		1.11.71	2	Derby	19 Jul
4.60	Ian Noble	U23	2.04.77	1	Cleckheaton	15 Aug
4.55	Paul Jones	U23	11.04.78	8=D	Arles, FRA	24 May
4.50	Warren Jousiffe	U23	27.05.77	1	Enfield	9 May
4.50	Chris Type 1-89	U17	5.10.81	1	Connahs Quay	4 Jul
4.50	Mark Beharrell	U20	10.01.81	1	Scunthorpe	31 Aug
4.40 i	Gareth Lease	U23	14.11.77	13	Birmingham	25 Jan
4.35				1	Redruth	27 May
	(50)					
4.40 i	Kevin Treen	U23	1.02.76	4	Glasgow	14 Mar
4.40				3	Sheffield (W)	16 May
4.40 i	Robin Hill	U23	23.02.77	3	Glasgow	15 Mar
4.10				1	Bolton	15 Aug
4.40	Iain Black		18.09.70	1	Greenock	26 Apr
4.40	Rob Laing		30.07.66	1	Wrexham	14 Jun
4.40	Alan Richardson	U20	15.01.81	1	Rotherham	21 Jun
4.40	Chris Boundy	U20	25.12.79	1	Wigan	4 Jul
4.40	Steve Leader		24.11.66	3	Bebington	4 Jul
4.40	Anthony Southward		31.01.71	1D	Sale	23 Jul
4.40	Chris Mills		12.11.75	2	Perivale	25 Jul
4.40	Wayne Weinman		2.05.66	1	London (Elt)	15 Aug
	(60)					
4.40	Alexis Sharp		31.10.72	10D	Kuala Lumpur, MAL	18 Sep
4.40	Steven Brown	U17	20.03.82	1	Southend	29 Sep
4.31	Alex Thomas	U20	3.12.79	1	Birmingham	14 Jun
4.30 i	Ian Gibb		8.01.75	2	Glasgow	25 Jan
4.30	Matthew Buck		5.04.74	1	St. Ives	29 Apr
4.30	Jamie Webb		18.12.75	11	Bedford	24 May
4.30	John Gullaksen	U20	24.02.80	1	Scunthorpe	4 Jul
4.30	Cameron Johnston	U17	22.10.82	2	Exeter	10 Jul
4.30	Andrew Corey	U17	15.10.81	1	Tessenderlo, BEL	19 Aug
4.30	Ian Parkinson	U20	17.02.79	2	London (He)	30 Aug
	(70)					
4.25	Paul Miles	U20	14.09.80	1	Birmingham	21 Jun
4.25	Dominic Shepherd	U23	11.12.76	1D	Birmingham	23 Aug
4.20 i	Daniel Broadhead	U17	19.04.82	3	Birmingham	22 Feb
4.20				1	Cudworth	9 May
4.20 i	Adam Walker	U20	16.11.79	1	Crawley	21 Mar
4.10				1	Crawley	10 May
4.20	Paul Howard		19.10.66	1	Woodford	18 Apr
4.20	Matthew Evans		19.11.75	2	Coventry	2 May
4.20	Tony Perry	U20	28.08.81	1	Cannock	9 May
4.20	Donovan Graham		18.9.61	1	Bury St. Edmonds	10 May

4.20	Steve Rogers		1.09.71	6	Sheffield (W)	16 May
4.20	Ian Wilding		3.03.75	7	Loughborough	17 May
	(80)					
4.20	Richard Stubbs		6.06.66	1	Cardiff	3 Jun
4.20	Jamie Skelton		75	1	Bracknell	6 Jun
4.20	Paul Thomas	U20	1.10.80	6	Cardiff	6 Jun
4.20	Darren Neport	U20	4.09.79	2	Enfield	14 Jun
4.20	Steven Atkinson	U20	12.04.79	11	Edinburgh	4 Jul
4.20	Glyn Price		12.09.65	3	Derby	4 Jul
4.20	Charles Rule	U20	22.05.80	1	Barry	14 Jul
4.20	Gary Jackson		28.04.68	1	Blackburn	12 Aug
4.20	Tom Abdy	U20	3.05.81	5	Bruges, BEL	23 Aug
4.20	David Ingram	U20	19.01.80	1	Woodford	23 Aug
	(90)					
4.15	Brendan McConville	U20	3.01.79	1	Belfast	27 Jun
4.10 i	Brychan Jones	V40	28.05.57	3=	Wakefield	2 May
4.10	Alan Hardy		4.09.58	1	London (WF)	9 May
4.10	Kevin Gray			1	Ashford	16 May
4.10	Richard Hull			2	London (TB)	20 May
4.10	Stephen Robertson		9.07.75	3	Grangemouth	3 Jun
4.10	Pat Campbell	U20	10.03.80	2	Antrim	20 Jun
4.10	Stephen Day	U17	10.02.82	1	Norwich	28 Jun
4.10	Adam Davis		19.11.72	3	Hayes	15 Jul
4.10	Mark Bishop		12.02.67	6=	Barking	8 Aug
	(100)					
4.10	Brian Hughes		6.01.70	2	Telford	13 Sep

Additional Under 17 (1 - 6 above)

4.00	Philip Wade		7.05.82	1	Stoke	20 Jun
3.90	Andrew MacDonald		19.05.83	1	Barnsley	28 Jun
3.89	Matthew Peerless		3.12.82	1	Dunfermline	8 Aug
3.80	John Hutchinson		3.05.82	1	Enfield	7 Jun
	(10)					
3.80	James Lamont		25.05.82	2	Edinburgh	20 Jun
3.80	Jason Fry		6.01.83	1	Thurrock	19 Jul
3.80	Steven James		9.02.82	1	Southampton	19 Jul
3.80	Richard Checkley		19.11.81	2	Birmingham	6 Sep
3.70	Ben Madden		4.10.82	1	Worcester	26 Apr
3.70	Matt Lewis		15.10.82	1	Bath	19 Jul
3.70	Ian Bowley		14.11.81	1	London (WF)	25 Jul
3.70	Luke Checkley		19.11.81	3	Peterborough	26 Jul
3.70	Alan Jervis	U15	27.07.84	1	Tessenderlo, BEL	19 Aug
3.65	Matthew Thompson		15.01.82	1	Birmingham	13 Jun
	(20)					
3.60	James Wright		2.04.82	1	Woodford	6 Jun
3.60	Daniel Elias		25.12.82	2	Woodford	6 Jun
3.60	Tim Holsgrove		11.12.82	2	Birmingham	5 Sep
3.60	Kevin Lawrence		28.12.81	4=	Birmingham	6 Sep
3.60	John Yates		17.12.82	4=	Birmingham	6 Sep

Additional Under 15 (1 above)

3.55	Greg Dillow		16.06.84	2	Exeter	10 Jul
3.50	Oliver Mahoney		21.10.83	1	Birmingham	5 Sep
3.35	James Mason		7.10.83	4	Exeter	10 Jul
3.30	Paul Stevens		15.11.83	1	Bingham	20 Jun
3.30	Richard Hurren		24.09.83	3	Sheffield	15 Aug
3.20	Byron Yeo		9.10.83	1	Thurrock	19 Jul
3.10	Michael Parker		29.10.83	2	Bingham	20 Jun
3.10	Tommy Saville			1	London (TB)	8 Aug
3.10	Joel Ward-Davies		9.02.84	5	Sheffield	15 Aug
	(10)					
3.10	Russell Thompson		9.09.83	4	Sheffield	15 Aug

3.10		Mark Watson	16.07.84	2	Birmingham	5 Sep
3.00		Craig MacKail-Smith	2.12.83	8	Exeter	10 Jul
3.00		Chris Carter	2.09.83	1	Bracknell	19 Jul
3.00		A. Turvey		1	Cannock	29 Aug
3.00		Jeff Osborne	22.09.83	2	Birmingham	6 Sep
2.95		Mark Garner	2.11.83	1	Cannock	19 Jul
2.95		David Thomson	1.10.83	1	York	25 Jul
2.90		Mike Cross	19.12.83	1	Hoo	28 Jun
2.90		Kit Branch	5.06.85		Telford	4 Jul
	(20)					
2.90		Chris Tremayne	11.11.84	2	Cannock	29 Aug
2.85		Philip Fisher	21.03.84	10	Exeter	10 Jul

Under 13

2.60	S. Lewis	20.05.86	1	Stoke	4 Aug
2.30	P. Yeomans				

Downhill Market Square

5.30	Kevin Hughes	30.04.73	1	Stafford	26 Sep
5.20	Mike Barber	19.10.73	2	Stafford	26 Sep
5.10	Christian North	2.02.74	3	Stafford	26 Sep

Foreign

4.80	*Andreas Ioannou (CYP)*	*73*	*1*	*Loughborough*	*13 May*
4.60	*Dylan McDermott (IRE)*	*1.12.70*	*1*	*Carshalton*	*16 May*
4.40	*Pierre Faber (RSA)*	*9.01.72*	*1*	*Enfield*	*14 Jun*
4.20 i	*Dirk Feil (GER)*	*9.03.65*	*1*	*Gateshead*	*19 Mar*
4.20			*4*	*Edinburgh*	*18 Jul*
4.20	*Alan Burke (IRE)*	*23.05.65*	*1*	*Feltham*	*2 May*
4.20	*Joe Naughton (IRE)*	*17.10.74*	*1*	*Barking*	*14 Jun*

LONG JUMP

8.11	1.5	Nathan Morgan	U23	30.06.78	1	Birmingham	24 Jul
8.04	1.4				1	Birmingham	18 Jul
8.04 w	3.3				1	Ljubljana, SLO	31 May
7.93	-0.6				3	St. Petersburg, RUS	27 Jun
7.86 w	2.1				1	Birmingham	6 Jun
7.67	1.0				*	Ljubljana, SLO	31 May
7.67	-0.1				1	Hexham	14 Jun
7.67	0.2				24Q	Budapest, HUN	18 Aug
7.50	1.5				*	Birmingham	6 Jun
8.03		Steve Phillips		17.03.72	1	Enfield	5 Aug
7.87 w	6.4				2	Bedford	25 May
7.79 w	5.2				1	Birmingham	22 Aug
7.75					1	Rugby	9 Jun
7.72 i					1	London (CP)	14 Feb
7.72					1	Corby	27 Jun
7.70					1	Rugby	12 Aug
7.69					1	Colwyn Bay	5 Sep
7.66					4	Rhede, GER	19 Jun
7.66 A	-0.2				8	Johannesburg, RSA	11 Sep
7.64	-0.1				7	Kuala Lumpur, MAL	20 Sep
7.62					1	Grantham	2 Aug
7.60	-0.3				Q	Kuala Lumpur, MAL	19 Sep
7.59					1	Leamington	9 May
7.59					1	Tamworth	6 Jun
7.55					1	Derby	19 Jul
7.51	0.2				32Q	Budapest, HUN.	18 Aug
7.50 w	3.5				1	Loughborough	17 May
7.48	1.9				3	Birmingham	24 Jul

7.89 w	3.1	Chris Davidson		4.12.75	1	Bedford	25 May
7.81 w	4.1				3	Ljubljana, SLO	31 May
7.71	1.5 ≈ 97				2	Birmingham	24 Jul
7.65	-0.3				1	Bath	4 May
7.63 w	3.4				1	Crawley	19 Jul
7.62	-0.2				8	Kuala Lumpur, MAL	20 Sep
7.55	1.1				2	Cork, IRE	27 Jun
7.53	0.0				Q	Kuala Lumpur, MAL	19 Sep
7.51	1.9				2	Birmingham	6 Jun
7.48	1.6				*	Crawley	19 Jul
7.47 w					2	Edinburgh	4 Jul
7.83 w	4.2	George Audu	U23	18.01.77	4	Amherst, USA	4 Jun
7.78 i	2.5?				2	Blacksburg, USA	13 Feb
7.72					1	Columbus, USA	23 May
7.67	1.1				2	University Park, USA	9 May
7.67	0.4				2	Harrisonburg, USA	16 May
7.59 w	5.5	Essop Merrick		24.05.74	2	Birmingham	22 Aug
7.37	-0.8				4	Bedford	29 Aug
7.58 w	2.1	Onochie Onuorah		16.10.73	6	Canberra, AUS	8 Feb
7.56	-0.2				2	Sydney, AUS	10 Jan
7.56	0.1	Darren Thompson 64	U20 16TH	6.11.79	1	Bedford	30 May
7.53	1.6	Julian Flynn		3.07.72	3	Cork, IRE	27 Jun
7.49	1.3				1	Bedford	29 Aug
7.48	1.5	Barrington Williams	V40	11.09.55	3	Birmingham	6 Jun
7.47		Fred Salle		10.09.64	1	Edinburgh	4 Jul
	(10)						
7.47		Stuart Wells 7·56-97	U20	26.07.79	1	Barking	8 Aug

53 performances to 7.45 by 11 athletes including 2 indoors and 12 wind assisted

7.39 w	2.8	James Leaver		15.09.75	Q	Bath	4 May
7.21					1	Bournemouth	9 May
7.38	0.8	John Munroe		6.01.69	5	Birmingham	24 Jul
7.34 w	7.0	Du'aine Ladejo		14.02.71	1D	Arles, FRA	23 May
7.16	2.0				10	Birmingham	24 Jul
7.30	1.3	Andy Lewis		9.03.68	6	Birmingham	24 Jul
7.30 w		Gary Smith		20.02.71	1	Peterborough	8 Mar
7.29 i					1	Bedford	25 Jan
7.10					2	Harrow	30 Aug
7.27 w	5.4	David Mountford	U17	23.06.82	1	Gran Canaria, SPA	25 Jul
6.94 i					2	Birmingham	21 Feb
6.90					1	Rotherham	20 Jun
7.25 w	6.3	Mark Awanah	U17	23.09.82	2	Gran Canaria, SPA	25 Jul
6.83	1.0				*	Sheffield	15 Aug
7.24 w	2.5	Jamie Quarry		15.11.72	2	Crawley	19 Jul
7.21					1	Loughborough	13 May
7.23 i		Chris Tomlinson	U20	15.09.81	1	Jarrow	13 Dec
6.95 i			U17		1	Birmingham	21 Feb
6.67	1.5		U17		6	Sheffield	15 Aug
	(20)						
7.22 w	2.3	Dominique Richards	U20	12.09.79	3	Bedford	5 Jul
7.05					1	London (TB)	29 Aug
7.21	1.1	Anthony Malcolm	U23	15.02.76	Q	Bath	4 May
7.20 w	2.9	Jan Irving	U23	4.03.77	5	Bedford	25 May
7.18	1.2				1	Dessau, GER	1 Aug
7.18 w	3.3	David Clerihew	U23	11.09.77	Q	Bath	4 May
7.14	1.7				4	Bath	4 May
7.17	1.3	Stuart Clark		16.10.75	3	Bath	4 May
7.16		Femi Akinsanya		29.11.69	2	Derby	4 Jul
7.15		Ken David	U23	13.03.78	1	St. Ives	2 May
7.15		Darren Ritchie		14.02.75	4	Edinburgh	4 Jul
7.14		Alvin Walker		30.04.65	2	Cosford	1 Jul

206

7.14 w	4.6	Barry Thomas		28.04.72	4D	Arles, FRA	23	May
6.91	1.1				Q	Bath	4	May
(30)								
7.14 w	2.6	Marlon Kerr	U20	3.04.81	4	Bedford	5	Jul
6.94	0.0				2	Hoo	13	Jun
7.14 w	3.6	Darrell Aldridge	U17	20.06.83	1	Sheffield	15	Aug
6.87					1	Cambridge	1	Aug
7.13		Mark Bushell	U23	22.10.76	1	Portsmouth	9	May
7.13 w	2.2	Alexis Sharp		31.10.72	D	Azusa, USA	16	Apr
7.10	1.5				12	Birmingham	24	Jul
7.13 w	3.5	Chris Dack	U17	28.11.82	2	Exeter	10	Jul
6.98	1.8				*	Exeter	10	Jul
7.12 i		Duncan Mathieson		8.03.69	1H	Glasgow	14	Feb
7.10 w?		Sam Nash		22.10.71	1	Enfield	14	Jun
7.09		Duncan Malins	U23	12.06.78	2	Barking	8	Aug
7.08	0.6	Matthew Bridle	U23	11.08.76	1	Enfield	6	Jun
7.08		Carl McMullen	U20	9.11.79	3	Colwyn Bay	5	Sep
(40)								
7.07		Simon Richardson		7.06.72	1	Cudworth	10	May
7.07 w	3.9	Chris Cotter		3.02.72	7	Bedford	25	May
7.05					1	Exeter	10	May
7.07 w	3.2	Allan Scott	U17	27.12.82	1	Ayr	18	Jul
6.96 i					1P	Glasgow	12	Dec
6.85					1P	Grangemouth	12	Jul
7.06		Gary Jones		15.07.72	1	Ormskirk	11	Jul
7.05		Dave Butler	U23	9.12.78	2	Tamworth	6	Jun
7.05		Simon Williams		9.05.72	1	London (Ha)	6	Jun
7.05	1.0	John King		13.02.63	13	Birmingham	24	Jul
7.04		Dave Ashton		24.01.70	1	Ormskirk	11	Jul
7.03 i		Andy Wooding	U20	2.06.79	6	Birmingham	7	Feb
7.03	0.4				1	Cwmbran	20	Jun
7.03 w	3.3	Andrew Morley			Q	Bath	4	May
6.95					2	Exeter	10	May
(50)								
7.03 w		Steven Shalders	U17	24.12.81	1	Cwmbran	13	Sep
7.02		Joe Sweeney		17.07.65	1	Bracknell	10	May
7.01		Fyn Corcoran	U23	17.03.78	1	Kingston	4	Jul
7.00		Nick Dowsett	U23	24.11.78	1	London (WF)	10	May
7.00	-0.8	Seni Edu		4.03.74	2	Watford	20	Jun
7.00	2.0	Charles Igbon	U20	20.04.79	6	Bedford	5	Jul
6.99		Martin Rossiter		4.09.69	1	St. Ives	9	May
6.99		Leo Barker	U23	26.12.78	2	Bebington	4	Jul
6.99		Adrian Phillips		29.07.75	1	Perivale	25	Jul
6.99		Jon French	U23	15.03.78	3	Barking	8	Aug
(60)				11.12.75				
6.99 w		Charles Madeira-Cole	U23	29.11.77	1	Aberdare	31	Aug
6.98		Adam Potter	U20	12.04.80	1	Yeovil	20	Jun
6.98		Dan Dugard		21.06.65	1	London (Elt)	15	Aug
6.98 w		Steven Maisey		11.05.74	2	Woodford	2	May
6.97		Jason McDade	U20	3.04.80	1	Bury St. Edmunds	9	May
6.97		Darren Hatton	U20	21.03.79	1	Hoo	13	Jun
6.96		Charles Ellis	U23	7.07.77	1	Jarrow	2	May
6.96		Mark Lawrence		26.01.71	3	Derby	4	Jul
6.96 w	4.5	James Gilbert		9.11.74	5	Edinburgh	18	Jul
6.95	1.2				*	Edinburgh	18	Jul
6.95		Paul Jones	U23	11.04.78	1	Brecon	5	Jul
(70)								
6.94		Glyn Chidlow		21.10.71	1	Yate	6	Jun
6.93	1.2	Nana Wilson	U20	14.01.79	3	London (Ha)	24	May
6.93 i		Mike Nesbeth	U20	1.03.79	2	London (CP)	19	Dec
6.93 w		Steven Finnie	U23	14.12.78	6	Edinburgh	4	Jul

Mark	Wind	Name	Cat	DOB	Pos	Venue	Date
6.92		Mark Faulkner	U20	14.11.79	1	Southampton	2 May
6.92		Bob Berriman		29.03.73	2	Cudworth	10 May
6.92 w	2.3	Nathan Palmer	U17	16.06.82	2	Aberdare	31 Aug
6.58	-2.0				*	Aberdare	31 Aug
6.90		Stuart Richmond		11.04.69	1	Welwyn	15 Aug
6.90 w		Leon Smith			3	Woodford	2 May
6.90 w	3.8	Lee Murphy		10.08.74	2	Liverpool	20 Jun

Additional Under 20 (1 - 21 above)

Mark	Wind	Name	Cat	DOB	Pos	Venue	Date
6.89		Leon Burnett	U17	12.09.81	1	Stafford	17 May
6.88 w	2.5	James Birks		5.01.81	4	Exeter	11 Jul
6.87 i		Craig Elder	U17	22.05.82	1	Glasgow	18 Jan
6.77					1	Dublin, IRE	8 Aug
6.82 w	3.0	Neil Barton		18.07.80	6	Exeter	11 Jul

Additional Under 17 (1 - 10 above)

Mark	Wind	Name	Cat	DOB	Pos	Venue	Date
6.70		Martin Taylor		31.01.82	P	Grangemouth	13 Jun
6.69		Chris Jenkins		2.03.82	1	Liverpool	7 Jun
6.68 w	2.5	Jordon Lau	U15 10	23.09.83	2	Sheffield	16 Aug
6.54	1.8				1	Exeter	11 Jul
6.67 w	2.3	Gary Hunter		10.09.81	1	Leeds	23 May
6.67 w	3.9	Simon Sebire		20.09.82	4	Exeter	10 Jul
6.57					1	Guernsey	9 Jun
6.66	1.7	Richard Danso		24.12.81	5	Exeter	10 Jul
6.65		M. Seeley			1	Worthing	24 May
6.64		Tom Roe		25.06.82	1	Norwich	13 Jun
6.63		Kris Davies		30.10.81	1	Brecon	4 Jul
6.60 w	3.2	Simon Tunnicliffe		2.03.83	6	Exeter	10 Jul
(20)							
6.59		Tim Lightfoot		1.05.83	1	Oxford	19 Jul
6.59		Michael Hunter		17.09.81	1	Pitreavie	8 Aug
6.56 w	3.6	Simon Heyes		14.03.82	7	Exeter	10 Jul
6.55		Jonathan Moore	U15 9	31.05.84	1	Stafford	17 May
6.55		Richard Piper		16.02.83	1	Kingston	20 Jun
6.55		A. Mazoka			2	Bingham	24 Jun
6.54		Gareth Morgan			2	Coventry	7 Jun
6.53		Leigh Smith		24.09.82	2	Cwmbran	26 Apr
6.53		Tim Greenwood		22.11.82	1	Abingdon	9 May
6.52		A. Hall			1	London (Elt)	29 Jul
(30)							
6.51		Martin O'Reilly			3	Dublin, IRE	8 Aug
6.50		John Davies		19.12.82	8	Sheffield	15 Aug
6.46		Dominic Girdler		6.03.82	1	Tamworth	31 Aug
6.43		Craig Thomas		28.09.81	3	Inverness	2 Aug
6.43		Kim Harland		21.02.82		Aberdare	31 Aug

Under 15 (1 - 2 above)

Mark	Wind	Name	Cat	DOB	Pos	Venue	Date
6.34		Chuka Enih-Snell 39TH		2.03.84	1P	Birmingham	23 Aug
6.33		Jermaine Bernard 43		1.12.84	1	Cambridge	16 Aug
6.30		Edward Dunford 53		15.09.84	1P	Hull	19 Sep
6.28	2.0	Richard Reader 59		4.01.84	2	Exeter	11 Jul
6.21 w	6.8	Matthew Walden		30.11.83	3	Sheffield	16 Aug
6.09	0.8				1	York	25 Jul
6.20 w	2.9	Minh Ho		3.01.84	2	Birmingham	6 Sep
6.16 w		James Smith		9.01.84	2	London (WF)	9 May
6.12 w	2.2	Quincy Belgrave			2	Birmingham	5 Sep
(10)							
6.11		Richard Burslem		4.01.84	1	Stoke	20 Jun
6.08		Neil Simpson		11.09.83	1	Hoo	26 Apr
6.06		David Whattley		5.09.83	1	Enfield	7 Jun
6.06		Alan Ruddock		12.09.83	2	York	25 Jul

6.06		Marlon Lewis		7.09.83	1	Tamworth	31	Aug
6.05		Darren Watson		9.09.83	2P	Hull	19	Sep
6.03	1.5	M. Husbands			4	Exeter	11	Jul
6.02		Frank Omorgie		9.10.83	1	Feltham	17	May
6.02		David Riley		27.09.83	2	Stoke	20	Jun
6.00		Adrian Dillon	*5.89 x 26*	10.09.83	3	Stoke	20	Jun
	(20)							
6.00 w	3.1	Chris Wilkins		20.12.83	3	Birmingham	6	Sep
5.99 w	3.4	Nicholas Sullivan		9.11.83	6	Exeter	11	Jul

Under 13

5.43		James Dunford *7TH*		14.01.86	1	Carshalton	20	Sep
5.30		William Fleckney *18TH*		19.10.85	1	Huntingdon	31	May
5.27		Bernard Yeboah *24TH*			1	Peterborough	19	Jul
5.24		Louis Moore *29TH*			1	Stoke	19	Jul
5.22		David McEwan *33RD*		29.06.86	1	Woking	6	Sep
		5-04 (10)						

Foreign

7.27		*Gary Munroe (CAN)*		12.04.69	1	*Copenhagen, DEN*	23	Jun
7.23 w	3.0	*Joe Naughton (IRE)*		17.10.74	1	*Dublin (S), IRE*	25	Jul
		6.90 i			1H	*Birmingham*	7	Feb
7.01 w	3.6	*Gareth Devlin (IRE)*	*U23*	2.06.76	3	*Dublin (S), IRE*	25	Jul
		7.00			2	*Loughborough*	13	May
7.00		*Olu Robbin-Cocker (SLE)*		27.11.75	1	*Bebington*	4	Jul

TRIPLE JUMP

18.01	0.4	Jonathan Edwards		10.05.66	1	Oslo, NOR	9	Jul
		17.99	0.5		1	Budapest, HUN	23	Aug
		17.75	-0.2		1	Zurich, SWZ	12	Aug
		17.65	1.8		1	Uniondale, USA	21	Jul
		17.64 i			1	Birmingham	15	Feb
		17.60	0.0		1	Rome, ITA	14	Jul
		17.43 i			1	Valencia, SPA	1	Mar
		17.37 A	0.6		1	Pietersburg, RSA	11	Mar
		17.29	1.7		1	St. Petersburg, RUS	28	Jun
		17.26 i			1	Stange, NOR	24	Jan
		17.23 i			1	Tampere, FIN	4	Feb
		17.22	0.4		1	Tallinn, EST	19	Jun
		17.18	1.3		1	Gateshead	19	Jul
		17.15 i			Q	Valencia, SPA	27	Feb
		17.14	1.6		1	Sheffield	2	Aug
		17.12	-1.6		1	Birmingham	26	Jul
		17.04	-0.3		1	Helsinki, FIN	13	Jun
		17.00	1.6		2	Lausanne, SWZ	25	Aug
		16.99	0.7		1	Stockholm, SWE	5	Aug
		16.97	0.1		Q	Budapest, HUN	22	Aug
		16.96 w	2.2		1	Leeds	7	Jun
		16.22 i			2	Maebashi, JAP	7	Mar
17.10	0.0	Larry Achike *6TH*		31.01.75	1	Kuala Lumpur, MAL	18	Sep
		17.07	0.0		2	Tallinn, EST	19	Jun
		16.85 w	2.9		1	Canberra, AUS	8	Feb
		16.79 w	2.1		1	Melbourne, AUS	15	Mar
		16.73	1.4		1	Hobart, AUS	21	Feb
		16.72 w	2.1		3	Gateshead	19	Jul
		16.69	1.2		4	Sheffield	2	Aug
		16.69 w	4.0		7	Johannesburg, RSA	12	Sep
		16.67	1.9		*	Gateshead	19	Jul
		16.66	1.9		*	Melbourne, AUS	15	Mar
		16.65	1.4		*	Canberra, AUS	8	Feb
		16.42	-0.2		2	Birmingham	26	Jul
		16.40 w	2.9		3	Leeds	7	Jun

Mark		Name	Cat	DOB	Pos	Venue	Date
(Achike)							
16.38	-0.6				*	Johannesburg, RSA	12 Sep
16.36	-0.3				3	Glasgow	30 Aug
16.31	0.6				3	Floro, NOR	23 May
16.89 i		Francis Agyepong		16.06.65	Q	Valencia, SPA	27 Feb
16.57 i					8	Valencia, SPA	1 Mar
16.31 i					2	Birmingham	8 Feb
16.27 i					1	Maebashi, JAP	7 Mar
16.89	0.5	Julian Golley		12.09.71	3	Tallinn, EST	19 Jun
16.89	0.0				5	Oslo, NOR	9 Jul
16.88	1.1				3	Sheffield	2 Aug
16.83	0.5				4	Kuala Lumpur, MAL	18 Sep
16.75	0.2				5	Lausanne, SWZ	25 Aug
16.72 w	6.1				2	Leeds	7 Jun
16.63	-0.5				1	Glasgow	30 Aug
16.55	1.0				4	Gateshead	19 Jul
16.51	-0.3				2	Budapest, HUN	5 Jul
16.49 i					1	Birmingham	8 Feb
16.41	1.2				1	Loughborough	17 May
16.34	0.6				4	Stockholm, SWE	5 Aug
16.32	-0.3				17Q	Budapest, HUN	22 Aug
16.28	0.3				3	Birmingham	26 Jul
16.27	-0.5				2	Baza, SPA	3 Jun
16.63 w	2.5	Tosi Fasinro		28.03.72	1	Watford	21 Jun
16.10 i					2	Birmingham	25 Jan
16.05	1.2				*	Watford	21 Jun
16.43 w	3.5	Tayo Erogbogbo		8.03.75	1	Jona, SWZ	12 Jul
16.12	0.3				5	Birmingham	26 Jul
16.35	1.6	Phillips Idowu *14TH*	U23 *12*	30.12.78	2	Watford	21 Jun
16.32 w	3.0	Femi Akinsanya		29.11.69	2	Jona, SWZ	12 Jul
16.16 i					1	Birmingham	25 Jan
16.16	-0.5				4	Birmingham	26 Jul

61 performances to 16.20 by 8 athletes including 10 wind assisted and 11 indoors

Mark		Name	Cat	DOB	Pos	Venue	Date
15.82 i	*46TH*	Charles Madeira-Cole	U23	29.11.77	1	Glasgow	15 Mar
15.81 w	3.3				2	Loughborough	17 May
15.79	2.0				*	Loughborough	17 May
15.82	2.0	Jon Wallace *47TH*	U20 *15*	1.01.79	1	Exeter	11 Jul
(10)							
15.71 w		Alvin Walker		30.04.65	1	Gateshead	9 May
15.56	0.0 *71*				7	Birmingham	26 Jul
15.70	1.3	Nick Thomas *66*	U20 *19*	4.04.79	2	Alicante, SPA	18 Jul
15.64 w		Paul Weston		6.10.67	1	Gloucester	11 Jul
15.34	1.8				1	Birmingham	22 Aug
15.62 w	2.6	Tosin Oke	U20 *54*	1.10.80	3	Bedford	4 Jul
15.16					1	London (Elt)	4 May
15.61	1.1	Rez Cameron		18.05.60	4	Watford	21 Jun
15.60 w	3.3	James Leaver		15.09.75	3	Bedford	24 May
15.18					1	Bournemouth	9 May
15.47 w		Steve Phillips		17.03.72	1	Tamworth	6 Jun
15.10					1	Derby	19 Jul
15.41		Stuart Richmond		11.04.69	1	Carshalton	20 Sep
15.40 w	2.5	Steven Shalders *356*	U17 *6*	24.12.81	1	Ayr	18 Jul
15.14	1.5				*	Ayr	18 Jul
15.36	2.0	Michael Brown		6.05.62	5	Watford	21 Jun
(20)							
15.33 w		Arif Shah	U23	29.11.78	2	Corby	27 Jun
15.03	0.9				1	Bedford	30 Aug
15.25 w	3.2	Mike McKernan	U23	28.11.78	2	Exeter	11 Jul
15.18 w?					3	Corby	27 Jun
14.94	1.4				*	Exeter	11 Jul
15.24 w	2.2	Joe Sweeney		17.07.65	4	Bedford	24 May
15.04					2	Derby	4 Jul

15.21		Michael McDonald		24.08.65	1	Antrim	15	Aug
15.13	0.3	Jon Hilton		11.01.74	3	Watford	16	May
15.03	0.7	Julian Flynn		3.07.72	3	Bedford	29	Aug
15.02 w		Ezra Clarke		9.12.74	2	Ashford	9	May
14.66					6	Birmingham	6	Jun
15.01 w 2.3		Martin Rossiter		4.09.69	7	Watford	21	Jun
14.97					2	Peterborough	31	Aug
15.01 w 3.6		Malwyn Gordon	U17	20.10.81	2	Sheffield	15	Aug
14.83	1.6				1	Exeter	10	Jul
14.98		George Audu	U23	18.01.77	7	Columbus, USA	23	May
(30)								
14.93	2.0	Peter Francis	U20	28.08.80	4	Bedford	4	Jul
14.93 w 2.7		Chris Tomlinson	U17	15.09.81	2	Ayr	18	Jul
14.67	-0.9				2	Exeter	11	Jul
14.90		James Peacock	U23	29.09.77	1	Barking	4	Jul
14.86		Ademola Oyediran		27.11.59	1	London (TB)	25	Jul
14.85		Dave McCalla			1	Copenhagen, DEN	23	Jun
14.82 w		Sam Bobb		29.08.75	3	Ashford	9	May
14.66 i					3	Glasgow	15	Mar
14.82 w 2.2		Marvin Bramble	U23	10.06.77	8	Watford	21	Jun
14.65					1	Woking	16	May
14.78		Michael Keeton	U23	14.12.76	2	Derby	19	Jul
14.75 i		Dave Sanderson		6.05.71	2	Sheffield	17	Jan
14.60 w 2.8					1	Liverpool	21	Jun
14.25					8	Edinburgh	4	Jul
14.75 w		Christopher Platt	U23	25.09.78	4	Bath	2	May
14.62 w?					6	Leeds	7	Jun
(40)								
14.74	2.0	Kori Stennett	U23	2.09.76	5	Birmingham	22	Aug
14.68 w 3.7		Dalton Grant		8.04.66	4	Enfield	16	May
14.25	1.8				*	Enfield	16	May
14.62		Delroy Hulme		14.09.72	4	Derby	4	Jul
14.54		Dean Taylor	U17	9.11.81	1	Cambridge	1	Aug
14.51		Courtney Charles		13.11.68	6	Edinburgh	4	Jul
14.47		Matt Randall		28.04.70	1	London (TB)	16	May
14.45		Mike Nesbeth	U20	1.03.79	1	Croydon	16	May
14.42		Chris Cotter		3.02.72	2	Exeter	9	Aug
14.39		Paul Curran	U23	5.04.77	7	Leeds	7	Jun
14.39	1.3	Shaun Lewis		5.01.73	6	Birmingham	23	Aug
(50)								
14.37		Matthew Muggeridge	U23	1.10.76	1	Yate	15	Aug
14.35		John Donnelly	U20	11.09.79	1	Antrim	23	Jun
14.32	1.5	Dale Garland	U20	13.10.80	4	Exeter	11	Jul
14.27	-1.7	James Etchells	U20	15.10.80	5	Exeter	11	Jul
14.27 w		Ian Rowe	U23	28.09.78	1	Portsmouth	9	May
13.99					6	Watford	4	Jul
14.26 w 2.2		Sayo Ojo	U20	9.05.80	6	Exeter	11	Jul
13.94					5	Liverpool	8	Aug
14.25	1.0	John Munroe		6.01.69	8	London (He)	8	Aug
14.23		Ruddy Farquharson		26.03.61	2	Cosford	1	Jul
14.23		Shola Casal	U20	20.06.80	1	Harrow	26	Jul
14.21 w 3.8		Oladipo Senbanjo	U17	20.03.82	4	Sheffield	15	Aug
13.71	1.0				*	Sheffield	15	Aug
(60)								
14.19		Dominic Gordon	U20	7.01.81	1	Stoke	20	Jun
14.18		Mark Lawrence		26.01.71	6	Stoke	16	May
14.16	1.2	Charles Igbon	U20	20.04.79	6	Watford	16	May
14.15		Keith Newton		12.12.68	2	Enfield	19	Jul
14.14		Martin Crabtree	U20	8.06.81	1	York	13	Jun
14.13		Simon Roper	U20	20.09.79	1	Derby	13	Jun
14.12 i		Steven Brown	U20	4.10.80	1	Jarrow	13	Dec

Mark	Name	Cat	DOB	Pos	Venue	Date
14.10	Junior Lewis		19.03.66	1	Dartford	16 May
14.09 w 3.5	Allan Scott	U17	27.12.82	4	Ayr	18 Jul
13.96				1	Dumfries	3 May
14.06	Stefan Rose		7.04.75	2	Portsmouth	9 May
(70)						
14.05	Denis Costello		3.12.61	3	Enfield	19 Jul
14.05	Dan Adejuwon	U23	27.11.76	1	Barking	8 Aug
14.05	Adam Potter	U20	12.04.80	2	Bath	6 Sep
14.03 w 4.9	Philip Ferdinand	U17	18.11.82	2	Birmingham	6 Sep
14.00	Gareth Davies		11.05.71	1	Oxford	1 Mar
13.97 w 2.1	Paul Revell	U20	18.11.80	2	Leeds	23 May
13.95	Joe Allison		16.09.59	1	London (Nh)	16 May
13.95	Robert Heaton	U20	6.05.81	1	Stretford	13 Jun
13.95 w 4.0	Steven Frost	U20	4.01.81	4	Bruges, BEL	23 Aug
13.94	James Porter	U20	12.01.81	1	Portsmouth	9 May
(80)						
13.94	Joe Parkes	U20	14.01.81	1	Bournemouth	13 Jun
13.92	Jon French *11.12.75*	U23	~~15.03.78~~	1	Great Yarmouth	16 Aug
13.90	Daniel Davies	U23	2.02.76	1	Loughborough	25 Apr

Additional Under 17 (1 - 7 above)

Mark	Name	Cat	DOB	Pos	Venue	Date
13.85	John Davies		19.12.82	1	Colchester	13 Jun
13.69 *1.3*	Chris Stobart		27.03.82	2	Leeds	23 May
13.65	Leon Burnett		12.09.81	1	Cwmbran	26 Apr
(10)						
13.63 *10L*	Quincy Phillips		12.12.81	1	Enfield	13 Jul
13.59	James Anthony		30.03.82	1	Newport	9 Sep
13.53	Gavin Gunputhram		21.03.82		Cannock	13 Sep
13.42	Peter Alexander		29.09.81	1	Hoo	13 Jun
13.37	Jamie Russell		1.10.81	1	Wakefield	7 Jun
13.31	Chris Weitz		28.04.83	2	Gateshead	29 Aug
13.30	Louis Evling-Jones		20.06.83	1	Lincoln	13 Jun
13.29 w	Lee Harris	U15	23.11.83	1	Bath	13 Jun
13.18 0.1				1	Exeter	10 Jul
13.25	Peter Favell		16.03.82	1	Corby	20 Jun

Additional Under 15 (1 above)

Mark	Name	Cat	DOB	Pos	Venue	Date
13.09	Keith Stoddart *38*		26.10.83	1	Livingston	5 Sep
13.03 -0.5	Andrew Harris *50*		21.09.83	2	Exeter	10 Jul
12.41 w 3.6	Robert Southey		23.10.83	3	Sheffield	16 Aug
12.34 0.1				3	Exeter	10 Jul
12.35 1.0	Richard Marshall		24.09.83	2	London (He)	30 Aug
12.35 w 2.1	Matthew Thurgood		29.12.83	4	Sheffield	16 Aug
12.22				1	Watford	10 May
12.34	Guto James			1	Brecon	4 Jul
12.31	Julien Adams		19.10.83	1	Reading	13 Jun
12.23	Stephen Alexander		6.10.84	1	Stretford	13 Jun
12.21	Edward Dunford		15.09.84	1	Gloucester	18 Jul
(10)						
12.18	Ian Carter		19.09.83	1	Portsmouth	10 May
12.11	Richard Gothard		6.09.83	1	Leeds	13 Jun
12.05 0.1	Alex Box		23.09.84	4	Exeter	10 Jul
12.03	Kieran Mckeever		16.08.84	5	Sheffield	16 Aug
12.00	G. Blair			1	Antrim	30 May
12.00 0.9	Simon Gregory		24.11.83	5	Exeter	10 Jul

Under 13

Mark	Name	Cat	DOB	Pos	Venue	Date
11.30	James Dunford *4TH*		14.01.86	1	Gloucester	18 Jul
10.52	William Fleckney		19.10.85	1	Luton	10 May

Foreign

Mark	Wind	Name	DOB	Pos	Venue	Date
14.86	*1.3*	*Olu Robbin-Cocker (SLE)*	*27.11.75*	*4*	*Birmingham*	*18 Jul*
14.64	*1.4*	*Sean Lonergan (IRE)*	*24.01.73*	*6*	*Kaunas, LIT*	*7 Jun*

SHOT

20.85 i	Mark Proctor		15.01.63	1	King's Lynn		25	Jan
	20.04			1	Cosford		1	Jul
	19.96			1	Bury St. Edmonds		4	Jul
	19.86			3	Gateshead		19	Jul
	19.84			3	Glasgow (S)		30	Aug
	19.66			5	Johannesburg, RSA	11	Sep
	19.50			2	Halle, GER		16	May
	19.50			1	Birmingham		26	Jul
	19.44			1	Hayes		15	Jul
	19.34			5	Bratislava, SVK		9	Jun
	19.28			1	Bury St. Edmonds		10	May
	19.15			1	Cosford		17	Jun
	19.13			2	Bedford		29	Aug
	19.12			1	London (He)		8	Aug
	19.06			1	Woodford		18	Apr
	19.02			1	Arles, FRA		24	May
	18.66 i			16Q	Valencia, SPA		28	Feb
	18.46			5	Ostrava, CZE		11	Jun
20.00	Shaun Pickering		14.11.61	1	Irvine, USA		2	May
	19.67			1	Stanford, USA		8	May
	19.47			1	Tivoli, ITA		30	May
	19.34			1	Modesto, USA		9	May
	19.33			3	Kuala Lumpur, MAL	21	Sep
	19.24			1	Luton		14	Jun
	19.21			1	Groningen, HOL		21	Jun
	19.20			3	Halle, GER		16	May
	19.14			1	Cwmbran		20	Jun
	19.04			9	Hengelo, HOL		1	Jun
	18.95 i			1	Birmingham		8	Feb
	18.93			4	Gateshead		19	Jul
	18.90			1	Cardiff		6	Jun
	18.87			2	Birmingham		26	Jul
	18.85			6	Walnut, USA		19	Apr
	18.84			1	Stanford, USA		28	Mar
	18.82 i			14Q	Valencia, SPA		28	Feb
	18.77			1	Cardiff		4	Aug
	18.73			1	Leiden, HOL		13	Jun
	18.54			1	Fullerton, USA		23	Apr
	18.46			2	Groningen, HOL		12	Jul
	18.28			1	Breda, HOL		6	Sep
19.46	Carl Myerscough	U20	21.10.79	1	Blackpool		6	Sep
	19.24			1	Bedford		4	Jul
	18.50			1	Mannheim, GER		13	Jun
	18.31 i			2	Birmingham		8	Feb
	18.28			1	Watford		12	Sep
	18.12			3	Annecy, FRA		1	Aug
	18.06			1	Blackpool		8	Aug
	18.05			Q	Annecy, FRA		31	Jul
18.88	Mark Edwards		2.12.74	1	Stretford		14	Jul
	18.52			3	Birmingham		26	Jul
	18.45			1	Telford		15	Aug
	18.14			1	Stretford		18	Aug
	18.13			1	Tamworth		31	Aug
	18.02			1	Loughborough		10	Jun
18.44	Matt Simson		28.05.70	3	Gainesville, USA		18	Apr
18.03	Stephan Hayward		30.07.74	4	Birmingham		26	Jul
	56 performances to 18.00 by 6 athletes including 5 indoors							
17.04	Gary Sollitt		13.01.72	2	Loughborough		17	May

Mark	Name	Cat	DOB	Pos	Venue	Date
17.03 i	Steve Whyte		14.03.64	3	Birmingham	8 Feb
15.90				6	Bedford	29 Aug
17.02 i	Emeka Udechuku	U20	10.07.79	1	Birmingham	22 Feb
16.92				1	Alicante, SPA	18 Jul
16.71	Dave Callaway		4.09.63	1	Portsmouth (RN)	26 Jun
	(10)					
16.65	Guy Marshall ¶		24.09.71	1	Derby	19 Jul
16.64	Lee Newman		1.05.73	3	Watford	16 May
16.15 i	Scott Hayes		4.01.73	2	London (CP)	19 Dec
15.01				1	Colchester	31 Aug
16.06	Neil Elliott		10.04.71	1	Linwood	18 Apr
16.04	Paul Reed		2.06.62	1	Gateshead	5 Aug
16.00	Chris Ellis		24.01.66	1	Tamworth	6 Jun
15.93	Laine Snook		2.07.68	1	Colwyn Bay	14 Jun
15.81	Keith Ansell		30.03.62	3	Bedford	25 May
15.80	Denzil McDonald		11.10.65	1	London (WF)	9 May
15.79	Bruce Robb	U23	27.07.77	1	Bedford	30 Aug
	(20)					
15.76	David Readle	U20	10.02.80	2	Watford	12 Sep
15.32	Iain McMullan	U23	15.06.78	4	Bedford	25 May
15.10	Simon Armstrong		29.05.62	1	Bournemouth	5 Apr
15.09 i	Scott Rider	U23	22.09.77	4	Glasgow	15 Mar
14.65				1	Crawley	12 Apr
15.05	Matthew Twigg		18.07.69	1	Peterborough	31 Aug
15.02	Phil Adams		3.11.71	2	Tamworth	6 Jun
14.88	Gary Herrington		31.03.61	1	Rugby	14 Jun
14.79	Rob Earle		15.09.60	3	Enfield	16 May
14.73	Kevin Brown		10.09.64	3	Istanbul, TUR	20 Jun
14.73	Simon Fricker		14.07.75	1	Bournemouth	30 Jul
	(30)					
14.70	Andy Turner		29.08.63	2	London (TB)	16 May
14.69	Mark Davies		10.01.71	1	Hoo	14 Jun
14.62	Andrew Wain		2.06.65	1	Peterborough	6 Jun
14.62	John Nicholls		1.09.65	1	Liverpool	20 Jun
14.51	George Baker	U23	14.08.76	1	Abingdon	9 May
14.51	Lyndon Woodward	U20	22.11.80	5	Birmingham	18 Jul
14.46	Antony Zaidman		18.03.62	1	Barking	8 Aug
14.46	Dean Macey	U23	12.12.77	1	Harrow	30 Aug
14.42	Mark Wiseman			2	Cosford	1 Jul
14.41	Andrew Rollins	U23	20.03.78	1	Stretford	3 May
	(40)					
14.38	Rafer Joseph		21.07.68	1D	Derby	30 May
14.38	Hamish Davidson	V40	25.05.54	2	Inverness	11 Jul
14.36	Guy Perryman		2.11.58	1	Worthing	15 Aug
14.25	Perris Wilkins		12.11.68	1	Redditch	27 Jun
14.24	Nick Owen	U20	17.07.80	1	Kingston	1 Jul
14.24	Daniel Brunt	U23	23.04.76	1	Grimsby	11 Jul
14.15	Scot Thompson	U20	10.08.81	1	Aberdeen	26 Jul
14.14	Malcolm Fenton	V40	12.02.56	2	Bury St. Edmonds	10 May
14.12	Simon Shirley		3.08.66	1	London (BP)	16 May
14.12	Glen Smith		21.05.72	6	Edinburgh	4 Jul
	(50)					
14.10	Andy Lewis		9.03.68	1	Newport	8 Aug
14.08	Paul Corrigan		19.01.66	2	Hexham	30 Aug
14.06	Iain Styles		2.10.75	1	Birmingham (Un)	6 Jun
14.05 i	Alexis Sharp		31.10.72	1H	Glasgow	14 Feb
13.73				2D	Azusa, USA	16 Apr
14.05	Craig Rogers	U23	14.02.76	7	Watford	16 May
14.04	Ian Lindley	V40	3.12.55	1	Cudworth	9 May
14.03	Du'aine Ladejo		14.02.71	11D	Bressanone, ITA	4 Jul
14.02	Gareth Cook		20.02.69	1	Sutton	16 May

13.97	Clayton Turner		9.01.68	1	London (TB)	2	May
13.97	Rory Birbeck		24.09.73	1	Blackpool	9	May
	(60)						
13.96	Graeme Allan	U20	24.09.80	1	Elgin	14	Jun
13.95	Justin Bryan		16.08.69	1	Aberdare	31	Aug
~~13.95~~	~~Steve Archer~~	~~V40~~	~~25.01.55~~	~~8~~	~~Cesenatico, ITA~~	~~13~~	~~Sep~~
13.94	William Renshaw	V45	7.08.49	1	Rotherham	6	Jun
13.94	James Muirhead		26.01.71	2	Bolton	15	Aug
13.93	Craig Anderson		19.06.71	2	Bearsden	13	Jun
13.90	S. King *STEPHEN*			1	Shotts	6	Jun
13.90	Bill Fuller	U23	19.10.76	1	Kingston	21	Jun
13.89	Jamie Quarry		15.11.72	1	Enfield	9	May
13.87	David Lovett	U23	13.09.78	3	Portsmouth (RN)	26	Jun
	(70)						
13.87	David Abernethy	V40	5.09.55	1	Blackpool	29	Aug
13.82	David Horne		9.03.68	3	Glenurquhart	29	Aug
13.81	Steve Head		21.10.58	2	Perivale	25	Jul
13.80	Andy Kruszewski		7.04.59	1	Birmingham		
13.76	Neil Griffin	V45	28.05.48	1	High Wycombe	9	May
13.71	Willie Falconer	U23	20.12.78	3	Grangemouth	17	May
13.69	Michael Jemi-Alade		13.10.64	7	Edinburgh	4	Jul
13.69	Andy Vince		9.05.59	3	Watford	12	Sep
13.64	Alex Kruger		18.11.63	9	Watford	16	May
13.61	Brett Heath		6.01.75	1	Barking	14	Jun
	(80)						
13.60	Colin Bryce		4.08.74	1	Brodick	8	Aug
13.60	Martin Wilson		3.03.71	1	Ormskirk	15	Aug
13.60	James Worland		3.02.72	1	Southend	15	Aug
13.59	Bill Fuller	V50	5.02.48	1	Kingston	4	Jul
13.58	Paul Howard		19.10.66	1	Enfield	16	May
13.58	Neville Thompson	V40	28.03.55	9	London (He)	8	Aug
13.58	Greg Richards	V40	25.04.56	1	London (FP)	15	Aug
13.57	Steve Bergin		17.06.66	2	Wakefield	2	May
13.57	Barry Thomas		28.04.72	D	Arles, FRA	23	May
13.56	Mark Quigley		6.11.74	1	Whitehaven	9	May
	(90)						
13.55	Peter Sochart		1.05.74	1	Gourock	10	May
13.55	Lester Williams	U23		2	Cosford	8	Jul
13.51	Tony Quinn	U20	14.01.81	3	Belfast	27	Jun
13.51	Anthony Southward		31.01.71	D	Sale	22	Jul
13.50	James South		4.01.75	9	Birmingham	6	Jun
13.49	Simon Bown		21.11.74	1	Great Yarmouth	2	Aug
13.46	Mark MacDonald		2.12.59	2	Gourock	10	May
13.46	John Painter ¶	V40	12.06.58	2	Great Yarmouth	2	Aug
13.45	Luke Rosenberg	U20	29.06.80	1	Woodford	25	Apr
13.45	Mike Small	V40	31.03.54	1	London (Col)	14	Jun
	(100)						
13.45	Sudip Burman-Roy	U23	15.01.78	3	Watford	4	Jul
13.45	Stuart Ryan		1.09.62	1	Middlesbrough	8	Aug
13.43	Paul Stronach		18.05.68	1	Yate	14	Jun
13.43	Bruce Shepherd		20.03.67	1	Nairn	15	Aug

Additional Under 20 (1- 9 above)

13.27	Simon Williams		5.10.80	5	Bedford	4	Jul
13.23	John Parkin		23.02.79	1	Stretford	22	Jun

Foreign

15.95	George Antonatos (GRE)		30.09.74	4	Loughborough	17	May
15.46	John Farrelly (IRE)		4.12.67	6	Dublin (S), IRE	25	Jul
15.09	Pierre Faber (RSA)		9.01.72	3	Bath	3	May
14.87	Tony Soalla-Bell (SLE)	U23	3.10.76	14	Kuala Lumpur, MAL	21	Sep
13.88	Jeroen Westmeijer (HOL)		5.07.70	1	London (Elt)	25	Jul
13.54	Pierre Charvet (FRA)		23.08.73	10	Watford	16	May

SHOT - Under 20 - 6.25kg

21.03	Carl Myerscough		21.10.79	1	Street	13 May
17.74	Emeka Udechuku		10.07.79	1	London (He)	9 Aug
16.49 i	Lyndon Woodward		22.11.80	1	Glasgow	29 Nov
	15.84			1	Cannock	29 Aug
15.80	Nick Owen		17.07.80	1	Sutton	20 Sep
15.79	David Readle		10.02.80	2	Stretford	10 Aug
15.61	Scot Thompson		10.08.81	1	Elgin	20 Sep
15.42	Graeme Allan		24.09.80	2	Cannock	13 Sep
15.06	Gregg Beard	U17	10.09.82	1	London (He)	31 Aug
14.30	Ben Roberts		15.01.80	1	Colwyn Bay	10 May
14.25 i	Adrian Cluskey		30.12.80	3	London (CP)	14 Dec
	13.81			3	Cannock	13 Sep
	(10)					
14.18	James Cottrell		19.12.80	1	Derby	13 Jun
14.08	David Parker		28.02.80	6	London (He)	9 Aug
14.07	Simon Williams		5.10.80	3	London (Ha)	23 May
14.04	David Blackmore			1	Cardiff	30 Apr
14.01	Andy Frost		17.04.81	1	Sandown, IOW	6 Sep
13.92	Jamie Hunt		29.11.79	5	Exeter	10 Jul
13.92	Adam Major	U17	2.11.81	3	Elgin	20 Sep
13.91	Robert Morris	U17	20.02.82	1	Luton	23 Aug
13.90	Steven Scott		29.05.79	1	Liverpool	26 Jul
13.84	Darren Hatton		21.03.79	D	Hull	20 Sep
	(20)					
13.72	John Parkin		23.02.79	1	Stretford	4 Aug

overage

14.08	David Lovett	U23	13.09.78	1	Portsmouth	13 Jun

SHOT - Under 17 - 5kg

16.80	Adam Major		2.11.81	1	Edinburgh	19 Jun
16.56	Gregg Beard		10.09.82	1	Crawley	30 Aug
16.23	Robert Morris		20.02.82	1	Welwyn	31 Aug
16.02	Geoffrey Reid-Hughes		14.10.81	2	Exeter	10 Jul
15.73	Deane Garrard		19.05.82	1	Thurrock	9 Aug
15.73	John Holtby		27.03.82	1O	Hull	20 Sep
15.30	Paul Archer		7.10.81	1	Ashford	5 Jul
15.19	Mark Tinwell		18.11.81	1	Stretford	26 Apr
15.19	Felice Miele		24.11.81	1	Enfield	9 May
14.80 i	James Anthony		30.03.82	2	Birmingham	22 Feb
	(10)					
14.47	Dylan Perryman		17.11.81	1	Reading	13 Jun
14.27	Jason Crawford		20.07.83	1	Sheffield (W)	19 Jul
14.23	Carl Saggers	U15	20.09.83	1	Sutton	20 Sep
14.13 i	Andy Chape		25.04.83	1	Jarrow	13 Dec
14.04	Dominic Girdler		6.03.82	1	Loughborough	2 Aug
13.98	Matt Peleszok		17.10.81	1	Birmingham	6 Sep
13.82	Adam Crane		1.06.82	6	Ayr	18 Jul

overage

17.50	Scot Thompson	U20	10.08.81	1	Dublin, IRE	8 Aug
16.38 i	John Holtby	U20	27.03.82	1P	Glasgow	12 Dec
15.55 i	Graeme Allan	U20	24.09.80	2	Glasgow	29 Jan
14.87 i	Dominic Girdler	U20	6.03.82	2P	Glasgow	12 Dec
14.52	Owen McCann	U20	15.07.81	1	Antrim	30 May

SHOT - Under 15 - 4kg

16.50	Carl Saggers		20.09.83	1	Watford	14 Jul
14.59	Martin Aram		2.12.83	2	Sheffield	15 Aug

216

14.48	Chris Levett		30.11.83	3	Sheffield NC	15	Aug
14.43	Derrick Squires 100TH		7.12.83	1	Birmingham AUX F	5	Sep
14.31	James Deacon-Brown		26.05.84	1P	Hexham	31	Aug
14.28	Crofton Alexander		7.01.84	1	Bracknell	19	Jul
13.84	Nsa Harrison		27.11.83	2	Stoke	20	Jun
13.68	Carl Fletcher		24.09.83	5	Exeter N S	10	Jul
13.45	I. Mason			1	Crawley	13	Jun
13.44	Andrew Mogford		29.09.83	2	Dublin, IRE	8	Aug
(10) (14.300)							
13.38	David Dawson		3.02.84	1	Yeovil	20	Jun
13.38	Garry Hagan		21.11.84	3	Dublin, IRE	8	Aug
13.34	Kevin Quinn		23.12.83	1	Bury	19	Apr
13.30	Richard Trimmer		7.09.83	1	Southampton	13	Sep
13.29	Edward Dunford		15.09.84	1	Exeter	29	Sep
13.24	Liam Farley		3.10.83	1	Kingston	20	Jun
13.22	Stuart Semple		3.11.83	2	London (He)	30	Aug
13.04	Nick Grundy		11.11.83	1	Cambridge	16	Aug

overage

| 13.96 i | Ewan Sime | U17 | 7.09.82 | 1 | Glasgow | 29 | Jan |
| 13.93 | Richard Oparka | U17 | 28.07.82 | 1 | Dundee | 18 | Jun |

SHOT - Under 13 - 3.25kg

| 12.12 | James Dunford | | 14.01.86 | 1 | Gloucester | | 5 | Sep |

DISCUS

66.64	Perris Wilkins		12.11.68 11.69	1	Birmingham (Un)	6	Jun
	62.30			1	Abingdon	10	May
	61.59			1	Bedford	24	May
	60.26			1	Birmingham	2	May
	59.82			1	Redditch	27	Jun
	58.65			2	Leamington	15	Aug
	58.54			9	Halle, GER	16	May
64.42	Robert Weir		4.02.61	1	Kuala Lumpur, MAL	17	Sep
	64.39			5	Johannesburg, RSA	12	Sep
	63.62			3	Salinas, USA	19	May
	62.82			1	Birmingham	25	Jul
	61.92			8	Budapest, HUN	23	Aug
	61.69			2	Edinburgh	4	Jul
	61.36			Q	Budapest, HUN	22	Aug
	61.32			2	Loughborough	7	Aug
	60.78			1	Leamington	15	Aug
	60.64			1	Stanford, USA	8	May
	60.56			1	Los Gatos, USA	13	Jun
	60.16			2	Glasgow	30	Aug
	59.93			1	London (He)	8	Aug
	59.76			2	Modesto, USA	9	May
	59.75			4	St. Petersburg, RUS	28	Jun
62.44	Glen Smith		21.05.72	1	Loughborough	7	Aug
	61.46			3	Edinburgh	4	Jul
	61.34			1	Istanbul, TUR	20	Jun
	60.62			1	Hechtel, BEL	1	Aug
	60.58			1	Loughborough	10	Jun
	60.56			2	Birmingham	25	Jul
	60.49			4	Kuala Lumpur, MAL	17	Sep
	60.27			5	Nuremberg, GER	11	Jul
	60.22			7	La Jolla, USA	28	Mar
	60.16			8	Halle, GER	16	May
	59.66			4	Ljubljana, SLO	31	May
	59.60			1	San Diego, USA	4	Apr

(Smith)	59.60			2	London (He)	8	Aug
	59.00			6	Walnut, USA	19	Apr
	58.97			15Q	Budapest, HUN	22	Aug
	58.88			1	Birmingham	18	Jul
	58.21			5	Lancaster, USA	16	Apr
60.97	Emeka Udechuku	U20	10.07.79	1	Bedford	5	Jul
	60.21			1	Enfield	16	May
	59.48			1	Loughborough	17	May
	58.08			1	Alicante, SPA	18	Jul
60.67	Kevin Brown		10.09.64	4	Helsingborg, SWE	4	Sep
	59.59			4	Helsingborg, SWE	6	Sep
	59.02			2	Bedford	24	May
	59.01			9	La Jolla, USA	28	Mar
	58.91			2	Lisse, HOL	2	May
	58.59			3	London (He)	8	Aug
	58.09			4	Edinburgh	4	Jul
60.43	Lee Newman		1.05.73	1	Enfield	23	Aug
	59.51			1	London (BP)	4	Jul
	59.38			1	Edinburgh	17	Jul
	59.37			1	Ashford	9	May
	58.81			3	Bedford	24	May
	58.58			1	Watford	16	May
60.19	Carl Myerscough	U20	21.10.79	1	Blackpool	8	Aug
	60.18			2	Bedford	5	Jul
	60.03			1	Watford	12	Sep
	59.90			3	Loughborough	7	Aug
	59.62			1	Mannheim, GER	13	Jun
	59.06			1	Cleckheaton	15	Aug
	58.52			2	San Diego, USA	4	Apr
	63 performances to 58.00 by 7 athletes						
54.91	Leith Marar		7.11.68	4	Loughborough	17	May
54.50	Mark Proctor		15.01.63	2	Bedford	29	Aug
54.20	Peter Gordon	V45	2.07.51	1	Jarrow	12	Aug
	(10)						
53.40	Gary Herrington		31.03.61	4	Stanford, USA	29	Mar
53.01	Paul Reed		2.06.62	3	Birmingham	18	Jul
52.11	Neville Thompson	V40	28.03.55	3	Bedford	29	Aug
51.95	Nick Woolcott		7.04.61	1	Luton	14	Jun
51.84	Denzil McDonald		11.10.65	3	Watford	16	May
49.78	Scott Hayes		4.01.73	4	Bedford	29	Aug
49.42	Bruce Robb 116	U23	27.07.77	3	Hexham	14	Jun
49.42	Steve Whyte		14.03.64	1	Inverness	2	Aug
49.23	Luke Rosenberg 114	U20	29.06.80	2	Liverpool	8	Aug
48.98	Ian Taylor		2.07.67	1	Tamworth	14	Jun
	(20)						
48.64	Rafer Joseph		21.07.68	1D	Bressanone, ITA	5	Jul
48.36	Simon Fricker		14.07.75	8	Bedford	24	May
48.14	Scott Rider 142	U23	22.09.77	2	London (BP)	18	Apr
48.13	Michael Jemi-Alade		13.10.64	5	Watford	16	May
47.48	Neil Elliott 151		10.04.71	3	Edinburgh	17	Jul
47.41	Scot Thompson 159	U20	10.08.81	4	Edinburgh	17	Jul
46.99	John Moreland	V40	13.09.58	2	Rugby	13	Sep
46.91	Alexis Sharp		31.10.72	5	Liverpool	8	Aug
46.70	Andy Kruszewski		7.04.59	3	Watford	4	Jul
46.68	Mark Quigley		6.11.74	1	Whitehaven	9	May
	(30)						
46.65	John Parkin 195	U20	23.02.79	2	Liverpool	18	Jul
46.64	Mark Davies		10.01.71	1	Brighton	16	May
46.48	Gareth Gilbert		24.08.72	1	Stretford	18	Aug
46.32	Matthew Twigg		18.07.69	1	Peterborough	31	Aug
46.31	James South		4.01.75	6	Birmingham	6	Jun

U18

45.90	Andrew Rollins ?²⁷	U23	20.03.78	1	Colwyn Bay	5	Sep
45.87	Robert Russell		5.08.74	2	Cudworth	10	May
45.74	Dean Macey 235	U23	12.12.77	1	Harrow	30	Aug
45.34	Neil Griffin	V50	28.05.48	2	Crawley	19	Jul
45.30	Mark Edwards		2.12.74	2	Telford	15	Aug
	(40)						
45.29	Justin Bryan		16.08.69	1	Wrexham	17	Aug
44.96	Iain Park		16.07.74	2	Grangemouth	17	May
44.94	Andy Turner		29.08.63	1	London (TB)	16	May
44.91	David Abernethy	V40	5.09.55	1	Carlisle	6	Sep
44.70	David Lovett	U23	13.09.78	1	London (Col)	6	Jun
44.68	Rory Birbeck		24.09.73	1	Blackpool	27	Sep
44.60	James Muirhead		26.01.71	7	Liverpool	8	Aug
44.34	Simon Williams	U20	5.10.80	6	Bedford	5	Jul
44.22	Mike Small	V40	31.03.54	1	London (TB)	23	May
44.13	Craig Munden	U23	24.12.76	1	Reading	14	Jun
	(50)						
44.00	Alex Kruger		18.11.63	1	Stellenbosch, RSA	7	Jan
44.00	Rob Earle		15.09.60	2	Colchester	31	Aug
43.97	Ashley Ward		1.08.64	1	Crawley	24	Jun
43.46	Anthony Southward		31.01.71	3	Bolton	15	Aug
43.43	Tom Hayman	U20	17.09.80	7	Bedford	5	Jul
43.29	Paul Head		1.07.65	3	Crawley	19	Jul
43.16	John Little	V45	14.04.53	8	Edinburgh	4	Jul
43.09	Greg Richards	V40	25.04.56	1	Peterborough	6	Jun
43.06	Matthew Allison		26.02.73	4	Blackpool	8	Aug
43.01	Jamie Quarry		15.11.72	4	Crawley	19	Jul
	(60)						
42.95	Gary Parsons		17.05.71	1	Cambridge	4	Jul
42.80	Paul Howard		19.10.66	14	Bedford	24	May
42.54	Daniel Brunt	U23	23.04.76	6	Birmingham	18	Jul
42.45	Gareth Cook		20.02.69	1	Andover	4	Jul
42.43	Martin Rowe	U20	23.07.80	8	Bedford	5	Jul
42.37	Ewart Hulse		21.01.62	1	Newport	3	May
42.22	Brett Heath		6.01.75	3	Bebington	4	Jul
42.21	Barry Thomas		28.04.72	3	Kingston	9	May
42.20	Neal Hart		15.04.68	1	Galashiels	30	Aug
42.17	P. Lekkas Tιτos (U23) 13.09.77			2	Inverness	2	Aug
	(70)						
42.07	Peter Russell		7.05.60	3	Belfast	27	Jun
42.00	Richard Czernik		12.08.72	1	Gloucester	11	Jul
41.98	Steve Stanford	U20	9.12.79	7	Enfield	16	May
41.78	Mike Conerney		30.10.72	1	Cambridge	18	Apr
41.67	Alun Williams		22.06.62	2	Brecon	5	Jul
41.66	Steven Hale	U23	20.04.77	2	Redditch	27	Jun
41.65	Liam McIntyre	U23	22.09.76	4	Grangemouth	17	May
41.64	Du'aine Ladejo		14.02.71	1	Portsmouth (RN)	15	Aug
41.60	Nicholas Crimmen		15.07.65	1	Grimsby	11	Jul
41.51	John Painter ¶		12.06.58	1	Great Yarmouth	9	May
	(80)						
41.40	Michael Ferne	V50	18.12.47	1	Southampton	11	Aug
41.28	Martin Wilson		3.03.71	2	Whitehaven	2	May
41.27	Craig Burrows		8.08.74	6	Watford	20	Jun
41.18	Gary Sollitt		13.01.72	2	Portsmouth	26	Jun
41.17	Peter Todd		14.10.61	1	Kingston	21	Jun
41.09	Peter Roberts		19.09.71	1	Neath	14	Jun
41.08	Mark Dumican		17.08.70	3	Blackburn	14	Jun
41.00	Duncan Mathieson		8.03.69	2	Stellenbosch, RSA	7	Jan
41.00	Paul Corrigan		19.01.66	3	Jarrow	16	Aug
40.98	Chris Bailey		18.09.69	2	Bebington	2	May
	(90)						

40.95	Willie Falconer		U23	20.12.78	4	Bath	2	May
40.91	Richard Healey		V40	17.11.54	3	Hayes	6	Jun
40.91	Paul Sutcliffe			8.12.70	1	Cleckheaton	30	Aug
40.72	Mark Wiseman				2	Cosford	1	Jul
40.58	Alan Rudkin		U23	5.11.78	5	Derby	4	Jul
40.50	James Worland			3.02.72	2	London (WP)	2	May
40.37	Graham Holder			16.01.72	2	Barking	15	Mar
40.37	Steven Lloyd			20.03.74	5	Liverpool	18	Jul
40.32	Jon Wilkinson			17.02.62	1	Stockport	4	Jul
40.28	Clayton Turner			9.01.68	1	London (TB)	2	May

(100)

40.26	Fyn Corcoran		U23	17.03.78	1	Carn Brea	5	Apr
40.23	Chris Howe			17.11.67	10	Enfield	16	May
40.07	Malcolm Fenton		V40	12.02.56	1	London (Ha)	6	Jun

handwritten: 20 ... 22 ... U20x9 ... U20 x 9

Foreign

47.71	John Farrelly (IRE)			4.12.67	3	Dublin (S), IRE	25	Jul
46.64	Pierre Faber (RSA)			9.01.72	Q	Bath	2	May
44.85	Garry Power (IRE)			1.09.62	2	Dublin, IRE	29	Jul
41.63	George Antonatos (GRE)			30.09.74	1	Cannock	9	May
41.51	Tony Soalla-Bell (SLE)		U23	3.10.76	2	London (TB)	19	Aug
40.88	Ken Souter (AUS)		V40	2.07.57	6	Edinburgh	17	Jul

DISCUS - Under 20 - 1.75kg

64.35	Emeka Udechuku			10.07.79	1	Basildon	21	Jun
61.81	Carl Myerscough			21.10.79	1	Stretford	18	Aug
51.13	Luke Rosenberg			29.06.80	1	Watford	12	Apr
50.82	Simon Williams			5.10.80	2	London (He)	9	Aug
50.78	Scot Thompson			10.08.81	1	Edinburgh	19	Jun
50.51	Steve Stanford			9.12.79	1	Stretford	19	May
50.04	John Parkin			23.02.79	1	Aberdare	31	Aug
47.54	Tom Hayman			17.09.80	1	Solihull	24	May
47.03	Adam Major		U17	2.11.81	2	Elgin	20	Sep
45.86	Andrew Waters			11.10.79	1	Worcester	12	Sep

(10) *handwritten: U18*

45.75	Graeme Allan			24.09.80	3	Basildon	21	Jun
45.42	Martin Rowe			23.07.80	2	Solihull	24	May
44.85	Michael Discala			5.04.81	4	London (He)	9	Aug
44.64	Darren Hatton			21.03.79	D	Ashford	28	Jun
44.59	Scott Metcalfe			8.10.79	3	Solihull	24	May
44.50	Nathan Jones			10.03.80	2	Portsmouth	9	May
44.38	Adam Hopcroft			3.08.79	3	London (Ha)	23	May
43.92	Robert Morris		U17	20.02.82	1	Luton	23	Aug
43.45	Brian Cooksley			5.04.80	2	Aberdare	31	Aug
43.27	Daniel Lethbridge			1.04.81	1	Crawley	24	Jun

(20)

42.95	David Blackmore				1	Cardiff	30	Apr
42.50	Martin Hayes			31.08.79	1	Rotherham	21	Jun
42.34	James Rumbold		U17	4.11.81	1	Exeter	5	Jul
42.07	Adrian Cluskey			30.12.80	4	Basildon	21	Jun
41.93	Chris Orr		U17	20.06.83	3	Birmingham	21	Jun
41.80	John Parnaby			8.10.79	1	Cudworth	10	May
41.69	Ross Kidner			12.09.80	1	Harrow	19	Apr
41.60	Chris Pritchard			13.12.80	1	Rotherham	21	Jun

handwritten: U18 5 ... 41.50 B. ROBERTS (80) ... 2 ... COL BAY ... 11 APR

overage

46.67	David Lovett		U23	13.09.78	3	Exeter	10	Jul

handwritten: 30 41.09 SAM LAKEY (EXE) ... 40 x 36

DISCUS - Under 17 - 1.5kg

53.98	Felice Miele *10TH*		24.11.81	1	Exeter	10	Jul
51.98	Robert Morris *19TH*		20.02.82	1	Bedford	9	Aug
47.94	Alan Brassington		27.09.81	1	Stoke	13	Jun
47.55	Adam Major		2.11.81	1	Grangemouth	23	Aug
47.27	James Rumbold		4.11.81	2	London (Ha)	24	May
46.80	Anthony Smith		11.01.83	1	Colchester	31	Aug
46.18	Mark Tinwell		18.11.81	2	Birmingham	6	Sep
46.04	Chris Orr *U18 10*		20.06.83	3	Sheffield	16	Aug
45.85	Peter Favell		16.03.82	1	Derby	13	Jun
45.04	Geoffrey Reid-Hughes		14.10.81	3	London (Ha)	24	May

47.863 (10)

44.69	Gregg Beard		10.09.82	1	Brighton	19	Aug
44.63	Alex Wilson		28.08.82	1	Harrow	7	Jun
43.76	James Taylor *U18 20*		24.04.82	1	York	25	Jul
43.66	David Onwubalili		5.12.82	5	Exeter	10	Jul
43.04	Tim Leaman		23.11.82	1	Worcester	13	Sep
42.54	Greg Urquhart		14.06.82	1	Hull	13	Jun
42.43	Adrian Hemery		6.08.82	1	Salisbury	10	May
41.60	Gary Winchcombe		26.07.82	1	Rotherham	28	Jun
41.40	John Holtby		27.03.82	O	Hull	19	Sep
40.70	Darrell Turner		22.10.82	1	Solihull	24	May

(20)

40.52	Jeff Bennett		4.04.83	1	Blackpool		9 May

46.02 JOHN BARNES 40x22

doubtful

51.68	Chris Orr		20.06.83	1	Whitehaven		9 May

overage

54.46	Scot Thompson	U20	10.08.81	1	Dublin, IRE		8 Aug

DISCUS - Under 15 - 1.25kg

45.84	Carl Saggers *24TH*		20.09.83	1	Colchester	31	Aug
43.66	Nick Grundy *57TH*		11.11.83	1	Peterborough	31	Aug
43.07	Chris Levett *66TH*		30.11.83	2	Peterborough	31	Aug
42.93	Simon Bulley *71ST*		19.09.84	2	Sheffield	15	Aug
39.90	Geoff Armstrong		6.08.84	1	Woking	6	Sep
39.81	Edward Dunford		15.09.84	1	Gloucester	5	Sep
39.62	Kevin Llewellyn			2	Dublin, IRE	8	Aug
38.71	Carl Bell		19.10.83	1	Jarrow	20	Jun
38.50	Tom Bivins		18.11.83	1	Leicester	13	Jun
38.25	Richard Hurren		24.09.83	1	Livingston	5	Sep

41.029 (10)

37.93	Ross Elliott		6.09.83	1	York	25	Jul
37.92	Stuart Semple		3.11.83	2	Woking	6	Sep
37.55	David Dawson		3.02.84	1	Exeter	13	Jun
37.42	Martin Aram		2.12.83	1	Douglas, IOM	29	Jul
37.26	Guy Heath		21.04.84	1	Blackpool	13	Jun
37.25	Kevin Quinn		23.12.83	3	London (Ha)	23	May
37.25	Gareth Browne *35x40*		19.04.84	1	Thurrock	19	Jul
37.04	K. Adu			2	Thurrock	19	Jul

5-8 30 36-99 5-16 40 *A. FROST 36-84 A. ROBERTSON 20*

overage

33.01	Simon Bissell *U13*		25.12.85	1	Nelson		6 Sep

DISCUS - Under 13 - 1kg

34.14	James Dunford *8TH*		14.01.86	1	Gloucester	5	Sep
34.06 ?	G. Williams *9TH OVER AGE*			1	Brecon	12	Jul
33.15	Samuel Herrington		2.10.86	1	Leamington	5	Aug
32.72	Charles Handley *12TH*		18.01.86	1	Cleckheaton	6	Sep

HAMMER

74.02	Mick Jones		23.07.63	2	Kuala Lumpur, MAL	18 Sep
73.47				1	Bedford	29 Aug
73.28				1	Birmingham	6 Jun
73.14				1	Thurrock	31 Aug
72.89				5	Johannesburg, RSA	12 Sep
72.88				1	London (He)	8 Aug
72.55				2	Belgrade, YUG	31 May
72.28				6	St. Petersburg, RUS	28 Jun
72.13				1	Birmingham	26 Jul
72.06				1	Liverpool	18 Jul
71.90				6	Halle, GER	16 May
71.72				1	Crawley	9 May
70.34				1	London (Col)	26 Apr
70.12				15Q	Budapest, HUN	5 Jun
73.50	David Smith		2.11.74	1	Cleckheaton	29 Aug
73.36				1	Cleckheaton	30 Aug
70.94				1	Watford	16 May
70.85				1	Leeds	7 Jun
70.84				2	London (He)	8 Aug
69.77				5	Kuala Lumpur, MAL	18 Sep
69.70				3	Birmingham	6 Jun
68.82				1	Bedford	25 May
68.46				6	Rehlingen, GER	1 Jun
67.74				1	Edinburgh	4 Jun
73.11	Paul Head		1.07.65	2	Birmingham	6 Jun
72.56				4	Halle, GER	16 May
71.16				2	Bedford	29 Aug
70.36				4	Kuala Lumpur, MAL	18 Sep
70.11				2	Thurrock	31 Aug
69.93				1	Watford	21 Jun
69.89				1	Enfield	23 Aug
69.82				3	London (He)	8 Aug
69.73				2	Ljubljana, SLO	31 May
69.46				2	Birmingham	26 Jul
68.89				1	Crawley	19 Jul
70.09	William Beauchamp		9.09.70	1	Enfield	19 Jul
69.44				1	Birmingham	18 Jul
69.22				1	Haslemere	22 Jul
68.81				2	London (Col)	26 Apr
68.20				1	Haslemere	14 Jul
67.36				1	Enfield	9 May
67.05				1	Loughborough	17 May
66.89				2	Watford	21 Jun
66.56				3	Birmingham	26 Jul
67.45	Steve Pearson		13.09.59	1B	Manchester	27 Jun
66.84				1A	Manchester	27 Jun
66.59				3	London (Col)	26 Apr
66.98	Steve Whyte		14.03.64	1	Walton	8 Jul
66.97	Chris Howe		17.11.67	1	Cardiff	6 Jun
66.66	John Pearson		30.04.66	1	Loughborough	9 May
66.59				1	Loughborough	9 May
	51 performances to 66.50 by 8 athletes					
66.35	Shane Peacock		5.03.63	2	Watford	16 May
64.64	Iain Park		16.07.74	1	Feltham	22 Jul
	(10)					
62.82	Craig Ellams		24.11.72	2B	Stoke	6 Sep
62.50	Russell Devine		24.04.68	2	Melbourne, AUS	14 Feb
62.43	Simon Bown		21.11.74	3	Birmingham	18 Jul
62.01	Mike Floyd	U23	26.09.76	1B	London (Col)	26 Apr

61.70	John Urquhart	U23	14.11.77	2	Edinburgh	18	Jul
61.62	Matthew Bell	U23	2.06.78	1	Peterborough	31	Aug
61.61	Graham Holder		16.01.72	1	Cwmbran	20	Jun
61.35	Malcolm Fenton	V40	12.02.56	1	Stevenage	4	Jul
61.28	Adrian Palmer		10.08.69	1	Yate	14	Jun
61.27	David Allan		17.10.70	1	Inverness (BP)	11	Jul
	(20)						
60.89	Steve Minnikin		4.01.72	1	Cudworth	12	Sep
59.76	Rob Earle		15.09.60	2	Colchester	31	Aug
59.68	Gareth Cook		20.02.69	1	Guildford	15	Aug
59.12	Andrew Grierson	U20	23.11.79	3	Alicante, SPA	18	Jul
58.93	Anthony Swain		17.01.75	1	Cudworth	9	May
58.68	Steve Sammut		3.05.67	2	Haslemere	22	Jul
58.38	Chris Walsh	U23	1.10.78	1	Gateshead	9	May
58.26	Glen Kerr		27.10.74	1	Bromley	15	Aug
58.04	Philip Bufton		10.11.67	1	Colwyn Bay	7	Jun
57.99	Peter Vivian		5.11.70	8	Watford	16	May
	(30)						
57.91	Paul Barnard		27.07.72	2	Gateshead	10	May
57.83	Alan McNicholas		10.12.74	1	Bedford	14	Jun
57.31	Robert Weir		4.02.61	9	Edinburgh	4	Jul
56.94	Rob Careless		7.09.74	5	Birmingham	22	Aug
56.76	David Nicholl		16.09.69	1	Dublin, IRE	3	May
56.58	David Smith		21.06.62	3	Grendon Hall	11	Oct
56.44	Wayne Clarke		24.12.75	4	Enfield	19	Jul
56.00	Stuart Thurgood	U23	17.05.76	1	Swindon	6	Jun
55.09	Sean Jones		21.03.69	1	Cosford	1	Jul
54.97	Steve McEvoy		23.05.63	3	Harrow	30	Aug
	(40)						
54.53	Chris Black	V45	1.01.50	2	Bellaria, ITA	16	Sep
54.50	Russell Payne		11.09.60	1	Leamington	9	May
54.43	Calum Bruce		28.02.75	1	Grangemouth	2	Sep
54.28	Matt Spicer		18.05.71	1	Watford	12	Sep
53.66	Ross Kidner	U20	12.09.80	1	London (PH)	6	Jun
53.57	Kevin Davies	U23	11.01.78	2	Cosford	25	Apr
53.54	Michael Madden		13.09.65	1	St. Albans	6	Jun
53.00	Andy Frost	U20	17.04.81	1	Sandown, IOW	15	Jul
52.76	Tom Eden	U20	16.05.79	1	Enfield	6	Jun
52.74	Mark Proctor		15.01.63	2	Cosford	1	Jul
	(50)						
52.55	Neil Curtis		30.07.74	2	Tamworth	6	Jun
52.55	Graeme Allan	U20	24.09.80	3	Bedford	4	Jul
52.42	Tim Wurr	U20	1.03.79	4	Bedford	4	Jul
52.37	Shaun Pickering		14.11.61	6	Cardiff	6	Jun
52.19	David Shenton	U23	20.10.77	1	Ormskirk	11	Jul
51.95	Paul Dickenson	V45	4.12.49	1	Bromley	6	Jun
51.86	Peter Fuller	U23	30.04.78	1	Kingston	14	Jun
51.48	Jason Dibble		15.02.71	3	Cannock	9	May
51.34	James Hawkins	U20	14.12.79	1	Hoo	14	Jun
51.25	Christopher Adams	U20	18.07.81	2	Newport	8	Aug
	(60)						
51.18	John Parkin	U20	23.02.79	5	Bedford	4	Jul
50.96	E. Reina			1	Perivale	16	May
50.91	Gary Herrington		31.03.61	4	Tamworth	6	Jun
50.88	Ewart Hulse		21.01.62	1	Colwyn Bay	10	May
50.67	Andy Turner		29.08.63	1	Bournemouth	9	May
50.45	Fyn Corcoran	U23	17.03.78	1	London (WP)	25	Jul
50.35	David Robinson	U23	12.01.78	2	Watford	2	Sep
50.30	Mark Roberson		21.03.75	3	Sutton	20	Sep
50.29	Peter Gordon	V45	2.07.51	1	Wakefield	2	May
50.13	Mark Sheridan		17.06.70	2	Enfield	6	Jun

50.09	Mark Miller		10.11.71	1	Derby	4	Jul
49.41	Rafer Joseph		21.07.68	3	Bedford	30	Aug
49.21	David Gisbey		2.05.60	2	Grangemouth	2	Sep
49.02	Neil Bulman	U23	7.09.77	2	Loughborough	25	Apr
49.02	Bruce Shepherd		20.03.67	1	Elgin	18	Jul
49.01	Michael Reiss		17.06.63	1	Croydon	16	May
48.98	Geoff Whaley		9.06.58	1	Exeter	10	May
48.73	Terry Lalley	V45	12.11.49	1	Exeter	21	Jun
48.59	Christopher Snook	U20	6.06.79	1	Middlesbrough	29	Aug
48.50	Barry Williams	V50	5.03.47	2	Crewe	10	May
	(80)						
48.45	S. White			4	Loughborough	13	May
48.45	Alan Woods	V45	27.03.51	3	Grendon Hall	10	Oct
48.41	Keith Robinson	V45	9.02.52	3	Enfield	6	Jun
48.30	Mike Small	V40	31.03.54	1	London (TB)	7	Nov
48.16	Brian Cooksley	U20	5.04.80	2	Cardiff	3	Jun
48.14	Nathan Marston		21.02.75	1	Oxford	16	May
47.98	Eric Kerr		9.12.64	2	Hemel Hempstead	15	Aug
47.95	Wayne Powell		27.07.71	1	Bath	6	Sep
47.90	Nicholas Fogg	U23	24.03.78	1	Watford	29	Jul
47.78	Martin Roberts		1.03.60	1	Wrexham	14	Jun
	(90)						
47.57	Chris Melluish	V50	15.07.44	2	London (Elt)	4	Jul
47.41	Robin Walker	U23	8.02.78	4	Cleckheaton	29	Aug
47.40	Matthew Hammond		26.09.68	2	Rotherham	6	Jun
47.33	Nick Woolcott		7.04.61	5	Watford	4	Jul
47.27	Martin Hayes	U20	31.08.79	1	Derby	9	May
47.22	David Little	U20	28.02.81	4	Middlesbrough	22	Aug
47.14	Mark Broughton		23.10.63	3	Bedford	22	Jul
46.55	Sam Broadley	U20	17.05.81	3	Cudworth	1	Aug
46.42	Leslie Mackintosh	U20	25.02.81	1	Blackpool	6	Sep
46.28	David Sole		19.01.65	4	Derby	4	Jul
	(100)						
46.18	John Little	V45	14.04.53	1	Middlesbrough	2	May
46.17	Jason Kingwell		8.10.70	2	London (He)	6	Jun
46.16	Anthony Doran		22.10.72	4	Stoke	16	May
46.16	Gareth Driscoll	U20	8.03.81	3	Newport	8	Aug
46.08	Mark Dumican		17.08.70	3	Wakefield	2	May
46.02	Peter Aston	V50	21.02.45	4	Liverpool	8	Aug

Foreign   45×13
| 57.49 | *Phil Spivey (AUS)* | | *15.05.61* | *1* | *Loughborough* | *20* | *May* |

HAMMER - Under 20 - 6.25kg

64.00	Matthew Sutton 21ˢᵗ	U17	8.09.81	1	Middlesbrough	22	Aug
62.12	Andrew Grierson		23.11.79	1	Windsor	14	Jun
60.35	Andy Frost 45ᵗᵘ		17.04.81	1	Hayes	26	Jul
59.90	Ross Kidner		12.09.80	2	London (Col)	26	Apr
59.87	Graeme Allan		24.09.80	1	London (He)	23	Aug
57.41	Christopher Adams		18.07.81	3	Windsor	14	Jun
57.31	Ross Thompson	U17	7.12.81	2	Middlesbrough	22	Aug
57.15	Tim Wurr		1.03.79	1	Solihull	23	May
56.48	Tom Eden		16.05.79	1	Stretford	2	Jun
55.45	David Little		28.02.81	3	Middlesbrough	23	Aug
59.004	(10)						
54.42	John Parkin		23.02.79	1	Colwyn Bay	11	Apr
53.98	James Hawkins		14.12.79	4	London (Ha)	23	May
53.67	Martin Hayes		31.08.79	1	Derby	13	Jun
53.38	Christopher Snook		6.06.79	1	Cudworth	1	Aug
52.40	John Barnes		6.05.82	1B	Grendon Hall	11	Oct
51.58	Brian Cooksley		5.04.80	1	Newport	9	Aug
51.39	Leslie Mackintosh		25.02.81	1	Cleckheaton	23	Aug

51.32	Danny Cunnane	U17	12.04.83	3	Wakefield	26	Jul
51.26	Tom Harrington		27.10.79	2	London (He)	30	Aug
50.51	Gareth Driscoll		8.03.81	3	Colwyn Bay	6	Sep
(20)							
49.68	Robert Taylor		9.06.80	2	Gateshead	23	Aug
49.29	Ashley Slater	U17	23.09.81	2	Stoke	23	Aug
49.14	Emeka Udechuku		10.07.79	3	Basildon	21	Jun
48.93	Ben Clare		21.09.80	6	Exeter	10	Jul
48.53	Tom Ash		29.11.79	1	Croydon	13	Jun
48.49	Sam Broadley		17.05.81	2	Leeds	13	Jun
48.17	Kirk Capeling		27.02.80	4	Harrow	26	Jul
46.02	Iain Holland		6.07.81	4	Barry	14	Jul

HAMMER - Under 17 - 5kg

73.76	Matthew Sutton		8.09.81	1	Windsor	14	Jun
67.21	Ross Thompson		7.12.81	2	Middlesbrough	22	Aug
63.08	Timmon Whitehead		20.04.82	1	Haslemere	22	Jul
61.46	Ashley Slater		23.09.81	3	Sheffield	15	Aug
60.13	Adam Beauford		24.10.81	1	Bristol	7	Jun
59.91	Nick Williams		2.02.82	1	Stretford	23	Aug
59.73	Damien Howard		23.11.81	1	Bury St. Edmonds	17	May
58.95	Peter Field		21.05.82	1	Stoke	27	Sep
58.22	John Barnes		6.05.82		Scunthorpe	8	Mar
56.26	Marc Landon		9.11.81	1	Corby	13	Jun
(10)							
54.50	Carl Saggers	U15	20.09.83	1	Sutton	20	Sep
53.93	Oliver Hoad		1.10.81	1	Peterborough	13	Jun
53.66	Christopher James		9.12.82	2	Sutton	20	Sep
52.35	Jason Smithson		23.09.82	4	Windsor	14	Jun
52.12	Alan Rodmell		23.09.81	1	Chester-Le-Street	28	Jun
51.73	Matthew Grindle		3.01.82	4	Ayr	18	Jul
51.48	John Hay		4.06.83	2	Corby	26	Apr
49.48	Matthew Newell		20.09.81	2	Stoke	6	Sep
49.06	Simon Gate		21.09.82	1	Carlisle	13	Jun
48.95	Mark Crawley		4.11.81	1	Middlesbrough	13	Jun
(20)							
47.70	Adam Major		2.11.81	9	Sheffield	15	Aug
47.64	Adrian Hemery		6.08.82	1	London (BP)	26	Apr
47.43	Peter Favell		16.03.82	1	Derby	9	May
47.41	Robert Watts		19.10.81	2	Yeovil	20	Jun

HAMMER - Under 15 - 4kg

60.15	Carl Saggers		20.09.83	1	Sheffield	16	Aug
57.15	Tom Dempsey		15.12.83	1	Birmingham	5	Sep
54.55	Derrick Squires		7.12.83	1C	Stoke	27	Sep
51.30	Chris Mason		6.04.84	1	Middlesbrough	11	Aug
48.77	Kamran Khan		2.10.83	2	Stoke	20	Jun
45.82	Daniel Boneham		9.12.83	1	Cwmbran	13	Sep
45.79	Daniel Allmark		11.05.84	1	Peterborough	31	Aug
45.12	Reece Drury		2.11.83	1	Hull	13	Jun
45.04	Nicholas Edwards		22.03.84	4	Sheffield	16	Aug
44.93	James Grindle		8.01.84	1	Worcester	19	Jul
(10)							
44.52	Paul Nash		13.02.84	1	Leamington	19	Jul
44.30	Gary Browne			5	Tullamore, IRE	6	Jun
44.29	Matthew Frampton		10.04.84	1	Portsmouth	28	Jun
44.23	Lee Hardy		1.11.83	3	Birmingham	6	Sep
43.87	Stephen Ashton		21.03.84	4	Birmingham	6	Sep
43.40	David Jones		26.09.83	5	Birmingham	6	Sep
42.50	Tom Bivins		18.11.83	4	Cwmbran	13	Sep

JAVELIN

89.89	Steve Backley	12.02.69	1	Gateshead	19	Jul
	89.72		1	Budapest, HUN	23	Aug
	89.22		2	Tartu, EST	11	Jun
	88.80		1	Sheffield	2	Aug
	88.71 A		1	Johannesburg, RSA	13	Sep
	87.58		1	Soini, FIN	24	May
	87.48		2	Helsinki, FIN	13	Jun
	87.45		Q	Budapest, HUN	21	Aug
	87.38		2	Kuala Lumpur, MAL	21	Sep
	85.79		1	Stockholm, SWE	5	Aug
	85.44		2	Oslo, NOR	9	Jul
	85.13		1	Glasgow	30	Aug
	84.78		1	Birmingham	26	Jul
	84.23		1	Brussels, BEL	28	Aug
	83.18		3	Lausanne, SWZ	25	Aug
	82.79		1	Leeds	7	Jun
86.92	Mick Hill	22.10.64	2	Budapest, HUN	23	Aug
	83.94		2	Sheffield	2	Aug
	83.80		3	Kuala Lumpur, MAL	21	Sep
	83.50		4	St. Petersburg, RUS	28	Jun
	82.85		1	Melbourne, AUS	25	Feb
	82.57		3	Glasgow	30	Aug
	82.33		4	Stockholm, SWE	5	Aug
	81.55		2	Birmingham	26	Jul
	81.51		7	Oslo, NOR	9	Jul
	81.41		3	Brussels, BEL	28	Aug
	81.24		2	Auckland, NZ	21	Feb
	81.06		3	Gateshead	19	Jul
	81.04		2	Leeds	7	Jun
	80.79		1	Sydney, AUS	28	Feb
	80.40		6	Lausanne, SWZ	25	Aug
	80.14		Q	Budapest, HUN	21	Aug
	79.94		4	Tartu, EST	11	Jun
	77.64		1	Santiago, CHI	25	Apr
	77.05		7	Soini, FIN	24	May
85.67	Mark Roberson 3	13.03.67	2	Gateshead	19	Jul
	84.37		2	Glasgow	30	Aug
	84.15		6	Budapest, HUN	23	Aug
	80.98		4	Kuala Lumpur, MAL	21	Sep
	80.78		2	Karlstad, SWE	13	Jun
	79.63		2Q	Budapest, HUN	21	Aug
	79.43		4	Sheffield	2	Aug
	79.13		1	Edinburgh	4	Jul
	78.99		1	L'Alfas Del Pi, SPA	18	Apr
	78.93		3	Birmingham	26	Jul
	78.70		1	Bedford	24	May
	78.61		3	Leeds	7	Jun
	78.51		1	Bedford	29	Aug
	78.26		4	Auckland, NZ	21	Feb
	77.88		3	Halle, GER	16	May
	77.79		1	Birmingham	6	Jun
	77.75		4	Sydney, AUS	28	Feb
	77.40		2	Ljubljana, SLO	31	May
	76.55		1	London (He)	8	Aug
78.73	Colin Mackenzie	30.06.63	1	Ashford	5	Apr
78.68	Nick Nieland	31.01.72	3	Karlstad, SWE	13	Jun
76.26	Nigel Bevan	3.01.68	1	University Park, USA	10	May

56 performances to 76.00 by 6 athletes

75.21	David Parker 14	U20²	28.02.80	1	York	13	Jun
74.20	Stuart Faben		28.02.75	2	L'Alfas Del Pi, SPA	18	Apr
72.85	Steve Harrison		19.12.72	Q	Bath	4	May
71.14	Dan Carter 23	U20 7	15.04.80	2	Exeter	11	Jul
(10)
70.90	Shane Lewis 24		22.08.72	1	Watford	6	Jun
68.91	Stuart Loughran 34	U23	19.02.76	6	Birmingham	26	Jul
68.53	Phill Sharpe 39	U20 11	6.03.81	1	Watford	16	May
68.33	Kevin Murch		11.11.58	1	Leamington	9	May
68.08	Tim Kitney 43	U20 14	26.04.80	2	Cannock	13	Sep
68.06	Peter Yates	V40	15.06.57	1	London (Elt)	4	Jul
68.02	Stefan Baldwin		26.04.70	2	Watford	6	Jun
67.77	Gary Jenson		14.02.67	1	London (WF)	9	May
67.19	Mark Francis	U23	23.09.77	2	Loughborough	17	May
66.37	Simon Carter 57		5.03.75	1	Enfield	16	May
(20)
66.21	Clifton Green 58	U20 19	10.10.79	1	Ware	4	May
65.44	David Hanna		13.12.75	1	Belfast	9	May
65.40	Phil Parry		4.10.65	1	Bournemouth	4	Jul
65.31	Sam Armstrong 65		17.02.74	1	Glasgow (S)	14	Jun
65.04	Keith Beard		8.11.61	4	Lisse, HOL	23	Aug
64.83	Paul Cooper	U23	4.12.76	1	Liverpool	8	Aug
64.38	Dwayne Marsden 79		25.10.73	1	Southampton	4	Jul
63.66	Tony Smith NOT →	V40	17.05.58	3	Watford	16	May
63.33	Daryl Brand		6.08.63	1	Hamilton, NZ	28	Nov
62.97	Trevor Ratcliffe		9.03.64	2	Bedford	30	Aug
(30)
62.13	Tim Phillips 116	U20 14	13.01.79	2	Bath	4	May
61.65	Mike Tarran 127	U20 28	10.12.80	6	Bedford	5	Jul
61.54	Ken Hayford		10.03.63	1	Bromley	15	Aug
61.37	Alistair Gidley		5.09.72	5	Watford	16	May
61.30	Simon Bennett		16.10.72	1	Cardiff	6	Jun
61.16	Emeka Udechuku 140	U20 53	10.07.79	7	Bedford	5	Jul
60.98	Livon Houslin		2.11.60	7	Watford	16	May
60.88	Gary Jones		9.07.72	4	Watford	21	Jun
60.87	Paul Howard		19.10.66	6	Bedford	24	May
60.86	Greg Markham 150	U23	28.11.78	2	Cudworth	10	May
(40)
60.86	Paul Morgan		5.07.65	1	Bedford	6	Jun
60.80	David Sketchley	U23	25.02.76	1	Crawley	19	Jul
60.48	Alex Gibson 161	U23	3.11.77	5	Loughborough	17	May
60.34	Chris Thomas	U20	11.01.80	1	Newport	2	May
60.34	Landley Darlington	U23	19.01.77	3	Bath	4	May
59.89	Stewart McMillan		12.09.69	8	Watford	16	May
59.89	Jeremy Smyth	U23	11.08.78	2	Grangemouth	17	May
59.73	Tom Dobbing		5.02.73	1	Woodford	18	Apr
59.73	Jonathan Clarke		20.11.67	3	Watford	6	Jun
59.65	Steve Jamieson	U20 16	4.02.79	4	Bath	4	May
(50)
59.56	Steve Rogers		1.09.71	1	Barking	8	Aug
59.41	Dean Smahon		8.12.61	1	Liverpool	18	Jul
59.32	Neil McLellan	U23	10.09.78	2	Watford	10	May
59.30	Gerard Plunkett	U20	30.06.80	1D	Hull	20	Sep
59.04	Tim Eldridge	U23	15.03.76	4	Edinburgh	4	Jul
58.95	Peter Fraser	U23	28.01.78	2	Greenock	26	Apr
58.82	Wayne Powell		27.07.71	1	Corby	15	Aug
58.80	Robert Charlesworth	U20	25.03.79	2	Newport	8	Aug
58.69	Fuat Fuat		20.09.71	1	Ashford	2	May
58.58	Rob Laing		30.07.66	1	Blackpool	6	Sep
(60)
58.49	Wesley Smith	U23	26.02.69	1	Redditch	27	Jun

58.37	Alexis Sharp		31.10.72	6D	Kuala Lumpur, MAL	18	Sep
58.33	Roger Killick	U23	20.11.76	1	Birmingham	2	May
58.30	Matthew Allison		26.02.73	2	Blackpool	6	Sep
58.17	Tony Norman		5.07.63	1	London (TB)	25	Jul
57.89	Richard Lainson	U17	5.11.81	1	Hayes	26	Jul
57.87	Peter Coxhead	U20	14.07.81	1	Colchester	16	Aug
57.83	Saul Perryman	U17	17.11.81	2	Hayes	26	Jul
57.74	Neil Christopherson		6.05.67	6	Enfield	16	May
57.74	Matthew Davies	U23	16.09.78	1	Brecon	4	Jul
	(70)						
57.44	James Apps	U20	29.04.80	3	Cannock	13	Sep
57.32	Simon Shirley		3.08.66	1	London (BP)	16	May
57.16	Nigel Carlisle		30.12.75	1	Antrim	23	Jun
57.10	Greg Hayward		28.01.64	1	Cosford	1	Jul
56.91	Darren Hatton	U20	21.03.79	D	Hull	20	Sep
56.70	James Peart	U20	1.08.79	1	Gloucester	29	Aug
56.60	Chris Oliver		16.07.71	2	Cosford	1	Jul
56.47	Lee Weaver	U23	9.03.76	1	Corby	27	Jun
56.47	Ian Burns	U23	20.09.77	2	Watford	12	Sep
56.43	Alistair Pagnameta	U23	12.10.76	1	Oxford	16	May
	(80)						
56.41	Simon Achurch		27.12.74	1	Peterborough	4	Jul
56.29	P. Poole			3	Cosford	1	Jul
56.22	Rafer Joseph		21.07.68	2D	Azusa, USA	17	Apr
55.95	Philips Olweny	U20	14.02.81	8	Exeter	11	Jul
55.90	Ciaran Doherty		14.01.75	6	Bath	4	Apr
55.90	Pawlo Ostapowycz	V45	1.07.52	3	Barking	8	Aug
55.76	Demetrio Barros		29.06.71	1	Feltham	20	Sep
55.71	Buster Watson	V40	19.11.57	3	Bedford	6	Jun
55.34	Greg Magee	U23	27.09.78	1	Belfast	16	Aug
55.29	Tim Newenham		1.04.60	1	Great Yarmouth	10	May
	(90)						
55.19	Andy Hayward		26.10.74	1	Hexham	8	Aug
55.16	Darren Gough	U20		1	Wrexham	14	Jul
55.08	William Wynn		15.02.73	2D	Derby	31	May
55.03	Dean Johnson		31.12.75	3	Sheffield (W)	16	May

Additional Under 20 (1 - 20 above)

54.72	Graeme Allan		24.09.80	1	Blackpool	6	Sep
54.53	Marc McCoy		5.06.81	1	Sheffield	13	Jun
54.30	Matthew Bond		13.07.81	1	Mansfield	19	Apr
54.21	Derek Hermann		7.04.79	1	Carmarthen	10	May
53.78	Matt Tribble		17.10.79	1	Bedford	3	Jun

Additional Under 17 (1 - 2 above)

49.26	Keith Simpson		19.10.81	3	Glasgow (S)	14	Jun

unconfirmed

62.28	Tom Dobbing		5.02.73				

Foreign

66.65	*Michael Allen (IRE)*	*U20*	*7.03.80*	*1*	*Tullamore, IRE*	*12*	*Jul*
63.52	*Ben Houghton (IRE)*	*U20*	*6.08.80*	*1*	*Antrim*	*25*	*Apr*
62.52	*Adam Read (AUS)*		*13.06.71*	*1*	*Grangemouth*	*17*	*May*
59.55	*Brian Scanlan (IRE)*			*1*	*Swindon*	*4*	*Jul*
58.67	*Pierre Faber (RSA)*		*9.01.72*	*5*	*Bath*	*4*	*May*
55.40	*Leon Karagounis*		*15.10.75*	*1*	*Derby*	*10*	*Jul*

JAVELIN - Under 17 - 700g

64.32	Richard Lainson		5.11.81	1	Portsmouth	9 May
59.94	Jonathan Lundman		7.12.81	1	Ashford	5 Jul
58.34	Anthony Lovett		20.09.82	2	Exeter	10 Jul
58.00	Saul Perryman		17.11.81	1	Oxford	19 Jul
57.41	William Maunder-Taylor		27.04.82	1	Watford	10 May
56.30	Thomas Coutts		1.09.81	1	Edinburgh	19 Jun
55.72	James Scaysbrook		1.01.82	1	Birmingham	6 Sep
55.69	Daniel Britton		25.09.81	1	Bournemouth	13 Jun
54.83	Alex Rowswell		18.03.82	6	Exeter	10 Jul
54.54	Alexander Hinchcliffe			1	York	25 Jul
	(10)					
54.50	Jason Hallett		29.03.82	2	Sheffield	15 Aug
54.06	Alex Simpson		19.01.82	1	Bromley	28 Jun
54.00	Owen Matthews		17.10.81	1	Luton	9 May
52.82	Tony Francis		6.07.83	2	Kingston	20 Jun
51.70	Ryan James		23.11.81	1	Corby	13 Jun
51.56	Sam Goddard		4.01.83	1	London (SP)	26 Sep
51.05	Keith Simpson		19.10.81	2	Edinburgh	19 Jun

overage

| 51.14 | Wilby Williamson | U20 | 8.08.81 | | Antrim | 30 May |

JAVELIN - Under 15 - 600g

53.46	James Deacon-Brown		26.05.84	1	Sheffield	16 Aug
53.30	Mike Groves		21.03.84	1	Brecon	4 Jul
50.60	Kunal Kapadia		30.09.83	1	Enfield	9 May
50.04	Stephen Berthier		19.07.84	1	Enfield	13 Jun
48.75	Matthew Crabb		29.09.83	1	Yeovil	26 Jul
47.61	Aaron Cramp		29.02.84	1	Stevenage	13 Sep
47.35	Nick Surtees		11.11.83	1	Bournemouth	20 Sep
46.99	Andrew Stevenson		7.09.83	1	Hoo	13 Jun
46.11	David Turner		4.07.84	1	Ormskirk	27 Jun
45.62	Craig Williams			1	Wrexham	22 Aug
	(10)					
45.47	William Murray			1	Bedford	9 Aug
45.27	David Regan		12.11.83	1	Kingston	13 Jun

JAVELIN - Under 13 - 400g

41.86	James Dunford		14.01.86	1	Exeter	29 Sep
40.60	Philip Mann		25.10.85		Rotherham	13 Sep
40.08	William Ferrier		15.04.86	1	Daventry	8 Aug
36.80	S. Osborne SAM			1	Bristol	10 May

DECATHLON

7654 w   Jamie Quarry   15.11.72   3   Arles, FRA   24 May
10.76W/6.0   7.09w/4.0   13.82   1.90   50.42   14.37w/3.0   41.24   4.65   44.36   4:29.06
7504   10   Bressanone, ITA   5   Jul
10.93/0.0   7.11/2.0   13.73   1.92   49.56   14.68/-0.7   40.13   4.30   45.40   4:32.01
7482   10   Kuala Lumpur, MAL   18 Sep
11.04   6.77/0.6   13.61   1.92   49.40   14.51/0.0   41.12   4.60   44.35   4:36.78
7635 w   Du'aine Ladejo   14.02.71   4   Arles, FRA   24 May
10.28W/6.0   7.34W/7.0 12.06   1.87   46.90   14.83w/3.2   38.51   3.95   50.20   4:28.86
7633   7   Kuala Lumpur, MAL   18 Sep
10.47/-0.6   6.97/-0.4   13.31   2.04   46.12   14.91/0.0   39.24   3.90   47.15   4:41.69
7003   24   Bressanone, ITA   5   Jul
10.45/-0.8   7.01/-0.2   14.03   1.98   46.73   14.63/-1.3   36.59   nh   49.28   4:45.85
7571   Alexis Sharp   31.10.72   1   Azusa, USA   17 Apr
10.5/0.3   7.13w/2.2 13.73   1.91   48.6   15.21/0.2   40.92   4.20   54.70   4:43.30
7542   9   Kuala Lumpur, MAL   18 Sep
11.00/-0.6   7.03/-0.1   13.02   1.95   50.05   15.24/0.0   46.45   4.40   58.37   4:59.99
7112   22   Bressanone, ITA   5   Jul
10.84/0.0   6.98w/2.8 12.77   1.92   49.35   15.49/-0.6   45.65   3.70   53.31   5:23.30
7479 w   Barry Thomas   28.04.72   6   Arles, FRA   24 May
11.05W/6.0   7.14W/4.6 13.57   1.93   52.14   14.91w/3.2   40.21   4.75   52.90   4:48.71
7447   Rafer Joseph   21.07.68   2   Azusa, USA   17 Apr
11.26/1.1   6.35/0.7   13.87   1.88   51.3   14.98w/2.8   47.92   4.80   56.22   4:52.29
7392 w   12   Bressanone, ITA   5   Jul
11.18/0.0   6.51W/7.6 14.17   1.86   51.43   15.04/0.4   48.64   4.30   55.95   4:46.91
7356   *   Bressanone, ITA   5   Jul
           6.35
7126   1   Derby   31 May
11.29/0.4   6.59w/2.7 14.38   1.86   51.35   15.1/2.0   45.92   4.60   56.04   5:37.33
7385   Anthony Southward   31.01.71   1   Sale   23   Jul
11.4/0.2   6.67w/2.3 13.51   1.95   50.2   14.8/-1.2   42.72   4.40   53.45   4:31.4
7052 w   Alex Kruger   18.11.63   10   Arles, FRA   24 May
11.52W/4.7   6.88W/4.7 13.34   2.02   53.71   15.28w/3.0   39.92   4.45   54.15   5:13.87
6901 w   Roger Hunter   U23   10.03.76   11   Arles, FRA   24 May
11.05W   6.79w   13.06   1.90   50.80   15.63W   37.62   3.95   50.54   5:04.74
6810   2   Wrexham   2 Aug
11.32   6.61   12.82   1.83   50.67   15.4   35.39   3.85   50.52   4:39.2
6700   William Wynn   15.02.73   3   Derby   31 May
11.51   6.60   11.47   1.80   50.99   15.2   33.56   3.90   55.08   4:41.23
6696 w   Paul Jones   U23   11.04.78   12   Arles, FRA   24 May
11.39W/5.6   6.69W/6.6 11.04   1.78   52.47   15.35W/4.6   31.79   4.55   51.68   4:49.67
6389   4   Wrexham   2 Aug
11.77   6.45   11.45   1.80   52.56   16.3   36.62   4.55   49.62   5:14.6
   (10)
6508 w   Darren Hatton   U20   21.03.79   13   Arles, FRA   24 May
11.29W/4.7   6.78w/3.7 12.12   1.78   50.26   16.17W/4.3   36.52   3.95   42.13   5:03.88
6477   1   Derby   31 May
11.49   6.57w   12.15   1.77   50.55   16.2   33.66   3.80   51.56   4:51.95
6503   Steve Garland   12.01.73   1   Enfield   2 Aug
11.61   6.19   11.30   1.83   50.85   16.07   34.40   3.90   47.27   4:31.1
6468   Leo Barker   U23   26.12.78   4   Derby   31 May
11.34   6.85   10.71   1.83   50.67   15.3   36.41   2.90   50.12   4:46.59
6456   3   Wrexham   2 Aug
11.26/-0.9   6.89/-0.9 11.69   1.77   51.71   15.3/-0.2   34.59   2.95   50.77   4:49.5
6427   Par Esegbona   16.04.68   2   Enfield   2 Aug
11.56   6.36   10.84   1.83   51.60   15.71   36.12   3.80   46.80   4:47.3
       25 performances to 6400 by 14 athletes
6366   Paul Curran   U23   5.04.77   3   Dublin (S), IRE   17 May
11.67   6.75   10.58   1.91   50.43   16.78w   30.55   3.30   45.95   4:25.69

6334	Dominic Shepherd	U23	11.12.76 5	Derby	31 May
	11.50	6.36	12.58 1.74	51.53 16.2	32.07 4.20 45.74 4:59.43
6265	David Bonsall		2.06.71 1	Cosford	28 Jul
	11.73	6.00	11.83 1.76	53.47 16.4	35.05 4.00 51.25 4:41.5
6241	Brendan McConville	U20	3.01.79 7	Wrexham	2 Aug
	12.26	6.06	10.78 1.92	52.67 16.44	31.73 3.95 46.37 4:27.8
6222 w	Ben Roberts	U20	15.01.80 14	Arles, FRA	24 May
	11.24W	6.41w	12.25 1.78	53.76 14.98W	28.51 3.95 48.25 5:29.43
6221	Scott Exley	U23	9.02.78 7	Derby	31 May
	11.18	6.13	10.42 1.83	50.86 15.8	34.53 3.50 37.30 4:40.19

(20)

6195	Matthew Gillard		11.07.75 2	Birmingham	23 Aug
	11.27	5.97 12.65	1.74	50.21 17.18	31.82 3.95 42.19 4:52.6
6168	Jason McDade	U20	3.04.80 8	Wrexham	2 Aug
	11.31	6.55	11.28 1.98	52.86 15.09	25.47 3.35 47.83 5:27.0
6148	Geoff Ingram		31.01.68 2	Cosford	28 Jul
	11.55	6.31	10.33 1.70	51.28 15.8	32.83 3.90 44.01 4:51.9
6091	Steve Bonnett	U23	13.07.78 2	Sale	23 Jul
	11.8	6.29	10.79 1.92	49.6 16.9	32.17 3.00 44.88 4:30.7
6075	Ciaran Doherty		14.01.75 7	Hexham	17 May
	11.90	6.65	11.66 1.93	54.45 15.29	32.52 3.10 51.32 5:28.50
5943	Richard Czernik		12.08.72 4	Birmingham	23 Aug
	11.48	6.11	11.51 1.77	52.25 16.66	38.16 3.25 42.92 5:12.0
5938	Gerard Plunkett	U20	30.06.80 3	Derby	31 May
	11.88	6.30	10.59 1.89	53.06 19.2	32.14 3.30 57.86 4:42.15
5913	Steven Maisey		11.05.74 8	Derby	31 May
	11.48	6.67	9.93 1.71	52.04 17.3	31.44 3.20 49.77 4:51.24
5884	Andrew Squire	U20	30.09.79 5	Birmingham	23 Aug
	11.75	6.81w	11.88 1.95	53.06 16.72	30.18 2.65 43.34 5:12.4
5875	Neil Fairlamb	U23	13.03.76 8	Hexham	17 May
	11.85	6.09	10.75 1.69	53.19 17.24	37.04 3.50 50.11 4:57.95

(30)

5846	Stephen Robertson		9.07.75 1	Glasgow (S)	3 May
	11.79w	6.41	9.54 1.74	51.25 16.64	23.44 3.80 42.50 4:45.86
5837	Richard Hunter		12.01.71 9	Derby	31 May
	11.83	6.12	10.72 1.74	53.33 15.5	33.32 3.40 36.80 4:49.75
5831	Stuart Caudery		19.11.66 4	Enfield	2 Aug
	12.18	5.97	9.65 1.83	54.43 16.19	33.81 4.00 37.60 4:49.8
5815	Mike Bull		6.06.70 10	Derby	31 May
	11.45	6.23	10.74 1.68	52.53 16.7	27.12 3.60 41.43 4:45.83
5787	Anthony Sawyer	U20	29.04.80 1	Basildon	27 Sep
	11.9	6.26 10.86	1.79	52.0 17.0	33.39 3.10 39.56 4:37.5
5695	Simon White		2.10.75 9	Hexham	17 May
	11.93	5.62	10.78 1.69	51.80 16.56	32.17 3.10 44.05 4:43.07
5669 w	Steve Gutteridge		5.07.71 16	Arles, FRA	24 May
	11.54W	6.72w	12.13 1.84	54.37 15.31W	33.68 nh 46.95 5:32.83
5660	Gavin Fordham	U20	1.02.79 4	Derby	31 May
	11.84	6.52w	9.10 1.89	52.63 17.3	25.43 3.70 37.81 5:01.43
5616	Dominic Chapman		10.02.72 1	Crawley	13 Sep
	12.4	5.74	12.73 1.64	55.1 17.2	33.38 3.40 54.66 5:17.9
5606	Chris Hindley	U23	21.01.76 7	Birmingham	23 Aug
	12.15	6.48	11.67 1.89	55.13 18.86	31.93 3.05 42.11 4:50.4

(40)

5573	Neal Killen		10.04.59 3	Cosford	28 Jul
	12.38	5.66	12.75 1.55	55.06 16.4	37.71 3.60 42.27 5:03.00
5526	Nigel Carlisle		30.12.75 2	Antrim	30 Aug
	11.8	6.11	9.62 1.72	51.1 18.1	29.33 2.90 50.50 4:49.8
5427	Steve Clark		24.05.72 3	Basildon	27 Sep
	12.5	5.50	10.35 1.79	55.3 17.3	33.93 3.60 44.51 4:53.4
5378	Nicholas Walker		24.02.64 12	Derby	31 May
	11.86	6.21w	10.35 1.62	53.63 18.0	33.18 3.50 40.04 5:15.82

231

Score	Name	Cat	DOB	Pos	Venue	Date
5371	Richard Nash		24.06.75	1	Hoo	9 Aug
	12.1	5.93	9.90	1.72	52.1	19.5	27.60	3.20	49.30	4:38.6
5352	Dale Daborn		14.11.66	4	Cosford	28 Jul
	12.26	5.36	8.07	1.67	52.24	16.1	30.59	3.20	43.80	4:49.8
5348	Gavin Showell		29.09.72	10	Hexham	17 May
	11.90	6.16	9.68	1.63	55.15	17.72	30.07	4.10	35.55	5:16.47
5289	Gavin Stott	U23	5.05.77	2	Glasgow (S)	3 May
	12.19w	6.10w	9.41	1.71	54.73	17.32	20.05	3.20	47.02	4:46.51
5287	Frank Chapman		17.01.70	2	Cosford	29 May
	12.0	6.03	11.64	1.72	53.97	16.4	32.74	2.50	34.90	5:08.61
5278	Philip Cantrell	U23	17.06.76	10	Vienna, AUT	28 Jun
	12.90	5.45	10.07	1.75	56.78	17.56	29.95	3.00	47.56	4:25.01

(50)

Score	Name	Cat	DOB	Pos	Venue	Date
5213	Lee Parkes	U23	23.12.76	1	Rotherham	13 Sep
	11.9	5.86	11.36	1.73	58.3	17.6	35.06	3.20	47.32	5:36.5
5186	David Powell	U23	11.09.78	11	Hexham	17 May
	12.28	6.03	10.03	1.69	52.77	18.93	31.42	3.20	39.50	5:08.91
5159	Troy Kennedy		17.08.73	13	Derby	31 May
	12.32	6.11w	11.02	1.59	54.94	17.8	30.96	2.90	42.22	5:02.51
5145	Gurmukh Sahans	U23	8.10.78	6	Enfield	2 Aug
	12.35	5.74	9.57	1.68	57.26	17.82	35.67	3.00	43.61	4:59.9
5100	Alastair Gordon	U23	16.04.78	2	Crawley	13 Sep
	11.4	6.18	8.42	1.58	50.9	17.0	21.11	2.50	33.38	4:42.8
5055	Ashley Pritchard	U20	14.07.79	12	Hexham	17 May
	12.40	5.92	8.51	1.57	53.55	17.05	26.56	3.00	37.42	4:46.80
5026	Stephen McDonnell	U20	24.07.80	12	Wrexham	2 Aug
	11.60	6.22	7.76	1.77	52.33	16.1	20.27	nh	34.72	4:48.7
4942	Jon Gregory		3.10.72	13	Hexham	17 May
	11.89	5.46	9.32	1.75	54.92	16.70	26.43	2.50	38.44	5:19.72
4929	Leigh Walker	U23	17.08.77	7	Enfield	2 Aug
	11.99	5.77	9.29	1.59	56.30	19.07	26.95	4.40	39.30	5:52.1
4914	Peter Coates		21.03.68	3	Hexham	31 Aug
	12.24	6.21	9.15	1.70	54.29	19.85	27.65	2.50	39.14	4:41.91

(60)

Score	Name	Cat	DOB	Pos	Venue	Date
4913	Brian Winning		7.02.67	3	Glasgow (S)	3 May
	11.53w	5.51	7.74	1.68	51.71	17.30	19.16	2.80	26.22	4:42.65

Foreign

Score	Name		DOB	Pos	Venue	Date
7247	*Pierre Faber (RSA)*		*9.01.72*	*1*	*Vienna, AUT*	*28 Jun*
	11.47	*6.89*	*14.44*	*1.99*	*50.96*	*15.97*	*42.26*	*4.40*	*54.91*	*5:03.39*
6996	*Joe Naughton (IRE)*		*17.10.74*	*1*	*Dublin (S), IRE*	*17 May*
	11.47w	*6.87*	*12.65*	*2.00*	*51.10*	*15.74w*	*36.29*	*3.90*	*46.39*	*4:27.15*

DECATHLON - Under 20 with Under 20 Implements

Score	Name	DOB	Pos	Venue	Date
6630	Jason McDade	3.04.80	1	Hull	20 Sep
	11.18	6.74	11.33	2.06	50.89	14.62	33.54	3.40	50.73	5:36.01
6543	Darren Hatton	21.03.79	1	Ashford	28 Jun
	11.9	6.83w	13.21	1.84	52.4	16.8	44.64	3.80	55.82	5:13.0
6514	Edward Coats	14.06.80	2	Hull	20 Sep
	11.72	6.47	11.57	1.85	50.89	16.14	39.89	3.70	44.87	4:42.43
6396	Gerard Plunkett	30.06.80	4	Hull	20 Sep
	12.19	6.31	11.58	1.91	54.04	16.69	36.76	3.50	59.30	4:33.85
6295	Anthony Sawyer	29.04.80	5	Hull	20 Sep
	11.46	5.91	12.42	1.82	50.68	15.96	36.98	3.40	38.89	4:39.49
6263	Brendan McConville	3.01.79	1	Glasgow (S)	3 May
	12.11	6.27	10.81	1.92	53.00	16.13	35.49	3.70	45.63	4:38.54
6252	Andrew East	25.07.81	6	Hull	20 Sep
	11.63	6.30	9.99	1.76	50.95	15.79	32.39	3.30	52.24	4:36.19
6157	John Heanley	25.09.80	7	Hull	20 Sep
	12.09	6.26	9.43	1.73	51.03	15.30	35.05	3.50	40.73	4:24.94

6046	Neil Thompson			23.04.79	1	Hexham			17 May
	11.56	6.78	11.20 1.96	54.73 15.12		32.20	3.00	37.94	5:11.19
6036	Robert Hollinger			11.10.80	8	Hull			20 Sep
	11.68	6.43	12.00 1.79	52.25 15.27		35.27	2.90	33.61	4:47.91
(10)									
5724	Edward Morris			3.03.80	9	Hull			20 Sep
	11.74	6.11	11.48 1.61	53.16 16.13		33.72	3.10	38.91	4:48.76
5718	Matt Tribble			17.10.79	2	St. Ives			28 Jun
	11.5	6.18	11.35 1.75	52.9 17.9		33.11	3.10	52.30	5:07.8
5717	Gavin Fordham			1.02.79	4	Enfield			2 Aug
	12.00	6.32	9.98 1.89	55.16 16.55		27.50	3.80	44.72	5:16.72
5704	Christopher Hunter			3.03.81	10	Hull			20 Sep
	11.73	6.30	9.51 1.88	52.09 15.75		24.90	3.20	34.00	4:55.45
5595	Neil Scrivener			18.09.80	3	St. Ives			28 Jun
	12.3	5.86	10.94 1.84	53.5 16.4		29.82	2.90	37.91	4:27.0
5593	Stephen Wilson			3.11.80	11	Hull			20 Sep
	11.52	6.15	11.17 1.70	51.33 17.22		29.53	2.20	43.94	4:47.01
5409	Tom Payn			18.10.79	12	Hull			20 Sep
	12.12	5.78	7.87 1.70	51.52 17.74		26.30	3.10	36.28	4:09.84
5389	Sam Laskey			28.05.80	1	Exeter			17 May
	12.1	6.17	11.49 1.78	55.2 19.5		39.24	3.10	42.52	5:05.2
5377	Ben Lock			23.05.81	4	Leeds			28 Jun
	11.7	6.14	9.26 1.63	55.2 16.6		27.04	3.60	41.84	5:00.4
5283	Stephen McDonnell			24.07.80	1	Antrim			30 Aug
	11.8	6.20	8.45 1.87	53.5 15.4		20.91	2.30	37.46	4:51.7
(20)									
5251	Mark Carnaghan			3.09.80	14	Hull			20 Sep
	12.31	5.69	10.10 1.61	53.46 17.06		31.93	2.80	34.94	4:34.74
5203	James Chatt			11.02.80	1	Hoo			9 Aug
	11.3	6.02	8.89 1.78	51.8 16.5		29.57	1.70	37.43	5:08.2
5195	Simon Eyre			30.10.80	1	Crawley			13 Sep
	11.9	5.55	9.30 1.67	52.7 16.8		22.63	2.90	36.07	4:26.6
5182	James Lowery			17.10.80	2	Wrexham			28 Jun
	12.0	6.02	10.11 1.80	55.88 16.8		30.89	3.10	39.74	5:33.6
5176	Ashley Pritchard			14.07.79	3	Birmingham			23 Aug
	12.18	5.76w	8.85 1.68	54.83 16.55		30.78	2.85	36.79	4:52.2
5133	Matthew Woodger			9.01.79	1	Carn Brea			28 Jun
	11.7	6.31	9.51 1.78	55.1 17.7		23.59	2.50	38.46	4:48.5
5113	Kenny Sanders			22.02.80	15	Hull			20 Sep
	12.14	6.05	9.13 1.67	54.59 15.60		26.06	2.40	35.30	4:59.41
5111	Lloyd Spicer			15.03.80	5	St. Ives			28 Jun
	11.6	6.29	10.32 1.84	55.5 17.3		25.12	2.40	39.00	5:19.4
5072	Bennett Brusch			2.06.79	2	Carn Brea			28 Jun
	12.1	6.47	9.62 1.81	55.1 17.7		26.04	2.30	40.88	5:04.2
5071	Chris Hodson			11.11.80	16	Hull			20 Sep
	11.93	5.74	9.28 1.76	53.67 15.51		22.85	2.50	33.67	5:14.76

OCTATHLON - Under 17

5500	Dominic Girdler			6.03.82	1	Hull			20 Sep
	6.31	37.12	44.38	50.04	13.56 1.99	13.53	4:48.87		(b)
5426	John Holtby			27.03.82	2	Hull			20 Sep
	6.20	41.40	43.62	50.61	14.47 1.69	15.73	4:36.61		(b)
5136	Jamie Russell			1.10.81	3	Hull			20 Sep
	6.17	34.15	38.55	51.79	15.43 1.99	11.17	4:19.69		(b)
5025	James Anthony			30.03.82	2	Birmingham			23 Aug
	14.0	6.26w	46.51	54.66	1.78 34.96	13.19	4:52.20		(a)
4937	Adrian Hemery			6.08.82	4	Hull			20 Sep
	5.74	41.21	36.55	53.76	14.77 1.78	12.07	4:30.97		(b)
4861	Chris Dack			28.11.82	2	Leeds			28 Jun
	14.1	6.26	40.44	51.9	1.82 29.86	12.22	5:00.3		(a)

4860	Simon Heyes			14.03.82	5	Hull		20 Sep
5.98	36.17	40.25	52.50	14.86	1.69	11.11	4:29.71	(b)
4698	Steven Hughes			25.02.82	6	Hull		20 Sep
5.86	32.09	39.74	54.62	14.34	1.75	12.28	4:50.71	(b)
4676	Chris Jenkins			2.03.82	2	Wrexham		28 Jun
6.58	29.76	42.89	54.28	14.5	1.77	11.99	5:18.0	(b)
4641	Alex Zulewski			6.06.82	7	Hull		20 Sep
5.65	32.72	35.40	52.43	14.31	1.78	10.08	4:42.83	(b)

(10)

4635	Owen Matthews			17.10.81	8	Hull		20 Sep
5.31	34.79	50.92	55.04	16.17	1.66	11.53	4:25.87	(b)
4634	Matt Peleszok			17.10.81	3	Wrexham		28 Jun
5.94	27.95	42.68	50.86	16.50	1.59	13.59	4:36.5	(b)
4628	Martin Taylor			31.01.82	1	Glasgow (S)		3 May
6.22	24.79	37.39	53.31	14.29	1.68	11.21	4:36.37	(b)
4606	Paul Roberts			15.09.81	1	Crawley		13 Sep
15.1	5.82	11.90	51.4	1.64	34.29	34.18	4:44.2	(c)
4601	Craig Elder			22.05.82	2	Glasgow (S)		3 May
5.73	34.98	33.96	53.08	14.53	1.80	11.76	5:07.85	(b)
4588	Peter Favell			16.03.82	10	Hull		20 Sep
6.06	38.90	45.27	56.44	16.07	1.72	12.45	5:09.05	(b)
4529	Daniel Armstrong			28.10.81	11	Hull		20 Sep
5.69	27.39	45.06	53.97	14.78	1.66	10.19	4:34.67	(b)
4527	Christopher Stanton			12.11.81	12	Hull		20 Sep
5.37	27.40	48.04	55.56	15.42	1.63	12.82	4:32.23	(b)
4443	Roger Skedd			3.09.82	4	Wrexham		28 Jun
5.89	36.91	35.66	55.66	14.8	1.77	12.33	5:27.8	(b)
4419	Steven Green			15.01.83	14	Hull		20 Sep
6.06	23.38	30.64	52.02	14.31	1.78	9.59	4:50.70	(b)

(20)

4413	Andy Clements			28.11.82	15	Hull		20 Sep
5.64	36.22	36.55	53.27	15.21	1.54	9.75	4:37.89	(b)
4408	Louis Evling-Jones			20.06.83	16	Hull		20 Sep
6.06	28.60	32.97	54.69	15.15	1.81	10.23	4:51.61	(b)
4405	James Roden			24.11.81	17	Hull		20 Sep
4.90	33.98	50.57	57.16	15.41	1.75	11.85	5:00.41	(b)
4365	Gary Tempest			16.04.82	2	Worcester		28 Jun
15.8	6.00	33.88	54.5	1.80	32.93	10.91	5:04.0	(a)
4364	David Harris			12.12.81	18	Hull		20 Sep
5.61	29.76	35.23	52.58	15.23	1.69	10.35	4:50.25	(b)
4356	Tim Greenwood			22.11.82	3	Worcester		28 Jun
15.0	6.23	36.85	55.7	1.80	31.14	10.69	5:20.0	(a)
4355	Lee Galligan			10.12.81	1	Derby		28 Jun
14.9	5.70	42.56	55.4	1.60	29.94	10.42	4:43.0	(a)
4344	Harry Webster			22.05.82	19	Hull		20 Sep
5.48	31.97	39.75	54.43	15.55	1.63	11.07	4:47.94	(b)
4332	Julian Pavey			16.05.83	2	Crawley		13 Sep
15.4	5.95	12.73	55.8	1.55	31.83	44.89	5:14.8	(c)
4275	Oliver Edwards			24.08.83	5	St. Ives		28 Jun
5.82	24.94	32.42	53.8	14.2	1.69	9.82	4:49.1	(b)

(30)

4259	Simon Tunnicliffe			2.03.83	4	Worcester		28 Jun
15.2	6.40	3NT	52.3	1.80	27.75	10.48	4:41.5	(a)
4253	Chris Hackett			1.03.83	6	Worcester		28 Jun
15.1	6.00	36.16	54.9	1.62	30.42	11.20	5:08.0	(a)
4234	Nick Hamilton			9.09.81	20	Hull		20 Sep
5.85	29.11	31.03	56.33	14.95	1.72	11.14	4:59.42	(b)

Order of Events   a)   100mH, LJ, JT, 400m, HJ, DT, SP, 1500m
                        b)   LJ, DT, JT, 400m, 100mH, HJ, SP, 1500m
                        c)   100mH, LJ, SP, 400m, HJ, DT, JT, 1500m

PENTATHLON - Under 15

3039	Chuka Enih-Snell				2.03.84	1	Birmingham	23 Aug
	11.80	10.20	6.34	1.91	2:21.6		(a)	
3037	Edward Dunford				15.09.84	1	Hull	19 Sep
	11.67	10.99	6.30	1.86	2:22.46		(a)	
2960	Matthew Walden				30.11.83	2	Hull	19 Sep
	11.89	11.86	6.07	1.65	2:14.11		(a)	
2865	Martin Roberts				20.09.83	3	Hull	19 Sep
	11.69	11.64	5.92	1.59	2:15.67		(a)	
2852	James Deacon-Brown				26.05.84	1	Hexham	31 Aug
	14.09	5.68	14.31	1.72	2:14.63		(b)	
2852	Oliver Brewer				14.09.83	4	Hull	19 Sep
	11.94	10.83	5.18	1.74	2:09.44		(a)	
2793	Colin Bailey				15.11.83	5	Hull	19 Sep
	12.50	10.24	5.33	1.89	2:17.45		(a)	
2701	Darren Watson				9.09.83	6	Hull	19 Sep
	12.85	9.24	6.05	1.65	2:13.69		(a)	
2643	Ross Elliott				6.09.83	3	Hexham	31 Aug
	11.91	5.35	12.39	1.60	2:25.14		(b)	
2629	Mark Garner				2.11.83	8	Hull	19 Sep
	11.73	9.84	5.33	1.65	2:18.94		(a)	
(10)								
2601	Gareth Pratt				12.11.83	9	Hull	19 Sep
	12.64	12.90	5.61	1.47	2:21.58		(a)	
2543	Matthew Roberts				8.07.84	1	Ashford	27 Jun
	11.9	8.70	5.47	1.60	2:16.3		(a)	
2529	Luke Williams				27.10.83	1	Carn Brea	27 Jun
	13.2	10.73	5.67	1.66	2:22.9		(a)	
2518	Adam Christie-Rees				9.09.83	2	Cardiff	20 Jun
	12.53	5.25	10.33	1.69	2:24.1		(b)	

Under 13

2444	James Dunford				14.01.86	2	Exeter	27 Sep
	12.6	5.21	9.67	1.62	2:19.6		(b)	

Order of Events

a) 80mH, SP, LJ, HJ, 800m
b) 80mH, LJ, SP, HJ, 800m

PENTATHLON - Under 13

2463	James Dunford				14.01.86	1	Woking	2 Aug
	12.6	10.70	5.29	1.51	2:17.8			

Order of Events   80mH (2'6"), SP, LJ, HJ, 800m

2000 Metres Walk - Track - Under 13

9:40.0	Luke Finch	21.09.85	3	Leicester	17 Sep
10:57.74	Sam McNally	26.03.86	2	Derby	30 May
11:05.7	Paul Graham	17.02.86	2	Bromsgrove	11 Oct
11:38.90	Oliver Fernandez	28.04.86	4	Bromsgrove	11 Oct

3000 Metres Walk - Track

Time	Name	Cat	DOB	Pos	Venue	Date
11:59.47	Martin Bell		9.04.61	1	Bedford	25 May
12:08.61 i				1	Birmingham	8 Feb
12:21.16 +				1m	Birmingham	25 Jul
12:06.8	Steve Partington		17.09.65	1	Douglas, IOM	12 Jul
12:10.5	Andi Drake		6.02.65	1	Leamington	9 May
12:19.24 i				1	Birmingham	25 Jan
12:23.13 i				3	Birmingham	8 Feb
12:28.8	Mark Easton		24.05.63	1	Kingston	10 May
12:31.50	Darrell Stone		2.02.68	1	Watford	20 Jun
12:36.35	Jamie O'Rawe		3.02.73	2	Watford	20 Jun
12:41.6	Michael Kemp	U20	23.12.79	1	Loughborough	10 May
12:44.4	Andy O'Rawe		8.09.63	2	Enfield	23 Aug
12:44.64	Lloyd Finch	U15	23.10.83	1	Solihull	24 May
12:58.0	Gareth Brown		10.05.68	1	Worthing	16 Jul
(10)						
12:59.09	Noel Carmody	V40	24.12.56	1	Newport	11 Jul
13:03.36	Richard Oldale		26.01.66	3	Bedford	25 May
13:03.7	Brian Adams	V45	13.03.49	2	Loughborough	10 May
13:05.0	Matthew Hales	U20	6.10.79	2	Worthing	16 Jun
13:05.43 i	Thomas Taylor	U20	30.01.81	2	Birmingham	22 Feb
13:06.68				1	London (He)	9 Aug
13:06.4	Chris Maddocks	V40	28.03.57	1	Exeter	9 Aug
13:10.3	Scott Taylor	U23	28.07.78	4	Loughborough	10 May
13:15.5	Ray Craggs		9.07.63	1	Hayes	15 Jul
13:16.23	Martin Young		11.07.72	4	Bedford	25 May
13:17.57	Don Bearman		16.04.66	3	Watford	20 Jun
(20)						
13:21.7	Nigel Whorlow	U20	26.11.80	1	Woodford	25 Jul
13:24.39	Bob Care	V50	8.04.47	2	Newport	11 Jul
13:25.2	Steve Allen	V40	22.01.58	2	Hayes	15 Jul
13:45.4	Andrew Goudie	U23	4.10.78	1	London (BP)	8 Jun

Additional Juniors

Time	Name	Cat	DOB	Pos	Venue	Date
14:06.5	Andrew Ball	U17	13.05.83	3	Ayr	18 Jul
14:12.5	Nathan Adams	U17	14.04.82	1	Rotherham	16 Jul
14:18.7	Dom King	U17	30.05.83	4	Ayr	18 Jul
14:24.58	Andrew Parker	U15	10.12.83	1	Hull	19 Sep
14:46.7	Dan King	U17	30.05.83	7	Woodford	17 Jun
15:41.71	James Davis	U15	10.10.84	3	Sheffield	16 Aug
15:54.0	Luke Finch	U13	21.09.85	1	Leicester	24 Jun
15:54.9	Ben Hibberd	U17	12.04.83	4	Loughborough	10 May
15:56.93	Philip Hollin	U17	14.11.81	4	Cudworth	9 May
16:04.84	Simeon Adams	U15	1.07.84	3	Sheffield	16 Aug
16:25.7	Paul Graham	U13	17.02.86	5	Woodford	16 Sep

3000 Metres Walk - Road - Juniors

Time	Name	Cat	DOB	Pos	Venue	Date
13:57	Nathan Adams	U17	14.04.82	6	Dublin, IRE	12 Sep
15:15	Ben Hibberd	U17	12.04.83	8	Dublin, IRE	12 Sep
15:16	James Davis	U15	10.10.84	1	Steyning	21 Nov

5000 Metres Walk - Track - Juniors

Time	Name	Cat	DOB	Pos	Venue	Date
21:42.44	Steve Hollier	U23	27.02.76	3	Hexham	14 Jun
21:53.0	Michael Kemp	U20	23.12.79	1	Leicester	24 Jun
22:31.84	Matthew Hales	U20	6.10.79	1	Hull	19 Sep
22:46.0	Thomas Taylor	U20	30.01.81	2	Leicester	24 Jun
22:54.0	Lloyd Finch	U15	23.10.83	1	Birmingham	15 Jul
23:31.15	Scott Taylor	U23	28.07.78	4	Hexham	14 Jun
24:09.44	Nigel Whorlow	U20	26.11.80	2	Hull	19 Sep
24:25.49	Nathan Adams	U17	14.04.82	1	Hull	19 Sep

24:26.14	Andrew Ball	U17	13.05.83	2	Derby	30 May
24:56.92	Dom King	U17	30.05.83	4	Derby	30 May

Road

21:36	Michael Kemp	U20	23.12.79	1	Steyning	21 Jun
23:27	Nigel Whorlow	U20	26.11.80	4	Steyning	21 Jun

10000 Metres Walk - Track

41:48.81	Martin Bell		9.04.61	1	Birmingham	26 Jul
43:47.6				1	Cwmbran	20 Jun
42:27.21	Steve Partington		17.09.65	2	Birmingham	26 Jul
42:46.26	Andi Drake		6.02.65	3	Birmingham	26 Jul
44:01.0	Gareth Brown		10.05.68	1	Brighton	24 Jan
44:04.41	Mark Easton		24.05.63	4	Birmingham	26 Jul
44:21.63	Martin Young		11.07.72	5	Birmingham	26 Jul
44:32.81	Jamie O'Rawe		3.02.73	6	Birmingham	26 Jul
44:53.0	Michael Kemp	U20	23.12.79	1	Leicester	4 Apr
44:55.16	Richard Oldale		26.01.66	7	Birmingham	26 Jul
45:08.97	Steve Hollier	U23	27.02.76	8	Birmingham	26 Jul
(10)						
45:56.16	Thomas Taylor	U20	30.01.81	1	Bedford	5 Jul
46:01.73	Andy O'Rawe		8.09.63	9	Birmingham	26 Jul
46:17.72	Allan King	V40	3.12.56	10	Birmingham	26 Jul
46:45.0	Matthew Hales	U20	6.10.79	2	Brighton	24 Jan
46:53.0	Don Bearman		16.04.66	3	Brighton	24 Jan
47:00.6	Noel Carmody	V40	24.12.56	2	London (BP)	29 Apr
47:08.62	Kevin Walmsley		6.09.67	3	Derby	30 May
47:27.42	Richard Miller		18.12.64	4	Derby	30 May
47:33.0	Brian Adams	V45	13.03.49	2	Leicester	4 Apr
47:39.32	Tim Watt		19.09.66	1	Enfield	2 Aug
(20)						
48:10.0	Mike Smith		20.04.63	1	Rugby	27 May
48:30.60	Scott Taylor	U23	28.07.78	6	Derby	30 May
48:46.19	Peter Kaneen		12.07.61	7	Derby	30 May
48:53.0	Guy Jackson		10.01.71	2	Rugby	27 May

Additional Juniors

50:38.65	Nigel Whorlow	U20	26.11.80	4	Bedford	5 Jul
51:56.0	Nathan Adams	U17	14.04.82	4	Leicester	4 April

10000 Metres Walk - Road - Juniors

43:53	Michael Kemp	U20	23.12.79	1	Sheffield	25 Apr
45:03	Thomas Taylor	U20	30.01.81	9	Senigallia, ITA	30 May
45:33	Matthew Hales	U20	6.10.79	2	London (VP)	31 Jan
47:17	Lloyd Finch	U17	23.10.83	1=	Leicester	21 Nov
48:49	Nathan Adams	U17	14.04.82	4	Birmingham	14 Nov
48:57	Nigel Whorlow	U20	26.11.80	7	London (VP)	31 Jan

20 Kilometres Walk

1:26:37	Darrell Stone		2.02.68	4	Kuala Lumpur, MAL	17 Sep
1:27:22	Martin Bell		9.04.61	1	Leicester	21 Mar
1:27:30				2	Szeged, HUN	4 Jul
1:29:17				1	Douglas, IOM	21 Feb
1:29:18				39	Dudince, SVK	26 Apr
1:29:20				7	Kuala Lumpur, MAL	17 Sep
1:28:01	Andi Drake		6.02.65	10	Senigallia, ITA	30 May
1:28:18				1	Burrator	4 May
1:28:44				1	East Molesey	18 Jul
1:30:25				2	Leicester	21 Mar

1:29:40	Chris Maddocks	V40	28.03.57	2	East Molesey	18	Jul
1:30:21				10	Kuala Lumpur, MAL	17	Sep
	12 performances to 1:31:00 by 4 athletes						
1:31:06	Andy Penn		31.03.67	2	Douglas, IOM	21	Feb
1:31:50	Steve Partington		17.09.65	4	Douglas, IOM	21	Feb
1:31:58	Chris Cheeseman		11.12.58	3	Leicester	21	Mar
1:32:20	Steve Hollier	U23	27.02.76	4	East Molesey	18	Jul
1:32:53	Les Morton	V40	1.07.58	5	East Molesey	18	Jul
1:33:00	Jamie O'Rawe		3.02.73	2	Burrator	4	May
1:33:07 (10)	Gareth Brown		10.05.68	3	Dublin, IRE	12	Sep
1:33:22	Richard Oldale		26.01.66	1	York	2	May
1:34:35	Andy O'Rawe		8.09.63	6	Dublin, IRE	12	Sep
1:34:54	Martin Young		11.07.72	7	Dublin, IRE	12	Sep
1:34:56	Don Bearman		16.04.66	4	Leicester	21	Mar
1:35:11	Graham White		28.03.59	5	Leicester	21	Mar
1:35:13	Allan King	V40	3.12.56	6	Leicester	21	Mar
1:35:16	Michael Kemp	U20	23.12.79	7	Leicester	21	Mar
1:35:32	Kevin Walmsley		6.09.67	8	Leicester	21	Mar
1:35:42 (20)	Karl Atton		14.09.71	9	Leicester	21	Mar
1:38:36	Tim Watt		19.09.66	9	East Molesey	18	Jul
1:39:39	Noel Carmody	V40	24.12.56	4	Colchester	31	May

30 Kilometres Walk

2:30.25	Allan King	V40	3.12.56	1	Leicester	19	Apr
2:39.06	Karl Atton		14.09.71	2	Leicester	19	Apr
2:42.57	Martin Young		11.07.72	3	Leicester	19	April

35 Kilometres Walk

2:47:28	Mark Easton		24.05.63	14	Senigallia, ITA	31	May
2:56:13	Chris Cheeseman		11.12.58	19	Senigallia, ITA	31	May

50 Kilometres Walk

4:03:53	Mark Easton		24.05.63	28	Dudince, SVK	25	Apr
4:05:17				1	Stockport	27	Jun
4:22:23				5	Kuala Lumpur, MAL	21	Sep
4:10:54	Chris Cheeseman		11.12.58	2	Stockport	27	Jun
4:17:17				1	Burrator	4	May
4:13:18	Graham White		28.03.59	3	Stockport	27	Jun
4:14:37	Steve Hollier	U23	27.02.76	4	Stockport	27	Jun
4:18:41				4	Kuala Lumpur, MAL	21	Sep
4:20:13				3	Burrator	4	May
4:28:00				9	Podebrady, CZE	29	Mar
4:17:44	Les Morton		1.07.58	2	Burrator	4	May
4:18:17				5	Stockport	27	Jun
4:22:33	Allan King	V40	3.12.56	4	Burrator	4	May
4:24:08	Karl Atton		14.09.71	6	Stockport	27	Jun
4:27:08	Tim Watt		19.09.66	18	Orense, SPA	22	Feb
	15 performances to 4:30:00 by 8 athletes						
4:49:40	Mike Smith		20.04.63	2	Holmewood	29	Aug
4:55:36	Peter Kaneen		12.07.61	1	Isle of Man	3	May
4:58:08 (10)	Chris Berwick	V50	1.05.46	3	Holmewood	29	Aug

100 Miles Walk - Track

19:22:26	Richard Brown	V50	18.11.46	1	Isle of Man	21	Jun
21:47:22	Chris Flint	V50	6.12.44	2	Isle of Man	21	Jun

4 x 100 METRES

38.09 A	National Team	1	Johannesburg, RSA	12	Sep
	(A Condon, M Devonish, J Golding, D Chambers)				
38.20	England	1	Kuala Lumpur, MAL	21	Sep
	(D Chambers, M Devonish, J Golding, D Campbell)				
38.47	National Team	1h1	Budapest, HUN	22	Aug
	(A Condon, D Campbell, M Devonish, D Chambers)				
38.52	National Team	1	Budapest, HUN	22	Aug
	(A Condon, D Campbell, D Walker, J Golding)				
38.56	National Team	1	St. Petersburg, RUS	27	Jun
	(A Condon, D Campbell, D Walker, J Golding)				
38.62	England	2h2	Kuala Lumpur, MAL	20	Sep
	(J Gardener, D Chambers, M Devonish , D Campbell)				
38.73	Wales	4	Kuala Lumpur, MAL	21	Sep
	(K Williams, D Turner, C Malcolm, J Henthorn)				
39.09	Wales	3h2	Kuala Lumpur, MAL	20	Sep
	(K Williams, D Turner, C Malcolm, J Henthorn)				
39.20	National Team	2	Glasgow	30	Aug
	(A Condon, J Regis, J Golding, D Chambers)				
39.31	National Team	1	Gateshead	19	Jul
	(A Condon, J Gardener, D Walker, O Dako)				
39.55	National U23 Team	U23	2	Gateshead	19	Jul
	(R Baillie, M Devonish, J Henthorn, D Greaves)				
39.68	Fast Lane	2	Walnut, USA	19	Apr
	(D Chambers, A Jarrett, D Braithwaite, J Golding)				
39.83	British All-Stars	3	Walnut, USA	19	Apr
	(Joselyn Thomas, Josephus Thomas, J Regis, N Stickings)				
40.09	National Team	1	Hexham	14	Jun
	(A Condon, D Campbell, D Walker, J Golding)				
40.11	National Under 23 Team	2	Hexham	14	Jun
	(D Money, M Devonish, J Henthorn, D Chambers)				
40.12	Wales	1	Cardiff	4	Aug
	(K Williams, D Turner, C Malcolm, J Henthorn)				
40.20	National Under 23 Team	2	Dessau, GER	1	Aug
	(R Baillie, J Henthorn, M Tietz, K Farrell)				
40.29	National Junior Team	U20	2	Alicante, SPA	18	Jul
	(C Lambert, T Benjamin, C Malcolm, J Barbour)				
40.40	England	2	Cardiff	4	Aug
	(J Gardener, J Regis, A Walcott, M Adam)				
40.43	Belgrave Harriers	1	London (He)	8	Aug
	(C Lambert, J Regis, A Walcott, J Fergus)				

Additional Club Teams (1 above)

40.7	Cardiff AAC	1	Watford	4	Jul
40.76	Woodford Green AC	2	Bedford	29	Aug
40.94	Newham & Essex Beagles AC	2	London (He)	8	Aug
40.99	PUMA TVH	1	Watford	16	May
40.99	Birchfield Harriers	3	Bedford	29	Aug
41.24	Sale Harriers Manchester	3	Watford	16	May
41.4	Blackheath Harriers	1	Liverpool	8	Aug
41.46	City of Edinburgh AC	4	London (He)	8	Aug
41.53	Brunel University	1	Bath	4	May
41.8	Windsor Slough & Eton AC	1	Watford	6	Jun
41.82	Shaftesbury Barnet Harriers	5	London (He)	8	Aug
41.88	Border Harriers	5	Watford	16	May
41.9	Team Solent	2	Crawley	19	Jul
42.0	Havering Mayesbrook AC	1	Enfield	6	Jun
42.0	Haringey AC	3	Watford	4	Jul
42.1	Rugby AC	2	Derby	19	Jul
42.16	Loughborough University	2	Bath	4	May

42.19	Coventry Godiva Harriers		1	Bedford	30	Aug
42.3	City of Norwich AC		1	Sheffield (W)	16	May
42.3	Liverpool HAC		4	Liverpool	8	Aug

Additional National Team

| 43.1 | Northern Ireland | | 1 | Antrim | 23 | Jun |

Additional Under 20 Teams (1 above)

40.67	National Junior Team		1	Loughborough	17	May
41.68	South		1	London (He)	9	Aug
41.9	Birchfield Harriers		1	Cannock	13	Sep
41.92	West Midlands Schools	U17	1h1	Exeter	11	Jul
41.92	Blackheath Harriers		1	Istanbul, TUR	26	Sep
41.94	England Schools	U17	1	Ayr	18	Jul
42.23	Wales		1	Bruges, BEL	23	Aug
42.28	Birchfield Harriers	U17	1	Birmingham	6	Sep
42.36	London Schools		1	Exeter	11	Jul

Additional Under 20 National Teams

| 42.96 | Scotland | | 3 | London (He) | 9 | Aug |
| 43.15 | Welsh Schools | | 1 | Barry | 14 | Jul |

Additional Under 20 Club Teams (1 - 2 above)

42.46	Trent College		1	Kettering	9	May
43.1	Coventry Godiva H	U17	1	Stafford	17	May
43.1	Belgrave Harriers		3	Cannock	13	Sep
43.4	Shaftesbury Barnet Harriers		4	Cannock	13	Sep
43.5	Liverpool HAC		1	Derby	20	Sep
43.6	Sale Harriers Manchester		5	Cannock	13	Sep
43.69	Mandale AC	U17	2	Birmingham	6	Sep
44.1	Motherwell & District H		1	Pitreavie	8	Aug

Additional Under 17 Teams (1 - 5 above)

42.85	Surrey Schools		2	Exeter	11	Jul
43.19	Scotland Schools		3	Ayr	18	Jul
43.59	Durham Schools		3	Exeter	11	Jul
43.70	Shropshire Schools		2h1	Exeter	11	Jul
43.80	London Schools		4	Exeter	11	Jul
43.84	Wales Schools		4	Ayr	18	Jul

Additional Under 17 Club Teams (1 - 3 above)

44.00	Sale Harriers Manchester		3	Birmingham	6	Sep
44.1	City of Stoke AC		2	Stafford	17	May
44.15	Blackheath Harriers		1	Birmingham	5	Sep
44.2 X	Royal Belfast AI		1	Antrim	30	May
44.39	Croydon Harriers		4	Birmingham	6	Sep
44.9	Uddingston Grammar School		1	Grangemouth	13	Jun
45.2	Havering & Mayesbrook AC		2	Peterborough	19	Jul

Under 15 Teams

45.48	Croydon Harriers		1	Birmingham	6	Sep
45.49	Surrey Schools		1	Exeter	11	Jul
45.73	Hampshire Schools		2h2	Exeter	11	Jul
46.10	Greater Manchester Schools		1h3	Exeter	11	Jul
46.23	N.Lincs & E.Yorks Schools		1h1	Exeter	11	Jul
46.23	Northamptonshire Schools		4	Exeter	11	Jul
46.55	Berkshire Schools		2h1	Exeter	11	Jul
46.73	Essex Schools		3h1	Exeter	11	Jul
46.96	Lincolnshire Schools		3h2	Exeter	11	Jul
46.98	West Midlands Schools		1	Stoke	20	Jun

Additional Under 15 Club Teams (1 above)

47.19	Sale Harriers Manchester	2	Birmingham	6	Sep
47.19	Birchfield Harriers	3	Birmingham	6	Sep
47.29	Blackheath Harriers	1	Birmingham	5	Sep
47.4	Ipswich Harriers	1	Peterborough	19	Jul
47.51	Shaftesbury Barnet Harriers	2	Birmingham	5	Sep
47.71	Borough of Enfield Harriers	4	Birmingham	6	Sep
47.8	Scunthorpe Harriers	1	Scunthorpe	28	Jun
48.0	Borough of Hounslow AC	1	Bournemouth	19	Jul
48.02	Mandale AC	5	Birmingham	6	Sep

Under 13 Club Teams

52.42	Harrow AC	1	Birmingham	6	Sep
52.43	Mandale AC	2	Birmingham	6	Sep
52.84	Sale Harriers Manchester	3	Birmingham	6	Sep
53.0	Croydon Harriers	1	Bromley	28	Jun
53.05 X	St Columb's College	1	Birmingham	5	Sep

4 x 200 METRES

1:22.30	Fast Lane	1	Walnut, USA	19	Apr
	(Joselyn Thomas, Josephus Thomas, J Regis, N Stickings)				
1:22.47	British All-Stars	2	Walnut, USA	19	Apr
	(M Findlay, D Braithwaite, A Jarrett, J Golding)				

Club Teams

1:27.27 i	Loughborough Students	1r1	Birmingham	25	Feb
1:27.72 i	Brunel University	1	Glasgow	15	Mar
1:29.7	Belgrave Harriers	1	London (TB)	19	Aug
1:30.06 i	Staffordshire University	2	Glasgow	15	Mar
1:30.3	Herne Hill Harriers	1	London (TB)	5	Aug
1:32.4	Cambridge University	1	Oxford	1	Mar
1:31.0 i	Strathclyde University	1	Glasgow	18	Nov
1:31.76 i	Birmingham University	3	Glasgow	15	Mar

Under 20 Teams

1:31.54 i	England Schools	U16	1	Birmingham	28	Feb
1:32.64 i	Digital Ayr Seaforth		1	Glasgow	22	Mar
1:32.95 i	Victoria Park AAC		2	Glasgow	22	Mar
1:33.9	Millfield School		1	Oxford	9	May
1:34.8	Epsom College		2	Oxford	9	May
1:34.93 i	Scottish Schools	U16	2	Birmingham	28	Feb
1:35.05 i	Airdrie Harriers		3	Glasgow	22	Mar

Under 17 Club Teams

1:35.24 i	Perth Strathtay	1h2	Glasgow	22	Mar
1:36.21 i	Victoria Park AAC	2	Glasgow	22	Mar
1:36.40 i	Whitemoss	3	Glasgow	22	Mar
1:37.6	Bedford Modern School	1	Oxford	9	May
1:37.6 X	St Columb's College	1r2	Antrim	17	May
1:38.44	Inverness H	1	Inverness	22	Aug
1:38.7 X	Lagan Valley AC	1r1	Antrim	17	May

Under 15 Teams

1:41.2	Wimbledon College	1	London (TB)	22	Jul
1:43.43 i	Digital Ayr Seaforth	1	Glasgow	22	Mar
1:43.4 X	Annadale Striders	1r2	Antrim	17	May
1:43.7	Scunthorpe H	1	Wakefield	24	May
1:44.4	Trinity School	1	Oxford	9	May
1:44.5	Hercules Wimbledon AC	2	London (TB)	22	Jul
1:44.69 i	Garscube Harriers	2	Glasgow	22	Mar

Under 13 Teams

1:56.0 X	St Columb's College	1r2	Antrim	17	May
1:58.0	Croydon Harriers	1	Croydon	5	Jul
2:00.3	Scottish Borders AC	1	Livingston	6	Sep
2:00.52 i	Airdrie Harriers	1h2	Glasgow	22	Mar
2:00.91	Bedford & County AC	1	Bedford	6	Sep

4 x 400 METRES

2:58.68   National Team   1   Budapest, HUN   23 Aug
(M Hylton 45.42, J Baulch 44.66, I Thomas 44.21, M Richardson 44.39)

2:59.71 A National Team   2   Johannesburg, RSA 13 Sep
(M Hylton 45.77, J Baulch 44.81, S Baldock 44.97, I Thomas 44.16)

3:00.82   England   2   Kuala Lumpur, MAL 21 Sep
(P Slythe 46.2, S Wariso 44.9, M Hylton 45.3, M Richardson 44.4)

3:00.95   National Team   1   St Petersburg, RUS 28 Jun
(R Black 45.57, J Baulch 45.09, I Thomas 44.82, M Richardson 45.47)

3:01.86   Wales   3   Kuala Lumpur, MAL 21 Sep
(P Gray 48.1, J Baulch 44.7, D Turner 45.1, I Thomas 44.0)

3:02.37   National Team   1h2   Budapest, HUN   22 Aug
(M Hylton 45.7, S Baldock 45.5, S Wariso 46.10, J Baulch 45.05)

3:03.58   England   2h1   Kuala Lumpur, MAL 20 Sep
(S Baldock 46.6, J Deacon 45.5, S Wariso 46.0, P Slythe 45.5)

3:03.63   Wales   3h1   Kuala Lumpur, MAL 20 Sep
(P Gray 48.9, J Baulch 44.4, M Elias 46.2, I Thomas 44.1)

3:05.29   National Team   2   Glasgow   30 Aug
(P Slythe, M Hylton, J Baulch, I Thomas)

3:06.32   National Junior Team   U20   5   Annecy, FRA   2 Aug
(D Naismith 47.24, D Caines 46.40, C Carson 46.49, A Wilson 46.19)

3:07.27   Northern Ireland   7h1   Kuala Lumpur, MAL 20 Sep
(B Forbes 47.8, M Douglas 46.2, E King 48.0, P McBurney 45.3)

3:07.48   National 'B' Team   3   Glasgow   30 Aug
(P McBurney, J Deacon, A Borsumato, M Douglas)

3:08.85   National Junior Team   U20   3h2   Annecy, FRA   1 Aug
(D Naismith 47.6, A Buckley 47.7, C Carson 47.13, A Wilson46.47)

3:09.26   Belgrave Harriers   1   Birmingham   6 Jun
(M Parper 48.8, G Dearman 47.0, M Douglas 47.4, S Baldock 46.1)

3:09.51   National Under 23 Team   3   Dessau, GER   1 Aug
(G Dearman, A Mitchell, P Brend, M Douglas)

3:10.43   British Universities   1   Loughborough   17 May

3:10.71   National Junior Team   U20   2   Loughborough   17 May
(A Wilson, M Elias, G Stevenson, D Caines)

3:10.76   National Junior Team   U20   1   Alicante, SPA   18 Jul
(D Naismith 48.73, A Buckley 47.88, C Carson 47.59, A Wilson 46.56)

3:10.89   Belgrave Harriers   4   Belgrade, YUG   31 May
(G Dearman, M Parper, M Douglas, S Baldock)

3:11.10   Newham & Essex Beagles AC   1   London (He)   8 Aug
(A Donaldson, T Williams, P McBurney, G Jennings)

3:11.16   Shaftesbury Barnet Harriers   2   Birmingham   6 Jun
(D Donovan, A Fugallo, C Carson, R Edu)

3:11.65   National Under 23 Team   1   Hexham   14 Jun
(G Dearman, M Douglas, S Baldock, M Hylton)

Additional Club Teams (1 - 3 above)

3:11.87	Loughborough Students	3	Loughborough	17	May
3:12.28	City of Edinburgh AC	2	Edinburgh	4	Jul
3:12.45	Sale Harriers Manchester	2	Bedford	29	Aug
3:12.9	Team Solent	1	Crawley	19	Jul

3:13.1	Woodford Green AC		1	Watford	4	Jul
3:13.43	Brunel University		2	Bath	4	May
3:13.90	Border Harriers		2	London (He)	8	Aug
3:15.3	Cardiff AAC		2	Cardiff	6	Jun
3:16.05	Blackheath Harriers	U20	1	Istanbul, TUR	26	Sep
3:16.2	Windsor Slough & Eton AC		1	Derby	4	Jul
3:16.26	PUMA TVH		4	Bedford	29	Aug
3:17.1	Morpeth Harriers		1	Gateshead	11	Jul
3:17.2	Borough of Hounslow AC		3	Derby	4	Jul
3:17.3	Swansea Harriers		1	Stoke	16	May
3:17.8	City of Norwich AC		2	Enfield	19	Jul
3:18.1	Havering Mayesbrook AC		3	Crawley	19	Jul

Additional Under 20 Teams (1 - 4 above)

3:13.88 i	National Junior Team	1	Birmingham	28	Feb
3:16.05	Blackheath Harriers	1	Istanbul, TUR	26	Sep
3:18.74	Wales	1	Bruges, BEL	23	Aug
3:19.42	Midlands	1	London (He)	9	Aug

Additional Under 20 Club Teams (1 above)

3:21.7	Liverpool HAC	1	Derby	20	Sep
3:22.2	Shaftesbury Barnet Harriers	1	London (He)	23	Aug
3:23.54	Medway AC	1	Ashford	20	Sep
3:23.6	Birchfield Harriers	3	Cannock	13	Sep
3:23.7	Wirral AC	2	Wirral	21	Jun
3:26.3	Mandale AC	2	Derby	20	Sep
3:26.8	Eton College	1	Oxford	9	May
3:26.9	Notts AC	1	Nottingham	26	Jul
3:27.2	Motherwell H	1	Pitreavie	8	Aug

Additional Under 17 Teams

3:23.46	England Schools	1	Ayr	18	Jul
3:24.82	Scotland Schools	2	Ayr	18	Jul
3:26.61	Wales Schools	3	Ayr	18	Jul
3:26.92	Birchfield Harriers	1	Birmingham	6	Sep
3:27.46	Borough of Enfield Harriers	2	Birmingham	6	Sep
3:27.63	Blackheath Harriers	1	Birmingham	5	Sep
3:29.68	Sale Harriers Manchester	3	Birmingham	6	Sep
3:29.7	City of Stoke AC	1	Stafford	17	May
3:31.1	Sussex	1	Ashford	5	Jul
3:32.3	Mandale AC	1	Middlesbrough	17	May

Additional Under 17 Club Teams (1 - 6 above)

3:32.7	Rotherham Harriers	1	Rotherham	28	Jun
3:33.31	Wirral AC	2	Birmingham	5	Sep
3:34.5	Croydon Harriers	1	Peterborough	19	Jul
3:34.51	Liverpool HAC	5	Birmingham	6	Sep

Under 15 Teams

3:37.7	Gloucester AC	1	Yeovil ·	28	Jun
3:38.04	Borough of Enfield Harriers	1	Birmingham	6	Sep
3:39.3	Thurrock Harriers	1	Hoo	28	Jun
3:40.19	Croydon Harriers	2	Birmingham	6	Sep
3:46.0	Wirral AC	1	Birmingham	5	Sep
3:46.1	Belgrave Harriers	1	Bracknell	19	Jul
3:47.2	Middlesbrough & C AC	1	Rotherham	28	Jun
3:47.6	Blackheath Harriers	1	London (He)	17	May
3:48.51	Sale Harriers Manchester	3	Birmingham	6	Sep
3:48.6	City of Stoke AC	1	Stoke	19	Jul

Under 13 Teams

4:32.20	Bexley Borough AC		1	Ashford	20 Sep
4:33.31	GEC Avionics AC		2	Ashford	20 Sep
4:38.2	Bournemouth AC		1	Southampton	5 Jul
4:38.6 X	Lagan Valley AC		1	Belfast	6 Jun
4:39.5	Basingstoke & Mid Hants AC		1	Andover	5 Jul

1600 METRES MEDLEY

3:32.97	Babcock Pitreavie		1	Dumfries	6 Jun
3:38.4	Kwik-Fit Corstorphine		1	Livingston	6 Sep
3:39.17	Blackheath Harriers		1	Ashford	20 Sep

Under 17 Team

3:53.5	Inverclyde		1	Linwood	25 Jul

3 x 800 METRES

Under 20 Teams

6:17.9	Blackburn Schools	U17	1	Blackburn	18 May
6:21.4	Lancaster Schools	U17	2	Blackburn	18 May
6:22.0	Blackburn Schools		1	Blackburn	18 May
6:26.3	Hyndburn Schools		2	Blackburn	18 May
6:26.6	Hyndburn Schools	U17	3	Blackburn	18 May

Under 17 Club Teams

6:29.4	Thurrock Harriers		1	Barking	10 Sep
6:34.0	Woodford Green AC	U15	1	Barking	2 Jul
6:34.3	Chelmsford AC		2	Barking	10 Sep
6:41.4	Croydon Harriers	U15	2	Barking	10 Sep
6:42.0	Newham & Essex Beagles	U15	2	Barking	2 Jul
6:43.8	East Grinstead AC		3	Barking	10 Sep
6:44.8	Havering Mayesbrook AC		4	Barking	10 Sep

Additional Under 15 Club Teams (1 - 3 above)

6:49.4	Basildon AC		3	Barking	10 Sep
6:53.72	Babcock Pitreavie		1	Edinburgh	18 Jul
6:57.5	Digital Ayr Seaforth		1	Ayr	1 Jul
6:58.4	Thurrock Harriers		4	Barking	10 Sep

Under 13 Teams

7:27.1	Norfolk Schools		1	Barking	10 Sep
7:36.4	Thurrock Harriers		2	Barking	10 Sep
7:36.7	Newham & Essex Beagles		1	Barking	2 Jul

4 x 800 METRES

7:39.2	Annadale Striders		1	Antrim	29 Aug

Under 20 Team

8:01.9	Millfield School		1	Oxford	9 May

Under 17 Team

8:23.95 X	Lagan Valley AC		1	Belfast	30 Jul

Under 15 Team

9:04.4X	St Columb's College		1	Belfast	30 Jul

4 x 1500 METRES

15:17.99	Loughborough Students		1	Rennes, FRA	12 Sep

(T Mayo 3:46.5 D Bullock 3:54.5 P Tulba 3:49.5 S Barden 3:47.5)

X Northern Ireland age groups and therefore possibly including older athletes.

1998 LISTS - WOMEN

55 METRES - Indoors

7.27	Lesley Owusu	U23	21.12.78		Lincoln, USA	24	Jan

60 METRES - Indoors

7.34	Joice Maduaka		30.09.73	1	Birmingham	7	Feb
	7.34			4h2	Valencia, SPA	27	Feb
	7.35			7	Birmingham	15	Feb
	7.36			1s1	Birmingham	7	Feb
	7.40			1	Birmingham	25	Jan
	7.43			1h2	Birmingham	7	Feb
	7.43			8s1	Valencia, SPA	27	Feb
	7.48			1h2	Birmingham	25	Jan
7.41	Diane Allahgreen		21.02.75	1	Glasgow	15	Mar
	7.47			1	Ghent, BEL	1	Feb
	7.48			1h1	Ghent, BEL	1	Feb
	7.48			1h1	Glasgow	15	Mar
7.46	Donna Fraser		7.11.72	1s2	Birmingham	7	Feb
	7.49			3	Birmingham	7	Feb
	7.53			8	Birmingham	15	Feb
7.50	Janine Whitlock		11.08.73	1h5	Birmingham	25	Jan
	7.50			1	Birmingham	1	Feb
	7.51			1h1	Sheffield	18	Jan
	7.53			1	Sheffield	18	Jan
7.51	Ashia Hansen		5.12.71	2h5	Birmingham	25	Jan
7.52	Shani Anderson		7.08.75	4	Birmingham	7	Feb
7.54	Aileen McGillivary		13.08.70	1h2	Glasgow	25	Jan
	7.55			1	Glasgow	25	Jan
	7.55			1	Glasgow	28	Jan
	7.55			2s2	Birmingham	7	Feb
7.54	Ellena Ruddock	U23	23.02.76	1	Birmingham	1	Mar
7.55	Rebecca White	U20	5.06.80	1	Birmingham	21	Feb
	27 performances to 7.55 by 9 athletes						
7.56	Catherine Murphy		21.09.75	1h3	Birmingham	25	Jan
	(10)						
7.56	Simmone Jacobs		5.09.66	3s2	Birmingham	7	Feb
7.56	Malgorzata Rostek	U23	25.03.77	4	Spala, POL	14	Feb
7.57	Christine Bloomfield		12.02.68	4s2	Birmingham	7	Feb
7.60	Susie Williams	U23	2.06.77	2	Birmingham	1	Feb
7.60	Rebecca Drummond	U23	18.04.78	5s2	Birmingham	7	Feb
7.60	Maria Bolsover	U20	5.06.80	2	Birmingham	21	Feb
7.61	Clova Court	V35	10.02.60	6	Birmingham	25	Jan
7.62	Zoe Wilson	U23	28.08.76	6s2	Birmingham	1	Mar
7.65	Shelley-Anne Bowen	U20	12.05.79	4	Birmingham	21	Feb
7.66	Tracy Joseph		29.11.69	2h1	Birmingham	25	Jan
	(20)						
7.66	Sarah Claxton	U20	23.09.79	5	Birmingham	21	Feb
7.66	Natalie Smellie	U17	16.01.82	1	Birmingham	21	Feb
7.68	Sue Rawlinson		13.10.70	3h3	Birmingham	25	Jan
7.68	Claire Spurway	U23	4.04.78	2h1	Birmingham	1	Mar
7.69	Rebecca Bird	U17	7.01.83	1	Birmingham	1	Mar
7.70	Libby Alder	U20	20.11.80	1	Birmingham	1	Mar
7.71	Carly Moody	U20	9.06.80	3h1	Birmingham	25	Jan
7.71	Jeanette Kwakye	U17	20.03.83	2	Birmingham	21	Feb
7.71	Liz Fairs	U23	1.12.77	1	Birmingham	25	Feb
7.72	Emma Whitter	U20	20.07.80	3	Birmingham	21	Feb
	(30)						
7.73	Kirstie Law	U23	31.01.78	1	Glasgow	18	Jan

7.74	Kelly Sotherton	U23	13.11.76	1rB	Birmingham	25	Feb
7.75	Nicola Gautier	U23	21.03.78	1h2	Sheffield	18	Jan
7.75	Heather McKay	U17	5.09.81	1	Glasgow	29	Jan
7.75	Danielle Freeman	U20	11.02.80	4s2	Birmingham	21	Feb
7.77	Kerry Jury		19.11.68	2h2	Sheffield	18	Jan
7.77	Lorraine Robins		13.05.70	8s2	Birmingham	7	Feb
7.77	Alex Bick	U17	4.01.83	3	Birmingham	21	Feb
7.77	Danielle Selley	U15	19.12.83	1	Birmingham	21	Feb
7.79	Sarah Zawada	U17	9.04.82	2	Birmingham	25	Jan
	(40)						
7.79	Louretta Thorne	U23	6.05.77	2h4	Birmingham	25	Jan
7.79	Kemesha Robinson	U20	27.11.80	4s2	Birmingham	21	Feb
7.79	Rachael Kay	U20	8.09.80	6s2	Birmingham	21	Feb

Additional Under 17 (1 - 6 above)

7.88	Lindsey Singer		4.06.83	3	Birmingham	25	Jan
7.89	Jan Little			1	Glasgow	29	Jan
7.90	Clare Russell		11.11.81	2h3	Birmingham	21	Feb
7.92	Nicola Sanders		23.06.82	1	Bedford	25	Jan
	(10)						
7.93	Kim Wall		21.04.83	2	Bedford	25	Jan
7.95	Rachel Redmond		7.12.81	2h4	Birmingham	21	Feb
7.96	Sharon Davidge		15.09.81	1P	Bedford	18	Jan
7.96	Alison Bennett		4.12.81	1	Glasgow	18	Jan
7.98	Hayley-Kate Baxter		25.06.82	2h2	Birmingham	21	Feb
7.99	Melissa Anderson		30.03.82	3h2	Birmingham	21	Feb

Under 15 (1 above)

7.86	Monique Parris		28.01.84	1h2	Birmingham	21	Feb
7.96	Cherie Pierre		15.05.84	4	Birmingham	21	Feb

Hand Timing

7.6	Andrea Coore		23.04.69	1rB	London (CP)	11	Feb
7.7	Sharon Williams		20.05.70	3	Birmingham	3	Jan
7.7	Sarah Zawada	U17	(7.79)	1	London (CP)	7	Feb
7.7	Kim Wall	U17	(7.93)	2	London (CP)	7	Feb
7.7	Lucy Atunumuo	U20	4.11.80	1	London (CP)	11	Feb
7.7	Jeanette Kwakye	U17	(7.71)	1s2	Birmingham	21	Feb
7.7	Emma Whitter	U20	(7.72)	1r3	London (CP)	16	Dec

Under 17

7.8	Jan Little		(7.89)	3	Birmingham	28	Feb

75 METRES - Under 13

9.8		Amy Spencer	19.09.85	1	Oldham	19	Jul
		9.83 -1.7		1	Birmingham	6	Sep
9.9		Charlene Lashley	1.09.85	1	Bournemouth	17	May
		10.02 -1.7		2	Birmingham	6	Sep
10.0		Lois Rudkin		2	Oldham	19	Jul
10.1		Safiya Greensword		1	Bromley	17	May
10.1		Katie Smith	19.02.86	2	Wakefield	28	Jun
10.2		Maria Garavand	30.06.86	2	Bromley	17	May
10.2		Karen Mylan	8.11.85	1h	Bromley	11	Jul
10.2		Lauren Hawkins-Taylor	29.10.86	1	Yate	19	Jul
10.2		Amalachukwu Onuora	16.03.86	1	Crawley	30	Aug
10.22	-1.7	Nicola Gossman	4.11.86	3	Birmingham	6	Sep

100 METRES

11.32	0.0	Joice Maduaka		30.09.73	2h2	Kuala Lumpur, MAL	16	Sep
11.35	0.6				4h4	Budapest, HUN	18	Aug
11.40	0.9				1	Birmingham	25	Jul
11.44	0.4				1s1	Birmingham	25	Jul
11.46	-0.6				3s1	Kuala Lumpur, MAL	17	Sep
11.49	1.3				7s1	Budapest, HUN	19	Aug
11.50	-0.3				7	Kuala Lumpur, MAL	17	Sep
11.63	-0.3				4	Cottbus, GER	27	May
11.40	1.5	Marcia Richardson		10.02.72	1	Bedford	29	Aug
11.45	-0.1				3h4	Kuala Lumpur, MAL	16	Sep
11.46	0.9				2	Birmingham	25	Jul
11.47	-0.1				5s2	Kuala Lumpur, MAL	17	Sep
11.49	1.0				1s2	Birmingham	25	Jul
11.56	-0.5				3	Hechtel, BEL	1	Aug
11.57	1.2				6	St. Petersburg, RUS	27	Jun
11.61	-4.5				1	Watford	20	Jun
11.63	-0.5				1h1	Hechtel, BEL	1	Aug
11.66	-1.8				1	Ljubljana, SLO	31	May
11.66	-1.1				1	Birmingham	6	Jun
11.43	0.0	Katharine Merry		21.09.74	5h2	Nuremberg, GER	11	Jul
11.56	0.0				8	Nuremberg, GER	11	Jul
11.65	-0.2				4	Helsinki, FIN	13	Jun
11.46	2.0	Simmone Jacobs		5.09.66	1h2	Birmingham	24	Jul
11.51	1.0				2s2	Birmingham	25	Jul
11.56	0.9				3	Birmingham	25	Jul
11.62	0.5				1	Claremont, USA	17	Apr
11.61	1.5	Andrea Coore		23.04.69	2	Bedford	29	Aug
11.63	1.9	Malgorzata Rostek	U23	25.03.77	1	Edinburgh	18	Jul
11.66	1.6				1h4	Birmingham	24	Jul
11.66	1.6	Aileen McGillivary		13.08.70	1h2	Edinburgh	18	Jul

30 performances to 11.66 by 7 athletes

11.67	1.4	Ellena Ruddock	U23	23.02.76	2	Hexham	14	Jun
11.67	1.6	Joanna Clark/Hill		11.02.73	2h2	Edinburgh	18	Jul
11.71	0.2	Sarah Wilhelmy	U20	2.02.80	1	Bedford	30	May
	(10)							
11.73	1.9	Tatum Nelson	U23	17.12.78	4	Edinburgh	18	Jul
11.77	1.6	Christine Bloomfield		12.02.68	3h4	Birmingham	24	Jul
11.78	1.0	Abi Oyepitan	U20	30.12.79	4s2	Birmingham	25	Jul
11.79	1.6	Sharon Williams		20.05.70	4h4	Birmingham	24	Jul
11.80	0.4	Samantha Davies	U20	20.09.79	3s1	Birmingham	25	Jul
11.81	1.4	Catherine Murphy		21.09.75	1h2	Cwmbran	20	Jun
11.82	0.2	Donna Fraser		7.11.72	3	Irvine, USA	2	May
11.85	1.9	Janine Whitlock		11.08.73	1h1	Cudworth	9	May
11.85	0.5	Laura Seston	U20	9.02.79	1	London (He)	30	Aug
11.88	1.5	Donna Maylor	U17	20.05.82	4	Bedford	29	Aug
	(20)							
11.89	-1.1	Michelle Thomas		16.10.71	3	Birmingham	6	Jun
11.93	-0.5	Tracy Joseph		29.11.69	1h1	Watford	20	Jun
11.93	0.4	Stephi Douglas		22.01.69	7s1	Birmingham	25	Jul
11.94	1.6	Nicole Crosby	U23	23.10.76	5h4	Birmingham	24	Jul
11.94	1.0	Melanie Purkiss	U20	11.03.79	7s2	Birmingham	25	Jul
11.97	1.6	Zoe Wilson	U23	28.08.76	6h4	Birmingham	24	Jul
11.98	2.0	Susie Williams	U23	2.06.77	2h3	Bath	2	May
11.98	-0.5	Michelle Turner	U23	25.12.77	2h1	Watford	20	Jun
12.02	1.6	Victoria Shipman	U23	31.03.77	7h4	Birmingham	24	Jul
12.03	1.4	Sarah Oxley		3.07.73	5	Hexham	14	Jun
	(30)							
12.04	-1.1	Sharon Tunaley		2.09.68	7	Birmingham	6	Jun
12.07	0.5	Maria Bolsover	U20	5.06.80	1h3	Cudworth	9	May

12.07		Libby Alder	U20	20.11.80	1	Solihull	23	May
12.07	0.6	Katherine Endacott	U20	29.01.80	3	Tessenderlo, BEL	30	Aug
12.09	1.5	Sue Rawlinson		13.10.70	1h2	Cudworth	9	May
12.10	1.9	Susan Christie	U20	7.03.79	6	Edinburgh	18	Jul
12.10	1.5	Julia White	U20	2.05.79	7	Bedford	29	Aug
12.10	0.4	Vicki Jamison	U23	19.05.77	4	Singapore, SIN	6	Sep
12.11	-0.5	Vicky Day		19.06.72	3h1	Watford	20	Jun
12.12	1.9	Natalie Hynd	U23	30.01.78	7	Edinburgh	18	Jul
	(40)							
12.12	1.2	Clare Russell	U17	11.11.81	2s2	Sheffield	15	Aug
12.13	1.2	Lowri Jones	U17	22.07.83	3s2	Sheffield	15	Aug
12.13	1.7	Danielle Selley	U15	19.12.83	1h2	Sheffield	15	Aug
12.13	-0.5	Kim Wall	U17	21.04.83	1	Birmingham	5	Sep
12.15		Bianca Liston	U23	28.05.78	1	Ashford	9	May
12.15	1.4	Nicola Sanders	U17	23.06.82	2h1	Sheffield	15	Aug
12.16		Sophie-Anne Williams	U20	29.03.80	1	Carmarthen	23	May
12.16	1.1	Adele Clarke	U17	29.08.83	1	York	25	Jul
12.19	0.4	Monique Parris	U15	28.01.84	1	London (Ha)	23	May
12.19	1.2	Alex Bick	U17	4.01.83	4s2	Sheffield	15	Aug
	(50)							
12.20	-1.1	Rebecca White	U20	5.06.80	3	London (He)	9	Aug
12.22		Kelly Sotherton	U23	13.11.76	2	Portsmouth	26	Jun
12.22	2.0	Hayley Clements		17.09.68	4h2	Birmingham	24	Jul
12.23	1.9	Emma Phillips	U20	31.01.81	2h1	Cudworth	9	May
12.23		Melanie Roberts	U23	2.03.78	6	Birmingham	18	Jul
12.24	2.0	Liz Ghojefa		24.02.69	3h3	Bath	2	May
12.24	1.8	Shelley-Anne Bowen	U20	12.05.79	2h1	London (Ha)	24	May
12.26	1.5	Elaine Sutcliffe		6.04.70	2h2	Cudworth	9	May
12.26	1.5	Melanie Pickersgill		20.04.73	3h2	Cudworth	9	May
12.27	1.1	Ann Brooks/Danson		4.05.71	1h	Cudworth	2	Aug
12.29	1.0	Jeanette Kwakye	U17	20.03.83	1	London (Ha)	24	May

Additional Under 17 (1 - 8 above)

12.31		Helen Griffin		30.09.82	5	Liverpool	23	May
12.36	-0.1	Gemma Ryde		23.06.83	2	Dublin (S), IRE	8	Aug
	(10)							
12.38	1.6	Rebecca Guthrie		19.03.83	3h3	Sheffield	15	Aug
12.41		Anna Boyle		29.03.83	2	Tullamore, IRE	6	Jun
12.42	1.2	Anne Tulloch		14.04.82	5s2	Sheffield	15	Aug
12.43	1.1	Melissa Anderson		30.03.82	3	York	25	Jul
12.44		Rebecca Bird		7.01.83	1	Solihull	24	May
12.44	1.3	Jackie Walters		17.12.81	2h1	Cudworth	2	Aug
12.44	1.6	Katie Metcalfe		10.02.83	4h3	Sheffield	15	Aug
12.51	1.4	Laura Watkins		1.01.82	4h1	Sheffield	15	Aug
12.53	1.5	Claire Rooney		23.08.83	1	Glasgow (S)	9	May
12.53		Elexi Walker		28.10.82	1h1	Solihull	23	May
	(20)							
12.54	1.2	Gemma Watson		28.11.82	1h3	London (Ha)	24	May
12.54		Jeni McCarthy		22.02.82	2	Colwyn Bay	5	Sep
12.56	1.5	Rhona MacKinnon		5.02.82	2	Glasgow (S)	9	May
12.56		Hayley-Kate Baxter		25.06.82	3	Carmarthen	23	May
12.57	1.0	Anisha Barnaby		9.07.83	2	London (Ha)	24	May
12.59		Lucy Evans		2.10.82	4	Carmarthen	23	May
12.59	-0.5	Karen Oughton		26.01.83	2	Birmingham	5	Sep

Wind Assisted

11.34	3.3	Simmone Jacobs		(11.46)	1	Cork, IRE	27	Jun
11.36	4.7	Marcia Richardson		(11.40)	1	Jona, SWZ	12	Jul
	11.41	2.5			1h1	Birmingham	24	Jul
	11.57	2.4			2	Cardiff	4	Aug
11.40	2.7	Maduaka		(11.32)	1h3	Birmingham	24	Jul
	11.57	2.6			1	Leeds	7	Jun

248

11.45	4.8	Rebecca White	U20	(12.20)	1	Bedford	4	Jul
11.45	4.8	Abi Oyepitan	U20	(11.78)	2	Bedford	4	Jul
		11.50	3.0		1	Alicante, SPA	18	Jul
		11.63	4.8		1	London (Ha)	24	May
11.50	3.0	Samantha Davies	U20	(11.80)	2	Alicante, SPA	18	Jul
		11.52	4.8		3	Bedford	4	Jul
		11.63	2.9		1r2	Cork, IRE	27	Jun
		11.65	2.7		2h3	Birmingham	24	Jul
11.53	3.4	Ellena Ruddock	U23	(11.67)	1	Bedford	25	May
		11.61	2.5		1h1	Bedford	25	May
11.58	2.2	Donna Fraser		(11.82)	1	Fullerton, USA	23	Apr
11.59	4.8	Maria Bolsover	U20	(12.07)	4	Bedford	4	Jul
11.61	3.7	Susie Williams	U23	(11.98)	1	Bath	2	May
11.61	4.8	Laura Seston	U20	(11.85)	5	Bedford	4	Jul
11.62	4.8	Donna Maylor	U17	(11.88)	6	Bedford	4	Jul
11.64	4.8	Melanie Purkiss	U20	(11.94)	7	Bedford	4	Jul
11.65	2.2	Rostek	U23	(11.63)	1h1	Edinburgh	18	Jul
11.66	4.3	Diane Allahgreen		21.02.75	1s1	Bath	2	May
24 performances to 11.66 by 15 athletes
11.70	2.5	Catherine Murphy		(11.81)	2h1	Birmingham	24	Jul
11.72	2.2	Tracy Joseph		(11.93)	3	Fullerton, USA	23	Apr
11.72	5.9	Jade Johnson	U20	7.06.80	2h3	Bedford	4	Jul
11.75	4.7	Christine Bloomfield		(11.77)	4	Jona, SWZ	12	Jul
11.81	3.4	Donna Hoggarth		14.10.73	4	Bedford	25	May
11.82	2.3	Jackie Walters	U17	(12.44)	1s2	Exeter	10	Jul
11.83	2.8	Angie Thorp		7.12.72	1h2	Bedford	25	May
11.86	3.6	Zoe Wilson	U23	(11.97)	2h2	Bath	2	May
11.86	5.9	Shelley-Anne Bowen	U20	(12.24)	3h3	Bedford	4	Jul
11.86	3.9	Libby Alder	U20	(12.07)	1rB	Bedford	4	Jul
11.87	4.8	Katherine Endacott	U20	(12.07)	3	London (Ha)	24	May
11.88	2.5	Stephi Douglas		(11.93)	5h1	Birmingham	24	Jul
11.89	3.9	Nicola Sanders	U17	(12.15)	2	Sheffield	15	Aug
11.92	3.4	Michelle Turner	U23	(11.98)	6	Bedford	25	May
11.93	3.9	Jeanette Kwakye	U17	(12.29)	3	Sheffield	15	Aug
11.95	2.3	Jacqueline Le Geyt	U17	17.08.82	2s2	Exeter	10	Jul
11.96	3.8	Emma Phillips	U20	(12.23)	3	Leeds	23	May
11.98	4.8	Natalie Gaynor	U20	7.11.79	5	London (Ha)	24	May
11.99	4.3	Helen Williams	U23	2.06.77	4s1	Bath	2	May
12.00	3.4	Helen Roscoe	U20	4.12.79	7	Bedford	25	May
12.00	3.9	Clare Russell	U17	(12.12)	4	Sheffield	15	Aug
12.02	2.3	Helen Griffin	U17	(12.31)	3s2	Exeter	10	Jul
12.06	4.8	Lucy Atunumuo	U20	4.11.80	6	London (Ha)	24	May
12.08	3.3	Lowri Jones	U17	(12.13)	1	Bruges, BEL	23	Aug
12.11	3.9	Natalie Smellie	U17	16.01.82	5rB	Bedford	4	Jul
12.14	3.8	Gemma Ryde	U17	(12.36)	4s1	Sheffield	15	Aug
12.15	2.5	Donita Benjamin		5.03.72	6h1	Birmingham	24	Jul
12.15	3.8	Elexi Walker	U17	(12.53)	5s1	Sheffield	15	Aug
12.16	2.8	Alex Bick	U17	(12.19)	2h2	Sheffield	15	Aug
12.18	2.7	Kadien Cameron	U20	24.02.80	4h1	Exeter	10	Jul
12.19	3.6	Claire Spurway	U23	4.04.78	4s2	Bath	2	May
12.20	3.0	Kelly Sotherton	U23	(12.22)	4	Portsmouth	9	May
12.20	2.8	Keeley Pallett		27.02.74	5h2	Bedford	25	May
12.20	5.9	Amina Ceesay	U20	19.11.79	6h3	Bedford	4	Jul
12.20	5.9	Syreena Pinel	U20	13.01.79	7h3	Bedford	4	Jul
12.20	2.3	Melissa Anderson	U17	(12.43)	4s2	Exeter	10	Jul
12.21	2.5	Katie Sketchley		9.07.73	5h1	Bedford	25	May

249

12.22	3.0	Sarah Nash	U20	10.11.80	3h2	Exeter	11	Jul
12.23	3.8	Sara Todd	U20	3.11.79	4	Leeds	23	May
12.23	2.7	Karlene Palmer	U20	23.10.80	5h1	Exeter	10	Jul
12.24	4.8	Sabrina Scott	U20	2.06.79	7	London (Ha)	24	May
12.24	2.2	Katrina Leys		11.09.73	4h1	Edinburgh	18	Jul
12.24	2.7	Melanie Pickersgill		(12.26)	7h3	Birmingham	24	Jul
12.27	3.2	Kate Denham	U20	18.03.80	1	Portsmouth	9	May
12.28	4.3	Serena Wilkins	U23	7.08.78	5s1	Bath	3	May
12.28	4.3	Michelle Walkes	U23	9.05.76	6s1	Bath	3	May
12.28	4.8	Tracy Bishop	U20	1.05.79	8	London (Ha)	24	May

Additional Under 17

12.32	2.3	Anya Pitters		18.12.82	6s2	Exeter	10	Jul
12.33	4.5	Danielle Norville		18.01.83	4s1	Exeter	10	Jul
12.34	4.5	Grace Smith		30.01.82	5s1	Exeter	10	Jul
12.36	3.0	Karen Oughton		(12.59)	1	Logrono, SPA	13	Jun
12.36	2.3	Denika St. Helen		10.09.82	7s2	Exeter	10	Jul
12.37	3.8	Laura Watkins		(12.51)	8s1	Sheffield	15	Aug
12.39	3.0	Anne Tulloch		(12.42)	3h4	Sheffield	15	Aug
12.41	3.6	Hayley-Kate Baxter		(12.56)	1h2	Carmarthen	23	May
12.42	4.5	Lucy Evans		(12.59)	6s1	Exeter	10	Jul
12.45	6.1	Rachel Redmond		7.12.81	1rB	Gran Canaria, SPA	27	Jul
12.47	2.5	Rhona MacKinnon		(12.56)	1	Edinburgh	19	Jun
12.48	2.3	Patricia Alexander		9.09.82	8s2	Exeter	10	Jul
12.53	2.8	Leonie Lightfoot		8.02.82	5h2	Sheffield	15	Aug
12.55	2.8	Anisha Barnaby		(12.57)	7h2	Sheffield	15	Aug
12.56	4.5	Samantha Wilson		28.09.81	7s1	Exeter	10	Jul
12.57	4.5	Sarah Tomlins		5.04.82	8s1	Exeter	10	Jul
12.59	2.4	Caroline Marsden		1.06.82	1rB	Birmingham	5	Sep

Hand Timing

11.2 w	3.0	Donna Fraser		(11.82)	1	Bellville, RSA	31	Jan
11.5 w	3.2	Richardson		(11.40)	1	Grangemouth	4	Jul
		11.6			1	Watford	15	Aug
11.6 w	2.5	Sarah Wilhelmy	U20	(11.71)	1	London (WF)	9	May
11.6 w?		Catherine Murphy		(11.81)	1	London (He)	22	May
		11.8	1.8		1rB	Watford	15	Aug
		5 performances to 11.6 by 4 athletes including 4 wind assisted						
11.7		Janine Whitlock		(11.85)	1	Lincoln	21	Jun
11.7		Christine Bloomfield		(11.77)	1	Portsmouth	5	Sep
11.7		Abi Oyepitan	U20	(11.78)	2	Portsmouth	5	Sep
11.7 w		Lesley Owusu	U23	21.12.78	1	Manhattan Ka, USA	9	May
		12.1			1	Perivale	27	Jun
11.7 w	9.8	Victoria Shipman	U23	(12.02)	1	Stoke	5	Jul
11.8		Melanie Purkiss	U20	(11.94)	1	Bath	12	Aug
11.8		Laura Seston	U20	(11.85)	1	Colchester	22	Aug
11.8 w	3.0	Kim Wall	U17	(12.13)	1	London (WF)	9	May
		12.0			1	Bromley	17	May
11.8 w	3.0	Jeanette Kwakye	U17	(12.29)	2	London (WF)	9	May
		12.2	0.0		2	Basildon	28	Jun
11.8 w		Rachel King	U23	11.05.76	1	Barry	10	May
		12.1			2	Derby	19	Jul
11.8 w		Louretta Thorne	U23	6.05.77	1	Worthing	27	Jun
		12.0			1	Bournemouth	22	Aug
11.8 w	3.2	Michelle Thomas		(11.89)	3	Grangemouth	4	Jul
11.8 w	9.8	Rebecca Drummond	U23	18.04.78	2	Stoke	5	Jul
11.8 w		Donna Maylor	U17	(11.88)	1	Telford	26	Jul
11.9 w?		Natalie Gaynor	U20	(11.98w)	1	Portsmouth	25	Apr

11.9 w	9.8	Liz Fairs	U23	1.12.77	3	Stoke	5	Jul
11.9 w	2.2	Melanie Roberts	U23	(12.23)	1rB	Coventry	5	Jul
12.0		Sarah Claxton	U20	23.09.79	1	Barking	5	Apr
12.0		Sarah Zawada	U17	9.04.82	1	Barking	25	Apr
12.0		Donna Hoggarth		(11.81w)	1	Blackpool	10	May
12.0		Libby Alder	U20	(12.07)	1	Worcester	10	May
12.0		Katherine Endacott	U20	(12.07)	1	Plymouth	30	May
12.0		Jade Johnson	U20	(11.72w)	1	Barking	14	Jun
12.0		Maria Bolsover	U20	(12.07)	2	Stretford	23	Jun
12.0		Donita Benjamin		(12.15w)	2	Bournemouth	27	Jun
12.0	1.7	Angie Thorp		(11.83w)	2	Coventry	5	Jul
12.0		Sharon Davidge	U17	15.09.81	1	Exeter	5	Sep
12.0 w	3.2	Sharon Tunaley		(12.04)	7	Grangemouth	4	Jul
12.1		Helen Roscoe	U20	(12.00w)	1	Loughborough	25	Apr
12.1		Rebecca White	U20	(12.20)	1	Blackburn	3	May
12.1		Tracy Bishop	U20	(12.28w)	2	Enfield	9	May
12.1		Milly Clements	U23	20.05.77	1	Abingdon	10	May
12.1		Helen Williams	U23	(11.99w)	1rB	Brighton	30	May
12.1		Sarah Nash	U20	(12.22w)	1	Leamington	13	Jun
12.1		Emily Freeman	U20	24.11.80	1rB	Whitley Bay	21	Jun
12.1		Nicole Bowring		27.01.74	1	Bracknell	27	Jun
12.1		Shelley-Anne Bowen	U20	(12.24)	2	Bracknell	27	Jun
12.1		Sinead Dudgeon	U23	9.07.76	1	Grangemouth	1	Jul
12.1		Lowri Jones	U17	(12.13)	1	Connah's Quay	4	Jul
12.1		Hayley Clements		(12.22)	1	Guildford	18	Jul
12.1	0.7	Natalie Hynd	U23	(12.12)	3	Stafford	12	Sep
12.1		Natalie Watson	U15	(12.46)	1h1	Telford	12	Sep
12.1 w	2.9	Katie Sketchley		(12.21w)	1	London (WF)	9	May
12.1 w	4.1	Monique Parris	U15	(12.19)	1h1	London (WF)	9	May
12.1 w	2.9	Vicky Day		(12.11)	2	London (WF)	9	May
12.1 w	2.5	Amina Ceesay	U20	(12.20w)	3	London (WF)	9	May
12.1 w	2.2	Louise Whitehead		26.03.75	2	Bebington	10	May
12.1 w		Katrina Leys		(12.24w)	1	Peterhead	24	May
12.1 w	9.8	Elaine Sutcliffe		(12.26)	4	Stoke	5	Jul
12.1 w	9.8	Ann Brooks/Danson		(12.27)	5	Stoke	5	Jul
12.1 w	2.2	Sue Briggs		26.03.67	2r2	Coventry	5	Jul
12.1 w		Liz Ghojefa		(12.24)	2	Carshalton	18	Jul

Additional Under 17

12.2		Anna Boyle		(12.41)	2	Tullamore, IRE	6	Jun
12.2	1.5	Karen Oughton		(12.59)	1h1	Logrono, SPA	13	Jun
12.2		Cath Jones		26.02.83	1	Carmarthen	14	Jun
12.2	0.9	Jacqueline Le Geyt		(11.95w)	1	Kingston	20	Jun
12.2	2.0	Grace Smith		(12.34w)	2h1	Exeter	10	Jul
12.2 w		Hayley Bowers		26.01.83	2	Peterhead	24	May
12.2 w		Susan Bovill		6.05.82	1rB	Carshalton	18	Jul
		12.3			3	Bournemouth	27	Jun
12.3		Heather McKay		5.09.81	1	Coatbridge	26	Apr
12.3		Gemma Ryde		(12.36)	1	Grangemouth	7	Jun
12.3		Jackie Walters		(12.44)	1	Derby	13	Jun
12.3		Gaby Howell		25.01.82	1	Enfield	27	Jun
12.3		Rachael Sutton		28.08.83	1	Bournemouth	2	Aug
12.3 w	3.0	Anya Pitters		(12.32w)	3	London (WF)	9	May
		12.4	2.0		3h1	Exeter	10	Jul
12.3 w	3.0	Danielle Norville		(12.33w)	3h4	Exeter	10	Jul
12.4		Rebecca Bird		(12.44)	1	Worcester	9	May
12.4		Natalie Smellie		(12.11w)	1rB	Bromley	17	May

12.4		Catherine Dockerty	9.01.83	1	Jarrow	13 Jun
12.4		Elexi Walker	(12.53)	2	Birmingham	14 Jun
12.4		Katie Metcalfe	(12.44)	1	Oldham	20 Jun
12.4		Lowri Roberts	9.10.81	1	Yate	19 Jul
12.4		Samantha Wilson	(12.56w)	2	Colchester	22 Aug
12.4 w	4.3	Lucy Evans	(12.59)	4h3	Exeter	10 Jul
12.4 w	4.2	Caroline Marsden	(12.59w)	2	Aberdare	31 Aug
12.4 w	4.2	Sarah Lane	24.11.82	3	Aberdare	31 Aug

Under 15 (1 - 2 above)

12.33 w 2.6		Deborah Okangi	6.05.84	1h3	Exeter	10 Jul
12.34	0.4	Cherie Pierre	15.05.84	2	London (Ha)	23 May
12.35 w 2.6		Tamsin Lees	24.04.84	2h3	Exeter	10 Jul
12.5				1	Worcester	12 Sep
12.37 w 2.4		Watson	(12.1)	1h2	Exeter	10 Jul
12.46				1h1	Solihull	23 May
12.4		Vernicha James	6.06.84	1	London (Elt)	30 May
12.4		Aimee John	20.09.83	2	Carmarthen	13 Jun
12.4		Kara Dunn	12.10.84	1	Perivale	27 Jun
12.45 w 2.6				3h3	Exeter	10 Jul
12.4		Kate Routledge	17.09.83	1	Whitehaven	22 Aug
12.58 w 3.3				2h1	Exeter	10 Jul
12.4		Amanda Applegarth	5.04.84			
	(10)					
12.46 w 3.3		Lauren McCarthy	30.08.84	1h1	Exeter	10 Jul
12.69	1.7			2h2	Sheffield	15 Aug
12.5		Gemma Bennett	4.01.84	2	Basingstoke	25 Apr
12.67	0.4			3	London (Ha)	23 May
12.6		Bernice Wilson	21.04.84	1	Lincoln	9 May
12.62 w 2.4				2h2	Exeter	10 Jul
12.68				4	Sheffield	15 Aug
12.6		Leanna Goode	24.04.84	1	Enfield	28 Jun
12.6		Kerry Everall	29.02.84	1	Yate	19 Jul
12.6		Michelle Johansen	1.02.84	2	Worcester	12 Sep
12.6 w		Kimberley Velvick	3.01.85	2	Carshalton	18 Jul
12.66 w 2.6		Laura Heslop	12.11.83	4h3	Exeter	10 Jul
12.66 w 3.3		Crystal Condie	28.08.84	3h1	Sheffield	15 Aug
	(20)					
12.68 w 3.3		Sarah Biggs	16.12.83	3h1	Exeter	10 Jul

doubtful timing

12.5		Siobhan McVie	6.07.84	1	Ayr	10 Jun

Under 13

12.9		Amy Spencer	19.09.85	2	Bebington	18 Jun
13.14	-1.9			3	York	25 Jul
13.0		Charlene Lashley	1.09.85	2	Woodford	30 May
13.0		Louise Hazel	6.10.85	1	Peterborough	22 Aug
13.1 w	3.6	Nicola Gossman	4.11.86	1	Grangemouth	11 Jul
13.2		Maria Garavand	30.06.86	1	Great Yarmouth	10 May
13.2		Natalie Cartwright	8.11.85	1h	Carmarthen	10 May
13.2		Faye Williamson	2.12.85	1	Telford	7 Jun
13.2		Samantha Day	8.02.86	2	Telford	7 Jun
13.2		Katie Flaherty		1	Stevenage	13 Sep
13.2		Leah Dunkley	11.11.85	1	Grimsby	27 Sep
	(10)					
13.2		Katie Smith	19.02.86	2	Grimsby	27 Sep

150 METRES - Under 13

19.2		Amy Spencer		19.09.85	1	Wakefield	28	Jun
19.47	-2.6				1	Birmingham	6	Sep
19.7		Natalie Bass			1	Telford	28	Jun
19.7		Katie Smith		19.02.86	2	Wakefield	28	Jun
19.8		Lauren Park		16.07.86	1	Grangemouth	7	Jun
19.8		Amalachukwu Onuora		16.03.86	1	Crawley	30	Aug
19.9		Charlene Lashley		1.09.85	1	Watford	28	Jun
20.0		Lois Rudkin			3	Wakefield	28	Jun
20.0		Samantha McGrath		14.04.86	1	Yate	19	Jul
20.0		Katie Flaherty			1	Norwich	19	Jul
20.06	1.0				1	Birmingham	5	Sep
20.1		Elley Derby		20.12.85	1	Derby	26	Apr
	(10)							
20.1		Natalie Spettie		22.10.85	2	Yate	19	Jul
20.2		Gemma Nicol		27.07.86	1	Grangemouth	28	Jun
20.2		Lisa Rock			2	Telford	28	Jun
20.2		Karen Mylan		8.11.85	1	Hoo	31	Aug

200 METRES

22.93	0.4	Katharine Merry		21.09.74	4	Sheffield	2	Aug
23.22	-0.9				5	St. Petersburg, RUS	28	Jun
23.23	-1.7				2h2	Budapest, HUN	20	Aug
23.32	0.7				1h1	Birmingham	25	Jul
23.33	-1.5				1	Loughborough	17	May
23.38	-1.1				5s2	Budapest, HUN	21	Aug
23.46	-1.2				1	Birmingham	26	Jul
23.60	-2.3				3	Gateshead	19	Jul
23.15 i		Donna Fraser		7.11.72	1	Birmingham	8	Feb
23.32 i					2h5	Valencia, SPA	28	Feb
23.36 i					1h1	Birmingham	8	Feb
23.39 i					2s3	Valencia, SPA	1	Mar
23.40	0.5				2h3	Watford	21	Jun
23.50	0.9				1	Irvine, USA	2	May
23.50	0.5				3	Bedford	30	May
23.53 i					5	Valencia, SPA	1	Mar
23.63	-2.3				4	Gateshead	19	Jul
23.73	-1.7				4	Glasgow	30	Aug
23.23	0.1	Sarah Wilhelmy	U20	2.02.80	2	Mannheim, GER	13	Jun
23.25	0.5				1	Bedford	30	May
23.25	1.9				1	Watford	21	Jun
23.52	0.7				1h3	Annecy, FRA	31	Jul
23.54 i					2	Birmingham	8	Feb
23.56	-1.1				3	Annecy, FRA	1	Aug
23.59 i					1	Birmingham	28	Feb
23.62	-0.6				2s1	Annecy, FRA	1	Aug
23.69	0.7				1q2	Annecy, FRA	31	Jul
23.33	-1.8	Allison Curbishley	U23	3.06.76	2	Prague, CZE	8	Jun
23.46	1.6				3	Cardiff	4	Aug
23.37	0.5	Joice Maduaka		30.09.73	2	Bedford	30	May
23.37	1.9				2	Watford	21	Jun
23.38	0.5				1h3	Watford	21	Jun
23.48	-1.2				2	Birmingham	26	Jul
23.50	-0.3				5s2	Kuala Lumpur, MAL	19	Sep
23.53	-0.2				2h3	Kuala Lumpur, MAL	18	Sep
23.54 i					3	Birmingham	8	Feb
23.61	0.3				1h2	Birmingham	25	Jul
23.66	0.4				8	Sheffield	2	Aug
23.70	-2.3				6	Gateshead	19	Jul
23.72	-1.7				3	Glasgow	30	Aug

Time	Wind	Name	Cat	DoB	Pos	Venue	Date	
23.55	-0.1	Marcia Richardson		10.02.72	1	Bedford	29	Aug
23.71	-1.2				3	Birmingham	26	Jul
23.73	-0.3				3h4	Kuala Lumpur, MAL	18	Sep
23.71	0.2	Simmone Jacobs		5.09.66	3h2	Kuala Lumpur, MAL	18	Sep
23.73	-0.5				5s1	Kuala Lumpur, MAL	19	Sep
		45 performances to 23.75 by 7 athletes including 8 indoors						
23.88	1.8	Clova Court	V35	10.02.60	1H	Bressanone, ITA	4	Jul
23.91 i		Catherine Murphy		21.09.75	4	Birmingham	8	Feb
24.22	0.7				2h1	Birmingham	25	Jul
23.93	1.9	Joanna Clark/Hill		11.02.73	1h2	Edinburgh	17	Jul
(10)								
23.94 i		Ellena Ruddock	U23	23.02.76	2h2	Birmingham	8	Feb
24.25	0.7				3h1	Birmingham	25	Jul
23.94	-0.1	Melanie Purkiss	U20	11.03.79	2	Bedford	29	Aug
24.02	0.1	Rebecca White	U20	5.06.80	3	Mannheim, GER	13	Jun
24.06	0.3	Christine Bloomfield		12.02.68	2h2	Birmingham	25	Jul
24.06	-0.4	Vicki Jamison	U23	19.05.77	3	Singapore, SIN	5	Sep
24.07	1.6	Janine Whitlock		11.08.73	1h1	Cudworth	10	May
24.07	1.9	Vicky Day		19.06.72	4	Watford	21	Jun
24.13	-0.4	Zoe Wilson	U23	28.08.76	1rB	Bedford	30	May
24.16		Tracy Joseph		29.11.69	1	Birmingham	18	Jul
24.17 i		Shani Anderson		7.08.75	2h1	Birmingham	8	Feb
(20)								
24.18	1.5	Emma Whitter	U20	20.07.80	2	Exeter	11	Jul
24.25	-0.4	Samantha Davies	U20	20.09.79	2rB	Bedford	30	May
24.26	-0.7	Sinead Dudgeon	U23	9.07.76	1	Grangemouth	23	Aug
24.29	-1.0	Laura Seston	U20	9.02.79	1	London (He)	30	Aug
24.30 i		Sarah Zawada	U17	9.04.82	1	Birmingham	22	Feb
24.67	-1.2				1	London (Ha)	23	May
24.31	1.5	Jade Johnson	U20	7.06.80	3	Exeter	11	Jul
24.33	1.9	Kerry Jury		19.11.68	1H	Bressanone, ITA	4	Jul
24.33	-0.1	Lorraine Hanson		22.04.65	4	Bedford	29	Aug
24.35	0.7	Nicole Crosby	U23	23.10.76	5h1	Birmingham	25	Jul
24.37	-0.3	Aileen McGillivary		13.08.70	1	Glasgow (S)	10	May
(30)								
24.41	1.8	Sharon Williams		20.05.70	2h1	Watford	21	Jun
24.44	1.5	Helen Roscoe	U20	4.12.79	4	Exeter	11	Jul
24.47 i		Emily Freeman	U20	24.11.80	3	Birmingham	22	Feb
24.50	1.2				1	Cudworth	2	Aug
24.47	2.0	Victoria Shipman	U23	31.03.77	1h1	Bath	3	May
24.47	0.0	Denise Lewis		27.08.72	2H	Kuala Lumpur, MAL	16	Sep
24.48	1.9	Susie Williams	U23	2.06.77	1	Bath	4	May
24.49	0.5	Maria Bolsover	U20	5.06.80	2	Cudworth	9	May
24.50	-2.3	Michelle Thomas		16.10.71	1	Birmingham	6	Jun
24.52	1.6	Sharon Tunaley		2.09.68	2h1	Bedford	24	May
24.52	1.2	Louise Whitehead		26.03.75	2	Cudworth	2	Aug
(40)								
24.54	1.0	Kim Wall	U17	21.04.83	1h2	Sheffield	16	Aug
24.57 i		Kelly Sotherton	U23	13.11.76	2h5	Birmingham	25	Jan
24.60	-0.4	Pauline Richards		30.06.68	3rB	Bedford	30	May
24.62	-1.3	Heather McKay	U17	5.09.81	1	Edinburgh	20	Jun
24.65	1.9	Hayley Clements		17.09.68	7	Watford	21	Jun
24.66	1.6	Claire O'Connor		24.09.74	4h1	Bedford	24	May
24.68	0.8	Malgorzata Rostek	U23	25.03.77	4h1	Wroclaw, POL	27	Jun
24.68	-1.1	Libby Alder	U20	20.11.80	6	London (He)	9	Aug
24.70	1.2	Jo Mahony	U23	22.10.76	3	Cudworth	2	Aug
24.73		Lesley Owusu	U23	21.12.78	3	Birmingham	18	Jul
(50)								
24.74	1.6	Julie Hollman	U23	16.02.77	2H	Bressanone, ITA	4	Jul
24.74	1.6	Melanie Neef		26.05.70	2h1	Edinburgh	17	Jul
24.75 i		Vernicha James	U15	6.06.84	1	Birmingham	1	Feb
24.75	-0.1	Ruth Watson	U20	29.11.79	6	Bedford	29	Aug

24.76 i		Sue Rawlinson		13.10.70	2h6	Birmingham	25 Jan
24.76	-1.5	Sarah Oxley		3.07.73	4	Loughborough	17 May
24.76	-1.2	Gaby Howell	U17	25.01.82	2	London (Ha)	23 May
24.80	1.6	Kelly Thomas	U20	9.01.81	5h1	Bedford	24 May
24.81	1.3	Lowri Jones	U17	22.07.83	1h4	Sheffield	16 Aug
24.82	1.2	Katherine Endacott	U20	29.01.80	1h2	London (Ha)	23 May
	(60)						
24.84	1.4	Katherine Livesey	U20	15.12.79	H	Wrexham	1 Aug
24.85	1.7	Alex Bick	U17	4.01.83	2	Dublin (S), IRE	8 Aug
24.88	1.2	Julia White	U20	2.05.79	4	Cudworth	2 Aug
24.90	-1.4	Melanie Roberts	U23	2.03.78	4	Liverpool	20 Jun
24.91 i		Ellie Mardle	U23	27.07.78	3h1	Birmingham	8 Feb
24.91	-0.4	Clare Russell	U17	11.11.81	1	Cudworth	2 Aug
24.96	2.0	Donna Maylor	U17	20.05.82	1H	Hull	20 Sep
24.99	0.6	Cherie Pierre	U15	15.05.84	1	London (Ha)	24 May
24.99		Stephanie Llewellyn		31.12.68	2	Belfast	27 Jun
25.00	-1.2	Jeanette Kwakye	U17	20.03.83	3	London (Ha)	23 May
	(70)						
25.06	0.7	Tracy Bishop	U20	1.05.79	3	London (Ha)	23 May
25.06	0.6	Nicola Gautier	U23	21.03.78	H	Val de Reuil, FRA	25 Jul
25.08 i		Rebecca Bird	U17	7.01.83	1	Birmingham	1 Mar
		25.30			1	Solihull	24 May
25.08	1.6	Melanie Pickersgill		20.04.73	2h1	Cudworth	10 May
25.08	0.7	Lucy Atunumuo	U20	4.11.80	4	London (Ha)	23 May
25.09	0.5	Tatum Nelson	U23	17.12.78	4h2	Watford	21 Jun
25.10	1.8	Helen Williams	U23	2.06.77	3h1	Watford	21 Jun
25.12 i		Emily Parr	U20	9.05.81	4	Birmingham	22 Feb
25.13 i		Louretta Thorne	U23	6.05.77	3h3	Birmingham	8 Feb
25.13		Michelle Pierre		30.09.73	6r2	Loughborough	17 May
	(80)						
25.13	0.3	Jenny Kelly		20.06.70	H	Val de Reuil, FRA	25 Jul
25.14	1.8	Claire Haslam		18.12.63	4h1	Watford	21 Jun
25.15 i		Jo Sloane	U23	2.12.76	3	Glasgow	15 Mar
25.15	0.5	Louisa Guthrie	U23	26.12.77	5h2	Watford	21 Jun
25.17	1.6	Natalie Hynd	U23	30.01.78	3h1	Edinburgh	17 Jul
25.18	1.9	Amina Ceesay	U20	19.11.79	4h1	Exeter	11 Jul
25.18	1.2	Nicola Sanders	U17	23.06.82	1H	Birmingham	23 Aug
25.21	-0.4	Adele Clarke	U17	29.08.83	2	Cudworth	2 Aug
25.21	2.0	Tina Thirwell	U17	5.09.81	2H	Hull	20 Sep
25.24	-0.9	Donna Porazinski	U20	28.01.81	1	Carmarthen	23 May
	(90)						
25.25 i		Danielle Norville	U17	18.01.83	2	Birmingham	1 Mar
25.26	1.0	Rachel Redmond	U17	7.12.81	3h2	Sheffield	16 Aug
25.27	1.6	Katrina Leys		11.09.73	4h1	Edinburgh	17 Jul

Additional Under 17 (1 - 15 above)

25.35	0.7	Susan Bovill		6.05.82	2h2	London (Ha)	23 May
25.36	-1.2	Natalie Smellie		16.01.82	4	London (Ha)	23 May
25.39	1.7	Louise Haugh		29.12.81	3	Dublin (S), IRE	8 Aug
25.40	-1.2	Sharon Davidge		15.09.81	5	London (Ha)	23 May
25.41	2.0	Claire Rooney		23.08.83	1	Glasgow (S)	10 May
	(20)						
25.49	2.0	Rhona MacKinnon		5.02.82	2	Glasgow (S)	10 May
25.49	1.0	Laura Watkins		1.01.82	4h2	Sheffield	16 Aug
25.52		Lynsey Munnoch		24.10.81	1	Inverness	31 May
25.55	-4.0	Jeni McCarthy		22.02.82	2	Ayr	18 Jul
25.56	-0.6	Gemma Ryde		23.06.83	1	Grangemouth	23 Aug
25.57		Dawn Wilson		16.12.81	1	Ashford	9 May
25.57	0.7	Anya Pitters		18.12.82	3h2	London (Ha)	23 May
25.57	-0.4	Melissa Anderson		30.03.82	3	Cudworth	2 Aug
25.59		Chevette Mais		22.09.82	2	Ashford	9 May

Wind Assisted

22.90	4.1	Allison Curbishley	U23	(23.33)	1	Edinburgh	17	Jul
23.03	2.5	Simmone Jacobs		(23.71)	1	Walnut, USA	19	Apr
		23.28	2.8		3	Cork, IRE	27	Jun
23.20	4.2	Sarah Wilhelmy	U20	(23.23)	2	Alicante, SPA	18	Jul
		23.21	2.8		2	Cork, IRE	27	Jun
		23.31	4.1		1	Bedford	5	Jul
23.39	3.0	Donna Fraser		(23.40)	1	Fullerton, USA	23	Apr
23.62	4.1	Joanna Clark/Hill		(23.93)	2	Edinburgh	17	Jul
23.67	4.2	Melanie Purkiss	U20	(23.94)	3	Alicante, SPA	18	Jul
		9 performances to 23.75 by 6 athletes						
23.80	3.9	Kerry Jury		(24.33)	1H	Arles, FRA	23	May
23.82	4.1	Rebecca White	U20	(24.02)	2	Bedford	5	Jul
23.84	4.4	Vicky Day		(24.07)	1	Bedford	24	May
23.93	4.4	Sharon Tunaley		(24.52)	2	Bedford	24	May
24.02	3.0	Tracy Joseph		(24.16)	2	Fullerton, USA	23	Apr
24.02	2.2	Samantha Davies	U20	(24.25)	1h3	Bedford	5	Jul
24.02	4.1	Abi Oyepitan	U20	30.12.79	3	Bedford	5	Jul
24.03	4.4	Louise Whitehead		(24.52)	4	Bedford	24	May
24.19	4.1	Melanie Neef		(24.74)	3	Edinburgh	17	Jul
24.25	3.1	Vernicha James	U15	6.06.84	1	Exeter	11	Jul
24.30	3.9	Pauline Richards		(24.60)	2H	Arles, FRA	23	May
24.33	3.9	Kelly Sotherton	U23	13.11.76	3H	Arles, FRA	23	May
24.34	5.0	Susie Williams	U23	(24.48)	4	Hexham	14	Jun
24.39	2.5	Maria Bolsover	U20	(24.49)	2	Leeds	23	May
24.43	4.1	Helen Roscoe	U20	(24.44)	6	Bedford	5	Jul
24.47	3.9	Julie Hollman	U23	(24.74)	H	Arles, FRA	23	May
24.48	4.4	Jeni McCarthy	U17	(25.55)	1	Exeter	11	Jul
24.49	4.4	Helen Williams	U23	(25.10)	5	Bedford	24	May
24.50	5.8	Karlene Palmer	U20	23.10.80	1rB	Bedford	5	Jul
24.52	2.2	Kim Wall	U17	(24.54)	1	Sheffield	16	Aug
24.56	4.4	Kelly Thomas	U20	(24.80)	6	Bedford	24	May
24.56	5.8	Lowri Jones	U17	(24.81)	2rB	Bedford	5	Jul
24.56	5.8	Lucy Atunumuo	U20	(25.08)	3rB	Bedford	5	Jul
24.64	2.4	Nicola Sanders	U17	(25.18)	1h3	Sheffield	16	Aug
24.68	5.8	Gaby Howell	U17	(24.76)	4rB	Bedford	5	Jul
24.71	3.7	Alex Bick	U17	(24.85)	1h1	Sheffield	16	Aug
24.72	2.7	Lesley Owusu	U23	(24.73)		Columbia, USA	11	Apr
24.73	3.7	Clare Russell	U17	(24.91)	2h1	Sheffield	16	Aug
24.74	4.2	Katherine Livesey	U20	(24.84)	4h1	Bedford	5	Jul
24.77	2.3	Katherine Endacott	U20	(24.82)	3h2	Bedford	5	Jul
24.81	4.4	Natalie Smellie	U17	(25.36)	3	Exeter	11	Jul
24.83	3.7	Adele Clarke	U17	(25.21)	1h4	Exeter	10	Jul
24.87	4.1	Natalie Hynd	U23	(25.17)	5	Edinburgh	17	Jul
24.89	3.9	Jenny Kelly		(25.13)	H	Arles, FRA	23	May
24.89	5.8	Amina Ceesay	U20	(25.18)	6rB	Bedford	5	Jul
24.92	4.5	Rachel Redmond	U17	(25.26)	2s2	Exeter	10	Jul
25.00	4.5	Rebecca Bird	U17	(25.30)	3s2	Exeter	10	Jul
25.04	3.5	Stephanie Spinks	U17	6.09.82	3h1	Exeter	10	Jul
25.05	2.5	Danielle Freeman	U20	11.02.80	2H	Arles, FRA	23	May
25.06	4.4	Charlene Barnes	U17	25.05.82	5	Exeter	11	Jul
25.15	3.7	Rhona MacKinnon	U17	(25.49)	3h1	Sheffield	16	Aug
25.21	4.7	Ellie Mardle	U23	(24.91i)	2h4	Bath	3	May
25.23	5.3	Katie Metcalfe	U17	10.02.83	2h2	Exeter	10	Jul
25.23	4.1	Katrina Leys		(25.27)	6	Edinburgh	17	Jul
25.26	3.6	Rebecca Guthrie	U17	19.03.83	3h3	Exeter	10	Jul
25.27	4.7	Claire Spurway	U23	4.04.78	3h4	Bath	3	May

DARREN CAMPBELL. A new European Champion.

CHRISTIAN MALCOLM. Double World Junior Champion.

DOUG WALKER. European 200m Champion, 400m to come?

JULIAN GOLDING. Another superb sprinting talent.

MARK RICHARDSON. A great season but overshadowed by Iwan.

COLIN JACKSON. European Champion and back to his best.

TONY JARRETT. Wins a major championship!

DALTON GRANT. The enigma.

NICK BUCKFIELD. A British Record in an injury hit season.

JONATHAN EDWARDS. World number one.

SHAUN PICKERING. A major medal to end his career.

CARL MYERSCOUGH. The future of shot putting looks secure.

ROBERT WEIR. Continues to produce great results.

EMEKA UDECHUKU. The future of the discus?

MICK HILL & STEVE BACKLEY. Still major world forces in world javelin throwing.

DAVID PARKER. World Junior Champion chasing the above.

PAULA RADCLIFFE. 10,000m Record and cross country success.

JULIE PRATT. World Junior Champion.

ASHIA HANSEN. World Indoor Record and Commonwealth Champion around a season missed through injury.

JANINE WHITLOCK. More British records!

DENISE LEWIS. Number one.

Additional Under 17

25.35	3.7	Anisha Barnaby		9.07.83	4h1	Sheffield	16	Aug
25.42	5.3	Alice Docherty		4.01.82	3h2	Sheffield	10	Jul
25.45	3.7	Charlene Williams		22.10.81	4h4	Exeter	10	Jul
25.52	2.4	Anya Pitters		(25.57)	5h3	Sheffield	16	Aug
25.53	3.6	Kirsty Millar		22.12.82	5h3	Exeter	10	Jul

Hand Timing

23.5 w	4.2	Fraser		(23.40)	1	Bellville, RSA	31	Jan
23.6	1.1	Richardson		(23.55)	1	Watford	15	Aug
23.6 w		Catherine Murphy		(24.22)	1	London (He)	22	Aug
		23.8	-1.3		1	Cwmbran	20	Jun
		3 performances to 23.6 by 3 athletes including 2 wind assisted						
24.0		Ellena Ruddock	U23	(24.25)	1	Nottingham	9	Aug
24.1 mx		Jenni Stoute		16.04.65	1	London (TB)	20	May
24.1	-0.5	Abi Oyepitan	U20	(24.02w)	1rB	Watford	15	Aug
24.1		Sharon Williams		(24.41)	1	Thurrock	31	Aug
24.1 w?		Louise Whitehead		(24.52)	1	Neath	14	Jun
		24.5	-1.3		2	Cwmbran	20	Jun
24.2		Samantha Davies	U20	(24.25)	1	Wigan	23	Aug
24.3	-0.8	Michelle Thomas		(24.50)	1	Leamington	9	May
24.3		Alison Thorne		25.09.72	1rB	Perivale	27	Jun
24.3		Kerry Jury		(24.33)	1	Wakefield	12	Jul
24.3 w	3.0	Kim Wall	U17	(24.54)	1	London (Nh)	4	May
		24.5	0.0		1	Thurrock	31	Aug
24.3 w	4.4	Susie Williams	U23	(24.48)	1	Kingston	10	May
		24.4			1	Worthing	27	Jun
24.3 w	2.2	Nicole Crosby	U23	(24.35)	1	Stafford	12	Sep
24.4		Sarah Zawada	U17	(24.67)	1	Crawley	12	Apr
24.4	0.0	Malgorzata Rostek	U23	(24.68)	1r2	Coatbridge	17	May
24.4		Louretta Thorne	U23	(25.13i)	1	Bournemouth	22	Aug
24.4 w	3.0	Jeanette Kwakye	U17	(25.00)	2	London (Nh)	4	May
24.5		Tatum Nelson	U23	(25.09)	1	Bath	30	May
24.5	1.3	Andrea Coore		23.04.69	1	Croydon	7	Jun
24.5		Sharon Tunaley		(24.52)	4	Grangemouth	4	Jul
24.5		Hayley Clements		(24.65)	1	Guildford	18	Jul
24.6		Alison Currie		15.07.68	1	Coatbridge	2	Aug
24.6		Nicola Sanders	U17	(25.18)	1	High Wycombe	31	Aug
24.7	1.6	Melanie Roberts	U23	(24.90)	2	Coventry	5	Jul
24.7		Nicole Bowring		27.01.74	2	St. Ives	5	Sep
24.7 w	4.4	Michelle Pierre		(25.13)	2	Kingston	10	May
		25.1	2.0		1h2	Kingston	10	May
24.8		Vernicha James	U15	(24.75i)	1	Crawley	25	Apr
24.8		Helen Williams	U23	(25.10)	1	Brighton	30	May
24.8		Kelly Sotherton	U23	(24.57i)	7	Grangemouth	4	Jul
24.9		Dawn Higgins		10.12.75	1	Yate	14	Jun
24.9		Kim Goodwin		16.05.70	1	Middlesbrough	14	Jun
24.9		Sandra Leigh		26.02.66	2	Thurrock	31	Aug
25.0		Alyson Layzell		16.12.66	1	Rugby	14	Jun
25.0		Sue Rawlinson		(24.76i)	1	Lincoln	14	Jun
25.0		Julie Money		26.04.64	2	Lincoln	14	Jun
25.0		Sue Briggs		26.03.67	1	Oldham	12	Jul
25.0		Monique Parris	U15	28.01.84	1	Perivale	19	Jul
25.0		Katrina Leys		(25.27)	2	Coatbridge	2	Aug
25.0		Nicola Sutton		4.03.74	1rB	Exeter	5	Sep
25.0 w		Joanna Reed	U20	13.11.79	1	Abingdon	18	Jul
25.1		Carey Easton	U20	16.11.79	2	Grangemouth	6	May
25.1		Rebecca Bird	U17	(25.30)	1	Worcester	9	May
25.1	-0.8	Helen Frost		12.03.74	5	Leamington	9	May

257

25.1	Rebecca Clark	U23	15.09.78	1rB	Solihull	17 May
25.1	Sian Adlam		8.11.70	2	Bath	30 May
25.1	Bibi Enwonwu		12.04.74	1	Norwich	30 May
25.1	Elizabeth Williams	U23	2.06.77	1rB	Norwich	30 May
25.1	Sarah Hancock	U23	2.02.78	1	London (WL)	30 May
25.1	Carmen Michalska		6.11.73	1	Perivale	27 Jun
25.1	Jennie Pearson/Matthews	V35	3.07.62	4	Thurrock	31 Aug

Additional Under 17

25.2	Susan Bovill		(25.35)	1rB	Portsmouth	25 Apr
25.2	Cath Jones		26.02.83	1	Yate	26 Jul
25.2 w	Jacqueline Le Geyt		17.08.82	2	Carshalton	18 Jul
25.3	Charlene Barnes		(25.06w)	2	Solihull	17 May
25.3	Danielle Norville		(25.25i)	1	Telford	28 Jun
25.3	Jeni McCarthy		(25.55)	1	Blackpool	5 Jul
25.3	Laura Watkins		(25.49)	3	Nottingham	9 Aug
25.3	Lynsey Munnoch		(25.52)	1	Coatbridge	30 Aug
25.3	Sharon Davidge		(25.40)	1	Exeter	5 Sep
25.4	Anya Pitters		(25.57)	2	Thurrock	31 Aug

Additional Under 15 (1 - 3 above)

25.51 w 2.7	Vicky Tunaley	4.06.84	1h3	Exeter	10 Jul
	25.95 -0.4		2	London (He)	30 Aug
25.59 i	Sarah Bell	20.09.83	1	Birmingham	24 Feb
	25.61 w 3.1		3	Exeter	11 Jul
	25.68 0.6		2	London (Ha)	24 May
25.6	Kate Routledge	17.09.83	1	Whitehaven	16 May
25.6	Natalie Watson	5.07.84	1	Corby	17 May
	25.74 w 2.4		3	Sheffield	16 Aug
	25.83 ?		1	Solihull	24 May
25.6	Lucy Millson-Watkins	19.10.83	1	Watford	23 Aug
25.7	Ellie Blackwell	28.09.84	1	Bromley	17 May
25.7	Sian Scott	20.03.84	1	Bournemouth	20 Sep
	25.85 -0.4		1	London (He)	30 Aug
(10)					
25.75 w 2.4	Laura Novis	22.01.84	2	Sheffield	16 Aug
	25.94 1.7		1h3	York	25 Jul
25.82 w 2.7	Natalie Street	8.11.83	2h3	Exeter	10 Jul
25.91 1.6	Deborah Okangi	6.05.84	1h4	Sheffield	16 Aug
25.94 1.9	Alanna Wain	27.04.85	3h2	Exeter	10 Jul
25.96 w 2.4	Amanda Applegarth	5.04.84	4	Sheffield	16 Aug
	26.02 1.6		2h2	Sheffield	16 Aug
26.05 0.6	Bernice Wilson	21.04.84	1	York	25 Jul

Under 13

25.87 0.9	Amy Spencer	19.09.85	1	Cudworth	2 Aug
26.7	Gemma Collier	25.11.85	2rB	Exeter	5 Sep
27.0	Elley Derby	20.12.85	1	Cannock	10 May
27.2	Charlotte Beckett	4.01.86	1	Southend	9 Aug
27.2	Leah Dunkley	11.11.85	1	Wakefield	20 Sep
27.27	Louise Hurst	27.10.85	1	Hexham	31 Aug
27.3	Louise Hazel	6.10.85	1	Kingston	26 Jul
27.3	Amalachukwu Onuora	16.03.86	1rB	Kingston	26 Jul
27.3	Samantha Day	8.02.86		Worcester	9 Aug
27.5	Katie Smith	19.02.86	1	Wakefield	24 May
(10)					
27.6	Lauren Park	16.07.86	1	Dunfermline	8 Aug
27.6	Nicola Gossman	4.11.86	1	Coatbridge	29 Aug
27.6	Lisa McManus	3.01.86	1	Peterborough	31 Aug

Foreign

25.15 -0.1	Margaret Veldman	7.06.74	7	Bedford	29 Aug

300 METRES

38.4	Kim Wall	U17	21.04.83	1	London (WF)	10	May
38.49				1	London (Ha)	24	May
38.75	Gaby Howell	U17	25.01.82	2	London (Ha)	24	May
39.04	Heather McKay	U17	5.09.81	1	Edinburgh	19	Jun
39.07	Nicola Sanders	U17	23.06.82	3	London (Ha)	24	May
39.08 i	Susie Williams	U23	2.06.77	1	Birmingham	25	Feb

Additional Under 17 (1 - 4 above)

39.77	Jeni McCarthy		22.02.82	1	Cudworth	2	Aug
39.79	Fiona Harrison		30.11.81	1	Cudworth	10	May
40.0	Natalie Smellie		16.01.82	2	London (WF)	9	May
40.34 i				3	Birmingham	21	Feb
40.05	Rebecca Scotcher		2.07.82	1	Birmingham	6	Sep
40.10	Lynsey Munnoch		24.10.81	5	Sheffield	15	Aug
40.1	Samantha Singer		8.05.82	2	Bromley	17	May
(10)							
40.26	Jo Owbridge		19.01.82	6	Sheffield	15	Aug
40.3	Lisa Miller		13.01.83	1	Hoo	31	Aug
41.28				5	Exeter	11	Jul
40.50	Alex Cooke		24.06.82	7	Sheffield	15	Aug
40.7	Ellie Childs		26.05.83	1	Norwich	19	Jul
40.8	Leah Tribe		3.09.81	2h2	Exeter	10	Jul
40.86				4	Exeter	11	Jul
40.87 i	Lowri Jones		22.07.83	2	Birmingham	28	Feb
40.87	Dawn Wilson		16.12.81	4	London (Ha)	24	May
40.9	Lynsey Turner		3.10.81	1	Grangemouth	12	Jul
41.06 i				1rB	Birmingham	21	Feb
41.34				1	Edinburgh	9	May
41.00	Laura Cowley		3.09.81	2h1	London (Ha)	23	May
41.09	Anna Glynn		18.12.81	1	Stoke	20	Jun
(20)							
41.1	Keeley Augustus		18.05.82	2	Hoo	31	Aug
41.13	Tracy Campbell		20.12.81	1	Glasgow (S)	9	May
41.18 i	Rhona MacKinnon		5.02.82	1h4	Birmingham	21	Feb
41.2	Katherine Porter		19.08.82	1	Ipswich	25	May
41.2	Clare Russell		11.11.81	1	Blackpool	27	Sep
41.3	Sarah Kerr		11.12.81	1	Jarrow	31	May
41.31	Helen Thieme		28.09.81	1	Solihull	23	May
41.4	Miranda Woodruff		6.09.82	1	Carshalton	3	May
41.4	Lindsey Singer		4.06.83	1	Leamington	10	May
41.4	Wendy Davidson		14.10.82	1	Aberdeen	26	Jul
(30)							
41.4	Catherine Riley		4.06.82	1	Stretford	4	Aug
41.4	Danielle Glover		26.07.82	1	Redditch	9	Aug
41.4	Susan Bovill		6.05.82	1	Woking	6	Sep
41.5	Nicola Gauld		28.03.82	2	Coatbridge	17	May
41.53	Sarita Franklin		27.09.81	3h1	Sheffield	15	Aug

400 METRES

50.71	Allison Curbishley	U23	3.06.76	2	Kuala Lumpur, MAL	18	Sep
50.73				1	Glasgow (S)	30	Aug
50.77				1	Gateshead	19	Jul
50.92				1	Birmingham	26	Jul
50.97				2	Milan, ITA	5	Jun
51.05				5	Budapest, HUN	21	Aug
51.10				2	Sheffield	2	Aug
51.35				2	Cottbus, GER	27	May
51.43				2s1	Budapest, HUN	20	Aug
51.45				2	Jena, GER	24	May

(Curbishley)	51.48			3	St. Petersburg, RUS	27	Jun
	51.64			3s2	Kuala Lumpur, MAL	17	Sep
	52.05			2h4	Budapest, HUN	19	Aug
	52.66			1h3	Kuala Lumpur, MAL	16	Sep
	53.14			1h1	Birmingham	25	Jul
	53.47			1	Hexham	14	Jun
50.85	Donna Fraser		7.11.72	2s2	Kuala Lumpur, MAL	17	Sep
	51.01			3	Kuala Lumpur, MAL	18	Sep
	51.19			3	Gateshead	19	Jul
	51.47			2	Birmingham	26	Jul
	51.50			3	Sheffield	2	Aug
	51.54			6	Budapest, HUN	21	Aug
	51.61			2	Walnut, USA	18	Apr
	52.05			4s2	Budapest, HUN	20	Aug
	52.09			1h2	Birmingham	25	Jul
	52.20			2h3	Budapest, HUN	19	Aug
	52.44			6	Bratislava, SVK	9	Jun
	52.49			2	Budapest, HUN	5	Jul
	52.65			3h1	Kuala Lumpur, MAL	16	Sep
51.02	Katharine Merry		21.09.74	2	Glasgow (S)	30	Aug
	51.7			1	Barry	10	May
	52.76			1	Cardiff	4	Aug
52.92 mx	Michelle Thomas		16.10.71	1	Jona, SWZ	12	Jul
	53.23			2	Tallinn, EST	19	Jun
	53.23			3h4	Kuala Lumpur, MAL	16	Sep
	53.25			3	Birmingham	26	Jul
	53.28			6	Hania, GRE	27	May
	53.30			7	Sheffield	2	Aug
	53.32			7s1	Kuala Lumpur, MAL	17	Sep
	53.39			1	Ljubljana, SLO	31	May
52.97	Vicki Jamison	U23	19.05.77	2	Dessau, GER	1	Aug
	53.04 i			1	Birmingham	8	Feb
	53.28 i			4	Birmingham	15	Feb
	53.31			1	Bedford	30	May
53.26	Natasha Danvers	U23	19.09.77	1	Watford	21	Jun
	45 performances to 53.5 by 6 athletes including 2 indoors						
53.52	Michelle Pierre		30.09.73	2	Watford	21	Jun
53.59	Lorraine Hanson		22.04.65	8	Sheffield	2	Aug
53.73	Vicky Day		19.06.72	2h3	Birmingham	25	Jul
53.79	Dawn Higgins		10.12.75	4	Birmingham	26	Jul
	(10)						
53.81	Alyson Layzell		16.12.66	1	Cwmbran	20	Jun
53.95	Aileen McGillivary		13.08.70	1	Glasgow (S)	9	May
54.25	Helen Frost		12.03.74	3h3	Birmingham	25	Jul
54.26	Lesley Owusu	U23	21.12.78	4	Gainesville, USA	2	May
54.28	Carey Easton	U20	16.11.79	5h1	Annecy, FRA	28	Jul
54.29	Stephanie Llewellyn		31.12.68	2	Birmingham	6	Jun
54.32	Louretta Thorne	U23	6.05.77	1rB	Dessau, GER	1	Aug
54.49 i	Kelly Sotherton	U23	13.11.76	2	Birmingham	8	Feb
	57.20			4h2	Watford	21	Jun
54.58	Melanie Neef		26.05.70	2	Istanbul, TUR	20	Jun
54.7	Gaby Howell	U17	25.01.82	1	Brighton	30	May
	56.58			3	London (He)	9	Aug
	(20)						
54.74	Lee McConnell	U23	9.10.78	2rB	Loughborough	17	May
54.87	Nicole Bowring		27.01.74	1	Bedford	30	Aug
54.9	Lisa Vannet		8.11.74	1	Grangemouth	4	Jul
	54.92			1	Edinburgh	18	Jul
55.11	Alison Thorne		25.09.72	5	Watford	21	Jun
55.13	Karen Gear	U20	30.09.79	4h1	Birmingham	25	Jul
55.21	Tania Taylor	U23	7.10.76	1rB	Birmingham	6	Jun

55.25 hur	Gowry Retchakan	V35	21.06.60	2	Kuala Lumpur, MAL	18 Sep
	57.4 (best flat performance !)			1	Southampton	27 Jun
55.29	Ruth Watson	U20	29.11.79	1	London (He)	30 Aug
55.32	Emily Parr	U20	9.05.81	1rB	Bedford	30 May
55.32	Sally Evans		14.05.75	4h2	Birmingham	25 Jul
(30)						
55.33 i	Keri Maddox		4.07.72	4	Birmingham	8 Feb
	55.5			3	Grangemouth	4 Jul
55.39	Kim Wall	U17	21.04.83	2	Alicante, SPA	18 Jul
55.4	Christine Amede	V35	7.08.63	1	Enfield	23 Aug
	55.70			2r2	Birmingham	6 Jun
55.41	Sandra Leigh		26.02.66	3	Bedford	25 May
55.45 i	Kim Goodwin		16.05.70	2s1	Birmingham	7 Feb
	55.5			1	Grimsby	7 Jun
	56.26			5	Bedford	25 May
55.8	Leigh Reade		15.08.72	1	Cannock	9 May
	56.07			3	Edinburgh	18 Jul
55.8	Kathryn Bright	U23	27.03.76	1	Newport	16 Aug
	56.01			6h3	Birmingham	25 Jul
55.82	Donna Porazinski	U20	28.01.81	3	Cwmbran	20 Jun
55.83 i	Abigail Naugher	U20	26.02.80	2	Birmingham	22 Feb
	56.76			3	Exeter	11 Jul
55.9	Samantha Singer	U17	8.05.82	1	Bromley	14 Jun
(40)						
55.9	Claire Raven		15.06.72	1	Stoke	9 Aug
55.9	Alison Currie		15.07.68	4	Watford	15 Aug
55.92	Jenny Meadows	U20	17.04.81	3r3	Loughborough	17 May
56.00 i	Jo Mahony	U23	22.10.76	3s1	Birmingham	7 Feb
56.02	Carmen Michalska		6.11.73	2	Edinburgh	18 Jul
56.1 i	Jo Sloane	U23	2.12.76	2	Birmingham	1 Feb
	57.35			4	Bath	4 May
56.1	Elizabeth Williams	U23	2.06.77	1	Kingston	9 May
	56.45			7	Bedford	25 May
56.1	Jacqui Parker		15.10.66	1	Croydon	7 Jun
56.17	Jo Mersh/Fenn		19.10.74	4rB	Nivelles, BEL	9 Aug
56.17	Catherine Murphy		21.09.75	4	Bedford	29 Aug
(50)						
56.30	Nicola Sanders	U17	23.06.82	2	London (He)	30 Aug
56.3	Rebecca Scotcher	U17	2.07.82	1	Norwich	30 May
	56.86			1	Bedford	14 Jun
56.3	Emma Davies	U23	9.10.78	2	Enfield	23 Aug
	56.60			8	Bedford	25 May
56.31	Zoe Arnold	U23	10.11.76	1	Tullamore, IRE	5 Jul
56.37	Syreeta Williams	U20	24.10.80	5	Bedford	29 Aug
56.5	Rosie Thorner		7.08.67	1	Yeovil	10 May
	57.36			5h2	Bedford	25 May
56.5	Rachel Newcombe		25.02.67	1	Wrexham	14 Jun
56.5	Lucy Chaffe	U20	25.03.79	2	Enfield	19 Jul
	56.54			5rB	Nivelles, BEL	9 Aug
56.5	Ellie Childs	U17	26.05.83	1	Harrow	26 Jul
56.56	Elaine Sutcliffe		6.04.70	6h2	Birmingham	25 Jul
(60)						
56.6	Mary McClung		19.12.71	1	Loughborough	20 May
	56.98			2	Poznan, POL	7 Sep
56.6	Emma Clapson		22.11.71	1	Walton	14 Jun
56.6	Jennie Pearson/Matthews	V35	3.07.62	1	Bedford	22 Jul
	57.25			2	Ashford	10 May
56.6	Melanie Pickersgill		20.04.73	1	Cudworth	9 Aug
56.7	Helen Windass		16.10.65	1	Glasgow (S)	26 Apr
56.7	Sharon Tunaley		2.09.68	1	Nottingham	9 May
	56.77			5	Alfaz Del Pi, SPA	18 Apr

56.7	Hayley Parry		17.02.73	2	Croydon	7	Jun
56.71	Linda Staines	V35	26.12.63	2	Bedford	30	Aug
56.75	Jane Wrighton		5.11.67	4rB	Birmingham	6	Jun
56.77 i	Sarah-Ann Davies	U23	22.04.76	2h1	Birmingham	1	Mar
(70)							
56.8	Jeina Mitchell		21.01.75	2	Kingston	9	May
56.8	Rachael Kay	U20	8.09.80	1	Wigan	31	May
56.8	Sarah Damm		12.09.70	2	Stoke	9	Aug
56.8	Louise Whitehead		26.03.75	1	Wrexham	22	Aug
57.21 i				2h2	Birmingham	25	Jan
56.8	Lorraine Phillips		27.01.75	3	Enfield	23	Aug
56.87	Wendy Davis	U20	7.11.79	2	Tullamore, IRE	6	Jun
56.88 i	Sharon Williams		20.05.70	1	Birmingham	3	Jan
56.9	Katharine Eustace		16.04.75	2	Yeovil	10	May
56.9	Diana Bennett		14.06.74	1	Kingston	27	Jun
56.9	Sharon Semper		26.11.68	2	Colchester	5	Sep
(80)							
56.93 i	Linda Gabriel		27.07.64	3h1	Birmingham	1	Mar
57.3				2	Coventry	5	Jul
57.51				4r2	Bedford	30	May
56.93	Amanda Crowe		21.10.73	6h1	Singapore, SIN	5	Sep
56.97	Zoe Crawford		1.03.75	3	Loughborough	17	May
57.0	Vicky Sterne		12.10.68	1	Watford	8	Jul
57.0 mx	Alice Beecroft		27.07.73	1	Stretford	1	Sep
57.56				2	Cudworth	2	Aug
57.03 i	Lois Cresswell	U20	12.01.81	1	Birmingham	1	Mar
57.03	Anne Hollman		18.02.74	5r2	Birmingham	6	Jun
57.09	Suzanne McGowan	U23	13.04.78	3	Glasgow (S)	9	May
57.1	Lisa Harvey		9.04.68	1r2	Coventry	17	May
57.1	Katie Jones	U23	4.01.77	1r2	Liverpool	16	Aug
(90)							
57.1	Clare Wise		22.08.69	1r2	Enfield	23	Aug
57.18	Christa Salt		17.06.64	1	Muttenz, SWZ	7	Jun
57.2	Tracy Fradley		20.03.75	2	Grimsby	7	Jun
57.2	Amanda Pritchard	U20	18.03.80	1	Yate	14	Jun
57.2	Sarah Roberts	U23	25.06.78	1	Hoo	14	Jun
57.2	Kelly McNeice	U23	17.06.78	1	Coatbridge	21	Jun
57.2	Josephine Peet		4.12.71	1	Guernsey	21	Jun
57.3	Dawn Gandy		28.07.65	1	Basingstoke	14	Jun
57.3	Lisa Miller	U17	13.01.83	2	Bromley	18	Jul
57.38	Elaine Wells	U23	30.05.78	1	Crawley	9	May
(100)							
57.4	Dyanna Clarke	V40	27.02.58	3	Enfield	9	May
57.5	Suzanne Everson		23.03.72	3	Liverpool	16	Aug
57.56				6h4	Birmingham	25	Jul
57.51	Rebecca King	U20	25.03.81	4	Exeter	11	Jul

Additional Under 17 (1 - 7 above)

57.6	Heather McKay		5.09.81	1	Greenock	24	May
57.88	Jeni McCarthy		22.02.82	1	Colwyn Bay	5	Sep
58.5	Laura Cowley		3.09.81	1	London (Elt)	30	May
(10)							
58.6	Jo Owbridge		19.01.82	1	Derby	20	Sep
58.7	Georgie Parnell		22.06.82	1	Street	4	May

First leg of Relay

52.6	Natasha Danvers	U23	19.09.77	h	Amherst, USA	4	Jun
52.87	Vicki Jamison	U23	19.05.77		St. Petersburg, RUS	27	Jun
52.9	Natasha Danvers	U23	19.09.77		Amherst, USA	6	Jun

Foreign

56.38	Orla Ryan (IRE)		7.09.69	2	Tullamore, IRE	9	Aug

600 METRES

1:29.4 +	Diane Modahl	17.06.66	2s1	Budapest, HUN	19	Aug
1:32.50	Christa Salt	17.06.64	1	Regensdorf, SWZ	18	Aug
1:34.7 mx	Vickie Lawrence	9.06.73		Blackpool	15	Mar

Under 13

1:43.4	Hayley Beard	2.12.85	1	Kingston	26	Jul
1:44.3	Rachael Thompson	15.11.85	1	Bebington	10	May
1:44.8	Kirsty Sammon	5.10.85	1	Bournemouth	2	Aug
1:45.5	Rebecca Keeping	17.09.85	1	Bournemouth	23	Aug
1:45.9	Faye Harding	7.09.85	1	Wrexham	22	Apr
1:45.9	Emma Hunt	25.04.86	1	Crawley	1	Sep
1:46.1	Emma Beck	22.11.85	1	Woking	20	Sep

800 METRES

1:58.81	Diane Modahl		17.06.66	3	Kuala Lumpur, MAL	19	Sep
	1:59.77			6	Monaco, MON	8	Aug
	2:00.08			5s1	Budapest, HUN	19	Aug
	2:00.17			2	Malmo, SWE	3	Aug
	2:00.52			4h1	Budapest, HUN	18	Aug
	2:00.97			5	Stockholm, SWE	5	Aug
	2:01.07			6	Athens, GRE	17	Jun
	2:01.92			4	Helsinki, FIN	13	Jun
	2:01.93			1	Solihull	5	Sep
	2:02.01			5	Uniondale,NY. USA	19	Jul
	2:02.61 i			4	Sindelfingen, GER	8	Mar
	2:02.70			8	Hengelo, HOL	1	Jun
	2:02.73			1	Birmingham	25	Jul
	2:02.97			2	Milan, ITA	5	Jun
	2:03.04			2s2	Kuala Lumpur, MAL	18	Sep
2:00.10	Tanya Blake		16.01.71	2	Eugene, USA	31	May
	2:02.06			6	St. Petersburg, RUS	27	Jun
	2:02.15			1	Eagle Rock, USA	9	May
	2:02.72			1	Portland, USA	16	May
	2:02.83			4	Linz, AUT	5	Jul
	2:03.83			2	Birmingham	25	Jul
	2:04.08			1	Irvine, USA	2	May
2:01.52 i	Hayley Parry		17.02.73	4	Birmingham	15	Feb
	2:02.91 i			1	Birmingham	8	Feb
	2:03.46			1	Berne, SWZ	13	Jun
	2:04.37 i			3h1	Valencia, SPA	27	Feb
2:01.83	Amanda Crowe		21.10.73	5s1	Kuala Lumpur, MAL	18	Sep
	2:02.7 mx			1	Belfast	14	Jul
	2:04.31			6	Lucerne, SWZ	2	Jul
	2:04.98			1	Belfast	9	May
2:02.39	Emma Davies	U23	9.10.78	4h2	Kuala Lumpur, MAL	17	Sep
	2:04.88			3	Dessau, GER	1	Aug
2:03.28	Rachel Newcombe		25.02.67	7s1	Kuala Lumpur, MAL	18	Sep
	2:03.58			4h4	Kuala Lumpur, MAL	17	Sep
	2:04.75			1	Cardiff	15	Jul
2:04.6	Angela Davies		21.10.70	1	Watford	5	Aug
2:04.61	Lynn Gibson		6.07.69	1	Swindon	24	Jun
	2:04.9			2	Watford	5	Aug
2:04.81	Vicky Sterne		12.10.68	2	Cardiff	15	Jul
2:04.98	Claire Raven		15.06.72	1rB	Hechtel, BEL	1	Aug

40 performances to 2:05.0 by 10 athletes including 4 indoors

2:05.2	Jo Mersh/Fenn	19.10.74	3	Watford	5	Aug
2:05.33	Bev Blakeman	4.04.74	2	Solihull	5	Sep
2:06.8	Alice Beecroft	27.07.73	4	Watford	5	Aug
2:07.08	Michelle Faherty	10.08.68	4h1	Birmingham	24	Jul

2:07.1 mx	Susan Scott	U23	26.09.77	1	Grangemouth	5	Aug
	2:07.77			5	Dessau, GER	1	Aug
2:07.2	Heidi Smith		20.05.74	1	Stretford	18	Aug
2:07.56	Rachel Jordan		29.01.72	2	Cork, IRE	27	Jun
2:07.56	Rachel Buller	U23	31.08.76	5	Solihull	5	Sep
2:07.62	Dianne Henaghan		6.08.65	1	Cudworth	2	Aug
2:07.99	Hayley Parkinson		5.12.75	1	Birmingham	6	Jun
	(20)						
2:08.01	Carolyn Smith	U23	3.10.77	2	Liverpool	20	Jun
2:08.01	Christa Salt		17.06.64	2rB	Lausanne, SWZ	25	Aug
2:08.11	Tanya Baker		23.11.74	4	Princeton, USA	2	May
2:08.2	Faith Aston		26.11.75	1	Stretford	19	May
2:08.2	Alex Carter	U20	1.04.80	3	Stretford	18	Aug
2:08.30	Helen Pattinson		2.01.74	6	Cardiff	15	Jul
2:08.4	Kerry Smithson	U23	13.09.76	2	Stretford	19	May
2:08.4 mx	Pauline Quinn/Thom		2.08.70	1	Belfast	26	Aug
	2:09.06			3	Tullamore, IRE	9	Aug
2:08.44	Julie Mitchell		3.10.74	7	Cardiff	15	Jul
2:08.58	Kelly McNeice	U23	17.06.78	1	Dublin (S), IRE	3	May
	(30)						
2:08.6	Jillian Jones		23.12.69	2	Watford	15	Aug
2:08.6	Amanda Parkinson		21.07.71	4	Stretford	18	Aug
2:08.7	Ellen O'Hare	U23	4.02.78	1	Oxford	16	May
2:08.85	Sharon King		27.01.72	4	Loughborough	17	May
2:09.4	Paula Fryer		14.07.69	1r2	Stretford	18	Aug
2:09.6	Esther Casson		24.11.75	2	Oxford	16	May
2:09.6 mx	Kelly Brownhill	U20	27.03.80	1	Stretford	1	Sep
	2:12.15			4	Bedford	29	Aug
2:09.61	Emma Brady		3.01.74	1r2	Cardiff	15	Jul
2:09.7	Rachael Ogden	U20	23.07.79	3	Loughborough	10	Jun
2:09.76	Sue Parker/Lamb		24.03.70	5	Liverpool	20	Jun
	(40)						
2:09.86 i	Shirley Griffiths		23.06.72	1	Birmingham	4	Jan
	2:10.6			4	Cudworth	9	May
2:09.96	Sonya Bowyer		18.09.72	3h1	Bedford	24	May
2:09.99 i	Joanna Ross	U20	18.02.81	1	Glasgow	18	Jan
	2:10.43			1	Glasgow	9	May
2:10.06 i	Gowry Retchakan	V35	21.06.60	2	Birmingham	4	Jan
2:10.06	Alison Potts		15.10.74	1r2	Birmingham	6	Jun
2:10.09	Sarah Knights		25.02.67	3	Watford	21	Jun
2:10.10	Candy Perkins		26.02.71	4	Watford	21	Jun
2:10.17	Sarah Mead	U20	16.10.79	4h2	Birmingham	24	Jul
2:10.5 mx	Catherine Riley	U17	4.06.82	1	Stretford	28	Apr
	2:11.9			2rB	Manchester	3	Jun
2:10.5	Karen McPherson		6.11.72	4	Stretford	14	Jul
	(50)						
2:10.52	Vickie Lawrence		9.06.73	2	Palma de Mallorca, SPA	28	May
2:10.6	Sally Evans		14.05.75	2r2	Watford	5	Aug
2:10.69	Diana Bennett		14.06.74	H	Wrexham	2	Aug
2:10.90	Alexandra Ercolani		18.08.75	4	Birmingham	6	Jun
2:10.9	Jenny Brown		27.02.70	1	Southampton	13	Sep
2:11.01	Georgie Parnell	U17	22.06.82	3	Dublin (S), IRE	8	Aug
2:11.1 mx	Claire Entwistle	U23	9.12.76	2	Stretford	4	Aug
2:11.21	Lisa Dobriskey	U15	23.12.83	1	London (Ha)	24	May
2:11.21	Lynne Gallagher		21.11.74	2r2	Cardiff	15	Jul
2:11.3	Sarah Damm		12.09.70	1	Leamington	9	May
	(60)						
2:11.36	Philippa McCrea	U23	1.03.78	2	Gateshead	29	Aug
2:11.4	Sarah Bull		4.06.75	2	Ashford	16	Aug
2:11.54	Jeina Mitchell		21.01.75	6	Birmingham	18	Jul
2:11.65	Simone Hardy	U20	9.11.79	8	Swindon	24	Jun

2:11.67	Mary McClung		19.12.71	3	Edinburgh	18	Jul
2:11.80 i	Jennifer Ward	U23	22.09.78	2h1	Birmingham	7	Feb
2:11.83	Jayne Puckeridge		23.10.71	5h3	Birmingham	24	Jul
2:11.97	Emily Hathaway	U20	22.12.79	1	Exeter	11	Jul
2:11.97	Karen Johns	U20	18.08.80	2	Exeter	11	Jul
2:12.00	Dawn Gandy		28.07.65	3	Bedford	29	Aug
	(70)						
2:12.0	Emma Ward	U17	2.01.82	1	Stoke	9	Aug
	2:12.08			1	Bedford	5	Jul
2:12.0	Joanne Colleran		1.09.72	1r2	Liverpool	16	Aug
2:12.02	Sharon Whitby	U20	29.09.80	3	Exeter	11	Jul
2:12.04	Olivia Hines	U15	19.10.83	2	London (Ha)	24	May
2:12.1	Sharon York-Morris		5.07.68	2	Ware	22	Aug
2:12.18	Vicki Andrews		31.08.69	1	Birmingham	23	Aug
2:12.20	Ruth Eddy		9.07.75	4h2	Watford	20	Jun
2:12.23	Charlotte Goff	U23	6.07.77	4h1	Watford	20	Jun
2:12.24	Wendy Davis	U20	7.11.79	2	Bedford	5	Jul
2:12.38 i	Sarah Wells		11.08.69	3h2	Birmingham	7	Feb
	(80)						
2:12.39	Samantha Singer	U17	8.05.82	4	Bedford	5	Jul
2:12.39	Barbara Dix	U20	23.11.80	4	Exeter	11	Jul
2:12.4	Maria Carville		8.12.73	6	London (BP)	14	Jun
2:12.4	Louise Damen	U17	12.10.82	1	Bournemouth	21	Jun
2:12.4	Kelly Caffell	U20	10.02.79	1	Watford	12	Aug
2:12.52	Claire Taylor	U17	25.10.82	1	Sheffield	16	Aug
2:12.7	Helen Daniel		24.10.63	1	Ashford	9	May
2:12.7	Sarah Bouchard		23.10.74	3r2	Stretford	18	Aug
2:12.8	Lucy Field/Doughty		1.05.71	7	London (BP)	14	Jun
2:12.8 mx	Laura McCabe	U20	24.01.80	1r7	Stretford	23	Jun
	(90)						
2:12.86	Sarah Simmons		12.01.75	9	Swindon	24	Jun
2:12.9	Pauline Powell		17.05.73	1	Blackburn	3	May
2:12.9	Jacqueline Kind		24.10.68	7	Stretford	14	Jul

Additional Under 17 (1 - 6 above)

2:13.04	Carley Wilson		6.12.81	1	Gateshead	9	May
2:13.29	Lisa Samuels		24.09.81	3	Exeter	11	Jul
2:13.8	Rebecca Scotcher		2.07.82	1	Basildon	28	Jun
2:13.82	Suzanne Hasler		7.04.82	3	Solihull	24	May
	(10)						
2:14.2	Lisa Miller		13.01.83	1	Bromley	18	Jul
2:14.63	Rebecca Lyne		4.07.82	1	Cudworth	10	May
2:14.99	Jenny Short		17.12.82	6	Exeter	11	Jul
2:15.2	Nikki Daniels		25.08.82	2	Coventry	17	May
2:15.27	Barbara Parker		8.11.82	2	London (Ha)	24	May
2:15.6	Ellie Childs		26.05.83	1	Hoo	26	Apr
2:15.6	Juliet Potter		24.10.81	1rB	Street	4	May
2:15.70	Katie Brennan		27.04.82	2rC	Manchester	3	Jun
2:15.92	Stephanie Cooper		16.09.82	8	Exeter	11	Jul
2:16.32	Louise Whittaker		29.11.82	3rC	Manchester	3	Jun
	(20)						
2:16.5	Sarah Herbert		29.08.83	1	Bath	13	Jun
2:16.74	Emily Hooper		16.05.82	7	Tessenderlo, BEL	30	Aug
2:16.8	Kate Reed		28.09.82	1	Worcester	2	Jul
2:17.0	Leah Harris		24.02.82	1	Exeter	9	Aug
2:17.5	Jade Wright		9.01.83	1	Watford	3	Jun
2:17.51	Kirsty Waterson		17.12.82	6	London (He)	30	Aug
2:17.54	Amy Shaw		2.07.83	2	Cudworth	2	Aug
2:17.8	Danielle Glover		26.07.82	1	Redditch	17	May
2:17.8	Sara Ann Stevenson		12.11.82	1	Grangemouth	23	Aug

Additional Under 15 (1 - 2 above)

2:14.4	Jemma Simpson	10.02.84	1	Telford	4	Jul
2:14.45	Sarah Pickering	26.10.83	3	Exeter	11	Jul
2:14.5	Charlotte Moore	4.01.85	1	Bournemouth	2	Aug
2:15.32	Kim Searle	27.12.83	1	Cudworth	2	Aug
2:15.47	Nisha Desai	5.08.84	2	Cudworth	2	Aug
2:15.56	Katie Clark	30.09.83	1	Gateshead	29	Aug
2:15.72	Claire Robson	9.01.84	4	Sheffield	15	Aug
2:16.42	Lisa Cater	16.01.84	1	Gateshead	19	Jul
(10)						
2:16.6	Faye Fullerton	31.05.84	1	Carshalton	20	Sep
2:16.81	Holly O'Connor	9.12.83	3	Cudworth	2	Aug
2:16.86	Lucy Jones	30.11.83	2h3	Exeter	10	Jul
2:16.96	Lauren Deadman	27.03.84	3	London (Ha)	24	May
2:17.65	Sally Oldfield	25.06.84	5	Exeter	11	Jul
2:17.9	Hannah Whitmore	24.02.84	1h5	Solihull	23	May
2:18.1	Zoe Jelbert	21.01.84	1	Carn Brea	2	Aug
2:18.2	Jessica Nugent	27.08.84	1	Watford	12	Aug
2:18.37	Jennifer Tunstill	16.05.84	4	Cudworth	2	Aug
2:18.56	Hayley Mottram	22.01.84	4	London (Ha)	24	May

Under 13

2:21.4	Megan Wright	19.02.87	1	Coatbridge	30	Aug
2:22.2	Kelly Rodmell	26.11.85	2	Carlisle	Jul	
2:22.4	Lynsey Jepson	12.01.87	1	Scunthorpe	31	Aug
2:23.3	Kirsty Sammon	5.10.85	1	Bournemouth	17	May
2:24.1	Jenny Bliss	6.07.86	1	Crawley	22	Jul
2:25.4	Hayley Beard	2.12.85	1	Bromley	18	Jul
2:26.3	Michelle Jessop	21.09.85	2	Bournemouth	17	May
2:27.0	Anna Warne		1	Watford	8	Jul
2:27.14	Rachael Thompson	15.11.85	1	Birmingham	6	Sep
2:27.2	Emma Hunt	25.04.86	1	St. Albans	31	May
(10)						
2:27.3	Jenna Hill	16.10.85	3	Warrington	1	Aug
2:27.6	Katrina Wooton	2.09.85	2	St. Albans	31	May

Foreign

2:10.19	*Wilemien Changuion (RSA)*	*11.02.75*	*5h2*	*Birmingham*	*24*	*Jul*

1000 METRES

2:50.25	Christa Salt	17.06.64	1	Berne, SWZ	13	May

Under 13

3:12.7	Claire Berry	23.02.86	1	Ashford	18	Apr
3:13.3	Lucy Copley	22.09.85	1	Woking	26	Jul
3:13.5	Rebecca Keeping	17.09.85	1	Bournemouth	31	May
3:14.7	Emma Hunt	25.04.86	1	Crawley	30	Aug

1200 METRES - Under 13

3:52.9	Emma Hunt	25.04.86	1	Bournemouth	17	May
3:56.5	Michelle Jessop	21.09.85	1	Watford	28	Jun
3:57.3	Megan Wright	19.02.87	1	Dunfermline	3	May
3:59.1	Jenna Hill	16.10.85	1	Liverpool	19	Jul
4:01.2	Charlie-Jo Devlin	28.09.85	1	Blackpool	27	Sep
4:01.4	Abby Lyons	18.12.85	1	Stockport	28	Jun
4:01.8	Emma Beck	22.11.85	2	Watford	28	Jun
4:02.0	Rebecca Keeping	17.09.85	1	Bournemouth	28	Jun
4:02.5	Helen Hudson	1.10.86	1	Sheffield	26	Apr
4:03.9	Emma Hopkins	16.09.86	1	Nottingham	28	Jun

1500 METRES

4:05.81	Paula Radcliffe		17.12.73	3	Hengelo, HOL	1	Jun
4:05.92				2	St. Petersburg, RUS	28	Jun
4:06.10	Kelly Holmes		19.04.70	2	Kuala Lumpur, MAL	21	Sep
4:10.68	Amanda Crowe		21.10.73	6	Kuala Lumpur, MAL	21	Sep
4:12.11				2	Gateshead	19	Jul
4:12.61	Helen Pattinson		2.01.74	9	Kuala Lumpur, MAL	21	Sep
4:12.87				2	Birmingham	25	Jul
4:14.53				5	Gateshead	19	Jul
4:14.84				5	Hechtel, BEL	1	Aug
4:15.0				1	Stretford	1	Sep
4:17.05				2	Solihull	5	Sep
4:17.31				3	Budapest, HUN	5	Jul
4:17.51				1	Swindon	24	Jun
4:17.52				3	Rhede, GER	17	Jun
4:17.85				1	Manchester	3	Jun
4:12.72	Lynn Gibson		6.07.69	1	Birmingham	25	Jul
4:13.35				10	Kuala Lumpur, MAL	21	Sep
4:14.72				6	Gateshead	19	Jul
4:14.84				1	Solihull	5	Sep
4:18.17				2	Manchester	3	Jun
4:13.55	Angela Davies		21.10.70	3	Birmingham	25	Jul
4:14.10				3	Hechtel, BEL	1	Aug
4:14.36				4	Gateshead	19	Jul
4:16.1				1	Watford	26	Aug
4:16.37				1	Jona, SWZ	12	Jul
4:16.84				1	Rhede, GER	19	Jun
4:18.1				1	Loughborough	10	Jun
4:14.19	Amanda Parkinson		21.07.71	4	Birmingham	25	Jul
4:16.60				8	Gateshead	19	Jul
4:19.96				4	Solihull	5	Sep
4:16.75	Debbie Gunning		31.08.65	2	Jona, SWZ	12	Jul
4:19.21				5	Birmingham	25	Jul
4:19.49				2	Watford	21	Jun
4:17.6	Kerry Smithson	U23	13.09.76	2	Stretford	1	Sep
4:18.2				1	Watford	5	Aug
4:18.17	Joanne Colleran		1.09.72	2	Dedham, USA	23	May
4:19.0 mx				1	Stretford	18	Aug
4:19.4				3	Stretford	1	Sep
4:19.59				3	Solihull	5	Sep
	(10)						
4:18.24	Andrea Whitcombe		8.06.71	1	Watford	21	Jun
4:19.96	Diane Modahl		17.06.66	2	Cape Town, RSA	20	Mar
41 performances to 4:20.0 by 12 athletes							
4:20.3	Shirley Griffiths		23.06.72	3	Watford	5	Aug
4:20.37	Susan Scott	U23	26.09.77	7	Birmingham	25	Jul
4:20.5	Sharon York-Morris		5.07.68	5	Watford	5	Aug
4:20.61	Jillian Jones		23.12.69	1	Cardiff	15	Jul
4:20.7	Sarah Young		2.01.70	1	Stretford	4	Aug
4:20.9	Sue Parker/Lamb		24.03.70	6	Watford	5	Aug
4:21.02	Sarah Bull		4.06.75	8	Birmingham	25	Jul
4:21.27	Hayley Parkinson		5.12.75	3h1	Birmingham	24	Jul
	(20)						
4:21.6 mx	Sonya Bowyer		18.09.72		Stretford	14	Jul
4:27.03				9h1	Birmingham	24	Jul
4:21.86	Ellen O'Hare	U23	4.02.78	4	Cardiff	15	Jul
4:22.2	Sarah Bentley		21.05.67	2	Watford	15	Aug
4:22.31	Pauline Quinn/Thom		2.08.70	4	Dublin (S), IRE	26	Jul
4:22.79	Sharon King		27.01.72	5	Cardiff	15	Jul
4:22.92	Julie Mitchell		3.10.74	5h2	Birmingham	24	Jul
4:22.96	Jilly Ingman	U23	17.08.78	9	Birmingham	25	Jul

4:23.0	Jenny Brown		27.02.70	1	Watford	9	Sep
4:23.40	Michelle Wannell		12.07.67	7	Swindon	24	Jun
4:23.5	Caroline Pimblett		28.01.75	2	Stretford	23	Jun
	(30)						
4:23.53	Bev Hartigan		10.06.67	2	Birmingham	6	Jun
4:23.7	Lucy Wright		17.11.69	2	Stretford	4	Aug
4:24.08	Tara Krzywicki		9.03.74	7	Solihull	5	Sep
4:24.2	Maria Carville		8.12.73	10	Watford	5	Aug
4:24.44	Wendy Farrow		25.12.71	1	Loughborough	17	May
4:24.5	Liz Talbot		5.12.74	1	Kingston	27	Jun
4:25.1	Caroline Walsh	U20	29.04.80	6	Watford	15	Aug
4:25.2 mx	Lucy Field/Doughty		1.05.71	1	Cwmbran	10	Jun
	4:25.52			4	Manchester	3	Jun
4:25.3	Alex Carter	U20	1.04.80	4	Stretford	23	Jun
4:25.56	Mara Myers		13.08.73	5	Watford	21	Jun
	(40)						
4:25.6	Karen McPherson		6.11.72	5	Stretford	23	Jun
4:25.65	Dianne Henaghan		6.08.65	5	Manchester	3	Jun
4:25.9	Sheila Fairweather	U23	24.11.77	7	Watford	15	Aug
4:26.10	Vikki McPherson		1.06.71	4	Edinburgh	18	Jul
4:26.2	Heather Heasman		27.09.63	2	Wigan	31	May
4:26.52	Tanya Baker		23.11.74		Holmdel, USA	11	Jun
4:27.44	Christa Salt		17.06.64	2	Yutz, SWZ	30	May
4:27.68	Vicky Sterne		12.10.68	10	Manchester	3	Jun
4:27.70	Lucy Elliott		9.03.66	5	Vilamoura, POR	30	May
4:27.75	Tommy Kemp	U20	5.03.80	4	Loughborough	17	May
	(50)						
4:27.81	Jane Groves	U23	17.05.77	12	Manchester	3	Jun
4:27.90	Emma Ford	U23	16.02.77	3	Bath	4	May
4:28.2	Dawn Hargan		14.04.71	1	Antrim	24	May
4:28.46	Julie Stacey		15.11.72	3	Bedford	25	May
4:28.96	Val Bothams		19.03.75	13	Manchester	3	Jun
4:29.1	Debbie Sullivan		24.01.72	1	Enfield	23	Aug
4:29.2	Charlotte Mayock		11.12.73	2	Tempe, USA	28	Mar
4:29.34	Sarah Salmon		9.09.74	1	Mississippi, USA	18	Apr
4:29.5 mx	Michelle Faherty		10.08.68	12rB	Stretford	14	Jul
4:29.79	Kelly Caffell	U20	10.02.79	2	London (Ha)	23	May
	(60)						
4:30.10	Penny Thackray		18.08.74	9	Swindon	24	Jun
4:30.1	Karen Hargrave		23.09.65		Rennes, FRA	26	Apr
4:30.24 i	Caroline Slimin		27.08.65	4	Birmingham	8	Feb
4:30.3	Ann Terek		22.09.64	1	Antrim	25	Apr
4:30.34	Rachel Jordan		29.01.72	2r2	Birmingham	6	Jun
4:30.52	Zahara Hyde/Hyde-Peters	V35	12.01.63	1	College Station, USA	9	May
4:30.6	Rachel Buller	U23	31.08.76	1	Cambridge	1	Aug
4:31.03	Rebecca Lovett	U23	11.05.78	9	Loughborough	17	May
4:31.45	Tanya Povey	U20	13.04.79		Columbia, USA	18	Apr
4:31.50	Rachel Jones		7.01.70	4	Liverpool	20	Jun
	(70)						
4:31.53	Hayley Yelling		3.01.74	1r2	Swindon	24	Jun
4:32.13	Amber Gascoigne	U20	5.09.79	2r2	Swindon	24	Jun
4:32.7	Candy Perkins		26.02.71	2	Ashford	16	Aug
4:32.7	Elizabeth Proctor		31.10.72	8	Stretford	1	Sep
4:33.0	Rachael Ogden	U20	23.07.79	1	Loughborough	13	May
4:33.03	Leanne Appleton	U20	3.03.81	2	Stoke	20	Jun
4:33.21	Carley Wilson	U17	6.12.81	4	London (He)	9	Aug
4:33.32	Julie Swann	V35	15.07.62	6	Edwardsville, USA	23	May
4:33.41	Amy Stiles		6.02.75	2r2	Solihull	5	Sep
4:33.5	Vicki Andrews		31.08.69	3	Stretford	4	Aug
	(80)						
4:33.6	Andrea Kershaw	U23	22.03.78	9	Stretford	1	Sep
4:33.70	Claire Entwistle	U23	9.12.76	12h1	Birmingham	24	Jul

Additional Under 17 (1 above)

4:33.9	Louise Damen	12.10.82	1	Kingston	20	Jun
4:35.25	Emma Ward	2.01.82	1	Exeter	11	Jul
4:35.33 i	Jenny Mockler	28.08.82	1	Birmingham	22	Feb
4:41.6			1	Bebington	9	May
4:38.32	Rebecca Lyne	4.07.82	3	Exeter	11	Jul
4:38.9	Claire Taylor	25.10.82	1	Gateshead	24	Jun
4:39.10	Joanna Ankier	5.08.82	1	London (Ha)	24	May
4:39.15	Hazel Lumb	23.11.82	3	Ayr	18	Jul
4:40.1	Kate Reed	28.09.82	9rB	Watford	5	Aug
4:41.22	Sophie Koehne	17.09.81	4	Exeter	11	Jul
(10)						
4:42.13	Sarah Herbert	29.08.83	1h1	Exeter	10	Jul
4:42.59	Kirsty Waterson	17.12.82	2	London (Ha)	24	May
4:42.72	Marika Hayward	12.11.82	3	London (Ha)	24	May
4:42.83	Diana Jeffery	9.03.83	4	London (Ha)	24	May
4:43.22	Collette Fagan	6.06.82	2	Dublin (S), IRE	8	Aug
4:44.3	Helen Zenner	15.08.82	6	Street	4	May
4:44.9	Barbara Parker	8.11.82	1	Norwich	19	Jul
4:45.90	Sadie Yousefian	3.02.83	3	Cudworth	2	Aug
4:46.24	Juliet Potter	24.10.81	3h1	Sheffield	15	Aug
4:46.80	Katie Brennan	27.04.82	3	York	25	Jul
(20)						
4:47.02	Jade Wright	9.01.83	7	London (Ha)	24	May
4:47.2	Louise Aaron	19.04.82	1	Nottingham	20	Jun
4:47.7	Ava Hutchinson	30.03.83	1	Watford	27	May
4:47.87	Susan Miles	1.11.81	5h1	London (Ha)	23	May

Under 15

4:36.48	Zoe Jelbert	21.01.84	1	Exeter	11	Jul
4:37.0	Charlotte Moore	4.01.85	1	Reading	31	Aug
4:38.1	Lisa Dobriskey	23.12.83	1	Ashford	13	May
4:38.21	Jessica Nugent	27.08.84	2	Exeter	11	Jul
4:38.89	Courtney Birch	5.10.84	3	Exeter	11	Jul
4:39.45	Faye Fullerton	31.05.84	2	London (He)	30	Aug
4:43.9	Lisa Cater	16.01.84	1	Bingham	20	Jul
4:45.76	Claire Robson	9.01.84	6	Exeter	11	Jul
4:46.79	Katie Clark	30.09.83	1	Cudworth	2	Aug
4:47.30	Vicki Turner	30.09.83	1h2	Exeter	10	Jul
(10)						
4:48.2	Helen Lee	10.12.84	1	London (Nh)	27	Jun
4:48.2	Alexa Joel	19.09.83	2	London (Nh)	27	Jun
4:48.47	Kim Searle	27.12.83	3	York	25	Jul
4:48.50	Victoria Leak	28.11.83	3h3	Exeter	10	Jul
4:48.6	Lucy Thomas	2.11.84	1	Swindon	19	Jul
4:49.34	Nisha Desai	5.08.84	1	Gateshead	9	May
4:49.7	Lauren Deadman	27.03.84	2	London (Nh)	4	May
4:50.0	Freya Murray	20.09.83	1	Grangemouth	11	Jul

Under 13

4:56.5	Emma Hunt	25.04.86	1	Watford	27	May
5:00.4	Toni Nally		2	Kingston	26	Jul
5:01.5	Michelle Jessop	21.09.85	1	London (WL)	24	May
5:03.0	Megan Wright	19.02.87	1	Dunfermline	4	Jun
5:03.9	Katrina Wooton	2.09.85	2	Luton	18	Jul
5:04.3	Lynsey Jepson	12.01.87	1	Solihull	26	Jul
5:05.1	Lucy Copley	22.09.85	3	Kingston	26	Jul
5:07.8	Cheryl Guiney	24.09.85	1	Belfast	13	Aug
5:08.1	Rebecca Gillespie	29.09.85	1	Carn Brea	21	Jul

Foreign

4:25.11	*Natalie Harvey (AUS)*	*17.01.75*	*1*	*Bedford*	*25*	*May*
4:26.9	*Wilemien Changuion (RSA)*	*11.02.75*	*1*	*Watford*	*29*	*Jul*

1 MILE

4:28.04	Kelly Holmes		19.04.70	1	Glasgow (S)	30	Aug
4:31.72	Paula Radcliffe		17.12.73	2	Glasgow (S)	30	Aug
4:32.99	Amanda Crowe		21.10.73	3	Glasgow (S)	30	Aug
4:44.11	Charlotte Mayock		11.12.73	5	Philadelphia, USA	25	Apr
4:44.16 i	Shirley Griffiths		23.06.72	3	Roxbury, USA	20	Feb
4:46.42 i	Sarah Salmon		9.09.74	1	Fort Worth, USA	21	Feb
4:47.08 i	Tanya Blake		16.01.71	3	Fairfax, USA	14	Feb
	4:47.50			10	Philadelphia, USA	25	Apr

2000 METRES

5:44.58 +	Paula Radcliffe	17.12.73	1m	Sheffield	2	Aug
5:59.0 +e	Sarah Young	2.01.70	7m	Sheffield	2	Aug
6:12.4	Dianne Henaghan	6.08.65	1	Jarrow	20	Apr

3000 METRES

8:38.84	Paula Radcliffe		17.12.73	1	Sheffield	2	Aug
	9:08.83 +			m	St. Petersburg, RUS	27	Jun
	9:12.54 +			m	Lisbon, POR	4	Apr
8:58.2	Joanne Pavey		20.09.73	1	Street	4	May
	9:12.10			10	Hengelo, HOL	1	Jun
9:04.27	Sarah Young		2.01.70	7	Sheffield	2	Aug
	9:08.6 mx			1	Stretford	18	Aug
	9:10.7			2	Street	4	May
9:10.23	Kelly Holmes		19.04.70	1	Bedford	22	Aug
9:10.7 mx	Andrea Whitcombe		8.06.71	1	Brighton	19	Aug
	9:14.9			1	Watford	1	Jul
9:15.25	Liz Talbot		5.12.74	1	Swindon	24	Jun
9:16.1 mx	Lucy Wright		17.11.69	2	Stretford	18	Aug
	9:16.93			8	Sheffield	2	Aug
9:16.5 mx	Heather Heasman	V35	27.09.63	1	Stretford	19	May
9:16.6	Debbie Gunning		31.08.65	3	Street	4	May
	9:17.39			2	Swindon	24	Jun
9:17.03	Angela Davies		21.10.70	7	St. Petersburg, RUS	28	Jun
	(10)						
9:18.6 mx	Caroline Pimblett		28.01.75	1	Stretford	14	Jul
	9:40.67			1	Birmingham	6	Jun
9:19.4 mx	Jilly Ingman	U23	17.08.78	2	Stretford	14	Jul
	9:35.96			1	Hexham	14	Jun
	20 performances to 9:20.0 by 12 athletes						
9:21.2 mx	Vikki McPherson		1.06.71	3	Stretford	18	Aug
	9:35.41 +			m	Birmingham	25	Jul
9:21.54	Tara Krzywicki		9.03.74	1	Loughborough	17	May
9:22.45	Sue Parker/Lamb		24.03.70	1	Bedford	29	Aug
9:22.72	Birhan Dagne	U23	7.10.77	9	Sheffield	2	Aug
	not elgible to compete for Britain (applies to other lists)						
9:22.87	Helen Pattinson		2.01.74	2	Loughborough	17	May
9:23.38	Sheila Fairweather	U23	24.11.77	3	Loughborough	17	May
9:23.79	Sarah Bentley		21.05.67	2	Bedford	29	Aug
9:24.26	Katie Skorupska	U23	3.11.78	3	Bedford	29	Aug
	(20)						
9:24.60	Lynn Gibson		6.07.69	4	Loughborough	17	May
9:25.95	Amber Gascoigne	U20	5.09.79	5	Loughborough	17	May
9:26.3	Amy Waterlow	U23	29.07.78	1	Watford	15	Aug
9:27.01 i	Emma Ford	U23	16.02.77	2	Glasgow	15	Mar
9:27.8	Michelle Wannell		12.07.67	4	Street	4	May
9:28.64	Louise Kelly	U20	20.09.80	3	Alicante, SPA	18	Jul
9:29.0 mx	Kerry Smithson	U23	13.09.76	5	Stretford	18	Aug
9:29.47 mx	Hayley Nash	V35	30.05.63	1	Cardiff	15	Jul
9:31.69	Zahara Hyde/Hyde-Peters	V35	12.01.63	3	Swindon	24	Jun

9:31.7	Sharon York-Morris		5.07.68	2	Kingston	27	Jun
(30)							
9:31.9	Amy Stiles		6.02.75	7	Street	4	May
9:31.96	Jenny Brown		27.02.70	5	Tessenderlo, BEL	30	Aug
9:32.20	Bev Jenkins		6.02.70	1	Cudworth	2	Aug
9:33.03 i	Catherine Berry		8.10.75		Indianapolis, USA	7	Mar
9:41.54				3	Raleigh, USA	28	Mar
9:33.99	Angela Joiner		14.02.69	8	Loughborough	17	May
9:34.6	Hayley Yelling		3.01.74	1	Stoke	5	Jul
9:34.74	Amanda Parkinson		21.07.71	1	Sheffield	15	Aug
9:34.8	Dawn James		4.01.67	2	Watford	15	Aug
9:35.04 i	Sarah Singleton		18.12.65	1	Birmingham	22	Feb
9:36.00	Penny Thackray		18.08.74	2	Cudworth	2	Aug
(40)							
9:36.50 i	Val Bothams		19.03.75	2	Birmingham	22	Feb
9:36.6 mx	Jill Hunter/Boltz		14.10.66	1	Jarrow	27	Jun
9:36.7	Pauline Quinn/Thom		2.08.70	1	Antrim	25	Apr
9:36.90	Debbie Sullivan		24.01.72	2	Sheffield	15	Aug
9:37.3	Lucy Field/Doughty		1.05.71	9	Street	4	May
9:37.7	Shirley Griffiths		23.06.72	2	Grimsby	7	Jun
9:38.9	Mara Myers		13.08.73	1	Enfield	14	Jun
9:39.18 i	Susan Harrison		6.08.71	3	Birmingham	22	Feb
9:39.79	Charlotte Mayock		11.12.73	1	Baton Rouge, USA	18	Apr
9:40.6	Lucy Elliott		9.03.66	1	Crawley	19	Jul
(50)							
9:41.5	Pauline Powell		17.05.73	1	Blackpool	9	May
9:42.72 i	Jennifer Cox		28.11.72	4	Birmingham	22	Feb
9:42.83	Jo Smith	U23	11.04.76	10	Loughborough	17	May
9:43.3	Caroline Walsh	U20	29.04.80	3	Watford	12	Apr
9:43.54 i	Joanne Colleran		1.09.72	3	New York, USA	10	Jan
9:43.6	Amanda Wright		14.07.68	1	Gloucester	30	May
9:44.11	Jo Dering		7.02.69	3	Birmingham	6	Jun
9:44.7	Debbie Percival	V35	22.04.62	3	Kingston	27	Jun
9:44.8	Michelle Ross		31.01.72	1	Colwyn Bay	14	Jun
9:45.2	Ellen O'Hare	U23	4.02.78	1	Watford	24	Jun
(60)							
9:45.31 i	Sarah Salmon		9.09.74	13	Indianapolis, USA	14	Mar
9:45.73	Hayley Parkinson		5.12.75	5	Hexham	14	Jun
9:45.80	Caroline Thomas		3.11.72	4	Birmingham	6	Jun
9:45.94	Catriona Morrison	U23	11.01.77	5	Birmingham	6	Jun
9:46.1	Dianne Henaghan		6.08.65	1	Jarrow	15	Jul
9:47.0	Amelia Griffiths	U23	19.07.76		Gainesville, USA		
9:47.16	Kate Ramsey		17.05.68	5	Swindon	24	Jun
9:49.0 mx	Michelle Mann	U23	6.02.77	4	Stretford	14	Jul
9:49.37	Andrea Kershaw	U23	22.03.78	4	Bedford	29	Aug
9:49.97	Karen Fletcher	U20	26.09.79	1	London (He)	9	Aug
(70)							
9:50.2	Wendy Farrow		25.12.71	4	Grimsby	7	Jun
9:50.8	Ceri Grech-Thomas		16.10.70	10	Street	4	May
9:51.78 i	Carolina Weatherill		13.05.68	6	Birmingham	22	Feb
9:51.79	Jo Thompson	V35	30.10.58	8	Swindon	24	Jun
9:52.1	Louise Brown	U23	6.05.78	2	Sheffield	19	Apr
9:52.5	Caroline Herbert		30.06.70	1	Crawley	27	May
9:53.10	Tanya Povey	U20	13.04.79		Lake Buena Vista, USA	4	Apr
9:53.76 i	Catherine Dugdale		29.11.74	7	Birmingham	22	Feb
9:53.9	Astrid Wingler		21.05.68	2	Ashford	16	Aug
9:53.93 i	Elaine Foster	V35	21.07.63	2	Birmingham	25	Jan
(80)							
9:54.78	Sonia Thomas	U20	16.05.79	14	Loughborough	17	May
9:55.1	Lisa Moody	U23	22.02.77	2	Grangemouth	5	Aug
9:55.20	Sharon Hatch		5.09.64	1	Belfast	17	Jun

9:55.71	Sue Reinsford		24.03.69	1	Bedford	14	Jun
9:55.93 i	Nikki Kearney		20.05.73	8	Birmingham	22	Feb
9:59.7				1	Reading	30	May
9:56.0	Julie Stacey		15.11.72	1	Hoo	3	May
9:56.13	Louise Damen	U17	12.10.82	16	Tessenderlo, BEL	30	Aug
9:56.2	Jenny Clague		6.08.73	1	Basildon	7	Jun
9:56.2	Rebecca Everett	U20	10.03.80	6	Watford	15	Aug
9:56.77	Paula Gowing	U23	31.05.78	15	Loughborough	17	May
(90)							
9:56.9	Meryl Dodd		12.04.69	1	Barnsley	9	Aug
9:57.2	Tracy Brindley		25.08.72	1	Aberdeen	9	Jun
9:57.22	Emma Brooker	U23	26.10.78	16	Loughborough	17	May
9:57.4	Clare Campbell	U20	21.10.80	2	Watford	13	May
9:59.4	Miranda Heathcote		18.09.72	1	London (Elt)	30	May
9:59.4	Kathryn Waugh		20.02.73	1	Stretford	1	Sep
9:59.9	Jodie Swallow	U20	23.06.81	1	Colchester	13	Jun
9:59.9	Lisa Webb		9.10.65	2	Enfield	23	Aug

Under 17 (1 above)

10:07.4	Louise Whittaker	29.11.82	1	Stretford	4	Aug
10:08.1	Juliet Potter	24.10.81	1	Mansfield	8	Aug
10:08.40	Kirsty Waterson	17.12.82	2	Exeter	11	Jul
10:10.75	Henrietta Freeman	12.07.83	3	Exeter	11	Jul
10:11.12	Hattie Dean	2.02.82	4	Exeter	11	Jul
10:22.2	Collette Fagan	6.06.82	1	Coatbridge	29	Aug
10:23.11	Ursula Counsell	7.12.82	1	Birmingham	23	Aug
10:25.2	Sarah Raven	22.11.82	2	Watford	3	Jun
10:25.61	Verity Spear	12.04.82	5	Exeter	11	May
(10)						
10:26.2	Jenny Mockler	28.08.82	1	Blackpool	26	Apr
10:28.4	Susan Miles	1.11.81	1	London (He)	13	Jun
10:28.6	Gemma Viney	7.01.83	1	Watford	9	Sep
10:29.2	Gemma Taylor	18.09.82	1	Gateshead	13	Jun
10:30.3	Sadie Yousefian	3.02.83	1	Stretford	28	Jun
10:33.7	Louise Aaron	19.04.82	1	Oldham	19	Jul
10:37.79	Nichola Coates	24.03.82	1	Gateshead	9	May
10:41.3	Jill Shannon	23.04.82	2	Antrim	29	May
10:41.5	Jill Christie	16.07.82	1	Watford	12	Apr
10:42.2	Victoria Kenny	3.04.83	1	Watford	26	Aug

Foreign

8:59.4 mx	*Natalie Harvey (AUS)*	*17.01.75*	*1*	*London (TB)*	*3*	*Jun*
9:50.82	*Kelley Wilder (USA)*	*30.07.71*	*7*	*Swindon*	*24*	*Jun*

2 MILES

9:49.62	Sarah Young	2.01.70	8	Cork, IRE	27	Jun
9:58.92	Lucy Wright	17.11.69	12	Cork, IRE	27	Jun
10:11.81	Vikki McPherson	1.06.71	13	Cork, IRE	27	Jun

5000 METRES

14:51.27	Paula Radcliffe	17.12.73	2	Stockholm, SWE	5	Aug
15:06.87			1	St. Petersburg, RUS	27	Jun
15:06.96			4	St. Denis, FRA	4	Jun
15:22.76 +			1m	Lisbon, POR	4	Apr
15:43.03	Andrea Whitcombe	8.06.71	1	Birmingham	25	Jul
15:53.43			3	Manchester	3	Jun
15:56.85			2	Kuala Lumpur, MAL	17	Sep
15:45.08	Sarah Young	2.01.70	2	Birmingham	25	Jul
15:53.81			4	Manchester	3	Jun
15:59.79			5	Kuala Lumpur, MAL	17	Sep
16:29.89			1	Liverpool	20	Jun

15:48.1 mx	Tara Krzywicki		9.03.74	1	Watford	5	Aug
15:53.28				3	Birmingham	25	Jul
16:00.1				1	London (BP)	14	Jun
16:00.84				6	Manchester	3	Jun
16:12.2				1	Birmingham	23	Aug
16:21.26				1	Bath	3	May
15:50.59	Angela Davies		21.10.70	1	Manchester	3	Jun
15:50.85	Liz Talbot		5.12.74	7	Hechtel, BEL	1	Aug
15:52.61				2	Manchester	3	Jun
16:06.88				8	Birmingham	25	Jul
15:55.81	Birhan Dagne	U23	7.10.77	4	Birmingham	25	Jul
16:05.54				3	Chiba, JAP	23	Nov
16:22.8				1	London (CP)	8	Jul
15:56.04	Vikki McPherson		1.06.71	5	Birmingham	25	Jul
16:07.7 mx				1	Southampton	7	Jul
15:57.24	Heather Heasman		27.09.63	5	Manchester	3	Jun
16:08.32				9	Birmingham	25	Jul
15:57.45	Amy Waterlow	U23	29.07.78	6	Birmingham	25	Jul
16:19.72				10	Manchester	3	Jun
16:27.47				3	Bath	3	May
(10)							
15:59.51	Lucy Wright		17.11.69	7	Birmingham	25	Jul
16:03.30				7	Manchester	3	Jun
16:20.5				2	Birmingham	23	Aug
16:01.41	Lynne MacDougall		18.02.65	7	Turku, FIN	1	Jul
16:04.10				4	Prague, CZE	8	Jun
16:21.8				1	Glasgow	11	Aug
16:07.34	Sheila Fairweather	U23	24.11.77	8	Manchester	3	Jun
16:23.39				2	Bath	3	May
16:10.08	Debbie Gunning		31.08.65	9	Manchester	3	Jun
16:15.36	Louise Kelly	U20	20.09.80	7h2	Annecy, FRA	31	Jul
16:20.51				10	Annecy, FRA	2	Aug
16:25.50	Mara Myers		13.08.73	10	Birmingham	25	Jul
16:29.57	Penny Thackray		18.08.74	11	Manchester	3	Jun
	44 performances to 16:30.0 by 17 athletes						
16:31.00	Emma Ford	U23	16.02.77	2	Liverpool	20	Jun
16:33.57	Angela Joiner		14.02.69	5	Vilamoura, POR	30	May
16:34.51	Caroline Pimblett		28.01.75	13	Manchester	3	Jun
(20)							
16:35.05	Hayley Nash	V35	30.05.63	12	Birmingham	25	Jul
16:35.86	Jilly Ingman	U23	17.08.78	3	Dessau, GER	1	Aug
16:37.03	Dawn James		4.01.67	13	Birmingham	25	Jul
16:42.87	Katie Skorupska	U23	3.11.78	9	Prague, CZE	8	Jun
16:43.02	Hayley Yelling		3.01.74	14	Birmingham	25	Jul
16:44.63	Tracy Brindley		25.08.72	15	Birmingham	25	Jul
16:47.10	Catriona Morrison	U23	11.01.77	1	Glasgow (S)	10	May
16:49.0	Zahara Hyde/Hyde-Peters	V35	12.01.63	1	Dedham, USA	6	Jun
16:49.50	Jo Smith	U23	11.04.76	4	Bath	3	May
16:50.8 mx	Jo Thompson	V35	30.10.58	2	Cwmbran	10	Jun
(30)							
16:52.5	Caroline Herbert		30.06.70	3	London (BP)	14	Jun
16:52.6 mx	Michelle Wannell		12.07.67	3	Cwmbran	10	Jun
17:05.40				19	Birmingham	25	Jul
16:53.65	Amy Stiles		6.02.75	14	Manchester	3	Jun
16:54.91	Debbie Sullivan		24.01.72	17	Birmingham	25	Jul
16:56.97	Fiona Lothian		2.12.65	2	Edinburgh	18	Jul
16:58.87	Tanya Povey	U20	13.04.79	13	Philadelphia, USA	23	Apr
17:00.15	Lindsay Cairns		1.06.71	4	Edinburgh	18	Jul
17:02.53	Jenny Clague		6.08.73	4	Liverpool	20	Jun
17:04.06	Louise Watson		13.12.71	18	Birmingham	25	Jul
17:07.39	Sarah Bradbury	V35	25.02.63	3	Poznan, POL	7	Sep

17:07.86	Meryl Dodd		12.04.69	20	Birmingham	25	Jul
17:09.8	Karen Fletcher	U20	26.09.79	4	Birmingham	23	Aug
17:10.2	Liz Francis-Thomas		22.12.63	5	Birmingham	23	Aug
17:14.03	Jane Groves	U23	17.05.77	6	Bath	3	May
17:15.53	Ann MacPhail		3.05.70	7	Edinburgh	18	Jul
17:16.8	Kate Ramsey		17.05.68	6	Birmingham	23	Aug
17:17.1	Alison Fletcher	V35	8.06.61	1	Enfield	2	Aug
17:22.97	Amber Gascoigne	U20	5.09.79	15	Manchester	3	Jun
17:23.9	Nicky Haines-Jones		21.05.65	4	Cwmbran	10	Jun
17:28.05	Louise Brown	U23	6.05.78	16	Manchester	3	Jun
	(50)						
17:29.06	Sharon Hatch		5.09.64	7	Dublin (S), IRE	25	Jul
17:29.18	Jessica Turnbull		4.07.75	7	Bath	3	May

Foreign
| *17:30.2* | *Kelley Wilder (USA)* | | *30.07.71* | *4* | *London (BP)* | *14* | *Jun* |

10000 METRES

30:48.58	Paula Radcliffe		17.12.73	2	Lisbon, POR	4	Apr
31:36.51				5	Budapest, HUN	19	Aug
32:38.48	Vikki McPherson		1.06.71	8	Lisbon, POR	4	Apr
34:05.11				4	Kuala Lumpur, MAL	20	Sep
33:30.27	Angela Joiner		14.02.69	15	Lisbon, POR	4	Apr
33:59.69	Sarah Bentley		21.05.67	17	Lisbon, POR	4	Apr
34:16.89	Sally Goldsmith	V35	18.01.61	3	Camaiore, ITA	3	May
34:21.91	Bev Hartigan		10.06.67	18	Lisbon, POR	4	Apr
34:28.8	Hayley Nash	V35	30.05.63	1	Barry	24	Jun
	9 performances to 34:30.0 by 7 athletes						
34:31.41	Tanya Povey	U20	13.04.79	7	Amherst, USA	3	Jun
34:37.04	Tara Krzywicki		9.03.74	1	Bedford	5	Jul
34:38.11	Birhan Dagne	U23	7.10.77	1	Palafrugell, SPA	26	May
	(10)						
34:39.98	Sheila Fairweather	U23	24.11.77	1	Bath	4	May
34:40.00	Katie Skorupska	U23	3.11.78	2	Bath	4	May
34:48.57	Penny Thackray		18.08.74	3	Bath	4	May
34:53.57	Mara Myers		13.08.73	4	Bedford	5	Jul
34:55.25	Jill Hunter/Boltz		14.10.66	5	Bedford	5	Jul
35:09.92	Miranda Heathcote		18.09.72	1	Bedford	24	May
35:14.76	Dawn James		4.01.67	6	Bedford	5	Jul
35:24.46	Zahara Hyde/Hyde-Peters	V35	12.01.63	7	Bedford	5	Jul
35:26.2 mx	Frances Gill	V35	13.01.60	1	Neath	20	May
35:33.72	Louise Watson		13.12.71	8	Bedford	5	Jul
	(20)						
35:46.42	Jo Thompson	V35	30.10.58	9	Bedford	5	Jul
35:53.04	Amy Stiles		6.02.75	3	Bedford	24	May
36:06.37	Debbie Sullivan		24.01.72	11	Bedford	5	Jul
36:45.26	Kate Ramsey		17.05.68	12	Bedford	5	Jul

10 KILOMETRES ROAD

33:02	Lucy Elliott		9.03.66	1	Totton	19	Apr
33:05	Marian Sutton		7.10.63	3	Mobile, USA	28	Mar
33:08				1	Swansea	6	Sep
33:10				1	Cardiff	27	Sep
33:05	Yvonne Murray-Mooney		4.10.64	1	Leeds	6	Dec
33:13	Liz McColgan		24.05.64	1	Belfast	6	Jun
33:22	Bev Hartigan		10.06.67	1	Crewe	3	May
33:32				4	Glasgow	17	May
33:23	Heather Heasman	V35	27.09.63	1	Basingstoke	18	Oct
33:28	Debbie Percival	V35	22.04.62	1	London (SP)	6	Sep
33:57				1	Eastleigh	15	Mar

33:32	Lynne MacDougall		18.02.65	1	Dewsbury	8 Feb
33:34	Birhan Dagne	U23	7.10.77	2	Dewsbury	8 Feb
	33:35			2	Cardiff	27 Sep
	33:36			2	Swansea	6 Sep
	33:46			5	Glasgow	17 May
33:37	Sarah Bentley		21.05.67	3	Dewsbury	8 Feb
	33:47			1	Birchwood	23 Aug
	(10)					
33:56	Helen Pattinson		2.01.74	1	Barnsley	1 Nov
33:57	Angharad Mair	V35	30.03.61	1	Pencoed	2 Aug
	20 performances to 34:00 by 12 athletes					
34:06	Miranda Heathcote		18.09.72	2	Barnsley	1 Nov
34:08	Jo Thompson	V35	30.10.58	2	Basingstoke	18 Oct
34:15	Sue Reinsford		24.03.69	1	Cranfield	7 Jun
34:17	Penny Thackray		18.08.74	5	Dewsbury	8 Feb
34:18	Wendy Jones	V35	10.03.62	1	Bourton	2 Feb
34:22	Caroline Herbert		30.06.70	2	Totton	18 Apr
34:23	Alison Wyeth		26.05.64	3	Swansea	6 Sep
34:28	Amy Waterlow	U23	29.07.78	2	Birchwood	23 Aug
	(20)					
34:29	Jill Hunter/Boltz		14.10.66	1	Darlington	30 Aug
34:29	Hayley Yelling		3.01.74	3	Basingstoke	18 Oct
34:30	Lucy Wright		17.11.69	3	Cardiff	27 Sep
34:32	Wendy Farrow		25.12.71	6	Dewsbury	8 Feb
34:33	Tara Krzywicki		9.03.74	1	Shepshed	1 Nov
34:34	Vicky Pincombe		19.06.66	1	Taunton	27 Sep
34:43	Maria Bradley	V35	2.01.63	1	Chichester	8 Feb
34:48	Tracy Swindell		8.11.66	1	Peterborough	13 Apr
34:48	Sheila Fairweather	U23	24.11.77	1	Helensburgh	21 May
34:49	Dawn James		4.01.67	2	Eastleigh	15 Mar
	(30)					
34:50	Steph Forrester			1	Sheffield	29 Nov
34:54	Caroline Horne	V40	7.11.56	1	Datchet	27 Jun
34:55	Rita Quill		12.03.67	2	Silverstone	28 Apr
34:55	Chaanah Fothergill/Patton		22.02.72	2	Sheffield	29 Nov
34:57	Evelyn Grant		22.01.64	7	Dewsbury	8 Feb
34:57	Zahara Hyde/Hyde-Peters	V35	12.01.63	1	Yateley	5 Aug
34:59	Michelle Wannell		12.07.67	4	Totton	19 Apr
34:59	Michelle Ross		31.01.72	2	Crewe	3 May

Relay Leg

| 33:53 | Marian Sutton | | 7.10.63 | | Yokohama, JAP | 1 Feb |
| 33:13 | Jo Thompson | V40 | 30.10.58 | 8 | Chiba, JAP | 23 Nov |

Short (236m)

| 34:04 sh | Fiona Lothian | | 2.12.65 | 1 | Glasgow | 7 Mar |
| 34:54 sh | Sandra Branney | V40 | 30.04.54 | 2 | Glasgow | 7 Mar |

Foreign

| *33:52* | *Teresa Duffy (IRE)* | | *6.07.69* | *1* | *Belfast* | *5 Sep* |
| *34:12* | *Anne Buckley (IRE)* | | *20.06.67* | *4* | *Dewsbury* | *8 Feb* |

15 KILOMETRES ROAD

49:34	Liz McColgan		24.05.64	2	Tampa, USA	14 Feb
51:12	Marian Sutton		7.10.63	5	Tampa, USA	14 Feb
54:10	Tracy Swindell		8.11.66	13	Tampa, USA	14 Feb

intermediate time

| 50:35 + | Alison Wyeth | | 26.05.64 | | The hague, HOL | 29 Mar |

10 MILES ROAD

| 53:31 | Marian Sutton | | 7.10.63 | 2 | Washington, USA | 5 Apr |
| | 54:17 | | | 1 | Portsmouth | 13 Sep |

53:55	Birhan Dagne	U23	7.10.77	1	Newry	20 Sep
	54:43			2	Portsmouth	13 Sep
54:30	Alison Wyeth		26.05.64	1	Woking	1 Mar
	55:55			1	Erewash	23 Aug
	55:59			5	Newry	20 Sep
54:32	Jo Thompson	V35	30.10.58	2	Newry	20 Sep
	55:47			4	Portsmouth	13 Sep
55:05	Liz Talbot		5.12.74	3	Portsmouth	13 Sep
55:19	Angharad Mair	V35	30.03.61	1	Brecon	26 Jul
55:58	Lynne MacDougall		18.02.65	1	Sale	2 Aug
55:59	Maria Bradley	V35	2.01.63	2	Erewash	23 Aug
56:07	Miranda Heathcote		18.09.72	6	Newry	20 Sep
56:29	Jill Hunter/Boltz		14.10.66	3	Erewash	23 Aug
	(10)					
56:39	Hayley Nash	V35	30.05.63	5	Erewash	23 Aug
56:40	Caroline Herbert		30.06.70	6	Erewash	23 Aug
57:04	Trudi Thomson	V35	18.01.59	8	Newry	20 Sep
57:27	Frances Gill	V35	13.01.60	3	Woking	1 Mar
57:31	Zahara Hyde/Hyde-Peters	V35	12.01.63	5	Portsmouth	13 Sep
57:34	Kath Bailey		25.03.68	1	Hayling Island	29 Nov
57:38	Mel Ellis		16.04.64	4	Woking	1 Mar
57:42	Amy Stiles		6.02.75	6	Portsmouth	13 Sep
57:46	Danielle Sanderson	V35	26.10.62	1	Harlow	2 Aug
57:48	Bronwen Cardy-Wise	V45	26.01.52	1	Llandudno	1 Nov
	(20)					
57:57	Lynne Maddison		17.08.67	2	Llandudno	1 Nov

downhill

| 57:27 | Tracy Brindley | | 25.08.72 | 1 | Motherwell | 5 Apr |

Foreign
| *56:49* | *Anne Buckley (IRE)* | | *20.06.67* | *1* | *Pocklington* | *22 Feb* |

HALF MARATHON

1:09:50	Liz McColgan		24.05.64	5	Lisbon, POR	15 Mar
1:10:54	Alison Wyeth		26.05.64	2	The Hague, HOL	29 Mar
1:13:22	Marian Sutton		7.10.63	5	Glasgow	23 Aug
1:13:31	Birhan Dagne	U23	7.10.77	6	Glasgow	23 Aug
1:14:01	Angharad Mair	V35	30.03.61	7	Glasgow	23 Aug
	1:14:12			2	Hardelot, FRA	5 Jul
1:14:31	Debbie Percival	V35	22.04.62	1	Fleet	22 Mar
1:14:58	Sally Goldsmith	V35	18.01.61	1	Ferrara, ITA	15 Feb
1:15:06	Liz Talbot		5.12.74	52	Uster, SWZ	27 Sep
1:15:14	Vicky Pincombe		19.06.66	4	South Shields	4 Oct
1:15:31	Sue Reinsford		24.03.69	3	Liverpool	30 Aug
	(10)					
1:15:34	Mel Ellis		16.04.64	1	Bath	8 Mar
1:15:56	Jo Thompson	V35	30.10.58	5	South Shields	4 Oct
1:15:59	Heather Heasman		27.09.63	1	Wilmslow	29 Mar
1:16:00	Maria Bradley	V35	2.01.63	1	Reading	15 Mar
1:16:00	Miranda Heathcote		18.09.72	6	South Shields	4 Oct
1:16:06	Amanda Wright		14.07.68	2	Wilmslow	29 Mar
1:16:21	Bev Jenkins		6.02.70	1	Tameside	23 Jul
1:16:26	Angela Allen		23.09.67	2	Helsby	18 Jan
1:16:33	Zahara Hyde/Hyde-Peters	V35	12.01.63	6	Liverpool	30 Aug
1:16:57	Kathy Charnock	V35	4.07.62	3	Helsby	18 Jan
	(20)					
1:17:11	Tracy Swindell		8.11.66	4	Wilmslow	29 Mar
1:17:16	Ruth Kingsborough		25.10.67	2	Reading	15 Mar
1:17:27	Frances Gill	V35	13.01.60	3	Reading	15 Mar

1:17:27	Andrea Whitcombe		8.06.71	7	South Shields	4	Oct
1:17:35	Emma Evans			1	Camberley	22	Feb
1:17:39	Danielle Sanderson	V35	26.10.62	1	Richmond	17	May
1:17:46	Amy Stiles		6.02.75	8	South Shields	4	Oct
1:17:54	Michelle Ross		31.01.72	1	Stratford	26	Apr
1:18:00	Beth Allott	U23	9.02.77	9	South Shields	4	Oct
1:18:03	Caroline Horne	V40	7.11.56	4	Reading	15	Mar
(30)							
1:18:14	Kath Bailey		25.03.68	1	Southampton	11	Oct
1:18:21	Lynne Maddison		17.08.67	1	Chester	24	May
1:18:22	Sandra Edwards	V35	14.03.61	11	Frankfurt, GER	1	Mar
1:18:28	Lisa Hollick		1.01.70	2	Fleet	22	Mar
1:18:36	Fiona Lothian		2.12.65	1	Inverness	8	Mar
1:18:36	Sandra Branney	V40	30.04.54	10	Glasgow	10	Aug
1:18:45	Alison Carr		30.08.66	2	Inverness	8	Mar
1:18:53	Nicola Brown		17.03.74	6	Reading	15	Mar
1:18:55	Julia McGowan/Cornford	V35	12.05.59	3	Fleet	22	Mar
1:18:56	Trish Sloan		22.03.66	6	Wilmslow	29	Mar

Unofficial intermediate times

1:13:53 +	Liz McColgan		24.05.64		London	26	Apr
1:13:53 +	Marian Sutton		7.10.63		London	26	Apr

Foreign

1:15:53	*Anne Buckley (IRE)*		*20.06.67*	*1*	*Leyland*	*22*	*Mar*
1:16:41	*Teresa Duffy (IRE)*		*6.07.69*	*1*	*Londonderry*	*26*	*Sep*
1:18:41	*Getenesh Tamirat (ETH)*	*U23*	*11.07.77*	*5*	*Reading*	*15*	*Mar*

MARATHON

2:26:54	Liz McColgan		24.05.64	2	London	26	Apr
2:32:14	Marian Sutton		7.10.63	10	London	26	Apr
2:35:41				10	Chicago, USA	11	Oct
2:39:54	Debbie Percival	V35	22.04.62	15	London	26	Apr
2:40:26				8	Frankfurt, GER	25	Oct
2:41:15	Gillian Horovitz	V40	7.06.55	16	Boston, USA	20	Apr
2:46:36				19	New York, USA	1	Nov
2:46:58				4	Kuala Lumpur, MAL	20	Sep
2:43:18	Nicola Brown		17.03.74	19	London	26	Apr
2:43:41	Tracy Swindell		8.11.66	20	London	26	Apr
2:44:33	Ruth Kingsborough		25.10.67	21	London	26	Apr
2:44:49	Amanda Wright		14.07.68	7	Belgrade, YUG	25	Apr
2:46:17	Anita Mellowdew		1.12.70	23	London	26	Apr
2:48:47	Sandra Branney	V40	30.04.54	24	London	26	Apr
	14 performances to 2:50:00 by 10 athletes						
2:50:10	Jo Lodge		6.01.68	25	London	26	Apr
2:50:12	Clare Pauzers	V35	2.08.62	1	Fort William	17	May
2:50:54	Danielle Sanderson	V35	26.10.62	6	Kuala Lumpur, MAL	20	Sep
2:51:02	Kathy Charnock	V35	4.07.62	3	Dublin, IRE	26	Oct
2:51:16	Lisa Hollick		1.01.70	26	London	26	Apr
2:51:17	Melanie Bradley	V35	12.03.63	12	Rotterdam, HOL	19	Apr
2:52:09	Joy Noad	V35	60	16	Berlin, GER	20	Sep
2:52:27	Sharon Dixon		22.04.68	33	Chicago, USA	11	Oct
2:52:39	Trudi Thomson	V35	18.01.59	4	Dublin, IRE	26	Oct
2:53:10	Zina Marchant	V45	30.09.50	28	London	26	Apr
(20)							
2:53:44	Zoe Lowe		7.07.65	29	London	26	Apr
2:53:45	Denise Pycroft		30.04.64	8	Amsterdam, HOL	1	Nov
2:53:56	Jackie Newton		28.08.64	1	Manchester	11	Oct
2:54:07	Julia McGowan/Cornford	V35	12.05.59	30	London	26	Apr
2:54:41	Trish Sloan		22.03.66	31	London	26	Apr

Time	Name	Cat		Pos	Location	Date	
2:54:42	Anna Jeeves	V40	19.09.54	32	London	26	Apr
2:54:44	Julianne White/Empfield			2	San Diego, USA	18	Jan
2:54:46	Gill O'Connor	V35	62	5	Dublin, IRE	26	Oct
2:54:48	Janice Moorekite	V40	1.05.57	33	London	26	Apr
2:54:55	Jane Boulton	V40	2.04.56	34	London	26	Apr
	(30)						
2:55:19	Beth Allott	U23	9.02.77	1	Sheffield	26	Apr
2:55:28	Kerrie Wood		66	2	Manchester	11	Oct
2:55:52	Kath Kaiser	V45	24.08.51	2	Sheffield	26	Apr
2:55:55	Heather Robinson	V35	31.08.61	35	London	26	Apr
2:57:29	Edwina Turner	V45	16.06.52	36	London	26	Apr
2:58:29	Sue Martin-Clarke	V40	13.09.55	38	London	26	Apr
2:58:33	Eleanor Robinson	V50	20.11.47	1	Gloucester	4	Oct
2:58:51	Linda Thomson		12.02.64	39	London	26	Apr
2:59:19	Nicole Docker		30.07.74	40	London	26	Apr
3:00:01	Libby Jones	V35	25.04.61	2	Nottingham	27	Sep
	(40)						
3:00:25	Rachel MacKenzie	V35	26.02.61	41	London	26	Apr
3:00:49	Alice Osbourne		27.02.67	43	London	26	Apr
3:00:54	Lisa Knights		12.07.71	44	London	26	Apr
3:00:54	Maggie Creber	V35	20.08.60	45	London	26	Apr
3:00:59	Maggie Thompson	V40	8.07.54	46	London	26	Apr
3:01:33	Marlene Pautard	V35	25.10.62	49	London	26	Apr
3:01:39	Carol Adams		27.11.63	50	London	26	Apr
3:02:11	Penny Buckingham		26.04.67	53	London	26	Apr
3:02:21	Debbie Maiden		27.05.67	54	London	26	Apr
3:02:40	Jane Burthem	V35	13.12.62	55	London	26	Apr
	(50)						
3:02:52	Alison Carpenter	V40	3.01.58	56	London	26	Apr
3:03:08	Frances Florence	V35	6.07.59	57	London	26	Apr
3:03:37	Marion Rayner	V45	14.01.50	58	London	26	Apr
3:03:51	Kay Leigh		3.12.60	59	London	26	Apr
3:03:51	Vicki Perry	V40	25.11.57	60	London	26	Apr
3:03:54	Lynn Jolley		26.11.73	61	London	26	Apr
3:04:05	Pat Affleck			1	Greenock	13	Sep
3:04:17	Paula Craig		2.07.73	63	London	26	Apr
3:04:24	Tracy Owen		29.04.64	64	London	26	Apr
3:04:33	Helen Barber		13.12.67	65	London	26	Apr
	(60)						
3:04:41	Rosie Nash	V40	58	67	London	26	Apr
3:04:45	Christine Naylor	V40	22.10.54	68	London	26	Apr
3:04:54	Liz Clarke	V40	14.02.57	81	London	26	Apr
3:04:57	Fiona Richardson	V35	8.12.58	71	London	26	Apr
3:05:16	H. Maskrey			1	Kingston	11	Oct
3:05:21	Lynn Williams		6.02.72	72	London	26	Apr
3:05:42	Susan Pavey		15.02.67	73	London	26	Apr
3:05:44	Lisa Godding-Felton		24.11.69	1	Abingdon	18	Oct
3:05:49	Aline Deleaval		31.10.71	74	London	26	Apr
3:05:56	Lucy Aron	U23	22.04.76	75	London	26	Apr
	(70)						
3:06:12	Helen Perkins		12.11.65	76	London	26	Apr
3:06:54	Susanna Harrison	V35	25.01.63	77	London	26	Apr
3:07:26	Anna Bannon		27.03.70	78	London	26	Apr
3:07:26	Kathy Drake	V35	25.05.60	1	Snowdonia	25	Oct
3:07:48	Jill McGee		16.04.64	79	London	26	Apr
3:07:50	Andrea Dennison	V35	22.04.63	80	London	26	Apr
3:07:56	Polly Rogers-Dixon		5.04.67	81	London	26	Apr
3:08:05	Susan Abbiss	V35	20.10.59	82	London	26	Apr
3:08:25	Yvonne Shashoua	V35	16.03.62	83	London	26	Apr
3:08:44	Penelope Clayton	U23	8.06.77	85	London	26	Apr
	(80)						

3:08:44	Philippa Leech			3	Sheffield	26 Apr
3:08:46	Tina Oldershaw		13.05.67	86	London	26 Apr
3:08:49	Christine Shouksmith	V35	12.09.58	87	London	26 Apr
3:08:55	Janet Thomas	V35	14.02.61	88	London	26 Apr
3:09:02	Helen Syms		20.06.66	89	London	26 Apr
3:09:22	Liz Craig	V35	7.07.60	90	London	26 Apr
3:09:45	Catherine Nevin	V40	12.11.55	91	London	26 Apr
3:09:47	Nikki Hanes			92	London	26 Apr
3:09:49	Erica Christie	V40	10.03.56	93	London	26 Apr
3:09:53	Lesley Turner		1.08.66	3	Nottingham	27 Sep
3:09:55	(90) Rachel West			94	London	26 Apr

unidentified athlete

2:57:04	Lawrence			26	Berlin, GER	20 Sep

Foreign

2:39:56	*Teresa Duffy (IRE)*		*6.07.69*	*1*	*Dublin, IRE*	*26 Oct*
3:04:01	*Jill Bruce (IRE)*		*25.07.73*	*62*	*London*	*26 Apr*

100 KILOMETRES - Road

8:16:07	Carolyn Hunter-Rowe		25.01.64	1	Nakamura, JAP	18 Oct
8:19:57	Eleanor Robinson	V50	20.11.47	2	Winschoten, HOL	12 Sep
8:33:35	Hilary Walker	V40	9.11.53	3	Winschoten, HOL	12 Sep
9:02:38	Sharon Gayter	V35	30.10.60	17	Torhout, BEL	19 Jun

24 HOURS - Track

193.346 km	Sandra Brown	V45	1.04.49	1	Doncaster	24 May
163.311 km	Ros Dwyer			3	London (TB)	11 Oct

24 HOURS - Road

212.606 km	Sharon Gayter	V35	30.10.60	5	Marquette, FRA	30 Aug
194.032 km	Sandra Brown	V45	1.04.49	7	Marquette, FRA	30 Aug
184.416 km	Hilary Walker	V40	9.11.53	9	Marquette, FRA	30 Aug

2000 METRES STEEPLECHASE (2'6" barriers?)

7:08.29	Tara Krzywicki		9.03.74	1	Bath	2 May
7:27.99	Lois Joslin	U20	1.03.79	2	Bath	2 May
7:34.66	Claire Martin	U23	12.07.76	3	Bath	2 May

60 METRES HURDLES - Indoors

8.02	Diane Allahgreen		21.02.75	3	Valencia, SPA	1 Mar
8.10				3h1	Valencia, SPA	1 Mar
8.21				1	Birmingham	7 Feb
8.26				1h1	Birmingham	7 Feb
8.29				1h1	Glasgow	15 Mar
8.34				4	Roxbury, USA	20 Feb
8.44				1	Glasgow	15 Mar
8.51				1h1	Ghent, BEL	1 Feb
8.38	Sarah Claxton	U20	23.09.79	1r2	Birmingham	28 Feb
8.39				1r1	Birmingham	28 Feb
8.53				1	Birmingham	21 Feb
8.40	Denise Lewis		27.08.72	2	Birmingham	7 Feb
8.48				2h2	Birmingham	7 Feb
8.41	Rachel King	U23	11.05.76	3	Birmingham	7 Feb
8.43				1	Birmingham	25 Jan
8.43				1h2	Ghent, BEL	1 Feb
8.45				2	Ghent, BEL	1 Feb
8.49				1h1	Birmingham	25 Jan
8.54				3h2	Birmingham	7 Feb

8.42	Clova Court	V35	10.02.60	1h2	Birmingham	7	Feb
	8.44			4	Birmingham	7	Feb
8.47	Keri Maddox		4.07.72	1	Birmingham	1	Mar
8.48	Liz Fairs	U23	1.12.77	2	Birmingham	25	Jan
	8.50			5	Birmingham	7	Feb
	8.53			2h1	Birmingham	7	Feb
	8.55			2h1	Glasgow	15	Mar
	8.57			1	Birmingham	25	Feb
	8.59			1	Sheffield	18	Jan
	8.59			2h1	Birmingham	25	Jan
8.55	Julie Pratt	U20	20.03.79	1h1	Birmingham	21	Feb
	8.56			2	Birmingham	21	Feb
8.59	Rachael Kay	U20	8.09.80	2h1	Birmingham	21	Feb

32 performances to 8.59 by 9 athletes

8.62	Kay Reynolds		15.09.67	4h2	Birmingham	7	Feb
	(10)						
8.64	Diana Bennett		14.06.74	1P	Birmingham	8	Feb
8.65	Nicola Gautier	U23	21.03.78	2	Sheffield	18	Jan
8.67	Natalie Murray	U23	24.03.76	1h2	Glasgow	15	Mar
8.71	Kerry Jury		19.11.68	3	Sheffield	18	Jan
8.72	Susan Jones	U23	8.06.78	1h1	Sheffield	18	Jan
8.72	Jenny Kelly		20.06.70	2P	Birmingham	8	Feb
8.72	Kelly Sotherton	U23	13.11.76	1	Birmingham	25	Feb
8.77	Julie Davis	U20	16.11.79	1h3	Birmingham	21	Feb
8.83	Julia Bennett		26.03.70	3P	Birmingham	8	Feb
8.89	Lorna Silver		10.01.74	2	Glasgow	25	Jan
	(20)						
8.90	Katherine Livesey	U20	15.12.79	2h3	Birmingham	21	Feb
8.96	Helen Worsey	U20	29.08.82	1	Birmingham	20	Dec
8.97	Katy Lestrange	U20	17.09.79	5	Birmingham	21	Feb
8.99	Julie Hollman	U23	16.02.77	2	Birmingham	25	Feb

exhibition

8.38	Denise Lewis		(8.40)		Birmingham	15	Feb

Under 17 - 2'6" Hurdles

8.49	Helen Worsey		29.08.82	1	Birmingham	1	Mar
	8.53			1	Birmingham	21	Feb
	8.57			1h3	Birmingham	21	Feb
8.66	Sharon Davidge		15.09.81	2h3	Birmingham	21	Feb
8.70	Stefanie Pullinger		3.04.83	3	Birmingham	21	Feb
8.73	Hayley Smith		14.01.82	4	Birmingham	21	Feb
8.78	Laura McShane		22.04.82	5	Birmingham	21	Feb
8.82	Sara McGreavy		13.12.82	1=h2	Birmingham	21	Feb
9.07	Katherine Porter		19.08.82	2s2	Bedford	25	Jan
9.07	Grace Smith		30.01.82	2r2	Birmingham	1	Feb
9.08	Pam Cook		25.10.82	3	Birmingham	1	Feb
9.09	Sian Polhill-Thomas		4.06.83	1h1	Birmingham	21	Feb
	(10)						
9.17	Zoe McKinnon		8.09.81	3h2	Birmingham	21	Feb
9.18	Lucy Michie		4.09.81	1	Glasgow	18	Jan
9.19	Lauren McLoughlin		8.09.82	5	Birmingham	1	Feb
9.20	Nicola Sanders		23.06.82	2s1	Bedford	25	Jan
9.20	Jemma Scott		14.03.83	2P	Glasgow	12	Dec
9.21	Kellie Smith		2.05.82	h	Sheffield	17	Jan
9.22	Sarah Bullock		6.12.81	4	Sheffield	17	Jan

overage

9.03 o	Karen Lowe		3.05.82	1P	Glasgow	12	Dec
9.22 o	Megan Freeth		1.02.82	3P	Glasgow	12	Dec
9.23 o	Samantha Adamson		27.03.82	4P	Glasgow	12	Dec

Under 15

8.94		Danielle Selley	19.12.83	1	Birmingham	21 Feb
9.04		Symone Belle	12.11.84	2	Birmingham	21 Feb
9.09		Melissa Harris	20.10.83	2h1	Birmingham	21 Feb
9.13		Gemma Bennett	4.01.84	1h3	Birmingham	21 Feb
9.14		Sarah Oldham	23.09.83	2	Birmingham	1 Mar
9.2		Monique Parris	28.01.84	1	London (CP)	7 Feb

70 METRES HURDLES - Under 13

11.1		Emma Makin	12.10.85	1	Bebington	26 May
		11.70		1	Crewe	10 May
11.4	0.4	Safiya Greensword		1	London (Nh)	4 May
11.4		Kelly Marshall	8.01.86	1	Grimsby	4 May
		11.51 1.6		1	Grangemouth	11 Jul
11.4		Lisa McManus	3.01.86	1	Cannock	29 Aug
11.5		Claire Sargent	11.03.86	2	Ipswich	25 May
11.5		Carly Dean	14.10.85	1	Bournemouth	2 Aug
11.6		Gemma Collier	25.11.85	1	Yeovil	14 Jun
11.6		Amy Fozzard	20.04.86	1	Wakefield	28 Jun
11.6		Leah McGuire	30.01.87	1	Great Yarmouth	16 Aug
11.6		Lucy Fisher	27.09.85	3	Cannock	29 Aug
	(10)					
11.7	1.5	Hannah Mathieson	28.10.85	1	Glasgow (S)	16 Aug
		11.73 -1.4		1	Inverness	13 Sep
11.71	-1.7	Staci Stewart	20.09.85	1	Birmingham	6 Sep
11.73	3.0	Lisa Burr	6.06.86	1	Edinburgh	10 May
11.77	1.6	Pamela Paterson	26.10.85	2	Grangemouth	11 Jul
11.78	1.8	Sarah Mathieson	28.10.85	1rB	Inverness	13 Sep

75 METRES HURDLES - Under 15

10.99 w 2.7		Symone Belle	12.11.84	1	Exeter	11 Jul
		11.11 0.7		1	London (Ha)	24 May
11.00		Danielle Selley	19.12.83	1P	Cardiff	20 Jun
11.07 w 2.7		Melissa Harris	20.10.83	2	Exeter	11 Jul
		11.17 1.9		2	Cwmbran	21 Jun
11.10 w 2.2		Lyndsey Russell	11.09.83	1	Grangemouth	11 Jul
		11.2 1.2		1	Grangemouth	24 Jun
		11.29 -1.0		2	Dublin (S), IRE	8 Aug
11.18 w 3.0		Sian Scott	20.03.84	2	Sheffield	15 Aug
		11.5		1	Watford	28 Jun
		11.53 0.7		3	London (He)	30 Aug
11.25 w 2.7		Hannah Elwiss	8.12.84	3	Exeter	11 Jul
		11.33 0.0		1	Cudworth	2 Aug
11.27 w 3.0		Holly Ferrier	13.07.84	3	Sheffield	15 Aug
		11.59 0.2		1h3	Exeter	10 Jul
11.3		Justine Roach	21.12.84	1	Redditch	17 May
		11.60 w 2.7		7	Exeter	11 Jul
11.32	1.9	Helen Davies	24.03.84	1	Connah's Quay	4 Jul
11.37 w 2.7		Sarah Oldham	23.09.83	4	Exeter	11 Jul
		11.5		2	Worcester	12 Sep
	(10)					
11.40 w 2.7		Lindsey Winter	19.03.84	5	Exeter	11 Jul
		11.6		2	Abingdon	18 Jul
		11.74 0.7		5	London (Ha)	24 May
11.44	1.5	Gemma Fergusson	20.08.84	2h1	Exeter	10 Jul
11.50	0.9	Jenni Molloy	23.09.83	2	London (Ha)	24 May
11.50	0.7	Gemma Bennett	4.01.84	2	London (He)	30 Aug
11.54 w 2.8		Rebecca Mitchell	10.12.83	2h4	Sheffield	15 Aug
		11.55 -1.0		3	Dublin (S), IRE	8 Aug
11.6 w		Catriona Pennet	10.10.83	2	Grangemouth	24 Jun
		11.62 1.2		1	Inverness	13 Sep

11.64 w 2.8		Aileen Wilson	30.03.84	3h4	Sheffield	15 Aug
11.70	0.3			P	Hull	20 Sep
11.67	0.9	Melissa Rogers	2.09.83	4	London (Ha)	24 May
11.70	0.9	Lara Carty	7.03.84	1	Birmingham	5 Sep
11.7		Melanie Canning	19.05.85	2	Enfield	10 May
(20)						
11.7		Monique Parris	28.01.84	1	London (Elt)	17 May
11.7		Leyna Hird	4.02.84	2	Exeter	13 Jun
11.7		Sarah Gallaway	14.11.84	3	Abingdon	18 Jul

80 METRES HURDLES - Under 17

10.96 w 2.3		Helen Worsey	29.08.82	1	Exeter	11 Jul
11.02	1.7			1	Sheffield	15 Aug
11.03	1.8			1h2	Sheffield	15 Aug
11.00 w 2.3		Sharon Davidge	15.09.81	2	Exeter	11 Jul
11.22	-1.9			1	Ayr	18 Jul
11.22 w 2.5		Stefanie Pullinger	3.04.83	1	London (Ha)	24 May
11.43	0.5			1h1	London (Ha)	24 May
11.28 w 2.3		Sara McGreavy	13.12.82	3	Exeter	11 Jul
11.7				1	Mansfield	17 May
11.77	1.1			2h1	Sheffield	15 Aug
11.34 w 2.3		Hayley Smith	14.01.82	1h2	London (Ha)	24 May
11.4				1	Ipswich	25 May
11.4		Zoe McKinnon	8.09.81	1	London (TB)	25 Apr
11.47 w 2.5				3	London (Ha)	24 May
11.48	0.5			2h1	London (Ha)	24 May
11.49 w 2.3		Louise O'Callaghan	12.12.81	5	Exeter	11 Jul
11.5		Katherine Porter	19.08.82	2	Ipswich	25 May
11.62 w 2.3				3h2	London (Ha)	24 May
11.72	1.7			5	Sheffield	15 Aug
11.51	1.7	Donna Maylor	20.05.82	3	Sheffield	15 Aug
11.6		Sian Polhill-Thomas	4.06.83	1	Bebington	13 Jun
11.68 w 2.3				8	Exeter	11 Jul
11.76	1.4			1	Leeds	23 May
(10)						
11.76	1.4	Lauren McLoughlin	8.09.82	1	Birmingham	5 Sep
11.8	-	Rebecca Mitchell	10.12.83	1	Dublin (S), IRE	27 Jun
11.81	-1.7	Wendy Davidson	14.10.82	2	Dublin (S), IRE	8 Aug
11.83	-0.1	Vicky O'Brien	15.11.82	2	Edinburgh	19 Jun
11.89	-0.1	Charlotte Todd	7.12.81	3	Edinburgh	19 Jun
11.89 w 3.5		Lisa Connolly	27.09.81	h	Leeds	23 May
12.05	1.4			3	Leeds	23 May
11.9		Grace Smith	30.01.82	1	Blackpool	3 May
12.04	1.1			6h1	Sheffield	15 Aug
11.9		Jennifer Oakes	14.08.82	1	Belfast	12 May
11.9		Nicola Sanders	23.06.82	1	Milton Keynes	13 Jun
11.96 w 2.5				2H	Birmingham	22 Aug
11.9		Jodie Hearne	17.09.81	1	Perivale	19 Jul
(20)						
11.94	1.1	Kellie Smith	2.05.82	3h1	Sheffield	15 Aug
11.95	1.4	Pam Cook	25.10.82	2	Leeds	23 May
11.95	1.1	Fliss Breens	6.11.81	4h1	Sheffield	15 Aug
11.95	1.4	Karen Lowe	3.05.82	2	Birmingham	5 Sep
11.96		Megan Freeth	1.02.82	1h	Connah's Quay	4 Jul
11.99 w 4.6		Jenny Wing	25.10.82	3h2	Exeter	10 Jul
12.0 w		Natalie Birney	21.09.81	2	Bebington	10 May
12.03	1.1	Kate Brewington	15.10.81	5h1	Sheffield	15 Aug
12.06	1.8	Laura McShane	22.04.82	5h2	Sheffield	15 Aug

100 METRES HURDLES - Under 17 (2' 6" Hurdles)

13.8	1.4	Helen Worsey	29.08.82	1r2	Peterborough	27 May

100 METRES HURDLES

13.11	1.2	Keri Maddox		4.07.72	1	Bedford	29	Aug
13.15	0.6				3h1	Kuala Lumpur, MAL	20	Sep
13.20	0.3				1h1	Birmingham	25	Jul
13.20	-0.6				1	Birmingham	25	Jul
13.21	0.5				1	Birmingham	18	Jul
13.21	0.0				6	Sheffield	2	Aug
13.30	-0.2				6	Kuala Lumpur, MAL	21	Sep
13.20	-0.3	Natasha Danvers	U23	19.09.77	2	Los Angeles (Ww), USA	2	May
13.32	1.6				2	Stanford, USA	24	May
13.20	1.2	Clova Court	V35	10.02.60	2	Bedford	29	Aug
13.34	-0.6				2	Birmingham	25	Jul
13.38	-1.0				1h2	Birmingham	25	Jul
13.42	1.0				1H	Derby	31	May
13.45	0.0				8	Sheffield	2	Aug
13.48	1.7				1H	Bressanone, ITA	4	Jul
13.61	-0.2				1H	Kuala Lumpur, MAL	16	Sep
13.43	0.6	Angie Thorp		7.12.72	1	Leeds	7	Jun
13.45	0.0				6	St. Petersburg, RUS	28	Jun
13.48	0.1				3r2	Tallinn, EST	19	Jun
13.51	0.3				5h2	Kuala Lumpur, MAL	20	Sep
13.58	1.1				1h1	Cudworth	10	May
13.59	1.3				1	Cudworth	10	May
13.62	-0.2				4r1	Tallinn, EST	19	Jun
13.52	1.3	Julie Pratt	U20	20.03.79	1h1	Bedford	5	Jul
13.57	1.8				1	London (Ha)	24	May
13.61	0.1				2h2	Annecy, FRA	2	Aug
13.64	1.1				1	London (He)	30	Aug
13.52	-0.6	Liz Fairs	U23	1.12.77	3	Birmingham	25	Jul
13.56	-1.0				1	Dessau, GER	1	Aug
13.57	0.3	Denise Lewis		27.08.72	2h1	Birmingham	25	Jul
13.59	-0.7				5H	Budapest, HUN	21	Aug
13.62	1.9	Sarah Claxton	U20	23.09.79	1	Alicante, SPA	18	Jul
		32 performances to 13.64 by 8 athletes						
13.65	-0.6	Melanie Wilkins		18.01.73	4	Birmingham	25	Jul
13.73	0.3	Rachel King	U23	11.05.76	6h2	Kuala Lumpur, MAL	20	Sep
	(10)							
13.78	0.5	Katie Sketchley		9.07.73	1h2	Watford	21	Jun
13.80	1.2	Jenny Kelly		20.06.70	3	Bedford	29	Aug
13.99	0.5	Kerry Jury		19.11.68	3H	Bressanone, ITA	4	Jul
14.04	0.4	Pauline Richards		30.06.68	2H	Kuala Lumpur, MAL	16	Sep
14.19	-0.6	Nicola Gautier	U23	21.03.78	H	Val de Reuil, FRA	25	Jul
14.23	1.6	Tamsin Stephens	U20	2.08.80	3	Bruges, BEL	23	Aug
14.24	-1.1	Julie Hollman	U23	16.02.77	2	Bath	4	May
14.25	0.6	Danielle Freeman	U20	11.02.80	5	Leeds	7	Jun
14.26	0.1	Jackie Brett		5.07.65	3	Tessenderlo, BEL	30	Aug
14.29	0.3	Kay Reynolds		15.09.67	4h1	Birmingham	25	Jul
	(20)							
14.30	-0.6	Bianca Liston	U23	28.05.78	3h3	Birmingham	25	Jul
14.31	-1.1	Kelly Sotherton	U23	13.11.76	3	Bath	4	May
14.31		Julie Davis	U20	16.11.79	1	Antrim	30	May
14.32	1.1	Sarah Porter	U20	11.12.79	2	London (He)	30	Aug
14.38	0.4	Diana Bennett		14.06.74	H	Val de Reuil, FRA	25	Jul
14.39	1.3	Sarah Akinbiyi	U20	23.08.81	2h1	Bedford	5	Jul
14.39	0.2	Katherine Livesey	U20	15.12.79	H	Hull	19	Sep
14.40	1.6	Kate Forsyth	U20	5.06.79	1	Leeds	23	May
14.41	1.8	Lorna Silver		10.01.74	1	Portsmouth	9	May
14.42	0.5	Leanne Buxton	U23	27.05.78	3h2	Watford	21	Jun
	(30)							
14.48		Clare Wise		22.08.69	1	Portsmouth	26	Jun

14.55	1.0	Kim Crowther		19.01.66	3H	Derby	30	May
14.56	-0.5	Non Evans		27.02.67	2	Cwmbran	20	Jun
14.57	-0.3	Katy Lestrange	U20	17.09.79	6	Bedford	30	May
14.58	1.2	Joanne Suddes	U23	27.01.77	5	Bedford	29	Aug
14.60	0.0	Natalie Murray	U23	24.03.76	1	Cudworth	2	Aug
14.62	1.2	Shani Anderson		7.08.75	6	Bedford	29	Aug
14.63	-0.6	Jocelyn Harwood	V40	21.11.57	5h3	Birmingham	25	Jul
14.64	1.6	Rebecca Gibb	U20	30.03.81	2	Leeds	23	May
14.72	1.2	Katie Jones	U23	4.01.77	7	Bedford	29	Aug
	(40)							
14.73	0.5	Clare Milborrow	U23	10.01.77	4h2	Watford	21	Jun
14.73	0.0	Donna Maylor	U17	20.05.82	1	Istanbul, TUR	26	Sep
14.79	1.3	Lowri Roberts	U17	9.10.81	5h1	Bedford	5	Jul
14.83		Katy Bartlett		6.05.73	4r2	Loughborough	17	May
14.86	0.2	Jo Thorn	U20	19.02.81	H	Hull	20	Sep
14.89	1.2	Natalie Butler	U23	25.11.78	8	Bedford	29	Aug
14.90	1.8	Tracey Duncan	U20	16.05.79	5	London (Ha)	24	May
14.92		Sarah Nicolle	U20	12.01.80	1	Solihull	24	May
14.93	1.6	Sara Todd	U20	3.11.79	3	Leeds	23	May
14.93		Cheryl Done		25.09.70	H	Cosford	28	Jul
	(50)							
14.96	1.3	Vicky Williams	U20	11.04.81	6h1	Bedford	5	Jul
14.98	-1.1	Lorraine Brackstone	U23	15.02.78	6	Bath	4	May
14.98	0.5	Samantha Male	U23	11.04.76	5h2	Watford	21	Jun
15.04	0.9	Gillian Stewart	U20	21.01.80	H	Glasgow (S)	2	May
15.04	-1.1	Liz Patrick	U23	29.08.77	7	Bath	4	May
15.06	1.3	Laura Foster	U20	22.07.81	7h1	Bedford	5	Jul
15.12	1.9	Jane Scott	U20	22.06.81	1	Edinburgh	19	Jun
15.13	1.9	Carolynne Sutherland	U20	4.09.80	2	Edinburgh	19	Jun
15.18	1.6	Allison English	U20	9.03.79	4	Leeds	23	May
15.20	1.5	Jackie Tindal	U20	21.01.79	1H	Derby	30	May
	(60)							
15.21	0.3	Nicola Duncalf	U20	6.05.81	2	Stoke	20	Jun
15.25		Suzy Hunt		26.09.75	3	Portsmouth	26	Jun
15.27		Amanda Wale		14.10.70	H	Wrexham	1	Aug

Additional Under 17 (1 - 2 above)

15.82		Amy Teale		30.12.82	1	Hexham	31	Aug

Wind Assisted

13.07	4.3	Keri Maddox		(13.11)	1	Cork, IRE	27	Jun
		13.37	2.8		1	Bedford	24	May
		13.57	2.6		1h2	Bedford	24	May
13.28	3.7	Sarah Claxton	U20	(13.62)	1	Bedford	5	Jul
13.36	3.4	Court	V35	(13.20)	1h1	Bedford	24	May
		13.42	2.8		2	Bedford	24	May
		13.44	4.3		3	Cork, IRE	27	Jun
13.42	3.4	Denise Lewis		(13.57)	2	Cardiff	4	Aug
13.44	3.8	Rachel King	U23	(13.73)	2rB	Palma de Mallorca, SPA	28	May
		13.52	3.4		4	Cardiff	4	Aug
13.47	2.4	Melanie Wilkins		(13.65)	1	Watford	21	Jun
		13.49	3.4		3	Cardiff	4	Aug
		13.50	2.1		1h1	Watford	21	Jun
13.48	3.7	Julie Pratt	U20	(13.52)	2	Bedford	5	Jul
13.57	4.4	Katie Sketchley		(13.78)	2	Maia, POR	14	Jun
		15 performances to 13.64 by 8 athletes						
13.79	5.8	Pauline Richards		(14.04)	H	Arles, FRA	23	May
13.83	5.5	Kerry Jury		(13.99)	H	Arles, FRA	23	May
13.95	4.6	Danielle Freeman	U20	(14.25)	2H	Arles, FRA	23	May
14.10	3.7	Sarah Akinbiyi	U20	(14.39)	3	Bedford	5	Jul

14.12	2.1	Jackie Brett		(14.26)	3h1	Watford	21	Jun
14.12	2.4	Sarah Porter	U20	(14.32)	1	Exeter	11	Jul
14.14	4.6	Julie Hollman	U23	(14.24)	H	Arles, FRA	23	May
14.23	4.6	Diana Bennett		(14.38)	H	Arles, FRA	23	May
14.23	3.9	Jocelyn Harwood	V40	(14.63)	2	Edinburgh	18	Jul
14.24	3.4	Clare Milborrow	U23	(14.73)	4h1	Bedford	24	May
14.29	2.4	Katherine Livesey	U20	(14.39)	2	Exeter	11	Jul
14.29	3.9	Sarah Richmond		6.01.73	3	Edinburgh	18	Jul
14.34	2.8	Lorna Silver		(14.41)	6	Bedford	24	May
14.39	2.3	Katy Lestrange	U20	(14.57)	2h2	Exeter	10	Jul
14.45	3.4	Non Evans		(14.56)	7	Cardiff	4	Aug
14.46	4.8	Sarah Nicolle	U20	(14.92)	2h1	Exeter	10	Jul
14.47	2.4	Yewande Ige	U20	21.03.80	4	Exeter	11	Jul
14.47	3.9	Joanne Suddes	U23	(14.58)	4	Edinburgh	18	Jul
14.52	4.6	Julia Bennett		26.03.70	H	Arles, FRA	23	May
14.53	4.8	Rebecca Gibb	U20	(14.64)	3h1	Exeter	10	Jul
14.56	3.4	Katie Jones	U23	(14.72)	6h1	Bedford	24	May
14.60	4.8	Jo Thorn	U20	(14.86)	4h1	Exeter	10	Jul
14.71	5.8	Gillian Stewart	U20	(15.04)	H	Arles, FRA	23	May
14.78	5.8	Chloe Cozens	U20	9.04.80	H	Arles, FRA	23	May
14.78	3.4	Natalie Butler	U23	(14.89)	7h1	Bedford	24	May
14.86	2.5	Caroline Pearce	U20	1.09.80	5h2	Bedford	5	Jul
14.93	2.6	Liz Patrick	U23	(15.04)	3s2	Bath	3	May
14.93	4.8	Allison English	U20	(15.18)	6h1	Exeter	10	Jul
14.96	2.3	Nicola Duncalf	U20	(15.21)	4h2	Exeter	10	Jul
15.02	2.3	Laura Foster	U20	(15.06)	6h2	Exeter	10	Jul
15.08	2.3	Clare O'Sullivan	U20	8.05.80	7h2	Exeter	10	Jul
15.15	4.8	Vicky Murphy	U20	5.07.81	8h1	Exeter	10	Jul
15.22	3.2	Lisa Williams	U23	11.04.78	3h3	Bath	3	May
15.23	2.6	Hannah Stares	U23	13.12.78	5s2	Bath	3	May
15.24	2.6	Abigail Ashby	U23	23.11.77	6s2	Bath	3	May
15.29	2.7	Sharon Price		10.12.75	5s1	Bath	3	May
15.29	3.9	Emma Reid	U20	5.01.81	6	Edinburgh	18	Jul

Hand Timing

13.4	1.5	Angie Thorp		(13.43)	1	Coventry	5	Jul
13.4 w	2.3	Maddox		(13.11)	1	Grangemouth	4	Jul
	13.5	1.9			1	Watford	15	Aug
3 performances to 13.5 by 2 athletes including 1 wind assisted								
14.0 w		Jackie Brett		(14.26)	1	Carn Brea	27	May
	14.1				1	Carn Brea	5	Sep
14.0 w		Kay Reynolds		(14.29)	1	Abingdon	18	Jul
	14.1				1	Woking	22	Aug
14.1	1.5	Nicola Gautier	U23	(14.19)	2	Coventry	5	Jul
14.2		Non Evans		(14.56)	1	Neath	14	Jun
14.2	-1.2	Bianca Liston	U23	(14.30)	3	Crawley	19	Jul
14.2 w	5.5	Jocelyn Harwood	V40	(14.63)	2	Stoke	5	Jul
14.2 w?		Diana Bennett		(14.38)	2	Woking	22	Aug
14.3		Janine Whitlock		11.08.73	2	Derby	19	Jul
14.4		Clare Milborrow	U23	(14.73)	1	Brighton	30	May
14.4		Lorna Silver		(14.41)	1	Dunfermline	31	May
14.4	1.5	Susan Jones	U23	8.06.78	1rB	Coventry	5	Jul
14.4		Katy Lestrange	U20	(14.57)	1	Telford	26	Jul
14.5		Natalie Murray	U23	(14.60)	1	Oldham	12	Jul
14.6		Sarah Nicolle	U20	(14.92)	1	Tamworth	14	Jun
14.6		Anne Hollman		18.02.74	1	Peterborough	22	Aug
14.7	-1.3	Sarah Richmond		(14.29w)	1	Edinburgh	9	May

285

14.7		Nichola Shereston	U20	1.09.79	1	Nottingham	9	May
14.7		Lowri Roberts	U17	(14.79)	2	Neath	14	Jun
14.7		Jennie Pearson/Matthews	V35	3.07.62	3	Stoke	5	Jul
14.7		Nicola Sutton		4.03.74	1	Exeter	5	Sep
14.7 w	2.4	Katy Bartlett		(14.83)	2	Enfield	9	May
14.7 w	5.2	Donna Maylor	U17	(14.73)	1rB	Cannock	13	Sep
14.8	1.8	Yewande Ige	U20	(14.47w)	2	Kingston	10	May
14.9		Alison Evans/Moseley		13.12.73	2	Tamworth	14	Jun
14.9		Vicky Williams	U20	(14.96)	H	Carn Brea	27	Jun
14.9		Jackie Tindal	U20	(15.20)	3rB	Watford	15	Aug
14.9 w		Lorraine Brackstone	U23	(14.98)	4	Stoke	5	Jul
14.9 w	4.2	Belinda Samuels	U23	29.11.78	1	Liverpool	18	Jul
14.9 w	4.2	Nicola Duncalf	U20	(15.21)	2	Liverpool	18	Jul
15.0					1rB	Telford	26	Jul
14.9 w	4.2	Wendy Laing	V35	29.12.62	3	Liverpool	18	Jul
15.1					3	Coventry	5	Jul
15.0		Julia Bennett		(14.52w)	2rB	Barking	25	Apr
15.0		Hannah Stares	U23	(15.23w)	1	Yeovil	10	May
15.0		Carolynne Sutherland	U20	(15.13)	1	Whitley Bay	21	Jun
15.0		Cicely Hall	U23	12.10.78	3	Woking	22	Aug
15.0		Katherine Porter	U17	19.08.82	1	Colchester	5	Sep
15.0		Jo Hyslop	U20	13.03.80	1	Derby	20	Sep
15.1		Gaye Clarke	V35	22.08.60	1	Peterborough	5	Apr
15.1		Chloe Cozens	U20	(14.78w)	2	Bournemouth	25	Apr

Additional Under 17

15.8		Nicola Sanders		23.06.82	2	St. Ives	5	Sep
15.8		Louise O'Callaghan		12.12.81	1	Kingston	13	Sep
15.9		Samantha Adamson		27.03.82	3	Ware	22	Aug
15.9 w	2.5	Helen Thieme		28.09.81	2	Cannock	13	Sep

Foreign

14.2		*Adri Van der Merwe (RSA)*	*U23*	*17.06.76*		*Grangemouth*	*4*	*Jul*
		14.48 -1.4			*1r2*	*Birmingham*	*6*	*Jun*

300 METRES HURDLES

43.37	Katherine Porter	U17	19.08.82	1	Exeter	11	Jul
43.38	Wendy Davidson	U17	14.10.82	1	Dublin (S), IRE	8	Aug
43.9	Lorna Silver		10.01.74	1	Bournemouth	5	Apr

Additional Under 17 (1 - 2 above)

44.20	Helen Thieme	28.09.81	2	Exeter	11	Jul
44.71	Hannah Wood	17.11.81	3	Exeter	11	Jul
44.73	Rebecca Scotcher	2.07.82	1	Birmingham	6	Sep
45.05	Natalia Naish	17.07.82	1	Norwalk, USA	23	May
45.07	Samantha Watts	13.10.81	4	Exeter	11	Jul
45.09	Amy Shaw	2.07.83	1	York	25	Jul
45.11	Abbie George	18.04.82	5	Exeter	11	Jul
45.13	Helen Worsey	29.08.82	3	Sheffield	16	Aug
(10)						
45.40	Helen Cooper	20.06.83	3	York	25	Jul
45.6	Natalie Birney	21.09.81	1	Bebington	10	May
	46.02		3h2	Exeter	10	Jul
45.6	Nicola Sanders	23.06.82	1	Bournemouth	17	May
45.81	Jemma Scott	14.03.83	2	Edinburgh	20	Jun
45.83	Luisa Giles	23.02.82	2h2	Exeter	10	Jul
45.9	Hana Carroll	19.09.81	1	Liverpool	18	Apr
46.08	Lisa Connolly	27.09.81	2	Cudworth	2	Aug
46.17	Sharon Davidge	15.09.81	4h2	Sheffield	16	Aug
46.18	Lindsey Maguire	15.01.82	1	Birmingham	5	Sep

46.28	Kristi Andrews		2.05.83	3h1	Sheffield	16	Aug
	(20)						
46.3	Cara Schofield		13.03.82	1	Crawley	13	Jun
46.36	Carly Austin		16.05.83	2h3	Exeter	10	Jul
46.43	Stacie King		19.01.82	7	Ayr	18	Jul
46.5	Jennifer Oakes		14.08.82	2	Antrim	13	Jun
46.5	Claire Brason		16.03.83	1	York	5	Jul
46.5	Tracy McDonnell		4.10.82	1	Yeovil	19	Jul
46.5	Sara McGreavy		13.12.82	1	Leamington	12	Sep
46.52	Lindsey Callum		13.04.82	4	York	25	Jul
46.65	Stephanie Little		5.11.81	4h1	Sheffield	16	Aug
46.75	Laura Daley		17.05.83	4h2	Exeter	10	Jul
	(30)						
46.8	Sarah Kerr		11.12.81	1	Jarrow	20	Jun
46.9	Katie Brooks		17.02.82	2	Bromley	17	May
46.9	Samantha Adamson		27.03.82	1	Hemel Hempstead	13	Jun
46.9	Louise O'Callaghan		12.12.81	1	Hoo	31	Aug

400 METRES HURDLES

55.25	Gowry Retchakan	V35	21.06.60	2	Kuala Lumpur, MAL	18	Sep
	56.29			1	Ljubljana, SLO	31	May
	56.4			1	Welwyn	31	Aug
	56.57			2	Birmingham	26	Jul
	56.7			1	Harrow	30	Aug
	56.86			4	Lucerne, SWZ	2	Jul
	57.1			1	Basildon	7	Jun
	57.37			2	Cardiff	4	Aug
	57.66			1	Tallinn, EST	19	Jun
	57.77			1h2	Birmingham	25	Jul
	57.98			1	Bedford	25	May
	58.2			1	London (BP)	25	Apr
	58.2			1	Enfield	9	May
	58.6			1	Liverpool	16	Aug
55.69	Natasha Danvers	U23	19.09.77	4	Gateshead	19	Jul
	56.27			1	Birmingham	26	Jul
	56.35			3	Amherst, USA	5	Jun
	56.39			5	Kuala Lumpur, MAL	18	Sep
	56.58			1	Eagle Rock, USA	9	May
	56.94			1h1	Stanford, USA	23	May
	57.14			1	Stanford, USA	28	Mar
	57.18			2	Dessau, GER	1	Aug
	57.19			6h3	Budapest, HUN	19	Aug
	57.70			1	San Luis Obispo, USA	21	Mar
	57.76			1h2	Amherst, USA	3	Jun
	57.9			1	Los Angeles, USA	4	Apr
	58.01			1	Stanford, USA	24	May
	58.06			1h1	Birmingham	25	Jul
	58.14			4	Budapest, HUN	5	Jul
56.38	Keri Maddox		4.07.72	4	Kuala Lumpur, MAL	18	Sep
	56.76			3	Birmingham	26	Jul
	56.95			2	Rhede, GER	19	Jun
	57.15			2	Cork, IRE	27	Jun
	57.22			1	Birmingham	6	Jun
	57.59			2	Bedford	29	Aug
	57.75			3	Leeds	7	Jun
	58.0			1	Watford	15	Aug
	58.03			1	Loughborough	17	May
	58.11			2h3	Birmingham	25	Jul
	58.30			3	Cardiff	4	Aug
	58.31			1	Birmingham	23	Aug

56.42	Vicki Jamison	U23	19.05.77	1	Tonsberg, NOR	20	Jun
	56.62			6	Kuala Lumpur, MAL	18	Sep
	56.92			1	Leeds	7	Jun
	56.98			1	Hexham	14	Jun
	57.16			6	Gateshead	19	Jul
	57.18			1h3	Birmingham	25	Jul
	57.51			5	St. Petersburg, RUS	27	Jun
	57.58			4	Birmingham	26	Jul
57.31	Alyson Layzell		16.12.66	2	Leeds	7	Jun
	58.08			3	Cork, IRE	27	Jun
	58.36			1	Bedford	30	May
57.46	Lorraine Hanson		22.04.65	1	Bedford	29	Aug
57.70	Jacqui Parker		15.10.66	1	Watford	20	Jun
	54 performances to 58.5 by 7 athletes						
58.54	Sinead Dudgeon	U23	9.07.76	5	Birmingham	26	Jul
58.72	Jennie Pearson/Matthews	V35	3.07.62	3h3	Birmingham	25	Jul
59.07	Clare Wise		22.08.69	7	Birmingham	26	Jul
	(10)						
59.39	Tracey Duncan	U20	16.05.79	5s2	Annecy, FRA	29	Jul
59.40	Nicola Sutton		4.03.74	2	Loughborough	17	May
59.43	Christine Amede	V35	7.08.63	4	Bedford	29	Aug
59.62	Rachael Kay	U20	8.09.80	2	Alicante, SPA	18	Jul
60.03	Jo Mahony	U23	22.10.76	2	Birmingham	18	Jul
60.2	Tanya Wilkinson		1.04.70	2	Stoke	9	Aug
	60.32			3	Bedford	25	May
60.21 mx	Alison Currie		15.07.68	1	Glasgow (S)	10	May
	60.38			4h2	Birmingham	25	Jul
60.53	Nusrat Ceesay	U20	18.03.81	1	London (He)	9	Aug
61.01	Julie Davis	U20	16.11.79	2	Tullamore, IRE	6	Jun
61.1	Sarah Damm		12.09.70	1rB	Derby	21	Jun
	61.70			5h1	Birmingham	25	Jul
	(20)						
61.26	Joanne Oates	U23	21.02.78	5h3	Birmingham	25	Jul
61.38	Katie Jones	U23	4.01.77	2	Cudworth	2	Aug
61.55	Michele Gillham		8.10.74	4	Watford	20	Jun
61.81	Cicely Hall	U23	12.10.78	3h3	Bedford	25	May
61.81	Anne Hollman		18.02.74	2h1	Watford	20	Jun
62.00	Sara Elson		8.05.70	2rB	Loughborough	17	May
62.20	Anya Hutchinson	U23	16.07.77	5	Birmingham	18	Jul
62.2	Caroline Wilkins		28.08.75	1	Solihull	17	May
	62.91			2	Cudworth	9	May
62.2	Lorna Silver		10.01.74	1	Dunfermline	31	May
	63.64			4h2	Bedford	25	May
62.2	Celia Brown	U23	22.01.77	1	Bromley	22	Aug
	62.63			6h3	Birmingham	25	Jul
	(30)						
62.22	Katy Bartlett		6.05.73	6	Vilamoura, POR	30	May
62.44	Laura Siddall	U20	10.09.80	2	Leeds	23	May
62.69	Elizabeth Waters	U23	19.02.77	1rB	Cosford	25	Apr
62.70	Lisa Thompson	U20	25.04.81	3	Bruges, BEL	23	Aug
62.7	Leanne Buxton	U23	27.05.78	1	Bromley	14	Jun
	63.57			5h1	Watford	20	Jun
62.79	Syreeta Williams	U20	24.10.80	3	Bedford	5	Jul
62.92	Helen Walker	U20	12.10.80	4	Exeter	11	Jul
63.0	Kate Williams	U23	10.11.77	2	Loughborough	25	Apr
	64.38			3s2	Bath	2	May
63.14	Kelly McNeice	U23	17.06.78	3	Tullamore, IRE	9	Aug
63.25	Linda Gabriel		27.07.64	6h2	Birmingham	25	Jul
	(40)						
63.27	Jane Low	V35	26.08.60	1	Calais, FRA	20	Jun
63.28	Rebecca Gibb	U20	30.03.81	3	London (He)	9	Aug

63.7	Sandra Leigh		26.02.66	1	Watford	10 May
63.7	Josephine Peet		4.12.71	2	Bath	5 Jul
64.04				5	Birmingham	23 Aug
63.7	Jo Hyslop	U20	13.03.80	3	Derby	19 Jul
64.01				6	Exeter	11 Jul
63.73	Carol Dawkins	V35	8.12.60	7	Bedford	29 Aug
63.81	Cheryl Done		25.09.70	1	Cosford	1 Jul
63.85	Sarah Smith	U23	18.08.76	1r2	Birmingham	6 Jun
63.9	Julia Bennett		26.03.70	1	Kingston	27 Jun
63.99	Louise Aylwin	U20	8.04.80	5	Exeter	11 Jul
	(50)					
64.09	Niki Pocock	U20	9.05.79	4	London (He)	9 Aug
64.2	Hazel Magrath	U20	5.08.81	1	Lincoln	20 Jun
64.3	Rebecca Wright	U23	20.12.77	3r2	Watford	15 Aug
64.31	Shona MacPherson	U20	31.08.80	4	Edinburgh	18 Jul
64.5	Jacqueline Elliott	U23	13.09.78	1	Jarrow	9 Aug
65.00				5	Edinburgh	18 Jul
64.5	Cara Schofield	U17	13.03.82	1	London (TB)	5 Sep
64.56	Kate Norman	U23	1.01.76	4s1	Bath	2 May
64.59	Lyndsay Fitzgerald	U20	31.01.80	2	London (Ha)	23 May
64.6	Charlotte Randall	U20	10.05.80	2	Guildford	18 Jul
64.98				7	Exeter	11 Jul
64.6	Laura Seston	U20	9.02.79	1	Colchester	5 Sep
	(60)					
64.74	Shelley Rudman	U20	23.03.81	1	London (He)	30 Aug
64.9	Lindsay Impett	U20	4.01.80	2	Yeovil	20 Jun
64.9	Katherine Porter	U17	19.08.82	1	Milton Keynes	27 Jun
65.0	Gael Davies	U20	5.02.79	4	Loughborough	25 Apr
65.0	Helen Nunn		15.09.71	3	Ashford	9 May
65.06	Rebecca Dougall	U20	11.05.81	1	Edinburgh	20 Jun
65.1	Pamela Johnstone	U20	16.03.79	1r2	Grangemouth	4 Jul
65.63				1	Edinburgh	9 May
65.14	Sarah Newman	U20	7.10.79	3	Barry	14 Jul
65.2	Dyanna Clarke	V40	27.02.58	2	London (TB)	25 Apr
65.33				1	Newport	11 Jul
65.2	Danielle Codd	U20	17.02.79	1	Wigan	31 May
	(70)					
65.3	Kelly Weall	U23	30.11.78	1	Middlesbrough	19 Apr
65.3	Donna Porazinski	U20	28.01.81	1	Yate	26 Jul
65.36	Pat Divine		21.10.67	6	Birmingham	6 Jun
65.4	Kelly Warner	U20	5.03.81	1	Watford	30 May
65.5	Alison McDonnell		28.06.72	1	Harrow	18 Jul
65.70				2	Bedford	30 Aug
65.6	Susie Williams	U23	2.06.77	1	Southampton	25 Apr
65.78	Jane O'Malley	U23	18.07.77	5r2	Loughborough	17 May
65.8	Helen Small	U23	10.10.78	2	Solihull	17 May
65.8	Ruth McCallum	U20	1.03.79	2	Dunfermline	31 May
65.94				1	Grangemouth	23 Aug
65.9	Heather Myers		5.12.64	1r2	Barking	25 Apr
	(80)					
65.9	Virginia Mitchell	V35	29.01.63	2	Woking	22 Aug
66.0	Angela Warburton		24.01.64	4	Grimsby	7 Jun

Additional Under 17 (1 - 2 above)

66.2	Kristi Andrews		2.05.83	1	Peterborough	26 Jul
66.3	Hannah Wood		17.11.81	3	Solihull	17 May
66.3	Samantha Adamson		27.03.82	2	Norwich	30 May
66.8	Katie Brooks		17.02.82	1	Harrow	26 Jul
67.0	Abbie George		18.04.82	1	Tamworth	17 May
67.2	Helen Thieme		28.09.81	3	Birmingham	21 Jun
67.7	Natalie Birney		21.09.81	1	Blackpool	19 Apr
68.0	Lindsey Maguire		15.01.82	1	Gateshead	23 Aug

60.13	Adri Van der Merwe (RSA)	U23	17.06.76	6	Cork, IRE	27	Jun
61.63	Margit Strand (NOR)	U23	22.01.78	1r2	Bedford	30	May
64.55	Kristina Hansen (NOR)	U23	30.05.77	5r2	Bedford	30	May
66.0	Caroline Heaney (IRE)	U23	3.04.76	2	Kingston	14	Jun

HIGH JUMP

1.92 i	Susan Jones IOTH	U23 5	8.06.78	6	Valencia, SPA	28	Feb
1.89 i				1	Birmingham	8	Feb
1.85				1	Loughborough	17	May
1.85				2	Birmingham	26	Jul
1.85				7	Kuala Lumpur, MAL	20	Sep
1.83				3	Birmingham	18	Jul
1.91	Jo Jennings		20.09.69	2	Kuala Lumpur, MAL	20	Sep
1.90				1	Barcelona, SPA	17	Jun
1.89				5	St. Petersburg, RUS	28	Jun
1.88				1	Leeds	7	Jun
1.88				1	Birmingham	26	Jul
1.88				1	Liverpool	16	Aug
1.86				1	Birmingham	18	Jul
1.85				1	Bedford	24	May
1.83				1	Cudworth	9	May
1.89 i	Debbie Marti		14.05.68	2	Birmingham	8	Feb
1.85 i				9	Valencia, SPA	28	Feb
1.89 i	Michelle Dunkley	U23	26.01.78	3	Birmingham	8	Feb
1.88				4=	Kuala Lumpur, MAL	20	Sep
1.86 i				1	Birmingham	25	Jan
1.86				1	Luton	14	Jun
1.86				2	Birmingham	18	Jul
1.85 i				11	Valencia, SPA	28	Feb
1.85 i				1	Glasgow	15	Mar
1.85				2	Istanbul, TUR	20	Jun
1.85				3	Birmingham	26	Jul
1.84 i	Julia Bennett		26.03.70	1P	Birmingham	8	Feb
1.83 i				2	Birmingham	25	Jan
1.83				1	Kingston	10	May
1.83	Denise Lewis		27.08.72	1	Cannock	9	May
1.83				2=H	Budapest, HUN	21	Aug
1.83	Lee McConnell 45	U23 35	9.10.78	1	Bedford	30	May
1.83	Julie Crane 46	U23 36	26.09.76	2	Bedford	30	May

33 performances to 1.83 by 8 athletes including 10 indoors

1.82	Natasha Danvers 56	U23	19.09.77	2	Stanford, USA	24	May
1.80 i	Hazel Melvin		19.11.73	1	Glasgow	18	Jan
1.80				1	Coatbridge	21	Jun
	(10)						
1.80 i	Diana Bennett 77		14.06.74	3	Birmingham	25	Jan
1.79				2	Long Beach, USA	18	Apr
1.80	Chloe Cozens 78	U20	9.04.80	4	Loughborough	17	May
1.80	Gillian Black	U20	27.10.79	2	Alicante, SPA	18	Jul
1.80	Julie Major/Peacock		19.08.70	1	Crawley	19	Jul
1.79	Julie Hollman	U23	16.02.77	H	Arles, FRA	23	May
1.79	Kerry Jury		19.11.68	H	Arles, FRA	23	May
1.79	Aileen Wilson 86 14	U15 8	30.03.84	1	Bedford	4	Jul
1.78	Emily Jackson 101 ST	U20	16.10.80	1	Jarrow	16	Aug
1.77	Rebecca Jones	U17 38	17.01.83	1	Dublin (S), IRE	8	Aug
1.76	Ursula Fay		23.09.67	4	Bedford	24	May
	(20)						
1.76	Judith Payne	U20	7.07.80	1	Derby	20	Sep
1.75 i	Alison Evans/Moseley		13.12.73	7=	Birmingham	8	Feb
1.72				1	Tamworth	14	Jun

1.75	Antonia Bemrose	U20	3.09.79	1	Portsmouth	9 May
1.75	Sophie McQueen	U17	3.12.81	1	Grimsby	26 Jul
1.75	Laura White	U20	5.09.79	1	Oldham	30 Aug
1.75	Samantha Adamson	U17	27.03.82	1H	Hull	19 Sep
1.73	Jenny Reader	U23	23.12.77	1	Southampton	25 Apr
1.73	Natalie Clark	U17	4.09.82	1	Exeter	11 Jul
1.73	Catherine Parmiter	U20	27.04.81	1	Exeter	9 Aug
1.73	Tracy Joseph		29.11.69	1	Bedford	30 Aug
	(30)					
1.72	Debbie Harrison	U23	13.11.78	1	Coventry	17 May
1.72	Lesley Buchanan	U17	25.11.81	1	Edinburgh	20 Jun
1.72	Denise Gayle	U20	11.09.79	4	Exeter	10 Jul
1.72	Leone Dickinson		5.11.75	2	Cudworth	9 Aug
1.72	Stephanie Higham	U15	26.12.83	2	Sheffield	15 Aug
1.71 i	Jenny Brown	V35	21.05.59	1P	Glasgow	28 Feb
1.71				1P	Bellaria, ITA	13 Sep
1.70	Natalie Hulse	U17	2.12.82	1	Cannock	9 May
1.70	Emma Kerr	U23	15.10.77	2	Glasgow (S)	9 May
1.70	Cathy Young	U17	14.03.82	1	Grantham	31 May
1.70	Jenny Walker		28.01.69	5	Birmingham	6 Jun
	(40)					
1.70	Beth Orford	U20	25.03.81	2	Coventry	5 Jul
1.70	Lindsey-Anne McDonnell	U20	13.08.79	1	London (CP)	5 Sep
1.69 i	Sonia Crawley	U15	7.12.83	2	Birmingham	21 Feb
1.65				1	Derby	26 Apr
1.69	Kirsty Roger	U23	24.03.78	H	Derby	30 May
1.69	Jennifer Hills	U20	25.03.81	1	Exeter	26 Jul
1.68 i	Debbie McIlroy	U23	18.12.77	5	Sheffield	18 Jan
1.65				3=	Ashford	16 Aug
1.68 i	Rachel Martin	U23	9.09.78	6	Sheffield	18 Jan
1.65				1	Middlesbrough	25 Apr
1.68	Sarah White	U20	25.12.80	1	London (PH)	25 Apr
1.68	Jemma Scott	U17	14.03.83	2	Edinburgh	20 Jun
1.68	Claire Sterry	U17	10.10.81	1	Ashford	21 Jun
	(50)					
1.68	Claire Wright	U15	9.09.83	1	Crewe	13 Jul
1.68	Danielle Freeman	U20	11.02.80	H	Cartagena, ITA	18 Jul
1.68	Sarah Humberstone	U20	6.07.81	2	Grimsby	26 Jul
1.68	Lisa Bennington	U23	12.12.78	1	York	9 Aug
1.68	Sharon Woolrich	U23	1.05.76	1	Portsmouth	22 Aug
1.68	Natalie Sims	U17	7.04.83	1	Derby	13 Sep
1.68	Karen Lowe	U17	3.05.82	1P	Glasgow	12 Dec
1.67	Pauline Richards		30.06.68	H	Arles, FRA	23 May
1.67	Kelly Sotherton	U23	13.11.76	H	Arles, FRA	23 May
1.67	Danielle Parkinson	U17	2.09.81	1	Stretford	13 Jun
	(60)					
1.67	Caroline Barber	U15	1.09.83	3	Exeter	10 Jul
1.67	Susannah Green	U17	5.12.81	3	Exeter	11 Jul
1.66 i	Laura Redmond	U20	19.04.81	1	Glasgow	29 Jan
1.65				2	Coatbridge	17 May
1.66 i	Hannah Stares	U23	13.11.78	4P	Birmingham	8 Feb
1.66	Angela Martin	U20	26.11.80	1	Whitehaven	16 May
1.66	Bev Howarth	U23	4.09.76	2	Birmingham	18 Jul
1.66	Dawn Walker	U15	29.09.83	1	Blackpool	29 Aug
1.66	Nicola Gautier	U23	21.03.78	H	Dordrecht, HOL	29 Aug
1.66	Jennie Woods	U15	28.01.84	1	Birmingham	6 Sep
1.66	Davina Ho	U15	20.11.83	2	Birmingham	6 Sep
	(70)					
1.66	Helen Thieme	U17	28.09.81	2H	Hull	19 Sep
1.65 i	Gillian Stewart	U20	21.01.80	2=	Glasgow	31 Jan
1.65 i	Katherine Silto	U17	12.08.83	1	Birmingham	1 Feb
1.65				1	Salisbury	10 May

1.65 i	Natalia Norford	U17	29.09.82	2	Birmingham	22	Feb
1.65				1	Bedford	9	Aug
1.65 i	Rachel Hogg	U17	11.06.82	3=	Birmingham	22	Feb
1.62				2H	Wrexham	28	Jun
1.65 i	Katherine Livesey	U20	15.12.79	5	Birmingham	22	Feb
1.65				H	Wrexham	1	Aug
1.65 i	Basilie Moffat	U23	8.04.78	3	Birmingham	25	Feb
1.65				4=	Cudworth	9	May
1.65 i	Jackie Powell		1.05.74	1	London (CP)	1	Mar
1.65 i	Kerry Saunders	U23	28.03.77	4	Glasgow	15	Mar
1.65				6	Bath	2	May
1.65	Jane Scott	U20	22.06.81	2	Glasgow (S)	9	May
(80)							
1.65	Claire Farquharson	U23	28.12.78	1	Crawley	9	May
1.65	Laura O'Sullivan	U17	30.07.82	2	Bebington	10	May
1.65	Katie Wigham	U15	27.05.84	1	Carlisle	20	May
1.65	Lisa Biscoe	U17	13.01.83	1	London (Ha)	23	May
1.65	Julie Hynan	U20	23.05.80	1	Wrexham	25	May
1.65	Ailsa Wallace	U23	12.03.77	1	Croydon	7	Jun
1.65	Kelly Moreton	U20	18.09.79	2	Cwmbran	20	Jun
1.65	Vicki Kellaway	U17	21.10.82	3	Kingston	28	Jun
1.65 i	Louise Irvine	U17	16.10.82	3	Grangemouth	12	Jul
1.65	Audrey Duncan		5.02.72	3	Edinburgh	18	Jul
(90)							
1.65	Frances Harris		1.06.72	4	Crawley	19	Jul
1.65	Emily Tugwell	U23	26.05.78	4	Enfield	19	Jul
1.65	Michelle Smith	U23	1.01.78	5	Crawley	19	Jul
1.65	Jodie Hearne	U17	17.09.81	2H	Enfield	1	Aug
1.65	Teresa Andrews	U23	4.01.77	H	Wrexham	1	Aug
1.65	Jennifer Glaysher	U17	3.05.83	3	Cudworth	2	Aug
1.65	Sarah Still		24.09.75	3	Coatbridge	29	Aug

Additional Under 17 (1 - 23 above)

1.63 i	Jennifer Saunders		21.10.81	2	London (CP)	1	Mar
1.63	Emma Kavanagh		3.12.82	1	Stevenage	31	May
1.63	Helen Weekes		4.10.81	1	Ashford	26	Jul
1.63	Donna Maylor		20.05.82	1	Cannock	13	Sep
1.63	Suzie Furlonger		30.09.81	1	Telford	13	Sep
1.63	Tina Thirwell		5.09.81	2H	Hull	20	Sep
1.63	Siobhan Dennehy		31.08.82	1H	Basildon	26	Sep

Additional Under 15 (1 - 9 above)

1.64	Jan Taylor		5.11.83	4	Exeter	10	Jul
(10)							
1.64	Alex Selwyn		20.09.83	5	Exeter	10	Jul
1.63	Lara Carty		7.03.84	1P	Enfield	2	Aug
1.63	Olivia Ross-Hurst		10.12.83	2P	Hull	20	Sep
1.62	Sarah Henderson		27.09.83	1	London (He)	18	Jul
1.61	India Hadland		7.01.85	6=	Exeter	10	Jul
1.60	Sam McCleggan		25.10.83	1	Stretford	18	Aug
1.60	Rebecca Mawer		31.01.84	1	Nottingham	12	Sep

Under 13

1.53	Staci Stewart		20.09.85	P	Grangemouth	13	Jun
1.51	Rebecca Bell		1.12.85	1	Bury St. Edmunds	20	Sep
1.50	Jadean Clarke		17.08.86	1	London (TB)	8	Aug
1.50	Sophie Upton		18.09.85	1	Solihull	13	Sep
1.49	Jade Halket		5.05.86	1	Ellon	27	Jul
1.47	Cheryl Shepherd		8.03.86	2	Coatbridge	2	Aug
1.46	Phyllis Agbo		16.12.85		Peterborough	22	Aug
1.46	J. Ellis			1	Nottingham	12	Sep

292

1.45	Katrina Peterson	6.08.86	1B	Redditch	9 Aug
1.45	Jenny Christie	28.09.85	1	Leamington	10 Sep
	(10)				
1.45	Vicki Allan	31.12.85	2	Grangemouth	13 Sep
1.44	Tanya Brook	20.02.87	1	Cleckheaton	6 Sep
1.44	Elen Davies		2	Bury St. Edmonds	20 Sep

Foreign

1.86 i	Dalia Mikneviciuté (ex LIT)	5.09.70	1	London (CP)	19 Dec
1.85 i			1	London (CP)	14 Feb
1.84 i			1	London (CP)	17 Jan
1.83 i			4	Birmingham	8 Feb
1.80			1	Kingston	20 May

POLE VAULT

4.31	Janine Whitlock	11.08.73	1	Bedford	30 May
4.30			4	Cottbus, GER	27 May
4.30			2	St. Petersburg, RUS	27 Jun
4.28 i			4	Sindelfingen, GER	8 Mar
4.25 i			4	Valencia, SPA	1 Mar
4.25			1	Loughborough	17 May
4.22			4	Sheffield	2 Aug
4.21 i			2	New York, USA	13 Feb
4.20 i			4	Berlin, GER	6 Mar
4.20			1	Arles, FRA	23 May
4.18 i			2	Bielefeld, GER	6 Feb
4.17			2	Arles, FRA	24 May
4.15 i			6	Erfurt,GER	4 Feb
4.12 i			1	Wakefield	10 Jan
4.11 i			1	Birmingham	8 Feb
4.10 i			Q	Valencia, SPA	27 Feb
4.10			1	Leeds	7 Jun
4.10			3	Linz, AUT	5 Jul
4.10			1	Birmingham	25 Jul
4.10			4	Kuala Lumpur, MAL	19 Sep
4.01			1	Stellenbosch, RSA	7 Jan
4.01			5=	Milan, ITA	5 Jun
4.00			3=	Ostrava, CZE	11 Jun
4.00			1	Birmingham	18 Jul
4.00			17=Q	Budapest, HUN	18 Aug
3.92			1	Cardiff	4 Aug
3.91	Emma Hornby 2ᴺᴰ	12.12.73	1	Belfast	27 Jun
3.81			1	Derby	21 Jun
3.80			1	Halesowen	13 Jul
3.80			1	Stoke	15 Jul
3.71			1	Worcester	9 May
3.70			2	Bedford	30 May
3.70			4	Birmingham	25 Jul
3.70			1	Stoke	9 Aug
3.85 A	Allie Murray-Jessee 5	13.01.67	1	Albuquerque, USA	16 Jun
3.83 A			1	El Paso, USA	26 Jun
3.60			5	Cardiff	4 Aug
3.82	Rhian Clarke	U23	19.04.77	4	Arles, FRA	24 May
3.82 sq			4	Hof, GER	10 Jul
3.80 i			2	Birmingham	8 Feb
3.80			2	Birmingham	25 Jul
3.80			11	Kuala Lumpur, MAL	19 Sep
3.70			3	Stellenbosch, RSA	7 Jan
3.70 i			1	Genoa, ITA	14 Feb
3.70			2	Irvine, USA	2 May
3.70			3	Leeds	7 Jun

1998

Height	Name	Cat	DOB	Pos	Venue	Date
(Clarke)	3.70			1	Cwmbran	20 Jun
	3.70			2	Rheinau-Freistett, GER	28 Jun
	3.70			4	Dessau, GER	1 Aug
3.80	Lucy Webber 6		5.02.72	1	Watford	21 Jun
	3.72			6	Arles, FRA	24 May
	3.71			2	Loughborough	17 May
	3.70			1	Fullerton, USA	23 Apr
	3.70			8	Arles, FRA	23 May
	3.70			5	Birmingham	25 Jul
3.80	Paula Wilson 7		20.11.69	3	Birmingham	25 Jul
	3.80			2	Cardiff	4 Aug
	3.70			2	Derby	21 Jun
	3.70			2	Stoke	15 Jul
	3.70			12	Kuala Lumpur, MAL	19 Sep
3.75	Louise Schramm 8		18.12.71	1	Crawley	19 Jul
	3.70			1	Kingston	27 Jun
3.75	Tracey Bloomfield 9	U20	13.09.79	1	London (He)	9 Aug
	3.72			1	London (Ha)	24 May
	3.70			1	Bedford	22 Aug
3.70	Linda Stanton		22.06.73	2	Leeds	7 Jun
	3.70			6	Birmingham	25 Jul

66 performances to 3.70 by 9 athletes including 11 indoors

Height	Name	Cat	DOB	Pos	Venue	Date
3.60 A	Krissy Owen 11		14.12.75	2	El Paso, USA	9 May
	3.52			1	Long Beach, USA	18 Apr
(10)						
3.60	Fiona Harrison 12	U17	30.11.81	2	Bedford	25 May
3.60	Clare Ridgley 13	U23	11.09.77	3	Bedford	25 May
3.60	Alison Davies 14	V35	6.04.61	1	Watford	29 Jul
3.55	Kim Rothman 15		6.09.64	4	Barcelona, SPA	17 Jun
3.50	Noelle Bradshaw 16	V35	18.12.63	11	Birmingham	25 Jul
3.41	Hilary Smith 17	U23	28.02.76	1	Carshalton	20 Sep
3.40	Maria Newton 19		22.07.66	1	Ashford	10 May
3.40	Danielle Codd 20	U20	17.02.79	5	Bedford	4 Jul
3.40	Becky Ridgley 21	U20	26.02.80	1	Bath	5 Jul
3.40	Laura Patterson 22	U20	31.01.81	1	London (He)	30 Aug
(20)						
3.35	Lindsay Hodges 23	U17	21.09.82	1	Yeovil	5 Sep
3.20 i	Jenny Cunnane	V40	23.02.57	11	Birmingham	8 Feb
	3.10			3	Cudworth	2 Aug
3.20 i	Kate Alexander		28.04.74	12=	Birmingham	8 Feb
	3.20			6	Watford	21 Jun
3.20 i	Suzanne Woods 30	U23	29.12.76	2	Glasgow	15 Mar
	3.20				Loughborough	10 Jun
3.20	Rebecca Roles=96	U20	14.12.79	2	Cwmbran	20 Jun
3.20	Ellie Spain 31	U17	23.08.82	1	Cannock	13 Sep
3.10	Dawn-Alice Wright	U23	20.01.76	3	Derby	21 Jun
3.10	Jo Hughes 37		7.12.71	4	Watford	29 Jul
3.10	Kate Rowe 38	U23	13.09.78	1	Peterborough	31 Aug
3.10 i	Kathryn Dowsett 39	U23	24.11.78	1	London (CP)	19 Dec
	3.00			3	Liverpool	16 Aug
(30)						
3.05 i	Sarah Hartley	U20	4.05.81	3	Birmingham	22 Feb
	2.90			1	Liverpool	26 Jul
3.05	Amy Rennison 40	U17	15.06.83	1	Stoke	4 Aug
3.05	Larissa Lowe	V35	19.08.63	1	Peterborough	22 Aug
3.03	Anna Watson 41	U17	30.04.82	1	Inverness	13 Sep
3.01 i	Louise Gauld 42	U20	24.08.80	1	Glasgow	16 Dec
	2.80			3	Edinburgh	17 Jul
3.00 i	Kia Wnuk	U17	31.10.81	1	London (CP)	28 Feb
	3.00			1	London (CP)	19 Apr
3.00	Ruth Anness	U23	3.10.78	1	King's Lynn	25 Apr

3.00	Jayne Collins	U20	27.03.80	1	Worcester	9 May
3.00	Fiona Peake	U23	31.05.77	7	Loughborough	17 May
3.00	Penny Hall	U23	13.01.77	4	Newport	16 Aug
(40)						
3.00	Eirion Owen	V35	30.07.63	2	Cesenatico, ITA	12 Sep
2.91	Alison Deuchars		20.01.67	1	Edinburgh	9 May
2.90	Jo-Anne Nightingale	U17	3.05.83	3	London (Ha)	24 May
2.90	Julie Hynan	U20	23.05.80	4	Liverpool	16 Aug
2.85	Caroline Nutt	U17	17.06.83	1	Derby	9 Aug
2.80 i	Hannah Gray	U20	15.06.81	2	Antwerp, BEL	10 Jan
2.70				4	London (Ha)	24 May
2.80 i	Rachel Foster	U23	1.09.76	1	Gateshead	19 Mar
2.80				1	Middlesbrough	9 Jun
2.80	Zoe Parsons	U17	11.02.83	1	Ashford	18 Apr
2.80	Kelly Ridgway	U17	14.04.82	1	York	25 Jul
2.80	Janet Yousden		25.11.68	2	Stoke	9 Aug
(50)						
2.80	Donna Hunter	U17	9.10.81	4=	Sheffield	15 Aug
2.80	Cariann Cutts	U15	1.02.85	1	Cudworth	30 Aug
2.80	Victoria Bramhall	U23	13.10.77	2	London (TB)	19 Sep
2.80	Amie Everitt	U23	1.11.78	3	Carshalton	20 Sep
2.70 i	Kathryn Burley	U20	5.02.79	9	Birmingham	25 Jan
2.50				1	London (Elt)	22 Aug
2.70	Helen Webb	U20	14.04.80	2	Solihull	23 May
2.70	Julia Cockram		1.01.68	1	London (WL)	30 May
2.70	Joanne Cozens	U20	9.04.80	4	Woodford	30 May
2.70	Michelle Smith	U20	28.05.80	2	Grangemouth	1 Jul
2.70 i	Kirsty Maguire	U17	5.07.83	3	Grangemouth	12 Jul
2.50				2=	Edinburgh	19 Jun
(60)						
2.70	Claudia Filce		11.11.72	2	Exeter	5 Sep
2.65	Susan Williams	U20	20.01.79	1	Barry	14 Jul
2.60 i	Kate Harrison	U17	21.07.82	3	Birmingham	4 Jan
2.60 i	Rebecca Morgan	U23	1.11.78	2	Birmingham	4 Jan
2.60 i	Liz Tapper	U23	2.06.78	1	Glasgow	18 Feb
2.60	Lindsay Miles	U17	17.10.81	1	Crawley	21 Mar
2.60	Elaine Murphy		2.09.75	5	Bath	2 May
2.60	Katie Skepes	U20	11.12.80	4	Croydon	7 Jun
2.60	Melissa Stamp	U20	5.07.81	1	Hull	13 Jun
2.60	Janet Lyon	V35	12.03.62	3	Aberdeen	26 Jul
(70)						
2.60	Natalie Warren	U20	28.08.81	2	Stoke	4 Aug
2.60	Rachel Kelly	U20	15.06.81	3	Exeter	9 Aug
2.60	Lynn Vale		9.01.71	2	Bedford	22 Aug
2.60 i	Sarah Randles	U20	6.06.80	2	Gateshead	15 Jan
2.60				1	Gateshead	29 Aug
2.60	Liz Hughes	U23	9.06.77	2	Bedford	30 Aug
2.60	Becky Stone	U17	27.11.82	3	Telford	12 Sep
2.60	Kelly Scrambler	U20	21.11.79	3	Cannock	13 Sep
2.60	Claire Dunstan	U17	15.10.81	1=	Derby	20 Sep
2.55	Megan Freeth	U17	1.02.82	1	Yate	26 Jul
2.50	Jemma Harding	U20	15.02.79	3	High Wycombe	25 Apr
(80)						
2.50	Emily Morris	U17	30.09.82	1	Rotherham	21 Jun
2.50	Louise Simpson	U23	18.12.77	3	Stoke	5 Jul
2.50	Nikki Witton		30.09.72	4	Bath	5 Jul
2.50	Jacqueline Marshall	U20	20.07.79	4	Aberdeen	26 Jul
2.50	Fiona McDougall	U20	1.08.81	3	Stoke	4 Aug
2.50	Kim Hobbs	U23	12.12.78	2	Derby	9 Aug
2.50	Carol Eames	V50	2.06.47	4	Ware	22 Aug
2.50	Catherine MacRae	U20	1.01.79	2	Crawley	22 Aug
2.50	Judy Turton	U15	26.05.84	1	Woking	6 Sep

Under 13

2.10		Laura Dawson 2ND		23.01.86	1	Scunthorpe	20	Jun
2.00		Natalie Olson		9.05.86	1	Ashford	24	Jun

Foreign

2.80		*Danielle MacCarthy (IRE) U17*		*13.09.81*	*8*	*Sheffield*	*15*	*Aug*
2.60		*Metra Meszarosova (SVK) U23*		*12.02.76*	*2*	*London (WL)*	*30*	*May*

LONG JUMP

6.63	0.0	Jo Wise		15.03.71	1	Kuala Lumpur, MAL	19	Sep
		6.58	0.9		6	Linz, AUT	5	Jul
		6.43 w	2.2		1	Cork, IRE	27	Jun
		6.39	1.6		6	Gateshead	19	Jul
		6.33	1.9		*	Cork, IRE	27	Jun
		6.31			1	Stoke	9	Aug
		6.23	0.1		4	Birmingham	25	Jul
		6.20			1	Peterborough	31	Aug
6.59	1.4	Denise Lewis		27.08.72	1H	Budapest, HUN	22	Aug
		6.52	0.1		1H	Kuala Lumpur, MAL	17	Sep
		6.44	0.3		1	Birmingham	25	Jul
		6.34	1.0		7	Gateshead	19	Jul
		6.30 i			8	Piraeus, GRE	21	Feb
		6.29 i			1	Birmingham	8	Feb
6.52	0.1	Sarah Claxton 16	U20	23.09.79	4	Annecy, FRA	31	Jul
		6.40 w	2.5		1	Loughborough	17	May
		6.34 w	2.1		1	Bedford	4	Jul
		6.32	1.1		7	St. Petersburg, RUS	28	Jun
		6.31	1.0		1	London (He)	9	Aug
		6.29	0.1		Q	Annecy, FRA	30	Jul
		6.27 w	2.2		2	Alicante, SPA	18	Jul
		6.22	0.6		1	Exeter	11	Jul
		6.21	1.8		*	Loughborough	17	May
		6.21 w	2.7		1	London (Ha)	23	May
6.39	1.4	Tracy Joseph 29		29.11.69	2	Cork, IRE	27	Jun
		6.38 w	4.6		2	Loughborough	17	May
		6.37 w	3.7		1	Bedford	25	May
		6.35	-2.0		1	Bedford	30	Aug
		6.35	-0.1		5	Kuala Lumpur, MAL	19	Sep
		6.34	0.9		*	Loughborough	17	May
		6.32			1	Kuala Lumpur, MAL	8	Sep
		6.28	0.8		1	Watford	21	Jun
		6.28 w			1	Portsmouth	10	May
		6.26 w	3.4		2	Ljubljana, SLO	31	May
		6.24	-0.4		2	Birmingham	25	Jul
		6.21 i			2	Birmingham	8	Feb
		6.20	1.4		*	Bedford	25	May
6.36	1.1	Andrea Coore 3(ST		23.04.69	1	Crawley	19	Jul
		6.31	0.2		1	Bedford	29	Aug
		6.25			6	Jena, GER	24	May
		6.23	0.2		3	Birmingham	25	Jul
6.29 w	4.0	Julie Hollman 65	U23	16.02.77	1	Bath	3	May
		6.17	1.8 65TH		4	Cork, IRE	27	Jun
6.28		Ruth Irving 72		20.07.74	1	Gateshead	9	May
		6.21 w	2.5		2	Bedford	25	May
6.28 w		Donita Benjamin		5.03.72	1	Abingdon	18	Jul
		6.09	-0.3 88		5	Birmingham	25	Jul
6.23	0.3	Ashia Hansen		5.12.71	4	Vilamoura, POR	30	May

46 performances to 6.20 by 9 athletes including 3 indoors and 12 wind assisted

6.16		Liz Ghojefa		24.02.69	1	Kingston	9	May

(10)

Mark	Wind	Name	Cat	DOB	Pos	Venue	Date
6.13 i		Julia Bennett 13		26.03.70	5P	Valencia, SPA	27 Feb
6.03					2	Kingston	9 May
6.08 w	4.8	Kerry Jury		19.11.68	H	Arles, FRA	24 May
5.96					1	Cudworth	10 May
6.08 w		Diana Bennett		14.06.74	1	Southampton	5 Sep
5.95					*	Southampton	5 Sep
6.07 i		Kelly Sotherton	U23	13.11.76	2	Birmingham	25 Feb
5.97 w	2.4				4	Loughborough	17 May
5.80							
6.06	-1.7	Connie Henry		15.04.72	7	Budapest, HUN	5 Jul
6.06 w	3.1	Syreena Pinel	U20	13.01.79	2	Bedford	4 Jul
5.88	1.1				6	Alicante, SPA	18 Jul
6.05	0.1	Danielle Freeman	U20	11.02.80	2	Exeter	11 Jul
6.04 w	2.1	Ann Brooks/Danson		4.05.71	1	Birmingham	18 Jul
5.95					1	Middlesbrough	14 Jun
6.01	1.1	Jackie White		12.01.71	1	Coventry	5 Jul
6.01 w	6.2	Jenny Kelly		20.06.70	H	Arles, FRA	24 May
5.86					H	Val de Reuil, FRA	26 Jul
(20)							
5.99		Gemma Holt		20.12.72	1	Hoo	22 Aug
5.97		Emma Hughes	U20	15.09.80	1	Braintree	21 Jun
5.94		Janine Whitlock		11.08.73	1	Derby	19 Jul
5.90	1.6	Pauline Richards		30.06.68	H	Bressanone, ITA	5 Jul
5.89		Michelle Dunkley	U23	26.01.78	1	Loughborough	26 Apr
5.89		Rachel Kirby		18.05.69	1	London (B)	21 Jun
5.88		Debbie Harrison	U23	13.11.78	1	Coventry	17 May
5.86		Sarah Wellstead	U20	22.10.79	1	Kingston	13 Jun
5.85		Adele Forester	U23	27.03.76	2	Gateshead	9 May
5.84 w	5.2	Aimee Cutler	U17	7.10.81	1	Sheffield	15 Aug
5.77					1	Brecon	8 Jul
(30)							
5.82		Kathryn Dowsett	U23	24.11.78	2	Loughborough	26 Apr
5.81 w	3.7	Denise Andrews	U20	1.07.80	1	Istanbul, TUR	26 Sep
5.78					*	Istanbul, TUR	26 Sep
5.80	-1.0	Monique Parris	U15	28.01.84	1	London (Ha)	23 May
5.79		Tammy McCammon	U23	17.10.76	1	Braintree	18 Jul
5.79	1.0	Caroline Black/Mercer		19.05.72	2	Edinburgh	18 Jul
5.77		Lucy Atunumuo	U20	4.11.80	1	Kingston	9 May
5.77		Katherine Livesey	U20	15.12.79	H	Wrexham	2 Aug
5.74 w	5.5	Elaine Smith	U17	16.05.83	1	Exeter	10 Jul
5.66 i					1	Jarrow	13 Dec
5.43					2	Leeds	23 May
5.73		Rachel Hogg	U17	11.06.82	1H	Wrexham	28 Jun
5.72 w	5.8	Chloe Cozens	U20	9.04.80	H	Arles, FRA	24 May
5.62					1	Bedford	22 Aug
(40)							
5.71		Fiona Westwood	U20	27.02.81	2	Cudworth	9 May
5.71 w		Caroline Stead		14.09.71	2	Coventry	5 Jul
5.68					2	Luton	14 Jun
5.70 w		Kerensa Denham		8.03.74	3	Coventry	5 Jul
5.70 w		Sarah Lane	U17	24.11.82	1	Aberdare	31 Aug
5.50					2	Brecon	8 Jul
5.67 w	5.4	Rachel Peacock	U17	18.05.82	2	Exeter	10 Jul
5.58	1.9				4	Sheffield	15 Aug
5.66		Catherine Parmiter	U20	27.04.81	1H	Carn Brea	27 Jun
5.66		Anna-Maria Thorpe		15.07.71	1	Southampton	27 Jun
5.65	1.0	Shani Anderson		7.08.75	7	Bedford	29 Aug
5.65	1.5	Jo Dear		8.06.75	8	Bedford	29 Aug
5.64		Charmaine Cameron	U20	9.09.80	1	Stoke	20 Jun
(50)							
5.64 w		Amanda Forrester	U23	29.09.78	2	Stoke	5 Jul

5.63	1.7	Vicky O'Brien	U17	15.11.82	1	Edinburgh	20	Jun
5.63		Helen Armishaw	U20	4.10.80	2	Stoke	20	Jun
5.63 w?		Claire Quigg	U17	13.10.81	3	Tullamore, IRE	6	Jun
5.62		Rebecca Baker	U20	7.02.79	1	London (WL)	30	May
5.62		Gemma Sargeant	U17	5.05.83	2	Luton	18	Jul
5.62		Debbie Rowe		8.09.72	2	Birmingham	23	Aug
5.61		Catriona Slater	U23	27.01.77	1	Braintree	25	Apr
5.60		Karen Skeggs		26.10.69	2	Hoo	27	Jun
5.60		Roz Gonse	U17	1.03.82	3	Kingston	28	Jun
	(60)							
5.60		Denise Gayle	U20	11.09.79	1	St. Albans	5	Sep
5.59		Angela Abrams		7.05.71	2	Portsmouth	22	Aug
5.59		Donna Maylor	U17	20.05.82	1H	Hull	20	Sep
5.59 w		Debbie Adams	U20	7.03.80	1	Cwmbran	10	May
5.54					1	Yate	26	Jul
5.58		Teresa Andrews	U23	4.01.77	1	Brecon	5	Jul
5.58		Hayley-Jane Cone	U20	16.07.80	1	Cambridge	16	Aug
5.58		Kim Crowther		19.01.66	1	Blackpool	6	Sep
5.58 w	5.0	Caroline Pearce	U20	1.09.80	6	Bedford	4	Jul
5.56	1.8				*	Bedford	4	Jul
5.57		Natalie Murray	U23	24.03.76	1	Crewe	9	May
5.56		Siobhan McVie	U15	6.07.84	1	Dublin (S), IRE	8	Aug
	(70)							
5.55		Rebecca White	U20	5.06.80	1	Blackburn	3	May
5.55		Clare Milborrow	U23	10.01.77	1	Brighton	30	May
5.55	0.9	Belinda Samuels	U23	29.11.78	7	Birmingham	6	Jun
5.55		Sharon Davidge	U17	15.09.81	1	Yeovil	14	Jun
5.55 w	3.2	Zainab Ceesay	U15	27.10.83	1	Sheffield	16	Aug
5.28	0.6				2	London (Ha)	23	May
5.54		Jackie Jenner	U23	25.10.76	2	Ashford	10	May
5.54		Vicky Williams	U20	11.04.81	1	Yeovil	10	May
5.54	0.6	Clova Court	V35	10.02.60	1H	Derby	31	May
5.54		Laura Patterson	U20	31.01.81	1	Hemel Hempstead	13	Jun
5.54	1.9	Michelle Johansen	U15	1.02.84	1	Worcester	12	Sep
	(80)							
5.53		Kate Rogers	U20	13.02.79	5	Bath	3	May
5.53		Tina Jones	U20	10.09.80	1	York	13	Jun
5.53		Rosie Curling	U20	5.09.80	2	Newport	16	Aug
5.53 w		Natalie Butler	U23	25.11.78	2	Southampton	5	Sep
5.51					2	London (He)	22	Aug
5.51		Rebecca Lewis	U23	31.12.77	1	Oxford	16	May
5.51		Mary Devlin	U20	14.09.79		Tullamore, IRE	6	Jun
5.51		Lisa Caryl		21.11.75	1	Wrexham	14	Jun
5.51		Nikki Gilding		16.05.72	1	Reading	18	Jul
5.51		Kirsty Corbett	U17	16.05.82	1	Bury St. Edmonds	13	Sep
5.50 i		Sarah Damm		12.09.70	1	Birmingham	4	Jan
	(90)							
5.50		Amelia Martin	U20	11.02.80	1	Croydon	30	May
5.50		Laura Smith	U20	16.11.80	1	Cudworth	5	Jul
5.50		Becky Folds		28.01.75	2	Abingdon	18	Jul

Additional Under 17 (1 - 12 above)

5.49		Kim Wall		21.04.83	1	Hoo	26	Apr
5.49		Stacey Martin		6.08.82	1	Brecon	12	Jul
5.49 w	2.7	Wendy Davidson		14.10.82	6	Sheffield	15	Aug
5.48	1.2				*	Sheffield	15	Aug
5.48 i		Vicky Hyland		27.10.81	3	Birmingham	22	Feb
5.33					1	Liverpool	19	Jul
5.45 i		Mandy Crompton		25.03.82	4	Birmingham	22	Feb
5.42					1	Middlesbrough	25	Apr
5.45 w	4.4	Shukurat Mumuni		27.01.82	8	Sheffield	15	Aug
5.37					1	London (CP)	19	Apr

5.44		Claire Pleavin	25.04.83	1	Stoke	20	Jun
5.43		Rebecca Jones	17.01.83	1	Wrexham	19	Jul
(20)							
5.41		Lucy Butler	18.11.81	1	Gateshead	9	May
5.40		Suzie Furlonger	30.09.81	1	Solihull	23	May
5.40		Sian Jones	20.01.83	1	Swansea	19	Jul
5.40		Cheryl McHardy	8.09.81	1	Aberdeen	26	Jul
5.40	1.5	Nadia Williams	17.11.81	3	Cannock	13	Sep
5.40 w	4.8	Rachel Redmond	7.12.81	2	Gran Canaria, SPA	27	Jul
5.39	1.6	Katie Richardson	12.09.82	2	York	25	Jul
5.37 i		Rebecca Bates	16.05.82	6	Birmingham	22	Feb
5.35				1	Stoke	9	Aug
5.37		Rebecca Lee	31.12.82	1	Corby	20	Jun
5.36		Tina Thirwell	5.09.81	2H	Hull	20	Sep
(30)							
5.36 w		Natalie Brant	11.12.82	3	Southampton	5	Sep
5.35		Alison Croad	10.06.82	1	London (TB)	25	Apr
5.35		Llinos Hughes	31.03.82	1	Barry	5	Jul
5.35		Laura Daley	17.05.83	1	Telford	26	Jul

Additional Under 15 (1 - 4 above)

5.44		Melissa Harris	20.10.83	2	Dublin (S), IRE	8	Aug
5.43		Danielle Selley	19.12.83	1	Brecon	8	Jul
5.43 w	2.4	Henrietta Paxton	19.09.83	2	Exeter	10	Jul
5.40				1P	Hull	20	Sep
5.35		Laura Paterson	8.09.83	2	Grangemouth	23	Aug
5.35 w	2.5	Alicia Bateson	6.11.83	4	Exeter	10	Jul
5.32				1	Stoke	20	Jun
5.33		Symone Belle	12.11.84	1	Carshalton	20	Sep
(10)							
5.32		Sarah Bratley	20.09.84	1	Nottingham	12	Sep
5.31		Helen Davies	24.03.84	2	Brecon	8	Jul
5.31 w	4.0	Kimberley Goodall	5.10.83	5	Exeter	10	Jul
5.28		Melissa Rogers	2.09.83	1	Watford	31	May
5.27		Chanelle Garnett	16.08.85	2	Carshalton	20	Sep
5.25		Danielle Humphreys	16.05.84	1	Mansfield	11	Sep
5.25 w	3.3	Sarah Henderson	27.09.83	6	Exeter	10	Jul
5.23		Megan Lishman	15.11.83	1	Whitehaven	16	May
5.20		Aileen Wilson	30.03.84	2P	Hull	20	Sep
5.19		Gemma Fergusson	20.08.84	1	York	25	Jul

overage

5.27 i		Lara Carty	7.03.84	2P	Glasgow	12	Dec

Under 13

5.28		Elley Derby	20.12.85	1	Cannock	10	May
4.83		Karen Mylan	8.11.85	1	Ilford	27	Jun
4.83		Sophie Newington	15.09.85	1	Brecon	15	Jul
4.80		Maria Garavand	30.06.86	1	Birmingham	6	Sep
4.73		Chloe Gee	1.12.85	1	Norwich	19	Jul
4.67		J. Scott		1	Mansfield	5	Apr
4.65	1.9	Kate Slade	26.11.85	1	Grangemouth	11	Jul
4.63		Louise Hazel	6.10.85	2	Kingston	26	Jul

Foreign

5.94 i		*Margaret Veldman*	7.06.74	1P	*Glasgow*	14	Feb
		5.83 *1.5*		3	*Bedford*	29	Aug
5.56		*Hilde Kaland (NOR)*	22.05.73	2	*Middlesbrough*	14	Jun

299

TRIPLE JUMP

Mark	Wind	Name	Cat	DOB	Pos	Venue	Day	Mon
15.16 i		Ashia Hansen		5.12.71	1	Valencia, SPA	28	Feb
14.85 i					1	Birmingham	15	Feb
14.73 i					2	Lievin, FRA	22	Feb
14.48 i					Q	Valencia, SPA	27	Feb
14.47 i					1	Ghent, BEL	8	Feb
14.32	0.1				1	Kuala Lumpur, MAL	21	Sep
14.31 i					2	Ostrava, CZE	29	Jan
14.30 imx						Birmingham	25	Jan
14.19 i					1	Birmingham	7	Feb
13.91					1	Kuala Lumpur, MAL	8	Sep
13.39	1.0				1	Bedford	29	Aug
13.95	0.5	Connie Henry		15.04.72	4	St. Petersburg, RUS	27	Jun
13.95					1	Thurrock	31	Aug
13.94	0.2				3	Kuala Lumpur, MAL	21	Sep
13.90	0.6				1	Birmingham	25	Jul
13.86	0.5				1	Melbourne, AUS	15	Mar
13.81	1.4				2	Tallinn, EST	19	Jun
13.77	0.8				20Q	Budapest, HUN	19	Aug
13.69	2.0				1	Sydney, AUS	14	Feb
13.63	-0.7				3	Vilamoura, POR	30	May
13.50					2	Waldshut-Tiengen, GER	2	Aug
13.49	1.6				2	Hobart, AUS	21	Feb
13.47	0.2				1	Brisbane, AUS	21	Mar
13.40 w	2.9				1	Loughborough	17	May
13.37	1.5				*	Loughborough	17	May
13.33	1.2				1	Canberra, AUS	8	Mar
13.26 w	2.8				1	Crawley	19	Jul
13.19	0.5				*	Crawley	19	Jul
13.15 w	2.4				1	Bedford	24	May
13.94		Michelle Griffith		6.10.71	1	Enfield	19	Jul
13.84	0.3				2	Birmingham	25	Jul
13.83					1	Waldshut-Tiengen, GER	2	Aug
13.77	0.5				5	Kuala Lumpur, MAL	21	Sep
13.71					1	Southampton	5	Sep
13.45 w	4.7				1	Grangemouth	4	Jul
13.42	0.4				1	Watford	20	Jun
13.40	0.6				1	Birmingham	6	Jun

37 performances to 13.00 by 3 athletes including 8 indoors and 4 wind assisted

Mark	Wind	Name	Cat	DOB	Pos	Venue	Day	Mon
12.69 w	2.1	Debbie Rowe		8.09.72	2	Bedford	29	Aug
12.61	1.9 14				*	Bedford	29	Aug
12.65 w	3.1	Kate Evans		4.02.74	2	Loughborough	17	May
12.56	0.9				1	Birmingham	18	Jul
12.61		Kerensa Denham 13		8.03.74	1	Luton	14	Jun
12.61 w	4.4	Judy Kotey	U20	20.05.80	1	Bedford	5	Jul
12.41 i	20TN				3	Birmingham	28	Feb
12.33	1.3				4	Loughborough	17	May
12.50		Julia Johnson 16	U20	21.09.79	1	Ashford	21	Jun
12.47		Anna-Maria Thorpe 17		15.07.71	1	Kingston	13	Sep
12.44		Karen Skeggs		26.10.69	1	Ashford	9	May
	(10)							
12.36	0.0	Liz Gibbens	U23	5.04.77	2	Bath	4	May
12.27		Nikki Barr 21		26.04.70	1	Coatbridge	17	May
12.26		Caroline Stead		14.09.71	1	Woodford	30	May
12.22	0.8	Liz Patrick 25	U23	29.08.77	3	Bath	4	May
12.22	0.4	Rachel Kirby		18.05.69	5	Birmingham	25	Jul
12.20	0.9	Jodie Hurst	U23	21.06.77	4	Bath	4	May
12.07 i		Justina Cruickshank	U23	27.09.77	1	Glasgow	18	Jan
11.68	1.2				6	Bath	4	May

Mark		Name	Cat	DOB	Pos	Venue	Date
12.07 w	5.1	Rachel Peacock	U17	18.05.82	1	Ayr	18 Jul
11.49	0.7				1	London (Ha)	24 May
11.88		Rachel Atkinson		26.05.73	1	Cudworth	9 May
11.87		Kirsty Payne	U23	22.10.77	1	Watford	15 Aug
(20)							
11.86		Kerry Jury		19.11.68	3	Enfield	19 Jul
11.85		Hayley Warrilow	U20	10.04.80	1	Stoke	13 Jun
11.83		Shani Anderson		7.08.75	2	Watford	15 Aug
11.73		Liz Ghojefa		24.02.69	1	Kingston	14 Jun
11.70 i		Pamela Anderson	U23	16.10.76	1	Glasgow	28 Jan
11.62	1.3				2	Glasgow (S)	10 May
11.69 w	2.2	Leandra Polius	U20	14.05.80	4	Bedford	5 Jul
11.62	0.6				4	Exeter	11 Jul
11.69 w	2.6	Claire Quigg	U17	13.10.81	3	Ayr	18 Jul
11.35					1	Tullamore, IRE	12 Jul
11.68 w	4.1	Rachel Hogg	U17	11.06.82	4	Ayr	18 Jul
11.44	1.7				1	Leeds	23 May
11.67		Rebecca White	U20	5.06.80	1	Blackpool	9 May
11.55 i		Milly Clements	U23	20.05.77	6	Glasgow	14 Mar
11.20					7	Bath	4 May
(30)							
11.54		Andrea Hall	U23	28.01.77	1	Bournemouth	25 Apr
11.48 w		Sarah Wellstead	U20	22.10.79	1	Sutton	18 Jul
11.13 i					1	London (CP)	14 Feb
11.00					1	Plymouth	30 May
11.47		Tolu Jegede	U20	25.09.80	2	Bournemouth	25 Apr
11.46		Joyce Adams	U20	25.03.80	1	Birmingham	21 Jun
11.45 w		Stephanie Aneto	U23	23.08.77	2	Sutton	18 Jul
11.40		Catherine Barnes	U23	28.09.77	1	Southampton	25 Apr
11.38		Louise Bryce	U20	19.04.81	2	Coatbridge	2 Aug
11.38 i		Joanne Stanley	U23	30.03.77	1	Jarrow	13 Dec
11.30 w	3.7				5	Liverpool	20 Jun
11.02	1.9				9	Bedford	24 May
11.38 w	3.7	Lisa Bennington	U23	12.12.78	3	Liverpool	20 Jun
11.20					2	Scunthorpe	10 May
11.34 w	3.8	Kerry Saunders	U23	28.03.77	4	Liverpool	20 Jun
11.27					1	Oldham	11 Jul
(40)							
11.33 w	4.9	Stacy McGivern	U23	14.12.76	8	Bedford	24 May
11.25					1	Milton Keynes	27 Jun
11.31		Bethan Page-Jones	U23	30.11.76	1	Oxford	16 May
11.30 i		Nicky Clark	U23	14.04.77	1	Sheffield	17 Jan
11.22					1	Scunthorpe	9 May
11.30		Sarah Fleetham	U20	9.01.79	4	Thurrock	31 Aug
11.27	0.2	Sharon Oakes	U17	26.08.82	2	Cannock	13 Sep
11.26	-0.5	Wendy Colman	U20	12.02.81	5	Exeter	11 Jul
11.25		Caroline Warden		16.09.72	1	Bebington	9 Aug
11.23		Catherine Burrows	U23	11.02.76	1	Blackburn	7 Jun
11.22 i		Rebecca Bates	U17	16.05.82	4	Birmingham	22 Feb
11.05 w	4.4				5	Sheffield	16 Aug
10.87					1	Cannock	9 May
11.22		Suzie Furlonger	U17	30.09.81	1	Galashiels	30 Aug
(50)							
11.21		Lisa Caryl		21.11.75	2	Cudworth	2 Aug
11.21 w		Jenny Brown	V35	21.05.59	3	Sutton	18 Jul
11.14					3	Ashford	16 Aug
11.20 w	4.1	Denise Howell	U17	16.07.82	3	Sheffield	16 Aug
11.08	0.3				2	Bedford	30 Aug
11.18 w	2.2	Hannah Moody	U20	26.07.79	2	Leeds	23 May
11.17					1	Leeds	13 Jun
11.17		Rebecca Baker	U20	7.02.79	1	London (WL)	30 May

11.17	1.0	Becky Ridgley	U20	26.02.80	2	Crawley	19	Jul
11.15		Kathryn Blackwood	U23	31.03.76	8	Bath	4	May
11.15		Hazel Carawardine	U20	6.11.80	1	Wigan	31	May
11.15		Maria Pringle	U20	18.12.80	1	Jarrow	20	Jun
11.15		Jessica Sample	U20	3.01.80	1	Cambridge	1	Aug
	(60)							
11.15	1.5	Natalie Brant	U17	11.12.82	1	Bedford	30	Aug
11.13		Maurine Okwue	U23	13.05.78	1	London (TB)	25	Apr
11.12		Natasha Brunning		10.03.73	1	Guildford	18	Jul
11.12	1.0	Angela Williams	U20	13.05.81	3	Crawley	19	Jul
11.12		Sarah Akinbiyi	U20	23.08.81	2	Kingston	13	Sep
11.11 w	2.5	Kelly Brow	U23	24.09.78	7	Liverpool	20	Jun
11.10					1	Blackpool	6	Sep
11.10		Laura Patterson	U20	31.01.81	1	High Wycombe	9	May
11.10		Emily Tugwell	U23	26.05.78	2	Exeter	9	Aug
11.10		Katie Jones	U23	4.01.77	3	Liverpool	16	Aug
11.10	1.4	Debbie Lloyd	U17	26.09.81	5	Bruges, BEL	23	Aug
	(70)							
11.09		Evette Finikin		25.09.63	1	London (He)	22	Aug
11.08		Debbie Flynn	U20	22.01.81	1	Tamworth	19	Apr
11.08		Natasha Faulkner		8.07.73	1	Birmingham	5	Aug
11.08		Gemma Holt		20.12.72	1	Exeter	5	Sep
11.07		Sarah Roberts	U23	25.06.78	1	Hoo	14	Jun
11.05		Clare Ridgley	U23	11.09.77	2	Oxford	16	May
11.05		Natalie Wright		13.11.73	2	London (Elt)	22	Aug
11.04 i		Sally Ash	U20	4.11.80	1	King's Lynn	28	Feb
11.04		Louise Gauld	U20	24.08.80	1	Coatbridge	21	Jun
11.04		Nikki Gilding		16.05.72	1	Reading	18	Jul
	(80)							
11.04	1.1	Alison Rough	U17	1.06.83	6	Sheffield	16	Aug
11.03 i		Ria Dickinson	U20	14.12.79	4	Birmingham	21	Feb
11.03		Sian Jones	U17	20.01.83	1	Yate	26	Jul
11.03 w		Louise Wood	U17	13.05.83	1	Braintree	18	Jul
11.03 w	3.8	Cheryl McHardy	U17	8.09.81	7	Sheffield	16	Aug
10.80					1	Aberdeen	5	Jul
11.02		Abigail Ashby	U23	23.11.77	3	Cudworth	9	May
11.02 w	2.6	Danielle Codd	U20	17.02.79	1	London (He)	9	Aug
11.01 i		Laura Eastwood	U20	7.04.81		Birmingham	4	Jan
11.00		Zoe McKinnon	U17	8.09.81	1	Portsmouth	22	Aug

Additional Under 17 (1 - 14 above)

10.99 w	3.8	Lara Richards	7.03.83	6	Ayr	18	Jul
10.88					Cardiff	1	Jul
10.98		Sarah Strevens	7.10.81	3	Hoo	22	Aug
10.96	0.6	Jennifer Glaysher	3.05.83	2	York	25	Jul
10.95		Megan Freeth	1.02.82	2	Yate	26	Jul
10.94 w	2.1	Helen Williams	13.01.83	3	York	25	Jul
10.66				1	Crewe	9	May
10.93		Jennifer Handley	8.06.83	1	Cleckheaton	30	Aug
	(20)						
10.89		Wendy Davidson	14.10.82	1	Grangemouth	5	Sep
10.87		Shirley Webb	28.09.81	1	York	5	Jul
10.86		Lindsey Christie	29.03.83	1	Ashford	9	May
10.85		Rebecca Shiel	16.01.82	1	Middlesbrough	25	Apr
10.85		Leanne Ogogo	26.09.82	1	Bury St. Edmonds	9	May
10.83 w	3.1	Tina Howell	16.07.82	4	London (Ha)	24	May
10.80		Julia Straker	25.11.82	1	Gateshead	29	Aug
10.74		Rebecca Scotcher	2.07.82	1	Peterborough	31	Aug
10.71		Katherine Silto	12.08.83	3	Exeter	9	Aug

Foreign

12.27 w	3.4	Hilde Kaland (NOR)	22.05.73	1	Liverpool	20	Jun
12.15	1.5			5	Bath	4	May

SHOT

18.83	Judy Oakes	V40	14.02.58	1	Kuala Lumpur, MAL	18	Sep
	18.79			1	Arles, FRA	24	May
	18.56 i			1	London (CP)	17	Jan
	18.46			3	Halle, GER	16	May
	18.42 i			6	Valencia, SPA	28	Feb
	18.38			2	St. Petersburg, RUS	28	Jun
	18.35			1	Croydon	7	Jun
	18.32 i			1	London (CP)	14	Feb
	18.28			1	Thurrock	31	Aug
	18.27			1	Kingston	14	Jun
	18.23 i			1	Birmingham	8	Feb
	18.12			6	Uniondale,NY. USA	19	Jul
	17.88			1	Watford	21	Jun
	17.82			1	Birmingham	25	Jul
17.69	Myrtle Augee		4.02.65	2	Thurrock	31	Aug
	17.39			2	Birmingham	25	Jul
	17.22			1	St. Ives	5	Sep
	17.16			2	Kuala Lumpur, MAL	18	Sep
	17.03			1	Crawley	19	Jul
	16.95			1	Bedford	30	Aug
	16.92			2	Arles, FRA	24	May
	16.69			1	Bromley	14	Jun
	16.12			2	Watford	21	Jun
15.81	Tracy Axten	V35	20.07.63	2	Crawley	19	Jul
15.76	Jo Duncan		27.12.66	1	Coventry	5	Jul
15.73	Maggie Lynes	V35	19.02.63	3	Birmingham	25	Jul
	15.55				Luton	14	Jun
27 performances to 15.50 by 5 athletes including 4 indoors							
15.27	Julie Dunkley	U20	11.09.79	4	Watford	21	Jun
15.27	Denise Lewis		27.08.72	1H	Budapest, HUN	21	Aug
15.10	Christina Bennett	U23	27.02.78	1	Barking	25	Apr
15.00 i	Philippa Roles	U23	1.03.78	1	London (CP)	19	Dec
	14.54			1	Wrexham	15	Aug
14.68	Eleanor Gatrell	U23	5.10.76	1	London (He)	18	Jul
(10)							
14.65 i	Jenny Kelly		20.06.70	1P	Birmingham	8	Feb
	14.27			2	Ashford	10	May
14.64 i	Vickie Foster		1.04.71	3	Birmingham	8	Feb
	14.61			7	Birmingham	25	Jul
14.57	Carol Parker		22.09.69	1	Derby	19	Jul
14.51	Pauline Richards		30.06.68	1H	Bressanone, ITA	4	Jul
14.31	Clova Court	V35	10.02.60	2H	Bressanone, ITA	4	Jul
14.22	Jennie Elphick		24.11.66	2	Bedford	24	May
13.94 i	Natasha Smith	U23	6.06.77	3	London (CP)	14	Feb
	13.64			1	Hayes	25	Apr
13.87	Alison Grey		12.05.73	4	Bedford	29	Aug
13.83	Nicola Gautier	U23	21.03.78	2H	Val de Reuil, FRA	25	Jul
13.66	Debbie Callaway		15.07.64	2	London (WF)	9	May
(20)							
13.58	Jayne Berry		18.07.70	2	Cwmbran	20	Jun
13.47	Helen Wilding	U23	25.10.76	2	Liverpool	20	Jun
13.46	Carol Bennett	U23	11.01.77	1	Hull	5	Apr
13.44	Jackie McKernan		1.07.65	1	Belfast	12	May
13.35	Navdeep Dhaliwal	U23	30.11.77	1	Linwood	18	Apr
13.34	Charmaine Johnson		4.06.63	4	Bath	4	May
13.32	Lorraine Shaw		2.04.68	5	Bedford	29	Aug
13.24	Eva Massey	U20	22.12.80	1	Belfast	26	Aug
13.18	Debbie Woolgar		10.03.65	2	Hayes	25	Apr
13.07	Julie McCorry	U20	7.11.79	2	Bedford	5	Jul

12.94	Claire Smithson	U17 ¹⁸	3.08.83	1	Crawley	12	Apr
12.86	Angela Lambourn		9.04.66	1	Solihull	17	May
12.79	Amy Wilson	U20	31.12.80	2	Exeter	11	Jul
12.74	Sharon Gibson	V35	31.12.61	2	Solihull	17	May
12.66	Fay Champion		27.09.66	7	Watford	15	Aug
12.65	Cathy-Ann Hill	U23	4.05.77	1	Southampton	5	Sep
12.50	Kim Crowther		19.01.66	3	Liverpool	20	Jun
12.50	Tracy Rea	U20	19.01.79	3	Exeter	11	Jul
12.43	Catherine Garden	U23	4.09.78	2	Edinburgh	9	May
12.36	Jackie Tindal	U20	21.01.79	1	Whitley Bay	21	Jun
(40)							
12.34	Shelley Drew		8.08.73	2	Portsmouth	25	Apr
12.34	Joanne Mortimer		18.12.71	1	Cudworth	2	Aug
12.31	Emma Merry		2.07.74	6	Bath	4	May
12.27	Elaine Cank	U20	5.12.79	1	Solihull	23	May
12.26	Vikki Shepherd	U20	26.01.80	2	Cudworth	2	Aug
12.17	Eleanor Garden	U23	20.11.76	3	Edinburgh	9	May
12.14	Leigh Dargan	U20	31.03.81	1	Crawley	13	Jun
12.09 i	Julia Bennett		26.03.70	9P	Valencia, SPA	27	Feb
	12.07			3	Kingston	10	May
12.06	Mhairi Walters	U20	19.06.81	2	Grangemouth	5	Sep
12.04	Sharon Nash		5.05.74	1	Hoo	30	May
(50)							
12.02	Shelley McLellan 80TH	U17	21.03.83	1	London (Ha)	24	May
12.00	Kerry Jury		19.11.68	H	Arles, FRA	23	May
12.00	Joanne Holloway	U23	10.05.76	4	Portsmouth	26	Jun
12.00	Amanda Sheppard		26.02.68	1	Blackpool	6	Sep
11.97	Liz Pidgeon	U23	27.04.77	3	Liverpool	16	Aug
11.95 i	Sarah Damm		12.09.70	2	Birmingham	4	Jan
	11.94			2	Liverpool	18	Jul
11.94 i	Shaunette Richards ¹⁰⁰	U17	15.08.83	2	Birmingham	22	Feb
	11.67			1	Stoke	20	Jun
11.94 i	Anna-Lisa Howard	U23	18.04.78	3	Glasgow	14	Mar
	11.69			1	Basingstoke	25	Apr
11.94	Diana Bennett		14.06.74	4	Kingston	10	May
11.93 i	Julie Hollman	U23	16.02.77	1	Birmingham	25	Feb
	11.83			3	High Wycombe	25	Apr
(60)							
11.91	Joan MacPherson	U20	18.09.80	1	Harrow	5	Sep
11.90	Clover Wynter-Pink	U23	29.11.77	H	Enfield	1	Aug
11.88	Lesley Brannan	U23	13.09.76	1	Colwyn Bay	5	Sep
11.86	Anne-Marie Cartmel/Green		18.11.73	1	Oldham	3	May
11.84	Kelly Sotherton	U23	13.11.76	2	High Wycombe	25	Apr
11.83	Noelle Bradshaw		18.12.63	2	Portsmouth	9	May
11.83	Frances Reid-Hughes	U20	18.03.80	2	London (Ha)	23	May
11.75	Lesley-Ann Roy	U17	3.01.82	1	Ayr	18	Jul
11.75	Angharad Lloyd	U20	11.09.80	6	Bruges, BEL	23	Aug
11.74	Karen Costello		21.10.68	8	Watford	15	Aug
(70)							
11.71	Rebecca Roles	U20	14.12.79	2	Wrexham	15	Aug
11.69	Lorraine Henry		16.09.67	1	Bedford	14	Jun
11.65	Esther Augee		1.01.64	2	Ware	22	Aug
11.57	Angie Nyhan	U23	13.04.78	1	Wakefield	24	May
11.50	Joanne Mees		28.09.73	1	Corby	21	Jun
11.49	Emma Carpenter	U17	16.05.82	1	Exeter	28	Apr
11.49	Sara Allen		7.12.70	4	Cudworth	2	Aug
11.46 i	Rebecca Chamberlain	U20	7.09.79	5	Birmingham	22	Feb
	11.26			1	Bournemouth	9	May
11.44 i	Elizabeth Bowyer	U17	8.09.81	3	Birmingham	22	Feb
	11.43			1	Bebington	13	Jun

11.41	Catherine Lane	U23	18.11.76	1	Watford	10	May
(80)							
11.41	Alyson Hourihan	V35	17.10.60	3	Cwmbran	20	Jun
11.39 i	Farah Louarradi	U20	11.10.79	1	Birmingham	1	Feb
11.32				1	Stoke	20	Jun
11.39	Joanne Street	U17	30.10.82	1	Tamworth	19	Apr
11.37	Lynne Barnett		12.08.74	5	Edinburgh	9	May
11.35	Fran Wilkins	U20	15.01.79	2	Telford	26	Jul
11.33 i	Rebecca Peake	U17	22.06.83	4	Birmingham	22	Feb
11.12				1	Cudworth	2	Aug
11.30	Chloe Cozens	U20	9.04.80	H	Arles, FRA	23	May
11.27 i	Julie Walton	U23	12.12.78	5	Glasgow	15	Mar
11.27	Sarah Moore		15.03.73	2	Coventry	17	May
11.27	Louise Batho	U23	27.11.76	5	Coventry	5	Jul
(90)							
11.27	Karen Smith	U23	25.12.78	H	Hull	19	Sep
11.25	Jane Aucott		10.10.68	4	Solihull	17	May
11.22	Rebecca Hardy		11.11.68	1	Luton	18	Jul
11.21	Alison Moffitt		6.10.69	10	Birmingham	6	Jun
11.21	Cheryl Done		25.09.70	1	Cosford	1	Jul
11.19	Gillian Stewart	U20	21.01.80	1	Coatbridge	17	May
11.18 i	Claire Cameron	V40	3.10.58	1	Glasgow	28	Feb

Additional Under 17 (1 - 8 above)

11.10	Joan Amaa		15.12.81	1	London (PH)	2	Jun
10.99	Sarah Manning		31.10.82	2	Portsmouth	22	Aug
(10)							
10.97	Lucy Marshall		28.11.81	1	Nottingham	28	Jun
10.94	Charlotte Spelzini		7.01.83	2	Cambridge	16	Aug
10.93	Liz Edwards		30.04.82	3	Dublin (S), IRE	8	Aug
10.91	Kim Cannon		27.07.82	1	London (WF)	9	May
10.81	Sarah Sasse		1.10.81	5	Exeter	10	Jul
10.78	Emma Morris		25.01.82	1	Derby	30	May
10.78	Lucy Newman		2.03.83	4	Kingston	14	Jun
10.77	Belinda Heil		8.03.82	2	Ashford	5	Jul
10.72	Katie Halford		4.10.82	2	Exeter	28	Apr
10.70	Joanna Bennett		6.08.83	9	Arles, FRA	23	May
(20)							
10.66	Olivia Reade		6.06.83	2	Yeovil	20	Jun
10.62	Sharon Wray		8.10.82	1	Wrexham	25	Jul
10.53	Clio Sigismondi		11.10.81	3	London (Ha)	24	May
10.50	Karen Lowe		3.05.82	1	Clayton-le-Moors	31	Aug
10.39	Kate Morris		18.01.83	2	Bromley	17	May
10.34	Kirsty Millar		22.12.82	1	Telford	4	Jul

Foreign

12.05	*Kelly Kane (IRE)*		28.10.74	1	*Blackpool*	5	*Jul*
11.28 i	*Linda Andreasson (SWE)*	*U23*	9.04.76	4	*Glasgow*	15	*Mar*

SHOT - Under 15 - 3.25kg

12.19	Shelley Moles		31.10.83	1	London (Nh)	27	Jun
11.91	Jody Cockcroft		14.09.83	2	Exeter	10	Jul
11.61	Louise Finlay		2.10.83	1	Aberdare	22	Aug
11.55	Kim Bridge		7.09.83	2	London (Ha)	24	May
11.52	Faye Brennan		13.05.84	3	Exeter	10	Jul
11.37	Kylie West		16.09.84	1	Birmingham	6	Sep
11.33	Saffie Perryman		26.03.84	1	Reading	18	Jul
11.32	Cherie Pierre		15.05.84	2	Sheffield	15	Aug
11.03	Nicola Dudman		5.10.83	4	London (Ha)	24	May
11.00	Jolene Marshall		22.10.83	1	Bromley	12	Jul
(10)							

10.95	Angela Lockley	7.10.84	1	Wrexham	21 Aug
10.91	Sarah Morgan	9.05.84	1	Nelson	6 Sep
10.90	Laura Smith	21.01.84	3	Sheffield	15 Aug
10.87	Gemma Avil	8.03.84	1	Oxford	27 Sep
10.83	Kerri Fardoe	22.11.83	4	Sheffield	15 Aug
10.82	Gemma Bennett	4.01.84	2	London (Nh)	27 Jun
10.80	Tanya Hunt	14.09.83	1	Colchester	5 Sep
10.75	Katy Herring	3.09.83	1	London (WF)	13 May
10.73	Charlotte Rees	14.06.84	1	Neath	19 Aug
10.70	Saffron Stoney	20.11.83	1	Solihull	23 May
	(20)				
10.67	Louisa Batey	30.11.83	1	Jarrow	8 Aug

SHOT - Under 13 - 2.72kg

10.03	Nimi Iniekio 22ND	25.10.86	1	Brighton	6 Aug
9.95	Lucy Fisher	27.09.85	1	Cannock	29 Aug
9.94	Lauren Therin	19.01.86	1	Bournemouth	20 Sep
9.75	Kate Franzke	26.09.85	2	Burnley	15 Aug
9.67	Rachel Bashford	10.01.86	1	Blackpool	29 Aug
9.64	Chioma Onwubalili	16.05.86	1	London (WL)	24 Jun
9.57	Hayley Hood		1	Birmingham	6 Sep
9.53	Samantha Day	8.02.86		Rugby	13 Sep
9.45	Lucy Sutton		2	Kingston	26 Jul
9.42 9.895	Laura Hudson		1		21 Jun
	(10)				
9.33	Amy Davis	28.01.86	1	Antrim	30 May
9.33	K. Just		1=	Leeds	28 Jun
9.32	Sarah McRobbie	8.11.86	1	Elgin	20 Sep

DISCUS

60.82	Shelley Drew	8.08.73	1	Birmingham	25 Jul
60.35			6	Sheffield	2 Aug
59.95			1	Watford	21 Jun
58.32			1	Bedford	25 May
57.94			8	Halle, GER	16 May
57.87			2	Loughborough	7 Aug
57.80			3	Budapest, HUN	5 Jul
57.43			7	La Jolla, USA	28 Mar
56.13			4	Kuala Lumpur, MAL	20 Sep
56.10			6	St. Petersburg, RUS	27 Jun
54.76			2	San Diego, USA	4 Apr
54.35			1	Birmingham	18 Jul
53.13			27Q	Budapest, HUN	19 Aug
52.60			1	Portsmouth	25 Apr
52.00			1	Basildon	5 Sep
58.05	Jackie McKernan	1.07.65	2	Bedford	25 May
58.02			1	Loughborough	7 Aug
57.92			7	Sheffield	2 Aug
57.10			4	Budapest, HUN	5 Jul
57.09			2	Birmingham	25 Jul
57.02			1	Singapore, SIN	5 Sep
56.66			1	Loughborough	17 May
56.20			4	Lancaster, USA	16 Apr
56.13			1	Cardiff	4 Aug
55.96			2	La Jolla, USA	11 Apr
55.32			1	Tullamore, IRE	9 Aug
55.16			5	Kuala Lumpur, MAL	20 Sep
54.88			1	San Diego, USA	4 Apr
53.16			1	Belfast	27 Jun

54.94	Debbie Callaway		15.07.64	1	Exeter	5	Sep
54.18				1	Southampton	11	Jul
52.43				4	Loughborough	7	Aug
52.16				3	Birmingham	18	Jul
54.14	Philippa Roles 10	U23	1.03.78	3	Birmingham	25	Jul
54.10				6	Kuala Lumpur, MAL	20	Sep
53.91				2	Dessau, GER	1	Aug
53.81				3	Loughborough	7	Aug
53.69				3	Bedford	25	May
53.66				3	Cardiff	4	Aug
53.42				2	Loughborough	17	May
53.38				1	Neath	20	May
52.86				1	Cwmbran	13	May
52.76				1	Hexham	14	Jun
52.73				1	Cardiff	8	Jul
52.68				1	Wrexham	15	Aug
52.60				1	Enfield	19	Jul
52.46				1	Bath	3	May
52.42				2	Birmingham	18	Jul
52.32				2	Singapore, SIN	5	Sep
54.03	Tracy Axten	V35	20.07.63	4	Birmingham	25	Jul
53.73				1	Bedford	29	Aug
53.33				1	Crawley	19	Jul
53.10				1	Watford	15	Aug
53.21	Emma Merry 24		2.07.74	1	Birmingham (Un)	26	Jun
52.57				1	Derby	19	Jul
52.35				4	Cardiff	4	Aug
52.32				7	Kuala Lumpur, MAL	20	Sep
52.30				5	Birmingham	25	Jul
52.31	Lauren Keightley 28	U20	2.08.79	2	Alicante, SPA	18	Jul
	59 performances to 52.00 by 7 athletes						
51.96	Lorraine Shaw		2.04.68	2	Bedford	29	Aug
51.71	Judy Oakes	V40	14.02.58	1	Kingston	14	Jun
47.96	Sarah Henton		4.05.73	3	Bath	3	May
	(10)						
47.37	Nicola Talbot		17.02.72	6	Birmingham	18	Jul
47.02	Vickie Foster		1.04.71	5	Watford	21	Jun
46.55	Emma Carpenter	U17	16.05.82	1	Exeter	5	Sep
45.27	Rebecca Roles 80	U20	14.12.79	1	Aberdare	31	Aug
45.12	Claire Smithson	U17	3.08.83	1	Brighton	30	May
44.76	Elaine Cank	U20	5.12.79	1	Telford	9	May
44.41	Sharon Andrews		4.07.67	2	Basildon	7	Jun
44.12	Rebecca Hardy		11.11.68	1	Birmingham	22	Aug
44.11	Susan Backhouse	U23	6.12.78	1	York	9	Aug
43.96	Eleanor Garden	U23	20.11.76	5	Watford	15	Aug
	(20)						
43.85	Navdeep Dhaliwal	U23	30.11.77	1	Linwood	18	Apr
43.75	Carly Burton	U20	14.10.80	1	Hoo	31	Aug
43.58	Joanna Bradley	U20	23.08.79	1	Ashford	16	Aug
43.47	Myrtle Augee		4.02.65	1	Bromley	14	Jun
43.18	Susan Freebairn		22.08.65	1	Carlisle	17	Jun
42.93	Jane Aucott		10.10.68	1	Rugby	21	Jun
42.81	Amanda Sheppard		26.02.68	1	Stretford	18	Aug
42.71	Tasha Saint-Smith		20.12.75	1	Loughborough	25	Apr
42.63	Kelly Mellis	U20	4.12.79	2	Worcester	12	Sep
42.59	Helen Wilding	U23	25.10.76	2	Coventry	5	Jul
	(30)						
42.54	Hannah Corneby	U20	22.01.81	1	Stafford	12	Sep
42.48	Jackie Wright	V40	8.10.53	2	Bracknell	27	Jun
42.33	Christina Bennett	U23	27.02.78	6	Bath	3	May
42.24	Rosanne Lister		9.05.69	3	Basildon	7	Jun

42.15	Joan MacPherson	U20	18.09.80	3	Bedford	5 Jul
42.08	Fay Champion		27.09.66	5	Watford	15 Aug
42.05	Angela Mitchell		17.08.65	7	Watford	21 Jun
41.69	Maggie Lynes	V35	19.02.63	3	Woodford	30 May
41.69	Sharon Nash		5.05.74	1	Hoo	30 May
41.50	Candie Lintern	U17	5.02.82	1	Crawley	5 Sep
(40)						
41.28	Laura Wood	U23	31.10.78	5	Bedford	29 Aug
41.19	Claire Cameron	V35	3.10.58	2	Bedford	22 Jul
41.13	Eva Massey	U20	22.12.80	1	Antrim	15 Aug
40.92	Kelly Roberts/Ricketts	U23	24.01.76	2	Aberdare	31 Aug
40.72	Catherine Lane	U23	18.11.76	4	Loughborough	20 May
40.61	Joanne Street	U17	30.10.82	1	Cannock	9 May
40.28	Victoria Bateman		6.09.72	4	Ashford	16 Aug
40.27	Alyson Hourihan	V35	17.10.60	1	Barry	9 May
39.95	Lynsey Herrington	U20	31.05.79	1	Southampton	21 Jun
39.94	Sandra Terry		28.04.69	2	Bedford	22 Aug
(50)						
39.80	Donna Williams	U23	7.10.78	10	Bedford	25 May
39.77	Jayne Berry		18.07.70	1	Brecon	5 Jul
39.75	Jenny Cooper	V35	1.09.62	2	Birmingham	23 Aug
39.64	Joanne John	U20	12.11.80	2	Carshalton	18 Jul
39.48	Suzanne Last		11.01.70	4	Ashford	10 May
39.46	Kate Semus		18.01.70	8	Watford	21 Jun
39.27	Alison Moffitt		6.10.69	3	Belfast	27 Jun
39.27	Julie Dunkley	U20	11.09.79	1	Portsmouth	5 Sep
39.23	Frances Reid-Hughes	U20	18.03.80	4	London (Ha)	23 May
39.11	Emma Sheridan	U17	24.02.82	1	Colchester	31 Aug
(60)						
38.84	Carol Parker		22.09.69	1	Liverpool	16 Aug
38.80	Heidi Gardt	U17	1.04.82	1	York	13 Jun
38.79	Lorraine Henry		16.09.67	5	Enfield	19 Jul
38.78	Catherine Garden	U23	4.09.78	3	Coatbridge	29 Aug
38.61	Noelle Bradshaw		18.12.63	12	Bedford	25 May
38.54	Lynsey Braddock	U23	14.10.77	3	Loughborough	25 Apr
38.54	Julie McCorry	U20	7.11.79	1	Antrim	30 May
38.52	Claire Moore	U17	29.03.82	1	Middlesbrough	25 Apr
38.00	Janine Crosby	U20	17.01.79	1	Leeds	23 May
37.99	Debbie Woolgar		10.03.65	3	Hayes	25 Apr
(70)						
37.71	Maria Hood	U20	20.12.79	5	Tessenderlo, BEL	30 Aug
37.65	Kathrin Ritchie	U20	8.03.79	1	Antrim	23 Jun
37.60	Jennie Elphick		24.11.66	2	Basingstoke	14 Jun
37.55	Debra Monds	U23	25.02.78	2	Colwyn Bay	5 Sep
37.53	Donna Calvert	U20	26.06.79	1	Rotherham	26 Jul
37.51	Amie Hill	U20	9.09.80	4	Hayes	25 Apr
37.44	Karen Sharp/Heweth	V35	29.11.59	1	Hull	5 Jul
37.09	Hayley Williams		30.01.75	2	Colwyn Bay	14 Jun
37.01	Irene Duffin	V35	10.08.60	2	Bournemouth	27 Jun
37.01	Janet Smith		7.10.64	3	Harrow	18 Jul
(80)						
36.84	Sara Allen		7.12.70	12	Grangemouth	4 Jul
36.56	Karen Ostersburg		23.09.65	6	Bedford	29 Aug
36.33	Eleanor Gatrell	U23	5.10.76	5	Exeter	5 Sep
36.33	Lori Payne	U17	17.12.82	1	Bournemouth	20 Sep
36.21	Vicky Gibbons	U20	19.12.80	1	Barry	14 Jul
36.17	Anwen James	U20	17.02.81	2	Carmarthen	23 May
36.15	Lucy Pierrot	U17	26.02.83	2	Bedford	14 Jun
36.09	Kirsty Perrett	U23	17.03.76	1	Gateshead	29 Aug
36.05	Carys Parry	U20	24.07.81		Barry	5 Jul
35.99	Vicky Williams	U20	11.03.81	3	Stoke	9 Aug

35.83	Jenny Duff	U17	29.07.82	2	Solihull	23 May
35.82	Kim Rawling	U17	22.07.83	1	Yeovil	24 May
35.73	Jo Evans/Powell		3.10.68	4	Solihull	17 May

Additional Under 17 (1 - 11 above)

35.72	Belinda Heil		8.03.82	1	Croydon	18 Jul
35.37	Paula Griffiths		10.02.82	6	Exeter	10 Jul
34.86	Ebony Hancock		17.03.82	1	Birmingham	13 Jun
34.64	Gemma Kelly		13.03.82	1	Blackburn	3 May
34.59	Katie Halford		4.10.82	7	Exeter	5 Sep
34.51	Lauren Procter		9.09.82	3	London (Ha)	24 May
34.32	Holly Owens		17.08.82	1	Glasgow (S)	7 Jun
33.90	Laura Douglas		4.01.83	1	Colwyn Bay	5 Sep
33.86	Emma Kirby		11.11.81	1	Bracknell	10 May
	(20)					
33.71	Lisa Thompson		3.12.82	5	Ayr	18 Jul
33.46	Kelly Goodman		16.03.82	1	Ipswich	20 Jun
33.18	Lowell Bryan		3.01.82	1	Portsmouth	9 May
33.14	Kate Morris		18.01.83	1	Bromley	17 May
32.78	Kate Green		19.11.81	9	Sheffield	16 Aug
32.68	Lucy Marshall		28.11.81	1	Nottingham	28 Jun
32.58	Vicky Haydock		24.08.83	1	Carlisle	28 Jun
32.45	Sharon Wray		8.10.82	1	Wrexham	25 Jul
32.38	Jo Armstrong		22.09.82	2	Bournemouth	20 Sep
32.25	Ffion Jones		19.07.83	1	Stockport	5 Jul

Under 15

34.03	Kylie West		16.09.84	1	Birmingham	6 Sep
33.66	Angela Lockley		7.10.84	1	Sheffield	15 Aug
31.66	Sian Howe		11.04.84	1	Ashford	5 Apr
31.52	Donna Swatheridge		4.03.85	1	Hoo	22 Aug
31.02	Laura Fox		25.10.84	2	Harrow	5 Sep
30.82	Faye Brennan		13.05.84	1	London (TB)	5 Sep
30.79	Candace Schofield		3.11.84	1	Yeovil	21 Jun
30.78	Emma Forrester		2.12.83	1	Exeter	10 Jul
30.70	Linsi Robinson		9.01.84	1	Corby	20 Jun
30.63	Louise Finlay		2.10.83	1	Aberdeen	22 Aug
	(10)					
30.26	Laura Smith		21.01.84	1	Carlisle	29 Mar
30.24	Alicia Copping		5.10.83	1	Birmingham	5 Sep
30.00	Rachel Houldsworth		18.06.84	1	Barnsley	5 Jul
29.41	Kate Grainger		17.02.84	6	Sheffield	15 Aug
29.20	Fallon Harrison		1.05.85	1	Leeds	18 Jun
29.16	Tracey Merrill			1	Worcester	12 Sep
29.15	Caroline Barrett		16.09.83	1	Scunthorpe	31 Aug
29.05	Shelley Moles		31.10.83	2	Birmingham	5 Sep

Foreign

44.23	*Alana Wallace (IRE)*		*28.07.65*	*2*	*Edinburgh*	*18 Jul*
40.36	*Clara Thompson (IRE)*	*U20*	*10.11.79*		*Dublin (S), IRE*	*25 Jul*

DISCUS - Under 13 - 0.75kg

29.35	Lauren Therin		19.01.86	1	St. Clement, JER	18 Jun
26.08	Sarah Davies		13.03.86	1	Bournemouth	23 Aug
25.61	Christina Carding		26.02.87	1	Bournemouth	20 Sep
25.30	Katie Pritchard			1	Telford	10 May
24.72	Kayleigh Pearce		4.09.85	1	Southampton	11 Aug
24.68	Lucy Sutton			1	Basingstoke	31 May
24.40	Laura Hudson			1	Aberdare	22 Aug
24.36	Laura Chalmers		1.05.86	1	Elgin	22 Aug
23.85	Victoria Newman		25.03.86	2	Bournemouth	31 May
23.39	Sarah Smith		17.09.85	2	Cannock	29 Sep

HAMMER

63.30	Lorraine Shaw		2.04.68	1	Bedford	29	Aug
63.13				1	Bedford	30	May
62.66				2	Kuala Lumpur, MAL	16	Sep
61.19				1	Watford	15	Aug
61.11				Q	Budapest, HUN	21	Aug
60.71				1	Birmingham	25	Jul
59.74				1	Birmingham	6	Jun
59.55				1	London (Col)	1	Aug
59.27				1	London (Col)	26	Apr
58.74				1	Liverpool	18	Jul
58.48				1	Cardiff	4	Aug
58.19				11	Budapest, HUN	22	Aug
58.02				5	St. Petersburg, RUS	27	Jun
61.66	Lyn Sprules		11.09.75	1	Woking	12	Aug
60.64				Q	Budapest, HUN	21	Aug
60.29				1	Enfield	9	May
60.03				1	Harrow	30	Aug
59.40				1	Watford	20	Jun
59.20				2	Birmingham	25	Jul
59.01				7	Kuala Lumpur, MAL	16	Sep
58.40				1	Feltham	22	Jul
58.34				1	Milton Keynes	27	Jun
58.30				1	London (WL)	30	May
58.20				8	Halle, GER	16	May
57.90				1	Leeds	7	Jun
57.68				12	Budapest, HUN	22	Aug
56.64				1	Feltham	18	Jul
57.97	Rachael Beverley 3	U20	23.07.79	3	Birmingham	25	Jul
56.35				1	Bedford	4	Jul
56.14				2	London (Col)	26	Apr
56.03				1	Loughborough	17	May
55.73				1	Bedford	24	May
55.68				2	Birmingham	6	Jun
55.67				1	Bath	2	May
55.34				11	Kuala Lumpur, MAL	16	Sep
55.20				4	Bedford	30	May
54.64				13Q	Annecy, FRA	28	Jul
57.95	Diana Holden 4		12.02.75	1	Birmingham	18	Jul
57.79				2	Bedford	30	May
56.36				1B	Windsor	14	Jun
56.27				3	Watford	20	Jun
56.18				2	London (Col)	1	Aug
55.85				1	Windsor	14	Jun
55.43				1	La Chaux de Fonds, SWZ	16	Aug
55.27				2	Leeds	7	Jun
55.26				5	Birmingham	25	Jul
54.88				2	Cardiff	4	Aug
54.85				4	London (Col)	26	Apr
54.80				12	Halle, GER	16	May
54.63				1	Stoke	5	Jul
57.56	Liz Pidgeon 5	U23	27.04.77	1	Lynchburg, USA	18	Apr
57.04				13	Amherst, USA	6	Jun
56.95				2	Watford	20	Jun
56.50				2	Chapel Hill, USA	10	May
56.38				5	Philadelphia, USA	23	Apr
55.96				1	Charleston, USA	7	Mar
55.96				3	Clemson, USA	15	May
55.78				4	Dessau, GER	1	Aug
55.73				1	Coventry	5	Jul

(Pidgeon)	55.70				3	Namur, BEL	7	Aug
	55.61				4	Birmingham	25	Jul
	55.51				2	Birmingham	18	Jul
	55.17				2	Hexham	14	Jun
	55.10				1	Atlanta, USA	23	May
	54.89				3	Nivelles, BEL	9	Aug
	54.27				2	Woking	12	Aug
	54.08				1	Liverpool	16	Aug
55.99	Sarah Moore			15.03.73	3	Bedford	30	May
	55.74				2	Lisse, HOL	2	May
	55.39				3	London (Col)	26	Apr
	54.94				3	Birmingham	18	Jul
	54.74				1	Newport	16	Aug
	54.20				1	Yate	14	Jun
55.60	Ann Gardner 8			11.10.68	1	Corby	9	May
	54.92				1	Peterborough	31	Aug
	54.70				3	Lisse, HOL	2	May
	54.08				1	Newport	21	Jun
	77 performances to 54.00 by 7 athletes							
53.37	Catherine Garden 10	U23	4.09.78		5	Dessau, GER	1	Aug
51.25	Zoe Derham 14	U20	24.11.80		1	Yate	26	Jul
50.35	Irene Duffin	V35	10.08.60		4	Bedford	24	May
(10)								
50.20	Janet Smith		7.10.64		1	Perivale	27	Jun
49.95	Esther Augee		1.01.64		2	Liverpool	16	Aug
49.86	Jean Clark		5.10.68		1	Derby	19	Jul
49.70	Helen Arnold	U23	5.10.78		1	Southampton	13	Sep
49.10	Carys Parry 21	U20	24.07.81		1	Aberdare	16	Aug
48.85	Suzanne Last		11.01.70		2	Ashford	9	May
48.38	Mhairi Walters 24	U20	19.06.81		1	Grangemouth	5	Sep
47.87	Philippa Roles 27	U23	1.03.78		3	Enfield	19	Jul
47.52	Vicki Clark 29	U20	23.09.80		2B	London (Col)	1	Aug
47.03	Suzanne Roberts	U23	19.12.78		9	Bedford	30	May
(20)								
46.83	Marina Peacock		12.07.64		5	Birmingham	6	Jun
	Not eligible to compete for Britain							
46.66	Christina Bennett 34	U23	27.02.78		2	Kingston	9	May
46.52	Andrea Jenkins		4.10.75		1	Wigan	31	May
46.35	Lesley Brannan	U23	13.09.76		5	Birmingham	18	Jul
45.82	Vicki Scott 36	U20	21.09.80		2	Liverpool	20	Jun
45.71	Lindsey Jones	U23	8.09.77		1	Cleckheaton	29	Aug
44.93	Jenny Cunnane 39	V40	23.02.57		1	Middlesbrough	22	Aug
44.87	Vickie Foster		1.04.71		4	Grangemouth	4	Jul
44.48	Helen Wilding 42	U23	25.10.76		5	Liverpool	20	Jun
44.43	Diane Smith	V35	15.11.60		2	Bellaria, ITA	14	Sep
(30)								
44.00	Natasha Smith 44	U23	6.06.77		2	Enfield	9	May
43.76	Julie Lavender		9.11.75		1	Hexham	30	Aug
43.57	Julie Kirkpatrick		14.07.72		2	Coatbridge	21	Jun
43.44	Janette Brown 48		19.02.73		1	Middlesbrough	7	Jul
43.10	Lucy Marshall 49	U17	28.11.81		1	Sheffield	15	Aug
42.86	Debbie Callaway		15.07.64		9	Watford	15	Aug
42.61	Leanne Jones/Taylor		13.05.74		2	Aberdare	16	Aug
42.49	Jenny Earle 54	V35	28.11.58		1	Newport	11	Jul
41.76	Sheena Parry	U23	16.11.77		8	Bath	2	May
41.34	Katy Lamb 6?	U17	21.08.82		1	Stevenage	5	Sep
(40)								
41.29	Marcelle Edwards	U23	9.01.78		1	Basingstoke	25	Apr
41.28	Clare Pardo	U20	9.08.81		1	Southampton	21	Jun
41.22	Louise Kay	U23	1.12.77		1	Blackburn	3	May
40.93	Rebecca Hardy 70		11.11.68		1	Kingston	14	Jun

40.85	Joan MacPherson	U20	18.09.80	1	Swindon	19	Apr
40.78	Rachael Dunn	U20	4.03.79	1	Worcester	21	Jun
40.73	Catherine Lane	U23	18.11.76	1	Loughborough	10	Jun
40.73	Kelly Roberts/Ricketts	U23	24.01.76	1	Colwyn Bay	14	Jun
40.68	Sharon Nash		5.05.74	3	Ashford	9	May
40.45	Rachel Stott		3.09.74	11	Watford	15	Aug
		(50)					
40.38	Janet Corlett		31.07.63	1	Mansfield	17	May
40.35	Karen Chambers		31.08.68	3	Grendon Hall	9	Oct
40.25	Llyn Jones	U20	21.02.79	1	Harrow	19	Apr
40.09	Karen Bell	U17	18.06.82	1	Grangemouth	5	Sep
39.94	Julia Delasaux		22.04.69	1	Croydon	30	May
39.51	Emma King	U20	25.07.81	1	Guernsey	31	Aug
39.19	Rachael Cox	U20	27.06.80	10	Birmingham	6	Jun
39.16	Sue Lawrence		25.11.70	1	Barking	14	Jun
39.13	Kirsty Perrett	U23	17.03.76	2	Hexham	30	Aug
38.88	Joanne Harding		12.04.64	7	Bedford	29	Aug
		(60)					
38.64	Carol Parker		22.09.69	1	Rugby	14	Jun
38.63	Rachel Owen	U20	24.02.81	1	York	19	Apr
38.59	Laura Douglas	U17	4.01.83	1	Colwyn Bay	10	May
38.45	Julie Dunkley	U20	11.09.79	4	Bournemouth	27	Jun
38.27	Katie Horne	U20	23.05.79	7	Bedford	4	Jul
37.97	Aline Cross		20.09.73	2	Coatbridge	2	Aug
37.96	Angela Lambourn		9.04.66	1	Solihull	17	May
37.86	Liz Bone	U20	22.11.79	1	Middlesbrough	14	Jun
37.81	Cassie Wilson	U23	24.09.77	1	Barnsley	9	Aug
37.58	Noelle Bradshaw		18.12.63	5	Enfield	23	Aug
		(70)					
37.37	Rachel Clough	U17	30.06.82	4	Ayr	18	Jul
37.19	Paula Cooper		6.08.75	4	Cudworth	10	May
37.15	Jenny Clarke	V45	19.10.52	2	Peterborough	31	Aug
37.11	Fay Champion		27.09.66	2	London (He)	22	Aug
37.09	Marian James		9.05.71	7	Liverpool	20	Jun
37.03	Kelly Shepherd		15.12.75	2	Newport	21	Jun
37.02	Myrtle Augee		4.02.65	1	St. Ives	5	Sep
37.00	Jennifer Ayero	U20	13.09.79	2	Kingston	14	Jun
37.00	Jenny Cooper	V35	1.09.62	3	Newport	21	Jun
37.00	Maria Hood	U20	20.12.79	3	Newport	16	Aug
		(80)					
36.85	Jacqui Loney	U20	17.04.79	2	Elgin	18	Jul
36.80	Sarah Etherton	U23	19.10.78	1	Crawley	12	Apr
36.76	Gemma Johnson	U23	21.07.78	1	Rugby	21	Jun
36.64	Helen Taylor	U17	19.07.82	2	Derby	20	Sep
36.56	Linda Low		20.01.71	1	Inverness	10	May
36.38	Carice Allen	U23	25.09.77	2	Telford	13	Sep
36.33	Lynette Bristow	U23	17.11.77	2	Yate	14	Jun
36.18	Joanne Holloway	U23	10.05.76	4	London (He)	23	Aug
36.16	Carly Burton	U20	14.10.80	3	Harrow	5	Sep
36.16	Claire Cameron	V35	3.10.58	5	Bellaria, ITA	14	Sep
		(90)					
36.15	Helen Gilbert	U17	1.03.82	1	Grantham	31	May
36.08	Susan Freebairn		22.08.65	9	Grangemouth	4	Jul
36.04	Ruth Finley	U20	23.11.80	3	Blackpool	6	Sep
36.03	Zoe Tristram		15.11.69	1	Rugby	12	Aug
35.84	Anna Town		22.04.75	1	Enfield	27	Jun
35.71	Tracey Williams	U17	31.10.82	1	Leamington	3	Sep
35.70	Eleanor Gatrell	U23	5.10.76	2	Woking	22	Aug
35.65	Siobhan Hart		15.06.75	4	Guildford	30	May
35.57	Lorraine Henry		16.09.67	3	Woking	22	Aug
35.41	Eva Massey	U20	22.12.80	7	Bruges, BEL	23	Aug

[00] 35.38 Kim Rawling U17 22.07.83 1 Par 27 Sep
35.30 Gemma Milden U17 31.05.82 3 London (He) 30 Aug
35.25 Belinda Heil U17 8.03.82 1 Carshalton 20 Sep
35.10 Laura Wood U23 31.10.78 8 Coventry 5 Jul
35.07 Jill Harnett U23 26.02.76 1 Ilford 27 Jun

Additional Under 17 (1 - 11 above)

34.54	Anna Howard		18.07.83	1	Crawley	5	Sep
34.53	Tammy Thompson		21.10.82	3	York	25	Jul
33.95	Shirley Webb		28.09.81	2	Grangemouth	5	Sep
33.58	Faye Blacktin		5.11.81	2	Portsmouth	25	Apr
33.52	Anna Smith		6.10.81	4	Birmingham	23	Aug
33.44	Diana Lewis		27.04.82	3	Carmarthen	23	May
33.42	Donna Powell		8.10.81	2	Stoke	23	Aug
33.42	Vikki Grime		21.08.82	3	Telford	13	Sep
32.31	Gemma Kelly		13.03.82	1	Whitehaven	9	May
	(20)						
32.28	Jo Barclay		28.07.82	1	Corby	21	Jun
30.49	Joanna Bennett		6.08.83	5	Woking	22	Aug

Note with 3.25kg
35.46 Kirsty Walters 2wⁿ U15 6.09.84 1 Elgin 20 Sep

Foreign

54.38	*Olivia Kelleher (IRE)*		*9.10.75*	*1*	*Tullamore, IRE*	*9*	*Aug*
49.14	*Clara Thompson (IRE)*	*U20*	*10.11.79*	*1B*	*Tullamore, IRE*	*9*	*Aug*
44.02	*Linda Andreasson (SWE)*	*U23*	*9.04.76*	*1*	*Gateshead*	*10*	*May*
	Note 47.91 in SWE						
42.96	*Margaret McCutcheon (USA)*		*30.12.68*	*1*	*Hemel Hempstead*	*21*	*Aug*

JAVELIN

58.39	Lorna Jackson	9.01.74	1	Birmingham	6	Jun
	57.89		1	Birmingham	25	Jul
	56.76		1	Karlstad, SWE	14	Jun
	56.71		1	Bedford	24	May
	55.79		1	Edinburgh	17	Jul
	55.10		3	Prague, CZE	8	Jun
	54.56		6	St. Petersburg, RUS	27	Jun
	54.51		1	Coatbridge	2	Aug
	54.30		1	Edinburgh	10	May
	53.72		6	Halle, GER	16	May
	53.42		1	Glasgow (S)	26	Apr
	52.97		4	Kuala Lumpur, MAL	19	Sep
	52.59		1	Watford	15	Aug
	52.41		1	Bedford	29	Aug
	52.36		1	Grangemouth	4	Jul
57.82	Karen Martin	24.11.74	2	Kuala Lumpur, MAL	19	Sep
	57.72		1	Loughborough	19	Apr
	55.89		1	Cosford	1	Jul
	55.67		1	Loughborough	17	May
	55.66		1	Derby	9	May
	55.44		1	Cosford	25	Apr
	54.66		2	Bedford	24	May
	54.65		5	Budapest, HUN	5	Jul
	53.17		3	Birmingham	25	Jul
	52.03		1	Lincoln	14	Jun
56.34	Kirsty Morrison	28.10.75	3	Kuala Lumpur, MAL	19	Sep
	56.3?		1	Thurrock	31	Aug
	56.13		1	Kingston	22	Mar
	55.66		5	Ludweiler, GER	9	May

(Morrison)	55.32				1	Ashford	5 Apr
	54.36				1	Liverpool	16 Aug
	53.46				3	Karlstad, SWE	13 Jun
	53.31				1	Watford	20 Jun
	53.05						
	52.43				1	Hoo	22 Aug
	52.14				1	Kingston	27 Jun
54.26	Sharon Gibson	V35		31.12.61	2	Alicante, SPA	10 Apr
54.16	Shelley Holroyd			17.05.73	2	Birmingham	25 Jul
	52.61				1	Birmingham	18 Jul
53.04	Kelly Morgan 28	U20 12TH		17.06.80	2	Loughborough	17 May
	40 performances to 52.00 by 6 athletes						
51.92	Goldie Sayers 37 5-18TH	U17		16.07.82	3	Loughborough	17 May
51.28	Denise Lewis			27.08.72	5	Birmingham	25 Jul
50.75	Nicola Emblem			27.03.71	1	Tulsa, USA	21 May
50.34	Katie Amos 52	U23		13.11.78	1	Bath	3 May
(10)							
49.36	Jenny Kemp 62	U20		18.02.80	1	Stretford	18 Aug
49.13	Caroline White			8.10.68	1	Basildon	7 Jun
48.60	Noelle Bradshaw			18.12.63	4	Bedford	24 May
48.41	Lucy Cook 75			11.09.75	2	Liverpool	16 Aug
48.09	Alison Moffitt			6.10.69	1	Dublin (S), IRE	3 May
48.00	Chloe Cozens 80	U20		9.04.80	2H	Annecy, FRA	1 Aug
47.80	Clova Court	V35		10.02.60	1H	Derby	31 May
47.18	Linda Gray			23.03.71	1	Bury St. Edmonds	17 May
46.17	Tammie Francis	U23		14.11.78	1	Basingstoke	30 May
46.12	Mandy Liverton			1.09.72	1	Exeter	5 Sep
(20)							
45.91	Katherine Evans	U23		19.11.77	5	Loughborough	17 May
45.10	Jenny Grimstone 143	U20		30.04.79	1	London (WF)	19 Apr
45.08	Katy Watts 144	U20		25.03.81	2	Exeter	11 Jul
44.84	Wendy Newman			31.08.71	4	Coventry	5 Jul
44.78	Rebecca Foster 149			14.04.71	2	Liverpool	20 Jun
44.60	Joanne Bruce	10 U23		26.10.78	1	Woking	24 Jun
44.56	Lucy Stevenson			30.01.73	1	Peterborough	31 Aug
44.38	Chissie Head	U20		18.12.79	1	Great Yarmouth	10 May
43.94	Michelle Kemp	U17 54		19.09.81	1	Carshalton	20 Sep
43.87	Karen Costello			21.10.68	1	Coatbridge	21 Jun
(30)							
43.82	Liz Pidgeon	U23		27.04.77	1	Lynchburg, USA	18 Apr
43.75	Paula Blank	U23		13.12.77	H	Wrexham	2 Aug
43.61	Nicola Gautier	U23		21.03.78	1H	Dordrecht, HOL	30 Aug
43.42	Clover Wynter-Pink	U23		29.11.77	1H	Enfield	2 Aug
43.21	Sian Lax	U20		4.08.79	1	Birmingham	21 Jun
43.18	Mari-Anne Daykin			16.02.73	1	Crawley	27 Jun
43.09	Jenna Allen	10 U20		2.05.79	7	Loughborough	17 May
43.05	Onyema Amadi			28.06.73	1	Yate	14 Jun
42.93	Lucy Rann	U20		5.09.80	3	London (He)	9 Aug
42.89	Amy Harvey	U17 75		23.04.82	4	Thurrock	31 Aug
(40)							
42.77	Samantha Lowe	U17 79		23.02.82	1	Stretford	13 Jun
42.76	Nicky Broome	U17 80		5.06.83	1	Bebington	21 Jun
42.75	Michelle Lonsdale	U17 81		29.10.81	1	Derby	30 May
42.44	Emma Lilley	U23		2.05.76	1	Blackburn	14 Jun
42.41	Judy Oakes	V40		14.02.58	1	Kingston	14 Jun
42.37	Natasha Campbell	U17 93		6.08.82	1	Ashford	5 Jul
42.33	Lynsay Munro	U23		1.02.77	3	Derby	19 Jul
42.32	Katie Granger			31.03.75	3	Harrow	5 Sep
42.18	Melanie Burrows	U23		7.08.76	1	Hoo	31 Aug
42.16	Clare Lockwood	U20		7.10.79	7	Bedford	4 Jul
(50)							

42.10	Carol Wallbanks	U17 [99] 9.12.82	1	Jarrow	20 Jun
42.02	Louise Smith	U23	11.07.77	4	Bath	3 May
41.61	Lynne Miles	U20	14.06.79	1	Solihull	24 May
41.33	Carol Costelloe	U23	14.01.76	1	Bedford	22 Jul
40.90	Joanne Harding		12.04.64	1	Oldham	12 Jul
40.73	Caroline Monk		7.09.75	1	Worcester	9 May
40.70	Teri Oboh		7.10.73	1	London (TB)	25 Apr
40.35	Samantha Redd	U15 [17] 16.02.84	1	Crawley	22 Aug
40.23	Jennifer Ayero	U20	13.09.79	3	London (Ha)	24 May
40.19	Alison Siggery	U15 [20] 14.09.83	1	Dublin (S), IRE	8 Aug
(60)
40.15	Rhian Hughes	U20	11.05.79	2	Carmarthen	23 May
39.93	Tammy Carless	U23	10.01.77	1	London (WL)	30 May
39.86	Elizabeth Austin		22.02.72	1	Crewe	9 May
39.85	Rachel Dunn	U17	14.11.82	6	Exeter	10 Jul
39.71	Georgina Hodgson	U17	23.11.81	2	Carshalton	18 Jul
39.70	Julie Nightingale		28.04.75	1	Tonbridge	22 Aug
39.63	Faye Bowring	U17	22.10.81	1	High Wycombe	19 Jul
39.63	Tracey Howard	U20	11.02.81	1	Yeovil	20 Sep
39.49	Nicky Cobb		2.11.71	1	Southampton	5 Sep
39.48	Alison Neall	U20	8.11.79	1	Kingston	9 May
(70)
39.42	Kerry Jury		19.11.68	6H	Kuala Lumpur, MAL	17 Sep
39.40	Danielle Mansfield	U17	18.10.81	5	Thurrock	31 Aug
39.38	Catherine O'Halloran	U17	17.09.81	2	Gran Canaria, SPA	23 Jul
39.31	Sally Green	U23	11.05.76	1	Hemel Hempstead	5 Sep
39.29	Claire Bennett	U17	4.02.83	1	Cannock	22 Jul
39.22	Diane Smith	V35	15.11.60	4	Cudworth	2 Aug
39.17	Sue Lawrence		25.11.70	1	Feltham	18 Jul
39.16	Carrie Macrae	U20	2.09.80	2	Leeds	23 May
39.11	Kerrie Atkin	U20	8.04.81	1	Great Yarmouth	2 Aug
39.01	Vicky James	U20	13.05.81	3	Birmingham	23 Aug
(80)
39.00	Anne-Marie Cartmel/Green		18.11.73	1	Whitehaven	9 May
38.82	Lauren Procter	U17	9.09.82	9	Exeter	10 Jul
38.76	Cathy Edgar	U20	27.02.80	4	Belfast	27 Jun
38.73	Isobel Donaldson		24.01.64	3	Barking	25 Apr
38.72	Siona Kelly		19.04.74	7	Grangemouth	4 Jul
38.66	Rebecca Roles	U20	14.12.79	3	Croydon	7 Jun
38.43	Jessica Brooker	U20	6.01.81	1	Yeovil	20 Jun
38.40	Anyha Kerr	U20	10.04.80	2	Derby	21 Jun
38.38	Angharad Richards	U23	9.12.76	1	Guildford	18 Jul
38.36	Charlotte Rees	U15 [38] 14.06.84	1	Neath	19 Aug
(90)
38.31	Laura Bolton	U20	22.01.79	6	Bath	3 May
38.21	Nightingale Anek	U23	25.01.78	2	Ashford	16 Aug
38.19	Emily Kitney	U20	25.04.81	1	Ashford	9 May
38.11	Yvette Greenhouse	U20	21.10.80	1	Worcester	13 Jun
38.11	Jo Davies		23.06.73	1	Neath	14 Jun

Additional Under 17 (1 - 15 above)

37.86	Joanna McGilchrist		27.08.83	3	Ayr	18 Jul
37.66	Lucy Newman		2.03.83	4	Ashford	5 Jul
36.88	Nicola Smith		6.03.82	1	Reading	5 Jul
36.84	Suzanne Finnis		12.08.83	1	Basildon	28 Jun
36.73	Gemma Gay		7.10.81	11	Exeter	10 Jul
(20)
36.54	Clare Warrington		28.07.82	3	Cudworth	2 Aug
36.47	Paula Hendricks		25.01.83	1H	Hull	20 Sep
36.44	Kathryn Stringer		24.09.81	3	Leeds	23 May
36.35	Amber Jackson		29.11.82	3	Carshalton	20 Sep
36.02	Jane McCandless		1.10.81	4	Dublin (S), IRE	8 Aug

35.89	Helen Gilbert	1.03.82	1	Rugby	24 May
35.84	Kathryn Redd	8.06.82	1	Crawley	31 Aug
35.78	Lisa Kenney	17.02.83	1	Nottingham	20 Jun
35.76	Kristine Ritchie	15.12.81		Tullamore, IRE	6 Jun
35.37	Freya Coombe	11.10.81	1	Milton Keynes	13 Jun
(30)					
35.23	Aimee Styles	1.05.82	2	Milton Keynes	13 Jun
35.16	Susan Theobald	4.03.83	2	Great Yarmouth	2 Aug
35.04	Rebecca Bailey	8.01.82	1	Carn Brea	19 Aug
35.01	Emma Thornton	27.11.82	2	Stretford	13 Jun
34.98	Gemma Walsh	2.07.83	5	Cudworth	2 Aug

Under 15 (1 - 3 above)

37.83	Colette Doran 52ND	20.09.83	1	Carlisle	13 Jun
36.65	Louise Matthews 73RD	27.12.83	1	London (He)	30 Aug
35.73	Kate Grainger 101	17.02.84	1	Inverness	13 Sep
35.23	Sarah Moss 134	17.11.83	1	Bournemouth	20 Sep
35.22	L. Bellwood 135		1	Yeovil	20 Jun
34.79	Laura Smith	21.01.84	2	Derby	31 May
34.67	Sarah Ashdown	18.10.83	5	Sheffield	16 Aug
(10)					
34.61	Rebecca Pyne	12.10.84	3	Exeter	13 Jun
34.48	Sarah Garrard	13.05.84	1	Colchester	22 Aug
34.31	Lisa Fryer	30.05.84	1	Tullamore, IRE	12 Jul
34.30	Sarah Ellis	27.10.83	1	Abingdon	18 Jul
34.16	Tanya Hunt	14.09.83	1	Southampton	13 Sep
34.06	Jo Chapman	10.01.85	1	Bury St. Edmonds	13 Jun
32.99	Siobhan Jenkins	14.06.84	1	Birmingham	6 Sep
32.26	Lindsay Hall	31.07.84	1	Grangemouth	11 Jul
32.24	Ria Buckley	25.09.83	1	Woking	6 Sep
31.96	Felicity Morgan		2	Connah's Quay	4 Jul
(20)					
31.80	A. Butcher		1	Antrim	30 May

Foreign

47.97	*Hilde Kaland (NOR)*	22.05.73	1	*Middlesbrough*	14 Jun
42.41	*Katrina Campbell (IRE)*	8.03.72	2	*Belfast*	27 Jun
38.55	*Linda Andreasson (SWE) U23*	9.04.76	1	*Gateshead*	9 May
	Note 40.75 in Sweden				

JAVELIN - Under 13 - 400 gram

33.90	Lauren Therin 2ND	19.01.86	1	St. Clement, JER	6 Sep
31.87	Georgina Field 7TH	8.04.86	1	Reading	31 Aug
29.17	Venetia Ellis	15.09.85	1	London (TB)	29 Aug
28.56	Samantha Case	5.01.86	1	Birmingham	29 Jun
27.30	Debbie Collinson	23.10.85	1	Hull	18 Jul
26.72	Sarah Snare	1.07.86	1		31 Aug
26.35	N. Griffiths		1	Carmarthen	14 Jun
25.54	Cheryl Shepherd	8.03.86	1	Coatbridge	2 Aug
25.40	Josie Jamieson	17.07.87	1	Grangemouth	11 Jul

New JAVELIN (Valid from 1.04.99)

47.37	Lorna Jackson	9.01.74	3	Karlstad, SWE	13 Jun

HEPTATHLON

6559	Denise Lewis				27.08.72	1	Budapest, HUN	22 Aug
	13.59/-0.7	1.83	15.27	24.75/-0.5	6.59/1.4	50.16	2:20.38	
6513						1	Kuala Lumpur, MAL	17 Sep
	13.77/0.4	1.82	15.09	24.47/0.0	6.52/0.1	51.22	2:21.90	
6005 w	Kerry Jury				19.11.68	2	Arles, FRA	24 May
	13.83W/5.5	1.79	12.00	23.80w/3.9	6.08W/4.8	37.60	2:15.89	
5692						5	Kuala Lumpur, MAL	17 Sep
	14.13/-0.2	1.76	10.57	24.59/0.1	5.81/0.3	39.42	2:17.03	
5686						6	Bressanone, ITA	5 Jul
	13.99/0.5	1.72	11.52	24.33/1.9	5.87/1.0	36.56	2:18.97	
5816 w	Julie Hollman	U23			16.02.77	3	Arles, FRA	24 May
	14.14W/4.6	1.79	11.72	24.47w/3.9	6.12w/3.2	34.03	2:16.51	
5557						13	Bressanone, ITA	5 Jul
	14.50/0.1	1.75	11.09	24.74/1.6	6.01/1.2	32.86	2:19.05	
5691 w	Pauline Richards				30.06.68	5	Arles, FRA	24 May
	13.79W/5.8	1.67	14.04	24.30w/3.9	5.87w/3.5	33.50	2:24.54	
5563						12	Bressanone, ITA	5 Jul
	14.17/0.7	1.57	14.51	24.65/1.0	5.90/1.6	33.66	2:22.01	
5456						7	Kuala Lumpur, MAL	17 Sep
	14.04/0.4	1.61	14.47	25.05/0.0	5.68/0.4	34.82	2:28.80	
5390						1	Glasgow (S)	3 May
	14.36/0.9	1.63	14.38	24.96w/2.9	5.61/-1.1	33.03	2:28.15	
5656	Clova Court	V35			10.02.60	9	Bressanone, ITA	5 Jul
	13.48/1.7	1.48	14.31	23.68/1.0	5.26/0.3	47.52	2:25.19	
5639						1	Derby	31 May
	13.42/1.0	1.48	13.83	24.19/0.9	5.54/0.6	47.80	2:29.27	
5421						8	Kuala Lumpur, MAL	17 Sep
	13.61/-0.2	1.52	13.17	24.01/0.1	5.37/-0.2	44.07	2:36.38	
5608 w	Jenny Kelly				20.06.70	6	Arles, FRA	24 May
	13.83W/4.6	1.64	13.43	24.89w/3.9	6.01W/6.2	34.69	2:25.55	
5584						4	Val de Reuil, FRA	26 Jul
	13.93/0.4	1.63	13.88	25.13/0.3	5.86/0.3	35.45	2:23.44	
5604 w	Julia Bennett				26.03.70	7	Arles, FRA	24 May
	14.52W/4.6	1.82	11.54	25.50w/2.5	5.93w/2.8	35.50	2:20.73	
5555 w	Diana Bennett				14.06.74	8	Arles, FRA	24 May
	14.23W/4.6	1.73	11.49	25.55W/6.1	5.80w/2.9	34.60	2:14.42	
5504						2	Dordrecht, HOL	30 Aug
	14.40/1.4	1.75	11.06	26.22/0.5	5.77/0.4	35.19	2:12.20	
5466						5	Val de Reuil, FRA	26 Jul
	14.38/0.4	1.75	11.15	26.11/0.3	5.66/-0.9	34.55	2:13.00	
5425						1	Wrexham	2 Aug
	14.49/-0.4	1.71	11.01	26.38/1.4	5.66/-1.1	35.77	2:10.69	
5497	Nicola Gautier	U23			21.03.78	3	Dordrecht, HOL	30 Aug
	14.28/1.4	1.66	13.58	25.57/0.5	5.39/0.6	43.61	2:25.82	
5368						6	Val de Reuil, FRA	26 Jul
	14.19/-0.6	1.63	13.83	25.06/0.3	5.43/0.6	32.57	2:23.52	
5358 w	Chloe Cozens	U20			9.04.80	10	Arles, FRA	24 May
	14.78W/5.8	1.73	11.30	25.87W/6.1	5.72W/5.8	41.06	2:27.95	
5220						16	Annecy, FRA	2 Aug
	15.47/-0.3	1.74	10.13	26.82/-0.4	5.54/1.2	48.00	2:26.46	
5129						1	Hull	20 Sep
	15.54/0.2	1.78	11.15	26.32/1.8	5.21/0.0	45.46	2:34.23	
(10)								
5237	Danielle Freeman	U20			11.02.80	1	Cartagena, SPA	19 Jul
	14.00w/2.1	1.68	10.42	25.24w/3.4	5.44/1.3	36.18	2:27.11	
5015	Katherine Livesey	U20			15.12.79	2	Wrexham	2 Aug
	14.69/-0.8	1.65	9.19	24.84/1.4	5.77/0.4	26.45	2:24.15	

28 performances to 5000 points by 12 athletes

4948	Kim Crowther		19.01.66	1	Birmingham	23 Aug
	14.64	1.62	12.23	26.49w	5.45	28.29	2:26.44
4809	Cheryl Done		25.09.70	1	Cosford	28 Jul
	14.93	1.54	11.12	26.52	5.18	37.71	2:29.06
4754	Clover Wynter-Pink	U23	29.11.77	1	Enfield	2 Aug
	15.81	1.56	11.90	26.85	5.21	43.42	2:37.71
4697	Leanne Buxton	U23	27.05.78	2	Enfield	2 Aug
	14.67	1.50	9.66	26.28	5.21	31.21	2:22.30
4670	Jackie Tindal	U20	21.01.79	1	Glasgow (S)	3 May
	15.39	1.51	11.50	25.62	4.96	33.10	2:29.05
4605	Jenny Brown	V35	21.05.59	1	Sheffield	23 Aug
	16.23	1.63	10.09	27.39	5.42	32.40	2:21.88
4590	Gillian Stewart	U20	21.01.80	2	Glasgow (S)	3 May
	15.04	1.63	10.57	26.60	5.06	36.16	2:46.46
4561	Natalie Butler	U23	25.11.78	3	Derby	31 May
	15.13	1.63	9.09	26.34	5.29	31.56	2:39.25

(20)

4559	Kirsty Roger	U23	24.03.78	4	Derby	31 May
	15.70	1.69	9.72	28.03	5.40	29.38	2:30.16
4546	Amanda Wale		14.10.70	4	Wrexham	2 Aug
	15.27	1.59	9.38	26.29	5.12	26.70	2:25.61
4460	Catherine Parmiter	U20	27.04.81	2	Carn Brea	28 Jun
	15.7	1.72	9.66	25.9	4.87	23.62	2:30.5
4458	Rebecca Foster		14.04.71	1	Rotherham	13 Sep
	15.3	1.46	10.29	27.5	5.40	44.20	2:47.4
4419	Laura White	U20	5.09.79	3	Hull	20 Aug
	15.62	1.72	8.69	26.59	5.30	21.35	2:35.02
4357	Lisa Thompson	U20	25.04.81	6	Wrexham	2 Aug
	15.89	1.59	8.13	27.02	5.23	24.19	2:21.97
4351	Angie Nyhan	U23	13.04.78	2	Rotherham	13 Sep
	15.7	1.52	10.76	27.4	5.42	33.73	2:44.4
4316	Caroline Pearce	U20	1.09.80	4	Hull	20 Sep
	15.67	1.57	8.93	27.43	5.24	25.03	2:28.22
4314	Tamsin Stephens	U20	2.08.80	7	Wrexham	2 Aug
	14.48	1.50	8.62	25.94	5.03	23.10	2:35.51
4309	Laura Curtis	U20	2.05.81	6	Hull	20 Sep
	16.32	1.57	9.43	27.24	4.82	29.09	2:23.43

(30)

4289	Vicky Williams	U20	11.04.81	2	Carn Brea	28 Jun
	14.9	1.48	9.45	26.6	5.16	28.13	2:37.3
4286	Kate Rogers	U20	13.02.79	3	Derby	31 May
	15.42	1.57	7.48	27.34	5.35	26.81	2:31.45
4272	Isobel Donaldson		24.01.64	3	Cosford	28 Jul
	16.74	1.51	8.74	27.57	4.84	37.86	2:24.77
4259	Jimenez Joseph		14.07.68	5	Derby	31 May
	16.38	1.57	10.09	27.52	4.99	30.65	2:34.26
4229	Teresa Andrews	U23	4.01.77	8	Wrexham	2 Aug
	17.02	1.65	11.05	28.42	5.12	25.74	2:32.88
4189	Jacqueline Elliott	U23	13.09.78	7	Hull	20 Sep
	16.53	1.42	8.45	25.87	5.20	23.20	2:21.45
4119	Hannah Stares	U23	13.11.78	3	Birmingham	23 Aug
	15.47	1.56	9.33	27.06w	4.91	24.10	2:41.46
4106 w	Helen Walker	U20	12.10.80	2	Hexham	17 May
	15.4	1.45	8.55	26.74W	4.83	23.99	2:29.14
	4096				1	Leeds	28 Jun
	15.5	1.49	8.84	27.2	5.18	23.78	2:34.1
4083	Lisa Caryl		21.11.75	6	Derby	31 May
	15.45	1.54	8.70	27.45	4.98	21.88	2:34.67
4081	Amelia Martin	U20	11.02.80	9	Hull	20 Sep
	16.47	1.45	8.96	26.01	5.40	29.21	2:49.73

4070	Nicola Jupp			26.10.75	10	Wrexham		2 Aug
	16.53	1.53	10.32	28.12	4.90	29.31	2:37.91	
4004	Vicky Consterdine			25.04.75	4	Birmingham		23 Aug
	15.74	1.47	8.14	27.74	5.00	23.38	2:29.47	
4004	Denise Gayle		U20	11.09.79	10	Hull		20 Sep
	18.86	1.66	8.39	25.84	5.07	22.31	2:33.55	
3943	Judy Kotey		U20	20.05.80	1	Ashford		28 Jun
	17.4	1.47	8.96	27.3	5.22w	36.10	2:47.9	
3932	Paula Blank		U23	13.12.77	11	Wrexham		2 Aug
	16.28	1.44	10.71	28.32	4.24	43.75	2:55.13	
3920	Judith Butler		U20	5.10.79	11	Hull		20 Sep
	16.73	1.57	7.88	27.09	4.89	24.17	2:37.74	
3916	Julia Sykes			27.05.75	9	Derby		31 May
	16.42	1.51	9.68	28.61	4.34	30.78	2:33.66	
3905	Jo Thorn		U20	19.02.81	12	Hull		20 Sep
	14.86	1.57	7.84	26.36	5.15	17.88	3:03.01	

incomplete

| 4599 dnf | Kelly Sotherton | | U23 | 13.11.76 | | Arles, FRA | | 24 May |
| | 14.56 | 1.67 | 11.39 | 24.33 | 5.95w | 30.13 | dns | |

Foreign

| 4817 | *Margaret Veldman* | | | *7.06.74* | *2* | *Birmingham* | | *23 Aug* |
| | *15.32* | *1.56* | *10.86* | *25.16w* | *5.51* | *28.73* | *2:28.36* | |

HEPTATHLON - Under 17

4666	Tina Thirwell			5.09.81	1	Hull		20 Sep
	12.42	1.63	8.77	25.21	5.36	27.78	2:26.41	
4629	Samantha Adamson			27.03.82	2	Hull		20 Sep
	12.37	1.75	9.30	26.53	4.87	30.15	2:27.54	
4497	Karen Lowe			3.05.82	3	Hull		20 Sep
	12.09	1.60	8.54	25.79	5.08	31.12	2:33.89	
4429	Paula Hendricks			25.01.83	4	Hull		20 Sep
	13.32	1.54	8.63	26.73	5.11	36.47	2:24.67	
4324	Cathy Young			14.03.82	5	Hull		20 Sep
	12.48	1.66	8.85	27.45	4.95	25.98	2:29.01	
4315	Claire Pleavin			25.04.83	2	Wrexham		28 Jun
	12.34	1.59	7.58	27.26	5.34	32.30	2:37.3	
4299	Helen Thieme			28.09.81	6	Hull		20 Sep
	12.40	1.66	8.44	26.05	4.94	22.74	2:34.12	
4298	Nicola Sanders			23.06.82	1	Birmingham		23 Aug
	11.96w	1.59	7.65	25.18	4.76	18.18	2:23.74	
4290	Sharon Davidge			15.09.81	1	Camborne		28 Jun
	11.4	1.57	7.73	25.8	5.25	20.41	2:37.3	
4258	Rachel Hogg			11.06.82	4	Wrexham		28 Jun
	12.50	1.62	7.82	25.96	5.73	22.98	2:50.0	
(10)								
4257	Suzie Furlonger			30.09.81	5	Wrexham		28 Jun
	12.70	1.62	8.33	27.00	5.38	26.51	2:23.95	
4255	Rebecca Jones			17.01.83	1	Wrexham		2 Aug
	12.42	1.65	8.53	27.67	5.33	26.37	2:40.64	
4233	Wendy Davidson			14.10.82	3	Birmingham		23 Aug
	11.99	1.59	7.74	26.03	5.33w	19.67	2:37.94	
4205	Donna Maylor			20.05.82	8	Hull		20 Sep
	11.96	1.60	10.13	24.96	5.59	20.98	3:19.61	
4151	Sara McGreavy			13.12.82	2	Worcester		28 Jun
	11.8	1.49	7.75	27.2	5.11	20.41	2:24.0	
4106	Natalie Hulse			2.12.82	4	Birmingham		23 Aug
	12.75	1.59	8.57	26.90	4.99w	22.33	2:34.86	
4083	Barbara Parker			8.11.82	9	Hull		20 Sep
	13.11	1.54	7.50	27.41	4.83	24.25	2:19.65	

4015	Siobhan Dennehy			31.08.82	1	Basildon		27 Sep
	12.4	1.63	7.69	27.2	4.87	24.75	2:42.9	
3994	Jemma Scott			14.03.83	1	Glasgow (S)		3 May
	12.64	1.57	7.01	27.13	4.89	20.16	2:28.06	
3963	Laura Biscoe			13.01.83	2	St. Ives		28 Jun
	13.3	1.65	7.31	27.6	5.16	17.15	2:30.2	
(20)								
3958	Stephanie Little			5.11.81	6	Birmingham		23 Aug
	12.35	1.50	8.10	27.40	4.84	22.28	2:33.28	
3931	Kim Wall			21.04.83		Basildon		27 Sep
	14.0	1.48	5.97	25.4	5.09	18.71	2:20.5	
3916	Jodie Hearne			17.09.81	2	Enfield		2 Aug
	12.28	1.65	8.02	27.85	4.95	21.61	2:51.28	
3911	Kate Brewington			15.10.81	3	Enfield		2 Aug
	12.11	1.59	7.82	27.81	5.01	24.21	2:52.25	
3885	Danielle Parkinson			2.09.81	7	Wrexham		28 Jun
	12.90	1.59	7.64	27.60	5.33	29.45	3:05.1	
3874	Kerry Swyer			2.12.82	1	Hexham		31 Aug
	14.30	1.60	8.14	27.65	4.77	24.08	2:31.90	
3870	Helen Cooper			20.06.83	10	Hull		20 Sep
	12.64	1.51	7.61	26.23	4.75	20.50	2:39.38	
3859	Abbey Nice			11.12.81	4	Enfield		2 Aug
	13.61	1.50	8.32	27.62	4.82	20.07	2:25.68	
3827	Cara Schofield			13.03.82	1	Crawley		13 Sep
	12.9	1.39	8.69	27.8	4.72	31.49	2:39.6	

PENTATHLON - Under 15

3509	Aileen Wilson			30.03.84	1	Hull	20 Sep
	11.70	9.77	1.78	5.20	2:28.01		
3063	Olivia Ross-Hurst			10.12.83	2	Hull	20 Sep
	12.28	8.33	1.63	5.13	2:34.84		
3045	Danielle Selley			19.12.83	1	Cardiff	20 Jun
	11.00	5.16	8.35	1.54	2:41.54		
2976	Stephanie Dalton			8.02.84	3	Hull	20 Sep
	12.07	8.85	1.54	4.95	2:34.06		
2972	Lara Carty			7.03.84	4	Hull	20 Sep
	11.98	8.49	1.57	4.88	2:34.61		
2972	Melissa Rogers			2.09.83	5	Hull	20 Sep
	12.12	9.07	1.54	4.97	2:35.58		
2966	Henrietta Paxton			19.09.83	6	Hull	20 Sep
	12.53	8.41	1.54	5.40	2:38.75		
2964	Hayley Jasper			1.05.84	7	Hull	20 Sep
	12.41	7.95	1.54	4.86	2:25.45		
2874	Katie Wigham			27.05.84	8	Hull	20 Sep
	12.74	9.48	1.51	5.04	2:39.11		
2854	Laura Taylor			22.04.84	9	Hull	20 Sep
	12.22	8.83	1.54	4.86	2:40.86		
(10)							
2810	Melissa Harris			20.10.83	10	Hull	20 Sep
	11.50	8.16	1.45	5.03	2:43.57		
2754	Catriona Pennet			10.10.83	2	Glasgow (S)	3 May
	4.69	11.87	1.45	8.22	2:37.10		
2748	Lyndsey Russell			11.09.83	1	Pitreavie	4 Jun
	1.35	26.5	12.1	8.50	2:50.4		
2748	Helen Davies			24.03.84	3	Birmingham	23 Aug
	4.87w	12.04	7.15	1.49	2:37.77		
2729	Carly Robson			5.12.83	5	Birmingham	23 Aug
	4.75	12.36	8.61	1.49	2:41.72		
2681	Cinzia Giancovich			10.01.85	11	Hull	20 Sep
	12.61	8.61	1.42	4.65	2:34.76		

2667	Louise Cook				7.01.84	3	Enfield	2 Aug
	5.01	12.17	8.65	1.42	2:49.02			
2659	Emma Nield				20.11.83	3	Glasgow (S)	3 May
	4.80	13.16	1.51	6.84	2:34.02			
2646	Rebecca Reid				9.12.83	12	Hull	20 Sep
	13.16	8.39	1.42	4.53	2:29.57			
2621	Nicola Britton				28.06.84	14	Hull	20 Sep
	12.86	10.49	1.54	4.55	2:59.50			
	(20)							
2602	Zainab Ceesay				27.10.83	15	Hull	20 Sep
	13.17	7.43	1.51	5.00	2:46.91			
2591	Catherine Crawford					1	Antrim	30 Aug
	12.3	4.43	7.37	1.45	2:36.6			
2584	Lucy Hunt				4.04.84	2	Carn Brea	28 Jun
	12.8	8.08	1.44	4.85	2:45.0			
2576	Jenny Egan				15.05.84	3	Carn Brea	28 Jun
	13.1	8.08	1.50	4.77	2:47.1			
2565	Imogen Robertson				2.10.83	16	Hull	20 Sep
	13.21	9.04	1.54	4.43	2:49.08			
2560	Gemma Evans				9.09.84	4	Carn Brea	28 Jun
	12.6	8.25	1.38	4.88	2:45.0			
2560	Louise Toward				27.03.84	17	Hull	20 Sep
	12.22	8.45	1.42	4.42	2:42.88			

non standard

2822	Joanne Erskine				28.05.85	1	Pitreavie	4 Jun
	14.4(100) 1.48		12.0(70H) 5.65		2:45.0			
2769	Kimberley Goodall				5.10.83	1	Guernsey	23 Aug
	14.45(100) 7.62		1.40	4.86	2:33.6			

PENTATHLON - Under 13

2329	Amy Fozzard				20.04.86	1	Glasgow (S)	3 May
	4.33	12.31	7.46	1.41	2:43.15			
2292	Gemma Collier				25.11.85	1	Exeter	27 Sep
	4.19	11.9	8.82	1.24	2:41.1			
2254	Staci Stewart				20.09.85	2	Glasgow (S)	3 May
	3.92	12.47	6.73	1.47	2:43.32			
2139	Emma Perkins					1	Crawley	13 Sep
	4.15	12.5	7.44	1.42	2:58.6			
2134	Nadia Bromley				21.09.86	3	Exeter	27 Sep
	4.08	12.7	7.56	1.33	2:46.9			
2121	Kelly Marshall				8.01.86	1	Woking	2 Aug
	4.25	11.7	6.39	1.22	2:44.1			
2091	Emma Smith				14.09.85	2	Woking	2 Aug
	4.01	12.7	6.36	1.28	2:38.0			
2081	Jenny Bliss				6.07.86	2	Crawley	13 Sep
	4.20	12.8	5.95	1.24	2:36.7			
2070	Jade Halket				5.05.86	4	Glasgow (S)	3 May
	4.30	13.11	5.54	1.35	2:44.84			
2041	Cathy Owbridge					1	Hull	25 Apr
	4.15	16.0	8.01	1.22	2:34.3			

2000 METRES WALK - Track - Under 13

11:08.37	Natasha Fox	21.09.85	1	Derby	30 May
11:08.93	Hayley Dyke	11.03.86	2	Derby	30 May
11:13.94	Charlotte Curtis		3	Derby	30 May
11:29.01	Joanna Hobson	22.01.87	4	Derby	30 May
11:32.81	Lianne Oldale	19.09.86	5	Derby	30 May
11:36.67	Gemma Evans	25.01.86	6	Derby	30 May

2500 METRES WALK - Track - Under 15

12:51.7	Kelly Mann		8.09.83	1	Leamington	9 May
13:19.8	Laura Fryer		3.12.83	4	Hoo	13 Jun
13:21.01	Hayley Hutchings		14.11.83	1	Crawley	9 May
13:35.20	Natalie Geens		27.12.84	2	Solihull	24 May
13:57.50	Nicky Reynolds		24.06.85	3	Solihull	24 May
13:58.25	Sophie Hales		30.03.85	2	Crawley	9 May

3000 METRES WALK - Track

13:02.5 mx	Lisa Kehler		15.03.67	1	Woodford	17 Jun
13:14.48 +				m	Birmingham	26 Jul
13:38.7 mx	Vicky Lupton		17.04.72	1	Sheffield	23 Aug
13:43.73				1	Bedford	25 May
13:50.71				1	Cudworth	9 May
13:56.6				1	Rotherham	16 Jul
13:50.58	Cal Partington		27.06.66	1	Birmingham	18 Jul
14:00.3				1	Douglas, IOM	12 Jul
14:01 +	Catherine Charnock		3.05.75	m	Birmingham	26 Jul
14:02.5				1	Whitehaven	9 May
14:21.55				2	Bedford	25 May
14:09.81	Amy Hales	U17	16.03.82	1	Hull	19 Sep
14:17.96 i	Katie Ford	U17	21.10.81	3	Birmingham	28 Feb
14:47.3				2	Sheffield	23 Aug
14:22.2	Karen Kneale		23.04.69	2	Douglas, IOM	12 Jul
14:23.2	Sharon Tonks (14:32.2?)		18.04.70	1	Worcester	9 May
14:23.48	Debbie Wallen	U20	28.05.79	1	Hexham	14 Jun
	16 performances to 14:25.0 by 9 athletes					
14:25.22	Lisa Crump	U23	30.03.76	2	Cudworth	9 May
(10)						
14:49.18	Sarah Bennett	U20	27.07.80	1	London (He)	9 Aug
15:06.06	Sally Warren	U23	29.01.78	3	Hexham	14 Jun
15:06.69	Kelly Mann	U15	8.09.83	1	Derby	30 May
15:07.8	Nikki Huckerby	U23	27.02.78	2	Bromsgrove	11 Oct
15:10.97	Karen Ratcliffe	V35	1.06.61	1	Newport	11 Jul
15:17.5	Louise Richmond	U17	15.12.81	2	Ayr	18 Jul
15:21.4	Nicola Phillips	U17	23.04.83	4	Ayr	18 Jul
15:35.0	Kate Horwill		26.01.75	3	Bromsgrove	11 Oct
15:39.55	Victoria Stainburn	U15	23.12.83	2	Hull	19 Sep
15:40.0	Helen Ford-Dunn	U23	20.10.77	1	Oxford	16 May
(20)						
15:41.71	Natalie Evans	U15	15.11.83	1	Sheffield	16 Aug
15:46.61	Lisa Airey	U20	19.12.80	3	London (He)	9 Aug
15:49.47	Hayley Hutchings	U15	14.11.83	3	Hull	19 Sep
15:57.19	Sian Woodcock	U20	13.01.80	4	Birmingham	18 Jul
15:59.68	Ann Lewis	V50	29.12.47	3	Bedford	25 May
16:00.26	Kirsty Coleman	U20	17.11.80	3	Crawley	9 May
16:03.33	Mary Wallen	V45	9.06.52	4	Bedford	25 May

Under 17 and Under 15

16:21.57	Laura Fryer	U15	3.12.83	2	Sheffield	16 Aug
16:28.53	Natalie Geens	U15	27.12.84	5	Derby	30 May
16:29.6	Natalie Watson	U17	29.01.83	7	Bromsgrove	11 Oct
16:31.01	Nicky Reynolds	U15	24.06.85	5	Hull	19 Sep

Road - Under 17 and Under 15

15:35	Laura Fryer	U15	3.12.83	2	Sheffield	25 Apr
15:38	Hayley Hutchings	U15	14.11.83	3	Sheffield	25 Apr
16:05	Natalie Watson	U17	29.01.83	6	Leamington	1 Mar
16:13	Sophie Hales	U15	30.03.85	1	Steyning	21 Jun
16:16	Natalie Geens	U15	27.12.84	1	Birkenhead	7 Nov

322

5000 METRES WALK - Track

22:01.53	Lisa Kehler		15.03.67	2	Birmingham	26	Jul
	22:08.69			1	Derby	30	May
23:32.03	Cal Partington		27.06.66	1	Liverpool	20	Jun
	23:42.48			3	Birmingham	26	Jul
23:32.48	Vicky Lupton		17.04.72	3	Birmingham	26	Jul
23:50.96	Catherine Charnock		3.05.75	4	Birmingham	26	Jul
	23:51.92			2	Liverpool	20	Jun
	24:09.02			2	Derby	30	May
24:20.07	Sharon Tonks		18.04.70	5	Birmingham	26	Jul
24:28.60	Debbie Wallen	U20	28.05.79	6	Birmingham	26	Jul
24:56.69	Nikki Huckerby	U23	27.02.78	2	Solihull	24	May
25:25.4	Katie Ford	U17	21.10.81	4	Alicante, SPA	18	Jul
25:36.61	Sally Warren	U23	29.01.78	4	Dessau, GER	1	Aug
25:37.69	Melanie Wright		5.04.64	3	Solihull	24	May
(10)							
26:01.4	Sarah Bennett	U20	27.07.80	6	Alicante, SPA	18	Jul
26:29.12	Lisa Airey	U20	19.12.80	6	Derby	30	May
26:33.56	Verity Snook		13.11.70	1	Enfield	2	Aug
26:58.7	Karen Ratcliffe	V35	1.06.61	1	Newport	12	Jul
27:00.0	Nicola Phillips	U17	23.04.83	1	Brighton	20	Dec
27:09.12	Ann Lewis	V50	29.12.47	7	Derby	30	May
27:22.77	Kirsty Coleman	U20	17.11.80	8	Derby	30	May
27:24.28	Louise Richmond	U17	15.12.81	9	Derby	30	May
27:25.63	Bridget Kaneen		15.08.65	10	Derby	30	May
27:42.65	Becky Tisshaw	U20	8.02.81	2	Hull	19	Sep
(20)							
27:46.0	Helen Ford-Dunn	U23	20.10.77	1	Horsham	21	Jul

Additional Under 17

28:30.76	Natalie Watson		29.01.83	13	Derby	30	May
29:10.72	Sam Campbell		22.11.81	14	Derby	30	May
29:17.47	Hayley Coleman		24.05.83	15	Derby	30	May

Road

21:55	Lisa Kehler		15.03.67	1hc	Earlsdon	13	Jul
	22:40 +				Budapest, HUN	20	Aug
	22:45 +				Dudince, SVK	26	Apr
	23:52 +			1m	East Molesey	18	Jul
	23:59			1	Leicester	7	Feb
22:35	Vicky Lupton		17.04.72	1	Sheffield	25	Apr
	23:54			1	Prestwich	7	Mar
23:58	Catherine Charnock		3.05.75	1	Birkenhead	7	Nov
24:35	Kim Braznell	V40	28.02.56	1	Hove	6	Jun
24:44	Kate Horwill		26.01.75	1	Tamworth	13	Dec
24:48	Katie Ford	U17	21.10.81	16	Senigallia, ITA	30	May
24:59	Sarah Bennett	U20	27.07.80	19	Senigallia, ITA	30	May
25:17	Amy Hales	U17	16.03.82	21	Senigallia, ITA	30	May
25:18	Sally Warren	U23	29.01.78	5	Sheffield	25	Apr
25:49	Karen Ratcliffe	V35	1.06.61	2	Coventry	13	Jul
(10)							
26:08	Helen Ford-Dunn	U23	20.10.77	2	London (VP)	31	Jan
26:25	Lisa Airey	U20	19.12.80	6	Sheffield	25	Apr
26:28	Kelly Mann	U17	8.09.83	3	Birkenhead	7	Nov
26:41	Louise Richmond	U17	15.12.81	4	Birkenhead	7	Nov
26:57	Nicola Phillips	U17	23.04.83	7	Sheffield	25	Apr

10000 METRES WALK - Track

56:36.0	Amy Hales	U17	16.03.82	1	Brighton	24	Jan
58:25.0	Kirsty Coleman	U20	17.11.80	1	Brighton	24	Jan

10000 METRES WALK - Road

45:03	Lisa Kehler		15.03.67	3	Kuala Lumpur, MAL	19	Sep
45:18				1	Rotterdam, HOL	15	May
45:42				18	Budapest, HUN	20	Aug
45:54				27	Dudince, SVK	25	Apr
46:25				1	East Molesey	18	Jul
47:10				1	Leicester	21	Mar
47:41	Vicky Lupton		17.04.72	2	East Molesey	18	Jul
48:27				7	Kuala Lumpur, MAL	19	Sep
48:38				2	Leicester	21	Mar
48:45				1	Sheffield	21	Feb
49:15				1	Leamington	1	Mar
49:49				1	Sheffield	20	Jan
48:09	Cal Partington		27.06.66	6	Kuala Lumpur, MAL	19	Sep
48:24				2	Stockport	27	Jun
49:50				1	Isle of Man	18	Jan
48:36	Kim Braznell	V40	28.02.56	1	Sheffield	25	Apr
48:55				3	East Molesey	18	Jul
49:10				17	Senigallia, ITA	31	May
49:27				3	Leicester	21	Mar
49:02	Catherine Charnock		3.05.75	3	Stockport	27	Jun
49:05				1	Birmingham	19	Dec
49:14				2	Dublin, IRE	12	Sep
49:20				4	East Molesey	18	Jul
49:47				1	Tamworth	13	Dec
49:51	Lisa Crump	U23	30.03.76	19	Senigallia, ITA	31	May

25 performances under 50:00 by 6 athletes

50:05	Karen Kneale		23.04.69	2	Sheffield	25	Apr
51:07	Nikki Huckerby	U23	27.02.78	5	Leicester	21	Mar
51:20	Sally Warren	U23	29.01.78	2	Tamworth	13	Dec
51:29	Kate Horwill		26.01.75	2	Birmingham	19	Dec
	(10)						
51:55	Sharon Tonks		18.04.70	4	Dublin, IRE	12	Sep
52:03	Melanie Wright		5.04.64	8	Leicester	21	Mar
52:24	Debbie Wallen	U20	28.05.79	9	Leicester	21	Mar
52:55	Katie Ford	U17	21.10.81	10	Leicester	21	Mar
53:53	Sarah Bennett	U20	27.07.80	4	Birmingham	19	Dec
54:20	Liz Corran	V40	23.09.55	1	Isle of Man	15	Mar
55:20	Kirsty Coleman	U20	17.11.80	3	East Molesey	11	Jan
55:35	Lynn Bradley		21.05.67	14	Leicester	21	Mar
55:41	Ann Lewis	V50	29.12.47	15	Leicester	21	Mar
55:47	Lisa Airey	U20	19.12.80	16	Leicester	21	Mar
	(20)						
56:12	Helen Ford-Dunn	U23	20.10.77	5	East Molesey	11	Jan
56:35	Jane Kennaugh			2	St. Johns, IOM	13	Dec
56:43	Maureen Cox	V45	7.09.50	18	Leicester	21	Mar

20 KILOMETRES WALK

1:44:35	Vicky Lupton		17.04.72	1	Holmewood	29	Aug
1:45:24	Catherine Charnock		3.05.75	2	Holmewood	29	Aug
1:58:14	Mary Wallen	V45	9.06.52	1	Sutton Coldfield	1	Aug
2:00:47	Ann Lewis	V50	29.12.47	2	Sutton Coldfield	1	Aug

50 KILOMETRES WALK

5:34:27	Jane Kennaugh			1	Isle of Man	3	May
5:41:36	Maureen Cox	V45	7.09.50	2	Bradford	25	May
5:41:36	Jackie Bairstow	V40	8.01.57	3	Bradford	25	May
5:45:58	Cath Reader	V40	19.10.54	1	Burrator	4	May
5:53:48	Pam Ficken	V55	25.07.41	1	Basildon	18	Apr
5:53:54	Kath Crilley	V50	8.09.47	2	Burrator	4	May

100 MILES WALK ROAD

| 19:32:26 | Sandra Brown | V45 | 1.04.49 | 1 | Isle of Man | 21 Jun |
| 22:22:30 | Jill Green | V55 | 10.10.41 | 3 | Isle of Man | 21 Jun |

24 HOURS WALK ROAD

| 186.922 km | Sandra Brown | V45 | 1.04.49 | 2 | Dijon, FRA | 23 May |

4 x 100 METRES

43.69	England		3	Kuala Lumpur, MAL	21 Sep
	(M Richardson, D Fraser, S Jacobs, J Maduaka)				
44.54	National Junior Team	U20	2	Alicante, SPA	18 Jul
	(A Oyepitan, S Wilhelmy, S Davies, R White)				
44.65	National Junior Team	U20	4	Annecy, FRA	2 Aug
	(A Oyepitan, S Wilhelmy, S Davies, R White)				
45.43	National Junior Team	U20	3h1	Annecy, FRA	2 Aug
	(A Oyepitan, S Wilhelmy, S Davies, M Purkiss)				
45.60	National Under 23 Team		3	Dessau, GER	1 Aug
	(M Rostek, E Ruddock, Z Wilson, T Nelson)				
45.72	Birchfield Harriers		1	Birmingham	6 Jun
	(,,, K Merry)				
45.84	National Junior Team	U20	1	Loughborough	17 May
	(N Gaynor, S Zawada, S Wilhelmy, R White)				
46.19	Shaftesbury Barnet Harriers		6	Vilamoura, POR	30 May
	(C Henry, A Hansen, C Murphy, S Jacobs)				
46.37	Team Solent		1	Bedford	29 Aug
	(A Coore, M Purkiss, H Joyce, K Sketchley)				
46.4	Windsor Slough & Eton AC		1	Enfield	19 Jul
46.55	Loughborough Students		2	Loughborough	17 May
46.64	AAA		3	Loughborough	17 May
46.68	Windsor Slough & Eton AC		2	Birmingham	6 Jun
46.68	National Under 23 Team		2	Hexham	14 Jun
46.70	Loughborough University		1	Bath	2/4 May
46.7	Essex Ladies		2	Enfield	19 Jul
46.74	British Universities		4	Loughborough	17 May
46.80	Birchfield Harriers	U20	1	Istanbul, TUR	26 Sep
	(K Robinson, D Maylor, E Walker, S Davies)				
46.91	Windsor Slough & Eton AC		2	Bedford	29 Aug
	(J Dear, M Richardson, M Clements, S Williams)				
46.98	North		1	Birmingham	18 Jul

Additional National Teams

47.60	Wales		1	Cardiff	4 Aug
49.20	Northern Ireland		1	Antrim	23 Jun

Additional Club Teams (1 - 6 above)

47.04	Trafford AC		3	Bedford	29 Aug
47.16	Brunel University		2	Bath	2/4 May
47.3	Edinburgh Woollen Mill		2	Grangemouth	4 Jul
47.3	Wakefield & District H		3	Enfield	19 Jul
47.50	Sale Harriers Manchester		5	Bedford	29 Aug
47.77	Peterborough AC		7	Bedford	29 Aug
47.8	Wigan and District Harriers		2	Coventry	5 Jul
47.84	Aldershot Farnham & District AC		4	Birmingham	6 Jun
48.03	City of Glasgow AC		6	Birmingham	6 Jun
48.1	Croydon Harriers		1	Kingston	14 Jun
48.1	Essex Ladies	U20	1	Basildon	21 Jun
48.2	Wycombe Phoenix Harriers		1	St Ives	5 Sep
48.3	City of Stoke AC		1	Liverpool	18 Jul
48.44	Walton AC		1	Bedford	30 Aug
48.6	Coventry Godiva Harriers		1	Stoke	9 Aug

Additional Under 20 Teams (1 - 5 above)

47.25	England Schools	U17	1	Ayr	18	Jul
	(N Smellie, J McCarthy, J Walters, D Maylor)					
47.55	London Schools		1h2	Exeter	11	Jul
	(D Gayle, E Whitter, A Hayles, J Johnson)					
47.6	Birchfield Harriers		1	Wigan	23	Aug
47.65	West Yorkshire Schools		2h2	Exeter	11	Jul
47.73	West Midlands Schools	U17	1h2	Exeter	11	Jul

Additional Under 20 Club Teams (1 - 2 above)

49.0	Wakefield Harriers		1	Whitley Bay	21	Jun
49.1	Edinburgh Woollen Mill		2	Wakefield	26	Jul
49.1	Birchfield Harriers	U17	1	Stoke	19	Jul
49.3	City of Stoke AC	U17	2	Stoke	19	Jul
49.6	Sale Harriers Manchester		2	Birmingham	21	Jun
49.66	Sale Harriers Manchester	U17	1	Birmingham	6	Sep
49.67	Swansea Harriers	U17	2	Birmingham	6	Sep
49.7	Torfaen AC	U17	1	Newport	28	Jun
49.7	Peterborough AC		1	Reading	20	Sep
49.8	Blackheath Harriers	U17	1	Bromley	17	May

Additional Under 17 Teams (1 - 2 above)

47.79	Cheshire Schools	1	Exeter	11	Jul
47.99	Shropshire Schools	1h3	Exeter	11	Jul
48.17	Greater Manchester Schools	2	Exeter	11	Jul
48.21	Essex Schools	4	Exeter	11	Jul
48.69	London Schools	2h3	Exeter	11	Jul
48.73	Surrey Schools	3h3	Exeter	11	Jul
49.04	Scotland Schools	3	Ayr	18	Jul
49.08	Greater Manchester AA	1	Cudworth	2	Aug

Additional Under 17 Club Teams (1 - 6 above)

49.82	Edinburgh Woollen Mill	1	Birmingham	5	Sep
50.1	Sutton & District AC	1	Sutton	3	May
50.1	Ilford AC	1	Thurrock	23	Jul
50.3	Oldham & Royton Harriers	1	Stretford	5	Jul

Under 15 Teams

49.60	Essex Schools	1h1	Exeter	11	Jul
50.31	Middlesex Schools	2	Exeter	11	Jul
50.33	Cambridge Harriers	1	Ashford	20	Sep
50.61	Warwickshire Schools	3	Exeter	11	Jul
50.84	Hertfordshire Schools	2h2	Exeter	11	Jul
50.89	Liverpool HAC	1	Birmingham	6	Sep
51.04	Cannock & Stafford AC	2	Birmingham	6	Sep
51.1	London Borough of Ealing	1	Kingston	13	Sep
51.12	Dyfed Schools	1	Deeside	4	Jul
51.18	Leicestershire Schools	2h1	Exeter	11	Jul

Additional Under 15 Club Teams (1 - 3 above)

51.3	Wolverhampton & Bilston AC	1	Corby	17	May
51.3	Coventry Godiva Harriers	1	Solihull	28	Jun
51.4	Dudley & Stourbridge Harriers	1	Derby	26	Apr
51.54	Wigan and District Harriers	3	Birmingham	6	Sep
51.67	Windsor Slough & Eton AC	4	Birmingham	6	Sep
51.7	Newham & Essex Beagles	1	Barking	2	Jul
51.7	Ipswich Harriers	2	Barking	10	Sep

Under 13 Teams

54.0	Essex AA	1	Kingston	26	Jul
54.3	Wigan and District Harriers	1	Blackpool	29	Aug

54.38	City of Glasgow AC		1	Birmingham	6	Sep
54.4	Wakefield Harriers		1	Wakefield	28	Jun
54.45	Liverpool HAC		2	Birmingham	6	Sep
54.5	Basildon AC		1	Norwich	19	Jul
54.8	Sussex AA		2	Kingston	26	Jul
54.9	Forth Valley League Div 1 Select		1	Livingston	5	Sep
54.91	Windsor Slough & Eton AC		4	Birmingham	6	Sep
55.0	South Yorkshire AA		1	Nottingham	12	Sep

4 x 200 METRES

1:39.1 i	Glasgow University		1	Glasgow	11	Nov
1:39.36 i	Brunel University		1	Glasgow	15	Mar
1:39.98 i	Loughborough University		2	Glasgow	15	Mar
1:41.55 i	England Schools	U16	1	Birmingham	28	Feb
1:42.78 i	Wales Schools	U16	2	Birmingham	28	Feb
1:43.18 i	Scotland Schools	U16	3	Birmingham	28	Feb
1:42.40 i	Staffordshire University		3	Glasgow	15	Mar
1:45.68	Medway AC		1	Ashford	20	Sep
1:46.10	Dartford Harriers		2	Ashford	20	Sep
1:48.41	Blackheath Harriers	U17	1	Ashford	20	Sep

Additional Under 17 Teams (1 - 4 above)

1:48.6	Bromley Ladies		1	Hoo	31	Aug
1:48.84 i	Victoria Park AAC		1	Glasgow	22	Mar
1:49.23 i	Digital Ayr Seaforth		2	Glasgow	22	Mar
1:50.1	Aberdeen AAC		1	Aberdeen	3	May
1:50.37 i	Law & District AC		3	Glasgow	22	Mar
1:50.48	Cambridge Harriers		2	Ashford	20	Sep

Under 15 Teams

1:48.5	Lincolnshire AA		1	Nottingham	12	Sep
1:49.8	Regent House School		1	Belfast	4	Jun
1:50.67	Dartford Harriers		1	Ashford	20	Sep
1:51.00 i	Digital Ayr Seaforth		1	Glasgow	22	Mar
1:51.9	Cambridge Harriers		1	Hoo	31	Aug
1:52.5 i	Falkirk Victoria Harriers		1	Glasgow	29	Mar
1:53.28	Ashford AC		2	Ashford	20	Sep
1:53.3	Lagan Valley AC		1r1	Antrim	17	May
1:53.47	Blackheath Harriers		3	Ashford	20	Sep
1:54.00 i	Avonside TC		1h2	Glasgow	22	Mar
1:54.3	Ealing Southall & Middlesex AC		1	Perivale	29	Aug

Under 13 Teams

2:00.09 i	Digital Ayr Seaforth		1	Glasgow	22	Mar
2:00.2	Aberdeen AAC		1	Aberdeen	3	May
2:01.6	Sparta AC		1r1	Antrim	17	May
2:04.8	Lasswade AC		1	Livingston	6	Sep
2:05.3	Lisburn AC		1	Belfast	6	Jun
2:05.33	Inverness H		1	Inverness	22	Aug
2:05.5	Dundee Hawkhill Harriers		1	Dundee	23	Aug
2:07.47 i	Airdrie Harriers		2	Glasgow	22	Mar
2:07.69	Corby AC		1	Bedford	6	Sep
2:07.8	Banchory Stonehaven		2	Dundee	23	Aug

4 x 400 METRES

3:25.66	National Team	3	Budapest, HUN	23	Aug
	(D Fraser 52.7, V Jamison 52.00, K Merry 50.37, A Curbishley 50.54)				
3:28.07	National Team	3	St. Petersburg, RUS	28	Jun
	(V Jamison 52.87, D Fraser 51.33, M Thomas 52.85, A Curbishley 51.02)				
3:29.28	England	2	Kuala Lumpur, MAL	21	Sep
	(M Thomas 53.4, M Pierre 52.8, V Day 52.8, D Fraser 50.2)				

3:29.90	National Team		3h1	Budapest, HUN	22	Aug

3:29.90 National Team 3h1 Budapest, HUN 22 Aug
(V Jamison 52.8, M Thomas 52.4, N Danvers 52.65, A Curbishley 52.05)
3:39.1 Windsor Slough & Eton AC 1 Enfield 19 Jul
3:40.10 National Under 23 Team 3 Dessau, GER 5 Aug
(S Dudgeon, L Owusu, L Thorne, V Jamison)
3:40.75 National Junior Team U20 1 Alicante, SPA 18 Jul
(A Naugher 56.83, K Gear 54.47, K Wall 55.07, C Easton 54.38)
3:42.62 National Under 23 Team 1 Hexham 14 Jun
(L Thorne, S Dudgeon, K Sotherton, V Jamison)
3:43.0 Birchfield Harriers 1 Watford 16 Aug
(L Hansen, S Damm, V Sterne, H Frost)
3:43.07 Birchfield Harriers 1 Birmingham 6 Jun
(H Frost, T Taylor, L Hanson, S Damm)
3:44.1 Sale Harriers Manchester 2 Watford 16 Aug
(S Evans, L Reade, K Maddox, F Aston)
3:44.2 Sale Harriers Manchester 1 Grangemouth 4 Jul
(S Evans, L Reade, K Maddox, P Smith 54.2)
3:44.47 British Universities 1 Loughborough 17 May
3:45.0 Windsor Slough & Eton AC 2 Grangemouth 4 Jul
(M.Griffith, , , A Thorne)
3:46.07 Wales 1 Birmingham 18 Jul
3:46.27 South 2 Birmingham 18 Jul
3:47.28 i National Junior Team U20 3 Birmingham 28 Feb
(A Naugher, J Meadows, K Gear, C Easton)
3:47.6 Wakefield & District Harriers 2 Enfield 19 Jul
3:47.90 Sale Harriers Manchester 1 Bedford 29 Aug
(S Evans, L Reade, K Maddox, A Parkinson)
3:48.3 Essex Ladies 1 Liverpool 16 Aug
3:48.9 Birchfield Harriers 3 Grangemouth 4 Jul
(D Lewis)
3:48.94 Peterborough AC 2 Bedford 29 Aug
(S Smith, J Kelly, A Hollman, R Watson)

Additional National Team
3:54.8 Northern Ireland U23 1 Antrim 23 Jun

Additional Club Teams (1 - 6 above)
3:49.8 Edinburgh Woollen Mill 3 Watford 16 Aug
3:49.9 Croydon Harriers 1 Kingston 14 Jun
3:50.80 Brunel University 1 Bath 4 May
3:50.90 Shaftesbury Barnet Harriers 6 Vilamoura, POR 30 May
3:50.9 City of Norwich AC 3 Enfield 19 Jul
3:51.14 Loughborough University 2 Bath 4 May
3:51.5 Ashford AC 1 Walton 14 Jun
3:51.6 Birchfield Harriers U20 1 Wigan 23 Aug
3:52.01 Trafford AC 5 Bedford 29 Aug
3:52.3 Basildon AC U20 1 Thurrock 23 Jul
3:52.4 Team Solent 1 Crawley 19 Jul
3:54.13 UWIC 3 Bath 4 May
3:54.6 City of Stoke AC 2 Stoke 9 Aug
3:55.5 Medway AC 2 Coventry 5 Jul
3:55.65 Aldershot Farnham & District AC 4 Birmingham 6 Jun

Additional Under 20 Teams (1 - 4 above)
3:50.20 National Junior Team 2 Loughborough 17 May
3:54.59 North 1 London (He) 9 Aug
3:57.59 Wales 2 Bruges, BEL 23 Aug
3:57.99 Midlands 2 London (He) 9 Aug
3:59.74 Nortern Ireland 4 Bruges, BEL 23 Aug
3:59.84 South 3 London (He) 9 Aug
4:00.4 Scottish Schools 1 Barry 14 Jul

Under 17 Teams

4:18.1 *	Newquay & Par AC	1	Carn Brea	2 Aug
4:19.3	Hertford & Ware AC	1	Ware	4 May
4:21.9	Verlea AC	2	Ware	4 May
4:22.7	Albertville Harriers	1	Belfast	6 Jun

* Includes under-age athletes

3 x 800 METRES

6:42.2	Vale Royal AC	1	Crewe	14 Jul

Under 17 Teams

7:15.80	Blackheath Harriers	1	Ashford	20 Sep
7:16.0	Basildon AC	1	Barking	10 Sep
7:20.1	Albertville Harriers	1	Belfast	30 Jul
7:22.33	Invicta East Kent AC	2	Ashford	20 Sep
7:23.2	Lagan Valley AC	2	Belfast	30 Jul
7:38.6	Havering Mayesbrook AC	2	Barking	10 Sep
7:39.7	Digital Ayr Seaforth	1	Ayr	1 Jul

Under 15 Teams

7:07.4	Basildon AC	1	Barking	2 Jul
7:08.6	Harlow RC	2	Barking	2 Jul
7:21.8	Havering Mayesbrook AC	1	Barking	10 Sep
7:30.04	GEC Avionics AC	1	Ashford	20 Sep
7:30.89	Lagan Valley AC	1	Belfast	30 Jul
7:32.44	Regent House School	2	Belfast	30 Jul
7:35.9	Huntingdon AC	4	Barking	10 Sep
7:37.3	Lancaster Schools	1	Blackburn	18 May
7:39.1	West Lancs Schools	2	Blackburn	18 May
7:39.50	Medway AC	2	Ashford	20 Sep
7:42.88	Lucozade Motherwell	1	Edinburgh	18 Jul
7:44.56	Kilbarchan AC	2	Edinburgh	18 Jul

Under 13 Teams

7:58.1	Vale Royal AC	1	Crewe	25 Jun
8:00.9	Lagan Valley AC	1	Belfast	30 Jul
8:01.4	Stockport H	2	Crewe	25 Jun
8:05.0	Basildon AC	1	Barking	2 Jul
8:08.18	City of Edinburgh AC	1	Edinburgh	18 Jul
8:14.4	Havering Mayesbrook AC	2	Barking	10 Sep
8:15.77	Blackheath Harriers	1	Ashford	20 Sep
8:17.0	Albertville Harriers	2	Belfast	30 Jul
8:23.3	Macclesfield H & AC	3	Crewe	25 Jun
8:24.21	Kirkintilloch Olympians	2	Edinburgh	18 Jul

4 x 800 METRES

9:44.3	Middlesbrough & Cleveland	1	Middlesbrough	21 Jul
10:02.6	Brentwood AC	1	Barking	10 Sep
10:24.7	Havering Mayesbrook AC	2	Barking	10 Sep

4 x 1500 METRES

20:58.13	Elswick Harriers	1	Hexham	31 Aug

MENS INDEX

ABDY Thomas U20 3.05.81, Northampton :
PV - 4.20
ABERNETHY David James V40 5.09.55,
Barrow & Furness :
SP - 13.87 (14.59-85), DT - 44.91 (46.70-85)
ABLITT Steven U15 16.11.83, Grantham :
1500 - 4:12.1, 3k - 9:21.5
ACHIKE Onochie 'Larry' 31.01.75, S B :
200 - 22.09 (21.6-96/21.68-97), TJ - 17.10
ACHURCH Simon 27.12.74, Peterborough :
JT - 56.41 (60.42-97)
ADAM Marcus 28.02.68, Haringey :
100 - 10.30w/10.45 (10.14w-90/10.23-91),
200 - 20.73 (20.10w-90/20.41-92), 400 - 48.3
ADAMS Allan 11.09.72, Clydesdale :
5k - 14:39.1 (14:21.3-97),
10kR - 29:38, 10MR - 49:28 (47:54dh-96)
ADAMS Brian V45 13.03.49, Leics WC :
3kW - 13:03.7 (12:02.2+-76/12:17.0-82),
10kW - 47:33.0 (42:40.0-75)
ADAMS Christopher U20 18.07.81, C of Stoke :
HT - 51.25, HTJ - 57.41
ADAMS Julien U15 19.10.83, Berks Sch :
TJ - 12.31
ADAMS Nathan U17 14.04.82, Sheffield RWC :
3kW - 14:12.5, 3kWR - 13:57, 5kW - 24:25.49,
10kW - 51:56.0, 10kWR - 48:49
ADAMS Philip 3.11.71, Charnwood :
SP - 15.02 (15.78-97)
ADAMS Raymond U17 5.11.81, Lagan Valley :
800 - 1:54.01, 1500 - 3:57.21
ADAMS Simeon U15 1.07.84, Sheffield RWC :
3kW - 16:04.84
ADEDZE Pierre 3.06.69, Portsmouth :
100 - 10.5wdt/10.8
ADEJUWON Dan U23 27.11.76, Sheffield :
TJ - 14.05
ADEPEGBA Sunny 6.06.71, Haringey :
60 - 6.94i, 100 - 10.7/10.80 (10.6-97),
200 - 21.51 (21.4w-95/21.5-90)
ADU K. U15, Haringey :
DTB - 37.04
AFILAKA Michael 16.11.71, Newham & EB :
60 - 6.96i (6.80i-95),
100 - 10.78w/10.88 (10.46w/10.63-95),
200 - 21.16w/21.47 (21.09w-93/21.2-95/21.22-94)
AFILAKA Tunde 'Carl' 13.07.68, Oxford C/TRI :
60 - 6.82i, 100 - 10.77 (10.5-96/10.76-97)
AGARD Trevor Alvin Jamieson U20 12.03.80,
Hounslow : 400H - 56.4
AGNEW Morton U15 07.84, Ballymena & A :
800 - 2:05.8
AGYEPONG Francis Keita 16.06.65, S B :
TJ - 16.89i (17.29wA/17.24w/17.18-95)
AIREY Martin 28.10.70, Blackheath :
800 - 1:52.3 (1:50.2-96),
1500 - 3:48.5 (3:48.0-96)
AKINSANYA Oluwafemi 29.11.69, Peterbro :
LJ - 7.16 (7.37-96),
TJ - 16.32w/16.16i/16.16 (16.58-96)
AKPOFURE O. U17 9.11.81, Derbs Sch :
100 - 10.7w/10.95
ALDRIDGE Darrell U17 20.06.83, Bedford & C :
100 - 10.90w LJ - 7.14w/6.87
ALDWINKLE Matthew 23.08.74, Notts :
400 - 48.63 (47.87-97)

ALEXANDER Crofton U15 7.01.84, Belgrave :
SPB - 14.28
ALEXANDER Peter U17 29.09.81, Medway :
TJ - 13.42 (13.56-97)
ALEXANDER Stephen U15 6.10.84, Trafford :
TJ - 12.23
ALFRED Ricky U23 20.12.77, Bedford & C :
100 - 10.98w (11.2-96)
ALI Ahmed U13 31.03.86, Newham & Essex B :
800 - 2:11.3, 1500 - 4:31.8
ALIX James U17 24.12.81, Dudley & Stourbr :
HJ - 2.06
ALLAN David Neil 17.10.70, C of Edinburgh :
HT - 61.27
ALLAN Graeme S. U20 24.09.80, S Barnet :
SP - 13.96, SPJ - 15.42,
SPY - 15.55io (16.01-97),
DTJ - 45.75, HT - 52.55, HTJ - 59.87,
ALLEN Clarence 1.04.64, Herne Hill :
110H - 15.4 (14.8-92/14.82-94)
ALLEN Mark 23.09.66, Border :
100 - 10.79 (10.6-92/10.63w-93/10.74-94),
200 - 21.66 (20.90-96)
ALLEN Michael U20 7.03.80, B & A/IRE :
JT - 66.65
ALLEN Steve V40 22.01.58, Ilford :
3kW - 13:25.2
ALLISON Joseph 16.09.59, Newham & EB :
TJ - 13.95 (15.93w-86/15.86-85)
ALLISON Matthew 26.02.73, Leeds :
DT - 43.06, JT - 58.30 (59.58-97)
ALLMARK Daniel U15 11.05.84, Corby :
HTB - 45.79
AMOS Guy 15.06.63, Norwich :
5k - 14:32.6
ANDERSON Craig 19.06.71, SGA (Prof) :
SP - 13.93
ANDERSON Keith V40 10.08.57, Bingley :
10MR - 49:45 (48:15-97),
Mar - 2:17:08
ANDERSON Mark U23 5.11.77, City of Stoke/
Sheff Univ : 400H - 54.7/55.43 (54.54-96)
ANDREWS Nicholas U17 3.10.81, S Devon :
400 - 50.4, 800 - 1:54.0
ANDREWS Nick U17 13.01.83, Telford :
1500 - 4:07.31, 3k - 9:01.20
ANGUS Daniel U17 15.07.82, Mandale :
100 - 10.83w/10.9/11.01 (10.8w-97),
200 - 22.04w/22.1/22.27 (22.1-97)
ANKERS Gary U17 2.06.82, Shildon :
200 - 22.5 (23.88-97), 400 - 49.01
ANSELL Keith 30.03.62, Woodford Green :
SP - 15.64
ANTHONY James U17 30.03.82, Neath :
100HY - 13.90, HJ - 1.95, TJ - 13.59,
SPY - 14.80i (12.65-97), OctY - 5025
ANTHONY Tristan U17 16.12.82, Verlea :
60 - 6.96i, 100 - 11.1 (11.11-97),
200 - 21.68w/22.02i/22.20,
400 - 49.48, 400H - 56.36
ANTONATOS George 30.09.74, Holbeach/
Staffs Univ/GRE : SP - 15.95, DT - 41.63
APPS James U20 29.04.80, Blackheath :
JT - 57.44 (58.22-97)
ARAM Martin U15 2.12.83, Western (I.O.M.) :
HJ - 1.85, SPB - 14.59, DTB - 37.42

ARCARI Paul U17 10.10.82, Kilbarchan :
3k - 8:56.09, 5k - 16:07.7
ARCHAMPONG James Quarshie U23
14.03.76, Swansea :
110H - 14.7w/14.80 (14.1w/14.14w-96/14.18-94)
ARCHBOLD Ian 10.06.65, Morpeth :
10k - 31:17.7 (29:47.16-92),
10MR - 49:50 (49:24-93)
ARCHER Paul Nicholas U17 7.10.81, Blackh :
SPY - 15.30
ARCHER Steve V40 25.01.55, Havering :
SP - 13.95
ARKLE Michael 31.03.73, Morpeth :
100 - 10.8/10.84, 200 - 21.69
ARMSTRONG Daniel U17 28.10.81, Border :
OctY - 4529
ARMSTRONG Geoffrey U15 6.08.84,Bas & MH :
DTB - 39.90,
ARMSTRONG Paul U20 20.10.79, Pitreavie :
400H - 54.80
ARMSTRONG Samuel 17.02.74, Bord/Law & D :
JT - 65.31
ARMSTRONG Simon John 29.05.62, Bournem :
SP - 15.10 (16.52-90)
ARRAND Andrew 20.01.66, Barnet/Army :
Mar - 2:23:36
ASH Tom U20 29.11.79, Shaftesbury Barnet :
HTJ - 48.53
ASHLEY Kevin U17 12.09.81, Charnwood :
200 - 22.57
ASHTON David 24.01.70, Stockport :
LJ - 7.04
ASHTON Sean U13, Leics Cor :
200 - 25.9, 70HC - 11.3,
80HC - 12.1
ASHTON Stephen U15 21.03.84, Sale :
HTB - 43.87
ASPDEN Richard U23 15.10.76, Belgrave :
HJ - 2.10i/2.10 (2.16-95)
ASTON Peter Robert George V50 21.02.45,
Woodford Green : HT - 46.02 (62.32-75)
ATKINS Gregory U17 20.10.81, Isle of Wight :
1.5kSt - 4:38.9 (4:38.2-97)
ATKINSON Steven U20 12.04.79, Border :
PV - 4.20
ATTON Karl Ronald 14.09.71, Roadhogs :
20kW - 1:35:42 (1:34:38-94), 30kW - 2:39.06,
50kW - 4:24:08 (4:16:30-97)
ATTWELL Robert U17 17.10.81, Cheltenham :
200 - 22.3, 400 - 49.77
AUDU George U23 18.01.77, Thames Valley/
Penn State Univ : 100 - 10.87,
LJ - 7.83w/7.78i/7.72, TJ - 14.98
AUSTIN James 9.08.65, Clydesdale :
3kSt - 9:24.9 (9:05.32-94)
AUSTIN Stuart U20 21.03.79, Blackheath :
800 - 1:51.9
AVIS Mark 22.10.71, Team Solent :
100 - 10.87 (10.7-96)
AWANAH Mark U17 23.09.82, Blackheath :
LJ - 7.25w/6.83
AYLESBURY Wayne Paul 24.03.64, Leeds :
3kSt - 9:17.87 (8:38.81-92)

*B*AARD Derrick 17.12.70, Herne Hill/RSA :
Mar - 2:32:28 (2:26:42-97)
BACCHUS Ross U20 6.06.81, Havering :
100 - 10.8 (11.12-97)

BACK Stuart U23 12.05.77, Harrow :
HJ - 1.95 (1.96-95)
BACKLEY Stephen James 12.02.69, Camb H :
JT - 89.89 (91.46-92)
BADDELEY Andrew U17 20.06.82, Wirral :
800 - 1:57.4, 1500 - 4:01.5, 3k - 8:57.50
BAILEY Christopher U15 28.09.83, Epsom & E :
HJ - 1.87
BAILEY Christopher J. 18.09.69, Liverpool H :
DT - 40.98 (47.64-89)
BAILEY Colin U15 15.11.83, Burnley :
HJ - 1.89, PenB - 2793
BAILEY Edward U15 14.02.84, City of Stoke :
400 - 53.30, 800 - 2:04.39
BAILEY Josef U23 2.12.77, City of Stoke :
110H - 15.48
BAILEY Stuart U23 6.08.78, Wigan :
800 - 1:49.51, 1500 - 3:45.6
BAILLIE Christopher U20 21.04.81, Vict Park/
Sale : 60H - 8.10i, 110HJ - 14.42,
110H - 14.55w/14.71
BAILLIE Ross U23 26.09.77, Vict Park /Sale :
100 - 10.35w (10.62-96), 110H - 13.80
BAIRD Lawrence U23 14.12.77, Cleethorpes :
100 - 10.62w (11.3-96), 200 - 21.9,
400 - 47.56i/47.85 (47.83-97)
BAKER George U23 14.08.76, Newham & E B :
SP - 14.51 (15.22-97)
BALDOCK Sean Michael U23 3.12.76, Belg/
Brunel Univ : 200 - 21.6/21.77w/21.85i/21.92
(21.1w-97/21.67-96), 400 - 45.45 (45.42-97)
BALDWIN David John U17 17.03.82, Mandale :
1500 - 4:06.07
BALDWIN Stefan Mark 26.04.70, Peterbro :
JT - 68.02 (72.92-93)
BALE Jason U20 12.12.79, Leics Cor :
100 - 10.8/10.98w (10.92-97)
BALL Andrew U17 13.05.83, Birchfield :
3kW - 14:06.5, 5kW - 24:26.14
BALLANTYNE Benedict 23.03.70, S B/STV :
Mar - 2:27:18 (2:24:56-97)
BALLANTYNE Pamenos 9.12.73, S B/STV :
5k - 14:31.5, 10k - 29:58.3, Mar - 2:15:37
BANDELE David 11.09.71, Norwich :
100 - 10.74, 200 - 21.6/21.92
BANNISTER Dominic 1.04.68, S Barnet :
1500 - 3:48.00
BANNISTER Simon U20 16.04.81, Peterbro :
HJ - 2.07
BANNON Clayton U23 15.03.77, Hounslow :
1500 - 3:49.5
BAPTISTE Shawn U20 16.04.81, Woodford Gr :
HJ - 1.95i/1.95 (1.95-97)
BARBER Michael W. 19.10.73, Bir/Staffs Univ :
PV - 5.20dhex/5.00 (5.45-97)
BARBOUR Jonathan U20 3.11.80, Croydon :
100 - 10.45w/10.5 (10.64-97),
200 - 21.6w (22.7-97)
BARDEN Spencer Christian 31.03.73, GEC/
Loughborough Studnts : 1500 - 3:39.64,
1M - 3:58.5, 3k - 7:55.50 (7:53.2-97),
5k - 13:45.31 (13:43.84-97), 10k - 30:14.11
BARGH Andrew U23 21.08.76, Team Solent :
200 - 22.16w, 110H - 15.1w/15.2
(15.0w-96/15.13w-97/15.20-96),
400H - 52.47 (52.4-96)
BARIKOR Bomene U17 22.05.82, Blackheath :
100 - 11.06w, HJ - 2.03 (2.03-97)

331

BARK Thomas U15 18.10.83, Corby :
1500 - 4:20.4
BARKER Carl 23.05.59, :
Mar - 2:32:29
BARKER Leo U23 26.12.78, Havering :
110H - 15.0w/15.1 (14.54w/14.6-97/15.32-96),
LJ - 6.99 (7.07-96),
BARNARD Paul 27.07.72, Birchfield :
HT - 57.91 (62.70-95)
BARNES John U17 6.05.82, Hull Springhead :
HTJ - 52.40, HTY - 58.22
BARNETSON David 1.07.71, C of Edinburgh :
HJ - 2.20i/2.05 (2.20-97)
BARNETT Edward U20 6.02.79, AF&D :
3kSt - 9:26.82
BARRETT Oliver U15 25.12.84, Ipswich :
800 - 2:02.90
BARROS Demetrio 29.06.71, Hounslow :
JT - 55.76 (66.92-93)
BARROW Mark 30.06.68, Liv.Pembroke Seft :
400H - 55.69 (55.0/55.58-97)
BARRY William U20 4.09.79, Preston :
800 - 1:54.3 (1:54.3-97)
BARTON Darren 11.10.69, Morpeth/RAF :
2kSt - 5:58.1, 3kSt - 9:12.05
BARTON Neil U20 18.07.80, Verlea :
LJ - 6.82w (6.91w/6.25-97)
BARTON Robert U17 5.11.82, Blackburn :
1.5kSt - 4:39.42
BARTON Tim D. 3.10.70, Charnwood :
60 - 6.92i, 100 - 10.55w/10.68 (10.67-97),
200 - 21.9 (21.8/21.84-97)
BASTOW Sebastian U17 11.10.81, Mandale :
100HY - 13.8/13.95
BATCHELOR Perry 11.12.75, Coventry G :
110H - 14.75w/15.1/15.32
(14.7w/14.9/15.10-94)
BATES Stephen U17 5.11.81, Rotherham :
800 - 1:57.6, 1500 - 4:01.42, 3k - 8:53.65
BAULCH James Steven 3.05.73, Cardiff :
100 - 10.72 (10.51-95), 200 - 21.07 (20.84-94),
400 - 44.83 (44.57-96)
BAXTER David U20 16.01.79, Sale :
2kSt - 6:08.3 (5:56.99-97),
3kSt - 9:50.61 (9:29.2-96)
BEARD Gareth U20 28.02.79, Dudley & Stour :
800 - 1:52.3, 1500 - 3:55.54
BEARD Gregory U17 10.09.82, GEC :
SPJ - 15.06, SPY - 16.56, DTY - 44.69
BEARD Keith 8.11.61, Leiden :
JT - 65.04 (76.10r-91/73.88-90)
BEARD Leigh 3.04.69, Phoenix :
Mar - 2:33:26
BEARMAN Donald J. 16.04.66, Steyning :
3kW - 13:17.57 (13:07.7-87),
10kW - 46:53.0 (45:37.0-86), 20kW - 1:34:56
BEASLEY Graham U23 24.10.77, Luton/
Brunel Univ : 60 - 6.93i, 150 - 15.6,
100 - 10.59w/10.8 (10.7-94/10.81-97),
200 - 21.38w/21.57 (21.20w-96/21.34-95)
BEASLEY Neil 28.09.73, Luton :
800 - 1:51.4
BEATTIE James 22.07.73, Pitreavie :
200 - 22.01w (22.02-94)
BEATTIE William U17 22.10.82, Nithsdale :
100HY - 13.29w/13.47
BEAUCHAMP William 9.09.70, Thames VH :
HT - 70.09

BEAUFORD Adam U17 24.10.81, Yeovil Oly :
HTY - 60.13
BEAUMONT Paul 27.03.63, Belgrave/Army :
400H - 54.90 (51.23-89)
BEAVERS Alan, Rowntrees :
Mar - 2:30:54 (2:27:47-97)
BECKWITH Andrew U20 22.04.79, Invicta :
1500 - 3:55.2, 3k - 8:27.05 (8:26.24-97),
5k - 14:55.88
BEDFORD Tom U15 12.12.83, Shaftesbury B :
3k - 9:35.1
BEEVERS Andrew 3.05.73, Leeds :
3kSt - 9:12.81 (9:12.33-97)
BEHARRELL Mark U20 10.01.81, City of Hull :
PV - 4.50
BELGRAVE Quincy U15, Blackheath :
LJ - 6.12w (5.23-97)
BELL Carl U15 19.10.83, Northumberland Sch :
DTB - 38.71
BELL John 10.09.73, Newham & Essex B/
Loughbro : 400H - 54.08 (53.70-92)
BELL Martin 9.04.61, Cardiff :
3kW - 11:59.47 (11:53.3-95),
10kW - 41:48.81 (41:13.65-95),
20kW - 1:27:22 (1:25:42-92)
BELL Matthew U23 2.06.78, Corby :
HT - 61.62
BELL Simon 26.12.66, Cambridge Harriers :
3kSt - 8:55.74 (8:53.39-96)
BELL Stuart 29.07.67, Chester Le Street :
5k - 14:29.0 (14:23.1-95),
10k - 30:46.19 (29:24.30-97), 10kR - 29:15
BELSHAM Matthew 11.10.71, Sale :
PV - 5.35 (5.40i-96/5.35-93)
BENJAMIN Timothy U17 2.05.82, Cardiff :
60 - 6.93i, 100 - 10.51w/10.71,
200 - 20.98w/21.19, 400 - 48.5
BENNETT Christopher U20 18.10.80, T Solent :
200 - 22.0w/22.12, 400 - 48.23
BENNETT Jeffrey U17 4.04.83, West (I.O.M.) :
DTY - 40.52
BENNETT Paul V40 18.01.58, Bridgend :
Mar - 2:26:11 (2:23:40-89)
BENNETT Simon 16.10.72, Team Solent :
JT - 61.30 (66.58-96)
BENT Colin 12.04.70, Shaftesbury B/RAF :
HJ - 2.12 (2.20-96)
BENTHAM Kermitt Edmund 16.04.60, TVH :
400 - 48.82 (46.57-87)
BENTLEY Robin 17.02.65, Army/Wx & Bath :
Mar - 2:29:19
BERGIN Steven 17.06.66, Gateshead :
SP - 13.57 (16.09-89)
BERNARD Jermaine U15 1.12.84, Ipswich :
LJ - 6.33
BERRIMAN Bob 29.03.73, Rowntrees :
LJ - 6.92
BERRY Robert 29.07.69, Liv.Pembroke Seft :
2kSt - 5:53.11 (5:48.08-96),
3kSt - 9:05.20 (9:04.36-97)
BERTHIER Stephen U15 19.07.84, Haringey :
100 - 11.6, JTB - 50.04
BERWICK Christopher V50 1.05.46, Leics WC :
50kW - 4:58:08 (4:23:22-86)
BEST Mark U20 9.09.79, AF&D :
800 - 1:53.8
BESWICK Paul A. 5.12.68, GEC :
PV - 4.60 (4.80ns-94/4.80-96)

BETTS Edward George 18.02.71, Thames VH :
400 - 48.42 (47.9-94), 400H - 51.55 (50.49-97)
BEVAN Nigel Charles 3.01.68, Birchfield :
JT - 76.26 (81.70-92)
BEYNON Daniel U17 23.01.82, Swansea :
1500 - 4:03.43
BIDWELL Mark U15 4.09.84, Chesterfield :
HJ - 1.85
BIGNALL Douglas 20.10.74, Haringey :
60 - 6.73i (6.7i/6.71i-97), 100 - 10.60 (10.49-97)
BILLINGHAM Russell U17 13.10.81, C of Plym :
400HY - 58.26
BILTON Darren 9.03.72, City of Hull :
Mar - 2:30:17
BINNS Christopher U17 7.05.82, Blackpool :
HJ - 1.90
BIRBECK Rory 24.09.73, Hyndburn :
SP - 13.97 (14.75-97), DT - 44.68 (45.84-97)
BIRCHALL Matthew John 1.11.71, Harrow :
400H - 54.9/54.97 (52.76-90)
BIRCHALL Robert 14.06.70, Birchfield :
5k - 14:36.10 (14:11.64-96), HMar - 1:05:46
BIRD Justin Paul 3.05.71, Morpeth :
400 - 48.19 (47.68-94)
BIRKS James U20 5.01.81, Worthing :
LJ - 6.88w (6.27-97)
BISHOP Mark Andrew Paul 12.02.67, Havering :
110H - 15.1 (14.2w/14.4-91/14.48-89),
PV - 4.10 (4.50-89)
BISSEL Simon U13 25.12.85, Burnley :
DTB - 33.01
BIVINS Tom U15 18.11.83, Charnwood :
DTB - 38.50, HTB - 42.50
BLACK Christopher Francis V45 1.01.50,
City of Edinburgh : HT - 54.53 (75.40-83)
BLACK Iain Russell 18.09.70,
City of Edinburgh : PV - 4.40 (4.51-97)
BLACK Roger Anthony 31.03.66, Team Solent :
100 - 10.58 (10.4-87/10.48-96),
300 - 32.51 (32.06+-91/32.08-86),
400 - 44.71 (44.37-96)
BLACKMAN Gary U20 24.09.80, Solihull & S H :
5k - 15:13.5, 2kSt - 5:54.64, 3kSt - 9:33.12
BLACKMAN Graham U15 25.03.85, Rushcliffe :
400 - 53.6/54.72
BLACKMORE Andrew U23 12.07.76, Telford :
800 - 1:50.82i (1:50.7-95)
BLACKMORE David U20, Cardiff Schools :
SPJ - 14.04, DTJ - 42.95
BLAGROVE Richard U17 29.12.81, Lincoln W :
800 - 1:54.5
BLAIR G. U15, Ulster Sch :
TJ - 12.00
BLISS Anthony 7.03.70, Brighton :
110H - 15.37w/15.4 (15.1/15.51-97)
BOBB Samuel 29.08.75, Blackh/Brunel Univ :
TJ - 14.82w/14.66i (14.98-97)
BODYS Christopher U15 29.12.83, Ayr Seafth :
800 - 2:05.51i
BOLT Christopher U20 21.09.80, Bracknell :
800 - 1:52.32, 1500 - 3:47.07
BOLTON Thomas U15 24.11.83, Bas & MH :
800 - 2:03.48, 1500 - 4:20.5, 3k - 9:37.28
BOND Matthew U20 13.07.81, Notts :
JT - 54.30
BONEHAM Daniel U15 9.12.83, Grantham :
HTB - 45.82
BONEHAM Ian U17 30.09.82, Grantham :
1500 - 4:02.56, 3k - 9:00.0

BONICH Daniel M. U23 22.11.78, Bexley :
100 - 10.6w/10.88 (10.6w-97/10.8-96),
200 - 22.0 (21.5w-97)
BONNETT Stephen U23 13.07.78, C of Stoke :
HJ - 1.95 (2.04-97), Dec - 6091 (6543-97)
BONSALL David 2.06.71, Royal Navy :
Dec - 6265
BOOTH Shane U17 16.01.82, Barnsley :
HJ - 1.93
BOOTHROYD Jason 26.11.69, Sale :
1500 - 3:48.18 (3:44.2-91)
BORSUMATO Anthony 13.12.73, Sale :
400 - 46.92, 400H - 49.79
BOTHWICK Daniel U15 22.02.84, Worcester :
800 - 2:01.1, 1500 - 4:19.1
BOTTOMLEY Andy 15.04.61, :
24HrT - 209.214km
BOUNDY Christopher U20 25.12.79, Gate :
PV - 4.40
BOWDEN Adam U17 5.08.82, Harrow :
1500 - 3:59.99, 3k - 8:56.3, 1.5kSt - 4:24.26
BOWDEN Alexander 16.11.73, Lanc & Morc :
3kSt - 9:29.8
BOWDITCH Kristen Robert 14.01.75,
City of Stoke : 1500 - 3:48.80 (3:44.2-97),
3k - 7:56.12, 5k - 13:36.24, 10k - 29:51.2
BOWLEY Ian U17 14.11.81, Bedford & Co :
PV - 3.70
BOWLING Luke U17 4.11.81, Peterborough :
100 - 10.70w/10.92, 200 - 22.1
BOWN Simon Paul 21.11.74, Newham & E B :
SP - 13.49, HT - 62.43
BOX Alex U15 23.09.84, London Schools :
TJ - 12.05
BOX Tobias 9.09.72, Birchfield :
100 - 10.61 (10.07w-94/10.32-95),
200 - 21.52 (20.72-94)
BRACE Steven 7.07.61, Bridgend :
HMar - 1:04:49 (1:02:03sh-93/1:02:33-91),
Mar - 2:16:34 (2:10:35-96)
BRACKSTONE David U17 13.03.82,
City of Stoke : 100HY - 13.58, 110HJ - 15.4
BRADBURY Michael U20 30.12.80, Rotherham :
200 - 21.9w/21.93w (22.60-97)
BRADLEY Dominic U23 22.12.76, Stockport/
Crewe & Alsager : 60 - 6.90i, 60H - 8.08i,
100 - 10.52w/10.6/10.63,
200 - 21.9 (23.34w-95), 110H - 14.07w/14.26
BRADLEY Michael V40 27.05.57, Chiltern :
Mar - 2:32:21 (2:23:36-88)
BRADSHAW Craig U15 14.04.84, Cramlington :
200 - 23.37w/23.59
BRAITHWAITE Darren 20.01.69, Haringey :
50 - 5.75i+, 60 - 6.57i (6.51i-95),
100 - 10.52i (10.12-95),
200 - 21.45i/21.87 (20.47-95)
BRAMBLE Marvin U23 10.06.77, Blackheath :
TJ - 14.82w/14.65 (15.31w-97/15.23-95)
BRANCH Kit U15 5.06.85, Basildon :
PV - 2.90
BRAND Daryl John 6.08.63, Blackheath :
JT - 63.33 (74.90-86)
BRANDOM Stuart U20 7.10.80, Bedford & Co :
110HJ - 15.4
BRANDWOOD Daniel U17 1.10.82, C of Hull :
400HY - 57.66
BRANNEN Anthony 16.09.68, City of Stoke :
110H - 14.9w/15.0 (14.2/14.25w-95/14.35-89)

BRASSINGTON Alan U17 27.09.81, C of Stoke :
DTY - 47.94
BREND Peter A. U23 2.02.77, Team Solent :
300 - 34.7 (34.48-97), 400 - 47.44
BREW Spencer U20 17.08.79, Liverpool H :
200 - 22.07w (23.06-96)
BREWER Daniel U20 10.08.80, Blackheath :
110HJ - 14.57 (14.57-97), 110H - 14.96
BREWER Oliver U15 14.09.83, Bingley :
80HB - 11.81, PenB - 2852
BRIDGER Peter U17 6.09.81, Luton :
800 - 1:57.31
BRIDGES Marcus 18.03.71, Bristol :
800 - 1:52.5
BRIDLE Matthew U23 11.08.76, Traff/Staffs Un :
200 - 21.86 (21.41w-93/21.6/21.83-94),
LJ - 7.08 (7.10-94)
BRIERLEY James U23 31.07.77, Ox Un/Telf :
HJ - 2.05 (2.26-96)
BRITTON Daniel U17 25.09.81, Bournemouth :
JTY - 55.69 (57.78-97)
BRIZZELL Paul U23 3.10.76, Ballymena & A/
Liverpool H/IRE :
100 - 10.55w/10.65, 200 - 20.81w/20.93
BROADHEAD Daniel U17 19.04.82, Rotherham :
PV - 4.20i/4.20
BROADLEY Sam U20 17.05.81, Bingley :
HT - 46.55, HTJ - 48.49
BROCKLEBANK Robert J. U23 12.10.76, Sale :
HJ - 2.10 (2.16-95)
BROOKS Jerome 9.08.73, Hercules Wimb :
5k - 14:33.9
BROOKS Steven 8.06.70, Bingley :
10kR - 29:45 (29:23-96),
HMar - 1:04:34 (1:01:28-97)
BROUGHTON Mark A. 23.10.63, Met. Police :
HT - 47.14 (54.28-93)
BROWELL Lee U17 16.02.82, Sunderland :
1500 - 4:05.14
BROWN Andrew U23 17.06.77, C of Edinburgh :
800 - 1:52.7
BROWN Gareth James 10.05.68, Steyning :
3kW - 12:58.0 (12:36.91-87),
10kW - 44:01.0 (43:54.25-87),
20kW - 1:33:07 (1:30:15-89)
BROWN John 2.02.69, Salford :
5k - 14:34.3, 3kSt - 8:55.6
BROWN Jonathan Michael 27.02.71, Sheff :
3k - 7:45.41, 5k - 13:19.03, 10k - 27:18.14,
HMar - 1:03:52+un (1:01:49-97),
Mar - 2:11:10 (2:10:13-97)
BROWN Kevin Dave 10.09.64, Belgrave :
SP - 14.73, DT - 60.67 (61.10-97)
BROWN Mark U20 1.08.79, Morpeth :
3k - 8:33.9
BROWN Mark U23 3.11.76, Newham & E B :
100 - 10.7w
BROWN Michael 6.05.62, Haringey :
TJ - 15.36 (16.15-89)
BROWN Patrick U20 2.09.79, Gateshead :
110HJ - 14.93w/15.10/15.1 (14.8w-97), 400H - 55.9
BROWN Paul U15 8.10.83, Charnwood :
800 - 2:01.7un/2:05.9
BROWN Richard U17 13.05.82, Havering :
HJ - 1.90
BROWN Richard V50 18.11.46, Surrey WC :
24HrT - 200.255km (220.183km-89),
100MWT - 19:22:26

BROWN Steven U17 20.03.82, Southend :
PV - 4.40
BROWN Steven U20 4.10.80, Gateshead :
TJ - 14.12i (13.53-97)
BROWN Stuart 27.11.72, Deeside :
HJ - 1.95 (2.05-95)
BROWNE Gareth U15 19.04.84, Haringey :
DTB - 37.25
BROWNE Gary U15, Annadale Striders :
HTB - 44.30
BRUCE Calum 28.02.75, Pitreavie :
HT - 54.43
BRUCE Daniel U23 29.09.76, Rowheath/
Loughborough Studnts : 400 - 48.9,
200 - 22.0/22.13w-95/22.31-96)
BRUNT Daniel U23 23.04.76, Sheff/Derby Un :
SP - 14.24 (14.49-97), DT - 42.54
BRUSCH Bennett U20 2.06.79, Devon Sch :
DecJ - 5072
BRYAN Justin 16.08.69, Torfaen :
SP - 13.95, DT - 45.29
BRYAN Lee U17 24.11.81, Coventry Godiva :
100 - 11.1 (11.52-97), 400 - 49.2,
200 - 22.18i/22.19w/22.59 (22.11w-97)
BRYCE Colin 4.08.74, Pitreavie :
SP - 13.60
BUCK Matthew 5.04.74, Woodford Green/
Cambridge University : PV - 4.30 (4.60-96)
BUCKFIELD Nicholas Jean 5.06.73, Crawley :
400 - 48.4 (47.4-96), PV - 5.80
BUCKLEY Adam U20 6.12.80, Wirral :
300 - 34.5, 400 - 47.93
BUCKNER Thomas Christopher 16.04.63, Hav :
3kSt - 9:27.80 (8:25.50-92)
BUDDEN Nicholas 17.11.75, Norwich/
Loughborough : 400 - 48.83 (46.34-96)
BUFTON Philip 10.11.67, Brecon :
HT - 58.04
BULL Andrew 26.06.69, Sheffield :
100 - 10.91 (10.6-96/10.77w-92),
200 - 21.5w/21.7/21.78w/22.06
(21.3-95/21.61w-93/21.78-92)
BULL Michael P. 6.06.70, Notts :
Dec - 5815 (6051-97)
BULLEN Richard 6.10.60, Les Croupiers :
Mar - 2:31:58 (2:25:58-86)
BULLEY Simon John U15 19.09.84, Wirral :
DTB - 42.93
BULLOCK David 18.12.74, Shaftesbury B :
800 - 1:50.62, 1500 - 3:45.43
BULLOCK Guy Ross 15.10.75, Wigan :
200 - 21.6 (21.25A-95/21.3-96/21.80w/21.82-93,
400 - 46.36 (45.76-96)
BULLOCK Simon U20 22.11.80, Cheltenham :
400 - 49.6 (49.76-97), 800 - 1:50.65
BULMAN Neil Andrew U23 7.09.77, Mandale :
HT - 49.02
BUNNEY Elliot John 11.12.66, C of Edinburgh :
100 - 10.20w/10.70 (10.20-86),
200 - 21.2/21.21 (21.08w-84/21.1-91/21.14-87)
BURGESS Paul William 10.11.70, Liverpool H :
800 - 1:52.04 (1:47.80-91),
1500 - 3:51.7 (3:46.83-89)
BURKE Alan P. 23.05.65, Hounslow/IRE :
PV - 4.20 (5.00-89)
BURKE David   68, London Irish/IRE :
3k - 8:17.60 (8:06.66-94)

BURKE John 18.05.70, London Irish/IRE :
5k - 14:15.6 (13:56.31-93), 10MR - 49:46
BURKE Raymond Nicholas 11.11.69, S B :
200 - 22.0 (21.4-91/21.87-92)
BURLEY Darren U20 13.01.80, Blackheath :
60 - 6.94i, 100 - 10.68w/10.83 (10.7db-96),
200 - 21.57w/21.67? (21.50w-96)
BURMAN-ROY Sudip U23 15.01.78, Blackh/
Cambridge University : SP - 13.45
BURNETT Leon U17 12.09.81, Birchfield :
LJ - 6.89, TJ - 13.65 (13.83-97)
BURNHOPE Mark E. 20.03.60, Tipton :
Mar - 2:27:55 (2:13:54-85)
BURNS Ian T. U23 20.09.77, Gateshead :
JT - 56.47
BURNS William 13.12.69, S. Ribble :
5k - 14:38.0, HMar - 1:05:49+un/1:06:24,
Mar - 2:16:11
BURRAWAY Paul 30.11.68, Hounslow :
HJ - 1.95 (2.10-93)
BURRELL Jonathan 24.11.75, Peterborough :
800 - 1:52.5
BURROWS Craig 8.08.74, Ilford :
DT - 41.27 (42.32-97)
BURROWS Darius 8.08.75, Birchfield :
1500 - 3:47.24 (3:46.1-96), 1M - 3:59.91,
3k - 8:04.06 (7:58.7-96),
5k - 14:05.11 (13:54.42-96)
BURSLEM Richard U15 4.01.84, Sale :
LJ - 6.11
BURTON Simon U20 23.04.79, Notts :
800 - 1:54.4 (1:54.3-97),
1500 - 3:54.57 (3:51.58-97)
BUSHELL Mark Anthony U23 22.10.76, N & E B :
110H - 15.46 (14.7w/14.72w-95/15.15-96),
LJ - 7.13 (7.51w-96/7.25-95)
BUTLER David U23 9.12.78, Charnwood :
LJ - 7.05
BUTLER K., Army :
Mar - 2:33:32
BUTLER Matthew Rhys U20 4.04.80, Cardiff :
110HJ - 14.7w/14.85, 110H - 15.30
BUZZA David Edward 6.12.62, Cornwall AC :
Mar - 2:14:59 (2:11:06-93)
BYRNE Colin U20 9.02.79, London Irish/IRE :
400H - 53.5

CADDY Neil 18.03.75, Newquay & Par :
800 - 1:51.3 (1:49.5-96),
1500 - 3:39.89 (3:39.1-96),
1M - 3:58.49 (3:55.84-96),
3k - 7:48.76, 2M - 8:54.43,
5k - 14:04.13 (13:48.91-97)
CADOGAN Gary Anthony 8.10.66, S B :
400 - 48.42A (46.37-87),
300H - 36.87i (36.48i-96),
400H - 51.01 (49.07-94)
CADWALLADER Paul 23.10.62, Liverpool H :
Mar - 2:28:22 (2:24:49-91)
CAINES Adrian 13.11.74, Birchfield :
60H - 8.53i (8.33i-95/8.4i-97),
110H - 14.88w/14.91 (14.51-96)
CAINES Daniel U20 15.05.79, R S Coldfield :
60 - 6.99i, 200 - 21.4/21.53, 400 - 47.13
CAIRNS Steven Mark 3.11.67, Border :
2kSt - 5:54.47 (5:47.7-97), 3kSt - 8:56.55
CALDWELL Ben U17 3.03.82, Bolton :
400 - 51.0 (50.79-97), 400H - 56.5, 400HY - 55.50

CALLAN Adrian 28.11.62, Shettleston :
5k - 14:24.07 (13:58.93-88), HMar - 1:06:01
CALLAWAY David John 4.09.63, S B :
SP - 16.71 (17.55-93)
CAMERON Leon U15 10.09.83, Sale :
100 - 11.31w (11.9/11.93-97), 200 - 23.70
CAMERON Niall U20 19.12.79, Forres :
3kSt - 9:35.2
CAMERON Rezlimond 18.05.60, Thames VH :
TJ - 15.61 (16.32w-89/16.20-88)
CAMPBELL Darren Andrew 12.09.73, Belgrave :
100 - 10.04, 200 - 20.48
CAMPBELL Ian 6.09.71, Har/Dundee HH :
800 - 1:50.81 (1:49.95-93), 1M - 4:07.9,
1500 - 3:47.65i/3:49.09 (3:41.75i-97/3:43.64-93)
CAMPBELL James 17.06.70, Annadale Str :
3k - 8:11.22 (7:57.66-93),
5k - 13:57.1 (13:48.9-94)
CAMPBELL Kenneth William 30.09.72, TVH/
C of Edin : 110H - 13.89w/14.22 (13.86-94)
CAMPBELL Leroy 10.08.66, Rugby :
100 - 10.8w/10.97
CAMPBELL Patrick U20 10.03.80, N Down :
PV - 4.10
CAMPBELL Paul A. U20 29.01.80, Mandale :
200 - 21.9/22.16
CAMPBELL Paul W. U20 26.03.80, Mandale :
100 - 10.6wdt (11.3/11.42w-96), 400 - 48.71
CANNON Brian 6.09.75, Harlow :
200 - 22.0
CANTRELL Philip U23 17.06.76, Oxford Univ :
Dec - 5278 (5396-97)
CAPELING Kirk U20 27.02.80, Medway :
HTJ - 48.17
CARE Robert G. V50 8.04.47, Rowheath :
3kW - 13:24.39 (12:46.03-90)
CARELESS Robert 7.09.74, Telford :
HT - 56.94 (57.08-97)
CARLISLE Nigel 30.12.75, Ballymena & A :
JT - 57.16, Dec - 5526
CARMODY Noel Philip V40 24.12.56, Camb H :
3kW - 12:59.09 (12:26.49-91),
10kW - 47:00.6 (44:45.63-91),
20kW - 1:39:39 (1:34:38-90)
CARNAGHAN Mark U20 3.09.80, Hallamshire :
DecJ - 5251
CARR Gary U17 24.09.82, Victoria Park AAC :
100 - 11.06w (12.4-97), 400 - 50.94
CARR Tyrone U20 30.07.80, Blackheath :
110HJ - 15.17 (14.44-97)
CARROLL Sean 8.08.74, Woodford Green :
110H - 14.40
CARSON Christopher U20 26.10.79, S B/Loch :
100 - 10.9w (10.7/10.78w/10.98-97),
200 - 22.0/22.03 (21.5-97/21.76-96),
400 - 47.09 (46.94-97)
CARTER Adrian R. 7.02.68, Thames Valley :
110H - 15.1/15.27w (14.72w/14.75-90)
CARTER Chris U15 2.09.83, Belgrave :
PV - 3.00
CARTER Daniel U20 15.04.80, Braintree :
JT - 71.14
CARTER Ian U15 19.09.83, Jersey :
1500 - 4:19.46, TJ - 12.18
CARTER Simon 5.03.75, GEC/Reading Univ :
JT - 66.37
CARTER Thomas U17 20.08.82, Vale Royal :
1500 - 4:03.2

CASAL Olushola U20 20.06.80, Shaftesbury B :
 TJ - 14.23
CASTILLO Richard U17 3.12.81, Notts :
 400HY - 56.79
CAUDERY Stuart 19.11.66, Cornwall AC :
 110H - 15.5 (15.2-94/15.62-97),
 Dec - 5831 (6118-97)
CAUSEY Paul 15.01.68, Wigan :
 800 - 1:52.5 (1:49.9-86)
CAVERS David 9.04.63, Border :
 HMar - 1:04:46, Mar - 2:16:06
CAWLEY Ian U23 21.11.78, Bournemouth :
 100 - 10.7wdt (11.64-96),
 110H - 15.1/15.31w/15.61 (14.81w/15.14-97)
CHALLENGER Benjamin U23 7.03.78, Bel :
 HJ - 2.28
CHAMBERS Dwain Anthony U23 5.04.78, Bel :
 60 - 6.58i, 100 - 10.03Art/10.10 (10.06-97),
 200 - 21.05
CHAPE Andrew U17 25.04.83, Mandale :
 SPY - 14.13i
CHAPMAN Dominic M. 10.02.72, Worthing :
 Dec - 5616 (5937-91)
CHAPMAN Frank 17.01.70, RAF :
 Dec - 5287 (5338-96)
CHARLES Courtney 13.11.68, Thames Valley :
 TJ - 14.51 (16.38w/16.09-90)
CHARLESWORTH Robert U20 25.03.79,
 Peterbro : JT - 58.80 (59.64-97)
CHARVET Pierre 23.08.73, Birch/Birm Un/FRA :
 SP - 13.54 (15.01i/14.33-96)
CHARVILLE Michael U17 7.05.82, Mandale :
 400 - 50.15
CHATT James U20 11.02.80, Dartford :
 60 - 6.9i/6.93i (6.9i-97), 300 - 34.6,
 100 - 10.67w/10.7/10.81 (10.7-97),
 200 - 21.63i/21.63w/21.76, DecJ - 5203
CHECKLEY Luke U17 19.11.81, Harrow :
 PV - 3.70
CHECKLEY Richard U17 19.11.81, Harrow :
 PV - 3.80
CHEESEMAN Christopher V40 11.12.58,
 Surrey WC/ Crawley/Thames H&H :
 20kW - 1:31:58 (1:29:11-94),
 35kW - 2:56:13, 50kW - 4:10:54 (4:10:23-97)
CHEPKWONY Hagai 13.08.69,
 Bromsgrove & R/KEN : 5k - 14:20.82
CHIDLOW Glyn 21.10.71, Worc/Oxford Univ :
 LJ - 6.94 (7.28w-95/7.25-94)
CHILDS Seriashe U17 2.09.82, Brecon :
 100 - 11.0w (11.94-97)
CHILTON Alan 16.04.71, Hounslow :
 10kR - 29:32, 10MR - 48:15,
 HMar - 1:04:43 (1:03:59-97), Mar - 2:17:07
CHIN Darren U20 30.06.81, Hounslow :
 60 - 6.96i, 100 - 10.8w/10.82w (11.1-97/11.27-96)
CHISHOLM Scott U23 20.10.77, Pitreavie :
 400H - 54.93
CHRISTIE Jeffrey U17 24.09.82, Leamington :
 400 - 50.5, 400HY - 54.64
CHRISTIE Linford 2.04.60, Thames Valley :
 100 - 10.38 (9.87-93)
CHRISTIE-REES Adam U15 9.09.83,
 Powys Sch : PenB - 2518
CHRISTOPHERSON Neil 6.05.67, Liv H :
 JT - 57.74
CLARE Ben U20 21.09.80, Middlesbro & C :
 HTJ - 48.93

CLARK Dean 20.12.73, Hillingdon :
 800 - 1:52.4 (1:50.6-96)
CLARK Stephen 24.05.72, Dacorum & Tring :
 Dec - 5427
CLARK Stuart 16.10.75, Belgrave :
 LJ - 7.17
SOLOMON/CLARKE Dafydd U20 18.09.79,
 Cardiff : 800 - 1:53.97
CLARKE Gordon U15, :
 HJ - 1.76
CLARKE Ian 6.11.72, Enfield :
 60 - 6.8i/6.88i,
 100 - 10.7w/10.8/10.82w (10.7w-93/10.8-91)
CLARKE Jonathan 20.11.67, Swansea :
 JT - 59.73 (68.74-86)
CLARKE Peter 9.07.65, Coventry Godiva :
 400 - 49.05i (47.90-94)
CLARKE S. Ezra 9.12.74, Shaftesbury Barnet :
 TJ - 15.02w/14.66 (15.75-97)
CLARKE Wayne A. R. 24.12.75, Peterbro :
 HT - 56.44 (59.86-97)
CLARKSON Alan, Clayton-Le-Moors :
 Mar - 2:31:39
CLARKSON Matthew J.S. 25.01.66, Birchfield :
 3k - 7:59.6, 5k - 13:52.4
CLEMENTS Andrew U17 28.11.82, AF&D :
 OctY - 4413
CLEMENTS Matthew Carlton U23 17.09.77, Har :
 60 - 6.77i, 60H - 7.88i, 110H - 14.12,
 100 - 10.50w/10.8 (10.7-97/10.85-94),
 200 - 21.8 (21.6-97/21.72w-94/21.86-97)
CLERIHEW David U23 11.09.77, C of Edin :
 LJ - 7.18w/7.14 (7.38i/7.30w/7.29-96)
CLIFFORD Richard U23 28.07.78, Blackpool :
 400 - 47.99
CLUSKEY Adrian U20 30.12.80, Blackheath :
 SPJ - 14.25i/13.81 (14.91-97),
 DTJ - 42.07 (43.02-97)
CLYNE Fraser J. V40 23.08.55, Aberdeen :
 Mar - 2:33:46 (2:11:50-84)
COATES Peter 21.03.68, Durham :
 Dec - 4914
COATS Edward M. U20 14.06.80, Guildford & G :
 DecJ - 6514
COHEN Scott 6.12.64, Leslie Deans RC :
 Mar - 2:34:18
COKER Michael G. V40 16.01.57, T Solent :
 110H - 15.3/15.44w (15.21-88),
 400H - 54.57 (53.8-88/53.93-89)
COKER Raymond 28.07.73, Sale :
 55 - 6.35i, 100 - 10.61 (10.51un/10.51-96),
 200 - 22.01i (21.19-96)
COLE John U17 13.11.81, Coventry Godiva :
 400HY - 55.51
COLEMAN Andy 29.09.74, Enfield :
 3k - 8:10.64, 3kSt - 8:52.35
COLEMAN Daniel U17 5.07.82, Mansfield :
 800 - 1:58.0
COLLINS Joseph U17 28.05.82, S B :
 800 - 1:55.1
COLLINS Liam James O'Neill U23 23.10.78, Sale :
 100 - 10.92w/10.97 (10.8w-97), 200 - 22.0,
 110HJ - 14.12o/14.13wo (14.0w/14.08-97),
 110H - 14.35w/14.8/14.88 (14.43-97)
COLLINS Mark 29.07.73, Hounslow :
 200 - 22.17w (21.80w/22.1-91), 400 - 48.73
COLVIN Andrew 23.08.72, Shaftesbury B/AUS :
 3k - 8:18.0, 5k - 14:12.7, 3kSt - 8:48.23

336

COMBE Michael U23 24.12.78, Borders :
800 - 1:51.30
COMERFORD Nick 23.04.66, Cardiff :
1500 - 3:46.8 (3:42.20-96), 1M - 4:03.2,
3k - 8:01.65 (8:00.54-95),
5k - 13:52.7, 10kR - 29:50
CONDON Allyn 24.08.74, Sale :
60 - 6.64i, 400 - 46.8 (47.43-94),
100 - 10.29w/10.4/10.42 (10.3-97/10.36-96),
200 - 20.53i/20.71 (20.63-97)
CONERNEY Michael T. 30.10.72, Braintree/
Cambridge University : DT - 41.78 (44.28-93)
CONOLLY Stuart U17 9.02.83, Morpeth :
200 - 22.50
CONROY Paul 24.08.71, Havering :
400H - 53.8/54.22
COOK Austin James Gareth 20.02.69, Sutt & D :
SP - 14.02 (14.59-90), DT - 42.45 (49.20-90),
HT - 59.68 (67.32-91)
COOK Philip 7.05.69, Cardiff :
3kSt - 9:29.9 (8:55.6-93)
COOKSLEY Brian U20 5.04.80, Cardiff :
DTJ - 43.45, HT - 48.16, HTJ - 51.58
COOPER Nicholas U23 4.02.77, Belgrave :
110H - 14.65w/14.7/14.79
COOPER Paul 30.01.75, Shaftesbury Barnet :
800 - 1:52.73 (1:51.9-94)
COOPER Paul U23 4.12.76, Woodford Green :
JT - 64.83 (65.34-95)
COOPER Rufus U20 24.02.79, Hounslow :
PV - 4.60 (4.70-97)
CORCORAN Fyn U23 17.03.78, Cornwall AC :
LJ - 7.01, DT - 40.26, HT - 50.45
COREY Andrew John U17 15.10.81, C of Stoke :
200 - 22.5/22.5, 400 - 50.40, PV - 4.30
CORNISH Glen U20 27.10.79, Sale :
5k - 15:22.47, 2kSt - 6:10.84
CORR Kevin U20 17.04.79, Jarrow & H :
800 - 1:52.66 (1:52.46-97)
CORRIGAN J. Paul 19.01.66, Gateshead :
SP - 14.08 (16.04-89), DT - 41.00 (44.08-95)
COSTELLO Denis Richard Michael 3.12.61,
Norwich : TJ - 14.05 (15.66-83)
COSTELLO Tom U23 16.12.76, Camb & C/
Oxford Univ : HJ - 2.00 (2.00-97)
COTTER Christopher 3.02.72, Shaftesbury B :
LJ - 7.07w/7.05 (7.67w/7.47-93),
TJ - 14.42 (15.19-93)
COTTON Michael 17.04.68, Potteries Mar :
Mar - 2:30:54
COTTRELL James U20 19.12.80, Derby & Co :
SPJ - 14.18
COULTHARD Michael U17 28.12.82, Barr & F :
800 - 1:56.6
COUTTS Thomas U17 1.09.81, :
JTY - 56.30
COWAN Lloyd 8.07.62, Shaftesbury Barnet :
60H - 8.23i (8.11i-88),
110H - 13.97w/14.03 (13.7w-95/13.75-94)
COX John 17.09.63, Les Croupiers :
Mar - 2:27:28
COXHEAD Peter U20 14.07.81, Braintree :
JT - 57.87
CRABB Matthew U15 29.09.83, Bridgewater :
JTB - 48.75
CRABTREE Martin U20 8.06.81, Goole :
TJ - 14.14

CRAGGS Ray 9.07.63, RAF :
3kW - 13:15.5 (13:08.9-96)
CRAIG Gary 15.02.75, Blackpool :
100 - 10.8w
CRAIG Ian 20.08.69, Border :
100 - 10.56 (10.3/10.41w-97),
200 - 21.49 (21.22w-96/21.4/21.43-97)
CRAMP Aaron U15 29.02.84, Basildon :
JTB - 47.61
CRANE Adam U17 1.06.82, Elgin :
SPY - 13.82
CRAWFORD Daniel U15 23.02.84, Dartford :
100 - 11.4/11.76w
CRAWFORD Jason U17 20.07.83, City of Hull :
SPY - 14.27
CRAWLEY Luke U17 5.09.81, Solihull & S H :
HJ - 2.03i/1.91
CRAWLEY Mark U17 4.11.81, Mandale :
HTY - 50.00?/44.56
CRAWSHAW Jonathon U17 28.09.81, Craw :
100HY - 13.45
CREIGHTON James U15 15.09.83, Liv H :
HJ - 1.81
CRICKMORE Adam U15 26.01.84, Hereford :
80HB - 11.6dt/12.03w
CRIMMEN Nicholas 15.07.65, Spenborough :
DT - 41.60 (46.00-86)
CRITCHLEY Kim 15.07.73, Sale :
1500 - 3:49.30 (3:45.17-96),
5k - 14:21.21 (14:10.04-94), 10kR - 29:49
CROASDALE Mark 10.01.60, Bingley :
10MR - 49:49 (49:04-94),
Mar - 2:31:33 (2:17:45-93)
CROLL Graeme 1.02.66, Cambuslang :
5k - 14:37.5 (14:05.3pace/14:17.3-95),
10MR - 49:31
CROSS Michael U15 19.12.83, Tonbridge :
HJ - 1.75, PV - 2.90
CROSSLEY Paul U20 30.03.79, Luton :
110HJ - 15.0 (14.7w/15.22-97),
110H - 15.6 (15.4/15.69-96),
400H - 54.53 (53.62-97)
CROWLEY Billy 1.01.63, Middleton H :
Mar - 2:29:52
CROWLEY Mark U15 15.11.83, St Albans :
HJ - 1.81
CROWLEY Patrick U20 4.11.80, Gloucester :
110HJ - 15.29w
CROWTHER Eric 23.01.75, Salford :
1500 - 3:50.55, 3k - 8:13.18, 10kR - 29:47
CRYER Martyn U17 16.10.81, Blackpool :
1500 - 4:02.8, 3k - 8:41.8
CUDDY Grant U23 6.01.77, Sale :
800 - 1:49.8 (1:47.2-97)
CUFF Jon U20 30.03.80, Stroud :
400H - 54.15
CULLEN Keith John 13.06.72, Chelmsford :
1500 - 3:47.42 (3:43.12-92),
5k - 13:22.31 (13:17.21-97), 10k - 27:53.52,
10kR - 29:08 (28:36-92)
CUNNANE Danny U17 12.04.83, Wakefield :
HTJ - 51.32
CUNNINGHAM John 19.09.63, Fife :
10k - 31:00.90
CURRAN Paul U23 5.04.77, North Down :
TJ - 14.39 (15.15-97), Dec - 6366
CURTIS Neil 30.07.74, Corby :
HT - 52.55 (55.62-94)

CURTIS Paul U20 29.05.80, Medway :
  400 - 48.39 (48.14-97)
CURZON Robert U23 7.12.78, Notts :
  HJ - 1.95 (2.00-97)
CZERNIK Richard 12.08.72, Birchfield :
  DT - 42.00, Dec - 5943 (6484-96)

D'ARCY Adam, U17 25.05.82, R S Coldf'ld :
  400HY - 57.33
DABORN Dale K.R. 14.11.66, Highgate H/RAF :
  400H - 54.97 (54.0-92/54.03-89),
  Dec - 5352 (5811-91)
DACK Christopher U17 28.11.82, Doncaster :
  100 - 10.97w/11.18, 100HY - 13.82,
  HJ - 1.94, LJ - 7.13w/6.98, OctY - 4861
DAKO Owusu 23.05.73, Sale :
  60 - 6.85i (6.83i-96), 200 - 20.99 (20.57-95),
  100 - 10.17w/10.36 (10.3-97/10.35-96)
DALMEDO Daniel U20 14.03.80, Hillingdon :
  3k - 8:35.08, 5k - 15:16.51
DALTON Timothy U20 18.01.79, Harrow :
  110HJ - 15.2 (14.7/15.09-97), 400H - 54.02
DALY Paul 27.10.68, Bracknell :
  Mar - 2:29:02
DALY Steven U20 29.12.79, Elan Valley :
  100 - 10.89w (10.85-97)
DANNAN John U20 5.12.80, Bedford & Co :
  110HJ - 15.20
DANSO Richard U17 24.12.81, Belgrave :
  LJ - 6.66 (6.86w/6.81-97)
DARLINGTON Landley Sean U23 19.01.77,
  Peterbro/Loughbro : JT - 60.34 (60.94-97)
DATEMA Cor 19.09.71, Team Solent/HOL :
  800 - 1:52.4, 1500 - 3:45.0
DAVID Andrew 9.09.69, Woodford Green :
  110H - 14.9w/15.1/15.12 (14.83-95)
DAVID Ken U23 13.03.78, Bedford & County :
  LJ - 7.15
DAVID Richard U23 15.08.77, Blackheath :
  200 - 22.0 (22.22-96),
  400 - 49.0 (48.7/48.85-96)
DAVIDSON Christopher 4.12.75, N & E B :
  200 - 21.62w (21.67-96),
  LJ - 7.89w (7.94w/7.71-97)
DAVIDSON Hamish M. V40 25.05.54,
  SGA (Prof) : SP - 14.38 (17.44-78)
DAVIDSON Mark 15.11.68, Aberdeen :
  400H - 53.5/55.33 (50.79-89)
DAVIES Adam U15 27.07.84, Gloucester AC :
  400 - 53.01, 800 - 2:04.17
DAVIES Alun Keith U20 23.08.80, Carmarthen :
  HJ - 2.00
DAVIES Ben U20 24.08.81, Wessex & Bath :
  HJ - 2.00i/2.00 (2.03-97)
DAVIES Berian Rhys 22.04.73, Swansea :
  400H - 52.92 (52.80-97)
DAVIES Christopher U15 2.09.83, Swansea :
  1500 - 4:21.29
DAVIES Christopher U23 19.10.76,
  Telf/Staffs Univ : 3k - 8:17.62,
  5k - 14:37.5 (14:07.9-97),
  2kSt - 5:58.07, 3kSt - 9:05.86 (8:59.1-97)
DAVIES Daniel U23 2.02.76, Torf/Loughbro :
  TJ - 13.90 (14.04-95)
DAVIES Gareth M. 11.05.71, Oxford Univ :
  TJ - 14.00 (14.73-94)
DAVIES John U17 19.12.82, Havering :
  LJ - 6.50, TJ - 13.85

DAVIES Kevin U23 11.01.78, Shaftesbury B :
  HT - 53.57
DAVIES Kris U17 30.10.81, Aberdare :
  LJ - 6.63
DAVIES Mark Howard 10.01.71, Tonbridge :
  SP - 14.69 (15.56-92), DT - 46.64 (53.06-92)
DAVIES Matthew 23.07.71, Woodford Green :
  800 - 1:52.7 (1:49.9-96),
  1500 - 3:46.5 (3:44.2-96)
DAVIES Matthew U23 16.09.78, Swansea :
  JT - 57.74
DAVIS Adam Gareth 19.11.72, Corby/RAF :
  PV - 4.10 (4.70-92)
DAVIS James U15 10.10.84, Portsmouth :
  3kW - 15:41.71, 3kWR - 15:16
DAVIS Luke U20 1.01.80, Shaftesbury Barnet :
  100 - 10.76 (10.40w/10.45-97)
DAVIS Mark Gavin U23 1.03.77, Corby :
  PV - 5.00 (5.10-96)
DAVIS Vincent U17 1.11.81, Sale :
  200 - 22.3/22.32
DAVOLLS Martin U15 9.04.85, Enfield :
  400 - 51.86
DAVOREN Patrick 13.03.72, Brighton/IRE :
  800 - 1:52.60 (1:52.0-96), 1500 - 3:43.99,
  1M - 4:08.08 (4:04.6-95), 3k - 8:14.4
DAVY Nick 26.12.74, Norwich :
  800 - 1:52.6 (1:52.3-97)
DAWKINS Chris U15 3.09.83, Trafford :
  100 - 11.37w/11.59
DAWSON David U15 3.02.84, Devon Sch :
  SPB - 13.38, DTB - 37.55
DAWSON Nicholas U23 11.05.78, Bel/Brunel U :
  200 - 22.0/22.03w (21.43w/21.48-97)
DAY Stephen U17 10.02.82, Shaftesbury B :
  PV - 4.10
DE EMMONY Denee U15, Belgrave :
  400 - 53.21
DEACON David William 19.03.65, Morpeth :
  400 - 48.7/48.82 (47.10-93)
DEACON Gareth 8.08.66, Coventry Godiva :
  10k - 31:12.2 (30:41.3-94)
DEACON Jared Mark 15.10.75, Morpeth :
  200 - 21.40 (21.14-96), 300 - 33.13 (32.78-96),
  400 - 46.32 (45.94-97)
DEACON-BROWN James U15 26.05.84, Gate :
  SPB - 14.31, JTB - 53.46, PenB - 2852
DEARMAN Geoffrey U23 4.08.77, Bel/Brunel U :
  100 - 10.6w, 200 - 21.5/22.08i,
  300 - 34.15i (34.30-96), 400 - 46.46
DELL Gregory J. 20.11.64, Woodstock R :
  Mar - 2:26:51
DEMPSEY Tom U15 15.12.83, Halesowen :
  HTB - 57.15
DENMARK Robert Neil 23.11.68, Basildon :
  1500 - 3:49.04 (3:37.99-95),
  5k - 13:48.48 (13:10.24-92),
  10k - 29:17.72 (28:03.34-94)
DENSLEY Martin Richard U20 1.05.81,
  Ealing,S & M : PV - 4.70
DENT Richard U23 2.11.78, Wakefield :
  HJ - 2.10 (2.10-97)
DESAI Ketan Kumar Hemant U17 1.12.82,
  Morpeth : 800 - 1:57.8
DEVINE James Russell 24.04.68, Inverness :
  HT - 62.50 (65.36-94)
DEVLIN Gareth U23 2.06.76, Loughbro
  /Sheffield/IRE : LJ - 7.01w/7.00 (7.30-96)

338

DEVONISH Marlon U23 1.06.76, Coventry G :
60 - 6.74i, 100 - 10.13,
200 - 20.92 (20.61w/20.65-97)
DEWSBERRY Matthew U17 9.10.81,
R S Coldfield : 400HY - 57.53
DIBBLE Jason 15.02.71, Cannock & Stafford :
HT - 51.48
DICKENSON Derek Paul V45 4.12.49,
Dacorum & Tring : HT - 51.95 (73.20-76)
DICKINSON S., New Marske :
Mar - 2:32:31
DICKINSON Tim 14.10.72, Blackheath :
10MR - 49:26
DICKSON Andrew U15 30.11.83, Camb & C :
HJ - 1.77
DICKSON Marlon U23 17.11.78, Belgrave :
100 - 10.77w (10.62w/10.65-96), 200 - 21.49
DILLON Adrian U15 10.09.83, Wolves & B :
100 - 11.59w (12.1-97), LJ - 6.00
DILLOW Greg U15 16.06.84, Woking :
PV - 3.55
DISCALA Michael U20 5.04.81, Liverpool H :
DTJ - 44.85
DIXON J. U13, Bedford & County :
100 - 12.4/12.58, 200 - 25.5/25.52
DIXON Matthew U23 26.12.78, Wigan :
1k - 2:22.7, 1500 - 3:45.90 (3:43.5-97)
DJAN Geoffrey U17 21.07.82, Birchfield:
400 - 49.21
DOBBING Thomas F. 5.02.73, Blackpool/RAF :
JT - 62.28un/59.73 (65.22-93)
DOBSON I., Army :
100 - 10.8
DOHERTY Ciaran 14.01.75, Cardiff :
110H - 14.8/14.89 (14.71w-97/14.85-95),
JT - 55.90 (58.72-97), Dec - 6075 (6648-97)
DOHERTY Paul U17 22.01.83, Clydesdale :
HJ - 1.90
DONALDSON Alasdair U23 21.06.77, N & E B/
Loughborough : 400 - 48.62, 800 - 1:48.6,
1500 - 3:51.60i (3:49.9-97)
DONKIN Bradley 6.12.71, Barton :
800 - 1:46.86, 1k - 2:22.4
DONNELLY Dermot 23.09.70, Annadale Str :
1500 - 3:48.92 (3:44.1-93),
3k - 8:00.38, 5k - 13:27.63,
10k - 28:43.17 (28:38.56-97), 10kR - 29:06
DONNELLY John U20 11.09.79, B & A :
TJ - 14.35
DONOVAN Daniel 8.10.70, Shaftesbury B :
100 - 10.8 (10.62w-97/10.8-95),
200 - 21.9/21.97 (21.18-97),
400 - 48.11 (47.20-97)
DORAN Anthony 22.10.72, Swansea :
HT - 46.16 (48.24-94)
DORGU Christopher 11.12.69, Hounslow :
110H - 15.2/15.54 (14.6-95/14.71-94)
DOSANJH Nathan U20 13.02.79, Sol & S H :
800 - 1:53.80, 1500 - 3:52.50
DOUBAL Robert U20 16.04.80, Scottish Sch :
400H - 56.40
DOUGLAS Matthew U23 26.11.76, Bel/Brunel U :
200 - 21.7 (21.68-97), 300 - 34.12i,
400 - 47.5/47.90 (47.64-97),
110H - 14.34 (14.32-97), 400H - 50.20
DOVELL Paul U23 5.05.77, Team Solent :
HJ - 2.00i (2.09-96)

DOWNES Philip U17 4.10.81, Morpeth :
1.5kSt - 4:32.23
DOWSE Richard U15 3.01.85, Scunthorpe :
800 - 2:03.01
DOWSETT Nicholas J.E. U23 24.11.78, Wood G :
LJ - 7.00 (7.15w-96/7.04i/7.02-97)
DOYLE Brian U23 12.03.77, Cumbernauld :
100 - 10.59, 200 - 21.9/22.12
DRAKE Andrew Paul 6.02.65, Coventry G :
3kW - 12:10.5 (11:31.0-90),
10kW - 42:46.26 (41:18.64-88),
20kW - 1:28:01 (1:24:53-87)
DRAPER Anthony 23.04.74, Blackheath :
400 - 49.0 (48.9-96), 800 - 1:49.6
DRISCOLL Gareth David U20 8.03.81, W Norf :
HT - 46.16, HTJ - 50.51
DRURY Reece U15 2.11.83, Grimsby :
HTB - 45.12
DUBERLEY Simon 2.09.67, Hillingdon :
100 - 10.8, 200 - 21.8/21.90w/22.03
DUBLIN Gavin U15 5.10.83, Croydon :
100 - 11.35w/11.46
DUDLEY David 2.05.65, Liv.Pembroke Sefton :
3k - 8:19.53 (8:08.3-92),
5k - 14:38.01 (14:21.0-92)
DUFFY Anthony V40 26.06.56, Bolton :
5k - 14:38.44, Mar - 2:25:41 (2:17:09-89)
DUGARD Daniel 21.06.65, Ilford :
LJ - 6.98 (7.15-89)
DUGGLEBY Philip U15 20.09.83, Sale :
400 - 52.4/52.86
DUKE Daniel James Maxwell 23.12.68, T V H :
3kSt - 9:27.22 (8:49.53-88)
DUMICAN Mark 17.08.70, Wigan :
DT - 41.08, HT - 46.08
DUNCAN Simon U23 20.05.77, Highgate H :
200 - 22.11 (22.0-97)
DUNFORD Edward U15 15.09.84, Birchfield :
80HB - 11.45, HJ - 1.86, LJ - 6.30, TJ - 12.21,
SPB - 13.29, DTB - 39.81, PenB - 3037
DUNFORD James U13 14.01.86, Birchfield :
100 - 12.4 (13.34-97), 400 - 58.0, 80HC - 12.6,
HJ - 1.68, LJ - 5.43, TJ - 11.30, SPC - 12.12,
DTC - 34.14, JTC - 41.86, PenB - 2444,
DUNSON Gregory Ian 2.12.63, RAF/S B :
60H - 8.31i (8.0i-92/8.04i-86),
110H - 14.6/14.73 (14.23w-89/14.29-86),
400H - 52.62 (50.88-92), HJ - 1.95 (2.06-88)
DUNWELL Mark 13.03.70, Notts :
100 - 10.97
(10.7w-93/10.8-94/10.90w-93/10.92-97)
DUPUY Jason 31.01.71, S B/Ayr Seaforth :
800 - 1:49.67, 1M - 4:09.96
DURRANI Ramon U15 9.10.83, Hercules W :
80HB - 11.71
DUVAL Spencer Gavin 5.01.70, Cannock & St :
2kSt - 5:40.6 (5:33.09-92),
3kSt - 8:36.37 (8:24.64-95)
DYBALL Gareth U20 16.03.81, Woodford Gr :
HJ - 2.00
DYMOND Terrance U15 24.10.83, Havering :
3k - 9:34.03
DZIKOWSKI Ray 6.03.63, Woodford Green :
Mar - 2:33:44 (2:27:47-95)

339

*E*ADIE David, 21.12.70 /AUS :
5k - 14:27.3?
EARLE Robert Bernard 15.09.60, Haringey :
SP - 14.79 (14.87i-93/14.80-86),
DT - 44.00 (45.12-90), HT - 59.76 (62.60-95)
EAST Andrew U20 25.07.81, Rowntrees :
DecJ - 6252
EAST Michael John U23 20.01.78, Portsmouth :
800 - 1:52.7 (1:52.48-97),
1500 - 3:44.86, 3k - 8:19.2,
4K - 11:20.7, 2kSt - 5:56.3
EASTMAN Gavin U20 28.06.80, Enfield :
100 - 10.75w/11.02, 200 - 22.0w
EASTON Mark Jonathan 24.05.63, Surrey WC :
3kW - 12:28.8 (11:24.4-89),
10kW - 44:04.41 (41:14.3-89),
35kW - 2:47:28 (2:42:13-93), 50kW - 4:03:53
ECCLES Martin V40 16.01.57, Orkney I :
24Hr - 200.280km (242.002km-89)
EDEN Tom U20 16.05.79, Trafford :
HT - 52.76 (52.84-97), HTJ - 56.48 (56.98-97)
EDGAR Raymond U15 15.05.84, Lanc & Morc :
3k - 9:35.67
EDGAR Tyrone U17 29.03.82, Highgate H :
100 - 10.58w/10.60, 200 - 21.55w/21.62
EDU Remi U23 14.12.78, S B/Loughbro :
400 - 47.82 (47.76-96), 400H - 51.3/51.37
EDU Seni 4.03.74, Shaftesbury Barnet :
100 - 10.76, 200 - 21.28, LJ - 7.00
EDWARDS Jonathan David 10.05.66, Gate :
50 - 5.9i, 60 - 6.73i,
TJ - 18.01 (18.43w/18.29-95)
EDWARDS Mark Simon 2.12.74, Charn/Lough :
SP - 18.88, DT - 45.30 (46.14-96)
EDWARDS Michael 19.10.68, Belgrave :
PV - 5.50 (5.52-93)
EDWARDS N., Royal Navy :
400H - 55.07
EDWARDS Nicholas U15 22.03.84, Salford :
HTB - 45.04
EDWARDS Noel 16.12.72, Leamington :
800 - 1:48.99
EDWARDS Oliver U17 24.08.83, Norwich :
OctY - 4275
EDWARDS Orlando 11.10.73, Shaftesbury B :
3kSt - 9:29.74
EGERTON Tim U15 19.01.84, Trafford :
1500 - 4:12.0, 3k - 9:13.7
ELDER Craig U17 22.05.82, Whitemoss :
LJ - 6.87i/6.77, OctY - 4601
ELDRIDGE Timothy U23 15.03.76, S B :
JT - 59.04 (64.00-97)
ELIAS Daniel U17 25.12.82, Woodford Green :
PV - 3.60
ELIAS Matthew U20 25.04.79, Cardiff :
400 - 47.83i (48.72-97),
400H - 51.5/52.34 (51.71-97)
ELLAMS Craig 24.11.72, City of Stoke :
HT - 62.82 (63.98-97)
ELLIOTT Mark U20 12.08.80, Avonside :
HJ - 1.95i/1.95
ELLIOTT Mensah U23 29.08.76, Blackh/Brunel U :
60H - 8.18i, 110H - 14.29w/14.3/14.59 (14.56-97)
ELLIOTT Neil 10.04.71, City of Edinburgh :
SP - 16.06, DT - 47.48
ELLIOTT Ross U15 6.09.83, Houghton & Plee :
80HB - 11.85w/11.9/11.91, DTB - 37.93,
PenB - 2643

ELLIS Charles Allan U23 7.07.77, Sunderland :
LJ - 6.96
ELLIS Christopher 24.01.66, Bristol :
SP - 16.00 (17.36i-84/17.26-86)
ELLIS Ieuan T. 11.05.60, Elswick :
Mar - 2:24:54 (2:13:21-86)
ELLIS Kevin U23 18.06.76, Peterborough :
60 - 6.9i, 100 - 10.8/10.91w (10.8/11.09-97)
ELLIS-SMITH James 11.09.72, Belgrave :
1500 - 3:47.48 (3:46.14-96)
ELLWOOD Wayne 26.09.74, Blackpool :
400 - 48.2/48.47 (47.50-97)
EMERY Julian 18.10.68, Westbury :
5k - 14:35.7
ENGLISH Desmond 6.06.67, Havering/IRE :
800 - 1:49.9 (1:48.4-91)
ENIH-SNELL Chuka U15 2.03.84, Swansea :
80HB - 11.80, HJ - 1.96, LJ - 6.34, PenB - 3039
ENRIGHT Stephen U15 5.09.84, Halifax :
1500 - 4:18.16
ENSBURY Scott U17 4.01.82, Rowntrees :
100HY - 13.86
EROGBOGBO Temitayo Faruq 8.03.75, Bir/Lough :
TJ - 16.43w/16.12 (16.44w-97/16.32-95)
ERSKINE Craig U15 26.09.83, Lochgelly :
100 - 11.6 (12.32-97), 200 - 23.22w/23.5/23.66,
400 - 49.96
ESEGBONA Unuakpor H. 16.04.68, C of Stoke :
Dec - 6427 (6494-96)
ESPIN David U17 27.01.83, Mansfield :
HJ - 1.90
ETCHELLS James U20 15.10.80, Copeland :
TJ - 14.27
EVANS Aaron U17 15.02.82, Blackheath :
200 - 22.55w (22.9/23.00-97), 400 - 48.73
EVANS Andrew U20 2.10.80, R S Coldfield :
800 - 1:54.88
EVANS G., RAF :
110H - 15.37
EVANS Matthew 19.11.75, Telford/Staffs Univ :
PV - 4.20 (4.60-96)
EVANS Paul William 13.04.61, Belgrave :
10MR - 47:01 (46:10+/46:35-97),
HMar - 1:03:23 (1:00:09un-95/1:01:18-97)
EVANS Steven U23 29.05.78, Colwyn Bay :
400H - 54.8
EVELYN Leroy U15 23.09.83, Ipswich :
100 - 11.38w
EVLING-JONES Louis U17 20.06.83, Holbeach :
TJ - 13.30, OctY - 4408
EXLEY Scott U23 9.02.78, Belgrave :
110H - 15.6 (16.38-96), Dec - 6221
EYRE Simon Peter U20 30.10.80, Crawley :
800 - 1:53.86, DecJ - 5195

*F*ABEN Stuart 28.02.75, Belgrave :
JT - 74.20 (76.66i-96/74.24-95)
FABER Pierre 9.01.72,
Dacorum & Tring/Oxford Univ/RSA :
HJ - 2.00 (2.06-96), PV - 4.40 (4.50-96),
SP - 15.09 (15.94-96), DT - 46.64,
JT - 58.67 (60.58-95), Dec - 7247 (7581-96)
FAIRCLOUGH Lee 23.06.70, Team Solent :
400 - 48.9 (47.2-96/47.30-97)
FAIRLAMB Neil U23 13.03.76, City of Stoke :
Dec - 5875
FALCONER William U23 20.12.78, Clydesdale :
SP - 13.71 (14.44-97), DT - 40.95

FALOLA Ayo 29.07.68, Woodford Green :
  60 - 6.88i (6.82i-95),
  100 - 10.2w/10.67w/10.7/10.77 (10.50-95),
  200 - 21.27 (20.93w-95/21.15-91),
  110H - 15.2 (14.80-97), 400H - 53.94
FANNING Robert U23 31.10.78, Milton K/IRE :
  400 - 48.05 (47.9-97)
FARAH Mohammed U17 13.03.83, Hounslow :
  1500 - 3:57.67, 3k - 8:33.51
FARLEY Liam U15 3.10.83, Surrey Sch :
  SPB - 13.24
FARMER Lea U20 22.01.80, Torfaen :
  400 - 48.50
FARQUHARSON Ruddy Anthony 26.03.61,
  Telford/RAF : TJ - 14.23 (15.59w/15.57-85)
FARRAN Martin J. 8.05.61, Longwood :
  Mar - 2:33:24 (2:26:23-90)
FARRAR Craig U15 11.10.83, Halifax :
  800 - 2:05.86
FARRELL Kevin U23 31.10.77, Havering :
  100 - 10.54, 200 - 21.3w/21.4/21.45
FARRELLY John 4.12.67, London Irish/IRE :
  SP - 15.46 (15.70-97), DT - 47.71 (48.80-97)
FARROW Kevin 8.09.75, Derby & Co/Iowa St U :
  1500 - 3:48.78 (3:48.44-96)
FARRUGIA Emmanuel U17 19.07.82, Muswell H :
  400 - 50.67i
FASINRO Ibrahim 'Tosi' 28.03.72, Haringey :
  TJ - 16.63w/16.10i/16.05 (17.30w/17.21-93)
FAULKNER Mark Peter U20 14.11.79, T Solent :
  LJ - 6.92 (7.33-97)
FAVELL Peter U17 16.03.82, Chesterfield :
  TJ - 13.25, DTY - 45.85,
  HTY - 47.43, OctY - 4588
FEASEY Terry U23 5.08.77, Bas & MH :
  800 - 1:50.77, 1500 - 3:43.5, 1M - 4:08.6
FEIL Dirk 9.03.65, Morpeth/GER :
  PV - 4.20i/4.20 (4.40-97)
FENN Ian U15 3.12.83, Worthing :
  HJ - 1.78
FENTON Malcolm Leonard V40 12.02.56,
  Newham & Essex B : SP - 14.14 (14.62-96),
  DT - 40.07 (47.40-79), HT - 61.35 (62.42-82)
FERDINAND Philip U17 18.11.82, Birchfield :
  TJ - 14.03w
FERGUS Jason Robert 11.10.73, Belgrave :
  100 - 10.4w/10.55w/10.61
    (10.34w-94/10.4-93/10.44-92),
  150 - 15.8, 200 - 21.01 (20.91-97)
FERGUSON Martin M. 17.09.64, C of Edin :
  Mar - 2:28:53 (2:26:45-95)
FERNANDEZ Oliver U13 28.04.86, Loughton :
  2kW - 11:38.90
FERNE Michael V50 18.12.47, Team Solent :
  DT - 41.40
FERNS Austin U20 12.01.81, Belgrave :
  110HJ - 15.1w, 400H - 53.80
FERRAND Adrian J. 5.02.68, Newham & E B :
  110H - 15.5 (15.06-94)
FERRIER William U13 15.04.86, :
  JTM - 40.08
FERRIN John 20.02.67, North Belfast :
  HMar - 1:06:05 (1:03:52-92)
FIELD Peter U17 21.05.82, City of Stoke :
  HTY - 58.95
FINCH Lloyd U15 23.10.83, Leics WC :
  3kW - 12:44.64, 5kW - 22:54.0,
  10kWR - 47:17

FINCH Luke U13 21.09.85, Leics WC :
  2kW - 9:40.0 (9:40.0-97),
  3kW - 15:54.0 (15:24.00-97)
FINCH Rodney 5.08.67, Team Solent/Army :
  1500 - 3:45.69 (3:37.97-93),
  3k - 7:59.07 (7:53.99i-94),
  5k - 13:27.75, 10k - 30:52.87
FINDLAY Mark U23 20.03.78, Blackheath :
  60 - 6.94i (6.79i-97), 100 - 10.55,
  200 - 21.20 (20.99w-97)
FINDLOW Richard David 4.12.66, Bradford :
  10kR - 29:45 (29:19-92)
FINNIE Steven U23 14.12.78, Border :
  LJ - 6.93w (6.99w-95/6.90-96)
FISHER Gavin U23 18.11.77, West Suffolk :
  HJ - 1.95 (2.00-96)
FISHER Paul U20 17.05.79, Milton Keynes :
  800 - 1:51.41, 1500 - 3:47.24,
  3k - 8:32.7 (8:30.0-97)
FISHER Philip U15 21.03.84, Wiltshire Sch :
  PV - 2.85
FITTALL Ross U20 4.09.79, Dursley :
  800 - 1:51.40
FITZGERALD Richard U15 6.06.84, Medway :
  80HB - 11.8/12.15w
FLECKNEY William U13 19.10.85, Beds & Co :
  LJ - 5.30, TJ - 10.52
FLEGG Frank U17, Carmarthen :
  1.5kSt - 4:39.2
FLEMMINGS Andre U15 6.01.84, Croydon :
  200 - 23.15w
FLETCHER Carl U15 24.09.83, Wigan :
  SPB - 13.68
FLETCHER John U13 15.07.86, Wakefield :
  HJ - 1.60,
FLETCHER Stephen J. 16.12.68, Notts :
  60 - 6.99i (6.95i-90)
FLINT Benjamin U23 16.09.78, Belgrave :
  PV - 5.16 (5.20-97)
FLINT Christopher V50 6.12.44, London Vid :
  100MWT - 21:47:22 (20:21:41-97)
FLINT Mark A. 19.02.63, Telford/RAF :
  3k - 8:19.47 (8:02.8-89),
  5k - 14:33.3 (13:54.5-90),
  HMar - 1:06:15 (1:01:56-93)
FLOYD Michael U23 26.09.76, Sale/Salford U :
  HT - 62.01
FLYNN Julian T. 3.07.72, Belgrave :
  LJ - 7.53 (7.71w/7.66-97), TJ - 15.03 (15.32-93)
FOGG Nicholas U23 24.03.78, Shaftesbury B :
  HT - 47.90 (49.54-97)
FOOKS Andrew 26.04.75, TVH/London Univ. :
  3kSt - 9:00.38 (8:56.83-95)
FORBES Brian 6.09.74, Mid Ulst/Bord/Qu Un :
  200 - 22.0, 400 - 47.41 (46.84-97)
FORDE Karl U17 15.04.83, Rowheath :
  100 - 11.0/11.02
FORDHAM Gavin U20 1.02.79, Bedford & Co :
  HJ - 1.96, Dec - 5660, DecJ - 5717
FORREST Anthony U23 22.12.76, Milton K :
  3kSt - 9:27.70 (9:19.60-97)
FORREST David 17.05.68, :
  Mar - 2:31:39
FOSTER Carl 24.10.75, Sheffield :
  400H - 54.3/54.96 (52.86-96)
FOSTER William R.G. V40 9.08.58, Blackh :
  10k - 30:14.47 (29:14.34-96)

341

FRAMPTON Matthew U15 10.04.84, Wimborne :
    HTB - 44.29
FRANCIS Anthony U17 6.07.83, Woking :
    JTY - 52.82
FRANCIS Mark U23 23.09.77, Sutton & Dist:
    JT - 67.19 (68.02-97)
FRANCIS Nick 29.08.71, Shaftesbury Barnet :
    5k - 14:31.87 (14:13.99-97),
    10k - 30:56.72 (30:40.8-94)
FRANCIS Peter U20 28.08.80, Blackheath :
    TJ - 14.93 (15.52w-97)
FRANCIS-FAMOUS James U15 14.12.83,
    Harrow : 80HB - 11.34
FRANKLIN Andrew U20 13.09.80, Sutton & D :
    2kSt - 6:03.25
FRANKLIN John 1.03.66, Woodford Green :
    110H - 15.6w (15.1w-90/15.13-91/15.2-95)
FRANKS David U23 27.04.78, Wigan :
    HJ - 1.95 (2.07-95)
FRASER Peter U23 28.01.78, Aberdeen :
    JT - 58.95
FREARY Paul 3.04.68, Bolton :
    3k - 8:18.2 (8:07.84-90),
    5k - 14:36.8 (13:55.34-96), 10kR - 29:40,
    10MR - 49:03 (48:37-94), HMar - 1:04:55
FREEMAN Oliver U13 11.01.86, Invicta :
    3k - 10:26.1
FREMPONG Kenneth U15 17.07.84, Herc W :
    80HB - 11.42w/11.7
FRENCH Jon U23 15.03.78, Norwich :
    LJ - 6.99 (7.22w/7.05-97),
    TJ - 13.92 (14.11-96)
FRICKER Simon David 14.07.75, T Solent :
    SP - 14.73 (15.29-96), DT - 48.36 (49.96-97)
FROST Andrew U20 17.04.81, Isle of Wight :
    SPJ - 14.01, HT - 53.00, HTJ - 60.35
FROST Liam U15 13.05.84, Derbs Sch :
    400 - 52.0/52.40
FROST Steven U20 4.01.81, Wrexham :
    TJ - 13.95w (13.18-97)
FROST Steven U17 12.12.81, Thurrock :
    800 - 1:54.8
FROUD Paul M. 6.04.66, Brighton :
    Mar - 2:25:57 (2:22:18-94)
FRY Jason U17 6.01.83, Southend :
    PV - 3.80
FUAT Fuat 20.09.71, Enfield :
    JT - 58.69 (59.60-97)
FUGALLO Alexander 28.01.70, Shaftesbury B :
    100 - 10.8 (10.42w-90/10.5-89/10.60-92),
    200 - 21.51 (21.20w-89/21.2/21.26-90),
    400 - 48.34 (46.39-94)
FULFORD Andrew U17 23.06.82, Swindon :
    600 - 1:23.0, 800 - 1:53.95, 1500 - 4:04.91
FULLER Peter U23 30.04.78, Epsom & Ewell :
    HT - 51.86
FULLER William U23 19.10.76, Epsom & E/
    Loughborough : SP - 13.90 (16.36-97)
FULLER William J. V50 5.02.48, Epsom & E :
    SP - 13.59 (17.87-72)
FURLONG Kevin 19.05.70, Manx H :
    110H - 14.9/15.22
FURSE Barry U15 13.05.84, Launceston :
    HJ - 1.75

G ALLAGHER Donal 5.12.72, Sparta :
    Mar - 2:29:52
GALLAGHER T. U15, :
    400 - 53.0
GALLIGAN Lee U17 10.12.81, Chesterfield :
    OctY - 4355
GALLIMORE Paige U13 18.01.86, Herne Hill :
    HJ - 1.60
GAMESTER Neil U17 15.02.83, Enfield :
    1.5kSt - 4:39.88
GAMMAGE Richard David 21.11.62,
    RAF/Colwyn Bay : PV - 4.61 (5.00-84)
GARDENER Jason 18.09.75, Wessex & Bath :
    60 - 6.56i (6.55i-96),
    100 - 10.0w/10.17w/10.30 (10.17w-97/10.25-94),
    200 - 21.1w (21.73-94)
GARDINER Richard 11.06.73, Cardiff :
    3k - 8:17.40, 4K - 11:22.6, 5k - 14:39.4
GARGAN Andrew U17 10.10.81, East Down :
    1.5kSt - 4:39.9 (4:29.7-97)
GARLAND Dale U20 13.10.80, Guernsey :
    400H - 56.4, TJ - 14.32
GARLAND Stephen 12.01.73, Liv.Pem Sefton :
    Dec - 6503
GARNER Mark U15 2.11.83, Mansfield :
    80HB - 11.69w/11.73, PV - 2.95, PenB - 2629
GARNER Vincent 2.07.66, AF&D :
    10MR - 49:40
GARRARD Deane U17 19.05.82, Ipswich :
    SPY - 15.73
GARRETT Lee U23 2.09.78, Mansfield :
    1500 - 3:48.2
GASCOIGNE Robert 5.10.74, Sale :
    400H - 55.89 (55.21-97)
GATE Simon U17 21.09.82, Border :
    HTY - 49.06
GATES Nigel G. V45 18.05.53, Brighton :
    10k - 31:05.69 (29:27.29-77)
GAWTHORPE Richard U20 28.01.81,
    Derby & Co : 400H - 55.6
GELMAN Bradley U17 18.01.82, Hertford & W :
    100 - 11.00w
GERRARD Gary 7.07.63, Wigan Ph/Army :
    Mar - 2:32:43
GHENT Brendon U23 7.09.76, Coventry G :
    60 - 6.78i, 100 - 10.46w/10.57,
    200 - 21.05w/21.30i/21.4/21.45
        (21.24i-97/21.28-96)
GIBB Bruce U17 10.10.81, Perth :
    200 - 22.47w/22.51, 400 - 50.49
GIBB Ian 8.01.75, Harmeny :
    PV - 4.30i/4.05 (4.20-96)
GIBLIN Chris U20 20.06.81, Liverpool H :
    HJ - 1.95i
GIBSON Alex U23 3.11.77, Brentwood/
    Loughborough Studnts : JT - 60.48
GIDLEY Alistair 5.09.72, Sale :
    JT - 61.37 (62.88-93)
GIDLEY Ian 13.11.70, Sale :
    HJ - 1.95i (2.05-93)
GIFFORD David 9.03.73, Cleethorpes :
    400H - 53.39 (53.34-94)
GILBERT Gareth 24.08.72, Cardiff/Liv Univ :
    DT - 46.48
GILBERT James 9.11.74, City of Edinburgh :
    LJ - 6.96w/6.95 (7.11-97)
GILBERT Paul U20 21.06.81, Phoenix :
    800 - 1:51.9

GILBY Clive Roger 24.02.66, Belgrave :
  800 - 1:52.60 (1:47.33-95),
  1500 - 3:49.18 (3:46.27-92)
GILDING Paul 2.10.75, Brighton :
  HJ - 1.96i/1.95 (2.03i/2.01-93)
GILHOOLY Anthony U23 26.03.76, C of Edin :
  HJ - 2.15i/2.10 (2.18i/2.15-97)
GILL Anthony U23 19.09.77, Bord/Trent Univ :
  110H - 14.47w/14.69
GILL Stephen U15 25.09.84, Middlesbro & C :
  400 - 52.87
GILLARD Matthew 11.07.75, Wakefield :
  Dec - 6195
GILLESPIE Andrew 16.10.71, Pitreavie :
  400 - 49.00
GILLESPIE Ian 18.05.70, Birchfield :
  1500 - 3:46.11 (3:39.8-97), 1M - 3:57.6,
  3k - 7:51.34 (7:48.28-97),
  5k - 13:28.57 (13:18.06-97)
GIRDLER Dominic U17 6.03.82, Charnwood :
  100 - 11.2, 400 - 50.04,
  100HY - 12.9w?/12.96w/12.99,
  HJ - 1.99, LJ - 6.46,
  SPY - 14.87io/14.04, OctY - 5500
GIRVAN Michael V40 16.03.54, Warrington :
  Mar - 2:30:46 (2:27:36-94)
GIRVAN Richard U23 26.07.76, Annadale Str/
  Oregon Univ. : 800 - 1:49.33 (1:49.13-97)
GISBEY David Edward 2.05.60, C of Edin :
  HT - 49.21 (55.70-95)
GITTENS Luke U20 4.01.81, Cardiff :
  110HJ - 14.69, 110H - 15.16w
GLENTON Bradford 2.11.69, Team Solent :
  800 - 1:52.6 (1:51.9-92), 1500 - 3:41.9,
  1M - 4:03.0 (4:01.85-93),
  3k - 8:14.6 (8:11.27-90), 5k - 14:21.5
GLOVER Danny U17 3.03.82, Basildon :
  400HY - 57.6/57.70
GLOVER Michael U20 20.12.81, Northampton :
  1.5kSt - 4:27.78
GODDARD Sam U17 4.01.83, Paddock Wood :
  JTY - 51.56
GODSELL Jospeh U15 27.10.83, Blackheath :
  800 - 2:05.37
GOLDING Alexander U17 3.12.81, Mandale :
  100 - 10.77w/10.99,
  200 - 22.18w/22.2/22.36
GOLDING Julian Antonio 17.02.75, Blackh :
  60 - 6.82i, 100 - 10.28 (10.28-97),
  200 - 20.18
GOLLEY Julian Quintin Patrick 12.09.71, TVH :
  TJ - 16.89 (17.06-94)
GOODLIFFE Nicholas U17 12.05.82, Holmfirth :
  3k - 8:57.5
GOODREM Greg U15 14.09.83, Southend :
  HJ - 1.75
GOODWIN Jon U23 22.09.76, Team Solent :
  400H - 54.03 (52.5/53.14-97)
GORDON Alastair U23 16.04.78, Worthing :
  100 - 10.8 (11.04-97), 200 - 21.77,
  400 - 48.2 (49.06-97), Dec - 5100
GORDON David 20.03.68, N & E B/Loughbro :
  PV - 4.60i/4.60
    (5.05iun-88/4.75-94/4.85Aun-93)
GORDON Dominic U20 7.01.81, Bristol :
  TJ - 14.19
GORDON Malwyn U17 20.10.81, Bristol :
  TJ - 15.01w/14.83

GORDON Peter V45 2.07.51, Gateshead :
  DT - 54.20 (61.62-91), HT - 50.29 (63.20-82)
GOTHARD Richard U15 6.09.83, W Yorks Sch :
  TJ - 12.11
GOUDIE Andrew U23 4.10.78, Belgrave :
  3kW - 13:45.4 (13:24.6-97)
GOUGH Darren U20, Cannock & Stafford :
  JT - 55.16
GOULD Leroy 16.06.64, Newham & Essex B :
  110H - 14.6db
GOW David Allan U20 9.02.79, Shettleston :
  800 - 1:53.5 (1:51.4-97)
GRAFFIN Allen Gordon U23 20.12.77,
  Tonbridge/Loughborough Studnts :
  1500 - 3:49.0, 1M - 4:04.0,
  3k - 8:03.22, 5k - 14:19.68 (14:16.8-95)
GRAFFIN Andrew Neill U23 20.12.77, Tonb :
  800 - 1:52.24 (1:50.0-97), 1500 - 3:45.3,
  1M - 4:02.05, 3k - 8:15.40 (8:11.1-97),
  5k - 14:06.73
GRAHAM Anthony 15.10.63, Tipton :
  10MR - 49:46,
  HMar - 1:06:01 (1:04:48-94), Mar - 2:20:13
GRAHAM Daniel Alexander U20 3.08.79,
  Liverpool H : HJ - 2.13 (2.15-96)
GRAHAM Donovan 18.08.61, Ipswich :
  PV - 4.20 (4.60-97)
GRAHAM Grant 27.12.72, Motherwell :
  800 - 1:47.85, 1k - 2:20.41, 1500 - 3:41.5
GRAHAM Jonathan U15 10.10.83, Gosforth :
  1500 - 4:16.1, 3k - 9:17.60
GRAHAM Paul U13 17.02.86, Blackheath :
  2kW - 11:05.7 (10:30.0-97), 3kW - 16:25.7
GRANT Dalton 8.04.66, Haringey :
  HJ - 2.34 (2.37i-94/2.36-91),
  TJ - 14.68w/14.25
GRANT Diarmuid 'Joe' U15, :
  1500 - 4:19.3
GRANT Dwayne U17 17.07.82, Blackheath :
  100 - 10.90w/11.0/11.17, 200 - 21.93w/22.02
GRANT Mark 17.05.71, Thames Valley :
  PV - 4.85 (5.10-95)
GRAY Glenn 21.04.68, Thames Valley :
  400H - 54.8/54.94 (52.80-97)
GRAY Kevin, Ashford :
  PV - 4.10
GRAY Paul 25.05.69, Cardiff :
  400 - 47.49 (47.4-97),
  110H - 13.54 (13.53-94), 400H - 49.16
GREAVES Damien David U23 19.09.77, N & E B :
  60 - 6.88i, 60H - 7.77i,
  110H - 13.84w/13.85 (13.82-97)
GREEN Ben U23 30.03.76, Haslemere :
  100 - 10.8/10.97w (10.86w-97/10.97-96),
  200 - 21.77w/21.8 (22.02-96)
GREEN Clifton Paul U20 10.10.79, Medway :
  JT - 66.21
GREEN David U17 24.12.82, Warrington :
  3k - 9:00.81
GREEN Leighton U23 10.01.78, Braintree :
  100 - 10.8w/10.89, 200 - 22.19
GREEN Mark 28.06.71, Hounslow :
  400H - 54.4 (53.1-95/53.16-97)
GREEN Paul 7.04.72, Sale :
  3k - 8:08.06,
  5k - 14:24.72 (13:56.27-97)
GREEN Royston U17 4.01.82, Brymore Sch :
  1.5kSt - 4:31.17

GREEN Stephen Harold 18.02.71, Trafford :
  1500 - 3:44.3 (3:39.19-94),
  1M - 4:02.9 (3:59.6i-94),
  3k - 8:10.2 (8:03.82i/8:05.45-95)
GREEN Stephen 28.07.70, Bingley :
  5k - 14:21.7 (14:17.2-94),
  10kR - 29:46 (29:46-97),
  HMar - 1:05:53 (1:04:45-95), Mar - 2:17:16
GREEN Steven U17 15.01.83, Cornwall AC :
  100HY - 13.9/13.98w/14.15, OctY - 4419
GREENWOOD Timothy U17 22.11.82, Ox C :
  100HY - 13.9, LJ - 6.53, OctY - 4356
GREEVES Jerry 14.09.67, RAF :
  Mar - 2:30:11
GREGORY Jonathan 3.10.72, Rowntrees/
  Loughborough : Dec - 4942 (5271-92)
GREGORY Simon U15 24.11.83, W Yorks Sch :
  TJ - 12.00
GRICE Lee U17 17.04.82, Sale :
  400HY - 57.79
GRIERSON Andrew U20 23.11.79, Reading :
  HT - 59.12, HTJ - 62.12 (63.78-97)
GRIFFIN David 5.12.63, Cardiff :
  400H - 55.6 (52.07-95)
GRIFFIN Mark 16.02.75, Walton :
  800 - 1:49.0, 1500 - 3:45.92 (3:43.5-96)
GRIFFIN Neil V50 28.05.48, Windsor S & E :
  SP - 13.76 (16.06-77),
  DT - 45.34 (51.66-80)
GRIFFITH Mark U17 25.11.81, Enfield :
  1500 - 4:00.8, 1.5kSt - 4:19.28,
  2kSt - 6:11.22
GRIFFITHS Andrew U17 26.09.81, Swansea :
  400HY - 57.6
GRIME Ian Stuart 29.09.70, N & E B/
  Loughborough : 1500 - 3:44.06 (3:40.1-96),
  1M - 4:07.39 (4:03.7-90),
  3k - 8:07.31 (7:55.4-96),
  5k - 14:23.26 (13:37.00-97), 10k - 30:22.88
GRINDLE James U15 8.01.84, Cardiff :
  HTB - 44.93
GRINDLE Matthew U17 3.01.82, Cardiff :
  HTY - 51.73
GRINNELL Luke U20 21.03.79, Bristol :
  60 - 6.97i
GRIPTON Paul U23 9.11.76, Bromsgrove & R :
  60H - 8.19i, 110H - 14.59
GRISTWOOD William E. 20.03.59, E, S & M :
  Mar - 2:29:17 (2:25:09-94)
GROVES Michael U15 21.03.84, Torfaen :
  200 - 23.55w/23.7, JTB - 53.30
GRUNDY Nick U15 11.11.83, Cambridge & C :
  SPB - 13.04, DTB - 43.66
GUITE Craig U23 19.08.77, Border :
  PV - 4.70i/4.62 (5.02i-97/4.90-96)
GULLAKSEN John U20 24.02.80, City of Hull :
  PV - 4.30
GUNPUTHRAM Gavin U17 21.03.82, Medway :
  HJ - 1.90, TJ - 13.53
GUTHRIE Alexander U20 6.07.79, Kilb/Bord:
  400 - 49.67
GUTTERIDGE Steven T. 5.07.71, Highgate H :
  110H - 15.31w/15.6 (15.04-93),
  Dec - 5669w (7047-94)
GYASI Koby U15 18.10.83, Notts :
  100 - 11.39

HACKETT Christopher U17 1.03.83, Ox C :
  OctY - 4253
HACKLEY Peter 19.02.71, Border :
  800 - 1:49.68 (1:47.59-93),
  1500 - 3:50.61 (3:48.5-93), 1M - 4:08.3
HADLER John 18.08.69, Cambridge Harriers :
  110H - 15.6 (14.8w/14.9-89/15.61-92)
HAGAN Garry U15 21.11.84, Clydesdale :
  SPB - 13.38
HAGGERTY Kristian U23 2.12.76, W S & E :
  800 - 1:52.7 (1:51.41-97)
HALE Darren 2.10.59, Rotherham/Army :
  Mar - 2:26:30 (2:22:09-97)
HALE Steven U23 20.04.77, Rowheath :
  DT - 41.66 (42.60-96)
HALES Matthew U20 6.10.79, Steyning :
  3kW - 13:05.0 (13:03.56i/13:05.0-97),
  5kW - 22:31.84, 10kW - 46:45.0,
  10kWR - 45:33
HALL A. U17, Cambridge Harriers :
  LJ - 6.52
HALL Brian U17 17.11.82, Bolton :
  HJ - 2.03
HALL Calvin U15, Birchfield :
  HJ - 1.85
HALL Dominic 21.02.71, Highgate Harriers :
  800 - 1:49.1
HALL Drew U20 31.08.81, Lagan Valley :
  400H - 56.9, 400HY - 55.89o
HALL Jonathon U15 18.11.83, Ayr Seaforth :
  400 - 51.67
HALL Samuel Thomas U13 15.10.85, S B :
  1500 - 4:35.3, 3k - 9:51.1
HALL-EVANS Michael U13 14.03.86,
  Dudley & Stourbridge : 800 - 2:15.6
HALLETT Jason U17 29.03.82, :
  JTY - 54.50
HAMILTON Aaron U17 7.08.82, Trafford :
  400HY - 57.59
HAMILTON Douglas W. 19.05.61, C of Edin :
  PV - 4.60 (4.75-87)
HAMILTON Nicholas U20 13.03.79, Blackh :
  400 - 49.20 (48.58-97)
HAMILTON Nick U17 9.09.81, Rotherham :
  OctY - 4234
HAMMOND Matthew 26.09.68, Scunthorpe :
  HT - 47.40 (52.24-97)
HANDLEY Charles U13 18.01.86, Wakefield :
  DTC - 32.72
HANNA David 13.12.75, Cardiff/Lagan Valley :
  JT - 65.44 (66.52-97)
HANNAY Mich 10.10.61, Manx H :
  Mar - 2:23:58
HARDIE James U17 16.04.82, Elgin :
  HJ - 1.95i/1.91
HARDY Alan P. V40 4.09.58, Blackheath :
  PV - 4.10 (4.50-92)
HARDY Lee U15 1.11.83, Croydon :
  HTB - 44.23
HARGRAVE Christopher U20 27.02.79, Bed & Co :
  60H - 8.35i (8.26i-97), 110H - 14.6/14.66
HARLAND Kim U17 21.02.82, Carmarthen :
  HJ - 1.96, LJ - 6.43
HARMAN Matthew U15 8.11.83, Mandale :
  200 - 23.68w/23.97
HARRIES Kirk 7.08.74, Thames Valley :
  110H - 14.63w/14.65 (14.45w-97)

HARRIES Philip James Charles 7.04.66,
  Derby & Co : 400H - 54.4 (50.01-88)
HARRINGTON Thomas U20 27.10.79, S B :
  HTJ - 51.26
HARRIS Andrew U15 21.09.83, Wx & Bath :
  200 - 23.53, TJ - 13.03
HARRIS Chris 2.03.72, Woking :
  400 - 48.8 (48.8-96)
HARRIS David U17 12.12.81, Cornwall AC :
  OctY - 4364
HARRIS Lee U15 23.11.83, Clevedon :
  TJ - 13.29w/13.18
HARRIS Lee 20.10.69, Wigan Phoenix :
  Mar - 2:31:18 (2:24:29-97)
HARRIS Mark U17 2.06.82, Swindon :
  3k - 9:01.6
HARRISON Ererton W. 8.04.66, Thames V H :
  110H - 14.52w/15.0/15.18 (14.11-91)
HARRISON Gary U13, Harrow :
  3k - 10:07.9
HARRISON Nsa U15 27.11.83, Worcester :
  SPB - 13.84
HARRISON Stephen 19.12.72, Blackh/Lond U :
  JT - 72.85 (75.32-95)
HART Andrew 13.09.69, Coventry Godiva :
  600 - 1:17.8, 800 - 1:45.71,
  1k - 2:22.33 (2:18.78-96),
  1500 - 3:42.55 (3:42.0-96), 1M - 4:01.7
HART Nathan Scott 1.07.73, Windsor S & E :
  60H - 8.43i (8.38i-97), 110H - 14.95,
  HJ - 2.00 (2.10-93)
HART Neal 15.04.68, Scottish Borders :
  DT - 42.20 (42.60-96)
HASSAN Malcolm U17 27.11.82, Sunderland :
  800 - 1:57.55, 1500 - 3:58.30, 3k - 8:56.15
HATTON Darren U20 21.03.79, Medway :
  LJ - 6.97 (7.01w-97), SPJ - 13.84,
  DTJ - 44.64, JT - 56.91 (57.30-97),
  Dec - 6508w/6477, DecJ - 6543 (6678-97)
HAUGHIAN Samuel 9.07.79, Hounslow :
  1500 - 3:52.7 (3:52.03-97),
  1M - 4:09.33, 5k - 14:17.2
HAWKEY Terry U15 6.01.84, Dartford :
  1500 - 4:17.26
HAWKINS Christopher Michael 24.10.61, Bing :
  3kSt - 9:03.90 (8:36.55-95)
HAWKINS Colin J. U15 23.03.84, Derby & Co :
  1500 - 4:17.30, 3k - 9:05.4
HAWKINS James U20 14.12.79, Medway :
  HT - 51.34, HTJ - 53.98 (54.00-97)
HAY John U17 4.06.83, Corby :
  HTY - 51.48
HAY Neil U15 10.05.84, Reading :
  HJ - 1.75i/1.72
HAYES Martin U20 31.08.79, Chesterfield :
  DTJ - 42.50 (43.28-97),
  HT - 47.27 (48.12-97), HTJ - 53.67
HAYES Scott 4.01.73, Thames Valley :
  SP - 16.15i/15.01 (15.62-95),
  DT - 49.78 (54.16-97)
HAYFORD Kenneth Nicholas 10.03.63,
  Cambridge H : JT - 61.54 (69.90-87)
HAYMAN Nigel 25.09.74, Bournemouth :
  110H - 15.4/15.65 (15.2/15.39-97)
HAYMAN Thomas U20 17.09.80, Mansfield :
  DT - 43.43, DTJ - 47.54
HAYWARD Andrew 26.10.74, Rowntrees :
  JT - 55.19 (60.38-95)

HAYWARD Gregory 28.01.64, Peterbro/RAF :
  JT - 57.10 (61.96-90)
HAYWARD Stephan 30.07.74, Sale/Sc Bord :
  SP - 18.03 (18.40-96)
HEAD Paul 1.07.65, Newham & Essex B :
  DT - 43.29 (44.12-89), HT - 73.11 (74.02-90)
HEAD Stephen V40 21.10.58, Newham & E B :
  SP - 13.81 (14.44-89)
HEALEY Richard V40 17.11.54, Portsmouth :
  DT - 40.91 (41.64-97)
HEANLEY John U20 25.09.80, Windsor S & E :
  110HJ - 15.30, DecJ - 6157
HEATH Brett 6.01.75, Havering :
  SP - 13.61 (13.73-96), DT - 42.22 (43.22-96)
HEATH Guy U15 21.04.84, Lancashire Sch :
  DTB - 37.26
HEATON Robert U20 6.05.81, Preston :
  TJ - 13.95
HEDMAN Graham U20 6.02.79, Braintree :
  100 - 10.7w/10.83w/10.89,
  200 - 21.9/21.95w/22.15,
  400 - 48.69 (48.47-97)
HEMERY Adrian U17 6.08.82, Windsor S & E :
  400HY - 58.21, DTY - 42.43,
  HTY - 47.64 (54.08-97), OctY - 4937
HENDRY James U20 12.05.79, Springburn :
  800 - 1:55.0
HENDRY Martyn John 10.04.75,
  City of Edinburgh/Strathclyde Univ :
  60H - 8.00i, 110H - 14.24w/14.39 (14.16-97)
HENNESSY Andrew U23 24.08.77, T Solent/
  Oxford Univ : 3kSt - 9:07.6
HENRY Corri U23 9.12.76, Notts :
  200 - 21.9 (20.8w/21.34-96),
  400 - 48.63 (46.50-96)
HENRY James U15 31.07.84, Spenborough :
  3k - 9:38.3
HENTHORN James U23 20.02.77, T Solent :
  60 - 6.78i,
  100 - 10.30w/10.46 (10.22w-97/10.41-95),
  200 - 20.99i/21.01 (21.0w-97)
HEPPLES Stephen U20 6.01.80, Loftus :
  3k - 8:32.51, 5k - 15:01.63
HERMANN Derek U20 7.04.79, Carmarthen :
  JT - 54.21 (56.42-97)
HERRING Christopher U20 3.03.81, Hartlepool :
  400H - 55.56
HERRINGTON Charles 28.07.71, Milton Keyn :
  10k - 31:18.06
HERRINGTON Gary Hugh 31.03.61, Rugby :
  SP - 14.88, DT - 53.40 (56.66-96),
  HT - 50.91
HERRINGTON Samuel Edward U13 2.10.86,
  Rugby : DTC - 33.15
HEYES Simon U17 14.03.82, Preston :
  LJ - 6.56w (5.91-97), OctY - 4860
HIBBERD Ben U17 12.04.83, Leics WC :
  3kW - 15:54.9, 3kWR - 15:15
HIBBERD Matthew J. 23.06.73, Thames V H :
  800 - 1:52.9 (1:49.2-92)
HIBBERT David U20 31.01.79, Trafford :
  1500 - 3:54.1,
  3k - 8:27.53 (8:25.3-97), 5k - 14:20.1
HIBBERT Paul N. 31.03.65, Birchfield :
  110H - 15.05w (15.02-96),
  400H - 52.18 (50.52-96)
HICKS Andrew U20 30.07.79, Banbury :
  110HJ - 14.8, 400H - 53.42 (53.36-97)

HIGGINBOTTOM Mike V40, Salford :
Mar - 2:30:40
HIGHAM Keith U13 7.11.85, Carlisle/Aspatria :
HJ - 1.60
HILL Graham 23.06.65, Stockport :
Mar - 2:21:38
HILL Matthew U17 15.12.82, Blackheath :
1.5kSt - 4:37.48
HILL Michael Christopher 22.10.64, Leeds :
JT - 86.92 (86.94-93)
HILL Robin U23 23.02.77, Sheffield/Sheff Un :
PV - 4.40i/4.10 (4.60-95)
HILL Walter, Crawley :
24HrT - 226.934km
HILLIER James U23 3.04.78, Newport/Birm U :
400H - 53.12
HILSTON James U20 25.02.79, Belgrave :
200 - 22.0 (21.9/22.05-97),
400 - 48.90 (47.24-97)
HILTON Jonathan 11.01.74, Sale :
TJ - 15.13 (15.37w/15.28-97)
HINCHCLIFFE Alexander U17, Oldham & R :
JTY - 54.54
HIND James U23 24.05.77, Leamington :
HJ - 2.00 (2.00i-96)
HINDLEY Christopher U23 21.01.76, Worksop :
Dec - 5606 (6514-94)
HIPKISS Brett U15 3.12.83, W Midland Sch :
400 - 53.17
HIRSCH Mark 31.03.63, Birchfield :
2kSt - 5:57.2, 3kSt - 9:23.4 (9:08.0-96)
HISCOTT Nick U15 19.09.83, Torfaen :
80HB - 11.53/11.8
HISCOX Darren 21.03.72, Bridgend :
5k - 14:33.3, 10MR - 49:56,
HMar - 1:06:18 (1:04:56-96), Mar - 2:21:16
HO Minh U15 3.01.84, Liverpool H :
80HB - 11.25w/11.8/12.00, LJ - 6.20w/5.97
HOAD Oliver U17 1.10.81, Cambridge & C :
HTY - 53.93
HODGE Andrew James 18.12.68, Blackheath :
HJ - 1.95 (2.10-93), 110H - 15.5
(14.9-94/15.2w-95/15.41w-92/15.56-95)
HODGKINSON Mark Roland 20.07.72, Bir :
PV - 4.60 (5.20-96)
HODSON Chris U20 11.11.80, West Norfolk :
110HJ - 14.69w/14.79,
110H - 15.5, DecJ - 5071
HOEY Michael 29.04.69, Bournemouth :
3kSt - 9:26.1 (9:06.6-95)
HOGG Colin S. 22.05.67, City of Edinburgh :
110H - 15.51w (14.91w/15.04-89)
HOLDEN Tom U15 2.02.84, Tipton :
1500 - 4:20.84
HOLDER Graham Paul 16.01.72, Bexley :
DT - 40.37, HT - 61.61
HOLEHOUSE Lee U17 23.12.81, Telford :
400 - 50.4/50.46
HOLGATE Martin C. 2.11.65, Woodford Gr :
400H - 54.9 (54.2/54.51-95)
HOLLADAY Robert 10.01.75, Roth/Loughbro :
10k - 31:18.85 (30:40.69-97)
HOLLAND Iain U20 6.07.81, Giffnock :
HTJ - 46.02
HOLLAND Kevin 11.09.75, Crawley :
10k - 31:11.2
HOLLIDAY Ian 9.12.73, Sale :
HJ - 2.16

HOLLIER Steven U23 27.02.76, Wolves & B :
5kW - 21:42.44 (21:27.0-97), 10kW - 45:08.97,
20kW - 1:32:20, 50kW - 4:14:37
HOLLIN Philip U17 14.11.81, Sheffield RWC :
3kW - 15:56.93
HOLLINGER Robert U20 11.10.80, Rotherham :
110HJ - 15.1/15.27, DecJ - 6036
HOLLOWAY Mark U15 6.10.83, Bracknell :
400 - 52.9,
HOLMES Stephen U20 17.10.80, Blackheath :
800 - 1:53.4
HOLSGROVE Tim U17 11.12.82, Wirral :
PV - 3.60
HOLT Andrew 23.02.64, Verlea :
Mar - 2:30:09 (2:24:26-93)
HOLTBY John U17 27.03.82, City of Hull :
400 - 50.34, SPY - 16.38io/15.73,
DTY - 41.40, OctY - 5426
HONEY Roger V40 10.02.55, Ilford :
110H - 15.4 (14.8-78/15.19-90)
HOOD Mark U17 6.09.81, Sunderland :
3k - 8:59.17
HOOD Samuel U15 17.10.83, Cardiff :
HJ - 1.80
HOOPER Ben U17 10.09.82, Yeovil Olympiads :
400HY - 56.8
HOOTON Robin 5.05.73, City of Edinburgh :
800 - 1:49.71 (1;47.7-96)
HOPCROFT Adam U20 3.08.79, Haringey :
DTJ - 44.38
HOPKINS Thomas U17 1.08.82, Crawley :
1500 - 4:02.4, 1.5kSt - 4:22.58
HOPTON Matt U15 2.03.84, AF&D :
100 - 11.18w/11.32, 200 - 23.0
HORNE P. David 9.03.68, SGA (Prof) :
SP - 13.82
HORSBURGH Ian Joseph U23 10.01.78,
City of Edinburgh/Heriot Watt :
400 - 47.75 (47.1/47.20-97)
HORSMAN James U13 27.09.85, Bedford & Co :
1500 - 4:38.6, 3k - 9:51.7
HOUGHTON Ben U20 6.08.80, B & Ant/IRE :
JT - 63.52 (64.34-97)
HOULIHAN Martin U17 19.09.81, Shildon :
100 - 11.1w/11.23, 200 - 22.1
HOUSLIN Livon 2.11.60, Thames Valley :
JT - 60.98 (63.92-92)
HOUSTON Craig U20 9.07.80, Penicuik :
800 - 1:54.8
HOWARD Damien U17 23.11.81, W Norfolk :
HTY - 59.73
HOWARD Paul 19.10.66, Woodford Green :
PV - 4.20 (4.40-90), SP - 13.58 (14.11-96),
DT - 42.80 (43.06-90), JT - 60.87 (65.10-91)
HOWE Christopher William 17.11.67,
Woodford Green/Loughborough Studnts :
DT - 40.23 (44.84-90), HT - 66.97
HUDSON Michael U15 13.03.84, Can & Staff :
80HB - 11.52w/11.9/12.03
HUDSON Stephen U23 13.08.76, Oxford City/
Loughborough Studnts : 400H - 55.3
HUDSPITH Ian 23.09.70, Morpeth :
3k - 8:13.1 (8:03.9-95),
5k - 14:11.4 (13:52.8-97),
10k - 29:42.08 (28:35.11-97),
HMar - 1:04:22 (1:02:53-96)

HUDSPITH Mark E. 19.01.69, Morpeth :
3k - 8:09.3 (7:58.72-93),
5k - 14:11.5 (13:51.73-91),
10k - 29:22.88 (29:02.38-92),
10MR - 49:49 (48:58-93),
HMar - 1:04:36 (1:02:50dh-95/1:03:19-97),
Mar - 2:14:19 (2:11:58-95)
HUGGINS Marlon Anthony 11.02.71, T V H :
HJ - 2.01 (2.12i-89/2.11-94)
HUGHES Andrew 10.07.67, RAF/S B :
60 - 6.89i, 100 - 10.67 (10.59db-95),
200 - 21.3/21.31
HUGHES Brian C. 6.01.70, Trafford :
PV - 4.10 (4.25-94)
HUGHES David U15 31.05.84, Scunthorpe :
80HB - 11.69w/12.0
HUGHES Kevin Michael 30.04.73, Haringey :
PV - 5.50
HUGHES Scott U23 20.11.78, Sale :
1500 - 3:51.89
HUGHES Steven U17 25.02.82, Scunthorpe :
OctY - 4698
HUGHES Thomas 8.01.60, Annadale Str/IRE :
Mar - 2:23:33 (2:13:59un-92/2:14:46-91)
HULA Martin 2.01.66, Bristol :
4K - 11:19.7, 5k - 14:23.0 (14:06.56-94),
10k - 30:35.15 (30:08.41-95)
HULL Gregory 16.11.65, Leeds :
10k - 31:07.2 (30:59.6-95)
HULL Richard, Croydon :
PV - 4.10
HULME Delroy 14.09.72, City of Stoke :
TJ - 14.62 (15.50w-91/15.26-90)
HULSE G.Ewart W. 21.01.62, Colwyn Bay :
DT - 42.37 (42.48-97), HT - 50.88 (54.62-91)
HUNT Jamie U20 29.11.79, Gresham :
SPJ - 13.92
HUNT Simon U20 22.07.81, Sutton & District :
110HJ - 14.83w/14.97
HUNTER Christopher U20 3.03.81, Jarrow & H :
DecJ - 5704
HUNTER Gary U17 10.09.81, West (I.O.M.) :
200 - 22.5 (23.25-97), LJ - 6.67w (5.90-97)
HUNTER Michael U17 17.09.81, Perth :
LJ - 6.59
HUNTER Richard 12.01.71, Gateshead :
110H - 15.35w/15.5 (14.79w-89/14.8/14.99-95),
Dec - 5837 (6092-92)
HUNTER Roger U23 10.03.76, Skyrac :
110H - 15.4/15.63w (15.0-96/15.33w-95),
Dec - 6901w/6810 (7159-97)
HURDWELL Duncan L. 24.04.62, Bournemouth :
Mar - 2:26:56 (2:26:56-94)
HURREN Richard U15 24.09.83, Falkirk :
PV - 3.30, DTB - 38.25,
HURST Craig 30.12.70, City of Stoke :
400 - 48.4 (49.04-97)
HURST Lee 29.07.72, Belgrave :
5k - 14:34.6, 2kSt - 5:48.2,
3kSt - 8:49.63 (8:48.34-96)
HUSBANDS M. U15, West Midland Sch :
LJ - 6.03
HUSSAIN Bashir 20.12.64, Stockport :
10MR - 49:54 (48:28-91),
Mar - 2:23:23 (2:19:00-97)
HUTCHINSON John U17 3.05.82, Enfield :
PV - 3.80

HUTCHINSON Michael Innes 5.10.65, Trafford :
3kSt - 9:25.1 (8:50.61-92)
HYDE Daniel U23 5.10.77, Torbay :
4K - 11:24.8
HYDE Tom U15 7.10.83, Bedford & County :
100 - 11.27, 200 - 22.40w/23.11
HYLTON Mark David U23 24.09.76, W S & E :
100 - 10.60 (11.02un-93), 300 - 32.26,
200 - 21.6 (21.04i-97/21.09-95), 400 - 45.24

IDDON Christopher U17 8.10.82, Bolt :
1500 - 4:06.61
IDESSANE Kheredine 1.12.69, Clydesdale :
800 - 1:51.80 (1:48.62-91)
IDOWU Phillips U23 30.12.78, Belgrave :
TJ - 16.35
IFILL Rowland A. 11.11.75, Vale of Aylesbury/
Loughbro : 100 - 10.82w, 400H - 56.0
IGBON Charles U20 20.04.79, Belgrave :
LJ - 7.00, TJ - 14.16 (14.63-97)
ILLIDGE Sam U23 4.02.77, Lincoln Well :
1500 - 3:47.5
INATIMI Ben U17 6.07.83, Liverpool H :
100 - 11.18, 200 - 22.42w/22.85
INGLE Andrew U20 19.02.80, Bideford :
800 - 1:54.93
INGRAM David U20 19.01.80, Brighton :
PV - 4.20
INGRAM Geoff 31.01.68, RAF :
Dec - 6148
IOANNOU Andreas   73, Haringey/CYP :
PV - 4.80
IRONMONGER Richard 11.07.67, Notts :
Mar - 2:30:56
IRVING Jan U23 4.03.77, Wirral :
LJ - 7.20w/7.18

JACKSON Colin Ray 18.02.67, Brecon :
100 - 10.31 (10.29-90),
110H - 13.02 (12.8w-90/12.91-93),
200H - 22.69 (22.63-91)
JACKSON Daniel P. U20 17.04.79, T Solent :
400H - 56.8 (59.39-96)
JACKSON Darren U23 21.10.78, Enfield :
200 - 21.8 (21.52w/22.24-97)
JACKSON Edward U17 4.04.82, Dorchester :
1500 - 4:06.5, 3k - 8:58.1
JACKSON Gary 28.04.68, Birchfield :
PV - 4.20 (4.90-86)
JACKSON Guy 10.01.71, Coventry RWC :
10kW - 48:53.0 (46:30.0-91)
JAMES Christopher U17 9.12.82, Milton K :
HTY - 53.66
JAMES Guto U15, :
TJ - 12.34
JAMES Michael, Chester Le Street :
1500 - 3:51.10
JAMES Ronnie 14.12.64, Cornwall AC :
Mar - 2:28:00 (2:25:33-97)
JAMES Ryan U17 23.11.81, Kettering :
JTY - 51.70
JAMES Steven U17 9.02.82, Southampton C :
PV - 3.80
JAMIESON Steven U20 4.02.79, Medway/
Loughborough Studnts : JT - 59.65
JARRETT Anthony Alexander 13.08.68, Har :
60 - 6.73i, 60H - 7.50i (7.42i-95),
110H - 13.25 (13.00-93)

347

JARVIS Bernard V50 28.10.44, :
24HrT - 205.990km
JEFFERIES Robert U20 4.10.79, Derby & Co :
800 - 1:54.0
JEFFREY Marcus U15 7.01.84, Shaftesbury B :
200 - 23.33w/23.88
JEMI-ALADE Michael 13.10.64, City of Edin :
SP - 13.69, DT - 48.13 (52.38-87)
JENKINS Christopher U17 2.03.82, Liv H :
LJ - 6.69, OctY - 4676
JENKINS William 13.07.71, Inverclyde :
5k - 14:27.82,
JENNER Andrew U15 2.02.84, Croydon :
800 - 2:04.3
JENNINGS Gary 21.02.72, Newham & E B :
400 - 48.31 (46.64-97),
400H - 50.12 (49.82-95)
JENNINGS Neil U23 18.09.77, Mandale :
400 - 47.46
JENSON Gary 14.02.67, :
JT - 67.77 (79.54r-91/78.54-89)
JERVIS Alan Peter U15 27.07.84, C of Stoke :
PV - 3.70
JOHN Jason 17.10.71, Birchfield :
100 - 10.40w/10.56 (10.08w/10.23-94),
200 - 21.4w/21.48 (20.51w-93/20.86-95)
JOHNSON Dean 31.12.75, Sheffield :
JT - 55.03 (60.50-93)
JOHNSON Mark 7.09.64, Haringey :
PV - 4.80i/4.80 (5.26-91)
JOHNSON Richard 13.10.71, Thames Valley :
100 - 10.7/10.77 (10.6/10.74-94),
200 - 21.46
JOHNSON Scott Alan U13 4.12.85, Yeovil Oly :
100 - 12.5,
JOHNSON Tatum U23 20.10.76, Woodford Gr :
800 - 1:52.7 (1:51.0-97)
JOHNSTON Anthony 23.08.68, RAF/Irvine :
1500 - 3:49.0i (3:45.6-96)
JOHNSTON Cameron B. U17 22.10.82, Croy :
PV - 4.30
JOHNSTON Colin 10.03.73, Shaftesbury B :
3kSt - 9:17.2 (9:11.61-97)
JOHNSTONE Kerr U17 3.09.82, Falkirk :
3k - 9:01.36
JONES Andres U23 3.02.77, Cardiff :
4K - 11:29.1, 5k - 14:29.1,
10k - 30:21.4 (30:06.01-96),
10kR - 29:38
JONES Brychan V40 28.05.57, Wakefield :
PV - 4.10i (4.50-85)
JONES David U15 26.09.83, Mandale :
HTB - 43.40
JONES Egryn 1.11.71, Cardiff :
PV - 4.60 (4.90-95)
JONES Gary 15.07.72, Liverpool H :
LJ - 7.06 (7.42-95)
JONES Gary 9.07.72, Verlea :
JT - 60.88 (61.48-97)
JONES Gary 6.01.72, Windsor S & E :
100 - 10.6w?/10.85w/10.98
(10.64w/10.7/10.88-97),
200 - 21.91w (21.83w/22.0/22.22-97)
JONES Gavin U20 4.03.80, Carmarthen :
400H - 56.07
JONES Matthew U20 5.12.80, Swindon :
200 - 22.20w (21.9w/22.4/22.64-97

JONES Matthew U17 10.10.82, City of Stoke :
1500 - 4:04.14, 3k - 8:55.50
JONES Michael David 23.07.63, Belgrave :
HT - 74.02
JONES Michael U17 1.02.82, Swansea :
1.5kSt - 4:39.5
JONES Nathan U20 10.03.80, Ryde :
DTJ - 44.50
JONES Neil U20 22.10.79, Warrington :
100 - 10.8w (11.4/11.50-97)
JONES Nick 10.07.74, Tipton :
10MR - 48:56 (48:40-97),
HMar - 1:05:58, Mar - 2:20:22
JONES Paul U23 11.04.78, Colwyn Bay :
60H - 8.48i, 110H - 15.35w/15.4,
PV - 4.55, LJ - 6.95,
JONES Sean 21.03.69, Cornwall AC/Army :
HT - 55.09
JORDAN Richard V40 14.07.57, :
Mar - 2:30:41
JORDAN Roger 26.05.72, Croydon :
400 - 47.5
JOSEPH Darren U23 10.04.78, Birchfield :
HJ - 2.05 (2.15i/2.10-96)
JOSEPH Rafer Ernest Lewis 21.07.68,
Dacorum & Tring : 60H - 8.45i (8.24i-94),
110H - 14.98w/15.04 (14.7-94/14.89-97),
PV - 4.80 (4.81-94), SP - 14.38 (14.68i-94),
DT - 48.64 (52.00-96), HT - 49.41,
JT - 56.22 (59.92-94), Dec - 7447 (7663-94)
JOUSIFFE Warren U23 27.05.77, Hounslow :
PV - 4.50 (4.70-96)
JOYCE Colin U17 21.10.81, Braintree :
400 - 50.46, 800 - 1:57.56
JOYCE Daniel 9.09.74, Thames Valley :
100 - 10.35w/10.43 (10.22w-97), 200 - 21.14
JUBB Michael 20.06.70, Derby & Co :
3kSt - 8:58.00 (8:50.37-96)
JUDGE Stuart 29.11.73, Peterborough :
HJ - 2.00 (2.00-94)

KANEEN Peter 12.07.61, Manx H :
10kW - 48:46.19, 50kW - 4:55:36
KANGUDI Joel U13, Shaftesbury Barnet :
100 - 12.48w
KAPADIA Kunal U15 30.09.83, Enfield :
JTB - 50.60
KARAGOUNIS Leon 15.10.75, Notts :
JT - 55.40
KARGBO Yassin U13, London Schools :
HJ - 1.60
KAY Richard U20, Morpeth :
3kSt - 9:55.1
KEENAN Scott U20 31.07.81, Ayr Seaforth :
400 - 48.58
KEETON Michael U23 14.12.76, Notts :
TJ - 14.78
KEITA Francis 23.07.70, Woodford Gr/SLE :
100 - 10.8w (10.5-92/10.61w/10.64-93)
KEITH Andrew 25.12.71, Hereford :
800 - 1:52.24 (1:47.56-92),
1500 - 3:45.7 (3:39.06-93),
1M - 3:58.80i (3:56.29i-94/3:57.96-95),
3k - 8:02.08i (7:49.83i-94/7:54.37-95)
KELLY Craig U15 20.03.84, Wirral :
800 - 2:05.28

KEMP Michael U20 23.12.79, Leics WC :
3kW - 12:41.6, 5kW - 21:53.0,
5kWR - 21:36, 10kW - 44:53.0,
10kWR - 43:53 (43:28-97),
20kW - 1:35:16 (1:33:45-97)
KENNARD Andrew 2.01.66, Walton :
400H - 53.8/54.60 (53.1-95/53.58-90)
KENNEDY Troy 17.08.73, Scunthorpe :
Dec - 5159
KEOGH Nigel 18.07.67, Blackheath/IRE :
400H - 53.75 (52.89-91)
KERR Eric 9.12.64, Luton :
HT - 47.98 (54.58-95)
KERR Glen 27.10.74, Bedford & County :
HT - 58.26 (58.38-96)
KERR Hugh U23 4.01.76, Har/Ayr Seaforth :
400 - 48.5/48.65 (47.69i/47.75-95)
KERR John V45 1.06.49, Steel City :
Mar - 2:31:24
KERR Marlon U20 3.04.81, Belgrave :
LJ - 7.14w/6.94
KERRY Rob U20 20.03.80, Coventry Godiva :
100 - 10.97w (11.5-96)
KESKA Karl 7.05.72, Birchfield/Oregon Univ. :
1500 - 3:47.63 (3:42.71-96),
3k - 7:50.04, 5k - 13:26.37
KHAN Kamran U15 2.10.83, Trafford :
HTB - 48.77
KIDD Derek U20 12.03.79, Larkhall :
HJ - 1.95i/1.95
KIDGER Joel U20 16.03.80, Crawley :
2kSt - 6:11.56, 3kSt - 9:49.0
KIDNER Ross David U20 12.09.80, T V H :
DTJ - 41.69, HT - 53.66, HTJ - 59.90
KILLEN Neal A. 10.04.59, Aldershot Serv/Army :
Dec - 5573 (7011w-87/6944-85)
KILLICK Roger U23 20.11.76, Banbury :
JT - 58.33
KING Allan V40 3.12.56, Roadhogs :
10kW - 46:17.72 (43:37.9-80),
20kW - 1:35:13 (1:28:30-85), 30kW - 2:30.25,
50kW - 4:22:33 (4:13:25-83)
KING Daniel U17 30.05.83, Colchester H :
3kW - 14:46.7
KING Dominic U17 30.05.83, Colchester H :
3kW - 14:18.7, 5kW - 24:56.92
KING Edward 26.11.75, Sale :
800 - 1:48.51 (1:48.22-97), 1500 - 3:46.37
KING John Stewart 13.02.63, Haringey :
LJ - 7.05 (7.94w-86/7.91-87)
KING Richard U17 5.04.82, Holmfirth :
1500 - 3:59.39
KING Shane 8.02.74, Kendal :
400 - 48.2 (48.80-96)
KING S., SGA (Prof) :
SP - 13.90
KINGMAN Robert 21.02.73, N & E B/RAF :
PV - 4.60 (5.02-94)
KINGSNORTH Tom U20 15.10.79, Wx & Bath :
2kSt - 5:55.39, 3kSt - 9:25.29
KINGWELL Jason, Verlea :
HT - 46.17 (48.38-97)
KINSELLA Paul 8.10.63, Cheltenham :
Mar - 2:32:40
KINSON Simon 3.12.70, Leamington :
Mar - 2:27:00 (2:25:17-95)
KIRBY Ross U17 16.12.81, GEC :
400HY - 57.4/58.23

KIRK Neil U23 14.09.78, GEC :
800 - 1:49.57
KITNEY Timothy J. U20 26.04.80, Belgrave :
JT - 68.08
KLOIBER Matthew 22.11.71, Belgrave :
400 - 48.6 (48.21-97),
800 - 1:52.21 (1:49.56-97)
KNELLER Steven 9.11.71, Richmond & T :
800 - 1:52.1
KNIGHT Andrew G. 26.10.68, Cambridge H :
800 - 1:50.8 (1:48.38-94)
KNIGHT Christopher Adam 3.01.69, GEC :
5k - 14:37.4, 3kSt - 9:11.0 (9:01.58-89)
KNOWLES Bradley U23 17.11.76, Birchfield :
HJ - 1.95 (2.05i-95/2.03-93)
KNOWLES Richard 12.11.75, Birchfield :
400 - 46.61 (45.84-97)
KNOX-HOOK Timothy U20 17.12.80, Enfield :
400H - 56.3, HJ - 2.05
KORJIE Haroun 17.02.72, Belgrave/SLE :
60 - 6.8i (6.77i-93),
100 - 10.5w/10.58w/10.66 (10.3-96/10.46-94)
KRUGER Alexander Eaton 18.11.63, Border :
110H - 15.28w (14.76-95),
HJ - 2.02 (2.20-88),
PV - 4.60 (4.90i/4.90-95),
SP - 13.64 (14.79i-95/14.76-94),
DT - 44.00 (45.46-96),
Dec - 7052w (8131-95)
KRUSZEWSKI Andrew P. 7.04.59, Haringey :
SP - 13.80 (15.21-90),
DT - 46.70 (51.26-92)
KUIPER Anthony U20 25.10.79, Liv.Pemb Seft :
HJ - 2.00 (2.05i-97/2.03-96)

L ADEJO Du'aine Thorne 14.02.71, Bel :
100 - 10.28w/10.45,
200 - 21.8 (20.96-93), 300 - 33.20 (32.73-94),
400 - 46.12 (44.66-96), 110H - 14.6/14.63,
HJ - 2.04, LJ - 7.34w/7.16, SP - 14.03,
DT - 41.64, Dec - 7635w/7633
LAING David 1.01.66, Ipswich Joggers :
Mar - 2:32:19 (2:31:29-96)
LAING Robert Howard 30.07.66, Liverpool H :
110H - 15.4w/15.6
(14.7w/14.8/14.82w-91/14.90-92),
PV - 4.40 (4.60-88), JT - 58.58 (67.48-87)
LAINSON Richard U17 5.11.81, Isle of Wight :
JT - 57.89, JTY - 64.32
LALLEY Terry V45 12.11.49, Cardiff :
HT - 48.73 (49.18-90)
LAMBERT Christopher U20 6.04.81, Belgrave :
100 - 10.52w/10.61, 200 - 21.38w/21.56
LAMBERT Rupert 26.06.74, Bedford & Co :
100 - 10.8
LAMMIE Graeme U17 3.10.81, Perth :
400H - 58.1, 400HY - 54.85
LAMONT James U17 25.05.82, Pitreavie :
PV - 3.80
LANDON Marc U17 9.11.81, Corby :
HTY - 56.26
LANE Nathaniel U23 10.04.76, Cardiff/
Oklahoma St Un : 3k - 8:18.98i,
5k - 14:29.46, 10k - 30:13.15
LANG Tim 8.12.73, Wigan/Manchester Univ :
400H - 55.94 (55.3/55.53-97)
LANGLEY Steven U15 16.12.83, Scunthorpe :
100 - 11.37w (13.4-97), 200 - 23.12w/23.64

LASHORE Akinola 28.03.73, Blackheath :
  60 - 6.77i, 100 - 10.4/10.46 (10.44-97),
  200 - 20.99 (20.99-97)
LASKEY Samuel U20 28.05.80, Exeter :
  DecJ - 5389 (5662-97)
LATHAM Mark U23 13.01.76, City of Stoke :
  HJ - 2.12i/2.10 (2.11-94)
LAU Jordon U15 23.09.83, Chelmsford :
  100 - 11.4w, LJ - 6.68w/6.54
LAUGHLIN Dale 28.12.66, Chelmsford :
  5k - 14:18.2 (13:43.29-91), 10MR - 48:41
LAVENDER Tom U17 7.12.81, Morpeth :
  400 - 50.13
LAWRENCE Kevin U17 28.12.81, Enfield :
  PV - 3.60
LAWRENCE Mark 26.01.71, Notts AC :
  LJ - 6.96 (7.33-93), TJ - 14.18 (14.52-93)
LAWS Oliver U20 18.03.80, Telford :
  5k - 14:51.60
LAWSON Matthew 22.07.71, Highgate H :
  800 - 1:52.8
LAWTON Christopher 6.01.73, Team Solent :
  400 - 48.6 (48.91-97)
LAWTON Ian U17 13.12.81, Liverpool H :
  1500 - 4:07.25
LEADER Steven 24.11.66, Enfield :
  110H - 15.6w (15.2-89/15.46-94),
  PV - 4.40 (4.90-90)
LEAMAN Timothy U17 23.11.82, Exeter :
  DTY - 43.04
LEASE Gareth U23 14.11.77, Bristol :
  PV - 4.40i/4.35
LEAVER James Robert 15.09.75, T Solent :
  HJ - 1.95 (2.11-95), LJ - 7.39w/7.21,
  TJ - 15.60w/15.27db??/15.18
LEDGERWOOD Daniel U17 24.03.83, AF&D :
  3k - 8:59.3
LEE Kirk U15 17.07.84, :
  800 - 2:05.0
LEES Simon U20 19.11.79, Solihull & S H :
  400 - 49.2, 800 - 1:47.69, 1500 - 3:47.82
LEGGATE Daniel 5.10.74, Harrow/Camb Un :
  5k - 14:27.7 (14:26.2-96)
LEIGH Anthony 27.12.65, City of Stoke :
  60 - 6.84i, 100 - 10.96 (10.71w/10.74-97),
  200 - 21.7 (21.60-97)
LEIGH Michael U23 14.12.77, Rotherham :
  HJ - 2.05
LEKKAS P., Aberdeen :
  DT - 42.17
LEMON Matthew U20 6.02.80, GEC :
  2kSt - 6:08.35, 3kSt - 9:47.4
LENDON Jason 17.03.75, Havering :
  3kSt - 9:11.5
LESLIE Dean U23 9.01.78, Crawley :
  110H - 15.6 (15.96-96)
LETHBRIDGE Daniel U20 1.04.81, Crawley :
  DTJ - 43.27
LEVETT Christopher U15 30.11.83, Birchfield :
  SPB - 14.48, DTB - 43.07
LEWIS Andrew 9.03.68, Hounslow/Brunel Un :
  100 - 10.84w (10.80w/10.89-94),
  LJ - 7.30 (7.54-97), SP - 14.10
LEWIS Benjamin U20 6.03.81, Birchfield :
  200 - 21.35w/21.7/21.89 (21.51-97)
LEWIS David U15 27.01.84, Mansfield :
  400 - 53.6, 800 - 2:03.5

LEWIS Gareth U23 5.10.78, Blackheath :
  400H - 55.3 (54.5/54.96-97)
LEWIS James 8.03.69, Swansea/IRE :
  HMar - 1:05:32 (1:04:11-94)
LEWIS Junior 19.03.66, Verlea :
  TJ - 14.10 (14.84-96)
LEWIS Leighton U17 10.09.81, Llanelli :
  400HY - 56.5
LEWIS Marlon U15 7.09.83, Rowheath :
  LJ - 6.06
LEWIS Matthew 11.11.75, Sale/Loughbro :
  100 - 10.8w (10.91-97), 200 - 21.72w/21.94,
  400 - 47.43
LEWIS Matthew U17 15.10.82, Wx & Bath :
  PV - 3.70
LEWIS Robert U23 2.09.78, Bedford & Co :
  400H - 53.9/54.15 (53.79-97)
LEWIS Shane 22.08.72, Swansea :
  JT - 70.90
LEWIS Shaun 5.01.73, :
  TJ - 14.39
LEWIS Steven U13 20.05.86, City of Stoke :
  PV - 2.60
LEWIS-FRANCIS Mark U17 4.09.82, Bir :
  60 - 6.79i, 100 - 10.36w/10.49,
  200 - 21.8/21.98
LIDDLE Jonathan U17 13.09.81, Wells :
  HJ - 1.91 (1.96-97)
LIGHTFOOT Tim U17 1.05.83, Reading :
  LJ - 6.59
LINDLEY Ian V40 3.12.55, Bingley :
  SP - 14.04 (17.87i/17.58-81)
LINDSEY Christopher U20 11.02.79,
  Wirral/Birmingham Univ. : 5k - 14:44.41
LING Christopher 5.08.63, Stowmarket :
  Mar - 2:30:16
LINNETT Ross U20 6.10.79, Gateshead :
  100 - 10.8/10.91w/10.97, 200 - 21.9/22.00
LINSELL Steven W. 13.10.63, Leeds :
  HJ - 1.96 (2.00-97)
LINSKEY Christian U20 14.06.80, S B :
  PV - 5.20
LIPMAN Paul U13 2.09.85, Dacorum & Tring :
  800 - 2:16.6
LITTLE David U20 28.02.81, Border :
  HT - 47.22, HTJ - 55.45
LITTLE John V45 14.04.53, Border :
  DT - 43.16 (43.70-95),
  HT - 46.18 (47.06-89)
LITTLE Matthew U17 22.07.83, Bedford & Co :
  HJ - 1.92
LIVESEY Christopher U20 8.08.80, Preston :
  800 - 1:52.6, 1500 - 3:46.5,
  3k - 8:19.5
LIVINGSTON ¶ Jason Christopher 17.03.71,
  Shaftesbury B : 60 - 6.66i (6.51i-92),
  100 - 10.24w/10.31 (10.09-92),
  200 - 21.97 (21.01-92)
LIVINGSTONE Stuart U20 29.08.79, C of Edin :
  HJ - 2.06 (2.08i-97)
LLEWELLYN Kevin U15, Preseli :
  DTB - 39.62
LLOYD Joseph 9.04.73, Swansea :
  400 - 48.5/48.77 (47.76-96)
LLOYD Mark 28.09.71, W Cheshire :
  200 - 21.6/21.87
LLOYD Martin Andrew U20 18.06.80, Bexley :
  HJ - 2.15i/2.15

350

LLOYD Robert U17 15.04.83, Peterborough :
  100HY - 14.10w/14.2
LLOYD Steven J. 20.03.74, Border :
  DT - 40.37 (43.94-94)
LOBB Huw U23 29.08.76, Bedford & County/
  Cambridge University : 3kSt - 9:15.0
LOBO Jason 18.09.69, Belgrave :
  800 - 1:47.48 (1:47.29-97),
  1k - 2:20.9 (2:20.45-90),
  1500 - 3:48.90 (3:44.14-93)
LOCK Benjamin U20 23.05.81, Morpeth :
  DecJ - 5377
LOCKE Darren U17 16.10.81, Scot Borders :
  HJ - 1.90i
LOCKER David Alan 28.03.75, City of Stoke :
  800 - 1:49.20, 1500 - 3:50.59 (3:47.8-96),
  1M - 4:08.70i (4:07.76i-96)
LOCKWOOD David U17 24.11.81, Holmfirth :
  400HY - 57.13
LOMAS Christopher U17 22.04.82, Luton :
  100HY - 13.83, 400HY - 56.16
LOMAS Richard U17 5.09.81, Rotherham :
  1.5kSt - 4:32.7
LONERGAN Sean 24.01.73, Border/IRE :
  TJ - 14.64
LONG Nicholas U20 1.02.79, Liverpool H :
  100 - 10.93 (10.83w-96/10.92-97)
LOUGH Gareth James 6.07.70, N & E B :
  1500 - 3:40.8 (3:34.76-95),
  1M - 3:57.58 (3:55.91-95),
  3k - 8:16.4 (7:49.45-95)
LOUGHRAN Stuart U23 19.02.76, Swansea :
  JT - 68.91
LOVELL Manuel U17 10.04.82, Phoenix :
  1.5kSt - 4:29.24
LOVETT Anthony U17 20.09.82, Enfield :
  JTY - 58.34
LOVETT David U23 13.09.78, Southampton C :
  SP - 13.87, SPJ - 14.08o (13.17-97),
  DT - 44.70, DTJ - 46.67o (45.86-97)
LOW Christopher U20 24.04.80, S B/Arbroath :
  60H - 8.28i, 100HY - 13.6odt (13.46-96),
  110HJ - 14.45, 110H - 15.35w/15.56 (14.96-97)
LOWE Stephen U23 10.01.76, Wakefield :
  800 - 1:52.2
LOWERY James U20 17.10.80, Cumbrian Sch :
  DecJ - 5182
LOWTHIAN Ian U20 10.10.80, Liverpool H :
  200 - 22.0 (22.76-97), 400 - 47.9/48.83
LUCAS John, :
  24HrT - 200.432km
LUNDMAN Jonathan U17 7.12.81, Blackheath :
  JTY - 59.94
LUSTGARTEN Anders 9.02.74, Thames V H :
  400 - 47.52 (46.93-96)
LYNCH Andrew 28.06.74, Thames Valley :
  HJ - 2.10 (2.18-95)
LYNCH Lawrence 1.11.67, Haringey :
  400 - 48.3 (47.02-93),
  400H - 51.2/51.28 (50.05-96)

M ACDONALD Andrew U17 19.05.83,
  Barnsley : PV - 3.90
MACDONALD Mark W. 2.12.59, SGA (Prof) :
  SP - 13.46 (15.98-90)
MACEY Dean U23 12.12.77, Harrow :
  SP - 14.46 (14.73-97), DT - 45.74

MACGEE William 9.06.68, Windsor S & E :
  100 - 10.92, 200 - 22.14w/22.15
MACINTOSH Robin U15 2.03.85, C of Edin :
  800 - 2:05.73
MACKAIL-SMITH Craig U15 2.12.83, Harrow :
  PV - 3.00
MACKENZIE Colin Thomas 30.06.63, N & E B :
  JT - 78.73 (82.60r-91/82.38-93)
MACKIE Ian 27.02.75, Pitreavie :
  100 - 10.00w/10.31 (10.17-96)
MACKINTOSH Leslie U20 25.02.81, Liv H :
  HT - 46.42, HTJ - 51.39
MACLEAN Angus U20 20.09.80, Team Solent :
  1500 - 3:53.8, 3k - 8:36.48
MACLEAN-DALEY Kingslee U15 1.12.83,
  London Schools : 100 - 11.46w
MACPHERSON Gavin U23 17.09.77, Blackpool :
  800 - 1:52.9 (1:52.0-97)
MADDEN Benjamin U17 4.10.82, Cann & St :
  PV - 3.70
MADDEN Michael J. 13.09.65, Newquay & P :
  HT - 53.54 (55.92-93)
MADDOCKS Christopher Lloyd V40 28.03.57,
  Plymouth C W : 3kW - 13:06.4 (11:45.1-87),
  20kW - 1:29:40 (1:22:12-92)
MADEIRA-COLE Charles H. U23 29.11.77,
  N & E B/Sheffield Univ : 100 - 10.88w,
  LJ - 6.99w (7.01-95), TJ - 15.82i/15.81w/15.79
MAGEE Greg U23 27.09.78, Scottish Borders :
  JT - 55.34
MAGNALL Andrew M. 1.03.62, Shaftesbury B :
  5k - 14:29.0
MAHONEY Oliver U15 21.10.83, Wirral :
  PV - 3.50
MAISEY Steven 11.05.74, Verlea :
  LJ - 6.98w, Dec - 5913
MAITLAND Peter 21.01.73, Newham & E B :
  100 - 10.60w/10.62 (10.42-95),
  200 - 21.75 (20.96-94),
  400 - 48.11 (47.2/47.29-95)
MAJOR Adam U17 2.11.81, Elgin :
  SPJ - 13.92, SPY - 16.80,
  DTJ - 47.03, DTY - 47.55, HTY - 47.70
MALCOLM Anthony U23 15.02.76, Cardiff/
  Loughbro : LJ - 7.21 (7.32w-96/7.21-95)
MALCOLM Christian Sean U20 3.06.79, Card:
  60 - 6.77i (6.67i-97),
  100 - 10.10w/10.12, 200 - 20.29
MALEY Gavin U23 19.05.78, Havering :
  800 - 1:52.5
MALINS Duncan U23 12.06.78, Crawley/
  Loughbro : 100 - 10.99, 60H - 8.12i,
  110H - 14.30, LJ - 7.09
MALLOCH Ewan U23 4.08.76, Cambridge Un :
  3kSt - 9:12.66
MALLOWS Andrew U17 18.01.82, Notts :
  1500 - 4:05.1
MANDY Mark 19.11.72, Birchfield/IRE :
  HJ - 2.23i/2.15 (2.26i-97/2.25-95)
MANN Philip U13 25.10.85, Barnsley :
  JTC - 40.60
MANNING Simon Paul U15 9.08.84, Leeds :
  800 - 2:05.85
MAPP Nick U20 18.03.79, Oadby & Wigston :
  3k - 8:29.92, 5k - 15:07.00
MARAR Leith 7.11.68, Belgrave :
  DT - 54.91 (55.68-96)

MARK Alastair U17 8.12.81, Northampton :
100 - 10.9w/11.0/11.13 (11.04-97),
200 - 22.2 (22.69-97)
MARKHAM Gregory U23 28.11.78, Rotherham :
JT - 60.86
MARRIOTT Adrian 24.09.72, Hercules Wimb :
3k - 8:16.62, 5k - 14:14.5, 10k - 30:19.66
MARRIOTT S. U15, Salford :
800 - 2:04.0
MARSDEN Barry 11.06.64, Wycombe :
110H - 15.3 (15.3/15.58-97)
MARSDEN Dwayne 25.10.73, Queens Park :
JT - 64.38
MARSHALL ¶ Guy 24.09.71, Birchfield :
SP - 16.65
MARSHALL Richard U15 24.09.83, Enfield :
TJ - 12.35
MARSTON Nathan 21.02.75, Cambridge Univ/
Sheffield : HT - 48.14
MARTIN Lee 21.05.64, Bury :
Mar - 2:31:34
MASON Chris U15 6.04.84, Mandale :
HTB - 51.30
MASON I. U15, Sussex Sch :
SPB - 13.45
MASON James U15 7.10.83, Southend :
PV - 3.35
MASSEY Ian U23 9.09.76, Liverpool H :
HJ - 2.05 (2.10-95)
MATARAZZO Antonio U20 27.03.80, Chelt :
100 - 10.9 (10.9-95/11.00w/11.13-97)
MATHIESON Duncan Graham 8.03.69, Aberdn :
60H - 8.41i (8.32i-97), DT - 41.00,
110H - 15.49w (14.81w-93/14.9-90/14.95-91),
HJ - 1.98i (2.07-90), LJ - 7.12i (7.62-95)
MATTHEWS Gary M. 9.04.60, East Cheshire :
Mar - 2:32:36 (2:22:32-92)
MATTHEWS Lawrence 11.08.65, Salf/Ox Un :
10MR - 49:18 (48:57-94),
HMar - 1:06:14 (1:03:45-93)
MATTHEWS Owen U17 17.10.81, Luton :
JTY - 54.00, OctY - 4635
MAUNDER-TAYLOR William U17 27.04.82,
Hertford & Ware : JTY - 57.41
MAWEMA Tennyson U17 12.12.82, Oxford C :
100HY - 14.1
MAYCOCK Robert U20 21.02.81, Sale :
1500 - 3:53.62, 5k - 15:07.42
MAYO James 24.02.75, Cannock & Stafford :
800 - 1:50.02 (1:48.2-96)
MAYO Thomas U23 2.05.77, Cannock & Staff :
800 - 1:51.44, 1500 - 3:41.2, 1M - 4:00.02
MAYOCK John Paul 26.10.70, Cannock & Staff :
800 - 1:47.8, 1500 - 3:32.82 (3:31.86-97),
1M - 3:51.99 (3:50.32-96),
3k - 7:47.43i (7:43.31i-97/7:47.28-95),
2M - 8:54.16 (8:32.54-91)
MAZOKA A. U17, :
LJ - 6.55
MCBURNEY Paul 14.03.72, N & E B/Lisburn :
200 - 21.20 (20.76w-97/20.81-94),
400 - 45.90 (45.85-97)
MCCALL Josie U15 12.11.83, Kilbarchan :
HJ - 1.77
MCCALLA Dave, Coventry Godiva/RAF :
TJ - 14.85
MCCALLUM Jonathan 19.11.75, Croydon :
800 - 1:51.7, 1500 - 3:43.82

MCCANN Owen U20 15.07.81, Annadale Str :
SPY - 14.52o
MCCARTHY Craig U20 13.10.80, Middlesbro & C :
110HJ - 15.1/15.12
MCCASH Lee U17 22.10.81, Pendle :
1500 - 3:57.5, 3k - 8:45.11
MCCONVILLE Brendan U20 3.01.79, N Down :
HJ - 2.02, PV - 4.15,
Dec - 6241, DecJ - 6263
MCCORMICK Nick U17 11.09.81, Tynedale :
800 - 1:57.1, 1500 - 3:58.24
MCCOURT Steven 6.05.71, Thames Valley :
200 - 21.7 (21.03w-94/21.28-95)
MCCOY Marc U20 5.06.81, Doncaster :
JT - 54.53
MCCRACKEN Gary U23 23.01.78, Border :
110H - 14.8w/15.14
MCCULLAGH Andrew U15 10.09.83, Scun :
100 - 11.34
MCDADE Jason U20 3.04.80, Ipswich :
110HJ - 14.26, 110H - 15.09, HJ - 2.15,
LJ - 6.97, Dec - 6168, DecJ - 6630
*MCDERMOTT Dylan 1.12.70, Epsom & E/IRE :
PV - 4.60 (4.91i-96/4.85-90)*
MCDONALD Denzil 11.10.65, Newham & E B :
SP - 15.80 (16.10-94), DT - 51.84 (55.04-95)
MCDONALD Jamie U20 11.06.79, Central :
3kSt - 9:50.6
MCDONALD Michael John Joseph 24.08.65,
Ballymena & Antrim/Border/Queen's Univ :
TJ - 15.21 (15.78-94)
MCDONALD Richard U20 11.01.80, S B :
400 - 48.84i/49.7 (49.3/49.53-96),
110HJ - 14.98, 400H - 52.13
MCDONNELL Stephen U20 24.07.80, Cuch :
110HJ - 15.14, 110H - 15.45w,
400H - 56.32, Dec - 5026, DecJ - 5283
MCEVOY Stephen 23.05.63, Met. Police :
HT - 54.97 (57.14-96)
MCEWAN David U13 29.06.86, N Devon :
LJ - 5.22
MCGEOCH Michael I. V40 15.08.55, Les Cr :
Mar - 2:32:30 (2:17:58-83)
MCGOWAN Liam U15 27.01.84, Gloucester :
400 - 53.54
MCGURK Ian 17.10.71, City of Edinburgh :
200 - 21.99, 400 - 47.19
MCILFATRICK Philip V40 5.02.54, Lisburn :
110H - 15.3 (14.7/14.99-84)
*MCILROY James U23 30.12.76, B & A/IRE :
800 - 1:45.32, 1500 - 3:46.00, 1M - 3:59.48*
MCILWHAM John 29.02.72, Blackpool :
400H - 53.3/53.74
MCINDOE Aaron U17 15.05.82, Ayr Seaforth :
800 - 1:55.21, 1500 - 4:07.5
MCINNES Duncan U23 1.05.78, Bord/E Kilb :
HJ - 2.00i/2.00 (2.05i/2.05-97)
MCINTYRE Liam U23 22.09.76, C of Edin :
DT - 41.65 (45.50-96)
MCINTYRE Mark 14.10.70, Shaftesbury B :
60 - 6.85i (6.79i-97),
100 - 10.70w/10.79 (10.3w-95/10.60-91),
200 - 22.19i
(21.3w-90/21.4-91/21.50w-95/21.63-91)
MCKAY Kevin John 9.02.69, Sale :
800 - 1:48.5 (1:45.35-92), 1k - 2:21.8 (2:17.63-89),
1500 - 3:37.22 (3:34.59-97),
1M - 3:58.52 (3:53.64-94)

352

MCKEE Paul U23 15.10.77, Liverpool H :
100 - 10.7dt, 400 - 47.92
MCKEEVER Kieran U15 16.08.84, Notts :
TJ - 12.03
MCKENZIE David Colin 3.09.70, Shaftesbury B :
400 - 48.9 (45.47-94)
MCKEOWN Kenneth U17 6.03.82, Ayr Seaforth :
HJ - 2.11i/2.11
MCKERNAN Michael U23 28.11.78, Cov G :
TJ - 15.25w/15.18w?
MCKINSON Kevin U20 6.09.80, Cambridge H :
HJ - 2.10
MCLAUGHLAN Nathan U15 6.10.84, Inverness :
LJ - 5.16
MCLEAN Colm U20 7.06.80, Cuchulainn/IRE :
800 - 1:49.64, 1500 - 3:43.46
MCLEAN-FOREMAN Alasdair U17 10.11.81
Bel : 800 - 1:55.6, 1500 - 4:02.22
MCLELLAN Neil U23 10.09.78, Steven & NH :
JT - 59.32 (60.44-97)
MCLENNAN Stephen U23 17.11.78, Houns :
PV - 4.60i/4.20 (4.70-96)
MCMASTER Colin U20 15.01.80, Law & Dist/
Shaftesbury B : HJ - 2.14i/2.05 (2.15-97)
MCMILLAN Stewart 12.09.69, Sale/Pitreavie :
JT - 59.89 (64.02-96)
MCMULLAN Iain U23 15.06.78, Lisb/Loughbro :
SP - 15.32
MCMULLAN Paul U20 11.07.81, B & A :
400HY - 57.9o
MCMULLEN Carl U20 9.11.79, Warrington :
100 - 10.8w (11.34-97), 200 - 22.0,
400 - 49.1 (49.97-97),
400H - 54.5/55.37 (54.3-97), LJ - 7.08
MCNALLY Sam U13 26.03.86, Belgrave :
2kW - 10:57.74
MCNICHOLAS Alan 10.12.74, Bedford & Co :
HT - 57.83 (58.24-96)
MCPHAIL Brian U17 6.05.82, Inverness :
400H - 58.4, 400HY - 58.05
MCRAE Leon U20 3.11.80, Wessex & Bath :
200 - 22.11w (23.5-96), 400H - 55.0/55.70
MELLOR Dean Ashley 25.11.71, Rotherham :
PV - 5.20 (5.30-95)
MELLUISH Christopher Jeremy V50 15.07.44,
Cambridge H : HT - 47.57 (62.10-74)
MERRICK Essop 24.05.74, Woodford Green :
LJ - 7.59w/7.37
METCALFE Scott U20 8.10.79, Northampton :
DTJ - 44.59
MIDDLETON Barry 10.03.75, Sale/Aberdeen :
400 - 48.9/49.09 (47.44i-97/48.3-96/48.48-97),
400H - 52.47 (51.18-96)
MIELE Felice U17 24.11.81, Haringey :
SPY - 15.19, DTY - 53.98
MILES David 16.11.65, Gateshead/Birchfield :
3k - 8:08.92 (8:02.03-94),
5k - 14:10.21 (13:46.66-94), 10k - 29:43.14,
10kR - 29:39 (29:00sh-96),
HMar - 1:05:40 (1:05:04-92)
MILES Paul U20 14.09.80, Birchfield :
PV - 4.25
MILFORD Shaun 13.07.63, Newquay & Par :
Mar - 2:26:48 (2:25:54-97)
MILLAR Barry U20 1.04.81, Inverclyde :
HJ - 1.95i (1.96-97)
MILLER James U20 29.03.80, Chesterfield :
100 - 10.7w/10.79

MILLER Lee U15 20.01.84, Hounslow :
100 - 11.44w/11.60
MILLER Mark 10.11.71, Enfield :
HT - 50.09 (57.12-97)
MILLER Patrick 21.02.67, Border :
3kSt - 9:16.67 (8:57.47-96)
MILLER Richard 18.12.64, AF&D :
10kW - 47:27.42
MILLER Tim U23 2.12.77, Torf/Univ. of Wales :
60 - 6.96i, 100 - 10.7w/10.79w (11.19-96),
200 - 22.0 (22.22-96)
MILLS Chris 12.11.75, Winchester :
PV - 4.40
MILLS Joseph 9.07.72, Blackheath :
800 - 1:50.2, 1500 - 3:45.4
MILOVSOROV Nick 16.03.64, Aberdeen :
10k - 31:18.8, Mar - 2:30:58
MINNIKIN Stephen 4.01.72, Doncaster :
HT - 60.89 (62.20-96)
MITCHELL Andrew U23 30.07.76, Kilb/Bor :
400 - 47.51
MITCHELL Ian U23 10.03.76, Longwood :
3k - 8:17.3, 5k - 14:33.9
MITCHELL Robert U20 14.09.80, Dac & Tring :
HJ - 2.07
MITCHINSON David U23 4.09.78, Swindon/
Loughbro : 3kSt - 9:14.83 (9:10.65-97)
MOGFORD Andrew U15 29.09.83, Preseli :
SPB - 13.44
MOHAMMED Abdusalam U20 20.03.79, Houn :
5k - 15:07.3 (15:06.8-97), 3kSt - 9:49.5
MOLE Adam 31.08.75, Hounslow :
800 - 1:51.84i (1:51.43-96)
MONCKTON Ian James U17 14.07.83,
Wolves & B : 100 - 11.0w/11.40
MONDS John U20 24.03.80, Wigan :
110HJ - 14.46w/14.8/14.81, 110H - 15.4/15.54
MONEY Daniel U23 7.10.76, Sale :
60 - 6.72i,
100 - 10.18w/10.65 (10.16w/10.32-97),
200 - 21.33 (20.75w/20.92-97)
MONTGOMERY Brian Eliot 19.07.74,
Club NW, CAN : 3kSt - 8:43.71
MOORE Colin 25.11.60, Bingley :
5k - 14:29.8 (13:33.95-90),
10kR - 29:41 (28:17-85),
HMar - 1:05:30 (1:02:06sh-93/1:02:22-85)
MOORE Daniel U17 8.11.81, Blackheath :
1.5kSt - 4:19.54
MOORE Jonathan U15 31.05.84, Birchfield :
LJ - 6.55
MOORE Louis U13, City of Stoke :
LJ - 5.24
MOORE Stephen R. V50 17.12.47, Herts & W :
Mar - 2:32:32 (2:27:30-90),
100kR - 6:55:48 (6:43:52-92)
MOORHOUSE Julian 13.11.71, Birchfield :
1500 - 3:46.5 (3:45.4-96),
1M - 4:09.24, 3k - 7:59.44, 5k - 13:48.5
MORBY Paul James U20 15.01.79, Sol & S H :
800 - 1:53.2 (1:52.5-97), 1500 - 3:47.36
MORELAND John R. V40 13.09.58, Rugby :
DT - 46.99 (51.76-95)
MORGAN Derek N. 4.04.69, Bristol :
100 - 10.8 (10.6-93/10.77-89)
MORGAN Gareth U17, Telford :
LJ - 6.54

MORGAN Mark 19.08.72, Swansea :
1500 - 3:48.1, 5k - 14:27.4 (13:59.46-94),
10kR - 29:40 (29:22-96), 10MR - 49:06
MORGAN Nathan U23 30.06.78, Birchfield :
100 - 10.49w (11.00-95),
200 - 21.4, LJ - 8.11
MORGAN Paul 5.07.65, Woodford Green :
JT - 60.86 (70.12-87)
MORGAN-LEE Andrew 1.03.69, Woodford Gr :
5k - 14:33.0 (14:19.5-95),
3kSt - 8:53.81 (8:50.40-96)
MORLEY Andrew, Exeter/Exeter Univ :
LJ - 7.03w/6.95
MORLEY Roger U23 20.09.77, Lincoln Well :
800 - 1:53.0 (1:52.59-95)
MORRIS Edward U20 3.03.80, Birchfield :
DecJ - 5724
MORRIS Matthew 5.04.75, Sale/Sheff Univ :
800 - 1:51.30 (1:50.5-97), 1500 - 3:51.04
MORRIS Michael 16.07.74, Chester Le Street/
Sheffield Univ : 800 - 1:50.8, 1500 - 3:47.5
MORRIS Robert U17 20.02.82, Hertford & W :
SPJ - 13.91, SPY - 16.23,
DTJ - 43.92, DTY - 51.98
MORTON Leslie V40 1.07.58, Sheffield RWC :
20kW - 1:32:53 (1:26:31un-93/1:27:10-89),
50kW - 4:17:44 (3:57:48-89)
MOSCROP Howard Wilson V40 16.12.57, Swin :
400H - 53.77 (51.4-84)
MOSES Alistair U23 5.07.78, Reigate :
1500 - 3:51.8 (3:49.74-97)
MOSS Alex 'Sandy' 21.09.72, TVH/Glas Univ :
10k - 31:06.70, 3kSt - 9:16.49-94)
MOSS Christopher U20 17.06.79, Blackheath :
800 - 1:48.43, 1500 - 3:48.3
MOULTON David U17 7.09.81, Blackheath :
400 - 50.54, 800 - 1:55.1
MOUNTFORD David U17 23.06.82, C of Stoke :
LJ - 7.27w/6.94i/6.90
MOWBRAY Philip 19.03.73, Strathclyde Univ/
C of Edin : 1500 - 3:48.99 (3:41.63-94),
3k - 7:59.97 (7:59.5-97),
5k - 14:02.41 (13:49.44-97)
MUGGERIDGE Matthew U23 1.10.76, Yate :
TJ - 14.37
MUIRHEAD James Cameron 26.01.71,
Liv H/Loughbro : SP - 13.94 (16.74-96),
DT - 44.60 (52.04-96)
MULLY Sam 4.09.64, Ilford/KEN :
Mar - 2:23:59
MULVANEY Christopher U20 25.05.81, Bord :
800 - 1:52.9, 1500 - 3:52.55
MUNDEN Craig U23 24.12.76, Bournemouth :
DT - 44.13
MUNRO Ian U15 5.09.83, Cambuslang :
800 - 2:04.34 (2:03.7-97)
MUNROE Gary 12.04.69, N & E B/RAF/CAN :
100 - 10.95, LJ - 7.27 (7.27-96)
MUNROE John 6.01.69, Thames Valley :
LJ - 7.38 (7.65i/7.64-95), TJ - 14.25 (14.38-92)
MURCH Kevin V40 11.11.58, Rugby :
JT - 68.33 (69.02-89)
MURDOCH Iain U20 10.07.80, Avonside :
3k - 8:31.22, 2kSt - 5:46.85, 3kSt - 8:58.15
MURPHY Lee 10.08.74, Bolton :
LJ - 6.90w (7.24w/7.18-92)
MURPHY Stephen U17 6.01.83, S B :
3k - 8:56.4, 1.5kSt - 4:33.8

MURRAY Thomas 18.05.61, Inverclyde :
5k - 14:35.0 (14:02.5-92),
10k - 29:46.45 (29:12.35-94),
10kR - 29:22sh/29:42 (29:09-97),
10MR - 48:38dh/49:42 (48:15dh-94),
HMar - 1:06:20 (1:05:34-92)
MURRAY William U15, Bedford & County :
JTB - 45.47
MUSSETT Adrian 14.04.72, Colchester H :
5k - 14:35.3 (14:13.7-97),
10k - 29:40.96, 10kR - 29:47, HMar - 1:06:28
MUTAI John U23 22.04.76, Brom & R/KEN :
HMar - 1:02:50 (1:02:36-97), Mar - 2:13:37
MYERS Richard U15 21.12.83, Tynedale :
80HB - 11.67w (12.5-97)
MYERS Sam U17 16.08.82, Liverpool H :
1.5kSt - 4:34.4
MYERSCOUGH Carl Andrew U20 21.10.79,
Blackpool : SP - 19.46, SPJ - 21.03,
DT - 60.19, DTJ - 61.81

NAGEL Gary Roderick 4.06.62, Gate :
5k - 14:33.3 (13:51.5-90)
NAISMITH David U20 15.12.79, Derby & Co :
400 - 47.17 (47.11-97)
NASH Kevin U23 6.02.77, Belgrave :
3kSt - 8:56.3 (8:43.21-96)
NASH Paul U15 13.02.84, Leamington :
HTB - 44.52
NASH Richard 24.06.75, Dartford :
Dec - 5371
NASH Samuel 22.10.71, Queens Park :
LJ - 7.10w?
NAUGHTON Joe 17.10.74, Havering/IRE :
110H - 15.53, HJ - 2.03i/2.01 (2.05-97),
PV - 4.20 (4.20-97),
LJ - 7.23w/6.90i, Dec - 6996
NAYLOR Donald 5.09.71, Swansea :
3kSt - 9:03.61
NEBLETT Gavin U20 27.12.79, Blackheath :
60 - 6.93i
NEELY Ian 29.12.74, Border :
110H - 15.52w/15.68, 400H - 52.34
NEILL Steven 11.08.66, Telford/RAF :
800 - 1:52.7, 1500 - 3:46.1, 1M - 4:07.32
NEPORT Darren U24 4.09.79, Enfield :
PV - 4.20 (4.40-96)
NERURKAR Richard David 6.01.64, Bingley :
10kR - 28:58 (28:25-94),
HMar - 1:03:25 (1:01:06-96),
Mar - 2:14:02 (2:08:36-97)
NESBETH Michael U20 1.03.79, Croydon :
LJ - 6.93i (6.61-96),
TJ - 14.45 (14.80w/14.79-96)
NEWELL Elisha U20 10.06.79, Richmond & T :
60 - 6.89i, 100 - 10.7w/10.95, 200 - 21.7
NEWELL Matthew U17 20.09.81, Tamworth :
HTY - 49.48
NEWENHAM Timothy O'Brien 1.04.60,
Norwich/Loughbro : JT - 55.29 (70.30-89)
NEWMAN Lee Jon 1.05.73, Belgrave :
SP - 16.64 (18.85-96), DT - 60.43 (60.48-97)
NEWPORT Spencer John 5.10.66, Blackheath :
3k - 8:03.55 (8:00.3-96),
5k - 14:07.57 (13:49.74-96),
10k - 30:07.82 (29:23.49-95),
10kR - 29:07, 10MR - 48:30,
Mar - 2:23:27, 3kSt - 9:04.1 (8:40.87-92)

NEWTON Keith 12.12.68, Woodford Green :
TJ - 14.15
NEWTON Keith 14.03.63, Brighton :
Mar - 2:33:13
NEWTON Robert U20 10.05.81, Mansfield :
60H - 8.40i, 110HJ - 14.16,
110H - 14.40w/14.56
NICHOL Graham U17 11.01.82, Border :
800 - 1:58.0, 1500 - 4:06.45
NICHOLL David 16.09.69, Border :
HT - 56.76 (57.06-97)
NICHOLLS John S. 1.09.65, Sale :
SP - 14.62 (15.48-95)
NICHOLLS Philip U15 29.09.83, Tipton :
1500 - 4:16.47, 3k - 9:12.72
NICHOLLS Russell U17 8.03.83, Enfield :
400 - 50.62
NICHOLLS Stephen U17 1.04.83, Sol & S H :
1.5kSt - 4:37.68
NICHOLSON Martin 9.12.70, Birchfield :
110H - 14.85 (13.8/14.14-94)
NICOLSON Christian 19.09.73, T Solent/Ark :
1500 - 3:44.87, 1M - 4:04.7,
3k - 8:15.83 (8:05.0-95),
5k - 14:00.43, 3kSt - 8:55.26?/8:56.40
NIELAND Nicholas 31.01.72, Shaftesbury B :
JT - 78.68 (83.06-96)
NIMMO Thomas 9.05.71, City of Edinburgh :
400 - 48.20 (47.99-92)
NITSCH Mark U23 3.03.78, Peterborough :
400H - 55.6
NIXON William 9.02.68, Southampton RR :
10MR - 49:32, Mar - 2:25:38
NOAD Ben U23 6.05.76, Bris/Providence Un :
3k - 8:18.82i, 5k - 14:08.84
NOBLE Ian U23 2.04.77, Leeds :
PV - 4.60 (4.70-96)
NOEL Tony, Richmond & Twick'ham :
100 - 10.6/10.82, 200 - 21.7/22.20
NOLAN David 25.07.69, Belgrave :
60 - 6.97i
NOLAN David 16.05.75, Swansea/Sheff Un :
HJ - 2.05 (2.06-94)
NORMAN Andrew U17 27.01.82, Newton Abb :
100 - 11.1, 200 - 22.5 (23.42w-96)
NORMAN Anthony Josephus 5.07.63, Woking :
JT - 58.17 (68.74-87)
NORMAN Oliver 6.09.73, Thames Valley :
3kSt - 9:09.9 (9:00.74-95)
NORTH Christian I.R. 2.02.74, Bristol :
PV - 5.10dhex/4.90 (4.90-92)
NORTHROP Paul 15.01.70, Enfield :
3kSt - 9:26.2 (8:51.25-90)
NUTLEY Ben U20 14.11.79, Richmond & T :
200 - 21.8/21.94w
NUTTALL John Barry 11.01.67, Preston :
1500 - 3:46.21 (3:40.6-90)
NWAOLISE Paul 31.05.73, Croy/Teeside Univ :
60 - 6.9i, 100 - 10.73w/10.8/10.89

O'BRIEN Anthony 14.11.70, Liv H :
HMar - 1:04:50 (1:04:46-96)
O'BRIEN Barry U13 21.04.86, Lochgelly :
75HC - 12.4/12.49
O'CONNOR Tony U20, Wigan :
400 - 49.5
O'DELL Timothy 29.05.70, Woodford Green :
200 - 21.7 (21.31-95), 400 - 46.34 (46.34-95)

O'DOWD Matthew U23 13.04.76, Swindon/
Loughboro : 3k - 8:15.16 (7:55.9-97),
5k - 14:12.83 (13:44.83-97),
10kR - 29:32, HMar - 1:05:23,
3kSt - 9:13.31 (8:44.26-96)
O'KEEFE Patrick 5.03.75, City of Edin/IRE :
5k - 14:32.62
O'LEARY David U20 3.08.80, Liverpool H :
110HJ - 15.0 (14.96-97), 400H - 55.48
O'NEILL Ian 30.12.65, North Belfast :
Mar - 2:32:10 (2:28:53-97)
O'RAWE Andrew 8.09.63, Roadhogs :
3kW - 12:44.4, 10kW - 46:01.73 (45:28.35-97),
20kW - 1:34:35 (1:34:05-96)
O'RAWE James 3.02.73, Roadhogs :
3kW - 12:36.35 (12:21.8-95),
10kW - 44:32.81 (43:25.2-96),
20kW - 1:33:00 (1:32:27-97)
O'REILLY Martin U17, :
LJ - 6.51
OBOH Laurence U15 14.05.84, Hounslow :
100 - 11.5, 200 - 22.74
OCTAVE Philip U23 12.06.78, Hillingdon :
400 - 48.8 (48.6/51.39-96)
OGUNYEMI Akeem 4.06.74, Haringey :
60 - 6.8i/6.82i, 100 - 10.6/10.75 (10.6-97)
OHRLAND Martin U20 19.11.79, Chelmsford :
HJ - 1.95
OHRLAND Stuart 6.09.75, N & E B/Loughbro :
HJ - 2.15 (2.20i-97/2.17-94)
OJEX Bola 26.08.72, Birchfield :
60 - 6.87i,
100 - 10.80w/10.8/10.92 (10.7/10.80-97)
OJO Sayo U20 9.05.80, Woodford Green :
TJ - 14.26w/13.94 (14.10-97)
OKE Tosin U20 1.10.80, Camb H/Man Univ :
TJ - 15.62w/15.16
OKOTIE McLean 31.07.69, Thames Valley :
60 - 6.85i (6.85i-97), 100 - 10.46, 200 - 21.4
OLABINRI Tokunbo 27.02.62, Thames Valley :
100 - 10.99
(10.5w-85/10.71w/10.72dsq-86/10.74-85),
200 - 21.87 (21.65w/21.7-81)
OLD Alan U20 1.12.79, Gateshead :
3k - 8:36.7
OLDALE Richard 26.01.66, Sheffield RWC :
3kW - 13:03.36 (12:21.22-96),
10kW - 44:55.16 (44:15.75-96),
20kW - 1:33:22 (1:33:17-96)
OLIVER Chris 16.07.71, Aldershot Serv/Army :
JT - 56.60 (59.12-91)
OLIVER Geoff V65 8.08.33, :
24HrT - 213.844km (222.720km-94)
OLWENY Philips U20 14.02.81,
Ealing,Southall & Mx : JT - 55.96
OMONUA Samson U23 16.06.76, Haringey :
100 - 10.92 (10.5/10.59-96),
200 - 21.8 (22.11-96)
OMORGIE Frank U15 9.10.83, Mornington :
LJ - 6.02
ONI Samson U20 25.06.81, Belgrave/NIG :
HJ - 2.10
ONIBUJE Fajo U15 25.09.83, Middlesex Sch :
400 - 53.52
ONUORAH Onochie Chukwuma 16.10.73, S B :
60 - 6.8i (6.85i-96),
100 - 10.76 (10.5/10.51-96),
LJ - 7.58w/7.56 (7.81w-95/7.67-96)

ONWUBALILI David U17 5.12.82, London Sch :
DTY - 43.66
OPARKA Jonathon U20 29.01.80, Dundee HH :
60 - 6.88i,
OPARKA Richard U17 28.07.82, Dundee HH :
SPB - 13.93o
OPENSHAW Michael 8.04.72, Chester Le St :
800 - 1:50.6 (1:49.9-97),
1500 - 3:39.7, 1M - 3:57.2,
3k - 7:58.92, 10kR - 29:22
ORR Christopher U17 20.06.83, Border :
DTJ - 41.93, DTY - 51.68db/46.04
OSBORNE Jeff U15 22.09.83, Enfield :
PV - 3.00
OSBORNE Patrick 5.06.74, Thames Valley :
60 - 6.9i/6.95i, 100 - 10.6
OSBORNE Robert 22.10.75, Cambridge Univ :
400H - 55.3
OSBORNE S. U13, Bristol :
JTC - 36.80
OSHAGBEMI Peter U20 26.01.81, Lagan Val :
100 - 10.84
OSMAN Mohammed U15 26.06.84, Hounslow :
3k - 9:35.98
OSTAPOWYCZ Pawlo H. V45 1.07.52, Traff :
JT - 55.90 (60.38-93)
OSUIDE Stanley 30.11.74, Thames Valley :
HJ - 2.15 (2.15-91)
OTTAWAY Ben U15 4.01.84, Bucks Sch :
400 - 53.01
OWEN Neil James 18.10.73, Belgrave :
110H - 14.10w/14.17 (13.5w-96/13.60-95)
OWEN Nicholas U20 17.07.80, Kingston & P :
SP - 14.24, SPJ - 15.80
OWENS Roger U17 26.10.81, Preseli :
HJ - 1.90 (1.90-97)
OXBOROUGH Wayne 10.11.66, Thames H&H :
10k - 30:51.33 (30:19.61-94)
OYEDIRAN Akinbode Ademola 27.11.59,
Herne Hill : TJ - 14.86 (15.91i/15.78-84)

PACE Kevin U17 21.10.81, Sunderland :
3k - 8:59.99
PAGE Christopher U20 13.11.80, Wx & Bath :
400 - 49.16
PAGE Gavin U15 25.06.84, Derby & Co :
800 - 2:05.64, 3k - 9:20.8
PAGKATIPUNAN Lolimar U17 17.11.82, Har :
100HY - 13.93w
PAGNAMETA Alistair U23 12.10.76,
Camb Univ/Richmond & T : JT - 56.43
PAINTER ¶ John James Thomas V40 12.06.58,
Norwich : SP - 13.46 (16.32i/16.09-89),
DT - 41.51 (50.36-88)
PAINTER Trevor 10.08.71, Wigan :
100 - 10.7, 200 - 21.8w (21.8-94),
400 - 47.08 (47.79A-95)
PALMER Adrian Mark 10.08.69, Cardiff :
HT - 61.28 (62.56-94)
PALMER Andrew U23 13.04.77, Team Solent :
HJ - 1.95 (2.00-95)
PALMER Colin 27.07.67, Team Solent/Army :
3kSt - 8:57.4
PALMER Martin U23 5.04.77, Yate :
5k - 14:18.00
PALMER Nathan U17 16.06.82, Cardiff :
100HY - 12.96w/13.1w?/13.11,
LJ - 6.92w/6.58

PALMER Neil U17 1.10.81, Sale :
400 - 50.9 (56.28-96)
PAMAH Anthony 11.11.63, Cambridge H :
400H - 55.07 (54.2-91/54.30-93)
PARDO Michael U17 29.07.82, Motherwell :
100 - 11.19, 200 - 22.59
PARK Dean U23 23.09.77, Newham & E B :
400 - 49.00 (49.15A-94), 400H - 53.95
PARK Iain 16.07.74, GEC/Falkirk :
DT - 44.96, HT - 64.64
PARKER Andrew U20 1.08.80, Newport :
100 - 10.7w/10.80w/10.8/10.93,
200 ñ 21.4w/21.55w/21.8/21.98
PARKER Andrew U15 10.12.83, Wolves & B :
3kW - 14:24.58
PARKER David U20 28.02.80, Shaftesbury B :
SPJ - 14.08, JT - 75.21
PARKER James U20 28.10.79, Millfield Sch :
800 - 1:52.36
PARKER Michael U15 29.10.83, City of Hull :
PV - 3.10
PARKES Christopher A. 17.04.64, Rotherham :
Mar - 2:21:09 (2:17:54-88)
PARKES Joe U20 14.01.81, Bournemouth :
TJ - 13.94 (14.08w-97)
PARKES Lee U23 23.12.76, Rotherham :
Dec - 5213 (5599-96)
PARKIN John U20 23.02.79, Sale :
SP - 13.23, SPJ - 13.72 (14.05-97),
DT - 46.65, DTJ - 50.04,
HT - 51.18, HTJ - 54.42 (55.60-97)
PARKINSON Ian Philip U20 17.02.79, Wyc :
PV - 4.30 (4.30-97)
PARNABY John U20 8.10.79, Scarborough :
DTJ - 41.80 (43.66-97)
PARPER Michael U23 20.05.78, Belgrave :
400 - 48.07i/48.49 (46.54-97)
PARRINGTON Russell U17 7.01.82, L & Morc :
3k - 9:01.4, 1.5kSt - 4:29.79
PARRY Philip John 4.10.65, Harrow :
JT - 65.40 (70.00-94)
PARRY Rhodri U17 24.11.81, :
HJ - 1.90
PARSELL Howard 13.11.60, Neath :
Mar - 2:28:48
PARSONS Gary 17.05.71, Cambridge & C :
DT - 42.95
PARSONS Geoffrey Peter 14.08.64, Lond AC :
HJ - 2.16 (2.31-94)
PARSONS Glenn U20 5.04.80, Shaftesbury B :
800 - 1:54.8
PARTINGTON Stephen Wyand 17.09.65, Manx H :
3kW - 12:06.8 (11:33.4-95),
10kW - 42:27.21 (41:14.61-95),
20kW - 1:31:50 (1:24:09sh-94/1:24:18-90)
PASSEY Adrian 2.09.64, Bromsgrove & R :
5k - 14:19 (13:20.09-97),
10kR - 29:33 (29:13-94)
PATERSON Jamie U17 5.04.82, Pitreavie :
1500 - 4:03.67
PATMORE Stephen U20 9.07.79, City of Hull :
3kSt - 9:31.6
PATRICK Adrian Leroy John 15.06.73,
Windsor S & E :
100 - 10.7 (10.3/10.38-96),
200 - 20.90w/20.9/21.63
(20.62w-95/20.9/21.02-96),
400 - 46.31 (45.63-95)

PAUL Jamie 17.07.70, Cambridge Harriers :
60 - 6.9i (6.9i-94), 100 - 10.4/10.49,
200 - 21.1/21.15w/21.34, 400 - 49.0
PAUL Robert U20 12.11.80, Epsom & Ewell :
HJ - 1.97
PAULLEY Adam U17 5.10.81, Newquay & Par :
200 - 22.60
PAVEY Gavin 13.09.71, Bristol :
4K - 11:21.6
PAVEY Julian U17 16.05.83, Eastbourne AC :
OctY - 4332
PAVIS Jon 4.10.66, Sale :
2kSt - 6:02.6 (5:58.80-95), 3kSt - 9:03.46
PAYN Tom U20 18.10.79, Colchester & T :
DecJ - 5409
PAYNE Russell H. 11.09.60, Birchfield :
HT - 54.50 (56.62-86)
PAYNE Stewart U17 15.03.82, Sale :
1.5kSt - 4:30.39
PEACOCK James U23 29.09.77, Thurrock :
TJ - 14.90 (15.74w/15.24-96)
PEACOCK Shane 5.03.63, Birchfield :
HT - 66.35 (71.60-90)
PEARCE Andrew U15 13.10.83, Middlesbro & C :
400 - 53.0/53.04
PEARCE Duncan James 21.10.70, Sale :
PV - 4.70 (4.90-96)
PEARSON Andrew 14.09.71, Bingley :
5k - 14:19 (13:40.16-97),
10k - 29:01.05 (28:32.0-96),
10MR - 48:37 (46:28+/47:32-97),
HMar - 1:06:04 (1:02:07-97)
PEARSON John Terry 30.04.66, Charnwood :
HT - 66.66 (70.24-97)
PEARSON Stephen Gordon 13.09.59, Sale :
HT - 67.45
PEART James U20 1.08.79, Stroud :
JT - 56.70
PEERLESS Matthew U17 3.12.82, Corst :
PV - 3.89
PEET James U17 2.12.82, Rowheath :
100HY - 13.61w/13.97
PELESZOK Matthew Jon U17 17.10.81,
City of Stoke : 400 - 50.7/50.82 (50.06-97),
SPY - 13.98, OctY - 4634
PELTIER-EMILE Kelvin U15 13.12.83,
Newham & Essex B : 100 - 11.56w/11.58
PENK Andrew U23 19.09.78, Cardiff :
HJ - 2.10 (2.15-97), PV - 4.80i/4.70
PENN Andrew Shaun 31.03.67, Coventry RWC :
20kW - 1:31:06 (1:23:34-92)
PERRY Anthony James Corbett U20 28.08.81,
City of Stoke : PV - 4.20
PERRYMAN Dylan U17 17.11.81, Reading :
SPY - 14.47
PERRYMAN Guy St. Denis Mansfield V40
2.11.58, Reading : SP - 14.36 (16.58-89)
PERRYMAN Saul U17 17.11.81, Reading :
JT - 57.83, JTY - 58.00
PETER R., :
60 - 6.9i
PETROS Daniel U15 8.08.85, Ealing,S & Mx :
400 - 51.86
PETTS Chris U20 22.01.80, Ashford :
HJ - 2.00
PHILLIPS Adrian 29.07.75, Ealing,S & Mx :
LJ - 6.99

PHILLIPS Quincy U17 12.12.81, Enfield :
TJ - 13.63 (13.79-97)
PHILLIPS Steven 17.03.72, Rugby :
60 - 6.85i, LJ - 8.03, TJ - 15.47w/15.10
PHILLIPS Thomas U15 12.10.83, Bucks Sch :
100 - 11.51w/11.54
PHILLIPS Tim U20 13.01.79, Ver/Brighton Un :
JT - 62.13
PHILLS Mark 26.07.64, Harrow :
100 - 10.88w (10.5w-95/10.55-91)
PICKERING Chris U20 23.09.79, Kent Sch :
2kSt - 6:10.55
PICKERING Shaun Desforges 14.11.61, Har :
SP - 20.00 (20.45-97), HT - 52.37 (68.64-84)
PIERCE Robert Ian 13.11.75, Tipton :
HMar - 1:06:18
PINNOCK Richard 31.10.70, Trafford :
100 - 10.7/10.81, 200 - 22.0
PIPER Richard U17 16.02.83, Eastbourne AC :
LJ - 6.55
PITTS Colin 5.04.60, Stowmarket :
Mar - 2:30:44
PLANK Daniel U17 27.04.82, Birchfield :
HJ - 2.05
PLANO Matthew U23 8.10.76, Traff/Staffs Un :
3kSt - 9:10.21
PLANT Raymond 13.05.68, City of Stoke :
2kSt - 5:50.6 (5:45.4-96),
3kSt - 9:01.1 (8:52.64-96)
PLATT Christopher U23 25.09.78, Bolton :
TJ - 14.75w/14.01i (14.49-97)
PLATTS Stephen J. 12.03.66, Morpeth :
5k - 14:35.9 (14:12.36-90)
PLUMMER Daniel U20 4.01.81, Blackheath :
60 - 6.99i,
200 - 22.09i (22.48-97)
PLUNKETT Gerard U20 30.06.80, Hallam :
HJ - 1.95, JT - 59.30,
Dec - 5938, DecJ - 6396
PONTING Mark David U23 28.04.77, Cardiff :
400 - 48.60i/48.89 (47.94-94)
POOLE Craig U17 28.03.83, Black Isle :
3k - 8:56.53
POOLE P., RAF/Swindon :
JT - 56.29 (56.50-97)
POORE Stuart 30.12.72, Team Solent :
1500 - 3:44.78 (3:43.0-96), 3k - 8:02.88,
5k - 14:05.45, 10kR - 29:41 (29:40-97)
PORTER James U20 12.01.81, Team Solent :
TJ - 13.94
POTTER Adam U20 12.04.80, Wessex & Bath :
LJ - 6.98, TJ - 14.05
POVEY Solomon U20 8.02.80, Bournemouth :
100 - 10.4wdt (10.98w/11.04-96)
POWELL Dalton Hugh 20.08.63, Belgrave :
200 - 22.09w (21.1dt/21.24w/21.26-92)
POWELL David U23 11.09.78, Richmond & Z :
Dec - 5186 (5906-96)
POWELL Wayne 27.07.71, Stroud :
HT - 47.95, JT - 58.82 (59.36-93)
POWER Garry 1.09.62, Herne Hill/IRE :
DT - 44.85 (48.98-86)
POWER Ryan U17 20.11.82, :
100 - 11.0 (11.98-96), 200 - 22.80
PRATT Gareth U15 12.11.83, Essex Sch :
PenB - 2601
PRATT Stephen 6.02.71, Queens Park :
400H - 55.2 (54.15-91)

PREDDY Ryan U15 30.01.84, Gloucester AC :
100 - 11.6 (12.14-97), 200 - 22.9/23.35i,
400 - 49.98, 800 - 1:57.5
PRESTON Ricky U15 18.09.83, Spenborough :
400 - 53.48
PRICE Gareth U20 27.11.79, Sutton & District/
Loughborough Studnts : 1500 - 3:52.37
PRICE Glyn A. 12.09.65, Swansea :
PV - 4.20 (4.80-90)
PRICE Malcolm 18.06.62, Sunderland :
5k - 14:21.1, 10k - 31:19.50 (29:31.64-97),
10kR - 29:17, 10MR - 48:34,
HMar - 1:04:24 (1:03:38-97), Mar - 2:17:43
PRICKETT Edward U17 28.01.83, Reigate :
1500 - 4:07.4
PRIDE Simon 20.07.67, Keith :
Mar - 2:29:04, 100kR - 6:57:28 (6:57:09-97)
PRITCHARD Ashley U20 14.07.79, Macc :
Dec - 5055, DecJ - 5176 (5441-97)
PRITCHARD Chris U20 13.12.80, Grimsby :
DTJ - 41.60
PROCTOR Mark Anthony 15.01.63, N & E B/
RAF : SP - 20.85i/20.04,
DT - 54.50 (55.08-97), HT - 52.74 (53.70-93)
PROPHETT Andrew 10.06.74, City of Stoke :
800 - 1:51.6, 1500 - 3:52.3
PROUDLOVE Michael 26.01.70, City of Stoke :
3k - 8:12.68, 2kSt - 6:01.5 (5:47.30-92),
3kSt - 9:17.5 (8:51.93-92)
PURVIS Martin 26.10.71, City of Edinburgh :
400H - 55.72
PUSEY Marcellus U20 28.04.79, Rowheath :
100 - 10.84w (11.3-97)
PYRAH Jeff 6.07.72, City of Edinburgh :
3kSt - 9:24.8 (9:17.58-96)

QUARRY James Stephen 15.11.72,
Harrow/Falkirk :
100 - 10.76w/10.93 (10.7-97/10.82-95),
110H - 14.16w/14.5/14.51 (14.10-94),
PV - 4.65, LJ - 7.24w/7.21 (7.40w-95),
SP - 13.89 (14.43-97),
QUIGLEY Mark 6.11.74, Border :
SP - 13.56 (14.41-97), DT - 46.68 (47.50-97)
QUINN Anthony U20 14.01.81, Annadale Str :
SP - 13.51
QUINN Kevin U15 23.12.83, Chelmsford :
SPB - 13.34, DTB - 37.25
QUINN Robert 10.12.65, Kilbarchan :
5k - 14:19.13 (14:00.91-95),
10k - 29:20.72 (29:14.23-95)

RAESIDE Bruce U17 2.12.81, Notts :
3k - 9:00.3
RAGAN David U17 26.03.83, Bas & MH :
1.5kSt - 4:35.67
RAGGETT Glen U15 30.07.84, Woking :
3k - 9:38.0
RAMSAY Iain U15 10.09.83, Inverness :
HJ - 1.75,
RANCE S. U23, Portsmouth :
HJ - 1.95
RANDALL Matthew 28.04.70, Hastings :
TJ - 14.47 (15.37-95)
RANGER Tom U23 20.11.77, Peterborough :
800 - 1:51.6
RATCLIFFE Ian U20 28.05.79, Bolton :
2kSt - 6:10.60, 3kSt - 9:49.96 (9:41.67-97)

RATCLIFFE Trevor 9.03.64, Dacorum & Tring :
JT - 62.97 (66.78-96)
RAWLINSON Christopher 19.05.72, Belgrave/
Loughbro : 200 - 21.9 (21.77-97),
300 - 34.06i, 400 - 48.10i (48.18-97),
60H - 8.26i (8.17i-97),
110H - 14.90 (14.2/14.25w-97/14.52-96),
400H - 49.81 (49.69-97)
READ Adam 13.06.71, City of Edinburgh/AUS :
HJ - 1.95 JT - 62.52
READ Graeme U20 24.10.79, Gateshead :
200 - 22.0 (22.44w-96/22.84-97)
READER Richard U15 4.01.84, Sale :
LJ - 6.28
READLE David U20 10.02.80, Liv.Pemb Seft :
SP - 15.76, SPJ - 15.79
REED Paul 2.06.62, Morpeth :
SP - 16.04 (17.04-88), DT - 53.01 (56.46-96)
REED Peter U17 31.12.81, Hereford :
100HY - 13.5db
REES Gareth U17 15.01.82, Blackpool :
100HY - 13.82, 400HY - 56.09
REES Martin V45 28.02.53, Swansea :
10MR - 49:36 (49:23-97)
REES Simon U15 23.01.84, Stockport :
400 - 53.2/54.48
REES-JONES Steve 24.12.74, Brighton :
800 - 1:51.28 (1:49.92-97)
REESE Ben U23 29.03.76, Wirral/E Mich Un :
1500 - 3:49.52 (3:41.87-97/3:47.4a-96),
3k - 8:18.6 (8:10.13i-97)
REGAN David U15 12.11.83, Croydon :
JTB - 45.27
REGIS John Paul Lyndon 13.10.66, Belgrave :
60 - 6.99i (6.71i-91),
100 - 10.60 (10.07w-90/10.15-93),
200 - 20.40 (19.87A-94/19.94-93),
400 - 48.03 (45.48-93)
REID Graeme U20 14.04.79, Clydesdale :
3k - 8:25.52i/8:28.05, 5k - 14:40.40
REID Stewart 15.11.73, Border :
1500 - 3:51.93
REID Stuart U20, Border :
800 - 1:54.30
REID-HUGHES Geoffrey U17 14.10.81, Bel :
SPY - 16.02, DTY - 45.04
REILLY Brendan Anthony John 23.12.72, Bel :
HJ - 2.28 (2.32i-94/2.31-92)
REINA E., Kent :
HT - 50.96
REISS Michael 17.06.63, Highgate Harriers :
HT - 49.01 (50.60-94)
RENAUD Pascal 20.04.70, Haringey/FRA :
60H - 8.3i (8.3i-94/8.34i-97),
110H - 15.3 (14.58-92)
RENFREE Andrew 18.05.75, Shaftesbury B :
1500 - 3:46.8 (3:45.61-97)
RENSHAW William V45 7.08.49, Rotherham :
SP - 13.94
REVELL Paul U20 18.11.80, Scarborough :
TJ - 13.97w (13.38-97)
REY Michael 19.07.68, Windsor S & E :
200 - 22.0 (21.14w-97/21.23-90)
REYNOLDS Chris U15 23.01.85, Woodford Gr :
1500 - 4:17.11, 3k - 9:31.37
RICE John U20 29.08.81, Liv.Pemb Sefton :
2kSt - 6:10.7

358

RICHARDS Dominique U20 12.09.79, Herne H :
   60 - 6.99i, 100 - 10.7/10.71w,
   200 - 21.4w/21.6/21.68, LJ - 7.22w/7.05
RICHARDS Gregory Roy V40 25.04.56, N Lond :
   SP - 13.58 (15.24-94), DT - 43.09 (50.66-91)
RICHARDS Henry U20 15.05.81, Charnwood :
   100 - 10.69w/10.75
RICHARDS Paul 13.02.65, Neath :
   Mar - 2:31:05
RICHARDS Thomas U23 13.11.78, N & E B/
   Cambridge Univ : PV - 4.90 (4.90-97)
RICHARDSON Alan U20 15.01.81, Clee :
   PV - 4.40
RICHARDSON Mark Austin 26.07.72, W S & E :
   100 - 10.35, 200 - 20.77 (20.6w-96/20.62-97),
   300 - 31.87, 400 - 44.37
RICHARDSON Simon 7.06.72, Sheffield :
   LJ - 7.07
RICHMOND Stuart Anthony 11.04.69, GEC :
   LJ - 6.90 (6.92-95), TJ - 15.41
RIDDELL Michael U20 3.08.79, Guildford & G :
   400 - 48.4/49.11
RIDER Scott U23 22.09.77, Enfield :
   SP - 15.09i/14.65, DT - 48.14
RILEY David U15 27.09.83, Cheshire Sch :
   LJ - 6.02
RILEY Malcolm U15 6.01.84, Stowe Sch :
   1500 - 4:20.0
RILEY Peter U20 6.07.79, Trafford :
   3k - 8:29.1 (8:28.4-97), 5k - 14:59.83
RIMMER Michael U13 3.02.86, Southport :
   800 - 2:16.8,
RING Nicholas U23   76, /IRE :
   400H - 53.72
RISA Svein 7.03.74, Bristol/NOR :
   5k - 14:26.8, 10k - 30:28.38, 3kSt - 9:07.1
RITCHIE Darren 14.02.75, Sale/Scottish Bord :
   LJ - 7.15 (7.86-96)
RITCHIE Donald Alexander V50 6.07.44,
   Moray RR : 24Hr - 234.083km
RITCHIE Grant U17 25.12.81, Arbroath :
   1.5kSt - 4:27.76
RIVERS Mark 8.10.73, Hastings :
   400 - 48.5/48.80
RIXON Dale 8.07.66, Bridgend :
   HMar - 1:05:21 (1:04:19-94),
   Mar - 2:18:11 (2:13:41-96)
ROBB Aaron U23 24.04.76, Avon/Law & Dist :
   HJ - 2.03
ROBB Bruce U23 27.07.77, Pitreavie :
   SP - 15.79 (15.99-97), DT - 49.42
ROBBIN-COCKER Olubunmi 27.11.75,
   Trafford/Fife/SLE : HJ - 2.05,
   LJ - 7.00 (7.14-95), TJ - 14.86 (14.94-95)
ROBBINS Michael John U23 14.03.76,
   Roth/NE Louisiana Un : 50H - 7.39i,
   110H - 13.96w/14.30 (14.2dt-97), 400H - 52.65,
   HJ - 2.13i/2.10 (2.19i-96/2.17-95)
ROBERSON Mark W. 21.03.75, Milton Keynes :
   HT - 50.30
ROBERSON Mark W. 13.03.67, N & E B :
   JT - 85.67
ROBERTS Ben U20 15.01.80, Colwyn Bay :
   60H - 8.50i,
   110HJ - 14.8w/14.9/15.15 (14.97w-97),
   110H - 14.98w/15.3 (16.30-97),
   SPJ - 14.30, Dec - 6222w (5867-97)

ROBERTS Colin U20 20.01.81, Norwich :
   110HJ - 14.64
ROBERTS Johnathan U23 28.09.77, Leeds/
   Royal Navy : HJ - 1.95 (1.98-96)
ROBERTS Mark 1.09.69, Kingston & Poly :
   110H - 15.3 (15.65-92)
ROBERTS Martin 1.03.60, Cannock & Staff :
   HT - 47.78 (53.08-88)
ROBERTS Martin U15 20.09.83, Scunthorpe :
   200 - 23.44w/23.78, 80HB - 11.69,
   PenB - 2865
ROBERTS Matthew U15 8.07.84, Crawley :
   200 - 23.47w (25.57-97),
   80HB - 11.49, PenB - 2543
ROBERTS Paul 24.12.69, Cardiff :
   800 - 1:52.1 (1:49.48-93)
ROBERTS Paul U17 15.09.81, Crawley :
   400 - 49.19, OctY - 4606
ROBERTS Peter 19.09.71, Swansea :
   DT - 41.09 (44.52-90)
ROBERTSON Stephen 9.07.75, Falkirk :
   PV - 4.10, Dec - 5846
ROBINSON Andrew U23 20.04.78, Horsham :
   3kSt - 9:05.73
ROBINSON David U23 12.01.78, Gateshead :
   HT - 50.35 (50.90-96)
ROBINSON Keith V45 9.02.52, Havering :
   HT - 48.41 (53.38-81)
ROBISON Christopher Mark 16.03.61,
   Inverclyde : 5k - 14:21.21 (13:54.66-84),
   10kR - 29:16 (29:10-96)
ROBSON Shaun U20 21.06.80, Newport :
   110HJ - 15.07 (15.0-97), 400H - 55.35
ROCHESTER Neil U17 4.10.81, Oswestry :
   100 - 11.0w (11.4-97),
   200 - 22.80w (22.9/23.82-97)
RODEN James U17 24.11.81, Chorley :
   OctY - 4405
RODEN Paul Anthony 18.04.65, Sale :
   HMar - 1:04:24 (1:03:19-93)
RODMELL Alan U17 23.09.81, Wallsend :
   HTY - 52.12
ROE Thomas U17 25.06.82, Norwich :
   100 - 11.0 (11.87-97), 400 - 49.5/49:77,
   LJ - 6.64
ROGERS Adam U17 10.04.83, Jarrow & H :
   200 - 22.66, 400 - 51.00
ROGERS Craig U23 14.02.76, Birchfield :
   SP - 14.05 (15.88-97)
ROGERS John 30.07.73, Annadale Striders :
   800 - 1:51.36
ROGERS Stephen A. 1.09.71, Liv.Pem Seft/
   Cambridge Univ : PV - 4.20 (4.60-95),
   JT - 59.56 (61.10-97)
ROLLINS Andrew U23 20.03.78, Peterborough :
   SP - 14.41, DT - 45.90
ROPER Simon U20 20.09.79, Derby & Co :
   TJ - 14.13 (14.47-97)
ROSATO Sebastian 19.11.72, GEC :
   110H - 15.4
      (14.79w-95/14.8db-93/14.8-94/14.97-95)
ROSCOE Martin Peter 19.09.64, Leeds :
   3kSt - 9:08.10 (8:53.2-89)
ROSE Andrew U17 17.08.82, Braintree :
   100 - 11.0w/11.13w (11.11w-96/11.13-97)
ROSE Stefan 7.04.75, Team Solent :
   TJ - 14.06

ROSENBERG Luke U20 29.06.80, Harrow :
SP - 13.45, DT - 49.23, DTJ - 51.13 (51.50-97)
ROSS John, :
Mar - 2:28:14
ROSSITER Martin R. 4.09.69, Peterborough :
LJ - 6.99, TJ - 15.01w/14.97 (15.20-97)
ROWE Alex V40 10.04.57, Wessex & Bath :
Mar - 2:32:11
ROWE Ian U23 28.09.78, Team Solent :
TJ - 14.27w (14.78w/14.32-97)
ROWE Martin U20 23.07.80, Telford :
DT - 42.43, DTJ - 45.42
ROWEN Daniel U20 30.12.79, Solihull & S H :
5k - 15:18.62
ROWLANDS Mark Stuart U23 18.04.78, Swan :
400H - 54.22 (51.63-97)
ROWLEY Lee U17 28.02.82, Dudley & Stour :
100HY - 13.81w/13.85
ROWSWELL Alex U17 18.03.82, Yeovil Oly :
HJ - 1.90, JTY - 54.83
ROYDEN Barry Mark 15.12.66, Medway :
5k - 14:29.4 (13:54.03-91),
HMar - 1:05:49+un/1:06:28 (1:02:25-94),
Mar - 2:19:57 (2:19:00-97)
RUBEN Alan V40 9.03.57, :
Mar - 2:29:54
RUBENIS Richard 10.11.73, Telford :
60 - 6.94i (6.89i-97),
200 - 22.15i (21.54w-95/21.6-94/21.94-97)
RUDDOCK Alan U15 12.09.83, Wakefield :
LJ - 6.06
RUDKIN Alan U23 5.11.78, Peterborough :
DT - 40.58 (42.88-97)
RULE Charles U20 22.05.80, C of Edinburgh :
PV - 4.20
RUMBOLD James U17 4.11.81, Wimborne :
DTJ - 42.34, DTY - 47.27
RUSHWORTH Brian 14.12.62, Sunderland :
5k - 14:31.0 (13:50.6-86),
HMar - 1:05:43 (1:03:35-90),
Mar - 2:27:41 (2:20:37-97)
RUSSELL Alaister 17.06.68, Bord/Law & Dist :
5k - 14:33.56 (14:17.1-96),
10k - 30:17.03 (29:52.16-95)
RUSSELL Jamie U17 1.10.81, Rotherham :
HJ - 2.07i/2.05, TJ - 13.37, OctY - 5136
RUSSELL Matthew U20 20.01.81, Havering :
100 - 10.6w/10.63w/10.76,
RUSSELL Peter 7.05.60, RUC :
DT - 42.07 (44.32-96)
RUSSELL Robert 5.08.74, Sale :
DT - 45.87 (53.76-96)
RUTHERFORD Tremayne 19.06.72, N & E B :
60 - 6.8i/6.82i (6.74i-95),
100 - 10.6w/10.74 (10.4w?/10.44-94),
200 - 21.71 (21.07-97)
RYAN Stuart M. 1.09.62, Jarrow & Hebburn :
SP - 13.45

S ABAN Dominic U17 27.02.82, Sutt & D :
100HY - 13.77w/14.02
SAGGERS Carl U15 20.09.83, Enfield :
SPY - 14.23, SPB - 16.50,
DTB - 45.84, HTY - 54.50, HTB - 60.15
SAHANS Gurmukh U23 8.10.78, Hounslow :
Dec - 5145 (5750-96)

SALAMI Raymond 11.04.75, Blackheath :
60 - 6.86i (6.8i/6.82i-97),
100 - 10.70w/10.82 (10.6-96/10.70-97),
200 - 21.66 (21.44-97)
SALES Richard 28.05.62, Norwich :
Mar - 2:33:22 (2:29:26-96)
SALLE Frederick Ebong 10.09.64, Belgrave :
LJ - 7.47 (8.10-94)
SALTER Tom U17 7.01.83, Cannock & Stafford :
HJ - 1.90
SAMMUT Steven 3.05.67, Team Solent :
HT - 58.68
SAMPSON Chris 30.09.75, Morpeth :
3kSt - 9:28.40 (9:19.01-97)
SAMPSON Paul U23 12.07.77, Wakefield :
200 - 21.9 (21.9/21.98-96)
SAMUEL Rohan 30.01.66, Harrow :
100 - 10.5w/10.88
(10.5w-89/10.58w-92/10.6/10.73-89)
SAMUYIWA David 4.08.72, Thames Valley :
60 - 6.86i,
100 - 10.2wdt/10.65w/10.70 (10.4/10.66-97),
200 - 21.48w/21.51 (21.2/21.46-97)
SANDERS Kenny U20 22.02.80, Frome :
DecJ - 5113
SANDERSON David 6.05.71, Sale :
TJ - 14.75i/14.60w/14.25 (15.72w-93/15.29-92)
SAVAGE David 13.11.72, Sale :
400 - 49.03 (47.12-96),
400H - 52.38 (50.97-96)
SAVILLE Tommy U15, Hercules Wimbledon :
PV - 3.10
SAWYER Anthony J. U20 29.04.80, Wycombe :
Dec - 5787, DecJ - 6295
SAXON Sean 11.12.71, Telford :
110H - 15.3w/15.4 (15.2-96)
SCALLY Brian J. 9.05.66, Shettleston :
10k - 30:58.33 (30:36.02-96),
Mar - 2:29:32
SCANLAN Brian, London Irish/IRE :
JT - 59.55
SCANLON Robert 13.04.74, Coventry Godiva :
800 - 1:50.9 (1:50.4-97),
1500 - 3:44.79 (3:41.3-96),
1M - 4:04.50, 3k - 8:08.67i (8:08.6-96)
SCAYSBROOK James U17 1.01.82, Birchfield :
JTY - 55.72
SCOTT Allan U17 27.12.82, Whitemoss :
100HY - 13.3/13.34,
LJ - 7.07w/6.96i/6.85, TJ - 14.09w/13.96
SCOTT Darren 7.03.69, Liverpool H :
60 - 6.96i, 300 - 34.5, 400 - 48.57i/48.9,
100 - 10.61w/10.8 (10.6w-96/10.74-95),
200 - 21.19w/21.46 (21.3/21.35-95)
SCOTT Ian U20 27.10.79, :
800 - 1:50.83
SCOTT Richard 14.09.73, Exeter :
110H - 15.5, 400H - 52.72
SCOTT Sandy U23 1.09.76, Shett/Glas Univ :
400 - 48.77
SCOTT Steven U20 5.06.79, Belgrave :
110HJ - 14.38w/14.40
(14.29w/14.3-96/14.40-97),
110H - 14.87w/15.39 (15.20-97)
SCOTT Steven U20 29.05.79, Liverpool H :
SPJ - 13.90
SCRIVENER Neil U20 18.09.80, Southend :
DecJ - 5595

SEAR Richard A. U20 21.08.79, Belgrave :
60H - 8.4i (8.45i-97),
110HJ - 15.0 (14.3/14.50-97),
110H - 14.52w/14.68 (14.37-97)
SEBIRE Simon U17 20.09.82, Guernsey :
LJ - 6.67w/6.57
SEELEY M. U17, :
LJ - 6.65
SEMPLE Stuart U15 3.11.83, Bas & MH :
SPB - 13.22, DTB - 37.92
SENBANJO Oladipo U17 20.03.82, Notts :
TJ - 14.21w/13.71 (13.73-97)
SESTON Tony U20 21.12.80, Ipswich :
400H - 55.00
SHAH Arif U23 29.11.78, Coventry G/Leics Un :
60 - 6.99i, TJ - 15.33w/15.03
SHALDERS Steven U17 24.12.81, Cardiff :
LJ - 7.03w, TJ - 15.40w/15.14
SHAM D. U15, Derby & Co :
HJ - 1.75
SHARKEY Andrew 13.12.74, C of Edinburgh :
3kSt - 9:07.47
SHARP Alexis 31.10.72, Blackh/London Univ. :
100 - 10.5/10.78w/10.84, 400 - 48.6 (48.57-97),
60H - 8.40i, 110H - 15.21, HJ - 1.95,
PV - 4.40, LJ - 7.13w/7.10 (7.23w-97),
SP - 14.05i/13.73 (13.92-97),
DT - 46.91 (48.56-96),
SHARP Fraser U23 11.03.78, C of Edinburgh :
100 - 10.84
SHARP Neil 21.08.75, Stockport :
200 - 21.5w
SHARP Stephen 31.12.75, Thames Valley :
800 - 1:52.8 (1:52.7-96), 1500 - 3:43.66
SHARPE Philip U20 6.03.81, Border :
JT - 68.53
SHENAVA John U20 5.02.81, Falkirk :
400H - 57.0
SHENTON David U23 20.10.77, Gateshead :
HT - 52.19 (52.34-96)
SHEPHERD Alan 28.04.69, Morpeth :
Mar - 2:27:11 (2:22:22-96)
SHEPHERD Bruce David 20.03.67, Aberdeen :
SP - 13.43 (14.50-93), HT - 49.02 (53.18-96)
SHEPHERD Dominic U23 11.12.76, C of Stoke :
PV - 4.25 (4.90-94), Dec - 6334
SHEPLEY Sebastian 23.11.67, Westbury :
Mar - 2:27:01
SHERIDAN Mark D. 17.06.70, Crawley :
HT - 50.13 (56.02-91)
SHERMAN Andrew U17 28.09.81, Swindon :
800 - 1:55.73, 1500 - 4:01.73,
1.5kSt - 4:24.87
SHIRLEY Simon 3.08.66, Belgrave :
SP - 14.12 (14.59-95), JT - 57.32 (65.00-93)
SHONE Matthew 10.07.75, Notts :
800 - 1:48.33, 1500 - 3:51.7
SHOWELL Gavin 29.09.72, Tamworth :
PV - 4.60, Dec - 5348
SIBBETT Peter 18.12.62, Bedford & County :
Mar - 2:33:06 (2:26:55-92)
SICHEL William V45 1.10.53, Orkney Islands :
24Hr - 240.291km
SILLAH-FRECKLETON Mohammed U20
11.09.80, Blackheath :
110HJ - 14.34, 110H - 14.76w/15.4
SIME Ewan U17 7.09.82, Inverness :
SPB - 13.96oi

SIMON Delroy U23 27.11.78, Harrow :
2kSt - 6:00.8, 3kSt - 9:19.8
SIMPKINS Matthew U17 9.05.82, Sol & S H :
800 - 1:58.4, 1500 - 3:59.76
SIMPSON Alexander U17 19.01.82, GEC :
JTY - 54.06
SIMPSON Jonathan U17 27.05.82, Falkirk :
400 - 49.26, 600 - 1:22.9
SIMPSON Keith U17 19.10.81, Aberdeen :
JT - 49.26, JTY - 51.05
SIMPSON Neil U15 11.09.83, Blackheath :
400 - 52.76i, LJ - 6.08
SIMPSON Scott E. U20 21.07.79, Wx & Bath :
PV - 4.75
SIMSON Matthew 28.05.70, Belgrave :
SP - 18.44 (19.49-94)
SINCLAIR Richard U20 25.06.79, Cann & St :
800 - 1:53.66 (1:53.4-97),
1500 - 3:51.38 (3:51.22-97)
SINCLAIR Timothy U15 26.12.83, Sutton & D :
80HB - 11.63w/11.7/11.72 (11.5-97)
SINER Neil U15 27.01.84, Liverpool H :
3k - 9:33.8
SKEDD Roger U17 3.09.82, City of Stoke :
OctY - 4443
SKEETE John U23 8.09.78, Blackh/Falkirk :
60 - 6.90i, 100 - 10.5w/10.67w/10.8/10.89,
200 - 21.66w/21.9 (21.78-95)
SKELTON James   75, Worthing :
PV - 4.20
SKETCHLEY David U23 25.02.76, T Solent :
JT - 60.80 (61.40-97)
SKINNER Michael U20 21.11.79, Blackheath :
800 - 1:52.5, 1500 - 3:52.4,
3k - 8:35.8 (9:09.3-97)
SLATER Ashley U17 23.09.81, Cannock & St :
HTJ - 49.29, HTY - 61.46
SLATER Darren U20 1.01.80, Bedford & Co :
HJ - 2.00 (2.00-97)
SLESSOR Daniel U23 5.10.78, Border :
HJ - 1.95i/1.95 (2.10i-97/2.07-96)
SLOCOMBE Tim U23 15.11.77, Bournemouth :
100 - 10.5wdt, 400 - 48.5 (48.86-95)
SLUE Leroy U17 11.12.81, Croydon :
100 - 11.06w, 200 - 22.48
SLYTHE Paul J. 5.09.74, GEC :
200 - 21.3w/21.4 (21.22-96), 400 - 45.94
SMAHON Dean Carey 8.12.61, Lisburn/Bord :
JT - 59.41 (67.60-94)
SMALL Michael V40 31.03.54, Belgrave :
SP - 13.45, DT - 44.22, HT - 48.30 (49.98-86)
SMALL Vernon U17 1.01.82, Enfield :
400 - 50.40
SMART Michael U13 18.11.85, Harrow :
800 - 2:11.8, 1500 - 4:32.9
SMITH Anthony U17 11.01.83, Thurrock :
DTY - 46.80
SMITH Ben U17 12.06.82, Shaftesbury B :
HJ - 2.00
SMITH Brendan U23 20.07.77, Sale :
800 - 1:52.7 (1:51.1-97),
1500 - 3:46.4 (3:43.1-97), 1M - 4:08.75,
SMITH Carl Anthony V40 17.05.58, S B :
JT - 63.66 (69.94r-91/69.90-96)
SMITH David U23 21.06.62, North East SH :
HT - 56.58 (77.30-85)
SMITH David W. 2.11.74, Belgrave :
HT - 73.50 (75.10-96)

SMITH David U17 15.10.81, Middlesbro & C :
200 - 22.3/22.48
SMITH Gary 20.02.71, S B/Stevenage & NH :
LJ - 7.30w/7.29i/7.10 (7.57w/7.49-97)
SMITH Glen Ernest 21.05.72, Birchfield :
SP - 14.12 (14.71-96), DT - 62.44 (62.80-97)
SMITH Gregory U15 29.01.84, Bournemouth :
80HB - 11.7/11.80
SMITH James U15 9.01.84, Havering :
LJ - 6.16w/5.48
SMITH Justin Michael U20 13.06.79, Swindon/
Ballymena & Antrim : 400H - 56.8 (56.80-97)
SMITH Leigh U17 24.09.82, Birchfield :
LJ - 6.53
SMITH Leon, Herne Hill :
LJ - 6.90w
SMITH Mark 14.09.74, Harrow :
HJ - 2.05 (2.07-91)
SMITH Matthew 26.12.74, Tipton :
1500 - 3:49.26 (3:45.59-97),
1M - 4:07.03i (4:06.74i-97),
3k - 7:58.15i/8:08.36,
5k - 14:02.41, 10kR - 29:49
SMITH Michael John 20.04.63, Coventry RWC :
10kW - 48:10.0 (44:39.0-87),
50kW - 4:49:40 (4:09:22-89)
SMITH Paul W. V40 12.08.54, Les Croupiers :
Mar - 2:31:30 (2:21:24-91)
SMITH Richard William U20 17.01.81, Peterbro :
PV - 4.60i/4.60 (4.70-97)
SMITH Richard U17 12.10.82, Middlesbro & C :
400HY - 57.85
SMITH Robert U15 25.01.84, Southampton C :
400 - 53.6/54.51
SMITH Rory U15 12.12.84, Wirral :
1500 - 4:19.34
SMITH Stephenson "Steve" James 29.03.73,
Liv H : HJ - 2.36i/2.30 (2.38i-94/2.37-92)
SMITH Stuart U23 2.08.76, Coventry Godiva :
HJ - 2.10 (2.20-97)
SMITH Wesley U23, Banbury :
JT - 58.49
SMITHSON Jason U17 23.09.82,
Houghton-le-Spring : HTY - 52.35
SMYTH Jeremy U23 11.08.78, Shettleston :
JT - 59.89
SNOOK Christopher U20 6.06.79, Mand/Cam U :
HT - 48.59, HTJ - 53.38
SNOOK Laine 2.07.68, Shrewsbury :
SP - 15.93
SNOW Michael U17 5.09.82, Northampton :
200 - 22.4 (23.67w-97), 400 - 49.67
SNOW Tom U13, Woodford Green :
1500 - 4:37.4, 3k - 10:21.0
SOALLA-BELL Anthony U23 3.10.76, Herne H/
SLE : SP - 14.87 (15.08-97), DT - 41.51
SOCHART Peter 1.05.74, Corstorphine :
SP - 13.55 (13.62-97)
SOLE David 19.01.65, Crawley :
HT - 46.28 (50.70-84)
SOLLITT Gary 13.01.72, Team Solent :
SP - 17.04 (17.14-97), DT - 41.18
SOLLY Jonathan 28.06.63, Herne Hill :
Mar - 2:24:49 (2:12:07-90)
SOOS Ricky U17 28.06.83, Mansfield :
1.5kSt - 4:35.9
SOUTER Kenneth V40 2.07.57, C of Edin/AUS :
DT - 40.88 (51.24-79)

SOUTH James 4.01.75, Shaftesbury Barnet :
SP - 13.50 (14.00-95), DT - 46.31 (48.32-94)
SOUTHEY Robert U15 23.10.83, Bridgewater :
TJ - 12.41w/12.34
SOUTHWARD Anthony 31.01.71, Trafford :
110H - 14.6w/14.7/14.98 (14.69-96),
HJ - 1.95 (1.98-96), PV - 4.40 (4.40-96),
SP - 13.51 (13.82-96), DT - 43.46,
Dec - 7385 (7425-96)
SPAWFORTH Darren 1.08.69, Wakefield :
3k - 8:14.21i (8:03.4-92)
SPEAIGHT Neil U23 9.09.78, Huntingdon :
800 - 1:50.46
SPENCER Alexander U15 25.10.83,
Liv.Pemb Seft : 800 - 2:01.8 (2:01.1-97)
SPENCER Robert U15 4.10.83, Skyrac :
3k - 9:29.82
SPICER Lloyd U20 15.03.80, Peterborough :
DecJ - 5111
SPICER Matthew William 18.05.71, Bristol :
HT - 54.28 (60.26jr?-90/59.68-96)
SPIKE Lee U20 20.02.80, Liverpool H :
HJ - 2.05 (2.05-96)
SPIVEY Philip 15.05.61, Belgrave/AUS :
HT - 57.49 (70.94-86)
SQUIRE Andrew U20 30.09.79, Cannock & St :
HJ - 1.95 (1.95-97), Dec - 5884
SQUIRES Derrick U15 7.12.83, Cannock & St :
SPB - 14.43, HTB - 54.55
STAINES Gary Martin 3.07.63, Belgrave :
5k - 14:04.4 (13:14.28-90),
10MR - 48:51 (46:11-93)
STAMP Terence 18.02.70, Newham & E B :
60 - 6.70i,
100 - 10.54w/10.67 (10.4-97/10.47-95),
200 - 21.74 (21.4-97)
STAMP Vince 22.11.59, Portsmouth :
Mar - 2:28:46
STANFORD Steven Gareth U20 9.12.79,
Liverpool H : DT - 41.98, DTJ - 50.51
STANLEY David U20 16.01.79, Bas & MH :
800 - 1:49.81, 1500 - 3:51.48
STANTON Christopher U17 12.11.81, Dor Sch :
OctY - 4527
STARLING James Mark 13.08.67, Woodford Gr :
10kR - 29:40
STEINLE Mark 22.11.74, Blackheath :
10k - 30:49.8 (29:07.33-95),
10MR - 48:25, HMar - 1:04:13
STENNETT Kori U23 2.09.76, Cheltenham :
TJ - 14.74 (15.02-94)
STEPHENSON Christian 22.07.74, Cardiff :
800 - 1:51.6, 1500 - 3:43.85, 1M - 4:01.7,
5k - 14:30.4 (13:48.31-97),
10kR - 29:28 (29:27-96), 3kSt - 8:32.76
STERN Mark 22.05.72, Shaftesbury Barnet :
400H - 52.6/52.90
STEVENS Paul U15 15.11.83, City of Hull :
PV - 3.30
STEVENSON Andrew U15 7.09.83, Blackheath :
JTB - 46.99
STEVENSON Gary U20 12.09.79, Kilbarchan :
400 - 48.5/48.61, 400H - 55.8
STEWART Glen 7.12.70, City of Edinburgh :
1M - 4:02.1 (3:59.56-96),
3k - 8:07.69 (8:02.63-97),
5k - 13:53.55, 10kR - 28:52sh

362

STEWART John U20 30.12.79, Middlesbro & C :
  100 - 10.67, 200 - 21.16w/21.6/21.62,
  300 - 33.93
STEWART Jonathan U20 22.05.80, Halifax :
  800 - 1:53.1, 1500 - 3:45.7
STEWART Kris George U20 11.04.80,
  Scot Borders/S B : 400 - 48.04 (47.31-97)
STICKINGS Nigel 1.04.71, :
  60 - 6.92i (6.85i-93),
  200 - 21.70i (20.84w-93/21.0-92/21.14-93),
  400 - 49.0i/49.05i
STIRK Nigel 13.03.72, Tipton :
  1500 - 3:50.1, 5k - 14:34.45 (14:21.76-93)
STOBART Christopher U17 27.03.82, Manx :
  100 - 10.7wdb?/10.8w/10.84w/10.89,
  TJ - 13.69
STODDART Dwayne U20 29.12.80, Reading :
  110HJ - 14.74w/15.17
STODDART Keith U15 26.10.83, C of Edin :
  TJ - 13.09
STOKES Stuart U23 15.12.76, Sale :
  3kSt - 8:56.39 (8:55.64-97)
STONE Darrell Richard 2.02.68, Steyning :
  3kW - 12:31.50 (11:49.0-90),
  20kW - 1:26:37 (1:23:27un-93/1:23:58-96)
STOPHER Brian U20 8.04.80, AF&D :
  800 - 1:53.1, 1500 - 3:55.6
STOTT Adrian V40 5.08.54, :
  24HrT - 218.016km
STOTT Gavin U23 5.05.77, Arbroath :
  Dec - 5289
STOVES Chris U15 20.02.84, Lanc & Morc :
  400 - 53.04, 800 - 1:59.92
STRAIN Michael U20 11.09.79, Victoria Park :
  400H - 56.0
STRONACH Paul A.G. 18.05.68, Severn :
  SP - 13.43 (13.96-89)
STUBBS Richard A.J. 6.06.66, Preseli :
  PV - 4.20
STYGALL Simon U17 20.09.82, Bristol :
  3k - 8:54.58
STYLES Iain 2.10.75, Cheltenham :
  SP - 14.06
SUFFLING Gareth U17 13.11.81, Luton :
  1500 - 4:02.90, 3k - 8:55.83
SUGGITT Mark U17 7.11.81, Gateshead :
  100 - 11.06w (11.4/11.83-97),
  150 - 15.7db, 200 - 22.16w/22.40
SULLIVAN Nicholas U15 9.11.83, Lanc & Morc :
  LJ - 5.99w/5.83
SURETY Steven U20 18.02.80, Basildon :
  100 - 10.7w/10.95, 200 - 21.89,
  400 - 49.5, 110HJ - 15.1 (15.39-97)
SURTEES Nicholas U15 11.11.83, Soton City :
  JTB - 47.35
SUTCLIFFE Paul 8.12.70, Wakefield :
  DT - 40.91
SUTTON Matthew U17 8.09.81, Wolves & B :
  HTJ - 64.00, HTY - 73.76
SWAIN Anthony Michael 17.01.75, Border/
  Huddersfield Univ. : HT - 58.93 (62.88-97)
SWAIN Ashley U20 3.10.80, Team Solent :
  PV - 4.80
SWARAY Tyrone U23 7.11.77, London AC :
  60 - 6.9i, 100 - 10.59w/10.8/10.92,
  200 - 22.0
SWEENEY Conor U17 28.12.81, Anna Str/IRE :
  800 - 1:53.1, 1500 - 3:57.44

SWEENEY Joseph Leonard 17.07.65, Wi S & E :
  LJ - 7.02 (7.41-87),
  TJ - 15.24w/15.04 (16.26-91)
SWEENEY Mark U23 26.02.77, Notts/Birm Un :
  110H - 15.13w/15.5/15.52 (14.9w-96/15.1-97,
  HJ - 1.95 (2.00i/2.00-97)
SWEETMAN David 27.01.71, Charnwood :
  110H - 14.22w/14.43
SWIFT-SMITH Justin 28.08.74, Shaftesbury B :
  800 - 1:49.7 (1:47.9-97),
  1500 - 3:46.21 (3:45.0-97)

TABARES Ruben U23 22.10.78, Blackh :
  400 - 48.1 (48.01-97),
  400H - 53.1/54.11 (52.5/52.95-97)
TADESSE Kassa 21.08.74, Belgrave/ETH :
  5k - 14:17 (14:05.8-97),
  10k - 30:34.13 (29:42.93-93),
  10kR - 29:28 (28:15sh-96/29:05-94),
  HMar - 1:04:02 (1:02:51-97)
TALHAOUI Kamel 18.03.71, Hounslow/ALG :
  400 - 48.3
TANSER Toby 21.07.68, Sparvagens :
  Mar - 2:31:35 (2:18:02-97)
TARGATT Michael U15 1.02.84, Neath :
  3k - 9:30.5
TARRAN Michael U20 10.12.80, Cheltenham :
  JT - 61.65
TATHAM Alan U23 29.04.76, Derby & Co/
  Loughbro : 800 - 1:52.4 (1:51.6-97),
  1500 - 3:48.56 (3:48.4-95)
TATTERSHALL James U17 25.11.81, Roth :
  100HY - 14.12w (14.59-97), 400HY - 56.85
TAWIAH Emmanuel U23 11.07.77, N & E B :
  100 - 10.7w (11.10-96)
TAYLOR David William 9.01.64, Blackheath :
  3k - 8:00.37i/8:12.41,
  10k - 29:24.15 (29:11.79-97),
  HMar - 1:04:14 (1:03:24-97),
  Mar - 2:20:30 (2:13:27-97)
TAYLOR David U17 28.10.81, Telford :
  1.5kSt - 4:31.9
TAYLOR Dean U17 9.11.81, Bedford & Co :
  TJ - 14.54
TAYLOR Ian J. 2.07.67, Telford :
  DT - 48.98 (49.44-93)
TAYLOR James U17 24.04.82, Hallamshire :
  DTY - 43.76
TAYLOR Martin U17 31.01.82, Victoria Park :
  100HY - 13.77, LJ - 6.70, OctY - 4628
TAYLOR Mike U15, :
  HJ - 1.75
TAYLOR Paul Thomas 9.01.66, Border :
  5k - 14:12.17 (13:45.31-89)
TAYLOR Richard 5.12.73, Coventry Godiva :
  3k - 8:10.20, 5k - 14:20.3 (14:14.15-96)
TAYLOR Robert Wesley James U20 9.06.80,
  Wakefield : HTJ - 49.68
TAYLOR Scott U23 28.07.78, Leics WC :
  3kW - 13:10.3, 5kW - 23:31.15 (23:07.5-96),
  10kW - 48:30.60
TAYLOR Thomas U20 30.01.81, Leics WC :
  3kW - 13:05.43i/13:06.68, 10kW - 45:56.16,
  5kW - 22:46.0, 10kWR - 45:03
TEAGUE David U17 20.01.82, Neath :
  400 - 50.18
TELFER Gary 10.01.65, Thames Valley :
  400H - 53.3/53.41 (51.29-95)

TEMPEST Gary U17 16.04.82, Sparkhill :
OctY - 4365
THACKERY Carl Edward 14.10.62, Hallam :
5k - 14:09.50 (13:42.98-87),
10k - 28:52.71 (27:59.24-87),
THANDA Lekeladio 'Bob' U13 22.09.85,
Barking Abbey : 100 - 12.3, 200 - 25.5,
400 - 58.2, 800 - 2:14.6,
THICKPENNY Robert U23 17.07.76, Peterbro/
Brunel Univ : PV - 4.60i (4.75-96)
THIE James U23 27.06.78, Cardiff :
1500 - 3:45.8, 1M - 4:03.9, 3k - 8:16.12
THOM Douglas 13.04.68, B & A/Border :
400 - 49.01i (48.61-96),
400H - 53.04 (52.18-97)
THOMAS Alexander U20 3.12.79, Rowheath :
PV - 4.31
THOMAS Andrew U20 29.01.81, Invicta :
2kSt - 6:10.07, 3kSt - 9:42.4
THOMAS Barry V.S. 28.04.72, Sheffield :
110H - 14.91w/15.6 (14.62w-95/14.81-92),
HJ - 1.95 (2.05-92), PV - 4.75 (5.00-92),
LJ - 7.14w/6.91 (7.44-92),
SP - 13.57 (14.06-96), DT - 42.21,
Dec - 7479w (7766-95)
THOMAS Chris U20 11.01.80, Torfaen :
JT - 60.34 (64.52-97)
THOMAS Craig U17 28.09.81, Airdrie :
LJ - 6.43 (6.52-97)
THOMAS Iwan Gwyn 5.01.74, Newham & E B :
200 - 21.32A (20.87-97),
300 - 32.36 (32.08+-97),
400 - 44.38 (44.36-97)
THOMAS Joselyn 11.07.71, Woodford Green :
60 - 6.77i,
100 - 10.3w/10.36w/10.52 (10.51-97),
200 - 21.10w/21.81i/21.9 (21.2/21.29-94)
THOMAS Josephus 11.07.71, Woodford Gr/
Army : 60 - 6.67i (6.66i-97),
100 - 10.19w/10.29 (10.2-96),
200 - 20.49w/21.26 (20.6-96/20.75-97)
THOMAS Martin U23 21.09.78, Liverpool H :
400H - 55.5 (53.52-97)
THOMAS Nicholas U20 4.04.79, Blackheath :
60 - 6.98i, 100 - 10.7w (10.98-97),
200 - 22.0 (21.97w/22.11-97), TJ - 15.70
THOMAS Paul U20 1.10.80, Team Solent :
PV - 4.20
THOMAS Simon U20 4.03.81, Southend :
HJ - 2.00 (2.00-97)
THOMAS Timothy Paul 18.11.73, Swansea :
PV - 5.20i/5.20 (5.40-97)
THOMPSON Chris U20 17.04.81, AF&D :
800 - 1:53.8, 1500 - 3:47.0, 3k - 8:16.91,
2kSt - 5:57.05, 3kSt - 9:06.20
THOMPSON Darren U20 6.11.79, Bel/Brunel U :
LJ - 7.56
THOMPSON Gavin U20 9.04.80, Crawley :
800 - 1:52.4, 1500 - 3:54.3
THOMPSON Matthew U17 15.01.82, Birchfield :
PV - 3.65
THOMPSON Michael 14.09.68, Sunderland :
Mar - 2:26:48
THOMPSON Neil U20 23.04.79, Border :
110HJ - 15.12, HJ - 1.97, DecJ - 6046
THOMPSON Neville Leigh V40 28.03.55, S B :
SP - 13.58 (15.26i-88/15.15-87),
DT - 52.11 (55.68-93)

THOMPSON Paul 22.03.72, Bir/Idaho Univ :
110H - 14.77, 400H - 51.05 (50.16-96)
THOMPSON Ross U17 7.12.81, Gateshead :
HTJ - 57.31, HTY - 67.21
THOMPSON Russell U15 9.09.83, Halesowen :
PV - 3.10
THOMPSON Scot W. U20 10.08.81, Nairn :
SP - 14.15, SPJ - 15.61, SPY - 17.50o,
DT - 47.41, DTJ - 50.78, DTY - 54.46o
THOMPSON Scott U17 21.02.82, Airdrie :
200 - 22.5/22.76
THOMPSON Stephen U17 5.12.82, Tonbridge :
1500 - 4:07.39
THOMPSON Tony U23 9.11.77, Border :
800 - 1:49.8
THOMSON David 18.09.59, Portsmouth :
Mar - 2:28:28
THOMSON David U15 1.10.83, Spenborough :
PV - 2.95
THOMSON Matthew U17 20.09.81, Yate :
800 - 1:55.1, 1500 - 3:58.41
THORNTON David 27.07.73, Hyndburn :
800 - 1:50.8
THORNTON N. U13, Longwood :
100 - 12.5
THURGOOD Matthew U15 29.12.83, Verlea :
HJ - 1.80, TJ - 12.35w/12.22
THURGOOD Stuart U23 17.05.76, Loughbro/
Newham & Essex B : HT - 56.00
TIBBETS Adam U23 14.12.78, Dudley & St/
Lough : 110H - 15.3/15.51 (14.93w-96/15.51-97)
TIETZ Michael U23 14.09.77, Birchfield :
60 - 6.84i, 100 - 10.51 (10.39w-97), 200 - 21.53
TINDALL Lee U20 19.02.80, Portsmouth :
110HJ - 14.91w/15.0/15.07,
110H - 15.30w/15.59
TINSLEY Ian U20 23.01.81, Wirral :
400 - 49.2 (49.15-97), 800 - 1:52.7
TINWELL Mark U17 18.11.81, Sale :
SPY - 15.19, DTY - 46.18
TOBIN Robert U15 20.12.83, Bas & MH :
800 - 2:04.3
TODD Peter 14.10.61, Annadale Striders :
DT - 41.17 (42.52-88)
TOHILL Paul U17 9.10.82, Mid Ulster :
HJ - 1.91
TOLCHER Stuart U23 18.10.77, Guernsey/
Birm Univ. : 400 - 48.78
TOMLINSON Christopher U17 15.09.81, Mand :
LJ - 7.23io/6.95i/6.67 (6.82w-97),
TJ - 14.93w/14.67
TONNER James 3.06.75, Kilmarnock/Border :
800 - 1:51.43 (1:50.9-97),
1500 - 3:49.64 (3:48.4-97)
TOPLISS Philip Stephen U23 17.07.78,
Peterbro (now WEBB) :
TOSH Henry U20 26.01.80, Yate :
100 - 10.8
TRAPMORE James 31.07.75, S B/Camb Univ :
1500 - 3:50.6 (3:49.1-97)
TREEN Kevin U23 1.02.76, Traff/Sheff Univ :
PV - 4.40i/4.40 (4.50i-94/4.40-93)
TREMAYNE Christopher U15 11.11.84,
Cannock & Stafford : PV - 2.90
TRESSIDER Ross U15 8.11.83, Thurrock :
80HB - 11.70
TRIBBLE Matthew U20 17.10.79, Bedford & Co :
JT - 53.78, DecJ - 5718 (5935-97)

TRIMMER Richard U15 7.09.83, Bournemouth :
SPB - 13.30,
TROMANS Ben U17 8.12.81, Halesowen :
400HY - 56.90
TROMANS Glynn 17.03.69, Coventry Godiva :
3k - 8:08.27 (7:59.27-95),
5k - 13:53.59 (13:48.0-97), 10k - 28:31.71,
10kR - 29:20 (28:54-97), 10MR - 47:25
TSHAYE Amanuel U15 5.11.83, Croydon :
1500 - 4:16.17
TUCKER Stephen 30.12.62, Shettleston :
60 - 6.93i, 100 - 10.83w
        (10.6w-88/10.70w-94/10.8/10.82-92),
200 - 22.0 (21.5w-87/21.7/21.97w-94/22.07-92)
TULBA Phillip William 20.09.73, Bas & MH/
Loughbro : 800 - 1:48.31, 1500 - 3:42.3,
1M - 3:59.7, 3k - 8:15.62i
TULLETT Ian Roger 15.08.69, Belgrave :
PV - 5.35
TULLOCH Andrew George 1.04.67, Belgrave :
60H - 7.55i, 110H - 13.57 (13.5w-96/13.52-94)
TUNE David 29.10.70, Rotherham :
3k - 8:16.9 (8:14.58-93),
5k - 14:32.4 (14:09.49-94),
10k - 29:39.23, 10kR - 29:15,
10MR - 47:46, HMar - 1:05:13 (1:04:48-96)
TUNNICLIFFE Simon U17 2.03.83, Nuneaton :
400 - 50.3, LJ - 6.60w/6.29, OctY - 4259
TURAY Sanusi 14.04.68, Thames Valley/SLE :
100 - 10.2w/10.47dq (10.24w/10.25-96),
200 - 21.50 (21.04A-92)
TURNBULL Alan 22.07.66, Bedford & Co/RAF :
Mar - 2:32:06
TURNBULL David U20 10.06.79, Ayr Seaforth :
60 - 6.88i, 100 - 10.77w/10.82 (10.8-97),
200 - 21.72i/21.89w/21.9/22.26 (21.9-97)
TURNBULL Gareth U20 14.05.79, Belf Sch/IRE :
800 - 1:50.65 (1:49.66-97),
1500 - 3:47.62 (3:42.8-97), 1M - 4:07.4
TURNER Andrew 29.08.63, Bournemouth :
SP - 14.70 (14.86i-96/14.74-94),
DT - 44.94 (47.40-95), HT - 50.67 (51.76-96)
TURNER Andrew U20 19.09.80, Notts :
110HJ - 14.24w/14.4/14.49
TURNER Clayton S. 9.01.68, Horsham BS :
SP - 13.97 (15.52-91), DT - 40.28 (45.26-91)
TURNER Daniel U23 27.11.78, Havant :
HJ - 2.10 (2.15-97)
TURNER Darrell U17 22.10.82, Mansfield :
DTY - 40.70
TURNER David U15 4.07.84, Blackpool :
JTB - 46.11
TURNER Douglas 2.12.66, Cardiff :
100 - 10.5 (10.26w-96/10.40-97),
200 - 20.51A/20.55 (20.36w-97/20.43-96)
TURNER Lee U17 30.06.82, City of Stoke :
1500 - 4:07.32
TURNER Sam U17 3.03.82, Shildon :
3k - 8:59.35
TURVEY A. U15, Halesowen :
PV - 3.00
TWIGG Matthew 18.07.69, :
SP - 15.05, DT - 46.32 (49.42-91)
TYE-WALKER Christopher U17 20.09.82,
Windsor S & E : 100HY - 13.53
TYPE Chris U17 5.10.81, Cardiff :
PV - 4.50

UDECHUKU Emeka U20 10.07.79, Blackh/
Loughbro : SP - 17.02i/16.92 (17.25-97),
SPJ - 17.74, DT - 60.97,
DTJ - 64.35, HTJ - 49.14, JT - 61.16
UGONO Uvie U23 8.03.78, Woodford Green :
60 - 6.8i/6.82i, 100 - 10.32w/10.40,
200 - 21.4 (21.29-96)
ULYATT Kent William 10.04.72, Norwich :
400 - 47.98i (46.31-95)
URQUHART Greg U17 14.06.82, Belgrave :
DTY - 42.54
URQUHART Ronald John U23 14.11.77, Bel :
HT - 61.70
URSELL Nangeloum U17 1.10.81, Blackheath :
100HY - 13.11w/13.19, 400H - 54.92,
400HY - 53.26

VARANAUSKAS Ginturas 17.04.72,
S B/LIT : HJ - 2.05
VAUX-HARVEY Matthew U23 30.03.76, Stour :
3k - 8:19.22, 5k - 14:35.5 (14:20.64-97)
VINCE Andrew Ivor 9.05.59, Falkirk :
SP - 13.69 (18.04-83)
VINT Richard U20 16.02.79, AF&D :
1500 - 3:49.72
VIVIAN Peter John Philip 5.11.70, T V H :
HT - 57.99 (71.28-95)

WADDINGTON Anthony 30.06.75,
Luton : 100 - 10.7w (10.8-96),
200 - 21.9 (21.8-95/22.10w-94/22.20-96)
WADE Philip U17 7.05.82, Wessex & Bath :
PV - 4.00
WADE Thomas U15 31.12.83, Liv.Pemb Seft :
1500 - 4:15.09
WAIN Andrew 2.06.65, Nene Vallley H :
SP - 14.62 (14.80i-96)
WALCOTT Andrew 11.01.75, Belgrave :
100 - 10.65 (10.58-97), 200 - 21.29 (21.15-96)
WALCOTT Mark 24.11.73, Birchfield :
100 - 10.6w (10.6w-92/10.67-94)
WALDEN Matthew U15 30.11.83, Scunthorpe :
80HB - 11.77, LJ - 6.21w/6.09, PenB - 2960
WALKER Adam U20 16.11.79, Crawley :
PV - 4.20i/4.10
WALKER Alvin 30.04.65, N & E B/Army :
LJ - 7.14 (7.38-97), TJ - 15.71w/15.56
WALKER David U23 24.11.78, Morpeth :
400H - 54.8/55.71 (54.08-97)
WALKER Dean U15 15.03.84, Trafford :
80HB - 11.83
WALKER Douglas 28.07.73, N & E B/
C of Edin : 100 - 10.01w/10.8 (10.31-97),
200 - 20.35, 300 - 31.56
WALKER Leigh U23 17.08.77, Craw/Loughbro :
PV - 4.70, Dec - 4929 (5048-97)
WALKER Nicholas O. 24.02.64, Severn :
Dec - 5378 (5510-92)
WALKER Paul 2.12.73, City of Edinburgh :
800 - 1:47.91 (1:46.4-97)
WALKER Robin U23 8.02.78, Scunthorpe :
HT - 47.41
WALL Darren U20 6.04.80, Team Solent :
100 - 10.71w/10.8, 200 - 21.65w/21.70
WALL Terry 12.06.70, Morpeth :
5k - 14:38.9 (14:18.9-97)
WALLACE John 9.10.68, Morpeth :
HJ - 2.05 (2.16-90)

365

WALLACE Jonathan U20 1.01.79, Birchfield :
  TJ - 15.82
WALLACE Mark U17 3.10.81, Birchfield :
  100 - 10.92w/11.17,
WALLING Andrew 3.04.73, Sale :
  800 - 1:51.94 (1:50.6-95)
WALMSLEY Kevin 6.09.67, Manx H :
  10kW - 47:08.62, 20kW - 1:35:32 (1:33:03-97)
WALSH Christopher U23 1.10.78, S B :
  HT - 58.38
WALSH Phillip U17 26.10.81, Belgrave :
  100HY - 13.70
WARD Ashley Keith 1.08.64, Crawley :
  DT - 43.97 (47.70-82)
WARD Ian U17 3.04.82, Chester Le Street :
  400HY - 57.26 (57.18-97)
WARD Jason U23 15.09.78, Hallamshire :
  3kSt - 9:24.88
WARD Richard James Stephen U17 5.05.82,
  Sutton & District : 800 - 1:56.7,
  1500 - 3:53.6, 3k - 8:39.88
WARD-DAVIES Joel U15 9.02.84, Hereford :
  PV - 3.10
WAREHAM Marc U20 9.08.80, Medway :
  110HJ - 14.85
WARISO Solomon Christopher 11.11.66, Har :
  60 - 6.85i (6.72i-94), 400 - 44.68
  100 - 10.7 (10.3-95/10.33-94),
  200 - 20.76 (20.50-95), 300 - 32.23,
WARMBY Mark U23 12.12.78, Longwood :
  3k - 8:32.7, 2kSt - 5:52.28 (5:49.25-97),
WARMINGTON Ben U20 20.03.79, S B/
  Loughbro : 60H - 8.20i, 110HJ - 14.1w/14.16,
  110H - 14.24w/14.25
WARREN Carl 28.09.69, Birchfield :
  3k - 8:15.2 (8:09.29i-94), 5k - 14:34.1 (14:34.1-95),
  3kSt - 9:03.15 (8:40.74-95)
WARREN David U20 5.12.79, Barrow & F :
  HJ - 1.97
WATERS Andrew U20 11.10.79, Oxford City :
  DTJ - 45.86
WATERS Anthony U17 18.07.82, Aberdare :
  1500 - 4:02.2
WATERS Rupert John 3.01.72, Sale :
  800 - 1:51.27 (1:47.9-96)
WATKINS Ben U23 12.11.78, Norwich :
  200 - 21.75
WATSON Darren U15 9.09.83, Blackheath :
  100 - 11.47, 200 - 22.98w/23.09,
  LJ - 6.05, PenB - 2701
WATSON Garth 20.04.73, Newham & E B :
  800 - 1:51.05 (1:50.2-95)
WATSON Graeme Lynton George 'Buster' V40
  19.11.57, Rich & T : JT - 55.71 (59.74-87)
WATSON James 4.10.67, City of Edinburgh :
  60 - 6.95i, 100 - 10.69w/10.84,
  200 - 21.66w/21.79
WATSON Mark U15 16.07.84, Wirral :
  PV - 3.10
WATSON Matthew U20 23.02.80, Bingley :
  3k - 8:33.28
WATSON N., Huntingdon :
  HJ - 1.95
WATSON Tim 28.06.73, Havant :
  3kSt - 9:27.+
WATT Timothy 19.09.66, Steyning :
  10kW - 47:39.32, 20kW - 1:38:36 (1:36:59-94),
  50kW - 4:27:08 (4:20:43-95)

WATTS Robert U17 19.10.81, Brymore Sch :
  HTY - 50.00?/46.37
WEATHERIDGE Nicholas 11.10.72, Basildon :
  5k - 14:01.5, 10kR - 29:45,
  HMar - 1:05:15 (1:04:46-97)
WEAVER Lee U23 9.03.76, Telford :
  JT - 56.47
WEAVER Matthew 14.11.73, Harrow :
  PV - 4.80 (4.90-94)
WEBB Jamie 18.12.75, Belgrave :
  PV - 4.30 (4.60-97)
WEBB Philip Stephen U23 17.07.78,
  Peterbro (formerly TOPLISS) :
  100 - 10.7 (10.61-97),
  200 - 21.31i/21.4/21.56 (21.01w/21.44-97
WEBSTER Harry U17 22.05.82, Brymore Sch :
  OctY - 4344
WEDLAKE Andrew 30.11.71, Bournemouth :
  3k - 8:09.65i/8:11.90 (8:05.06i-94),
  5k - 14:21.14 (14:11.37-94),
  10k - 30:21.19 (30:01.20-95)
WEINMAN Wayne 2.05.66, Ilford :
  PV - 4.40 (4.65-85)
WEIR Robert Boyd 4.02.61, Birchfield :
  DT - 64.42 (64.60-97), HT - 57.31 (75.08-82)
WEITZ Chris U17 28.04.83, Gateshead :
  TJ - 13.31
WELLS Ian 18.02.62, Belgrave :
  400H - 55.9/55.92 (53.3-91/53.34-95)
WELLS John U15 19.04.84, Belgrave :
  400 - 53.56
WELLS Louis U23 6.02.78, Enfield :
  800 - 1:52.4
WELLS Stuart U20 26.07.79, Havering :
  LJ - 7.47 (7.56-97)
WELSH Graeme 8.10.75, Border :
  100 - 10.51w/10.56, 200 - 21.72 (21.70-96)
WEST Terence 19.11.68, Gosforth :
  800 - 1:52.1 (1:47.70-96),
  1500 - 3:45.32 (3:43.39i-94)
WESTMEIJER Jeroen 5.07.70, E & E/HOL :
  SP - 13.88
WESTON Andrew D. 4.12.73, Reading/
  Loughbro : PV - 5.00
WESTON Paul 6.10.67, Bristol :
  TJ - 15.64w/15.34 (15.46-92)
WHALEY Geoffrey Jackson V40 9.06.58,
  City of Plymouth : HT - 48.98 (62.16-80)
WHALLEY Robert Simon 11.02.68, C of Stoke :
  3k - 8:17.10i (7:51.4-97), 4K - 11:03.2,
  5k - 14:07.73 (13:41.08-97)
WHATTLEY David U15 5.09.83, Enfield :
  200 - 23.44w/23.5/24.02 (23.91-97), LJ - 6.06
WHEELER Craig U23 14.06.76, Trafford :
  1500 - 3:48.2, 3k - 8:13.0, 3kSt - 8:42.83
WHEELER Neil U15 6.09.83, Gloucester Sch :
  100 - 11.60w/11.82
WHITBY Benedict U23 6.01.77, Hounslow :
  1500 - 3:48.8, 3k - 8:13.28i,
  5k - 14:31.8, 3kSt - 8:41.79
WHITE Adrian Paul 1.09.74, Thames Valley :
  100 - 10.3w/10.7/10.78 (10.40-95),
  200 - 21.59 (20.79-96)
WHITE Edward 16.11.73, Sale :
  60 - 6.9i/6.91i, 100 - 10.53w/10.59,
  200 - 21.06 (21.02-97)
WHITE Graham 28.03.59, Brighton :
  20kW - 1:35:11 (1:29:27-97), 50kW - 4:13:18

WHITE Jonathon U15 23.10.83, Team Solent :
200 - 23.6w/23.77w/24.00
WHITE S., Loughborough Studnts :
HT - 48.45
WHITE Simon 2.10.75, Blackheath :
Dec - 5695
WHITE Stephen 2.10.75, Blackh/Brunel Univ :
400H - 55.9
WHITEHEAD Lee U15 7.03.84, Oldham & R :
400 - 52.8/52.96
WHITEHEAD Peter Kenneth 3.12.64, Skyrac :
10MR - 48:14 (47:51-93)
WHITEHEAD Timmon U17 20.04.82, G & G :
HTY - 63.08
WHITEMAN Anthony 13.11.71, GEC :
800 - 1:47.5 (1:47.16-97),
1k - 2:18.82 (2:18.8i-96), 1M - 3:51.90,
1500 - 3:32.69 (3:32.34-97), 3k - 7:43.61
WHITTINGHAM Simon U23 18.09.78, Watford :
HJ - 1.97
WHORLOW Nigel U20 26.11.80, Belgrave :
3kW - 13:21.7 (13:11.5-97),
5kW - 24:09.44 (23:04.0i-97),
5kWR - 23:27 (23:25-97),
10kW - 50:38.65 (49:18.4-97),
10kWR - 48:57 (47:05-97)
WHYTE Stephen Anthony 14.03.64, T V H :
SP - 17.03i/15.90 (17.78-89),
DT - 49.42 (50.40-94), HT - 66.98 (67.82-89)
WILD Jonathan 30.08.73, Sale/Oklah St Un :
3k - 7:59.59 (7:53.10i-96/7:55.16-95),
5k - 14:29.87 (13:45.1-96), 10kR - 29:36
WILDING Ian 3.03.75, Newham & Essex B :
PV - 4.20 (5.00ns-94/5.00-96)
WILKINS Chris U15 20.12.83, Birchfield :
LJ - 6.00w/5.60
WILKINS Perris 12.12.69, Banbury : 12-12-69
SP - 14.25, DT - 66.64
WILKINSON Jonathon 17.02.62, Spenborough :
DT - 40.32
WILKINSON Simon U23 27.08.77, Dudley & St :
5k - 14:26.7
WILLERS Edward T. U20 18.09.79, Millfld Sch:
HJ - 2.15
WILLIAMS Alun 22.06.62, Torfaen/RAF :
DT - 41.67 (43.78-96)
WILLIAMS Anthony Richard 1.05.72, N & E B :
400 - 47.63, 400H - 51.16 (50.31-95)
WILLIAMS Barrington Chester V40 11.09.55,
Birchfield : LJ - 7.48 (8.05i/8.01-89)
WILLIAMS Barry V50 5.03.47, Trafford :
HT - 48.50 (73.86-76)
WILLIAMS Brett U15 23.10.83, Wirral :
HJ - 1.75
WILLIAMS Craig U15, Wrexham :
JTB - 45.62
WILLIAMS Delvyn U15 8.12.83, Mx Sch :
100 - 11.52
WILLIAMS Edward 1.10.70, Thames Valley :
400 - 48.4 (46.84-94),
800 - 1:51.65 (1:49.41-96)
WILLIAMS G. U13, Cardiff :
DTC - 34.06?
WILLIAMS James U17 17.07.82, Mercury :
1.5kSt - 4:31.47
WILLIAMS Kevin 15.12.71, Cardiff :
60 - 6.69i (6.63i-97), 200 - 21.50 (21.30-97),
100 - 10.43 (10.30w/10.34-97)

WILLIAMS Lester U23, :
SP - 13.55
WILLIAMS Luke U15 27.10.83, AVON S :
PenB - 2529
WILLIAMS Matthew U15 31.01.84, Wolves & B :
80HB - 11.84
WILLIAMS Nicholas U17 2.02.82, Trafford :
HTY - 59.91
WILLIAMS Richard U17 22.10.81, S B :
3k - 8:53.7, 1.5kSt - 4:28.1
WILLIAMS Simon 9.05.72, Yeovil Olympiads :
LJ - 7.05 (7.05-97)
WILLIAMS Simon David U20 5.10.80,
Bas & MH : SP - 13.27, SPJ - 14.07,
DT - 44.34, DTJ - 50.82
WILLIAMSON Paul Lee 16.06.74, T V H/
Staffs Univ : PV - 5.30 (5.50-96)
WILLIAMSON Wilby U20 8.08.81, Lagan Val :
JTY - 51.14o
WILLS Chris U23 18.05.76, Birchfield :
PV - 4.80
WILSON Alex U17 28.08.82, Harrow :
DTY - 44.63
WILSON Alloy U20 25.01.80, Blackheath :
60 - 6.93i, 100 - 10.8w, 400 - 46.64
WILSON Ian U17 6.02.82, Hartlepool :
1.5kSt - 4:31.40
WILSON Martin 3.03.71, Barrow & Furness :
SP - 13.60 (14.24-90), DT - 41.28 (44.86-91)
WILSON Nana U20 14.01.79, Belgrave :
100 - 10.88, LJ - 6.93 (7.02-97)
WILSON Simon 30.04.74, GEC :
400H - 54.9 (55.76-97)
WILSON Stephen U20 3.11.80, Preston :
DecJ - 5593
WILSON Vincent 1.04.73, Morpeth :
400 - 48.98, 800 - 1:48.68,
1500 - 3:44.63 (3:43.38-96), 1M - 4:03.3
WINCHCOMBE Gary U17 26.07.82, Rotherham :
DTY - 41.60
WINNING Brian 7.02.67, Corstorphine :
Dec - 4913
WINROW Craig Nicholas 22.12.71, Wigan :
800 - 1:49.05 (1:45.69-96)
WINSTANLEY Shaun, Bilderston Bounders :
Mar - 2:33:11
WINTER Neil Stephen 21.03.74, S B :
PV - 5.10 (5.60-95)
WISCOMBE Lee U20 12.07.80, Jarrow & H :
400 - 48.74, 400H - 53.92
WISCOMBE Mark 25.01.74, Yeovil Olympiads :
800 - 1:50.82, 1500 - 3:51.9 (3:50.6-97)
WISEMAN Mark, Army/Basingstoke & MH :
SP - 14.42 (14.90-97), DT - 40.72 (48.84-95)
WITCHALLS Bruno 22.03.75, Dork & Mole V/
Loughbro : 1500 - 3:48.92 (3:41.51-95),
3kSt - 9:01.19
WODU Ejike 15.12.74, Blackheath :
100 - 10.91 (10.38w/10.55-93)
WOLSTENCROFT Lee U20 19.07.81, Trafford :
3kSt - 9:51.5
WOOD Joshua 19.04.74, Herne Hill :
100 - 10.7/10.92, 200 - 22.0 (22.0-97)
WOODD Charles 16.11.71, Bristol :
10k - 31:13.71 (31:06.44-97)
WOODGER Matthew U20 9.01.79, Newton Ab :
DecJ - 5133

WOODHOUSE Mark 1.11.75, Norwich/
Loughborough Studnts :
100 - 10.7w/10.71w
(10.4w?-95/10.6-96/10.61w-93/10.68-95),
200 - 21.60w/21.7/22.43 (21.1w/21.35-97)
WOODING Andrew U20 2.06.79, Colwyn Bay :
LJ - 7.03i/7.03 (7.16-97)
WOODS Alan Peter V45 27.03.51, Birchfield :
HT - 48.45 (57.24-78)
WOODWARD Barry U20 20.11.80, Mansfield :
800 - 1:54.98
WOODWARD Lyndon U20 22.11.80, Can & St :
SP - 14.51, SPJ - 16.49i/15.84
WOOLCOTT Nicholas David 7.04.61, Har :
DT - 51.95 (55.34-88), HT - 47.33 (49.14-81)
WORKMAN Richard J. 31.05.71, Trafford :
400 - 47.81
WORLAND James 3.02.72, Southend :
SP - 13.60, DT - 40.50
WRIGHT James U17 2.04.82, Woodford Gr :
PV - 3.60
WURR Simon U23 7.01.77, Leam/Durham Un :
2kSt - 5:54.1, 3kSt - 9:13.25 (8:57.52-97)
WURR Timothy U20 1.03.79, Leamington :
HT - 52.42, HTJ - 57.15 (58.52-97)
WYNN William 15.02.73, Croydon :
110H - 15.10w/15.2 (15.1-97/15.37-96),
JT - 55.08, Dec - 6700 (6800w/6790-96)

Y AMBASU Aiah 10.11.73, T V H :
60 - 6.89i, 100 - 10.8/10.88 (10.7-96)
YATES John James U17 17.12.82, Sale :
PV - 3.60
YATES Matthew Stewart 4.02.69, Belgrave :
800 - 1:48.28 (1:45.05-92),
1500 - 3:37.04 (3:34.00-91),
1M - 4:03.65 (3:52.75-93)

YATES Peter Derek V40 15.06.57, Dac & Tring :
JT - 68.06 (77.84-87)
YEBOAH Bernard U13, Croydon :
LJ - 5.27
YELLING Martin 7.02.72, Bedford & County :
3kSt - 8:57.03 (8:54.63-97)
YEO Byron U15 9.10.83, Southend :
PV - 3.20
YEOMANS P. U13, Watford :
PV - 2.30
YIEND Bradley U20 25.10.80, Birchfield :
400H - 56.05
YOUNG Andrew U23 20.06.77, Victoria Park/
Loughbro : 800 - 1:49.13
YOUNG Blair 5.04.71, City of Edinburgh :
400 - 46.89, 400H - 50.57
YOUNG Colin U20 11.12.79, Mansfield :
400 - 49.1 (52.13-95)
YOUNG Martin 11.07.72, Roadhogs :
3kW - 13:16.23 (12:16.10i-96/12:20.38-95),
10kW - 44:21.63 (43:39.0-96),
20kW - 1:34:54 (1:29:48-96),
30kW - 2:42.57
YOUNG Neil U23 20.02.77, S B/Bath Univ. :
PV - 5.10 (5.20-97)
YOUNG P., Hallamshire :
Mar - 2:32:30

Z AIDMAN Antony Adam 18.03.62, Enf :
SP - 14.46 (17.87i-83/17.22-81)
ZAREI Rab'ali 'James' V50 13.01.44, Croy :
24Hr - 210.199km (243.564km-89)
ZULEWSKI Alex U17 6.06.82, Braintree :
100HY - 13.94, OctY ñ 4641

With the change of age group descriptions it is obvious that changes must be made to the names of the events. Whilst this is easy to organanize in the main lists, it is much more difficult with the index where a concise code is required. I have, therefore, decided to keep the previous descriptions of the events. This should not cause any confusion since the age group of each athlete is clearly shown in the new form eg U15 but some examples will clarify this.

A **J** after an event is used to designate an Under 20 event
eg 110HJ - 110 metres hurdles with 3'3" hurdles

A **Y** or an **I** is an Under 17 event (men and women)
eg 100HY - 100 metres hurdles with 3' 0" hurdles Heptl - Heptathlon with Under 17 implements

A **B** or a **G** is an Under 15 event (men and women)
eg JTB - 600 gram Javelin SPG - 3.25kg Shot

A **C** or an **M** is an Under 13 event (men and women)
eg SPC - 3.25kg Shot SPM - 2.72kg Shot

WOMENS INDEX

AARON Louise U17 19.04.82, Hull Spr :
1500 - 4:47.2 (4:41.6-97),
3k - 10:33.7 (10:13.94-97)
ABBISS Susan V35 20.10.59, Chester Le Str :
Mar - 3:08:05 (2:51:33-94)
ABRAMS Angela 7.05.71, Belgrave :
LJ - 5.59 (5.70-90)
ADAMS Carol 27.11.63, Central :
Mar - 3:01:39
ADAMS Debbie U20 7.03.80, Newport :
LJ - 5.59w/5.54
ADAMS Joyce U20 25.03.80, Birchfield :
TJ - 11.46
ADAMSON Samantha U17 27.03.82, Herts & W :
60HI - 9.23o, 100H - 15.9 (15.9-97),
300H - 46.9 (46.59-97), 400H - 66.3,
HJ - 1.75 (1.75-97), Hepl - 4629
ADLAM Sian 8.11.70, Yate :
200 - 25.1
AFFLECK Pat, Gala :
Mar - 3:04:05
AGBO Phyllis U13 16.12.85, Thames Valley :
HJ - 1.46
AIREY Lisa U20 19.12.80, Birchfield :
3kW - 15:46.61, 5kW - 26:29.12,
5kWR - 26:25, 10kWR - 55:47
AKINBIYI Sarah U20 23.08.81, Tower Haml :
100H - 14.10w/14.39, TJ - 11.12
ALDER Elizabeth U20 20.11.80, Cheltenham :
60 - 7.70i (7.70i-96),
100 - 11.86w/12.0/12.07, 200 - 24.68
ALEXANDER Kate 28.04.74, Shaftesbury B :
PV - 3.20i/3.20 (3.30-96)
ALEXANDER Patricia U17 9.09.82, Tower H :
100 - 12.48w (12.88-97)
ALLAHGREEN Diane 21.02.75, Liverpool H :
60 - 7.41i (7.38i-95),
100 - 11.66w (11.7-94/11.84-97), 60H - 8.02i
ALLAN Vicki U13 31.12.85, Giffnock :
HJ - 1.45
ALLEN Angela 23.09.67, City of Plymouth :
HMar - 1:16:26
ALLEN Carice U23 25.09.77, Telford :
HT - 36.38 (39.80-95)
ALLEN Jenna U20 2.05.79, Charnwood :
JT - 43.09 (43.64-96)
ALLEN Sara 7.12.70, Sale :
SP - 11.49 (12.65-95), DT - 36.84 (42.90-95)
ALLOTT Beth U23 9.02.77, Salford :
HMar - 1:18:00, Mar - 2:55:19
AMAA Joan U17 15.12.81, Barnet :
SP - 11.10
AMADI Onyema 28.06.73, Cardiff :
JT - 43.05 (49.04-94)
AMEDE Christine F. V35 7.08.63, W S & E :
400 - 55.4/55.70 (55.53-90), 400H - 59.43
AMOS Katie U23 13.11.78, Thurrock :
JT - 50.34
ANDERSON Melissa U17 30.03.82, Cram :
60 - 7.99i, 100 - 12.20w/12.43 (12.39-96),
200 - 25.57 (25.44-97)
ANDERSON Pamela U23 16.10.76, C of Glas :
TJ - 11.70i/11.62 (12.55-96)
ANDERSON Shani 7.08.75, S B/Brunel Univ :
60 - 7.52i (7.6-97), 200 - 24.17i (23.9w-97),
100H - 14.62, LJ - 5.65 (5.91-97),
TJ - 11.83 (13.03-96)

ANDREASSON Linda U23 9.04.76, Gate/SWE :
SP - 11.28i, HT - 44.02, JT - 38.55
ANDREWS Denise U20 1.07.80, Birchfield :
LJ - 5.81
ANDREWS Kristi U17 2.05.83, Braintree :
300H - 46.28, 400H - 66.2
ANDREWS Sharon Vivian 4.07.67, Essex L :
DT - 44.41 (56.24-94)
ANDREWS Teresa U23 4.01.77, Preseli :
HJ - 1.65 (1.79-94), Hep - 4229 (4456w-94),
LJ - 5.58 (5.69-96/5.61-95),
ANDREWS Vicki 31.08.69, Wolves & B :
800 - 2:12.18 (2:09.4-95),
1500 - 4:33.5 (4:32.6-97/4:33.8mx-96)
ANEK Nightingale U23 25.01.78, Hounslow :
JT - 38.21
ANETO Stephanie U23 23.08.77, Essex L :
TJ - 11.45w (12.06w/12.03-97)
ANKIER Joanna U17 5.08.82, Shaftesbury B :
1500 - 4:39.10
ANNESS Ruth U23 3.10.78, West Suffolk :
PV - 3.00
APPLEGARTH Amanda U15 5.04.84, S Devon :
100 - 12.4, 200 - 25.96w/26.02
APPLETON Leanne U20 3.03.81, Bristol :
1500 - 4:33.03
ARMISHAW Helen U20 4.10.80, Sale :
LJ - 5.63
ARMSTRONG Joanne U17 22.09.82,
Basingstoke & MH : DT - 32.38
ARNOLD Helen Louise U23 5.10.78,
City of Portsmouth : HT - 49.70 (54.72-97)
ARNOLD Zoe U23 10.11.76, Lagan Valley :
400 - 56.31 (56.21-97)
ARON Lucy U23 22.04.76, :
Mar - 3:05:56
ASH Sally U20 4.11.80, Norwich :
TJ - 11.04i (10.85-97)
ASHBY Abigail U23 23.11.77, Rowntrees :
100H - 15.24w (14.6/14.67-97), TJ - 11.02
ASHCROFT S. U13, Barnsley :
PV - 1.50
ASTON Faith 26.11.75, Sale :
800 - 2:08.2
ATKIN Kerrie U20 8.04.81, Great Yarmouth :
JT - 39.11
ATKINSON Rachel 26.05.73, Sale/Leeds Univ :
TJ - 11.88 (12.20w-96)
ATUNUMUO Lucy U20 4.11.80, Hercules W :
60 - 7.7i (7.82i-97), LJ - 5.77
100 - 12.06w (12.28-97),
200 - 24.56w/25.08 (24.9/24.96-97),
AUCOTT Jane Christine 10.10.68, Rugby :
SP - 11.25 (12.99i-86/12.89-93),
DT - 42.93 (55.52-90)
AUGEE Esther 1.01.64, Essex L :
SP - 11.65 (11.89-97),
HT - 49.95 (56.76-93)
AUGEE Myrtle Sharon Mary 4.02.65, Bromley :
SP - 17.69 (19.03-90),
DT - 43.47 (49.44-95), HT - 37.02 (46.64-95)
AUGUSTUS Keeley U17 18.05.82, Medway :
300 - 41.1
AUSTIN Carly U17 16.05.83, Radley :
300H - 46.36

369

AUSTIN Elizabeth 22.02.72, Trafford :
JT - 39.86 (41.38-97)
AVIL Gemma U15 8.03.84, Oxford City :
SPG - 10.87
AXTEN Tracy V35 20.07.63, Shaftesbury B :
SP - 15.81, DT - 54.03 (58.18-97)
AYERO Jennifer U20 13.09.79, Ealing,S & Mx :
HT - 37.00 (37.36-97), JT - 40.23
AYLWIN Louise U20 8.04.80, Bracknell :
400H - 63.99

BACKHOUSE Susan U23 6.12.78, Leeds :
DT - 44.11
BAILEY Kathryn 25.03.68, Havant :
10MR - 57:34 (55:48-93),
HMar - 1:18:14 (1:14:07-95)
BAILEY Rebecca U17 8.01.82, Cornwall AC :
JT - 35.04 (36.88-96)
BAIRSTOW Jackie V40 8.01.57, Manx H :
50kW - 5:41:36
BAKER Rebecca U20 7.02.79, Thames Valley :
LJ - 5.62, TJ - 11.17
BAKER Tanya 23.11.74, Andover :
800 - 2:08.11, 1500 - 4:26.52 (4:20.87-97)
BANNON Anna 27.03.70, :
Mar - 3:07:26
BARBER Caroline U15 1.09.83, Swindon :
HJ - 1.67
BARBER Helen 13.12.67, Horsforth :
Mar - 3:04:33
BARCLAY Jo U17 28.07.82, Northampton :
HT - 32.28
BARNABY Anisha U17 9.07.83, Blackheath :
100 - 12.55w/12.57, 200 - 25.35w
BARNES Catherine U23 28.09.77, Winchester :
TJ - 11.40 (11.49-95)
BARNES Charlene U17 25.05.82, R S C :
200 - 25.06w/25.3 (25.81-97)
BARNETT Lynne 12.08.74, Perth :
SP - 11.37 (12.83-93)
BARR Nicola 26.04.70, Edinburgh WM :
TJ - 12.27 (12.42w-97)
BARRETT Caroline U15 16.09.83, Lincs Sch :
DT - 29.15
BARTLETT Katherine 6.05.73, Shaftesbury B :
100H - 14.7w/14.83 (14.5w-96/14.54-94),
400H - 62.22 (60.75-97)
BASHFORD Rachel U13 10.01.86, Blackpool :
SPM - 9.67
BASS Natalie U13, Leamington :
150 - 19.7
BATEMAN Victoria 6.09.72, City of Stoke :
DT - 40.28 (40.44-97)
BATES Rebecca U17 16.05.82, City of Stoke :
LJ - 5.37i/5.35 (5.60-97),
TJ - 11.22i/11.05w/10.87
BATESON Alicia U15 6.11.83, W Ches :
LJ - 5.35w/5.32
BATEY Louisa U15 30.11.83, Middlesbro & C :
SPG - 10.67
BATHO Louise U23 27.11.76, Thurrock :
SP - 11.27 (11.88-94)
BAXTER Hayley-Kate U17 25.06.82, Brecon :
60 - 7.98i, 100 - 12.41w/12.56
BEARD Hayley U13 2.12.85, Stevenage & NH :
600 - 1:43.4, 800 - 2:25.4
BECK Emma U13 22.11.85, Windsor S & E :
600 - 1:46.1, 1200 - 4:01.8

BECKETT Charlotte U13 4.01.86, Milton K :
200 - 27.2
BEECROFT Alice 27.07.73, Wakefield :
400 - 57.0mx/57.56 (55.6/55.81-97),
800 - 2:06.8 (2:04.9mx-97)
BELL Karen U17 18.06.82, Elgin :
HT - 40.09
BELL Rebecca U13 1.12.85, Norwich :
HJ - 1.51
BELL Sarah U15 20.09.83, Parkside :
200 - 25.59i/25.61w/25.68
BELLE Symone U15 12.11.84, Tower Hamlets :
60HG - 9.04i, 75HG - 10.99w/11.11, LJ - 5.33
BELLWOOD L. U15, Gloucester Sch :
JT - 35.22
BEMROSE Antonia Marie U20 3.09.79, AF&D :
HJ - 1.75 (1.76-96)
BENJAMIN Donita 5.03.72, Radley :
100 - 12.0/12.15w, LJ - 6.28w/6.09
BENNETT Alison U17 4.12.81, Law & Dist :
60 - 7.96i
BENNETT Carol Jane U23 11.01.77, Hull Spr :
SP - 13.46 (14.24-97)
BENNETT Christina Jayne U23 27.02.78, E & E :
SP - 15.10, DT - 42.33, HT - 46.66
BENNETT Claire U17 4.02.83, Cannock & St :
JT - 39.29
BENNETT Diana Faye 14.06.74, Epsom & E :
400 - 56.9 (56.5-93), 800 - 2:10.69,
60H - 8.64i, 100H - 14.2w?/14.23w/14.38,
HJ - 1.80i/1.79, LJ - 6.08w/5.95 (6.07-97),
SP - 11.94 (12.00-97),
Hep - 5555w/5504 (5550-97)
BENNETT Gemma U15 4.01.84, N & E B :
100 - 12.5/12.67, 60HG - 9.13i,
75HG - 11.50 (11.43-97), SPG - 10.82
BENNETT Joanna U17 6.08.83, Epsom & E :
SP - 10.70, HT - 30.49
BENNETT Julia Margaret 26.03.70, Epsom & E :
60H - 8.83i, 400H - 63.9 (61.7/61.84-97),
100H - 14.52w/15.0 (14.43w/14.7-96/14.74-95),
HJ - 1.84i/1.83 (1.92i-90/1.89-94),
LJ - 6.13i/6.03, SP - 12.09i/12.07,
Hep - 5604w (5747w-96/5496-95)
BENNETT Sarah U20 27.07.80, Birchfield :
3kW - 14:49.18 (14:39.24i-96),
5kW - 26:01.4 (25:34.1-97),
5kWR - 24:59, 10kWR - 53:53
BENNINGTON Lisa U23 12.12.78, Grimsby :
HJ - 1.68 (1.70-96),
TJ - 11.38w/11.20 (11.32-97)
BENTLEY Sarah 21.05.67, Birchfield :
1500 - 4:22.2, 3k - 9:23.79 (9:04.4-96),
10k - 33:59.69, 10kR - 33:37 (33:30-96)
BERRY Catherine 8.10.75, Kingston & Poly :
3k - 9:33.03i/9:41.54 (9:25.86-94)
BERRY Claire U13 23.02.86, Blackheath :
1k - 3:12.7
BERRY Jayne N. 18.07.70, Brecon :
SP - 13.58 (15.09-93),
DT - 39.77 (43.22-92)
BEVERLEY Rachael Ann U20 23.07.79, Sale :
HT - 57.97
BICK Alexandria U17 4.01.83, Cardiff :
60 - 7.77i, 100 - 12.16w/12.19,
200 - 24.71w/24.85
BIGGS Sarah U15 16.12.83, Peterborough :
100 - 12.68w (13.0-97)

BIRCH Courtney U15 5.10.84, Liv.Pemb Seft :
  1500 - 4:38.89
BIRD Rebecca U17 7.01.83, Cheltenham :
  60 - 7.69i, 100 - 12.4/12.44,
  200 - 25.00w/25.08i/25.1/25.30
BIRNEY Natalie U17 21.09.81, Southport :
  80HI - 12.0w (12.7-97), 300H - 45.6/46.02,
  400H - 67.7
BISCOE Lisa U17 13.01.83, Southend :
  HJ - 1.65, HepI - 3963
BISHOP Tracy U20 1.05.79, Parkside :
  100 - 12.1/12.28w (12.52-96),
  200 - 25.06 (24.87w-96/24.92-95)
BLACK Caroline E. 19.05.72, Edinburgh WM :
  (see MERCER)
BLACK Gillian Elizabeth U20 27.10.79,
  City of Glasgow : HJ - 1.80 (1.81-97)
BLACKTIN Faye U17 5.11.81, Hertford & Ware :
  HT - 33.58
BLACKWELL Eleanor U15 28.09.84, Bromley :
  200 - 25.7
BLACKWOOD Kathryn U23 31.03.76, Roth :
  TJ - 11.15 (11.80w-93/11.69-94)
BLAKE Tanya-Gee 16.01.71, Reebok East :
  800 - 2:00.10 (2:01.9mx-97),
  1M - 4:47.08i/4:47.50
BLAKEMAN Beverley 4.04.74, Sunderland :
  800 - 2:05.33 (2:18c-97)
BLANK Paula U23 13.12.77, Verlea :
  JT - 43.75 (45.20-96),
  Hep - 3932 (4057-94)
BLISS Jenny U13 6.07.86, Brighton :
  800 - 2:24.1, PenM - 2081
BLOOMFIELD Christine Beverley 12.02.68,
  Essex L : 60 - 7.57i,
  100 - 11.7/11.75w/11.77 (11.59-93),
  200 - 24.06 (23.70-93)
BLOOMFIELD Tracey U20 13.09.79, G & G :
  PV - 3.75
BLUNDELL Gemma U15, Medway :
  PenG - 2507
BOLSOVER Maria Teresa U20 5.06.80,
  Hallamshire : 60 - 7.60i,
  100 - 11.59w/12.0/12.07 (12.0-96),
  200 - 24.39w/24.49
BOLTON Laura U20 22.01.79, Newquay & Par :
  JT - 38.31
BOLTZ Jill 14.10.66, Blaydon (nee Hunter) :
  3k - 9:36.6mx (8:47.36-88),
  10k - 34:55.25 (31:07.88-91),
  10kR - 34:29 (31:42-89),
BONE Liz U20 22.11.79, Middlesbro & C :
  HT - 37.86
BOSTOCK Claire 24.02.73, Rugby (nee White) :
  100H - 15.1 (14.6/15.11w-95/15.18-96)
BOTHAMS Valerie 19.03.75, City of Glasgow :
  1500 - 4:28.96 (4:22.7-97), 3k - 9:36.50i
BOUCHARD Sarah 23.10.74, Trafford :
  800 - 2:12.7 (2:08.94-93)
BOULTON Jane V40 2.04.56, Crowborough :
  Mar - 2:54:55 (2:52:36-97)
BOVILL Susan U17 6.05.82, Sutton & District :
  100 - 12.2w/12.3 (12.3/12.46w-97),
  200 - 25.2/25.35 (25.35-97), 300 - 41.4
BOWEN Shelley-Anne U20 12.05.79, Reading :
  60 - 7.65i, 100 - 11.86w/12.1/12.24 (11.95-96)
BOWERS Hayley U17 26.01.83, Aberdeen :
  100 - 12.2w

BOWRING Faye U17 22.10.81, Bournemouth :
  JT - 39.63
BOWRING Nicole 27.01.74, Bromley :
  100 - 12.1, 200 - 24.7 (25.05w-97),
  400 - 54.87
BOWYER Elizabeth U17 8.09.81, Wirral :
  SP - 11.44i/11.43
BOWYER Sonya 18.09.72, Sale/Loughbro :
  800 - 2:09.96 (2:01.67-95),
  1500 - 4:21.6mx/4:27.03 (4:10.7mx/4:17.4-96)
BOYLE Anna U17 29.03.83, Ballymena & A :
  100 - 12.2/12.41
BRACKSTONE Lorraine U23 15.02.78, Stoke :
  100H - 14.9w/14.98 (14.3w/14.78-96)
BRADBURY Sarah V35 25.02.63, AF&D :
  5k - 17:07.39 (17:07.24-95)
BRADDOCK Lynsey U23 14.10.77, Bracknell :
  DT - 38.54 (39.02-94)
BRADLEY Joanna U20 23.08.79, Ashford :
  DT - 43.58
BRADLEY Lynn 21.05.67, Sheffield RWC :
  10kWR - 55:35 (53:54-96)
BRADLEY Maria V35 2.01.63, Overton :
  10kR - 34:43, 10MR - 55:59, HMar - 1:16:00
BRADLEY Melanie V35 12.03.63, Army/AF&D :
  Mar - 2:51:17
BRADSHAW Noelle Elizabeth V35 18.12.63,
  AF&D : PV - 3.50, SP - 11.83 (12.26-95),
  DT - 38.61, HT - 37.58 (38.82-94),
  JT - 48.60 (52.40-93)
BRADY Emma 3.01.74, Sale :
  800 - 2:09.61 (2:09.1-97)
BRAMHALL Victoria U23 13.10.77, Guild & G :
  PV - 2.80
BRANNAN Lesley U23 13.09.76, Sale :
  SP - 11.86 (12.10-95), HT - 46.35 (47.08-96)
BRANNEY Sandra V40 30.04.54, City of Glas :
  10kR - 34:54sh (31:58un-89/33:43-92),
  HMar - 1:18:36 (1:12:22-86),
  Mar - 2:48:47 (2:35:03-89)
BRANT Natalie U17 11.12.82, Epsom & Ewell :
  LJ - 5.36w (5.26-97), TJ - 11.15
BRASON Claire U17 16.03.83, North Shields P :
  300H - 46.5
BRATLEY Sarah U15 20.09.84, Hull Spr :
  LJ - 5.32
BRAZNELL Kimberley V40 28.02.56, Dud & St :
  5kWR - 24:35 (24:35-93), 10kWR - 48:36
BREENS Felicity J. U17 6.11.81, Leics Cor :
  80HI - 11.95
BRENNAN Faye U15 13.05.84, Worthing :
  SPG - 11.52, DT - 30.82
BRENNAN Katie U17 27.04.82, Warrington :
  800 - 2:15.70, 1500 - 4:46.80
BRETT Jacquelyn Charis 5.07.65, Newq & Par :
  100H - 14.0w/14.1/14.12w/14.26 (13.86-87)
BREWINGTON Kate U17 15.10.81, Havering :
  80HI - 12.03, HepI - 3911 (3977-97)
BRIDGE Kim U15 7.09.83, AF&D :
  SPG - 11.55
BRIGGS Susan 26.03.67, Trafford :
  100 - 12.1w (11.6w-85/11.8-88/11.82w-89/12.00-93),
  200 - 25.0 (24.02i-92/24.1/24.1w-89/24.18-94
BRIGHT Kathryn U23 27.03.76, Newport :
  400 - 55.8/56.01
BRINDLEY Tracy 25.08.72, Aberdeen :
  3k - 9:57.2 (9:53.2-97), 5k - 16:44.63,
  10MR - 57:27dh

371

BRISTOW Lynette U23 17.11.77, Worcester :
HT - 36.33
BRITTON Nicola U15 28.06.84, West Norfolk :
PenG - 2621
BROMLEY Nadia U13 21.09.86, Wakefield :
PenM - 2134
BROOK Tanya U13 20.02.87, Parkside :
HJ - 1.44
BROOKER Emma U23 26.10.78, S Barnet/
Cambridge Univ : 3k - 9:57.22
BROOKER Jessica U20 6.01.81, Exeter :
JT - 38.43
BROOKS Ann Elizabeth 4.05.71, City of Hull :
(see DANSON)
BROOKS Katie U17 17.02.82, Shaftesbury B :
300H - 46.9, 400H - 66.8
BROOME Nicola U17 5.06.83, Wirral :
JT - 42.76
BROW Kelly U23 24.09.78, Bingley :
TJ - 11.11w/11.10 (11.53w-97/11.24-96)
BROWN Celia U23 22.01.77, Chelmsford :
400H - 62.2/62.63
BROWN Janette 19.02.73, Mandale :
HT - 43.44
BROWN Jennifer A. V35 21.05.59, Ashford :
HJ - 1.71i/1.71 (1.73-89),
TJ - 11.21w/11.14 (11.56-97),
Hep - 4605 (4803w-89/4757-90)
BROWN Jennifer A. 27.02.70, Bournemouth :
800 - 2:10.9 (2:10.5-91),
1500 - 4:23.0, 3k - 9:31.96
BROWN Louise U23 6.05.78, Scarborough :
3k - 9:52.1, 5k - 17:28.05
BROWN Nicola 17.03.74, Tynedale :
HMar - 1:18:53, Mar - 2:43:18
BROWN Sandra V45 1.04.49, Surrey WC :
24HrT - 193.346km (215.068km-93),
24Hr - 194.032km,
100MW - 19:32:26 (18:50:29-92),
BROWNHILL Kelly U20 27.03.80, Trafford :
800 - 2:09.6mx/2:12.15
BRUCE Jill 25.07.73, Dromore/IRE :
Mar - 3:04:01
BRUCE Joanne U23 26.10.78, Woking :
JT - 44.60 (46.54-97)
BRUNNING Natasha 10.03.73, AF&D :
TJ - 11.12
BRYAN Lowell U17 3.01.82, Ryde :
DT - 33.18
BRYCE Louise U20 19.04.81, Edinburgh WM :
TJ - 11.38
BUCHANAN Lesley U17 25.11.81, East Kilb :
HJ - 1.72
BUCKINGHAM Penny 26.04.67, Guernsey :
Mar - 3:02:11 (3:00:11-97)
BUCKLEY Anne 20.06.67, Pudsey & Bram/IRE :
10kR - 34:12, 10MR - 56:49 (55:38dh-93),
HMar - 1:15:53
BUCKLEY Ria U15 25.09.83, AF&D :
JT - 32.24
BULL Sarah 4.06.75, Derby LAC :
800 - 2:11.4 (2:09.82-96), 1500 - 4:21.02
BULLER Rachel U23 31.08.76, Norwich :
800 - 2:07.56, 1500 - 4:30.6
BULLOCK Sarah U17 6.12.81, Middlesbro & C :
60HI - 9.22i

BURGE Kate, Staffs H :
HMar - 1:19:21 (1:18:57-96)
BURLEY Kathryn Jane U20 5.02.79, King & P :
PV - 2.70i/2.50 (2.70-97)
BURR Lisa 6.06.86, Aberdeen :
70HM - 11.73
BURROWS Catherine U23 11.02.76, Wigan :
TJ - 11.23 (11.79w/11.72i/11.69-95)
BURROWS Melanie U23 7.08.76, Ashford :
JT - 42.18
BURTHEM Jane V35 13.12.62, Warrington :
Mar - 3:02:40
BURTON Carly U20 14.10.80, Ashford :
DT - 43.75, HT - 36.16
BUTCHER A. U15, :
JT - 31.80
BUTLER Judith U20 5.10.79, Oadby & Wig :
Hep - 3920
BUTLER Lucy U17 18.11.81, Gateshead :
LJ - 5.41 (5.50-96)
BUTLER Natalie U23 25.11.78, Windsor S & E :
100H - 14.78w/14.89,
LJ - 5.53w/5.51 (5.51-94),
Hep - 4561
BUXTON Leanne U23 27.05.78, Brighton :
100H - 14.42, 400H - 62.7/63.57 (63.03-96),
Hep - 4697

CAFFELL Kelly U20 10.02.79, Oxford C :
800 - 2:12.4, 1500 - 4:29.79
CAIRNS Lindsay 1.06.71, Kilmarnock :
5k - 17:00.15 (16:40.6-97),
HMar - 1:19:15 (1:18:38-96)
CALLAWAY Deborah Ann 15.07.64, AF&D :
SP - 13.66 (14.88-93),
DT - 54.94 (58.56-96), HT - 42.86 (44.64-96)
CALLUM Lindsey U17 13.04.82, Cleethorpes :
300H - 46.52
CALVERT Donna U20 26.06.79, Wombwell :
DT - 37.53
CAMERON Charmaine U20 9.09.80, Newcastle :
LJ - 5.64
CAMERON Claire V40 3.10.58, City of Glas :
SP - 11.18i (11.80-88),
DT - 41.19 (46.34-85), HT - 36.16
CAMERON Kadien U20 24.02.80, Birchfield :
100 - 12.18w
CAMPBELL Clare U20 21.10.80, Shaftesbury B :
3k - 9:57.4
CAMPBELL Katrina 8.03.72, Lisburn/IRE :
JT - 42.41 (45.02-95)
CAMPBELL Natasha U17 6.08.82, Medway :
JT - 42.37
CAMPBELL Samantha U17 22.11.81, Dartford :
5kW - 29:10.72
CAMPBELL Tracy U17 20.12.81, City of Glas :
300 - 41.13
CANK Elaine U20 5.12.79, Telford :
SP - 12.27, DT - 44.76
CANNING Melanie U15 19.05.85, E, S & Mx :
75HG - 11.7
CANNON Kim U17 27.07.82, Basildon :
SP - 10.91
CARAWARDINE Hazel U20 6.11.80, Bolton :
TJ - 11.15
CARDING Christina U13 26.02.87, Bas & MH :
DTM - 25.61

372

CARDY-WISE Bronwen G. V45 26.01.52,
Brom & R : 10MR - 57:48 (55:55-86),
HMar - 1:19:15 (1:14:06un-86)
CARLESS Tammy U23 10.01.77, Braintree :
JT - 39.93 (45.62-96)
CARPENTER Alison J. V40 3.01.58,
Thames H & H : Mar - 3:02:52
CARPENTER Emma U17 16.05.82, Exeter :
SP - 11.49, DT - 46.55
CARR Alison 30.08.66, Dundee HH :
HMar - 1:18:45
CARROLL Hana U17 19.09.81, Liverpool H :
300H - 45.9
CARTER Alexandra U20 1.04.80, Vale Royal :
800 - 2:08.2 (2:13.4mx-96), 1500 - 4:25.3
CARTMEL Anne-Marie 18.11.73, Copeland :
(see GREEN)
CARTWRIGHT Natalie U13 8.11.85, Swansea :
100 - 13.2
CARTY Lara U15 7.03.84, Basildon :
75HG - 11.70, HJ - 1.63,
LJ - 5.27io, PenG - 2972
CARVILLE Maria 8.12.73, Thames Valley :
800 - 2:12.4 (2:08.73-95), 1500 - 4:24.2
CARYL Lisa 21.11.75, Liverpool H :
LJ - 5.51 (5.56-97), TJ - 11.21 (11.26w-93),
Hep - 4083 (4160-93)
CASE Samantha U13 5.01.86, Guildford & G :
JTM - 28.56
CASSON Esther 24.11.75, Middlesbro & C/
Cambridge Univ : 800 - 2:09.6
CATER Lisa U15 16.01.84, Mansfield :
800 - 2:16.42, 1500 - 4:43.9
CEESAY Amina U20 19.11.79, N & E B :
100 - 12.1w/12.20w (12.4-96),
200 - 24.89w/25.18
CEESAY Nusrat U20 18.03.81, N & E B :
400H - 60.53
CEESAY Zainab U15 27.10.83, N & E B :
LJ - 5.55w/5.28, PenG - 2602
CHAFFE Lucy U20 25.03.79, Essex L :
400 - 56.5/56.54 (55.93-97)
CHALMERS Laura U13 1.05.86, Elgin :
DTM - 24.36
CHAMBERLAIN Rebecca U20 7.09.79,
Bournemouth : SP - 11.46i/11.26
CHAMBERS Karen Louise 31.08.68, Sale :
HT - 40.35 (47.10-93)
CHAMPION Fay 27.09.66, Windsor S & E :
SP - 12.66 (13.30-95),
DT - 42.08 (44.64-95), HT - 37.11 (38.44-96)
CHANGUION Wilemien 11.02.75, S B/RSA :
800 - 2:10.19, 1500 - 4:26.9
CHAPMAN Jo U15 10.01.85, West Suffolk :
JT - 34.06
CHARNOCK Catherine 3.05.75, Barrow & F :
3kW - 14:01+/14:02.5, 5kW - 23:50.96,
5kWR - 23:58, 10kWR - 49:02, 20kW - 1:45:24
CHARNOCK Kathryn V35 4.07.62, Wigan Ph :
HMar - 1:16:57 (1:15:46-97), Mar - 2:51:02
CHILDS Ellie U17 26.05.83, Basildon :
300 - 40.7, 400 - 56.5, 800 - 2:15.6
CHRISTIE Erica M. V40 10.03.56, Victoria Pk :
Mar - 3:09:49 (3:06:31-95)
CHRISTIE Jenny U13 28.09.85, Leamington :
HJ - 1.45
CHRISTIE Jill U17 16.07.82, Hillingdon :
3k - 10:41.5

CHRISTIE Lindsey U17 29.03.83, Dartford :
TJ - 10.86
CHRISTIE Susan U20 7.03.79, Motherwell :
100 - 12.10
CLAGUE Jennifer 6.08.73, Liverpool H :
3k - 9:56.2 (9:21.54-93),
5k - 17:02.53 (16:11.61i-92)
CLAPSON Emma 22.11.71, Ashford :
400 - 56.6 (54.25-88)
CLARK Jean 5.10.68, Edinburgh WM :
HT - 49.86 (50.34-97)
CLARK Joanna 11.02.73, AF&D : (see HILL)
CLARK Katie U15 30.09.83, Border :
800 - 2:15.56, 1500 - 4:46.79
CLARK Lynsey U13 2.09.86, Havering :
DTM - 23.30
CLARK Natalie U17 4.09.82, Hull Springhead :
HJ - 1.73
CLARK Nicola U23 14.04.77, Hull Springhead :
TJ - 11.30i/11.22 (11.66w/11.62-97)
CLARK Rebecca U23 15.09.78, Rugby :
200 - 25.1 (25.57-94)
CLARK Vicki U20 23.09.80, Ashford :
HT - 47.52
CLARKE Adele U17 29.08.83, Hallamshire :
100 - 12.16, 200 - 24.83w/25.21
CLARKE Dianne Olivia V40 27.02.58, T V H :
400 - 57.4 (52.98-79),
400H - 65.2/65.33 (62.9-94)
CLARKE Elizabeth M. V40 14.02.57, Les Cr :
Mar - 3:04:54 (2:53:29-91)
CLARKE Gay V35 22.08.60, Ryston :
100H - 15.1
CLARKE Jadean U13 17.08.86, Herne Hill :
HJ - 1.50
CLARKE Jennifer V45 19.10.52, Peterbro :
HT - 37.15 (37.82-96)
CLARKE Rhian U23 19.04.77, Essex L :
PV - 3.82 (3.90i/3.90-97)
CLAXTON Sarah U20 23.09.79, Colchester & T :
60 - 7.66i (7.63i-96), 60H - 8.38i,100 - 12.0
(11.7w-96/11.88w-94/12.0-95/12.19-94),
100H - 13.28w/13.62, LJ - 6.52 (6.53w-97)
CLAYTON Penelope U23 8.06.77, :
Mar - 3:08:44
CLEMENTS Hayley Diane 17.09.68, Dartford :
100 - 12.1/12.22 (11.77-85),
200 - 24.5/24.65 (23.4w-85/23.8/23.90-86)
CLEMENTS Melinda U23 20.05.77, W S & E :
100 - 12.1 (12.43w-93),
TJ - 11.55i/11.20 (11.94w/11.66-97)
CLOUGH Rachel U17 30.06.82, Colwyn Bay :
HT - 37.37 (38.08-97)
COATES Nichola U17 24.03.82, Cramlington :
3k - 10:37.79 (10:05.52-97)
COBB Nicola 2.11.71, Windsor S & E :
JT - 39.49 (43.38-96)
COCKCROFT Jody U15 14.09.83, Andover :
SPG - 11.91
COCKRAM Julia 1.01.68, Belgrave :
PV - 2.70 (2.90i-95/2.85-96)
CODD Danielle U20 17.02.79, Trafford :
400H - 65.2 (66.48-96), PV - 3.40, TJ - 11.02w
COLEMAN Hayley U17 24.05.83, Steyning :
5kW - 29:17.47 (28:54.9-97)
COLEMAN Kirsty U20 17.11.80, Steyning :
3kW - 16:00.26 (15:51.21-97),
5kW - 27:22.77 (27:11.0-97),
10kW - 58:25.0 (57:37.4-97), 10kWR - 55:20

COLLERAN Joanne 1.09.72, Liverpool H :
800 - 2:12.0 (2:08.7-97/2:11.3mx-95),
1500 - 4:18.17/4:19.0mx/4:19.4, 3k - 9:43.54i
COLLIER Gemma U13 25.11.85, Exeter :
200 - 26.7, 70HM - 11.6, PenM - 2292
COLLINS Jayne U20 27.03.80, Halesowen :
PV - 3.00
COLLINSON Debbie U13 23.10.85, Hull Spr :
JTM - 27.30
COLMAN Wendy U20 12.02.81, Wells :
TJ - 11.26 (11.37-97)
CONDIE Crystal Remi U15 28.08.84,
Vale of Aylesbury : 100 - 12.66w
CONE Hayley-Jane U20 16.07.80, Camb & C :
LJ - 5.58
CONNOLLY Lisa U17 27.09.81, Liverpool H :
80HI - 11.89w/12.05 (12.0/12.04-97),
300H - 46.08
CONSTERDINE Victoria 25.04.75, Stockport :
Hep - 4004
COOK Louise U15 7.01.84, West Norfolk :
PenG - 2667 (2679-97)
COOK Lucy 11.09.75, Medway :
JT - 48.41
COOK Pamela U17 25.10.82, Wirral :
60HI - 9.08i, 80HI - 11.95
COOKE Alexandra U17 24.06.82, Leighton B :
300 - 40.50
COOMBE Freya U17 11.10.81, Enfield :
JT - 35.37
COOPER Helen U17 20.06.83, Blackpool :
300H - 45.40, Hepl - 3870
COOPER Jennifer V35 1.09.62, Wolves & B :
DT - 39.75 (43.94-90), HT - 37.00 (37.94-92)
COOPER Paula 6.08.75, Rotherham :
HT - 37.19
COOPER Stephanie U17 16.09.82, Peterbro :
800 - 2:15.92
COORE Andrea Anne 23.04.69, Team Solent :
60 - 7.6i (7.48i-97), 100 - 11.61 (11.48-97),
200 - 24.5 (23.7mx/24.27-97), LJ - 6.36
COPLEY Lucy U13 22.09.85, AF&D :
1k - 3:13.3, 1500 - 5:05.1
COPPING Alicia U15 5.10.83, Coventry G :
DT - 30.24
CORBETT Kirsty U17 16.05.82, Ilford :
LJ - 5.51
CORLETT Janet V35 31.07.63, Leamington :
HT - 40.38
CORNEBY Hannah U20 22.01.81, Cann & St :
DT - 42.54
CORNFORD Julia Helen V35 12.05.59,
Brighton (nee MCGOWAN) :
HMar - 1:18:55 (1:12:48sh-86/1:14:45-84),
Mar - 2:54:07 (2:36:31-86)
CORRAN Elizabeth V40 23.09.55, Manx H :
10kWR - 54:20 (51:37hc-96/51:38-95)
COSTELLO Karen 21.10.68, C of Glas/ H Watt :
SP - 11.74 (12.64-94), JT - 43.87 (54.50-94)
COSTELLOE Carol U23 14.01.76, Bed & Co :
JT - 41.33
COUNSELL Ursula U17 7.12.82, Bristol :
3k - 10:23.11
COURT Clova V35 10.02.60, Birchfield :
60 - 7.61i (7.47i-94/7.6-88/7.6i-89),
200 - 23.88 (23.57-90), 60H - 8.42i (8.12i-94),
100H - 13.20 (13.04-94), LJ - 5.54 (6.10-92),
SP - 14.31 (14.44-97), JT - 47.80 (55.30-91),
Hep - 5656 (6022-91)

COWLEY Laura U17 3.09.81, Verlea :
300 - 41.00, 400 - 58.5 (58.4-97)
COX Jennifer 28.11.72, Enfield :
3k - 9:42.72i (9:49.4-92)
COX Maureen V45 7.09.50, Manx H :
10kWR - 56:43 (56:08-95), 50kW - 5:41:36
COX Rachael U20 27.06.80, Birchfield :
HT - 39.19 (40.56-96)
COZENS Chloe U20 9.04.80, Bedford & Co :
100H - 14.78w/15.1 (16.01-97), HJ - 1.80,
LJ - 5.72w/5.62, SP - 11.30,
JT - 48.00, Hep - 5358w/5220
COZENS Joanne U20 9.04.80, Bedford & Co :
PV - 2.70 (2.80-97)
CRAIG Elizabeth F. V35 7.07.60, Serpentine :
Mar - 3:09:22 (3:04:29-94)
CRAIG Paula 2.07.73, St Albans :
Mar - 3:04:17
CRANE Julie U23 26.09.76, Notts :
HJ - 1.83
CRAWFORD Catherine U15, :
PenG - 2591
CRAWFORD Zoe 1.03.75, City of Hull :
400 - 56.97 (56.8-96)
CRAWLEY Sonia U15 7.12.83, Solihull & S H :
HJ - 1.69i/1.65
CREBER Maggie V35 20.08.60, Edinburgh WM :
Mar - 3:00:54
CRESSWELL Lois U20 12.01.81, R S Coldfield :
400 - 57.03i
CRILLEY Kath V50 8.09.47, Surrey WC :
50kW - 5:53:54 (5:53:41-93)
CRIPPS Faith U15 23.09.83, Vale of Aylesbury :
PenG - 2546
CROAD Alison U17 10.06.82, Wimborne :
LJ - 5.35
CROMPTON Mandy U17 25.03.82, Oldh & R :
LJ - 5.45i/5.42
CROSBY Janine U20 17.01.79, Bingley :
DT - 38.00
CROSBY Nicole U23 23.10.76, Bingley :
100 - 11.94, 200 - 24.3w/24.35
CROSS Aline 20.09.73, City of Edinburgh :
HT - 37.97 (38.92-91)
CROWE Amanda 21.10.73, Lisburn :
400 - 55.0, 800 - 2:01.83,
1500 - 4:10.68, 1M - 4:32.99
CROWTHER Kimberley 19.01.66, Middleb & C :
100H - 14.55 (14.2-96/14.22w-94/14.30-86),
LJ - 5.58 (5.95w/5.79-88),
SP - 12.50, Hep - 4948 (5297-86)
CRUICKSHANK Justina U23 27.09.77, Trafford :
TJ - 12.07i/11.68/11.41 (12.21w/12.18-96)
CRUMP Lisa Jane U23 30.03.76, Sheff RWC :
3kW - 14:25.22, 10kWR - 49:51
CUNNANE Jennifer V40 23.02.57, Wakefield :
PV - 3.20i/3.10 (3.20-97), HT - 44.93
CURBISHLEY Allison U23 3.06.76, Edin WM :
200 - 22.90w/23.33 (23.4-97), 400 - 50.71
CURLING Roseanne U20 5.09.80, Bristol :
LJ - 5.53 (5.60-97)
CURRIE Alison 15.07.68, City of Glasgow :
200 - 24.6 (24.86w-87), 400 - 55.9 (56.33-97),
400H - 60.21mx/60.38 (59.78-97)
CURTIS Charlotte U13, Dartford :
2kW - 11:13.94
CURTIS Laura U20 2.05.81, Hull Springhead :
Hep - 4309

374

CUTLER Aimee Louise U17 7.10.81, Torfaen :
LJ - 5.84w/5.77
CUTTS Cariann U15 1.02.85, Barnsley :
PV - 2.80

DAGNE Birhan U23 7.10.77, Essex L :
3k - 9:22.72 (9:21.0-96),
5k - 15:55.81,
10k - 34:38.11, 10kR - 33:34,
10MR - 53:55, HMar - 1:13:31
DALEY Laura U17 17.05.83, Telford :
300H - 46.75, LJ - 5.35
DALTON Stephanie U15 8.02.84, Sheffield :
PenG - 2976
DAMEN Louise U17 12.10.82, Bournemouth :
800 - 2:12.4, 1500 - 4:33.9, 3k - 9:56.13
DAMM Sarah Grace 12.09.70, Birchfield :
400 - 56.8 (56.4-95/57.39i-96), 800 - 2:11.3,
400H - 61.1/61.70 (61.1-95),
LJ - 5.50i (5.94w-96/5.89-95),
SP - 11.95i/11.94 (12.98i-96/12.44-95)
DANIEL Helen Jane V35 24.10.63, Camb H :
800 - 2:12.7 (2:01.86-87)
DANIELS Nikki U17 25.08.82, City of Stoke :
800 - 2:15.2 (2:11.6-96)
DANSON Ann Elizabeth 4.05.71, City of Hull
(nee BROOKS) :
100 - 12.1w/12.27 (11.8w-94/11.91-95),
LJ - 6.04w/5.95 (6.38w-94/6.16-95)
DANVERS Natasha U23 19.09.77, Croydon :
400 - 52.6R/53.26, 100H - 13.20,
400H - 55.69, HJ - 1.82
DARGAN Leigh U20 31.03.81, Epsom & Ewell :
SP - 12.14
DAVIDGE Sharon U17 15.09.81, Exeter :
60 - 7.96i, 100 - 12.0 (12.92-96),
200 - 25.3/25.40, 60HI - 8.66i,
80HI - 11.00w/11.22, 300H - 46.17, LJ - 5.55
DAVIDSON Wendy U17 14.10.82, Ellon :
300 - 41.4, 80HI - 11.81, 300H - 43.38,
LJ - 5.49w/5.48, TJ - 10.89, HepI - 4233
DAVIES Alison V35 6.04.61, Woking :
PV - 3.60
DAVIES Angela 21.10.70, Basingstoke & MH/
Loughbro : 800 - 2:04.6 (2:03.67-94),
1500 - 4:13.55 (4:09.29-94),
3k - 9:17.03 (9:14.1-94), 5k - 15:50.59
DAVIES Elen U13, Norwich :
HJ - 1.44
DAVIES Emma U23 9.10.78, Andover :
400 - 56.3/56.60 (55.48-97), 800 - 2:02.39
DAVIES Gael U20 5.02.79, Gloucester L :
400H - 65.0 (64.22-97)
DAVIES Helen U15 24.03.84, Colwyn Bay :
75HG - 11.32, LJ - 5.31, PenG - 2748
DAVIES Joanne 23.06.73, Swansea :
JT - 38.11 (41.18-91)
DAVIES Samantha U20 20.09.79, Birchfield :
100 - 11.50w/11.80,
200 - 24.02w/24.2/24.25 (24.22-97)
DAVIES Sarah U13 13.03.86, Bournemouth :
DTM - 26.08
DAVIES Sarah-Ann U23 22.04.76, S & S H :
400 - 56.77i
DAVIS Amy U13 28.01.86, Lagan Valley :
SPM - 9.33
DAVIS Julie U20 16.11.79, Lagan Valley :
60H - 8.77i, 100H - 14.31 (14.3-97), 400H - 61.01

DAVIS Wendy U20 7.11.79, Lagan Valley :
400 - 56.87, 800 - 2:12.24
DAWKINS Carol Ann V35 8.12.60, T Solent :
400H - 63.73 (58.28-85)
DAWSON Laura U13 23.01.86, Scunthorpe :
PV - 2.10
DAY Samantha U13 8.02.86, Tamworth :
100 - 13.2, 200 - 27.3, SPM - 9.53
DAY Victoria 19.06.72, Essex L :
100 - 12.1w/12.11 (12.1-93),
200 - 23.84w/24.07, 400 - 53.73
DAYKIN Mari-Anne L. 16.02.73, Tonbridge :
JT - 43.18 (46.08-93)
DEADMAN Lauren U15 27.03.84, Havering :
800 - 2:16.96, 1500 - 4:49.7
DEAN Carly U13 14.10.85, Dorchester :
70HM - 11.5
DEAN Harriet U17 2.02.82, Radley :
3k - 10:11.12
DEAR Joanne Mary 8.06.75, Windsor S & E :
LJ - 5.65 (6.33-93)
DELASAUX Julia 22.04.69, Blackheath :
HT - 39.94 (42.80-97)
DELEAVAL Aline 31.10.71, :
Mar - 3:05:49
DENHAM Kate U20 18.03.80, Southampton C :
100 - 12.27w (12.16w-96/12.2-95/12.23-97)
DENHAM Kerensa 8.03.74, Essex L :
LJ - 5.70w (5.89-94), TJ - 12.61
DENNEHY Siobhan U17 31.08.82, Brentwood :
HJ - 1.63, HepI - 4015
DENNISON Andrea M. V35 22.04.63, Bradford :
Mar - 3:07:50 (3:06:19-94)
DERBY Elley U13 20.12.85, Birchfield :
150 - 20.1 (19.8-97), 200 - 27.0, LJ - 5.28
DERHAM Zoe U20 24.11.80, Yate :
HT - 51.25
DERING Joanne 7.02.69, Windsor S & E :
3k - 9:44.11 (8:59.45-90)
DESAI Nisha U15 5.08.84, Morpeth :
800 - 2:15.47, 1500 - 4:49.34
DEUCHARS Jane Alison 20.01.67, Edin WM :
PV - 2.91
DEVLIN Charlie-Jo U13 28.09.85, Lanc & Morc :
1200 - 4:01.2
DEVLIN Mary U20 14.09.79, Ballinascreen :
LJ - 5.51
DHALIWAL Navdeep U23 30.11.77, S B :
SP - 13.35, DT - 43.85
DICKINSON Leone 5.11.75, Bingley :
HJ - 1.72 (1.76-97)
DICKINSON Ria U20 14.12.79, Bingley :
TJ - 11.03i (11.10-97)
DIVINE Patricia 21.10.67, Edinburgh WM :
400H - 65.36 (63.8-97)
DIX Barbara Helen U20 23.11.80, Preston :
800 - 2:12.39
DIXON Sharon Jane 22.04.68, Parkside :
Mar - 2:52:27
DOBRISKEY Lisa U15 23.12.83, Ashford :
800 - 2:11.21, 1500 - 4:38.1
DOCHERTY Alice U17 4.01.82, Dacorum & T :
200 - 25.42w
DOCKER Nicole 30.07.74, Hounslow :
Mar - 2:59:19 (2:58:38-97)
DOCKERTY Catherine U17 9.01.83, Jarr & H :
100 - 12.4

DODD Meryl 12.04.69, Bingley :
  3k - 9:56.9 (9:48.0-96),
  5k - 17:07.86 (16:50.28-96)
DOLAN Sue V35, Imperial/IRE :
  HMar - 1:19:05
DONALDSON Isobel 24.01.64, AF&D/WRAF :
  JT - 38.73 (42.78-85), Hep - 4272 (5038-93)
DONE Cheryl 25.09.70, West (I.O.M.)/WRAF :
  100H - 14.93 (14.7-96), 400H - 63.81,
  SP - 11.21 (12.20i-97/11.80-96), Hep - 4809
DORAN Colette U15 20.09.83, Carlisle/Asp :
  JT - 37.83
DOUGALL Rebecca U20 11.05.81, Aberdeen :
  400H - 65.06
DOUGHTY Lucy 1.05.71, Bristol (nee FIELD) :
  800 - 2:12.8 (2:11.9-97), 3k - 9:37.3 (9:37.1-97),
  1500 - 4:25.52 (4:21.07-97)
DOUGLAS L. Stephanie 22.01.69, Sale :
  100 - 11.88w/11.93 (11.27-91)
DOUGLAS Laura U17 4.01.83, Deeside :
  DT - 33.90, HT - 38.59
DOWSETT Kathryn U23 24.11.78, Essex L :
  PV - 3.10i/3.00, LJ - 5.82
DRAKE Kathryn V35 25.05.60, Spenborough :
  Mar - 3:07:26 (2:47:18-90)
DREW Shelley Jean 8.08.73, Sutton & District/
  Birm Un : SP - 12.34 (12.34-96), DT - 60.82
DRUMMOND Rebecca Louise U23 18.04.78,
  Stoke : 60 - 7.60i (7.43i-97),
  100 - 11.8w/12.37 (11.50w-94/11.59-95)
DUDGEON Sinead Marie U23 9.07.76, E WM :
  100 - 12.1 (11.8-94/11.88w-93/11.93-95),
  200 - 24.26 (23.9w-94/24.17w-95/24.22-94),
  400H - 58.54
DUDMAN Nicola U15 5.10.83, Verlea :
  SPG - 11.03
DUFF Jennifer U17 29.07.82, Coventry Godiva :
  DT - 35.83
DUFFIN Irene Maria V35 10.08.60, S B :
  DT - 37.01 (44.90-87), HT - 50.35 (50.38-97)
DUFFY Teresa 6.07.69, Essex L/IRE :
  10kR - 33:52 (33:34-97), HMar - 1:16:41,
  Mar - 2:39:56
DUGDALE Catherine 29.11.74, Cardiff :
  3k - 9:53.76i (9:44.82-96)
DUNCALF Nicola U20 6.05.81, Sale :
  100H - 14.9w/14.96w/15.0/15.21
DUNCAN Audrey 5.02.72, Solihull & S Heath :
  HJ - 1.65
DUNCAN Joanne 27.12.66, Essex L :
  SP - 15.76
DUNCAN Tracey U20 16.05.79, Essex L :
  100H - 14.90 (14.79-97), 400H - 59.39
DUNKLEY Julie U20 11.09.79, Shaftesbury B :
  SP - 15.27, DT - 39.27, HT - 38.45
DUNKLEY Leah U13 11.11.85, Barnsley :
  100 - 13.2, 200 - 27.2
DUNKLEY Michelle Lisa U23 26.01.78, Ex L :
  HJ - 1.89i/1.88 (1.89i-97), LJ - 5.89
DUNN Kara U15 12.10.84, Ealing,S & Mx :
  100 - 12.4/12.45w
DUNN Rachael U20 4.03.79, Gloucester L :
  HT - 40.78 (41.22-97)
DUNN Rachel U17 14.11.82, Huntingdon :
  JT - 39.85
DUNSTAN Claire U17 15.10.81, Wakefield :
  PV - 2.60

DWYER Ros, :
  24HrT - 163.311km
DYKE Hayley U13 11.03.86, Solihull & S Heath :
  2kW - 11:08.93

EAMES Carol V50 2.06.47, Bournemouth :
  PV - 2.50
EARLE Jennifer V40 28.11.58, Guildford & G :
  HT - 42.49
EASTON Carey U20 16.11.79, Hamilton :
  200 - 25.1, 400 - 54.28
EASTWOOD Laura U20 7.04.81, Deeside :
  TJ - 11.01i
EDDY Ruth 9.07.75, Colchester H :
  800 - 2:12.20
EDGAR Catherine U20 27.02.80, Lagan Valley :
  JT - 38.76
EDWARDS Elizabeth U17 30.04.82, Wrexham :
  SP - 10.93
EDWARDS Marcelle U23 9.01.78, Essex L :
  HT - 41.29 (41.30-96)
EDWARDS Sandra V35 14.03.61, Lincoln Well :
  HMar - 1:18:22 (1:16:21-97)
EGAN Jenny U15 15.05.84, Dorset Sch :
  PenG - 2576
ELLEKER Helen V40 21.03.56, Sheffield RWC :
  10kWR - 57:08 (47:26-91)
ELLIOTT Jacqueline U23 13.09.78, Elswick :
  400H - 64.5/65.00 (64.12-97),
  Hep - 4189
ELLIOTT Lucy Helen 9.03.66, Shaftesbury B :
  1500 - 4:27.70 (4:18.54-91),
  3k - 9:40.6 (9:19.2-97), 10kR - 33:02
ELLIS J. U13, S Yorks Sch :
  HJ - 1.46
ELLIS Melanie 16.04.64, Shaftesbury Barnet :
  10MR - 57:38, HMar - 1:15:34
ELLIS Sarah U15 27.10.83, Havant :
  JT - 34.30
ELLIS Venetia U13 15.09.85, London Schools :
  JTM - 29.17
ELPHICK Jennifer 24.11.66, Team Solent :
  SP - 14.22, DT - 37.60 (40.44-86)
ELSON Sara Jo-Anne 8.05.70, Gateshead :
  400H - 62.00 (58.19-92)
ELWISS Hannah U15 8.12.84, Preston :
  75HG - 11.25w/11.33
EMBLEM Nicola 27.03.71, Edinburgh WM :
  JT - 50.75 (56.96-90)
EMPFIELD Julianne, (nee WHITE) :
  Mar - 2:54:44
ENDACOTT Katherine U20 29.01.80,
  City of Plymouth : 100 - 11.87w/12.0/12.07,
  200 - 24.77w/24.82 (24.72-95)
ENGLISH Allison U20 9.03.79, Hull Springhead :
  100H - 14.93w/15.18 (14.64w/14.76-97)
ENTWISTLE Claire U23 9.12.76, Wigan :
  800 - 2:11.1mx (2:09.73-97), 1500 - 4:33.70
ENWONWU Bibi T. 12.04.74, Shaftesbury B :
  200 - 25.1 (24.62w-91)
ERCOLANI Alexandra 18.08.75, C of Glasgow :
  800 - 2:10.90
ERSKINE Joanne U15 28.05.85, Lochgelly :
  PenG - 2822ns
ETHERTON Sarah U23 19.10.78, Dartford :
  HT - 36.80
EUSTACE Katharine 16.04.75, Bristol :
  400 - 56.9 (54.91-97)

EVANS Alison C. 13.12.73, Solihull & S Heath :
(see MOSELY)
EVANS Emma, Bridgend :
HMar - 1:17:35
EVANS Gemma U13 25.01.86, Wirral :
2kW - 11:36.67
EVANS Gemma U15 9.09.84, Somerset Sch :
PenG - 2560
EVANS Joanne 3.10.68, Cardiff :
(see POWELL)
EVANS Kate Victoria 4.02.74, Birchfield :
TJ - 12.65w/12.56 (13.03-97)
EVANS Katherine U23 19.11.77, Coventry G :
JT - 45.91 (47.68-96)
EVANS Lucy Hannah U17 2.10.82, Sale :
100 - 12.4w/12.42w/12.59
EVANS Natalie U15 15.11.83, Wolves & B :
3kW - 15:41.71
EVANS Non 27.02.67, Swansea :
100H - 14.2/14.45w/14.56
(14.0w-96/14.2/14.28-95)
EVANS Sally 14.05.75, Sale :
400 - 55.32, 800 - 2:10.6
EVERALL Kerry U15 29.02.84, Yate :
100 - 12.6
EVERETT Rebecca U20 10.03.80, Birchfield :
3k - 9:56.2
EVERITT Amie U23 1.11.78, Huntingdon :
PV - 2.80
EVERSON Suzanne 23.03.72, Medway :
400 - 57.5/57.56 (57.4-96)

FAGAN Collette U17 6.06.82, C of Glas :
1500 - 4:43.22 (4:41.45i-97), 3k - 10:22.2
FAHERTY Michelle Mary 10.08.68, Skyrac :
800 - 2:07.08
(2:03.72i-97/2:04.4mx-96/2:05.3-95),
1500 - 4:29.5mx (4:14.19-96)
FAIRS Elizabeth U23 1.12.77, Hallamshire :
60 - 7.71i, 100 - 11.9w (12.4-94),
60H - 8.48i, 100H - 13.52
FAIRWEATHER Sheila U23 24.11.77,
C of Glasgow : 1500 - 4:25.9, 3k - 9:23.38,
5k - 16:07.34, 10k - 34:39.98, 10kR - 34:48
FARDOE Kerri U15 22.11.83, Shrewsbury :
SPG - 10.83
FARQUHARSON Claire U23 28.12.78,
Horsham BS : HJ - 1.65 (1.70-95)
FARROW Wendy 25.12.71, Derby LAC :
1500 - 4:24.44 (4:21.4-96),
3k - 9:50.2 (9:31.91-94), 10kR - 34:32
FAULKNER Natasha 8.07.73, Weymouth :
TJ - 11.08 (11.13-96)
FAY Ursula 23.09.67, Belfast L/Ulster Univ. :
HJ - 1.76 (1.84-83)
FENN Joanne 19.10.74, Essex L (nee MERSH):
400 - 56.17, 800 - 2:05.2
FERGUSSON Gemma U15 20.08.84, N S P :
75HG - 11.44, LJ - 5.19
FERRIER Holly U15 13.07.84, Stamford & D :
75HG - 11.27w/11.59
FICKEN Pam V55 25.07.41, Surrey WC :
50kW - 5:53:48 (5:53:16-96)
FIELD Georgina U13 8.04.86, Bas & MH :
JTM - 31.87
FIELD Lucy 1.05.71, Bristol : (see DOUGHTY)
FILCE Claudia Dawn 11.11.72, AF&D :
PV - 2.70 (3.00-95)

FINIKIN Evette V35 25.09.63, Shaftesbury B :
TJ - 11.09 (13.46-91)
FINLAY Louise U15 2.10.83, Rhondda :
SPG - 11.61, DT - 30.63
FINLEY Ruth U20 23.11.80, Border :
HT - 36.04
FINNIS Suzanne U17 12.08.83, Essex L :
JT - 36.84
FISHER Lucy U13 27.09.85, Crewe & Alsager :
70HM - 11.6, SPM - 9.95
FITZGERALD Lyndsay U20 31.01.80, Houns :
400H - 64.59
FLAHERTY Katie U13, Basildon :
100 - 13.2, 150 - 20.0/20.06
FLEETHAM Sarah U20 9.01.79, Braintree :
TJ - 11.30
FLETCHER Alison Kay V35 8.06.61, Camb H :
5k - 17:17.1 (17:10.54-97)
FLETCHER Karen U20 26.09.79, Kirk Hallam :
3k - 9:49.97, 5k - 17:09.8
FLINT Stacy U13 18.10.85, City of Hull :
70HM - 11.8
FLORENCE Frances V35 6.07.59, Shettleston :
Mar - 3:03:08
FLYNN Debbie U20 22.01.81, Banbury :
TJ - 11.08
FOLDS Rebecca 28.01.75, Exeter :
LJ - 5.50 (5.73-93)
FORD A. U13, Wigan :
70HM - 11.8
FORD Emma U23 16.02.77, Liverpool H :
1500 - 4:27.90, 3k - 9:27.01i, 5k - 16:31.00
FORD Katie U17 21.10.81, Sheffield RWC :
3kW - 14:17.96i/14:47.3,
5kW - 25:25.4 (25:20.0-97),
5kWR - 24:48 (26:22o-96), 10kWR - 52:55
FORD-DUNN Helen U23 20.10.77, Steyning/
Cambridge Un : 5kW - 27:46.0 (27:33.0-95),
3kW - 15:40.0, 5kWR - 26:08, 10kWR - 56:12
FORESTER Adele U23 27.03.76, Middles & C :
LJ - 5.85 (6.05-94)
FORRESTER Amanda U23 29.09.78,
City of Stoke : LJ - 5.64w
FORRESTER Emma U15 2.12.83, Telford :
DT - 30.78
FORRESTER Stephanie Emma 30.04.69,
Milton : 10kR - 34:50
FORSYTH Kate U20 5.06.79, North Shields P :
100H - 14.40 (13.72w/13.94-97)
FOSTER Elaine Claire V35 21.07.63, Charn/
Loughbro : 3k - 9:53.93i (9:21.18-92)
FOSTER Laura U20 22.07.81, Hallamshire :
100H - 15.02w/15.06
FOSTER Rachel U23 1.09.76, Barnsley :
PV - 2.80i/2.80
FOSTER Rebecca 14.04.71, Wakefield :
JT - 44.78, Hep - 4458 (5165-93)
FOSTER Vickie 1.04.71, AF&D :
SP - 14.64i/14.61, DT - 47.02 (48.62-93),
HT - 44.87 (45.46-97)
FOTHERGILL Chaanah 22.02.72, Hallamshire/
Cambridge University : (see PATTON)
FOX Laura U15 25.10.84, Ashford :
DT - 31.02
FOX Natasha U13 21.09.85, Dartford :
2kW - 11:08.37
FOZZARD Amy U13 20.04.86, Wakefield :
70HM - 11.6, PenM - 2329

FRADLEY Tracy 20.03.75, City of Stoke :
400 - 57.2
FRANCIS Tamara U23 14.11.78, Bournemouth :
JT - 46.17 (48.30-97)
FRANCIS-THOMAS Elizabeth V35 22.12.63,
Cardiff : 5k - 17:10.2
FRANKLIN Sarita U17 27.09.81, Bromley :
300 - 41.53
FRANZKE Kate U13 26.09.85, Pendle :
SPM - 9.75
FRASER Donna Karen 7.11.72, Croydon :
60 - 7.46i, 400 - 50.85,
100 - 11.2w/11.58w/11.82 (11.32w/11.66-97),
200 - 23.15i/23.39w/23.40 (22.90w/22.96i/23.25-97)
FREEBAIRN Susan 22.08.65, C of Glasgow :
DT - 43.18 (46.70-94), HT - 36.08 (37.30-95)
FREEMAN Danielle U20 11.02.80, Leeds :
60 - 7.75i, 200 - 25.05w,
100H - 13.95w/14.25, HJ - 1.68,
LJ - 6.05 (6.20w/6.15-97), Hep - 5237
FREEMAN Emily U20 24.11.80, Wakefield :
100 - 12.1 (12.42w-97/12.55-96),
200 - 24.47i/24.50 (24.19i-97)
FREEMAN Henrietta U17 12.07.83, Invicta :
3k - 10:10.75
FREETH Megan U17 1.02.82, Swansea :
60HI - 9.22o, 80HI - 11.96,
PV - 2.55, TJ - 10.95
FROST Helen Paula 12.03.74, Birchfield :
200 - 25.1 (24.75w-92/25.53-89), 400 - 54.25
FRYER Laura U15 3.12.83, Belgrave :
2.5kW - 13:19.8 (13:12.2-97),
3kW - 16:21.57 (15:53.90-97), 3kWR - 15:35
FRYER Lisa U15 30.05.84, Lagan Valley :
JT - 34.31
FRYER Paula Tracy 14.07.69, Sale :
800 - 2:09.4 (1:59.76-91)
FULLERTON Faye U15 31.05.84, Havering :
800 - 2:16.6, 1500 - 4:39.45
FURLONGER Susan U17 30.09.81, Oswestry :
HJ - 1.63 (1.64-97), LJ - 5.40,
TJ - 11.22, Hepl - 4257

GABRIEL Linda 27.07.64, Trafford :
400 - 56.93i/57.3/57.51,
400H - 63.25 (62.7/62.96-97)
GALLAGHER Lynne 21.11.74, Shaftesbury B :
800 - 2:11.21
GALLAWAY Sarah U15 14.11.84, Havant :
75HG - 11.7
GANDY Dawn Suzanne 28.07.65, T Solent :
400 - 57.3 (53.8/53.98-87),
800 - 2:12.00 (2:01.87-88)
GARAVAND Maria U13 30.06.86, Norwich :
75 - 10.2, 100 - 13.2, LJ - 4.80
GARDEN Catherine U23 4.09.78, Pitreavie :
SP - 12.43 (12.50-97),
DT - 38.78 (42.72-94), HT - 53.37
GARDEN Eleanor U23 20.11.76, Edin WM :
SP - 12.17 (12.60-97), DT - 43.96 (44.42-97)
GARDNER Ann 11.10.68, Corby :
HT - 55.60
GARDT Heidi U17 1.04.82, Skipton :
DT - 38.80
GARNETT Chanelle U15 16.08.85, Herne Hill :
LJ - 5.27
GARRARD Sarah U15 13.05.84, S London :
JT - 34.48

GASCOIGNE Amber U20 5.09.79, Wells :
1500 - 4:32.13 (4:31.47-97),
3k - 9:25.95, 5k - 17:22.97
GATRELL Eleanor U23 5.10.76, Woking :
SP - 14.68, DT - 36.33, HT - 35.70
GAULD Louise U20 24.08.80, C of Edinburgh :
PV - 3.01i/2.80, TJ - 11.04
GAULD Nicola U17 28.03.82, Aberdeen :
300 - 41.5 (43.35-97), TJ - 10.68
GAUTIER Nicola Louise U23 21.03.78, Traff :
60 - 7.75i, 200 - 25.06 (24.81-97), 60H - 8.65i,
100H - 14.1/14.19, HJ - 1.66 (1.68-96),
SP - 13.83 (14.71i/14.37-97),
JT - 43.61, Hep - 5497
GAY Gemma U17 7.10.81, Bristol :
JT - 36.73
GAYLE Denise U20 11.09.79, Barnet :
HJ - 1.72, LJ - 5.60, Hep - 4004
GAYNOR Natalie U20 7.11.79, Sutton & Dist :
100 - 11.9w?/11.98w (12.19-97)
GAYTER Sharon V35 30.10.60, Mandale :
100kR - 9:02:38 (8:12:03-95),
24Hr - 212.606km
GEAR Karen U20 30.09.79, N Devon :
400 - 55.13
GEE Chloe U13 1.12.85, Essex L :
LJ - 4.73
GEENS Natalie U15 27.12.84, Solihull & S H :
· 2.5kW - 13:35.20, 3kW - 16:28.53, 3kWR - 16:16
GEORGE Abbie U17 18.04.82, Stourport :
300H - 45.11, 400H - 67.0
GHOJEFA Elizabeth 24.02.69, Epsom & Ewell :
100 - 12.1w/12.24 (12.1-93),
LJ - 6.16 (6.32w-94/6.27-95),
TJ - 11.73 (12.64-93)
GIANCOVICH Cinzia U15 10.01.85, Verlea :
PenG - 2681
GIBB Rebecca U20 30.03.81, Middlesbro & C :
100H - 14.53w/14.64, 400H - 63.28
GIBBENS Elizabeth Jane U23 5.04.77, Brom :
TJ - 12.36 (12.42-95)
GIBBONS Victoria U20 19.12.80, Llanelli :
DT - 36.21
GIBSON Lynn Marie 6.07.69, Oxford City :
800 - 2:04.61 (2:02.34-92),
1500 - 4:12.72 (4:05.75-94),
3k - 9:24.60 (9:09.1-92)
GIBSON Sharon Angelia V35 31.12.61, Notts :
SP - 12.74 (13.50-82), JT - 54.26 (62.32-87)
GILBERT Helen U17 1.03.82, Grantham :
HT - 36.15, JT - 35.89
GILDING Nicola 16.05.72, Brighton :
LJ - 5.51 (5.84-89), TJ - 11.04 (11.20-94)
GILES Luisa U17 23.02.82, City of Stoke :
300H - 45.83
GILL Frances V35 13.01.60, Neath :
10k - 35:26.2mx (35:06.8-97),
10MR - 57:27, HMar - 1:17:27
GILLESPIE Rebecca U13 29.09.85, Corn AC :
1500 - 5:08.1
GILLHAM Michele 8.10.74, Ashford :
400H - 61.55 (60.18-97)
GLAYSHER Jennifer U17 3.05.83, Preston :
HJ - 1.65 (1.65-97), TJ - 10.96
GLOVER Danielle U17 26.07.82, Northampton :
100 - 41.4, 800 - 2:17.8 (2:14.74-97)
GLYNN Anna U17 18.12.81, Wigan :
300 - 41.09

378

GODDING-FELTON Lisa 24.11.69, White H :
  Mar - 3:05:44 (3:00:29-93)
GOFF Charlotte U23 6.07.77, Peterborough :
  800 - 2:12.23
GOLDSMITH Sally J. V35 18.01.61, Edin WM :
  10k - 34:16.89, HMar - 1:14:58 (1:13:13-96)
GONSE Rosalyn U17 1.03.82, Bedford & Co :
  LJ - 5.60, TJ - 10.69
GOODALL Kimberley U15 5.10.83, Guernsey :
  LJ - 5.31w, PenG - 2769ns
GOODE Leanna U15 24.04.84, S London :
  100 - 12.6
GOODMAN Kelly U17 16.03.82, Peterborough :
  DT - 33.46
GOODWIN Kim Louise 16.05.70, City of Hull :
  200 - 24.9 (24.25w/24.49-96),
  400 - 55.45i/55.5/56.26 (54.64-95)
GOSSMAN Nicola U13 4.11.86, C of Glasgow :
  75 - 10.22, 100 - 13.1w,
  200 - 27.6
GOWING Paula U23 31.05.78, Bristol :
  3k - 9:56.77
GRAINGER Kate U15 17.02.84, Inverness :
  DT - 29.41, JT - 35.73
GRANGER Katie 31.03.75, Exeter :
  JT - 42.32 (50.32-93)
GRANT Evelyn M. 22.01.64, City of Glasgow :
  10kR - 34:57
GRAY Hannah U20 15.06.81, Exeter :
  PV - 2.80i/2.70 (2.70-97)
GRAY Linda 23.03.71, Peterborough :
  JT - 47.18 (47.94-97)
GRECH-THOMAS Ceri 16.10.70, Cardiff :
  3k - 9:50.8
GREEN Anne-Marie 18.11.73, Copeland
  (nee CARTMEL) :
  SP - 11.86, JT - 39.00 (40.14-93)
GREEN Jill V55 10.10.41, London Vidarians :
  100MW - 22:22:30
GREEN Kate U17 19.11.81, Hallamshire :
  DT - 32.78
GREEN Sally U23 11.05.76, Dacorum & Tring :
  JT - 39.31 (40.64-97)
GREEN Susannah U17 5.12.81, Liverpool H :
  HJ - 1.67
GREENHOUSE Yvette U20 21.10.80, Hereford :
  JT - 38.11 (38.52-97)
GREENSWORD Safiya U13, Essex L :
  75 - 10.1, 70HM - 11.4
GREER Jane U15 19.07.84, Oxford City :
  PenG - 2531
GREY Alison Helen 12.05.73, Edinburgh WM :
  SP - 13.87 (15.85i/15.69-94)
GRIFFIN Helen U17 30.09.82, Sale :
  100 - 12.02w/12.31
GRIFFITH Michelle Amanda 6.10.71, W S & E :
  TJ - 13.94 (14.08-94)
GRIFFITHS Amelia U23 19.07.76, Ipswich :
  3k - 9:47.0
GRIFFITHS N. U13, Carmarthen :
  JTM - 26.35
GRIFFITHS Paula U17 10.02.82, Parkside :
  DT - 35.37
GRIFFITHS Shirley 23.06.72, Wakefield :
  800 - 2:09.86i/2:10.6 (2:07.3-96),
  1500 - 4:20.3 (4:14.41i-97/4:15.68-96),
  1M - 4:44.16i (4:44.60-96),
  3k - 9:37.7 (9:23.8-93)

GRIME Vikki U17 21.08.82, Hyndburn :
  HT - 33.42
GRIMSTONE Jenny U20 30.04.79, S Barnet :
  JT - 45.10
GROVES Jane U23 17.05.77, Vale Royal :
  1500 - 4:27.81 (4:27.12-97), 5k - 17:14.03
GUINEY Cheryl U13 24.09.85, Lagan Valley :
  1500 - 5:07.8
GUNNING Deborah 31.08.65, Essex L :
  1500 - 4:16.75 (4:12.69-90),
  3k - 9:16.6 (9:12.12-94), 5k - 16:10.08
GUTHRIE Louisa U23 26.12.77, Bromley :
  200 - 25.15
GUTHRIE Rebecca U17 19.03.83, Leamington :
  100 - 12.38, 200 - 25.26w (25.69-97)

HADLAND India U15 7.01.85, N Devon :
  HJ - 1.61
HAINES-JONES Nicola 21.05.65, Newport :
  5k - 17:23.9 (17:21.5-97)
HALES Amy U17 16.03.82, Steyning :
  3kW - 14:09.81, 5kWR - 25:17,
  10kW - 56:36.0
HALES Sophie U15 30.03.85, Steyning :
  2.5kW - 13:58.25, 3kWR - 16:13
HALFORD Katie U17 4.10.82, Exeter :
  SP - 10.72, DT - 34.59
HALKET Jade U13 5.05.86, Ellon :
  HJ - 1.49, PenM - 2070
HALL Andrea U23 28.01.77, Bedford & Co :
  TJ - 11.54
HALL Cicely U23 12.10.78, Norwich :
  100H - 15.0, 400H - 61.81 (60.83-97)
HALL Lindsay U15 31.07.84, Ayr Seaforth :
  JT - 32.26
HALL Penny U23 13.01.77, Cardiff :
  PV - 3.00
HALL Sally 14.02.71, Birchfield :
  10kWR - 57:04
HANCOCK Ebony U17 17.03.82, Birchfield :
  DT - 34.86
HANCOCK Sarah U23 2.02.78, Braintree :
  200 - 25.1 (24.98w-97)
HANDLEY Jennifer U17 8.06.83, Wakefield :
  TJ - 10.93
HANES Nikki, :
  Mar - 3:09:47
HANSEN Ashia 5.12.71, Shaftesbury Barnet :
  60 - 7.51i, LJ - 6.23 (6.47A-96/6.27-94),
  TJ - 15.16i/14.32 (15.15-97)
HANSEN Kristina U23 30.05.77, Thurrock/NOR :
  400H - 64.55
HANSON Lorraine I. 22.04.65, Birchfield :
  200 - 24.33 (24.2-91), 400 - 53.59 (50.93-91),
  400H - 57.46 (56.70-89)
HARDING Faye U13 7.09.85, Wrexham :
  600 - 1:45.9
HARDING Jemma U20 15.02.79, Wycombe :
  PV - 2.50 (2.50-97)
HARDING Joanne 12.04.64, Trafford :
  HT - 38.88, JT - 40.90 (55.04-87)
HARDY Rebecca Jana 11.11.68, Highgate H :
  SP - 11.22 (11.50-89),
  DT - 44.12 (45.20-97), HT - 40.93
HARDY Simone U20 9.11.79, Kettering :
  800 - 2:11.65 (2:10.12i/2:11.0-97)
HARGAN Dawn 14.04.71, Finn Valley :
  1500 - 4:28.2 (4:23.37-87)

379

HARGRAVE Karen 23.09.65, :
  1500 - 4:30.1 (4:09.46-89)
HARNETT Jill U23 26.02.76, S London :
  HT - 35.07
HARRIS Frances 1.06.72, Newham & Essex B :
  HJ - 1.65
HARRIS Leah U17 24.02.82, Newquay & Par :
  800 - 2:17.0
HARRIS Melissa U15 20.10.83, Oswestry :
  60HG - 9.09i, 75HG - 11.07w/11.17,
  LJ - 5.44, PenG - 2810
HARRISON Deborah U23 13.11.78, Birchfield :
  HJ - 1.72, LJ - 5.88 (6.00w-96)
HARRISON Fallon U15 1.05.85, Chesterfield :
  DT - 29.20
HARRISON Fiona Jane U17 30.11.81, Barns :
  300 - 39.79, PV - 3.60,
HARRISON Kate U17 21.07.82, Wells :
  PV - 2.60i (2.70-97)
HARRISON Susan 6.08.71, Leam/Leeds Poly :
  3k - 9:39.18i (9:25.5-94)
HARRISON Susanna J. V35 25.01.63, Woking :
  Mar - 3:06:54
HART Siobhan 15.06.75, Guildford & G :
  HT - 35.65 (36.32-97)
HARTIGAN Beverley Marie 10.06.67, Birchfield :
  1500 - 4:23.53 (4:05.66-90),
  10k - 34:21.91, 10kR - 33:22 (33:02-95)
HARTLEY Sarah U20 4.05.81, Spenborough :
  PV - 3.05i/2.90 (3.15-97)
HARVEY Amy U17 23.04.82, Braintree :
  JT - 42.89
HARVEY Lisa 9.04.68, Bristol :
  400 - 57.1 (56.5-96/56.67-97)
HARVEY Natalie 17.01.75, S London/AUS :
  1500 - 4:25.11, 3k - 8:59.4mx
HARWOOD Jocelyn Anne V40 21.11.57, M & C :
  100H - 14.2w/14.23w/14.63 (13.79-89)
HASLAM Claire Maria V35 18.12.63, W S & E :
  200 - 25.14 (24.4-91/24.76-97)
HASLER Suzanne U17 7.04.82, R S Coldfield :
  800 - 2:13.82 (2:11.51-97)
HATCH Sharon 5.09.64, Sparta :
  3k - 9:55.20 (9:47.8-88), 5k - 17:29.06
HATHAWAY Emily U20 22.12.79, R S Coldfield :
  800 - 2:11.97
HAUGH Louise U17 29.12.81, Ballymena & A :
  200 - 25.39 (25.3-97)
HAWKINS-TAYLOR Lauren U13 29.10.86,
  Radcliffe : 75 - 10.2
HAYDOCK Victoria U17 24.08.83, Pendle :
  DT - 32.58
HAYWARD Marika U17 12.11.82, Invicta :
  1500 - 4:42.72
HAZEL Louise U13 6.10.85, Peterborough :
  100 - 13.0, 200 - 27.3, 70HM - 11.8, LJ - 4.63
HEAD Christine U20 18.12.79, Norwich :
  JT - 44.38
HEANEY Caroline U23 3.04.76, E, S & M/IRE :
  400H - 66.0 (65.41-97)
HEARNE Jodie U17 17.09.81, Ilford :
  80HI - 11.9 (12.61-97),
  HJ - 1.65, Hepl - 3916 (3949-97)
HEASMAN Heather V35 27.09.63, Altrincham :
  1500 - 4:26.2, 3k - 9:16.5mx (9:38.9-91),
  5k - 15:57.24 (15:53.84-96),
  10kR - 33:23 (32:31-94),
  HMar - 1:15:59 (1:14:06-94)

HEATHCOTE Miranda 18.09.72, Tonbridge :
  3k - 9:59.4, 10k - 35:09.92,
  10kR - 34:06, 10MR - 56:07, HMar - 1:16:00
HEIL Belinda U17 8.03.82, Croydon :
  SP - 10.77, DT - 35.72, HT - 35.25
HENAGHAN Dianne 6.08.65, Morpeth :
  800 - 2:07.62 (2:03.1mx/2:05.4-97),
  1500 - 4:25.65 (4:16.17-97),
  2k - 6:12.4, 3k - 9:46.1 (9:26.6-96)
HENDERSON Sarah U15 27.09.83, Woking :
  HJ - 1.62, LJ - 5.25w
HENDRICKS Caroline U17 25.01.83, Wolves & B :
  JT - 36.47, Hepl - 4429
HENRY Corinne Cynthia 15.04.72, S Barnet :
  LJ - 6.06 (6.12w-93), TJ - 13.95
HENRY Lorraine 16.09.67, Norwich :
  SP - 11.69 (13.09-88),
  DT - 38.79 (43.88-90), HT - 35.57
HENTON Sarah 4.05.73, Birchfield/Birm Univ. :
  DT - 47.96 (50.98-97)
HERBERT Caroline 30.06.70, Arena :
  3k - 9:52.5 (9:51.1-96), 5k - 16:52.5,
  10kR - 34:22 (34:01-96), 10MR - 56:40
HERBERT Sarah U17 29.08.83, Bristol :
  800 - 2:16.5, 1500 - 4:42.13
HERRING Katy U15 3.09.83, Havering :
  SPG - 10.75
HERRINGTON Lynsey U20 31.05.79, AF&D :
  DT - 39.95 (42.62-96/41.86dh-95)
HESKETH Joanne 16.06.69, Steyning :
  10kWR - 57:06
HESLOP Laura U15 12.11.83, Wirral :
  100 - 12.66w
HEWETH Karen V35 29.11.59, Hull Achilles
  (nee SHARP):
  DT - 37.44 (38.82-93)
HIGGINS Dawn 10.12.75, Cardiff :
  200 - 24.9 (25.57-97), 400 - 53.79
HIGHAM Stephanie U15 26.12.83, Carlisle/Asp :
  HJ - 1.72
HILL Amie U20 9.09.80, Oxford City :
  DT - 37.51 (40.72-96)
HILL Cathy-Ann U23 4.05.77, Team Solent :
  SP - 12.65 (13.10-96)
HILL Jenna U13 16.10.85, Sale :
  800 - 2:27.3, 1200 - 3:59.1
HILL Joanna 11.02.73, AF&D (nee CLARK):
  100 - 11.67,
  200 - 23.62w/23.93 (24.2-97)
HILLS Jennifer U20 25.03.81, Yeovil Oly :
  HJ - 1.69
HINES Olivia U15 19.10.83, Hercules Wimb :
  800 - 2:12.04
HIRD Leyna U15 4.02.84, Exeter :
  75HG - 11.7/11.79
HO Davina U15 20.11.83, City of Glasgow :
  HJ - 1.66
HOBBS Kim U23 12.12.78, Hull Achilles :
  PV - 2.50 (2.80-97)
HOBSON Joanna U13 22.01.87, Steyning :
  2kW - 11:29.01
HODGES Lindsay U17 21.09.82, Yeovil Oly :
  PV - 3.35
HODGSON Georgina U17 23.11.81, Sutton & D :
  JT - 39.71
HOGG Rachel U17 11.06.82, Copeland :
  HJ - 1.65i/1.62 (1.66-97), LJ - 5.73,
  TJ - 11.68w/11.44, Hepl - 4258 (4279-97)

HOGGARTH Donna Louise 14.10.73, Preston :
100 - 11.81w/12.0 (11.55w/11.61-92)
HOLDEN Diana 12.02.75, Hounslow :
HT - 57.95
HOLDSWORTH C. U13, Colchester H :
70HM - 11.8
HOLLICK Lisa 1.01.70, Shaftesbury Barnet :
HMar - 1:18:28 (1:17:28-96), Mar - 2:51:16
HOLLMAN Anne Marie 18.02.74, Peterborough :
400 - 57.03, 100H - 14.6 (14.1/14.30-96),
400H - 61.81 (61.56-93)
HOLLMAN Julie Caroline U23 16.02.77,
Peterborough : 200 - 24.47w/24.74,
60H - 8.99i, 100H - 14.14w/14.24,
HJ - 1.79 (1.81-97),
LJ - 6.29w/6.17 (6.29w-97), SP - 11.93i/11.83,
Hep - 5816w/5557 (5595-97)
HOLLOWAY Joanne U23 10.05.76, W S & E :
SP - 12.00 (12.02i-96), HT - 36.18
HOLMES Kelly 19.04.70, Ealing,Southall & Mx :
1500 - 4:06.10 (3:58.07-97),
1M - 4:28.04, 3k - 9:10.23 (9:08.7-95)
HOLROYD Shelley Ann 17.05.73, Essex L :
JT - 54.16 (60.12-96)
HOLT Gemma 20.12.72, AF&D :
LJ - 5.99, TJ - 11.08 (11.14-97)
HOOD Hayley U13, Sale :
SPM - 9.57
HOOD Maria U20 20.12.79, Bournemouth :
DT - 37.71, HT - 37.00
HOOPER Emily U17 16.05.82, N Devon :
800 - 2:16.74
HOPKINS Emma U13 16.09.86, Leics Cor :
1200 - 4:03.9
HORNBY Emma 12.12.73, Birchfield :
PV - 3.91
HORNE Caroline A. V40 7.11.56, Crawley :
10kR - 34:54 (33:08-85),
HMar - 1:18:03 (1:13:43sh/1:14:00-84)
HORNE Katie U20 23.05.79, City of Glasgow :
HT - 38.27
HOROVITZ Gillian P. V40 7.06.55, AF&D :
Mar - 2:41:15 (2:36:52-92)
HORWILL Katherine 26.01.75, Dudley & St :
3kW - 15:35.0 (14:41.0-93),
5kWR - 24:44 (24:44-96),
10kWR - 51:29 (51:20-95)
HOULDSWORTH Rachel U15 18.06.84, Bing :
DT - 30.00
HOURIHAN Alyson J. V35 17.10.60, Cardiff :
SP - 11.41 (12.41-92), DT - 40.27 (43.58-92)
HOWARD Anna U17 18.07.83, Oxford City :
HT - 34.54
HOWARD Anna-Lisa U23 18.04.78, Norwich :
SP - 11.94i/11.69 (13.03-96)
HOWARD Tracey U20 11.02.81, Bournemouth :
JT - 39.63
HOWARTH Beverley U23 4.09.76, Sale :
HJ - 1.66 (1.73-93)
HOWE Sian U15 11.04.84, Invicta :
DT - 31.66
HOWELL Denise U17 16.07.82, Walton :
TJ - 11.20w/11.08 (11.16-97)
HOWELL Gabrielle U17 25.01.82, Brighton :
100 - 12.3 (12.20w/12.2/12.82-97), 300 - 38.75,
200 - 24.68w/24.76, 400 - 54.7/56.58
HOWELL Tina U17 16.07.82, Walton :
TJ - 10.83w

HUCKERBY Nicola U23 27.02.78, Birchfield :
3kW - 15:07.8 (14:49.0-97),
5kW - 24:56.69, 10kWR - 51:07
HUDSON Helen. U13 1.10.86, East Cheshire :
1200 - 4:02.5
HUDSON Laura U13, Cleddau :
SPM - 9.42, DTM - 24.40
HUGHES Elizabeth U23 9.06.77, Bromley :
PV - 2.60 (3.00-96)
HUGHES Emma L. U20 15.09.80, Luton :
LJ - 5.97
HUGHES Jo 7.12.71, Shaftesbury Barnet :
PV - 3.10
HUGHES Llinos U17 31.03.82, Ynys Mon :
LJ - 5.35
HUGHES Rhian U20 11.05.79, Colwyn Bay :
JT - 40.15
HULSE Natalie U17 2.12.82, City of Stoke :
HJ - 1.70, Hepl - 4106
HUMBERSTONE Sarah U20 6.07.81, Clee :
HJ - 1.68
HUMPHREYS Danielle U15 16.05.84,
Mansfield : LJ - 5.25
HUNT Emma U15 25.04.86, Milton Keynes :
600 - 1:45.9, 800 - 2:27.2,
1k - 3:14.7, 1200 - 3:52.9, 1500 - 4:56.5
HUNT Lucy U15 4.04.84, Cheltenham :
PenG - 2584
HUNT Suzy 26.09.75, Windsor S & E :
100H - 15.25
HUNT Tanya U15 14.09.83, Salisbury :
SPG - 10.80, JT - 34.16
HUNTER Donna U17 9.10.81, Central :
PV - 2.80
HUNTER Jill 14.10.66, Blaydon : (see BOLTZ)
HUNTER-ROWE Carolyn 25.01.64, Pud & B
/Knaves : 100kR - 8:16:07 (7:27:19-93)
HURST Jodie U23 21.06.77, City of Stoke :
TJ - 12.20 (12.42w/12.26-97)
HURST Louise U13 27.10.85, Wallsend :
200 - 27.27
HUTCHINGS Hayley U15 14.11.83, Steyning :
2.5kW - 13:21.01, 3kW - 15:49.47,
3kWR - 15:38
HUTCHINSON Anya U23 16.07.77, Notts :
400H - 62.20
HUTCHINSON Ava U17 30.03.83, AF&D :
1500 - 4:47.7
HYDE Zahara V35 12.01.63, Havant :
(see HYDE- PETERS)
HYDE-PETERS Zahara V35 12.01.63, Havant
(nee HYDE) :
1500 - 4:30.52 (4:19.36-93),
3k - 9:31.69 (9:05.49-91),
5k - 16:49.0 (16:04.12-96),
10k - 35:24.46 (33:23.25-94),
10kR - 34:57 (33:46-95),
10MR - 57:31 (56:11-94), HMar - 1:16:33
HYLAND Victoria U17 27.10.81, Sale :
LJ - 5.48i/5.33
HYNAN Julie U20 23.05.80, Liverpool H :
HJ - 1.65 (1.73-97), PV - 2.90
HYND Natalie U23 30.01.78, Pitreavie :
100 - 12.1/12.12 (11.93w-96/12.00-95),
200 - 24.87w/25.17 (24.51w/24.61-96)
HYSLOP Joanne U20 13.03.80, Coventry G :
100H - 15.0, 400H - 63.7/64.01

381

GE Yewande U20 21.03.80, Sutton & Dist :
100H - 14.47w/14.8

IMPETT Lindsay U20 4.01.80, Wimborne :
400H - 64.9 (63.2-97)

INGMAN Jilly U23 17.08.78, Barnsley :
1500 - 4:22.96,
3k - 9:19.4mx/9:35.96, 5k - 16:35.86

INIEKIO Nimi U13 25.10.86, Brighton :
SPM - 10.03

IRVINE Louise U17 16.10.82, C of Glasgow :
HJ - 1.65i

IRVING Ruth 20.07.74, Wirral :
LJ - 6.28

JACKSON Amber U17 29.11.82, Verlea :
JT - 36.35

JACKSON Emily U20 16.10.80, Gateshead :
HJ - 1.78

JACKSON Lorna 9.01.74, Edinburgh WM :
NJT - 47.37, JT - 58.39

JACOBS Kim Simmone Geraldine 5.09.66,
Shaftesbury B : 60 - 7.56i (7.33i-85),
100 - 11.34w/11.46 (11.18w-97/11.31-88),
200 - 23.03w/23.71 (22.95-96)

JAMES Anwen U20 17.02.81, Swansea :
DT - 36.17 (36.76-97)

JAMES Dawn 4.01.67, AF&D :
3k - 9:34.8, 5k - 16:37.03,
10k - 35:14.76, 10kR - 34:49

JAMES Marian 9.05.71, Edinburgh WM :
HT - 37.09

JAMES Vernicha U15 6.06.84, Cambridge H :
100 - 12.4,
200 - 24.25w/24.75i/24.8

JAMES Vicky U20 13.05.81, Cheltenham :
JT - 39.01

JAMIESON Josie U13 17.07.87, Shetland :
JTM - 25.40

JAMISON Victoria U23 19.05.77, Lagan Valley :
100 - 12.10 (11.93-97), 200 - 24.06,
400 - 52.87R/52.97, 400H - 56.42

JASPER Hayley Laurette U15 1.05.84, Hunt :
PenG - 2964

JEEVES Anna V40 19.09.54, Shaftesbury B :
Mar - 2:54:42

JEFFERY Diana U17 9.03.83, Invicta :
1500 - 4:42.83

JEGEDE Tolu U20 25.09.80, Newham & E B :
TJ - 11.47 (11.59-96)

JELBERT Zoe U15 21.01.84, Newquay & Par :
800 - 2:18.1, 1500 - 4:36.48

JENKINS Andrea 4.10.75, Bedford & County :
HT - 46.52 (48.58-97)

JENKINS Beverley 6.02.70, Salford :
3k - 9:32.20, HMar - 1:16:21

JENKINS Siobhan U15 14.06.84, Liverpool H :
JT - 32.99

JENNER Jackie U23 25.10.76, Tonbridge :
LJ - 5.54 (5.56-96)

JENNINGS Joanne 20.09.69, Essex L :
HJ - 1.91 (1.94i-93)

JEPSON Lynsey U13 12.01.87, Leics Cor :
800 - 2:22.4, 1500 - 5:04.3

JESSOP Michelle U13 21.09.85, Milton Keynes :
800 - 2:26.3, 1200 - 3:56.5, 1500 - 5:01.5

JOEL Alexa U15 19.09.83, Basildon :
1500 - 4:48.2

JOHANSEN Michelle U15 1.02.84, Oxford City :
100 - 12.6, LJ - 5.54

JOHN Aimee U15 20.09.83, Carmarthen :
100 - 12.4

JOHN Joanne E. U20 12.11.80, Ealing, & Mx :
DT - 39.64

JOHNS Karen U20 18.08.80, Shildon :
800 - 2:11.97 (2:11.19-94)

JOHNSON Charmaine Rachael V35 4.06.63,
Windsor S & E : SP - 13.34 (14.29-93)

JOHNSON Emma U17 3.03.82, Trafford :
HJ - 1.62

JOHNSON Gemma Lynne U23 21.07.78, Notts :
HT - 36.76 (37.70-97)

JOHNSON Jade U20 7.06.80, Herne Hill :
100 - 11.72w/12.0, 200 - 24.31

JOHNSON Julia U20 21.09.79, Invicta :
TJ - 12.50

JOHNSTONE Pamela U20 16.03.79, Edin WM :
400H - 65.1/65.63 (61.93-96)

JOINER Angela 14.02.69, Shaftesbury Barnet :
3k - 9:33.99 (9:33.0-97),
5k - 16:33.57 (16:25.22-97), 10k - 33:30.27

JOLLEY Lynn 26.11.73, Salford :
Mar - 3:03:54

JONES Catherine T. U17 26.02.83, Swansea :
100 - 12.2 (12.76-97), 200 - 25.2 (26.16-97)

JONES Elizabeth V35 25.04.61, Arena :
Mar - 3:00:01 (2:54:03-95)

JONES Ffion U17 19.07.83, Deeside :
DT - 32.25

JONES Jillian Avril 23.12.69, AF&D :
800 - 2:08.6 (2:04.97-93),
1500 - 4:20.61 (4:16.0-93)

JONES Katie U23 4.01.77, Trafford :
400 - 57.1 (56.35-96),
100H - 14.56w/14.72,
400H - 61.38 (61.19-96),
TJ - 11.10 (11.18-96)

JONES Leanne 13.05.74, Rhondda :
(see TAYLOR)

JONES Lindsey U23 8.09.77, Wakefield :
HT - 45.71 (49.10-97)

JONES Llyn U20 21.02.79, Braintree :
HT - 40.25

JONES Lowri U17 22.07.83, Torfaen :
100 - 12.08w/12.1/12.13,
200 - 24.56w/24.81, 300 - 40.87i

JONES Lucy U15 30.11.83, Bristol :
800 - 2:16.86

JONES Rachel 7.01.70, Blackpool :
1500 - 4:31.50

JONES Rebecca U17 17.01.83, Wrexham :
HJ - 1.77, LJ - 5.43, Hepl - 4255

JONES Sian U17 20.01.83, Swansea :
LJ - 5.40, TJ - 11.03

JONES Susan Eva U23 8.06.78, Wigan :
60H - 8.72i, 100H - 14.4 (13.95-97),
HJ - 1.92i/1.85 (1.91-97)

JONES Tina U20 10.09.80, Rowntrees :
LJ - 5.53

JONES Wendy C. V35 10.03.62, Ryston :
10kR - 34:18

JORDAN Rachel 29.01.72, Birchfield :
800 - 2:07.56 (2:06.7-97),
1500 - 4:30.34 (4:22.7-97)

JOSEPH Jimenez 14.07.68, Richmond & T :
Hep - 4259

JOSEPH Tracy Carol 29.11.69, Bas & MH :
  60 - 7.66i (7.42i-89),
  100 - 11.72w/11.93 (11.66w-97/11.79-96),
  200 - 24.02w/24.16 (23.57w-96/23.59-97),
  HJ - 1.73, LJ - 6.39 (6.44w-97)
JOSLIN Lois U20 1.03.79, Enfield :
  2KSTW - 7:27.99
JUPP Nicola 26.10.75, Preseli :
  Hep - 4070 (4257w/4186-93)
JURY Kerry 19.11.68, Wakefield :
  60 - 7.77i (7.76i-97),
  200 - 23.80w/24.3/24.33 (24.33-97),
  60H - 8.71i, 100H - 13.83w/13.99,
  HJ - 1.79 (1.81-97), LJ - 6.08w/5.96,
  TJ - 11.86, SP - 12.00, JT - 39.42,
  Hep - 6005w/5692 (5719-97)
JUST K. U13, Kendal :
  SPM - 9.33

KAISER Kath M. V45 24.08.51, Valli :
  Mar - 2:55:52 (2:55:03-94)
KALAND Hilde 22.05.73, Middlesbro & C/NOR :
  LJ - 5.56, TJ - 12.27w/12.15, JT - 47.97
KANE Kelly 28.10.74, Blackpool/IRE :
  SP - 12.05 (13.70-93)
KANEEN Bridget 15.08.65, Manx H :
  5kW - 27:25.63,
  10kWR - 57:05 (56:30-97)
KAVANAGH Emma U17 3.12.82, Hertford & W :
  HJ - 1.63
KAY Louise U23 1.12.77, Bolton :
  HT - 41.22 (42.86-96)
KAY Rachael U20 8.09.80, Wigan :
  60 - 7.79i (7.77i-97), 400 - 56.8,
  60H - 8.59i, 400H - 59.62
KEARNEY Nikki 20.05.73, Portsmouth :
  3k - 9:55.93i/9:59.7 (9:46.6-97)
KEEPING Rebecca U13 17.09.85, Soton City :
  600 - 1:45.5, 1k - 3:13.5, 1200 - 4:02.0
KEHLER Lisa Martine 15.03.67, Wolves & B :
  3kW - 13:02.5mx/13:14.48+ (13:11.0-90),
  5kW - 22:01.53 (21:57.68-90),
  5kWR - 21:55, 10kWR - 45:53
KEIGHTLEY Lauren U20 2.08.79, Bracknell :
  DT - 52.31
KELLAWAY Victoria U17 21.10.82, Medway :
  HJ - 1.65
KELLEHER Olivia 9.10.75, Windsor S & E/IRE :
  HT - 54.38 (56.22-97)
KELLY Gemma U17 13.03.82, Barrow & F :
  DT - 34.64, HT - 32.31
KELLY Jennifer Angela 20.06.70, Peterbro :
  200 - 24.89w/25.13 (24.70-94), 60H - 8.72i,
  100H - 13.80, LJ - 6.01w/5.86 (6.09-93),
  SP - 14.65i/14.27 (14.88i-90/14.73-91),
  Hep - 5608w/5584 (5826-94)
KELLY Louise U20 20.09.80, Barrow & F :
  3k - 9:28.64, 5k - 16:15.36
KELLY Rachel U20 15.06.81, Dorchester :
  PV - 2.60
KELLY Siona 19.04.74, Sale :
  JT - 38.72 (43.46-94)
KEMP Jennifer U20 18.02.80, Liv.Pemb Seft :
  JT - 49.36
KEMP Michelle U17 19.09.81, Sutton & Dist :
  JT - 43.94
KEMP Thomasin U20 5.03.80, Yeovil Oly :
  1500 - 4:27.75

KENNAUGH Jane, Manx H :
  10kWR - 56:35, 50kW - 5:34:27
KENNEY Lisa U17 17.02.83, Hull Springhead :
  JT - 35.78
KENNY Victoria U17 3.04.83, Ipswich :
  3k - 10:42.2
KERR Anyha U20 10.04.80, Bristol :
  JT - 38.40
KERR Emma U23 15.10.77, Ayr Seaforth :
  HJ - 1.70 (1.70-95)
KERR Sarah U17 11.12.81, Black Hill :
  300 - 41.3, 300H - 46.8
KERSHAW Andrea U23 22.03.78, Trafford :
  1500 - 4:33.6 (4:30.9-97), 3k - 9:49.37
KIND Jacqueline 24.10.68, Derby LAC :
  800 - 2:12.9
KING Emma U20 25.07.81, Guernsey :
  HT - 39.51
KING Rachel U23 11.05.76, Cardiff :
  100 - 11.8w/12.1 (11.8w/12.0/12.12-97),
  60H - 8.41i, 100H - 13.44w/13.73 (13.52-97)
KING Rebecca U20 25.03.81, Crawley :
  400 - 57.51
KING Sharon Marie 27.01.72, Sale :
  800 - 2:08.85 (2:07.1mx-96/2:07.7-97),
  1500 - 4:22.79 (4:19.83-96)
KING Stacie U17 19.01.82, Cardiff :
  300H - 46.43
KINGSBOROUGH Ruth 25.10.67, Overton :
  HMar - 1:17:16, Mar - 2:44:33
KIRBY Emma U17 11.11.81, Bracknell :
  DT - 33.86 (35.88-96)
KIRBY Rachel 18.05.69, Essex L :
  LJ - 5.89 (6.02-94), TJ - 12.22 (13.64-94)
KIRKPATRICK Julie 14.07.72, Lisburn :
  HT - 43.57 (48.90-96)
KITNEY Emily U20 25.04.81, Medway :
  JT - 38.19 (38.32-96)
KNEALE Karen 23.04.69, Manx H :
  3kW - 14:22.2 (14:05.1-95),
  10kWR - 50:05 (48:18un?-97/49:37-96)
KNIGHTS Lisa 12.07.71, Notts Poly :
  Mar - 3:00:54
KNIGHTS Sarah 25.02.67, Norwich :
  800 - 2:10.09
KOEHNE Sophie U17 17.09.81, S Barnet :
  1500 - 4:41.22
KOTEY Judy U20 20.05.80, St Albans :
  TJ - 12.61w/12.41i/12.33, Hep - 3943
KRZYWICKI Tara 9.03.74, Charnwood :
  1500 - 4:24.08, 3k - 9:21.54,
  5k - 15:48.1mx/15:53.28,
  10k - 34:37.04, 10kR - 34:33 (34:25-97),
  2KSTW - 7:08.29
KWAKYE Jeanette U17 20.03.83, Essex L :
  60 - 7.7i/7.71i,
  100 - 11.8w/11.93w/12.2/12.29 (12.11-97),
  200 - 24.4w/25.00
KINGSBOROUGH Ruth 25.10.67, Overton :
  Mar - 2:46:53
KIRBY Lucy U17 7.05.81, Cardiff :
  1500 - 4:45.31
KIRBY Stacey U15 19.09.83, Sale :
  800 - 2:18.08
KIRKPATRICK Julie 14.07.72, Birchfield :
  HT - 43.80 (48.90-96)
KITNEY Emily U17 25.04.81, Medway :
  JT - 37.94 (38.32-96)

KNEALE Karen 23.04.69, Manx H :
5kWR - 24:36 (24:21-95),
10kWR - 51:42 (49:37-96)
KOTEY Judy U20 20.05.80, St Albans :
TJ - 12.37i/12.36w/12.21
KRZYWICKI Tara 9.03.74, :
10kR - 34:25
KUENSTLINGER Erika U17 4.10.81, Blackh :
LJ - 5.39w/5.30
KWAKYE Jeanette U15 20.03.83, Essex L :
100 - 12.11, 200 - 25.3 (27.29-96)

LAING Wendy Jean V35 29.12.62, Liv H :
100H - 14.9w/15.1
(14.14w-93/14.2-81/14.35-86)
LAMB Katy U17 21.08.82, Dartford :
HT - 41.34
LAMB Susan 24.03.70, Sale (nee PARKER) :
800 - 2:09.76 (2:04.9mx-96/2:05.50-93),
1500 - 4:20.9 (4:11.57-96),
3k - 9:22.45 (9:06.2-92)
LAMBOURN Angela Jean 9.04.66, Rugby :
SP - 12.86 (13.75-91), HT - 37.96
LANE Catherine U23 18.11.76, Dacorum & T :
SP - 11.41, DT - 40.72, HT - 40.73
LANE Sarah E. U17 24.11.82, Swansea :
100 - 12.4w,
LJ - 5.70w/5.50
LASHLEY Charlene U13 1.09.85, W S & E :
75 - 9.9/10.02, 100 - 13.0,
150 - 19.9 (20.94-97)
LAST Suzanne F. 11.01.70, Medway :
DT - 39.48, HT - 48.85 (49.48-97)
LAVENDER Julie 9.11.75, Sunderland :
HT - 43.76 (51.62-94)
LAW Kirstie U23 31.01.78, City of Glasgow :
60 - 7.73i
LAWRENCE ., :
Mar - 2:57:04
LAWRENCE Susan 25.11.70, Thurrock :
HT - 39.16, JT - 39.17 (39.50-92)
LAWRENCE Victoria 9.06.73, Edinburgh WM :
600 - 1:34.7mx (1:32.83i+-96),
800 - 2:10.52 (2:03.52-96)
LAX Sian U20 4.08.79, Telford :
JT - 43.21 (45.74-96)
LAYZELL Alyson Elizabeth 16.12.66, Chelt :
200 - 25.0, 400 - 53.81,
400H - 57.31 (56.43-96)
LE GEYT Jacqueline U17 17.08.82, Sutton & D :
100 - 11.95w/12.2 (12.1/12.19-97),
200 - 25.2w (25.54-97)
LEAK Victoria U15 28.11.83, Yeovil Olympiads :
1500 - 4:48.50
LEE Helen U15 10.12.84, Parkside :
1500 - 4:48.2
LEE Rebecca U17 31.12.82, Banbury :
LJ - 5.37
LEECH Phillipa, Hallamshire :
Mar - 3:08:44
LEES Tamsin U15 24.04.84, Newton Abbot :
100 - 12.35w/12.5
LEIGH Kay, 3.12.60, Todmorden :
Mar - 3:03:51
LEIGH Sandra Christine 26.02.66, S & NH :
200 - 24.9 (24.0-91/24.09w?-90/24.13-91),
400 - 55.41 (52.75-91), 400H - 63.7 (61.8-93)

LESTRANGE Katy U20 17.09.79, Sale :
60H - 8.97i (8.86i-96),
100H - 14.39w/14.4/14.57 (14.36w/14.52-97)
LEWIS Ann V50 29.12.47, AF&D :
3kW - 15:59.68 (15:52.71i/15:55.0-96),
5kW - 27:09.12 (26:55.75-97),
10kWR - 55:41, 20kW - 2:00:47 (1:56:14-96)
LEWIS Denise 27.08.72, Birchfield :
200 - 24.47 (24.06w-96/24.10-97),
60H - 8.38iex/8.40i (8.2i/8.30i-97),
100H - 13.42w/13.57 (13.18-96),
HJ - 1.83 (1.84-96), Hep - 6559 (6736-97)
LJ - 6.59 (6.77w-97/6.67-95),
SP - 15.27, JT - 51.28 (56.50-96)
LEWIS Diana U17 27.04.82, Carmarthen :
HT - 33.44
LEWIS Rebecca U23 31.12.77, Sale/Camb U :
LJ - 5.51 (6.03w-96/5.73-94)
LEYS Katrina 11.09.73, Aberdeen :
100 - 12.1w/12.24w (12.1w-92/12.3-89),
200 - 25.0/25.23w/25.27
LIGHTFOOT Leonie U17 8.02.82, C of Stoke :
100 - 12.53w (12.44w/12.63-96)
LILLEY Emma U20 2.05.76, Bingley :
JT - 42.44 (44.08-95)
LINTERN Candie U17 5.02.82, Crawley :
DT - 41.50
LISHMAN Megan U15 15.11.83, Cockermouth :
LJ - 5.23
LISTER Rosanne 9.05.69, Medway :
DT - 42.24 (53.66-91)
LISTON Bianca U23 28.05.78, Bromley :
100 - 12.15, 100H - 14.2/14.30 (14.18-97)
LITTLE Jan U17, Scottish Schools :
60 - 7.8i/7.89i
LITTLE Stephanie U17 5.11.81, Newport :
300H - 46.65, HepI - 3958 (4009-97)
LIVERTON Amanda Jayne 1.09.72, Exeter :
JT - 46.12 (57.84-90)
LIVESEY Katherine U20 15.12.79, Blackpool :
200 - 24.74w/24.84 (24.70w/24.78-97),
60H - 8.90i, 100H - 14.29w/14.39 (14.25-97),
HJ - 1.65i/1.65 (1.75-96),
LJ - 5.77, Hep - 5015 (5215-97)
LLEWELLYN Stephanie 31.12.68, S Barnet :
200 - 24.99 (24.1-97/24.38-95),
400 - 54.29 (52.4/52.54-95)
LLOYD Amy U15 30.11.83, Wakefield :
PenG - 2546
LLOYD Angharad U20 11.09.80, Carmarthen :
SP - 11.75 (11.85-97)
LLOYD Debbie U17 26.09.81, Colwyn Bay :
TJ - 11.10
LOCKLEY Angela U15 7.10.84, E Cheshire :
SPG - 10.95, DT - 33.66
LOCKWOOD Clare U20 7.10.79, Colwyn Bay :
JT - 42.16
LODGE Joanna 6.01.68, Hounslow :
HMar - 1:19:15, Mar - 2:50:10
LONEY Jacqui U20 17.04.79, Elgin :
HT - 36.85
LONSDALE Michelle U17 29.10.81, Wakefield :
JT - 42.75
LOTHIAN Fiona 2.12.65, Fife :
5k - 16:56.97, 10kR - 34:04sh (33:51-97sh),
HMar - 1:18:36
LOUARRADI Farah U20 11.10.79, Wx & Bath :
SP - 11.39i/11.32

384

LOVETT Rebecca U23 11.05.78, Medway :
1500 - 4:31.03
LOW Jane Kathryn V35 26.08.60, C of Glas :
400H - 63.27 (58.43-94)
LOW Linda 20.01.71, Aberdeen :
HT - 36.56 (41.32-94)
LOWE Karen U17 3.05.82, Blackpool :
60HI - 9.03o, 80HI - 11.95, HJ - 1.68,
SP - 10.50, Hepl - 4497
LOWE Larissa V35 19.08.63, Reading :
PV - 3.05 (3.20-96)
LOWE Samantha U17 23.02.82, Sale :
JT - 42.77
LOWE Zoe A. 7.07.65, St Albans :
Mar - 2:53:44 (2:49:28-95)
LUMB Hazel U17 23.11.82, Huntingdon :
1500 - 4:39.15
LUPTON Victoria Anne 17.04.72, Sheff RWC :
3kW - 13:38.7mx/13:43.73 (12:59.3-95),
5kW - 23:32.48 (21:52.4-95),
5kWR - 22:35 (21:36-92),
10kWR - 47:41 (45:28sh-93/45:48-94),
20kW - 1:44:35 (1:42:47-95)
LYNE Rebecca U17 4.07.82, Hallamshire :
800 - 2:14.63,
1500 - 4:38.32 (4:36.83-97)
LYNES Margaret Tracey V35 19.02.63, Ex L :
SP - 15.73 (16.57-94), DT - 41.69 (44.76-93)
LYON Janet V35 12.03.62, Aberdeen :
PV - 2.60
LYONS Abby U13 18.12.85, Liverpool H :
1200 - 4:01.4

*M*ACCARTHY Danielle U17 13.09.81,
Wessex & Bath/IRE : PV - 2.80
MACDOUGALL Lynne 18.02.65, C of Glasgow :
5k - 16:01.41 (15:45.03-97),
10kR - 33:32, 10MR - 55:58
MACKENZIE Rachel V35 26.02.61, Serpentine :
Mar - 3:00:25
MACKINNON Rhona U17 5.02.82, C of Glas :
100 - 12.47w/12.56 (12.5-97),
200 - 25.15w/25.49, 300 - 41.18i (40.87i-97)
MACPHAIL Ann 3.05.70, City of Glasgow :
5k - 17:15.53 (16:55.83-97)
MACPHERSON Joan U20 18.09.80, Bas & MH :
SP - 11.91, DT - 42.15, HT - 40.85
MACPHERSON Shona U20 31.08.80,
City of Glasgow : 400H - 64.31
MACRAE Carrie U20 2.09.80, Blackpool :
JT - 39.16
MACRAE Catherine U20 1.01.79, Hounslow :
PV - 2.50
MADDISON Lynne 17.08.67, Traff/Prestatyn :
10MR - 57:57 (57:52-97), HMar - 1:18:21
MADDOX Keri 4.07.72, Sale/Staffs Univ :
400 - 55.33i/55.5 (55.2-92),
60H - 8.47i (8.47i-92),
100H - 13.07w/13.11, 400H - 56.38
MADUAKA Joice 30.09.73, Essex L :
60 - 7.34i, 100 - 11.32, 200 - 23.37
MAGRATH Hazel U20 5.08.81, Norwich :
400H - 64.2
MAGUIRE Kirsty U17 5.07.83, Edinburgh WM :
PV - 2.70i/2.50
MAGUIRE Lindsey U17 15.01.82, Edin WM :
300H - 46.18, 400H - 68.0

MAHONY Joanne U23 22.10.76, Trafford :
200 - 24.70, 400 - 56.00i, 400H - 60.03
MAIDEN Debbie 27.05.67, Hounslow :
Mar - 3:02:21
MAIR Angharad V35 30.03.61, Newport :
10kR - 33:57, 10MR - 55:19 (55:16-97),
HMar - 1:14:01
MAIS Chevette U17 22.09.82, GEC :
200 - 25.59
MAJOR Julie 19.08.70, Shaftesbury Barnet :
(see PEACOCK)
MAKIN Emma U13 12.10.85, Warrington :
70HM - 11.1/11.70
MALE Kirsty U17 7.07.82, Edinburgh WM :
DT - 32.16
MALE Samantha U23 11.04.76, AF&D :
100H - 14.98 (14.4w-96/14.64w-95/14.7/14.79-96)
MANN Kelly U15 8.09.83, Solihull & S Heath :
2.5kW - 12:51.7, 3kW - 15:06.69,
5kWR - 26:28
MANN Michelle Louise U23 6.02.77, Preston :
3k - 9:49.0mx (9:30.5mx/9:43.23-96)
MANNING Sarah U17 31.10.82, Portsmouth :
SP - 10.99
MANSFIELD Danielle U17 18.10.81, Thurrock :
JT - 39.40
MARCHANT Zina D. V45 30.09.50, Wx & Bath :
HMar - 1:19:42 (1:13:38-90),
Mar - 2:53:10 (2:39:26-91)
MARDLE Eleanor U23 27.07.78, Exeter :
200 - 24.91i/25.21w (24.57-97)
MARSDEN Caroline U17 1.06.82, Cardiff :
100 - 12.4w/12.59w
MARSHALL Jacqueline U20 20.07.79, Edin U :
PV - 2.50
MARSHALL Jolene U15 22.10.83, GEC :
SPG - 11.00
MARSHALL Kelly U13 8.01.86, Dudley & St :
70HM - 11.4/11.51, PenM - 2121
MARSHALL Lucy U17 28.11.81, Charnwood :
SP - 10.97, DT - 32.68, HT - 43.10
MARTI Debora Jane 14.05.68, Bromley :
HJ - 1.89i (1.95i-97/1.94-96)
MARTIN Amelia U20 11.02.80, Blackheath :
LJ - 5.50 (5.50i-96), Hep - 4081
MARTIN Angela U20 26.11.80, Border :
HJ - 1.66 (1.67-97)
MARTIN Claire U23 12.07.76, Newport/Ox Un :
2KSTW - 7:34.66
MARTIN Karen Lesley 24.11.74, Derby/WRAF :
JT - 57.82
MARTIN Rachel U23 9.09.78, Sale :
HJ - 1.68i/1.65 (1.76-97)
MARTIN Stacey U17 6.08.82, Torfaen :
LJ - 5.49
MARTIN-CLARKE Susan J. V40 13.09.55,
Medway : Mar - 2:58:29 (2:42:32-89)
MASKREY H., Belgrave :
Mar - 3:05:16
MASSEY Eva U20 22.12.80, North Down :
SP - 13.24, DT - 41.13, HT - 35.41
MATHIESON Hannah U13 28.10.85, Aberdeen :
70HM - 11.7/11.73
MATHIESON Sarah U13 28.10.85, Aberdeen :
70HM - 11.78

MATTHEWS Jennifer Ann V35 3.07.62,
Ashford (nee PEARSON) :
200 - 25.1 (24.6-86/25.06w-89),
400 - 56.6/57.25 (54.6-88/55.62i-93/55.89-89),
100H - 14.7 (14.78-91/14.99w-94),
400H - 58.72 (57.41-88)
MATTHEWS Louise U15 27.12.83, Thurrock :
JT - 36.65
MAWER Rebecca U15 31.01.84, Grimsby :
HJ - 1.60
MAYLOR Donna U17 20.05.82, Birchfield :
100 - 11.62w/11.8w/11.88, 200 - 24.96,
80HI - 11.51, 100H - 14.7w/14.73, Hepl - 4205
HJ - 1.63 (1.65-97), LJ - 5.59 (5.86w-96)
MAYOCK Charlotte 11.12.73, Barnsley :
1500 - 4:29.2 (4:19.5-97),
1M - 4:44.11 (4:36.96-97),
3k - 9:39.79 (9:25.58-97)
MCCABE Laura Ann U20 24.01.80, Vale Royal :
800 - 2:12.8mx (2:11.99-97)
MCCALLUM Ruth U20 1.03.79, Black Isle :
400H - 65.8/65.94 (62.59-97)
MCCAMMON Tammy U23 17.10.76, Hillingdon :
LJ - 5.79 (5.89i-95/5.86-91)
MCCANDLESS Jane U17 1.10.81, B & A :
JT - 36.02
MCCARTHY Jeni U17 22.02.82, Warrington :
100 - 12.54 (12.4-97),
200 - 24.48w/25.3/25.55 (25.0/25.13-97),
300 - 39.77, 400 - 57.88
MCCARTHY Lauren U15 30.08.84, Cann & St :
100 - 12.46w/12.69
MCCLEGGAN Samantha U15 25.10.83, Traff :
HJ - 1.60
MCCLUNG Mary 19.12.71, Edinburgh WM :
400 - 56.6/56.98 (55.6/56.06-97),
800 - 2:11.67 (2:05.64-95)
MCCOLGAN Elizabeth 24.05.64, Dundee HH :
10kR - 33:13 (30:39-89),
15kR - 49:34 (47:43-88),
MCCONNELL Lee U23 9.10.78, S Barnet :
400 - 54.74, HJ - 1.83
MCCORRY Julie U20 7.11.79, Ballymena & A :
SP - 13.07, DT - 38.54
MCCREA Philippa U23 1.03.78, Gateshead :
800 - 2:11.36 (2:09.3-96)
MCCUTCHEON Margaret 30.12.68, Rad/USA :
HT - 42.96
MCDONNELL Alison 28.06.72, Parkside :
400H - 65.5/65.70 (62.7/63.02-96)
MCDONNELL Lindsey-Anne U20 13.08.79,
N Devon : HJ - 1.70 (1.73-97)
MCDONNELL Tracy U17 4.10.82, Yeovil Oly :
300H - 46.5
MCDOUGALL Fiona U20 1.08.81, Walton :
PV - 2.50
MCGEE Jill 16.04.64, Lancaster & Morcambe :
Mar - 3:07:48 (3:00:18-97)
MCGHEE Catherine U13 11.09.85,
Newquay & Par : PV - 1.50
MCGILCHRIST Joanna U17 27.08.83, Arbroath :
JT - 37.86
MCGILLIVARY Aileen 13.08.70, Edinburgh WM :
60 - 7.54i (7.36i-95),
100 - 11.66 (11.43w-93/11.54-92),
200 - 24.37 (23.29-93), 400 - 53.95
MCGIVERN Stacy U23 14.12.76, Peterborough :
TJ - 11.33w/11.25 (11.64-95)

MCGOWAN Julia Helen V35 12.05.59,
Brighton : (see CORNFORD)
MCGOWAN Suzanne U23 13.04.78, Motherw :
400 - 57.09
MCGRATH Samantha U13 14.04.86, Yate :
150 - 20.0
MCGREAVY Sara U17 13.12.82, Leamington :
60HI - 8.82i, 80HI - 11.28w/11.7/11.77,
300H - 46.5, Hepl - 4151
MCGUIRE Leah U13 30.01.87, Gr Yarmouth :
70HM - 11.6
MCHARDY Cheryl Ann U17 8.09.81, Ellon :
LJ - 5.40, TJ - 11.03w/10.80
MCILROY Debra U23 18.12.77, Middlesbro & C :
HJ - 1.68i/1.65 (1.70-93)
MCKAY Heather U17 5.09.81, Lochgelly :
60 - 7.75i, 100 - 12.3 (12.3/12.76-97),
200 - 24.62, 300 - 39.04, 400 - 57.6
MCKERNAN Jacqueline Lena 1.07.65, Lisburn/
Loughbro : SP - 13.44 (14.40-97),
DT - 58.05 (60.72-93)
MCKINNON Zoe U17 8.09.81, Horsham BS :
60HI - 9.17i, 80HI - 11.4/11.47w/11.48,
TJ - 11.00
MCLELLAN Shelley U17 21.03.83, S & NH :
SP - 12.02
MCLOUGHLIN Lauren U17 8.09.82, Cardiff :
60HI - 9.19i, 80HI - 11.76
MCMANUS Lisa U13 3.01.86, Leics Cor :
200 - 27.6, 70HM - 11.4
MCNEICE Kelly U23 17.06.78, Lisburn :
400 - 57.2 (57.0-97), 800 - 2:08.58,
400H - 63.14 (62.42-97)
MCPHERSON Karen 6.11.72, Trafford :
800 - 2:10.5 (2:06.3-91),
1500 - 4:25.6 (4:24.8-97)
MCPHERSON Victoria 1.06.71,
C of Glasgow/Glasgow Un : 2M - 10:11.81,
1500 - 4:26.10 (4:25.3-92),
3k - 9:21.2mx/9:35.41+ (9:10.1-92),
5k - 15:56.04,
10k - 32:38.48 (32:32.42-93)
MCQUEEN Sophie U17 3.12.81, Cleethorpes :
HJ - 1.75
MCROBBIE Sarah U13 8.11.86, Ellon :
SPM - 9.32
MCSHANE Laura U17 22.04.82, Hallamshire :
60HI - 8.78i, 80HI - 12.06 (11.81-97)
MCVIE Siobhan U15 6.07.84, Ayr Seaforth :
100 - 12.5dt, LJ - 5.56
MEAD Sarah U20 16.10.79, Torfaen :
800 - 2:10.17
MEADOWS Jennifer U20 17.04.81, Wigan :
400 - 55.92 (55.6-97)
MEES Joanne 28.09.73, Halesowen :
SP - 11.50 (11.53-97)
MELLIS Kelly U20 4.12.79, Banbury :
DT - 42.63 (44.86-97)
MELLOWDEW Anita 1.12.70, Epsom & Ewell :
HMar - 1:19:03, Mar - 2:46:17
MELVIN Hazel 19.11.73, City of Glasgow :
HJ - 1.80i/1.80 (1.85-97)
MERCER Caroline E. 19.05.72, Edinburgh WM
(nee BLACK): LJ - 5.79 (6.05w-97/6.00-92)
MERRILL Tracey U15, Reading :
DT - 29.16
MERRY Emma Louise 2.07.74, Coventry God :
SP - 12.31 (13.62-93), DT - 53.21

MERRY Katharine 21.09.74, Birchfield :
100 - 11.43 (11.27w/11.34-94),
200 - 22.93 (22.77-97), 400 - 51.02
MERSH Joanne 19.10.74, Ex L :
(see FENN)
MESZAROSOVA Metra U23 12.02.76,
Thames Valley/SVK : PV - 2.60
METCALFE Katie U17 10.02.83, Halifax :
100 - 12.4/12.44,
200 - 25.23w
MICHALSKA Carmen 6.11.73, E,S & Mx/Army :
200 - 25.1 (25.53un-96), 400 - 56.02
MICHIE Lucy U17 4.09.81, Ayr Seaforth :
60HI - 9.18i
MIKNEVICIUTE Dalia 5.09.70, S Barnet/exLIT :
HJ - 1.86i/1.80 (1.89-97)
MILBORROW Clare U23 10.01.77, Horsham :
100H - 14.24w/14.4/14.73, LJ - 5.55
MILDEN Gemma U17 31.05.82, Exeter :
HT - 35.30
MILES Lindsay U17 17.10.81, Ashford :
PV - 2.60 (2.60-97)
MILES Lynne U20 14.06.79, Birchfield :
JT - 41.61
MILES Susan U17 1.11.81, Hillingdon :
1500 - 4:47.87, 3k - 10:28.4 (10:20.6-97)
MILLAR Kirtsy U17 22.12.82, C of Plymouth :
200 - 25.53w, SP - 10.34
MILLER Lisa U17 13.01.83, Cambridge H :
300 - 40.3/41.28, 400 - 57.3, 800 - 2:14.2
MILLSON-WATKINS Lucy U15 19.10.83,
Wycombe : 200 - 25.6
MITCHELL Angela 17.08.65, Parkside :
DT - 42.05
MITCHELL Jeina Sophia 21.01.75, Croydon :
400 - 56.8 (55.9-97),
800 - 2:11.54 (2:03.36-97)
MITCHELL Julie 3.10.74, Brighton :
800 - 2:08.44, 1500 - 4:22.92 (4:22.52-97)
MITCHELL Rebecca U15 10.12.83, Regent H :
75HG - 11.54w/11.55
MITCHELL Virginia V35 29.01.63, Woking :
400H - 65.9 (64.05-95)
MITTLEBERGER Hayley 28.06.68, :
1500 - 4:29.5mx
MOCKLER Jennifer U17 28.08.82, Liverpool H :
1500 - 4:35.33i/4:41.6 (4:31.0-97),
3k - 10:26.2 (9:54.6-97)
MODAHL Diane Dolores 17.06.66, Sale :
600 - 1:29.4+ (1:22.99+'-89/1:26.18-87),
800 - 1:58.81 (1:58.65-90),
1500 - 4:19.96 (4:12.3-89)
MOFFAT Basilie U23 8.04.78, Bingley :
HJ - 1.65i/1.65 (1.70-96)
MOFFITT Alison J. 6.10.69, Windsor S & E :
SP - 11.21 (11.96-96),
DT - 39.27 (47.22-91), JT - 48.09 (49.10-96)
MOLES Shelley U15 31.10.83, Basildon :
SPG - 12.19, DT - 29.05
MOLLOY Jennifer U15 23.09.83, Bournemouth :
75HG - 11.50
MONDS Debra U23 25.02.78, Wigan :
DT - 37.55
MONEY Julie 26.04.64, Derby LAC :
200 - 25.0 (24.7w-91/24.8-90/24.89-88)
MONK Caroline 7.09.75, Halesowen :
JT - 40.73

MOODY Carly U20 9.06.80, Braintree :
60 - 7.71i (7.66i-97)
MOODY Hannah U20 26.07.79, Skyrac :
TJ - 11.18w/11.17
MOODY Lisa U23 22.02.77, City of Glasgow :
3k - 9:55.1 (9:54.87-96)
MOORE Charlotte U15 4.01.85, Bournemouth :
800 - 2:14.5, 1500 - 4:37.0
MOORE Claire U17 29.03.82, Gateshead :
DT - 38.52
MOORE Sarah Louise 15.03.73, Bristol :
SP - 11.27 (11.99-91), HT - 55.99 (56.60-97)
MOOREKITE Janice D. V40 1.05.57, Invicta :
Mar - 2:54:48 (2:48:06-95)
MORETON Kelly U20 18.09.79, Newport :
HJ - 1.65 (1.71-95)
MORGAN Felicity U15, :
JT - 31.96
MORGAN Kelly U20 17.06.80, Windsor S & E :
JT - 53.04
MORGAN Rebecca U23 1.11.78, Brecon :
PV - 2.60i (2.70-97)
MORGAN Sarah U15 9.05.84, Mandale :
SPG - 10.91
MORRIS Emily U17 30.09.82, City of Hull :
PV - 2.50
MORRIS Emma U17 25.01.82, Burnley :
SP - 10.78 (10.84-97)
MORRIS Kate U17 18.01.83, Dartford :
SP - 10.39, DT - 33.14
MORRISON Catriona U23 11.01.77, C of Glas :
3k - 9:45.94, 5k - 16:47.10
MORRISON Kirsty 28.10.75, Medway :
JT - 56.34 (59.36-93)
MORTIMER Joanne 18.12.71, Sale :
SP - 12.34 (13.18-92)
MOSELY Alison C. 13.12.73, Solihull & S H
(nee EVANS) :
100H - 14.9, HJ - 1.75i/1.72 (1.80-96)
MOSS Sarah U15 17.11.83, Southampton City :
JT - 35.23
MOTTRAM Hayley U15 22.01.84, Basildon :
800 - 2:18.56
MUMUNI Shukurat U17 27.01.82, Herne Hill :
LJ - 5.45w/5.37 (5.50-97)
MUNNOCH Lynsey U17 24.10.81, Falkirk :
200 - 25.3/25.52, 300 - 40.10
MUNRO Lynsay U23 1.02.77, Edinburgh WM :
JT - 42.33
MURPHY Catherine Ann 21.09.75, S Barnet :
60 - 7.56i (7.54i-97), 400 - 56.17,
100 - 11.6w?/11.70w/11.8/11.81
(11.6-96/11.63w-94/11.69A/11.77-96,
200 - 23.6w/23.8/23.91i/24.22 (23.40-95)
MURPHY Elaine 2.09.75, Bedford & County :
PV - 2.60
MURPHY Victoria U20 5.07.81, Wirral :
100H - 15.15w
MURRAY Freya U15 20.09.83, Lasswade :
1500 - 4:50.0
MURRAY Natalie U23 24.03.76, Stockport :
60H - 8.67i, LJ - 5.57,
100H - 14.5/14.60 (14.4w/14.51-97)
MURRAY-JESSEE Alison 13.01.67, C of Glas :
PV - 3.85A/3.60
MURRAY-MOONEY Yvonne Carole Grace
4.10.64, Motherwell :
10kR - 33:05 (32:24-97/33:00+-96)

MYERS Heather Ruth 5.12.64, AF&D :
  400H - 65.9 (59.46-94)
MYERS Mara 13.08.73, Parkside :
  1500 - 4:25.56, 3k - 9:38.9 (9:26.10-96),
  5k - 16:25.50, 10k - 34:53.57 (34:41.28-96)
MYLAN Karen U13 8.11.85, Cambridge H :
  75 - 10.2, 150 - 20.2, LJ - 4.83

N AISH Natalia U17 17.07.82, S Calif Univ :
  300H - 45.05
NALLY Toni U13, Worthing :
  1500 - 5:00.4
NASH Hayley L. V35 30.05.63, Newport :
  3k - 9:29.47mx (9:13.65-92),
  5k - 16:35.05 (16:25.7-92),
  10k - 34:28.8 (34:07.24-92),
  10MR - 56:39 (55:32-94)
NASH Rosie V40   58, Bro Dysynni :
  Mar - 3:04:41
NASH Sarah U20 10.11.80, Leamington :
  100 - 12.1/12.22w (12.94-97)
NASH Sharon 5.05.74, GEC :
  SP - 12.04 (12.67-93),
  DT - 41.69 (44.32-93), HT - 40.68 (41.94-94)
NAUGHER Abigail U20 26.02.80, Sunderland :
  400 - 55.83i/56.76
NAYLOR Christine V40 22.10.54, Arena :
  Mar - 3:04:45 (3:04:31-92)
NEALL Alison U20 8.11.79, Croydon :
  JT - 39.48 (40.60-97)
NEEF Melanie 26.05.70, City of Glasgow :
  200 - 24.19w/24.74 (23.35-95),
  400 - 54.58 (51.18-95)
NELSON Tatum U23 17.12.78, GEC :
  100 - 11.73 (11.63-97),
  200 - 24.5/25.09 (24.35w/24.51-93)
NEVIN Catherine E. V40 12.11.55,
  Penny Lane Str. : Mar - 3:09:45 (3:07:00-95)
NEWCOMBE Rachel 25.02.67, Liverpool H :
  400 - 56.5 (55.19-92), 800 - 2:03.28
NEWINGTON Sophie U13 15.09.85, Swansea :
  LJ - 4.83
NEWMAN Lucy U17 2.03.83, Horsham BS :
  SP - 10.78, JT - 37.66
NEWMAN Sarah U20 7.10.79, Preseli :
  400H - 65.14
NEWMAN Victoria U13 25.03.86, Bournemouth :
  DTM - 23.85
NEWMAN Wendy 31.08.71, Ex L/Brunel Un :
  JT - 44.84 (46.02-97)
NEWTON Jackie 28.08.64, Stockport :
  HMar - 1:19:46 (1:16:09-97),
  Mar - 2:53:56 (2:47:28-96)
NEWTON Maria Angela 22.07.66, Ashford :
  PV - 3.40
NICE Abbey U17 11.12.81, Thurrock :
  Hepl - 3859
NICHOLS Angie U15 22.09.84, Wycombe :
  PV - 2.00
NICOL Gemma U13 27.07.86, Lochgelly :
  150 - 20.2
NICOLLE Sarah U20 12.01.80, Telford :
  100H - 14.46w/14.6/14.92
NIELD Emma U15 20.11.83, Lanark & Lesg :
  PenG - 2659
NIGHTINGALE Jo-Anne U17 3.05.83, Wyc :
  PV - 2.90

NIGHTINGALE Julie 28.04.75, Eastbourne GS :
  JT - 39.70 (42.80-95)
NOAD Joy V35   60, Maidenhead :
  Mar - 2:52:09
NORFORD Natalia U17 29.09.82, Beds & Co :
  HJ - 1.65i/1.65
NORMAN Katrina U23 1.01.76, Walton :
  400H - 64.56 (60.15-95)
NORVILLE Danielle U17 18.01.83, Telford :
  100 - 12.3w/12.33w (12.49-97),
  200 - 25.25i/25.3
NOVIS Laura U15 22.01.84, Hull Springhead :
  200 - 25.75w/25.94
NUGENT Jessica Natalie Rosemary U15
  27.08.84, Shaftesbury Barnet :
  800 - 2:18.2, 1500 - 4:38.21
NUNN Helen 15.09.71, Ashford :
  400H - 65.0 (64.0/64.36-97)
NUTT Caroline U17 17.06.83, Scunthorpe :
  PV - 2.85
NYHAN Angela U23 13.04.78, Rowntrees :
  SP - 11.57 (11.95-96), Hep - 4351 (4805-96)

O 'BRIEN Vicky U17 15.11.82, Inverness :
  80HI - 11.83, LJ - 5.63
O'CALLAGHAN Louise U17 12.12.81, Camb H :
  80HI - 11.49w (11.9/12.00-97),
  100H - 15.8, 300H - 46.9 (45.2-97)
O'CONNOR Claire 24.09.74, Lisburn :
  200 - 24.66 (24.53-94)
O'CONNOR Gill V35   62, RRC :
  Mar - 2:54:46
O'CONNOR Holly U15 9.12.83, St Helens :
  800 - 2:16.81
O'HALLORAN Catherine U17 17.09.81, Bingley :
  JT - 39.38
O'HARE Ellen U23 4.02.78, Circ/Oxford Univ :
  800 - 2:08.7 (2:06.59-96),
  1500 - 4:21.86 (4:20.17-97), 3k - 9:45.2
O'MALLEY Jane U23 18.07.77, Hull Achilles :
  400H - 63.78 (63.80-95)
O'SULLIVAN Clare U20 8.05.80, Sutton & D :
  100H - 15.08w (15.0w-97)
O'SULLIVAN Laura U17 30.07.82, Liverpool H :
  HJ - 1.65 (1.68-97)
OAKES Jennifer U17 14.08.82, North Down :
  80HI - 11.9, 300H - 46.5
OAKES Judith Miriam V40 14.02.58, Croydon :
  SP - 18.83 (19.36-88),
  DT - 51.71 (53.44-88), JT - 42.41 (46.66-86)
OAKES Sharon U17 26.08.82, Medway :
  TJ - 11.27
OATES Joanne U23 21.02.78, Bingley :
  400H - 61.26
OBOH Oteri 7.10.73, Herne Hill :
  JT - 40.70 (48.30-92)
OGDEN Rachael U20 23.07.79, Rowntrees :
  800 - 2:09.7 (2:07.93-97),
  1500 - 4:33.0 (4:30.51-97)
OGOGO Leanne U17 26.09.82, Waveney :
  TJ - 10.85
OKANGI Deborah U15 6.05.84, Cambridge H :
  100 - 12.33w, 200 - 25.91
OKWUE Maurine U23 13.05.78, Thames V H :
  TJ - 11.13 (11.31-96)
OLDALE Lianne U13 19.09.86, Sheffield RWC :
  2kW - 11:32.81

OLDERSHAW Tina 13.05.67, Paddock Wood :
  Mar - 3:08:46
OLDFIELD Sally U15 25.06.84, Kettering :
  800 - 2:17.65
OLDHAM Sarah U15 23.09.83, Dudley & St :
  60HG - 9.14i,
  75HG - 11.37w/11.5 (11.58-97), PenG - 2513
OLSON Natalie U13 9.05.86, Ashford :
  PV - 2.00
ONUORA Amalachukwu U13 16.03.86,
  Eastbourne : 75 - 10.2, 150 - 19.8, 200 - 27.3
ONWUBALILI Chioma U13 16.05.86,
  London Schools : SPM - 9.64
ORFORD Beth U20 25.03.81, Coventry G :
  HJ - 1.70 (1.73-96)
OSBOURNE Alice 27.02.67, Canterbury H :
  Mar - 3:00:49
OSTERSBURG Karen 23.09.65, Birchfield :
  DT - 36.56 (38.74-93)
OUGHTON Karen U17 26.01.83, Coventry G :
  100 - 12.2/12.36w/12.59
OWBRIDGE Cathy U13, Hull Sch :
  PenM - 2041
OWBRIDGE Joanne U17 19.01.82, Hull Spr :
  300 - 40.26, 400 - 58.6
OWEN Eirion Sian V35 30.07.63, Brecon :
  PV - 3.00
OWEN Krissy 14.12.75, Eryri :
  PV - 3.60A/3.52
OWEN Rachel U20 24.02.81, Wakefield :
  HT - 38.63
OWEN Tracy A. 29.04.64, Arena :
  Mar - 3:04:24 (3:03:32-94)
OWENS Holly U17 17.08.82, City of Glasgow :
  DT - 34.32
OWUSU Lesley U23 21.12.78, Windsor S & E :
  55 - 7.27i, 100 - 11.7w/12.1 (12.10-93),
  200 - 24.72w/24.73
      (24.2-96/24.34w/24.41-95), 400 - 54.26
OXLEY Sarah E. 3.07.73, Birchfield :
  100 - 12.03 (11.51-97), 200 - 24.76 (23.20-97)
OYEPITAN Abiodun U20 30.12.79, S Barnet :
  100 - 11.45w/11.7/11.78,
  200 - 24.02w/24.1

PAGE-JONES Bethan U23 30.11.76,
  Cambridge Univ : TJ - 11.31
PALLETT Keeley 27.02.74, Corby :
  100 - 12.20w
PALMER Karlene J. U20 23.10.80, W S & E :
  100 - 12.23w (11.96w/12.12-97),
  200 - 24.50w (24.41w/24.42-97)
PARDO Clare U20 9.08.81, Guildford & G :
  HT - 41.28
PARK Lauren U13 16.07.86, City of Edinburgh :
  150 - 19.8, 200 - 27.6
PARKER Barbara U17 8.11.82, Norwich :
  800 - 2:15.27, 1500 - 4:44.9, Hepl - 4083
PARKER Carol Ann 22.09.69, Coventry Godiva :
  SP - 14.57 (14.76i-91/14.71-90),
  DT - 38.84 (44.70-89), HT - 38.64 (39.08-95)
PARKER Jacqueline T. 15.10.66, Team Solent :
  400 - 56.1 (54.07-89),
  400H - 57.70 (56.15-91)
PARKER Susan 24.03.70, Sale : (see LAMB)
PARKINSON Amanda 21.07.71, Sale :
  800 - 2:08.6, 1500 - 4:14.19 (4:12.9unmx-95),
  3k - 9:34.74 (9:17.4mx-94/9:19.6-96)

PARKINSON Danielle U17 2.09.81, Rochdale :
  HJ - 1.67, Hepl - 3885 (4269-97)
PARKINSON Hayley 5.12.75, Edinburgh WM :
  800 - 2:07.99, 1500 - 4:21.27, 3k - 9:45.73
PARMITER Catherine U20 27.04.81, Taunton :
  HJ - 1.73, LJ - 5.66, Hep - 4460
PARNELL Georgina U17 22.06.82, Newport :
  400 - 58.7, 800 - 2:11.01
PARR Emily U20 9.05.81, Norwich :
  200 - 25.12i, 400 - 55.32
PARRIS Monique U15 28.01.84, Ilford :
  60 - 7.86i, 100 - 12.1w/12.19, 200 - 25.0,
  60HG - 9.2i, 75HG - 11.7, LJ - 5.80
PARRY Carys U20 24.07.81, Rhondda :
  DT - 36.05, HT - 49.10
PARRY Hayley 17.02.73, Swansea :
  400 - 56.7 (55.6-97),
  800 - 2:01.52i/2:03.46 (2:02.18-97)
PARRY Sheena U23 16.11.77, Rhondda :
  HT - 41.76 (42.92-97)
PARSONS Zoe Marie U17 11.02.83, Ashford :
  PV - 2.80
PARTINGTON Carolyn 27.06.66, Manx :
  3kW - 13:50.58 (13:13.3-95),
  5kW - 23:32.03 (22:41.19-95),
  10kWR - 48:09 (46:26-95)
PARTRIDGE Susan U20 4.01.80, E Kilbride :
  3k - 10:07.6
PATERSON Laura U15 8.09.83, Ayr Seaforth :
  LJ - 5.35
PATERSON Pamela U13 26.10.85, Edin WM :
  70HM - 11.77
PATRICK Elizabeth U23 29.08.77, Kingst & P :
  100H - 14.93w/15.04, TJ - 12.22
PATTERSON Laura U20 31.01.81, Wycombe :
  PV - 3.40, LJ - 5.54, TJ - 11.10
PATTINSON Helen Teresa 2.01.74, Preston :
  800 - 2:08.30 (2:07.8-97/2:09.5mx-96),
  1500 - 4:12.61, 3k - 9:22.87, 10kR - 33:56
PATTON Chaanah 22.02.72, Hallamshire/
  Cambridge Univ (nee FOTHERGILL) :
  10kR - 34:55 (34:51-94)
PAUTARD Marlene V35 25.10.62, Ranelagh :
  Mar - 3:01:33
PAUZERS Clare V35 2.08.62, Herne Hill/
  London RR : Mar - 2:50:12 (2:43:27-97)
PAVEY Joanne 20.09.73, Bristol :
  3k - 8:58.2
PAVEY Susan 15.02.67, Altrincham :
  Mar - 3:05:42
PAXTON Henrietta U15 19.09.83, Salisbury :
  LJ - 5.43w/5.40, PenG - 2966
PAYNE Judith U20 7.07.80, Wakefield :
  HJ - 1.76
PAYNE Kirsty U23 22.10.77, Birchfield :
  TJ - 11.97
PAYNE Lori U17 17.12.82, Basingstoke & MH :
  DT - 36.33
PEACOCK Julie 19.08.70, Shaftesbury Barnet
  (nee MAJOR) : HJ - 1.80 (1.85-94)
PEACOCK Marina 12.07.64, Birchfield :
  HT - 46.83 (48.20-96)
PEACOCK Rachel U17 18.05.82, Bournemouth :
  LJ - 5.67w/5.58 (5.66-97),
  TJ - 12.07w/11.49 (11.64-97)
PEAKE Fiona U23 31.05.77, Woking :
  PV - 3.00 (3.10-96)

PEAKE Rebecca U17 22.06.83, Derby LAC :
SP - 11.33i/11.12
PEARCE Caroline U20 1.09.80, Huntingdon :
100H - 14.86w,
LJ - 5.58w/5.56 (5.68w/5.61-97), Hep - 4316
PEARCE Kayleigh U13 4.09.85, Soton City :
DTM - 24.72
PEARSON Jennifer Ann V35 3.07.62, Ashford :
(see MATTHEWS)
PEET Josephine 4.12.71, Bristol :
400 - 57.2, 400H - 63.7/64.04 (62.6-97/63.51-96)
PENNET Catriona U15 10.10.83, Aberdeen :
75HG - 11.6w/11.62, PenG - 2754
PERCIVAL Deborah J. V35 22.04.62, Medway :
3k - 9:44.7, 10kR - 33:28,
HMar - 1:14:31 (1:14:13-97),
Mar - 2:39:54 (2:39:05-97)
PERKINS Candy 26.02.71, Ashford :
800 - 2:10.10, 1500 - 4:32.7
PERKINS Emma U13, Worthing :
PenM - 2139
PERKINS Helen 12.11.65, Wimbledon :
Mar - 3:06:12
PERRETT Kirsty U23 17.03.76, Middleb & C :
DT - 36.09 (37.34-94), HT - 39.13 (39.58-97)
PERRY Victoria A. V40 25.11.57, Stockport :
Mar - 3:03:51
PERRYMAN Saffron U15 26.03.84, Reading :
SPG - 11.33
PETERSON Katrina U13 6.08.86, Kettering :
HJ - 1.45
PHILLIPS Emma U20 31.01.81, Wakefield :
100 - 11.96w/12.23 (12.2-97)
PHILLIPS Lorraine 27.01.75, Newbury :
400 - 56.8
PHILLIPS Nicola U17 23.04.83, Dartford :
3kW - 15:21.4, 5kW - 27:00.0,
5kWR - 26:57 (26:40-97)
PHILP Hazel U15 21.10.83, Arbroath :
200 - 26.0w/42.3 (27.53-97)
PICKERING Sarah U15 26.10.83, Cann & Staff :
800 - 2:14.45
PICKERSGILL Melanie Jane 20.04.73, Barns :
100 - 12.24w/12.26, 200 - 25.08,
400 - 56.6 (56.15-92)
PIDGEON Elizabeth S. U23 27.04.77, Essex L :
SP - 11.97 (12.90i-97), HT - 57.56, JT - 43.82
PIERRE Cherie U15 15.05.84, S Barnet :
60 - 7.96i, 100 - 12.34, 200 - 24.99,
SPG - 11.32
PIERRE Michelle 30.09.73, Croydon :
200 - 24.7w/25.1/25.13 (24.4w-96/24.8-95),
400 - 53.52 (52.77-97)
PIERROT Lucy U17 26.02.83, Milton Keynes :
DT - 36.15
PIMBLETT Caroline 28.01.75, Sale :
1500 - 4:23.5 (4:21.3-96),
3k - 9:18.6mx/9:40.67 (9:25.8-97),
5k - 16:34.51
PINCOMBE Vicky 19.06.66, Minehead :
10kR - 34:34, HMar - 1:15:14
PINEL Syreena U20 13.01.79, Leics Cor :
100 - 12.20w (12.4/12.41-95), LJ - 6.06w/5.88
PITTERS Anya U17 18.12.82, Ilford :
100 - 12.3w/12.32w/12.4,
200 - 25.4/25.52w/25.57
PLEAVIN Claire U17 25.04.83, Warrington :
LJ - 5.44, Hepl - 4315

POCOCK Nicola U20 9.05.79, AF&D :
400H - 64.09 (63.8-97)
POLHILL-THOMAS Sian U17 4.06.83, Wirral :
60HI - 9.09i, 80HI - 11.6/11.68w/11.76
POLIUS Leandra U20 14.05.80, N & E B :
TJ - 11.69w/11.62
PORAZINSKI Donna-Marie U20 28.01.81,
Newport : 200 - 25.24, 400 - 55.82,
400H - 65.3 (64.5-97)
PORTER Katherine U17 19.08.82, Blackheath :
300 - 41.2, 60HI - 9.07i,
80HI - 11.5/11.62w/11.72,
100H - 15.0, 300H - 43.37, 400H - 64.9
PORTER Sarah U20 11.12.79, Sutton & Dist :
100H - 14.12w/14.32
POTTER Jayne U17 31.05.83, Bournemouth :
PV - 2.45
POTTER Juliet U17 24.10.81, Rushcliffe :
800 - 2:15.6, 1500 - 4:46.24, 3k - 10:08.1
POTTS Alison 15.10.74, City of Glasgow :
800 - 2:10.06
POVEY Tanya U20 13.04.79, South West RR/
S Carol Univ : 1500 - 4:31.45,
3k - 9:53.10 (9:37.6-96),
5k - 16:58.87, 10k - 34:31.41
POWELL Donna U17 8.10.81, Tamworth :
HT - 33.42
POWELL Jacqueline 1.05.74, Paddock Wood :
HJ - 1.65i (1.74-90)
POWELL Joanne 3.10.68, Cardiff (nee EVANS) :
DT - 35.73 (39.94-94)
POWELL Pauline 17.05.73, Blackburn :
800 - 2:12.9, 3k - 9:41.5
PRATT Julie U20 20.03.79, Essex L :
60H - 8.55i, 100H - 13.48w/13.52
PRICE Sharon 10.12.75, R Sutton Coldfield :
100H - 15.1/15.29w
(14.4w-95/14.43w-93/14.61-95)
PRINGLE Maria U20 18.12.80, Copeland :
TJ - 11.15
PRITCHARD Amanda U20 18.03.80, Cardiff :
400 - 57.2 (54.60-97)
PRITCHARD Katie U13, Telford :
DTM - 25.30
PROCTER Lauren U17 9.09.82, Bournemouth :
DT - 34.51, JT - 38.82
PROCTOR Elizabeth 31.10.72, Bolton :
1500 - 4:32.7
PUCKERIDGE Jayne Diane 23.10.71, Medway/
Loughbro : 800 - 2:11.83
PULLINGER Stefanie U17 3.04.83, Bracknell :
60HI - 8.70i, 80HI - 11.22w/11.43
PURKISS Melanie U20 11.03.79, T Solent :
100 - 11.64w/11.8/11.94 (11.80-97),
200 - 23.67w/23.94
PYCROFT Denise 30.04.64, Wootton RR :
Mar - 2:53:45
PYNE Rebecca U15 12.10.84, Tonbridge :
JT - 34.61

QUIGG Claire U17 13.10.81,
Ballymena & Antrim :
LJ - 5.63w? (5.62-97), TJ - 11.69w/11.35
QUILL Rita 12.03.67, Shaftesbury Barnet :
10kR - 34:55
QUINN Pauline 2.08.70, Edinburgh WM :
(see THOM)

RADCLIFFE Paula Jane 17.12.73,
Beds & Co : 1500 - 4:05.81,
1M - 4:31.72 (4:24.94-96),
2k - 5:44.58+ (5:39.20-93),
3k - 8:38.84 (8:35.28-97),
5k - 14:51.27 (14:45.51-97), 10k - 30:48.58
RAMSEY Kate 17.05.68, Charnwood :
3k - 9:47.16 (9:16.24-93),
5k - 17:16.8, 10k - 36:45.26
RANDALL Charlotte U20 10.05.80,
C of Plymouth : 400H - 64.6/64.98
Sarah U20 6.06.80, Gateshead :
PV - 2.60i/2.60
RANKINE Anne-Louise U15 30.03.85, :
PenG - 2547ns
RANN Lucy U20 5.09.80, Isle of Wight :
JT - 42.93 (45.32-96)
RATCLIFFE Karen V35 1.06.61, Cov RWC :
3kW - 15:10.97 (14:02.29-93),
5kW - 26:58.7 (24:12.11-93),
5kWR - 25:49 (24:03-94)
RAVEN Claire Heather 15.06.72, Coventry G/
Loughbro : 400 - 55.9 (53.99-92),
800 - 2:04.98 (2:03.15-97)
RAVEN Sarah U17 22.11.82, Southend :
3k - 10:25.2
RAWLING Kimberley U17 22.07.83, Newq & P :
DT - 35.82, HT - 35.38
RAWLINSON Susan 13.10.70, Rotherham/
Leeds Poly : 60 - 7.68i (7.64i-94),
100 - 12.09 (11.7w-97/11.8/11.89-94),
200 - 24.76i/25.0 (23.5/23.80w/24.13-94)
RAYNER Marion V45 14.01.50, West 4 :
Mar - 3:03:37
REA Tracy U20 19.01.79, Coventry Godiva :
SP - 12.50
READE Leigh 15.08.72, Sale :
400 - 55.8/56.07 (54.76-94)
READE Olivia U17 6.06.83, Wilts Sch :
SP - 10.66
READER Catherine V40 19.10.54, Ryston :
50kW - 5:45:58 (5:22:04-93)
READER Jennifer U23 23.12.77, Soton City :
HJ - 1.73
REDD Kathryn U17 8.06.82, Brighton :
JT - 35.84
REDD Samantha U15 16.02.84, Brighton :
JT - 40.35
REDMOND Laura A. U20 19.04.81, Edin WM :
HJ - 1.66i/1.65 (1.69io-97)
REDMOND Rachel U17 7.12.81, City of Stoke :
60 - 7.95i (7.95i-97), LJ - 5.40w,
100 - 12.45w (12.06w/12.21-96),
200 - 24.92w/25.26 (25.1-96)
REED Joanna U20 13.11.79, Havant :
200 - 25.0w (24.90w/25.30-97)
REED Kate U17 28.09.82, Bristol :
800 - 2:16.8 (2:16.56-97), 1500 - 4:40.1
REES Charlotte U15 14.06.84, Neath :
SPG - 10.73, JT - 38.36
REID Emma U20 5.01.81, Pitreavie :
100H - 15.29w
REID Rebecca U15 9.12.83, Barrow & Furness :
PenG - 2646
REID-HUGHES Frances U20 18.03.80,
Tonbridge : SP - 11.83, DT - 39.23
REINSFORD Sue 24.03.69, Bedford & County :
3k - 9:55.71 (9:52.7-87),
10kR - 34:15, HMar - 1:15:31

RENNISON Amy U17 15.06.83, Wolves & B :
PV - 3.05
RETCHAKAN Gowry P. V35 21.06.60, Thurr :
400 - 57.4 (54.63Hur-92/55.1-91),
800 - 2:10.06i (2:07.37i-93/2:08.3mx/2:11.3-96),
400H - 55.25 (54.63-92)
REYNOLDS Kay 15.09.67, Radley :
60H - 8.62i,
100H - 14.0w/14.1/14.29 (14.0w-97)
REYNOLDS Nicky U15 24.06.85, Birchfield :
2.5kW - 13:57.50, 3kW - 16:31.01
RICHARDS Angharad U23 9.12.76, G & G :
JT - 38.38 (46.20-93)
RICHARDS Lara U17 7.03.83, Newport :
TJ - 10.99w/10.88
RICHARDS Pauline 30.06.68, Bir/C of Edin :
200 - 24.30w/24.60, 100H - 13.79w/14.04,
HJ - 1.67, LJ - 5.90/5.87w (5.93-95),
SP - 14.51, Hep - 5691w/5563
RICHARDS Shaunette U17 15.08.83, Birchfield :
SP - 11.94i/11.67
RICHARDSON Fiona V35 8.12.58, :
Mar - 3:04:57
RICHARDSON Katie U17 12.09.82, Wakefield :
LJ - 5.39
RICHARDSON Marcia Maureen 10.02.72,
Windsor S & E : 100 - 11.36w/11.40,
200 - 23.55 (23.4-93/23.53-95)
RICHMOND Louise U17 15.12.81, S & S H :
3kW - 15:17.5, 5kW - 27:24.28,
5kWR - 26:41 (26:29o-96)
RICHMOND Sarah 6.01.73, Pitr/Glasgow Un :
100H - 14.29w/14.7 (14.02w/14.2/14.29-94)
RICKETTS Kelly U23 24.01.76, Wrexham
(nee ROBERTS) : DT - 40.92, HT - 40.73
RIDGLEY Clare Louise U23 11.09.77, T Sol/
Ox Un : PV - 3.60 (3.55ex-97), TJ - 11.05
RIDGLEY Rebecca U20 26.02.80, T Solent :
PV - 3.40, TJ - 11.17 (11.36w-96)
RIDGWAY Kelly U17 14.04.82, Barnsley :
PV - 2.80
RILEY Catherine U17 4.06.82, Parkhill HS :
300 - 41.4, 800 - 2:10.5mx/2:11.9 (2:09.9-97)
RITCHIE Kathrin U20 8.03.79, Edinburgh WM :
DT - 37.65
RITCHIE Kristine U17 15.12.81, Lisburn :
JT - 35.76
ROACH Justine U15 21.12.84, Leics Cor :
75HG - 11.3/11.60w/11.77
ROBERTS Kelly U23 24.01.76, Wrexham :
(see RICKETTS)
ROBERTS Lowri U17 9.10.81, Newport :
100 - 12.4, 100H - 14.7/14.79
ROBERTS Melanie U23 2.03.78, Wigan :
100 - 11.9w/12.23, 200 - 24.7/24.90
ROBERTS Sarah U23 25.06.78, Belgrave :
400 - 57.2 (55.97-97), TJ - 11.07
ROBERTS Suzanne U23 19.12.78, Bingley :
HT - 47.03 (48.18-97)
ROBERTSON Imogen U15 2.10.83, Som Sch :
PenG - 2565
ROBINS Lorraine A. 13.05.70, Hounslow :
60 - 7.77i (7.5i-93/7.52i-94)
ROBINSON Eleanor M. V50 20.11.47, Border :
Mar - 2:58:33 (2:45:12-90),
100kR - 8:19:57 (7:48:33-89)
ROBINSON Heather V35 31.08.61, Chester L S :
Mar - 2:55:55

ROBINSON Kemesha U20 27.11.80, Birchfield :
60 - 7.79i
ROBINSON Linsi U15 9.01.84, Nuneaton :
DT - 30.70
ROBSON Carly U15 5.12.83, Dacorum & Tring :
PenG - 2729
ROBSON Claire U15 9.01.84, Teesdale :
800 - 2:15.72, 1500 - 4:45.76
ROCK Lisa U13, Wolverhampton & B :
150 - 20.2
RODMELL Kelly U13 26.11.85, Tynedale :
800 - 2:22.2
ROGER Kirsty U23 24.03.78, City of Glasgow :
HJ - 1.69 (1.70i/1.70-97),
Hep - 4559 (4778w/4723-97)
ROGERS Kate U20 13.02.79, Skyrac :
LJ - 5.53 (5.86w-96/5.70-97),
Hep - 4286 (4598-97)
ROGERS Melissa Ann U15 2.09.83, Verlea :
75HG - 11.67, LJ - 5.28, PenG - 2972
ROGERS-DIXON Polly 5.04.67, Wimbledon :
Mar - 3:07:56
ROLES Philippa U23 1.03.78, Swansea :
SP - 15.00i/14.54 (14.60-96),
DT - 54.14, HT - 47.87
ROLES Rebecca U20 14.12.79, Swansea :
PV - 3.20 (3.20-96), SP - 11.71,
DT - 45.27, JT - 38.66
ROONEY Claire U17 23.08.83, East Kilbride :
100 - 12.53, 200 - 25.41
ROSCOE Helen U20 4.12.79, Liverpool H :
100 - 12.00w/12.1 (11.9/12.27-97),
200 - 24.43w/24.44 (24.31w-96/24.4-97)
ROSS Joanna U20 18.02.81, Victoria Park :
800 - 2:09.99i/2:10.43
ROSS Michelle 31.01.72, City of Stoke :
3k - 9:44.8 (9:43.9-97),
10kR - 34:59, HMar - 1:17:54
ROSS-HURST Olivia U15 10.12.83, Verlea :
HJ - 1.63, PenG - 3063
ROSTEK Malgorzata U23 25.03.77, C of Glas :
60 - 7.56i (7.52i-96),
100 - 11.63, 200 - 24.4/24.68
ROTHMAN Kimberly 6.09.64, Windsor S & E :
PV - 3.55
ROUGH Alison U17 1.06.83, City of Glasgow :
TJ - 11.04
ROUTLEDGE Kate U15 17.09.83, Seaton :
100 - 12.4/12.58w, 200 - 25.6
ROWE Deborah 8.09.72, Birchfield :
LJ - 5.62 (5.81w?-92/5.78-93),
TJ - 12.69w/12.61 (12.76w-97)
ROWE Kate U23 13.09.78, Peterborough :
PV - 3.10
ROY Lesley-Ann U17 3.01.82, Pitreavie :
SP - 11.75
RUDDOCK Ellena U23 23.02.76, Rugby :
60 - 7.54i, 100 - 11.53w/11.67,
200 - 23.94i/24.0/24.25 (23.71-97)
RUDKIN Lois U13, Gateshead :
75 - 10.0, 150 - 20.0
RUDMAN Shelley U20 23.03.81, Swindon :
400H - 64.74
RUSSELL Clare U17 11.11.81, Oldham & R :
60 - 7.90i, 100 - 12.00w/12.12,
200 - 24.73w/24.91, 300 - 41.2
RUSSELL Lyndsey U15 11.09.83, Fife :
75HG - 11.10w/11.2/11.29, PenG - 2748

RYAN Orla 7.09.69, Ealing,Southall & Mx/IRE :
400 - 56.38 (55.9/56.17-96)
RYDE Gemma U17 23.06.83, Central :
100 - 12.14w/12.3/12.36, 200 - 25.56

S AINT-SMITH Tasha 20.12.75, Enfield :
DT - 42.71 (44.68-94)
SALMON Sarah 9.09.74, Newquay & Par :
1500 - 4:29.34 (4:24.00-96),
1M - 4:46.42i (4:44.79-96),
3k - 9:45.31i (9:30.24i-97/9:40.87-96)
SALT Christa 17.06.64, Basel :
400 - 57.18 (56.90-96),
600 - 1:32.50 (1:32.47-97),
800 - 2:08.01 (2:06.97-96),
1k - 2:50.25 (2:47.22-95),
1500 - 4:27.44 (4:22.96-97)
SAMMON Kirsty U13 5.10.85, Bournemouth :
600 - 1:44.8, 800 - 2:23.3
SAMPLE Jessica U20 3.01.80, St Albans :
TJ - 11.15 (11.31-97)
SAMUELS Belinda U23 29.11.78, Birchfield :
100H - 14.9w (14.68w/15.13-97),
LJ - 5.55 (5.62-97)
SAMUELS Lisa U17 24.09.81, Stevenage & NH :
800 - 2:13.29 (2:12.20-97)
SANDERS Nicola U17 23.06.82, Wycombe :
60 - 7.92i, 100 - 11.89w/12.15,
200 - 24.6/24.64w/25.18 (25.11-97),
300 - 39.07, 400 - 56.30, 60HI - 9.20i,
80HI - 11.9/11.96w (12.29-97),
100H - 15.8, 300H - 45.6, Hepl - 4298
SANDERSON Danielle V35 26.10.62, Watford :
10MR - 57:46 (55:42-94),
HMar - 1:17:39 (1:13:11-94),
Mar - 2:50:54 (2:36:29-94)
SARGEANT Gemma U17 5.05.83, Ilford :
LJ - 5.62
SARGENT Claire U13 11.03.86, Havering :
70HM - 11.5
SASSE Sarah U17 1.10.81, Sutton & District :
SP - 10.81
SAUNDERS Jennifer U17 21.10.81, GEC :
HJ - 1.63i
SAUNDERS Kerry U23 28.03.77, Derby LAC :
HJ - 1.65i/1.65 (1.73-97),
TJ - 11.34w/11.27 (11.47w/11.45-97)
SAYERS Goldie K. D. U17 16.07.82, Peterbro :
JT - 51.92
SCHOFIELD Candace U15 3.11.84, Worthing :
DT - 30.79, PenG - 2533
SCHOFIELD Cara U17 13.03.82, Worthing :
300H - 46.3,
400H - 64.5, Hepl - 3827
SCHRAMM Louise Halina 18.12.71, E & E :
PV - 3.75
SCOTCHER Rebecca U17 2.07.82, Norwich :
300 - 40.05, 400 - 56.3/56.86,
800 - 2:13.8, 300H - 44.73, TJ - 10.74
SCOTT J. U13, Worksop :
LJ - 4.67
SCOTT Jane U20 22.06.81, Stewartry :
100H - 15.12, HJ - 1.65 (1.66-97)
SCOTT Jemma U17 14.03.83, Arbroath :
60HI - 9.20i, 300H - 45.81,
HJ - 1.68, Hepl - 3994
SCOTT Sabrina U20 2.06.79, Belgrave :
100 - 12.24w (12.68-97)

SCOTT Sian U15 20.03.84, Bournemouth :
200 - 25.7/25.85, 75HG - 11.18w/11.5/11.53
SCOTT Susan U23 26.09.77, City of Glasgow :
800 - 2:07.1mx/2:07.77, 1500 - 4:20.37
SCOTT Victoria U20 21.09.80, Liverpool H :
HT - 45.82
SCRAMBLER Kelly U20 21.11.79, Birchfield :
PV - 2.60
SEARLE Kim U15 27.12.83, Hull Springhead :
800 - 2:15.32, 1500 - 4:48.47
SELLEY Danielle U15 19.12.83, Preseli :
60 - 7.77i, 100 - 12.13, 60HG - 8.94i,
75HG - 11.00, LJ - 5.43, PenG - 3045
SELWYN Alex U15 20.09.83, Coventry Godiva :
HJ - 1.64
SEMPER Sharon 26.11.68, Ilford :
400 - 56.9
SEMUS Kate 18.01.70, Parkside :
DT - 39.46 (40.20-97)
SESTON Laura U20 9.02.79, Ipswich :
100 - 11.61w/11.8/11.85,
200 - 24.29, 400H - 64.6
SHANNON Jill U17 23.04.82, Lagan Valley :
3k - 10:41.3
SHARP Karen V35 29.11.59, Hull Achilles :
(see HEWETH)
SHARP Sue, WRNS :
HMar - 1:19:00
SHASHOUA Yvonne R. V35 16.03.62,
East London : Mar - 3:08:25 (3:07:44-94)
SHAW Amy U17 2.07.83, Halifax :
800 - 2:17.54, 300H - 45.09
SHAW Lorraine A. 2.04.68, Sale :
SP - 13.32 (14.21-94),
DT - 51.96 (55.04-94), HT - 63.30 (64.90-95)
SHEPHERD Cheryl U13 8.03.86, Arbroath :
HJ - 1.47, JTM - 25.54
SHEPHERD Kelly 15.12.75, Charnwood :
HT - 37.03
SHEPHERD Victoria U20 26.01.80, Wakefield :
SP - 12.26 (12.35-96)
SHEPPARD Amanda 26.02.68, Wakefield :
SP - 12.00 (12.05-92), DT - 42.81
SHERESTON Nichola U20 1.09.79, Newark :
100H - 14.7
SHERIDAN Emma U17 24.02.82, Essex L :
DT - 39.11
SHIEL Rebecca U17 16.01.82, Gateshead :
TJ - 10.85
SHIPMAN Victoria U23 31.03.77, Derby LAC :
100 - 11.7w/12.02 (11.5-96/11.84-97),
200 - 24.47 (23.87-97)
SHORT Jenny U17 17.12.82, Basildon :
800 - 2:14.99
SHOUKSMITH Christine V35 12.09.58, Knaves :
Mar - 3:08:49
SIDDALL Laura U20 10.09.80, Barnsley :
400H - 62.44
SIGGERY Alison U15 14.09.83, Carmarthen :
JT - 40.19
SIGISMONDI Clio U17 11.10.81, Basildon :
SP - 10.53
SILTO Katherine U17 12.08.83, Swindon :
HJ - 1.65i/1.65, TJ - 10.71
SILVER Lorna Jane 10.01.74, C of Glasgow :
60H - 8.89i (8.88i-95),
100H - 14.34w/14.4/14.41 (14.3w-95/14.4-97,
300H - 43.9, 400H - 62.2/63.64 (59.9/60.58-94)

SIMMONS Sarah 12.01.75, Hounslow :
800 - 2:12.86 (2:10.87-97),
SIMPSON Jemma U15 10.02.84, Newquay & P :
800 - 2:14.4
SIMPSON Louise U23 18.12.77, City of Hull :
PV - 2.50 (2.60-97)
SIMS Natalie U17 7.04.83, Derby LAC :
HJ - 1.68
SINGER Lindsey U17 4.06.83, R S Coldfield :
60 - 7.88i, 300 - 41.4
SINGER Samantha U17 8.05.82, Blackheath :
300 - 40.1 (41.28-97),
400 - 55.9, 800 - 2:12.39
SINGLETON Sarah 18.12.65, Liverpool H :
3k - 9:35.04i (9:34.0-97)
SKEGGS Karen 26.10.69, Ashford :
LJ - 5.60 (6.29w-89/6.08-90),
TJ - 12.44 (12.93w/12.89-92)
SKEPES Katie U20 11.12.80, Croydon :
PV - 2.60
SKETCHLEY Katie 9.07.73, Team Solent :
100 - 12.1w/12.21w (12.14w-96),
100H - 13.57w/13.78
SKORUPSKA Katie U23 3.11.78, Edin WM :
3k - 9:24.26, 5k - 16:42.87 (16:41.9-96),
10k - 34:40.00
SLADE Kate U13 26.11.85, Falkirk :
LJ - 4.65
SLATER Catriona U23 27.01.77, Chelmsford :
LJ - 5.61 (5.70-95)
SLIMIN Caroline 27.08.65, Basingstoke & MH :
1500 - 4:30.24i (4:18.61-94)
SLOAN Patricia A. 22.03.66, Salford :
HMar - 1:18:56, Mar - 2:54:41
SLOANE Joanne U23 2.12.76, Coventry G :
200 - 25.15i (24.49w-92/24.50-93),
400 - 56.1i/57.35 (54.59-95)
SMALL Helen U23 10.10.78, Telford :
400H - 65.8 (65.84-97)
SMELLIE Natalie U17 16.01.82, Essex L :
60 - 7.66i, 100 - 12.11w/12.4 (12.51-97),
200 - 24.81w/25.36 (25.00-97),
300 - 40.0/40.34i
SMITH Anna U17 6.10.81, Hereford :
HT - 33.52
SMITH Carolyn U23 3.10.77, Liverpool H :
800 - 2:08.01
SMITH Diane V35 15.11.60, Hull Spartan :
HT - 44.43 (46.00-96), JT - 39.22
SMITH Elaine U17 16.05.83, Mandale :
LJ - 5.74w/5.66i/5.43
SMITH Emma M. U13 14.09.85, West Norfolk :
PenM - 2091
SMITH Grace U17 30.01.82, Sale :
100 - 12.2/12.34w (12.77-96),
60HI - 9.07i, 80HI - 11.9/12.04
SMITH Hayley U17 14.01.82, Norwich :
60HI - 8.73i, 80HI - 11.34w/11.4 (11.73-97)
SMITH Heidi 20.05.74, Liv.Pembroke Sefton :
800 - 2:07.2
SMITH Hilary U23 28.02.76, Halesowen :
PV - 3.41
SMITH Janet Carole 7.10.64, Windsor S & E :
DT - 37.01, HT - 50.20 (50.62-97)
SMITH Jo U23 11.04.76, Dark Peak :
3k - 9:42.83, 5k - 16:49.50
SMITH Karen U23 25.12.78, Medway :
SP - 11.27 (11.92-97)

SMITH Katie U13 19.02.86, Wakefield :
75 - 10.1, 100 - 13.2,
150 - 19.7, 200 - 27.5
SMITH Kellie U17 2.05.82, Wirral :
60HI - 9.21i, 80HI - 11.94 (11.8-97)
SMITH Laura U20 16.11.80, Hull Springhead :
LJ - 5.50 (6.04w/5.90w?/5.88-97)
SMITH Laura U15 21.01.84, Kendal :
SPG - 10.90, DT - 30.26, JT - 34.79
SMITH Louise U23 11.07.77, Ipswich :
JT - 42.02 (47.04-96)
SMITH Michelle Louise U23 1.01.78, T Solent :
HJ - 1.65 (1.70-94)
SMITH Michelle U20 28.05.80, Edinburgh WM :
PV - 2.70
SMITH Natasha U23 6.06.77, Hounslow :
SP - 13.94i/13.64 (14.12-97), HT - 44.00
SMITH Nicola U17 6.03.82, AF&D :
JT - 36.88
SMITH Sarah A. U13 17.09.85, Chesterfield :
DTM - 23.39
SMITH Sarah U23 18.08.76, Peterborough :
400H - 63.85
SMITHSON Claire U17 3.08.83, Brighton :
SP - 12.94, DT - 45.12
SMITHSON Kerry U23 13.09.76, Sale :
800 - 2:08.4 (2:09.5mx-96),
1500 - 4:17.6, 3k - 9:29.0mx
SNARE Sarah J. U13 1.07.86, Ashford :
JTM - 26.72
SNOOK Verity Beatrice 13.11.70, AF&D :
5kW - 26:33.56 (23:22.52-94)
SOTHERTON Kelly Jade U23 13.11.76,
Peterborough : 60 - 7.74i,
100 - 12.20w/12.22 (11.80w/11.85-97),
200 - 24.33w/24.57i/24.8 (24.03-97),
400 - 54.49i/57.20 (54.17-97),
60H - 8.72i, 100H - 14.31 (14.21-97),
HJ - 1.67 (1.75-94),
LJ - 6.07i/5.97w/5.80 (6.16w/6.10-97),
SP - 11.84, Hep - 4599dnf (5585-97)
SPAIN Elizabeth U17 23.08.82, S Barnet :
PV - 3.20
SPEAR Verity U17 12.04.82, City of Plymouth :
3k - 10:25.61
SPELZINI Charlotte U17 7.01.83, Camb & C :
SP - 10.94
SPENCER Amy U13 19.09.85, Wigan :
75 - 9.8/9.83, 100 - 12.9/13.14 (13.14-97),
150 - 19.2/19.47, 200 - 25.87
SPETTIE Natalie U13 22.10.85, Cardiff :
150 - 20.1
SPINKS Stephanie U17 6.09.82, West Norfolk :
200 - 25.04w
SPRULES Lyn 11.09.75, Hounslow :
HT - 61.66 (61.70-97)
SPURWAY Claire U23 4.04.78, Cannock & St :
60 - 7.68i, 200 - 25.27w (25.16-93),
100 - 12.19w/12.48 (12.08w/12.24-97)
ST. HELEN Denika U17 10.09.82, Enfield :
100 - 12.36w (12.55-97)
STACEY Julie 15.11.72, Bromley :
1500 - 4:28.46 (4:21.70-91),
3k - 9:56.0 (9:20.70i-93/10:13.3un-88)
STAINBURN Victoria U15 23.12.83, Bingley :
3kW - 15:39.55
STAINES Linda V35 26.12.63, Bas & MH :
400 - 56.71 (50.98-91)

STAMP Melissa U20 5.07.81, Scunthorpe :
PV - 2.60
STANLEY Joanne Marie U23 30.03.77, Elswick :
TJ - 11.38i/11.30w/11.02 (11.37-96)
STANTON Linda Mary 22.06.73, Sale :
PV - 3.70 (3.72-95)
STARES Hannah U23 13.11.78, Yate :
100H - 15.0/15.23w, HJ - 1.66i,
Hep - 4119 (4278-97)
STEAD Caroline 14.09.71, Essex L :
LJ - 5.71w/5.68 (5.71-95),
TJ - 12.26 (12.67-96)
STEPHENS Tamsin U20 2.08.80, Lagan Val :
100H - 14.23, Hep - 4314 (4344-97)
STERN Annette U23 9.09.76, Shaftesbury B :
100H - 15.1 (15.0w/15.16-95)
STERNE Victoria Louise 12.10.68, Birchfield :
400 - 57.0 (56.7-96),
800 - 2:04.81 (2:04.63-96),
1500 - 4:27.68 (4:24.4-97)
STERRY Claire U17 10.10.81, Croydon :
HJ - 1.68
STEVENSON Lucy 30.01.73, Sale :
JT - 44.56 (52.00-92)
STEVENSON Sara Ann U17 12.11.82, Giffnock :
800 - 2:17.8
STEWART Gillian U20 21.01.80, Edin WM :
100H - 14.71w/15.04 (14.7w-96/14.97-97),
HJ - 1.65i (1.69-97),
SP - 11.19, Hep - 4590 (4806-97)
STEWART Staci U13 20.09.85, C of Glasgow :
70HM - 11.71, HJ - 1.53, PenM - 2254
STILES Amy 6.02.75, Crawley/Westbury :
1500 - 4:33.41, 3k - 9:31.9,
5k - 16:53.65, 10k - 35:53.04,
10MR - 57:42, HMar - 1:17:46
STILL Sarah 24.09.75, Aberdeen :
HJ - 1.65 (1.65-94)
STONE Becky U17 27.11.82, Telford :
PV - 2.60
STONEY Saffron U15 20.11.83, Cannock & St :
SPG - 10.70
STOTT Rachel 3.09.74, Peterborough :
HT - 40.45 (43.60-97)
STOUTE Jennifer Elaine 16.04.65, Essex L :
200 - 24.1mx (22.73-92)
STRAKER Julia U17 25.11.82, Morpeth :
TJ - 10.80
STRAND Margit U23 22.01.78, Essex L/NOR :
400H - 61.63
STREATFIELD Cahterine U17 28.07.83,
Southampton City : TJ - 10.66
STREET Joanne U17 30.10.82, Tamworth :
SP - 11.39, DT - 40.61
STREET Natalie U15 8.11.83, Essex L :
200 - 25.82w
STREVENS Sarah U17 7.10.81, N & E B :
TJ - 10.98
STRINGER Kathryn U17 24.09.81, Rotherham :
JT - 36.44
STYLES Aimee U17 1.05.82, Dacorum & Tring :
JT - 35.23
SUDDES Joanne U23 27.01.77, Edinburgh WM :
100H - 14.47w/14.58
SULLIVAN Deborah 24.01.72, Havering :
1500 - 4:29.1 (4:25.52-97),
3k - 9:36.90 (9:34.30-97),
5k - 16:54.91 (16:28.14-97), 10k - 36:06.37

SUTCLIFFE Elaine 6.04.70, Wakefield :
100 - 12.1w/12.26 (11.8/11.94w/12.03-90),
400 - 56.56 (54.35-95)
SUTHERLAND Carolynne U20 4.09.80, E WM :
100H - 15.0/15.13 (15.0-97)
SUTTON Lucy U13, Oxford City :
SPM - 9.45, DTM - 24.68, PenM - 2028
SUTTON Marian R. V35 7.10.63, Westbury :
10kR - 33:05 (32:38-97),
15kR - 51:12 (49:01+-97/50:42-91),
10MR - 53:31 (52:15-97),
HMar - 1:13:22 (1:09:41-97),
Mar - 2:32:14 (2:29:03-97)
SUTTON Nicola 4.03.74, Exeter :
200 - 25.0, 100H - 14.7, 400H - 59.40
SUTTON Rachael U17 28.08.83, Oxford City :
100 - 12.3
SWALLOW Jodie U20 23.06.81, Brentwood :
3k - 9:59.9 (9:47.84-97)
SWANN Julie V35 15.07.62, Wolves & B :
1500 - 4:33.32 (4:26.07i-94/4:27.0-93)
SWATHERIDGE Donna U15 4.03.85,
Basingstoke & MH : DT - 31.52
SWINDELL Tracy 8.11.66, Thurrock :
10kR - 34:48 (34:43-97), 15kR - 54:10,
HMar - 1:17:11 (1:16:34-97),
Mar - 2:43:41 (2:40:22-97)
SWYER Kerry U17 2.12.82, Gateshead :
Hepl - 3874
SYKES Julia 27.05.75, Hallamshire :
Hep - 3916 (4240-96)
SYMS Helen 20.06.66, :
Mar - 3:09:02

TALBOT Elizabeth 5.12.74, Beds & Co :
1500 - 4:24.5 (4:19.09-95), 3k - 9:15.25,
5k - 15:50.85, 10MR - 55:05, HMar - 1:15:06
TALBOT Nicola 17.02.72, Birchfield :
DT - 47.37 (54.24-93)
TAMIRAT Getenesh U23 11.07.77, Ex L/ETH :
HMar - 1:18:41
TAPPER Elizabeth U23 2.06.78, Charnwood :
PV - 2.60i (2.70-96)
TAYLOR Claire U17 25.10.82, North Shields P :
800 - 2:12.52, 1500 - 4:38.9
TAYLOR Gemma U17 18.09.82, Morpeth :
3k - 10:29.2
TAYLOR Helen U17 19.07.82, Wakefield :
HT - 36.64
TAYLOR Jan U15 5.11.83, Cheltenham :
HJ - 1.64
TAYLOR Laura U15 22.04.84, Radley :
PenG - 2854
TAYLOR Leanne 13.05.74, Rhondda
(nee JONES) : HT - 42.61 (46.86-97)
TAYLOR Tania U23 7.10.76, Birchfield :
400 - 55.21
TEALE Amy U17 30.12.82, North Shields P :
100H - 15.82
TEREK Ann 22.09.64, Lisburn :
1500 - 4:30.3 (4:20.6-96)
TERRY Sandra 28.04.69, Ealing,Southall & Mx :
DT - 39.94
THACKRAY Penny 18.08.74, Hallamshire :
1500 - 4:30.10 (4:22.4-97),
3k - 9:36.00 (9:23.5mx-96/9:35.76-94),
5k - 16:29.57 (16:16.01-97),
10k - 34:48.57, 10kR - 34:17 (34:10-97)

THEOBALD Susan U17 4.03.83, Braintree :
JT - 35.16 (35.42-96)
THERIN Lauren U13 19.01.86, Jersey :
SPM - 9.94, DTM - 29.35, JTM - 33.90
THIEME Helen U17 28.09.81, Birchfield :
300 - 41.31 (39.72-97), 100H - 15.9w,
300H - 44.20 (43.84-97), 400H - 67.2,
HJ - 1.66 (1.68-97), Hepl - 4299
THIRWELL Tina M. U17 5.09.81, Sale :
200 - 25.21, HJ - 1.63,
LJ - 5.36 (5.46w-96), Hepl - 4666
THOM Pauline 2.08.70, Edinburgh WM
(nee QUINN) : 800 - 2:08.4mx/2:09.06,
1500 - 4:22.31, 3k - 9:36.7
THOMAS Caroline 3.11.72, Peterborough :
3k - 9:45.80
THOMAS Janet V35 14.02.61, :
Mar - 3:08:55
THOMAS Kelly U20 9.01.81, Dartford :
200 - 24.56w/24.80
THOMAS Lucy A. U15 2.11.84, Neath :
1500 - 4:48.6
THOMAS Michelle 16.10.71, Birchfield :
100 - 11.8w/11.89,
200 - 24.3/24.50 (23.98-97),
400 - 52.92mx/53.23 (52.88-97)
THOMAS Sonia U20 16.05.79, Wallsend :
3k - 9:54.78
THOMPSON Clara U20 10.11.79, /IRE :
DT - 40.36, HT - 49.14
THOMPSON Joanne Mary V40 30.10.58,
Wx & Bath : 3k - 9:51.79 (9:15.54-93),
5k - 16:50.8mx (16:13.43-94),
10k - 35:46.42 (33:38.36-97),
10kR - 33:13R/34:08 (33:10-93),
10MR - 54:32, HMar - 1:15:56
THOMPSON Lisa U20 25.04.81, Colwyn Bay :
400H - 62.70, Hep - 4357
THOMPSON Lisa U17 3.12.82, Nairn :
DT - 33.71
THOMPSON Margaret V40 8.07.54, Pott Mar :
Mar - 3:00:59 (2:53:45-97)
THOMPSON Rachael U13 15.11.85, Liv H :
600 - 1:44.3, 800 - 2:27.14
THOMPSON Tammy U17 21.10.82, Skyrac :
HT - 34.53
THOMSON Carol-Ann 30.09.68, C of Glasgow :
HMar - 1:19:36
THOMSON Linda 12.02.64, Law & Dist :
Mar - 2:58:51 (2:58:08-96)
THOMSON Trudi V35 18.01.59, Pitreavie :
10MR - 57:04, Mar - 2:52:39 (2:38:23-95)
THORN Joanna U20 19.02.81, Yate :
100H - 14.60w/14.86, Hep - 3905
THORNE Alison 25.09.72, Windsor S & E :
200 - 24.3 (24.97-93), 400 - 55.11
THORNE Louretta U23 6.05.77, Wycombe :
60 - 7.79i, 100 - 11.8w/12.0 (12.24-94),
200 - 24.4/25.13i (24.39-94),
400 - 54.32 (54.27-94)
THORNER Rosie 7.08.67, Bristol :
400 - 56.5/57.36 (55.86-95)
THORNTON Emma U17 27.11.82, Bolton :
JT - 35.01
THORP Angela Caroline 7.12.72, Wigan :
100 - 11.83w/12.0 (11.48w-96/11.98-97),
100H - 13.4/13.43 (12.80-96)

395

THORPE Anna-Maria 15.07.71, Queens Park :
   LJ - 5.66 (5.88-92), TJ - 12.47
TINDAL Jacqueline U20 21.01.79, Edin WM :
   100H - 14.9/15.20 (15.19w-96),
   SP - 12.36, Hep - 4670
TISSHAW Rebecca U20 8.02.81, Dartford :
   5kW - 27:42.65 (25:26.41-97)
TODD Charlotte U17 7.12.81, Edinburgh WM :
   80HI - 11.89
TODD Sarah L. U20 3.11.79, Jarrow & H :
   100 - 12.23w (12.5-96/12.61-94), 100H - 14.93
TOMLINS Sarah U17 5.04.82, Brighton :
   100 - 12.57w (13.36-97)
TONKS Sharon Jayne 18.04.70, Brom & R :
   3kW - 14:23.2, 5kW - 24:20.07, 10kWR - 51:55
TOWARD Louise U15 27.03.84, Blackpool :
   PenG - 2560
TOWN Anna 22.04.75, Verlea :
   HT - 35.84 (36.48-94)
TRIBE Leah U17 3.09.81, Portsmouth :
   300 - 40.8/40.86 (39.5/39.87-97)
TRISTRAM Zoe 15.11.69, Rugby :
   HT - 36.03
TUGWELL Emily U23 26.05.78, Swansea :
   HJ - 1.65 (1.66-96),
   TJ - 11.10 (11.23?/11.13-96)
TULLOCH Anne U17 14.04.82, Wycombe :
   100 - 12.39w/12.42
TUNALEY Sharon Jane 2.09.68, Sale :
   100 - 12.0w/12.04
      (11.5w-85/11.53w-86/11.6-87/11.80-85),
   200 - 23.93w/24.5/24.52 (23.6w-95/23.91-97),
   400 - 56.7/56.77 (53.58-95)
TUNALEY Vicky U15 4.06.84, Ipswich :
   200 - 25.51w/25.95
TUNSTILL Jennifer U15 16.05.84, Parkhill HS :
   800 - 2:18.37
TUOHY Teresa V35 1.06.59, London Oly/IRE :
   HMar - 1:19:35 (1:18:04-92)
TURNBULL Jessica 4.07.75, Bury :
   5k - 17:29.18 (16:57.5-95)
TURNER Edwina V45 16.06.52, Les Croupiers :
   Mar - 2:57:29 (2:53:01-97)
TURNER Lesley 1.08.66, Rowheath :
   Mar - 3:09:53 (2:41:09-93)
TURNER Lynsey U17 3.10.81, Edinburgh WM :
   300 - 40.9/41.06i/41.34
TURNER Michelle U23 25.12.77, Parkside :
   100 - 11.92w/11.98
TURNER Vicktoria U15 30.09.83, Bracknell :
   1500 - 4:47.30
TURTON Judy U15 26.05.84, Wycombe :
   PV - 2.50

U PTON Sophie U13 18.09.85, S & S H :
   HJ - 1.50

V ALE Lynn 9.01.71, Havant :
   PV - 2.60
VAN DER MERWE Adri U23 17.06.76, Peterbro/
   RSA : 100H - 14.2/14.48, 400H - 60.13 (58.30-94)
VANNET Lisa 8.11.74, Edinburgh WM :
   400 - 54.9/54.92 (54.54-96)
VELDMAN Margaret 7.06.74, Sale/HOL :
   200 - 25.15, LJ - 5.94i, Hep - 4817 (5038-92)
VELVICK Kimberley U15 3.01.85, Ashford :
   100 - 12.6w
VINEY Gemma U17 7.01.83, Blackheath :
   3k - 10:28.6

W AIN Alanna U15 27.04.85, C of Stoke :
   200 - 25.94
WALE Amanda 14.10.70, Wrexham :
   100H - 15.27, Hep - 4546
WALKER Dawn U15 29.09.83, Barrow & F :
   HJ - 1.66
WALKER Elexi U17 28.10.82, Birchfield :
   100 - 12.15w/12.4/12.53
WALKER Helen U20 12.10.80, Middlesbro & C :
   400H - 62.92, Hep - 4106w/4096
WALKER Hilary C. V45 9.11.53, Serpentine :
   100kR - 8:33:35 (7:50:09-93),
   24Hr - 184.416km (236.453km-88)
WALKER Jennifer 28.01.69, Windsor S & E :
   HJ - 1.70 (1.76-88)
WALKES Michelle U23 9.05.76, Bedford & Co :
   100 - 12.28w
WALL Kim U17 21.04.83, Basildon :
   60 - 7.7i/7.93i, 100 - 11.8w/12.0/12.13,
   200 - 24.3w/24.5/24.52w/24.54,
   300 - 38.4/38.49, 400 - 55.39,
   LJ - 5.49, HepI - 3931
WALLACE Ailsa U23 12.03.77, Cardiff :
   HJ - 1.65 (1.73i/1.70-94)
WALLACE Alana 28.07.65, Windsor S & E/IRE :
   DT - 44.23
WALLBANKS Carol U17 9.12.82, Copeland :
   JT - 42.10
WALLEN Deborah U20 28.05.79, AF&D :
   3kW - 14:23.48, 5kW - 24:28.60,
   10kWR - 52:24
WALLEN Mary V45 9.06.52, AF&D :
   3kW - 16:03.33, 10kWR - 57:45,
   20kW - 1:58:14
WALSH Caroline U20 29.04.80, S Barnet :
   1500 - 4:25.1, 3k - 9:43.3
WALSH Gemma U17 2.07.83, Wigan :
   JT - 34.98
WALTERS Jacqueline U17 17.12.81, Derby :
   100 - 11.82w/12.3/12.44 (12.35-97)
WALTERS Kirsty U15 6.09.84, Whitemoss :
   HT - 35.46
WALTERS Mhairi U20 19.06.81, C of Glasgow :
   SP - 12.06, HT - 48.38
WALTON Julie U23 12.12.78, Coventry Godiva :
   SP - 11.27i (11.27-97)
WANNELL Michelle 12.07.67, Exeter :
   1500 - 4:23.40, 3k - 9:27.8,
   5k - 16:52.6mx/17:05.40, 10kR - 34:59
WARBURTON Angela 24.01.64, City of Hull :
   400H - 66.0 (63.5-92/64.00-94)
WARD Emma U17 2.01.82, City of Stoke :
   800 - 2:12.0 (2:09.97-97),
   1500 - 4:35.25 (4:32.04-97)
WARD Jennifer U23 22.09.78, C of Glasgow :
   800 - 2:11.80i (2:07.82-97)
WARDEN Caroline 16.09.72, Preston :
   TJ - 11.25 (12.31w-94/12.11i-96/12.06-94)
WARNE Anna U13, Harborough :
   800 - 2:27.0
WARNER Kelly U20 5.03.81, Radley :
   400H - 65.4
WARREN Natalie U20 28.08.81, Walton :
   PV - 2.60
WARREN Sally U23 29.01.78, Birchfield :
   3kW - 15:06.06, 5kW - 25:36.61,
   5kWR - 25:18, 10kWR - 51:20

WARRILOW Hayley U20 10.04.80, C of Stoke :
TJ - 11.85
WARRINGTON Clare U17 28.07.82, Warr :
JT - 36.54
WATERLOW Amy U23 29.07.78, Sale :
3k - 9:26.3, 5k - 15:57.45, 10kR - 34:28
WATERS Elizabeth U23 19.02.77, Kettering :
400H - 62.69
WATERSON Kirsty U17 17.12.82, Ipswich :
800 - 2:17.51, 1500 - 4:42.59, 3k - 10:08.40
WATKINS Laura U17 1.01.82, Telford :
100 - 12.37w/12.51 (12.3-96),
200 - 25.3/25.49 (25.08w/25.1/25.44-96)
WATSON Anna U17 30.04.82, Inverness :
PV - 3.03
WATSON Gemma U17 28.11.82, Herne Hill :
100 - 12.54
WATSON Louise Carole 13.12.71, GEC/
Loughbro : 5k - 17:04.06 (15:57.06-95),
10k - 35:33.72 (33:21.46-96)
WATSON Natalie U17 29.01.83, Solihull & S H :
3kW - 16:29.6 (15:16.4-96),
3kWR - 16:05 (15:48o-95/15:56-96),
5kW - 28:30.76
WATSON Natalie U15 5.07.84, Wolves & B :
100 - 12.1/12.37w/12.46,
200 - 25.6/25.74w/25.83?
WATSON Ruth U20 29.11.79, Peterborough :
200 - 24.75, 400 - 55.29
WATTS Katy U20 25.03.81, Basingstoke & MH :
JT - 45.08
WATTS Samantha U17 13.10.81, Wigan :
300H - 45.07
WAUGH Kathryn 20.02.73, Liverpool H :
3k - 9:59.4
WEALL Kelly U23 30.11.78, Middlesbro & C :
400H - 65.3 (62.5/63.80-97)
WEATHERILL Carolina 13.05.68, S Barnet :
3k - 9:51.78i (9:23.1-95)
WEBB Helen U20 14.04.80, Halesowen :
PV - 2.70
WEBB Lisa Jane 9.10.65, Shaftesbury Barnet :
3k - 9:59.9 (9:11.45-88)
WEBB Shirley U17 28.09.81, North Shields P :
TJ - 10.87, HT - 33.95
WEBBER Claire U15 13.12.83, Arbroath :
PenG - 2544
WEBBER Lucy 5.02.72, Brighton :
PV - 3.80
WEEKES Helen U17 4.10.81, Ashford :
HJ - 1.63
WELLS Elaine U23 30.05.78, Crawley :
400 - 57.38 (57.3-97)
WELLS Sarah 11.08.69, Worthing :
800 - 2:12.38i (2:10.67-97)
WELLSTEAD Sarah U20 22.10.79, Sutton & D :
LJ - 5.86,
TJ - 11.48w/11.13i/11.00 (11.63-97)
WEST Kylie U15 16.09.84, Cannock & Stafford :
SPG - 11.37, DT - 34.03
WEST Rachel, :
Mar - 3:09:55
WESTWOOD Fiona U20 27.02.81, Wakefield :
LJ - 5.71
WHITBY Sharon U20 29.09.80, Crawley :
800 - 2:12.02

WHITCOMBE Andrea 8.06.71, Parkside :
1500 - 4:18.24 (4:14.56-90),
3k - 9:10.7mx/9:14.9 (8:58.59-91),
5k - 15:43.03, HMar - 1:17:27
WHITE Caroline Helen 8.10.68, Trafford :
JT - 49.13 (56.50-91)
WHITE Jacqueline 12.01.71, Coventry Godiva :
LJ - 6.01 (6.11w-95/6.08-96)
WHITE Julia U20 2.05.79, Peterborough :
100 - 12.10 (12.0/12.05-97), 200 - 24.88
WHITE Laura U20 5.09.79, Hyndburn/
Camb Un : HJ - 1.75, Hep - 4419
WHITE Rebecca U20 5.06.80, Blackburn :
60 - 7.55i, 100 - 11.45w/12.1/12.20 (12.00-97),
200 - 23.82w/24.02,
LJ - 5.55 (5.57-97), TJ - 11.67
WHITE Claire 24.02.73, Rugby :
(see BOSTOCK)
WHITE Julianne, : (see EMPFIELD)
WHITE Sarah U20 25.12.80, Andover :
HJ - 1.68
WHITEHEAD Louise 26.03.75, Swansea :
100 - 12.1w (12.1-93),
200 - 24.03w/24.1w?/24.5/24.52
(24.1-93/24.24-97),
400 - 56.8/57.21i (54.92-95)
WHITLOCK Janine 11.08.73, Trafford :
60 - 7.50i (7.45i-97), 100 - 11.7/11.85,
200 - 24.07 (23.87-97),
100H - 14.3 (14.0w-96/14.1/14.47-95),
PV - 4.31, LJ - 5.94
WHITMORE Hannah U15 24.02.84, Oadby & W :
800 - 2:17.9
WHITTAKER Louise U17 29.11.82, Sale :
800 - 2:16.32 (2:15.1-97), 3k - 10:07.4
WHITTER Emma U20 20.07.80, Herne Hill :
60 - 7.7i/7.72i, 200 - 24.18
WIGHAM Katie U15 27.05.84, Border :
HJ - 1.65, PenG - 2874
WILDER Kelley 30.07.71, Oxford Univ/USA :
3k - 9:50.82, 5k - 17:30.2
WILDING Helen U23 25.10.76, Trafford :
SP - 13.47 (13.88-95),
DT - 42.59 (42.90-95), HT - 44.48
WILHELMY Sarah U20 2.02.80, Southend :
100 - 11.6w/11.71 (11.83"-95),
200 - 23.20w/23.23
WILKINS Caroline 28.08.75, Cardiff :
400H - 62.2/62.91 (61.32-97)
WILKINS Frances U20 15.01.79, Birchfield :
SP - 11.35
WILKINS Melanie 18.01.73, AF&D :
100H - 13.47w/13.65
(13.1-95/13.23w-96/13.34-95)
WILKINS Serena U23 7.08.78, Yate :
100 - 12.28w (12.2-96)
WILKINSON Tanya 1.04.70, City of Stoke :
400H - 60.2/60.32
WILLIAMS Angela U20 13.05.81, Dartford :
TJ - 11.12 (11.15-96)
WILLIAMS Charlene U17 22.10.81, Herne Hill :
200 - 25.45w
WILLIAMS Donna Maria U23 7.10.78, Sale :
DT - 39.80 (48.08-96)
WILLIAMS Elizabeth U23 2.06.77, Walton :
200 - 25.1, 400 - 56.1/56.45 (55.47-95)
WILLIAMS Hayley 30.01.75, City of Stoke :
DT - 37.09

WILLIAMS Helen U23 2.06.77, Walton :
  100 - 11.99w/12.1,
  200 - 24.49w/24.8/25.10 (25.07-95)
WILLIAMS Helen U17 13.01.83, Vale Royal :
  TJ - 10.94w/10.66
WILLIAMS Kathryn U23 10.11.77, Swansea :
  400H - 63.0/64.38 (60.21-96)
WILLIAMS Lisa S. U23 11.04.78, Telford :
  100H - 15.22w (14.81-96)
WILLIAMS Lynn 6.02.72, Arena :
  Mar - 3:05:21
WILLIAMS Nadia U17 17.11.81, S Barnet :
  LJ - 5.40
WILLIAMS Sharon Bernadette 20.05.70, W S & E :
  60 - 7.7i (7.42i-96), 100 - 11.79 (11.53-95),
  200 - 24.1/24.41 (23.80w/23.9/23.91-95),
  400 - 56.88i (55.8-95/56.07-89)
WILLIAMS Sophie-Anne U20 29.03.80,
  Wessex & Bath : 100 - 12.16 (12.05dt-97)
WILLIAMS Susan U20 20.01.79, Deeside :
  PV - 2.65
WILLIAMS Susan U23 2.06.77, Walton :
  60 - 7.60i, 100 - 11.61w/11.98 (11.89-97),
  200 - 24.3w/24.34w/24.4/24.48
    (24.11w-94/24.2-95/24.27-94),
  300 - 39.08i/39.4 (39.72-96),
  400H - 65.6 (63.5-97)
WILLIAMS Syreeta U20 24.10.80, Birchfield :
  400 - 56.37 (55.92-97), 400H - 62.79
WILLIAMS Tracey U17 31.10.82, Leamington :
  HT - 35.71
WILLIAMS Victoria U20 11.04.81, Clevedon :
  100H - 14.9/14.96,
  LJ - 5.54 (5.54-97), Hep - 4289
WILLIAMS Victoria U20 11.03.81, Cann & St :
  DT - 35.99 (38.70-97)
WILLIAMSON Faye U13 2.12.85, Dudley & St :
  100 - 13.2
WILSON Aileen J. U15 30.03.84, Peterborough :
  75HG - 11.64w/11.70, HJ - 1.79,
  LJ - 5.20, PenG - 3509
WILSON Amy U20 31.12.80, Ipswich :
  SP - 12.79
WILSON Bernice U15 21.04.84, Grantham :
  100 - 12.6/12.62w/12.68, 200 - 26.05
WILSON Carley U17 6.12.81, Morpeth :
  800 - 2:13.04 (2:12.9-97), 1500 - 4:33.21
WILSON Cassie U23 24.09.77, Bingley :
  HT - 37.81
WILSON Dawn U17 16.12.81, Bromley :
  200 - 25.57, 300 - 40.87
WILSON Paula Anneke 20.11.69, Birchfield :
  PV - 3.80
WILSON Samantha U17 28.09.81, S London :
  100 - 12.4/12.56w
WILSON Zoe U23 28.08.76, Birchfield :
  60 - 7.62i (7.60i-97),
  100 - 11.86w/11.97 (11.9-96), 200 - 24.13
WINDASS Helen 16.10.65, Aberdeen :
  400 - 56.7 (55.8/56.03-92)
WING Jenny U17 25.10.82, Staffs Sch :
  80HI - 11.99w
WINGLER Astrid 21.05.68, Hallamshire :
  3k - 9:53.9 (9:39.8mx-96/9:45.8-97)
WINTER Lindsey U15 19.03.84, Exeter :
  75HG - 11.40w/11.6/11.74
WISE Clare L. 22.08.69, AF&D :
  400 - 57.1, 100H - 14.48, 400H - 59.07

WISE Joanne 15.03.71, Coventry Godiva :
  LJ - 6.63 (6.70i-97/6.69w-88)
WITTON Nikki 30.09.72, Newport :
  PV - 2.50
WNUK Kia U17 31.10.81, Croydon :
  PV - 3.00i/3.00
WOOD Hannah U17 17.11.81, Solihull & S H :
  300H - 44.71, 400H - 66.3
WOOD Kerrie   66, Manchester YMCA :
  Mar - 2:55:28
WOOD Laura U23 31.10.78, Trafford :
  DT - 41.28, HT - 35.10 (36.54-96)
WOOD Louise U17 13.05.83, Braintree :
  TJ - 11.03w
WOODCOCK Sian U20 13.01.80, Bingley :
  3kW - 15:57.19 (15:33.17-97)
WOODRUFF Miranda U17 6.09.82, Sutton & D :
  300 - 41.4
WOODS Jennie U15 28.01.84, Liverpool H :
  HJ - 1.66
WOODS Suzanne U23 29.12.76, Basildon/
  Loughbro : PV - 3.20i/3.20
WOOLGAR Deborah Caroline 10.03.65, Worth :
  SP - 13.18 (14.18-89), DT - 37.99 (40.92-91)
WOOLRICH Sharon U23 1.05.76, C of Portsm :
  HJ - 1.68 (1.70-94)
WOOTON Katrina U13 2.09.85, Luton :
  800 - 2:27.6, 1500 - 5:03.9
WORSEY Helen U17 29.08.82, Leics Cor :
  60H - 8.96i, 60HI - 8.49I,
  80HI - 10.96w/11.02,
  100HI - 13.8, 300H - 45.13
WRAY Sharon U17 8.10.82, Oswestry :
  SP - 10.62, DT - 32.45
WRIGHT Amanda 14.07.68, Birchfield :
  3k - 9:43.6 (9:06.7-92),
  HMar - 1:16:00 (1:14:00-97),
  Mar - 2:44:49 (2:40:43-97)
WRIGHT Claire U15 9.09.83, Vale Royal :
  HJ - 1.68
WRIGHT Dawn-Alice U23 20.01.76, Cov G :
  PV - 3.10 (3.10-94)
WRIGHT Jacqueline G. V45 8.10.53, Bracknell :
  DT - 42.48 (49.58-75)
WRIGHT Jade U17 9.01.83, S Barnet :
  800 - 2:17.5, 1500 - 4:47.02
WRIGHT Lucy 17.11.69, Leeds :
  1500 - 4:23.7, 3k - 9:16.1mx/9:16.93,
  2M - 9:58.92, 5k - 15:59.51, 10kR - 34:30
WRIGHT Megan U13 19.02.87, C of Edin :
  800 - 2:21.4, 1200 - 3:57.3, 1500 - 5:03.0
WRIGHT Melanie 5.04.64, Nuneaton :
  5kW - 25:37.69 (23:47.6-94),
  10kWR - 52:03 (47:40sh-93/48:18-92)
WRIGHT Natalie 13.11.73, Richmond & T :
  TJ - 11.05
WRIGHT Rebecca U23 20.12.77, W S & E/
  Cambridge University : 400H - 64.3
WRIGHTON Jane 5.11.67, Shaftesbury B :
  400 - 56.75
WYETH Alison 26.05.64, Parkside :
  10kR - 34:23 (32:56-94),
  10MR - 54:30, 15kR - 50:35, HMar - 1:10:54
WYNTER-PINK Clover U23 29.11.77, W S & E :
  SP - 11.90 (11.91-96),
  JT - 43.42 (44.20-93), Hep - 4754 (5143-95)

YELLING Hayley 3.01.74, Hounslow :
 1500 - 4:31.53 (4:30.2-96),
 3k - 9:34.6 (9:26.12-96),
 5k - 16:43.02 (16:32.04-96), 10kR - 34:29
YORK-MORRIS Sharon 5.07.68, Hertford & W :
 800 - 2:12.1, 1500 - 4:20.5, 3k - 9:31.7
YOUNG Catherine U17 14.03.82, Stamford & D :
 HJ - 1.70, HepI - 4324
YOUNG Sarah 2.01.70, Salford :
 1500 - 4:20.7, 2k - 5:59.0+e,
 3k - 9:04.27, 2M - 9:49.62, 5k - 15:45.08

YOUSDEN Janet 25.11.68, Coventry Godiva :
 PV - 2.80
YOUSEFIAN Sadie U17 3.02.83, Stockport :
 1500 - 4:45.90, 3k - 10:30.3

ZAWADA Sarah U17 9.04.82, AF&D :
 60 - 7.7i/7.79i (7.79i-97),
 100 - 12.0 (11.87w/12.25-95),
 200 - 24.30i/24.4/24.67 (24.1w/24.20-97)
ZENNER Helen U17 15.08.82, Team Solent :
 1500 - 4:44.3

AMENDMENTS TO BRITISH ATHLETICS 1998
From Peter Matthews, Martin Rix, members of NUTS and readers

RECORDS & ALL TIME
Martin Rix has again examined the records and All Time lists, this year's lists contain the latest known entries, in particular the Under 13 Men has been extensively revised.

RESULTS
p.89: AAA U15 Indoor 800m: Aaron (not Alloy) Wilson
p.97: U20 v GER: 110mh r1 6. Malins 14.75
p.111: date of Combined Events at Hemel Hempstead 23-24 August
p.113: NI Women's JT: Moffitt 46.50
p.114: Southern champions: 10,000m: Adrian Marriott 30:33.82, 3000mW: Mark Easton 12:31.53

MERIT RANKINGS
Men's 10,000m: Jon Brown (5y, 1)
Men's HT: Floyd (0y, -)
Women's 800m: Tanya Blake was British and therefore ranks 4th, with the rest moving down one place.
Women's PV: Fiona Harrison 3.40 twice
Women's HT: Beverley add 54.04

MEN 1997
Some athletes were wrongly shown as V40 or V45 – which comes into effect only from the athlete's birthday. So delete V40 from: SP 14.11 Aldridge, 13.78 Smith; DT: 40.18 Drzwiecki, JT: 69.04 Yates (but note 68.68 1 London (Elt) 5 Jul), 55.40 Watson, and change V45 for V40 for 58.24 Ostapowycz

60:	6.88 Ojex b. 26.8.72 (also in 100m), 6.9 Newell 10.6.79
100:	10.83 1.4 Kyaw Htoo Aung MYA 4h3 Jakarta, INA 13 Oct (from 10.89);
	U13: 12.2 Scruton 1 Bebington 11 May, Romain Henry (& 200m) 1st
200:	21.68 Kyaw Htoo Aung MYA 7 Singapore 27 Sep (note 21.36w- 91) (from 22.02),
	21.7w/21.9 Bandele 11.9.71
300:	note 32.08+ Thomas m (in 400m) Athens, GRE 5 Aug
800:	1:57.4 McIndoe 2:11.6 Barrett 1 Watford 16 Jul, 2:15.1 Murdock
10km Road:	29:17 Murray, 29:21 Ross, 29:26 Coyle, 29:39 MacKay - course short by 236m in
	Glasgow - and women: 33:51 Lothian and 34:55 Brindley
	(and 1996: 29:26 Stewart, 29:31 Quinn, 29:36 Ross)

Half Marathon:

64:25	Gareth Davies		21	South Shields	14	Sep
64:46	Nick Wetheridge		22	South Shields	14	Sep
64:48	Malcolm Campbell	3.01.71	2	Naples, USA	19	Jan
64:52	Alan Shepherd	28.04.69	23	South Shields	14	Sep

100km: all road except Sichel
3000mSt: 9:26.97 Mason not U20; delete 8:54.3 Donald Lennon-Jones –he claimed 8:54.3,
but results had 9:54.3, and that has now been confirmed by the second placed man.
Season's best 9:25.24 13h1 Birmingham 11 Jul

75HC:	delete 11.9 Scott
80HB::	11.5 Jones (11.61w) best legal 11.77 1 Brecon 5 Jul
100HY:	13.9 Gawthorpe - add 13.92 O Derby 21 Sep,
	14.16 Peter Watson 30.6.81 O Derby 21 Sep
110HJ:	15.45 Butler 4.4.80
110H:	14.71w Doherty - 14.85 0.4 3 Cardiff 31 May;
	delete 15.40 Coker and 15.58 Scholes as these made over 3'3" hurdles
HJ:	2.00 Tom Costello (Oxford Univ) not Dennis Costello
PV:	4.60 Donovan Graham 18.8.61, 4.35 Lease 14.11.77, 4.30 Parkinson 17.2.79
TJ:	15.37w Hilton - best legal 15.28 2 Solihull 5 Jul (delete 15.32 *),
	U13: 10.64 0.1 Blair 20 Jun
SPB:	13.32 Adam Hall 1 Carshalton 17 Aug (from 13.01)
DT:	54.16 Hayes at Barking, 42.38 Menhenitt at St Peter Port
Dec:	5218 Stephens U23 12.9.77
PenB:	Derby on 20 not 21 Sep
3000W:	12:31.53 Easton 22 Jun, 12:49.41 (not .4 i) O'Rawe;
	delete 14:52.58 Deacon and Moulds
5000W:	22:51.1 Taylor (not 22:25.6), 23:24.01 Whorlow
4x100:	41.08 GB U18 - 23 Jul
4x200:	1:25.41i GB U23 - 1 Mar
4x400:	3:19.47 (not 3:14.97) English Schools 19 Jul, 3:20.28 (not .38) Scottish Schools

WOMEN 1997

200:	24.78 -1.1 Stephanie Douglas 22.1.69 7 Valencia, SPA 31 May
1500:	4:20.87 Tanya Baker 23.11.74 (not Blake)
3000:	9:36.4+e Yvonne Murray 4.10.64 2 Birmingham 13 Jul
10M:	57:52 Lynne Madison
Marathon:	2:39:05 Percival 22.4.62 (she says) (and other events),
	2:55:21 Anita Mellowdew 1.12.70 (Epsom & Ewell)
100km:	Road not Track
24 Hr:	193,448 Gayter V35 30.10.60
2000mSt:	note 7:20.85 Colebrook over 2'6" barriers
60H:	delete 8.5 Worsey (was 8.9)
100H:	14.18 0.0 Liston 6r1
LJ:	5.93/6.22w Benjamin 5.3.72, (also have 7.3.72??) 6.16w Sotherton 10 May
TJ:	11.56 1.0 Brown
HT:	42.18 Sara-Jane Cattermole (AUS 43.30 -96), 38.66 King at St Peter Port,
	35.78 Margaret McCutcheon (USA) 30.12.68
Heptathlon:	4616 Jenny Brown 1 Durban, RSA 17 Jul
	(16.41, 1.66, 11.13, 27.51, 5.23, 32.10, 2:26.91) (from 4594)
3000W:	14:15.72 Amy Hales,14:56.3 Ford; **Road**: 16:13 Shipley 2 Tamworth 14 Dec
5000W:	27:11.0 Kirsty Coleman (from 28:17.70) 1 and 27:21.0
	Jo Hesketh 2 Brighton 14 Dec; **Road**: 25:09 Bennett on 25 May
4x1 Mile:	Swallow 4:57.4

INDEX
Martin Rix has examined the index and made numerous small changes which are now reflected in this year's index.

1998 List
Donovan Grahm's dob 18.08.61 does not appear in the lists but is shown in the index.

PREVIOUS ANNUALS

1978 Lists: Women's 400mh: doubtful 60.6 Amanda Stacey
1982 Lists: Women's Hep: 4867 Mullin
1988 Lists: Women 400mh: delete 60.8 Amanda Moseley
1992 Lists: Men HJ: Steve Smith - delete 2.25 on 11 Jun
1993 Lists: Men 60mh: Colin Jackson 7.49 not 7.43 1h1 Karlsruhe 6 Mar
1994 Lists: Men 200m: 21.68i Ross Baillie,
                4x100m: 39.92 National Juniors – team was Gardener, Devonish, Mark, Cameron
1996 Lists: Men 300m: 32.85 David McKenzie